2011 Federal Tax Handbook   S0-BKI-201

After the 2011 Federal Tax Handbook went to press, there was a need to clarify some recently updated information in ¶2363. As a service to our customers, we are including the following substitute for that paragraph. For yet-to-be enacted legislation that may affect the 2010 or 2011 tax years, please visit the RIA Federal Tax Handbook homepage at *http://ria.thomsonreuters.com/federaltaxhandbook*. It is our mission to provide Federal Tax Handbook customers with the most accurate and up-to-date information possible.

¶ 2363 Nonbusiness energy property credit for 2010—Form 5695.
For property placed in service in 2009 and 2010 (Code Sec. 25C(g)), a taxpayer can claim (on Form 5695) a credit equal to 30% of the cost of: (1) qualified energy efficiency improvements, and (2) residential energy property expenditures. The aggregate credit is $1,500 for both years together. (Code Sec. 25C(a), Code Sec. 25C(b)) The expenses must be made on or in connection with a dwelling unit located in the U.S. owned and used by taxpayer as his principal residence (under Code Sec. 121) at the time of installation. (Code Sec. 25C(c), Code Sec. 25C(d)) (See FTC ¶A-4751; USTR ¶25C4; Tax Desk ¶569,551.)

Qualified energy efficiency improvements are energy efficient building envelope components such as insulation materials or systems specifically and primarily designed to reduce heat loss/gain; exterior windows, skylights or doors; and certain metal or asphalt roofs installed on a dwelling unit with pigmented coatings or cooling granules to reduce heat gain, that meet criteria established by the 2000 International Energy Conservation Code (or Energy Star program requirements, for a metal or asphalt roof). (Code Sec. 25C(c)) Taxpayers can rely on an appropriate manufacturer's certification that a component meets energy requirements, unless IRS withdraws it before taxpayer's purchase. Also, the component must be expected to last for at least five years. (Code Sec. 25C(c)(1)(C)) This requirement is met if the manufacturer offers a two-year warranty to repair or replace at no extra charge. (See FTC ¶A-4752; USTR ¶25C4; Tax Desk ¶569,552.)

Residential energy property expenses are expenses for qualified energy property (including labor costs for onsite preparation, assembly, or original installation) that meet specific standards set forth in Code Sec. 25C(d)(2)(B) and Code Sec. 25C(d)(2)(C). This property includes:
. . . energy-efficient building property (electric heat pump water heater, electric heat pump; central air conditioner; natural gas, propane or oil water heater; or a stove burning biomass fuel to heat or provide hot water to a taxpayer's residence in the U.S.) that meets specific energy efficiency standards;
. . . a qualified natural gas, propane, or oil furnace; or qualified natural gas, propane, or oil hot water boiler; or
. . . an advanced main air circulating fan. (Code Sec. 25C(d)) (See FTC ¶A-4753; USTR ¶25C4; Tax Desk ¶569,553.)

An expense won't fail to qualify just because it was made for two or more dwelling units; the credit is computed separately for the expenses for each dwelling unit. (Code Sec. 25C(e)(2)(B)) (See FTC ¶A-4755; USTR ¶25C4; Tax Desk ¶569,555.) If the credit is allowed for an expense for a property, the increase in the property's basis that would otherwise result is reduced by the credit allowed (¶2478). (Code Sec. 25C(f), Code Sec. 1016(a)(33)) (See FTC ¶A-4757; USTR ¶25C4; Tax Desk ¶569,557.)

RIA *caution:* Check http://ria.thomsonreuters.com/federaltaxhandbook for the credit's extension.

RIA Federal Tax Handbook Quick Reference Card
2010 Income and Gift Tax Rates

Single Taxpayers

Taxable income	Amount of tax
Not over $ 8,375	10% of taxable income
Over $ 8,375 but not over $ 34,000	$ 837.50 plus 15% of the amount over $ 8,375
Over $ 34,000 but not over $ 82,400	$ 4,681.25 plus 25% of the amount over $ 34,000
Over $ 82,400 but not over $ 171,850	$ 16,781.25 plus 28% of the amount over $ 82,400
Over $ 171,850 but not over $ 373,650	$ 41,827.25 plus 33% of the amount over $ 171,850
Over $ 373,650	$ 108,421.25 plus 35% of the amount over $ 373,650

Married Taxpayers Filing Joint Returns and Qualified Widows and Widowers

Taxable income	Amount of tax
Not over $ 16,750	10% of taxable income
Over $ 16,750 but not over $ 68,000	$ 1,675 plus 15% of the amount over $ 16,750
Over $ 68,000 but not over $ 137,300	$ 9,362.50 plus 25% of the amount over $ 68,000
Over $ 137,300 but not over $ 209,250	$ 26,687.50 plus 28% of the amount over $ 137,300
Over $ 209,250 but not over $ 373,650	$ 46,833.50 plus 33% of the amount over $ 209,250
Over $ 373,650	$ 101,085.50 plus 35% of the amount over $ 373,650

Married Taxpayers Filing Separate Returns

Taxable income	Amount of tax
Not over $ 8,375	10% of taxable income
Over $ 8,375 but not over $ 34,000	$ 837.50 plus 15% of the amount over $ 8,375
Over $ 34,000 but not over $ 68,650	$ 4,681.25 plus 25% of the amount over $ 34,000
Over $ 68,650 but not over $ 104,625	$ 13,343.75 plus 28% of the amount over $ 68,650
Over $ 104,625 but not over $ 186,825	$ 23,416.75 plus 33% of the amount over $ 104,625
Over $ 186,825	$ 50,542.75 plus 35% of the amount over $ 186,825

Heads Of Household

Taxable income	Amount of tax
Not over $ 11,950	10% of taxable income
Over $ 11,950 but not over $ 45,550	$ 1,195 plus 15% of the amount over $ 11,950
Over $ 45,550 but not over $ 117,650	$ 6,235 plus 25% of the amount over $ 45,550
Over $ 117,650 but not over $ 190,550	$ 24,260 plus 28% of the amount over $ 117,650
Over $ 190,550 but not over $ 373,650	$ 44,672 plus 33% of the amount over $ 190,550
Over $ 373,650	$ 105,095 plus 35% of the amount over $ 373,650

Estates and Trusts

Taxable income	Amount of tax
Not over $ 2,300	15% of taxable income
Over $ 2,300 but not over $ 5,350	$ 345 plus 25% of the amount over $ 2,300
Over $ 5,350 but not over $ 8,200	$ 1,107.50 plus 28% of the amount over $ 5,350
Over $ 8,200 but not over $ 11,200	$ 1,905.50 plus 33% of the amount over $ 8,200
Over $ 11,200	$ 2,895.50 plus 35% of the amount over $ 11,200

Bankruptcy estates use the rate schedules for married taxpayers filing separate returns.

Standard Deductions

Basic*
Single or married filing separate	$ 5,700
Married filing joint and surviving spouses	$ 11,400
Head of household	$ 8,400

Additional (for 65 or over and/or blind)
Unmarried (including head of household)	$ 1,400
Married or surviving spouse (whether or not joint return)	$ 1,100

* Limited to greater of $ 950 or the sum of $ 300 plus earned income for individuals who can be claimed as a dependent by another taxpayer.

Capital Gains and qualified dividend income*— Individuals, Estates & Trusts

Net short-term (held one year or less) capital gain is taxed at: Ordinary income rates

Long-term (more than one year) **capital gain** and **qualified dividend income*** are taxed at: 15% (0% for gain otherwise taxable at ordinary 10% or 15% rate)

Except the maximum tax on:

Unrecaptured section 1250 gain (attributable to real estate depreciation) is:	25%
Collectibles gain (on works of art, rugs, antiques, etc.) is:	28%
Section 1202 gain (from the sale of small business stock eligible for partial exclusion from gross income) is:	28%

* Dividends from domestic corporations and qualified foreign corporations that meet specified holding period requirements. Exclusions may apply.

Standard Mileage Rates

Business use of auto	50¢ a mile
Charitable	14¢
Medical	16.5¢
Moving expenses	16.5¢

RIA Federal Tax Handbook Quick Reference Card
2010 Income and Gift Tax Rates

Itemized Deductions Percentage Limitations

Medical expenses	7.5% of adjusted gross income (AGI)—floor
Personal interest	0%
Net nonbusiness casualty losses	10% of AGI (after $100 per casualty limitation) -- floor
Charitable contributions	50%* of AGI—ceiling on deductible amount
Miscellaneous itemized deductions	2% of AGI—floor

* Other limits apply depending on type of gift and/or recipient.

Personal Exemption

Exemption amount	$3,650

Alternative Minimum Tax

AMT rates (on taxable excess – i.e., alternative minimum taxable income less exemption amount):

Individual, estate, trust:*	26% of taxable excess that doesn't exceed $175,000 ($87,500 for married filing separately)
	28% of taxable excess that exceeds $175,000 ($87,500 for married filing separately)
Corporation (other than an exempt small corporation):	20% of taxable excess**

*Tax rate on net capital gain is the same as for regular tax.

**Special rates apply for certain corporations with qualified timber gain.

AMT Exemption Amounts*		Phaseout range
Single**	$33,750	$112,500 – 247,500
Married filing separate***	22,500	75,000 – 165,000
Joint filers or surviving spouse	45,000	150,000 – 330,000
Estate, trust	22,500	75,000 – 165,000
Corporation	40,000	150,000 – 310,000

* Congress may increase individuals' exemption (and phaseout) amounts, retroactively for 2010, as it has for the past several tax years.

** Special calculations apply to child subject to the kiddie tax.

*** Must also add to AMTI the lesser of $22,500 or 25% of the excess of AMTI (without regard to the exemption reduction) over $165,000.

2010 Social Security Tax

FICA	Tax base	Rate	Maximum tax
Social Security	$106,800	6.2%	$6,621.60
Medicare	no limit	1.45%	no limit

2010 Self-Employment Tax

FICA	Tax base	Rate	Maximum tax
Social Security	$106,800	12.4%	$13,243.20
Medicare	no limit	2.9%	no limit

Corporations

Taxable income	Amount of tax
Not over $50,000	15% of taxable income
Over $50,000 but not over $75,000	$7,500 plus 25% of the amount over $50,000
Over $75,000 but not over $100,000	$13,750 plus 34% of the amount over $75,000
Over $100,000 but not over $335,000	$22,250 plus 39% of the amount over $100,000
Over $335,000 but not over $10,000,000	$113,900 plus 34% of the amount over $335,000
Over $10,000,000 but not over $15,000,000	$3,400,000 plus 35% of the amount over $10,000,000
Over $15,000,000 but not over $18,333,333.33	$5,150,000 plus 38% of the amount over $15,000,000
Over $18,333,333.33	$6,416,666.67 plus 35% of the amount over $18,333,333.33

Capital gains are taxable at regular corporate rates. The tax on qualified personal service corporations is 35% of taxable income.

Gift Tax Rates

For 2010, there is no estate tax, but the gift tax continues to apply. The unified estate and gift tax schedule has been replaced with the seperate gift tax rate schedule below.

If the amount with respect to which the tentative tax to be computed is:	The tentative tax is
Not over $10,000	18% of such amount
Over $10,000 but not over $20,000	$1,800, plus 20% of the excess over $10,000
Over $20,000 but not over $40,000	$3,800, plus 22% of the excess over $20,000
Over $40,000 but not over $60,000	$8,200, plus 24% of the excess over $40,000
Over $60,000 but not over $80,000	$13,000, plus 26% of the excess over $60,000
Over $80,000 but not over $100,000	$18,200, plus 28% of the excess over $80,000
Over $100,000 but not over $150,000	$23,800, plus 30% of the excess over $100,000
Over $150,000 but not over $250,000	$38,800, plus 32% of the excess over $150,000
Over $250,000 but not over $500,000	$70,800, plus 34% of the excess over $250,000
Over $500,000	$155,800, plus 35% of the excess over $500,000

Subject to a credit of $330,800 allowed to U.S. citizens and residents.

RIA® Book-Based Self-Study

Presented in Partnership with PPC

Expert coverage of tax and accounting issues from Thomson Reuters

For more than 70 years, RIA has delivered accurate, insightful and accessible research and productivity-enhancing solutions to tax, accounting and corporate finance professionals.

Visit ria.thomson.com to learn more about additional products available such as the 2011 RIA FEDERAL TAX HANDBOOK, the premier source for today's federal tax law.

Rely on RIA's must-have Federal Tax Review

RIA Federal Tax Review Course 2011

The RIA *Federal Tax Review 2011* CPE Course is comprised of three modules: Individual Taxes (9 CPE), Business Taxes (10 CPE), and Special Situations (9 CPE). A general refresher in federal taxation, this course will reinforce basic tax law interpretations to keep you up to date on the latest and most important changes for both the 2010 and 2011 tax years.

Grading fee of $95 for each module, with discounts available if you complete two or all three modules—see website for details.

Immediate RIA course access plus Online Grading

Download PDF version of this course at no charge!

At cl.thomsonreuters.com, click on the Course Finder tab and search for RIA courses.

Online Grading for immediate results!

The Checkpoint Learning Online Grading Center provides convenient access to self-study course exams, with real-time test results as soon as you complete your courses. Print CPE certificates with a simple mouse click—the Online Grading Center retains all of your certificates and exam results for retrieval at any time!

For more CPE information and to access the PDF download of this course or the online grading tool for this course, visit cl.thomsonreuters.com.

RBBI010

TAX & ACCOUNTING

THOMSON REUTERS

CPE & Training Solutions *Powered by Checkpoint Learning!*

800.231.1860 | cl.thomsonreuters.com

ONLINE LEARNING

Checkpoint Learning *New!*
With the combined power of MicroMash, PASS Online, PPC and Reqwired, we are pleased to introduce you to the next level in online learning! Checkpoint Learning provides reporting, learning reminders and prompts, CPE compliance tracking, and much more—including the ability to purchase and complete hundreds of courses directly from Checkpoint Learning.

MicroMash
A trusted provider of technology-based CPE and training for over 20 years. Choose from over 130 courses on hot topics that will help you stay on top of your field—now available through Checkpoint Learning!

PASS Online
A CPE provider since 1990, PASS Online offers more than 180 electronic courses covering a variety of accounting and tax topics, including industry-leading state ethics training courses for accountants. Now available through Checkpoint Learning!

Reqwired
Online CPE tracking for CPAs, customized learning plans for staff and accountants, self-service tools, and more! Call 800.800.0064 for more information.

LIVE SEMINARS & CONFERENCES

Gear Up Live Seminars & Conferences
A leading provider of tax and accounting education for 39 years, with nationwide seminars and exciting conferences! Week-long conferences take place throughout the year in Chicago, Las Vegas, and Orlando.

PPC and AuditWatch Conferences
PPC and AuditWatch offer in-depth learning at conferences created to meet the needs of professionals nationwide, and combines nationally recognized speakers, cutting-edge content, and outstanding accommodations.

AuditWatch Live Seminars
AuditWatch offers specialized auditing seminars in locations nationwide, including AuditWatch University, AuditWatch University Yellow Book, and TaxWatch University.

IN-HOUSE TRAINING

PPC In-House Seminars
PPC offers on-site customized training on over 50 topics related to accounting and tax professions. This learning experience is custom-tailored to meet your needs, taught by highly rated instructors, and features current, relevant course content. For more information call 800.387.1120.

Practitioners Monthly Video Digest
A convenient and cost-effective way for firms to provide timely, leading-edge in-house training. Every month (excluding February and March) your firm will receive a training module that contains a high-quality instructional DVD and related course materials including an instructor's guide and participant materials.

Webinar Learning Network
You'll find webinars (with live streaming video) on the latest developments in tax, accounting, auditing, finance and more!

AuditWatch
AuditWatch has an intense focus on serving the audit and accounting profession with leading experts to train and consult with firms that provide auditing services. Call 800.775.9866 for more information.

SELF-STUDY COURSES

Gear Up Self-Study
Gear Up offers standalone and seminar-based self-study courses in a variety of formats.

PPC Self-Study
Learn with the company that provides the industry-leading PPC Guides—convenient self-study courses are available on a variety of accounting & auditing and tax topics.

Quickfinder | Gear Up Self-Study CPE
Quickfinder's trusted content combined with Gear Up's 39-year history as a leader in tax & accounting professional education—a winning combination for your training needs!

RIA Self-Study CPE
See reverse for more information on RIA's Federal Tax Review 2011 CPE Course. Download PDF at no cost from Checkpoint Learning!

For more CPE information on all of these solutions and products, visit cl.thomsonreuters.com.

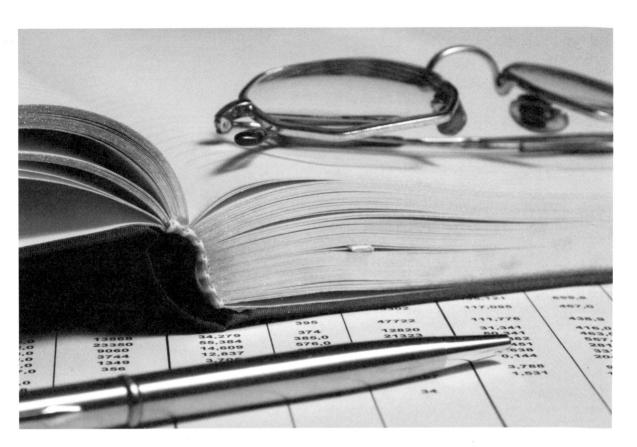

MAKE YOUR FEDERAL TAX
HANDBOOK WORK FOR YOU.

RIA Federal Tax Handbook **RIA**

2011 RIA Federal Tax Handbook

The 2011 edition of the RIA Federal Tax Handbook is designed to answer the tax questions and resolve the tax problems that arise in everyday business and personal transactions. It helps in preparing 2010 federal income tax returns, and provides specific guidance to tax consequences of transactions occurring in 2011. It is prepared by the professional staff that prepares the comprehensive federal tax service, RIA's Federal Tax Coordinator 2d, and the complete income tax service, RIA's Analysis of Federal Taxes: Income, and is derived from these tax services and RIA's Tax Desk and Tax Guide.

The 2011 RIA Federal Tax Handbook reflects federal tax legislation to the date of print publication. It also reflects other key developments (such as new regulations, rulings and revenue procedures) affecting the 2010 return and the 2011 tax year.

caution: After we go to print with the 2011 Edition of the RIA Federal Tax Handbook, Congress may enact legislation modifying or deferring the EGTRRA sunset rules (¶1114) and extending expired tax provisions. For highlights of later-enacted tax laws that affect the 2011 edition, consult the homepage dedicated to users of the RIA Federal Tax Handbook (http://www.ria.thomsonreuters.com/federaltaxhandbook).

The Handbook discusses and explains the common tax problems in clear, concise, nontechnical language. And, where appropriate, the Handbook includes:

illustration: To clarify the tax rules and problems discussed, with simple easy-to-follow illustrations.

caution: To warn of dangers that arise in particular tax situations and, where appropriate, to indicate what should be done.

recommendation: To provide specific, carefully studied guides to action which will keep taxes at a legal minimum.

observation: For professional analysis or commentary that is not part of cited authorities.

Forms to use: The Handbook explains which IRS forms to use to report transactions, pay taxes, make elections, etc. For a complete list of all official forms discussed, with references to the paragraph where they are discussed, see the "Forms" entry in the Topic Index.

References: The Handbook uses the following references:

. . . "Code Sec." references are to sections of the Internal Revenue Code.

. . . "Reg § " references are to sections of the federal tax regulations. "Prop Reg § " references are to proposed regulations, which are only cited in the text where IRS has indicated that "Taxpayers may rely" on them.

. . . Footnote references beginning with a single letter are to paragraphs in RIA's Federal Tax Coordinator 2d and RIA's Analysis of Federal Taxes: Income. However, RIA's Analysis of Federal Taxes: Income doesn't include coverage of estate, gift and excise taxes. Accordingly, references to ¶Q-1000 *et seq.* (gift tax), ¶R-1000 *et seq.* (estate tax), and ¶W-1000 *et seq.* (excise taxes) are only to paragraphs in RIA's Federal Tax Coordinator 2d. References beginning with numbers are to paragraphs in RIA's United States Tax Reporter. References beginning with the letters "TD" are to paragraphs in RIA's Tax Desk.

¶101. Highlights of the 2011 Edition.

The 2011 RIA Federal Tax Handbook reflects federal tax legislation to the date of publication, including the Worker, Homeownership, and Business Assistance Act of 2009 (WHBAA, P.L. 111-92, 11/6/2009); the Hiring Incentives to Restore Employment Act (HIRE Act, P.L. 111-147, 3/18/2010); the Patient Protection and Affordable Care Act (2010 Health Care Act, P.L. 111-148, 3/23/2010); the Health Care and Education Reconciliation Act of 2010 (Reconciliation Act, P.L. 111-152, 3/30/2010); the Continuing Extension Act of 2010 (P.L. 111–157); the Education Jobs and Medicaid Assistance Act (PL 111-226, 8/10/2010); the 2010 Firearms Excise Tax Act; the 2010 Aviation Extension Act (PL 111-216, 8/1/2010); the Homebuyer Assistance and Improvement Act (PL 111-198, 7/2/2010); the Preservation of Access to Care for Medicare Beneficiaries and Pension Relief Act of 2010 (PL 111-192, 6/25/2010); and the Small Business Jobs Act of 2010 (P.L. 111-240, 9/27/2010). The Handbook also reflects other key developments (such as new regulations, rulings and revenue procedures) affecting the 2010 return and the 2011 tax year.

What's new in the 2011 Edition. The 2011 RIA Federal Tax Handbook reflects the new tax developments listed below. *Note that provisions of the health care reform legislation affecting 2012 through 2018 are summarized at ¶ 101.1, at the end of this list of new developments.*

- "What's new on the 2010 IRS Form 1040." (¶105)
- 2010 income tax rate brackets for individuals and estates and trusts. (¶1100 *et seq.*)
- 2010 and 2011 wage bases and rates for Social Security and Medicare taxes, for employers, employees and self-employed taxpayers. (¶1107 *et seq.*)
- If state law extends full community property treatment to registered domestic partners, each reports half of the community property on the federal income tax return. (¶1203)
- A Medicare Part D coverage gap ("donut hole") rebate is not taxable. (¶1206)
- A Smart Grid Investment Grant made to a corporation is a nontaxable, nonshareholder contribution to capital if the corporation properly reduces the basis of its property. (¶1206)
- The maximum fair market value (FMV) for 2010 for which the fleet-average valuation method can be used is $20,300 for a passenger auto and $21,000 for a truck or van. (¶1235)
- The maximum FMV for 2010 for which the cents-per-mile valuation method can be used is $15,300 for a passenger auto and $16,000 for a truck or van. (¶1238)
- Low value clothing bearing the employer's name and which must be worn by the employee is a de minimis fringe benefit. (¶1248)
- For 2010, an employee may exclude up to $230 a month of qualified parking, and up to $230 for employer-provided transit and vanpooling benefits. (¶1249)
- For 2010, the maximum exclusion for employer-provided adoption assistance is $13,170 per child (for both non-special needs and special needs adoptions); for 2011, it's $13,360. The phaseout ranges based on adjusted gross income (AGI) increase. (¶1256)
- Effective Mar. 30, 2010, the exclusion for employer reimbursement of employee medical care also applies to any child of an employee who hasn't attained age 27 as of the end of the year. (¶1257)
- A delay or acceleration in the payment of nonqualified deferred compensation to comply with a Troubled Asset Relief Program (TARP) advisory opinion won't violate Code Sec. 409A; neither will certain document failures. (¶1277)
- For amounts received in tax years beginning after Dec. 31, 2010, taxpayers may partially annuitize a nonqualified annuity, endowment, or life insurance contract. (¶1367)
- Higher 2010 and 2011 limits apply for the exclusion of benefits from long-term care insurance. (¶1381)
- After 2010, medicine or drugs are qualified medical expenses for Archer MSA (¶1382), HSA (¶1383) and HRA (¶1384) purposes only if prescribed (whether or not over-the-counter) or if insulin.
- After 2010, premature distributions from an Archer MSA (¶1382) or HSA (¶1383) that aren't used to pay for qualified medical expenses are subject to a 20% additional tax.

- For amounts received in tax years beginning after 2008, there's an exclusion for any State loan repayment or loan forgiveness program intended to provide for the increased availability of health care services in underserved or health professional shortage areas (as determined by the State). (¶1392)
- Temporary regs on the deferral and ratable exclusion for debt instruments reacquired in 2009 and 2010 explain the acceleration rule for entities. (¶1399)
- Start-up cost deduction increased to $10,000 (with $60,000 phaseout threshold) only for 2010. (¶1501)
- Inflation-indexed definition of a high deductible health plan and limit on contributions for 2010 and 2011 for MSA (¶1528) and HSA (¶1529) purposes are provided.
- The up-to-15-month 65% federal COBRA subsidy is extended for involuntary terminations through May 31, 2010. (¶1531)
- For the first plan year beginning on or after Sept. 23, 2010, group health plans and health insurance issuers providing dependent coverage of children generally must continue to provide dependent coverage of children to an adult child until age 26. (¶1532)
- Self-employed individual's health insurance deduction also applies, effective Mar. 30, 2010, to any child of the taxpayer who has not attained age 27 as of the end of the year. (¶1533)
- Final regs explain deduction of travel expenses by state legislators. (¶1544)
- The standard mileage rate for business travel is 50 cents per mile. (¶1561)
- The simplified (high-low) per diem rates for 2010 are reflected. (¶1576)
- The optional meal or incidental expenses allowances for 2010 are reflected. (¶1582)
- For the moving expense deduction, a taxpayer using his own car to travel to the new location may deduct 16.5 cents per mile for 2010. (¶1647)
- IRS extends temporary suspension of applicable high yield discount obligation (AHYDO) rules. (¶1753)
- IRS approves worthless stock deduction on merger of subsidiary into parent. (¶1782)
- IRS provides safe harbor for casualty loss deduction of corrosive drywall. (¶1796)
- Passive activity loss (PAL) activity groupings and regroupings must be reported to IRS. (¶1825)
- IRS acquiesces in decision holding limited liability company (LLC) interest not equivalent to a limited partnership interest for passive activity loss (PAL) purposes. (¶1830)
- Former closely held C corporation could carry back NOLs against prior portfolio income. (¶1841)
- Property held primarily for sale wasn't depreciable even if sometimes rented to others before sale. (¶1902)
- Support vessels used in offshore oil and gas operations are five-year MACRS property whether or not used in connection with drilling. (¶1914)
- Street light assets of an electric utility are seven-year property. (¶1915)
- Permanently anchored mobile homes were 27.5-year residential rental property. (¶1919)
- 50% bonus depreciation is extended to apply to property placed in service before 2011 (2012 for certain long-production-period property and aircraft). (¶1933)
- Code Sec. 179 expensing limit is set at $500,000, and the investment-based phase-out level for the expensing is set at $2,000,000 for tax years beginning in 2010 and 2011. (¶1941)
- Right to revoke or alter a Code Sec. 179 expensing election without IRS consent is extended to cover tax years beginning in 2011. (¶1941)
- Eligibility of off-the-shelf computer software for Code Sec. 179 expensing is extended to cover tax years beginning in 2011. (¶1946)
- Up to $250,000 of certain qualified real property is eligible for Code Sec. 179 expensing

for tax years beginning in 2010 and 2011. (¶1946)

- Clearly marked public safety officer vehicles are added to the list of vehicles treated as qualified nonpersonal use vehicles. (¶1949)

- Cellular telephones and similar telecommunications equipment aren't "listed property" for tax years beginning after Dec. 31, 2009. (¶1949)

- Autos, trucks and vans placed in service in 2010 are subject to revised auto depreciation and expensing dollar caps. (¶1954)

- Autos, trucks and vans leased in 2010 are subject to revised income inclusion amounts. (¶1959)

- Facilities using a dry mill process to produce ethanol from corn can qualify for expensing as qualified refinery property. (¶1968)

- Covenant not to compete agreed to by the seller in connection with a corporation's repurchase of 23% of its stock was a section 197 intangible. (¶1977)

- Costs of creating, as opposed to acquiring, customer relationships weren't section 197 intangibles. (¶1978)

- Designation as an American viticultural area was a section 197 intangible. (¶1978)

- Deductible amounts for insubstantial benefit to donors of charitable contributions increase. (¶2104)

- Taxpayer opting to have his credit card rebate paid to charity has charitable deduction. (¶2106)

- Special rules for deducting donations to aid Haiti earthquake victims (¶2133)

- Sex-change costs qualify as medical expense, except for breast augmentation undertaken for cosmetic reasons. (¶2145)

- Cost of service animal used in mental health therapy qualifies as medical expense (¶2145)

- In vitro fertilization costs for taxpayer who was not infertile do not qualify as medical expense (¶2145)

- Maximum premiums paid for a qualified long-term care insurance contract, deductible as medical expense, increase. (¶2146)

- Mileage rate for use of a car for qualified medical transportation set at 16.5 cents for 2010. (¶2149)

- Workers must file Schedule M to claim Making Work Pay Credit for 2010 even if they received the credit through reduced withholding during the year. (¶2343)

- For 2010, the maximum earned income credit amount increases. (¶2344)

- The earned income credit advance payment option isn't available after 2010. (¶2349)

- Starting in 2010, the adoption expense credit is refundable. The maximum credit for the adoption of a child (including a special-needs child) increases for 2010 and 2011, as does the AGI-based phaseout thresholds. (¶2359)

- The credits for advanced lean burn technology and hybrid motor vehicles are reduced for Volkswagens sold after June 30, 2010. (¶2366)

- New qualified plug-in electric drive motor vehicle credit is claimed on Form 8936, qualified electric vehicle credit on Form 8834. (¶2367)

- The first-time homebuyer credit (FTHBC) is extended to apply to a principal residence purchased (a) before May 1, 2010, and (b) before Oct. 1, 2010 by a taxpayer who entered into a written binding contract before May 1, 2010, to close on the purchase of the principal residence before July 1, 2010. (¶2369)

- Liberalized FTHBC rules apply for service members on qualified official extended duty. (¶2370)

- For purchases after Nov. 6, 2009, (1) the FTHBC phases out for individual taxpayers with modified AGI between $125,000 and $145,000 ($225,000 and $245,000 for joint filers) for the year of purchase; (2) an individual (and, if married, his spouse) who has maintained the same principal residence for any 5-consecutive year period during the 8-year period ending on the date he purchases a later principal residence is treated as a first-time homebuyer for the later residence (the maximum allowable FTHBC for such purchasers is $6,500 ($3,250 for marrieds filing separately)); (3) the FTHBC can't be claimed for buying a residence if its purchase price exceeds $800,000; and (4) the FTHBC isn't allowed if the taxpayer can't be claimed as a dependent by another taxpayer for the tax year of purchase, or if the taxpayer (or his spouse, if married) hasn't attained age 18 as of the purchase date. (¶2369)

- The AGI amounts used in computing the "saver's" credit for elective deferrals and IRA contributions are increased for 2010 and 2011. (¶2371)

- For bonds issued after Mar. 18, 2010, issuers of certain tax credit bonds can elect to receive a refundable credit from IRS in lieu of any tax credit otherwise allowable to the bond holder. (¶2374)

- For credits determined in tax years starting in 2010, eligible small business (ESB) credits can offset the alternative minimum tax. (¶2303)

- A five-year carryback is allowed for ESB credits. (¶2304)

- Employers can claim an up-to-$1,000 increase to the general business credit for certain retained workers hired after Mar. 8, 2010. (¶2317)

- Eligible small employers can claim a general business credit equal to a percentage of nonelective contributions used to buy health insurance for their employees. (¶2334)

- Foreign tax credit is suspended until the underlying foreign income is taken into account for U.S. tax purposes. (¶2377)

- Foreign tax credit is eliminated for foreign taxes attributable to basis differences in certain basis step-up acquisitions. (¶2377)

- Separate application of foreign tax credit limitation for items resourced under a treaty. (¶2381)

- Limitation imposed on foreign income taxes deemed paid with respect to Code Sec. 956 inclusions to the amount that an actual dividend would carry up the corporate chain. (¶2384)

- Swap of emissions credits may qualify for tax deferral as like-kind exchange. (¶2419)

- Safe harbor method available where time limits for deferred like-kind exchange not met because of default by qualified intermediary. (¶2423)

- Depreciation part of standard mileage rate increases to $.23 in 2010 from $.21 in 2009. (¶2476)

- Basis of shares in dividend reinvestment plan purchased after 2010 is determined in accordance with rules for sales of shares in mutual funds, see ¶2498. (¶2494)

- Double-category method of determining average basis of shares sold in mutual fund not allowed for sales after Mar. 31. 2011. (¶2498)

- All of gain can be excluded on sale of qualified small business stock held more than five years that was acquired after Sep. 27, 2010 and before 2011. (¶2648)

- Taxpayer's foreign currency call option wasn't a Code Sec. 1256 foreign currency contract. (¶2657)

- For tax years beginning after July 21, 2010, Code Sec. 1256 contracts do not include interest rate swaps, currency swaps, basis swaps, interest rate caps, interest rate floors, etc. (¶2657)

- IRS revised change in accounting method request Form 3115. (¶2840)

- In applying the percentage of completion method, 50% bonus depreciation in 2010 isn't taken into account. (¶2852)

- Income thresholds for exemption from withholding for employees who are dependents are not changed for 2010 and 2011. (¶3017)

- W-2 form to include information on value of health insurance provided to employee; but such reporting is optional for 2011. (¶3021)

- Qualified employers are exempted from paying the employer 6.2% share of Social Security (OASDI) employment taxes on wages paid in 2010 to a newly hired qualified individual who begins work after Feb. 3, 2010 and before Jan. 1, 2011. (¶3025)
- New Form W-11 has been issued for Social Security payroll tax holiday for new hires. (¶3025)
- Threshold amount for cash payments to domestic service employees (e.g., nannies) to be subject to FICA remains at $1,700 in 2011. (¶3031)
- The standard deduction amounts are listed. (¶3112)
- For 2010, the phaseout of itemized deductions for high income individuals doesn't apply. (¶3114)
- For 2010, the personal exemption amount is $3,650 ($3700 for 2011). (¶3115) The phaseout for high income individuals doesn't apply.
- Under the kiddie tax, the parents' highest tax rate applies to a child's unearned income over $1,900 for 2010 and 2011. (¶3135)
- For 2010, the income tax deduction allowed to self-employed individuals for health insurance costs is also allowed in computing self-employment tax. (¶3143)
- For 2011, the dollar thresholds for the optional methods of computing net earnings from self-employment remain the same as for 2010, $4,480 and $6,720. (¶3149)
- Additional payment options (Debit card, Electronic Fund Withdrawal (EFT)) are available for estimated tax. (¶3151)
- An alternative tax net operating loss (ATNOL) deduction attributable to an NOL for a tax year beginning in 2008 or 2009, for which the taxpayer has made a Code Sec. 172(b)(1)(H) increased carryback period election, can offset up to 100% (instead of 90%) of alternative minimum taxable income (AMTI). (¶3212)
- Certain stock distributions from publicly traded REITs and RICs declared no later than 12/31/2012 for tax years ending on or before 12/31/2011, will be treated as dividend distributions. (¶3335)
- Final regs on AMT and apportionment for controlled and consolidated groups. (¶3341)
- Court ruled that IRS can recharacterize dividends paid to S corporation shareholder/employee as additional compensation subject to employment taxes. (¶3370)
- E&P of foreign acquiring corporation in Code Sec. 304 related party redemption is ignored if more than 50% of the dividends would not be subject to U.S. tax and not included in the CFC's E&P. (¶3533)
- Modified regs recharacterize parties to a Code Sec. 304 transaction when there is a principal purpose to avoid application of Code Sec. 304 to a particular corporation. (¶3533)
- IRS finalizes regs on D reorganizations without distributions ("all-boot reorgs") including deemed issuances. (¶3547)
- Prepaid income is not built-in gain under final regs on corporate ownership changes. (¶3567)
- Long-term tax exempt rates for Code Sec. 382 limitation updated. (¶3569)
- Married couples conducting qualified joint ventures can elect to avoid partnership treatment and report their income on separate Schedule Cs instead. Real estate rental income will not be self-employment income. (¶3701)
- Anti-abuse rules for allocations related to property contributed by a partner to a partnership are tightened by final regs. (¶3752).
- Effective Mar. 18, 2010, there is a rebuttable presumption that a foreign trust has U.S. beneficiaries, unless the transferor demonstrates otherwise to IRS's satisfaction. (¶3962)
- Effective Mar. 18, 2010, a loan of cash or marketable securities (or the use of any other trust property) to or by any U.S. person will cause a foreign trust to be treated as having a U.S. beneficiary, unless the U.S. person repays the loan at a market rate of interest (or pays the fair market value of the use of the property) within a reasonable period of time. (¶3962)

- For 2010 and 2011, the limit on 401(k) plan elective deferrals is $16,500. (¶4317)
- For 2010 and 2011, compensation for "highly compensated employee" status is $110,000. (¶4327)
- For 2010 and 2011, the limit on annual additions to a defined compensation plan is $49,000. (¶4328)
- For 2010 and 2011, the maximum annual benefit from a defined benefit plan is $195,000. (¶4317)
- For 2008 to 2011 plan years, sponsors may elect extended (nine-year or 15-year) amortization periods for their defined benefit plans' shortfall amortization bases. (¶4331)
- U.S. beneficiaries of foreign trusts are subject to additional income inclusion rules after Mar. 18, 2010. (¶4620)
- Dividend equivalent payments by domestic corporations are treated as U.S. source income on or after Sept 14, 2010. (¶4648)
- Withholding is required on post-2012 payments to foreign financial institutions and other foreign entities unless steps are taken to prevent U.S. persons from using foreign accounts to avoid U.S. taxes. (¶4672)
- Individuals must disclose interests in specified foreign financial assets over $50,000 in tax years beginning after Mar. 18. 2010. (¶4673)
- Individual return filing thresholds are increased. (¶4701)
- Beginning with the 2010 tax year, domestic corporations and foreign corporations with both uncertain tax positions and at least $100 million of assets have to file Schedule UTP if they or a related party have issued audited financial statements. (¶4726)
- Use of paper federal tax deposit (FTD) coupons are to be eliminated after 2010. (¶4730)
- Income tax return filing threshold for a bankruptcy estate of an individual is increased for 2011. (¶4736)
- Information reporting will be required for a trade or business payor of $600 or more to a payee for property or services after 2011. (¶4743)
- Information reporting will be required for payments of $600 or more for property or services to a non-tax-exempt corporation after 2011. (¶4743)
- After 2010, preparers who aren't CPAs (or LPAs in certain states as listed on irs.gov), attorneys, or enrolled agents have to satisfy competency testing requirements, continuing education requirements, and standards of conduct set by Circular 230. (¶4750)
- In 2009, IRS audited 1% of individual returns filed. (¶4803)
- The name of IRS's Large and Mid-Size Business Division (LMSB) was changed effective Oct. 1, 2010 to the Large Business and International Division (LB&I). (¶4806)
- The First Circuit holds tax accrual workpapers aren't protected by the work product privilege. (¶4810)
- For restitution ordered by a court after Aug. 26, 2010, IRS can assess and collect restitution for unpaid taxes owed by defendants in criminal cases as if it were a tax. Court-ordered restitution can be assessed, or a court proceeding for the amount can be begun without assessment, at any time. (¶4829)
- For returns filed after Mar. 18, 2010 and for any other return for which the assessment period has not yet expired as of Mar. 18, 2010, a six-year limitations period applies for assessment of tax on understatements of income attributable to foreign financial assets. (¶4834)
- For returns filed after Mar. 18, 2010 and for any other return for which the assessment period has not yet expired as of Mar. 18, 2010, certain information reporting requirements with regard to passive foreign investment companies and specified foreign financial assets are added to the rule suspending the three-year assessment limitations period until required information is furnished to IRS and the suspension rule is modified so that, if the failure is due to reasonable cause and not willful neglect, the rule applies only to items related to that failure. (¶4837)

- For refunds of withheld taxes for: (1) returns due after Mar. 18, 2010, (2) claims for refund filed after Mar. 18, 2010, and (3) IRS initiated adjustments if the refunds are paid after Mar. 18, 2010, the grace period during which the government isn't required to pay interest on overpayments is increased from 45 days to 180 days for overpayments resulting from excess amounts deducted and withheld under provisions relating to withholding on nonresident aliens and foreign corporations and withholding to enforce reporting on certain foreign accounts. (¶4855)
- Overpayment (¶4855) and underpayment (¶4867) interest rates for the last three quarters of 2009 are extended without change to Dec. 31, 2010.
- Regs explain the denial, with respect to listed and undisclosed reportable transactions, of the suspension of interest and penalties that generally applies where IRS fails to notify individual taxpayers of liability within 36 months after the return is filed (or after the due date if that is later). (¶4872)
- For tax years beginning after Mar. 18, 2010, a 40% penalty is imposed on any under-statement attributable to an undisclosed foreign financial asset. (¶4880)
- For transactions entered into after Mar. 30, 2010, the reasonable basis exception to the erroneous refund penalty doesn't apply to transactions lacking economic substance. (¶4885)
- The amount of the penalty for failure to report reportable transactions was retroactively reduced for penalties assessed after 2006. The amount is 75% of the decrease in tax shown on the return resulting from the transaction (or which would have resulted if the transaction were respected) subject to a maximum of $10,000 for natural persons and $50,000 for others (increased to $100,000 and $200,000 respectively if a listed transaction is involved). (¶4892)
- For underpayments due to transactions entered into after Mar. 30, 2010, the reasonable cause exception doesn't apply to any part of a reportable transaction understatement which is attributable to a transaction that lacks economic substance and the penalty itself doesn't apply to any part of an understatement on which the 40% penalty for transactions that lack economic substance is imposed. (¶4893)
- For underpayments due to transactions entered into after Mar. 30, 2010, a 20% penalty applies to any disallowance of claimed tax benefits because of a transaction lacking economic substance. (¶4896)
- For returns due after Mar. 18, 2010, failures by financial institutions to file certain returns on magnetic media can trigger a penalty without regard to the number of returns involved. (¶4897)
- For information returns required to be filed after 2010, the penalties for failure to furnish information returns and payee statements are increased. (¶4897)
- For instruments tendered after July 2, 2010, the bad check penalty applies to electronic payments. (¶4898)
- There is no estate tax for 2010 but under the EGTRRA sunset rule (¶1114) the estate tax returns in 2011 with harsher terms. (¶5000)
- Gross-up rule reaches deemed gifts under Code Sec. 2519 but not gifts by nonresident aliens. (¶5004)
- Transfers to family limited partnerships held not to be includible in transferor's estate. (¶5007)
- Deduction for state death taxes sunsets in 2011 under the EGTRRA sunset rule. (¶5007)
- Rules for qualified conservation easements would be changed for estates of individuals dying after 2010 if the EGTRRA sunset rule kicks in. (¶5027)
- For 2011, the potential saving from estate-tax special use valuation is increased as a result of indexing. (¶5028)
- For estates of decedents dying in 2011, the unified credit exempts $1 million from estate tax. (¶5029)
- For estates of decedents dying in 2011, an estate tax return need 'be filed only if the decedent's gross estate exceeds $1 million. (¶5033)

- Annual per-donee gift tax exclusion is $13,000 for 2010 and 2011. (¶5037)

- For 2011, $136,00 ($134,000 for 2010) may be transferred to a noncitizen spouse free of gift tax. (¶5046)

- The GST tax does not apply for estates of decedents dying in 2010 but there is uncertainty over how it will apply after 2010. (¶5055)

¶ 101.1.Timeline of post-2011 tax changes in health care reform legislation

In March of 2010, Congress passed and the President signed into law legislation that overhauls the U.S. health care system and affects nearly all taxpayers, many employers, and many elements of the health care industry (the Patient Protection and Affordable Care Act, P.L. 111-148, 3/23/2010, and the Health Care and Education Reconciliation Act of 2010, P.L 111-152, 3/30/2010). This massive overhaul contains a host of tax changes, many of which are both complex and novel. To compound the challenge, the tax changes go into effect over an unusually long number of years.

Tax changes in the health care overhaul legislation that are effective in 2011 or earlier tax years are reflected in place in the 2011 edition of RIA's Federal Tax Handbook. Tax changes in the health care overhaul legislation that are slated to go into effect in 2012 through 2018 are highlighted in this paragraph.

caution: Congress may tinker further with rules introduced by the health care overhaul legislation, and IRS guidance may defer deadlines.

TAX CHANGES TAKING EFFECT IN 2012

Information reporting expanded. For payments made after Dec. 31, 2011, businesses that pay any amount greater than $600 during the year to providers (including non-tax-exempt corporate providers) of property and services will have to file an information report with each provider and with IRS. (Code Sec. 6040(a), Code Sec. 6041(h))

TAX CHANGES TAKING EFFECT IN 2013

Increased HI tax for high-earning workers and self-employed taxpayers. For tax years beginning after 2012, an additional 0.9% hospital insurance (HI) tax applies under Code Sec. 3101(b)(2) to wages received with respect to employment in excess of: $250,000 for joint returns; $125,000 for married taxpayers filing a separate return; and $200,000 in all other cases. Under Code Sec. 1401(b)(2), the additional 0.9% HI tax also applies to self-employment income for the tax year in excess of the above figures. (Code Sec. 6051(a)(14))

Surtax on unearned income of higher-income individuals. For tax years beginning after Dec. 31, 2012, an unearned income Medicare contribution tax is imposed on individuals, estates, and trusts. (Code Sec. 1411) For an individual, the tax is 3.8% of the lesser of either (1) net investment income or (2) the excess of modified adjusted gross income over the threshold amount ($250,000 for a joint return or surviving spouse, $125,000 for a married individual filing a separate return, and $200,000 for all others). For surtax purposes, gross income doesn't include excluded items, such as interest on tax-exempt bonds, veterans' benefits, and excluded gain from the sale of a principal residence.

Higher threshold for deducting medical expenses. For tax years beginning after Dec. 31, 2012, unreimbursed medical expenses will be deductible by taxpayers under age 65 only to the extent they exceed 10% of adjusted gross income (AGI) for the tax year. (Code Sec. 213(a)) If the taxpayer or his or her spouse has reached age 65 before the close of the tax year, a 7.5% floor applies through 2016 and a 10% floor applies for tax years ending after Dec. 31, 2016. (Code Sec. 213(f))

Dollar cap on contributions to health FSAs. For tax years beginning after Dec. 31, 2012, for a health FSA to be a qualified benefit under a cafeteria plan, the maximum amount available for reimbursement of incurred medical expenses of an employee (and dependents and other eligible beneficiaries) under the health FSA for a plan year (or other 12-month coverage period) can't exceed $2,500. (Code Sec. 125(i)) (Code Sec. 213(f))

Deduction eliminated for retiree drug coverage. Sponsors of qualified retiree prescription drug plans are eligible for subsidy payments from the Secretary of Health and Human Services (HHS) for a portion of each qualified covered retiree's gross covered prescription drug costs ("qualified retiree prescription drug plan subsidy"). These qualified retiree prescription drug plan subsidies are excludable from the taxpayer's (plan sponsor's) gross income for regular income tax and alternative minimum tax (AMT) purposes. For tax years beginning before 2013, a taxpayer may claim a business deduction for covered retiree prescription drug expenses, even though it excludes qualified retiree prescription drug plan subsidies allocable to those expenses. But for tax years beginning after Dec. 31, 2012, under Code Sec. 139A, the amount otherwise allowable as a deduction for retiree prescription drug expenses will be reduced by the amount of the excludable subsidy payments received.

Fee on health plans. For each policy year ending after Sept. 30, 2012, each specified health insurance policy and each applicable self-insured health plan will have to pay a fee equal to the product of $2 ($1 for policy years ending during 2013) multiplied by the average number of lives covered under the policy. The issuer of the health insurance policy or the self-insured health plan sponsor is liable for and must pay the fee. (Code Sec. 4375, Code Sec. 4376, and Code Sec. 4377)

$500,000 compensation deduction limit for health insurance issuers. For tax years beginning after Dec. 31, 2012, for services performed during that year, a covered health insurance provider isn't allowed a compensation deduction for an "applicable individual" (officers, employees, directors, and other workers or service providers such as consultants) in excess of $500,000. (Code Sec. 162(m)(6)(A)) A complex rule may reach compensation attributable to services performed in a tax year beginning after Dec. 31, 2009.

Excise tax on medical device manufacturers. For sales after Dec. 31, 2012, a 2.3% excise tax applies under Code Sec. 4191 to sales of taxable medical devices intended for humans. The excise tax, paid by the manufacturer, producer, or importer of the device, won't apply to eyeglasses, contact lenses, hearing aids, and any other medical device determined by IRS to be of a type that is generally purchased by the general public at retail for individual use.

TAX CHANGES TAKING EFFECT IN 2014

Larger employers not offering affordable health insurance coverage must pay penalty. Under Code Sec. 4980H, for months beginning after Dec. 31, 2013, a large employer (generally, one with at least 50 full-time employees) that (1) doesn't offer health care coverage for all its full-time employees, (2) offers minimum essential coverage that is unaffordable (coverage with a premium required to be paid by the employee that is more than 9.5% of the employee's household income, as defined for purposes of certain premium tax credit rules), or (3) offers minimum essential coverage that consists of a plan under which the plan's share of the total allowed cost of benefits is less than 60%, must pay a penalty if any full-time employee is certified to the employer as having purchased health insurance through a state exchange with respect to which a tax credit or cost-sharing reduction is allowed or paid to the employee.

Individuals not carrying health insurance face a penalty. For tax years beginning after Dec. 31, 2013, nonexempt U.S. citizens and legal residents must pay a penalty if they do not maintain minimum essential coverage, which includes government sponsored programs (e.g., Medicare, Medicaid, Children's Health Insurance Program), eligible employer-sponsored plans, plans in the individual market, certain grandfathered group health plans and other coverage as recognized by HHS in coordination with IRS. (Code Sec. 5000A) There are a number of exceptions, such as one for certain lower-income individuals.

Some employers must offer "free choice" vouchers for basic coverage. Effective for periods after Dec. 31, 2013, employers offering minimum essential coverage through an eligible employer-sponsored plan and paying a portion of that coverage must provide qualified employees with a "free choice" voucher whose value can be applied to purchase of a health plan through an Insurance Exchange. (Code Sec. 139D) The employer treats the free choice voucher as an amount for compensation for personal services actually rendered. (Code Sec. 162(a)) In general, qualified employees are those who do not participate in the employer sponsored plan; whose required contribution for employer sponsored minimum essential coverage (if they did participate in the plan) exceeds 8%, but does not exceed 9.8% of household income; and whose total household income does not exceed 400% of the poverty line for the family.

Refundable tax credit for low- or moderate-income families buying certain health insurance. For tax years ending after Dec. 31, 2013, a new refundable tax credit (the "premium assistance credit") under Code Sec. 36B applies to qualifying taxpayers who get health insurance coverage by enrolling in a qualified health plan through a State-established American Health Benefit Exchange.

"Qualified health plans" may be offered through cafeteria plans by "qualified employers." For tax years beginning after Dec. 31, 2013, a reimbursement (or direct payment) for the premiums for coverage under any "qualified health plan" through a health insurance Exchange is a qualified benefit under a cafeteria plan if the employer is a qualified employer (generally, smaller businesses). (Code Sec. 125(f)(3)(B)) In very broad terms, a qualified health plan is one that meets certain certification requirements, provides "an essential health benefits package," and is offered by an insurer meeting detailed requirements. And a health insurance "Exchange" is a federally supervised marketplace for health insurance policies meeting specific eligibility and benefit criteria, to be made available not later than Jan. 1, 2014, to qualifying individuals and employer groups of graduated sizes.

New information reporting of employer provided health coverage. For periods beginning after Dec. 31, 2013, new information reporting and related statement obligations apply under Code Sec. 6056 for (1) certain applicable large employers required to offer their full-time employees and their dependents the opportunity to enroll in minimum essential coverage under an eligible employer-sponsored plan and (2) offering employers (those offering minimum essential coverage to employees and paying any portion of the such coverage, but only if the required employer contribution of any employee exceeds 8% of the employee's wages).

Excise tax on health insurance providers. For calendar years beginning after Dec. 31, 2013, an annual fee applies to health insurance providers. The aggregate annual flat fee for the industry (e.g., $8 billion for 2014) will be allocated based on a health provider's market share of net premiums written for a U.S. health risk for calendar years beginning after Dec. 31, 2012. The fee will not apply to companies whose net premiums written are $25 million or less. For purposes of the fee, health insurance does not include: coverage only for a specified disease or illness; hospital indemnity or other fixed indemnity insurance; insurance for long-term care; or any Medicare supplemental health insurance. (Sec. 9010 of 111–148, as amended by Sec. 10905 and Sec. 1406 of P.L. 111–152)

Accelerated estimated tax payments for large corporations. The estimated tax payment due for large corporations (assets of at least $1 billion at the end of the previous tax year) in July, August, or September 2014 is increased from 157.75% to 173.50% of the payment otherwise due, and the amount of the next required installment is appropriately reduced. (Sec. 1410 of P.L. 111–152)

TAX CHANGE TAKING EFFECT IN 2018

Excise tax applies to high-cost employer provided health insurance coverage. For tax years beginning after Dec. 31, 2017, a 40% nondeductible excise tax will be levied on insurance companies and plan administrators for employer-sponsored health coverage to the extent that annual premiums exceed $10,200 for single coverage and $27,500 for family coverage. (Code Sec. 4980I) An additional threshold amount of $1,650 for single coverage and $3,450 for family coverage will apply for retired individuals age 55 and older and for plans that cover employees engaged in high risk professions.

¶105. What's New on the 2010 Form 1040?

Here are the changes with the greatest impact on the preparation of 2010 individual returns, cross-referenced to where they are discussed in the Handbook, and referenced to the appropriate lines on the Form 1040 and related Schedules as available in final or draft versions at press-time.

☼caution: A number of provisions that expired at the end of 2009 may be retroactively extended by Congress after we go to press, including the deduction for educator expenses, the deduction for tuition and fees, and the District of Columbia homebuyer credit. Additionally, Congress may enact another AMT patch for 2010 (increasing AMT exemptions and allowing personal credits to offset AMT). Congress may also act to defer or modify the EGTRRA sunset rules, see ¶1114. For highlights of later-enacted tax laws that affect the 2010 return, consult the homepage dedicated to users of the RIA Federal Tax Handbook (http://www.ria.thomsonreuters.com/federaltaxhandbook).

FORM 1040, INDIVIDUAL INCOME TAX RETURN FOR 2010

GROSS INCOME

Line 13. Capital gain or (loss).	As part of the estate tax repeal that applies for individuals dying in 2010, the income tax basis rules for property acquired from a decedent in 2010 are similar to the gift tax carryover basis rules but with many opportunities for heirs to get increases in basis. For example, it is possible to increase the basis of assets received from an individual dying in 2010 by $1.3 million and by an additional $3 million for assets going to a spouse. (¶2522) Under the EGTRRA sunset rule, the step-up in basis rules are slated to return for 2011. (¶2512)
Line 15. IRA distributions.	Required minimum distributions (RMDs) must be made for calendar year 2010. (¶4345)
	For tax years beginning after 2009, the rule that barred taxpayers with more than $100,000 of modified AGI from converting traditional IRAs to Roth IRAs is eliminated. Additionally, married taxpayers filing a separate return may convert amounts in a traditional IRA into a Roth IRA (before 2010 they were barred from doing so). (¶4371)
	The Code Sec. 408(d)(8) rule allowing taxpayers who are age 70 ½ or older to make tax-free distributions to charity from an Individual Retirement Account (IRA) of up to $100,000 per taxpayer, per tax year does not apply for tax years beginning after 2009. (¶4357)
Line 16. Pensions and Annuities.	RMDs must be made for calendar year 2010. (¶4345)
	Rollovers in 2010 from an eligible retirement plan to a Roth IRA are included in gross income ratably over 2011 and 2012, unless the taxpayer elects out of the deferral. (¶4371)
	For distributions made after Sept. 27, 2010, where a plan so allows, participants may transfer an eligible rollover distribution from their 401(k) (or 403(b)) plan to a designated Roth account in the plan. The transfer is included in gross income ratably over 2011 and 2012, unless the taxpayer elects out of the deferral. (¶4375)

Line 19. Unemployment compensation.	All unemployment compensation received by an individual is included in gross income. (¶1283)
Line 21 Other income.	The first time homebuyer tax credit claimed for homes bought after Apr. 8, 2008 and before Jan. 1, 2009, generally must be recaptured in equal installments over a 15-year period that begins in 2010. (¶2369)
Exclusions from income.	For amounts received in tax years beginning after Dec. 31, 2008, individuals may exclude any amount under any State loan repayment or loan forgiveness program intended to provide for the increased availability of health care services in underserved or health professional shortage areas (as determined by the State). (¶1392)
	Effective on Mar. 30, 2010, the general exclusion for reimbursements for medical care expenses under an employer-provided accident or health plan is extended to any child of an employee who hasn't attained age 27 as of the end of the tax year. (¶1257)
	For tax years beginning after Dec. 31, 2009, the maximum exclusion for employer-provided adoption assistance is increased to $13,170 per eligible child. (¶1256)

ADJUSTED GROSS INCOME

Line 23. Educator expenses.	The $250 above-the-line tax deduction under Code Sec. 62(a)(2) for teachers and other school professionals for expenses paid or incurred for books, certain supplies, computer equipment, other equipment, and supplementary materials used by the educator in the classroom does not apply for tax years beginning after 2009. (¶2232)
Line 26. Moving expenses.	The deduction for moving expenses is 16.5¢ per mile for 2010. (¶1647)
Line 32. IRA deduction.	A taxpayer may be able to take an IRA deduction if he was covered by a retirement plan and his 2010 modified AGI is less than $66,000 ($109,000 if married filing jointly or qualifying widow(er)). If the taxpayer's spouse was covered by a retirement plan, but the taxpayer was not, he may be able to take an IRA deduction if his 2010 modified AGI is less than $177,000. (¶4352)
	The extra $3,000 IRA deduction for employees of bankrupt companies does not apply for tax years beginning after 2009. (¶4352)
Line 34. Tuition and fees deduction.	The Code Sec. 222 above-the-line tax deduction for qualified tuition and related expenses does not apply for tax years beginning after 2009. (¶2223)

TAX AND CREDITS

Line 40. Itemized deductions or standard deduction.	For 2010, the standard deduction is $5,700 for single filers and for married persons filing separately, $11,400 for joint filers and qualifying widow(er)s, and $8,400 for heads of household. (¶3112)
	The Code Sec. 63(c)(1)(C) additional standard deduction for State and local real property taxes does not apply for tax years beginning after 2009. (¶3112)

	The Code Sec. 63(c)(1)(D) additional standard deduction for disaster losses does not apply for tax years beginning after 2009. (¶3112)
	For 2010, taxpayers with higher levels of AGI no longer face a reduction in their itemized deductions.(¶3114)
Line 42. Exemptions.	The exemption for 2010 is $3,650. (¶3115) For tax years beginning after 2009, the rules phasing out personal exemptions of higher income taxpayers no longer apply. (¶3117)
Line 45. Alternative minimum tax.	Under Code Sec. 55(d), the AMT exemption amount for 2010 is $33,750 ($45,000 if married filing jointly or a qualifying widow(er); $22,500 if married filing separately). (¶3203) Additionally, under Code Sec. 26(a)(1), many personal nonrefundable credits are allowed only to the extent that their aggregate amount doesn't exceed the excess of: (a) the taxpayer's regular tax liability, over (b) his tentative minimum tax, determined without regard to the AMT tax foreign tax credit. (¶3201)
Line 53 Other credits.	For tax years beginning after Dec. 31, 2009, there's a tax credit for an eligible small employer who makes qualifying contributions to buy health insurance for his employees. (¶2334)
	There's a retention credit equal to the lesser of $1,000, or 6.2% of the wages paid to certain "retained workers." (¶2317)
	For expenses paid or incurred after Dec. 31, 2008, there's a 50% nonrefundable investment tax credit for qualified investments in qualifying therapeutic discovery projects. (¶2314)
	The Code Sec. 1400C District of Columbia first-time homebuyer credit does not apply for homes purchased after 2009. (¶2368)
	Eligible small business credits that are determined in a taxpayer's first tax year beginning in 2010 but are unused are eligible for 5-year carryback. (¶2304)
	Eligible small business credits determined in tax years beginning in 2010 can offset AMT liability and, to an increased extent, regular tax liability for credits determined in tax years beginning after 2009. (¶2303)

OTHER TAXES

Line 56. Self-employment tax.	Maximum amount of self-employment income subject to FICA tax is $106,800; no ceiling on Medicare wage base. (¶1108)
	Health insurance costs for a taxpayer and his family are deductible in computing 2010 self-employment tax. (¶3143)
	An individual may use the farm optional method only if (a) his gross farm income was not more than $6,720 or (b) his net farm profits were less than $4,851. Using this method, farm self-employment earnings equals the smaller of (1) 66 ⅔ % of gross farm income, or (2) $4,480. (¶3149)

An individual may use the nonfarm optional method only if (a) his net nonfarm profits were less than $4,851 and also less than 72.189% of his gross nonfarm income and (b) he had net earnings from self-employment of at least $400 in 2 of the prior 3 years. Individuals may compute their self-employment earnings as the smaller of two-thirds of gross nonfarm income or $4,480. (¶3149)

A self-employed individual with both farm and nonfarm incomes is allowed to use both optional computation methods if the farm income qualifies for the farm optional method and the nonfarm income qualifies for the nonfarm optional method. If both optional methods are used to compute net earnings from self-employment, the maximum combined total net earnings from self-employment for any tax year can't be more than $4,480. (¶3149)

Line 60. Total tax.	A recapture rule applies if a premium subsidy is provided for COBRA continuation coverage of the taxpayer (or spouse or any dependent) during the tax year and the taxpayer's modified adjusted gross income (MAGI) exceeds $125,000 ($250,000 for joint return filers). If the MAGI limit is exceeded, the taxpayer's income tax for the tax year is increased by part or all of the amount of the premium subsidy. The full amount of the subsidy must be repaid as an additional tax if a taxpayer's MAGI exceeds $145,000 ($290,000 for joint return filers). The recaptured amount is included in the total tax on this line and is to be shown on the dotted line. (¶1531)

PAYMENTS

Line 63. Making work pay.	The making working pay credit is available to eligible individuals for tax years beginning 2010. The credit, which is refundable, is the lesser of (1) 6.2% of an individual's earned income or (2) $400 ($800 for a joint return). It is phased out for higher income taxpayers. Schedule M is used to compute the amount of the credit, which generally was paid in advance through reduced withholding. (¶2343)
Line 64. Earned income credit (EIC).	The maximum credit is higher, and the AGI-based phaseout figures are revised. (¶2344)
Line 67. First-time homebuyer credit.	On the 2010 return, an eligible first time homebuyer (and a qualifying long-term resident treated as a first time homebuyer) may claim a first time homebuyer credit for a home costing $800,000 or less bought (1) after Dec. 31, 2009, and before May 1, 2010, or (2) after Apr. 30, 2010, and before Oct. 1, 2010, and he entered into a binding contract before May 1, 2010, to purchase the property before July 1, 2010. The maximum credit is the lesser of 10% of the home's purchase price or $8,000 ($4,000 for married individuals filing separately), or for qualifying long-term residents the lesser of 10% of the purchase price or $6,500 ($3,250 for a married individual filing separately). (¶2369)

Line 69. Excess social security and RRTA tax withheld.	Maximum Social Security (OASDI) tax for 2010 is $6,621.60 (computed on the first $106,800 of wages) for purposes of credit for excess tax withheld. (¶1108)
Line 71. Credits from Form 2439, 8839, 8801, 8885.	For tax years beginning after Dec. 31, 2009, the maximum adoption credit is increased to $13,170 per eligible child for both non-special needs adoptions and special needs adoptions and the adoption credit is made refundable. (¶2359)

FORM 1040, SCHEDULE A ITEMIZED DEDUCTIONS 2010

Line 1. Medical and dental expenses.	The standard mileage rate for medically-related use of an auto is 16.5¢ per mile for 2010. (¶2149)
Line 5. State and local income taxes.	The Code Sec. 164(b)(5) election to take an itemized deduction for State and local general sales taxes instead of the itemized deduction permitted for State and local income taxes does not apply for tax years beginning after 2009. (¶1756)
Line 20. Casualty or theft losses.	For 2010, a personal casualty or theft loss must only exceed $100 to be deductible. (¶1796)
Line 21. Unreimbursed employee expenses.	The standard mileage rate is 50¢ per mile for 2010. (¶1561)
Line 29. Total itemized deductions.	For 2010, taxpayers with higher levels of AGI no longer face a reduction in their itemized deductions. (¶3114)

FORM 1040, SCHEDULE B INTEREST AND DIVIDEND INCOME 2010

Line 1. Interest.	Accrued interest on Series E or EE U.S. savings bonds issued in '80 is taxable. (¶1336)
Line 3. Excludable interest on Series EE or Series I U.S. savings bonds.	The exclusion for education related savings bond interest phases out at higher income levels. For 2010, the phaseout begins at modified adjusted gross income above $70,100 ($105,100 on a joint return). (¶2220)

FORM 1040, SCHEDULE C PROFIT OR LOSS FROM BUSINESS 2010

Part I. Income.	For debt discharges in tax years ending after Dec. 31, 2008, a taxpayer can elect to have debt discharge income from the reacquisition of an applicable debt instrument after Dec. 31, 2008, and before Jan. 1, 2011, included in gross income ratably over five tax years, beginning with, for repurchases occurring in 2010, the fourth tax year following the tax year the debt is reacquired. (¶1399)
Part II. Expenses. Line 9. Car and truck expenses.	The standard mileage rate is 50¢ per mile for business travel during 2010. (¶1561)
Part II. Expenses. Line 13. Depreciation and section 179 expense.	See entries for Form 4562, below.

FORM 4562, DEPRECIATION AND AMORTIZATION 2010

Part I. Election to expense certain tangible property under Sec. 179.	For tax years beginning in 2010 (or 2011), the amount that may be expensed under Code Sec. 179 is $500,000, with the investment-based phaseout beginning at $2,000,000. (¶1941)

	For a tax year beginning in 2010 or 2011, a taxpayer may elect to treat up to $250,000 of qualified real property (qualified leasehold improvement property, qualified restaurant property, and qualified retail improvement property) as Code Sec. 179 property. (¶1941)
Part II. Special depreciation allowance.	Taxpayers may claim a 50% bonus depreciation deduction for qualified property. (¶1933)
Part V. Listed property.	First-year luxury auto limits for vehicles first placed in service in 2010 are $11,060 for autos and $11,160 for light trucks or vans (for vehicles ineligible for bonus depreciation, or if taxpayer elects out, $3,060 and $3,160, respectively). (¶1954)
	For tax years beginning after Dec. 31, 2009, cellular telephones (cell phones) and other similar telecommunications equipment are removed from the categories of "listed property" under Code Sec. 280F. (¶1949)
Part VI. Amortization.	An increased startup expense deduction ($10,000 limit, with $60,000 phaseout threshold) applies for tax years beginning after 2009 and before 2011. (¶1954)

FORM 1040, SCHEDULE D CAPITAL GAINS AND LOSSES 2010

For QSBS acquired after Sept. 27, 2010 and before Jan. 1, 2011, no regular tax or AMT is imposed on the sale of QSBS held for more than five years. (¶2648)

FORM 1040, SCHEDULE F PROFIT OR LOSS FROM FARMING

Line 36, Net farm profit (or loss).	For tax years beginning after 2009, the farming loss of a non-C corporation taxpayer, is limited for any tax year in which certain government subsidies are received. The loss is limited to the greater of (a) $300,000 ($150,000 for a married person filing separately), or (b) the taxpayer's total net farm income for the prior five tax years. (¶4504)

¶1000. Tax Calendar—2011 Due Dates.

Here are the principal 2011 tax due dates. The effect of Saturdays, Sundays, and federal (but not State) holidays has been taken into account.

January 18, 2011

Individuals.

Make a payment of your estimated tax for 2010, if you didn't pay your income tax for the year through withholding (or didn't pay in enough tax that way). Use Form 1040-ES or pay by credit card or by EFTPS. This is the final installment date for 2010 estimated tax. However, you don't have to make this payment if you file your 2010 return (Form 1040) and pay any tax due by Jan. 31, 2011.

Farmers and fishermen.

Pay your estimated tax for 2010 using Form 1040-ES or pay by credit card or by EFTPS. You can then file your 2010 income tax return (Form 1040) by Apr. 18. If you don't pay at this time, your 2010 return will be due Mar. 1, 2011.

January 31, 2011

All employers.

Give your employees their copies of Form W-2 for 2010.

All businesses.

Give an annual information statement to recipients of certain payments you made during 2010. (You can use a copy of the appropriate Form 1099.)

Individuals.

File your income tax return (Form 1040) for 2010 if you didn't pay your last installment of estimated tax by Jan. 18. Filing your return now prevents any penalty for late payment of the last installment.

February 15, 2011

Individuals.

If you claimed exemption from income tax withholding for 2010 on the Form W-4 you gave your employer, you must file a new Form W-4 by this date to continue your exemption for another year.

All businesses.

Give an annual information statement to recipients of certain payments (e.g., proceeds from broker and barter transactions) you made during 2010. (You can use a copy of the appropriate Form 1099.)

February 28, 2011

All businesses.

File an information return (Form 1099) with IRS for certain payments you made during 2010. There are different versions of Form 1099 for different types of payments. Use a separate Form 1096 to summarize and transmit each separate version. For a 30-day extension of time to file, use Form 8809. The due date for electronic filers is Mar. 31, 2011.

All employers.

File Form W-3 along with Copy A of all the Form W-2s you issued for 2010. The due date for electronic filers is Mar. 31, 2011.

Large food and beverage establishment employers.

File Form 8027 to report tip income and allocated tips. Use Form 8027-T to summarize and transmit Form 8027 if you have more than one establishment. The due date for electronic filers is Mar. 31, 2011.

March 1, 2011

Farmers and fishermen.

File your 2010 income tax return (Form 1040) and pay any tax due. However, you have until Apr. 18, if you paid your 2010 estimated tax by Jan. 18, 2011.

March 15, 2011

C corporations and S corporations.

File a 2010 calendar year income tax return (Form 1120 or Form 1120S) and pay any tax still due. If you want an automatic 6-month extension, file Form 7004 and deposit what you estimate you owe.

S elections.

File Form 2553 to choose to be treated as an S corporation, beginning with calendar year 2011. If Form 2553 is filed late, S treatment will begin with calendar year 2012 (unless IRS determines there was reasonable cause for failure to file on time).

Electing large partnerships.

Provide each partner with a copy of Schedule K-1 of Form 1065-B.

March 31, 2011

Electronic filers of information returns.

File information returns listed under Feb. 28 (e.g., Form 1099s, Form W-2s, etc.), which is the due date for non-electronic filers.

April 18, 2011

Individuals.

File an income tax return for 2010 (Form 1040, Form 1040A, or Form 1040EZ), and pay any tax due. Taxpayers who can't make payments should request (on Form 9465) an agreement to pay in installments. If you want an automatic 6-month extension to file, file Form 4868 and estimate your tax or pay by credit card. Then file Form 1040 or Form 1040A by Oct. 17.

If you paid cash wages of $1,700 or more in 2010 to a household employee you must file Schedule H with your income tax return (Form 1040) and report any employment taxes and withheld income taxes for those employees.

Contributions to an IRA for 2010 must be made by this date.

If you aren't paying your 2011 income tax through withholding (or won't pay in enough tax during the year that way), pay the first installment of your 2011 estimated tax by this date. Use Form 1040-ES or pay by credit card or by EFTPS.

Partnerships.

File a 2010 calendar year return (Form 1065) and provide each partner with a copy of Schedule K-1. If you want an automatic 5-month extension to file the return and provide Schedule K-1 or a substitute Schedule K-1, file Form 7004. Then file Form 1065 by Sept. 15.

Electing large partnerships.

File a 2010 calendar year return (Form 1065-B). If you want an automatic 6-month extension to file the return and provide Schedule K-1 or a substitute Schedule K-1, file Form 7004. Then file Form 1065-B by Oct. 17.

Corporations.

Deposit the first installment of estimated income tax for 2011.

June 15, 2011

Individuals.

If you are a U.S. citizen or resident alien living and working (or on military duty) outside the U.S. and Puerto Rico, file your 2010 Form 1040 and pay any tax, interest and penalties due. Otherwise, see April 18, above. However, if you are a participant in a combat zone you may be able to further extend the filing deadline.

Make the second installment payment of your 2011 estimated tax, if you aren't paying your income tax for the year through withholding (or won't pay in enough tax that way). Use Form 1040-ES or pay by credit card or by EFTPS.

Corporations.

Deposit the second installment of estimated income tax for 2011.

August 1, 2011

All employers.

If you maintain an employee benefit plan, such as a pension, profit-sharing, or stock bonus plan, file Form 5500 or Form 5500-EZ for calendar year 2010. If you use a fiscal year as your plan year, file the form by the last day of the seventh month after the plan year ends.

September 15, 2011

Individuals.

Make the third installment payment of your 2011 estimated tax, if you aren't paying your income tax for the year through withholding (or won't pay in enough tax that way). Use Form 1040-ES or pay by credit card or by EFTPS.

C corporations and S corporations.

File a 2010 calendar year income tax return (Form 1120 or Form 1120S) and pay any tax due if you were given an automatic 6-month extension.

Corporations.

Deposit the third installment of estimated income tax for 2011.

Partnerships.

File a 2010 calendar year return (Form 1065) if you were given an automatic 5-month extension.

October 17, 2011

Individuals.

If you have an automatic 6-month extension to file your income tax return for 2010, file Form 1040 and pay any tax, interest, and penalties due.

Electing large partnerships.

File a 2010 calendar year return (Form 1065-B) if you were given an automatic 6-month extension.

During November, 2010

Income tax withholding.

Request employees whose withholding exemptions will be different in 2012 to fill out a new Form W-4.

December 15, 2011

Corporations.

Deposit the fourth installment of estimated income tax for 2011.

2011 RIA FEDERAL TAX HANDBOOK

Contents

Table of Contents—Main Topics

Chapter 1   Tax Rates and Tables

¶ 1100   Tax Rates and Tables

Federal tax rates for income, gift, excise and other taxes are set forth in this Chapter. Also included are current income tax tables. The rate brackets for individuals and estates and trusts are adjusted annually for cost-of-living increases based on the average consumer price index (CPI) for the 12-month period ending the previous Aug. 31. Similar adjustments are made to other key figures.

¶ 1101   Income tax rates for individuals.

Different rates apply to:

. . . single taxpayers (¶1102);

. . . married persons filing joint returns and qualified widows and widowers (¶1103);

. . . married persons filing separate returns (¶1104); and

. . . heads of households (¶1105).

Bankruptcy estates of individuals compute their tax using the same rate schedule as married individuals filing separate tax returns.

Individuals with taxable income under a ceiling amount ($100,000) compute their tax using tax tables (Code Sec. 3), reproduced at ¶1110.

For capital gains rates, see ¶2600 *et seq.*

caution: As we go to press with the 2011 RIA Federal Tax Handbook, it is uncertain what the tax rate brackets for individuals will be for tax year 2011. Unless Congress acts in the "lame duck" session that begins after we go to press, under the EGTRRA sunset rule, the tax rate brackets will revert to their pre-2001 levels, as adjusted for inflation (see ¶1114). Congress may set aside (perhaps temporarily) the EGTRRA sunset rule for tax rates, in which case tax rates for 2011 would be similar to those in effect for 2010, but adjusted for inflation. Alternatively, Congress may keep the basic rate structure in effect for 2010 for most people, but increase tax rates for higher-income individuals. For highlights of later-enacted tax laws that affect the 2011 edition, consult the homepage dedicated to users of the RIA Federal Tax Handbook (http://www.ria.thomsonreuters.com/federaltaxhandbook).

¶ 1102   Single individuals.

Taxpayers who aren't married *at year's end* and who don't qualify as surviving spouses or heads of household, and certain married taxpayers living apart compute their tax under the following tax rates for single persons if they can't use the tax tables.

The rates for 2010 are:

If taxable income is:	The tax is:
Not over $8,375	10% of taxable income
Over $8,375 but not over $34,000	$837.50 plus 15% of the excess over $8,375
Over $34,000 but not over $82,400	$4,681.25 plus 25% of the excess over $34,000
Over $82,400 but not over $171,850	$16,781.25 plus 28% of the excess over $82,400

References beginning with a single letter are to paragraphs in RIA's Federal Tax Coordinator 2d and RIA's Analysis of Federal Taxes: Income. Those beginning with numbers are to paragraphs in RIA's United States Tax Reporter. Those beginning with TD are to paragraphs in RIA's Tax Desk.

27

Over $171,850 but not over $373,650	$41,827.25 plus 33% of the excess over $171,850
Over $373,650	$108,421.25 plus 35% of the excess over $373,650

¶ 1103 Married filing joint returns and surviving spouses.

Married taxpayers filing joint returns and surviving spouses who can't use the tax tables compute their tax on the basis of the rates indicated below.

The rates for 2010 are:

If taxable income is:	The tax is:
Not over $16,750	10% of taxable income
Over $16,750 but not over $68,000	$1,675.00 plus 15% of the excess over $16,750
Over $68,000 but not over $137,300	$9,362.50 plus 25% of the excess over $68,000
Over $137,300 but not over $209,250	$26,687.50 plus 28% of the excess over $137,300
Over $209,250 but not over $373,650	$46,833.50 plus 33% of the excess over $209,250
Over $373,650	$101,085.50 plus 35% of the excess over $373,650

¶ 1104 Married filing separate returns.

Married taxpayers filing separate returns who can't use the tax tables compute their tax on the basis of the rates indicated below.

The rates for 2010 are:

If taxable income is:	The tax is:
Not over $8,375	10% of taxable income
Over $8,375 but not over $34,000	$837.50 plus 15% of the excess over $8,375
Over $34,000 but not over $68,650	$4,681.25 plus 25% of the excess over $34,000
Over $68,650 but not over $104,625	$13,343.75 plus 28% of the excess over $68,650
Over $104,625 but not over $186,825	$23,416.75 plus 33% of the excess over $104,625
Over $186,825	$50,542.75 plus 35% of the excess over $186,825

¶ 1105 Head of household.

Unmarried persons maintaining households who can't use the tax tables compute their tax on the basis of the rates indicated below.

The rates for 2010 are:

If taxable income is:	The tax is:
Not over $11,950	10% of taxable income
Over $11,950 but not over $45,550	$1,195.00 plus 15% of the excess over $11,950

Over $45,550 but not over $117,650	$6,235.00 plus 25% of the excess over $45,550
Over $117,650 but not over $190,550	$24,260.00 plus 28% of the excess over $117,650
Over $190,550 but not over $373,650	$44,672.00 plus 33% of the excess over $190,550
Over $373,650	$105,095.00 plus 35% of the excess over $373,650

¶ 1106   Income tax rates for trusts and estates.

The income tax on trusts and decedent's estates is imposed at graduated rates on their taxable income. (Code Sec. 1(e)) For capital gains rates, see ¶2600.

The rates for 2010 are:

If taxable income is:	The tax is:
Not over $2,300	15% of taxable income
Over $2,300 but not over $5,350	$345.00 plus 25% of the excess over $2,300
Over $5,350 but not over $8,200	$1,107.50 plus 28% of the excess over $5,350
Over $8,200 but not over $11,200	$1,905.50 plus 33% of the excess over $8,200
Over $11,200	$2,895.50 plus 35% of the excess over $11,200

¶ 1107   FICA (Social Security and Medicare) tax.

A 7.65% FICA tax for employers and employees is imposed: the 6.20% Social Security tax plus the 1.45% Medicare tax. (Code Sec. 3101(a), Code Sec. 3101(b), Code Sec. 3111(a), Code Sec. 3111(b))

For 2010 and 2011 the 6.20% Social Security tax is computed on the first $106,800 of the employee's wages. Thus, the maximum Social Security tax for 2010 and 2011 is $6,621.60 (6.20% of $106,800). The 1.45% Medicare tax is computed on the employee's total wages (no ceiling).

¶ 1108   Self-employment tax.

A self-employment tax is imposed on self-employed people at a rate of 15.30%: a combination of a 12.40% Old Age, Survivors, and Disability Insurance tax (OASDI, the equivalent of the Social Security tax at ¶1107), and a 2.90% Medicare tax. (Code Sec. 1401(a), Code Sec. 1401(b))

For 2010 and 2011, the 12.40% OASDI tax is computed on the first $106,800 of self-employment income. Thus, the maximum OASDI tax for 2010 and 2011 is $13,243.20 (12.40% of $106,800). The 2.90% Medicare tax is computed on the entire self-employment income (no ceiling).

observation: Sole proprietors and partners are subject to the Medicare tax on their entire self-employment income even if the income isn't distributed (unlike shareholders in an S corporation, who aren't subject to the self-employment tax on their share of the corporation's net income, whether distributed or not, see ¶3143).

29

¶ 1109   Federal unemployment tax (FUTA).

The tax is 6.2% through June of 2011, and 6.0% for the remainder of calendar year 2011 and later years (Code Sec. 3301), of the first $7,000 paid each employee as wages during the calendar year. (Code Sec. 3306(b))

The employer gets a credit against FUTA tax for contributions paid into state unemployment funds. The credit can't exceed 5.4% of the first $7,000 of wages. (Code Sec. 3302)

¶ 1110 Tax Table for Individuals

2010
Tax Table

See the instructions for line 44 on page 35 to see if you must use the Tax Table below to figure your tax.

Example. Mr. and Mrs. Brown are filing a joint return. Their taxable income on Form 1040, line 43, is $25,300. First, they find the $25,300–25,350 taxable income line. Next, they find the column for married filing jointly and read down the column. The amount shown where the taxable income line and filing status column meet is $2,961. This is the tax amount they should enter on Form 1040, line 44.

Sample Table

At least	But less than	Single	Married filing jointly	Married filing separately	Head of a household
			Your tax is—		
25,200	25,250	3,365	2,946	3,365	3,186
25,250	25,300	3,373	2,954	3,373	3,194
25,300	25,350	3,380	2,961	3,380	3,201
25,350	25,400	3,388	2,969	3,388	3,209

If line 43 (taxable income) is— At least	But less than	Single	Married filing jointly *	Married filing separately	Head of a household
			Your tax is—		
0	5	0	0	0	0
5	15	1	1	1	1
15	25	2	2	2	2
25	50	4	4	4	4
50	75	6	6	6	6
75	100	9	9	9	9
100	125	11	11	11	11
125	150	14	14	14	14
150	175	16	16	16	16
175	200	19	19	19	19
200	225	21	21	21	21
225	250	24	24	24	24
250	275	26	26	26	26
275	300	29	29	29	29
300	325	31	31	31	31
325	350	34	34	34	34
350	375	36	36	36	36
375	400	39	39	39	39
400	425	41	41	41	41
425	450	44	44	44	44
450	475	46	46	46	46
475	500	49	49	49	49
500	525	51	51	51	51
525	550	54	54	54	54
550	575	56	56	56	56
575	600	59	59	59	59
600	625	61	61	61	61
625	650	64	64	64	64
650	675	66	66	66	66
675	700	69	69	69	69
700	725	71	71	71	71
725	750	74	74	74	74
750	775	76	76	76	76
775	800	79	79	79	79
800	825	81	81	81	81
825	850	84	84	84	84
850	875	86	86	86	86
875	900	89	89	89	89
900	925	91	91	91	91
925	950	94	94	94	94
950	975	96	96	96	96
975	1,000	99	99	99	99

1,000

At least	But less than	Single	Married filing jointly	Married filing separately	Head of a household
1,000	1,025	101	101	101	101
1,025	1,050	104	104	104	104
1,050	1,075	106	106	106	106
1,075	1,100	109	109	109	109
1,100	1,125	111	111	111	111
1,125	1,150	114	114	114	114
1,150	1,175	116	116	116	116
1,175	1,200	119	119	119	119
1,200	1,225	121	121	121	121
1,225	1,250	124	124	124	124
1,250	1,275	126	126	126	126
1,275	1,300	129	129	129	129

If line 43 (taxable income) is— At least	But less than	Single	Married filing jointly *	Married filing separately	Head of a household
			Your tax is—		
1,300	1,325	131	131	131	131
1,325	1,350	134	134	134	134
1,350	1,375	136	136	136	136
1,375	1,400	139	139	139	139
1,400	1,425	141	141	141	141
1,425	1,450	144	144	144	144
1,450	1,475	146	146	146	146
1,475	1,500	149	149	149	149
1,500	1,525	151	151	151	151
1,525	1,550	154	154	154	154
1,550	1,575	156	156	156	156
1,575	1,600	159	159	159	159
1,600	1,625	161	161	161	161
1,625	1,650	164	164	164	164
1,650	1,675	166	166	166	166
1,675	1,700	169	169	169	169
1,700	1,725	171	171	171	171
1,725	1,750	174	174	174	174
1,750	1,775	176	176	176	176
1,775	1,800	179	179	179	179
1,800	1,825	181	181	181	181
1,825	1,850	184	184	184	184
1,850	1,875	186	186	186	186
1,875	1,900	189	189	189	189
1,900	1,925	191	191	191	191
1,925	1,950	194	194	194	194
1,950	1,975	196	196	196	196
1,975	2,000	199	199	199	199

2,000

At least	But less than	Single	Married filing jointly	Married filing separately	Head of a household
2,000	2,025	201	201	201	201
2,025	2,050	204	204	204	204
2,050	2,075	206	206	206	206
2,075	2,100	209	209	209	209
2,100	2,125	211	211	211	211
2,125	2,150	214	214	214	214
2,150	2,175	216	216	216	216
2,175	2,200	219	219	219	219
2,200	2,225	221	221	221	221
2,225	2,250	224	224	224	224
2,250	2,275	226	226	226	226
2,275	2,300	229	229	229	229
2,300	2,325	231	231	231	231
2,325	2,350	234	234	234	234
2,350	2,375	236	236	236	236
2,375	2,400	239	239	239	230
2,400	2,425	241	241	241	241
2,425	2,450	244	244	244	244
2,450	2,475	246	246	246	246
2,475	2,500	249	249	249	249
2,500	2,525	251	251	251	251
2,525	2,550	254	254	254	254
2,550	2,575	256	256	256	256
2,575	2,600	259	259	259	259
2,600	2,625	261	261	261	261
2,625	2,650	264	264	264	264
2,650	2,675	266	266	266	266
2,675	2,700	269	269	269	269

If line 43 (taxable income) is— At least	But less than	Single	Married filing jointly *	Married filing separately	Head of a household
			Your tax is—		
2,700	2,725	271	271	271	271
2,725	2,750	274	274	274	274
2,750	2,775	276	276	276	276
2,775	2,800	279	279	279	279
2,800	2,825	281	281	281	281
2,825	2,850	284	284	284	284
2,850	2,875	286	286	286	286
2,875	2,900	289	289	289	289
2,900	2,925	291	291	291	291
2,925	2,950	294	294	294	294
2,950	2,975	296	296	296	296
2,975	3,000	299	299	299	299

3,000

At least	But less than	Single	Married filing jointly	Married filing separately	Head of a household
3,000	3,050	303	303	303	303
3,050	3,100	308	308	308	308
3,100	3,150	313	313	313	313
3,150	3,200	318	318	318	318
3,200	3,250	323	323	323	323
3,250	3,300	328	328	328	328
3,300	3,350	333	333	333	333
3,350	3,400	338	338	338	338
3,400	3,450	343	343	343	343
3,450	3,500	348	348	348	348
3,500	3,550	353	353	353	353
3,550	3,600	358	358	358	358
3,600	3,650	363	363	363	363
3,650	3,700	368	368	368	368
3,700	3,750	373	373	373	373
3,750	3,800	378	378	378	378
3,800	3,850	383	383	383	383
3,850	3,900	388	388	388	388
3,900	3,950	393	393	393	393
3,950	4,000	398	398	398	398

4,000

At least	But less than	Single	Married filing jointly	Married filing separately	Head of a household
4,000	4,050	403	403	403	403
4,050	4,100	408	408	408	408
4,100	4,150	413	413	413	413
4,150	4,200	418	418	418	418
4,200	4,250	423	423	423	423
4,250	4,300	428	428	428	428
4,300	4,350	433	433	433	433
4,350	4,400	438	438	438	438
4,400	4,450	443	443	443	443
4,450	4,500	448	448	448	448
4,500	4,550	453	453	453	453
4,550	4,600	458	458	458	458
4,600	4,650	463	463	463	463
4,650	4,700	468	468	468	468
4,700	4,750	473	473	473	473
4,750	4,800	478	478	478	478
4,800	4,850	483	483	483	483
4,850	4,900	488	488	488	488
4,900	4,950	493	493	493	493
4,950	5,000	498	498	498	498

* This column must also be used by a qualifying widow(er).

Caution: Draft as of 09/13/2010

2010 Tax Table—*Continued*

If line 43 (taxable income) is—		And you are—			
At least	But less than	Single	Married filing jointly*	Married filing separately	Head of a household
		Your tax is—			

5,000

At least	But less than	Single	Married filing jointly*	Married filing separately	Head of a household
5,000	5,050	503	503	503	503
5,050	5,100	508	508	508	508
5,100	5,150	513	513	513	513
5,150	5,200	518	518	518	518
5,200	5,250	523	523	523	523
5,250	5,300	528	528	528	528
5,300	5,350	533	533	533	533
5,350	5,400	538	538	538	538
5,400	5,450	543	543	543	543
5,450	5,500	548	548	548	548
5,500	5,550	553	553	553	553
5,550	5,600	558	558	558	558
5,600	5,650	563	563	563	563
5,650	5,700	568	568	568	568
5,700	5,750	573	573	573	573
5,750	5,800	578	578	578	578
5,800	5,850	583	583	583	583
5,850	5,900	588	588	588	588
5,900	5,950	593	593	593	593
5,950	6,000	598	598	598	598

6,000

At least	But less than	Single	Married filing jointly*	Married filing separately	Head of a household
6,000	6,050	603	603	603	603
6,050	6,100	608	608	608	608
6,100	6,150	613	613	613	613
6,150	6,200	618	618	618	618
6,200	6,250	623	623	623	623
6,250	6,300	628	628	628	628
6,300	6,350	633	633	633	633
6,350	6,400	638	638	638	638
6,400	6,450	643	643	643	643
6,450	6,500	648	648	648	648
6,500	6,550	653	653	653	653
6,550	6,600	658	658	658	658
6,600	6,650	663	663	663	663
6,650	6,700	668	668	668	668
6,700	6,750	673	673	673	673
6,750	6,800	678	678	678	678
6,800	6,850	683	683	683	683
6,850	6,900	688	688	688	688
6,900	6,950	693	693	693	693
6,950	7,000	698	698	698	698

7,000

At least	But less than	Single	Married filing jointly*	Married filing separately	Head of a household
7,000	7,050	703	703	703	703
7,050	7,100	708	708	708	708
7,100	7,150	713	713	713	713
7,150	7,200	718	718	718	718
7,200	7,250	723	723	723	723
7,250	7,300	728	728	728	728
7,300	7,350	733	733	733	733
7,350	7,400	738	738	738	738
7,400	7,450	743	743	743	743
7,450	7,500	748	748	748	748
7,500	7,550	753	753	753	753
7,550	7,600	758	758	758	758
7,600	7,650	763	763	763	763
7,650	7,700	768	768	768	768
7,700	7,750	773	773	773	773
7,750	7,800	778	778	778	778
7,800	7,850	783	783	783	783
7,850	7,900	788	788	788	788
7,900	7,950	793	793	793	793
7,950	8,000	798	798	798	798

8,000

At least	But less than	Single	Married filing jointly*	Married filing separately	Head of a household
8,000	8,050	803	803	803	803
8,050	8,100	808	808	808	808
8,100	8,150	813	813	813	813
8,150	8,200	818	818	818	818
8,200	8,250	823	823	823	823
8,250	8,300	828	828	828	828
8,300	8,350	833	833	833	833
8,350	8,400	838	838	838	838
8,400	8,450	845	843	845	843
8,450	8,500	853	848	853	848
8,500	8,550	860	853	860	853
8,550	8,600	868	858	868	858
8,600	8,650	875	863	875	863
8,650	8,700	883	868	883	868
8,700	8,750	890	873	890	873
8,750	8,800	898	878	898	878
8,800	8,850	905	883	905	883
8,850	8,900	913	888	913	888
8,900	8,950	920	893	920	893
8,950	9,000	928	898	928	898

9,000

At least	But less than	Single	Married filing jointly*	Married filing separately	Head of a household
9,000	9,050	935	903	935	903
9,050	9,100	943	908	943	908
9,100	9,150	950	913	950	913
9,150	9,200	958	918	958	918
9,200	9,250	965	923	965	923
9,250	9,300	973	928	973	928
9,300	9,350	980	933	980	933
9,350	9,400	988	938	988	938
9,400	9,450	995	943	995	943
9,450	9,500	1,003	948	1,003	948
9,500	9,550	1,010	953	1,010	953
9,550	9,600	1,018	958	1,018	958
9,600	9,650	1,025	963	1,025	963
9,650	9,700	1,033	968	1,033	968
9,700	9,750	1,040	973	1,040	973
9,750	9,800	1,048	978	1,048	978
9,800	9,850	1,055	983	1,055	983
9,850	9,900	1,063	988	1,063	988
9,900	9,950	1,070	993	1,070	993
9,950	10,000	1,078	998	1,078	998

10,000

At least	But less than	Single	Married filing jointly*	Married filing separately	Head of a household
10,000	10,050	1,085	1,003	1,085	1,003
10,050	10,100	1,093	1,008	1,093	1,008
10,100	10,150	1,100	1,013	1,100	1,013
10,150	10,200	1,108	1,018	1,108	1,018
10,200	10,250	1,115	1,023	1,115	1,023
10,250	10,300	1,123	1,028	1,123	1,028
10,300	10,350	1,130	1,033	1,130	1,033
10,350	10,400	1,138	1,038	1,138	1,038
10,400	10,450	1,145	1,043	1,145	1,043
10,450	10,500	1,153	1,048	1,153	1,048
10,500	10,550	1,160	1,053	1,160	1,053
10,550	10,600	1,168	1,058	1,168	1,058
10,600	10,650	1,175	1,063	1,175	1,063
10,650	10,700	1,183	1,068	1,183	1,068
10,700	10,750	1,190	1,073	1,190	1,073
10,750	10,800	1,198	1,078	1,198	1,078
10,800	10,850	1,205	1,083	1,205	1,083
10,850	10,900	1,213	1,088	1,213	1,088
10,900	10,950	1,220	1,093	1,220	1,093
10,950	11,000	1,228	1,098	1,228	1,098

11,000

At least	But less than	Single	Married filing jointly*	Married filing separately	Head of a household
11,000	11,050	1,235	1,103	1,235	1,103
11,050	11,100	1,243	1,108	1,243	1,108
11,100	11,150	1,250	1,113	1,250	1,113
11,150	11,200	1,258	1,118	1,258	1,118
11,200	11,250	1,265	1,123	1,265	1,123
11,250	11,300	1,273	1,128	1,273	1,128
11,300	11,350	1,280	1,133	1,280	1,133
11,350	11,400	1,288	1,138	1,288	1,138
11,400	11,450	1,295	1,143	1,295	1,143
11,450	11,500	1,303	1,148	1,303	1,148
11,500	11,550	1,310	1,153	1,310	1,153
11,550	11,600	1,318	1,158	1,318	1,158
11,600	11,650	1,325	1,163	1,325	1,163
11,650	11,700	1,333	1,168	1,333	1,168
11,700	11,750	1,340	1,173	1,340	1,173
11,750	11,800	1,348	1,178	1,348	1,178
11,800	11,850	1,355	1,183	1,355	1,183
11,850	11,900	1,363	1,188	1,363	1,188
11,900	11,950	1,370	1,193	1,370	1,193
11,950	12,000	1,378	1,198	1,378	1,199

12,000

At least	But less than	Single	Married filing jointly*	Married filing separately	Head of a household
12,000	12,050	1,385	1,203	1,385	1,206
12,050	12,100	1,393	1,208	1,393	1,214
12,100	12,150	1,400	1,213	1,400	1,221
12,150	12,200	1,408	1,218	1,408	1,229
12,200	12,250	1,415	1,223	1,415	1,236
12,250	12,300	1,423	1,228	1,423	1,244
12,300	12,350	1,430	1,233	1,430	1,251
12,350	12,400	1,438	1,238	1,438	1,259
12,400	12,450	1,445	1,243	1,445	1,266
12,450	12,500	1,453	1,248	1,453	1,274
12,500	12,550	1,460	1,253	1,460	1,281
12,550	12,600	1,468	1,258	1,468	1,289
12,600	12,650	1,475	1,263	1,475	1,296
12,650	12,700	1,483	1,268	1,483	1,304
12,700	12,750	1,490	1,273	1,490	1,311
12,750	12,800	1,498	1,278	1,498	1,319
12,800	12,850	1,505	1,283	1,505	1,326
12,850	12,900	1,513	1,288	1,513	1,334
12,900	12,950	1,520	1,293	1,520	1,341
12,950	13,000	1,528	1,298	1,528	1,349

13,000

At least	But less than	Single	Married filing jointly*	Married filing separately	Head of a household
13,000	13,050	1,535	1,303	1,535	1,356
13,050	13,100	1,543	1,308	1,543	1,364
13,100	13,150	1,550	1,313	1,550	1,371
13,150	13,200	1,558	1,318	1,558	1,379
13,200	13,250	1,565	1,323	1,565	1,386
13,250	13,300	1,573	1,328	1,573	1,394
13,300	13,350	1,580	1,333	1,580	1,401
13,350	13,400	1,588	1,338	1,588	1,409
13,400	13,450	1,595	1,343	1,595	1,416
13,450	13,500	1,603	1,348	1,603	1,424
13,500	13,550	1,610	1,353	1,610	1,431
13,550	13,600	1,618	1,358	1,618	1,439
13,600	13,650	1,625	1,363	1,625	1,446
13,650	13,700	1,633	1,368	1,633	1,454
13,700	13,750	1,640	1,373	1,640	1,461
13,750	13,800	1,648	1,378	1,648	1,469
13,800	13,850	1,655	1,383	1,655	1,476
13,850	13,900	1,663	1,388	1,663	1,484
13,900	13,950	1,670	1,393	1,670	1,491
13,950	14,000	1,678	1,398	1,678	1,499

Caution: Draft as of 09/13/2010

* This column must also be used by a qualifying widow(er).

2010 Tax Table – *Continued*

If line 43 (taxable income) is — At least	But less than	Single	Married filing jointly*	Married filing separately	Head of a household
14,000					
14,000	14,050	1,685	1,403	1,685	1,506
14,050	14,100	1,693	1,408	1,693	1,514
14,100	14,150	1,700	1,413	1,700	1,521
14,150	14,200	1,708	1,418	1,708	1,529
14,200	14,250	1,715	1,423	1,715	1,536
14,250	14,300	1,723	1,428	1,723	1,544
14,300	14,350	1,730	1,433	1,730	1,551
14,350	14,400	1,738	1,438	1,738	1,559
14,400	14,450	1,745	1,443	1,745	1,566
14,450	14,500	1,753	1,448	1,753	1,574
14,500	14,550	1,760	1,453	1,760	1,581
14,550	14,600	1,768	1,458	1,768	1,589
14,600	14,650	1,775	1,463	1,775	1,596
14,650	14,700	1,783	1,468	1,783	1,604
14,700	14,750	1,790	1,473	1,790	1,611
14,750	14,800	1,798	1,478	1,798	1,619
14,800	14,850	1,805	1,483	1,805	1,626
14,850	14,900	1,813	1,488	1,813	1,634
14,900	14,950	1,820	1,493	1,820	1,641
14,950	15,000	1,828	1,498	1,828	1,649
15,000					
15,000	15,050	1,835	1,503	1,835	1,656
15,050	15,100	1,843	1,508	1,843	1,664
15,100	15,150	1,850	1,513	1,850	1,671
15,150	15,200	1,858	1,518	1,858	1,679
15,200	15,250	1,865	1,523	1,865	1,686
15,250	15,300	1,873	1,528	1,873	1,694
15,300	15,350	1,880	1,533	1,880	1,701
15,350	15,400	1,888	1,538	1,888	1,709
15,400	15,450	1,895	1,543	1,895	1,716
15,450	15,500	1,903	1,548	1,903	1,724
15,500	15,550	1,910	1,553	1,910	1,731
15,550	15,600	1,918	1,558	1,918	1,739
15,600	15,650	1,925	1,563	1,925	1,746
15,650	15,700	1,933	1,568	1,933	1,754
15,700	15,750	1,940	1,573	1,940	1,761
15,750	15,800	1,948	1,578	1,948	1,769
15,800	15,850	1,955	1,583	1,955	1,776
15,850	15,900	1,963	1,588	1,963	1,784
15,900	15,950	1,970	1,593	1,970	1,791
15,950	16,000	1,978	1,598	1,978	1,799
16,000					
16,000	16,050	1,985	1,603	1,985	1,806
16,050	16,100	1,993	1,608	1,993	1,814
16,100	16,150	2,000	1,613	2,000	1,821
16,150	16,200	2,008	1,618	2,008	1,829
16,200	16,250	2,015	1,623	2,015	1,836
16,250	16,300	2,023	1,628	2,023	1,844
16,300	16,350	2,030	1,633	2,030	1,851
16,350	16,400	2,038	1,638	2,038	1,859
16,400	16,450	2,045	1,643	2,045	1,866
16,450	16,500	2,053	1,648	2,053	1,874
16,500	16,550	2,060	1,653	2,060	1,881
16,550	16,600	2,068	1,658	2,068	1,889
16,600	16,650	2,075	1,663	2,075	1,896
16,650	16,700	2,083	1,668	2,083	1,904
16,700	16,750	2,090	1,673	2,090	1,911
16,750	16,800	2,098	1,679	2,098	1,919
16,800	16,850	2,105	1,686	2,105	1,926
16,850	16,900	2,113	1,694	2,113	1,934
16,900	16,950	2,120	1,701	2,120	1,941
16,950	17,000	2,128	1,709	2,128	1,949

If line 43 (taxable income) is — At least	But less than	Single	Married filing jointly*	Married filing separately	Head of a household
17,000					
17,000	17,050	2,135	1,716	2,135	1,956
17,050	17,100	2,143	1,724	2,143	1,964
17,100	17,150	2,150	1,731	2,150	1,971
17,150	17,200	2,158	1,739	2,158	1,979
17,200	17,250	2,165	1,746	2,165	1,986
17,250	17,300	2,173	1,754	2,173	1,994
17,300	17,350	2,180	1,761	2,180	2,001
17,350	17,400	2,188	1,769	2,188	2,009
17,400	17,450	2,195	1,776	2,195	2,016
17,450	17,500	2,203	1,784	2,203	2,024
17,500	17,550	2,210	1,791	2,210	2,031
17,550	17,600	2,218	1,799	2,218	2,039
17,600	17,650	2,225	1,806	2,225	2,046
17,650	17,700	2,233	1,814	2,233	2,054
17,700	17,750	2,240	1,821	2,240	2,061
17,750	17,800	2,248	1,829	2,248	2,069
17,800	17,850	2,255	1,836	2,255	2,076
17,850	17,900	2,263	1,844	2,263	2,084
17,900	17,950	2,270	1,851	2,270	2,091
17,950	18,000	2,278	1,859	2,278	2,099
18,000					
18,000	18,050	2,285	1,866	2,285	2,106
18,050	18,100	2,293	1,874	2,293	2,114
18,100	18,150	2,300	1,881	2,300	2,121
18,150	18,200	2,308	1,889	2,308	2,129
18,200	18,250	2,315	1,896	2,315	2,136
18,250	18,300	2,323	1,904	2,323	2,144
18,300	18,350	2,330	1,911	2,330	2,151
18,350	18,400	2,338	1,919	2,338	2,159
18,400	18,450	2,345	1,926	2,345	2,166
18,450	18,500	2,353	1,934	2,353	2,174
18,500	18,550	2,360	1,941	2,360	2,181
18,550	18,600	2,368	1,949	2,368	2,189
18,600	18,650	2,375	1,956	2,375	2,196
18,650	18,700	2,383	1,964	2,383	2,204
18,700	18,750	2,390	1,971	2,390	2,211
18,750	18,800	2,398	1,979	2,398	2,219
18,800	18,850	2,405	1,986	2,405	2,226
18,850	18,900	2,413	1,994	2,413	2,234
18,900	18,950	2,420	2,001	2,420	2,241
18,950	19,000	2,428	2,009	2,428	2,249
19,000					
19,000	19,050	2,435	2,016	2,435	2,256
19,050	19,100	2,443	2,024	2,443	2,264
19,100	19,150	2,450	2,031	2,450	2,271
19,150	19,200	2,458	2,039	2,458	2,279
19,200	19,250	2,465	2,046	2,465	2,286
19,250	19,300	2,473	2,054	2,473	2,294
19,300	19,350	2,480	2,061	2,480	2,301
19,350	19,400	2,488	2,069	2,488	2,309
19,400	19,450	2,495	2,076	2,495	2,316
19,450	19,500	2,503	2,084	2,503	2,324
19,500	19,550	2,510	2,091	2,510	2,331
19,550	19,600	2,518	2,099	2,518	2,339
19,600	19,650	2,525	2,106	2,525	2,346
19,650	19,700	2,533	2,114	2,533	2,354
19,700	19,750	2,540	2,121	2,540	2,361
19,750	19,800	2,548	2,129	2,548	2,369
19,800	19,850	2,555	2,136	2,555	2,376
19,850	19,900	2,563	2,144	2,563	2,384
19,900	19,950	2,570	2,151	2,570	2,391
19,950	20,000	2,578	2,159	2,578	2,399

If line 43 (taxable income) is — At least	But less than	Single	Married filing jointly*	Married filing separately	Head of a household
20,000					
20,000	20,050	2,585	2,166	2,585	2,406
20,050	20,100	2,593	2,174	2,593	2,414
20,100	20,150	2,600	2,181	2,600	2,421
20,150	20,200	2,608	2,189	2,608	2,429
20,200	20,250	2,615	2,196	2,615	2,436
20,250	20,300	2,623	2,204	2,623	2,444
20,300	20,350	2,630	2,211	2,630	2,451
20,350	20,400	2,638	2,219	2,638	2,459
20,400	20,450	2,645	2,226	2,645	2,466
20,450	20,500	2,653	2,234	2,653	2,474
20,500	20,550	2,660	2,241	2,660	2,481
20,550	20,600	2,668	2,249	2,668	2,489
20,600	20,650	2,675	2,256	2,675	2,496
20,650	20,700	2,683	2,264	2,683	2,504
20,700	20,750	2,690	2,271	2,690	2,511
20,750	20,800	2,698	2,279	2,698	2,519
20,800	20,850	2,705	2,286	2,705	2,526
20,850	20,900	2,713	2,294	2,713	2,534
20,900	20,950	2,720	2,301	2,720	2,541
20,950	21,000	2,728	2,309	2,728	2,549
21,000					
21,000	21,050	2,735	2,316	2,735	2,556
21,050	21,100	2,743	2,324	2,743	2,564
21,100	21,150	2,750	2,331	2,750	2,571
21,150	21,200	2,758	2,339	2,758	2,579
21,200	21,250	2,765	2,346	2,765	2,586
21,250	21,300	2,773	2,354	2,773	2,594
21,300	21,350	2,780	2,361	2,780	2,601
21,350	21,400	2,788	2,369	2,788	2,609
21,400	21,450	2,795	2,376	2,795	2,616
21,450	21,500	2,803	2,384	2,803	2,624
21,500	21,550	2,810	2,391	2,810	2,631
21,550	21,600	2,818	2,399	2,818	2,639
21,600	21,650	2,825	2,406	2,825	2,646
21,650	21,700	2,833	2,414	2,833	2,654
21,700	21,750	2,840	2,421	2,840	2,661
21,750	21,800	2,848	2,429	2,848	2,669
21,800	21,850	2,855	2,436	2,855	2,676
21,850	21,900	2,863	2,444	2,863	2,684
21,900	21,950	2,870	2,451	2,870	2,691
21,950	22,000	2,878	2,459	2,878	2,699
22,000					
22,000	22,050	2,885	2,466	2,885	2,706
22,050	22,100	2,893	2,474	2,893	2,714
22,100	22,150	2,900	2,481	2,900	2,721
22,150	22,200	2,908	2,489	2,908	2,729
22,200	22,250	2,915	2,496	2,915	2,736
22,250	22,300	2,923	2,504	2,923	2,744
22,300	22,350	2,930	2,511	2,930	2,751
22,350	22,400	2,938	2,519	2,938	2,759
22,400	22,450	2,945	2,526	2,945	2,766
22,450	22,500	2,953	2,534	2,953	2,774
22,500	22,550	2,960	2,541	2,960	2,781
22,550	22,600	2,968	2,549	2,968	2,789
22,600	22,650	2,975	2,556	2,975	2,796
22,650	22,700	2,983	2,564	2,983	2,804
22,700	22,750	2,990	2,571	2,990	2,811
22,750	22,800	2,998	2,579	2,998	2,819
22,800	22,850	3,005	2,586	3,005	2,826
22,850	22,900	3,013	2,594	3,013	2,834
22,900	22,950	3,020	2,601	3,020	2,841
22,950	23,000	3,028	2,609	3,028	2,849

Caution: Draft as of 09/13/2010

* This column must also be used by a qualifying widow(er).

2010 Tax Table–*Continued*

If line 43 (taxable income) is—		And you are—			
At least	But less than	Single	Married filing jointly *	Married filing separately	Head of a household
		Your tax is—			

23,000

At least	But less than	Single	Married filing jointly	Married filing separately	Head of a household
23,000	23,050	3,035	2,616	3,035	2,856
23,050	23,100	3,043	2,624	3,043	2,864
23,100	23,150	3,050	2,631	3,050	2,871
23,150	23,200	3,058	2,639	3,058	2,879
23,200	23,250	3,065	2,646	3,065	2,886
23,250	23,300	3,073	2,654	3,073	2,894
23,300	23,350	3,080	2,661	3,080	2,901
23,350	23,400	3,088	2,669	3,088	2,909
23,400	23,450	3,095	2,676	3,095	2,916
23,450	23,500	3,103	2,684	3,103	2,924
23,500	23,550	3,110	2,691	3,110	2,931
23,550	23,600	3,118	2,699	3,118	2,939
23,600	23,650	3,125	2,706	3,125	2,946
23,650	23,700	3,133	2,714	3,133	2,954
23,700	23,750	3,140	2,721	3,140	2,961
23,750	23,800	3,148	2,729	3,148	2,969
23,800	23,850	3,155	2,736	3,155	2,976
23,850	23,900	3,163	2,744	3,163	2,984
23,900	23,950	3,170	2,751	3,170	2,991
23,950	24,000	3,178	2,759	3,178	2,999

24,000

At least	But less than	Single	Married filing jointly	Married filing separately	Head of a household
24,000	24,050	3,185	2,766	3,185	3,006
24,050	24,100	3,193	2,774	3,193	3,014
24,100	24,150	3,200	2,781	3,200	3,021
24,150	24,200	3,208	2,789	3,208	3,029
24,200	24,250	3,215	2,796	3,215	3,036
24,250	24,300	3,223	2,804	3,223	3,044
24,300	24,350	3,230	2,811	3,230	3,051
24,350	24,400	3,238	2,819	3,238	3,059
24,400	24,450	3,245	2,826	3,245	3,066
24,450	24,500	3,253	2,834	3,253	3,074
24,500	24,550	3,260	2,841	3,260	3,081
24,550	24,600	3,268	2,849	3,268	3,089
24,600	24,650	3,275	2,856	3,275	3,096
24,650	24,700	3,283	2,864	3,283	3,104
24,700	24,750	3,290	2,871	3,290	3,111
24,750	24,800	3,298	2,879	3,298	3,119
24,800	24,850	3,305	2,886	3,305	3,126
24,850	24,900	3,313	2,894	3,313	3,134
24,900	24,950	3,320	2,901	3,320	3,141
24,950	25,000	3,328	2,909	3,328	3,149

25,000

At least	But less than	Single	Married filing jointly	Married filing separately	Head of a household
25,000	25,050	3,335	2,916	3,335	3,156
25,050	25,100	3,343	2,924	3,343	3,164
25,100	25,150	3,350	2,931	3,350	3,171
25,150	25,200	3,358	2,939	3,358	3,179
25,200	25,250	3,365	2,946	3,365	3,186
25,250	25,300	3,373	2,954	3,373	3,194
25,300	25,350	3,380	2,961	3,380	3,201
25,350	25,400	3,388	2,969	3,388	3,209
25,400	25,450	3,395	2,976	3,395	3,216
25,450	25,500	3,403	2,984	3,403	3,224
25,500	25,550	3,410	2,991	3,410	3,231
25,550	25,600	3,418	2,999	3,418	3,239
25,600	25,650	3,425	3,006	3,425	3,246
25,650	25,700	3,433	3,014	3,433	3,254
25,700	25,750	3,440	3,021	3,440	3,261
25,750	25,800	3,448	3,029	3,448	3,269
25,800	25,850	3,455	3,036	3,455	3,276
25,850	25,900	3,463	3,044	3,463	3,284
25,900	25,950	3,470	3,051	3,470	3,291
25,950	26,000	3,478	3,059	3,478	3,299

26,000

At least	But less than	Single	Married filing jointly	Married filing separately	Head of a household
26,000	26,050	3,485	3,066	3,485	3,306
26,050	26,100	3,493	3,074	3,493	3,314
26,100	26,150	3,500	3,081	3,500	3,321
26,150	26,200	3,508	3,089	3,508	3,329
26,200	26,250	3,515	3,096	3,515	3,336
26,250	26,300	3,523	3,104	3,523	3,344
26,300	26,350	3,530	3,111	3,530	3,351
26,350	26,400	3,538	3,119	3,538	3,359
26,400	26,450	3,545	3,126	3,545	3,366
26,450	26,500	3,553	3,134	3,553	3,374
26,500	26,550	3,560	3,141	3,560	3,381
26,550	26,600	3,568	3,149	3,568	3,389
26,600	26,650	3,575	3,156	3,575	3,396
26,650	26,700	3,583	3,164	3,583	3,404
26,700	26,750	3,590	3,171	3,590	3,411
26,750	26,800	3,598	3,179	3,598	3,419
26,800	26,850	3,605	3,186	3,605	3,426
26,850	26,900	3,613	3,194	3,613	3,434
26,900	26,950	3,620	3,201	3,620	3,441
26,950	27,000	3,628	3,209	3,628	3,449

27,000

At least	But less than	Single	Married filing jointly	Married filing separately	Head of a household
27,000	27,050	3,635	3,216	3,635	3,456
27,050	27,100	3,643	3,224	3,643	3,464
27,100	27,150	3,650	3,231	3,650	3,471
27,150	27,200	3,658	3,239	3,658	3,479
27,200	27,250	3,665	3,246	3,665	3,486
27,250	27,300	3,673	3,254	3,673	3,494
27,300	27,350	3,680	3,261	3,680	3,501
27,350	27,400	3,688	3,269	3,688	3,509
27,400	27,450	3,695	3,276	3,695	3,516
27,450	27,500	3,703	3,284	3,703	3,524
27,500	27,550	3,710	3,291	3,710	3,531
27,550	27,600	3,718	3,299	3,718	3,539
27,600	27,650	3,725	3,306	3,725	3,546
27,650	27,700	3,733	3,314	3,733	3,554
27,700	27,750	3,740	3,321	3,740	3,561
27,750	27,800	3,748	3,329	3,748	3,569
27,800	27,850	3,755	3,336	3,755	3,576
27,850	27,900	3,763	3,344	3,763	3,584
27,900	27,950	3,770	3,351	3,770	3,591
27,950	28,000	3,778	3,359	3,778	3,599

28,000

At least	But less than	Single	Married filing jointly	Married filing separately	Head of a household
28,000	28,050	3,785	3,366	3,785	3,606
28,050	28,100	3,793	3,374	3,793	3,614
28,100	28,150	3,800	3,381	3,800	3,621
28,150	28,200	3,808	3,389	3,808	3,629
28,200	28,250	3,815	3,396	3,815	3,636
28,250	28,300	3,823	3,404	3,823	3,644
28,300	28,350	3,830	3,411	3,830	3,651
28,350	28,400	3,838	3,419	3,838	3,659
28,400	28,450	3,845	3,426	3,845	3,666
28,450	28,500	3,853	3,434	3,853	3,674
28,500	28,550	3,860	3,441	3,860	3,681
28,550	28,600	3,868	3,449	3,868	3,689
28,600	28,650	3,875	3,456	3,875	3,696
28,650	28,700	3,883	3,464	3,883	3,704
28,700	28,750	3,890	3,471	3,890	3,711
28,750	28,800	3,898	3,479	3,898	3,719
28,800	28,850	3,905	3,486	3,905	3,726
28,850	28,900	3,913	3,494	3,913	3,734
28,900	28,950	3,920	3,501	3,920	3,741
28,950	29,000	3,928	3,509	3,928	3,749

29,000

At least	But less than	Single	Married filing jointly	Married filing separately	Head of a household
29,000	29,050	3,935	3,516	3,935	3,756
29,050	29,100	3,943	3,524	3,943	3,764
29,100	29,150	3,950	3,531	3,950	3,771
29,150	29,200	3,958	3,539	3,958	3,779
29,200	29,250	3,965	3,546	3,965	3,786
29,250	29,300	3,973	3,554	3,973	3,794
29,300	29,350	3,980	3,561	3,980	3,801
29,350	29,400	3,988	3,569	3,988	3,809
29,400	29,450	3,995	3,576	3,995	3,816
29,450	29,500	4,003	3,584	4,003	3,824
29,500	29,550	4,010	3,591	4,010	3,831
29,550	29,600	4,018	3,599	4,018	3,839
29,600	29,650	4,025	3,606	4,025	3,846
29,650	29,700	4,033	3,614	4,033	3,854
29,700	29,750	4,040	3,621	4,040	3,861
29,750	29,800	4,048	3,629	4,048	3,869
29,800	29,850	4,055	3,636	4,055	3,876
29,850	29,900	4,063	3,644	4,063	3,884
29,900	29,950	4,070	3,651	4,070	3,891
29,950	30,000	4,078	3,659	4,078	3,899

30,000

At least	But less than	Single	Married filing jointly	Married filing separately	Head of a household
30,000	30,050	4,085	3,666	4,085	3,906
30,050	30,100	4,093	3,674	4,093	3,914
30,100	30,150	4,100	3,681	4,100	3,921
30,150	30,200	4,108	3,689	4,108	3,929
30,200	30,250	4,115	3,696	4,115	3,936
30,250	30,300	4,123	3,704	4,123	3,944
30,300	30,350	4,130	3,711	4,130	3,951
30,350	30,400	4,138	3,719	4,138	3,959
30,400	30,450	4,145	3,726	4,145	3,966
30,450	30,500	4,153	3,734	4,153	3,974
30,500	30,550	4,160	3,741	4,160	3,981
30,550	30,600	4,168	3,749	4,168	3,989
30,600	30,650	4,175	3,756	4,175	3,996
30,650	30,700	4,183	3,764	4,183	4,004
30,700	30,750	4,190	3,771	4,190	4,011
30,750	30,800	4,198	3,779	4,198	4,019
30,800	30,850	4,205	3,786	4,205	4,026
30,850	30,900	4,213	3,794	4,213	4,034
30,900	30,950	4,220	3,801	4,220	4,041
30,950	31,000	4,228	3,809	4,228	4,049

31,000

At least	But less than	Single	Married filing jointly	Married filing separately	Head of a household
31,000	31,050	4,235	3,816	4,235	4,056
31,050	31,100	4,243	3,824	4,243	4,064
31,100	31,150	4,250	3,831	4,250	4,071
31,150	31,200	4,258	3,839	4,258	4,079
31,200	31,250	4,265	3,846	4,265	4,086
31,250	31,300	4,273	3,854	4,273	4,094
31,300	31,350	4,280	3,861	4,280	4,101
31,350	31,400	4,288	3,869	4,288	4,109
31,400	31,450	4,295	3,876	4,295	4,116
31,450	31,500	4,303	3,884	4,303	4,124
31,500	31,550	4,310	3,891	4,310	4,131
31,550	31,600	4,318	3,899	4,318	4,139
31,600	31,650	4,325	3,906	4,325	4,146
31,650	31,700	4,333	3,914	4,333	4,154
31,700	31,750	4,340	3,921	4,340	4,161
31,750	31,800	4,348	3,929	4,348	4,169
31,800	31,850	4,355	3,936	4,355	4,176
31,850	31,900	4,363	3,944	4,363	4,184
31,900	31,950	4,370	3,951	4,370	4,191
31,950	32,000	4,378	3,959	4,378	4,199

Caution: Draft as of 09/13/2010

* This column must also be used by a qualifying widow(er).

2010 Tax Table–*Continued*

32,000 / 35,000 / 38,000 — If line 43 (taxable income) is — And you are —

At least	But less than	Single	Married filing jointly*	Married filing separately	Head of a household
32,000					
32,000	32,050	4,385	3,966	4,385	4,206
32,050	32,100	4,393	3,974	4,393	4,214
32,100	32,150	4,400	3,981	4,400	4,221
32,150	32,200	4,408	3,989	4,408	4,229
32,200	32,250	4,415	3,996	4,415	4,236
32,250	32,300	4,423	4,004	4,423	4,244
32,300	32,350	4,430	4,011	4,430	4,251
32,350	32,400	4,438	4,019	4,438	4,259
32,400	32,450	4,445	4,026	4,445	4,266
32,450	32,500	4,453	4,034	4,453	4,274
32,500	32,550	4,460	4,041	4,460	4,281
32,550	32,600	4,468	4,049	4,468	4,289
32,600	32,650	4,475	4,056	4,475	4,296
32,650	32,700	4,483	4,064	4,483	4,304
32,700	32,750	4,490	4,071	4,490	4,311
32,750	32,800	4,498	4,079	4,498	4,319
32,800	32,850	4,505	4,086	4,505	4,326
32,850	32,900	4,513	4,094	4,513	4,334
32,900	32,950	4,520	4,101	4,520	4,341
32,950	33,000	4,528	4,109	4,528	4,349
33,000					
33,000	33,050	4,535	4,116	4,535	4,356
33,050	33,100	4,543	4,124	4,543	4,364
33,100	33,150	4,550	4,131	4,550	4,371
33,150	33,200	4,558	4,139	4,558	4,379
33,200	33,250	4,565	4,146	4,565	4,386
33,250	33,300	4,573	4,154	4,573	4,394
33,300	33,350	4,580	4,161	4,580	4,401
33,350	33,400	4,588	4,169	4,588	4,409
33,400	33,450	4,595	4,176	4,595	4,416
33,450	33,500	4,603	4,184	4,603	4,424
33,500	33,550	4,610	4,191	4,610	4,431
33,550	33,600	4,618	4,199	4,618	4,439
33,600	33,650	4,625	4,206	4,625	4,446
33,650	33,700	4,633	4,214	4,633	4,454
33,700	33,750	4,640	4,221	4,640	4,461
33,750	33,800	4,648	4,229	4,648	4,469
33,800	33,850	4,655	4,236	4,655	4,476
33,850	33,900	4,663	4,244	4,663	4,484
33,900	33,950	4,670	4,251	4,670	4,491
33,950	34,000	4,678	4,259	4,678	4,499
34,000					
34,000	34,050	4,688	4,266	4,688	4,506
34,050	34,100	4,700	4,274	4,700	4,514
34,100	34,150	4,713	4,281	4,713	4,521
34,150	34,200	4,725	4,289	4,725	4,529
34,200	34,250	4,738	4,296	4,738	4,536
34,250	34,300	4,750	4,304	4,750	4,544
34,300	34,350	4,763	4,311	4,763	4,551
34,350	34,400	4,775	4,319	4,775	4,559
34,400	34,450	4,788	4,326	4,788	4,566
34,450	34,500	4,800	4,334	4,800	4,574
34,500	34,550	4,813	4,341	4,813	4,581
34,550	34,600	4,825	4,349	4,825	4,589
34,600	34,650	4,838	4,356	4,838	4,596
34,650	34,700	4,850	4,364	4,850	4,604
34,700	34,750	4,863	4,371	4,863	4,611
34,750	34,800	4,875	4,379	4,875	4,619
34,800	34,850	4,888	4,386	4,888	4,626
34,850	34,900	4,900	4,394	4,900	4,634
34,900	34,950	4,913	4,401	4,913	4,641
34,950	35,000	4,925	4,409	4,925	4,649
35,000					
35,000	35,050	4,938	4,416	4,938	4,656
35,050	35,100	4,950	4,424	4,950	4,664
35,100	35,150	4,963	4,431	4,963	4,671
35,150	35,200	4,975	4,439	4,975	4,679
35,200	35,250	4,988	4,446	4,988	4,686
35,250	35,300	5,000	4,454	5,000	4,694
35,300	35,350	5,013	4,461	5,013	4,701
35,350	35,400	5,025	4,469	5,025	4,709
35,400	35,450	5,038	4,476	5,038	4,716
35,450	35,500	5,050	4,484	5,050	4,724
35,500	35,550	5,063	4,491	5,063	4,731
35,550	35,600	5,075	4,499	5,075	4,739
35,600	35,650	5,088	4,506	5,088	4,746
35,650	35,700	5,100	4,514	5,100	4,754
35,700	35,750	5,113	4,521	5,113	4,761
35,750	35,800	5,125	4,529	5,125	4,769
35,800	35,850	5,138	4,536	5,138	4,776
35,850	35,900	5,150	4,544	5,150	4,784
35,900	35,950	5,163	4,551	5,163	4,791
35,950	36,000	5,175	4,559	5,175	4,799
36,000					
36,000	36,050	5,188	4,566	5,188	4,806
36,050	36,100	5,200	4,574	5,200	4,814
36,100	36,150	5,213	4,581	5,213	4,821
36,150	36,200	5,225	4,589	5,225	4,829
36,200	36,250	5,238	4,596	5,238	4,836
36,250	36,300	5,250	4,604	5,250	4,844
36,300	36,350	5,263	4,611	5,263	4,851
36,350	36,400	5,275	4,619	5,275	4,859
36,400	36,450	5,288	4,626	5,288	4,866
36,450	36,500	5,300	4,634	5,300	4,874
36,500	36,550	5,313	4,641	5,313	4,881
36,550	36,600	5,325	4,649	5,325	4,889
36,600	36,650	5,338	4,656	5,338	4,896
36,650	36,700	5,350	4,664	5,350	4,904
36,700	36,750	5,363	4,671	5,363	4,911
36,750	36,800	5,375	4,679	5,375	4,919
36,800	36,850	5,388	4,686	5,388	4,926
36,850	36,900	5,400	4,694	5,400	4,934
36,900	36,950	5,413	4,701	5,413	4,941
36,950	37,000	5,425	4,709	5,425	4,949
37,000					
37,000	37,050	5,438	4,716	5,438	4,956
37,050	37,100	5,450	4,724	5,450	4,964
37,100	37,150	5,463	4,731	5,463	4,971
37,150	37,200	5,475	4,739	5,475	4,979
37,200	37,250	5,488	4,746	5,488	4,986
37,250	37,300	5,500	4,754	5,500	4,994
37,300	37,350	5,513	4,761	5,513	5,001
37,350	37,400	5,525	4,769	5,525	5,009
37,400	37,450	5,538	4,776	5,538	5,016
37,450	37,500	5,550	4,784	5,550	5,024
37,500	37,550	5,563	4,791	5,563	5,031
37,550	37,600	5,575	4,799	5,575	5,039
37,600	37,650	5,588	4,806	5,588	5,046
37,650	37,700	5,600	4,814	5,600	5,054
37,700	37,750	5,613	4,821	5,613	5,061
37,750	37,800	5,625	4,829	5,625	5,069
37,800	37,850	5,638	4,836	5,638	5,076
37,850	37,900	5,650	4,844	5,650	5,084
37,900	37,950	5,663	4,851	5,663	5,091
37,950	38,000	5,675	4,859	5,675	5,099
38,000					
38,000	38,050	5,688	4,866	5,688	5,106
38,050	38,100	5,700	4,874	5,700	5,114
38,100	38,150	5,713	4,881	5,713	5,121
38,150	38,200	5,725	4,889	5,725	5,129
38,200	38,250	5,738	4,896	5,738	5,136
38,250	38,300	5,750	4,904	5,750	5,144
38,300	38,350	5,763	4,911	5,763	5,151
38,350	38,400	5,775	4,919	5,775	5,159
38,400	38,450	5,788	4,926	5,788	5,166
38,450	38,500	5,800	4,934	5,800	5,174
38,500	38,550	5,813	4,941	5,813	5,181
38,550	38,600	5,825	4,949	5,825	5,189
38,600	38,650	5,838	4,956	5,838	5,196
38,650	38,700	5,850	4,964	5,850	5,204
38,700	38,750	5,863	4,971	5,863	5,211
38,750	38,800	5,875	4,979	5,875	5,219
38,800	38,850	5,888	4,986	5,888	5,226
38,850	38,900	5,900	4,994	5,900	5,234
38,900	38,950	5,913	5,001	5,913	5,241
38,950	39,000	5,925	5,009	5,925	5,249
39,000					
39,000	39,050	5,938	5,016	5,938	5,256
39,050	39,100	5,950	5,024	5,950	5,264
39,100	39,150	5,963	5,031	5,963	5,271
39,150	39,200	5,975	5,039	5,975	5,279
39,200	39,250	5,988	5,046	5,988	5,286
39,250	39,300	6,000	5,054	6,000	5,294
39,300	39,350	6,013	5,061	6,013	5,301
39,350	39,400	6,025	5,069	6,025	5,309
39,400	39,450	6,038	5,076	6,038	5,316
39,450	39,500	6,050	5,084	6,050	5,324
39,500	39,550	6,063	5,091	6,063	5,331
39,550	39,600	6,075	5,099	6,075	5,339
39,600	39,650	6,088	5,106	6,088	5,346
39,650	39,700	6,100	5,114	6,100	5,354
39,700	39,750	6,113	5,121	6,113	5,361
39,750	39,800	6,125	5,129	6,125	5,369
39,800	39,850	6,138	5,136	6,138	5,376
39,850	39,900	6,150	5,144	6,150	5,384
39,900	39,950	6,163	5,151	6,163	5,391
39,950	40,000	6,175	5,159	6,175	5,399
40,000					
40,000	40,050	6,188	5,166	6,188	5,406
40,050	40,100	6,200	5,174	6,200	5,414
40,100	40,150	6,213	5,181	6,213	5,421
40,150	40,200	6,225	5,189	6,225	5,429
40,200	40,250	6,238	5,196	6,238	5,436
40,250	40,300	6,250	5,204	6,250	5,444
40,300	40,350	6,263	5,211	6,263	5,451
40,350	40,400	6,275	5,219	6,275	5,459
40,400	40,450	6,288	5,226	6,288	5,466
40,450	40,500	6,300	5,234	6,300	5,474
40,500	40,550	6,313	5,241	6,313	5,481
40,550	40,600	6,325	5,249	6,325	5,489
40,600	40,650	6,338	5,256	6,338	5,496
40,650	40,700	6,350	5,264	6,350	5,504
40,700	40,750	6,363	5,271	6,363	5,511
40,750	40,800	6,375	5,279	6,375	5,519
40,800	40,850	6,388	5,286	6,388	5,526
40,850	40,900	6,400	5,294	6,400	5,534
40,900	40,950	6,413	5,301	6,413	5,541
40,950	41,000	6,425	5,309	6,425	5,549

Caution: Draft as of 09/13/2010

* This column must also be used by a qualifying widow(er).

2010 Tax Table–*Continued*

41,000 – 43,000

At least	But less than	Single	Married filing jointly *	Married filing separately	Head of a household
41,000					
41,000	41,050	6,438	5,316	6,438	5,556
41,050	41,100	6,450	5,324	6,450	5,564
41,100	41,150	6,463	5,331	6,463	5,571
41,150	41,200	6,475	5,339	6,475	5,579
41,200	41,250	6,488	5,346	6,488	5,586
41,250	41,300	6,500	5,354	6,500	5,594
41,300	41,350	6,513	5,361	6,513	5,601
41,350	41,400	6,525	5,369	6,525	5,609
41,400	41,450	6,538	5,376	6,538	5,616
41,450	41,500	6,550	5,384	6,550	5,624
41,500	41,550	6,563	5,391	6,563	5,631
41,550	41,600	6,575	5,399	6,575	5,639
41,600	41,650	6,588	5,406	6,588	5,646
41,650	41,700	6,600	5,414	6,600	5,654
41,700	41,750	6,613	5,421	6,613	5,661
41,750	41,800	6,625	5,429	6,625	5,669
41,800	41,850	6,638	5,436	6,638	5,676
41,850	41,900	6,650	5,444	6,650	5,684
41,900	41,950	6,663	5,451	6,663	5,691
41,950	42,000	6,675	5,459	6,675	5,699
42,000					
42,000	42,050	6,688	5,466	6,688	5,706
42,050	42,100	6,700	5,474	6,700	5,714
42,100	42,150	6,713	5,481	6,713	5,721
42,150	42,200	6,725	5,489	6,725	5,729
42,200	42,250	6,738	5,496	6,738	5,736
42,250	42,300	6,750	5,504	6,750	5,744
42,300	42,350	6,763	5,511	6,763	5,751
42,350	42,400	6,775	5,519	6,775	5,759
42,400	42,450	6,788	5,526	6,788	5,766
42,450	42,500	6,800	5,534	6,800	5,774
42,500	42,550	6,813	5,541	6,813	5,781
42,550	42,600	6,825	5,549	6,825	5,789
42,600	42,650	6,838	5,556	6,838	5,796
42,650	42,700	6,850	5,564	6,850	5,804
42,700	42,750	6,863	5,571	6,863	5,811
42,750	42,800	6,875	5,579	6,875	5,819
42,800	42,850	6,888	5,586	6,888	5,826
42,850	42,900	6,900	5,594	6,900	5,834
42,900	42,950	6,913	5,601	6,913	5,841
42,950	43,000	6,925	5,609	6,925	5,849
43,000					
43,000	43,050	6,938	5,616	6,938	5,856
43,050	43,100	6,950	5,624	6,950	5,864
43,100	43,150	6,963	5,631	6,963	5,871
43,150	43,200	6,975	5,639	6,975	5,879
43,200	43,250	6,988	5,646	6,988	5,886
43,250	43,300	7,000	5,654	7,000	5,894
43,300	43,350	7,013	5,661	7,013	5,901
43,350	43,400	7,025	5,669	7,025	5,909
43,400	43,450	7,038	5,676	7,038	5,916
43,450	43,500	7,050	5,684	7,050	5,924
43,500	43,550	7,063	5,691	7,063	5,931
43,550	43,600	7,075	5,699	7,075	5,939
43,600	43,650	7,088	5,706	7,088	5,946
43,650	43,700	7,100	5,714	7,100	5,954
43,700	43,750	7,113	5,721	7,113	5,961
43,750	43,800	7,125	5,729	7,125	5,969
43,800	43,850	7,138	5,736	7,138	5,976
43,850	43,900	7,150	5,744	7,150	5,984
43,900	43,950	7,163	5,751	7,163	5,991
43,950	44,000	7,175	5,759	7,175	5,999

44,000 – 46,000

At least	But less than	Single	Married filing jointly *	Married filing separately	Head of a household
44,000					
44,000	44,050	7,188	5,766	7,188	6,006
44,050	44,100	7,200	5,774	7,200	6,014
44,100	44,150	7,213	5,781	7,213	6,021
44,150	44,200	7,225	5,789	7,225	6,029
44,200	44,250	7,238	5,796	7,238	6,036
44,250	44,300	7,250	5,804	7,250	6,044
44,300	44,350	7,263	5,811	7,263	6,051
44,350	44,400	7,275	5,819	7,275	6,059
44,400	44,450	7,288	5,826	7,288	6,066
44,450	44,500	7,300	5,834	7,300	6,074
44,500	44,550	7,313	5,841	7,313	6,081
44,550	44,600	7,325	5,849	7,325	6,089
44,600	44,650	7,338	5,856	7,338	6,096
44,650	44,700	7,350	5,864	7,350	6,104
44,700	44,750	7,363	5,871	7,363	6,111
44,750	44,800	7,375	5,879	7,375	6,119
44,800	44,850	7,388	5,886	7,388	6,126
44,850	44,900	7,400	5,894	7,400	6,134
44,900	44,950	7,413	5,901	7,413	6,141
44,950	45,000	7,425	5,909	7,425	6,149
45,000					
45,000	45,050	7,438	5,916	7,438	6,156
45,050	45,100	7,450	5,924	7,450	6,164
45,100	45,150	7,463	5,931	7,463	6,171
45,150	45,200	7,475	5,939	7,475	6,179
45,200	45,250	7,488	5,946	7,488	6,186
45,250	45,300	7,500	5,954	7,500	6,194
45,300	45,350	7,513	5,961	7,513	6,201
45,350	45,400	7,525	5,969	7,525	6,209
45,400	45,450	7,538	5,976	7,538	6,216
45,450	45,500	7,550	5,984	7,550	6,224
45,500	45,550	7,563	5,991	7,563	6,231
45,550	45,600	7,575	5,999	7,575	6,241
45,600	45,650	7,588	6,006	7,588	6,254
45,650	45,700	7,600	6,014	7,600	6,266
45,700	45,750	7,613	6,021	7,613	6,279
45,750	45,800	7,625	6,029	7,625	6,291
45,800	45,850	7,638	6,036	7,638	6,304
45,850	45,900	7,650	6,044	7,650	6,316
45,900	45,950	7,663	6,051	7,663	6,329
45,950	46,000	7,675	6,059	7,675	6,341
46,000					
46,000	46,050	7,688	6,066	7,688	6,354
46,050	46,100	7,700	6,074	7,700	6,366
46,100	46,150	7,713	6,081	7,713	6,379
46,150	46,200	7,725	6,089	7,725	6,391
46,200	46,250	7,738	6,096	7,738	6,404
46,250	46,300	7,750	6,104	7,750	6,416
46,300	46,350	7,763	6,111	7,763	6,429
46,350	46,400	7,775	6,119	7,775	6,441
46,400	46,450	7,788	6,126	7,788	6,454
46,450	46,500	7,800	6,134	7,800	6,466
46,500	46,550	7,813	6,141	7,813	6,479
46,550	46,600	7,825	6,149	7,825	6,491
46,600	46,650	7,838	6,156	7,838	6,504
46,650	46,700	7,850	6,164	7,850	6,516
46,700	46,750	7,863	6,171	7,863	6,529
46,750	46,800	7,875	6,179	7,875	6,541
46,800	46,850	7,888	6,186	7,888	6,554
46,850	46,900	7,900	6,194	7,900	6,566
46,900	46,950	7,913	6,201	7,913	6,579
46,950	47,000	7,925	6,209	7,925	6,591

47,000 – 49,000

At least	But less than	Single	Married filing jointly *	Married filing separately	Head of a household
47,000					
47,000	47,050	7,938	6,216	7,938	6,604
47,050	47,100	7,950	6,224	7,950	6,616
47,100	47,150	7,963	6,231	7,963	6,629
47,150	47,200	7,975	6,239	7,975	6,641
47,200	47,250	7,988	6,246	7,988	6,654
47,250	47,300	8,000	6,254	8,000	6,666
47,300	47,350	8,013	6,261	8,013	6,679
47,350	47,400	8,025	6,269	8,025	6,691
47,400	47,450	8,038	6,276	8,038	6,704
47,450	47,500	8,050	6,284	8,050	6,716
47,500	47,550	8,063	6,291	8,063	6,729
47,550	47,600	8,075	6,299	8,075	6,741
47,600	47,650	8,088	6,306	8,088	6,754
47,650	47,700	8,100	6,314	8,100	6,766
47,700	47,750	8,113	6,321	8,113	6,779
47,750	47,800	8,125	6,329	8,125	6,791
47,800	47,850	8,138	6,336	8,138	6,804
47,850	47,900	8,150	6,344	8,150	6,816
47,900	47,950	8,163	6,351	8,163	6,829
47,950	48,000	8,175	6,359	8,175	6,841
48,000					
48,000	48,050	8,188	6,366	8,188	6,854
48,050	48,100	8,200	6,374	8,200	6,866
48,100	48,150	8,213	6,381	8,213	6,879
48,150	48,200	8,225	6,389	8,225	6,891
48,200	48,250	8,238	6,396	8,238	6,904
48,250	48,300	8,250	6,404	8,250	6,916
48,300	48,350	8,263	6,411	8,263	6,929
48,350	48,400	8,275	6,419	8,275	6,941
48,400	48,450	8,288	6,426	8,288	6,954
48,450	48,500	8,300	6,434	8,300	6,966
48,500	48,550	8,313	6,441	8,313	6,979
48,550	48,600	8,325	6,449	8,325	6,991
48,600	48,650	8,338	6,456	8,338	7,004
48,650	48,700	8,350	6,464	8,350	7,016
48,700	48,750	8,363	6,471	8,363	7,029
48,750	48,800	8,375	6,479	8,375	7,041
48,800	48,850	8,388	6,486	8,388	7,054
48,850	48,900	8,400	6,494	8,400	7,066
48,900	48,950	8,413	6,501	8,413	7,079
48,950	49,000	8,425	6,509	8,425	7,091
49,000					
49,000	49,050	8,438	6,516	8,438	7,104
49,050	49,100	8,450	6,524	8,450	7,116
49,100	49,150	8,463	6,531	8,463	7,129
49,150	49,200	8,475	6,539	8,475	7,141
49,200	49,250	8,488	6,546	8,488	7,154
49,250	49,300	8,500	6,554	8,500	7,166
49,300	49,350	8,513	6,561	8,513	7,179
49,350	49,400	8,525	6,569	8,525	7,191
49,400	49,450	8,538	6,576	8,538	7,204
49,450	49,500	8,550	6,584	8,550	7,216
49,500	49,550	8,563	6,591	8,563	7,229
49,550	49,600	8,575	6,599	8,575	7,241
49,600	49,650	8,588	6,606	8,588	7,254
49,650	49,700	8,600	6,614	8,600	7,266
49,700	49,750	8,613	6,621	8,613	7,279
49,750	49,800	8,625	6,629	8,625	7,291
49,800	49,850	8,638	6,636	8,638	7,304
49,850	49,900	8,650	6,644	8,650	7,316
49,900	49,950	8,663	6,651	8,663	7,329
49,950	50,000	8,675	6,659	8,675	7,341

Caution: Draft as of 09/13/2010

* This column must also be used by a qualifying widow(er).

2010 Tax Table–Continued

If line 43 (taxable income) is—		And you are—			
At least	But less than	Single	Married filing jointly*	Married filing separately	Head of a household
		Your tax is—			
50,000					
50,000	50,050	8,688	6,666	8,688	7,354
50,050	50,100	8,700	6,674	8,700	7,366
50,100	50,150	8,713	6,681	8,713	7,379
50,150	50,200	8,725	6,689	8,725	7,391
50,200	50,250	8,738	6,696	8,738	7,404
50,250	50,300	8,750	6,704	8,750	7,416
50,300	50,350	8,763	6,711	8,763	7,429
50,350	50,400	8,775	6,719	8,775	7,441
50,400	50,450	8,788	6,726	8,788	7,454
50,450	50,500	8,800	6,734	8,800	7,466
50,500	50,550	8,813	6,741	8,813	7,479
50,550	50,600	8,825	6,749	8,825	7,491
50,600	50,650	8,838	6,756	8,838	7,504
50,650	50,700	8,850	6,764	8,850	7,516
50,700	50,750	8,863	6,771	8,863	7,529
50,750	50,800	8,875	6,779	8,875	7,541
50,800	50,850	8,888	6,786	8,888	7,554
50,850	50,900	8,900	6,794	8,900	7,566
50,900	50,950	8,913	6,801	8,913	7,579
50,950	51,000	8,925	6,809	8,925	7,591
51,000					
51,000	51,050	8,938	6,816	8,938	7,604
51,050	51,100	8,950	6,824	8,950	7,616
51,100	51,150	8,963	6,831	8,963	7,629
51,150	51,200	8,975	6,839	8,975	7,641
51,200	51,250	8,988	6,846	8,988	7,654
51,250	51,300	9,000	6,854	9,000	7,666
51,300	51,350	9,013	6,861	9,013	7,679
51,350	51,400	9,025	6,869	9,025	7,691
51,400	51,450	9,038	6,876	9,038	7,704
51,450	51,500	9,050	6,884	9,050	7,716
51,500	51,550	9,063	6,891	9,063	7,729
51,550	51,600	9,075	6,899	9,075	7,741
51,600	51,650	9,088	6,906	9,088	7,754
51,650	51,700	9,100	6,914	9,100	7,766
51,700	51,750	9,113	6,921	9,113	7,779
51,750	51,800	9,125	6,929	9,125	7,791
51,800	51,850	9,138	6,936	9,138	7,804
51,850	51,900	9,150	6,944	9,150	7,816
51,900	51,950	9,163	6,951	9,163	7,829
51,950	52,000	9,175	6,959	9,175	7,841
52,000					
52,000	52,050	9,188	6,966	9,188	7,854
52,050	52,100	9,200	6,974	9,200	7,866
52,100	52,150	9,213	6,981	9,213	7,879
52,150	52,200	9,225	6,989	9,225	7,891
52,200	52,250	9,238	6,996	9,238	7,904
52,250	52,300	9,250	7,004	9,250	7,916
52,300	52,350	9,263	7,011	9,263	7,929
52,350	52,400	9,275	7,019	9,275	7,941
52,400	52,450	9,288	7,026	9,288	7,954
52,450	52,500	9,300	7,034	9,300	7,966
52,500	52,550	9,313	7,041	9,313	7,979
52,550	52,600	9,325	7,049	9,325	7,991
52,600	52,650	9,338	7,056	9,338	8,004
52,650	52,700	9,350	7,064	9,350	8,016
52,700	52,750	9,363	7,071	9,363	8,029
52,750	52,800	9,375	7,079	9,375	8,041
52,800	52,850	9,388	7,086	9,388	8,054
52,850	52,900	9,400	7,094	9,400	8,066
52,900	52,950	9,413	7,101	9,413	8,079
52,950	53,000	9,425	7,109	9,425	8,091

If line 43 (taxable income) is—		And you are—			
At least	But less than	Single	Married filing jointly*	Married filing separately	Head of a household
		Your tax is—			
53,000					
53,000	53,050	9,438	7,116	9,438	8,104
53,050	53,100	9,450	7,124	9,450	8,116
53,100	53,150	9,463	7,131	9,463	8,129
53,150	53,200	9,475	7,139	9,475	8,141
53,200	53,250	9,488	7,146	9,488	8,154
53,250	53,300	9,500	7,154	9,500	8,166
53,300	53,350	9,513	7,161	9,513	8,179
53,350	53,400	9,525	7,169	9,525	8,191
53,400	53,450	9,538	7,176	9,538	8,204
53,450	53,500	9,550	7,184	9,550	8,216
53,500	53,550	9,563	7,191	9,563	8,229
53,550	53,600	9,575	7,199	9,575	8,241
53,600	53,650	9,588	7,206	9,588	8,254
53,650	53,700	9,600	7,214	9,600	8,266
53,700	53,750	9,613	7,221	9,613	8,279
53,750	53,800	9,625	7,229	9,625	8,291
53,800	53,850	9,638	7,236	9,638	8,304
53,850	53,900	9,650	7,244	9,650	8,316
53,900	53,950	9,663	7,251	9,663	8,329
53,950	54,000	9,675	7,259	9,675	8,341
54,000					
54,000	54,050	9,688	7,266	9,688	8,354
54,050	54,100	9,700	7,274	9,700	8,366
54,100	54,150	9,713	7,281	9,713	8,379
54,150	54,200	9,725	7,289	9,725	8,391
54,200	54,250	9,738	7,296	9,738	8,404
54,250	54,300	9,750	7,304	9,750	8,416
54,300	54,350	9,763	7,311	9,763	8,429
54,350	54,400	9,775	7,319	9,775	8,441
54,400	54,450	9,788	7,326	9,788	8,454
54,450	54,500	9,800	7,334	9,800	8,466
54,500	54,550	9,813	7,341	9,813	8,479
54,550	54,600	9,825	7,349	9,825	8,491
54,600	54,650	9,838	7,356	9,838	8,504
54,650	54,700	9,850	7,364	9,850	8,516
54,700	54,750	9,863	7,371	9,863	8,529
54,750	54,800	9,875	7,379	9,875	8,541
54,800	54,850	9,888	7,386	9,888	8,554
54,850	54,900	9,900	7,394	9,900	8,566
54,900	54,950	9,913	7,401	9,913	8,579
54,950	55,000	9,925	7,409	9,925	8,591
55,000					
55,000	55,050	9,938	7,416	9,938	8,604
55,050	55,100	9,950	7,424	9,950	8,616
55,100	55,150	9,963	7,431	9,963	8,629
55,150	55,200	9,975	7,439	9,975	8,641
55,200	55,250	9,988	7,446	9,988	8,654
55,250	55,300	10,000	7,454	10,000	8,666
55,300	55,350	10,013	7,461	10,013	8,679
55,350	55,400	10,025	7,469	10,025	8,691
55,400	55,450	10,038	7,476	10,038	8,704
55,450	55,500	10,050	7,484	10,050	8,716
55,500	55,550	10,063	7,491	10,063	8,729
55,550	55,600	10,075	7,499	10,075	8,741
55,600	55,650	10,088	7,506	10,088	8,754
55,650	55,700	10,100	7,514	10,100	8,766
55,700	55,750	10,113	7,521	10,113	8,779
55,750	55,800	10,125	7,529	10,125	8,791
55,800	55,850	10,138	7,536	10,138	8,804
55,850	55,900	10,150	7,544	10,150	8,816
55,900	55,950	10,163	7,551	10,163	8,829
55,950	56,000	10,175	7,559	10,175	8,841

If line 43 (taxable income) is—		And you are—			
At least	But less than	Single	Married filing jointly*	Married filing separately	Head of a household
		Your tax is—			
56,000					
56,000	56,050	10,188	7,566	10,188	8,854
56,050	56,100	10,200	7,574	10,200	8,866
56,100	56,150	10,213	7,581	10,213	8,879
56,150	56,200	10,225	7,589	10,225	8,891
56,200	56,250	10,238	7,596	10,238	8,904
56,250	56,300	10,250	7,604	10,250	8,916
56,300	56,350	10,263	7,611	10,263	8,929
56,350	56,400	10,275	7,619	10,275	8,941
56,400	56,450	10,288	7,626	10,288	8,954
56,450	56,500	10,300	7,634	10,300	8,966
56,500	56,550	10,313	7,641	10,313	8,979
56,550	56,600	10,325	7,649	10,325	8,991
56,600	56,650	10,338	7,656	10,338	9,004
56,650	56,700	10,350	7,664	10,350	9,016
56,700	56,750	10,363	7,671	10,363	9,029
56,750	56,800	10,375	7,679	10,375	9,041
56,800	56,850	10,388	7,686	10,388	9,054
56,850	56,900	10,400	7,694	10,400	9,066
56,900	56,950	10,413	7,701	10,413	9,079
56,950	57,000	10,425	7,709	10,425	9,091
57,000					
57,000	57,050	10,438	7,716	10,438	9,104
57,050	57,100	10,450	7,724	10,450	9,116
57,100	57,150	10,463	7,731	10,463	9,129
57,150	57,200	10,475	7,739	10,475	9,141
57,200	57,250	10,488	7,746	10,488	9,154
57,250	57,300	10,500	7,754	10,500	9,166
57,300	57,350	10,513	7,761	10,513	9,179
57,350	57,400	10,525	7,769	10,525	9,191
57,400	57,450	10,538	7,776	10,538	9,204
57,450	57,500	10,550	7,784	10,550	9,216
57,500	57,550	10,563	7,791	10,563	9,229
57,550	57,600	10,575	7,799	10,575	9,241
57,600	57,650	10,588	7,806	10,588	9,254
57,650	57,700	10,600	7,814	10,600	9,266
57,700	57,750	10,613	7,821	10,613	9,279
57,750	57,800	10,625	7,829	10,625	9,291
57,800	57,850	10,638	7,836	10,638	9,304
57,850	57,900	10,650	7,844	10,650	9,316
57,900	57,950	10,663	7,851	10,663	9,329
57,950	58,000	10,675	7,859	10,675	9,341
58,000					
58,000	58,050	10,688	7,866	10,688	9,354
58,050	58,100	10,700	7,874	10,700	9,366
58,100	58,150	10,713	7,881	10,713	9,379
58,150	58,200	10,725	7,889	10,725	9,391
58,200	58,250	10,738	7,896	10,738	9,404
58,250	58,300	10,750	7,904	10,750	9,416
58,300	58,350	10,763	7,911	10,763	9,429
58,350	58,400	10,775	7,919	10,775	9,441
58,400	58,450	10,788	7,926	10,788	9,454
58,450	58,500	10,800	7,934	10,800	9,466
58,500	58,550	10,813	7,941	10,813	9,479
58,550	58,600	10,825	7,949	10,825	9,491
58,600	58,650	10,838	7,956	10,838	9,504
58,650	58,700	10,850	7,964	10,850	9,516
58,700	58,750	10,863	7,971	10,863	9,529
58,750	58,800	10,875	7,979	10,875	9,541
58,800	58,850	10,888	7,986	10,888	9,554
58,850	58,900	10,900	7,994	10,900	9,566
58,900	58,950	10,913	8,001	10,913	9,579
58,950	59,000	10,925	8,009	10,925	9,591

Caution: Draft as of 09/13/2010

* This column must also be used by a qualifying widow(er).

2010 Tax Table–*Continued*

59,000

If line 43 (taxable income) is— At least	But less than	Single	Married filing jointly	Married filing separately *	Head of a household
59,000	59,050	10,938	8,016	10,938	9,604
59,050	59,100	10,950	8,024	10,950	9,616
59,100	59,150	10,963	8,031	10,963	9,629
59,150	59,200	10,975	8,039	10,975	9,641
59,200	59,250	10,988	8,046	10,988	9,654
59,250	59,300	11,000	8,054	11,000	9,666
59,300	59,350	11,013	8,061	11,013	9,679
59,350	59,400	11,025	8,069	11,025	9,691
59,400	59,450	11,038	8,076	11,038	9,704
59,450	59,500	11,050	8,084	11,050	9,716
59,500	59,550	11,063	8,091	11,063	9,729
59,550	59,600	11,075	8,099	11,075	9,741
59,600	59,650	11,088	8,106	11,088	9,754
59,650	59,700	11,100	8,114	11,100	9,766
59,700	59,750	11,113	8,121	11,113	9,779
59,750	59,800	11,125	8,129	11,125	9,791
59,800	59,850	11,138	8,136	11,138	9,804
59,850	59,900	11,150	8,144	11,150	9,816
59,900	59,950	11,163	8,151	11,163	9,829
59,950	60,000	11,175	8,159	11,175	9,841

60,000

At least	But less than	Single	Married filing jointly	Married filing separately *	Head of a household
60,000	60,050	11,188	8,166	11,188	9,854
60,050	60,100	11,200	8,174	11,200	9,866
60,100	60,150	11,213	8,181	11,213	9,879
60,150	60,200	11,225	8,189	11,225	9,891
60,200	60,250	11,238	8,196	11,238	9,904
60,250	60,300	11,250	8,204	11,250	9,916
60,300	60,350	11,263	8,211	11,263	9,929
60,350	60,400	11,275	8,219	11,275	9,941
60,400	60,450	11,288	8,226	11,288	9,954
60,450	60,500	11,300	8,234	11,300	9,966
60,500	60,550	11,313	8,241	11,313	9,979
60,550	60,600	11,325	8,249	11,325	9,991
60,600	60,650	11,338	8,256	11,338	10,004
60,650	60,700	11,350	8,264	11,350	10,016
60,700	60,750	11,363	8,271	11,363	10,029
60,750	60,800	11,375	8,279	11,375	10,041
60,800	60,850	11,388	8,286	11,388	10,054
60,850	60,900	11,400	8,294	11,400	10,066
60,900	60,950	11,413	8,301	11,413	10,079
60,950	61,000	11,425	8,309	11,425	10,091

61,000

At least	But less than	Single	Married filing jointly	Married filing separately *	Head of a household
61,000	61,050	11,438	8,316	11,438	10,104
61,050	61,100	11,450	8,324	11,450	10,116
61,100	61,150	11,463	8,331	11,463	10,129
61,150	61,200	11,475	8,339	11,475	10,141
61,200	61,250	11,488	8,346	11,488	10,154
61,250	61,300	11,500	8,354	11,500	10,166
61,300	61,350	11,513	8,361	11,513	10,179
61,350	61,400	11,525	8,369	11,525	10,191
61,400	61,450	11,538	8,376	11,538	10,204
61,450	61,500	11,550	8,384	11,550	10,216
61,500	61,550	11,563	8,391	11,563	10,229
61,550	61,600	11,575	8,399	11,575	10,241
61,600	61,650	11,588	8,406	11,588	10,254
61,650	61,700	11,600	8,414	11,600	10,266
61,700	61,750	11,613	8,421	11,613	10,279
61,750	61,800	11,625	8,429	11,625	10,291
61,800	61,850	11,638	8,436	11,638	10,304
61,850	61,900	11,650	8,444	11,650	10,316
61,900	61,950	11,663	8,451	11,663	10,329
61,950	62,000	11,675	8,459	11,675	10,341

62,000

At least	But less than	Single	Married filing jointly	Married filing separately *	Head of a household
62,000	62,050	11,688	8,466	11,688	10,354
62,050	62,100	11,700	8,474	11,700	10,366
62,100	62,150	11,713	8,481	11,713	10,379
62,150	62,200	11,725	8,489	11,725	10,391
62,200	62,250	11,738	8,496	11,738	10,404
62,250	62,300	11,750	8,504	11,750	10,416
62,300	62,350	11,763	8,511	11,763	10,429
62,350	62,400	11,775	8,519	11,775	10,441
62,400	62,450	11,788	8,526	11,788	10,454
62,450	62,500	11,800	8,534	11,800	10,466
62,500	62,550	11,813	8,541	11,813	10,479
62,550	62,600	11,825	8,549	11,825	10,491
62,600	62,650	11,838	8,556	11,838	10,504
62,650	62,700	11,850	8,564	11,850	10,516
62,700	62,750	11,863	8,571	11,863	10,529
62,750	62,800	11,875	8,579	11,875	10,541
62,800	62,850	11,888	8,586	11,888	10,554
62,850	62,900	11,900	8,594	11,900	10,566
62,900	62,950	11,913	8,601	11,913	10,579
62,950	63,000	11,925	8,609	11,925	10,591

63,000

At least	But less than	Single	Married filing jointly	Married filing separately *	Head of a household
63,000	63,050	11,938	8,616	11,938	10,604
63,050	63,100	11,950	8,624	11,950	10,616
63,100	63,150	11,963	8,631	11,963	10,629
63,150	63,200	11,975	8,639	11,975	10,641
63,200	63,250	11,988	8,646	11,988	10,654
63,250	63,300	12,000	8,654	12,000	10,666
63,300	63,350	12,013	8,661	12,013	10,679
63,350	63,400	12,025	8,669	12,025	10,691
63,400	63,450	12,038	8,676	12,038	10,704
63,450	63,500	12,050	8,684	12,050	10,716
63,500	63,550	12,063	8,691	12,063	10,729
63,550	63,600	12,075	8,699	12,075	10,741
63,600	63,650	12,088	8,706	12,088	10,754
63,650	63,700	12,100	8,714	12,100	10,766
63,700	63,750	12,113	8,721	12,113	10,779
63,750	63,800	12,125	8,729	12,125	10,791
63,800	63,850	12,138	8,736	12,138	10,804
63,850	63,900	12,150	8,744	12,150	10,816
63,900	63,950	12,163	8,751	12,163	10,829
63,950	64,000	12,175	8,759	12,175	10,841

64,000

At least	But less than	Single	Married filing jointly	Married filing separately *	Head of a household
64,000	64,050	12,188	8,766	12,188	10,854
64,050	64,100	12,200	8,774	12,200	10,866
64,100	64,150	12,213	8,781	12,213	10,879
64,150	64,200	12,225	8,789	12,225	10,891
64,200	64,250	12,238	8,796	12,238	10,904
64,250	64,300	12,250	8,804	12,250	10,916
64,300	64,350	12,263	8,811	12,263	10,929
64,350	64,400	12,275	8,819	12,275	10,941
64,400	64,450	12,288	8,826	12,288	10,954
64,450	64,500	12,300	8,834	12,300	10,966
64,500	64,550	12,313	8,841	12,313	10,979
64,550	64,600	12,325	8,849	12,325	10,991
64,600	64,650	12,338	8,856	12,338	11,004
64,650	64,700	12,350	8,864	12,350	11,016
64,700	64,750	12,363	8,871	12,363	11,029
64,750	64,800	12,375	8,879	12,375	11,041
64,800	64,850	12,388	8,886	12,388	11,054
64,850	64,900	12,400	8,894	12,400	11,066
64,900	64,950	12,413	8,901	12,413	11,079
64,950	65,000	12,425	8,909	12,425	11,091

65,000

At least	But less than	Single	Married filing jointly	Married filing separately *	Head of a household
65,000	65,050	12,438	8,916	12,438	11,104
65,050	65,100	12,450	8,924	12,450	11,116
65,100	65,150	12,463	8,931	12,463	11,129
65,150	65,200	12,475	8,939	12,475	11,141
65,200	65,250	12,488	8,946	12,488	11,154
65,250	65,300	12,500	8,954	12,500	11,166
65,300	65,350	12,513	8,961	12,513	11,179
65,350	65,400	12,525	8,969	12,525	11,191
65,400	65,450	12,538	8,976	12,538	11,204
65,450	65,500	12,550	8,984	12,550	11,216
65,500	65,550	12,563	8,991	12,563	11,229
65,550	65,600	12,575	8,999	12,575	11,241
65,600	65,650	12,588	9,006	12,588	11,254
65,650	65,700	12,600	9,014	12,600	11,266
65,700	65,750	12,613	9,021	12,613	11,279
65,750	65,800	12,625	9,029	12,625	11,291
65,800	65,850	12,638	9,036	12,638	11,304
65,850	65,900	12,650	9,044	12,650	11,316
65,900	65,950	12,663	9,051	12,663	11,329
65,950	66,000	12,675	9,059	12,675	11,341

66,000

At least	But less than	Single	Married filing jointly	Married filing separately *	Head of a household
66,000	66,050	12,688	9,066	12,688	11,354
66,050	66,100	12,700	9,074	12,700	11,366
66,100	66,150	12,713	9,081	12,713	11,379
66,150	66,200	12,725	9,089	12,725	11,391
66,200	66,250	12,738	9,096	12,738	11,404
66,250	66,300	12,750	9,104	12,750	11,416
66,300	66,350	12,763	9,111	12,763	11,429
66,350	66,400	12,775	9,119	12,775	11,441
66,400	66,450	12,788	9,126	12,788	11,454
66,450	66,500	12,800	9,134	12,800	11,466
66,500	66,550	12,813	9,141	12,813	11,479
66,550	66,600	12,825	9,149	12,825	11,491
66,600	66,650	12,838	9,156	12,838	11,504
66,650	66,700	12,850	9,164	12,850	11,516
66,700	66,750	12,863	9,171	12,863	11,529
66,750	66,800	12,875	9,179	12,875	11,541
66,800	66,850	12,888	9,186	12,888	11,554
66,850	66,900	12,900	9,194	12,900	11,566
66,900	66,950	12,913	9,201	12,913	11,579
66,950	67,000	12,925	9,209	12,925	11,591

67,000

At least	But less than	Single	Married filing jointly	Married filing separately *	Head of a household
67,000	67,050	12,938	9,216	12,938	11,604
67,050	67,100	12,950	9,224	12,950	11,616
67,100	67,150	12,963	9,231	12,963	11,629
67,150	67,200	12,975	9,239	12,975	11,641
67,200	67,250	12,988	9,246	12,988	11,654
67,250	67,300	13,000	9,254	13,000	11,666
67,300	67,350	13,013	9,261	13,013	11,679
67,350	67,400	13,025	9,269	13,025	11,691
67,400	67,450	13,038	9,276	13,038	11,704
67,450	67,500	13,050	9,284	13,050	11,716
67,500	67,550	13,063	9,291	13,063	11,729
67,550	67,600	13,075	9,299	13,075	11,741
67,600	67,650	13,088	9,306	13,088	11,754
67,650	67,700	13,100	9,314	13,100	11,766
67,700	67,750	13,113	9,321	13,113	11,779
67,750	67,800	13,125	9,329	13,125	11,791
67,800	67,850	13,138	9,336	13,138	11,804
67,850	67,900	13,150	9,344	13,150	11,816
67,900	67,950	13,163	9,351	13,163	11,829
67,950	68,000	13,175	9,359	13,175	11,841

Caution: Draft as of 09/13/2010

* This column must also be used by a qualifying widow(er).

2010 Tax Table – *Continued*

If line 43 (taxable Income) is — / **And you are —** / **Your tax is —**

At least	But less than	Single	Married filing jointly *	Married filing separately	Head of a household
68,000					
68,000	68,050	13,188	9,369	13,188	11,854
68,050	68,100	13,200	9,381	13,200	11,866
68,100	68,150	13,213	9,394	13,213	11,879
68,150	68,200	13,225	9,406	13,225	11,891
68,200	68,250	13,238	9,419	13,238	11,904
68,250	68,300	13,250	9,431	13,250	11,916
68,300	68,350	13,263	9,444	13,263	11,929
68,350	68,400	13,275	9,456	13,275	11,941
68,400	68,450	13,288	9,469	13,288	11,954
68,450	68,500	13,300	9,481	13,300	11,966
68,500	68,550	13,313	9,494	13,313	11,979
68,550	68,600	13,325	9,506	13,325	11,991
68,600	68,650	13,338	9,519	13,338	12,004
68,650	68,700	13,350	9,531	13,351	12,016
68,700	68,750	13,363	9,544	13,365	12,029
68,750	68,800	13,375	9,556	13,379	12,041
68,800	68,850	13,388	9,569	13,393	12,054
68,850	68,900	13,400	9,581	13,407	12,066
68,900	68,950	13,413	9,594	13,421	12,079
68,950	69,000	13,425	9,606	13,435	12,091
69,000					
69,000	69,050	13,438	9,619	13,449	12,104
69,050	69,100	13,450	9,631	13,463	12,116
69,100	69,150	13,463	9,644	13,477	12,129
69,150	69,200	13,475	9,656	13,491	12,141
69,200	69,250	13,488	9,669	13,505	12,154
69,250	69,300	13,500	9,681	13,519	12,166
69,300	69,350	13,513	9,694	13,533	12,179
69,350	69,400	13,525	9,706	13,547	12,191
69,400	69,450	13,538	9,719	13,561	12,204
69,450	69,500	13,550	9,731	13,575	12,216
69,500	69,550	13,563	9,744	13,589	12,229
69,550	69,600	13,575	9,756	13,603	12,241
69,600	69,650	13,588	9,769	13,617	12,254
69,650	69,700	13,600	9,781	13,631	12,266
69,700	69,750	13,613	9,794	13,645	12,279
69,750	69,800	13,625	9,806	13,659	12,291
69,800	69,850	13,638	9,819	13,673	12,304
69,850	69,900	13,650	9,831	13,687	12,316
69,900	69,950	13,663	9,844	13,701	12,329
69,950	70,000	13,675	9,856	13,715	12,341
70,000					
70,000	70,050	13,688	9,869	13,729	12,354
70,050	70,100	13,700	9,881	13,743	12,366
70,100	70,150	13,713	9,894	13,757	12,379
70,150	70,200	13,725	9,906	13,771	12,391
70,200	70,250	13,738	9,919	13,785	12,404
70,250	70,300	13,750	9,931	13,799	12,416
70,300	70,350	13,763	9,944	13,813	12,429
70,350	70,400	13,775	9,956	13,827	12,441
70,400	70,450	13,788	9,969	13,841	12,454
70,450	70,500	13,800	9,981	13,855	12,466
70,500	70,550	13,813	9,994	13,869	12,479
70,550	70,600	13,825	10,006	13,883	12,491
70,600	70,650	13,838	10,019	13,897	12,504
70,650	70,700	13,850	10,031	13,911	12,516
70,700	70,750	13,863	10,044	13,925	12,529
70,750	70,800	13,875	10,056	13,939	12,541
70,800	70,850	13,888	10,069	13,953	12,554
70,850	70,900	13,900	10,081	13,967	12,566
70,900	70,950	13,913	10,094	13,981	12,579
70,950	71,000	13,925	10,106	13,995	12,591

At least	But less than	Single	Married filing jointly *	Married filing separately	Head of a household
71,000					
71,000	71,050	13,938	10,119	14,009	12,604
71,050	71,100	13,950	10,131	14,023	12,616
71,100	71,150	13,963	10,144	14,037	12,629
71,150	71,200	13,975	10,156	14,051	12,641
71,200	71,250	13,988	10,169	14,065	12,654
71,250	71,300	14,000	10,181	14,079	12,666
71,300	71,350	14,013	10,194	14,093	12,679
71,350	71,400	14,025	10,206	14,107	12,691
71,400	71,450	14,038	10,219	14,121	12,704
71,450	71,500	14,050	10,231	14,135	12,716
71,500	71,550	14,063	10,244	14,149	12,729
71,550	71,600	14,075	10,256	14,163	12,741
71,600	71,650	14,088	10,269	14,177	12,754
71,650	71,700	14,100	10,281	14,191	12,766
71,700	71,750	14,113	10,294	14,205	12,779
71,750	71,800	14,125	10,306	14,219	12,791
71,800	71,850	14,138	10,319	14,233	12,804
71,850	71,900	14,150	10,331	14,247	12,816
71,900	71,950	14,163	10,344	14,261	12,829
71,950	72,000	14,175	10,356	14,275	12,841
72,000					
72,000	72,050	14,188	10,369	14,289	12,854
72,050	72,100	14,200	10,381	14,303	12,866
72,100	72,150	14,213	10,394	14,317	12,879
72,150	72,200	14,225	10,406	14,331	12,891
72,200	72,250	14,238	10,419	14,345	12,904
72,250	72,300	14,250	10,431	14,359	12,916
72,300	72,350	14,263	10,444	14,373	12,929
72,350	72,400	14,275	10,456	14,387	12,941
72,400	72,450	14,288	10,469	14,401	12,954
72,450	72,500	14,300	10,481	14,415	12,966
72,500	72,550	14,313	10,494	14,429	12,979
72,550	72,600	14,325	10,506	14,443	12,991
72,600	72,650	14,338	10,519	14,457	13,004
72,650	72,700	14,350	10,531	14,471	13,016
72,700	72,750	14,363	10,544	14,485	13,029
72,750	72,800	14,375	10,556	14,499	13,041
72,800	72,850	14,388	10,569	14,513	13,054
72,850	72,900	14,400	10,581	14,527	13,066
72,900	72,950	14,413	10,594	14,541	13,079
72,950	73,000	14,425	10,606	14,555	13,091
73,000					
73,000	73,050	14,438	10,619	14,569	13,104
73,050	73,100	14,450	10,631	14,583	13,116
73,100	73,150	14,463	10,644	14,597	13,129
73,150	73,200	14,475	10,656	14,611	13,141
73,200	73,250	14,488	10,669	14,625	13,154
73,250	73,300	14,500	10,681	14,639	13,166
73,300	73,350	14,513	10,694	14,653	13,179
73,350	73,400	14,525	10,706	14,667	13,191
73,400	73,450	14,538	10,719	14,681	13,204
73,450	73,500	14,550	10,731	14,695	13,216
73,500	73,550	14,563	10,744	14,709	13,229
73,550	73,600	14,575	10,756	14,723	13,241
73,600	73,650	14,588	10,769	14,737	13,254
73,650	73,700	14,600	10,781	14,751	13,266
73,700	73,750	14,613	10,794	14,765	13,279
73,750	73,800	14,625	10,806	14,779	13,291
73,800	73,850	14,638	10,819	14,793	13,304
73,850	73,900	14,650	10,831	14,807	13,316
73,900	73,950	14,663	10,844	14,821	13,329
73,950	74,000	14,675	10,856	14,835	13,341

At least	But less than	Single	Married filing jointly *	Married filing separately	Head of a household
74,000					
74,000	74,050	14,688	10,869	14,849	13,354
74,050	74,100	14,700	10,881	14,863	13,366
74,100	74,150	14,713	10,894	14,877	13,379
74,150	74,200	14,725	10,906	14,891	13,391
74,200	74,250	14,738	10,919	14,905	13,404
74,250	74,300	14,750	10,931	14,919	13,416
74,300	74,350	14,763	10,944	14,933	13,429
74,350	74,400	14,775	10,956	14,947	13,441
74,400	74,450	14,788	10,969	14,961	13,454
74,450	74,500	14,800	10,981	14,975	13,466
74,500	74,550	14,813	10,994	14,989	13,479
74,550	74,600	14,825	11,006	15,003	13,491
74,600	74,650	14,838	11,019	15,017	13,504
74,650	74,700	14,850	11,031	15,031	13,516
74,700	74,750	14,863	11,044	15,045	13,529
74,750	74,800	14,875	11,056	15,059	13,541
74,800	74,850	14,888	11,069	15,073	13,554
74,850	74,900	14,900	11,081	15,087	13,566
74,900	74,950	14,913	11,094	15,101	13,579
74,950	75,000	14,925	11,106	15,115	13,591
75,000					
75,000	75,050	14,938	11,119	15,129	13,604
75,050	75,100	14,950	11,131	15,143	13,616
75,100	75,150	14,963	11,144	15,157	13,629
75,150	75,200	14,975	11,156	15,171	13,641
75,200	75,250	14,988	11,169	15,185	13,654
75,250	75,300	15,000	11,181	15,199	13,666
75,300	75,350	15,013	11,194	15,213	13,679
75,350	75,400	15,025	11,206	15,227	13,691
75,400	75,450	15,038	11,219	15,241	13,704
75,450	75,500	15,050	11,231	15,255	13,716
75,500	75,550	15,063	11,244	15,269	13,729
75,550	75,600	15,075	11,256	15,283	13,741
75,600	75,650	15,088	11,269	15,297	13,754
75,650	75,700	15,100	11,281	15,311	13,766
75,700	75,750	15,113	11,294	15,325	13,779
75,750	75,800	15,125	11,306	15,339	13,791
75,800	75,850	15,138	11,319	15,353	13,804
75,850	75,900	15,150	11,331	15,367	13,816
75,900	75,950	15,163	11,344	15,381	13,829
75,950	76,000	15,175	11,356	15,395	13,841
76,000					
76,000	76,050	15,188	11,369	15,409	13,854
76,050	76,100	15,200	11,381	15,423	13,866
76,100	76,150	15,213	11,394	15,437	13,879
76,150	76,200	15,225	11,406	15,451	13,891
76,200	76,250	15,238	11,419	15,465	13,904
76,250	76,300	15,250	11,431	15,479	13,916
76,300	76,350	15,263	11,444	15,493	13,929
76,350	76,400	15,275	11,456	15,507	13,941
76,400	76,450	15,288	11,469	15,521	13,954
76,450	76,500	15,300	11,481	15,535	13,966
76,500	76,550	15,313	11,494	15,549	13,979
76,550	76,600	15,325	11,506	15,563	13,991
76,600	76,650	15,338	11,519	15,577	14,004
76,650	76,700	15,350	11,531	15,591	14,016
76,700	76,750	15,363	11,544	15,605	14,029
76,750	76,800	15,375	11,556	15,619	14,041
76,800	76,850	15,388	11,569	15,633	14,054
76,850	76,900	15,400	11,581	15,647	14,066
76,900	76,950	15,413	11,594	15,661	14,079
76,950	77,000	15,425	11,606	15,675	14,091

Caution: Draft as of 09/13/2010

* This column must also be used by a qualifying widow(er).

2010 Tax Table–*Continued*

If line 43 (taxable income) is— At least	But less than	Single	Married filing jointly *	Married filing separately	Head of a house-hold
77,000					
77,000	77,050	15,438	11,619	15,689	14,104
77,050	77,100	15,450	11,631	15,703	14,116
77,100	77,150	15,463	11,644	15,717	14,129
77,150	77,200	15,475	11,656	15,731	14,141
77,200	77,250	15,488	11,669	15,745	14,154
77,250	77,300	15,500	11,681	15,759	14,166
77,300	77,350	15,513	11,694	15,773	14,179
77,350	77,400	15,525	11,706	15,787	14,191
77,400	77,450	15,538	11,719	15,801	14,204
77,450	77,500	15,550	11,731	15,815	14,216
77,500	77,550	15,563	11,744	15,829	14,229
77,550	77,600	15,575	11,756	15,843	14,241
77,600	77,650	15,588	11,769	15,857	14,254
77,650	77,700	15,600	11,781	15,871	14,266
77,700	77,750	15,613	11,794	15,885	14,279
77,750	77,800	15,625	11,806	15,899	14,291
77,800	77,850	15,638	11,819	15,913	14,304
77,850	77,900	15,650	11,831	15,927	14,316
77,900	77,950	15,663	11,844	15,941	14,329
77,950	78,000	15,675	11,856	15,955	14,341
78,000					
78,000	78,050	15,688	11,869	15,969	14,354
78,050	78,100	15,700	11,881	15,983	14,366
78,100	78,150	15,713	11,894	15,997	14,379
78,150	78,200	15,725	11,906	16,011	14,391
78,200	78,250	15,738	11,919	16,025	14,404
78,250	78,300	15,750	11,931	16,039	14,416
78,300	78,350	15,763	11,944	16,053	14,429
78,350	78,400	15,775	11,956	16,067	14,441
78,400	78,450	15,788	11,969	16,081	14,454
78,450	78,500	15,800	11,981	16,095	14,466
78,500	78,550	15,813	11,994	16,109	14,479
78,550	78,600	15,825	12,006	16,123	14,491
78,600	78,650	15,838	12,019	16,137	14,504
78,650	78,700	15,850	12,031	16,151	14,516
78,700	78,750	15,863	12,044	16,165	14,529
78,750	78,800	15,875	12,056	16,179	14,541
78,800	78,850	15,888	12,069	16,193	14,554
78,850	78,900	15,900	12,081	16,207	14,566
78,900	78,950	15,913	12,094	16,221	14,579
78,950	79,000	15,925	12,106	16,235	14,591
79,000					
79,000	79,050	15,938	12,119	16,249	14,604
79,050	79,100	15,950	12,131	16,263	14,616
79,100	79,150	15,963	12,144	16,277	14,629
79,150	79,200	15,975	12,156	16,291	14,641
79,200	79,250	15,988	12,169	16,305	14,654
79,250	79,300	16,000	12,181	16,319	14,666
79,300	79,350	16,013	12,194	16,333	14,679
79,350	79,400	16,025	12,206	16,347	14,691
79,400	79,450	16,038	12,219	16,361	14,704
79,450	79,500	16,050	12,231	16,375	14,716
79,500	79,550	16,063	12,244	16,389	14,729
79,550	79,600	16,075	12,256	16,403	14,741
79,600	79,650	16,088	12,269	16,417	14,754
79,650	79,700	16,100	12,281	16,431	14,766
79,700	79,750	16,113	12,294	16,445	14,779
79,750	79,800	16,125	12,306	16,459	14,791
79,800	79,850	16,138	12,319	16,473	14,804
79,850	79,900	16,150	12,331	16,487	14,816
79,900	79,950	16,163	12,344	16,501	14,829
79,950	80,000	16,175	12,356	16,515	14,841

If line 43 (taxable income) is— At least	But less than	Single	Married filing jointly *	Married filing separately	Head of a house-hold
80,000					
80,000	80,050	16,188	12,369	16,529	14,854
80,050	80,100	16,200	12,381	16,543	14,866
80,100	80,150	16,213	12,394	16,557	14,879
80,150	80,200	16,225	12,406	16,571	14,891
80,200	80,250	16,238	12,419	16,585	14,904
80,250	80,300	16,250	12,431	16,599	14,916
80,300	80,350	16,263	12,444	16,613	14,929
80,350	80,400	16,275	12,456	16,627	14,941
80,400	80,450	16,288	12,469	16,641	14,954
80,450	80,500	16,300	12,481	16,655	14,966
80,500	80,550	16,313	12,494	16,669	14,979
80,550	80,600	16,325	12,506	16,683	14,991
80,600	80,650	16,338	12,519	16,697	15,004
80,650	80,700	16,350	12,531	16,711	15,016
80,700	80,750	16,363	12,544	16,725	15,029
80,750	80,800	16,375	12,556	16,739	15,041
80,800	80,850	16,388	12,569	16,753	15,054
80,850	80,900	16,400	12,581	16,767	15,066
80,900	80,950	16,413	12,594	16,781	15,079
80,950	81,000	16,425	12,606	16,795	15,091
81,000					
81,000	81,050	16,438	12,619	16,809	15,104
81,050	81,100	16,450	12,631	16,823	15,116
81,100	81,150	16,463	12,644	16,837	15,129
81,150	81,200	16,475	12,656	16,851	15,141
81,200	81,250	16,488	12,669	16,865	15,154
81,250	81,300	16,500	12,681	16,879	15,166
81,300	81,350	16,513	12,694	16,893	15,179
81,350	81,400	16,525	12,706	16,907	15,191
81,400	81,450	16,538	12,719	16,921	15,204
81,450	81,500	16,550	12,731	16,935	15,216
81,500	81,550	16,563	12,744	16,949	15,229
81,550	81,600	16,575	12,756	16,963	15,241
81,600	81,650	16,588	12,769	16,977	15,254
81,650	81,700	16,600	12,781	16,991	15,266
81,700	81,750	16,613	12,794	17,005	15,279
81,750	81,800	16,625	12,806	17,019	15,291
81,800	81,850	16,638	12,819	17,033	15,304
81,850	81,900	16,650	12,831	17,047	15,316
81,900	81,950	16,663	12,844	17,061	15,329
81,950	82,000	16,675	12,856	17,075	15,341
82,000					
82,000	82,050	16,688	12,869	17,089	15,354
82,050	82,100	16,700	12,881	17,103	15,366
82,100	82,150	16,713	12,894	17,117	15,379
82,150	82,200	16,725	12,906	17,131	15,391
82,200	82,250	16,738	12,919	17,145	15,404
82,250	82,300	16,750	12,931	17,159	15,416
82,300	82,350	16,763	12,944	17,173	15,429
82,350	82,400	16,775	12,956	17,187	15,441
82,400	82,450	16,788	12,969	17,201	15,454
82,450	82,500	16,802	12,981	17,215	15,466
82,500	82,550	16,816	12,994	17,229	15,479
82,550	82,600	16,830	13,006	17,243	15,491
82,600	82,650	16,844	13,019	17,257	15,504
82,650	82,700	16,858	13,031	17,271	15,516
82,700	82,750	16,872	13,044	17,285	15,529
82,750	82,800	16,886	13,056	17,299	15,541
82,800	82,850	16,900	13,069	17,313	15,554
82,850	82,900	16,914	13,081	17,327	15,566
82,900	82,950	16,928	13,094	17,341	15,579
82,950	83,000	16,942	13,106	17,355	15,591

If line 43 (taxable income) is— At least	But less than	Single	Married filing jointly *	Married filing separately	Head of a house-hold
83,000					
83,000	83,050	16,956	13,119	17,369	15,604
83,050	83,100	16,970	13,131	17,383	15,616
83,100	83,150	16,984	13,144	17,397	15,629
83,150	83,200	16,998	13,156	17,411	15,641
83,200	83,250	17,012	13,169	17,425	15,654
83,250	83,300	17,026	13,181	17,439	15,666
83,300	83,350	17,040	13,194	17,453	15,679
83,350	83,400	17,054	13,206	17,467	15,691
83,400	83,450	17,068	13,219	17,481	15,704
83,450	83,500	17,082	13,231	17,495	15,716
83,500	83,550	17,096	13,244	17,509	15,729
83,550	83,600	17,110	13,256	17,523	15,741
83,600	83,650	17,124	13,269	17,537	15,754
83,650	83,700	17,138	13,281	17,551	15,766
83,700	83,750	17,152	13,294	17,565	15,779
83,750	83,800	17,166	13,306	17,579	15,791
83,800	83,850	17,180	13,319	17,593	15,804
83,850	83,900	17,194	13,331	17,607	15,816
83,900	83,950	17,208	13,344	17,621	15,829
83,950	84,000	17,222	13,356	17,635	15,841
84,000					
84,000	84,050	17,236	13,369	17,649	15,854
84,050	84,100	17,250	13,381	17,663	15,866
84,100	84,150	17,264	13,394	17,677	15,879
84,150	84,200	17,278	13,406	17,691	15,891
84,200	84,250	17,292	13,419	17,705	15,904
84,250	84,300	17,306	13,431	17,719	15,916
84,300	84,350	17,320	13,444	17,733	15,929
84,350	84,400	17,334	13,456	17,747	15,941
84,400	84,450	17,348	13,469	17,761	15,954
84,450	84,500	17,362	13,481	17,775	15,966
84,500	84,550	17,376	13,494	17,789	15,979
84,550	84,600	17,390	13,506	17,803	15,991
84,600	84,650	17,404	13,519	17,817	16,004
84,650	84,700	17,418	13,531	17,831	16,016
84,700	84,750	17,432	13,544	17,845	16,029
84,750	84,800	17,446	13,556	17,859	16,041
84,800	84,850	17,460	13,569	17,873	16,054
84,850	84,900	17,474	13,581	17,887	16,066
84,900	84,950	17,488	13,594	17,901	16,079
84,950	85,000	17,502	13,606	17,915	16,091
85,000					
85,000	85,050	17,516	13,619	17,929	16,104
85,050	85,100	17,530	13,631	17,943	16,116
85,100	85,150	17,544	13,644	17,957	16,129
85,150	85,200	17,558	13,656	17,971	16,141
85,200	85,250	17,572	13,669	17,985	16,154
85,250	85,300	17,586	13,681	17,999	16,166
85,300	85,350	17,600	13,694	18,013	16,179
85,350	85,400	17,614	13,706	18,027	16,191
85,400	85,450	17,628	13,719	18,041	16,204
85,450	85,500	17,642	13,731	18,055	16,216
85,500	85,550	17,656	13,744	18,069	16,229
85,550	85,600	17,670	13,756	18,083	16,241
85,600	85,650	17,684	13,769	18,097	16,254
85,650	85,700	17,698	13,781	18,111	16,266
85,700	85,750	17,712	13,794	18,125	16,279
85,750	85,800	17,726	13,806	18,139	16,291
85,800	85,850	17,740	13,819	18,153	16,304
85,850	85,900	17,754	13,831	18,167	16,316
85,900	85,950	17,768	13,844	18,181	16,329
85,950	86,000	17,782	13,856	18,195	16,341

Caution: Draft as of 09/13/2010

* This column must also be used by a qualifying widow(er).

2010 Tax Table–*Continued*

86,000

At least	But less than	Single	Married filing jointly*	Married filing separately	Head of a household
86,000	86,050	17,796	13,869	18,209	16,354
86,050	86,100	17,810	13,881	18,223	16,366
86,100	86,150	17,824	13,894	18,237	16,379
86,150	86,200	17,838	13,906	18,251	16,391
86,200	86,250	17,852	13,919	18,265	16,404
86,250	86,300	17,866	13,931	18,279	16,416
86,300	86,350	17,880	13,944	18,293	16,429
86,350	86,400	17,894	13,956	18,307	16,441
86,400	86,450	17,908	13,969	18,321	16,454
86,450	86,500	17,922	13,981	18,335	16,466
86,500	86,550	17,936	13,994	18,349	16,479
86,550	86,600	17,950	14,006	18,363	16,491
86,600	86,650	17,964	14,019	18,377	16,504
86,650	86,700	17,978	14,031	18,391	16,516
86,700	86,750	17,992	14,044	18,405	16,529
86,750	86,800	18,006	14,056	18,419	16,541
86,800	86,850	18,020	14,069	18,433	16,554
86,850	86,900	18,034	14,081	18,447	16,566
86,900	86,950	18,048	14,094	18,461	16,579
86,950	87,000	18,062	14,106	18,475	16,591

87,000

At least	But less than	Single	Married filing jointly*	Married filing separately	Head of a household
87,000	87,050	18,076	14,119	18,489	16,604
87,050	87,100	18,090	14,131	18,503	16,616
87,100	87,150	18,104	14,144	18,517	16,629
87,150	87,200	18,118	14,156	18,531	16,641
87,200	87,250	18,132	14,169	18,545	16,654
87,250	87,300	18,146	14,181	18,559	16,666
87,300	87,350	18,160	14,194	18,573	16,679
87,350	87,400	18,174	14,206	18,587	16,691
87,400	87,450	18,188	14,219	18,601	16,704
87,450	87,500	18,202	14,231	18,615	16,716
87,500	87,550	18,216	14,244	18,629	16,729
87,550	87,600	18,230	14,256	18,643	16,741
87,600	87,650	18,244	14,269	18,657	16,754
87,650	87,700	18,258	14,281	18,671	16,766
87,700	87,750	18,272	14,294	18,685	16,779
87,750	87,800	18,286	14,306	18,699	16,791
87,800	87,850	18,300	14,319	18,713	16,804
87,850	87,900	18,314	14,331	18,727	16,816
87,900	87,950	18,328	14,344	18,741	16,829
87,950	88,000	18,342	14,356	18,755	16,841

88,000

At least	But less than	Single	Married filing jointly*	Married filing separately	Head of a household
88,000	88,050	18,356	14,369	18,769	16,854
88,050	88,100	18,370	14,381	18,783	16,866
88,100	88,150	18,384	14,394	18,797	16,879
88,150	88,200	18,398	14,406	18,811	16,891
88,200	88,250	18,412	14,419	18,825	16,904
88,250	88,300	18,426	14,431	18,839	16,916
88,300	88,350	18,440	14,444	18,853	16,929
88,350	88,400	18,454	14,456	18,867	16,941
88,400	88,450	18,468	14,469	18,881	16,954
88,450	88,500	18,482	14,481	18,895	16,966
88,500	88,550	18,496	14,494	18,909	16,979
88,550	88,600	18,510	14,506	18,923	16,991
88,600	88,650	18,524	14,519	18,937	17,004
88,650	88,700	18,538	14,531	18,951	17,016
88,700	88,750	18,552	14,544	18,965	17,029
88,750	88,800	18,566	14,556	18,979	17,041
88,800	88,850	18,580	14,569	18,993	17,054
88,850	88,900	18,594	14,581	19,007	17,066
88,900	88,950	18,608	14,594	19,021	17,079
88,950	89,000	18,622	14,606	19,035	17,091

89,000

At least	But less than	Single	Married filing jointly*	Married filing separately	Head of a household
89,000	89,050	18,636	14,619	19,049	17,104
89,050	89,100	18,650	14,631	19,063	17,116
89,100	89,150	18,664	14,644	19,077	17,129
89,150	89,200	18,678	14,656	19,091	17,141
89,200	89,250	18,692	14,669	19,105	17,154
89,250	89,300	18,706	14,681	19,119	17,166
89,300	89,350	18,720	14,694	19,133	17,179
89,350	89,400	18,734	14,706	19,147	17,191
89,400	89,450	18,748	14,719	19,161	17,204
89,450	89,500	18,762	14,731	19,175	17,216
89,500	89,550	18,776	14,744	19,189	17,229
89,550	89,600	18,790	14,756	19,203	17,241
89,600	89,650	18,804	14,769	19,217	17,254
89,650	89,700	18,818	14,781	19,231	17,266
89,700	89,750	18,832	14,794	19,245	17,279
89,750	89,800	18,846	14,806	19,259	17,291
89,800	89,850	18,860	14,819	19,273	17,304
89,850	89,900	18,874	14,831	19,287	17,316
89,900	89,950	18,888	14,844	19,301	17,329
89,950	90,000	18,902	14,856	19,315	17,341

90,000

At least	But less than	Single	Married filing jointly*	Married filing separately	Head of a household
90,000	90,050	18,916	14,869	19,329	17,354
90,050	90,100	18,930	14,881	19,343	17,366
90,100	90,150	18,944	14,894	19,357	17,379
90,150	90,200	18,958	14,906	19,371	17,391
90,200	90,250	18,972	14,919	19,385	17,404
90,250	90,300	18,986	14,931	19,399	17,416
90,300	90,350	19,000	14,944	19,413	17,429
90,350	90,400	19,014	14,956	19,427	17,441
90,400	90,450	19,028	14,969	19,441	17,454
90,450	90,500	19,042	14,981	19,455	17,466
90,500	90,550	19,056	14,994	19,469	17,479
90,550	90,600	19,070	15,006	19,483	17,491
90,600	90,650	19,084	15,019	19,497	17,504
90,650	90,700	19,098	15,031	19,511	17,516
90,700	90,750	19,112	15,044	19,525	17,529
90,750	90,800	19,126	15,056	19,539	17,541
90,800	90,850	19,140	15,069	19,553	17,554
90,850	90,900	19,154	15,081	19,567	17,566
90,900	90,950	19,168	15,094	19,581	17,579
90,950	91,000	19,182	15,106	19,595	17,591

91,000

At least	But less than	Single	Married filing jointly*	Married filing separately	Head of a household
91,000	91,050	19,196	15,119	19,609	17,604
91,050	91,100	19,210	15,131	19,623	17,616
91,100	91,150	19,224	15,144	19,637	17,629
91,150	91,200	19,238	15,156	19,651	17,641
91,200	91,250	19,252	15,169	19,665	17,654
91,250	91,300	19,266	15,181	19,679	17,666
91,300	91,350	19,280	15,194	19,693	17,679
91,350	91,400	19,294	15,206	19,707	17,691
91,400	91,450	19,308	15,219	19,721	17,704
91,450	91,500	19,322	15,231	19,735	17,716
91,500	91,550	19,336	15,244	19,749	17,729
91,550	91,600	19,350	15,256	19,763	17,741
91,600	91,650	19,364	15,269	19,777	17,754
91,650	91,700	19,378	15,281	19,791	17,766
91,700	91,750	19,392	15,294	19,805	17,779
91,750	91,800	19,406	15,306	19,819	17,791
91,800	91,850	19,420	15,319	19,833	17,804
91,850	91,900	19,434	15,331	19,847	17,816
91,900	91,950	19,448	15,344	19,861	17,829
91,950	92,000	19,462	15,356	19,875	17,841

92,000

At least	But less than	Single	Married filing jointly*	Married filing separately	Head of a household
92,000	92,050	19,476	15,369	19,889	17,854
92,050	92,100	19,490	15,381	19,903	17,866
92,100	92,150	19,504	15,394	19,917	17,879
92,150	92,200	19,518	15,406	19,931	17,891
92,200	92,250	19,532	15,419	19,945	17,904
92,250	92,300	19,546	15,431	19,959	17,916
92,300	92,350	19,560	15,444	19,973	17,929
92,350	92,400	19,574	15,456	19,987	17,941
92,400	92,450	19,588	15,469	20,001	17,954
92,450	92,500	19,602	15,481	20,015	17,966
92,500	92,550	19,616	15,494	20,029	17,979
92,550	92,600	19,630	15,506	20,043	17,991
92,600	92,650	19,644	15,519	20,057	18,004
92,650	92,700	19,658	15,531	20,071	18,016
92,700	92,750	19,672	15,544	20,085	18,029
92,750	92,800	19,686	15,556	20,099	18,041
92,800	92,850	19,700	15,569	20,113	18,054
92,850	92,900	19,714	15,581	20,127	18,066
92,900	92,950	19,728	15,594	20,141	18,079
92,950	93,000	19,742	15,606	20,155	18,091

93,000

At least	But less than	Single	Married filing jointly*	Married filing separately	Head of a household
93,000	93,050	19,756	15,619	20,169	18,104
93,050	93,100	19,770	15,631	20,183	18,116
93,100	93,150	19,784	15,644	20,197	18,129
93,150	93,200	19,798	15,656	20,211	18,141
93,200	93,250	19,812	15,669	20,225	18,154
93,250	93,300	19,826	15,681	20,239	18,166
93,300	93,350	19,840	15,694	20,253	18,179
93,350	93,400	19,854	15,706	20,267	18,191
93,400	93,450	19,868	15,719	20,281	18,204
93,450	93,500	19,882	15,731	20,295	18,216
93,500	93,550	19,896	15,744	20,309	18,229
93,550	93,600	19,910	15,756	20,323	18,241
93,600	93,650	19,924	15,769	20,337	18,254
93,650	93,700	19,938	15,781	20,351	18,266
93,700	93,750	19,952	15,794	20,365	18,279
93,750	93,800	19,966	15,806	20,379	18,291
93,800	93,850	19,980	15,819	20,393	18,304
93,850	93,900	19,994	15,831	20,407	18,316
93,900	93,950	20,008	15,844	20,421	18,329
93,950	94,000	20,022	15,856	20,435	18,341

94,000

At least	But less than	Single	Married filing jointly*	Married filing separately	Head of a household
94,000	94,050	20,036	15,869	20,449	18,354
94,050	94,100	20,050	15,881	20,463	18,366
94,100	94,150	20,064	15,894	20,477	18,379
94,150	94,200	20,078	15,906	20,491	18,391
94,200	94,250	20,092	15,919	20,505	18,404
94,250	94,300	20,106	15,931	20,519	18,416
94,300	94,350	20,120	15,944	20,533	18,429
94,350	94,400	20,134	15,956	20,547	18,441
94,400	94,450	20,148	15,969	20,561	18,454
94,450	94,500	20,162	15,981	20,575	18,466
94,500	94,550	20,176	15,994	20,589	18,479
94,550	94,600	20,190	16,006	20,603	18,491
94,600	94,650	20,204	16,019	20,617	18,504
94,650	94,700	20,218	16,031	20,631	18,516
94,700	94,750	20,232	16,044	20,645	18,529
94,750	94,800	20,246	16,056	20,659	18,541
94,800	94,850	20,260	16,069	20,673	18,554
94,850	94,900	20,274	16,081	20,687	18,566
94,900	94,950	20,288	16,094	20,701	18,579
94,950	95,000	20,302	16,106	20,715	18,591

Caution: Draft as of 09/13/2010

* This column must also be used by a qualifying widow(er).

2010 Tax Table—*Continued*

95,000

If line 43 (taxable income) is— At least	But less than	Single	Married filing jointly	Married filing separately	Head of a household
95,000	95,050	20,316	16,119	20,729	18,604
95,050	95,100	20,330	16,131	20,743	18,616
95,100	95,150	20,344	16,144	20,757	18,629
95,150	95,200	20,358	16,156	20,771	18,641
95,200	95,250	20,372	16,169	20,785	18,654
95,250	95,300	20,386	16,181	20,799	18,666
95,300	95,350	20,400	16,194	20,813	18,679
95,350	95,400	20,414	16,206	20,827	18,691
95,400	95,450	20,428	16,219	20,841	18,704
95,450	95,500	20,442	16,231	20,855	18,716
95,500	95,550	20,456	16,244	20,869	18,729
95,550	95,600	20,470	16,256	20,883	18,741
95,600	95,650	20,484	16,269	20,897	18,754
95,650	95,700	20,498	16,281	20,911	18,766
95,700	95,750	20,512	16,294	20,925	18,779
95,750	95,800	20,526	16,306	20,939	18,791
95,800	95,850	20,540	16,319	20,953	18,804
95,850	95,900	20,554	16,331	20,967	18,816
95,900	95,950	20,568	16,344	20,981	18,829
95,950	96,000	20,582	16,356	20,995	18,841

96,000

At least	But less than	Single	Married filing jointly	Married filing separately	Head of a household
96,000	96,050	20,596	16,369	21,009	18,854
96,050	96,100	20,610	16,381	21,023	18,866
96,100	96,150	20,624	16,394	21,037	18,879
96,150	96,200	20,638	16,406	21,051	18,891
96,200	96,250	20,652	16,419	21,065	18,904
96,250	96,300	20,666	16,431	21,079	18,916
96,300	96,350	20,680	16,444	21,093	18,929
96,350	96,400	20,694	16,456	21,107	18,941
96,400	96,450	20,708	16,469	21,121	18,954
96,450	96,500	20,722	16,481	21,135	18,966
96,500	96,550	20,736	16,494	21,149	18,979
96,550	96,600	20,750	16,506	21,163	18,991
96,600	96,650	20,764	16,519	21,177	19,004
96,650	96,700	20,778	16,531	21,191	19,016
96,700	96,750	20,792	16,544	21,205	19,029
96,750	96,800	20,806	16,556	21,219	19,041
96,800	96,850	20,820	16,569	21,233	19,054
96,850	96,900	20,834	16,581	21,247	19,066
96,900	96,950	20,848	16,594	21,261	19,079
96,950	97,000	20,862	16,606	21,275	19,091

97,000

At least	But less than	Single	Married filing jointly	Married filing separately	Head of a household
97,000	97,050	20,876	16,619	21,289	19,104
97,050	97,100	20,890	16,631	21,303	19,116
97,100	97,150	20,904	16,644	21,317	19,129
97,150	97,200	20,918	16,656	21,331	19,141
97,200	97,250	20,932	16,669	21,345	19,154
97,250	97,300	20,946	16,681	21,359	19,166
97,300	97,350	20,960	16,694	21,373	19,179
97,350	97,400	20,974	16,706	21,387	19,191
97,400	97,450	20,988	16,719	21,401	19,204
97,450	97,500	21,002	16,731	21,415	19,216
97,500	97,550	21,016	16,744	21,429	19,229
97,550	97,600	21,030	16,756	21,443	19,241
97,600	97,650	21,044	16,769	21,457	19,254
97,650	97,700	21,058	16,781	21,471	19,266
97,700	97,750	21,072	16,794	21,485	19,279
97,750	97,800	21,086	16,806	21,499	19,291
97,800	97,850	21,100	16,819	21,513	19,304
97,850	97,900	21,114	16,831	21,527	19,316
97,900	97,950	21,128	16,844	21,541	19,329
97,950	98,000	21,142	16,856	21,555	19,341

98,000

At least	But less than	Single	Married filing jointly	Married filing separately	Head of a household
98,000	98,050	21,156	16,869	21,569	19,354
98,050	98,100	21,170	16,881	21,583	19,366
98,100	98,150	21,184	16,894	21,597	19,379
98,150	98,200	21,198	16,906	21,611	19,391
98,200	98,250	21,212	16,919	21,625	19,404
98,250	98,300	21,226	16,931	21,639	19,416
98,300	98,350	21,240	16,944	21,653	19,429
98,350	98,400	21,254	16,956	21,667	19,441
98,400	98,450	21,268	16,969	21,681	19,454
98,450	98,500	21,282	16,981	21,695	19,466
98,500	98,550	21,296	16,994	21,709	19,479
98,550	98,600	21,310	17,006	21,723	19,491
98,600	98,650	21,324	17,019	21,737	19,504
98,650	98,700	21,338	17,031	21,751	19,516
98,700	98,750	21,352	17,044	21,765	19,529
98,750	98,800	21,366	17,056	21,779	19,541
98,800	98,850	21,380	17,069	21,793	19,554
98,850	98,900	21,394	17,081	21,807	19,566
98,900	98,950	21,408	17,094	21,821	19,579
98,950	99,000	21,422	17,106	21,835	19,591

99,000

At least	But less than	Single	Married filing jointly	Married filing separately	Head of a household
99,000	99,050	21,436	17,119	21,849	19,604
99,050	99,100	21,450	17,131	21,863	19,616
99,100	99,150	21,464	17,144	21,877	19,629
99,150	99,200	21,478	17,156	21,891	19,641
99,200	99,250	21,492	17,169	21,905	19,654
99,250	99,300	21,506	17,181	21,919	19,666
99,300	99,350	21,520	17,194	21,933	19,679
99,350	99,400	21,534	17,206	21,947	19,691
99,400	99,450	21,548	17,219	21,961	19,704
99,450	99,500	21,562	17,231	21,975	19,716
99,500	99,550	21,576	17,244	21,989	19,729
99,550	99,600	21,590	17,256	22,003	19,741
99,600	99,650	21,604	17,269	22,017	19,754
99,650	99,700	21,618	17,281	22,031	19,766
99,700	99,750	21,632	17,294	22,045	19,779
99,750	99,800	21,646	17,306	22,059	19,791
99,800	99,850	21,660	17,319	22,073	19,804
99,850	99,900	21,674	17,331	22,087	19,816
99,900	99,950	21,688	17,344	22,101	19,829
99,950	100,000	21,702	17,356	22,115	19,841

$100,000
or over —
use the Tax
Computation
Worksheet

Caution: Draft as of 09/13/2010

¶ 1111 Earned Income Credit Table

2010 Earned Income Credit (EIC) Table
Caution. This is **not** a tax table.

1. To find your credit, read down the "At least - But less than" columns and find the line that includes the amount you were told to look up from your EIC Worksheet.

2. Then, go to the column that includes your filing status and the number of qualifying children you have. Enter the credit from that column on your EIC Worksheet.

Example. If your filing status is single, you have one qualifying child, and the amount you are looking up from your EIC Worksheet is $2,455, you would enter $842.

If the amount you are looking up from the worksheet is—	And your filing status is— Single, head of household, or qualifying widow(er) and you have—			
	No children	One child	Two children	Three children
At least But less than	Your credit is—			
2,400 2,450	186	825	970	1,091
2,450 2,500	189	842	990	1,114

If the amount you are looking up from the worksheet is—		And your filing status is—							
		Single, head of household, or qualifying widow(er) and you have—				Married filing jointly and you have—			
		No Children	One Child	Two Children	Three Children	No Children	One Child	Two Children	Three Children
At least	But less than	Your credit is—				Your credit is—			
$1	$50	$2	$9	$10	$11	$2	$9	$10	$11
50	100	6	26	30	34	6	26	30	34
100	150	10	43	50	56	10	43	50	56
150	200	13	60	70	79	13	60	70	79
200	250	17	77	90	101	17	77	90	101
250	300	21	94	110	124	21	94	110	124
300	350	25	111	130	146	25	111	130	146
350	400	29	128	150	169	29	128	150	169
400	450	33	145	170	191	33	145	170	191
450	500	36	162	190	214	36	162	190	214
500	550	40	179	210	236	40	179	210	236
550	600	44	196	230	259	44	196	230	259
600	650	48	213	250	281	48	213	250	281
650	700	52	230	270	304	52	230	270	304
700	750	55	247	290	326	55	247	290	326
750	800	59	264	310	349	59	264	310	349
800	850	63	281	330	371	63	281	330	371
850	900	67	298	350	394	67	298	350	394
900	950	71	315	370	416	71	315	370	416
950	1,000	75	332	390	439	75	332	390	439
1,000	1,050	78	349	410	461	78	349	410	461
1,050	1,100	82	366	430	484	82	366	430	484
1,100	1,150	86	383	450	506	86	383	450	506
1,150	1,200	90	400	470	529	90	400	470	529
1,200	1,250	94	417	490	551	94	417	490	551
1,250	1,300	98	434	510	574	98	434	510	574
1,300	1,350	101	451	530	596	101	451	530	596
1,350	1,400	105	468	550	619	105	468	550	619
1,400	1,450	109	485	570	641	109	485	570	641
1,450	1,500	113	502	590	664	113	502	590	664
1,500	1,550	117	519	610	686	117	519	610	686
1,550	1,600	120	536	630	709	120	536	630	709
1,600	1,650	124	553	650	731	124	553	650	731
1,650	1,700	128	570	670	754	128	570	670	754
1,700	1,750	132	587	690	776	132	587	690	776
1,750	1,800	136	604	710	799	136	604	710	799
1,800	1,850	140	621	730	821	140	621	730	821
1,850	1,900	143	638	750	844	143	638	750	844
1,900	1,950	147	655	770	866	147	655	770	866
1,950	2,000	151	672	790	889	151	672	790	889
2,000	2,050	155	689	810	911	155	689	810	911
2,050	2,100	159	706	830	934	159	706	830	934
2,100	2,150	163	723	850	956	163	723	850	956
2,150	2,200	166	740	870	979	166	740	870	979
2,200	2,250	170	757	890	1,001	170	757	890	1,001
2,250	2,300	174	774	910	1,024	174	774	910	1,024
2,300	2,350	178	791	930	1,046	178	791	930	1,046
2,350	2,400	182	808	950	1,069	182	808	950	1,069
2,400	2,450	186	825	970	1,091	186	825	970	1,091
2,450	2,500	189	842	990	1,114	189	842	990	1,114

Caution: Draft as of 09/13/2010

2010 Earned Income Credit (EIC) Table—*Continued*   (**Caution.** This is **not** a tax table.)

If the amount you are looking up from the worksheet is—		Single, head of household, or qualifying widow(er) and you have—				Married filing jointly and you have—			
At least	But less than	No Children	One Child	Two Children	Three Children	No Children	One Child	Two Children	Three Children
		Your credit is—				Your credit is—			
2,500	2,550	193	859	1,010	1,136	193	859	1,010	1,136
2,550	2,600	197	876	1,030	1,159	197	876	1,030	1,159
2,600	2,650	201	893	1,050	1,181	201	893	1,050	1,181
2,650	2,700	205	910	1,070	1,204	205	910	1,070	1,204
2,700	2,750	208	927	1,090	1,226	208	927	1,090	1,226
2,750	2,800	212	944	1,110	1,249	212	944	1,110	1,249
2,800	2,850	216	961	1,130	1,271	216	961	1,130	1,271
2,850	2,900	220	978	1,150	1,294	220	978	1,150	1,294
2,900	2,950	224	995	1,170	1,316	224	995	1,170	1,316
2,950	3,000	228	1,012	1,190	1,339	228	1,012	1,190	1,339
3,000	3,050	231	1,029	1,210	1,361	231	1,029	1,210	1,361
3,050	3,100	235	1,046	1,230	1,384	235	1,046	1,230	1,384
3,100	3,150	239	1,063	1,250	1,406	239	1,063	1,250	1,406
3,150	3,200	243	1,080	1,270	1,429	243	1,080	1,270	1,429
3,200	3,250	247	1,097	1,290	1,451	247	1,097	1,290	1,451
3,250	3,300	251	1,114	1,310	1,474	251	1,114	1,310	1,474
3,300	3,350	254	1,131	1,330	1,496	254	1,131	1,330	1,496
3,350	3,400	258	1,148	1,350	1,519	258	1,148	1,350	1,519
3,400	3,450	262	1,165	1,370	1,541	262	1,165	1,370	1,541
3,450	3,500	266	1,182	1,390	1,564	266	1,182	1,390	1,564
3,500	3,550	270	1,199	1,410	1,586	270	1,199	1,410	1,586
3,550	3,600	273	1,216	1,430	1,609	273	1,216	1,430	1,609
3,600	3,650	277	1,233	1,450	1,631	277	1,233	1,450	1,631
3,650	3,700	281	1,250	1,470	1,654	281	1,250	1,470	1,654
3,700	3,750	285	1,267	1,490	1,676	285	1,267	1,490	1,676
3,750	3,800	289	1,284	1,510	1,699	289	1,284	1,510	1,699
3,800	3,850	293	1,301	1,530	1,721	293	1,301	1,530	1,721
3,850	3,900	296	1,318	1,550	1,744	296	1,318	1,550	1,744
3,900	3,950	300	1,335	1,570	1,766	300	1,335	1,570	1,766
3,950	4,000	304	1,352	1,590	1,789	304	1,352	1,590	1,789
4,000	4,050	308	1,369	1,610	1,811	308	1,369	1,610	1,811
4,050	4,100	312	1,386	1,630	1,834	312	1,386	1,630	1,834
4,100	4,150	316	1,403	1,650	1,856	316	1,403	1,650	1,856
4,150	4,200	319	1,420	1,670	1,879	319	1,420	1,670	1,879
4,200	4,250	323	1,437	1,690	1,901	323	1,437	1,690	1,901
4,250	4,300	327	1,454	1,710	1,924	327	1,454	1,710	1,924
4,300	4,350	331	1,471	1,730	1,946	331	1,471	1,730	1,946
4,350	4,400	335	1,488	1,750	1,969	335	1,488	1,750	1,969
4,400	4,450	339	1,505	1,770	1,991	339	1,505	1,770	1,991
4,450	4,500	342	1,522	1,790	2,014	342	1,522	1,790	2,014
4,500	4,550	346	1,539	1,810	2,036	346	1,539	1,810	2,036
4,550	4,600	350	1,556	1,830	2,059	350	1,556	1,830	2,059
4,600	4,650	354	1,573	1,850	2,081	354	1,573	1,850	2,081
4,650	4,700	358	1,590	1,870	2,104	358	1,590	1,870	2,104
4,700	4,750	361	1,607	1,890	2,126	361	1,607	1,890	2,126
4,750	4,800	365	1,624	1,910	2,149	365	1,624	1,910	2,149
4,800	4,850	369	1,641	1,930	2,171	369	1,641	1,930	2,171
4,850	4,900	373	1,658	1,950	2,194	373	1,658	1,950	2,194
4,900	4,950	377	1,675	1,970	2,216	377	1,675	1,970	2,216
4,950	5,000	381	1,692	1,990	2,239	381	1,692	1,990	2,239
5,000	5,050	384	1,709	2,010	2,261	384	1,709	2,010	2,261
5,050	5,100	388	1,726	2,030	2,284	388	1,726	2,030	2,284
5,100	5,150	392	1,743	2,050	2,306	392	1,743	2,050	2,306
5,150	5,200	396	1,760	2,070	2,329	396	1,760	2,070	2,329
5,200	5,250	400	1,777	2,090	2,351	400	1,777	2,090	2,351
5,250	5,300	404	1,794	2,110	2,374	404	1,794	2,110	2,374
5,300	5,350	407	1,811	2,130	2,396	407	1,811	2,130	2,396
5,350	5,400	411	1,828	2,150	2,419	411	1,828	2,150	2,419
5,400	5,450	415	1,845	2,170	2,441	415	1,845	2,170	2,441
5,450	5,500	419	1,862	2,190	2,464	419	1,862	2,190	2,464

Caution: Draft as of 09/13/2010

2010 Earned Income Credit (EIC) Table—*Continued* (**Caution.** This is **not** a tax table.)

If the amount you are looking up from the worksheet is—		Single, head of household, or qualifying widow(er) and you have—				Married filing jointly and you have—			
At least	But less than	No Children	One Child	Two Children	Three Children	No Children	One Child	Two Children	Three Children
		Your credit is—				Your credit is—			
5,500	5,550	423	1,879	2,210	2,486	423	1,879	2,210	2,486
5,550	5,600	426	1,896	2,230	2,509	426	1,896	2,230	2,509
5,600	5,650	430	1,913	2,250	2,531	430	1,913	2,250	2,531
5,650	5,700	434	1,930	2,270	2,554	434	1,930	2,270	2,554
5,700	5,750	438	1,947	2,290	2,576	438	1,947	2,290	2,576
5,750	5,800	442	1,964	2,310	2,599	442	1,964	2,310	2,599
5,800	5,850	446	1,981	2,330	2,621	446	1,981	2,330	2,621
5,850	5,900	449	1,998	2,350	2,644	449	1,998	2,350	2,644
5,900	5,950	453	2,015	2,370	2,666	453	2,015	2,370	2,666
5,950	6,000	457	2,032	2,390	2,689	457	2,032	2,390	2,689
6,000	6,050	457	2,049	2,410	2,711	457	2,049	2,410	2,711
6,050	6,100	457	2,066	2,430	2,734	457	2,066	2,430	2,734
6,100	6,150	457	2,083	2,450	2,756	457	2,083	2,450	2,756
6,150	6,200	457	2,100	2,470	2,779	457	2,100	2,470	2,779
6,200	6,250	457	2,117	2,490	2,801	457	2,117	2,490	2,801
6,250	6,300	457	2,134	2,510	2,824	457	2,134	2,510	2,824
6,300	6,350	457	2,151	2,530	2,846	457	2,151	2,530	2,846
6,350	6,400	457	2,168	2,550	2,869	457	2,168	2,550	2,869
6,400	6,450	457	2,185	2,570	2,891	457	2,185	2,570	2,891
6,450	6,500	457	2,202	2,590	2,914	457	2,202	2,590	2,914
6,500	6,550	457	2,219	2,610	2,936	457	2,219	2,610	2,936
6,550	6,600	457	2,236	2,630	2,959	457	2,236	2,630	2,959
6,600	6,650	457	2,253	2,650	2,981	457	2,253	2,650	2,981
6,650	6,700	457	2,270	2,670	3,004	457	2,270	2,670	3,004
6,700	6,750	457	2,287	2,690	3,026	457	2,287	2,690	3,026
6,750	6,800	457	2,304	2,710	3,049	457	2,304	2,710	3,049
6,800	6,850	457	2,321	2,730	3,071	457	2,321	2,730	3,071
6,850	6,900	457	2,338	2,750	3,094	457	2,338	2,750	3,094
6,900	6,950	457	2,355	2,770	3,116	457	2,355	2,770	3,116
6,950	7,000	457	2,372	2,790	3,139	457	2,372	2,790	3,139
7,000	7,050	457	2,389	2,810	3,161	457	2,389	2,810	3,161
7,050	7,100	457	2,406	2,830	3,184	457	2,406	2,830	3,184
7,100	7,150	457	2,423	2,850	3,206	457	2,423	2,850	3,206
7,150	7,200	457	2,440	2,870	3,229	457	2,440	2,870	3,229
7,200	7,250	457	2,457	2,890	3,251	457	2,457	2,890	3,251
7,250	7,300	457	2,474	2,910	3,274	457	2,474	2,910	3,274
7,300	7,350	457	2,491	2,930	3,296	457	2,491	2,930	3,296
7,350	7,400	457	2,508	2,950	3,319	457	2,508	2,950	3,319
7,400	7,450	457	2,525	2,970	3,341	457	2,525	2,970	3,341
7,450	7,500	457	2,542	2,990	3,364	457	2,542	2,990	3,364
7,500	7,550	454	2,559	3,010	3,386	457	2,559	3,010	3,386
7,550	7,600	450	2,576	3,030	3,409	457	2,576	3,030	3,409
7,600	7,650	446	2,593	3,050	3,431	457	2,593	3,050	3,431
7,650	7,700	443	2,610	3,070	3,454	457	2,610	3,070	3,454
7,700	7,750	439	2,627	3,090	3,476	457	2,627	3,090	3,476
7,750	7,800	435	2,644	3,110	3,499	457	2,644	3,110	3,499
7,800	7,850	431	2,661	3,130	3,521	457	2,661	3,130	3,521
7,850	7,900	427	2,678	3,150	3,544	457	2,678	3,150	3,544
7,900	7,950	423	2,695	3,170	3,566	457	2,695	3,170	3,566
7,950	8,000	420	2,712	3,190	3,589	457	2,712	3,190	3,589
8,000	8,050	416	2,729	3,210	3,611	457	2,729	3,210	3,611
8,050	8,100	412	2,746	3,230	3,634	457	2,746	3,230	3,634
8,100	8,150	408	2,763	3,250	3,656	457	2,763	3,250	3,656
8,150	8,200	404	2,780	3,270	3,679	457	2,780	3,270	3,679
8,200	8,250	400	2,797	3,290	3,701	457	2,797	3,290	3,701
8,250	8,300	397	2,814	3,310	3,724	457	2,814	3,310	3,724
8,300	8,350	393	2,831	3,330	3,746	457	2,831	3,330	3,746
8,350	8,400	389	2,848	3,350	3,769	457	2,848	3,350	3,769
8,400	8,450	385	2,865	3,370	3,791	457	2,865	3,370	3,791
8,450	8,500	381	2,882	3,390	3,814	457	2,882	3,390	3,814

Caution: Draft as of 09/13/2010

2010 Earned Income Credit (EIC) Table—*Continued*   (**Caution.** This is **not** a tax table.)

If the amount you are looking up from the worksheet is—		Single, head of household, or qualifying widow(er) and you have—				Married filing jointly and you have—			
At least	But less than	No Children	One Child	Two Children	Three Children	No Children	One Child	Two Children	Three Children
		Your credit is—				Your credit is—			
8,500	8,550	378	2,899	3,410	3,836	457	2,899	3,410	3,836
8,550	8,600	374	2,916	3,430	3,859	457	2,916	3,430	3,859
8,600	8,650	370	2,933	3,450	3,881	457	2,933	3,450	3,881
8,650	8,700	366	2,950	3,470	3,904	457	2,950	3,470	3,904
8,700	8,750	362	2,967	3,490	3,926	457	2,967	3,490	3,926
8,750	8,800	358	2,984	3,510	3,949	457	2,984	3,510	3,949
8,800	8,850	355	3,001	3,530	3,971	457	3,001	3,530	3,971
8,850	8,900	351	3,018	3,550	3,994	457	3,018	3,550	3,994
8,900	8,950	347	3,035	3,570	4,016	457	3,035	3,570	4,016
8,950	9,000	343	3,050	3,590	4,039	457	3,050	3,590	4,039
9,000	9,050	339	3,050	3,610	4,061	457	3,050	3,610	4,061
9,050	9,100	335	3,050	3,630	4,084	457	3,050	3,630	4,084
9,100	9,150	332	3,050	3,650	4,106	457	3,050	3,650	4,106
9,150	9,200	328	3,050	3,670	4,129	457	3,050	3,670	4,129
9,200	9,250	324	3,050	3,690	4,151	457	3,050	3,690	4,151
9,250	9,300	320	3,050	3,710	4,174	457	3,050	3,710	4,174
9,300	9,350	316	3,050	3,730	4,196	457	3,050	3,730	4,196
9,350	9,400	313	3,050	3,750	4,219	457	3,050	3,750	4,219
9,400	9,450	309	3,050	3,770	4,241	457	3,050	3,770	4,241
9,450	9,500	305	3,050	3,790	4,264	457	3,050	3,790	4,264
9,500	9,550	301	3,050	3,810	4,286	457	3,050	3,810	4,286
9,550	9,600	297	3,050	3,830	4,309	457	3,050	3,830	4,309
9,600	9,650	293	3,050	3,850	4,331	457	3,050	3,850	4,331
9,650	9,700	290	3,050	3,870	4,354	457	3,050	3,870	4,354
9,700	9,750	286	3,050	3,890	4,376	457	3,050	3,890	4,376
9,750	9,800	282	3,050	3,910	4,399	457	3,050	3,910	4,399
9,800	9,850	278	3,050	3,930	4,421	457	3,050	3,930	4,421
9,850	9,900	274	3,050	3,950	4,444	457	3,050	3,950	4,444
9,900	9,950	270	3,050	3,970	4,466	457	3,050	3,970	4,466
9,950	10,000	267	3,050	3,990	4,489	457	3,050	3,990	4,489
10,000	10,050	263	3,050	4,010	4,511	457	3,050	4,010	4,511
10,050	10,100	259	3,050	4,030	4,534	457	3,050	4,030	4,534
10,100	10,150	255	3,050	4,050	4,556	457	3,050	4,050	4,556
10,150	10,200	251	3,050	4,070	4,579	457	3,050	4,070	4,579
10,200	10,250	247	3,050	4,090	4,601	457	3,050	4,090	4,601
10,250	10,300	244	3,050	4,110	4,624	457	3,050	4,110	4,624
10,300	10,350	240	3,050	4,130	4,646	457	3,050	4,130	4,646
10,350	10,400	236	3,050	4,150	4,669	457	3,050	4,150	4,669
10,400	10,450	232	3,050	4,170	4,691	457	3,050	4,170	4,691
10,450	10,500	228	3,050	4,190	4,714	457	3,050	4,190	4,714
10,500	10,550	225	3,050	4,210	4,736	457	3,050	4,210	4,736
10,550	10,600	221	3,050	4,230	4,759	457	3,050	4,230	4,759
10,600	10,650	217	3,050	4,250	4,781	457	3,050	4,250	4,781
10,650	10,700	213	3,050	4,270	4,804	457	3,050	4,270	4,804
10,700	10,750	209	3,050	4,290	4,826	457	3,050	4,290	4,826
10,750	10,800	205	3,050	4,310	4,849	457	3,050	4,310	4,849
10,800	10,850	202	3,050	4,330	4,871	457	3,050	4,330	4,871
10,850	10,900	198	3,050	4,350	4,894	457	3,050	4,350	4,894
10,900	10,950	194	3,050	4,370	4,916	457	3,050	4,370	4,916
10,950	11,000	190	3,050	4,390	4,939	457	3,050	4,390	4,939
11,000	11,050	186	3,050	4,410	4,961	457	3,050	4,410	4,961
11,050	11,100	182	3,050	4,430	4,984	457	3,050	4,430	4,984
11,100	11,150	179	3,050	4,450	5,006	457	3,050	4,450	5,006
11,150	11,200	175	3,050	4,470	5,029	457	3,050	4,470	5,029
11,200	11,250	171	3,050	4,490	5,051	457	3,050	4,490	5,051
11,250	11,300	167	3,050	4,510	5,074	457	3,050	4,510	5,074
11,300	11,350	163	3,050	4,530	5,096	457	3,050	4,530	5,096
11,350	11,400	160	3,050	4,550	5,119	457	3,050	4,550	5,119
11,400	11,450	156	3,050	4,570	5,141	457	3,050	4,570	5,141
11,450	11,500	152	3,050	4,590	5,164	457	3,050	4,590	5,164

Caution: Draft as of 09/13/2010

2010 Earned Income Credit (EIC) Table–*Continued* (**Caution.** This is **not** a tax table.)

If the amount you are looking up from the worksheet is—		Single, head of household, or qualifying widow(er) and you have—				Married filing jointly and you have—			
At least	But less than	No Children	One Child	Two Children	Three Children	No Children	One Child	Two Children	Three Children
		Your credit is—				Your credit is—			
11,500	11,550	148	3,050	4,610	5,186	457	3,050	4,610	5,186
11,550	11,600	144	3,050	4,630	5,209	457	3,050	4,630	5,209
11,600	11,650	140	3,050	4,650	5,231	457	3,050	4,650	5,231
11,650	11,700	137	3,050	4,670	5,254	457	3,050	4,670	5,254
11,700	11,750	133	3,050	4,690	5,276	457	3,050	4,690	5,276
11,750	11,800	129	3,050	4,710	5,299	457	3,050	4,710	5,299
11,800	11,850	125	3,050	4,730	5,321	457	3,050	4,730	5,321
11,850	11,900	121	3,050	4,750	5,344	457	3,050	4,750	5,344
11,900	11,950	117	3,050	4,770	5,366	457	3,050	4,770	5,366
11,950	12,000	114	3,050	4,790	5,389	457	3,050	4,790	5,389
12,000	12,050	110	3,050	4,810	5,411	457	3,050	4,810	5,411
12,050	12,100	106	3,050	4,830	5,434	457	3,050	4,830	5,434
12,100	12,150	102	3,050	4,850	5,456	457	3,050	4,850	5,456
12,150	12,200	98	3,050	4,870	5,479	457	3,050	4,870	5,479
12,200	12,250	94	3,050	4,890	5,501	457	3,050	4,890	5,501
12,250	12,300	91	3,050	4,910	5,524	457	3,050	4,910	5,524
12,300	12,350	87	3,050	4,930	5,546	457	3,050	4,930	5,546
12,350	12,400	83	3,050	4,950	5,569	457	3,050	4,950	5,569
12,400	12,450	79	3,050	4,970	5,591	457	3,050	4,970	5,591
12,450	12,500	75	3,050	4,990	5,614	457	3,050	4,990	5,614
12,500	12,550	72	3,050	5,010	5,636	455	3,050	5,010	5,636
12,550	12,600	68	3,050	5,036	5,666	451	3,050	5,036	5,666
12,600	12,650	64	3,050	5,036	5,666	447	3,050	5,036	5,666
12,650	12,700	60	3,050	5,036	5,666	443	3,050	5,036	5,666
12,700	12,750	56	3,050	5,036	5,666	439	3,050	5,036	5,666
12,750	12,800	52	3,050	5,036	5,666	436	3,050	5,036	5,666
12,800	12,850	49	3,050	5,036	5,666	432	3,050	5,036	5,666
12,850	12,900	45	3,050	5,036	5,666	428	3,050	5,036	5,666
12,900	12,950	41	3,050	5,036	5,666	424	3,050	5,036	5,666
12,950	13,000	37	3,050	5,036	5,666	420	3,050	5,036	5,666
13,000	13,050	33	3,050	5,036	5,666	417	3,050	5,036	5,666
13,050	13,100	29	3,050	5,036	5,666	413	3,050	5,036	5,666
13,100	13,150	26	3,050	5,036	5,666	409	3,050	5,036	5,666
13,150	13,200	22	3,050	5,036	5,666	405	3,050	5,036	5,666
13,200	13,250	18	3,050	5,036	5,666	401	3,050	5,036	5,666
13,250	13,300	14	3,050	5,036	5,666	397	3,050	5,036	5,666
13,300	13,350	10	3,050	5,036	5,666	394	3,050	5,036	5,666
13,350	13,400	7	3,050	5,036	5,666	390	3,050	5,036	5,666
13,400	13,450	3	3,050	5,036	5,666	386	3,050	5,036	5,666
13,450	13,500	0	3,050	5,036	5,666	382	3,050	5,036	5,666
13,500	13,550	0	3,050	5,036	5,666	378	3,050	5,036	5,666
13,550	13,600	0	3,050	5,036	5,666	374	3,050	5,036	5,666
13,600	13,650	0	3,050	5,036	5,666	371	3,050	5,036	5,666
13,650	13,700	0	3,050	5,036	5,666	367	3,050	5,036	5,666
13,700	13,750	0	3,050	5,036	5,666	363	3,050	5,036	5,666
13,750	13,800	0	3,050	5,036	5,666	359	3,050	5,036	5,666
13,800	13,850	0	3,050	5,036	5,666	355	3,050	5,036	5,666
13,850	13,900	0	3,050	5,036	5,666	352	3,050	5,036	5,666
13,900	13,950	0	3,050	5,036	5,666	348	3,050	5,036	5,666
13,950	14,000	0	3,050	5,036	5,666	344	3,050	5,036	5,666
14,000	14,050	0	3,050	5,036	5,666	340	3,050	5,036	5,666
14,050	14,100	0	3,050	5,036	5,666	336	3,050	5,036	5,666
14,100	14,150	0	3,050	5,036	5,666	332	3,050	5,036	5,666
14,150	14,200	0	3,050	5,036	5,666	329	3,050	5,036	5,666
14,200	14,250	0	3,050	5,036	5,666	325	3,050	5,036	5,666
14,250	14,300	0	3,050	5,036	5,666	321	3,050	5,036	5,666
14,300	14,350	0	3,050	5,036	5,666	317	3,050	5,036	5,666
14,350	14,400	0	3,050	5,036	5,666	313	3,050	5,036	5,666
14,400	14,450	0	3,050	5,036	5,666	309	3,050	5,036	5,666
14,450	14,500	0	3,050	5,036	5,666	306	3,050	5,036	5,666

Caution: Draft as of 09/13/2010

2010 Earned Income Credit (EIC) Table—*Continued*   **(Caution.** This is **not** a tax table.)

If the amount you are looking up from the worksheet is—		Single, head of household, or qualifying widow(er) and you have—				Married filing jointly and you have—			
At least	But less than	No Children	One Child	Two Children	Three Children	No Children	One Child	Two Children	Three Children
		Your credit is—				Your credit is—			
14,500	14,550	0	3,050	5,036	5,666	302	3,050	5,036	5,666
14,550	14,600	0	3,050	5,036	5,666	298	3,050	5,036	5,666
14,600	14,650	0	3,050	5,036	5,666	294	3,050	5,036	5,666
14,650	14,700	0	3,050	5,036	5,666	290	3,050	5,036	5,666
14,700	14,750	0	3,050	5,036	5,666	286	3,050	5,036	5,666
14,750	14,800	0	3,050	5,036	5,666	283	3,050	5,036	5,666
14,800	14,850	0	3,050	5,036	5,666	279	3,050	5,036	5,666
14,850	14,900	0	3,050	5,036	5,666	275	3,050	5,036	5,666
14,900	14,950	0	3,050	5,036	5,666	271	3,050	5,036	5,666
14,950	15,000	0	3,050	5,036	5,666	267	3,050	5,036	5,666
15,000	15,050	0	3,050	5,036	5,666	264	3,050	5,036	5,666
15,050	15,100	0	3,050	5,036	5,666	260	3,050	5,036	5,666
15,100	15,150	0	3,050	5,036	5,666	256	3,050	5,036	5,666
15,150	15,200	0	3,050	5,036	5,666	252	3,050	5,036	5,666
15,200	15,250	0	3,050	5,036	5,666	248	3,050	5,036	5,666
15,250	15,300	0	3,050	5,036	5,666	244	3,050	5,036	5,666
15,300	15,350	0	3,050	5,036	5,666	241	3,050	5,036	5,666
15,350	15,400	0	3,050	5,036	5,666	237	3,050	5,036	5,666
15,400	15,450	0	3,050	5,036	5,666	233	3,050	5,036	5,666
15,450	15,500	0	3,050	5,036	5,666	229	3,050	5,036	5,666
15,500	15,550	0	3,050	5,036	5,666	225	3,050	5,036	5,666
15,550	15,600	0	3,050	5,036	5,666	221	3,050	5,036	5,666
15,600	15,650	0	3,050	5,036	5,666	218	3,050	5,036	5,666
15,650	15,700	0	3,050	5,036	5,666	214	3,050	5,036	5,666
15,700	15,750	0	3,050	5,036	5,666	210	3,050	5,036	5,666
15,750	15,800	0	3,050	5,036	5,666	206	3,050	5,036	5,666
15,800	15,850	0	3,050	5,036	5,666	202	3,050	5,036	5,666
15,850	15,900	0	3,050	5,036	5,666	199	3,050	5,036	5,666
15,900	15,950	0	3,050	5,036	5,666	195	3,050	5,036	5,666
15,950	16,000	0	3,050	5,036	5,666	191	3,050	5,036	5,666
16,000	16,050	0	3,050	5,036	5,666	187	3,050	5,036	5,666
16,050	16,100	0	3,050	5,036	5,666	183	3,050	5,036	5,666
16,100	16,150	0	3,050	5,036	5,666	179	3,050	5,036	5,666
16,150	16,200	0	3,050	5,036	5,666	176	3,050	5,036	5,666
16,200	16,250	0	3,050	5,036	5,666	172	3,050	5,036	5,666
16,250	16,300	0	3,050	5,036	5,666	168	3,050	5,036	5,666
16,300	16,350	0	3,050	5,036	5,666	164	3,050	5,036	5,666
16,350	16,400	0	3,050	5,036	5,666	160	3,050	5,036	5,666
16,400	16,450	0	3,050	5,036	5,666	156	3,050	5,036	5,666
16,450	16,500	0	3,046	5,031	5,660	153	3,050	5,036	5,666
16,500	16,550	0	3,038	5,020	5,650	149	3,050	5,036	5,666
16,550	16,600	0	3,030	5,010	5,639	145	3,050	5,036	5,666
16,600	16,650	0	3,022	4,999	5,629	141	3,050	5,036	5,666
16,650	16,700	0	3,014	4,989	5,618	137	3,050	5,036	5,666
16,700	16,750	0	3,006	4,978	5,608	133	3,050	5,036	5,666
16,750	16,800	0	2,998	4,968	5,597	130	3,050	5,036	5,666
16,800	16,850	0	2,990	4,957	5,587	126	3,050	5,036	5,666
16,850	16,900	0	2,982	4,946	5,576	122	3,050	5,036	5,666
16,900	16,950	0	2,974	4,936	5,565	118	3,050	5,036	5,666
16,950	17,000	0	2,966	4,925	5,555	114	3,050	5,036	5,666
17,000	17,050	0	2,958	4,915	5,544	111	3,050	5,036	5,666
17,050	17,100	0	2,950	4,904	5,534	107	3,050	5,036	5,666
17,100	17,150	0	2,942	4,894	5,523	103	3,050	5,036	5,666
17,150	17,200	0	2,934	4,883	5,513	99	3,050	5,036	5,666
17,200	17,250	0	2,926	4,873	5,502	95	3,050	5,036	5,666
17,250	17,300	0	2,918	4,862	5,492	91	3,050	5,036	5,666
17,300	17,350	0	2,910	4,852	5,481	88	3,050	5,036	5,666
17,350	17,400	0	2,902	4,841	5,471	84	3,050	5,036	5,666
17,400	17,450	0	2,894	4,831	5,460	80	3,050	5,036	5,666
17,450	17,500	0	2,886	4,820	5,450	76	3,050	5,036	5,666

Caution: Draft as of 09/13/2010

2010 Earned Income Credit (EIC) Table—*Continued* (**Caution.** This is **not** a tax table.)

If the amount you are looking up from the worksheet is—		Single, head of household, or qualifying widow(er) and you have—				Married filing jointly and you have—			
At least	But less than	No Children	One Child	Two Children	Three Children	No Children	One Child	Two Children	Three Children
		Your credit is—				Your credit is—			
17,500	17,550	0	2,878	4,810	5,439	72	3,050	5,036	5,666
17,550	17,600	0	2,870	4,799	5,429	68	3,050	5,036	5,666
17,600	17,650	0	2,862	4,789	5,418	65	3,050	5,036	5,666
17,650	17,700	0	2,854	4,778	5,408	61	3,050	5,036	5,666
17,700	17,750	0	2,846	4,767	5,397	57	3,050	5,036	5,666
17,750	17,800	0	2,838	4,757	5,386	53	3,050	5,036	5,666
17,800	17,850	0	2,830	4,746	5,376	49	3,050	5,036	5,666
17,850	17,900	0	2,822	4,736	5,365	46	3,050	5,036	5,666
17,900	17,950	0	2,814	4,725	5,355	42	3,050	5,036	5,666
17,950	18,000	0	2,806	4,715	5,344	38	3,050	5,036	5,666
18,000	18,050	0	2,798	4,704	5,334	34	3,050	5,036	5,666
18,050	18,100	0	2,790	4,694	5,323	30	3,050	5,036	5,666
18,100	18,150	0	2,782	4,683	5,313	26	3,050	5,036	5,666
18,150	18,200	0	2,774	4,673	5,302	23	3,050	5,036	5,666
18,200	18,250	0	2,766	4,662	5,292	19	3,050	5,036	5,666
18,250	18,300	0	2,758	4,652	5,281	15	3,050	5,036	5,666
18,300	18,350	0	2,750	4,641	5,271	11	3,050	5,036	5,666
18,350	18,400	0	2,742	4,631	5,260	7	3,050	5,036	5,666
18,400	18,450	0	2,734	4,620	5,250	3	3,050	5,036	5,666
18,450	18,500	0	2,726	4,610	5,239	*	3,050	5,036	5,666
18,500	18,550	0	2,718	4,599	5,229	0	3,050	5,036	5,666
18,550	18,600	0	2,710	4,588	5,218	0	3,050	5,036	5,666
18,600	18,650	0	2,702	4,578	5,207	0	3,050	5,036	5,666
18,650	18,700	0	2,694	4,567	5,197	0	3,050	5,036	5,666
18,700	18,750	0	2,686	4,557	5,186	0	3,050	5,036	5,666
18,750	18,800	0	2,678	4,546	5,176	0	3,050	5,036	5,666
18,800	18,850	0	2,670	4,536	5,165	0	3,050	5,036	5,666
18,850	18,900	0	2,662	4,525	5,155	0	3,050	5,036	5,666
18,900	18,950	0	2,654	4,515	5,144	0	3,050	5,036	5,666
18,950	19,000	0	2,646	4,504	5,134	0	3,050	5,036	5,666
19,000	19,050	0	2,638	4,494	5,123	0	3,050	5,036	5,666
19,050	19,100	0	2,630	4,483	5,113	0	3,050	5,036	5,666
19,100	19,150	0	2,622	4,473	5,102	0	3,050	5,036	5,666
19,150	19,200	0	2,614	4,462	5,092	0	3,050	5,036	5,666
19,200	19,250	0	2,606	4,452	5,081	0	3,050	5,036	5,666
19,250	19,300	0	2,598	4,441	5,071	0	3,050	5,036	5,666
19,300	19,350	0	2,590	4,431	5,060	0	3,050	5,036	5,666
19,350	19,400	0	2,582	4,420	5,049	0	3,050	5,036	5,666
19,400	19,450	0	2,574	4,409	5,039	0	3,050	5,036	5,666
19,450	19,500	0	2,566	4,399	5,028	0	3,050	5,036	5,666
19,500	19,550	0	2,558	4,388	5,018	0	3,050	5,036	5,666
19,550	19,600	0	2,550	4,378	5,007	0	3,050	5,036	5,666
19,600	19,650	0	2,542	4,367	4,997	0	3,050	5,036	5,666
19,650	19,700	0	2,534	4,357	4,986	0	3,050	5,036	5,666
19,700	19,750	0	2,526	4,346	4,976	0	3,050	5,036	5,666
19,750	19,800	0	2,518	4,336	4,965	0	3,050	5,036	5,666
19,800	19,850	0	2,510	4,325	4,955	0	3,050	5,036	5,666
19,850	19,900	0	2,502	4,315	4,944	0	3,050	5,036	5,666
19,900	19,950	0	2,494	4,304	4,934	0	3,050	5,036	5,666
19,950	20,000	0	2,487	4,294	4,923	0	3,050	5,036	5,666
20,000	20,050	0	2,470	4,283	4,913	0	3,050	5,036	5,666
20,050	20,100	0	2,471	4,273	4,902	0	3,050	5,036	5,666
20,100	20,150	0	2,463	4,262	4,892	0	3,050	5,036	5,666
20,150	20,200	0	2,455	4,252	4,881	0	3,050	5,036	5,666
20,200	20,250	0	2,447	4,241	4,870	0	3,050	5,036	5,666

Caution: Draft as of 09/13/2010

*If the amount you are looking up from the worksheet is at least $18,450 but less than $18,470, your credit is $1. Otherwise, you cannot take the credit.

2010 Earned Income Credit (EIC) Table–*Continued*   (**Caution.** This is **not** a tax table.)

At least	But less than	No Children	One Child	Two Children	Three Children	No Children	One Child	Two Children	Three Children
20,250	20,300	0	2,439	4,230	4,860	0	3,050	5,036	5,666
20,300	20,350	0	2,431	4,220	4,849	0	3,050	5,036	5,666
20,350	20,400	0	2,423	4,209	4,839	0	3,050	5,036	5,666
20,400	20,450	0	2,415	4,199	4,828	0	3,050	5,036	5,666
20,450	20,500	0	2,407	4,188	4,818	0	3,050	5,036	5,666
20,500	20,550	0	2,399	4,178	4,807	0	3,050	5,036	5,666
20,550	20,600	0	2,391	4,167	4,797	0	3,050	5,036	5,666
20,600	20,650	0	2,383	4,157	4,786	0	3,050	5,036	5,666
20,650	20,700	0	2,375	4,146	4,776	0	3,050	5,036	5,666
20,700	20,750	0	2,367	4,136	4,765	0	3,050	5,036	5,666
20,750	20,800	0	2,359	4,125	4,755	0	3,050	5,036	5,666
20,800	20,850	0	2,351	4,115	4,744	0	3,050	5,036	5,666
20,850	20,900	0	2,343	4,104	4,734	0	3,050	5,036	5,666
20,900	20,950	0	2,335	4,094	4,723	0	3,050	5,036	5,666
20,950	21,000	0	2,327	4,083	4,713	0	3,050	5,036	5,666
21,000	21,050	0	2,319	4,073	4,702	0	3,050	5,036	5,666
21,050	21,100	0	2,311	4,062	4,691	0	3,050	5,036	5,666
21,100	21,150	0	2,303	4,051	4,681	0	3,050	5,036	5,666
21,150	21,200	0	2,295	4,041	4,670	0	3,050	5,036	5,666
21,200	21,250	0	2,287	4,030	4,660	0	3,050	5,036	5,666
21,250	21,300	0	2,279	4,020	4,649	0	3,050	5,036	5,666
21,300	21,350	0	2,271	4,009	4,639	0	3,050	5,036	5,666
21,350	21,400	0	2,263	3,999	4,628	0	3,050	5,036	5,666
21,400	21,450	0	2,255	3,988	4,618	0	3,050	5,036	5,666
21,450	21,500	0	2,247	3,978	4,607	0	3,050	5,036	5,666
21,500	21,550	0	2,239	3,967	4,597	0	3,039	5,022	5,652
21,550	21,600	0	2,231	3,957	4,586	0	3,031	5,012	5,641
21,600	21,650	0	2,223	3,946	4,576	0	3,023	5,001	5,631
21,650	21,700	0	2,215	3,936	4,565	0	3,015	4,991	5,620
21,700	21,750	0	2,207	3,925	4,555	0	3,007	4,980	5,610
21,750	21,800	0	2,199	3,915	4,544	0	2,999	4,970	5,599
21,800	21,850	0	2,191	3,904	4,534	0	2,991	4,959	5,589
21,850	21,900	0	2,183	3,893	4,523	0	2,983	4,949	5,578
21,900	21,950	0	2,175	3,883	4,512	0	2,975	4,938	5,568
21,950	22,000	0	2,167	3,872	4,502	0	2,968	4,928	5,557
22,000	22,050	0	2,159	3,862	4,491	0	2,960	4,917	5,547
22,050	22,100	0	2,151	3,851	4,481	0	2,952	4,906	5,536
22,100	22,150	0	2,143	3,841	4,470	0	2,944	4,896	5,525
22,150	22,200	0	2,135	3,830	4,460	0	2,936	4,885	5,515
22,200	22,250	0	2,127	3,820	4,449	0	2,928	4,875	5,504
22,250	22,300	0	2,119	3,809	4,439	0	2,920	4,864	5,494
22,300	22,350	0	2,111	3,799	4,428	0	2,912	4,854	5,483
22,350	22,400	0	2,103	3,788	4,418	0	2,904	4,843	5,473
22,400	22,450	0	2,095	3,778	4,407	0	2,896	4,833	5,462
22,450	22,500	0	2,087	3,767	4,397	0	2,888	4,822	5,452
22,500	22,550	0	2,079	3,757	4,386	0	2,880	4,812	5,441
22,550	22,600	0	2,071	3,746	4,376	0	2,872	4,801	5,431
22,600	22,650	0	2,063	3,736	4,365	0	2,864	4,791	5,420
22,650	22,700	0	2,055	3,725	4,355	0	2,856	4,780	5,410
22,700	22,750	0	2,047	3,714	4,344	0	2,848	4,770	5,399
22,750	22,800	0	2,039	3,704	4,333	0	2,840	4,759	5,389
22,800	22,850	0	2,031	3,693	4,323	0	2,832	4,749	5,378
22,850	22,900	0	2,023	3,683	4,312	0	2,824	4,738	5,368
22,900	22,950	0	2,015	3,672	4,302	0	2,816	4,727	5,357
22,950	23,000	0	2,007	3,662	4,291	0	2,808	4,717	5,346
23,000	23,050	0	1,999	3,651	4,281	0	2,800	4,706	5,336
23,050	23,100	0	1,991	3,641	4,270	0	2,792	4,696	5,325
23,100	23,150	0	1,983	3,630	4,260	0	2,784	4,685	5,315
23,150	23,200	0	1,975	3,620	4,249	0	2,776	4,675	5,304
23,200	23,250	0	1,967	3,609	4,239	0	2,768	4,664	5,294

Caution: Draft as of 09/13/2010

2010 Earned Income Credit (EIC) Table—*Continued* (**Caution.** This is **not** a tax table.)

If the amount you are looking up from the worksheet is—		Single, head of household, or qualifying widow(er) and you have—				Married filing jointly and you have—			
		No Children	One Child	Two Children	Three Children	No Children	One Child	Two Children	Three Children
At least	But less than	Your credit is—					Your credit is—		
23,250	23,300	0	1,959	3,599	4,228	0	2,760	4,654	5,283
23,300	23,350	0	1,951	3,588	4,218	0	2,752	4,643	5,273
23,350	23,400	0	1,943	3,578	4,207	0	2,744	4,633	5,262
23,400	23,450	0	1,935	3,567	4,197	0	2,736	4,622	5,252
23,450	23,500	0	1,927	3,557	4,186	0	2,728	4,612	5,241
23,500	23,550	0	1,919	3,546	4,176	0	2,720	4,601	5,231
23,550	23,600	0	1,911	3,535	4,165	0	2,712	4,591	5,220
23,600	23,650	0	1,903	3,525	4,154	0	2,704	4,580	5,210
23,650	23,700	0	1,895	3,514	4,144	0	2,696	4,570	5,199
23,700	23,750	0	1,887	3,504	4,133	0	2,688	4,559	5,188
23,750	23,800	0	1,879	3,493	4,123	0	2,680	4,548	5,178
23,800	23,850	0	1,871	3,483	4,112	0	2,672	4,538	5,167
23,850	23,900	0	1,863	3,472	4,102	0	2,664	4,527	5,157
23,900	23,950	0	1,855	3,462	4,091	0	2,656	4,517	5,146
23,950	24,000	0	1,847	3,451	4,081	0	2,648	4,506	5,136
24,000	24,050	0	1,839	3,441	4,070	0	2,640	4,496	5,125
24,050	24,100	0	1,831	3,430	4,060	0	2,632	4,485	5,115
24,100	24,150	0	1,823	3,420	4,049	0	2,624	4,475	5,104
24,150	24,200	0	1,815	3,409	4,039	0	2,616	4,464	5,094
24,200	24,250	0	1,807	3,399	4,028	0	2,608	4,454	5,083
24,250	24,300	0	1,799	3,388	4,018	0	2,600	4,443	5,073
24,300	24,350	0	1,791	3,378	4,007	0	2,592	4,433	5,062
24,350	24,400	0	1,783	3,367	3,996	0	2,584	4,422	5,052
24,400	24,450	0	1,775	3,356	3,986	0	2,576	4,412	5,041
24,450	24,500	0	1,767	3,346	3,975	0	2,568	4,401	5,031
24,500	24,550	0	1,759	3,335	3,965	0	2,560	4,391	5,020
24,550	24,600	0	1,751	3,325	3,954	0	2,552	4,380	5,009
24,600	24,650	0	1,743	3,314	3,944	0	2,544	4,369	4,999
24,650	24,700	0	1,735	3,304	3,933	0	2,536	4,359	4,988
24,700	24,750	0	1,727	3,293	3,923	0	2,528	4,348	4,978
24,750	24,800	0	1,719	3,283	3,912	0	2,520	4,338	4,967
24,800	24,850	0	1,711	3,272	3,902	0	2,512	4,327	4,957
24,850	24,900	0	1,703	3,262	3,891	0	2,504	4,317	4,946
24,900	24,950	0	1,695	3,251	3,881	0	2,496	4,306	4,936
24,950	25,000	0	1,688	3,241	3,870	0	2,488	4,296	4,925
25,000	25,050	0	1,680	3,230	3,860	0	2,480	4,285	4,915
25,050	25,100	0	1,672	3,220	3,849	0	2,472	4,275	4,904
25,100	25,150	0	1,664	3,209	3,839	0	2,464	4,264	4,894
25,150	25,200	0	1,656	3,199	3,828	0	2,456	4,254	4,883
25,200	25,250	0	1,648	3,188	3,817	0	2,448	4,243	4,873
25,250	25,300	0	1,640	3,177	3,807	0	2,440	4,233	4,862
25,300	25,350	0	1,632	3,167	3,796	0	2,432	4,222	4,852
25,350	25,400	0	1,624	3,156	3,786	0	2,424	4,212	4,841
25,400	25,450	0	1,616	3,146	3,775	0	2,416	4,201	4,830
25,450	25,500	0	1,608	3,135	3,765	0	2,408	4,190	4,820
25,500	25,550	0	1,600	3,125	3,754	0	2,400	4,180	4,809
25,550	25,600	0	1,592	3,114	3,744	0	2,392	4,169	4,799
25,600	25,650	0	1,584	3,104	3,733	0	2,384	4,159	4,788
25,650	25,700	0	1,576	3,093	3,723	0	2,376	4,148	4,778
25,700	25,750	0	1,568	3,083	3,712	0	2,368	4,138	4,767
25,750	25,800	0	1,560	3,072	3,702	0	2,360	4,127	4,757
25,800	25,850	0	1,552	3,062	3,691	0	2,352	4,117	4,746
25,850	25,900	0	1,544	3,051	3,681	0	2,344	4,106	4,736
25,900	25,950	0	1,536	3,041	3,670	0	2,336	4,096	4,725
25,950	26,000	0	1,528	3,030	3,660	0	2,328	4,085	4,715
26,000	26,050	0	1,520	3,020	3,649	0	2,320	4,075	4,704
26,050	26,100	0	1,512	3,009	3,638	0	2,312	4,064	4,694
26,100	26,150	0	1,504	2,998	3,628	0	2,304	4,054	4,683
26,150	26,200	0	1,496	2,988	3,617	0	2,296	4,043	4,673
26,200	26,250	0	1,488	2,977	3,607	0	2,288	4,032	4,662

Caution: Draft as of 09/13/2010

2010 Earned Income Credit (EIC) Table–*Continued*　　　　(**Caution.** This is **not** a tax table.)

If the amount you are looking up from the worksheet is–		Single, head of household, or qualifying widow(er) and you have–				Married filing jointly and you have–			
		No Children	One Child	Two Children	Three Children	No Children	One Child	Two Children	Three Children
At least	But less than	Your credit is–				Your credit is–			
26,250	26,300	0	1,480	2,967	3,596	0	2,280	4,022	4,651
26,300	26,350	0	1,472	2,956	3,586	0	2,272	4,011	4,641
26,350	26,400	0	1,464	2,946	3,575	0	2,264	4,001	4,630
26,400	26,450	0	1,456	2,935	3,565	0	2,256	3,990	4,620
26,450	26,500	0	1,448	2,925	3,554	0	2,248	3,980	4,609
26,500	26,550	0	1,440	2,914	3,544	0	2,240	3,969	4,599
26,550	26,600	0	1,432	2,904	3,533	0	2,232	3,959	4,588
26,600	26,650	0	1,424	2,893	3,523	0	2,224	3,948	4,578
26,650	26,700	0	1,416	2,883	3,512	0	2,216	3,938	4,567
26,700	26,750	0	1,408	2,872	3,502	0	2,208	3,927	4,557
26,750	26,800	0	1,400	2,862	3,491	0	2,200	3,917	4,546
26,800	26,850	0	1,392	2,851	3,481	0	2,192	3,906	4,536
26,850	26,900	0	1,384	2,840	3,470	0	2,184	3,896	4,525
26,900	26,950	0	1,376	2,830	3,459	0	2,176	3,885	4,515
26,950	27,000	0	1,368	2,819	3,449	0	2,169	3,875	4,504
27,000	27,050	0	1,360	2,809	3,438	0	2,161	3,864	4,494
27,050	27,100	0	1,352	2,798	3,428	0	2,153	3,853	4,483
27,100	27,150	0	1,344	2,788	3,417	0	2,145	3,843	4,472
27,150	27,200	0	1,336	2,777	3,407	0	2,137	3,832	4,462
27,200	27,250	0	1,328	2,767	3,396	0	2,129	3,822	4,451
27,250	27,300	0	1,320	2,756	3,386	0	2,121	3,811	4,441
27,300	27,350	0	1,312	2,746	3,375	0	2,113	3,801	4,430
27,350	27,400	0	1,304	2,735	3,365	0	2,105	3,790	4,420
27,400	27,450	0	1,296	2,725	3,354	0	2,097	3,780	4,409
27,450	27,500	0	1,288	2,714	3,344	0	2,089	3,769	4,399
27,500	27,550	0	1,280	2,704	3,333	0	2,081	3,759	4,388
27,550	27,600	0	1,272	2,693	3,323	0	2,073	3,748	4,378
27,600	27,650	0	1,264	2,683	3,312	0	2,065	3,738	4,367
27,650	27,700	0	1,256	2,672	3,302	0	2,057	3,727	4,357
27,700	27,750	0	1,248	2,661	3,291	0	2,049	3,717	4,346
27,750	27,800	0	1,240	2,651	3,280	0	2,041	3,706	4,336
27,800	27,850	0	1,232	2,640	3,270	0	2,033	3,696	4,325
27,850	27,900	0	1,224	2,630	3,259	0	2,025	3,685	4,315
27,900	27,950	0	1,216	2,619	3,249	0	2,017	3,674	4,304
27,950	28,000	0	1,208	2,609	3,238	0	2,009	3,664	4,293
28,000	28,050	0	1,200	2,598	3,228	0	2,001	3,653	4,283
28,050	28,100	0	1,192	2,588	3,217	0	1,993	3,643	4,272
28,100	28,150	0	1,184	2,577	3,207	0	1,985	3,632	4,262
28,150	28,200	0	1,176	2,567	3,196	0	1,977	3,622	4,251
28,200	28,250	0	1,168	2,556	3,186	0	1,969	3,611	4,241
28,250	28,300	0	1,160	2,546	3,175	0	1,961	3,601	4,230
28,300	28,350	0	1,152	2,535	3,165	0	1,953	3,590	4,220
28,350	28,400	0	1,144	2,525	3,154	0	1,945	3,580	4,209
28,400	28,450	0	1,136	2,514	3,144	0	1,937	3,569	4,199
28,450	28,500	0	1,128	2,504	3,133	0	1,929	3,559	4,188
28,500	28,550	0	1,120	2,493	3,123	0	1,921	3,548	4,178
28,550	28,600	0	1,112	2,482	3,112	0	1,913	3,538	4,167
28,600	28,650	0	1,104	2,472	3,101	0	1,905	3,527	4,157
28,650	28,700	0	1,096	2,461	3,091	0	1,897	3,517	4,146
28,700	28,750	0	1,088	2,451	3,080	0	1,889	3,506	4,135
28,750	28,800	0	1,080	2,440	3,070	0	1,881	3,495	4,125
28,800	28,850	0	1,072	2,430	3,059	0	1,873	3,485	4,114
28,850	28,900	0	1,064	2,419	3,049	0	1,865	3,474	4,104
28,900	28,950	0	1,056	2,409	3,038	0	1,857	3,464	4,093
28,950	29,000	0	1,048	2,398	3,028	0	1,849	3,453	4,083
29,000	29,050	0	1,040	2,388	3,017	0	1,841	3,443	4,072
29,050	29,100	0	1,032	2,377	3,007	0	1,833	3,432	4,062
29,100	29,150	0	1,024	2,367	2,996	0	1,825	3,422	4,051
29,150	29,200	0	1,016	2,356	2,986	0	1,817	3,411	4,041
29,200	29,250	0	1,008	2,346	2,975	0	1,809	3,401	4,030

Caution: Draft as of 09/13/2010

2010 Earned Income Credit (EIC) Table—*Continued*   (**Caution.** This is **not** a tax table.)

If the amount you are looking up from the worksheet is—		Single, head of household, or qualifying widow(er) and you have—				Married filing jointly and you have—			
At least	But less than	No Children	One Child	Two Children	Three Children	No Children	One Child	Two Children	Three Children
		Your credit is—				Your credit is—			
29,250	29,300	0	1,000	2,335	2,965	0	1,801	3,390	4,020
29,300	29,350	0	992	2,325	2,954	0	1,793	3,380	4,009
29,350	29,400	0	984	2,314	2,943	0	1,785	3,369	3,999
29,400	29,450	0	976	2,303	2,933	0	1,777	3,359	3,988
29,450	29,500	0	968	2,293	2,922	0	1,769	3,348	3,978
29,500	29,550	0	960	2,282	2,912	0	1,761	3,338	3,967
29,550	29,600	0	952	2,272	2,901	0	1,753	3,327	3,956
29,600	29,650	0	944	2,261	2,891	0	1,745	3,316	3,946
29,650	29,700	0	936	2,251	2,880	0	1,737	3,306	3,935
29,700	29,750	0	928	2,240	2,870	0	1,729	3,295	3,925
29,750	29,800	0	920	2,230	2,859	0	1,721	3,285	3,914
29,800	29,850	0	912	2,219	2,849	0	1,713	3,274	3,904
29,850	29,900	0	904	2,209	2,838	0	1,705	3,264	3,893
29,900	29,950	0	896	2,198	2,828	0	1,697	3,253	3,883
29,950	30,000	0	889	2,188	2,817	0	1,689	3,243	3,872
30,000	30,050	0	881	2,177	2,807	0	1,681	3,232	3,862
30,050	30,100	0	873	2,167	2,796	0	1,673	3,222	3,851
30,100	30,150	0	865	2,156	2,786	0	1,665	3,211	3,841
30,150	30,200	0	857	2,146	2,775	0	1,657	3,201	3,830
30,200	30,250	0	849	2,135	2,764	0	1,649	3,190	3,820
30,250	30,300	0	841	2,124	2,754	0	1,641	3,180	3,809
30,300	30,350	0	833	2,114	2,743	0	1,633	3,169	3,799
30,350	30,400	0	825	2,103	2,733	0	1,625	3,159	3,788
30,400	30,450	0	817	2,093	2,722	0	1,617	3,148	3,777
30,450	30,500	0	809	2,082	2,712	0	1,609	3,137	3,767
30,500	30,550	0	801	2,072	2,701	0	1,601	3,127	3,756
30,550	30,600	0	793	2,061	2,691	0	1,593	3,116	3,746
30,600	30,650	0	785	2,051	2,680	0	1,585	3,106	3,735
30,650	30,700	0	777	2,040	2,670	0	1,577	3,095	3,725
30,700	30,750	0	769	2,030	2,659	0	1,569	3,085	3,714
30,750	30,800	0	761	2,019	2,649	0	1,561	3,074	3,704
30,800	30,850	0	753	2,009	2,638	0	1,553	3,064	3,693
30,850	30,900	0	745	1,998	2,628	0	1,545	3,053	3,683
30,900	30,950	0	737	1,988	2,617	0	1,537	3,043	3,672
30,950	31,000	0	729	1,977	2,607	0	1,529	3,032	3,662
31,000	31,050	0	721	1,967	2,596	0	1,521	3,022	3,651
31,050	31,100	0	713	1,956	2,585	0	1,513	3,011	3,641
31,100	31,150	0	705	1,945	2,575	0	1,505	3,001	3,630
31,150	31,200	0	697	1,935	2,564	0	1,497	2,990	3,620
31,200	31,250	0	689	1,924	2,554	0	1,489	2,979	3,609
31,250	31,300	0	681	1,914	2,543	0	1,481	2,969	3,598
31,300	31,350	0	673	1,903	2,533	0	1,473	2,958	3,588
31,350	31,400	0	665	1,893	2,522	0	1,465	2,948	3,577
31,400	31,450	0	657	1,882	2,512	0	1,457	2,937	3,567
31,450	31,500	0	649	1,872	2,501	0	1,449	2,927	3,556
31,500	31,550	0	641	1,861	2,491	0	1,441	2,916	3,546
31,550	31,600	0	633	1,851	2,480	0	1,433	2,906	3,535
31,600	31,650	0	625	1,840	2,470	0	1,425	2,895	3,525
31,650	31,700	0	617	1,830	2,459	0	1,417	2,885	3,514
31,700	31,750	0	609	1,819	2,449	0	1,409	2,874	3,504
31,750	31,800	0	001	1,809	2,438	0	1,401	2,864	3,493
31,800	31,850	0	593	1,798	2,428	0	1,393	2,853	3,483
31,850	31,900	0	585	1,787	2,417	0	1,385	2,843	3,472
31,900	31,950	0	577	1,777	2,406	0	1,377	2,832	3,462
31,950	32,000	0	569	1,766	2,396	0	1,370	2,822	3,451
32,000	32,050	0	561	1,756	2,385	0	1,362	2,811	3,441
32,050	32,100	0	553	1,745	2,375	0	1,354	2,800	3,430
32,100	32,150	0	545	1,735	2,364	0	1,346	2,790	3,419
32,150	32,200	0	537	1,724	2,354	0	1,338	2,779	3,409
32,200	32,250	0	529	1,714	2,343	0	1,330	2,769	3,398

Caution: Draft as of 09/13/2010

2010 Earned Income Credit (EIC) Table—*Continued*   (**Caution.** This is **not** a tax table.)

If the amount you are looking up from the worksheet is—		Single, head of household, or qualifying widow(er) and you have—				Married filing jointly and you have—			
At least	But less than	No Children	One Child	Two Children	Three Children	No Children	One Child	Two Children	Three Children
		Your credit is—				Your credit is—			
32,250	32,300	0	521	1,703	2,333	0	1,322	2,758	3,388
32,300	32,350	0	513	1,693	2,322	0	1,314	2,748	3,377
32,350	32,400	0	505	1,682	2,312	0	1,306	2,737	3,367
32,400	32,450	0	497	1,672	2,301	0	1,298	2,727	3,356
32,450	32,500	0	489	1,661	2,291	0	1,290	2,716	3,346
32,500	32,550	0	481	1,651	2,280	0	1,282	2,706	3,335
32,550	32,600	0	473	1,640	2,270	0	1,274	2,695	3,325
32,600	32,650	0	465	1,630	2,259	0	1,266	2,685	3,314
32,650	32,700	0	457	1,619	2,249	0	1,258	2,674	3,304
32,700	32,750	0	449	1,608	2,238	0	1,250	2,664	3,293
32,750	32,800	0	441	1,598	2,227	0	1,242	2,653	3,283
32,800	32,850	0	433	1,587	2,217	0	1,234	2,643	3,272
32,850	32,900	0	425	1,577	2,206	0	1,226	2,632	3,262
32,900	32,950	0	417	1,566	2,196	0	1,218	2,621	3,251
32,950	33,000	0	409	1,556	2,185	0	1,210	2,611	3,240
33,000	33,050	0	401	1,545	2,175	0	1,202	2,600	3,230
33,050	33,100	0	393	1,535	2,164	0	1,194	2,590	3,219
33,100	33,150	0	385	1,524	2,154	0	1,186	2,579	3,209
33,150	33,200	0	377	1,514	2,143	0	1,178	2,569	3,198
33,200	33,250	0	369	1,503	2,133	0	1,170	2,558	3,188
33,250	33,300	0	361	1,493	2,122	0	1,162	2,548	3,177
33,300	33,350	0	353	1,482	2,112	0	1,154	2,537	3,167
33,350	33,400	0	345	1,472	2,101	0	1,146	2,527	3,156
33,400	33,450	0	337	1,461	2,091	0	1,138	2,516	3,146
33,450	33,500	0	329	1,451	2,080	0	1,130	2,506	3,135
33,500	33,550	0	321	1,440	2,070	0	1,122	2,495	3,125
33,550	33,600	0	313	1,429	2,059	0	1,114	2,485	3,114
33,600	33,650	0	305	1,419	2,048	0	1,106	2,474	3,104
33,650	33,700	0	297	1,408	2,038	0	1,098	2,464	3,093
33,700	33,750	0	289	1,398	2,027	0	1,090	2,453	3,082
33,750	33,800	0	281	1,387	2,017	0	1,082	2,442	3,072
33,800	33,850	0	273	1,377	2,006	0	1,074	2,432	3,061
33,850	33,900	0	265	1,366	1,996	0	1,066	2,421	3,051
33,900	33,950	0	257	1,356	1,985	0	1,058	2,411	3,040
33,950	34,000	0	249	1,345	1,975	0	1,050	2,400	3,030
34,000	34,050	0	241	1,335	1,964	0	1,042	2,390	3,019
34,050	34,100	0	233	1,324	1,954	0	1,034	2,379	3,009
34,100	34,150	0	225	1,314	1,943	0	1,026	2,369	2,998
34,150	34,200	0	217	1,303	1,933	0	1,018	2,358	2,988
34,200	34,250	0	209	1,293	1,922	0	1,010	2,348	2,977
34,250	34,300	0	201	1,282	1,912	0	1,002	2,337	2,967
34,300	34,350	0	193	1,272	1,901	0	994	2,327	2,956
34,350	34,400	0	185	1,261	1,890	0	986	2,316	2,946
34,400	34,450	0	177	1,250	1,880	0	978	2,306	2,935
34,450	34,500	0	169	1,240	1,869	0	970	2,295	2,925
34,500	34,550	0	161	1,229	1,859	0	962	2,285	2,914
34,550	34,600	0	153	1,219	1,848	0	954	2,274	2,903
34,600	34,650	0	145	1,208	1,838	0	946	2,263	2,893
34,650	34,700	0	137	1,198	1,827	0	938	2,253	2,882
34,700	34,750	0	129	1,187	1,817	0	930	2,242	2,872
34,750	34,800	0	121	1,177	1,806	0	922	2,232	2,861
34,800	34,850	0	113	1,166	1,796	0	914	2,221	2,851
34,850	34,900	0	105	1,156	1,785	0	906	2,211	2,840
34,900	34,950	0	97	1,145	1,775	0	898	2,200	2,830
34,950	35,000	0	90	1,135	1,764	0	890	2,190	2,819
35,000	35,050	0	82	1,124	1,754	0	882	2,179	2,809
35,050	35,100	0	74	1,114	1,743	0	874	2,169	2,798
35,100	35,150	0	66	1,103	1,733	0	866	2,158	2,788
35,150	35,200	0	58	1,093	1,722	0	858	2,148	2,777
35,200	35,250	0	50	1,082	1,711	0	850	2,137	2,767

Caution: Draft as of 09/13/2010

2010 Earned Income Credit (EIC) Table–*Continued* (**Caution.** This is **not** a tax table.)

If the amount you are looking up from the worksheet is–		Single, head of household, or qualifying widow(er) and you have–				Married filing jointly and you have–			
At least	But less than	No Children	One Child	Two Children	Three Children	No Children	One Child	Two Children	Three Children
		Your credit is–				Your credit is–			
35,250	35,300	0	42	1,071	1,701	0	842	2,127	2,756
35,300	35,350	0	34	1,061	1,690	0	834	2,116	2,746
35,350	35,400	0	26	1,050	1,680	0	826	2,106	2,735
35,400	35,450	0	18	1,040	1,669	0	818	2,095	2,724
35,450	35,500	0	10	1,029	1,659	0	810	2,084	2,714
35,500	35,550	0	*	1,019	1,648	0	802	2,074	2,703
35,550	35,600	0	0	1,008	1,638	0	794	2,063	2,693
35,600	35,650	0	0	998	1,627	0	786	2,053	2,682
35,650	35,700	0	0	987	1,617	0	778	2,042	2,672
35,700	35,750	0	0	977	1,606	0	770	2,032	2,661
35,750	35,800	0	0	966	1,596	0	762	2,021	2,651
35,800	35,850	0	0	956	1,585	0	754	2,011	2,640
35,850	35,900	0	0	945	1,575	0	746	2,000	2,630
35,900	35,950	0	0	935	1,564	0	738	1,990	2,619
35,950	36,000	0	0	924	1,554	0	730	1,979	2,609
36,000	36,050	0	0	914	1,543	0	722	1,969	2,598
36,050	36,100	0	0	903	1,532	0	714	1,958	2,588
36,100	36,150	0	0	892	1,522	0	706	1,948	2,577
36,150	36,200	0	0	882	1,511	0	698	1,937	2,567
36,200	36,250	0	0	871	1,501	0	690	1,926	2,556
36,250	36,300	0	0	861	1,490	0	682	1,916	2,545
36,300	36,350	0	0	850	1,480	0	674	1,905	2,535
36,350	36,400	0	0	840	1,469	0	666	1,895	2,524
36,400	36,450	0	0	829	1,459	0	658	1,884	2,514
36,450	36,500	0	0	819	1,448	0	650	1,874	2,503
36,500	36,550	0	0	808	1,438	0	642	1,863	2,493
36,550	36,600	0	0	798	1,427	0	634	1,853	2,482
36,600	36,650	0	0	787	1,417	0	626	1,842	2,472
36,650	36,700	0	0	777	1,406	0	618	1,832	2,461
36,700	36,750	0	0	766	1,396	0	610	1,821	2,451
36,750	36,800	0	0	756	1,385	0	602	1,811	2,440
36,800	36,850	0	0	745	1,375	0	594	1,800	2,430
36,850	36,900	0	0	734	1,364	0	586	1,790	2,419
36,900	36,950	0	0	724	1,353	0	578	1,779	2,409
36,950	37,000	0	0	713	1,343	0	571	1,769	2,398
37,000	37,050	0	0	703	1,332	0	563	1,758	2,388
37,050	37,100	0	0	692	1,322	0	555	1,747	2,377
37,100	37,150	0	0	682	1,311	0	547	1,737	2,366
37,150	37,200	0	0	671	1,301	0	539	1,726	2,356
37,200	37,250	0	0	661	1,290	0	531	1,716	2,345
37,250	37,300	0	0	650	1,280	0	523	1,705	2,335
37,300	37,350	0	0	640	1,269	0	515	1,695	2,324
37,350	37,400	0	0	629	1,259	0	507	1,684	2,314
37,400	37,450	0	0	619	1,248	0	499	1,674	2,303
37,450	37,500	0	0	608	1,238	0	491	1,663	2,293
37,500	37,550	0	0	598	1,227	0	483	1,653	2,282
37,550	37,600	0	0	587	1,217	0	475	1,642	2,272
37,600	37,650	0	0	577	1,206	0	467	1,632	2,261
37,650	37,700	0	0	566	1,196	0	459	1,621	2,251
37,700	37,750	0	0	555	1,185	0	451	1,611	2,240
37,750	37,800	0	0	545	1,174	0	443	1,600	2,230
37,800	37,850	0	0	534	1,164	0	435	1,590	2,219
37,850	37,900	0	0	524	1,153	0	427	1,579	2,209
37,900	37,950	0	0	513	1,143	0	419	1,568	2,198
37,950	38,000	0	0	503	1,132	0	411	1,558	2,187

Caution: Draft as of 09/13/2010

*If the amount you are looking up from the worksheet is at least $35,500 but less than $35,535, your credit is $3. Otherwise, you cannot take the credit.

2010 Earned Income Credit (EIC) Table–*Continued*   (**Caution.** This is **not** a tax table.)

If the amount you are looking up from the worksheet is–		Single, head of household, or qualifying widow(er) and you have–				Married filing jointly and you have–			
		No Children	One Child	Two Children	Three Children	No Children	One Child	Two Children	Three Children
At least	But less than	Your credit is–				Your credit is–			
38,000	38,050	0	0	492	1,122	0	403	1,547	2,177
38,050	38,100	0	0	482	1,111	0	395	1,537	2,166
38,100	38,150	0	0	471	1,101	0	387	1,526	2,156
38,150	38,200	0	0	461	1,090	0	379	1,516	2,145
38,200	38,250	0	0	450	1,080	0	371	1,505	2,135
38,250	38,300	0	0	440	1,069	0	363	1,495	2,124
38,300	38,350	0	0	429	1,059	0	355	1,484	2,114
38,350	38,400	0	0	419	1,048	0	347	1,474	2,103
38,400	38,450	0	0	408	1,038	0	339	1,463	2,093
38,450	38,500	0	0	398	1,027	0	331	1,453	2,082
38,500	38,550	0	0	387	1,017	0	323	1,442	2,072
38,550	38,600	0	0	376	1,006	0	315	1,432	2,061
38,600	38,650	0	0	366	995	0	307	1,421	2,051
38,650	38,700	0	0	355	985	0	299	1,411	2,040
38,700	38,750	0	0	345	974	0	291	1,400	2,029
38,750	38,800	0	0	334	964	0	283	1,389	2,019
38,800	38,850	0	0	324	953	0	275	1,379	2,008
38,850	38,900	0	0	313	943	0	267	1,368	1,998
38,900	38,950	0	0	303	932	0	259	1,358	1,987
38,950	39,000	0	0	292	922	0	251	1,347	1,977
39,000	39,050	0	0	282	911	0	243	1,337	1,966
39,050	39,100	0	0	271	901	0	235	1,326	1,956
39,100	39,150	0	0	261	890	0	227	1,316	1,945
39,150	39,200	0	0	250	880	0	219	1,305	1,935
39,200	39,250	0	0	240	869	0	211	1,295	1,924
39,250	39,300	0	0	229	859	0	203	1,284	1,914
39,300	39,350	0	0	219	848	0	195	1,274	1,903
39,350	39,400	0	0	208	837	0	187	1,263	1,893
39,400	39,450	0	0	197	827	0	179	1,253	1,882
39,450	39,500	0	0	187	816	0	171	1,242	1,872
39,500	39,550	0	0	176	806	0	163	1,232	1,861
39,550	39,600	0	0	166	795	0	155	1,221	1,850
39,600	39,650	0	0	155	785	0	147	1,210	1,840
39,650	39,700	0	0	145	774	0	139	1,200	1,829
39,700	39,750	0	0	134	764	0	131	1,189	1,819
39,750	39,800	0	0	124	753	0	123	1,179	1,808
39,800	39,850	0	0	113	743	0	115	1,168	1,798
39,850	39,900	0	0	103	732	0	107	1,158	1,787
39,900	39,950	0	0	92	722	0	99	1,147	1,777
39,950	40,000	0	0	82	711	0	91	1,137	1,766
40,000	40,050	0	0	71	701	0	83	1,126	1,756
40,050	40,100	0	0	61	690	0	75	1,116	1,745
40,100	40,150	0	0	50	680	0	67	1,105	1,735
40,150	40,200	0	0	40	669	0	59	1,095	1,724
40,200	40,250	0	0	29	658	0	51	1,084	1,714
40,250	40,300	0	0	18	648	0	43	1,074	1,703
40,300	40,350	0	0	8	637	0	35	1,063	1,693
40,350	40,400	0	0	*	627	0	27	1,053	1,682
40,400	40,450	0	0	0	616	0	19	1,042	1,671
40,450	40,500	0	0	0	606	0	11	1,031	1,661
40,500	40,550	0	0	0	595	0	**	1,021	1,650
40,550	40,600	0	0	0	585	0	0	1,010	1,640
40,600	40,650	0	0	0	574	0	0	1,000	1,629
40,650	40,700	0	0	0	564	0	0	989	1,619
40,700	40,750	0	0	0	553	0	0	979	1,608

Caution: Draft as of 09/13/2010

*If the amount you are looking up from the worksheet is at least $40,350 but less than $40,363, your credit is $1. Otherwise, you cannot take the credit.
**If the amount you are looking up from the worksheet is at least $40,500 but less than $40,545, your credit is $4. Otherwise, you cannot take the credit.

2010 Earned Income Credit (EIC) Table–*Continued*   (**Caution.** This is **not** a tax table.)

If the amount you are looking up from the worksheet is–		And your filing status is–							
		Single, head of household, or qualifying widow(er) and you have–				Married filing jointly and you have–			
		No Children	One Child	Two Children	Three Children	No Children	One Child	Two Children	Three Children
At least	But less than	Your credit is–				Your credit is–			
40,750	40,800	0	0	0	543	0	0	968	1,598
40,800	40,850	0	0	0	532	0	0	958	1,587
40,850	40,900	0	0	0	522	0	0	947	1,577
40,900	40,950	0	0	0	511	0	0	937	1,566
40,950	41,000	0	0	0	501	0	0	926	1,556
41,000	41,050	0	0	0	490	0	0	916	1,545
41,050	41,100	0	0	0	479	0	0	905	1,535
41,100	41,150	0	0	0	469	0	0	895	1,524
41,150	41,200	0	0	0	458	0	0	884	1,514
41,200	41,250	0	0	0	448	0	0	873	1,503
41,250	41,300	0	0	0	437	0	0	863	1,492
41,300	41,350	0	0	0	427	0	0	852	1,482
41,350	41,400	0	0	0	416	0	0	842	1,471
41,400	41,450	0	0	0	406	0	0	831	1,461
41,450	41,500	0	0	0	395	0	0	821	1,450
41,500	41,550	0	0	0	385	0	0	810	1,440
41,550	41,600	0	0	0	374	0	0	800	1,429
41,600	41,650	0	0	0	364	0	0	789	1,419
41,650	41,700	0	0	0	353	0	0	779	1,408
41,700	41,750	0	0	0	343	0	0	768	1,398
41,750	41,800	0	0	0	332	0	0	758	1,387
41,800	41,850	0	0	0	322	0	0	747	1,377
41,850	41,900	0	0	0	311	0	0	737	1,366
41,900	41,950	0	0	0	300	0	0	726	1,356
41,950	42,000	0	0	0	290	0	0	716	1,345
42,000	42,050	0	0	0	279	0	0	705	1,335
42,050	42,100	0	0	0	269	0	0	694	1,324
42,100	42,150	0	0	0	258	0	0	684	1,313
42,150	42,200	0	0	0	248	0	0	673	1,303
42,200	42,250	0	0	0	237	0	0	663	1,292
42,250	42,300	0	0	0	227	0	0	652	1,282
42,300	42,350	0	0	0	216	0	0	642	1,271
42,350	42,400	0	0	0	206	0	0	631	1,261
42,400	42,450	0	0	0	195	0	0	621	1,250
42,450	42,500	0	0	0	185	0	0	610	1,240
42,500	42,550	0	0	0	174	0	0	600	1,229
42,550	42,600	0	0	0	164	0	0	589	1,219
42,600	42,650	0	0	0	153	0	0	579	1,208
42,650	42,700	0	0	0	143	0	0	568	1,198
42,700	42,750	0	0	0	132	0	0	558	1,187
42,750	42,800	0	0	0	121	0	0	547	1,177
42,800	42,850	0	0	0	111	0	0	537	1,166
42,850	42,900	0	0	0	100	0	0	526	1,156
42,900	42,950	0	0	0	90	0	0	515	1,145
42,950	43,000	0	0	0	79	0	0	505	1,134
43,000	43,050	0	0	0	69	0	0	494	1,124
43,050	43,100	0	0	0	58	0	0	484	1,113
43,100	43,150	0	0	0	48	0	0	473	1,103
43,150	43,200	0	0	0	37	0	0	463	1,092
43,200	43,250	0	0	0	27	0	0	452	1,082
43,250	43,300	0	0	0	16	0	0	442	1,071
43,300	43,350	0	0	0	6	0	0	431	1,061
43,350	43,400	0	0	0	0	0	0	421	1,050
43,400	43,450	0	0	0	0	0	0	410	1,040
43,450	43,500	0	0	0	0	0	0	400	1,029
43,500	43,550	0	0	0	0	0	0	389	1,019
43,550	43,600	0	0	0	0	0	0	379	1,008
43,600	43,650	0	0	0	0	0	0	368	998
43,650	43,700	0	0	0	0	0	0	358	987
43,700	43,750	0	0	0	0	0	0	347	976

Caution: Draft as of 09/13/2010

2010 Earned Income Credit (EIC) Table—*Continued* (**Caution.** This is **not** a tax table.)

If the amount you are looking up from the worksheet is—		Single, head of household, or qualifying widow(er) and you have—				Married filing jointly and you have—			
		No Children	One Child	Two Children	Three Children	No Children	One Child	Two Children	Three Children
At least	But less than	Your credit is—				Your credit is—			
43,750	43,800	0	0	0	0	0	0	336	966
43,800	43,850	0	0	0	0	0	0	326	955
43,850	43,900	0	0	0	0	0	0	315	945
43,900	43,950	0	0	0	0	0	0	305	934
43,950	44,000	0	0	0	0	0	0	294	924
44,000	44,050	0	0	0	0	0	0	284	913
44,050	44,100	0	0	0	0	0	0	273	903
44,100	44,150	0	0	0	0	0	0	263	892
44,150	44,200	0	0	0	0	0	0	252	882
44,200	44,250	0	0	0	0	0	0	242	871
44,250	44,300	0	0	0	0	0	0	231	861
44,300	44,350	0	0	0	0	0	0	221	850
44,350	44,400	0	0	0	0	0	0	210	840
44,400	44,450	0	0	0	0	0	0	200	829
44,450	44,500	0	0	0	0	0	0	189	819
44,500	44,550	0	0	0	0	0	0	179	808
44,550	44,600	0	0	0	0	0	0	168	797
44,600	44,650	0	0	0	0	0	0	157	787
44,650	44,700	0	0	0	0	0	0	147	776
44,700	44,750	0	0	0	0	0	0	136	766
44,750	44,800	0	0	0	0	0	0	126	755
44,800	44,850	0	0	0	0	0	0	115	745
44,850	44,900	0	0	0	0	0	0	105	734
44,900	44,950	0	0	0	0	0	0	94	724
44,950	45,000	0	0	0	0	0	0	84	713
45,000	45,050	0	0	0	0	0	0	73	703
45,050	45,100	0	0	0	0	0	0	63	692
45,100	45,150	0	0	0	0	0	0	52	682
45,150	45,200	0	0	0	0	0	0	42	671
45,200	45,250	0	0	0	0	0	0	31	661
45,250	45,300	0	0	0	0	0	0	21	650
45,300	45,350	0	0	0	0	0	0	10	640
45,350	45,400	0	0	0	0	0	0	*	629
45,400	45,450	0	0	0	0	0	0	0	618
45,450	45,500	0	0	0	0	0	0	0	608
45,500	45,550	0	0	0	0	0	0	0	597
45,550	45,600	0	0	0	0	0	0	0	587
45,600	45,650	0	0	0	0	0	0	0	576
45,650	45,700	0	0	0	0	0	0	0	566
45,700	45,750	0	0	0	0	0	0	0	555
45,750	45,800	0	0	0	0	0	0	0	545
45,800	45,850	0	0	0	0	0	0	0	534
45,850	45,900	0	0	0	0	0	0	0	524
45,900	45,950	0	0	0	0	0	0	0	513
45,950	46,000	0	0	0	0	0	0	0	503
46,000	46,050	0	0	0	0	0	0	0	492
46,050	46,100	0	0	0	0	0	0	0	482
46,100	46,150	0	0	0	0	0	0	0	471
46,150	46,200	0	0	0	0	0	0	0	461
46,200	46,250	0	0	0	0	0	0	0	450
46,250	46,300	0	0	0	0	0	0	0	439
46,300	46,350	0	0	0	0	0	0	0	429
46,350	46,400	0	0	0	0	0	0	0	418
46,400	46,450	0	0	0	0	0	0	0	408
46,450	46,500	0	0	0	0	0	0	0	397

Caution: Draft as of 09/13/2010

*If the amount you are looking up from the worksheet is at least $45,350 but less than $45,373, your credit is $2. Otherwise, you cannot take the credit.

2010 Earned Income Credit (EIC) Table—*Continued* (**Caution.** This is **not** a tax table.)

If the amount you are looking up from the worksheet is—		Single, head of household, or qualifying widow(er) and you have—				Married filing jointly and you have—			
		No Children	One Child	Two Children	Three Children	No Children	One Child	Two Children	Three Children
At least	But less than	Your credit is—				Your credit is—			
46,500	46,550	0	0	0	0	0	0	0	387
46,550	46,600	0	0	0	0	0	0	0	376
46,600	46,650	0	0	0	0	0	0	0	366
46,650	46,700	0	0	0	0	0	0	0	355
46,700	46,750	0	0	0	0	0	0	0	345
46,750	46,800	0	0	0	0	0	0	0	334
46,800	46,850	0	0	0	0	0	0	0	324
46,850	46,900	0	0	0	0	0	0	0	313
46,900	46,950	0	0	0	0	0	0	0	303
46,950	47,000	0	0	0	0	0	0	0	292
47,000	47,050	0	0	0	0	0	0	0	282
47,050	47,100	0	0	0	0	0	0	0	271
47,100	47,150	0	0	0	0	0	0	0	260
47,150	47,200	0	0	0	0	0	0	0	250
47,200	47,250	0	0	0	0	0	0	0	239
47,250	47,300	0	0	0	0	0	0	0	229
47,300	47,350	0	0	0	0	0	0	0	218
47,350	47,400	0	0	0	0	0	0	0	208
47,400	47,450	0	0	0	0	0	0	0	197
47,450	47,500	0	0	0	0	0	0	0	187
47,500	47,550	0	0	0	0	0	0	0	176
47,550	47,600	0	0	0	0	0	0	0	166
47,600	47,650	0	0	0	0	0	0	0	155
47,650	47,700	0	0	0	0	0	0	0	145
47,700	47,750	0	0	0	0	0	0	0	134
47,750	47,800	0	0	0	0	0	0	0	124
47,800	47,850	0	0	0	0	0	0	0	113
47,850	47,900	0	0	0	0	0	0	0	103
47,900	47,950	0	0	0	0	0	0	0	92
47,950	48,000	0	0	0	0	0	0	0	81
48,000	48,050	0	0	0	0	0	0	0	71
48,050	48,100	0	0	0	0	0	0	0	60
48,100	48,150	0	0	0	0	0	0	0	50
48,150	48,200	0	0	0	0	0	0	0	39
48,200	48,250	0	0	0	0	0	0	0	29
48,250	48,300	0	0	0	0	0	0	0	18
48,300	48,350	0	0	0	0	0	0	0	8
48,350	48,362	0	0	0	0	0	0	0	1

Caution: Draft as of 09/13/2010

¶ 1112   Corporate income tax rates.

The rates for domestic corporations (other than qualified personal service corporations) are: (Code Sec. 11(b))[1]

Taxable income over—	But not over—	The tax is:	Of the amount over—
0	$ 50,000	15%	0
$ 50,000	75,000	$ 7,500 + 25%	$ 50,000
75,000	100,000	13,750 + 34%	75,000
100,000	335,000	22,250 + 39%	100,000
335,000	10,000,000	113,900 + 34%	335,000
10,000,000	15,000,000	3,400,000 + 35%	10,000,000
15,000,000	18,333,333	5,150,000 + 38%	15,000,000
18,333,333	—	35%	0

A qualified personal service corporation (as defined in Code Sec. 448(d)(2)) is taxed at a flat 35% of its taxable income. (Code Sec. 11(b)(2))[2]

Special taxes or rates on corporations include the alternative minimum tax, see ¶3200 *et seq.*; the accumulated earnings tax, see ¶3316; and the personal holding company tax, see ¶3323.

For tax rates on foreign corporations, see ¶4638 *et seq.*

¶ 1113   Gift tax rates.

The gift tax is based on the cumulative value of current and prior gifts (after a specified exclusion) after specified deductions, see ¶5037 *et seq.* (Code Sec. 2001, Code Sec. 2501)[3]

For gifts made in 2010, the gift tax rate schedule is as follows:

Gift Tax Rate Schedule

If the amount with respect to which the tentative tax to be computed is:	The tentative tax is:
Not over $10,000.	18% of such amount.
Over $10,000 but not over $20,000.	$1,800, plus 20% of the excess over $10,000.
Over $20,000 but not over $40,000.	$3,800, plus 22% of the excess over $20,000.
Over $40,000 but not over $60,000.	$8,200, plus 24% of the excess over $40,000.
Over $60,000 but not over $80,000.	$13,000, plus 26% of the excess over $60,000.
Over $80,000 but not over $100,000.	$18,200, plus 28% of the excess over $80,000.
Over $100,000 but not over $150,000.	$23,800, plus 30% of the excess over $100,000.
Over $150,000 but not over $250,000.	$38,800, plus 32% of the excess over $150,000.
Over $250,000 but not over $500,000.	$70,800, plus 34% of the excess over $250,000.
Over $500,000.	$155,800, plus 35% of the excess over $500,000.

The top gift tax rate for gifts made in 2010 is 35%.

The federal estate tax does not apply to decedents dying in 2010.

caution: For EGTRRA sunset rules, see ¶1114.

---

1. ¶D-1003; ¶114.01; TD ¶600,503
2. ¶D-1006; ¶114.02; TD ¶600,901

3. ¶s Q-8003 *et seq.*, R-7000 *et seq.*; ¶20,014 *et seq.*, ¶25,024 *et seq.* (Estate & Gift); TD ¶s 751,000, 744,002

¶ 1114   Post-2010 sunset provisions.

Unless Congress acts, the provisions of the Economic Growth and Tax Relief Reconciliation Act of 2001 (EGTRRA, PL 107-16), other than those made permanent or extended by subsequent legislation, sunset and won't apply to tax or limitation years beginning after 2010. In the case of Title V of EGTRRA, relating to estate, gift and generation skipping transfer taxes, the EGTRRA provisions sunset and won't apply to estates of decedents dying, gifts made, or generation skipping transfers, after 2010. (Sec. 901(a) of EGTRRA) The Internal Revenue Code of '86 will be applied and administered to tax or limitation years beginning after 2010, and to estates of decedents dying, gifts made, or generation skipping transfers, after 2010 as if the provisions of, and amendments made by, EGTRRA had never been enacted. (Sec. 901(b) of EGTRRA)

observation: Thus, upon sunset of EGTRRA, the Code would revert to its status before EGTRRA's enactment, except for those provisions made permanent or extended by subsequent legislation (the Pension Protection Act of 2006 (PL 109-280) repealed the sunset provisions of PL 107-16 as they relate to pension and IRA provisions and qualified tuition plans).

caution: Congress is widely expected either to defer the EGTRRA sunset provisions or modify them for 2011. However, as of Nov. 2, 2010, the date that the 2011 Federal Tax Handbook was sent to the printer, Congress had not yet acted. Thus, as of Nov. 2, 2010, the Code provides for many automatic, EGTRRA related rule changes for 2011. These EGTRRA sunset changes are summarized below, with cross references to the 2011 Federal Tax Handbook paragraphs where the subjects are discussed. Note that post-2010 sunsets under the Jobs and Growth Tax Relief Reconciliation Act of 2003 (JGTRRA, PL 108-27), such as those related to taxation of capital gains and dividends, also are included here. Check http://ria.thomsonreuters.com/federaltaxhandbook for new law updates.

Tax Provision	Post-2010 Changes Under EGTRRA Sunset Rules
Tax brackets (¶1100 to ¶1105)	(1) 10% bracket disappears (lowest bracket is 15%). (2) Size of the 15% tax bracket for joint filers & qualified surviving spouses is 167% (rather than 200%) of the 15% tax bracket for individual filers. (3) Top four brackets rise from 25%, 28%, 33% and 35% to 28%, 31%, 36% and 39.6%.
Taxation of capital gains (¶2600 to ¶2603) and qualified dividends (¶1288 to ¶1290)	Long-term capital gain is taxed at a maximum rate of 20% (18% for assets held more than five years); dividends paid to individuals are taxed at the same rates that apply to ordinary income. Repeal of requirement for individuals to treat stock loss as long-term capital loss to the extent extraordinary dividends are taxed as capital gains.
Rules for passthrough of qualified dividend income by RICs and REITs (¶1300, ¶1301)	Rules no longer apply.

Tax Provision	Post-2010 Changes Under EGTRRA Sunset Rules
Rule excluding qualified dividend income from investment income for investment interest deduction limit unless taxpayers elects to include it (¶1729)	Rule no longer applies.
Coverdell Education Saving Accounts (CESAs), formerly called education IRAs (¶2205 to ¶2208)	Annual per-beneficiary contribution limit drops to $500. Lower phaseout range for marrieds filing jointly. Restricted definition of qualifying education expenses (e.g., only for higher education). No special rules for special needs beneficiaries. The rule allowing corporations and other entities to make CESA contributions sunsets.
Exclusion for employer provided educational assistance under Code Sec. 127 (¶2215)	Exclusion ends after 2010 (so does the rule that allowed exclusion for graduate level education).
Payments for teaching or research (¶2218)	The exemption from the payments-for-services rule for amounts received under certain Government health professions scholarship programs sunsets after 2010.
Above-the-line student loan interest deduction (¶2225 to ¶2227)	Deduction phases out over lower modified AGI ranges. Deduction applies only to interest paid during the first 60 months in which interest payments are required.
Credit for employer-provided child care facilities (¶2332)	Credit sunsets after 2010.
Earned income tax (EITC) credit (¶2344 to ¶2348)	Beginning of phaseout range for joint returns drops. Phaseout computed with reference to modified AGI (rather than AGI). Earned income for EITC purposes includes exempt income. EITC reduced by AMT.
Credit for household and dependent care expenses (¶2354 to ¶2358)	Creditable expenses drop from $3,000 (1 qualifying individual) and $6,000 (2 or more) to $2,400 and $4,800 respectively. Maximum credit percentage drops from 35% to 30% and AGI-based percentage reduction begins at $10,000 (instead of $15,000).
Child credit (¶2360 to ¶2361)	Maximum credit drops from $1,000 to $500. Credit not allowed against AMT. More restrictive rules apply to refundable child credit.
Use of Code Sec. 121 homesale exclusion by heirs, estates, and qualified revocable trusts (¶2445)	No longer applicable.
Basis of inherited property (¶2512 and ¶2523)	Basis rules that applied for decedents dying before 2010 will apply again for decedents dying after 2010.
Basis of property acquired from a decedent (¶2523)	After 2010, property acquired from a decedent generally receives a stepped up (i.e., fair market value) basis.
Minimum withholding rate on supplemental wages under flat rate method (¶3011)	Rises to 28%. (For supplemental wage payments totalling more than $1 million, rate rises to 39.6%.

Tax Provision	Post-2010 Changes Under EGTRRA Sunset Rules
Backup withholding rate on gambling winnings (¶3034)	Rises to 28%.
Backup withholding rate on reportable payments (¶3045)	Rises to 31%.
Standard deduction (¶3112)	Standard deduction for married taxpayers filing jointly (and qualified surviving spouses) is 167% (rather than 200%) of the standard deduction for single taxpayers. Standard deduction for marrieds filing separately is half the joint filer amount.
Reduction in itemized deductions (¶3114)	Most itemized deductions of higher-income taxpayers are reduced by 3% of AGI above an inflation-adjusted figure, but reduction can't exceed 80%.
Phaseout of personal exemptions (¶3117)	A higher-income taxpayer's personal exemptions are phased out when AGI exceeds an inflation-adjusted threshold.
Voluntary withholding rate on certain federal payments (¶3119)	Rises to 7%, 15%, 28%, 31%.
Voluntary withholding rate on unemployment benefits (¶3119)	Rises to 15%.
Parent's election to include child's unearned income on parent's return (¶3139)	Parent includes child's gross income in excess of an inflation indexed figure, plus 15% of the lesser of (a) inflation adjusted standard deduction for dependent child, or (b) the excess of the child's gross income over the amount in (a).
Noncorporate taxpayer's net capital gain and qualified dividend income taxed for AMT purposes at the same rates that apply for regular tax purposes (¶3201)	This rule no longer applies.
AMT preference for excluded gain on QSBS stock (¶3209)	AMT preference is increased.
Accumulated earnings tax rate (¶3320)	Rises to 39.6%.
Personal holding company tax rate (¶3323)	Rises to 39.6%.
Repeal of collapsible corporation rules (¶3587)	Collapsible corporation rules reinstated.
Gain on transfer of property to satisfy pecuniary bequest (¶3918)	Estate recognizes gain or loss to extent of difference between bequest dollar amount and estate's basis for the property (gain limited in case of certain special use property).
Transfer at death to nonresident alien (¶4638)	No gain recognized on transfers of appreciated property.

Tax Provision	Post-2010 Changes Under EGTRRA Sunset Rules
Who must file individual income tax returns (¶4701)	Standard deduction (1) for joint filers (and qualified surviving spouses) is 167% (rather than 200%) of the standard deduction for single taxpayers, and (2) for marrieds filing separately is half joint filer amount. This affects minimum gross income thresholds for married taxpayers (filing jointly or separately) and for qualifying surviving spouses.
Estate tax (¶5000, ¶5026, and ¶5029)	Reinstated with top rate of 55%. A 5% surtax on the wealthiest of estates phases out the benefit of graduated rates, with (a) a unified credit exemption equivalent of $1 million, (b) reinstated Code Sec. 2057 deduction for family owned businesses, and (c) credit against State death taxes allowed (instead of deduction allowed in 2009 and earlier years).
Certain transfer-tax related information statements (¶4745)	No longer apply.
GST tax (¶5000)	Reinstated, with top rate of 55%, and GST exemption amount set at $1 million.
Gift tax (¶1113 and ¶5000)	Top rate increased to 55%.
Treatment of transfers to non-grantor trusts as taxable gifts (¶5039)	This rule no longer applies.

¶ 1115   Excise tax rates (nonpenalty).

Here are selected "nonpenalty" excise tax rates. [4] For penalty-type excise taxes, see the entries under "Excise taxes" in the Topic Index.

Retail excise taxes

Trucks, trailers, etc.

- auto truck chassis and bodies (for vehicles weighing more than 33,000 lbs),

- truck trailer and semi-trailer chassis and bodies (for vehicles weighing more than 26,000 lbs)

- tractors used chiefly for highway transportation, in combination with a trailer or semi-trailer (for tractors weighing more than 19,500 lbs and in combination with trailer or semi-trailer weighing more than 33,000 lbs)

- accessories sold with one of the above or installed within 6 months after one of the above is placed in service

12% of first retail sale amount. Tax scheduled to expire after 9/30/2011.

---

4. ¶s W-3100 *et seq.*, W-1500 *et seq.*, W-2000 *et seq.*; ¶s 40,009.05   *et seq.*, 40,609 *et seq.* (Excise)

Transportation fuel taxes

Gasoline other than aviation gasoline; gasohol	Through 9/30/2011, on removal at terminal: 18.4¢ per gal. After 9/30/2011: 4.3¢ per gal.
Aviation gasoline	Through 12/31/2010[1], on removal at terminal: 19.4¢ per gal. 1/1/2011-9/30/2011, 4.4¢ per gal. After 9/30/2011: 4.3¢ per gal.
Diesel fuel[2]; diesohol	Through 9/30/2011, on removal at terminal or retail sale: 24.4¢ per gal. After 9/30/2011: 4.3¢ per gal.
• Diesel-water fuel emulsion	Through 9/30/2011, on removal at terminal: 19.8¢ per gal. After 9/30/2011, see diesel fuel rate above
• Dyed diesel fuel, other than for export	Through 9/30/2011, on removal at terminal or retail sale: .1¢ per gal.
Kerosene	Through 9/30/2011, on removal at terminal or retail sale, generally: 24.4¢ per gal. After 9/30/2011: 4.3¢ per gal.
• Noncommercial aviation use—on removal directly into noncommercial aircraft's fuel tank	Through 12/31/2010[1]: 21.9¢ per gal. 1/1/2011-9/30/2011: 4.4¢ per gal. After 9/30/2011: 4.3¢ per gal.
• Commercial aviation use—on removal directly into commercial aircraft's fuel tank	Through 9/30/2011: 4.4¢ per gal. After 9/30/2011: 4.3¢ per gal.
• Retail sale for aviation use (where fuel not previously taxed)	Through 9/30/2011, for noncommercial aviation: 21.9¢ per gal.; for commercial aviation: 4.4¢ per gal. After 9/30/2011: 21.8¢ per gal. and 4.3¢ per gal., respectively
• Dyed kerosene, other than for export	Through 9/30/2011, on removal at terminal or retail sale: .1¢ per gal.
Alternative fuels	
• Special motor fuels (other than LPG and LNG)	Through 9/30/2011, on retail sale or use, for motor vehicle or motorboat use: 18.4¢ per gal. After 9/30/2011: 4.3¢ per gal.
• Liquefied petroleum gas (LPG) (e.g., propane, butane)	18.3¢ per gal.
• Liquefied natural gas (LNG)	24.3¢ per gal.
• Liquid fuel (other than ethanol or methanol) derived from coal, liquid hydrocarbons derived from biomass	Through 9/30/2011: 24.4¢ per gal. After 9/30/2011: 24.3¢ per gal.
• Partially exempt ethanol and methanol	Through 9/30/2011, for retail sale or use, of: partially exempt ethanol, 11.4¢ per gal.; partially exempt methanol, 9.25¢ per gal. After 9/30/2011, for partially exempt ethanol, 4.3¢ per gal.; for partially exempt methanol, 2.15¢ per gal.
Compressed natural gas (CNG)	18.3¢ per energy equivalent of a gal. of gasoline

Fuel used in commercial transportation on inland waterways

Through 9/30/2011, 20.1¢ per gal. After 9/30/2011, 20¢ per gal.

---

[1] Congress may extend application of this rate as it considers broader changes to FAA funding.
[2] Special rates apply to diesel fuel used in certain buses and trains.

Selected manufacturers and other excise taxes

Coal (except lignite)

- From underground mines

  Lower of $1.10 per ton or 4.4% of selling price

- From surface mines

  Lower of 55¢ per ton or 4.4% of selling price

Tires (of type used in highway vehicles, wholly or in part made of rubber)

9.45¢ (4.725¢ for biasply or super single tires) for each 10 lbs. the tire's maximum rated load capacity exceeds 3,500 lbs. Tax scheduled to expire after 9/30/2011.

Sport fishing equipment

10% of mfrs. price of specified sport fishing equipment (up to max. of $10 on fishing rods and poles); 3% for electric outboard motors and fishing tackle boxes

Gas guzzling passenger autos, as follows:

If the fuel economy of the model type in which the automobile falls is:	*The tax is:*
At least 22.5	0
At least 21.5 but less than 22.5	$1,000
At least 20.5 but less than 21.5	1,300
At least 19.5 but less than 20.5	1,700
At least 18.5 but less than 19.5	2,100
At least 17.5 but less than 18.5	2,600
At least 16.5 but less than 17.5	3,000
At least 15.5 but less than 16.5	3,700
At least 14.5 but less than 15.5	4,500
At least 13.5 but less than 14.5	5,400
At least 12.5 but less than 13.5	6,400
Less than 12.5	7,700

Indoor tanning, after June 30, 2010

10% of amount paid for services.

¶ 1116 Applicable Federal Rates. ▬▬▬▬▬▬

The IRS tables below show the Applicable one-month Federal Rates (AFRs). The tables provide short-term (obligations not exceeding three years), mid-term (over three years but not over nine years) and long-term (over nine years) rates (in percentages) based on annual, semiannual, quarterly and monthly compounding assumptions.[5]

Applicable Federal Rate	Annual	Semiannual	Quarterly	Monthly
November 2010				
Short-Term				
AFR	.35%	.35%	.35%	.35%
110% AFR	.39%	.39%	.39%	.39%
120% AFR	.42%	.42%	.42%	.42%
130% AFR	.46%	.46%	.46%	.46%
Mid-Term				
AFR	1.59%	1.58%	1.58%	1.57%
110% AFR	1.75%	1.74%	1.74%	1.73%
120% AFR	1.91%	1.90%	1.90%	1.89%
130% AFR	2.06%	2.05%	2.04%	2.04%
150% AFR	2.38%	2.37%	2.36%	2.36%
175% AFR	2.79%	2.77%	2.76%	2.75%
Long-Term				
AFR	3.35%	3.32%	3.31%	3.30%
110% AFR	3.68%	3.65%	3.63%	3.62%
120% AFR	4.02%	3.98%	3.96%	3.95%
130% AFR	4.37%	4.32%	4.30%	4.28%
October 2010				
Short-Term				
AFR	.41%	.41%	.41%	.41%
110% AFR	.45%	.45%	.45%	.45%
120% AFR	.49%	.49%	.49%	.49%
130% AFR	.53%	.53%	.53%	.53%
Mid-Term				
AFR	1.73%	1.72%	1.72%	1.71%
110% AFR	1.90%	1.89%	1.89%	1.88%
120% AFR	2.07%	2.06%	2.05%	2.05%
130% AFR	2.25%	2.24%	2.23%	2.23%
150% AFR	2.60%	2.58%	2.57%	2.57%
175% AFR	3.03%	3.01%	3.00%	2.99%
Long-Term				
AFR	3.32%	3.29%	3.28%	3.27%
110% AFR	3.65%	3.62%	3.60%	3.59%
120% AFR	3.99%	3.95%	3.93%	3.92%
130% AFR	4.33%	4.28%	4.26%	4.24%
September 2010				
Short-Term				
AFR	.46%	.46%	.46%	.46%
110% AFR	.51%	.51%	.51%	.51%
120% AFR	.55%	.55%	.55%	.55%
130% AFR	.60%	.60%	.60%	.60%
Mid-Term				
AFR	1.94%	1.93%	1.93%	1.92%
110% AFR	2.13%	2.12%	2.11%	2.11%
120% AFR	2.33%	2.32%	2.31%	2.31%
130% AFR	2.53%	2.51%	2.50%	2.50%
150% AFR	2.92%	2.90%	2.89%	2.88%
175% AFR	3.41%	3.38%	3.37%	3.36%

Applicable Federal Rate	Annual	Semiannual	Quarterly	Monthly
Long-Term				
AFR	3.66%	3.63%	3.61%	3.60%
110% AFR	4.03%	3.99%	3.97%	3.96%
120% AFR	4.41%	4.36%	4.34%	4.32%
130% AFR	4.78%	4.72%	4.69%	4.67%
August 2010				
Short-Term				
AFR	.53%	.53%	.53%	.53%
110% AFR	.58%	.58%	.58%	.58%
120% AFR	.64%	.64%	.64%	.64%
130% AFR	.69%	.69%	.69%	.69%
Mid-Term				
AFR	2.18%	2.17%	2.16%	2.16%
110% AFR	2.40%	2.39%	2.38%	2.38%
120% AFR	2.62%	2.60%	2.59%	2.59%
130% AFR	2.84%	2.82%	2.81%	2.80%
150% AFR	3.29%	3.26%	3.25%	3.24%
175% AFR	3.84%	3.80%	3.78%	3.77%
Long-Term				
AFR	3.79%	3.75%	3.73%	3.72%
110% AFR	4.17%	4.13%	4.11%	4.09%
120% AFR	4.55%	4.50%	4.47%	4.46%
130% AFR	4.94%	4.88%	4.85%	4.83%
July 2010				
Short-Term				
AFR	.61%	.61%	.61%	.61%
110% AFR	.67%	.67%	.67%	.67%
120% AFR	.73%	.73%	.73%	.73%
130% AFR	.79%	.79%	.79%	.79%
Mid-Term				
AFR	2.35%	2.34%	2.33%	2.33%
110% AFR	2.59%	2.57%	2.56%	2.56%
120% AFR	2.83%	2.81%	2.80%	2.79%
130% AFR	3.06%	3.04%	3.03%	3.02%
150% AFR	3.54%	3.51%	3.49%	3.48%
175% AFR	4.14%	4.10%	4.08%	4.07%
Long-Term				
AFR	3.94%	3.90%	3.88%	3.87%
110% AFR	4.34%	4.29%	4.27%	4.25%
120% AFR	4.73%	4.68%	4.65%	4.64%
130% AFR	5.13%	5.07%	5.04%	5.02%
June 2010				
Short-Term				
AFR	.74%	.74%	.74%	.74%
110% AFR	.81%	.81%	.81%	.81%
120% AFR	.89%	.89%	.89%	.89%
130% AFR	.96%	.96%	.96%	.96%
Mid-Term				
AFR	2.72%	2.70%	2.69%	2.68%
110% AFR	2.99%	2.97%	2.96%	2.95%
120% AFR	3.27%	3.24%	3.23%	3.22%

5. ¶J-4192; ¶12,714.01; TD ¶153,030

Applicable Federal Rate	Annual	Semiannual	Quarterly	Monthly
130% AFR	3.54%	3.51%	3.49%	3.48%
150% AFR	4.09%	4.05%	4.03%	4.02%
175% AFR	4.79%	4.73%	4.70%	4.68%
Long-Term				
AFR	4.30%	4.25%	4.23%	4.21%
110% AFR	4.73%	4.68%	4.65%	4.64%
120% AFR	5.17%	5.10%	5.07%	5.05%
130% AFR	5.61%	5.53%	5.49%	5.47%

May 2010

Short-Term	Annual	Semiannual	Quarterly	Monthly
AFR	.79%	.79%	.79%	.79%
110% AFR	.87%	.87%	.87%	.87%
120% AFR	.95%	.95%	.95%	.95%
130% AFR	1.03%	1.03%	1.03%	1.03%
Mid-Term				
AFR	2.87%	2.85%	2.84%	2.83%
110% AFR	3.16%	3.14%	3.13%	3.12%
120% AFR	3.45%	3.42%	3.41%	3.40%
130% AFR	3.74%	3.71%	3.69%	3.68%
150% AFR	4.33%	4.28%	4.26%	4.24%
175% AFR	5.05%	4.99%	4.96%	4.94%
Long-Term				
AFR	4.47%	4.42%	4.40%	4.38%
110% AFR	4.92%	4.86%	4.83%	4.81%
120% AFR	5.37%	5.30%	5.27%	5.24%
130% AFR	5.83%	5.75%	5.71%	5.68%

April 2010

Short-Term	Annual	Semiannual	Quarterly	Monthly
AFR	.67%	.67%	.67%	.67%
110% AFR	.74%	.74%	.74%	.74%
120% AFR	.80%	.80%	.80%	.80%
130% AFR	.87%	.87%	.87%	.87%
Mid-Term				
AFR	2.70%	2.68%	2.67%	2.67%
110% AFR	2.97%	2.95%	2.94%	2.93%
120% AFR	3.25%	3.22%	3.21%	3.20%
130% AFR	3.51%	3.48%	3.46%	3.46%
150% AFR	4.06%	4.02%	4.00%	3.99%
175% AFR	4.74%	4.69%	4.66%	4.64%
Long-Term				
AFR	4.40%	4.35%	4.33%	4.31%
110% AFR	4.85%	4.79%	4.76%	4.74%
120% AFR	5.29%	5.22%	5.19%	5.16%
130% AFR	5.74%	5.66%	5.62%	5.59%

March 2010

Short-Term	Annual	Semiannual	Quarterly	Monthly
AFR	.64%	.64%	.64%	.64%
110% AFR	.70%	.70%	.70%	.70%
120% AFR	.77%	.77%	.77%	.77%
130% AFR	.83%	.83%	.83%	.83%
Mid-Term				
AFR	2.69%	2.67%	2.66%	2.66%
110% AFR	2.96%	2.94%	2.93%	2.92%
120% AFR	3.23%	3.20%	3.19%	3.18%
130% AFR	3.50%	3.47%	3.46%	3.45%
150% AFR	4.05%	4.01%	3.99%	3.98%
175% AFR	4.72%	4.67%	4.64%	4.63%
Long-Term				
AFR	4.35%	4.30%	4.28%	4.26%
110% AFR	4.79%	4.73%	4.70%	4.68%

Applicable Federal Rate	Annual	Semiannual	Quarterly	Monthly
120% AFR	5.23%	5.16%	5.13%	5.11%
130% AFR	5.67%	5.59%	5.55%	5.53%

February 2010

Short-Term	Annual	Semiannual	Quarterly	Monthly
AFR	.72%	.72%	.72%	.72%
110% AFR	.79%	.79%	.79%	.79%
120% AFR	.86%	.86%	.86%	.86%
130% AFR	.94%	.94%	.94%	.94%
Mid-Term				
AFR	2.82%	2.80%	2.79%	2.78%
110% AFR	3.10%	3.08%	3.07%	3.06%
120% AFR	3.39%	3.36%	3.35%	3.34%
130% AFR	3.67%	3.64%	3.62%	3.61%
150% AFR	4.24%	4.20%	4.18%	4.16%
175% AFR	4.96%	4.90%	4.87%	4.85%
Long-Term				
AFR	4.44%	4.39%	4.37%	4.35%
110% AFR	4.89%	4.83%	4.80%	4.78%
120% AFR	5.34%	5.27%	5.24%	5.21%
130% AFR	5.79%	5.71%	5.67%	5.64%

January 2010

Short-Term	Annual	Semiannual	Quarterly	Monthly
AFR	.57%	.57%	.57%	.57%
110% AFR	.63%	.63%	.63%	.63%
120% AFR	.68%	.68%	.68%	.68%
130% AFR	.74%	.74%	.74%	.74%
Mid-Term				
AFR	2.45%	2.44%	2.43%	2.43%
110% AFR	2.70%	2.68%	2.67%	2.67%
120% AFR	2.95%	2.93%	2.92%	2.91%
130% AFR	3.20%	3.17%	3.16%	3.15%
150% AFR	3.69%	3.66%	3.64%	3.63%
175% AFR	4.32%	4.27%	4.25%	4.23%
Long-Term				
AFR	4.11%	4.07%	4.05%	4.04%
110% AFR	4.53%	4.48%	4.46%	4.44%
120% AFR	4.94%	4.88%	4.85%	4.83%
130% AFR	5.36%	5.29%	5.26%	5.23%

December 2009

Short-Term	Annual	Semiannual	Quarterly	Monthly
AFR	.69%	.69%	.69%	.69%
110% AFR	.76%	.76%	.76%	.76%
120% AFR	.83%	.83%	.83%	.83%
130% AFR	.90%	.90%	.90%	.90%
Mid-Term				
AFR	2.64%	2.62%	2.61%	2.61%
110% AFR	2.90%	2.88%	2.87%	2.86%
120% AFR	3.16%	3.14%	3.13%	3.12%
130% AFR	3.44%	3.41%	3.40%	3.39%
150% AFR	3.97%	3.93%	3.91%	3.90%
175% AFR	4.64%	4.59%	4.56%	4.55%
Long-Term				
AFR	4.17%	4.13%	4.11%	4.09%
110% AFR	4.59%	4.54%	4.51%	4.50%
120% AFR	5.02%	4.96%	4.93%	4.91%
130% AFR	5.44%	5.37%	5.33%	5.31%

¶ 1117   MACRS Tables. ▬▬▬▬▬▬▬▬▬▬▬▬▬▬▬▬▬▬▬▬▬

Here are MACRS depreciation (cost recovery) tables.

The tables reproduced are the MACRS tables (general depreciation as well as alternative depreciation system (ADS)), plus the listed property tables used to determine income inclusion amounts by lessees of listed property other than automobiles. The depreciation amounts for automobiles under the luxury auto restrictions are carried at ¶1954; the income inclusion amounts for lessees of automobiles carried at ¶1118 are explained at ¶1959 *et seq.*

Under the general depreciation system (GDS) of MACRS, the table rates are based on: (1) the 200% declining balance method for 3-, 5-, 7-, and 10-year personal property; (2) the 150% declining balance method for 15-, and 20-year personal property; and (3) the straight-line method for residential and nonresidential realty. Under the alternative depreciation system (ADS) of MACRS, the table rates for personal and real property are based on the straight-line method. The use of the tables is discussed in ¶1911. (IRS alternative minimum tax tables and the tables for straight line depreciation under the midquarter convention are not reproduced in this Handbook. For those tables, see the Appendix to Federal Tax Coordinator 2d Chapter L-7400.)

Table 1

General Depreciation System
Applicable Depreciation Method: 200 or 150 Percent
Declining Balance Switching to Straight Line
Applicable Recovery Periods: 3, 5, 7, 10, 15, 20 years
Applicable Convention: Half-year

If the Recovery Year is:	and the Recovery Period is:					
	3-year	5-year	7-year	10-year	15-year	20-year
			the Depreciation Rate is:			
1	33.33	20.00	14.29	10.00	5.00	3.750
2	44.45	32.00	24.49	18.00	9.50	7.219
3	14.81	19.20	17.49	14.40	8.55	6.677
4	7.41	11.52	12.49	11.52	7.70	6.177
5		11.52	8.93	9.22	6.93	5.713
6		5.76	8.92	7.37	6.23	5.285
7			8.93	6.55	5.90	4.888
8			4.46	6.55	5.90	4.522
9				6.56	5.91	4.462
10				6.55	5.90	4.461
11				3.28	5.91	4.462
12					5.90	4.461
13					5.91	4.462
14					5.90	4.461
15					5.91	4.462
16					2.95	4.461
17						4.462
18						4.461
19						4.462
20						4.461
21						2.231

Table 2

General Depreciation System
Applicable Depreciation Method: 200 or 150 Percent
Declining Balance Switching to Straight Line
Applicable Recovery Periods: 3, 5, 7, 10, 15, 20 years
Applicable Convention: Mid-quarter
(property placed in service in first quarter)

If the Recovery Year is:	and the Recovery Period is:					
	3-year	5-year	7-year	10-year	15-year	20-year
			the Depreciation Rate is:			
1	58.33	35.00	25.00	17.50	8.75	6.563
2	27.78	26.00	21.43	16.50	9.13	7.000
3	12.35	15.60	15.31	13.20	8.21	6.482
4	1.54	11.01	10.93	10.56	7.39	5.996
5		11.01	8.75	8.45	6.65	5.546
6		1.38	8.74	6.76	5.99	5.130
7			8.75	6.55	5.90	4.746
8			1.09	6.55	5.91	4.459
9				6.56	5.90	4.459
10				6.55	5.91	4.459
11				0.82	5.90	4.459
12					5.91	4.460
13					5.90	4.459
14					5.91	4.460
15					5.90	4.459
16					0.74	4.460
17						4.459
18						4.460
19						4.459
20						4.460
21						0.557

Table 3

General Depreciation System
Applicable Depreciation Method: 200 or 150 Percent
Declining Balance Switching to Straight Line
Applicable Recovery Periods: 3, 5, 7, 10, 15, 20 years
Applicable Convention: Mid-quarter
(property placed in service in second quarter)

If the Recovery Year is:	and the Recovery Period is:					
	3-year	5-year	7-year	10-year	15-year	20-year
			the Depreciation Rate is:			
1	41.67	25.00	17.85	12.50	6.25	4.688
2	38.89	30.00	23.47	17.50	9.38	7.148
3	14.14	18.00	16.76	14.00	8.44	6.612
4	5.30	11.37	11.97	11.20	7.59	6.116
5		11.37	8.87	8.96	6.83	5.658
6		4.26	8.87	7.17	6.15	5.233
7			8.87	6.55	5.91	4.841
8			3.33	6.55	5.90	4.478
9				6.56	5.91	4.463
10				6.55	5.90	4.463
11				2.46	5.91	4.463
12					5.90	4.463
13					5.91	4.463
14					5.90	4.463
15					5.91	4.462
16					2.21	4.463
17						4.462
18						4.463
19						4.462
20						4.463
21						1.673

Table 4

General Depreciation System
Applicable Depreciation Method: 200 or 150 Percent
Declining Balance Switching to Straight Line
Applicable Recovery Periods: 3, 5, 7, 10, 15, 20 years
Applicable Convention: Mid-quarter
(property placed in service in third quarter)

If the Recovery Year is:	and the Recovery Period is:					
	3-year	5-year	7-year	10-year	15-year	20-year
			the Depreciation Rate is:			
1	25.00	15.00	10.71	7.50	3.75	2.813
2	50.00	34.00	25.51	18.50	9.63	7.289
3	16.67	20.40	18.22	14.80	8.66	6.742
4	8.33	12.24	13.02	11.84	7.80	6.237
5		11.30	9.30	9.47	7.02	5.769
6		7.06	8.85	7.58	6.31	5.336
7			8.86	6.55	5.90	4.936
8			5.53	6.55	5.90	4.566
9				6.56	5.91	4.460
10				6.55	5.90	4.460
11				4.10	5.91	4.460
12					5.90	4.460
13					5.91	4.461
14					5.90	4.460
15					5.91	4.461
16					3.69	4.460
17						4.461
18						4.460
19						4.461
20						4.460
21						2.788

Table 5

General Depreciation System
Applicable Depreciation Method: 200 or 150 Percent
Declining Balance Switching to Straight Line
Applicable Recovery Periods: 3, 5, 7, 10, 15, 20 years
Applicable Convention: Mid-quarter
(property placed in service in fourth quarter)

If the Recovery Year is:	and the Recovery Period is:					
	3-year	5-year	7-year	10-year	15-year	20-year
			the Depreciation Rate is:			
1	8.33	5.00	3.57	2.50	1.25	0.938
2	61.11	38.00	27.55	19.50	9.88	7.430
3	20.37	22.80	19.68	15.60	8.89	6.872
4	10.19	13.68	14.06	12.48	8.00	6.357
5		10.94	10.04	9.98	7.20	5.880
6		9.58	8.73	7.99	6.48	5.439
7			8.73	6.55	5.90	5.031
8			7.64	6.55	5.90	4.654
9				6.56	5.90	4.458
10				6.55	5.91	4.458
11				5.74	5.90	4.458
12					5.91	4.458
13					5.90	4.458
14					5.91	4.458
15					5.90	4.458
16					5.17	4.458
17						4.458
18						4.459
19						4.458
20						4.459
21						3.901

Table 6

General Depreciation System
Applicable Depreciation Method: Straight Line
Applicable Recovery Period: 27.5 years
Applicable Convention: Mid-month

If the Recovery Year is:	And the Month in the First Recovery Year the Property is Placed in Service is:											
	1	2	3	4	5	6	7	8	9	10	11	12
						the Depreciation Rate is:						
1	3.485	3.182	2.879	2.576	2.273	1.970	1.667	1.364	1.061	0.758	0.455	0.152
2-9	3.636	3.636	3.636	3.636	3.636	3.636	3.636	3.636	3.636	3.636	3.636	3.636
10	3.637	3.637	3.637	3.637	3.637	3.637	3.636	3.636	3.636	3.636	3.636	3.636
11	3.636	3.636	3.636	3.636	3.636	3.636	3.637	3.637	3.637	3.637	3.637	3.637
12	3.637	3.637	3.637	3.637	3.637	3.637	3.636	3.636	3.636	3.636	3.636	3.636
13	3.636	3.636	3.636	3.636	3.636	3.636	3.637	3.637	3.637	3.637	3.637	3.637
14	3.637	3.637	3.637	3.637	3.637	3.637	3.636	3.636	3.636	3.636	3.636	3.636
15	3.636	3.636	3.636	3.636	3.636	3.636	3.637	3.637	3.637	3.637	3.637	3.637
16	3.637	3.637	3.637	3.637	3.637	3.637	3.636	3.636	3.636	3.636	3.636	3.636
17	3.636	3.636	3.636	3.636	3.636	3.636	3.637	3.637	3.637	3.637	3.637	3.637
18	3.637	3.637	3.637	3.637	3.637	3.637	3.636	3.636	3.636	3.636	3.636	3.636
19	3.636	3.636	3.636	3.636	3.636	3.636	3.637	3.637	3.637	3.637	3.637	3.637
20	3.637	3.637	3.637	3.637	3.637	3.637	3.636	3.636	3.636	3.636	3.636	3.636
21	3.636	3.636	3.636	3.636	3.636	3.636	3.637	3.637	3.637	3.637	3.637	3.637
22	3.637	3.637	3.637	3.637	3.637	3.637	3.636	3.636	3.636	3.636	3.636	3.636
23	3.636	3.636	3.636	3.636	3.636	3.636	3.637	3.637	3.637	3.637	3.637	3.637
24	3.637	3.637	3.637	3.637	3.637	3.637	3.636	3.636	3.636	3.636	3.636	3.636
25	3.636	3.636	3.636	3.636	3.636	3.636	3.637	3.637	3.637	3.637	3.637	3.637
26	3.637	3.637	3.637	3.637	3.637	3.637	3.636	3.636	3.636	3.636	3.636	3.636
27	3.636	3.636	3.636	3.636	3.636	3.636	3.637	3.637	3.637	3.637	3.637	3.637
28	1.970	2.273	2.576	2.879	3.182	3.485	3.636	3.636	3.636	3.636	3.636	3.636
29	0.000	0.000	0.000	0.000	0.000	0.000	0.152	0.455	0.758	1.061	1.364	1.667

Table 7

General Depreciation System
Applicable Depreciation Method: Straight Line
Applicable Recovery Period: 31.5 years
Applicable Convention: Mid-month

If the Recovery Year is:	And the Month in the First Recovery Year the Property is Placed in Service is:											
	1	2	3	4	5	6	7	8	9	10	11	12
	the Depreciation Rate is:											
1	3.042	2.778	2.513	2.249	1.984	1.720	1.455	1.190	0.926	0.661	0.397	0.132
2-7	3.175	3.175	3.175	3.175	3.175	3.175	3.175	3.175	3.175	3.175	3.175	3.175
8	3.175	3.174	3.175	3.174	3.175	3.174	3.175	3.175	3.175	3.175	3.175	3.175
9	3.174	3.175	3.174	3.175	3.174	3.175	3.174	3.175	3.174	3.175	3.174	3.175
10	3.175	3.174	3.175	3.174	3.175	3.174	3.175	3.174	3.175	3.174	3.175	3.174
11	3.174	3.175	3.174	3.175	3.174	3.175	3.174	3.175	3.174	3.175	3.174	3.175
12	3.175	3.174	3.175	3.174	3.175	3.174	3.175	3.174	3.175	3.174	3.175	3.174
13	3.174	3.175	3.174	3.175	3.174	3.175	3.174	3.175	3.174	3.175	3.174	3.175
14	3.175	3.174	3.175	3.174	3.175	3.174	3.175	3.174	3.175	3.174	3.175	3.174
15	3.174	3.175	3.174	3.175	3.174	3.175	3.174	3.175	3.174	3.175	3.174	3.175
16	3.175	3.174	3.175	3.174	3.175	3.174	3.175	3.174	3.175	3.174	3.175	3.174
17	3.174	3.175	3.174	3.175	3.174	3.175	3.174	3.175	3.174	3.175	3.174	3.175
18	3.175	3.174	3.175	3.174	3.175	3.174	3.175	3.174	3.175	3.174	3.175	3.174
19	3.174	3.175	3.174	3.175	3.174	3.175	3.174	3.175	3.174	3.175	3.174	3.175
20	3.175	3.174	3.175	3.174	3.175	3.174	3.175	3.174	3.175	3.174	3.175	3.174
21	3.174	3.175	3.174	3.175	3.174	3.175	3.174	3.175	3.174	3.175	3.174	3.175
22	3.175	3.174	3.175	3.174	3.175	3.174	3.175	3.174	3.175	3.174	3.175	3.174
23	3.174	3.175	3.174	3.175	3.174	3.175	3.174	3.175	3.174	3.175	3.174	3.175
24	3.175	3.174	3.175	3.174	3.175	3.174	3.175	3.174	3.175	3.174	3.175	3.174
25	3.174	3.175	3.174	3.175	3.174	3.175	3.174	3.175	3.174	3.175	3.174	3.175
26	3.175	3.174	3.175	3.174	3.175	3.174	3.175	3.174	3.175	3.174	3.175	3.174
27	3.174	3.175	3.174	3.175	3.174	3.175	3.174	3.175	3.174	3.175	3.174	3.175
28	3.175	3.174	3.175	3.174	3.175	3.174	3.175	3.174	3.175	3.174	3.175	3.174
29	3.174	3.175	3.174	3.175	3.174	3.175	3.174	3.175	3.174	3.175	3.174	3.175
30	3.175	3.174	3.175	3.174	3.175	3.174	3.175	3.174	3.175	3.174	3.175	3.174
31	3.174	3.175	3.174	3.175	3.174	3.175	3.174	3.175	3.174	3.175	3.174	3.175
32	1.720	1.984	2.249	2.513	2.778	3.042	3.175	3.174	3.175	3.174	3.175	3.174
33	0.000	0.000	0.000	0.000	0.000	0.000	0.132	0.397	0.661	0.926	1.190	1.455

Table 7a

General Depreciation System
Applicable Depreciation Method: Straight Line
Applicable Recovery Period: 39 years
Applicable Convention: Mid-month

Year	Month property placed in service											
	1	2	3	4	5	6	7	8	9	10	11	12
1	2.461%	2.247%	2.033%	1.819%	1.605%	1.391%	1.177%	0.963%	0.749%	0.535%	0.321%	0.107%
2-39	2.564	2.564	2.564	2.564	2.564	2.564	2.564	2.564	2.564	2.564	2.564	2.564
40	0.107	0.321	0.535	0.749	0.963	1.177	1.391	1.605	1.819	2.033	2.247	2.461

Table 8

General and Alternative Depreciation Systems
Applicable Depreciation Method: Straight Line
Applicable Recovery Periods: 2.5-50 years
Applicable Convention: Half-year

If the Recovery Year is:	and the Recovery Period is: the Depreciation Rate is:															
	2.5	3.0	3.5	4.0	4.5	5.0	5.5	6.0	6.5	7.0	7.5	8.0	8.5	9.0	9.5	10.0
1	20.00	16.67	14.29	12.50	11.11	10.00	9.09	8.33	7.69	7.14	6.67	6.25	5.88	5.56	5.26	5.00
2	40.00	33.33	28.57	25.00	22.22	20.00	18.18	16.67	15.39	14.29	13.33	12.50	11.77	11.11	10.53	10.00
3	40.00	33.33	28.57	25.00	22.22	20.00	18.18	16.67	15.38	14.29	13.33	12.50	11.76	11.11	10.53	10.00
4		16.67	28.57	25.00	22.23	20.00	18.18	16.67	15.39	14.28	13.33	12.50	11.77	11.11	10.53	10.00
5				12.50	22.22	20.00	18.19	16.66	15.38	14.29	13.34	12.50	11.76	11.11	10.52	10.00
6						10.00	18.18	16.67	15.39	14.28	13.33	12.50	11.77	11.11	10.53	10.00
7								8.33	15.38	14.29	13.34	12.50	11.76	11.11	10.52	10.00
8										7.14	13.33	12.50	11.77	11.11	10.53	10.00
9											6.25	11.76	11.11	10.52	10.00
10													5.56	10.53	10.00
11																5.00

If the Recovery Year is:	and the Recovery Period is: the Depreciation Rate is:															
	10.5	11.0	11.5	12.0	12.5	13.0	13.5	14.0	14.5	15.0	15.5	16.0	16.5	17.0	17.5	18.0
1	4.76	4.55	4.35	4.17	4.00	3.85	3.70	3.57	3.45	3.33	3.23	3.13	3.03	2.94	2.86	2.78
2	9.52	9.09	8.70	8.33	8.00	7.69	7.41	7.14	6.90	6.67	6.45	6.25	6.06	5.88	5.71	5.56
3	9.52	9.09	8.70	8.33	8.00	7.69	7.41	7.14	6.90	6.67	6.45	6.25	6.06	5.88	5.71	5.56
4	9.53	9.09	8.69	8.33	8.00	7.69	7.41	7.14	6.90	6.67	6.45	6.25	6.06	5.88	5.71	5.55
5	9.52	9.09	8.70	8.33	8.00	7.69	7.41	7.14	6.90	6.67	6.45	6.25	6.06	5.88	5.72	5.56
6	9.53	9.09	8.69	8.33	8.00	7.69	7.41	7.14	6.89	6.67	6.45	6.25	6.06	5.88	5.71	5.55
7	9.52	9.09	8.70	8.34	8.00	7.69	7.41	7.14	6.90	6.67	6.45	6.25	6.06	5.88	5.72	5.56
8	9.53	9.09	8.69	8.33	8.00	7.69	7.41	7.15	6.89	6.66	6.45	6.25	6.06	5.88	5.71	5.55
9	9.52	9.09	8.70	8.34	8.00	7.69	7.41	7.14	6.90	6.67	6.45	6.25	6.06	5.88	5.72	5.56
10	9.53	9.09	8.69	8.33	8.00	7.70	7.40	7.15	6.89	6.66	6.45	6.25	6.06	5.88	5.71	5.55
11	9.52	9.09	8.70	8.34	8.00	7.69	7.41	7.14	6.90	6.67	6.45	6.25	6.06	5.89	5.72	5.56
12		4.55	8.69	8.33	8.00	7.70	7.40	7.15	6.89	6.66	6.45	6.25	6.06	5.88	5.71	5.55
13				4.17	8.00	7.69	7.41	7.14	6.90	6.67	6.45	6.25	6.06	5.89	5.72	5.56
14						3.85	7.40	7.15	6.89	6.66	6.46	6.25	6.06	5.88	5.71	5.55
15								3.57	6.90	6.67	6.45	6.25	6.06	5.89	5.72	5.56
16										3.33	6.46	6.25	6.06	5.88	5.71	5.55
17												3.12	6.07	5.89	5.72	5.56
18														2.94	5.71	5.55
19																2.78

Table 8

General and Alternative Depreciation Systems
Applicable Depreciation Method: Straight Line
Applicable Recovery Periods: 2.5-50 years
Applicable Convention: Half-year
(continued)

If the Recovery Year is:	and the Recovery Period is:															
	18.5	19.0	19.5	20.0	20.5	21.0	21.5	22.0	22.5	23.0	23.5	24.0	24.5	25.0	25.5	26.0
							the Depreciation Rate is:									
1	2.70	2.63	2.56	2.500	2.439	2.381	2.326	2.273	2.222	2.174	2.128	2.083	2.041	2.000	1.961	1.923
2	5.41	5.26	5.13	5.000	4.878	4.762	4.651	4.545	4.444	4.348	4.255	4.167	4.082	4.000	3.922	3.846
3	5.41	5.26	5.13	5.000	4.878	4.762	4.651	4.545	4.444	4.348	4.255	4.167	4.082	4.000	3.922	3.846
4	5.41	5.26	5.13	5.000	4.878	4.762	4.651	4.545	4.445	4.348	4.255	4.167	4.082	4.000	3.922	3.846
5	5.40	5.26	5.13	5.000	4.878	4.762	4.651	4.546	4.444	4.348	4.255	4.167	4.082	4.000	3.922	3.846
6	5.41	5.26	5.13	5.000	4.878	4.762	4.651	4.545	4.445	4.348	4.255	4.167	4.082	4.000	3.921	3.846
7	5.40	5.26	5.13	5.000	4.878	4.762	4.651	4.546	4.444	4.348	4.255	4.167	4.082	4.000	3.922	3.846
8	5.41	5.26	5.13	5.000	4.878	4.762	4.651	4.545	4.445	4.348	4.255	4.167	4.082	4.000	3.921	3.846
9	5.40	5.27	5.13	5.000	4.878	4.762	4.651	4.546	4.444	4.348	4.255	4.167	4.081	4.000	3.922	3.846
10	5.41	5.26	5.13	5.000	4.878	4.762	4.651	4.545	4.445	4.348	4.255	4.167	4.082	4.000	3.921	3.846
11	5.40	5.27	5.13	5.000	4.878	4.762	4.651	4.546	4.444	4.348	4.256	4.166	4.081	4.000	3.922	3.846
12	5.41	5.26	5.13	5.000	4.878	4.762	4.651	4.545	4.445	4.348	4.255	4.167	4.082	4.000	3.921	3.846
13	5.40	5.27	5.13	5.000	4.878	4.762	4.651	4.546	4.444	4.348	4.256	4.166	4.081	4.000	3.922	3.846
14	5.41	5.26	5.13	5.000	4.878	4.762	4.651	4.545	4.445	4.348	4.255	4.167	4.082	4.000	3.921	3.846
15	5.40	5.27	5.13	5.000	4.878	4.762	4.651	4.546	4.444	4.348	4.256	4.166	4.081	4.000	3.922	3.846
16	5.41	5.26	5.12	5.000	4.878	4.762	4.651	4.545	4.445	4.348	4.255	4.167	4.082	4.000	3.921	3.846
17	5.40	5.27	5.13	5.000	4.878	4.762	4.652	4.546	4.444	4.347	4.256	4.166	4.081	4.000	3.922	3.846
18	5.41	5.26	5.12	5.000	4.878	4.762	4.651	4.545	4.445	4.348	4.255	4.167	4.082	4.000	3.921	3.846
19	5.40	5.27	5.13	5.000	4.878	4.761	4.652	4.546	4.444	4.347	4.256	4.166	4.081	4.000	3.922	3.846
20		2.63	5.12	5.000	4.879	4.762	4.651	4.545	4.445	4.348	4.255	4.167	4.082	4.000	3.921	3.847
21			2.500	4.878	4.761	4.652	4.546	4.444	4.347	4.256	4.166	4.081	4.000	3.922	3.846
22					2.381	4.651	4.545	4.445	4.348	4.255	4.167	4.082	4.000	3.921	3.847
23							2.273	4.444	4.347	4.256	4.166	4.081	4.000	3.922	3.846
24								2.174	4.255	4.167	4.082	4.000	3.921	3.847
25									2.083	4.081	4.000	3.922	3.846
26										2.000	3.921	3.847	3.846
27												1.923

If the Recovery Year is:	and the Recovery Period is:															
	26.5	27.0	27.5	28.0	28.5	29.0	29.5	30.0	30.5	31.0	31.5	32.0	32.5	33.0	33.5	34.0
							the Depreciation Rate is:									
1	1.887	1.852	1.818	1.786	1.754	1.724	1.695	1.667	1.639	1.613	1.587	1.563	1.538	1.515	1.493	1.471
2-6	3.774	3.704	3.636	3.571	3.509	3.448	3.390	3.333	3.279	3.226	3.175	3.125	3.077	3.030	2.985	2.941
7	3.773	3.704	3.636	3.572	3.509	3.448	3.390	3.333	3.279	3.226	3.175	3.125	3.077	3.030	2.985	2.941
8	3.774	3.704	3.636	3.571	3.509	3.448	3.390	3.333	3.279	3.226	3.175	3.125	3.077	3.030	2.985	2.941
9	3.773	3.704	3.637	3.572	3.509	3.448	3.390	3.333	3.279	3.226	3.174	3.125	3.077	3.030	2.985	2.941
10	3.774	3.704	3.636	3.571	3.509	3.448	3.390	3.333	3.279	3.226	3.174	3.125	3.077	3.030	2.985	2.941
11	3.773	3.704	3.637	3.572	3.509	3.448	3.390	3.333	3.279	3.226	3.175	3.125	3.077	3.030	2.985	2.941
12	3.774	3.704	3.636	3.571	3.509	3.448	3.390	3.333	3.279	3.226	3.174	3.125	3.077	3.030	2.985	2.941
13	3.773	3.703	3.637	3.572	3.509	3.448	3.390	3.334	3.279	3.226	3.175	3.125	3.077	3.030	2.985	2.941
14	3.773	3.704	3.636	3.571	3.509	3.448	3.390	3.333	3.270	0.220	3.174	3.125	3.077	3.030	2.985	2.941
15	3.774	3.703	3.637	3.572	3.509	3.449	3.390	3.334	3.278	3.226	3.175	3.125	3.077	3.031	2.985	2.941
16	3.773	3.704	3.636	3.571	3.509	3.448	3.390	3.333	3.279	3.226	3.174	3.125	3.077	3.030	2.985	2.941
17	3.774	3.703	3.637	3.572	3.509	3.449	3.390	3.334	3.278	3.226	3.175	3.125	3.077	3.031	2.985	2.941
18	3.773	3.704	3.636	3.571	3.508	3.448	3.390	3.333	3.279	3.226	3.175	3.125	3.077	3.030	2.985	2.941
19	3.774	3.703	3.637	3.572	3.509	3.449	3.390	3.334	3.278	3.226	3.175	3.125	3.077	3.031	2.985	2.941
20	3.773	3.704	3.636	3.571	3.508	3.448	3.390	3.333	3.279	3.226	3.174	3.125	3.077	3.030	2.985	2.941
21	3.774	3.703	3.637	3.572	3.509	3.449	3.389	3.334	3.278	3.225	3.175	3.125	3.077	3.031	2.985	2.941
22	3.773	3.704	3.636	3.571	3.508	3.448	3.390	3.333	3.279	3.226	3.174	3.125	3.077	3.030	2.985	2.941
23	3.774	3.703	3.637	3.572	3.509	3.449	3.389	3.334	3.278	3.225	3.175	3.125	3.077	3.031	2.985	2.941
24	3.773	3.704	3.636	3.571	3.508	3.448	3.390	3.333	3.279	3.226	3.174	3.125	3.077	3.030	2.985	2.941
25	3.774	3.703	3.637	3.572	3.509	3.449	3.389	3.334	3.278	3.225	3.175	3.125	3.077	3.031	2.985	2.942
26	3.773	3.704	3.636	3.571	3.508	3.448	3.390	3.333	3.279	3.226	3.174	3.125	3.077	3.030	2.985	2.941
27	3.774	3.703	3.637	3.572	3.509	3.449	3.389	3.334	3.278	3.225	3.175	3.125	3.077	3.030	2.985	2.942
28		1.852	3.636	3.571	3.508	3.448	3.390	3.333	3.279	3.226	3.174	3.125	3.077	3.031	2.985	2.941
29				1.786	3.509	3.449	3.389	3.334	3.278	3.225	3.175	3.125	3.077	3.030	2.985	2.942
30						1.724	3.390	3.333	3.279	3.226	3.174	3.125	3.077	3.031	2.985	2.941
31								1.667	3.278	3.225	3.175	3.125	3.076	3.031	2.986	2.942
32									1.613	3.174	3.125	3.077	3.030	2.985	2.941

Table 8

General and Alternative Depreciation Systems
Applicable Depreciation Method: Straight Line
Applicable Recovery Periods: 2.5-50 years
Applicable Convention: Half-year
(continued)

33	1.562	3.076	3.031	2.986	2.942
34			1.515	2.985	2.941
35					1.471

If the Recovery Year is:	34.5	35.0	35.5	36.0	36.5	37.0	37.5	38.0	38.5	39.0	39.5	40.0	40.5	41.0	41.5	42.0
						and the Recovery Period is: the Depreciation Rate is:										
1	1.449	1.429	1.408	1.389	1.370	1.351	1.333	1.316	1.299	1.282	1.266	1.250	1.235	1.220	1.205	1.190
2	2.899	2.857	2.817	2.778	2.740	2.703	2.667	2.632	2.597	2.564	2.532	2.500	2.469	2.439	2.410	2.381
3	2.899	2.857	2.817	2.778	2.740	2.703	2.667	2.632	2.597	2.564	2.532	2.500	2.469	2.439	2.410	2.381
4	2.899	2.857	2.817	2.778	2.740	2.703	2.667	2.632	2.597	2.564	2.532	2.500	2.469	2.439	2.410	2.381
5	2.899	2.857	2.817	2.778	2.740	2.703	2.667	2.632	2.597	2.564	2.532	2.500	2.469	2.439	2.410	2.381
6	2.899	2.857	2.817	2.778	2.740	2.703	2.667	2.632	2.597	2.564	2.532	2.500	2.469	2.439	2.410	2.381
7	2.898	2.857	2.817	2.778	2.740	2.703	2.667	2.632	2.597	2.564	2.532	2.500	2.469	2.439	2.410	2.381
8	2.899	2.857	2.817	2.778	2.740	2.703	2.667	2.631	2.597	2.564	2.532	2.500	2.469	2.439	2.410	2.381
9	2.898	2.857	2.817	2.778	2.740	2.703	2.667	2.632	2.597	2.564	2.532	2.500	2.469	2.439	2.410	2.381
10	2.899	2.857	2.817	2.778	2.740	2.703	2.667	2.631	2.598	2.564	2.532	2.500	2.469	2.439	2.410	2.381
11	2.898	2.857	2.817	2.778	2.740	2.703	2.667	2.632	2.597	2.564	2.532	2.500	2.469	2.439	2.410	2.381
12	2.899	2.857	2.817	2.778	2.740	2.703	2.667	2.631	2.598	2.564	2.532	2.500	2.469	2.439	2.410	2.381
13	2.898	2.857	2.817	2.778	2.740	2.703	2.667	2.632	2.597	2.564	2.532	2.500	2.469	2.439	2.410	2.381
14	2.899	2.857	2.817	2.778	2.740	2.703	2.667	2.631	2.598	2.564	2.531	2.500	2.469	2.439	2.409	2.381
15	2.898	2.857	2.817	2.778	2.740	2.703	2.666	2.632	2.597	2.564	2.532	2.500	2.469	2.439	2.410	2.381
16	2.899	2.857	2.817	2.778	2.740	2.703	2.667	2.631	2.598	2.564	2.531	2.500	2.469	2.439	2.409	2.381
17	2.898	2.857	2.817	2.778	2.740	2.703	2.666	2.632	2.597	2.564	2.532	2.500	2.469	2.439	2.410	2.381
18	2.899	2.857	2.817	2.778	2.740	2.702	2.667	2.631	2.598	2.564	2.531	2.500	2.469	2.439	2.409	2.381
19	2.898	2.857	2.817	2.778	2.739	2.703	2.666	2.632	2.597	2.564	2.532	2.500	2.469	2.439	2.410	2.381
20	2.898	2.857	2.817	2.778	2.740	2.702	2.667	2.631	2.598	2.564	2.531	2.500	2.469	2.439	2.409	2.381
21	2.899	2.857	2.817	2.778	2.739	2.703	2.666	2.632	2.597	2.564	2.532	2.500	2.469	2.439	2.410	2.381
22	2.898	2.857	2.817	2.777	2.740	2.702	2.667	2.631	2.598	2.564	2.531	2.500	2.469	2.439	2.409	2.381
23	2.899	2.857	2.817	2.778	2.739	2.703	2.666	2.632	2.597	2.564	2.532	2.500	2.469	2.439	2.410	2.381
24	2.898	2.857	2.817	2.777	2.740	2.702	2.667	2.631	2.598	2.564	2.531	2.500	2.469	2.439	2.409	2.381
25	2.899	2.857	2.817	2.778	2.739	2.703	2.666	2.632	2.597	2.564	2.532	2.500	2.469	2.439	2.410	2.381
26	2.898	2.857	2.817	2.777	2.740	2.702	2.667	2.631	2.598	2.564	2.531	2.500	2.469	2.439	2.409	2.381
27	2.899	2.857	2.817	2.778	2.739	2.703	2.666	2.632	2.597	2.564	2.532	2.500	2.469	2.439	2.410	2.381
28	2.898	2.858	2.817	2.777	2.740	2.702	2.667	2.631	2.598	2.564	2.531	2.500	2.469	2.439	2.409	2.381
29	2.899	2.857	2.817	2.778	2.739	2.703	2.666	2.632	2.597	2.564	2.532	2.500	2.469	2.439	2.410	2.381
30	2.898	2.858	2.817	2.777	2.740	2.702	2.667	2.631	2.598	2.564	2.531	2.500	2.469	2.439	2.409	2.381
31	2.899	2.857	2.817	2.778	2.739	2.703	2.666	2.632	2.597	2.564	2.532	2.500	2.469	2.439	2.410	2.381
32	2.898	2.858	2.816	2.777	2.740	2.702	2.667	2.631	2.598	2.564	2.531	2.500	2.470	2.439	2.409	2.381
33	2.899	2.857	2.817	2.778	2.739	2.703	2.666	2.632	2.597	2.565	2.532	2.500	2.469	2.439	2.410	2.381
34	2.898	2.858	2.816	2.777	2.740	2.702	2.667	2.631	2.598	2.564	2.531	2.500	2.470	2.439	2.409	2.381
35	2.899	2.857	2.817	2.778	2.739	2.703	2.666	2.632	2.597	2.565	2.532	2.500	2.469	2.439	2.410	2.381
36		1.429	2.816	2.777	2.740	2.702	2.667	2.631	2.598	2.564	2.531	2.500	2.470	2.439	2.409	2.381
37				1.389	2.739	2.703	2.666	2.632	2.597	2.565	2.532	2.500	2.469	2.439	2.410	2.381
38						1.351	2.667	2.631	2.598	2.564	2.531	2.500	2.469	2.439	2.410	2.381
39								1.316	2.597	2.565	2.532	2.500	2.469	2.439	2.410	2.381
40										1.282	2.531	2.500	2.470	2.439	2.409	2.381
41												1.250	2.469	2.439	2.410	2.380
42														1.220	2.409	2.381
43																1.190

Table 8

General and Alternative Depreciation Systems
Applicable Depreciation Method: Straight Line
Applicable Recovery Periods: 2.5-50 years
Applicable Convention: Half-year
(continued)

If the Recovery Year is:	42.5	43.0	43.5	44.0	44.5	45.0	45.5	46.0	46.5	47.0	47.5	48.0	48.5	49.0	49.5	50.0
					and the Recovery Period is: the Depreciation Rate is:											
1	1.176	1.163	1.149	1.136	1.124	1.111	1.099	1.087	1.075	1.064	1.053	1.042	1.031	1.020	1.010	1.000
2	2.353	2.326	2.299	2.273	2.247	2.222	2.198	2.174	2.151	2.128	2.105	2.083	2.062	2.041	2.020	2.000
3	2.353	2.326	2.299	2.273	2.247	2.222	2.198	2.174	2.151	2.128	2.105	2.083	2.062	2.041	2.020	2.000
4	2.353	2.326	2.299	2.273	2.247	2.222	2.198	2.174	2.151	2.128	2.105	2.083	2.062	2.041	2.020	2.000
5	2.353	2.326	2.299	2.273	2.247	2.222	2.198	2.174	2.151	2.128	2.105	2.083	2.062	2.041	2.020	2.000
6	2.353	2.326	2.299	2.273	2.247	2.222	2.198	2.174	2.151	2.128	2.105	2.083	2.062	2.041	2.020	2.000
7	2.353	2.326	2.299	2.273	2.247	2.222	2.198	2.174	2.150	2.128	2.105	2.083	2.062	2.041	2.020	2.000
8	2.353	2.326	2.299	2.273	2.247	2.222	2.198	2.174	2.151	2.128	2.105	2.083	2.062	2.041	2.020	2.000
9	2.353	2.325	2.299	2.273	2.247	2.222	2.198	2.174	2.150	2.128	2.105	2.083	2.062	2.041	2.020	2.000
10	2.353	2.326	2.299	2.273	2.247	2.222	2.198	2.174	2.151	2.128	2.105	2.083	2.062	2.041	2.020	2.000
11	2.353	2.325	2.299	2.273	2.247	2.222	2.198	2.174	2.150	2.128	2.105	2.083	2.062	2.041	2.020	2.000
12	2.353	2.326	2.299	2.273	2.247	2.222	2.198	2.174	2.151	2.128	2.105	2.083	2.062	2.041	2.020	2.000
13	2.353	2.325	2.299	2.273	2.247	2.222	2.198	2.174	2.150	2.128	2.105	2.083	2.062	2.041	2.020	2.000
14	2.353	2.326	2.299	2.273	2.247	2.222	2.198	2.174	2.151	2.128	2.105	2.083	2.062	2.041	2.020	2.000
15	2.353	2.325	2.299	2.273	2.247	2.222	2.198	2.174	2.150	2.128	2.105	2.083	2.062	2.041	2.020	2.000
16	2.353	2.326	2.299	2.273	2.247	2.222	2.198	2.174	2.151	2.128	2.105	2.083	2.062	2.041	2.020	2.000
17	2.353	2.325	2.299	2.273	2.247	2.222	2.198	2.174	2.150	2.127	2.105	2.083	2.062	2.041	2.020	2.000
18	2.353	2.326	2.299	2.273	2.247	2.222	2.198	2.174	2.151	2.128	2.105	2.083	2.062	2.041	2.020	2.000
19	2.353	2.325	2.299	2.273	2.247	2.222	2.198	2.174	2.150	2.127	2.105	2.084	2.062	2.041	2.020	2.000
20	2.353	2.326	2.299	2.273	2.247	2.222	2.198	2.174	2.151	2.128	2.105	2.083	2.062	2.041	2.020	2.000
21	2.353	2.325	2.299	2.273	2.247	2.222	2.198	2.174	2.150	2.127	2.105	2.084	2.062	2.041	2.020	2.000
22	2.353	2.326	2.299	2.273	2.247	2.222	2.198	2.174	2.151	2.128	2.105	2.083	2.062	2.041	2.020	2.000
23	2.353	2.325	2.299	2.272	2.247	2.222	2.198	2.174	2.150	2.127	2.105	2.083	2.062	2.041	2.020	2.000
24	2.353	2.326	2.299	2.273	2.247	2.222	2.198	2.174	2.151	2.128	2.105	2.083	2.062	2.041	2.020	2.000
25	2.353	2.325	2.299	2.272	2.247	2.222	2.198	2.174	2.150	2.127	2.105	2.084	2.062	2.041	2.020	2.000
26	2.353	2.326	2.299	2.273	2.247	2.222	2.198	2.174	2.151	2.128	2.106	2.083	2.062	2.041	2.020	2.000
27	2.353	2.325	2.299	2.272	2.247	2.223	2.198	2.174	2.150	2.127	2.105	2.084	2.062	2.041	2.020	2.000
28	2.353	2.326	2.299	2.273	2.247	2.222	2.198	2.174	2.151	2.128	2.106	2.083	2.062	2.041	2.020	2.000
29	2.353	2.325	2.299	2.272	2.247	2.223	2.198	2.174	2.150	2.127	2.105	2.084	2.062	2.041	2.020	2.000
30	2.353	2.326	2.299	2.273	2.248	2.222	2.197	2.174	2.151	2.128	2.106	2.083	2.062	2.041	2.020	2.000
31	2.353	2.325	2.299	2.272	2.247	2.223	2.198	2.174	2.150	2.127	2.105	2.084	2.062	2.041	2.021	2.000
32	2.353	2.326	2.299	2.273	2.248	2.222	2.197	2.174	2.151	2.128	2.106	2.083	2.062	2.041	2.020	2.000
33	2.353	2.325	2.298	2.272	2.247	2.223	2.198	2.174	2.150	2.127	2.105	2.084	2.062	2.041	2.021	2.000
34	2.353	2.326	2.299	2.273	2.248	2.222	2.197	2.174	2.151	2.128	2.106	2.083	2.062	2.040	2.020	2.000
35	2.353	2.325	2.298	2.272	2.247	2.223	2.198	2.174	2.150	2.127	2.105	2.084	2.062	2.040	2.021	2.000
36	2.353	2.326	2.299	2.273	2.248	2.222	2.197	2.174	2.151	2.128	2.106	2.083	2.062	2.040	2.020	2.000
37	2.353	2.325	2.298	2.272	2.247	2.223	2.198	2.174	2.150	2.127	2.105	2.084	2.061	2.041	2.021	2.000
38	2.353	2.326	2.299	2.273	2.248	2.222	2.197	2.174	2.151	2.128	2.106	2.083	2.062	2.040	2.020	2.000
39	2.353	2.325	2.298	2.272	2.247	2.223	2.198	2.174	2.150	2.127	2.105	2.084	2.061	2.041	2.021	2.000
40	2.353	2.326	2.299	2.273	2.248	2.222	2.197	2.173	2.151	2.128	2.106	2.083	2.062	2.040	2.020	2.000
41	2.352	2.325	2.298	2.272	2.247	2.223	2.198	2.174	2.150	2.127	2.105	2.084	2.061	2.041	2.021	2.000
42	2.353	2.326	2.299	2.273	2.248	2.222	2.197	2.173	2.151	2.128	2.106	2.083	2.062	2.040	2.020	2.000
43	2.352	2.325	2.298	2.272	2.247	2.223	2.198	2.174	2.150	2.127	2.105	2.084	2.061	2.041	2.021	2.000
44		1.163	2.299	2.273	2.248	2.222	2.197	2.173	2.151	2.128	2.106	2.083	2.062	2.040	2.020	2.000
45				1.136	2.247	2.223	2.198	2.174	2.150	2.127	2.105	2.084	2.061	2.041	2.021	2.000
46						1.111	2.197	2.173	2.151	2.128	2.106	2.083	2.062	2.040	2.020	2.000
47								1.087	2.150	2.127	2.105	2.084	2.061	2.041	2.021	2.000
48										1.064	2.106	2.083	2.062	2.040	2.020	2.000
49												1.042	2.061	2.041	2.021	2.000
50														1.020	2.020	2.000
51																1.000

Table 9

Alternative Depreciation System
Applicable Depreciation Method: Straight Line
Applicable Recovery Period: 40 years
Applicable Convention: Mid-month

If the Recovery Year is:	And the Month in the First Recovery Year the Property is Placed in Service is:											
	1	2	3	4	5	6	7	8	9	10	11	12
	the Depreciation Rate is:											
1	2.396	2.188	1.979	1.771	1.563	1.354	1.146	0.938	0.729	0.521	0.313	0.104
2 to 40	2.500	2.500	2.500	2.500	2.500	2.500	2.500	2.500	2.500	2.500	2.500	2.500
41	0.104	0.312	0.521	0.729	0.937	1.146	1.354	1.562	1.771	1.979	2.187	2.396

Table I
Leased MACRS Business Listed Property

Income Inclusion Amounts—Step (1) Computation Rates—for
Business Listed Property (Except Autos) Leased After '86
(Reg §1.280F-7T(b)(2)(i)(C))

Type of Property	First Taxable Year During Lease in Which Business Use Percentage is 50% or Less											
	1	2	3	4	5	6	7	8	9	10	11	12 & Later
Property with a Recovery Period of Less Than 7 Years under the Alternative Depreciation System (Such as Computers, Trucks and Airplanes)	0.0%	10.0%	22.0%	21.2%	12.7%	12.7%	12.7%	12.7%	12.7%	12.7%	12.7%	12.7%
Property with a 7- to 10-Year Recovery Period under the Alternative Depreciation System (Such as Recreation Property)	0.0%	9.3%	23.8%	31.3%	33.8%	32.7%	31.6%	30.5%	25.0%	15.0%	15.0%	15.0%
Property with Recovery Period of more Than 10 Years under the Alternative Depreciation System (Such as Certain Property with No Class Life)	0.0%	10.1%	26.3%	35.4%	39.6%	40.2%	40.8%	41.4%	37.5%	29.2%	20.8%	12.5%

Table II
Leased MACRS Business Listed Property

Income Inclusion Amounts—Step (2) Computation Rates—for
Business Listed Property (Except Autos) Leased After '86
(Reg §1.280F-7T(b)(2)(i)(C))

Type of Property	First Taxable Year During Lease in Which Business Use Percentage is 50% or Less											
	1	2	3	4	5	6	7	8	9	10	11	12 & Later
Property with a Recovery Period of Less Than 7 Years under Alternative Depreciation System (Such as Computers, Trucks and Airplanes)	2.1%	−7.2%	−19.8%	−20.1%	−12.4%	−12.4%	−12.4%	−12.4%	−12.4%	−12.4%	−12.4%	−12.4%
Property with a 7- to 10-Year Recovery Period under the Alternative Depreciation System (Such as Recreation Property)	3.9%	−3.8%	−17.7%	−25.1%	−27.8%	−27.2%	−27.1%	−27.6%	−23.7%	−14.7%	−14.7%	−14.7%
Property with a Recovery Period of More Than 10 Years under the Alternative Depreciation System (Such as Certain Property with No Class Life)	6.6%	−1.6%	−16.9%	−25.6%	−29.9%	−31.1%	−32.8%	−35.1%	−33.3%	−26.7%	−19.7%	−12.2%

¶ 1118   Income Inclusion Amounts for Autos, Trucks and Vans ▐███████████▌

REV. PROC. 2010-18 TABLE 3
DOLLAR AMOUNTS FOR PASSENGER AUTOMOBILES
(THAT ARE NOT TRUCKS OR VANS) WITH A LEASE TERM
BEGINNING IN CALENDAR YEAR 2010

Fair Market Value of Passenger Automobile		Tax Year During Lease				
Over	Not Over	1st	2nd	3rd	4th	5th & later
$ 16,700	$ 17,000	3	7	10	11	14
17,000	17,500	4	8	13	15	16
17,500	18,000	5	10	16	19	21
18,000	18,500	6	13	18	23	26
18,500	19,000	7	15	22	26	31
19,000	19,500	8	17	25	30	35
19,500	20,000	9	19	29	34	39
20,000	20,500	10	21	32	38	44
20,500	21,000	11	23	35	42	48
21,000	21,500	12	26	38	45	53
21,500	22,000	13	28	41	50	57
22,000	23,000	14	31	46	56	63
23,000	24,000	16	36	52	63	73
24,000	25,000	18	40	59	71	81
25,000	26,000	20	44	66	78	90
26,000	27,000	22	49	71	86	100
27,000	28,000	24	53	78	94	108
28,000	29,000	26	57	85	101	118
29,000	30,000	28	61	92	109	126
30,000	31,000	30	66	97	117	135
31,000	32,000	32	70	104	125	144
32,000	33,000	34	74	111	132	153
33,000	34,000	36	79	117	140	161
34,000	35,000	38	83	123	148	171
35,000	36,000	40	87	130	156	179
36,000	37,000	42	92	136	163	188
37,000	38,000	44	96	143	170	198
38,000	39,000	46	100	149	179	206
39,000	40,000	48	105	155	186	215
40,000	41,000	50	109	162	194	224
41,000	42,000	52	113	169	201	233
42,000	43,000	54	118	174	210	241
43,000	44,000	56	122	181	217	251
44,000	45,000	58	126	188	225	259
45,000	46,000	60	131	194	232	269
46,000	47,000	61	135	201	240	277
47,000	48,000	63	140	207	248	286
48,000	49,000	65	144	213	256	295
49,000	50,000	67	148	220	263	304
50,000	51,000	69	153	226	271	313
51,000	52,000	71	157	232	279	322
52,000	53,000	73	161	239	287	331
53,000	54,000	75	166	245	294	340
54,000	55,000	77	170	252	302	348
55,000	56,000	79	174	258	310	358
56,000	57,000	81	178	265	318	366
57,000	58,000	83	183	271	325	375

Fair Market Value of Passenger Automobile		Tax Year During Lease				
Over	Not Over	1st	2nd	3rd	4th	5th & later
58,000	59,000	85	187	278	333	384
59,000	60,000	87	191	284	341	393
60,000	62,000	90	198	294	352	406
62,000	64,000	94	207	306	368	424
64,000	66,000	98	215	320	382	443
66,000	68,000	102	224	332	398	460
68,000	70,000	106	232	346	413	478
70,000	72,000	110	241	358	429	496
72,000	74,000	114	250	371	444	513
74,000	76,000	118	258	384	460	531
76,000	78,000	122	267	396	476	549
78,000	80,000	126	276	409	491	566
80,000	85,000	132	291	432	518	598
85,000	90,000	142	313	464	556	643
90,000	95,000	152	334	497	594	687
95,000	100,000	162	356	528	634	731
100,000	110,000	177	388	577	691	798
110,000	120,000	196	432	641	768	887
120,000	130,000	216	475	705	846	976
130,000	140,000	236	518	770	922	1,065
140,000	150,000	256	561	834	1,000	1,154
150,000	160,000	275	605	898	1,077	1,243
160,000	170,000	295	648	963	1,153	1,333
170,000	180,000	315	691	1,027	1,231	1,421
180,000	190,000	334	735	1,091	1,308	1,510
190,000	200,000	354	778	1,155	1,386	1,599
200,000	210,000	374	821	1,220	1,462	1,688
210,000	220,000	393	865	1,284	1,539	1,777
220,000	230,000	413	908	1,348	1,617	1,866
230,000	240,000	433	951	1,413	1,693	1,956
240,000	and up	453	995	1,476	1,771	2,044

REV. PROC. 2010-18 TABLE 4
DOLLAR AMOUNTS FOR TRUCKS AND VANS WITH A LEASE TERM
BEGINNING IN CALENDAR YEAR 2010

Fair Market Value of Truck or Van		Tax Year During Lease				
Over	Not Over	1st	2nd	3rd	4th	5th & later
17,000	17,500	3	6	9	10	11
17,500	18,000	4	8	12	14	16
18,000	18,500	5	10	15	18	21
18,500	19,000	6	12	19	22	24
19,000	19,500	7	15	21	26	29
19,500	20,000	8	17	25	29	34
20,000	20,500	9	19	28	33	38
20,500	21,000	10	21	31	37	43
21,000	21,500	11	23	35	41	47
21,500	22,000	12	25	38	45	51
22,000	23,000	13	29	42	51	58
23,000	24,000	15	33	49	58	67
24,000	25,000	17	37	56	66	76

Fair Market Value of Truck or Van		Tax Year During Lease				
Over	Not Over	1st	2nd	3rd	4th	5th & later
25,000	26,000	19	42	62	73	85
26,000	27,000	21	46	68	82	93
27,000	28,000	23	50	75	89	103
28,000	29,000	25	55	81	97	111
29,000	30,000	27	59	88	104	121
30,000	31,000	29	63	94	113	129
31,000	32,000	31	68	100	120	138
32,000	33,000	33	72	107	127	148
33,000	34,000	35	76	114	135	156
34,000	35,000	37	81	119	143	165
35,000	36,000	39	85	126	151	174
36,000	37,000	41	89	133	158	183
37,000	38,000	43	94	139	166	191
38,000	39,000	45	98	145	174	201
39,000	40,000	47	102	152	182	209
40,000	41,000	49	106	159	189	218
41,000	42,000	51	111	164	198	227
42,000	43,000	53	115	171	205	236
43,000	44,000	55	119	178	213	245
44,000	45,000	57	124	184	220	254
45,000	46,000	59	128	190	228	263
46,000	47,000	60	133	197	235	272
47,000	48,000	62	137	203	244	280
48,000	49,000	64	142	209	251	290
49,000	50,000	66	146	216	259	298
50,000	51,000	68	150	223	266	308
51,000	52,000	70	154	229	275	316
52,000	53,000	72	159	235	282	325
53,000	54,000	74	163	242	290	334
54,000	55,000	76	167	249	297	343
55,000	56,000	78	172	254	305	352
56,000	57,000	80	176	261	313	361
57,000	58,000	82	180	268	320	370
58,000	59,000	84	185	274	328	378
59,000	60,000	86	189	280	336	388
60,000	62,000	89	195	291	347	401
62,000	64,000	93	204	303	363	418
64,000	66,000	97	213	315	379	436
66,000	68,000	101	221	329	394	454
68,000	70,000	105	230	341	410	472
70,000	72,000	109	239	354	424	490
72,000	74,000	113	247	367	440	508
74,000	76,000	117	256	380	455	526
76,000	78,000	121	264	393	471	543
78,000	80,000	125	273	406	486	561
80,000	85,000	131	289	428	513	592
85,000	90,000	141	310	461	552	636
90,000	95,000	151	332	492	591	681
95,000	100,000	161	353	525	629	726
100,000	110,000	176	386	573	686	793
110,000	120,000	195	430	637	763	882
120,000	130,000	215	473	701	841	971
130,000	140,000	235	516	766	918	1,059

Fair Market Value of Truck or Van		Tax Year During Lease				
Over	Not Over	1st	2nd	3rd	4th	5th & later
140,000	150,000	255	559	830	995	1,149
150,000	160,000	274	603	894	1,072	1,238
160,000	170,000	294	646	958	1,150	1,326
170,000	180,000	314	689	1,023	1,226	1,416
180,000	190,000	333	733	1,087	1,303	1,505
190,000	200,000	353	776	1,151	1,381	1,594
200,000	210,000	373	819	1,216	1,457	1,683
210,000	220,000	392	863	1,280	1,534	1,772
220,000	230,000	412	906	1,344	1,612	1,861
230,000	240,000	432	949	1,409	1,689	1,949
240,000	250,000	452	992	1,473	1,766	2,039

Chapter 2   Income—Taxable and Exempt

¶ 1200   Gross Income. ▬▬▬▬▬▬▬▬▬▬▬▬▬▬▬▬▬▬▬▬▬

Gross income consists of all income, from all sources, such as compensation for services, business income, interest, rents, dividends and gains from the sale of property. Only items specifically exempt may be excluded.

Gross income is the starting point in determining tax liability and is broadly defined. (Code Sec. 61)[1]

¶ 1201   Assignment of income.

The person who earns and is entitled to receive income is taxed on it. He can't avoid tax on it by assigning it to another.[2] But if a taxpayer assigns or transfers income-producing *property* before the income is earned, the assignee will be taxed on the income.[3]

¶ 1202   Income from co-owned property—joint tenancies, etc.

In a tenancy in common (co-owners without survivorship), each co-owner is taxable on that part of the income attributable to his share.[4] Co-owners who are joint tenants (with survivorship) split income from their property according to their ownership interests.[5]

Similarly, any gain (or loss) from sale of jointly-owned property is divided among the co-owners unless the joint ownership was created to save taxes on the sale, in which case the original owner is taxed on the full amount of the gain.[6]

Co-owners who are husband and wife and file joint returns report their combined income, gains and losses from the jointly-owned property. If they file separately, the income, etc., from the property is split equally if they so share it under state law.[7]

¶ 1203   Community property and income.

Federal tax law recognizes the principle of community income in community property states (AZ, CA, ID, LA, NV, NM, TX, WA and WI) or countries, which treats half of community income and expenses as belonging to each spouse.[8] Community income is all the income from community property (including business property) and salaries, etc., for the services of either or both spouses. Income from separate property during marriage is community income only in ID, LA, TX and WI.[9] If state law extends full community property treatment to registered domestic partners, each partner must report one-half of the community property on his/her federal income tax return, whether received in the form of compensation for personal services or income from property.[10]

If one spouse acts as if he's solely entitled to the community income and fails to notify his spouse of the nature and amount of the income before the return due date (with extensions), IRS may deny him any community property benefit. (Code Sec. 66(b))[11]

Community property income for a calendar year is taxed to the spouse who earned it if in that year the couple lived apart for the entire year, filed separate returns *and* one or both spouses had earned income no part of which was transferred between them. (Code Sec. 66(a), Code Sec. 66(d)(1))[12]

A divorced individual who resided in a community property state was taxable on amounts

---

1. ¶s J-1000 *et seq.*; ¶614; TD ¶101,000
2. ¶J-8151 *et seq.*; ¶s 614.185, 614.192; TD ¶201,001
3. ¶J-8172 *et seq.*; ¶s 614.192, 1024; TD ¶201,001
4. ¶J-8103; ¶614.202; TD ¶204,003
5. ¶s J-8101, J-8102; ¶614.202; TD ¶204,002
6. ¶J-8107; ¶614.202; TD ¶204,007
7. ¶J-8100 *et seq.*; ¶614.202; TD ¶204,005
8. ¶A-5001; ¶79,006.51; TD ¶573,501
9. ¶A-5008; TD ¶573,506
10. ¶A-5017
11. ¶A-5026; ¶664; TD ¶573,512
12. ¶A-5022; ¶664; TD ¶573,514

References beginning with a single letter are to paragraphs in RIA's Federal Tax Coordinator 2d and RIA's Analysis of Federal Taxes: Income. Those beginning with numbers are to paragraphs in RIA's United States Tax Reporter. Those beginning with TD are to paragraphs in RIA's Tax Desk.

he paid from his wages to his ex-spouse as ordered by a state court.[13]

Relief for separate return liability. A spouse who did not file a joint return for the tax year for which he seeks relief and omits from gross income his share of community income (¶1203) is relieved from tax liability on that omitted income if he establishes lack of knowledge or reason to know of the omitted item and, under all the facts and circumstances, it's inequitable to include the omitted item in his gross income ("traditional relief"). (Code Sec. 66(c); Reg § 1.66-4(a)(1))[14]

IRS may grant equitable relief to a separately-filing spouse from liability attributable to a community income item for which relief isn't available under the above provision ("equitable relief"). (Code Sec. 66(c); Reg § 1.66-4(b))

Traditional relief applies only to deficiencies arising out of items of omitted income but equitable relief includes relief for underpayments of tax or any deficiency, including those arising from disallowed deductions or credits. (Reg § 1.66-4(c))

A spouse requesting relief under the above provisions does so by filing Form 8857. (Reg § 1.66-4(j)(1))[15] For joint filers, see ¶4710.

¶ 1204   Claim of right.

Income received without restriction—income the taxpayer has dominion and control over—must be reported in the year received, even if there's a possibility it may have to be repaid in a later year.[16] For deduction in the repayment year, see ¶2860 *et seq.*

¶ 1205   The "tax benefit rule"—recoveries attributable to an earlier year's deduction or credit.

The recovery of an amount deducted or credited in an earlier tax year is included in a taxpayer's income in the current (recovery) year, except to the extent the deduction or credit *didn't* reduce federal income tax (or alternative minimum tax, but not the accumulated earnings or personal holding company "penalty" taxes (Code Sec. 111(d)(1))[17] imposed in the earlier year. (Code Sec. 111(a))[18]

Similarly, if there's a downward price adjustment (e.g., price reduction) during the tax year that affects an amount paid or incurred on which a credit (other than the investment credit or the foreign tax credit) was allowed in an earlier year, taxpayer's tax for the adjustment year is increased by the amount of credit attributable to the adjustment, to the extent it reduced his tax in the earlier year. (Code Sec. 111(b))[19]

This "tax benefit rule" applies to recoveries of both itemized deductions (i.e., taxes, medical expenses and other items deductible on Form 1040, Schedule A) and non-itemized deductions (e.g., bad debts). The taxable amount is limited to the itemized deduction amount that reduced the tax in the earlier year. A taxpayer who recovers an amount he deducted in an earlier year as an itemized deduction is taxed on the *lesser* of the amount recovered, or the amount deducted on Schedule A. A taxpayer who wasn't required to itemize deductions in the earlier year is taxed on the *lesser* of his itemized deduction recoveries or the amount by which his itemized deductions exceeded the standard deduction.[20]

Illustration: B's itemized deductions on his Year 1 return were $6,250. The standard deduction B could have claimed for that year was $5,150. In Year 2, B recovers $2,400 of his Year 1 itemized deductions. B must include $1,100 of the recoveries in his Year 2 income, since that's the smaller of his itemized deduction recoveries ($2,400) or the excess of his itemized

13. ¶A-5013; TD ¶573,513
14. ¶A-5029; ¶664; TD ¶573,609
15. ¶A-5034; ¶664; TD ¶573,613
16. ¶J-8001 *et seq.*; ¶4514.069 *et seq.*; TD ¶203,001

17. ¶J-5526, ¶J-5527; ¶1114; TD ¶181,004
18. ¶J-5500 *et seq.*; ¶1114 *et seq.*; TD ¶181,001
19. ¶J-5511; ¶1114.02; TD ¶181,001
20. ¶J-5512; ¶1114.02; TD ¶181,020

deductions over the standard deduction ($6,250 − $5,150 = $1,100).[21]

If taxpayer had negative taxable income for the year the items were deducted, the otherwise includable amount of the recovery is reduced by the negative amount.[22]

The tax benefit rule applies to state income taxes deducted in an earlier year where there's a refund or credit of taxes paid or the cancellation of taxes accrued.[23]

If an earlier year's itemized deductions were reduced under the 3%/80% rule (see ¶3114), a later recovery of previously deducted amounts is generally fully includible in gross income. Specifically, the taxpayer is taxed on the difference between the earlier year's reduced itemized deductions, and his reduced itemized deductions (or standard deduction, if greater) had he paid the proper amount in the earlier year and not received the recovery.[24]

The increase of a carryover that hasn't expired as of the start of the tax year of the recovery (deduction) or adjustment (credit item) is treated as a reduction of tax imposed. (Code Sec. 111(c))[25]

The tax rates for the recovery (or adjustment) year are used to compute the tax on the portion that isn't excludible.[26] A recovery of amounts, e.g., bad debts, deducted in more than one tax year must be allocated pro rata between those years. (Reg § 1.111-1(a)(3))[27]

To claim any part of a recovery is tax-free, attach a schedule to the return showing the right to the exclusion. (Reg § 1.111-1(b)(1))[28]

¶ 1206   Miscellaneous taxable and exempt income.

Here is the taxable or exempt status of items not covered elsewhere in this Handbook:

. . . Alaska Permanent Fund Dividend. Taxable.[29]

. . . Alcohol fuel credit. Includable in gross income. (Code Sec. 87)[30]

. . . Barter, or the swapping of goods and services, results in gross income to each party to the swap to the extent of the fair market value of the goods or services received. The dollar value of barter "credits" received by members of barter clubs for goods or services rendered to other members is taxable.[31] For information returns of barter exchanges, see ¶4745.

. . . Car pool expenses reimbursed by fellow members. Nontaxable unless received as part of a trade or business of transporting workers.[32] For exclusion as a qualified transportation fringe benefit, see ¶1249.

. . . Damages recovered for faulty home construction are tax free to the extent of basis. They reduce basis and are taxable to the extent they exceed basis.[33]

. . . Elderly in-home care payments by a state agency to caregiver to help elderly live at home instead of nursing home were tax-free (under so-called "general welfare exclusion"). [34]

. . . Employer-provided death benefits of specified victims of terrorism and astronauts who die in the line of duty. Excludable from gross income. (Code Sec. 101(i)(1))[35]

. . . Energy conservation subsidies provided (directly or indirectly) by a public utility to customers for buying or installing "energy conservation measures" for dwelling units are not taxable. (Code Sec. 136)[36]

. . . Escrow funds or property, and the income from them. Not taxable to the stakeholder but may be taxable to the ultimate recipient when paid to him.[37]

21. ¶J-5512; ¶1114.02; TD ¶181,020
22. ¶J-5512; TD ¶181,020
23. ¶J-5701 *et seq.*; ¶1114; TD ¶183,001
24. ¶J-5513; ¶1114.02; TD ¶181,022
25. ¶J-5524; ¶1114; TD ¶181,008
26. ¶J-5530; ¶1114.02; TD ¶181,030
27. ¶J-5603; ¶1114.02; TD ¶181,017
28. ¶J-5528; TD ¶181,003
29. ¶J-1493

30. ¶L-17505; ¶874
31. ¶s J-1010, J-1012; TD ¶112,003
32. ¶J-1398; TD ¶196,003
33. ¶J-5820; TD ¶182,011
34. ¶J-1480A; TD ¶198,201
35. ¶C-9674; ¶1014.10; TD ¶579,624
36. ¶J-1401 *et seq.*; ¶1364; TD ¶198,510
37. ¶J-1371; ¶4514.087

. . . Executor's or administrator's fees or commissions that are waived. Not taxed to executor, etc., who files a formal waiver within six months after appointment, or whose conduct amounts to an implied waiver.[38]

. . . Financial counseling fees paid by employer to family members of terminally ill employees (taxable to employees) and survivors of deceased employees (taxable to survivors).[39]

. . . Foster care payments by state or licensed/certified placement agency to individual foster care provider. Not taxable, if payments are for caring for qualified foster individual (child or adult) in care provider's home (where provider resides), or are "difficulty-of-care payments." (Code Sec. 131)[40]

. . . Frequent flyer miles earned or received in connection with business travel are not included in taxable income.[41]

. . . Grants to homeowners under a city program to preserve old neighborhoods. Taxable.[42]

. . . 25% of qualifying gain from conservation sales of qualifying mineral or geothermal interests. Excludable from gross income. (TRHCA § 403(c)(1)(Div. C, Title IV))[43]

. . . Illegal income. Taxable whether from an illegal business, an actual crime, or immoral or unethical practices, e.g., embezzlement. (Repayment is an itemized deduction.)[44]

. . . "Insider's" short-term stock sale profits which SEC requires be turned over to corporation. Taxable to corporation on receipt.[45]

. . . Insurance reimbursement for living expenses incurred due to the loss of use of (or government's denial of access to) principal residence (owned or rented) resulting from a fire, storm or other casualty. Nontaxable, to extent it covers additional living expenses (but balance of reimbursement is taxable). (Code Sec. 123; Reg § 1.123-1)[46] Use and occupancy insurance reimbursements for loss of profits if business is suspended are taxable.[47]

. . . Leave-donor who deposits leave in an employer-sponsored leave bank under a major disaster leave-sharing plan. Nontaxable, if plan treats payments made by the employer to leave recipients as wages.[48]

. . . Leaves under employer-sponsored leave-sharing plan which permits employees with a medical emergency to receive leave that other employees surrender or deposit into a leave bank. Taxable to recipient-employee as compensation.[49]

. . . Medicare (Part A and Part B). Not taxable (except for Part B amounts attributable to medical deductions taken in an earlier year). Medicare Part D coverage gap ("donut hole") rebate also is not taxable.[50]

. . . Mortgage assistance payments by a federal agency to a mortgagee on mortgagor's behalf. Not taxable to the mortgagor unless *not* made for the general welfare (e.g., interest reduction payments to mortgagee). Pay-for-Performance Success Payments that reduce principal balance of taxpayer's home mortgage under Home Affordable Modification Program aren't taxable.[1]

. . . Property tax rebates are taxable to the extent they exceed the property tax paid. Rebates received after the year of payment are subject to the tax benefit rule, see ¶1205. Rebates received in the year of payment reduce the amount of tax paid for that year. Where the tax was paid over two years, the rebate is apportioned over the two years.[2] However, state property tax credits are treated as a reduction in a taxpayer's property tax liability for the year the credit is claimed or for the year the credit is carried forward to.

. . . Rate reduction or nonrefundable credit provided by utility to customer for participation in energy conservation program. Not taxable.[3]

---

38. ¶J-1419; ¶4514.042; TD ¶198,511
39. ¶H-1701
40. ¶J-1500 *et seq.*; ¶s 1314.01, 1314.02; TD ¶196,501
41. ¶J-1393; TD ¶134,600
42. ¶J-1480
43. ¶I-8851; TD ¶229,901
44. ¶J-1600 *et seq.*; ¶614.176; TD ¶197,501
45. ¶J-5829; TD ¶182,018

46. ¶J-1311 *et seq.*; ¶1234; TD ¶195,501
47. ¶J-5830; ¶614.167; TD ¶182,019
48. ¶H-1013.1
49. ¶H-1013; TD ¶198,521
50. ¶J-1307; TD ¶194,506
1. ¶J-1489
2. ¶J-1394.1
3. ¶J-1431; TD ¶198,522

. . . Rebates of part of purchase price to retail customers. Payment wasn't income but instead an adjustment to the purchase price of acquiring the property. Not taxable.[4]

. . . Relocation payments and similar government subsidies for moving expenses and actual direct losses of property because of displacement from personal residences, as a result of urban renewal projects. Not taxable, to extent payments are made by government to compensate for (and are actually so used for) these expenses.[5] Taxable, to extent payments are made by nongovernmental landlords as part of co-op or condo conversion.[6]

. . . Restitution (generally, money or property received as a result of an individual's persecution by the Nazis) received by Holocaust survivors or their heirs is excludable.[7]

. . . Security deposits received. If purpose is to guarantee performance of an obligation, not taxable where repayment is required if the obligation is performed. Taxed to the recipient when he becomes entitled to retain them because of a default.[8] If purpose is to protect taxpayer's interest in property and not to secure payment, it's not taxable.[9]

. . . Smart Grid Investment Grant made to a corporation, nontaxable, nonshareholder contribution to capital if corporation properly reduces the basis of its property.[10]

. . . Subsidies received from Social Security by sponsors of qualified retiree prescription drug plans under the Medicare Prescription Drug Act of 2003 for certain covered retiree drug costs are not taxable.[11]

. . . Whistleblower's settlement under a Federal False Claims Act action against his former employer, taxable.[12]

¶ 1207 Exclusion for qualified disaster relief or mitigation payments.

A qualified disaster relief payment isn't included in gross income. It also isn't earnings for self-employment tax purposes or wages for employment tax purposes. (Code Sec. 139) The exclusion doesn't apply to amounts received for the sale or disposition of property, but the involuntary conversion rules may apply to such amounts, see ¶2430.[13]

A qualified disaster relief payment is any amount (to the extent not compensated by insurance or otherwise) paid to or for the benefit of an individual:

(1) to reimburse or pay reasonable and necessary personal, family, living, or funeral expenses incurred as a result of a qualified disaster (defined below),

(2) to reimburse or pay reasonable and necessary expenses incurred to repair or rehabilitate a personal residence (including a rented residence) or repair or replace its contents to the extent that the need for the work results from a qualified disaster,

(3) by a person who provides or sells transportation as a common carrier because of the death or personal physical injuries arising from a qualified disaster, or

(4) if the amount is paid by a federal, state, or local government, or an agency or instrumentality of those governments, in connection with a qualified disaster in order to promote the general welfare (but not if payments are made to businesses or for income replacement or unemployment compensation).

A qualified disaster is a disaster which results from a terroristic or military action, a Federally declared disaster, a disaster resulting from an accident involving a common carrier, or from any other event, that is determined by IRS to be of a catastrophic nature, or for payments by a federal, state, or local government, or an agency or instrumentality of those governments, a disaster that is determined by the appropriate governmental authority (as determined by IRS) to warrant assistance from the governmental authority.[14]

4. ¶J-1391; TD ¶196,005
5. ¶J-1492; ¶614.006
6. ¶J-1492; TD ¶198,521
7. ¶J-1476; ¶614.0065
8. ¶J-1371; ¶4514.166; TD ¶121,008
9. ¶G-2490; ¶4514.166; TD ¶121,008
10. ¶F-1914.1
11. ¶J-1480.2; ¶139A4
12. ¶J-1485.3; TD ¶198,210
13. ¶J-1296; ¶1394; TD ¶193,600
14. ¶J-1290 *et seq.*; TD ¶193,601

Qualified disaster mitigation payments are excluded from gross income. (Code Sec. 139(g)) These include payments under the Flood Mitigation Assistance Program, Pre-Disaster Mitigation Program, and Hazard Mitigation Grant Program. The exclusion does not apply to amounts received for the sale or disposition of property, but the involuntary conversion rules may apply to such amounts, see ¶2430.[15]

¶ 1208 Pre-2011 exclusion for volunteer emergency medical responders.

For tax years beginning before 2011, any qualified State or local tax benefit and any qualified payment is excluded from the gross income of members of qualified volunteer emergency response organizations. (Code Sec. 139B(a)) These amount also aren't subject to social security or unemployment tax, or withholding. (Code Sec. 3121(a)(23), Code Sec. 3306(b)(20), Code Sec. 3401(a)(23)) A qualified State or local tax benefit is any reduction or rebate of State or local income, real property, or personal property taxes on account of services performed by individuals as members of a qualified volunteer emergency response organization. (Code Sec. 139B(c)(1)) The amount of State or local taxes taken into account by a taxpayer in determining his deduction for taxes under Code Sec. 164 (see ¶1755) is reduced by the amount of any qualified State or local tax benefit. (Code Sec. 139B(b)(1))[16]

A qualified payment is a payment provided by a State or political subdivision on account of the performance of services as a member of a qualified volunteer emergency response organization. The excludable amount of these payments is limited to $30 multiplied by the number of months during the year that the taxpayer performs such services. (Code Sec. 139B(c)(2)) Expenses paid or incurred by the taxpayer in connection with the performance of services are taken into account for a charitable contribution deduction by him only to the extent they exceed the amount of excluded qualified payments. (Code Sec. 139B(b)(2))

A qualified volunteer emergency response organization is one: (1) organized and operated to provide firefighting or emergency medical services for persons in the State or its political subdivision; and (2) required (by written agreement) by the State or political subdivision to furnish firefighting or emergency medical services in the State or political subdivision. (Code Sec. 139B(c)(3))

caution: Check http://ria.thomsonreuters.com/federaltaxhandbook to see if this provision has been extended.

¶ 1209 Compensation Income. ▬▬▬▬▬▬▬▬▬▬▬▬▬▬▬▬▬▬▬▬▬

All forms of compensation received for personal services are included in gross income.

¶ 1210 Compensation includible in gross income.

Gross income includes compensation for services including: wages, salaries, fees, tips (¶1212), salesperson's commissions (including on sales to self or family), percentage of profits paid as compensation, commissions on insurance premiums, bonuses (including Christmas bonuses, see ¶1214), termination or severance pay, golden parachute payments (excess golden parachute payments subject the recipient to a 20% excise tax (Code Sec. 4999(a)),[17] rewards, jury duty fees (Code Sec. 61(a)(1); Reg § 1.61-2(a)(1)),[18] and fringe benefits not excluded by statute (see ¶1230 *et seq.*). (Code Sec. 61(a)(1)) Vacation pay also is taxable.[19] The employee is taxed even if the employer can't deduct part or all of the compensation because it's "unreasonable." (¶1517). (Reg § 1.162-8)[20]

Pension or retirement allowances to employees (reported to recipients on Form 1099-R) generally are taxable to the recipient, see ¶4338 *et seq.* (Reg § 1.61-11(a))[21] For rules for

15. ¶J-1296; ¶1394; TD ¶193,600
16. ¶H-3050; ¶139B4; TD ¶138,600
17. ¶H-3003; ¶49,994; TD ¶132,504
18. ¶H-1001 *et seq.*; ¶614.007; TD ¶111,002

19. ¶s H-1001, H-1012; TD ¶130,505
20. ¶H-1021; ¶614.014; TD ¶130,513
21. ¶H-3245; ¶s 614.007, 4014; TD ¶141,000

certain military pensions, see ¶1286.

Amounts withheld from an employee's pay by his employer for income and social security taxes, savings bonds, union dues, etc., represent compensation constructively received by the employee and must be included in his income for the year in which withheld.[22]

¶ 1211 Reporting compensation and self-employment income.

The amount of wages, salaries, tips, etc., that's includible in income (¶1210), which should be shown on a Form W-2 issued by the employer, is reported on Form 1040.[23]

Income (or loss) subject to self-employment tax (¶3140) from a business operated, or a profession practiced, as a sole proprietor is reported on Form 1040, Schedule C or C-EZ. If an individual operates more than one business as a sole proprietor, a separate Schedule C or C-EZ must be prepared for each business. An individual can't report his income on Schedule C or C-EZ if he earns it as an "employee." [24] For farm income, see ¶4501.

¶ 1212 Tips and similar payments.

Tips and similar payments for special services are income. (Reg § 1.61-2(a)(1)) But a waiter may deduct the portion of tips that he turns over to assistants.[25] A tipped employee must maintain sufficient evidence to establish the amount of tip income he receives in a tax year. (Reg § 31.6053-4(a))[26]

¶ 1213 Compensation distinguished from gift.

Although gifts are generally excluded from the recipient's gross income (¶1373), transfer by or for an employer to or for the benefit of an employee can't be excluded as a gift. (Code Sec. 102(c)(1)) Extraordinary transfers to the natural objects of an employer's bounty (e.g., an employee who is the employer's son) aren't transfers to or for the benefit of the employee if he can show the transfer wasn't made in recognition of his employment.[27] For holiday gifts of nominal value, see ¶1214. For de minimis fringe benefits, see ¶1248.

¶ 1214 Holiday gifts.

If, as a means of promoting goodwill, an employer makes a general distribution to employees of hams, turkeys or other merchandise of nominal value at Christmas or a comparable holiday, the value of the gifts isn't included in the employees' income. But if an employer distributes cash, gift certificates or similar items of readily convertible cash value, the value of the gifts is additional wages or salary, *regardless* of the value.[28]

¶ 1215 Below-market interest rate loans from employer.

An employee or independent contractor who receives a below-market (¶1308) compensation-related loan (except certain de minimis loans), recognizes compensation income equal to:

. . . on a compensation-related demand loan, the forgone interest (interest at the applicable federal rate (¶1116) over actual interest payable), and

. . . on any other compensation-related loan, the excess of the amount borrowed over the present value of all payments required to be made under the terms of the loan. (Code Sec. 7872(a)(1), Code Sec. 7872(b)(1))[29]

Certain employee-relocation loans are exempt from these rules. (Reg § 1.7872-5T(b)(6))[30]

---

22. ¶H-2152; TD ¶141,000
23. ¶H-1001.1; TD ¶102,002
24. ¶H-1001.1; TD ¶102,002
25. ¶s H-1009, H-4342; TD ¶131,006
26. ¶H-4343; ¶60,534; TD ¶131,003

27. ¶H-1027.1 *et seq.*; ¶s 614.016, 1024; TD ¶132,010
28. ¶H-1033; ¶1324.06; TD ¶132,002
29. ¶s H-2002, H-2004; ¶78,724.14; TD ¶136,503
30. ¶H-2014; ¶78,724.20; TD ¶136,512

¶ 1216   Vacation trips for salespersons; other noncash compensation.

If services rendered by the taxpayer are paid for in property or services rather than money, the fair market value (FMV) of the property or services must be included in income. For example, if a vacation trip is awarded to salespersons as a prize, the FMV of the trip is income. Where a price has been specified for the services being rendered, that price is considered the FMV of the property or services received if there's no evidence showing a different value. (Code Sec. 83; Reg § 1.61-2(d))[31]

¶ 1217   Notes receivable as compensation.

Notes and other evidences of indebtedness received in payment for services or in settlement of a claim for compensation are taxable as compensation in the amount of their fair market value when received. When a taxpayer receives as compensation a non-interest-bearing note regarded as good for its face value at maturity, he treats as income its fair discounted value computed at the prevailing rate. As note payments are received, he includes in income that portion of each payment representing the proportionate part of the discount originally taken on the entire note. (Reg § 1.61-2(d)(4))[32]

¶ 1218   Bargain purchase from employer.

If property, including stock, is transferred by an employer to an employee for less than its fair market value, the difference is compensation. (Code Sec. 83(a); Reg § 1.83-1(a))[33] For stock options, see ¶1221 *et seq.*

If an employee pays with a recourse note for stock acquired from his employer under a nonqualified stock option, and the employer later reduces the amount due on the note, the debt reduction is treated as compensation income.[34]

¶ 1219   Restricted stock or other property—Section 83 rules.

A person receiving a beneficial interest in stock or other property for his services has compensation income equal to the value of that property at the time of receipt. But if his interest in the property is subject to substantial risk of forfeiture (is "restricted") and can't be transferred free of that risk, then income is deferred until the interest in the property either: (1) is no longer subject to that risk, *or* (2) becomes transferable free of the risk, whichever occurs earlier. (Code Sec. 83)[35] For election not to defer income, see ¶1220.

But the employee (or other owner of the property) has income if he sells or disposes of the property before (1) or (2), above. (Code Sec. 83(a))[36]

The amount included in income (in the year in which (1) or (2) occurs) is the excess of: the fair market value of the property in that year (figured without regard to restrictions other than those that by their terms will never lapse), over the amount, if any, paid for the property. (Code Sec. 83(a))[37]

A substantial risk of forfeiture exists if a person's rights to full enjoyment of the property are conditioned, directly or indirectly, upon the future performance (or refraining from performance) of substantial services by any individual. (Code Sec. 83(c)(1); Reg § 1.83-3(c)(1)) Examples: a requirement that the property be returned to the employer if total earnings don't increase (Reg § 1.83-3(c)(2)),[38] and SEC restrictions, such as the "short swing" rule (insider must pay over profits if stock is sold within six months of receipt). (Code Sec. 83(c)(3))[39] The

31. ¶H-2500 *et seq.*; ¶s 614.007, 614.027; TD ¶136,001
32. ¶H-2513; ¶614.034; TD ¶136,003
33. ¶H-2509; ¶614.030; TD ¶136,005
34. ¶H-2535
35. ¶s H-2500, H-2517 *et seq.*; ¶834 *et seq.*; TD ¶136,006

36. ¶H-2547 *et seq.*; ¶834.01; TD ¶136,006
37. ¶H-2532 *et seq.*; ¶834.01; TD ¶136,007
38. ¶H-2521; ¶834.02; TD ¶135,014
39. ¶s H-2530, H-2531; ¶834.02; TD ¶135,018

six-month period under the short swing rule is measured from the date a nonstatutory option to acquire the stock is granted, and not from the date of exercise.[40]

¶ 1220   Election not to defer income from restricted stock or other property.

An employee or other person who receives restricted stock or other property (¶1219) may elect to recognize the income immediately instead of deferring it. (Code Sec. 83(b)(1))[41]

The amount of compensation income included in the year the property is received is the excess of: the fair market value of the property at receipt (without regard to restrictions other than those that by their terms will never lapse), over the amount, if any, paid for the property. (Code Sec. 83(b)(1))[42]

✓recommendation: Elect if the income taxed at grant would be negligible. This defers tax on any post-grant appreciation until sale, makes it eligible for capital gain rates, and may eliminate additional income tax completely if the property is held until death.

If the stock or other property is forfeited after the election is made, the employee can't get a deduction or refund of tax previously paid on income reported. (Code Sec. 83(b)(1))[43] The employee will have capital loss at the time of forfeiture. (Reg § 1.83-2(a))[44]

Elect within 30 days after the property is transferred to the employee. (Code Sec. 83(b)(2)) To elect, file a statement (specified in the regs) with the IRS office where the person who performs the services files his return. Attach a copy of the statement to the return for the year the property was transferred. (Reg § 1.83-2(c))[45]

IRS will consent to a revocation if the election was filed under a mistake of fact in the underlying transaction and the revocation is requested within 60 days of discovering the mistake of fact. Request to revoke the election within the 30 day period for making the election will generally be granted.[46]

¶ 1221   Nonstatutory stock options.

An option—other than an option under an employee stock purchase plan (see ¶1222) or an incentive stock option (ISO, see ¶1223)—which is granted in connection with the performance of services, to buy stock at a bargain, results in compensation income to the employee (or independent contractor) grantee. (Code Sec. 83) If the option has a readily ascertainable fair market value (FMV) at grant, it's subject to the restricted property rules of Code Sec. 83 (¶1219 *et seq.*) when the option is granted. (Code Sec. 83; Reg § 1.83-7(a))[47]

An option "ordinarily" has a readily ascertainable FMV only if it (or a substantially identical option) is actively traded on an established market. If not so traded, it has value only if certain conditions specified in the regs exist. (Reg § 1.83-7(b))[48]

If the option doesn't have a readily ascertainable FMV when granted, the employee doesn't realize compensation until the optioned property is transferred at exercise. The amount of compensation is the FMV of the property at transfer less any amount paid for the property. (Reg § 1.83-7(a))[49] (For the employer's compensation deduction, see ¶1525.)

The above treatment for nonstatutory options without a readily ascertainable FMV doesn't apply where the option is transferred before exercise to a "related person." (Reg § 1.83-7(a))[50]

Under an exception, the exercise of an option is treated as the grant of another option, instead of a transfer of shares, where the amount paid for the exercise is a debt secured by the shares on which there is no personal liability. (Reg § 1.83-3(a)(2)) However, this exception

---

40. ¶H-2530
41. ¶H-2540; ¶834.03; TD ¶135,016
42. ¶H-2541; ¶834.03; TD ¶135,016
43. ¶M-3503; ¶834.03; TD ¶135,016
44. ¶I-1020; ¶834.03; TD ¶135,016
45. ¶H-2542 *et seq.*; ¶834.03; TD ¶135,016

46. ¶H-2545
47. ¶s H-2853, H-2857; ¶s 834.07, 4214.03; TD ¶135,202
48. ¶H-2872; ¶834.07; TD ¶135,203
49. ¶H-2861; ¶834.07; TD ¶135,206
50. ¶H-2864.1; ¶834.07; TD ¶135,207

doesn't apply simply because options are exercised through a margin loan, and income will be realized on the exercise of options without a readily ascertainable FMV.[1]

¶ 1222   Employee stock purchase plan (ESPP) options.

These are options issued to employees under an employer plan to buy stock in the employer. The employee pays no tax on the option or the stock until he disposes of the stock. If the option price at least equals the stock's fair market value (FMV) at grant, gain is capital gain. But gain is ordinary compensation income (to the extent of the spread between option price and FMV of stock when option is exercised) if the stock is sold within two years after the option was granted or within one year after its exercise. (Code Sec. 423(a), Code Sec. 423(c); Reg § 1.423-1, Reg § 1.423-2[2]

If the option price is less than 100% (but at least 85%) of the stock's FMV at grant, and the above holding period is met, the amount treated as ordinary income (rather than capital gain) is the *lesser* of: (1) the FMV of the stock when the option was granted, minus the option price, or (2) the excess of the FMV at the time of disposition or optionee's death, over the amount paid for the share under the option. (Code Sec. 423(c); Reg § 1.423-2(k))[3]

An executive branch federal employee (or spouse or dependent child) who acquired stock through the exercise of an employee stock purchase plan option (or ISO, see ¶1223) and sells the stock in order to comply with Code Sec. 1043 federal conflict-of-interest requirements is deemed to satisfy the Code Sec. 423(a)(1) (or Code Sec. 422(a)(1)) holding period requirement. (Code Sec. 421(d))

The plan must be nondiscriminatory, i.e., available to all employees (with certain exceptions). (Code Sec. 423(b)(4))[4]

¶ 1223   Incentive stock options (ISOs).

An ISO is granted to an employee by an employer corporation (or its parent or sub) to buy stock or ownership interests in one of those corporations (a term that takes in S corporations, foreign corporations, and limited liability companies treated as corporations for federal tax purposes). (Reg § 1.421-1(d)(3), Reg § 1.421-1(i)(1)) There are no regular income tax consequences when an ISO is granted or exercised; the employee has capital gain when the stock is sold at a gain. (Code Sec. 421(a))[5] To qualify, an ISO must meet various requirements. (Code Sec. 422(b))[6]

Stock acquired through the exercise of an ISO generally can't be disposed of within two years after the option is granted or one year after the stock is transferred to the employee. (Code Sec. 422(a)(1)) Also, for the entire time from the date an ISO is granted until three months (one year in case of total and permanent disability) before its exercise, the option holder must be an employee of the option grantor (or its parent or sub or certain successor corporations). (Code Sec. 422(a)(2), Code Sec. 422(c)(6))[7] For executive branch federal employee holding period rules, see ¶1222.

If there is a disqualifying disposition of a share of stock, Code Sec. 421 does not apply to the transfer of the share. Instead, the exercise of the option is governed by Code Sec. 83 and its regs. Thus, in the tax year in which the disqualifying disposition occurs, the individual recognizes compensation income (and gets a basis increase) equal to the FMV of the stock on the date the stock is transferred less the exercise price (determined without reduction for any brokerage fees or other disposition costs). (Reg § 1.421-2(b)) If the disqualifying disposition would trigger an allowable loss (e.g., not a sale to a related taxpayer), then the amount includible in the employee's income (and deductible by the employer, see ¶1525) as a result of

1. ¶H-2508.1; TD ¶135,012
2. ¶H-2952 *et seq.*; ¶4234.01; TD ¶136,101
3. ¶H-2953; ¶4234.01; TD ¶136,101
4. ¶H-2972; ¶4234.02; TD ¶136,103

5. ¶H-2750; ¶4224.01; TD ¶136,001
6. ¶H-2767; ¶4224.02; TD ¶136,004
7. ¶H-2795 *et seq.*; ¶4224.01; TD ¶136,006

that disqualifying disposition can't be more than the amount realized on the sale, minus the employee's adjusted basis in the stock. (Code Sec. 422(c)(2); Reg § 1.422-1(b)(2)(i))[8]

⚫*caution:* For alternative minimum tax treatment, see ¶3209.

¶ 1224 Sale or cancellation of employment contract.

Proceeds from an employee's sale of rights under an employment contract to be performed are ordinary income. The same is true of amounts received from an employer in cancellation of an employment contract.[9]

¶ 1225 Members of Armed Forces.

The pay of Armed Forces members is taxable (Reg § 1.61-2(a)(1)), with exceptions:[10]

Gross income doesn't include any "qualified military benefit," which is any allowance or in-kind benefit (other than personal use of an automobile) received by a member or former member of the uniformed services of the U.S., or his dependent, and which was excludable from gross income on Sept. 9, '86 under any provision of law, reg or administrative practice (other than the Code) in effect on that date. (Code Sec. 134(b)) It includes any bonus payment made by a state or political subdivision to any member or former member of the U.S. uniformed services, or his dependent, because of his service in a combat zone. (Code Sec. 134(b)(6)) Excludable allowances include (within certain limitations): veteran's benefits (¶1226), medical benefits, disability benefits, dependent care assistance program benefits, professional education, moving and storage, group-term life insurance, survivor and retirement protection plan premiums, subsistence, uniform, housing, overseas cost-of-living, evacuation, family separation allowances, death gratuities, interment allowance, various travel allowances and dependent benefits.[11] Specifically, dislocation allowances, temporary lodging allowances and expenses and move-in housing allowances provided in connection with permanent changes of station are excludible from income. (Reg § 1.61-2(b)(2))[12] For treatment of retirement pay, see ¶1286. A "qualified military base realignment and closure" fringe benefit is excluded and isn't subject to FICA. This benefit is a payment (subject to a maximum allowance) received under the Homeowner's Assistance Program (HAP) (as in effect on 2/17/2009, for payments after that date). (Code Sec. 132(a)(8))[13]

The recipient of a tax-free military housing allowance isn't thereby prevented from deducting mortgage interest or real estate taxes on a personal residence. (Code Sec. 265(a)(6)(A))[14]

The Code also excludes combat-zone compensation (limited, for commissioned officers, to the maximum enlisted amount). (Code Sec. 112; Reg § 1.112-1) Areas designated as combat zones include: Pakistan; Tajikistan; Jordan; Uzbekistan; Kyrgyzstan; the Afghanistan area; Serbia/Montenegro; Albania; the Adriatic Sea; the Ionian Sea (north of the 39th parallel); the Persian Gulf area; the Red Sea; the Gulf of Oman; parts of the Arabian Sea; the Gulf of Aden; the total land areas of Iraq, Kuwait, Saudi Arabia, Oman, Bahrain, Qatar, and the United Arab Emirates.[15]

For various deadline extensions for a member of the Armed Forces serving in a designated "combat zone," see ¶4719. For tax relief for military and civilian employees of the U.S. dying in combat or terrorist attacks, see ¶4715.

¶ 1226 VA and state benefits to veterans.

Benefits under any law, regulation, or practice in effect on Sept. 9, '86 and administered by the Department of Veterans' Affairs are excludable from the recipient's gross income, (Code

8. ¶H-2799; ¶4224.01; TD ¶136,008
9. ¶H-1048 *et seq.*; TD ¶182,009
10. ¶H-3101; ¶614.040; TD ¶138,001
11. ¶H-3102; ¶1344; TD ¶138,002

12. ¶H-3103; TD ¶138,003
13. ¶H-3104; ¶1324.11; TD ¶138,003.5
14. ¶K-9009; ¶2654
15. ¶H-3106 *et seq.*; ¶1124.01; TD ¶138,005

Sec. 140(a)(3)) including interest earned on dividends left on deposit with the VA. It also includes amounts received under a VA administered work therapy program.[16] State bonuses to veterans for service rendered to the U.S. are also exempt.[17]

¶ 1227   Government employees' compensation.

Federal, state and municipal employees, including federal judges, are taxable on their salary, wages and other compensation the same as other employees.[18] Payments under the Civil Service Retirement System are taxed like annuities, see ¶1357 *et seq.*[19] For tax relief for military and civilian employees of the U.S. dying in combat or terrorist attacks, see ¶4715.

¶ 1228   Members of clergy.

Members of the clergy are taxable on the salaries and fees they receive, and on any offerings they receive for marriages, funerals, masses, etc., *but not* on offerings made to the religious institution. (Reg § 1.61-2(a))[20]

A current or retired member of the clergy who is a "minister of the gospel" [21] can exclude from gross income:

. . . the rental value of a home (parsonage), including utilities, furnished to him as part of his compensation; (Code Sec. 107(1); Reg § 1.107-1(a)) or

. . . the rental allowance (parsonage allowance) paid to him as compensation, to the extent it's used in the year received to rent or provide a home and to the extent it does not exceed the fair rental value of the home, including furnishings and appurtenances such as a garage, plus the cost of utilities. (Code Sec. 107(2)) The employer church or organization must designate the payment as a rental allowance before the payment is made. (Reg § 1.107-1(b))[22]

The rental allowance exclusion doesn't prevent a minister from deducting mortgage interest or real estate taxes on a personal residence. (Code Sec. 265(a)(6)(B))[23]

¶ 1229   Compensation of minors.

The income of a minor from compensation earned by him or received in respect of his services is income to him, even if received by the parent. (Code Sec. 73(a))[24]

🅡ⁱᵃ observation: If the child is subject to the kiddie tax rules, the rate of tax on his unearned income may depend on the parent's tax rate, see ¶3135.

¶ 1230   Fringe Benefits. ▬▬▬▬▬▬▬▬▬▬▬▬▬▬▬▬▬▬▬▬▬▬▬▬▬▬▬▬▬▬▬▬

Fringe benefits received by an employee are taxable unless specifically excluded.

¶ 1231   Taxation of fringe benefits.

A fringe benefit provided to any person in connection with the performance of services is treated as compensation for those services. (Reg § 1.61-21(a)(3))[25] Unless it's specifically excluded (¶1244), the benefit is includible in the gross income of the person performing the services, even if it's furnished to someone else. (Code Sec. 61(a)(1); Reg § 1.61-21(a)(4))[26]

---

16. ¶H-3128; ¶614.041; TD ¶138,029
17. ¶H-3129; TD ¶138,030
18. ¶H-3130; ¶614.036; TD ¶138,031
19. ¶J-5052; ¶724.26; TD ¶141,006
20. ¶H-3151; ¶614.007; TD ¶138,501
21. ¶H-3163; ¶1074.02; TD ¶138,511

22. ¶H-3153 *et seq.*; ¶1074; TD ¶138,502 *et seq.*
23. ¶H-3160; ¶s 1074.03, 2654; TD ¶138,505
24. ¶H-3180; ¶734.01; TD ¶836,009
25. ¶H-1051; ¶614.027; TD ¶134,002
26. ¶H-1051, ¶H-1053; ¶614.027; TD ¶134,001; TD ¶134,002

¶ 1232 Valuation of taxable fringe benefits—general rule.

An employee who is taxed on a fringe benefit (¶1231) must include in gross income the fair market value (FMV) of the benefit minus: (1) any payment for the benefit, and (2) any amount specifically excluded by a Code provision. (Reg § 1.61-21(b)(1))[27] The FMV of a fringe benefit generally is the amount that an individual would have to pay for the particular benefit in an arm's-length transaction. (Reg § 1.61-21(b)(2))[28]

Unless a special valuation rule (¶1234) applies, an employer-provided vehicle is valued at the comparable lease cost (¶1235) (Reg § 1.61-21(b)(4)),[29] and flights on an employer-provided aircraft at comparable charter or lease cost. (Reg § 1.61-21(b)(6), Reg § 1.61-21(b)(7))[30]

Chauffeur services are valued separately from vehicle availability, at comparable arm's-length transaction costs or by reference to the chauffeur's compensation (including any non-taxable lodging, see ¶1269). (Reg § 1.61-21(b)(5))[31]

¶ 1233 Transportation furnished because of unsafe conditions.

Transportation or reimbursement for such (e.g., cab fare) furnished by an employer under a written policy solely because of unsafe conditions for employee commuting is valued at $1.50 per one-way commute (i.e., from home to work, or work to home) for each qualifying employee. (Reg § 1.61-21(k)(3))[32]

¶ 1234 Special valuation rules for autos, other vehicles and airflights.

Special valuation rules may be used under certain circumstances for certain commonly provided fringe benefits (e.g., automobiles, noncommercial flights, commuting). (Reg § 1.61-21(b), Reg § 1.61-21(c)(1), Reg § 1.61-21(c)(3))[33] Where the special rules aren't used, either by choice or because they aren't permitted, or where they're improperly applied, the value of the fringe benefit must be determined under the general valuation principles at ¶1232. (Reg § 1.61-21(c)(5))[34]

An employee can't use a special valuation rule to value a fringe benefit unless the employer uses the same rule to value it. (Reg § 1.61-21(c)(2))[35]

¶ 1235 Annual lease value method for automobiles—use of IRS table.

To compute an auto's annual lease value, first determine fair market value (FMV) as of the first date it is made available to *any* employee for personal use. Under safe harbor rules, where the auto is bought at arm's length by the employer, the FMV is the cost, including sales tax, title fees and other purchase expenses. Where leased, it's the suggested retail price less 8%, the retail value as reported in a nationally recognized publication that regularly reports such values (Reg § 1.61 21(d)(5)), or the manufacturer's invoice price plus 4%.[36] Then, find the dollar range in column (1) of the table below that includes the auto's FMV. The corresponding amount in column (2) is its annual lease value. (Reg § 1.61-21(d)(2)(iii))

27. ¶H-1055; ¶614.027; TD ¶134,003
28. ¶H-1056; ¶614.027; TD ¶134,003
29. ¶H-2232; ¶614.027; TD ¶134,502
30. ¶H-2302 *et seq.*; ¶614.027; TD ¶134,570
31. ¶H-2289 *et seq.*; ¶614.027
32. ¶H-2201 *et seq.*; TD ¶134,606

33. ¶s H-1056 *et seq.*, H-2200 *et seq.*, H-2300 *et seq.*; ¶614.027; TD ¶134,500
34. ¶H-1057; ¶614.027; TD ¶134,502
35. ¶H-1060; ¶614.027; TD ¶134,555
36. ¶H-2240; ¶614.027; TD ¶134,510

Automobile fair market value (1)	Annual lease value (2)	Automobile fair market value (1)	Annual lease value (2)
$0 to 999	$600	22,000 to 22,999	6,100
1,000 to 1,999	850	23,000 to 23,999	6,350
2,000 to 2,999	1,100	24,000 to 24,999	6,600
3,000 to 3,999	1,350	25,000 to 25,999	6,850
4,000 to 4,999	1,600	26,000 to 27,999	7,250
5,000 to 5,999	1,850	28,000 to 29,999	7,750
6,000 to 6,999	2,100	30,000 to 31,999	8,250
7,000 to 7,999	2,350	32,000 to 33,999	8,750
8,000 to 8,999	2,600	34,000 to 35,999	9,250
9,000 to 9,999	2,850	36,000 to 37,999	9,750
10,000 to 10,999	3,100	38,000 to 39,999	10,250
11,000 to 11,999	3,350	40,000 to 41,999	10,750
12,000 to 12,999	3,600	42,000 to 43,999	11,250
13,000 to 13,999	3,850	44,000 to 45,999	11,750
14,000 to 14,999	4,100	46,000 to 47,999	12,250
15,000 to 15,999	4,350	48,000 to 49,999	12,750
16,000 to 16,999	4,600	50,000 to 51,999	13,250
17,000 to 17,999	4,850	52,000 to 53,999	13,750
18,000 to 18,999	5,100	54,000 to 55,999	14,250
19,000 to 19,999	5,350	56,000 to 57,999	14,750
20,000 to 20,999	5,600	58,000 to 59,999	15,250
21,000 to 21,999	5,850		

For autos with a FMV in excess of $59,999, the annual lease value equals: (.25 × auto FMV) + $500.[37]

illustration: On Jan. 1, of Year 1, X Co. provides a car worth $20,500 free to its employee E. None of the fringe benefit exclusions applies. The annual lease value (see chart above) is $5,600. This is the value of E's benefit for Year 1. E must include $5,600 in income.

This method takes into account the value of insuring and maintaining the auto, but not the value of fuel, which if provided in kind can be valued based on all facts and circumstances, or alternatively at 5½¢ per mile for all miles driven (in the U.S., Canada or Mexico) by the employee. (Reg § 1.61-21(d)(3))[38]

The annual lease values computed above are determined on the basis of an assumed four-year lease term (beginning on the first date this method is used and ending on Dec. 31 of the following fourth full calendar year). The annual lease value for each next four-year period is determined on the basis of the FMV on the Jan. 1 after the preceding period, using the lease valuation table. (Reg § 1.61-21(d)(2)(iv))[39]

Subject to certain restrictions, an employer with a fleet of 20 or more autos may determine the annual lease value of each auto in the fleet as if its FMV were equal to the "fleet-average value." (Reg § 1.61-21(d)(5)) This method can't be used for autos with a FMV greater than $20,300 for 2010 ($21,000 for trucks or vans).[40]

¶ 1236 Prorated annual lease value.

Where an employer-provided auto is continuously available to the employee for periods of 30 or more days, but less than an entire calendar year, the value of the availability of the auto is the prorated annual lease value, computed by multiplying the annual lease value

37. ¶s H-2238, H-2239; TD ¶134,508   39. ¶H-2246; ¶614.027; TD ¶134,516
38. ¶H-2253; ¶614.027; TD ¶134,521   40. ¶H-2260; ¶614.027; TD ¶134,527

(¶1236) by a fraction: the numerator is the number of days of availability, and the denominator is 365. (Reg § 1.61-21(d)(4))[41]

¶ 1237 Daily lease value.

Where an employer-provided auto is continuously available to the employee for at least one but less than 30 days, the value of the use of the auto is its daily lease value, calculated by multiplying the auto's annual lease value (¶1236) by a fraction: the numerator is four times the number of days of the auto's availability, and the denominator is 365. A 30-day period may be used even if availability is less than 30 days if this produces a lower valuation. (Reg § 1.61-21(d)(4))[42]

¶ 1238 Cents-per-mile valuation method.

Under this method, the value of an employer-provided auto equals the total number of miles the employee drove it for personal purposes in the tax year times the optional standard mileage rate, see ¶1561.[43] This method takes into account the value of insuring and maintaining the vehicle, and the value of fuel provided by the employer. If fuel isn't provided, the cents-per-mile rate may be reduced by no more than 5.5¢ per mile. (Reg § 1.61-21(e)(3))[44] The cents-per-mile method can't be used if the auto's fair market value, as of the date it's first made available to any employee for personal use, exceeds an annually-adjusted amount, $15,300 for 2010 ($16,000 for a truck or van).[45]

¶ 1239 Commuting value method—$1.50 per one-way commute.

Under this method, the value of an employee's use of a vehicle, including an automobile, for commuting purposes only is computed as $1.50 per one-way commute (e.g., from home to work, or work to home). If there's more than one employee who commutes in a single vehicle, the commuting benefit is still $1.50 per one way commute for each employee. (Reg § 1.61-21(f)(3))[46] Various requirements must be satisfied. For example, the employee must be required to commute in the auto for bona-fide noncompensatory business reasons. The method can't be used for "control employees" (certain owner-employees, higher-paid employees, and directors) (Reg § 1.61-21(f)(1)), or to value the commuting use of any chauffeur-driven vehicle, except for the commuting use by the chauffeur. (Reg § 1.61-21(f)(2))[47]

¶ 1240 Employer-provided airflights.

Airflights provided by an employer for an employee's personal purposes are fringe benefits includible in the employee's gross income. (Reg § 1.61-21(a)(1))[48]

Special valuation methods are available to value noncommercial flights on employer-provided aircraft (¶1241 *et seq.*), and "space available" flights on commercial aircraft (¶1243). Use of a special method is optional. But if an employer uses either special rule, he must generally use it to value all flights taken by employees in a calendar year. (Reg § 1.61-21(g)(14)(i), Reg § 1.61-21(h)(5)(i))[49]

If an employee takes a trip on an employer-provided aircraft primarily for his employer's business which includes both personal flights and business flights, the value of the personal flights is a taxable fringe benefit. The value of the benefit equals the excess of the value of all the flights comprising the trip, over the value of the flights the employee would have taken had he travelled only for business. If the employee combines personal and business flights on a trip that's primarily personal, the amount includible is the value of the personal flights that

41. ¶H-2243; ¶614.027; TD ¶134,513
42. ¶H-2245; ¶614.027; TD ¶134,515
43. ¶H-2268; ¶614.027; TD ¶134,536
44. ¶H-2277 *et seq.*; ¶614.027; TD ¶134,543
45. ¶H-2272; ¶614.027; TD ¶134,540

46. ¶H-2282; ¶614.027; TD ¶134,549
47. ¶H-2283; ¶614.027; TD ¶134,550
48. ¶H-2301; ¶614.027; TD ¶134,570
49. ¶H-2301 *et seq.*; ¶614.027; TD ¶134,570

would have been taken had there been only personal flights. The value of all these flights may be computed under the special valuation rules (¶1241 *et seq.*). (Reg § 1.61-21(g)(4))[50]

¶ 1241 SIFL formula for noncommercial flights.

Value is determined by multiplying the "base aircraft valuation formula" —also known as the Standard Industry Fair Level (SIFL) formula (cents-per-mile rates that are revised semi-annually)—in effect at the time of the flight by the "aircraft multiple" (based on the takeoff weight of the plane) and adding the applicable "terminal charge." (Reg § 1.61-21(g)(5))[1]

¶ 1242 "Seating capacity" (zero inclusion) rule for noncommercial flights.

The "seating capacity" rule is available for noncommercial flights on employer-provided aircraft where at least half of the aircraft's passenger seating capacity is occupied by employees whose flights are primarily for the employer's business (and whose flights are excludable as a working condition fringe, see ¶1247). In this situation, the includible value of the flight taken by the employee for personal purposes is zero. (Reg § 1.61-21(g)(12))[2]

¶ 1243 "Space-available" rule for commercial flights.

If an employer provides an employee (as specially defined at Reg § 1.132-1(b)(1)) with a flight on a commercial aircraft for the employee's personal purposes, the flight is a taxable fringe benefit whose value must be included in the employee's gross income (¶1240). If the flight is a "space-available flight" on a commercial airline, its value for certain current or former airline employees may be computed under a special rule: 25% of the actual carrier's highest unrestricted coach fare for the flight taken. (Reg § 1.61-21(h)(1))[3]

¶ 1244 Excludable fringe benefits.

A fringe benefit isn't included in gross income if it's excluded under a specific Code Section (see below) (Code Sec. 61(a)), or qualifies as one of the following: (Code Sec. 132(a))[4]

. . . no additional cost service (¶1245);

. . . qualified employee discount (¶1246);

. . . working condition fringe (¶1247);

. . . de minimis fringe (¶1248);

. . . qualified transportation fringe (¶1249);

. . . qualified moving expense reimbursement (¶1250);

. . . employer-provided retirement advice (¶1252).

For qualified military base realignment and closure fringe benefit, see ¶1225.

A fringe benefit that's expressly provided for in any other Code Section can't be excluded from gross income under the Code Sec. 132 rules, except as a de minimis fringe or as a qualified moving expense reimbursement. (Code Sec. 132(l))[5] Fringe benefits excluded under a specific Code Section include: holiday and other gifts of nominal value (¶1214); stock options (¶1221); clergy member's home ("parsonage allowance," ¶1228); employee achievement awards (¶1253); on-premises athletic facilities (¶1254); adoption assistance (¶1256); educational assistance (¶2215); medical care coverage, including accident and health insurance (¶1257 *et seq.*); group-term life insurance (¶1264); meals and lodging (¶1269); qualified campus lodging (¶1270); cafeteria (flexible benefit) plans (¶1271); dependent care assistance programs (¶1272); scholarships (¶2216); and cost of living allowances to certain U.S. government

50. ¶s H-2314, H-2315; ¶614.027
1. ¶s H-2304, H-2307 *et seq.*; ¶614.027; TD ¶134,570
2. ¶H-2319; ¶614.027; TD ¶134,570

3. ¶H-2337; ¶614.027; TD ¶134,570
4. ¶H-1051; ¶1324; TD ¶134,001
5. ¶H-1052; ¶1324; TD ¶134,001

employees (¶4619).[6]

¶ 1245   No-additional-cost services.

No-additional-cost services are excluded from an employee's gross income (see ¶1244). (Code Sec. 132(a)(1))[7] These are services provided by an employer to an employee for personal use by the employee, his spouse or dependent children, if:

(1) the services are ordinarily offered for sale to nonemployee customers in the ordinary course of the line of business in which the employee works,

(2) the employer incurs no substantial additional cost (including foregone revenue) in providing the services to the employee—computed without regard to any amounts paid by the employee for the services (Code Sec. 132(b)),[8] and

(3) special nondiscrimination rules are satisfied. (Code Sec. 132(j)(1))[9]

No-additional-cost services include services that would remain unused if the employee customers didn't use them, e.g., hotel accommodations, transportation by air, train, bus, subway or cruise line, and telephone services. (Reg § 1.132-2(a)(2))[10]

¶ 1246   Qualified employee discounts.

A qualified employee discount is excluded from an employee's gross income (see ¶1244). (Code Sec. 132(a)(2))[11] This is an "employee discount" allowed with respect to "qualified property or services" provided by an employer to an employee, his spouse or dependent children, to the extent the discount doesn't exceed the limits described below. (Code Sec. 132(c)(1))[12]

An "employee discount" is the excess of: (a) the price at which property or services are offered by an employer for sale to nonemployee customers, over (b) the price at which the employer offers the same property or services to employees for use by those employees. (Code Sec. 132(c)(3))[13]

"Qualified property or services" means any property (other than real property, or personal property of a kind held for investment) or services that are offered for sale to nonemployee customers in the ordinary course of the employer's line of business in which the employee works. (Code Sec. 132(c)(4), Code Sec. 132(k))[14]

Limitations. The excludable amount of a qualified employee discount with respect to property is limited to the gross profit percentage of the price at which that property is offered by the employer to customers. (Code Sec. 132(c)(1)(A)) Gross profit percentage equals the aggregate sales price of the property sold by the employer to all customers, whether employees or nonemployees (Reg § 1.132-3(c)(1)(i)), over the aggregate cost of the property (Code Sec. 132(c)(2)(A)(i)), divided by the aggregate sales price. (Code Sec. 132(c)(2)(A)(ii))[15]

The excludable amount for services is limited to 20% of the price at which the employer offers the service to nonemployee customers. (Code Sec. 132(c)(1)(B), Code Sec. 132(k))[16]

¶ 1247   Working condition fringes.

Working condition fringes are excluded from the employee's gross income (see ¶1244). (Code Sec. 132(a)(3))[17] A "working condition fringe" is any property or services provided to an employee by the employer to the extent the cost of the property or services would have been deductible by the employee under either Code Sec. 162 (as trade or business expenses) or

---

6. ¶H-1052; ¶614.027; TD ¶134,018
7. ¶H-1871; ¶1324.03; TD ¶134,004
8. ¶H-1871; ¶1324.03; TD ¶134,004
9. ¶H-1930 *et seq.*; ¶1324.01; TD ¶134,007
10. ¶H-1872; ¶1324.03
11. ¶H-1901; ¶1324.04; TD ¶134,008

12. ¶H-1902; ¶1324.04; TD ¶134,009
13. ¶H-1904; ¶1324.04
14. ¶H-1903; ¶1324.04; TD ¶134,008
15. ¶H-1909; ¶1324.04; TD ¶134,009
16. ¶H-1914; ¶1324.04; TD ¶134,009
17. ¶H-1701; ¶1324.05; TD ¶134,010

Code Sec. 167 (as depreciation expenses) if the employee had paid for the property or services himself. (Code Sec. 132(d))[18] Examples are: employer-paid business travel and the use of employer-provided vehicles for business purposes.[19]

Certain benefits qualify as working condition fringes only if special requirements are satisfied. These include: the use of consumer goods manufactured for sale to nonemployee customers and provided to employees for product testing and evaluation outside the employer's work place (Reg § 1.132-5(n)(1));[20] the personal use of vehicles otherwise used in connection with the business of farming (Reg § 1.132-5(g));[21] job placement assistance;[22] employer-paid club dues (Reg § 1.132-5(s));[23] employer-paid expenses of a companion on a business trip (Reg § 1.132-5(t));[24] "qualified automobile demonstration use" by automobile salespersons (Code Sec. 132(j)(3); Reg § 1.132-5(o));[25] the use of employer-owned aircraft for business travel (Reg § 1.132-5(k));[26] certain forms of transportation and other employer-provided security measures provided because of bona fide business-oriented security concerns (Reg § 1.132-5(m));[27] and the use of "qualified nonpersonal use vehicles." (Reg § 1.132-5(h))[28]

If an employer provides the use of a vehicle and includes the entire amount in the employee's income (without excluding any working condition fringe benefit amount), the employee can deduct the value multiplied by the percentage of business use as a miscellaneous itemized deduction (subject to the 2% floor, see ¶3110). This deduction can't be computed under a cents-per-mile method. (Reg § 1.162-25(b))[29]

¶ 1248 De minimis fringe benefits.

De minimis fringe benefits are excluded from the recipient's gross income (see ¶1244). (Code Sec. 132(a)(4)) A de minimis fringe is any property or service whose value is so small that accounting for it is unreasonable or administratively impracticable, taking into account the frequency with which similar fringe benefits are provided by the employer to its employees. (Code Sec. 132(e)(1))

Examples of de minimis fringes include: occasional meals, supper money, or local transportation provided because of overtime work (Reg § 1.132-6(d)(2)); meals at employer-operated eating facilities (see below); transportation (e.g., taxi fare) where other available means of transportation are unsafe, in excess of value over $1.50 per each one-way commute (¶1233) (Reg § 1.132-6(d)(2)); occasional cocktail parties or picnics; traditional holiday gifts of property (not cash) with a low FMV; flowers, fruit, etc., provided under special circumstances, such as sickness or outstanding performance; (Reg § 1.132-6(e)(1)); low-value clothing bearing employer's name, which must be worn by the employee; and electronically filing the employee's income tax return (but not paying someone to prepare his return).[30]

No qualified transportation fringe benefit (¶1249) (including amounts in excess of the dollar limit) may be excluded as a de minimis fringe benefit. (Code Sec. 132(f)(7))[31] However, partners, more-than-2% S corporation shareholders and independent contractors (but not employees) can exclude transit passes, tokens and fare cards if not in excess of $21 per month.[32]

Meals at employer-operated eating facilities are de minimis fringes if the facility's annual revenues normally equal or exceed its direct operating costs and certain nondiscrimination rules are met. Employees who are entitled (under the rules at ¶1269) to exclude the value of a meal provided at the facility are treated as having paid an amount for the meal equal to the direct operating costs of the facility attributable to the meal. (Code Sec. 132(e)(2);

18. ¶H-1701; ¶1324.05; TD ¶134,010
19. ¶H-1701; ¶1324.05; TD ¶134,012
20. ¶H-1712; ¶1324.05; TD ¶134,012
21. ¶H-2370; ¶1324.05; TD ¶134,012
22. ¶H-1711; ¶1324.05; TD ¶134,012
23. ¶H-2153.1; TD ¶136,529
24. ¶H-2153.2; TD ¶136,530
25. ¶H-2364; ¶1324.05; TD ¶134,568

26. ¶H-2351; ¶1324.05; TD ¶134,012
27. ¶H-2373 *et seq.*; ¶1324.05; TD ¶134,012
28. ¶H-2354; ¶1324.05; TD ¶134,012
29. ¶s H-2363, L-1912; ¶s 1624.283, 2744.17; TD ¶293,019
30. ¶H-1802 *et seq.*; ¶1324.06; TD ¶134,013
31. ¶H-2202; ¶1324.08; TD ¶134,596
32. ¶H-1806; TD ¶134,014

Reg § 1.132-7(a)(2), Reg § 1.132-7(c))[33] Direct operating costs are the costs of the food and beverages served and the labor for related services performed primarily on the facility's premises. (Reg § 1.132-7(b)(1))[34]

¶ 1249 Qualified transportation fringe benefits.

An employee (other than a self-employed person) may exclude from income qualified transportation fringe benefits up to specified dollar amounts (below). (Code Sec. 132(a)(5), Code Sec. 132(f)(5)) These benefits include:

(1) Transportation in a commuter highway vehicle (van pool), if in connection with travel between the employee's residence and place of employment. A commuter highway vehicle has a seating capacity of 6 adults (excluding the driver) for which 80% of the mileage must be reasonably expected to be for employee commuting and to be for trips where the vehicle is half full (excluding the driver).

(2) Transit passes for use on a mass transit facility (e.g., rail, bus or ferry) or a commuter highway vehicle.

(3) Qualified parking at or near the employer's business premises or a location from which the employee commutes to work by mass transit or hired commuter vehicle. Any parking at or near the employee's residence isn't qualified parking. (Code Sec. 132(f)(1), Code Sec. 132(f)(5); Reg § 1.132-9(b))

(4) Qualified bicycle commuting reimbursements, i.e., for any calendar year, any employer reimbursement during the 15-month period beginning with the first day of that calendar year for reasonable expenses incurred by the employee during that calendar year for the purchase of a bicycle and improvements, repair, or storage. The exclusion is limited to $20 per month a bicycle is regularly used for a substantial portion of the employee's commute. This benefit can't be used with commuter highway vehicle transportation, transit passes, or parking benefits. (Code Sec. 132(f)(5)(F))[35]

For 2010, an employee can exclude up to $230 a month of qualified parking and up to $230 for employer-provided transit and vanpooling benefits. (Code Sec. 132(f)(2))[36]

caution: Check http://ria.thomsonreuters.com/federaltaxhandbook to see if this provision has been changed for 2011.

Cash reimbursements (but *not* cash advances) are excludable. But reimbursements for transit passes are excludable only where vouchers, etc. (which may be exchanged only for transit passes) aren't readily available for direct distribution by the employer to the employee. (Code Sec. 132(f)(3); Reg § 1.132-9(b))[37]

No amount is included in an employee's gross income solely because he may choose between any qualified transportation fringe and otherwise includible compensation. (Code Sec. 132(f)(4)) But if he chooses cash instead of a qualified transportation fringe, he will be taxed.[38] If he elects fringes rather than cash, he won't be taxed on any exchanged cash if requirements are met. (Reg § 1.132-9(b))[39]

The qualified transportation fringe exclusion doesn't apply to any arrangement that results in the reimbursement of an expense the employee hasn't actually incurred, e.g., where the employee is reimbursed for an item he paid for through a tax-free salary reduction.[40]

Partners, 2% S corporation shareholders and independent contractors can't exclude qualified transportation fringes. (Code Sec. 132(f)(5)(E))[41]

---

33. ¶H-1821; ¶1324.06; TD ¶131,510
34. ¶H-1823; ¶1324.06; TD ¶131,510
35. ¶H-2205; ¶1324.08; TD ¶134,016
36. ¶H-2217.1; ¶1324.08; TD ¶134,591
37. ¶H-2212, H-2216; ¶1324.08; TD ¶134,578

38. ¶H-2216.1; ¶1324.08; TD ¶134,016
39. ¶H-2216.1; ¶1324.08; TD ¶134,584 *et seq.*
40. ¶H-2216
41. ¶H-2206; ¶1324.08; TD ¶134,572

¶ 1250 Qualified moving expense reimbursement.

A taxpayer excludes from gross income any qualified moving expense reimbursement. (Code Sec. 132(a)(6))[42] A qualified moving expense reimbursement is any amount received (directly or indirectly) by the taxpayer from an employer as a payment of (or reimbursement for) moving expenses that would have been deductible had the taxpayer paid them directly (for employee's moving expense deduction, see ¶1645 *et seq.*). Expenses aren't excludable if the taxpayer actually deducted them in an earlier year. (Code Sec. 132(g))[43] Otherwise an employer's payment or reimbursement is income to the employee. (Code Sec. 82)[44] The employer reports moving expense reimbursements (but not qualifying payments to third parties or qualifying services furnished in kind) to the employee on Form W-2.[45]

¶ 1251 Reimbursement of employee in connection with sale of his home.

An employer's reimbursement for an employee's loss on sale of the employee's home is income to the employee.[46] However, if the employer buys the employee's home at its fair market value (FMV), the employee has no income other than gain on the sale. Where, as an alternative to reimbursing an employee for the loss, the employer buys the home for more than its FMV, that *excess* is taxable to the employee.[47]

¶ 1252 Employer-provided retirement advice.

Qualified retirement planning services are excluded from the income of the employee receiving the services. (Code Sec. 132(a)(7)) Qualified retirement planning services are any retirement planning services provided to an employee and his spouse by an employer maintaining a qualified employer plan (as defined in Code Sec. 219(g)(5)). (Code Sec. 132(m))[48]

¶ 1253 Employee achievement awards.

Employee achievement awards are excludable only to the extent the employer can deduct the cost of the award—generally limited to $400 for any one employee, or $1,600 for a "qualified plan award," see ¶1591. (Code Sec. 74(c)(2))[49]

¶ 1254 On-premises athletic facilities.

The value of an on-premises athletic facility provided by an employer is excluded from an employee's gross income. (Code Sec. 132(j)(4)(A))[50]

¶ 1255 Employer payment of employee's personal expenses.

Where an employer pays the debts or personal expenses of an employee, or reimburses the employee's payment, the employee must include the employer's payment or reimbursement in his (employee's) income.[1] For medical expenses, see ¶1257.

An employer's payment of an employee's income taxes (federal or state) or other taxes is income to the employee. Pyramiding of income, and of tax, results where the employer agrees to pay all the employee's tax. (Reg § 1.61-14)[2]

42. ¶H-1971; ¶1324.09; TD ¶136,541
43. ¶H-1971; ¶1324.09; TD ¶136,541
44. ¶H-4418; ¶824; TD ¶136,535
45. ¶S-3170; ¶60,514; TD ¶812,012
46. ¶s H-2161, H-2162; ¶824.01; TD ¶136,536
47. ¶H-2162; TD ¶136,536
48. ¶H-1980; ¶1324.10
49. ¶L-2317 *et seq.*; ¶744.03; TD ¶132,007
50. ¶H-1951; ¶1324.07; TD ¶134,017
1. ¶H-2151; ¶s 614.007, 614.146; TD ¶136,527
2. ¶H-2157; ¶614.147; TD ¶198,506

¶ 1256 Employer-provided adoption assistance.

An employee may exclude amounts paid or expenses incurred by his employer for qualified adoption expenses (¶2359) connected with the employee's adoption of a child, if the amounts are furnished under an adoption assistance program in existence (and known to the employee) before the expenses are incurred. For the adoption of a child with special needs the exclusion applies regardless of whether the employee has qualified adoption expenses. (Code Sec. 137(a), Code Sec. 137(b), Code Sec. 137(f))[3]

The excludable amount is phased out for taxpayers with adjusted gross income (AGI, as specially computed) over $182,520 in 2010 ($185,210 in 2011), adjusted for inflation annually, and is fully eliminated when AGI reaches $222,520 in 2010 ($225,210 in 2011). (Code Sec. 137(b)(2), Code Sec. 137(f)) To compute the excluded employer-provided adoption benefits, use Form 8839.[4]

Amounts are excludable in the year in which the employer pays for qualified adoption expenses of an eligible child who is a U.S. citizen or resident when the adoption commenced. If the eligible child isn't a U.S. citizen or resident, the exclusion is available only for adoptions that become final, and only in the year that they are finalized. Where expenses of a foreign eligible child are paid in a year before the adoption becomes final, the employee includes the employer's assistance in income for that year, and claims the otherwise available exclusion in the year the adoption becomes final. A taxpayer may claim both an adoption expense credit (see ¶2359) and an exclusion for the adoption of an eligible child, but cannot claim a credit and an exclusion for the same expense.[5]

For 2010, the maximum exclusion for employer-provided adoption assistance is $13,170 per child (for both non-special needs and special needs adoptions); for 2011, it's $13,360. (Code Sec. 137) The credit maximum and phaseout thresholds are adjusted for inflation in tax years beginning after 2010. (Code Sec. 137(f)) The sunset provisions of EGTRRA (see ¶1114)—under which the exclusion wouldn't apply—are delayed for one year to tax years beginning after Dec. 31, 2011. (Health Care Act § 10909(c), P.L. 111-148, 3/23/2010)

¶ 1257 Employee's medical expenses reimbursed or insured by employer.

An employee can exclude from gross income amounts received from his employer, directly or indirectly, as reimbursement for expenses for the medical care of himself, his spouse, and his dependents. Effective Mar. 30, 2010, the exclusion also applies to any child of an employee who hasn't attained age 27 as of the end of the year. (Code Sec. 105(b)) (These amounts are excludable even where a sole proprietor employer is the employee's spouse, and the amounts received are for the employer-spouse's medical care.)[6] However, reimbursement is includible in the employee's income to the extent it exceeds medical expenses or it's attributable to medical expense deductions he took in a previous year. (Code Sec. 105(b); Reg § 1.105-2)[7]

An employee also excludes the cost (i.e., premiums paid) of employer-provided *coverage* under an accident or health plan. (Code Sec. 106)[8] However, if the employer-provided policy, trust, etc., provides other benefits, only the portion of the employer contributions for the accident and health coverage is excludable. (Reg § 1.106-1)[9]

Where a plan allows reimbursements of a nonqualifying beneficiary's medical expense, no payment from the plan during the year to any person—including the employee, his spouse or dependents—is excluded from income.[10]

Insurance premiums paid for partners and more-than-2% S corporation shareholders (who

3. ¶H-1450 et seq.; ¶1374; TD ¶133,600 et seq.
4. ¶H-1453; ¶1374; TD ¶133,603
5. ¶H-1451 et seq.; ¶1374; TD ¶133,602; 133,608
6. ¶H-1110; TD ¶133,036
7. ¶H-1110 et seq.; ¶1054.01; TD ¶133,036
8. ¶H-1102; ¶1064; TD ¶133,032
9. ¶H-1106; ¶1064; TD ¶133,034
10. ¶H-1349.3

are treated as partners) are not excludable.[11]

Highly compensated individuals (as defined in Code Sec. 105(h)(5)) who benefit from an employer's "self-insured" medical reimbursement plan that discriminates in their favor must include "excess reimbursements" (reimbursements for benefits not available to other plan participants) in income. (Code Sec. 105(h))[12]

¶ 1258   Employer contributions to Archer medical savings account (Archer MSA).

Small-employer contributions to an employee's Archer medical savings account (Archer MSA) are treated as excludable employer-provided coverage for medical expenses under an accident or health plan (¶1257) to the extent the amounts don't exceed the applicable statutory limits (see ¶1528). (Code Sec. 106(b)(1))[13] Generally, small employers are those that employed on average no more than 50 employees during either of the two preceding years. An employer that grows past the 50-employee limit in a succeeding year may continue MSA contributions until the year after the first year in which it has more than 200 employees. (Code Sec. 220(c)(4))[14] For treatment of Archer MSA distributions, see ¶1382. Employer Archer MSA contributions aren't excludable if made at the employee's election under a salary reduction arrangement under a cafeteria plan. (Code Sec. 125(f))

Employers that provide high deductible health plan coverage plus an MSA and make employer contributions must make available a comparable contribution on behalf of all employees with comparable coverage during the same period. A 35% penalty applies for noncompliance. (Code Sec. 4980E)[15]

For the cutoff date for Archer MSA contributions, see ¶1528.

¶ 1259   Employer contributions to health savings accounts (HSA).

Employer contributions to a health savings account (HSA) of the employee are treated as employer-provided coverage for medical expenses under an accident or health plan (¶1257) to the extent the amounts don't exceed the statutory limits (see ¶1529) applicable to the employee for the tax year, and are deductible by the employer in the year they are paid. (Code Sec. 106(d)(2)) Employer contributions to an HSA on behalf of an eligible individual are excludable from income.[16] The contributions must be reported on the employee's Form W-2, Box 12.[17] For HSA distributions, see ¶1383. However, where contributions exceed the limits and the employer doesn't recoup the amount, the excess must be included in the employee's income and reported on his Form W-2.[18]

There is no constructive receipt of income solely because the employee may choose between employer contributions to an HSA and to another health plan. (Code Sec. 106(d)(2)) Employer contributions to an HSA are excludable if made at the employee's election under a salary reduction arrangement in a cafeteria plan (see ¶1271). (Code Sec. 125(d)(2))

¶ 1260   Employer's payments for employee's loss of limb, disfigurement, etc.

Amounts received under an employer plan as payment for permanent loss or loss of use of a member or function of the body, or permanent disfigurement, of the employee, his spouse or his dependent are tax-free, but only if the payment is based on the nature of the injury without regard to the period the employee is absent from work. (Code Sec. 105(c))[19]

---

11. ¶H-1126; ¶1064; TD ¶133,026
12. ¶H-1138 *et seq.*; ¶1054.05; TD ¶133,013
13. ¶H-1101.1 et seq., ¶1064, TD ¶133,040
14. ¶s H-1333, H-1333.1; ¶2204.01; TD ¶288,102
15. ¶H-1336.3; ¶4980E4; TD ¶288,104

16. ¶H-1101.5; ¶1064; TD ¶133,051
17. ¶S-3152; ¶60,514; TD ¶812,002
18. ¶H-1350.8D
19. ¶H-1201; ¶1054.02; TD ¶133,048

¶ 1261　Worker's compensation.

Amounts received under a worker's compensation act or similar law for personal injuries or sickness are excludable from the employee's (or survivor's) income. But worker's compensation is includible in income to the extent it's attributable to medical expense deductions taken in an earlier year. (Code Sec. 104(a)(1); Reg § 1.104-1(b))[20]

¶ 1262　Annuities paid to survivors of public safety officers killed in line of duty.

Survivor annuity benefits paid on account of the death of a public safety officer (including law enforcement officers, firefighters, rescue squad workers and ambulance crew members) killed in the line of duty are excluded if: (1) the annuity is provided under a governmental plan which meets the requirements of Code Sec. 401(a) to the officer's spouse, former spouse, or child; and (2) to the extent the annuity is attributable to the officer's service as a public safety officer. (Code Sec. 101(h)(1)) The exclusion doesn't apply under certain circumstances (e.g., if the death was caused by the officer's intentional misconduct). (Code Sec. 101(h)(2))[21]

¶ 1263　Employer-paid individual life insurance policies.

Premiums paid by an employer for policies on the life of an employee are taxable to the employee if the proceeds are payable to the employee's beneficiary (except for group-term insurance, see ¶1264) but not where the employer is the beneficiary. (Reg § 1.61-2(d)(2))[22]

¶ 1264　Group-term life insurance premiums.

An employee isn't taxed on premiums paid by the employer on insurance covering the employee's life under a group-term life insurance policy, if the employee's total coverage under all such plans of all his employers doesn't exceed $50,000. If his total coverage does exceed $50,000, he's taxed on the "cost" (¶1265) of coverage over $50,000 minus the amount he paid. (Code Sec. 79(a))[23] For coverage of employee's spouse and dependents, see ¶1266.

An employee whose total coverage exceeds $50,000 for only part of the year includes the employer's payments for that part of the year coverage, even if his average coverage for the year is under this ceiling. (Code Sec. 79(a))[24]

A disabled terminated employee isn't taxable on group term coverage even if it exceeds $50,000. (Code Sec. 79(b)(1))[25]

Retired employees (except certain employees who reached 55 or retired before Jan. 2, '84) are treated the same as other employees. (Code Sec. 79(e))[26]

The exclusion doesn't apply to any insurance protection in excess of the maximum allowed by state law for employee group insurance. (Reg § 1.79-1(e))[27]

The exclusion is available to a key employee only if the plan doesn't discriminate in favor of key employees (at any time in the key employee's tax year) (Reg § 1.79-4T, Q&A-11) as to eligibility to participate and in the type and amount of benefits available. (Code Sec. 79(d))[28] If the plan is discriminatory, each key employee must include the *greater of* (a) the actual cost of the insurance (determined by apportioning the net premium allocable to the group-term coverage during the key employee's tax year among the covered employees (Reg § 1.79-4T, Q&A-6(b)), *or* (b) the cost determined from IRS's premium table. (Code Sec. 79(d)(1)(B))[29]

---

20. ¶H-1351; ¶1044.01; TD ¶133,049
21. ¶H-1650 *et seq.*; ¶1014.09; TD ¶141,090
22. ¶H-1501 *et seq.*; ¶614.031; TD ¶137,000
23. ¶H-1518; ¶794; TD ¶137,007
24. ¶H-1520; ¶794.01; TD ¶137,009

25. ¶H-1552; ¶794.03; TD ¶137,041
26. ¶s H-1555, H-1556; ¶794.06; TD ¶137,043
27. ¶H-1537
28. ¶H-1564; ¶794.05; TD ¶137,024
29. ¶H-1565; ¶794.05; TD ¶137,023; 137,025

¶ 1265   "Cost" of taxable group-term insurance—IRS uniform premium table.

The employer must compute the "cost" of taxable group-term coverage (¶1264) and notify the employee on Form W-2 of the amount included in his income. The employee computes the cost only where he has two or more employers who provide him with coverage.

The cost of group-term life insurance is determined on the basis of uniform premiums (computed on the basis of five-year age brackets) prescribed by IRS. (Code Sec. 79(c)) The cost for each month of coverage is the number of thousands of dollars of coverage over $50,000 (to the nearest tenth) times the amount in IRS's table for the employee's attained age on the last day of the employee's tax year. (Reg § 1.79-3(d)(2))[30] Under the table, the cost per $1,000 of protection per month is 5¢ for under age 25; 6¢ for 25 through 29; 8¢ for 30 through 34; 9¢ for 35 through 39; 10¢ for 40 through 44; 15¢ for 45 through 49; 23¢ for 50 through 54; 43¢ for 55 through 59; 66¢ for 60 through 64; $1.27 for 65 through 69; and $2.06 for 70 and older.

If the employee contributes to the plan, all his contributions for the tax year are considered made for that part of his coverage over $50,000. (Code Sec. 79(a)(2))[31]

illustration: J, a 57-year-old employee, is provided with a $250,000 group-term life insurance policy by his employer for the year. For this coverage, J contributes 20¢ per $1,000 of coverage per month. The amount included in J's income for the $200,000 excess coverage ($250,000 – $50,000) is $432—the cost of the insurance above the excludable amount (43¢ monthly cost from the IRS table × 12 months × 200 [excess insurance]) less J's employee contribution (20¢ × 12 × 250 total insurance).

¶ 1266   Group-term coverage of employee's spouse and dependents.

The cost (as determined at ¶1265) of group-term life insurance on the life of an individual other than an employee (e.g., the employee's spouse or dependent) provided in connection with the performance of services by the employee is includible in the employee's gross income. (Reg § 1.61-2(d)(2)(ii)(b)) If, however, the face amount of employer-provided group-term insurance payable on the death of an employee's spouse or dependent doesn't exceed $2,000, it's an excludable de minimis fringe (¶1248).[32]

¶ 1267   Group-permanent insurance premiums.

Group-permanent insurance premiums that an employer pays on an employee's life are included in the employee's income. Where a group term policy provides permanent benefits, the amount included in income for the permanent benefits is computed under a complex formula. (Reg § 1.79-1(d))[33]

¶ 1268   Split-dollar life insurance.

Under a "split-dollar" insurance arrangement, the employer pays part of the premium for a life insurance policy on the life of the employee (to the extent of the annual increase in cash surrender value) and the employee pays the rest. Out of the insurance proceeds, the employer gets either the cash surrender value or the amount it paid; the employee can designate the beneficiary of the balance.[34] For arrangements entered into (or materially modified) after Sept. 17, 2003, there are two mutually exclusive regimes for taxing split-dollar life insurance arrangements.

Under the economic benefit regime, the policy owner is treated as providing economic benefits to the non-owner (as valued in the regs). This regime governs the taxation of what

30. ¶H-1521; ¶794.01; TD ¶137,010
31. ¶H-1522; ¶794.01; TD ¶137,011
32. ¶H-1560 *et seq.*; ¶s 614.031, 1324.06; TD ¶137,044

33. ¶H-1545; ¶794.04; TD ¶137,016
34. ¶H-1601; ¶614.033; TD ¶137,030

are known as endorsement split-dollar arrangements (e.g., employer owns the policy and employee's rights are derived from the employer's endorsement in the contract of those rights to him). This regime automatically applies if the arrangement is (1) entered into in connection with the performance of services, and the employee or other service provider is not the contract owner, or (2) a gift situation, and the donee is not the contract owner. (Reg § 1.61-22)

Under the loan regime, the non-owner of the life insurance contract is treated as loaning premium payments to the contract owner. Unless specifically excepted, the loan regime applies to any split-dollar loan. The loan regime also governs what are known as collateral assignment split-dollar life insurance arrangements (e.g., employee owns the policy, which is used as collateral for employer's right to recover the premiums it pays). (Reg § 1.7872-15)

The employer (or donor in a gift arrangement) is treated as the owner of a split-dollar life insurance contract if the only economic benefit that the employee (or donee) has under the arrangement is current life insurance protection. (Reg § 1.61-22(c)(1))

Unless the non-owner's payments are made in consideration of economic benefits, then general income, employment, and gift tax principles apply to the arrangement. For example, if an employee/contract owner's repayment obligation to an employer were waived or cancelled, both parties have to account for the amount as compensation. (Reg § 1.61-22(b)(6))

In a split-dollar life insurance arrangement taxed under the economic benefit regime, the policy owner is treated as providing economic benefits to the non-owner, and those benefits have to be accounted for fully and consistently by both the owner and the non-owner. The value of the economic benefits, less any consideration paid by the non-owner, is treated as transferred from the owner to the non-owner. The tax consequences of that transfer depend on the relationship between the owner and the non-owner. Thus, depending on the circumstances, it might be treated as compensation, a dividend, or a gift. (Reg § 1.61-22(d)(1))

A payment made under a split-dollar life insurance arrangement is a split-dollar loan, and the policy owner and non-owner are treated, respectively, as borrower and lender, if: the payment is made directly or indirectly by the non-owner to the owner; the payment either is a loan under general tax law principles or if a reasonable person would expect the payment to be repaid in full to the non-owner; and repayment is to be made from, or secured by, the policy's death benefit or cash surrender value, or both. (Reg § 1.7872-15(a)(2))

Because split-dollar life insurance arrangements typically provide for deferred compensation, Code Sec. 409A (¶1277) generally applies. But Code Sec. 409A doesn't apply for earnings on amounts deferred under a split-dollar life insurance arrangement in tax years beginning before 2005 (unless the plan is materially modified after Oct. 3, 2004), including increases in the policy cash value—but not including increases attributable to continued services performed, compensation earned, or premium payments or other contributions made on or after 2005.[35]

For arrangements entered into before Sept. 18, 2003 and not materially modified on or after that date (unless rules similar to the above rules are relied on by taxpayers), an employee is taxed on the value of the insurance protection he receives, less any premium he paid; the taxable amount is determined under IRS's Table 2001 (carried in IRS Notice 2002–8), and *not* under the group-term table at ¶1265), plus cash dividends or other benefits received, reduced by any part of the premiums he paid. (But in some cases, an insurer's published gross premium rates for initial-issue standard-risk insurance can be used for policies issued by that insurer, or, for certain pre-Jan. 28, 2002 arrangements, the PS 58 rates may be used). Insurance proceeds received by the employer and the employee's beneficiaries are tax-free.[36]

For split-dollar life insurance arrangements entered into before Jan. 28, 2002 under which an employer has made premium payments and has received, or is entitled to receive, full repayment of all of its payments, IRS won't assert that there has been a taxable transfer of

---

35. ¶H-3200.6; ¶409A4.01; TD ¶135,504.1   36. ¶H-1647 *et seq.*; ¶614.033; TD ¶137,031

property to a benefited person upon termination of the arrangement if for all periods beginning on or after Jan.1, 2004, all payments by the employer from inception of the arrangement (less any repayments) are treated as loans for tax purposes, and the parties report the tax treatment consistently with this loan treatment. Any payments by the employer not previously treated as loans must be treated as loans entered into at the beginning of that first year in which the payments are treated as loans.[37]

¶ 1269 Meals and lodging furnished by or on behalf of employer.

Meals or lodging (including utilities) furnished to an employee and his family (spouse and dependents) is nontaxable to the employee if (Code Sec. 119):

(1) the meals and lodging are furnished by or on behalf of the employer for the convenience of the employer (e.g., meals supplied because eating places near work are scarce, or because employees must for valid business reasons remain on-premises until their shifts end) (Reg § 1.119-1(a)(2)), and

(2) (a) in the case of *meals,* they are furnished on the employer's business premises, or (b) in the case of *lodging,* the employee is required to accept the lodging as a condition of his employment (i.e., to properly perform his duties). (Reg § 1.119-1(b))[38] This means the employee's presence must be required from a business standpoint—e.g., ranches, hotels, motels and resorts.[39] For faculty housing, see ¶1270.

The value (not the cost) of meals or lodging that fails to meet these tests generally is income to the employee. (Reg § 1.61-2(d)(3), Reg § 1.119-1(a)(1))[40] However, all meals furnished on the employer's business premises to its employees are treated as furnished for the employer's convenience—and so are excludable from the employees' income—if *more than half* of the employees to whom the meals are furnished on the premises are furnished the meals for the convenience of the employer. (Code Sec. 119(b)(4))[41]

observation: In other words, if the more-than-half test is met, all employees may exclude the value of meals provided on premises, even those who weren't supplied the meals for the convenience of the employer.

Cash allowances for meals are taxable.[42] If the employee can take either cash, or meals or lodging furnished in kind, the value of meals or lodging furnished is income. But occasional "supper money" paid to overtime employees is excludable as a de minimis fringe, see ¶1248.[43]

¶ 1270 Faculty housing—qualified campus lodging.

The value of qualified campus lodging furnished to an employee of an educational institution is excludable (with limits, below) from his gross income. (Code Sec. 119(d))[44]

Qualified campus lodging is lodging that isn't eligible for the exclusion at ¶1269, that's located on or near a campus of a tax-exempt educational institution (or a qualifying academic health center), and that's furnished by the institution to an employee, his spouse, and his dependents for use as a residence. (Code Sec. 119(d)(3), Code Sec. 119(d)(4))[45]

The exclusion isn't a total one. The employee must include the excess of: (1) the lesser of (a) 5% of the appraised value (as of the close of the tax year) of the qualified campus lodging, or (b) the average of the rentals paid by individuals other than employees or students for comparable lodging provided by the institution; over (2) the rent paid by the employee. (Code Sec. 119(d)(2))[46]

37. ¶H-1647.10
38. ¶H-1751; ¶1194.01; TD ¶131,501
39. ¶H-1776; ¶1194.02; TD ¶131,511
40. ¶s H-1751, H-1785; ¶s 614.027, 1194 *et seq.*; TD ¶131,511
41. ¶H-1754; ¶1194.02

42. ¶H-1790; ¶1194.03; TD ¶131,506
43. ¶H-1791; ¶1324.06; TD ¶131,507
44. ¶H-1797; ¶1194.06; TD ¶131,525
45. ¶H-1799; ¶1194.06; TD ¶131,525
46. ¶H-1797; ¶1194.06; TD ¶131,525

¶ 1271   Cafeteria plans (including flexible spending accounts).

No amount is included in the gross income of the participant in a cafeteria plan solely because, under the plan, the participant may choose among the benefits of the plan. (Code Sec. 125(a))[47] Cafeteria plans are generally the sole method of employers providing nontaxable benefits where employees can elect between taxable compensation and nontaxable benefits. (Prop Reg. § 1.125-1(b)(1) ["Taxpayers may rely"])

A "cafeteria plan" (also referred to as a flexible benefit plan) is a written plan under which participants (all employees) may choose their own "menu" of benefits consisting of "cash" and "qualified benefits". (Code Sec. 125(d))[48] For this purpose, cash means cash from current compensation (including salary reduction), payment for annual leave, sick leave, or other paid time off, severance pay, property, and certain after-tax employee contributions; distributions from qualified retirement plans are not cash. (Prop Reg. § 1.125-1(a)(2) ["Taxpayers may rely"]) A qualified benefit, which generally must be excludible from employees' gross income under a specific Code section—and must not defer compensation (with some exceptions) (Code Sec. 125(d)(2))—includes: group-term life insurance on an employee's life (up to the excludable $50,000 amount, see ¶1264); employer-provided accident and health plans (¶1257) (including health flexible spending arrangements (FSAs), and accidental death and dismemberment policies); a dependent care assistance program (¶1272); an adoption assistance program (¶1256); contributions to a Code Sec. 401(k) plan (¶4317); contributions to certain plans maintained by educational organizations, contributions to Health Savings Accounts (HSAs, see ¶1259); and long-term and short-term disability coverage. (Code Sec. 125(f); Prop Reg. § 1.125-1(a)(3) ["Taxpayers may rely"]) [49]

In the case of a "highly compensated participant," the exclusion won't apply to any benefit attributable to a plan year for which the plan discriminates in favor of highly compensated participants as to contributions, benefits or eligibility to participate. (Code Sec. 125(b)(1))[50] An individual is a "highly compensated participant" if he is an officer or more-than-5% shareholder of the employer, a highly compensated employee or a spouse or dependent of such a person. (Code Sec. 125(e)(1))[1]

In the case of a key employee (defined in Code Sec. 416(i)(1)), the exclusion won't apply to any plan year if the qualified benefits provided to key employees under the plan exceed 25% of the total of such benefits provided for all employees under the plan. (Code Sec. 125(b)(2))[2]

FSAs. A cafeteria plan also can include one or more "flexible spending accounts" (FSAs). An FSA is a benefit designed to reimburse employees for expenses incurred for certain qualified benefits, up to a maximum amount not substantially in excess of the salary reduction and employer flex-credits allocated for the benefit. The maximum amount of reimbursement reasonably available must be less than five times the value of the coverage. (Prop Reg. § 1.125-5(a) ["Taxpayers may rely"]) Employer flex-credits are non-elective contributions that an employer makes available for every employee eligible to participate in the cafeteria plan, to be used at the employee's election only for one or more qualified benefits (but not as cash or other taxable benefits). (Prop Reg. § 1.125-5(b) ["Taxpayers may rely"]) The three types of FSAs are dependent care assistance, adoption assistance and medical care reimbursements (health FSA).

A health FSA may be limited to a subset of permitted Code Sec. 213(d) medical expenses, or it may be a health saving account (HSA) compatible limited-purpose health FSA or postdeductible health FSA. (Prop Reg. § 1.125-5(m) ["Taxpayers may rely"]) A health FSA may not reimburse premiums for accident and health insurance or long-term care insurance. (Code Sec. 125(f))

47. ¶H-2401; ¶1254; TD ¶133,045
48. ¶H-2405; ¶1254.01; TD ¶133,042
49. ¶H-2413 *et seq.*; ¶1254.01; TD ¶133,042

50. ¶H-2450; ¶1254.06; TD ¶133,045.
1. ¶H-2455; ¶1254.06
2. ¶H-2456; ¶1254.06; TD ¶133,045

Use-it-or-lose-it rule. Unused cafeteria plan amounts left over at the end of a plan year generally have to be forfeited (use-it-or-lose-it rule). But a cafeteria plan can provide an optional grace period immediately following the end of each plan year, extending the period for incurring expenses for qualified benefits to the 15th day of the third month after the end of the plan year. It may apply to one or more qualified benefits but can't apply to paid time off or elective contributions to Code Sec. 401(k) plans. Unused benefits or contributions for one qualified benefit may only be used to reimburse expenses incurred during the grace period for that same qualified benefit. Benefits or contributions not used as of the end of the grace period are forfeited. (Prop Reg. § 1.125-1(e)(1) ["Taxpayers may rely"]) [3] An exception allows FSAs to make distributions of all or part of unused health FSA benefits after June 17, 2008 to military reservists who are called to active duty for a period exceeding 179 days (or an indefinite period). The distribution must be made during the period beginning with the call to active duty and ending on the last day of the coverage period of the FSA that includes the date of the call to active duty. (Code Sec. 125(h))

¶ 1272   Dependent care assistance payments.

Payments incurred by an employer for dependent care assistance under a written plan are excluded from an employee's gross income. (Code Sec. 129(a)(1))[4]

The amount an employee can exclude (computed on Form 2441 with Form 1040 or Form 1040A) can't exceed the employee's earned income (excluding employer dependent care assistance payments) or, for married employees, the earned income of the lower earning spouse. (Code Sec. 129(b))[5] The aggregate exclusion is further limited to $5,000 ($2,500 for a married individual filing separately). (Code Sec. 129(a)(2)(A)) Any excess is includible in the tax year the dependent care services are provided. (Code Sec. 129(a)(2)(B))[6]

Dependent care assistance is the payment for or provision of services that if paid for by the employee would be considered employment-related expenses under the child care credit rules (see ¶2356). (Code Sec. 129(e)(1))[7] For eligible dependents, see ¶2355. An employee includes a self-employed individual who can be covered under a self-employed retirement plan. An individual who owns the entire interest in an unincorporated trade or business is treated as his own employer. A partnership is treated as the employer of each partner who is eligible to be included in a self-employed retirement plan. (Code Sec. 129(e)(3), Code Sec. 129(e)(4))[8]

No amount is excludable unless the name, address and (except in the case of a tax-exempt service-provider) taxpayer identifying number (TIN) of the person providing the dependent care services are included on the employee's return. The employee can use Form W-10 to ask for this information from the service provider. Failure to provide this information is excused if the employee exercised due diligence in trying to do so. (Code Sec. 129(e)(9))[9]

The plan must satisfy specific nondiscrimination rules and certain other requirements. (Code Sec. 129(d))[10] If an otherwise qualified program fails to meet these requirements, the program will be a dependent care assistance program under which expenses are still excludable for nonhighly compensated employees. (Code Sec. 129(d)(1))[11]

For how excludable dependent care assistance affects the dependent care credit, see ¶2354.

¶ 1273   Time for Reporting Compensation. ■■■■■■■■■■■■■■■

Compensation income is reported according to the recipient's accounting method, subject to constructive receipt, repaid income and deferred income rules.

3. ¶H-2417.1; TD ¶133,045.1
4. ¶H-1401; ¶1294 *et seq.*; TD ¶133,504
5. ¶H-1402; ¶1294; TD ¶133,505
6. ¶H-1402 *et seq.*; ¶1294; TD ¶133,503
7. ¶H-1419; ¶1294.02; TD ¶133,516

8. ¶H-1413 *et seq.*; ¶1294.02; TD ¶133,504
9. ¶H-1406 *et seq.*; ¶1294.03; TD ¶133,501
10. ¶H-1428 *et seq.*; ¶1294.01; TD ¶133,518
11. ¶H-1418; ¶1294.01; TD ¶133,515

¶ 1274   Cash basis taxpayers.

Cash basis taxpayers report compensation for the tax year they actually receive it.[12]

Compensation paid by check is reported for the year the check is received, even if the check covers past or future services, or isn't cashed until the following year.[13]

Compensation income must be reported for the year it's constructively received (see ¶2822), even though it's not actually received until a later year. Income is constructively received for the year it's credited to the taxpayer's account, set apart for him, or otherwise made available so he can draw upon it at any time, or could have drawn upon it during the tax year if he had given notice of intention to withdraw. (Reg § 1.451-2(a))[14] For advances, see ¶1276.

¶ 1275   Accrual basis taxpayers.

Accrual basis taxpayers report compensation for the tax year in which it accrues. Compensation accrues when all events have occurred that fix the right to receive the income and its amount can be determined with reasonable accuracy. (Reg § 1.451-1(a))[15]

If the right to compensation for services or its amount can't be determined until the services are completed, the amount of compensation ordinarily isn't reported until the tax year the services are completed and the determination can be made. (Reg § 1.451-1(a))[16]

¶ 1276   Advances and drawing accounts.

A cash basis taxpayer who receives advances against commissions that haven't been earned reports the advances as income for the year they are received, if he isn't required to repay the amounts received in excess of commissions. If he must repay the excess drawings, those amounts aren't income until offset by a credit for commissions earned.[17]

¶ 1277   Deferred compensation plans.

All amounts deferred under a nonqualified deferred compensation (NQDC) plan for all tax years are currently includible in gross income to the extent not subject to a substantial risk of forfeiture and not previously included in gross income, unless the plan:

... meets specified distribution, acceleration of benefit, and election requirements; and

... is operated in accordance with these requirements. (Code Sec. 409A(a)(1)(A)(i))[18]

If a NQDC plan doesn't comply with the Code Sec. 409A rules, all amounts deferred under the plan for the tax year and all prior tax years, by any participant to whom the failure relates, are included in income for that year to the extent not subject to a substantial risk of forfeiture and not previously included in income. This amount is also subject to: (1) interest (at the underpayment rate plus one percentage point) on the tax underpayments that would have occurred had the amount been included in income for the tax year when first deferred, or if later, when not subject to a substantial risk of forfeiture; and (2) a penalty of 20% of the compensation required to be included in income. (Code Sec. 409A(a)(1)(B))

For inclusion in income of deferred compensation from tax-indifferent corporations and partnerships, see ¶1279.

Compensation is subject to a substantial risk of forfeiture if entitlement to it is conditioned on a person's performance of substantial future services or the occurrence of a condition related to the compensation's purpose (e.g., an amount conditioned on involuntary separation

---

12. ¶H-3501; ¶s 614.023, 4514.003; TD ¶130,526
13. ¶H-3502; ¶s 614.023, 4514.004; TD ¶130,527
14. ¶H-3508; ¶4514.036; TD ¶130,531
15. ¶G-2471; ¶4514.011; TD ¶441,701
16. ¶H-3526; ¶4514.011; TD ¶441,702
17. ¶H-3515; ¶614.023; TD ¶130,518
18. ¶H-3200; ¶409A4.01; TD ¶135,508

from service without cause), and the possibility of forfeiture is substantial. An amount isn't subject to a substantial risk of forfeiture merely because the right to the amount is conditioned upon the refraining from performance of services, such as a noncompete clause. (Reg § 1.409A-1(d)(1))[19]

A NQDC plan is any plan that provides for the deferral of compensation, other than (1) a qualified employer plan (a qualified retirement plan, tax-deferred annuity, simplified employee pension, SIMPLE plan, qualified governmental excess benefit arrangement under Code Sec. 415(m), or eligible deferred compensation plan under Code Sec. 457(b)), and (2) any bona fide vacation leave, sick leave, compensatory time, disability pay, or death benefit plan. (Code Sec. 409A(d)) It also doesn't include annual bonuses, or other annual compensation amounts, paid within 2 ½ months after the later of a service recipient's or service provider's tax year. (Reg § 1.409A-1(b)(4))[20] IRS won't treat as subject to Code Sec. 409A common arrangements in which school teachers, who provide services during a ten-month school year, elect to be paid ratably over 12 months.[21]

Incentive stock options (ISOs) and options granted under an employee stock purchase plan (ESPP) aren't subject to Code Sec. 409A. Nonqualified stock options and stock appreciation rights (SARs) are similarly excepted if the exercise price may never be less than the fair market value (FMV) of the underlying stock when the option or right is granted, the number of shares subject to the option are fixed on the grant date, and there is no other deferral feature; in addition, the receipt, transfer or exercise of the stock option must be subject to tax under Code Sec. 83, and only the service recipient's stock may be delivered upon a SAR's exercise. (Reg § 1.409A-1(b)(5))[22]

The distribution requirement is met if a NQDC plan provides that compensation deferred under the plan cannot be distributed earlier than (1) the participant's separation from service; (2) the date the participant becomes disabled; (3) the participant's death; (4) a time specified, or a schedule fixed, under the plan as of the date of the deferral of the compensation (amounts payable on the occurrence of an event are not treated as payable at a specified time); (5) a change in the ownership or effective control of the corporation, or in the ownership of a substantial portion of the assets of the corporation; or (6) the occurrence of an unforeseeable emergency such as a severe financial hardship resulting from illness, casualty loss, etc. (Code Sec. 409A(a)(2); Reg § 1.409A-3(a))[23]

The acceleration of benefits requirement is met if a NQDC plan doesn't allow the acceleration of the time or schedule of any payment under the plan, except as provided in IRS regs. (Code Sec. 409A(a)(3)) Changes in the form of distribution that accelerate payments generally are subject to this rule. But payments made in accordance with plan provisions for acceleration in the event of a service provider's separation from service, death or disability, or in the event of a change in control do not violate these rules.[24] Nor do payments under a domestic relations order,[25] or to comply with a certificate of divestiture for a conflict-of-interest,[26] or de minimis nonelective payments to terminate a participant's entire interest in the plan ($16,500 or less for 2010).[27] (Reg § 1.409A-3(j))

The election requirements are met if the plan provides that compensation for services performed during a tax year can be deferred at the participant's election only if the initial deferral election is made (1) not later than the close of the preceding tax year; or (2) at another time provided in IRS regs. For performance-based compensation (e.g., bonuses), based on services performed over a period of at least 12 months, the initial deferral election must be made no later than six months before the end of the period. The time and form of distributions have to be specified at the time of initial deferral. An election made after the initial election (a redeferral election) generally must not take effect until at least 12 months

19. ¶H-3200.50; ¶409A4.01; TD ¶135,511
20. ¶H-3200.27; ¶409A4.01; TD ¶135,508.1
21. ¶H-3307.1
22. ¶H-3200.28 *et seq.*; ¶409A4.01; TD ¶135,520
23. ¶H-3200.56; ¶409A4.01; TD ¶135,514

24. ¶H-3200.66; ¶409A4.01; TD ¶135,513.1
25. ¶H-3200.67
26. ¶H-3200.68
27. ¶H-3200.69

after the date on which the election is made and must require deferral for a period of not less than five years from the date on which payment would otherwise have been made. (Code Sec. 409A(a)(4))[28]

Relief provisions. Under IRS relief, if there is an unintentional operational failure to comply with specified Code Sec. 409A(a) requirements (e.g., incorrect amount treated as deferred compensation) that is corrected within the year, no amount is generally included in income under Code Sec. 409A(a). Relief is conditioned on timely filing and information reporting and taking commercially reasonable steps to avoid a recurrence of the failure. For other specified unintentional operational failures that aren't corrected in the same year, the amount included in income, and the resulting additional tax, is limited. A delay or acceleration in the payment of NQDC to comply with a Troubled Asset Relief Program (TARP) advisory opinion won't violate Code Sec. 409A. Neither will certain document failures.[29]

¶ 1278　Rabbi trusts and funding triggers.

Amounts deferred under nonqualified deferred compensation (NQDC) plans (¶1277) generally are not includible in income if the deferred compensation is payable from general corporate funds that are subject to the claims of general creditors. Arrangements known as "rabbi trusts" generally are irrevocable and don't permit the employer to use the assets for purposes other than payment of deferred compensation. However, the trust assets are subject to the claims of the employer's creditors in the case of insolvency or bankruptcy. Because of this feature, rabbi trusts are not considered to be funded and so compensation is deferred.

Assets directly or indirectly set aside in a trust for purposes of paying nonqualified deferred compensation are treated, for Code Sec. 83 purposes, as property transferred in connection with the performance of services (see ¶1219), whether or not the assets are available to satisfy claims of general creditors (1) at the time set aside, if the assets are located outside of the U.S.; or (2) at the time transferred, if the assets are later transferred outside of the U.S. (Code Sec. 409A(b)(1))

There is also a transfer of property, for Code Sec. 83 purposes, as of the earlier of (1) the date on which a NQDC plan first provides that assets will become restricted to the provision of benefits under the plan in connection with a change in the employer's financial health; or (2) the date on which assets are so restricted. (Code Sec. 409A(b)(2))[30]

Interest and a 20% penalty apply with regard to the off-shore rabbi trust and financial trigger rules.

For assets set aside, transferred or restricted before Mar. 22, 2006, taxpayers aren't subject to income inclusion or penalties if, before 2008, the NQDC plan is brought into conformity with Code Sec. 409A(b) (see ¶1277) and any guidance issued before that date.[31]

¶ 1279　Deferred compensation from tax-indifferent corporations and partnerships.

For deferred amounts attributable to services performed after Dec. 31, 2008, any compensation that is deferred under a nonqualified deferred compensation (NQDC) plan of a nonqualified entity is includible in gross income when there is no substantial risk of forfeiture of the rights to the compensation. (Code Sec. 457A(a))[32] A person's rights to compensation are subject to a substantial risk of forfeiture only if those rights are conditioned on the future performance of substantial services by any individual. (Code Sec. 457A(d)(1)) A nonqualified entity is: (1) any foreign corporation unless substantially all of its income is either effectively connected with the conduct of a trade or business in the U.S. or subject to a comprehensive foreign income tax; and (2) any partnership (either domestic or foreign), unless substantially all of its income is allocated to persons other than foreign persons for whom that income isn't

---

28. ¶H-3200.72 *et seq.*; ¶409A4.01; TD ¶135,515
29. ¶H-3200.18 *et seq.*; ¶409A4.01; TD ¶135,507
30. ¶H-3233; ¶409A4.20; TD ¶135,507

31. ¶H-2503.2
32. ¶H-3401; ¶457A4; TD ¶135,801

subject to a comprehensive foreign income tax (as defined in Code Sec. 457A(d)(2)); or organizations that are exempt from U.S. income tax. (Code Sec. 457A(b))

A NQDC plan is generally one described in Code Sec. 409A(d) (see ¶1277), except that it includes any plan that provides a right to compensation based on the appreciation in value of a specified number of equity units of the service recipient (e.g., stock appreciation rights (SARs)). Compensation (other than that based on gain on an investment asset) isn't treated as deferred if the service provider receives payment not later than 12 months after the end of the service recipient's tax year during which the right to the payment of the compensation is no longer subject to a substantial risk of forfeiture. (Code Sec. 457A(d)(3)) For foreign corporations with income that is effectively connected with the conduct of a U.S. trade or business, Code Sec. 457A doesn't apply to compensation that the corporation could have deducted against its effectively connected income if it had been paid in cash on the date that it ceased to be subject to a substantial risk of forfeiture. (Code Sec. 457A(d)(4)) Code Sec. 457A doesn't apply to a NQDC plan if the compensation is: (a) payable to an employee of a domestic subsidiary of the entity and (b) reasonably expected to be deductible by that subsidiary under Code Sec. 404(a)(5) (¶1539) when it is includible in the employee's income.[33]

If an amount of compensation is not determinable when it is otherwise includible in income under Code Sec. 457A, it is taken into account when it becomes determinable, subject to an additional 20% tax and an interest charge at the Code Sec. 6621 underpayment rate plus one percentage point, from the tax year first deferred or, if later, the first tax year not subject to a substantial risk of forfeiture. (Code Sec. 457A(c)) An amount isn't determinable if, at the time it is no longer subject to a substantial risk of forfeiture, it varies depending on the satisfaction of an objective condition.[34]

To the extent provided in regs, if compensation is determined solely by reference to the amount of gain recognized on the disposition of an investment asset, that compensation is treated as subject to a substantial risk of forfeiture until the date of the disposition. An investment asset is any single asset, other than an investment fund or similar entity, that's acquired directly by an investment fund or similar entity for which neither the entity nor any person related participates in the active management of that asset (or if that asset is an interest in an entity, in the active management of the activities of the entity), and substantially all of any gain on the disposition of that asset (other than the NQDC) is allocated to investors in the entity. (Code Sec. 457A(d)(1))

Inclusion of pre-2009 amounts. For a deferred amount to which Code Sec. 457A doesn't apply solely because it's attributable to services performed before 2009, to the extent not includible in gross income in a tax year beginning before 2018, it is includible in the later of (1) the last tax year beginning before 2018; or (2) the tax year in which there is no substantial risk of forfeiture of the rights to the compensation. (Sec. 801(d)(2) of Division C, P.L. 110-343, 10/3/2008) Earnings on deferred amounts attributable to services performed before 2009, are subject to Code Sec. 457A only to the extent that the amounts to which the earnings relate are subject to Code Sec. 457A. (§801(d) EESA, DivC, PL 110-343, 10/3/2008)[35]

¶ 1280   Social Security, Unemployment and Certain Disability Payments. ▰▰▰

Social security benefits may be partly taxable. Unemployment benefits are fully taxable. Payments under military and government disability pensions may be excludible from income.

For voluntary withholding on social security and certain other federal payments, and on unemployment compensation payments, see ¶3009.

---

33. ¶H-3401; ¶457A4; TD ¶135,801
34. ¶H-3421; ¶457A4; TD ¶135,814.1

35. ¶H-3401; ¶457A4; TD ¶135,801

¶ 1281 Social security payments—the Tier I and Tier II taxes.

A taxpayer whose "provisional income" —i.e., modified adjusted gross income (modified AGI, see below) plus one half of the social security benefits (including Tier 1 Railroad Retirement benefits) received—for a tax year exceeds either of two threshold amounts is taxed on a portion of social security benefits received that year, as follows:

Tier I: If provisional income exceeds a "base amount," include in gross income the *lesser* of:

. . . 50% of the social security benefits received that year; (Code Sec. 86(a)(1)(A)) or

. . . 50% of the excess of provisional income over the "base amount." (Code Sec. 86(a)(1)(B))[36]

"Modified AGI" means AGI: (1) determined without regard to the social security benefits; the deduction for qualified education loan interest (¶2225); the pre-2010 deduction for higher-education expenses (¶2224); the exclusions for foreign earned income and housing costs (¶4612 *et seq.*), savings bond proceeds for education expenses (¶2220), employer-provided adoption assistance (¶1256), and income from sources within U.S. possessions and Puerto Rico, and (2) increased by the amount of tax-exempt interest received or accrued by taxpayer during the tax year. (Code Sec. 86(b)(2))[37]

The "base amount" is $32,000 for married individuals filing a joint return; zero for a married individual filing a separate return who doesn't live apart from his spouse for the entire tax year; and $25,000 for all other individuals (Code Sec. 86(c)(1)), such as those filing as single, head of household or qualifying widow(er).[38]

illustration: G's modified AGI for the tax year consists of pension income of $15,000 and $3,000 of taxable interest and dividends. His social security benefit is $12,000. He's married and files a joint return. His wife has no income. The sum of their modified AGI ($18,000) plus one-half of his social security benefit ($6,000) is $24,000. This is less than their base amount ($32,000), so no part of his social security benefit is taxable.

Tier II: If provisional income exceeds an "adjusted base amount," include in gross income the *lesser* of:

. . . 85% of the social security benefits received that year; or

. . . the sum of: (a) the amount included under the above 50% rule or, if less, one-half of the difference between taxpayer's "adjusted base amount" and "base amount," plus (b) 85% of the excess of provisional income over the "adjusted base amount." (Code Sec. 86(a)(2))

The "adjusted base amount" is $44,000 for married individuals filing jointly; zero for a married individual filing separately who doesn't live apart from his spouse for the entire tax year); and $34,000 for all other individuals. (Code Sec. 86(c)(2))

caution: Any spike in income, e.g., from the sale of stock or a mutual fund, or a retirement plan distribution, may subject a taxpayer to an unexpected tax on his social security benefits, if the extra income causes him to exceed his base or adjusted base amount.

Benefits a taxpayer repays during a tax year reduce the benefits taxed that year, whether the repayment is for overpayments received that repayment year or any earlier year. (Code Sec. 86(d)(2)(A))[39]

If any portion of a lump-sum social security benefit received during a tax year is attributable to an earlier year, the taxpayer can elect (write "LSE" on the return) to include in gross income with respect to that portion, the sum of the increases in gross income that would have resulted had the portion been paid in the earlier year. (Code Sec. 86(e)(1))[40]

36. ¶J-1456; ¶864.04; TD ¶146,001
37. ¶J-1459; ¶864.02; TD ¶146,004
38. ¶J-1457; ¶864.03; TD ¶146,002

39. ¶J-1467; ¶864.05; TD ¶146,011
40. ¶J-1469; ¶864.08; TD ¶146,012

¶ 1282   Railroad Retirement Act benefits other than Tier 1 benefits.

Railroad Retirement Act benefits (other than Tier 1 benefits, see ¶1281) are treated as benefits provided under an employer plan that meets the requirements of Code Sec. 401(a) (a "qualified plan," see ¶4319 et seq.). (Code Sec. 72(r)(1), Code Sec. 72(r)(3)) Lump-sum termination (early retirement) payments have been held to be taxable under these rules.[41]

¶ 1283   Unemployment compensation.

Unemployment compensation (reported to recipients on Form 1099-G) is fully taxable. (Code Sec. 85(a)) (Up to $2,400 of unemployment compensation benefits received in 2009 was excluded.) (Code Sec. 85(c)) Unemployment compensation includes any amount received under a law of the U.S. or a state that's in the nature of unemployment compensation. (Code Sec. 85(b)) It also includes disability benefits paid under federal or state law as a substitute for unemployment benefits to those who are ineligible for unemployment benefits because they're disabled.[42]

¶ 1284   Unemployment benefits paid by employers.

Unemployment benefits (not described at ¶1283) paid directly by an employer are includible in the employee's income. Amounts received by an employee from an employer under a "guaranteed annual wage plan" during periods of unemployment are taxable as wages.[43]

¶ 1285   Strike and lockout benefits.

Strike and lockout benefits paid to an employee by a union, from union dues, including both cash and the fair market value of goods received, are included in the employee's income unless the facts clearly show they're intended as a gift. To be excluded, at a minimum, the union must inquire into the recipient's personal needs and make payments accordingly.[44]

¶ 1286   Certain military and government disability pensions.

Eligible members of the armed forces of any country, the National Oceanic and Atmospheric Administration, or the Public Health Service, and individuals who receive a disability annuity under section 808 of the Foreign Service Act of 1980, exclude from gross income amounts received as pension, annuity or similar allowance for personal injuries or sickness resulting from active service. Those eligible are primarily individuals with combat-related injuries or sickness or entitled to disability compensation from the Department of Veterans Affairs. (Code Sec. 104(a)(4))[45] While armed forces retirement pay based on length of service is taxable, that pay is excludible to the extent it could be received as a disability pension.[46]

¶ 1287   Dividends.

When a corporation distributes its earnings to its shareholders, the distribution is usually a dividend. If the dividend is "qualified" it is taxable at rates that apply to net capital gain; otherwise it is taxable as ordinary income. But not all corporate distributions are dividends. And some transactions that don't appear to be dividends may be taxed as constructive dividends.

For stock redemptions, see ¶3526 et seq. For liquidations, see ¶3574 et seq.

---

41. ¶J-1471; ¶724.26; TD ¶146,014
42. ¶H-3007 et seq.; ¶854.01; TD ¶132,506
43. ¶H-3005; ¶854.01; TD ¶132,501

44. ¶H-3009; TD ¶132,509
45. ¶H-3120; ¶s 614.041, 1044.04; TD ¶138,020
46. ¶H-3123; ¶s 614.040, 1044.04; TD ¶138,023

¶ 1288 How dividends are taxed to shareholders.

Dividends (defined at ¶1289) are taxable to the person who has the present, enforceable right to receive them, whether or not he's the owner of the underlying stock.[47] Dividends received by an agent are taxable to his principal.[48] If the stock is sold before a dividend is declared and paid, or between the declaration and record (or "ex dividend") dates, the dividends are taxed to the buyer. Dividends on stock sold on or after the record date are taxed to the seller. (Reg § 1.61-9(c))[49]

Dividends are taxable in the year received or unqualifiedly made subject to the shareholder's demand. This applies to both cash and accrual shareholders. Thus, if a corporation pays a dividend on Dec. 30 last year, and the shareholder receives the check on Jan. 2 this year, the shareholder reports it on this year's return. (Reg § 1.301-1(b))[50] For RIC (mutual fund) dividends, see ¶1300. For REIT dividends, see ¶1301.

Dividends received before 2011 are taxed to shareholders at the rates that apply to net capital gain (i.e., 15% or 0%, see ¶2604) if they constitute "qualified dividend income" (¶1290) paid to noncorporate shareholders (Code Sec. 1(h)(11)) and otherwise at ordinary income rates, to the extent the distributing corporation has earnings and profits (E&P, ¶3522). (Code Sec. 301(c)(1))

caution: For sunset rule, see ¶1114.

The part of a distribution in excess of E&P is treated as a tax-free return of capital and is applied against (reduces) the shareholder's basis in the stock. (Code Sec. 301(c)(2)) Any remaining excess (once basis is reduced to zero) is treated as payment for the stock, i.e., as capital gain if the stock is a capital asset in the shareholder's hands. (Code Sec. 301(c)(3))[1]

¶ 1289 Dividend defined.

A dividend is a distribution of property by a corporation to its shareholders with respect to its stock, out of accumulated or current earnings and profits (E&P, see ¶3522). (Code Sec. 316(a)) The distribution must be made in the ordinary course of the corporation's business, but it may be extraordinary in amount. (Reg § 1.316-1(a)(1))[2]

A dividend needn't be proportionate[3] and needn't be formally declared.[4]

"Property" includes money, securities and any other property (except the corporation's own stock or rights to that stock, see ¶1297). (Code Sec. 317(a)) Property also includes any economic benefit the corporation gives its shareholders, in whatever form (Reg § 1.317-1), e.g., paying their debts (see ¶1291).[5]

¶ 1290 Qualified dividend income defined.

For dividends received before 2011, qualified dividend income is dividend income received from domestic corporations and qualified foreign corporations (U.S. possession corporations and corporations eligible for benefits of a comprehensive income tax treaty with the U.S. that includes an exchange of information program, but not passive foreign investment companies.) (Code Sec. 1(h)(11)(B)(i)) Dividends paid by other foreign corporations also are qualified if paid on stock or ADRs readily tradable on an established U.S. securities market. (Code Sec. 1(h)(11)(C))

caution: For sunset rule, see ¶1114.

47. ¶J-2401; ¶3014.05; TD ¶172,013
48. ¶J-2405; ¶3014.05; TD ¶172,014
49. ¶J-2406; ¶3014.05; TD ¶172,021
50. ¶J-2451; ¶s 3014.07, 4514.036; TD ¶172,005
1. ¶J-2350 *et seq.*; ¶3014; TD ¶172,001

2. ¶J-2356; ¶3164 *et seq.*; TD ¶171,001
3. ¶J-2366; ¶3014; TD ¶171,001
4. ¶J-2360; ¶3014.01; TD ¶171,001
5. ¶s J-2357, J-2365; ¶s 3014.01, 3174; TD ¶171,002

Qualified dividend income does not include: (1) dividends paid on stock unless the stock has been held for more than 60 days during the 121 day period beginning 60 days before the ex-dividend date (more than 90 days during the 181 day period beginning 90 days before the ex-dividend date for preferred stock dividends attributable to a period of more than 366 days) (Code Sec. 1(h)(11)(B)(iii)(I)); (2) dividends on stock to the extent that the taxpayer is under an obligation to make related payments with respect to positions in substantially similar or related property (Code Sec. 1(h)(11)(B)(iii)(II)); (3) any amount that the taxpayer elects to treat as investment income to support an investment interest deduction (Code Sec. 1(h)(11)(D)(i)) (see ¶1729); (4) dividends from corporations that for the distribution year or the preceding year are exempt from tax under Code Sec. 501 (see ¶4100) or Code Sec. 521 (exempt farmers' cooperatives, see ¶4206 *et seq.*) (Code Sec. 1(h)(11)(B)(ii)(I)); (5) dividends deductible under Code Sec. 591 by mutual savings banks (Code Sec. 1(h)(11)(B)(ii)(II)); and (6) dividends paid on employer securities owned by an employee stock ownership plan (ESOP), which are deductible under Code Sec. 404(k). (Code Sec. 1(h)(11)(B)(ii)(III))[6]

Qualified dividend income does not include payments in lieu of dividends (typically made to owners of stock that has been lent in connection with a short sale). However, if a payment in lieu of dividends is reported as dividend income on a Form 1099-DIV, the recipient may treat the payment for tax purposes as a dividend, and not as a payment in lieu of dividends, unless he knows, or has reason to know, of the actual character of the payment.[7]

Before 2011, if an individual, trust, or estate receives extraordinary dividends (within the meaning of Code Sec. 1059(c)) that are qualified dividend income, any loss on the dividend-paying stock is a long-term capital loss to the extent of the extraordinary dividends. (Code Sec. 1(h)(11)(D)(ii))[8]

⊘ caution: For sunset rule, see ¶1114.

For dividends from RICs, see ¶1300. For dividends from REITs, see ¶1301.

¶ 1291 Constructive or disguised dividends.

When a corporation pays excessive or unreasonably large amounts to a shareholder or a member of his family as salary (Reg § 1.162-7(b)(1)) or rent,[9] or for a purchase price,[10] the excess is a constructive dividend (assuming sufficient E&P, see ¶3522). Similarly, constructive dividends include a corporation's payments of a shareholder's debts[11] or personal expenses.[12] A dividend may also result without a direct payment to the shareholder, if the corporation makes a payment to a third party that's for the shareholder's benefit and made with respect to his stock.[13]

¶ 1292 Loan vs. dividend.

A shareholder may borrow money from the corporation with or without interest, and with or without security. If the agreement and the genuine intent (at withdrawal) is that the amount be repaid to the corporation, and there's persuasive evidence of both that intent *and* the shareholder's ability to carry it out, the amount received is treated as a loan (i.e., nontaxable), and not as a dividend[14] (unless a below-market interest rate is involved, see ¶1293).

¶ 1293 Dividends from below-market loans between corporation and shareholder.

For any below-market interest rate loan (¶1308) (directly or indirectly) between a corporation and a shareholder, the corporation/lender is treated as having paid a dividend, equal to the amount of the foregone interest, that's includible in the shareholder/borrower's income.

6. ¶I-5115; ¶14.085; TD ¶223,345
7. ¶I-5115.4; TD ¶223,349
8. ¶I-5104.1; ¶14.087; TD ¶223,304.1
9. ¶J-2726; ¶3014.09 *et seq.* TD ¶175,052
10. ¶J-2730; ¶3014.11; TD ¶175,044

11. ¶J-2749; ¶3014.14; TD ¶175,038
12. ¶J-2757; ¶3014.13; TD ¶175,007
13. ¶J-2700 *et seq.*; ¶3014.14; TD ¶175,002
14. ¶J-2707 *et seq.*; ¶3014.14; TD ¶175,014

De minimis ($10,000 or less) and certain other loans are excepted. (Code Sec. 7872(a))[15]

¶ 1294 Determining the amount of a dividend (cash and in-kind).

The amount of a dividend is the sum of the cash plus the fair market value (FMV), at distribution, of any other property received (Code Sec. 301(b)(1), Code Sec. 301(b)(3)), reduced (but not below zero) by the amount of any liability of the corporation that the shareholder assumes in connection with the distribution, or to which the property is subject. (Code Sec. 301(b)(2))[16] But the amount taxable as a dividend in kind can't exceed the distributing corporation's E&P (¶3522). (Reg § 1.316-1(a)(2))[17]

A dividend consisting of the corporation's obligations equals the FMV of the notes. (Reg § 1.301-1(d)) For stock dividends, see ¶1298.

These rules apply to both corporate (U.S. or foreign) and noncorporate shareholders[18] (but a corporate shareholder may get a dividends-received deduction, see ¶3306 *et seq.*), and to dividends from a foreign corporation to its U.S. corporate shareholder. (Code Sec. 301(b)(1))[19]

¶ 1295 Basis of distributed property to shareholder-distributee.

The basis to the shareholder (corporate or individual) for property received as a dividend (¶1289) is the property's fair market value at distribution (Code Sec. 301(d)), i.e., the amount treated as a dividend (see ¶1294), but without the reduction for liabilities.[20]

¶ 1296 Holding period for property received as a taxable dividend.

The shareholder's holding period for property received as a taxable dividend begins on the date of receipt (actual or constructive). (Code Sec. 1223(2))[21]

¶ 1297 Distributions of stock or rights to stock.

With certain exceptions (see ¶1298), a stock dividend—i.e., a corporation's distribution of its *own* stock, or rights (e.g., options or warrants) to buy its stock, that's made to shareholders with respect to their stock (i.e., not as compensation)—isn't taxable to the shareholder. (Code Sec. 305) But a corporation's distribution of stock, or rights to buy stock, in *another* corporation (even if affiliated) is a regular dividend in kind, taxed under the rules at ¶1288 *et seq.*[22]

Stock splits are treated as stock dividends if identical stock is distributed on stock held.[23]

For stock (rights) received in connection with corporate organizations, reorganizations or divisions, see ¶3554.

¶ 1298 Taxable stock (or rights) dividends.

Where a stock (or rights) dividend is taxable, the dividend amount is the fair market value (FMV) at distribution of the stock (rights), under the "regular" dividend-in-kind rules, see ¶1294.[24] Where the dividend is taxable because of a cash election, the "dividend" equals: (1) the cash received, for shareholders electing cash, and (2) the FMV of the stock (rights) at distribution, for those receiving stock (rights). (Reg § 1.305-1(b))[25]

These stock (or rights) dividends are *not* tax-free:

(1) A distribution in which *any* shareholder has the option to take cash or other property instead of the stock (or rights); (Code Sec. 305(b)(1); Reg § 1.305-2)[26]

15. ¶J-2721 *et seq.*; ¶78,724.16; TD ¶172,011
16. ¶J-2482; ¶3014.02; TD ¶173,503
17. ¶J-2361; ¶3164.01; TD ¶173,501
18. ¶J-2482; ¶s 3014, 3014.02
19. ¶3014.02
20. ¶P-5401; ¶3014.03; TD ¶217,501

21. ¶s I-8903, I-8918; TD ¶223,508
22. ¶J-2478; ¶3054.01; TD ¶174,009
23. ¶J-2501; ¶3054.02; TD ¶174,001
24. ¶J-2504, J-2506; ¶3054.02; TD ¶173,501
25. ¶J-2507; ¶3054.02; TD ¶174,006
26. ¶s J-2508 *et seq.*, J-2501; ¶3054.02; TD ¶174,017

(2) A "disproportionate" distribution that results in the receipt of property by some shareholders and, for others, an increase in their proportionate interests in the corporation's assets or earnings and profits; (Code Sec. 305(b)(2); Reg § 1.305-3)[27]

(3) A distribution that results in the receipt of preferred stock by some common shareholders and the receipt of common stock by others; (Code Sec. 305(b)(3); Reg § 1.305-4)[28]

(4) Any distributions on preferred stock, including a redemption premium treated as a distribution (for preferred stock issued after Oct. 9, '90, the premium is included as OID, see ¶1316 *et seq.*), *other than* an increase in the conversion ratio of convertible preferred stock made solely to take into account a stock dividend or stock split with respect to the stock into which the preferred is convertible; (Code Sec. 305(b)(4); Reg § 1.305-5)[29]

(5) Any distribution of convertible preferred stock unless IRS is satisfied it won't have the result in (2), above; (Code Sec. 305(b)(5); Reg § 1.305-6)[30]

(6) A constructive stock distribution, e.g., a change in conversion ratio or redemption price, or a redemption premium (difference between redemption price and issue price). (Code Sec. 305(c); Reg § 1.305-5(b), Reg § 1.305-7)[31]

¶ 1299 Cash for fractional shares.

Where a corporation's purpose in distributing cash (instead of scrip or fractional shares) in a distribution that otherwise qualifies as a nontaxable stock dividend (¶1297) is to save trouble, expense and inconvenience, and not to give any shareholder(s) an increased interest, the distribution is treated as if the fractional shares had been issued and then redeemed by the corporation. (Reg § 1.305-3(c)) The cash received is treated as an amount realized on the sale of a fractional share. Gain or loss is the cash received minus the basis of the share sold. (Reg § 1.305-3(c)(2))[32]

¶ 1300 Dividends from regulated investment companies (mutual funds).

Ordinary dividends a regulated investment company (RIC or mutual fund, see ¶4201) distributes to its shareholders generally are taxed to them just like other corporate dividends (¶1288, ¶1294). (Code Sec. 852; Reg § 1.852-4(a))[33] However, if the amount of dividends eligible for qualified dividend income treatment (i.e., taxable at the capital gain rates) (¶1288) received by a RIC for a tax year is less than 95% of its gross income (as specially computed) then only the amount of qualified dividend income received by the RIC for the tax year may be distributed to its shareholders as qualified dividend income. (Code Sec. 1(h)(11)(D)(iii), Code Sec. 854(b)(1)(B)) But capital gain dividends, which the RIC need not actually distribute, result in capital gain income (see ¶4201) (Code Sec. 852(b)(3)(D)),[34] and exempt-interest dividends are treated as tax-exempt interest (¶1333). (Code Sec. 852(b)(5)(B))[35] Capital gain dividends are not treated as qualified dividend income (¶1290). (Code Sec. 854(a)) The amount of RIC dividends that are qualifying dividend income must be reported to RIC shareholders within 60 days after the close of the RIC's tax year. (Code Sec. 854(b)(2))

caution: For sunset rule, see ¶1114.

A dividend the RIC pays after the close of its tax year generally is treated as received by the shareholder in the year actually paid, even if the RIC elects to treat it as paid in the preceding year (see ¶4203). (Code Sec. 855(b))[36] But dividends the RIC declares in Oct., Nov. or Dec. are treated as received by the shareholder on Dec. 31 if the RIC actually pays them during the following Jan. (Code Sec. 852(b)(7))[37]

27. ¶J-2510 *et seq.*; ¶3054.02; TD ¶174,020
28. ¶J-2515; ¶3054.02; TD ¶174,024
29. ¶J-2501, J-2516 *et seq.*; ¶3054.02; TD ¶174,025
30. ¶s J-2501, J-2526; ¶3054.02; TD ¶174,027
31. ¶s J-2501, J-2527 *et seq.*; ¶3054.02; TD ¶174,013
32. ¶J-2514; ¶3054.01; TD ¶174,014

33. ¶E-6150 *et seq.*; ¶8524.02; TD ¶172,005
34. ¶E-6152; ¶8524.02
35. ¶E-6160; ¶8524.02
36. ¶E-6201; ¶8554.01
37. ¶E-6202; ¶8554.01; TD ¶172,005

caution: Since dividends paid in Jan. may have to be picked up in the preceding year's income, that year's Form 1099, and not the RIC's monthly statements, should be used to determine the dividends to report for that year.

A RIC can designate a dividend as a capital gain dividend and can make additional designations of its capital gain dividend distributions corresponding to the various maximum rates at which net capital gains may be taxed (¶2603). Limitations apply, e.g., the additional designation cannot exceed the maximum distributable amount in that class.[38]

Qualified dividend income is calculated without any reduction for expenses. In addition, where a RIC has several types of income that must be specially designated, the RIC may designate the maximum amount that may be designated in each category even if the aggregate of all the amounts so designated exceeds the total amount of the RIC's dividend distributions. Each shareholder may then apply these designations to the dividends he receives up to his share of these amounts, even though his designations differ from the designations applied by other shareholders.[39]

¶ 1301 Dividends from real estate investment trusts (REITs).

Real estate investment trusts (REITs, see ¶4202) distribute ordinary dividends and capital gain dividends which (as with RICs, see ¶1300) the beneficiaries or shareholders (investors) treat, respectively, as ordinary income (except there's no dividends-received deduction) (Code Sec. 857(c)) and capital gain. (Code Sec. 857(b)(3)(B))[40] The only REIT dividends that are eligible for qualified dividend income treatment (¶1288) are those that the REIT received as qualified dividend income, such as dividends paid to the REIT from a taxable REIT subsidiary. (Code Sec. 1(h)(11)(D)(iii), Code Sec. 857(c)(2)) For undistributed capital gains of REITs, see ¶4202. A deficiency dividend the REIT pays for any year is taxed to the shareholder in the year it's paid, not the year *for which* it's paid. (Reg § 1.860-2(a)(3)(i))[41] But any dividend declared by the REIT in Oct., Nov. or Dec. and payable to shareholders of record on a specified date in that month is considered received by the shareholder on Dec. 31 if the REIT actually pays it the next Jan. (Code Sec. 857(b)(8)(A))[42]

caution: For sunset rule, see ¶1114.

REITs are subject to the same capital gain designation rules as RICs (see ¶1300).[43]

¶ 1302 Dividends to co-op patrons; patronage dividends.

Distributions made by a co-op (¶4206) on its stock or other proprietary interests are taxed under the "regular" dividend rules (see ¶1294), but the dividends-received deduction doesn't apply if the co-op is exempt. (Code Sec. 246(a)(1))[44]

Patronage dividends and per-unit retain allocations (¶4207) received in money are included in income by the patron in the year received. Qualified written notices of allocation and qualified per-unit retain certificates (¶4207) are included in income at their stated dollar amount when received. Other property (but not nonqualified allocations or nonqualified per-unit retain certificates) is included at its fair market value when received. (Code Sec. 1385)[45]

But the amount of any patronage dividend isn't included in income to the extent it is: (1) properly taken into account as an adjustment to basis of property, or (2) attributable to personal, living or family items. (Code Sec. 1385(b))[46]

38. ¶E-6153.1; ¶8524.02; TD ¶173,000.1
39. ¶E-6163.1
40. ¶E-6616; ¶8574.02; TD ¶173,006
41. ¶E-6304; ¶8604
42. ¶E-6704; ¶8574.02; TD ¶172,005

43. ¶E-6617.1; ¶8574.02; TD ¶173,000.1
44. ¶J-2608; ¶2434.04; TD ¶600,513
45. ¶J-2609 *et seq.*; ¶13,814.13; TD ¶171,042
46. ¶J-2612; ¶13,814.13

¶ 1303   Interest Income. ■■■■■■■■■■■■■■■■■■■■■■■■■■■■

Whatever the name given to the amounts or the form of the transaction, the receipt or accrual of interest is taxable as ordinary income, unless specifically exempt.

¶ 1304   Taxation of interest.

Unless specifically exempt, any interest received by or credited to a taxpayer is taxable as ordinary income. (Code Sec. 61(a)(4); Reg § 1.61-7(a))[47] The interest is taxable even if it's usurious unless applicable state law automatically converts the illegal portion into a payment of principal. (Reg § 1.61-7(a))[48]

¶ 1305   What is interest?

Interest is the price paid for the use of another's money or for the right to defer payment of money owed to another, regardless of the form of the transaction.[49] Interest generally includes the FMV of gifts or services received for opening or adding to accounts in financial institutions, but not if it's a de minimis premium (for a deposit of less than $5,000, the premium costs the bank $10 or less; for a deposit of $5,000 or more, it costs $20 or less).[50]

To be interest, generally a payment must be made with respect to a bona fide debt.[1] But other "interest" payments imposed by law, e.g., on judgments, tax refunds, installment sales, etc., are also interest.[2] And IRS may use the Code Sec. 482 allocation rules (¶2858) to "create" interest.[3]

¶ 1306   Interest on defaulted mortgage.

Amounts paid to a mortgagee as a result of the sale of property on foreclosure (or voluntary conveyance in lieu of foreclosure) of the mortgage, that represent accrued interest due on the mortgage, are taxable interest.[4] For mortgagee's gain or loss, see ¶1788.

For mortgage interest recipient's reporting requirements, see ¶4744.

¶ 1307   "Points" and other loan-related fees.

Payments made to a bank or other lender to get a loan are interest, to the extent they are made for the use or forbearance of money rather than for services rendered. Thus, "points" (i.e., charges connected with mortgages that the borrower pays in addition to the stated interest) are interest, while commitment and service fees (for escrow, recording, credit inspection, appraisal) aren't.[5] For recipient's reporting requirements, see ¶4744.

¶ 1308   Below-market interest-rate loans.

The forgone interest on a "below-market" loan is taxed to the lender as interest income. (Code Sec. 7872)[6] A "below-market" loan is:

. . . *a demand loan* where interest is payable on the loan at a rate less than the applicable federal rate (AFR, see ¶1312), (Code Sec. 7872(e)(1)(A))[7] or

. . . *a term loan* where the amount loaned exceeds the present value of all payments due under the loan. (Code Sec. 7872(e)(1)(B))[8]

For a below-market demand loan, the "interest" for any period is the excess of: (1) the

47. ¶J-2801; ¶614.067; TD ¶151,001
48. ¶J-2814; ¶614.068; TD ¶151,010
49. ¶J-2802 *et seq.*; TD ¶151,002
50. ¶J-2820; TD ¶811,513
1. ¶J-2803; ¶614.068; TD ¶151,003
2. ¶J-2834 *et seq.*; ¶614.068 *et seq.*; TD ¶151,030

3. ¶J-2817; ¶s 4824, 614.148;
4. ¶J-2819; ¶614.083
5. ¶J-2818; ¶1634.005; TD ¶151,013
6. ¶J-2900; ¶78,724 *et seq.*; TD ¶151,504
7. ¶J-2939 *et seq.*; ¶78,724.04; TD ¶155,010
8. ¶J-2947 *et seq.*; ¶78,724.06; TD ¶155,015

interest that would have been payable on the loan if it accrued annually at the AFR, over (2) any interest payable on the loan and properly allocable to the period. (Code Sec. 7872(e)(2)) For below-market term loans, the "interest" (treated as original issue discount (OID), see ¶1315 *et seq.*) is the excess of: (a) the amount loaned, over (b) the present value of all payments required to be made under the loan. (Code Sec. 7872(b)(2)(B))[9]

These rules don't apply to certain de minimis ($10,000 or less) loans (Code Sec. 7872(c)(2), Code Sec. 7872(c)(3)),[10] amounts treated as "unstated interest" (see ¶1309) (Code Sec. 7872(f)(8)),[11] or certain loans under a written continuing care contract to a qualified continuing care facility. (Code Sec. 7872(g))[12]

¶ 1309 Unstated (imputed) interest on deferred payment sales.

For certain deferred payment or installment sales (¶1310) where the sales contract fails to provide for interest at a minimum rate specified by the Code or by IRS, part of the payments received is treated as interest ("unstated interest") that's taxable to the seller despite any contrary intention of the parties. (Code Sec. 483)[13]

¶ 1310 Payments subject to unstated interest rules.

With certain exceptions (¶1314), the unstated interest rules (¶1309) apply to any payment where *all* the following requirements are met:

(1) The payment must be made on account of the sale or exchange of property.

(2) The payment must be part of the sales price under the contract.

(3) The "sales price" (determined at the time of sale) must be more than $3,000. "Sales price" includes the amount of any down payment, any liability encumbering the property and any amount treated as unstated interest under these rules, but not any *stated* interest payments.

(4) The payment must be due (under the contract) more than six months after the date of the sale or exchange.

(5) At least one payment under the contract must be due more than one year after the date of the sale or exchange.

(6) There must be total unstated interest (¶1311) under the contract. (Code Sec. 483(c)(1), Code Sec. 483(d)(2); Reg § 1.483-1(b)(1))[14]

A debt instrument of the buyer given in exchange for property isn't itself treated as a payment. Rather, any payment due under the instrument is treated as due under the sales contract. (Code Sec. 483(c)(2))[15]

¶ 1311 What is "total unstated interest"?

There's "total unstated interest" under the contract (see ¶1310) if the sum of all payments (other than *stated* interest payments) due under it more than six months after the date of the sale or exchange exceeds the sum of: (1) the present value of all those payments, plus (2) the present value of all interest payments due under the contract (regardless of when due). The total unstated interest equals the excess, if any. (Code Sec. 483(b))[16]

The present value of a payment is determined as of the date of the sale, etc., using a "test" rate prescribed by IRS. This test rate, which depends on the type of property sold, is a discount rate equal to the then applicable federal rate (AFR, see ¶1312), compounded semiannually. (Code Sec. 483(b), Code Sec. 1274(b)(2))[17]

9. ¶s J-2902, J-2904; ¶s 78,724.04, 78,724.06; TD ¶155,004
10. ¶J-2961; ¶78,724.12 *et seq.*; TD ¶155,027
11. ¶J-2918; ¶78,724.20; TD ¶155,021
12. ¶J-2988; ¶78,724.20; TD ¶155,056
13. ¶J-3750 *et seq.*; ¶4834; TD ¶152,001
14. ¶J-3800 *et seq.*; ¶s 4834, 4834.01; TD ¶152,221
15. ¶J-3806; ¶4834.01; TD ¶152,226
16. ¶J-3814; ¶4834; TD ¶152,233
17. ¶J-3814 *et seq.*; ¶4834.01; TD ¶152,234

These discount rates are used to determine the amount of unstated interest the seller must report as interest income:

(1) For sales or exchanges of property (not described below), the discount rate may not exceed 9% compounded semiannually if the stated principal amount of the debt instrument doesn't exceed a specified amount, as adjusted for inflation ($5,115,100 for sales and exchanges in 2010). If the stated principal amount is over the specified amount, the discount rate is 100% of the AFR, compounded semiannually. (Code Sec. 483(b), Code Sec. 1274A(a))[18]

(2) For sales or exchanges of new investment credit property, the discount rate is 100% of the AFR, compounded semiannually. (Code Sec. 483(b))[19]

(3) For sales or exchanges where part of the sold property is leased back to the seller, the discount rate is 110% of the AFR, compounded semiannually. (Code Sec. 1274(e))[20]

(4) For sales, etc., of land between family members where the aggregate sales price for all land sales between those individuals in that calendar year isn't over $500,000, the discount rate can't exceed 6% compounded semiannually. (Code Sec. 483(e))[21]

¶ 1312 Applicable federal rate (AFR).

IRS issues monthly tables (reproduced at ¶1116 for the most recent 12 months available as we went to press) showing the AFRs to be used in determining whether there is unstated interest (¶1311) (or OID in some cases, see ¶1320) on a sale or exchange of property, and if there is, the amount of that unstated interest.[22] The rate to use on a particular sale or exchange depends on the term over which the payments are to be made. If the term is three years or less, use the short-term rate (from the tables). If it's more than three years but not more than nine years, use the mid-term rate. If it's more than nine years, use the long-term rate. (Code Sec. 1274(d)(1)(A))[23] The rate to use also depends on when the contract was made. (Code Sec. 1274(d)(2))[24]

¶ 1313 Allocating total unstated interest.

For any payment subject to the unstated interest rules (¶1309), that part of the total unstated interest under the contract (¶1311) which is properly allocable to that payment is treated as interest. This "interest" amount is determined in a manner consistent with the method used to compute the amount of currently includible OID (¶1323) (Code Sec. 483(a)) so that unstated interest income must be reported on an economic accrual basis.[25]

¶ 1314 Exceptions to unstated interest rules.

Even if all the requirements listed at ¶1310 are met, there's no unstated interest on:

(1) sales or exchanges where the sales price (¶1310) is $3,000 or less; (Code Sec. 483(d)(2))[26]

(2) any debt instrument (given in connection with a sale or exchange of property) whose issue price is figured under the OID rules (¶1315 et seq.); (Code Sec. 483(d)(1))[27]

(3) any amount received on the sale of patent rights described in Code Sec. 1235(a) that's contingent on the productivity, use or disposition of those rights; (Code Sec. 483(d)(4))[28]

(4) amounts received under certain annuity contracts;[29]

(5) lump-sum divorce payments and property settlements payable in installments;[30] and

---

18. ¶J-3816 et seq.; ¶4834.01; TD ¶152,234
19. ¶J-3818; ¶4834.01; TD ¶152,234
20. ¶J-3819; ¶12,714.03; TD ¶152,234
21. ¶J-3820; ¶4834.01; TD ¶152,234
22. ¶J-4181 et seq.; ¶4834.01; TD ¶153,030
23. ¶J-4181; ¶4834.01; TD ¶153,030
24. ¶J-4190 et seq.; ¶12,714.03; TD ¶153,030

25. ¶J-3951; ¶s 4834.01, 4464.01; TD ¶152,010
26. ¶J-3901; ¶4834.01; TD ¶152,005
27. ¶J-3902; ¶4834.01; TD ¶152,005
28. ¶J-3903; ¶4834.01; TD ¶152,005
29. ¶J-3905; ¶4834.01; TD ¶152,005
30. ¶J-3906; ¶4834.01; TD ¶152,005

(6) certain acquisitions of amortizable section 197 intangibles (¶1975). (Reg § 1.197-2(f)(3)(iv)(B)(3))[31]

(7) payments under options to buy or sell property (Reg § 1.483-1(c)(3)(v)).[32]

(8) assumptions of debt in connection with sales or exchanges and acquisitions of property subject to debt (Code Sec. 1274(c)(4)).[33]

(9) below-market interest rate loans (¶1308) (Code Sec. 7872(f)(8)).[34]

¶ 1315 Current inclusion of original issue discount (OID) as interest income.

If a debt instrument is acquired from an issuer for an amount less than what the issuer will have to pay the holder when the instrument matures, the difference is original issue discount (OID, see ¶1316). No matter which method of accounting the holder uses, he must report part of the OID as interest income in each tax year the debt instrument is held (¶1323), even though the OID won't be paid until maturity. (Code Sec. 1272)[35]

The OID current inclusion rules apply to all debt instruments issued with OID (Code Sec. 1272)[36] *other than:*

(1) Tax-exempt obligations (unless stripped). (Code Sec. 1272(a)(2)(A), Code Sec. 1286(d))

(2) U.S. savings bonds. (Code Sec. 1272(a)(2)(B))

(3) Short-term obligations (i.e., with a fixed maturity date not more than one year from the date of issue). (Code Sec. 1272(a)(2)(C))

(4) Debt instruments issued by natural persons before Mar. 2, '84. (Code Sec. 1272(a)(2)(D))

(5) Certain nonbusiness loans of $10,000 or less between natural persons. (Code Sec. 1272(a)(2)(E))[37]

"Debt instruments" are bonds, debentures, notes, certificates or other instruments or contractual arrangements that are "indebtedness" under tax law principles, e.g., certificates of deposit or loans (Code Sec. 1275(a)(1); Reg § 1.1275-1(d)),[38] and REMIC interests and some similar instruments where payment may be accelerated. (Code Sec. 1272(a)(6)(C))[39] A debt instrument doesn't include a life annuity, or certain annuities issued by insurance companies. (Code Sec. 1275(a)(1)(B); Reg § 1.1275-1(j))[40]

The OID current inclusion rules also apply to bonds, and preferred stock bought (after being stripped) after Apr. 30, '93. (Code Sec. 305(e), Code Sec. 1286(a))[41]

The OID current inclusion rules don't apply to a holder who buys a debt instrument at a premium (Code Sec. 1272(c)(1))[42] (except as described at ¶1325).

¶ 1316 OID defined.

OID (see ¶1315) is the excess (if any) of: (1) a debt instrument's stated redemption price at maturity (¶1318) over (2) its issue price (¶1319). (Code Sec. 1273(a)(1))[43]

But the OID is treated as zero if that excess is less than: 0.25% of the stated redemption price at maturity, times the number of years to maturity. (Code Sec. 1273(a)(3)) In this case, all stated interest (including amounts that would otherwise be OID) is treated as "qualified stated interest" (¶1317). (Reg § 1.1273-1(d)(1))[44]

31. ¶J-3903.1
32. ¶J-3904; ¶4834.01
33. ¶J-3909; ¶4834.01
34. ¶J-3910; ¶4834.01
35. ¶J-4000 et seq.; ¶12,714 et seq.; TD ¶153,001
36. ¶J-4051; ¶s 12,714, 12,714.01; TD ¶153,003
37. ¶J-4060 et seq.; ¶12,714.01; TD ¶153,003
38. ¶s J-4054, J-4055; ¶12,714; TD ¶153,002
39. ¶J-4343; ¶12,714.01; TD ¶153,010
40. ¶J-4057; ¶12,714; TD ¶153,002
41. ¶J-4400 et seq.; ¶12,864; TD ¶153,501
42. ¶J-4005; ¶12714.01; TD ¶153,001
43. ¶J-4100 et seq.; ¶12,714; TD ¶153,004
44. ¶J-4102; ¶12,714.01; TD ¶153,004

¶ 1317   "Qualified stated interest" defined.

"Qualified stated interest" is stated interest that's unconditionally payable in cash or property (other than the issuer's debt instruments), or will be constructively received under Code Sec. 451 (¶2822) at least annually at a single fixed rate. (Reg § 1.1273-1(c)(1))[45]

¶ 1318   Stated redemption price at maturity.

For OID purposes, an instrument's *stated redemption price at maturity* is usually its face value. It includes interest payable at maturity *but not* interest payable at a fixed rate at periodic intervals of a year or less during the entire term of the instrument (Code Sec. 1273(a)(2)), or "qualified stated interest" (¶1317). (Reg § 1.1273-1(b))[46]

¶ 1319   Issue price.

A debt instrument's issue price depends on whether it's issued for cash or property, and if issued for property, whether the instrument or property is publicly traded, as follows:

. . . For a *publicly offered debt instrument issued for money,* the issue price is the initial offering price to the public at which a substantial amount of the instruments is sold. (Code Sec. 1273(b)(1); Reg § 1.1232-3(b)(2)(i))[47]

. . . For a *privately offered debt instrument issued for money,* the issue price is the price paid by the first buyer of that instrument (Code Sec. 1273(b)(2)) or the first price at which a substantial amount of instruments in the issue is sold. (Reg § 1.1273-2(a)(1))[48]

. . . For a *debt instrument issued for property where there's public trading,* the issue price is the instrument's fair market value (FMV) as of the issue date, if it's publicly traded. If the instrument itself isn't publicly traded but is issued for property (i.e., stock or securities) that is, its issue price is the FMV of that property. (Code Sec. 1273(b)(3); Reg § 1.1232-3(b)(2)(iii), Reg § 1.1273-2(b)(1))[49]

. . . For a *nonpublicly traded debt instrument issued for nonpublicly traded property,* the issue price is its stated principal amount (total payments due under the instrument, less stated interest payments or payments designated as interest or points) if the instrument pays adequate stated interest (¶1320), or its imputed principal amount (¶1321) if it doesn't. (Code Sec. 1274(a); Reg § 1.1274-2(b)(1))[50] For exceptions, see ¶1322.

. . . For *Treasury securities,* the issue price is the average price of the securities sold (price sold at auction, if sold before Mar. 13, 2001). (Reg § 1.1275-2(d))[1]

. . . For a *debt instrument that provides for one or more contingent payments,* issued after Aug. 12, '96, the issue price is the lesser of the instrument's noncontingent principal payments, or the sum of the present values of the noncontingent payments. (Reg § 1.1274-2(g))[2]

. . . For a *tax-exempt obligation* issued after Aug. 12, '96, the issue price is (a) the greater of the obligation's FMV or its stated principal amount, or (b) for contingent obligations, its FMV. (Reg § 1.1274-2(j))[3]

The issue price of a debt instrument issued in a potentially abusive situation (e.g., a tax shelter) is the FMV of the property received in exchange for the instrument, reduced by the sum of the money plus the FMV of any property or rights (other than the instrument) that are given for the sale or exchange. (Reg § 1.1274-2(b)(3))[4]

---

45. ¶J-4112; TD ¶153,006
46. ¶J-4111; TD ¶153,005
47. ¶J-4130; TD ¶153,021
48. ¶J-4138; TD ¶153,023
49. ¶J-4140; TD ¶153,024

50. ¶J-4151; ¶12,714.03; TD ¶153,025
1. ¶J-4131; TD ¶153,022
2. ¶J-4151.2; ¶12,714.037; TD ¶153,026
3. ¶J-4151.3, J-4151.4
4. ¶J-4151.5; TD ¶152,235

¶ 1320 Adequate stated interest.

There's adequate stated interest for a debt instrument if the sum of the present values (using the discount rate at ¶1311) of all payments of principal and interest due under it equals or exceeds its stated principal amount (¶1319) (Code Sec. 1274(c)(2)), or if the instrument has a single fixed rate of interest that's paid or compounded at least annually and is at least equal to the test rate. (Reg § 1.1274-2(c))[5]

¶ 1321 Imputed principal amount.

The imputed principal amount is the sum of the present values of all payments of principal and interest due under a debt instrument, computed as of the date of the sale or exchange using the discount rates at ¶1311. (Code Sec. 1274(b)(2); Reg § 1.1274-2(c)(1))[6]

The imputed principal amount of a variable rate debt instrument that provides for stated interest at a qualified floating rate(s) generally is determined by assuming that the instrument provides for a fixed rate of interest for each accrual period to which a qualified floating rate applies. (Reg § 1.1274-2(f)(1)(i))[7]

In a potentially abusive situation (e.g., tax shelter), the imputed principal amount of an instrument received in exchange for property is the property's fair market value, adjusted for other considerations in the transaction. (Code Sec. 1274(b)(3)(A); Reg § 1.1274-3(a))[8]

¶ 1322 Exceptions to OID rules for nonpublicly traded debt instruments.

The issue price of a nonpublicly traded debt instrument issued for nonpublicly traded property is its stated redemption price at maturity (so there's no OID, see ¶1316), instead of the amount determined under the rules at ¶1319, in these cases: (Code Sec. 1273(b)(4))[9]

(1) sales or exchanges involving total payments of $250,000 or less; (Code Sec. 1274(c)(3)(C))

(2) sales or exchanges by an individual of his principal residence; (Code Sec. 1274(c)(3)(B))

(3) sales or exchanges of certain farms where the sales price cannot exceed $1,000,000; (Code Sec. 1274(c)(3)(A))

(4) certain sales of patents; (Code Sec. 1274(c)(3)(E))

(5) certain transfers of land between family members where the total price for all land sales between them for the year is not more than $500,000; (Code Sec. 1274(c)(3)(F))

(6) sales or exchanges where, in exchange for property, a nonaccrual method buyer (other than a dealer) issues a "cash method debt instrument" —i.e., a debt instrument whose principal amount doesn't exceed a specified amount ($3,658,600 for sales and exchanges in 2010), if the "regular" issue price rules otherwise would apply *and* buyer and seller jointly elect cash method treatment for the instrument; (Code Sec. 1274A(c))[10]

(7) sales or exchanges of personal use property (to the issuer) that evidence a below-market loan (¶1308); (Reg § 1.1274-1(b)(3)(i))[11]

(8) transactions involving "demand" below-market loans; (Reg § 1.1274-1(b)(3)(ii))[12] or

(9) transfers between spouses or incident to divorce. (Reg § 1.1274-1(b)(3)(iii))[13]

> **RIA** *observation:* Even if there's no OID, there may be unstated interest (see ¶1309).

5. ¶J-4153 *et seq.*; ¶12,714.03; TD ¶153,027
6. ¶J-4154 *et seq.*; ¶12,714.03; TD ¶153,028
7. ¶J-4157
8. ¶J-4173 *et seq.*; ¶12,714.03; TD ¶153,029
9. ¶J-4196; ¶12,714.03; TD ¶153,031

10. ¶J-4207
11. ¶J-4202; ¶12,714.03; TD ¶153,031
12. ¶J-4203; ¶12,714.03; TD ¶153,031
13. ¶J-4204; ¶12,714.03; TD ¶153,031

¶ 1323   Determining amount of currently includible OID.

A holder of a debt instrument issued with OID (¶1316) who is required to include part of the OID in gross income currently must include in gross income for his tax year, an amount equal to the sum of the daily portions of the OID for each day he held the instrument during that year. (Code Sec. 1272(a)(1))[14] For accrual under the constant yield method, see ¶1324.

To determine the daily OID portion, allocate to each day in any "accrual period" (below) that day's ratable portion of the increase (during that period) in the instrument's adjusted issue price (below). This increase equals the excess of: (1) the adjusted issue price at the start of the accrual period times the yield to maturity (based on compounding at the end of each accrual period), over (2) the sum of the amounts payable as interest on the instrument during that accrual period. (Code Sec. 1272(a)(3))[15]

The adjusted issue price of a debt instrument at the start of any accrual period is the sum of its issue price (¶1319), plus all adjustments (i.e., OID inclusions) in that issue price for all earlier accrual periods. (Code Sec. 1272(a)(4))[16]

Accrual period generally means a six-month period (or shorter period from date of issuance) ending on a day in the calendar year corresponding to the debt instrument's maturity date, or a date six months before that date. (Code Sec. 1272(a)(5))[17]

For *inflation-indexed debt instruments,* OID is computed using the coupon bond method or the discount bond method (see ¶1335). (Reg § 1.1275-7(a))[18]

¶ 1324   Accrual of OID using constant yield method.

Under the constant yield method, the amount of OID includible in the holder's income for a tax year (¶1323) is determined as follows:

(1) Determine the instrument's yield to maturity. This is the discount rate that, when used to compute the present value of all payments under the instrument, produces an amount equal to the instrument's issue price. The yield must be constant over the instrument's term and must be calculated to at least two decimal places. (Reg § 1.1272-1(b)(1)(i))

(2) Determine the accrual period, which may be any length (based on any reasonable accounting convention), but can't exceed one year. Each scheduled payment must occur either on the first or last day of an accrual period. The simplest OID computation is where the accrual periods correspond to the intervals between payment dates set forth by the instrument. (Reg § 1.1272-1(b)(1)(ii))

(3) Determine the OID allocable to each accrual period. This is the instrument's adjusted issue price at the start of the accrual period, times the instrument's yield, less the "qualified stated interest" (¶1317) allocable to the period. (Reg § 1.1272-1(b)(1)(iii))

(4) Determine the daily portions of OID, by allocating to each day in an accrual period the ratable portion of the OID allocable to that period. The holder includes in income the daily portions of OID for each day in the tax year on which he held the instrument. (Reg § 1.1272-1(b)(1)(iv))[19]

The constant yield method may not be used for certain interests held by a REMIC, certain instruments with payments subject to acceleration or that provide for contingent payments, or certain variable rate instruments. (Reg § 1.1272-1(b)(2))[20]

14. ¶J-4301; ¶12,714.01; TD ¶153,008
15. ¶J-4301; ¶12,714.01; TD ¶153,008
16. ¶J-4324; ¶12,714.01; TD ¶153,008
17. ¶J-4301; TD ¶153,008

18. ¶J-4379 *et seq.*; ¶12,714.037; TD ¶153,043 *et seq.*
19. ¶J-4302; ¶12,714.01; TD ¶153,009
20. ¶J-4303; ¶12,714.01; TD ¶153,010

¶ 1325   OID inclusion reduced where holder paid acquisition premium.

If the holder of a debt instrument bought it from someone other than the original issuer, paying an acquisition premium (i.e., an amount in excess of the original issue price plus all OID required to be included in the gross income of earlier holders), the holder's current OID inclusion (¶1323) is reduced. This is done by reducing each daily includible OID portion by this constant fraction: the acquisition premium, divided by the total OID (before reduction) allocable to the days after the purchase date and ending on the date of maturity. However, the reduction applies only to the OID inclusion and isn't taken into account in computing the instrument's adjusted issue price at the start of an accrual period. (Code Sec. 1272(a)(7))[21]

¶ 1326   Accrued market discount on disposition of "market discount bonds."

Gain on the disposition of a market discount bond (¶1328) is ordinary income to the extent of the accrued market discount on the bond (Code Sec. 1276(a)(1)) (unless the holder elects to include the discount currently, see ¶1329). This ordinary income is treated as interest income, with exceptions. (Code Sec. 1276(a)(4))[22] For partial principal payments, see ¶1327.

The accrued market discount interest is computed under a ratable accrual method or, at taxpayer's election, a constant interest rate method. (Code Sec. 1276(b))[23]

Dispositions by gift and transfers to controlled corporations also can result in interest income under this rule. (Code Sec. 1276(d)(1)(A))[24] If the disposition is other than by sale, exchange or involuntary conversion, the amount realized is equal to the bond's fair market value. (Code Sec. 1276(a)(2))[25]

Interest treatment applies even if the gain wouldn't otherwise be recognized. Regs may allow nonrecognition in certain nontaxable transactions. (Code Sec. 1276(a)(1), Code Sec. 1276(d)(1))[26]

¶ 1327   Accrued market discount when partial principal payments are made.

If the principal on a market discount bond (¶1328) (acquired after Oct. 22, '86) is paid in more than one installment, any partial principal payment is included as ordinary income to the extent of the accrued market discount on the bond (Code Sec. 1276(a)(3)(A))[27] (unless the holder elects to include the discount currently, see ¶1329).

Any amount that has been included in gross income under this rule reduces the amount of any accrued market discount that's included on any later disposition of (¶1326), or further partial principal payments on, the bond. (Code Sec. 1276(a)(3)(B))[28]

If bond principal can be paid in two or more payments, the accrued market discount is to be determined under regs. (Code Sec. 1276(b)(3))[29]

¶ 1328   What are market discount bonds.

Market discount bonds are any "bonds" having a market discount *other than* short-term obligations (one year or less), tax-exempt obligations bought before May, 1, '93, U.S. savings bonds and certain installment obligations. (Code Sec. 1278(a)(1)(A), Code Sec. 1278(a)(1)(B))[30]

Market discount is the excess (if any) of the bond's stated redemption price at maturity (¶1318) over taxpayer's basis for the bond immediately after acquiring it. (Code Sec. 1278(a)(2))[31] The market discount is zero if it's less than 0.25% of the bond's stated

21. ¶J-4349; ¶12,714.01; TD ¶153,019
22. ¶J-4551; ¶12,764 *et seq.*; TD ¶154,001
23. ¶J-4560; ¶12,764.01; TD ¶154,004
24. ¶J-4570; ¶12,764.01; TD ¶154,007
25. ¶J-4551; ¶12,764.01; TD ¶154,001
26. ¶s J-4551, J-4569; ¶12,764.01; TD ¶154,007

27. ¶J-4566; ¶12,764.01; TD ¶154,006
28. ¶J-4567; ¶12,764.01; TD ¶154,006
29. ¶J-4568; TD ¶154,006
30. ¶s J-4552, J-4556; ¶12,764.01; TD ¶154,002
31. ¶J-4553; ¶12,764.01; TD ¶154,003

redemption price at maturity times the number of years to maturity after the taxpayer acquires the bond. (Code Sec. 1278(a)(2)(C))[32]

Special rules determine the stated redemption price at maturity for this purpose if the bond was issued with OID. (Code Sec. 1278(a)(4))[33]

¶ 1329   Election to include accrued market discount in income currently.

Instead of including a bond's accrued market discount on disposition (¶1326) or partial payment of principal (¶1327), taxpayer may elect to include the discount as interest income for the tax years to which it is attributable, i.e., currently. Taxpayer may use either the ratable accrual method or the constant interest rate method. (Code Sec. 1278(b)(1))[34]

Elect by attaching to a timely filed income tax return, a statement that market discount has been included in gross income under Code Sec. 1278(b), describing the method used to determine the amount attributable to that tax year.[35]

¶ 1330   Acquisition discount on short-term obligations—mandatory accrual.

Certain holders (below) of short-term obligations (not more than one year) are currently taxed on their daily portions of the "acquisition discount" (for government obligations, or nongovernment obligations if the holder so elects) or OID (for nongovernment obligations), for each day during the year that they hold the obligation. (Code Sec. 1281(a)(1), Code Sec. 1283(c)) Any other interest payable on the obligation also must be taken into account as it accrues. (Code Sec. 1281(a)(2))[36]

An obligation's "acquisition discount" is the excess of its stated redemption price at maturity (¶1318) over taxpayer's basis in it. (Code Sec. 1283(a)(2))[37]

The daily portion of the acquisition discount is computed using the ratable accrual method or, if taxpayer so elects, the constant interest method. (Code Sec. 1283(b))[38]

This mandatory accrual rule applies only to these holders of short-term obligations:

(1) Accrual basis taxpayers;

(2) Taxpayers who hold the obligations primarily for sale to customers in the ordinary course of their trade or business. (Code Sec. 1281(b)(1))[39] This doesn't include banks that make short-term loans to customers in the ordinary course of business;[40]

(3) Regulated investment companies (mutual funds, ¶4201) or common trust funds (¶4210);

(4) Taxpayers who identify the obligations as part of a Code Sec. 1256 hedging transaction;

(5) Taxpayers whose short-term obligations are stripped bonds or stripped coupons that taxpayer stripped. (Code Sec. 1281(b)(1))[41]

The mandatory accrual rules doesn't apply to the ordinary investor.[42]

observation: The mandatory accrual rule doesn't apply to a cash basis holder who isn't a dealer in these obligations and isn't subject to the Code Sec. 1256 hedging rules.

Special rules apply to obligations held by pass-through entities. (Code Sec. 1281(b)(2))[43]

¶ 1331   Interest on bonds sold between interest dates.

When fixed-interest bonds (not in default) are sold between interest dates, the amount the buyer pays that represents interest accrued as of the sale date is taxable interest to the seller.

32. ¶J-4554; ¶12,764.01; TD ¶154,003
33. ¶J-4553; ¶12,764.01; TD ¶154,003
34. ¶J-4573; ¶12,764.02; TD ¶154,005
35. ¶J-4574; ¶12,764.02; TD ¶154,005
36. ¶s J-4501, J-4506; ¶12,814; TD ¶153,801
37. ¶J-4501; ¶12,814.01; TD ¶153,803
38. ¶J-4500; ¶12,814.01; TD ¶153,804
39. ¶J-4502; ¶12,814; TD ¶153,802
40. ¶J-4501; TD ¶153,802
41. ¶J-4502; ¶12,814; TD ¶153,802
42. ¶J-4502
43. ¶J-4502; ¶12,814; TD ¶153,802

(Reg § 1.61-7(d)) Interest accrued after the sale date is taxable to the buyer on receipt.[44]

Bonds in default are usually traded "flat" (no part of the selling price is allocated between interest and principal). If there's accrued interest, the part of the selling price that represents interest accrued before the sale isn't taxable to the buyer until it exceeds the buyer's basis.[45]

¶ 1332 Interest credited to frozen deposits.

Interest credited to a frozen deposit (i.e., in a bankrupt or insolvent (actual or threatened) financial institution) during a calendar year, that's includible in the depositor's income for the year, can't exceed the sum of the net withdrawals during the year plus the amount withdrawable at the end of the year. (Code Sec. 451(g)(1))[46]

¶ 1333 Tax-exempt interest.

Interest on state and local bonds (i.e., obligations of a state, the District of Columbia, a U.S. possession, certain Indian tribal governments or any political subdivision of the foregoing) is exempt from federal income tax (Code Sec. 103(a), Code Sec. 103(c), Code Sec. 7871(a)(4))[47] (with certain exceptions, see ¶1334). For "educational expense" exclusion for certain U.S. savings bonds, see ¶2220 *et seq.* For Build America Bonds and other tax credit bonds, see ¶2374.

RIA *observation:* Even if interest isn't subject to federal income tax, it may have to be taken into account, e.g., in calculating the taxable portion of social security benefits (¶1281), for alternative minimum tax purposes for certain bonds (¶3208), in calculating earnings and profits (¶3525), and for certain other purposes.

RIA *caution:* There's also a bar against deducting interest on debt incurred or continued to buy or carry tax-exempt bonds (¶1723).

Every person required to file a return must report on it all tax-exempt interest received or accrued during the tax year. (Code Sec. 6012(d))[48]

¶ 1334 Taxable interest from private activity bonds, hedge bonds, arbitrage bonds.

Private activity bonds aren't eligible for the interest exemption described at ¶1333 unless the bond meets detailed requirements *and* is one of seven specified types of bonds (exempt facility, mortgage, veterans' mortgage, small issue, scholarship funding, redevelopment, or Code Sec. 501(c)(3) bonds). (Code Sec. 103(b)(1), Code Sec. 141(e))[49] Pre-Aug. 16, '86 industrial development bonds are subject to similar "qualification" rules.[50]

Hedge bonds (i.e., issued to "hedge" another bond) aren't exempt unless 85% of the bond's spendable proceeds (i.e., net of issuance expenses and certain reserves) are reasonably expected to be spent within specified periods, and at least 95% of the issuance costs (which can't be contingent) are paid within 180 days after issuance. (Code Sec. 149(g))[1]

Arbitrage bonds aren't exempt. (Code Sec. 103(b)(2)) This means a bond forming part of an issue any part of whose proceeds is reasonably expected to be used, directly or indirectly, to acquire (or refinance) nontemporary investments with a materially higher yield (more than ⅛ of 1 percentage point) than the bond itself, unless a required rebate is paid. (Code Sec. 148(a), Code Sec. 148(f); Reg § 1.148-2(d)(2)) If an issuer enters a transaction for a principal purpose of getting a material financial advantage based on the difference between tax-exempt and taxable rates, IRS has discretion to clearly reflect the economic substance of the transaction. (Reg § 1.148-10(e)) An issuer can't avoid having a bond treated as an arbitrage bond by

44. ¶J-2827; ¶614.080; TD ¶151,020
45. ¶J-2828 *et seq.*; ¶614.081; TD ¶151,021
46. ¶J-3711; ¶4514.185; TD ¶151,507
47. ¶J-3000; ¶1034; TD ¶158,001
48. ¶J-3001.1; ¶60,124; TD ¶158,003

49. ¶s J-3000 *et seq.*, J-3100, J-3252 *et seq.*, J-3600; ¶1414 *et seq.*; TD ¶158,009
50. ¶s J-3153 *et seq.*, J-3227 *et seq.*, J-3251; ¶1034.01; TD ¶158,009
1. ¶J-3667 *et seq.*; ¶1494.06; TD ¶158,001

giving away the prohibited arbitrage bond profit, e.g., by buying investments at other than fair market value ("yield burning"). [2]

¶ 1335   Inflation-indexed debt instruments; Treasury Inflation-Indexed Securities.

There are two methods of accounting for stated interest and inflation adjustments on inflation-indexed debt instruments (issued after Jan. 1, '97). Inflation-indexed debt instruments are issued for cash, indexed for inflation and deflation using a general price or wage index, and are not otherwise contingent payment debt instruments. (Reg § 1.1275-7(c)(1), Reg § 1.1275-7(h)) These rules apply to Treasury Inflation-Indexed Securities (TIPS), but not certain debt instruments, e.g., U.S. savings bonds and bonds issued by qualified tuition programs. (Reg § 1.1275-7(b))[3]

(1) The coupon bond method is a simplified method that applies if (a) the debt instrument is issued at par, and (b) all stated interest on it is qualified stated interest (i.e., it's unconditionally payable in cash at least annually, see ¶1317). The coupon bond method applies to TIPS that aren't stripped. Under this method, the stated interest is taxable to the holder when received or accrued, in accordance with his accounting method. Any increase in the inflation-adjusted principal amount is treated as OID (¶1316) for the period in which it occurs. (Reg § 1.1275-7(d))[4]

☞ *observation:* Assuming there's some inflation and principal continues to be adjusted upward, holders will have to include amounts not yet realized as interest income.

A decrease in a bond's inflation-indexed principal first reduces the interest income attributable to the interest payments for the year of the adjustment. If the decrease exceeds that income, the excess generally is an ordinary deduction to the extent taxpayer previously included interest from the bond in income. Any remaining decrease is carried forward to reduce interest income in future years. A taxpayer generally has a capital loss if he sells the bond, or it matures, before he has used all the decrease. (Reg § 1.1275-7(f)(1), Reg § 1.1275-7(d)(4))[5]

(2) The discount bond method is used if the instrument doesn't qualify for the coupon bond method (e.g., because it is issued at a discount). Under this method, taxpayers make current adjustments to their OID accruals to account for changes in the inflation-adjusted principal amount. If the daily portions for an accrual period are positive amounts, they are taken into account under Code Sec. 1272 by the holder (¶1315). If the daily portions are negative, they are taken into account under the rules for deflation adjustments described above. (Reg § 1.1275-7(e)) The discount bond method applies to TIPS that are stripped under the Treasury's STRIPS program. (Reg § 1.1286-2)[6]

¶ 1336   Interest on U.S. savings bonds.

Interest on U.S. savings bonds now being issued is earned in three ways: On Series HH "face amount" bonds (not issued after Aug. 31, 2004), it's paid semiannually by check. On Series EE "discount" bonds, it's reflected as an increase in the bond's value over stated periods. On Series I inflation-indexed face amount bonds, it's credited monthly (at a fixed rate for the 30-year life of the bond and a semiannual variable inflation rate) and paid when the bond is cashed. The interest on these bonds (and on any unmatured or extended Series E and Series H bonds now outstanding) is fully taxable unless the exclusion at ¶2219 applies.[7]

Cash basis taxpayers report the interest on Series HH (or H) bonds in the year received.[8]

A cash basis owner of Series EE bonds (and outstanding Series E bonds) and Series I bonds

---

2. ¶J-3400 *et seq.*; ¶1484 *et seq.*; TD ¶158,001
3. ¶J-4056.1, J-4379.1 *et seq.*; ¶12,714.037; TD ¶153,043 *et seq.*
4. ¶J-4379.1 *et seq.*; ¶12,714.037; TD ¶153,044
5. ¶J-4379.1 *et seq.*; ¶12,714.037; TD ¶153,044

6. ¶J-4379.5; ¶12,714.037; TD ¶153,045
7. ¶s J-3014, J-3719 *et seq.*; ¶4544.01; TD ¶156,001
8. ¶s J-3720, J-3721; ¶4544.01; TD ¶156,008

may either: (1) defer reporting any interest (i.e., the bond's increase in value) until the year of final maturity, redemption, or other disposition, whichever is earlier, or (2) elect to report the annual increase in value in each year's return.[9]

Some Series E bonds can, at the owner's option, be held up to 30 years beyond their original maturity ("final maturity"). A cash basis owner who hasn't elected to report the interest on a Series E bond annually (under (2), above) must report all of the interest on the bond in the year in which the bond is redeemed or disposed of or, if earlier, the year in which it reaches "final maturity." (Code Sec. 454(a); Reg § 1.454-1(a)(1))[10]

observation: Series E bonds issued before Dec., '65 reach final maturity 40 years after their issue date. Series E bonds issued after Nov., '65, and all Series EE bonds, reach final maturity 30 years after their issue dates. This means that any accrued interest on Series E or EE bonds issued in '80 is taxable in 2010 (the last Series E bonds stop paying interest in 2010).

Accrual basis taxpayers include the interest on the above bonds as it accrues.[11]

For the exclusion of income earned on qualified U.S. savings bonds by a payor of higher education expenses, see ¶2219 *et seq.*

¶ 1337 When to report interest income (other than OID).

Cash basis taxpayers report interest in the tax year it's actually or constructively received, regardless of when the interest is accrued on the debtor's books.[12] Generally, interest isn't constructively received if taxpayer's control of its receipt is subject to substantial limits or restrictions. (Reg § 1.451-2(a))[13] Thus, interest on a six-month certificate that isn't credited or made available before maturity without penalty isn't taxable until the certificate is redeemed or matures.[14]

Savings institution interest, or interest on life insurance dividends left to accumulate, is considered received when credited to the depositor's (policyholder's) account and subject to his withdrawal.[15]

Where a bank charges a penalty for premature withdrawals from a time savings account, the gross amount of interest paid or credited during the withdrawal year is reported as interest that year, even if the penalty partially or completely offsets the interest.[16] For deduction of forfeited interest, see ¶2171.

Matured interest coupons are constructively received in the year they mature unless it can be shown that there are no funds available for payment of the interest during the year.[17]

Accrual basis taxpayers report interest in the tax year in which the right to receive the interest becomes fixed, regardless of when it is received.[18] But if it appears reasonably certain the interest won't be paid because the debtor is insolvent, the creditor can delay reporting the interest until its collection appears reasonably certain.[19]

For cash and accrual taxpayers, there are special rules on when to include "interest" on below-market rate loans (¶1308), (Code Sec. 7872(a)(2), Code Sec. 7872(b)(2)(A))[20] "points" (¶1338), and unstated interest (¶1339).

caution: These rules don't apply to debt issued with original issue discount (¶1315).

---

9. ¶J-3719; ¶4544 *et seq.*; TD ¶156,003
10. ¶s J-3721, J-3722; ¶4544 *et seq.*; TD ¶156,003
11. ¶J-3719 *et seq.*; ¶4544.01; TD ¶156,008
12. ¶J-3703; ¶614.067; TD ¶151,501
13. ¶J-3706; ¶s 4514.036, 4514.053; TD ¶441,005
14. ¶J-3710; ¶4514.053; TD ¶151,015

15. ¶s J-3709, J-3717; ¶s 4514.036, 4514.053; TD ¶151,501
16. ¶J-2822; TD ¶151,501
17. ¶J-3715; ¶4514.053; TD ¶151,501
18. ¶J-3701; ¶4514.011; TD ¶151,502
19. ¶J-3702; ¶4514.023; TD ¶151,502
20. ¶J-3708; ¶78,724 *et seq.*; TD ¶155,000

¶ 1338   When "points" are included in income.

"Points" (¶1307) in the form of discount are taken into account under the "principal-reduction method"—i.e., as stated principal payments on the loan are made. "Points" paid out of funds not from the lender are included on receipt.[21]

¶ 1339   When to report unstated interest income.

A cash method seller includes unstated interest allocated to a payment (¶1309) as interest income in the tax year the payment is received. An accrual method seller includes the unstated interest in the tax year the payment is due. (Reg § 1.483-2(a)(1)(ii))[22]

¶ 1340   Rents and Royalties.

Rent is the payment for the use of real or tangible personal property. Royalties are payments for the use of certain rights, e.g., intangible rights such as patents. Both are includible in gross income.

¶ 1341   Rents.

Rents are includible in gross income, whether paid in cash or property. (Code Sec. 61(a)(5); Reg § 1.61-1(a)) If paid in property, the property's fair market value (at receipt) is the amount taxed as rent.[23]

Rents are reported by cash basis taxpayers when received, and by accrual basis taxpayers when due unless they're considered uncollectible.[24] For advance rentals, see ¶1343.

¶ 1342   Bonuses; lease cancellation payments.

A bonus or extra payment by the tenant to the lessor or sublessor on the execution of the lease is taxable as rent to the lessor or sublessor.[25]

If the tenant pays the landlord for permission to cancel the lease, the payments are rent to the landlord (whether cash or accrual basis) in the year received. (Reg § 1.61-8(a)) Payments to the landlord for modifying a lease or consenting to a sublease are also considered rent.[26] Where the lessor pays the tenant to cancel the lease, see ¶1598.

¶ 1343   Advance rentals and security deposits.

An advance rental is currently taxable (Reg § 1.61-8(b)), even if it's refundable or can be applied against the purchase price.[27] But a security deposit (¶1206) isn't taxable rent.[28]

¶ 1344   Deferred rentals.

Where the rules on deferred payment leases over $250,000 apply (see ¶1600), the lessor has a "constant accrual" of rental income in the same way that rental expenses are deductible by the lessee. (Code Sec. 467)[29]

¶ 1345   Tenant's payment of landlord's expenses.

Where a tenant is required under the lease to pay interest, property taxes, mortgage principal, etc., thus satisfying the *landlord's* own payment obligation, the payments are

21. ¶E-3004 *et seq.*; ¶4614.75; TD ¶151,503
22. ¶J-3758; ¶4834.01; TD ¶152,007
23. ¶J-2200 *et seq.*; ¶614.084 *et seq.*; TD ¶121,000
24. ¶J-2276; ¶s 4514.001, 4514.023; TD ¶121,002
25. ¶J-2278; TD ¶121,004

26. ¶J-2215 *et seq.*; ¶4514.022; TD ¶121,005
27. ¶J-2218; ¶4514.193; TD ¶121,003
28. ¶J-2277; ¶4514.194; TD ¶121,008
29. ¶L-6800 *et seq.*; ¶4674; TD ¶261,001

treated as rent paid by the tenant to the landlord. (Reg § 1.61-8(c))[30]

¶ 1346 Tenant's improvements to the leased property; construction allowances from lessor.

Where a tenant erects a building or makes other improvements to leased property, the resulting increase in the property's value isn't income to the landlord either at the time the improvements are made or at the end of the lease term. (Code Sec. 109) But the landlord does have rental income if the improvements are made as rent substitutes.[31]

A lessee may exclude any amount received in cash (or as a rent reduction) from a lessor under a short-term lease (15 years or less) of retail space, that's for the purpose of the lessee's constructing or improving qualified long-term real property for use in the lessee's trade or business at the leased space. The construction allowance is excludible to the extent the lessee uses it for that purpose, within 8½ months after the end of the tax year it was received. Qualified long-term real property is nonresidential real property which is part of or otherwise present at the retail space and reverts to the lessor at lease termination. The lessor treats any qualified long-term real property that's constructed or improved with an allowance excluded under these rules as its own nonresidential real property (¶1923). (Code Sec. 110; Reg § 1.110-1)[32]

¶ 1347 Royalties.

Royalties (payments received for the use of copyrights, patents, trademarks, secret processes and similar intangibles, and for the right to exploit mineral or other natural resources) are taxable as ordinary income (Code Sec. 61(a)(6)), regardless of the name given to them by the parties or the form of payment (e.g., lump sum or property such as stock).[33]

Royalties are included by cash basis taxpayers on receipt (actual or constructive), and by accrual basis taxpayers when their rights to them are fixed.[34]

¶ 1348 Life Insurance Proceeds.

Life insurance proceeds payable by reason of the insured's death are fully excludable or, if paid later than death under an interest option or in installments, partially excludable, from the recipient's gross income. All or part of the exclusion may be lost if the contract is transferred during the insured's life. Certain accelerated death benefits received by terminally or chronically ill insureds are excludable. Special requirements apply for employer-owned life insurance.

¶ 1349 How life insurance proceeds are taxed.

Amounts received under a "life insurance contract" (¶1350), that are paid by reason of the insured's death aren't included in the gross income of the recipient (i.e., beneficiary) (Code Sec. 101(a)) (unless the policy was transferred for value, see ¶1355). The exclusion applies to lump sum payments made at the time of the insured's death, and to amounts paid later to the extent the payment doesn't exceed the amount payable at death. (Reg § 1.101-1(a)(1))[35] For dividends and other lifetime payments, see ¶1353. For accelerated death benefits, see ¶1354.

For life insurance contracts that don't qualify, the exclusion is limited to the excess of the death benefits over the contract's net surrender value (i.e., value on surrender). (Code Sec. 7702(g)(2)) The net surrender value is treated as an annuity payment (¶1357 et seq.). Also, the owner of the contract is taxed (in the year it fails to qualify) on the income earned on it. This income equals the excess, for the year, of: (1) the sum of the net surrender value

30. ¶J-2210 *et seq.*; ¶614.094; TD ¶121,007
31. ¶J-2250 *et seq.*; ¶1094.01 *et seq.*; TD ¶121,013
32. ¶J-2261 *et seq.*; ¶1104

33. ¶J-2300 *et seq.*; ¶614.084 *et seq.*; TD ¶122,001
34. ¶s J-2305, J-2306; ¶4514.001; TD ¶122,003
35. ¶J-4700 *et seq.*; ¶1014; TD ¶148,501

increase plus the cost of life insurance protection provided, over (2) premiums paid. (Code Sec. 7702(g)(1)(B))[36]

¶ 1350   Life insurance contract defined.

To qualify as a life insurance contract, a contract must be a life insurance (or endowment) contract under local law *and* satisfy either (a) a cash value accumulation test, or (b) a combined guideline premium requirement/cash value corridor test. (Code Sec. 101(f), Code Sec. 7702(a), Code Sec. 7702(h))[37] Pre-'85 contracts must entail risk shifting and risk distribution.[38]

¶ 1351   Proceeds paid in installments.

If the life insurance proceeds payable on the insured's death are paid in installments or for life, only part (below) of each payment is excluded. Any amount that exceeds the excluded portion is taxable when received. But if the amount of the total anticipated payments can't exceed the total amount payable at the insured's death, then each payment is fully excludable, whenever it's made. (Code Sec. 101(d)(1); Reg § 1.101-4(a)(1)(i))[39]

The excludable portion of each payment is: (1) the excludable amount held by the insurer with respect to the particular beneficiary, divided by (2) the number of payments to be made or, if payments are for life, the number of payments anticipated over the life expectancy of the beneficiary. This same prorated amount of each payment is excludable, regardless of how many payments are made (Reg § 1.101-4) (i.e., even if the beneficiary exceeds his anticipated life expectancy). The excludable amount is the present value to the beneficiary (as of the date of death) of the settlement.[40]

A beneficiary who is the spouse of an insured who died before Oct. 23, '86, may exclude an *additional* $1,000 each year of amounts received by reason of the insured's death.[41]

¶ 1352   Proceeds left at interest.

Where excludable life insurance proceeds are held by the insurer under an agreement to pay interest, the interest is taxable to the recipient, whether the interest option was chosen by the insured or by his beneficiaries or estate. No part of this interest may be excluded under the proration rules (¶1351). (Code Sec. 101(c); Reg § 1.101-3(a))[42]

¶ 1353   Proceeds paid before death of insured—loans, refunds, dividends, policy surrenders.

Payments made under life insurance or endowment contracts before the death of the insured (e.g., loans, refunds, dividends, and amounts received on surrender, redemption or maturity of a contract) generally are treated as amounts "not received" under an annuity contract (¶1369). (Code Sec. 72(a))[43] For accelerated death benefits received by terminally or chronically ill individuals, see ¶1354.

Thus, a transferee generally recognizes ordinary income in the amount received on the surrender of a life insurance policy (cash surrender value) less his adjusted basis in contract (aggregate premiums paid).[44]

36. ¶J-4900 *et seq.*; ¶s 1014, 77,024.07; TD ¶148,504
37. ¶J-4800 *et seq.*; ¶s 1014, 77,024; TD ¶149,001
38. ¶J-4950 *et seq.*; ¶1014; TD ¶149,001
39. ¶J-4718; ¶1014.04; TD ¶148,505
40. ¶J-4720; ¶1014.04; TD ¶148,505

41. ¶J-4719; ¶1014.05; TD ¶148,505
42. ¶J-4717; ¶1014.03; TD ¶148,503
43. ¶J-5055 *et seq.*; ¶724 *et seq.*; TD ¶148,900 *et seq.*
44. ¶J-5058; TD ¶146,528

¶ 1354   Accelerated death benefits—terminally or chronically ill insureds—viatical settlements.

Amounts received under a life insurance contract on the life of individuals who are certified terminally or chronically ill are excluded from gross income as amounts paid by reason of the death of an insured (¶1349). (Code Sec. 101(g)(1)) A similar exclusion applies to amounts received for the sale or assignment of any portion of a death benefit under a life insurance contract to a viatical settlement provider (one that regularly buys or takes assignments of life insurance contracts on the lives of the terminally ill and meets detailed standards) if the insured under the life insurance contract is either terminally or chronically ill. (Code Sec. 101(g)(2)(A))[45] In the case of chronically ill individuals, the exclusions apply only if detailed requirements are met. (Code Sec. 101(g)(3))[46]

¶ 1355   Death benefits exclusion where contract was transferred.

If a life insurance contract is transferred for valuable consideration, e.g., by sale, during the insured's lifetime, the transferee's exclusion for the life insurance proceeds he receives under the contract by reason of the insured's death (¶1349) is limited to the value of the consideration he paid for the contract, plus the net premiums and "other amounts" he paid later. (Code Sec. 101(a)(2))[47] For contracts issued after June 8, '97, "other amounts" includes interest paid or accrued by the transferee on debt with respect to a life insurance contract (or to an interest in one) that was transferred for valuable consideration, if the interest is disallowed under Code Sec. 264(a)(4) (see ¶1718). (Code Sec. 101(a)(2))

Thus, IRS explained that a transferee generally recognizes income in the amount received over his adjusted basis in contract (i.e., aggregate premiums paid minus cost of insurance already provided). The cost of insurance is determined by the reduction in the contract's cash surrender value at the time of sale. Inside build-up immediately prior to sale (cash surrender value minus aggregate premiums paid) is ordinary income while any remaining amount is capital gain. On the sale of a term life contract with no cash surrender value, a transferee recognized capital gain on the excess of the amount realized on the sale over his adjusted basis of contract, with the reduction for the cost of insurance that's been provided each month presumed to be equal to monthly premium paid.[48] For the sale or assignment of any portion of the death benefit to a viatical settlement provider, see ¶1354.

If only an interest in the contract is transferred, the limit applies only to the part of the proceeds attributable to the transferred interest.[49]

This limitation doesn't apply if:

. . . the transfer is to the insured, his partner, his partnership or a corporation in which he is a shareholder or officer; (Code Sec. 101(a)(2)(B)) or

. . . the transferee's basis for the contract (or interest) is determined in whole or in part by reference to the transferor's basis (Code Sec. 101(a)(2)(A))[50] as in a tax-free reorganization. (Reg § 1.101-1(b)(5), Ex 2)[1]

Where the transfer is gratuitous, i.e., a gift, the above limitation doesn't apply. The full death benefits exclusion is preserved. (Reg § 1.101-1(b)(2))[2]

¶ 1356   Employer-owned life insurance—Form 8925.

For contracts issued after Aug. 17, 2006 (except for tax-free Code Sec. 1035 exchanges), an employer in a trade or businesses treats proceeds payable to it from an employer-owned life

---

45. ¶J-4750 *et seq.*, ¶J-4818; ¶1014.015; TD ¶148,900 *et seq.*
46. ¶J-4754 *et seq.*; ¶1014.015; TD ¶148,905 *et seq.*
47. ¶J-4729; ¶1014.02; TD ¶148,528
48. ¶J-5307; TD ¶146,624

49. ¶J-4731; ¶1014.02; TD ¶148,528
50. ¶J-4730; ¶1014.02; TD ¶148,528
1. ¶J-4742; ¶1014.02; TD ¶148,530
2. ¶J-4732; ¶1014.02; TD ¶148,529

insurance contract on an employee as income, excluding as a death benefit only the premiums and other amounts it paid for the contract. (Code Sec. 101(j)(1))[3] This rule doesn't apply for a contract for which notice and consent requirements are met, if:

(1) the insured was an individual who was an employee within 12 months of his death;

(2) at the time the contract was issued, the insured was a director; a "highly compensated employee," i.e., a more-than-5% owner or employee who for the preceding year received in excess of $110,000 for 2010 (¶4326); or a "highly compensated individual," i.e., one of the 5 highest paid officers, a shareholder owning more than 10%, or anyone else in the top 35% of employees ranked by pay;

(3) the amount is paid to: a family member of the insured (under Code Sec. 267(c)(4)), an individual who is a designated beneficiary under the contract (other than the policyholder), a trust established for either the family member's or beneficiary's benefit, or the insured's estate; or

(4) the amount is used to buy an equity (or partnership capital or profits) interest in the policyholder from the family member, beneficiary, trust or estate. (Code Sec. 101(j)(2)) It's intended that this amount be paid or used by the due date of the tax return for the policyholder's tax year in which the proceeds are received as a death benefit under the insurance contract, so that who is paid and what purchases are made with proceeds are known in the tax year in which the exception from the income inclusion rule is claimed.[4]

The notice and consent requirements are met if, before the issuance of the contract, the employee is notified (and consents) in writing to the employer insuring him with the employer as a beneficiary. The employee must be told the maximum face amount of the life insurance and if coverage continues after his termination. (Code Sec. 101(j)(4)) In guidance, IRS says it won't challenge an inadvertent notice and consent failure if: (1) the policyholder made a good faith effort to satisfy the requirements; and (2) the failure was inadvertent, and was discovered and corrected no later than the due date of the tax return for the tax year of the applicable policyholder in which the employer-owned life insurance contract was issued.[5]

Annual reporting (on Form 8925) and recordkeeping by policyholders that own one or more employer-owned life insurance contracts is also required. (Code Sec. 6039I; Reg § 1.6039I-1)

¶ 1357   Taxation of Annuity Payments.

Annuity payments consist generally of two parts: nontaxable return of investment (based on an exclusion ratio), and taxable interest. Other amounts (e.g., withdrawals, dividends) are taxable to the extent they exceed the contract's cost.

¶ 1358   How annuities are taxed.

Gross income includes any amount received "as an annuity" that's paid under an annuity, life insurance or endowment contract. (Code Sec. 72(a))[6] For exclusion under the "annuity rule," see ¶1359. For "nonannuity" payments under the contract (e.g., loans, dividends), see ¶1369. For private annuities, see ¶1372. For annuities paid to survivors of certain public safety officers, see ¶1262. For partial annuitization rule, see ¶1367.

¶ 1359   The annuity rule—"exclusion ratio" for amounts received "as an annuity."

If a payment under an annuity, life insurance or endowment contract is received "as an annuity" (i.e., a sum of money (or property) payable at regular intervals over a period of more than one full year from the starting date (¶1366) (Reg § 1.72-2(b)), all or part of it may be tax-free (for "natural person" holders, see ¶1360). The part of each "annuity" payment that

3. ¶J-4744; ¶1014.11; TD ¶148,536
4. ¶J-4744; ¶1014.11; TD ¶148,536
5. ¶J-4744; ¶1014.11; TD ¶148,536
6. ¶J-5001; ¶724 *et seq.*; TD ¶146,501

represents return of investment (e.g., premiums paid) is excludable from the recipient's income until the entire investment is recovered. Excess receipts are fully taxable. (Code Sec. 72(b)(1); Reg § 1.72-4(a))[7]

The excludable portion is computed by multiplying each payment received by an "exclusion ratio," determined by dividing the investment in the contract (¶1364) by the contract's expected return (¶1365), as of the annuity starting date, and rounding to the nearest tenth. (Code Sec. 72(b); Reg § 1.72-4(a)) But the excludable portion of any payment can't exceed the amount of investment in the contract that is unrecovered immediately before the payment is received. (Code Sec. 72(b)(2))[8] (For employee annuities, see ¶1368.)

Once computed, the exclusion ratio is applied to each "annuity" payment received under the contract, until the total investment has been recovered tax-free. (Code Sec. 72(b); Reg § 1.72-4(a))[9] But the ratio must be recomputed if the contract is transferred for valuable consideration, matures, is surrendered, or is exchanged. (Reg § 1.72-4(a)(4))[10]

If there was no investment in the contract, all payments are taxable in full. If investment exceeds total expected return, all payments are tax-free. (Reg § 1.72-4(d))[11]

Where the annuitant's death causes the annuity payments (starting after Jan. 1, '86) to stop, the amount of any investment in the contract that the annuitant hasn't yet recovered tax-free may be deducted on his final income tax return. (Code Sec. 72(b)(3)(A))[12] For after-death distribution requirements, see ¶1361.

For annuities that started before '87, the exclusion ratio, once computed, applies to all payments no matter how long the annuitant lives (unless the contract is modified or exchanged). (Reg § 1.72-4(a))[13]

¶ 1360 Annuity rule exclusion available only to natural persons.

If an annuity contract is held by a person who isn't a natural person, the annuity rule (¶1359) doesn't apply. The income on the contract (for the holder's tax year) must be treated as ordinary income received or accrued by the holder during that year. (Code Sec. 72(u)(1))[14] A natural person doesn't include a trust or corporation. But holding by a trust, etc., *as agent* for a natural person is disregarded. (Code Sec. 72(u)(1))[15]

However, an *employer* that's the nominal owner (agent) of an annuity contract whose beneficial owners are (the employer's) employees is considered to hold the contract.[16]

The natural person rule *doesn't apply* to contracts: acquired by an estate by reason of the decedent's death; held by a qualified plan or IRA; that are "qualified funding assets" (¶1387); bought by an employer on termination of a qualified plan and held until all amounts under the contract are distributed to the employee (or his beneficiary) for whom the contract was bought; or that are immediate annuities. (Code Sec. 72(u)(3))[17]

¶ 1361 After-death distribution requirements for annuity contracts.

Payments under a contract aren't entitled to the partial exclusion under the annuity rule *unless* the contract provides that: (1) if any holder ("primary annuitant" for contracts not held by an individual) dies on or after the annuity starting date (¶1366) (and before the entire interest in the contract has been distributed), the balance will be distributed at least as rapidly as it was at the date of death, and (2) if any holder dies before the starting date, the entire interest must be distributed within five years of his death. (Code Sec. 72(s)(1))[18]

7. ¶J-5100 *et seq.;* ¶724; TD ¶146,541
8. ¶J-5105; ¶724.06; TD ¶146,545
9. ¶J-5104; ¶724.06; TD ¶146,545
10. ¶J-5106; ¶724.06; TD ¶146,547
11. ¶J-5104; ¶724.06; TD ¶146,545
12. ¶J-5109; ¶s 724, 724.06; TD ¶146,551

13. ¶J-5104; ¶724.06; TD ¶146,541
14. ¶s J-5005, J-5006; ¶724.25; TD ¶146,506
15. ¶J-5005; ¶724.25; TD ¶146,506
16. ¶J-5005; ¶724.25; TD ¶146,506
17. ¶J-5007; ¶724.25; TD ¶146,508
18. ¶s J-5014, J-5015; ¶724.01; TD ¶146,515

However, distributions that are payable to (or for) a designated beneficiary can be made for the beneficiary's life or a period not ending past his life expectancy. As long as the payments begin within one year of the holder's death, they'll be considered distributed on that starting date. (Code Sec. 72(s)(2)) A beneficiary who is the holder's surviving spouse will be considered the holder. (Code Sec. 72(s)(3))[19]

⚫/observation: Treating the surviving spouse/beneficiary as the holder means that the after-death distribution provisions must be satisfied with respect to the *spouse's* death.

The after-death distribution rules *don't apply to:* contracts provided under qualified pension, profit-sharing, stock bonus or annuity plans; tax-sheltered annuities; individual retirement annuities (or contracts provided under IRAs); qualified funding assets (¶1387), regardless of any qualified assignment (Code Sec. 72(s)(5))[20] or contracts issued before Jan. 19, '85.[21]

¶ 1362 Variable annuities.

A variable annuity contract is one where the amount paid varies depending on investment experience, cost of living indexes, market fluctuations, etc. The excludable portion of each payment is computed by dividing the investment in the contract (¶1364) by the total number of anticipated payments. (Reg § 1.72-2(b)(3), Reg § 1.72-4(d)(3))[22]

The excludable amount stays the same regardless of changes in the amount received. (Reg § 1.72-2(b)(3))[23] But if the amount received in a tax year is *less* than the excludable amount, taxpayer may elect (attach a specified statement to the return) to recompute the exclusion ratio for later years' payments. (Reg § 1.72-4(d)(3)(ii), Reg § 1.72-4(d)(3)(iv))[24]

¶ 1363 Joint and survivor annuity contracts.

Under a joint and survivor annuity contract, payments are made during the lives of two annuitants and, after the death of one, during the life of the survivor. A single exclusion ratio (¶1359), based on the aggregate expected return to both annuitants, is applied to the payments received by both annuitants. (Reg § 1.72-2(a)(2))[25]

¶ 1364 Investment in the contract.

For annuity rule purposes (¶1359), the "investment in the contract" is, in general, the net cost of the contract as of the annuity starting date (¶1366) or, if later, the date of the first contract payment. It equals the aggregate amount of premiums and other consideration paid (as of that date) for the contract, minus the aggregate amount previously received under the contract that was excluded from income. (Code Sec. 72(c)(1))[26] It must also be reduced to account for any refund feature. (Code Sec. 72(c)(2))[27] Separate computations may be required for pre-July '86 and post-June '86 investments. (Reg § 1.72-6(d))[28]

For an employee annuity, investment in the contract includes certain employer contributions that were taxable to the owner (employee). (Reg § 1.72-8(a))[29] Where the annuity began after Nov. 18, '96 (¶1368), or the safe-harbor method is elected for annuities beginning before Nov. 19, '96, no refund feature adjustment is required.[30]

For an employee annuity where the decedent died before Aug. 21, '96, the survivor-annuitant's investment in the contract also includes prior law's $5,000 death benefit exclusion, if applicable. (Reg § 1.72-8(b))[31]

19. ¶J-5014; ¶724.01; TD ¶146,515
20. ¶J-5016; ¶724.01; TD ¶146,515
21. ¶J-5014; ¶724.01; TD ¶146,517
22. ¶J-5143; ¶724.08; TD ¶146,582
23. ¶J-5143; ¶724.08; TD ¶146,582
24. ¶J-5145; ¶724.08; TD ¶146,584
25. ¶J-5132 *et seq.*; ¶724.15; TD ¶146,572

26. ¶J-5113; ¶724.10; TD ¶141,033
27. ¶J-5122; ¶724.12; TD ¶141,038
28. ¶J-5117 *et seq.*; ¶724.10; TD ¶146,558
29. ¶H-11032 *et seq.*; ¶724.11; TD ¶141,034
30. ¶H-11047; ¶4024.02
31. ¶H-11037; ¶724.12; TD ¶141,034

¶ 1365 Expected return from the contract.

For annuity rule purposes (¶1359), the "expected return from the contract" is the total amount to be received (or estimated to be received) under the contract. It is computed as of the annuity starting date (¶1366) (Code Sec. 72(b)(1)) and doesn't take into account any amount for dividends or other payments *not* received as an annuity (¶1369). (Code Sec. 72(c)(3); Reg § 1.72-7(a))[32]

If the annuity is for a fixed term and doesn't depend on any life expectancy, the expected return is the amount of the payment specified for each period multiplied by the number of periods. (Reg § 1.72-5(c))[33]

If the annuity is payable for life or joint lives, the expected return is the amount of the *annual* payment multiplied by the number of years of life expectancy using IRS actuarial tables. (Code Sec. 72(c)(3)(A); Reg § 1.72-5(a))[34]

If the annuity is for an amount certain payable in periodic installments, the expected return is the total amount guaranteed. (Reg § 1.72-5(d))[35]

¶ 1366 Annuity starting date.

The "annuity starting date" is the first day of the first period for which an amount is received *as an annuity* (¶1359) under the contract. This is the date the contractual obligation becomes fixed or, if later, the first day of the period (year, quarter, etc., depending on whether the payments are to be made annually, quarterly, etc.) that ends on the date of the first annuity payment. (Code Sec. 72(c)(4); Reg § 1.72-4(b)(1))[36] Special rules apply if the contract is transferred or exchanged. (Code Sec. 72(g)(3))[37]

¶ 1367 Partial annuitization of annuities.

For amounts received in tax years beginning after Dec. 31, 2010, taxpayers may partially annuitize a nonqualified annuity, endowment, or life insurance contract. (Code Sec. 72(a)(2)) If any amount is received as an annuity for a period of 10 years or more, or during one or more lives, under any portion of an annuity, endowment, or life insurance contract:

(1) that portion will be treated as a separate contract for annuity taxation purposes;

(2) for purposes of applying Code Sec. 72(b) (calculation of the exclusion ratio for annuity distributions, ¶1359), Code Sec. 72(c) (investment in contract, expected return, and annuity starting date, ¶1364–¶1366), and Code Sec. 72(e) (taxation of distributions from an annuity, endowment, or life insurance contract, that aren't received as an annuity, ¶1369), the investment in the contract is allocated pro rata between each portion of the contract from which amounts are received as an annuity, and the portion of the contract from which amounts are not received as an annuity, and

(3) a separate annuity starting date under Code Sec. 72(c)(4) (annuity starting date) is determined for each portion of the contract from which amounts are received as an annuity. (Code Sec. 72(a)(2))

Thus, holders of nonqualified annuities can elect to receive a portion of an annuity contract in the form of a stream of annuity payments, leaving the remainder of the contract to accumulate income on a tax-deferred basis.

The partial annuitization rule is not intended to change the rules for amounts received as an annuity (or as a lump sum) from Code Sec. 401(a) qualified plans, Code Sec. 403(a) annuity plans, Code Sec. 403(b) annuity plans, or individual retirement plans.

---

32. ¶J-5124 *et seq.*; ¶724.14; TD ¶146,564
33. ¶J-5130; ¶724.14; TD ¶146,570
34. ¶J-5126 *et seq.*; ¶724.14; TD ¶146,564
35. ¶J-5131; ¶724.14; TD ¶146,571
36. ¶J-5110; ¶724.09; TD ¶141,019
37. ¶J-5112; ¶724.09; TD ¶146,553

¶ 1368   Employee annuities—simplified method for computing nontaxable portion.

The nontaxable portion of amounts received as an annuity (¶1359) under a Code Sec. 401(a) qualified employee plan, a Code Sec. 403(a) qualified employee annuity or a Code Sec. 403(b) tax-sheltered annuity is computed under a simplified method, by dividing the investment in the contract (¶1364) as of the annuity starting date (¶1366) by a designated number of monthly payments. (Code Sec. 72(d)(1)(B))

For an annuity payable over the life of a single individual, the number of payments is 360 if the age of the annuitant on the annuity starting date is not more than 55; 310 payments if the age is more than 55 but not more than 60; 260 payments if more than 60 but not more than 65; 210 payments if more than 65 but not more than 70; and 160 payments if more than 70. (Code Sec. 72(d)(1)(B)(iii))[38]

For an annuity payable over the lives of more than one individual, the number of payments is 410 if the combined age of the annuitants on the annuity starting date is not more than 110; 360 payments if more than 110 but not more than 120; 310 payments if more than 120 but not more than 130; 260 payments if more than 130 but not more than 140; and 210 payments if more than 140. (Code Sec. 72(d)(1)(B)(iv))[39]

Appropriate adjustments must be made if payments are not made on a monthly basis. (Code Sec. 72(d)(1)(F))[40]

The simplified method doesn't apply if the primary annuitant is 75 or older on the annuity starting date, unless there are fewer than 5 years of guaranteed payments under the annuity. (Code Sec. 72(d)(1)(E))[41]

A lump-sum payment received in connection with the start of annuity payments is taxable under Code Sec. 72(e) as if received before the annuity starting date (see ¶1369), and the investment in the contract is determined by taking into consideration the receipt of this lump-sum payment. (Code Sec. 72(d)(1)(D))[42]

For annuity starting dates before Jan. 1, '98 and after Nov. 18, '96, the designated number of payments is based on the age of the primary annuitant, and there is no separate table for annuities based on the life of more than one individual.[43]

For annuity starting dates before Nov. 19, '96, the regular annuity rules apply (¶1357 *et seq.*) unless the employee elects a simplified safe-harbor method.[44]

¶ 1369   Amounts "not" received as an annuity—cash withdrawals, dividends, etc.

Payments under life insurance, endowment and annuity contracts (other than modified endowment contracts, see ¶1371) that aren't "annuities" (e.g., cash withdrawals, loans, dividends, etc.) are fully taxable if received *on or after* the annuity starting date (¶1366). (Code Sec. 72(e)(2)(A), Code Sec. 72(e)(3)(A))[45]

"Nonannuity" amounts received *before* the annuity starting date are: (1) *not taxable,* to the extent that, as of the date of distribution, they don't exceed the cost of the contract (i.e., accumulated net premiums paid) and (2) *taxable,* to the extent allocable to income (i.e., excess of the contract's cash value over the owner's investment) at that time. (Code Sec. 72(e)(2)(B), Code Sec. 72(e)(3)(B))[46] (Veteran's insurance dividends are tax-free, regardless of cost.)[47]

caution: The pre-annuity starting date withdrawal may be subject to the premature distribution penalty (¶1370).

38. ¶H-11012; ¶4024.02; TD ¶141,016
39. ¶H-11012; ¶4024.02; TD ¶141,016
40. ¶H-11012; ¶4024.02; TD ¶141,016
41. ¶H-11012; ¶4024.02; TD ¶141,016
42. ¶H-11012; ¶4024.02; TD ¶141,016
43. ¶H-11012; ¶4024.02; TD ¶141,016
44. ¶H-11012 *et seq.*; ¶724.07; TD ¶146,595
45. ¶J-5053; ¶724.17; TD ¶146,523
46. ¶724.17; TD ¶146,523
47. ¶J-5055; TD ¶146,525

Receipts less than on insurance or endowment contract's cost don't give rise to a deductible loss.[48]

The contract's cost is reduced by the nontaxable amount of the dividend, etc., for purposes of computing the taxable portion of later payments. (Code Sec. 72(e)(6)(B))[49]

For these purposes, all contracts (other than immediate annuities or qualified plan annuities) issued by the same company (or its affiliates) to the same policyholder during any one calendar year are treated as a single contract. (Code Sec. 72(e)(11))[50]

¶ 1370 10% penalty on premature distributions from annuity contracts.

A penalty is imposed (except as noted below) on a person who receives any nonannuity distribution (¶1369) before the annuity starting date (¶1366) in the tax year the distribution is received. The penalty equals 10% of the taxable portion of the distribution. (Code Sec. 72(q)(1))[1] Calculate and pay the penalty on Form 5329.[2]

This 10% penalty *doesn't apply* to any distribution:

(1) made on or after the date taxpayer (recipient) reaches age 59½;

(2) made on or after the death of the holder (or the primary annuitant, where the holder isn't an individual);

(3) attributable to recipient's total and indefinite disability;

(4) that's part of a series of substantially equal periodic payments (not less frequently than annually) made for the life (or life expectancy) of taxpayer or the joint lives (or joint life expectancies) of taxpayer and his designated beneficiary;

(5) made from a Code Sec. 401(a) qualified employee plan, a Code Sec. 403(a) qualified annuity plan, a Code Sec. 403(b) tax-sheltered annuity plan or a Code Sec. 818(a)(3) retirement plan for life insurance company employees (but for the separate penalty on premature distributions from these plans, see ¶4344);

(6) made from an individual retirement account or annuity (but for the separate penalty on premature distributions from these plans, see ¶4344);

(7) made under an annuity contract which is purchased by an employer on termination of a qualified plan (bonus, pension, profit-sharing or annuity) and which is held by the employer until the employee separates from service;

(8) under an immediate annuity;

(9) under a "qualified funding asset" (¶1387), regardless of any qualified assignment;

(10) to which the Code Sec. 72(t) tax on premature distributions from qualified plans applies (without regard to the Code Sec. 72(t)(2) exceptions), see ¶4344;

(11) allocable to pre-Aug. 14, '82 investment in the contract. (Code Sec. 72(q)(2))[3]

¶ 1371 Modified endowment contracts.

A modified endowment contract is a life insurance contract (entered into after June 20, '88) that fails to meet a "7-pay test" (or that is exchanged for such a contract). The test is failed if the accumulated amount paid under the contract during the first seven years exceeds the net level premiums that would have been paid as paid-up future benefits. (Code Sec. 7702A(a), Code Sec. 7702(b))[4]

Payments under a modified endowment contract that are received before the annuity starting date (¶1366) are includible in gross income to the extent allocable to income on the

---

48. ¶J-5308; TD ¶146,626
49. ¶J-5063; ¶724.10; TD ¶146,533
50. ¶J-5064; ¶724.17; TD ¶146,534
1. ¶J-5017; ¶724.21; TD ¶146,518

2. ¶S-2510; TD ¶146,519
3. ¶J-5018; ¶724.21; TD ¶146,520
4. ¶J-5066 *et seq.*; ¶s 724.17, 77,02A4; TD ¶146,536

contract, as described at ¶1369. (Code Sec. 72(e)(10)(A)(i))[5] This applies to any amount received as a loan, or assigned or pledged on the value of the contract, unless the loan, etc., is made solely to cover burial expenses or prearranged funeral expenses where the maximum death benefit under the contract doesn't exceed $25,000. (Code Sec. 72(e)(10)(B)) However, taxpayer's investment in the contract (¶1364) is increased by the amount taxed to him (as a loan or assignment). (Code Sec. 72(e)(4)(A))[6]

Certain amounts received under a modified endowment contract that are includible in income are subject to a 10% penalty tax (Code Sec. 72(v)(1), Code Sec. 72(v)(2))[7] (use Form 5329).[8]

¶ 1372   Private annuities.

A private annuity generally involves the transfer of money or property to an individual or organization in exchange for the transferee's promise to make lifetime payments to the transferor. These transfers typically are made: to family members, controlled entities, or unrelated purchasers; to charitable organizations; and in settlement of a will contest.[9]

Transfer of an "unsecured" private annuity arrangement doesn't result in immediate taxable gain (or loss). Instead, any gain is reportable ratably over the lifetime of the transferor (i.e., annuitant). The gain equals the excess of the present value of the annuity (determined under regs) over the transferor's adjusted basis in the transferred property. Any loss may be disallowed if the arrangement is between related parties (¶2446 *et seq.*).[10]

If the arrangement is "secured" (i.e., the property transferred also is collateral for the payments), it's taxed (except for gift tax aspects) under the rules for commercial annuities, (¶1357 *et seq.*).[11] In applying those rules, the annuitant's basis in the property he transferred for the annuity is used as his investment in the contract.[12]

The value of annuities issued by charities is determined under IRS tables.[13]

¶ 1373   Gifts and Inheritances.

Property received as a gift, bequest, devise or inheritance is exempt from income tax.

¶ 1374   Gifts of property.

A gift of property isn't taxable to a recipient (Code Sec. 102; Reg § 1.102-1)[14] other than an employee, see ¶1213. For gifts of income, see ¶1376. For employee awards, see ¶1253. For gift tax, see ¶5037 *et seq.*

¶ 1375   Inheritances.

Tax-free bequests, devises and inheritances are money and any property that pass on the death of a person by his will or under intestacy, including amounts received in settlement of a will contest.[15] For bequests of income, see ¶1376. For estate tax, see ¶5000 *et seq.*

¶ 1376   Gifts and bequests of income.

Gifts and bequests of *income,* and the income from property that is received as a gift or bequest, are taxable to the recipient, whether paid periodically or in a lump sum. (Code Sec. 102(b); Reg § 1.102-1(c))[16] For an exception for income paid or credited as a gift or bequest of specific property or money, see ¶3950.

5. ¶J-5065; ¶724.17; TD ¶146,535
6. ¶J-5063; ¶724.17; TD ¶146,529
7. ¶J-5076; ¶724.17; TD ¶146,540
8. ¶S-2510; TD ¶146,519
9. ¶J-5252; ¶724.01; TD ¶146,601
10. ¶J-5256 *et seq.*; ¶724.05; TD ¶146,602
11. ¶J-5257; TD ¶146,606
12. ¶J-5254; ¶724.05; TD ¶146,603
13. ¶P-6615, P-6674 *et seq.*; TD ¶146,612
14. ¶J-6000 *et seq.*; ¶1024; TD ¶178,001
15. ¶J-6000 *et seq.*; ¶1024.02; TD ¶178,010
16. ¶J-6004, ¶J-6005; ¶1024; TD ¶178,004

¶ 1377 Prizes and Awards. ▬▬▬▬▬▬▬▬▬▬▬▬▬▬▬▬▬▬▬▬▬▬▬▬▬▬▬▬

Prizes and awards generally are taxable.

¶ 1378 Prizes and awards.

All prizes and awards (with exceptions for qualified scholarships, see ¶2216) are includible in gross income (Code Sec. 74(a); Reg § 1.74-1(b)) *unless:* the prize is primarily for religious, charitable, scientific, educational, artistic, literary, etc., achievement; the recipient was selected without any action on his part, and thus isn't required to render substantial future services; *and* it's transferred by the payor to a governmental unit or charity the recipient designated (Code Sec. 74(b))[17] before getting any benefit from it.[18] IRS specifies the requirements of the designation (including model language).[19] For employee awards, see ¶1253.

For a prize paid in property or services, the taxable amount is the prize's current fair market (resale) value. (Reg § 1.74-1(a)(2))[20]

Under the principle of constructive receipt (¶2822), the winner of a contest (e.g., a lottery, jackpot) who is given the option of receiving either a lump sum or an annuity has to include the value of the award in gross income, even if he or she takes the annuity. However, in the case of a cash basis individual, a "qualified prize option" (to choose either cash or an annuity not later than 60 days after becoming entitled to the prize) is disregarded in determining the tax year for which any portion of a "qualified prize" (one payable over at least 10 years and that meets other requirements) is included in income. (Code Sec. 451(h)) That is, the individual doesn't have to include the value of the prize in income immediately merely by having had the option to choose cash.[21]

¶ 1379 Accident and Health Insurance Benefits. ▬▬▬▬▬▬▬▬▬▬▬▬▬▬▬▬

Benefits received from accident and health insurance are excluded from gross income, unless the benefits compensate for medical expense deductions from an earlier year. Benefits from long-term care insurance policies are subject to special rules.

¶ 1380 Exclusion for benefits received through accident or health insurance.

Amounts received through accident or health insurance (or through an arrangement having the effect of accident or health insurance) for personal injuries or sickness are generally excluded from income, except to the extent attributable to medical expenses that were deducted in a previous year. This exclusion doesn't apply to amounts received by an employee to the extent the amounts are (1) attributable to employer contributions that weren't includible in the employee's gross income, or (2) are paid by the employer. (Code Sec. 104(a)(3))[22]

Where an employer-provided disability plan allows employees to elect annually to pay for coverage out of pre- or post-tax dollars, disability benefits paid to an employee who elected the post-tax option for the plan year in which he became disabled are excludable from gross income.[23]

¶ 1381 Exclusion for benefits from long-term care insurance—per diem limit.

Qualified long-term care insurance contracts (see ¶2146) issued after '96 are treated as accident and health insurance contracts. (Code Sec. 7702B(a)(1)) Pre-'97 contracts that met applicable state long-term care insurance requirements also qualify. (Reg § 1.7702B-2)[24] Amounts (other than policyholder dividends, as defined in Code Sec. 808 or premium refunds) received from such contracts are treated as amounts received for personal injury or sickness

17. ¶J-1201 *et seq.*; ¶744; TD ¶194,001
18. ¶J-1208; ¶744.01; TD ¶194,006
19. ¶J-1210; ¶744.01; TD ¶194,008
20. ¶J-1223; ¶744.04; TD ¶194,019

21. ¶G-2424.2; ¶4514.043; TD ¶441,012
22. ¶J-1301; ¶1044.03; TD ¶194,501
23. ¶H-1115 *et seq.*; ¶1044.03; TD ¶194,501
24. ¶K-2141.6; ¶77,02B4; TD ¶346,304

and as reimbursement for expenses actually incurred for medical care, and are excludable (see ¶1380), subject to a per diem limit, below.[25]

If the total of (1) the periodic payments received for any period under all qualified long-term care insurance contracts treated as made for qualified long-term care services for an insured and (2) the periodic payments received for the period which are treated under Code Sec. 101(g) (see ¶1354) as paid by reason of the death of the insured, exceeds the per diem limit for the period, the excess is includible in gross income. A payment isn't taken into account under (2) if the insured is a terminally ill individual at the time the payment is received. (Code Sec. 7702B(d)(1))[26]

The per diem limit for any period is the excess (if any) of: (a) the greater of (i) $290 per day for 2010 ($300 in 2011), or the equivalent amount when payments are made on another periodic basis, or (ii) the costs incurred for qualified long-term care services provided for the insured for the period, over (b) the total payments received as reimbursement (by insurance or otherwise) for qualified long-term care services provided for the insured during the period. (Code Sec. 7702B(d)(2)) If payments exceed this limit, the excess is excludible only to the extent of actual costs incurred for long-term care services; amounts with respect to which no such actual costs are incurred are fully includible.[27]

¶ 1382   Exclusion for Archer medical savings account (MSA) distributions.

Distributions from an Archer medical savings account (MSA, see ¶1528 for limitations) are excludable from gross income if used exclusively to pay the qualified medical expenses of the individual (account holder) or his spouse or dependents. (Code Sec. 220(f)(1))[28] Otherwise, they are (1) included in gross income (Code Sec. 220(f)(2)) and (2) subject to an additional tax of 15% (20% for post-2010 distributions) reported on Form 8853 unless made after the individual attains age 65, dies, or becomes disabled. (Code Sec. 220(f)(4))[29]

Qualified medical expenses are for medical care as defined under the medical expense deduction rules (see ¶2145), but only to the extent not reimbursed by insurance or otherwise. (Code Sec. 220(d)(2)(A)) For amounts paid with respect to tax years beginning after Dec. 31, 2010, medicine or drugs are qualified medical expenses only if prescribed (whether or not over-the-counter) or if insulin. (Code Sec. 220(d)(2)(A)) Qualified medical expenses don't include insurance premiums other than premiums for qualified long-term care insurance (¶2146), health care continuation coverage (COBRA), and coverage while receiving unemployment compensation. (Code Sec. 220(d)(2)(B))[30]

In any year for which an MSA contribution is made, distributions from that MSA to pay medical expenses are included in gross income if, for the month in which the expense was incurred, the individual for whom the expense was incurred wasn't covered under a "high deductible health plan" or had ineligible coverage. (Code Sec. 220(d)(2)(C))[31]

¶ 1383   Exclusion for health savings account (HSA) distributions.

Distributions from a health savings account (HSA) (see ¶1529) that are used exclusively to pay the qualified medical expenses of an eligible individual (account holder) or his spouse or dependents are excludable from gross income. (Code Sec. 223(f)) For this purpose, an individual may qualify as a dependent without regard to whether he: (1) is subject to the general rule that a dependent of a taxpayer shall be treated as himself having no dependents; (2) is married and files a joint return; and (3) has gross income that exceeds an otherwise applicable gross income limitation. (Code Sec. 223(d)(2)(A))

Qualified medical expenses are expenses paid for medical care as defined under the medical

---

25. ¶J-1308; ¶7702B4.04; TD ¶194,507
26. ¶J-1308; ¶7702B4.04; TD ¶194,507
27. ¶J-1308; ¶7702B4.04; TD ¶194,507
28. ¶H-1337 et seq.; ¶2204.01; TD ¶288,101 et seq.
29. ¶H-1338 et seq.; ¶2204.01; TD ¶288,101 et seq.
30. ¶H-1337.1 et seq.; ¶2204.01; TD ¶288,101 et seq.
31. ¶H-1337.2; ¶2204.01

expense deduction rules (see ¶2145), but only to the extent they're not reimbursed by insurance or otherwise. (Code Sec. 223(d)(2)) For reimbursements of expenses incurred with respect to tax years beginning after Dec. 31, 2010, medicine or drugs are qualified medical expenses only if prescribed (whether or not over-the-counter) or if insulin. (Code Sec. 223(d)(2)(A)) Qualified medical expenses, which must be incurred after the HSA is established, don't include insurance premiums other than premiums for qualified long-term care insurance (¶2146), health care continuation coverage (COBRA) (see ¶1531), and coverage while the eligible individual is receiving unemployment compensation. (Code Sec. 223(d)(2)(B))[32]

Distributions not used for qualified medical expenses are subject to tax, they also are subject to an additional 10% tax (20% for post-2010 distributions) reported on Form 8853 unless made after the individual attains age 65, dies, or becomes disabled. (Code Sec. 223(f))[33]

Contributions for a year exceeding the deduction limit (see ¶1529) can be withdrawn tax-free if the distribution is: (1) completed by the extended tax return due date; and (2) accompanied by the net income (includible in the individual's income) attributable to the excess contribution. (Code Sec. 223(f)(3)(A))[34]

¶ 1384 Exclusion for benefits received through health reimbursement arrangements (HRAs).

Amounts received by an employee under a health reimbursement arrangement (HRA) are excluded from gross income as amounts received under an accident and health plan (¶1380). An HRA is a type of employee benefit plan reimbursing employees for medical expenses not covered by other forms of insurance. For reimbursements of expenses incurred with respect to tax years beginning after Dec. 31, 2010, medicine or drugs are qualified medical expenses only if prescribed (whether or not over-the-counter) or if insulin. (Code Sec. 106(f)) Benefits are paid up to a specific dollar amount from funds provided exclusively by the employer (and not through a salary reduction or otherwise under a cafeteria plan (¶1271)). Balances remaining in the employee's account at the end of a coverage period may be carried forward if the plan so provides. An HRA may use debit cards, credit cards, or other electronic media to support and document the tax-free reimbursement of an employee's claimed medical or dental expenses if proper safeguards and substantiation methods are used.[35]

¶ 1385 Damages.

Compensatory damages received on account of personal physical injuries or personal physical sickness are tax-free (but punitive damages generally are not excludable).

¶ 1386 Nonbusiness damages—personal physical injury or sickness.

Damages other than punitive damages received (by suit or agreement, in a lump-sum or as periodic payments) as compensation for personal *physical*injury or personal *physical* sickness are excluded from income (Code Sec. 104(a)(2); Prop Reg. § 1.104-1 [Taxpayers may apply]) If an action has its origin in a physical injury or physical sickness, then all nonpunitive damages from that injury or sickness are excluded, whether or not the recipient is the injured party. Emotional distress is not considered a physical injury or physical sickness, but the exclusion does apply to damages received up to the amount paid for medical care attributable to emotional distress. (Code Sec. 104(a)) Thus, the exclusion doesn't apply to damages (other than for medical expenses attributable to emotional distress) based on a claim of employment discrimination or injury to reputation accompanied by a claim of emotional distress and does apply to nonpunitive damages received based on a claim of emotional distress, that are attributable to a physical injury or physical sickness.[36] The exclusion does not apply to "delay

---

32. ¶H-1350.1 *et seq.*; ¶2234; TD ¶289,103 *et seq.*
33. ¶H-1350.11 *et seq.*; ¶2234.01; TD ¶289,111 *et seq.*
34. ¶H-1350.10; ¶2234.04; TD ¶289,110

35. ¶H-1349 *et seq.*; TD ¶289,000
36. ¶J-5801; ¶1044.02; TD ¶182,001

damages," i.e., damages awarded due to the delay in payment, which have been held to be in the nature of interest.[37]

Punitive damages generally are taxable, regardless of the nature of the claim. (Code Sec. 104(a)(2)) But under an exception, punitive damages received in connection with a physical injury or sickness are tax-free if received in a civil wrongful death action, and under applicable state law (as in effect on Sept. 13, '95, and without regard to later modification) which provides (or has been construed by a court to provide) that only punitive damages may be awarded in the action. (Code Sec. 104(c))[38]

Where a lump-sum award is specifically allocated by the parties between compensatory and punitive damages, or between personal and business injury, that allocation generally controls. But if no allocation is made, the courts look to the nature of the claims (e.g., primary nature of the harm inflicted) and the payor's intent.[39]

¶ 1387 Amounts received for accepting assignment of personal injury liability.

Amounts received by an assignee (e.g., insurance company) for accepting assignment of a liability to make periodic payments as damages for personal injury or sickness (in a case involving *physical* injury or sickness), including a liability to pay workers' compensation, are excludable from the assignee's gross income, up to the aggregate cost of any "qualified funding asset" used to satisfy the liability. A "qualified funding asset" is a commercial annuity contract, or a U.S. obligation, having payment periods corresponding to those of the liability, which the assignee: (1) purchased within 60 days before or after the date of the assignment, and (2) uses to satisfy that liability. (Code Sec. 130(c))[40]

¶ 1388 Business damages.

Damages received for injury to business that represent compensation for lost profits (including business interruption insurance proceeds) are taxable as ordinary income. This applies to awards for breach of a contract of sale and for business slander. Amounts received for injury to capital (e.g., injury to good will, fraudulent stock sale) are tax-free to the extent of basis; any excess is capital gain.[41] Punitive damages (e.g., insiders' profits, treble damages under antitrust laws) are taxable. (Reg § 1.61-14(a))[42]

There is a special deduction for certain expired net operating losses that resulted from the same injury. (Code Sec. 186(d))[43]

¶ 1389 Attorney's fees payable out of judgment.

Except as provided below, the full amount of the judgment or settlement awarded to the taxpayer belongs to him (and is therefore includable in his gross income), and attorney's fees payable from the award are deductible only as a miscellaneous itemized deduction regardless of whether the fees are contingent or noncontingent.[44]

observation: Since miscellaneous itemized deductions are not deductible for AMT purposes (see ¶3209), attorney's fees not allowable as an above-the-line deduction under Code Sec. 62(a)(19) cannot be deducted in computing AMT.

But attorney fees and court costs paid in connection with the following are deductible from gross income to determine adjusted gross income: (1) a claim of unlawful discrimination; (2) a claim of a violation of subchapter III of chapter 37 of title 31, United States Code (Claims Against the U.S. Government); or (3) a claim made under section 1862(b)(3)(A) of the Social Security Act (private cause of action under the Medicare Secondary Payer statute). (Code

---

37. ¶J-5817; ¶1044.02; TD ¶151,027
38. ¶J-5816.1 *et seq.*; TD ¶182,006
39. ¶J-5810; ¶1044.02; TD ¶182,004
40. ¶J-5833 *et seq.*; ¶s 1304, 1304.01; TD ¶182,008

41. ¶J-5819 *et seq.*; ¶614.170 *et seq.*; TD ¶182,013
42. ¶J-5829; ¶614.168; TD ¶182,018
43. ¶K-8501 *et seq.*; ¶1864 *et seq.*
44. ¶J-8258; TD ¶201,086

Sec. 62(a)(19))[45]

⚫️observation: The deduction applies whether or not eligible legal fees are paid on a contingency basis.

¶ 1390 Income Realized on Discharge or Cancellation of Indebtedness. ▬▬▬▬

Gross income includes income from discharge of indebtedness.

For information reporting by banks, etc., that discharge indebtedness, see ¶4745.

¶ 1391 Debtor has income on discharge of debt—COD income.

Reduction or cancellation of debt (recourse or nonrecourse) is income to the debtor. (Code Sec. 61(a)(12))[46] Cancellation of debt (COD) income thus can result where a creditor accepts less than full payment as a complete discharge of the debt, or where events or circumstances make its collection unlikely.[47] But if the debtor's payment of the liability would have given rise to a deduction, the debtor won't have income from the discharge. (Code Sec. 108(e)(2))[48]

¶ 1392 Cancellation of debt under student loan programs.

There is no income (COD income, see ¶1391) from the cancellation of all or part of certain government student loans (or certain loans made by tax-exempt educational organizations), or loans made by exempt educational organizations or other exempt organizations to refinance any student loan, if the debtor is required to perform public service work for a period of time in certain professions for any of a broad range of employers. (Code Sec. 108(f)(1))[49]

Nor does gross income include any amount received under: (a) Sec. 338B(g) of the Public Health Service Act (relating to the National Health Service Corps Loan Repayment Program); (b) a state program described in Sec. 338I of that Act; or (c) for amounts received in tax years beginning after 2008, any State loan repayment or loan forgiveness program intended to provide for the increased availability of health care services in underserved or health professional shortage areas (as determined by the State). (Code Sec. 108(f)(4))[50]

¶ 1393 Discharge of indebtedness of solvent debtors outside bankruptcy.

Any discharge of indebtedness of a debtor, other than in a bankruptcy case (¶1395), or where the debtor is insolvent (¶1394), results in the current (i.e., year of discharge) recognition of income (COD income, see ¶1391) in the amount of the discharge (Reg § 1.61-12(a))[1] except for certain farm (¶1396) or real property (¶1397) indebtedness.

¶ 1394 Insolvent debtor outside bankruptcy—"insolvency exception"—Form 982

If the indebtedness is discharged when the debtor is insolvent (but not in a bankruptcy case), the discharge is excluded from the debtor's gross income up to the amount of the insolvency. (Code Sec. 108(a)(1)(B), Code Sec. 108(a)(2)(A), Code Sec. 108(a)(3))[2]

The amount excluded under this "insolvency exception" must be applied to reduce the debtor's tax attributes such as loss or credit carryovers or basis in assets. (Credit carryovers are reduced 33⅓¢ per dollar of debt discharge amount; other tax attributes are reduced dollar for dollar.) (Code Sec. 108(b)(3)) (Use Form 982 to report the reduction of tax attributes.) Or the debtor can elect (on Form 982) to apply any or all of the excluded amount *first* to reduce his basis in *depreciable* assets (or real property held as inventory). (Code Sec. 108(b)(5)(A), Code Sec. 1017(b)(3); Reg § 1.108-4(b))[3]

---

45. ¶A-2628; ¶624.04; TD ¶560,715.2
46. ¶J-7001; ¶614.114; TD ¶186,001
47. ¶J-7001 *et seq.*; ¶614.114; TD ¶186,015
48. ¶J-7504; ¶1084.04; TD ¶188,003
49. ¶J-7508; ¶1084.04; TD ¶188,006

50. ¶J-7510.1; ¶1084.04; TD ¶188,008.1
1. ¶s J-7001, J-7200 *et seq.* ¶s 1084, 1084.01; TD ¶188,011
2. ¶J-7401; ¶1084.01; TD ¶188,011
3. ¶J-7404; ¶1084.02; TD ¶188,011

Any balance of the discharged debt (excess over the amount the debtor is insolvent) is COD income, as for a wholly solvent debtor (¶1393). (Code Sec. 108(a)(2)(B), Code Sec. 108(a)(3))[4]

A debtor is insolvent for this purpose if, immediately before the debt is discharged, his liabilities exceed the fair market value of his assets. (Code Sec. 108(d)(3))[5]

If a reorganization or other transaction described in Code Sec. 381(a) ends a year in which the distributor or transferor corporation excludes COD income under Code Sec. 108(a), any tax attributes to which the acquiring corporation succeeds and the basis of property acquired by the acquiring corporation must reflect the reductions required by Code Sec. 108 and Code Sec. 1017. (Reg § 1.108-7(c), Reg § 1.1017-1(b)(4))

For partners and S corporations, see ¶1398.

¶ 1395 Discharge of indebtedness of bankrupt debtor—Form 982.

No amount is included in a debtor's gross income by reason of a discharge of indebtedness in a bankruptcy case (Code Sec. 108(a)(1)(A)), even if the debtor is solvent after the discharge. (Code Sec. 108(a)(2))[6]

The amount of discharged debt that is excluded under this rule must be applied to reduce certain of the debtor's tax attributes (Code Sec. 108(b)(1)) (use Form 982) unless the debtor elects (on Form 982) to apply any or all of the excluded amount *first* to reduce his basis in depreciable assets (or real property held as inventory). (Code Sec. 108(b)(5)(A), Code Sec. 1017(b)(3); Reg § 1.1017-1(c))[7] For partners and S corporations, see ¶1398.

¶ 1396 Discharge of "qualified farm indebtedness" of solvent farmers.

A solvent taxpayer whose "qualified farm indebtedness" is discharged (outside bank-ruptcy) by certain unrelated lenders doesn't have COD income (see ¶1391), to the extent the discharge doesn't exceed the sum of his adjusted tax attributes plus the aggregate adjusted bases (as of the start of the year after discharge) of his business or income-producing prop-erty. (Code Sec. 108(a)(1)(C), Code Sec. 108(g)(1), Code Sec. 108(g)(3)) Any excess is COD income (but the insolvency (¶1394) or bankruptcy (¶1395) rules have precedence). (Code Sec. 108(a)(2))[8]

"Qualified farm indebtedness" is debt incurred directly in connection with taxpayer's farm business if at least 50% of taxpayer's total gross receipts for the three tax years preceding the tax year of the discharge is attributable to farming. (Code Sec. 108(g)(2))[9] For partners and S corporations, see ¶1398.

¶ 1397 Discharge of "qualified real property business indebtedness"—Form 982.

A solvent taxpayer other than a C corporation whose "qualified real property business indebtedness" (QRPBI) is discharged (outside bankruptcy) can elect to exclude the discharged amount from income, to the extent of the excess (if any) of (1) the outstanding principal amount of the QRPBI immediately before the discharge over (2) the fair market value (at discharge) of the property securing the QRPBI less the outstanding principal amount of any other QRPBI secured by the property at that time. (Code Sec. 108(a)(1)(D), Code Sec. 108(c)(2)(A), Code Sec. 108(c)(3)(C); Reg § 1.108-6(a))[10] The excluded amount must be applied (on Form 982) to reduce the basis of taxpayer's depreciable real property. (Code Sec. 108(c)(1)(A))[11]

QRPBI is indebtedness (other than qualified farm indebtedness, ¶1396) incurred or as-sumed by taxpayer in connection with real property used in a trade or business and secured

---

4. ¶J-7401; ¶1084.01; TD ¶188,014   8. ¶J-7405 *et seq.*; ¶1084.01; TD ¶188,018
5. ¶J-7403; ¶1084.01; TD ¶188,014   9. ¶J-7406; ¶1084.01; TD ¶188,019
6. ¶J-7402; ¶1084.01; TD ¶188,013   10. ¶J-7409; ¶1084.01; TD ¶188,022
7. ¶J-7404; ¶1084.02; TD ¶188,016   11. ¶J-7411; ¶1084.01; TD ¶188,024

by the real property (Code Sec. 108(c)(3)(A)) that:

... if incurred or assumed by the taxpayer after '92, is "qualified acquisition indebtedness" (Code Sec. 108(c)(3)(B))—i.e., indebtedness incurred or assumed to acquire, construct, re-construct, or substantially improve the property (Code Sec. 108(c)(4)); and

... taxpayer elects to treat as "qualified real property business indebtedness" (Code Sec. 108(c)(3)(C))[12] on Form 982 attached to the return for the tax year of discharge. (Code Sec. 108(d)(9)(A); Reg § 1.108-5)[13]

QRPBI also includes indebtedness incurred to refinance QRPBI, but only to the extent it doesn't exceed the amount of the indebtedness being refinanced. (Code Sec. 108(c)(3))[14]

¶ 1398 How COD income exclusions apply to partnership or S corporation debt.

For partnership debt, the insolvency (¶1394), bankruptcy (¶1395), qualified farm indebted-ness (¶1396), and qualified real property indebtedness (¶1397) exclusions are applied at the partner level, not at the partnership level. (Code Sec. 108(d)(6))[15] For an S corporation's debt, the exclusions are applied at the corporate level, not at the shareholder level. (Code Sec. 108(d)(7)(A))[16]

¶ 1399 Discounted purchase of debtor's own obligations.

When a debtor buys or otherwise acquires his own obligations for less than face value (i.e., at a discount), he usually realizes taxable income to the extent of the discount. (Reg § 1.61-12(a))[17] This also applies if a party related to the debtor acquires the debtor's indebtedness from an unrelated party. (Code Sec. 108(e)(4)(A); Reg § 1.108-2)[18]

A corporation that repurchases its own bonds (directly or indirectly) has cancellation of debt (COD) income (¶1391) to the extent of the excess of the adjusted issue price over the repurchase price. (Reg § 1.61-12(c)(2))[19]

For the debtor to be taxed, the obligation must require the unconditional payment of a fixed amount. If the obligation really represents an equity interest, a corporate debtor will be, in effect, acquiring its own stock and thus won't be taxed on the "discount." [20]

Deferral and ratable inclusion for debt instrument reacquired in 2009 and 2010. At the taxpayer's election, debt discharge income from the reacquisition of a discounted applicable debt instrument by the taxpayer or a related party after 2008 and before 2011 is deferred for up to five years, and then included in income ratably over five years. For reacquisitions occurring in 2009, income is includible over the 5-year period beginning with the fifth tax year following the tax year in which it's reacquired; and for reacquisitions occurring in 2010, beginning with the fourth tax year following the tax year in which it's reacquired. (Code Sec. 108(i)(1)) An applicable debt instrument is any debt instrument that was issued by a C corporation or by any other person in connection with the conduct of a trade or business by that person. Debt instruments include a bond, debenture, note, certificate, or any other instrument or contractual arrangement constituting indebtedness under Code Sec. 1275(a)(1) (¶1315). (Code Sec. 108(i)(3))[21]

The election is made by including a statement that clearly identifies the instrument and amount of deferred income with the timely filed return (including extensions) for the tax year in which the debt instrument is reacquired. It's made on an instrument-by-instrument basis, and for partnerships, S corporations, or other pass-through entities, the election is made by the partnership, corporation, or other entity. Once made, the election is irrevocable. (Code

12. ¶J-7410; ¶1084.01; TD ¶188,023
13. ¶J-7412; ¶1084.01; TD ¶188,025
14. ¶J-7410; ¶1084.01; TD ¶188,023
15. ¶J-7415; ¶1084.03; TD ¶188,027
16. ¶J-7416; ¶1084.03; TD ¶188,028
17. ¶J-7011; ¶614.114; TD ¶186,020
18. ¶J-7016 et seq.; ¶1084.04; TD ¶186,024
19. ¶J-7204.1; ¶614.136; TD ¶186,003
20. ¶J-7007; TD ¶186,014
21. ¶J-7421; ¶1084.01; TD ¶188,032

Sec. 108(i)(5)(B))

A taxpayer may make an election for any part of debt discharge income realized from the reacquisition of any applicable debt instrument and may exclude the remaining income under other Code Sec. 108 provisions, if applicable. A partnership that elects to defer less than all income realized may determine, in any manner, the part, if any, of a partner's debt discharge income amount that is the partner's deferred amount and the portion, if any, of a partner's debt discharge income amount that is the partner's included amount. For example, one partner's deferred amount may be zero while another partner's deferred amount may equal that partner's COD income amount (or any part of it).[22]

In the case of the taxpayer's death, the liquidation or sale of substantially all the taxpayer's assets (including in a Title 11 or similar case), the cessation of business by the taxpayer, or similar circumstances, any item of income or deduction that is deferred under the deferral rules (and hasn't previously been taken into account) is taken into account in the tax year in which that event occurs (or in a Title 11 case, the day before the bankruptcy petition is filed). This acceleration rule also applies to the sale, exchange or redemption of an interest in a partnership, S corporation, or other passthrough entity by a partner, shareholder, or other person holding an ownership interest in the entity. (Code Sec. 108(i)(5)(D)) Under Reg § 1.108(i)-1T, in general, an electing corporation's deferred COD income is accelerated only if it: (1) changes its tax status, (2) ceases its corporate existence in a transaction to which Code Sec. 381(a) does not apply, or (3) engages in a transaction impairing its ability to pay the tax liability associated with its deferred COD income. Under Reg § 1.108(i)-2T, in general, deferred items allocated to owners of a passthrough are accelerated if the entity: liquidates; sells, exchanges, transfers, or gifts substantially all of its assets; ceases doing business; files a petition in a Title 11 or similar case; or for an S corporation, its election under Code Sec. 1362(a) is terminated.[23]

¶ 1400 Satisfaction of debt with property or services (including "stock for debt").

If a debtor transfers property (other than debt) to, or performs services for, a creditor (or third party) in full satisfaction of the debt, and the property or services are worth the amount owed, there's no *cancellation* of the debt since it was actually paid. But a debtor who satisfies debt with services has taxable *compensation* equal to the debt. (Reg § 1.61-12(a))[24]

A debtor who transfers property (other than debt) in satisfaction of the debt has gain (or loss) to the extent the fair market value (FMV) of the property transferred exceeds (or is less than) his basis in it. The type of gain (or loss), or whether any loss is deductible, is determined under the regular sale or exchange rules (¶2400 *et seq.*). If the property transferred is worth less than the face amount of the debt, the difference is cancellation of debt (COD) income to the debtor.[25]

If a debtor corporation transfers stock, or a debtor partnership transfers a capital or profits interest in that partnership, to a creditor in satisfaction of its recourse or nonrecourse debt, the corporation or partnership is treated as having satisfied the debt with an amount of money equal to the FMV of the stock or the interest. In the case of a partnership, any discharge of debt income recognized under this rule is included in the distributive shares of taxpayers that were partners in the partnership immediately before the discharge. (Code Sec. 108(e)(8)) So the debtor has taxable income to the extent the principal of the debt exceeds the value of the stock or interest.[26]

---

22. ¶J-7424.1
23. ¶J-7427; ¶1084.01; TD ¶188,038
24. ¶J-7040; ¶614.114; TD ¶186,033
25. ¶J-7206; ¶10,014.76; TD ¶221,401
26. ¶J-7015; ¶1084.04; TD ¶186,021

¶ 1401 Debt-for-debt exchanges.

A debtor may satisfy an outstanding "old" debt by issuing a "new" debt. The old debt is treated as having been satisfied with an amount of money equal to the issue price of the new debt. (Code Sec. 108(e)(10)(A)) The excess (if any) of the "old" adjusted issue price over the "new" issue price is COD income (¶1391) to the debtor.[27]

For this purpose, "issue price" is determined under the OID rules (¶1319). (Code Sec. 108(e)(10)(B)) However, if the Code Sec. 483 unstated interest rules (¶1309 *et seq.*) (rather than the OID rules) apply, the new debt's issue price is its stated redemption price at maturity (¶1318) less the unstated interest.[28]

¶ 1402 Home mortgage debt forgiveness—Form 982.

For indebtedness discharged before Jan. 1, 2013, gross income doesn't include any discharge of qualified principal residence indebtedness. (Code Sec. 108(a)(1)(E)) Qualified principal residence indebtedness is acquisition indebtedness under Code Sec. 163(h)(3)(B) with respect to the taxpayers's principal residence (see ¶1733), but with a $2 million limit ($1 million for married individuals filing separately). (Code Sec. 108(h)(2)) It includes indebtedness incurred in the acquisition, construction, or substantial improvement of a principal residence that is secured by the residence. It also includes refinancing of debt to the extent the amount doesn't exceed the amount of the refinanced indebtedness. "Principal residence" has the same meaning as under the homesale exclusion rules of Code Sec. 121 (see ¶2442). (Code Sec. 108(h)(5)) A taxpayer can have only one principal residence at any one time.[29]

The basis of the taxpayer's principal residence is reduced by the excluded amount, but not below zero. (Code Sec. 108(h)(1))[30]

If any loan is discharged, in whole or in part, and only part of the loan is qualified principal residence indebtedness, the mortgage forgiveness exclusion (claimed on Form 982) applies only to so much of the amount discharged as exceeds the amount of the loan (as determined immediately before the discharge) which is not qualified principal residence indebtedness. (Code Sec. 108(h)(4))

The exclusion doesn't apply to the discharge of a loan if the discharge is on account of services performed for the lender or any other factor not directly related to a decline in the value of the residence or to the taxpayer's financial condition.[31] The exclusion also doesn't apply to a taxpayer in a Title 11 bankruptcy (see ¶1395). (Code Sec. 108(h)(3)) An insolvent taxpayer (other than one in a Title 11 bankruptcy) can elect to have the mortgage forgiveness exclusion not apply and can instead rely on the Code Sec. 108(a)(1)(B) exclusion for insolvent taxpayers (see ¶1394). (Code Sec. 108(a)(2))[32]

---

27. ¶J-7205; ¶1084.04; TD ¶186,004
28. ¶J-7205; ¶1084.04; TD ¶186,004
29. ¶J-7417; ¶1084.01; TD ¶188,029

30. ¶P-3006.2; ¶1084.01; TD ¶215,504.1
31. ¶J-7419; ¶1084.01; TD ¶188,031
32. ¶J-7420; ¶1084.01; TD ¶188,029

Chapter 3 Deductions—Expenses of a Business

¶ 1500   Start-Up Expenditures. ▬▬▬▬▬▬▬▬▬▬▬▬

Start-up expenditures must be capitalized, unless a taxpayer elects to expense up to $10,000 in tax years beginning in 2010 ($5,000 in later years) of the cost and amortize the balance over a 180-month period.

¶ 1501   Tax treatment of start-up expenditures.

Start-up expenditures must be amortized and can't be deducted unless the taxpayer elects (¶1502) to expense up to $10,000 of these costs (in tax years beginning in 2010; $5,000 in later years) with the $10,000 cap being reduced by the excess of total start-up expenditures over $60,000 (in tax years beginning in 2010; $50,000 in later years) in the tax year in which the trade or business begins. The remainder of the start-up expenditures may be amortized (deducted ratably) over a 15-year period. (Code Sec. 195(b)(1))[1]

Start-up expenditures are amounts paid or incurred in connection with:

. . . investigating the creation, acquisition, or establishment of an active trade or business, (Code Sec. 195(c)(1)(A)(i)) but not costs incurred after a taxpayer decides whether to enter a new business, and which new business it will enter or acquire;[2]

. . . creating an active trade or business (Code Sec. 195(c)(1)(A)(ii)); or

. . . any activity engaged in for profit and for the production of income before the day the active trade or business begins, in anticipation of that activity becoming an active trade or business. (Code Sec. 195(c)(1)(A)(iii))

The expenditure must be one that, if paid or incurred in connection with the operation of an existing active trade or business (in the same field as the taxpayer's new business), would be deductible for the year in which paid or incurred. (Code Sec. 195(c)(1)(B))[3]

Start-up expenses don't include any amounts deductible under Code Sec. 163(a) (i.e., as interest expenses); Code Sec. 164 (i.e., as taxes); or Code Sec. 174 (i.e., as research and experimental expenses). (Code Sec. 195(c)(1))[4]

¶ 1502   Election to expense/amortize start-up expenditures—Form 4562.

A taxpayer (1) is deemed to have elected to expense/amortize start-up costs under Code Sec. 195(b) (¶1501) for the tax year in which the active trade or business begins, but (2) may forgo the deemed election by clearly electing to capitalize start-up expenditures on a timely filed Federal income tax return (including extensions) for the tax year in which the active trade or business begins. The choice of expensing/amortizing or capitalizing start-up expenditures is irrevocable and applies to all start-up expenditures related to the active trade or business. (Reg § 1.195-1T(b))

¶ 1503   Treatment of deferred start-up expenses on disposition of business.

If the trade or business is disposed of before the end of the amortization period, any deferred expenses not yet deducted may be deducted to the extent the disposition results in a loss under Code Sec. 165. (Code Sec. 195(b)(2))[5]

---

1. ¶L-5001; ¶1954; TD ¶301,001
2. ¶L-5013; ¶1954.01; TD ¶301,009
3. ¶L-5011; ¶s 1954, 1954.01; TD ¶301,012

4. ¶L-5011; ¶1954.01; TD ¶301,008
5. ¶L-5023; ¶1954.04; TD ¶301,015

References beginning with a single letter are to paragraphs in RIA's Federal Tax Coordinator 2d and RIA's Analysis of Federal Taxes: Income. Those beginning with numbers are to paragraphs in RIA's United States Tax Reporter. Those beginning with TD are to paragraphs in RIA's Tax Desk.

¶ 1504 Fruitless searches for new ventures.

A corporation that makes expenditures in fruitlessly searching for or investigating a new venture may deduct them as a loss when it abandons the effort.[6] A noncorporate taxpayer not engaged in the business of locating or promoting new ventures can't deduct expenditures made in fruitlessly searching for or investigating a new venture. However, once a taxpayer has focused on the acquisition of a specific business or investment, unsuccessful start-up expenses that are related to an attempt to acquire that business or investment are deductible as business or investment losses under Code Sec. 165 (¶1774).[7]

¶ 1505 Expanding an existing business.

A taxpayer can deduct expenditures made to expand an existing business. The taxpayer must show that the business contemplated and the one already conducted are closely related or "intramural," *and* that the expenditures are ordinary and necessary expenses of the business conducted when the expenses were incurred, and not capital expenditures.

Expansion costs must be capitalized if they provide the taxpayer with long-term benefits, or create separate and distinct assets, or relate to a change in the nature of the taxpayer's activities (e.g., wholesaler opening retail outlet).[8]

¶ 1506 Ordinary and Necessary Business Expenses. ■■■■■■■■■■■■■■■■■■■■■■■

Individuals, corporations and other taxpayers generally can deduct ordinary and necessary expenses paid or incurred during the tax year in carrying on any trade or business. Various limits (e.g., percentage limit on meal and entertainment deductions, see ¶1570) may apply.

¶ 1507 "Ordinary and necessary" requirement.

A deductible business expense must be both ordinary and necessary in relation to the taxpayer's industry. (Code Sec. 162(a))[9]

An expense is *ordinary* if it's customary or usual in the taxpayer's business.[10] But an unusual expense may be ordinary if it's reasonably related to the taxpayer's trade or business.[11] A *necessary* expense is one that's appropriate and helpful in developing and maintaining the taxpayer's business. It need not be essential or indispensable. Usually the taxpayer's judgment as to what's necessary will be accepted.[12] Expenditures are deductible as ordinary and necessary even if they are unwise.[13]

Some courts have held that to be deductible under Code Sec. 162, an expense must not only be ordinary and necessary, but also reasonable in amount and reasonable in relation to its purpose.[14] It has been held that depreciation deductions are not to be considered in assessing if business expenses are reasonable under Code Sec. 162.[15]

¶ 1508 Connection to taxpayer's trade or business.

To be deductible as a business expense, an item must be directly connected with or pertain to a trade or business carried on by the taxpayer. (Code Sec. 162(a); Reg § 1.162-1(a))[16]

Serving as an employee is a business (see ¶1628 for deduction limitations).[17] A trade or business need not be the taxpayer's principal occupation; a sideline can qualify.[18]

---

6. ¶L-5019; ¶1954; TD ¶301,013
7. ¶L-5020; ¶1954; TD ¶301,014
8. ¶L-5101; ¶1624 *et seq.*; TD ¶301,016
9. ¶L-1200 *et seq.*; ¶1624.012; TD ¶255,512
10. ¶L-1201; ¶1624.012; TD ¶255,512
11. ¶s L-1201, L-1209; ¶1624.012; TD ¶255,512
12. ¶L-1201; ¶1624.012; TD ¶255,512
13. ¶L-1210; TD ¶255,522
14. ¶L-1202; ¶1624.013; TD ¶255,513
15. ¶L-1211
16. ¶L-1002; ¶1624; TD ¶256,001
17. ¶L-3900; ¶1624; TD ¶256,005
18. ¶L-1100 *et seq.*; ¶1624.002

¶ 1509   Expense must benefit person claiming deduction.

A deductible expense must be an expense of *the taxpayer's* business. Expenses incurred on another's behalf aren't deductible.[19]

A corporation can't deduct payment of the personal expenses of its shareholders.[20] Nor can it deduct payment of the personal expenses of its officers and employees, except to the extent the payment represents reasonable compensation (¶1517) or is made for business reasons to provide benefits to employees in general.[21]

A corporate officer can't deduct an expenditure he makes to pay an expense of the corporation.[22]

If a taxpayer pays the debts or other obligations of another, the payment may sometimes qualify as a business expense.[23] Deductions have been allowed where such a payment is made for a good business reason, e.g., preserve sales-force morale and customer goodwill; reestablish or protect credit standing; avoid loss of business patronage, etc.[24]

¶ 1510   Right to deduction—*Cohan* rule.

Where a taxpayer's records or other proof aren't adequate to substantiate expense deductions, he may be allowed to deduct an estimated amount under the *Cohan* rule. But a court may allow a much smaller deduction than claimed, bearing heavily against a taxpayer whose inexactitude is of his own making.[25] The *Cohan* rule doesn't apply to travel or entertainment expenses, listed property, or business gifts, see ¶1580.

¶ 1511   Expenses of membership organizations.

Organizations that aren't exempt from tax under the rules discussed at ¶ 4100 *et seq.*, which are operated primarily to furnish services or goods to members, can deduct expenses of furnishing services, insurance, goods, or other items to members only to the extent of income derived during the year from members or transactions with members. (Code Sec. 277(a))[26] Any excess of expenses over income isn't deductible, but may be carried over to the following tax year. (Code Sec. 277(a))[27]

¶ 1512   Advertising and business promotion costs.

Advertising and business promotion costs relating to an existing business can be deducted currently, even though the business benefit they generate may extend over a period beyond the year they are incurred or paid.[28]

Production costs of a business catalog that will remain unchanged for several years must be capitalized according to IRS, but some courts disagree.[29] Display equipment (cabinets, signs, etc.) must be capitalized if it has a useful life beyond the tax year.[30] IRS says that package design costs (e.g., physical construction of a package containing a consumer product) must be capitalized. A court has held that graphic design costs making up the overall visual display of a product may be deducted currently as advertising expenses, but IRS disagrees.[31]

¶ 1513   Costs of determining or contesting tax liability.

Costs relating to tax matters that are ordinary and necessary in the course of the conduct of taxpayer's trade or business, including costs of tax advice, are deductible. The deduction

---

19. ¶L-4400; ¶1624.104; TD ¶256,500
20. ¶L-1214; ¶1624.104; TD ¶256,517
21. ¶L-4414; ¶1624.205; TD ¶256,517
22. ¶L-4405; ¶1624.009; TD ¶256,505
23. ¶L-1214; ¶1624.104; TD ¶256,500
24. ¶L-1214 *et seq.*; ¶s 1624.015, 1624.026; TD ¶255,515
25. ¶L-4509 *et seq.*; ¶1624.014; TD ¶257,007

26. ¶L-4301; ¶2774; TD ¶307,724
27. ¶L-4301; ¶2774; TD ¶307,727
28. ¶L-2201; ¶1624.355; TD ¶300,500
29. ¶L-2205; ¶1624.355; TD ¶300,510
30. ¶L-2206; ¶1624.355; TD ¶300,511
31. ¶L-5629

applies to expenses incurred in: (1) preparing tax returns, (2) determining tax liability, (3) contesting tax liability, (4) securing tax counsel. (Code Sec. 62(a)(1); Reg § 1.62-1T(d)) This includes expenses incurred by an individual taxpayer in:[32]

- preparing that portion of the individual's tax return that relates to the taxpayer's business as sole proprietor,
- preparing schedules relating to income or loss from rentals or royalties, or farm income and expenses, and
- resolving asserted tax deficiencies relating to a business, to rental or royalty income, or to a farm.

For deduction of nonbusiness tax determination costs as miscellaneous itemized deductions subject to the 2%-of-AGI floor, see ¶3110. For deductibility of interest on taxes, see ¶1708.

¶ 1514 Other deductible costs of carrying on a trade or business.

These include:[33]

. . . cost of materials and supplies not consumed in the process of manufacturing;[34]

. . . annual license and regulatory fees;[35]

. . . amounts paid to cancel burdensome contracts;[36]

. . . cost of moving business equipment and machinery;[37]

. . . current membership fees (but not admission fees), dues (but for social club dues, see ¶1569) and assessments paid for business association, etc.;[38]

. . . restaurant's cost of smallware (glassware, flatware, etc.);[39]

. . . training costs; and[40]

. . . certain education expenses, see ¶2228 *et seq.*

¶ 1515 Compensation Deduction.

Reasonable amounts that are paid or incurred in connection with a trade or business as compensation for personal services actually rendered are deductible, subject to a limit for top officers. Payments for fringe benefits are deductible as compensation, subject to some limits.

¶ 1516 Compensation paid for personal services.

Compensation (including severance pay)[41] paid or incurred for personal services rendered is deductible as a trade or business expense. (Code Sec. 162(a)(1)) Deductible compensation includes amounts paid to independent contractors, as well as employees.[42]

A parent can deduct reasonable wages he pays his unemancipated minor child for personal services actually rendered as a bona fide employee in the business.[43]

For deductibility of amounts paid for fringe benefits, see ¶1524 *et seq.* For when compensation can be deducted, see ¶1538 *et seq.*

¶ 1517 Reasonableness of compensation.

Compensation is deductible only to the extent it's *reasonable*. Compensation paid to employee-shareholders also must be paid purely for services, or have a purely compensatory purpose, in order to be deductible. (Code Sec. 162(a)(1))[44] The question of reasonableness

32. ¶L-3000 *et seq.*; ¶2124.14; TD ¶307,201
33. ¶L-4200 *et seq.*; ¶1624.404; TD ¶307,700 *et seq.*
34. ¶L-4207 *et seq.*; TD ¶307,718
35. ¶L-4216 *et seq.*; TD ¶307,717
36. ¶L-4213 *et seq.*; TD ¶307,714
37. ¶L-4209 *et seq.*; ¶1624.052; TD ¶307,711
38. ¶L-4231; ¶1624.061; TD ¶307,721
39. ¶L-4207.1; ¶4465.22(5)
40. ¶L-4232.3; TD ¶256,201
41. ¶H-3600 *et seq.*; ¶1624.205; TD ¶276,000 *et seq.*
42. ¶H-3600 *et seq.*; ¶1624.205; TD ¶276,000
43. ¶H-3755; ¶1624.212; TD ¶276,045
44. ¶1624.229; TD ¶276,022

rarely arises unless the payments are made to a person "related" to the taxpayer —that is, to the members of an employer's family, or to stockholders of the employer, or to members of a stockholder's family.[45]

The unreasonable portion of compensation is nondeductible. If the recipient is a shareholder, the unreasonable portion may be treated as a dividend. (Reg § 1.162-7(b)(1))[46]

¶ 1518 Factors determining reasonableness.

Reasonable compensation is the amount that would ordinarily be paid for like services by like enterprises under like circumstances. (Reg § 1.162-7(b)(3))[47] Other factors determining reasonableness include: (1) duties performed by the employee; (2) character and amount of responsibility; (3) amount of time required; (4) ability and achievements of the employee; (5) volume of business handled by the employee; (6) complexities of the business; (7) relationship of compensation to gross and net income of the business; (8) living conditions in locality; (9) compensation history of the employee; and (10) salary policy as to all employees.[48]

The Seventh Circuit applies a single independent-investor test in evaluating if a stockholder-employee's pay is reasonable (i.e., would an outside investor have paid the compensation amount based on performance). Other courts employ the independent-investor test in conjunction with an analysis of the above factors.[49]

The test of whether compensation is reasonable is normally applied to the compensation paid to the particular individual and not to the total compensation paid to a group of employees.[50] Services rendered in earlier years can be taken into account in determining the reasonableness of compensation paid during the current year.[1] Reasonableness of compensation for part-time services is determined under the usual reasonableness rules. Generally, salaries that are reasonable for an employee's full-time services aren't reasonable for his part-time services.[2]

¶ 1519 Deduction limit for compensation paid to top officers.

A publicly held corporation can't deduct applicable employee remuneration (defined below) in excess of $1 million per year paid to a covered employee (Code Sec. 162(m)(1))[3] —the principal executive officer (or someone acting in that capacity) and the three highest paid officers (other than the principal executive officer or principal financial officer). (Code Sec. 162(m)(3); Reg § 1.162-27(c)(2))[4] The $1 million limit is reduced (but not below zero) by the amount, if any, paid to the executive but not deductible under the golden parachute rules (¶1536). (Code Sec. 162(m)(4)(F); Reg § 1.162-27(g))[5]

Applicable employee remuneration means a covered employee's aggregate remuneration for services performed (either during the deduction year or during another tax year) which would be deductible entirely for the tax year if the $1 million limit didn't apply. (Code Sec. 162(m)(4)(A)) But it doesn't include commissions generated directly by the executive's performance (Code Sec. 162(m)(4)(B); Reg § 1.162-27(d)), certain other performance-based compensation (Code Sec. 162(m)(4)(C); Reg § 1.162-27(e)), certain grandfathered contracts (Code Sec. 162(m)(4)(D)), qualified plan contributions and certain excludable employee fringe benefits. (Code Sec. 162(m)(4)(E); Reg § 1.162-27(c)(3)(ii))[6]

The above Code Sec. 162(m) deduction limit is reduced to $500,000 for remuneration paid to covered executives (generally, CEO, CFO, and the 3 highest paid other officers) by an employer that is a TARP recipient—i.e., any entity that has received or will receive financial assistance under the Troubled Asset Relief Program established under §101, Div. A., PL 110-343, 10/3/2008. This limit applies to executive remuneration paid by a TARP recipient during

45. ¶s H-3725 *et seq.*, H-3752 *et seq.*; ¶1624.229; TD ¶276,044
46. ¶H-3607; ¶1624.268; TD ¶276,009
47. ¶H-3701; ¶1624.229; TD ¶276,023
48. ¶H-3706; ¶1624.229; TD ¶276,041
49. ¶H-3721; TD ¶276,027
50. ¶H-3705; ¶1624.229; TD ¶276,026

1. ¶H-3745; ¶1624.229; TD ¶276,062
2. ¶H-3715; ¶1624.229; TD ¶276,036
3. ¶H-3776; ¶1624.009; TD ¶276,001.1
4. ¶H-3780; ¶1624.009; TD ¶276,001.1
5. ¶H-3809; ¶1624.009; TD ¶276,001.1
6. ¶H-3781 *et seq.*; ¶1624.009; TD ¶276,001.1

the period in which any obligation arising from financial assistance provided under TARP remains outstanding. (Code Sec. 162(m)(5), §7001, PL 111-5, 2/17/2009)[7]

¶ 1520   Services rendered to another.

A taxpayer can't deduct payments for services rendered to someone other than the taxpayer—for example, payments by a shareholder to employees of the corporation for services to the corporation, or by a corporation to its officers for services to subsidiaries and related corporations, or by a corporation to employees of a sub. But salary paid by a parent corporation to its own executives for supervising the operations of a sub is deductible by the parent as an expense of the parent's business.[8]

¶ 1521   Payment of employee debts or expenses.

An employer's payment of an employee's debts or personal expenses is deductible by the employer as compensation paid (if reasonable, see ¶1517), just as if the employee had been paid directly and he had used the money to pay his debts or expenses.[9]

¶ 1522   Contingent compensation.

An employer can deduct contingent compensation, where it's freely bargained for between the employer and the individual before the services are rendered, and not influenced by any consideration on the part of the employer other than that of securing the individual's services on fair and advantageous terms. This is so even though the arrangement results in higher compensation than would otherwise be allowed as a deduction. The reasonableness of the amount is determined by the circumstances at the date the contract for services is made, not when the contract is questioned. (Reg § 1.162-7(b)(2), Reg § 1.162-7(b)(3))[10]

¶ 1523   Payment in property other than cash.

The deduction for compensation paid in property, including a bargain sale and including restricted property, is the amount included in the income of the person who performed the services, to the extent the compensation is reasonable. (Code Sec. 83(h))[11] The "amount included" in income is the amount reported by the service provider on an original or amended return, or included in income as a result of an IRS audit. It includes excluded group-term life insurance and foreign income. (Reg § 1.83-6(a)(1))

Under a "deemed inclusion rule," however, a deduction may be taken by an employer (service recipient) if he timely complies with the applicable information reporting requirements. Thus, an employee is *deemed* to have included the property received in income, and a deduction can be claimed by the employer if he timely satisfies the Code Sec. 6041 or Code Sec. 6041A reporting requirements (Reg § 1.83-6(a)(2)), i.e., by timely reporting the transaction to the service provider and federal government on Form W-2 or Form 1099-MISC, whichever applies. If this rule isn't satisfied, an employer must demonstrate that the compensation amount deducted was actually included in the service provider's income.[12]

The deemed inclusion rule can be used where the service provider is a corporation by issuing Form 1099-MISC even though there would otherwise be a general reporting exemption for a service provider that's a corporation. (Reg § 1.83-6(a)(2))

If a transfer is less than $600 in any tax year (in which case the reporting requirements don't apply), or if the transfer is eligible for any other reporting exemption (applicable to a noncorporate service provider), no Form 1099 reporting is required in order for the service recipient to rely on the deemed inclusion rule.[13]

7. ¶H-3821; ¶1624.009; TD ¶276,001.1
8. ¶H-3613; ¶1624.104; TD ¶276,001
9. ¶H-4014; ¶1624.273; TD ¶136,527
10. ¶H-3732; ¶1624.229; TD ¶276,053

11. ¶H-3650 *et seq.*; ¶s 834.04, 1624.273; TD ¶277,001
12. ¶H-3650 *et seq.*; ¶s 834.04, 1624.273, TD ¶277,003
13. ¶H-3654; ¶834.04; TD ¶277,003

In addition, to be deductible a transfer can't be a capital expenditure, a deferred expense, or part of inventory. (Reg § 1.83-6(a)(4))[14]

If payment is in employer stock, no gain or loss results. (Code Sec. 1032)[15] If payment is in property other than the employer's stock, and the value of the property exceeds the employer's basis for the property, the excess is income to the employer (capital gain or ordinary income, depending on the character of the property used). (Reg § 1.83-6(b)) The employer has a loss deduction where the basis of the property exceeds its fair market value[16] (subject to related-taxpayer restrictions on losses).[17]

The deduction is allowed for the tax year of the employer in which, or with which, the employee's tax year ends. (Code Sec. 83(h))[18]

illustration: Corporation X, which is on a Sept. 30 fiscal year, pays calendar year employee J in stock on July 1, Year 1. J reports the income on his return for Year 1. X deducts the payment on its return for the year ending Sept. 30, Year 2, because that is X's tax year in which the tax year of J, in which the amounts are included in income, ends.

For restricted property, see ¶1219; for noncash fringe benefits, see ¶1524.

¶ 1524   Compensation paid as noncash fringe benefits.

If an employer furnishes a noncash fringe benefit to an employee as compensation, the employer may deduct only the costs it incurs in providing the property to its employees, not the property's value. The employer may claim a depreciation deduction if it owns the property or a deduction for leasing costs if it rents the property. (Reg § 1.162-25T(a))[19]

Furnishing property to an employee for his personal use is additional compensation to him and gives rise to a deduction by the employer. For example, the employer can deduct depreciation and maintenance expenses it pays on a car, house, etc., furnished for an employee's personal use and treated by the employer as compensation. (Code Sec. 274(e)(2))[20]

For deduction limits on entertainment expenses of officers, directors, and 10%-or-more owners, see ¶1573.

¶ 1525   Stock options.

An employer's deduction for a nonstatutory stock option is determined under the Code Sec. 83 payment-in-property rules at ¶1523 (and thus, the employer would deduct the amount the employee must include in income on exercise of the option, where the option has no readily ascertainable value at grant, see ¶1221).[21] The employer isn't allowed a compensation deduction for stock transferred under an incentive stock option or an employee stock purchase plan, unless the employee has income by reason of a disqualified (premature) disposition of the stock (¶1222 *et seq.*). (Code Sec. 421(a), Code Sec. 421(b))[22]

¶ 1526   Premiums on company-owned life insurance, endowment or annuity contracts.

A taxpayer can't deduct premiums on any life insurance policy, or endowment or annuity contract if it is directly or indirectly a beneficiary under the policy or contract. (Code Sec. 264(a)(1)) However, this rule doesn't apply to Code Sec. 72(s)(5) annuity contracts (certain qualified pension plans, retirement annuities, individual retirement annuities and qualified funding assets) or to any annuity contract to which Code Sec. 72(u) (annuity contracts held by other than natural persons) applies. (Code Sec. 264(b)(2)) Premiums are deductible as a noncash fringe benefit where only the insured employee or his beneficiaries will get the

14. ¶H-3650 *et seq.*; ¶s 834.04, 1624.273; TD ¶277,008
15. ¶H-3659; ¶10,324; TD ¶277,010
16. ¶H-3659; TD ¶277,010
17. ¶H-3659; TD ¶277,010
18. ¶H-3653; ¶834.04; TD ¶277,002

19. ¶H-4002; ¶1624.283; TD ¶278,303
20. ¶s H-2150 *et seq.*, H-2160; ¶1624.283; TD ¶277,000 *et seq.*
21. ¶H-2883
22. ¶H-2960; ¶4214.01 *et seq.*; TD ¶136,102

proceeds. For contracts issued before June 9, '97, the deduction disallowance only applies to premiums on the life of an officer, employee or any person financially interested in any trade or business carried on by the taxpayer if the taxpayer is directly or indirectly a beneficiary of any part of the policy.[23]

Premiums on group term life insurance are deductible (if the employer isn't directly or indirectly a beneficiary) even though the employee isn't taxed (¶1264) on group term coverage of $50,000 or less.[24]

For interest on business life insurance loans, see ¶1718.

¶ 1527 Health and accident insurance premiums and direct payment or reimbursement of medical expenses under a plan for employees.

The employer's payment of health and accident insurance premiums for employees and their families, or the employer's direct payment or reimbursement of actual expenses if under a plan, is deductible. (Reg § 1.162-10(a))[25] Reimbursements are deductible even where the employee is the spouse of a sole proprietor, and the medical expenses incurred on behalf of the employee's family include those of the sole proprietor (as the employee's spouse).[26] IRS treats these amounts as additional compensation deductible by the employer to the extent that it, when added to other compensation, is reasonable.[27]

¶ 1528 Contributions to Archer medical savings account (MSA)—Form 8853.

Eligible small employers (see ¶1258), their employees, and self-employed individuals may deduct contributions to an Archer medical savings account (MSA). (Code Sec. 106, Code Sec. 220) An eligible self-employed claims deductions for MSAs above the line, to arrive at adjusted gross income. (Code Sec. 62(a)(16)) After 2007, no new contributions can be made to MSAs, except by or for individuals who previously had MSA contributions and employees who are employed by a participating employer. (Code Sec. 220(i))[28]

MSAs are available to employees covered under a high deductible health plan (HDHP) of a small employer (¶1258) and to self-employed individuals covered by a HDHP. An individual isn't eligible for an MSA if he's entitled to benefits under Medicare or covered under any other health plan, unless the other coverage is permitted insurance (e.g., insurance for a specified disease or illness, or fixed payment for hospitalization) or coverage for accidents, disability, dental care, vision care, or long-term care. For employees, contributions can be made by the employee or the employer, but not by both for the same year. An MSA is a tax-exempt entity but is subject to the tax on unrelated business income. (Code Sec. 220(c), Code Sec. 220(d))[29]

For 2010, a HDHP is a health plan with an annual deductible of at least $2,000 and not more than $3,000 for individual coverage ($4,050 and not more than $6,050 for family coverage); in addition, the maximum out-of-pocket expenses can't exceed $4,050 for individual coverage ($7,400 for family coverage). For 2011, a HDHP is a health plan with an annual deductible of at least $2,050 and not more than $3,050 for individual coverage ($4,100 and not more than $6,150 for family coverage); in addition, the maximum out-of-pocket expenses can't exceed $4,100 for individual coverage ($7,500 for family coverage). (Code Sec. 220(c)(2))[30]

The maximum annual contribution for individual coverage is 65% of the HDHP (75% for family coverage). The annual contribution limit is the sum of the limits determined separately for each month the individual is MSA-eligible. (Code Sec. 220(b)(1))[31] A self-employed's deduction for contributions to an MSA can't exceed his earned income from the trade or

23. ¶H-4031; ¶2644; TD ¶278,505
24. ¶H-4037; ¶s 614.031, 794; TD ¶278,507
25. ¶s H-4071, H-4073; ¶1624.277; TD ¶278,901
26. ¶L-3510; TD ¶278,902
27. ¶L-3509; ¶1624.229; TD ¶278,901

28. ¶H-1326 *et seq.*; ¶2204 *et seq.*; TD ¶288,100 *et seq.*
29. ¶H-1331.1 *et seq.*, ¶H-1335.4; ¶2204.01; TD ¶288,108
30. ¶H-1332; ¶2204.01; TD ¶288,103
31. ¶s H-1335, H-1335.1; ¶2204.01; TD ¶288,101

business that established the HDHP (Code Sec. 220(b)(4)(B)),[32] and an employee's contributions to an MSA can't exceed his compensation from the employer that set up the plan. (Code Sec. 220(b)(4)(A))[33] Contributions can be made until the unextended tax return due date. Excess contributions are subject to a 6% penalty tax (on Form 5329). (Code Sec. 4973(a)(2), Code Sec. 4973(d))[34]

For treatment of MSA distributions, see ¶1382.

¶ 1529 Contributions to health savings accounts (HSAs).

Eligible individuals may, subject to statutory limits, make deductible contributions to a health savings account (HSA). Other persons (e.g., family members) also may contribute on behalf of eligible individuals, as may employers (see ¶1259). (Code Sec. 106, Code Sec. 223) An account holder may deduct contributions to his HSA even if another (e.g., family member) makes the contributions. (Code Sec. 62(a)(19)) An HSA is a tax-exempt entity but is subject to the tax on unrelated business income. (Code Sec. 223(e)(1))

For tax-free HSA distributions for qualifying medical expenses see ¶1383.

Eligible individuals. These are individuals who are covered under a high deductible health plan (HDHP) (see below) and are not covered under any other health plan which is not a HDHP, unless the other coverage is permitted insurance (for worker's compensation, torts, ownership and use of property such as auto insurance, insurance for a specified disease or illness, or providing a fixed payment for hospitalization) or coverage for accidents, disability, dental care, vision care, or long-term care. (Code Sec. 223(c))[35] HSA contributions for an individual aren't deductible if he is claimed as a dependent by another taxpayer for the year. (Code Sec. 223(b)(6)) There's no deduction for an HSA contribution for any month an individual is eligible for and enrolled in Medicare. (Code Sec. 223(b)(7))

HDHP. For 2010 and 2011, a HDHP is a health plan with an annual deductible that is not less than $1,200 for individual coverage ($2,400 for family coverage), and maximum out-of-pocket expenses of $5,950 for individual coverage ($11,900 for family coverage). (Code Sec. 223(c)(2))[36] However, an HDHP may have a zero preventive care deductible or a preventive care deductible below the minimum annual deductible. (Code Sec. 223(c)(2)(C)) Preventive care does not generally include any service or benefit intended to treat an existing illness, injury, or condition.

Other coverage. Health flexible spending accounts (FSAs, see ¶1271) and health reimbursement arrangements (HRAs, see ¶1384) are "other coverage" that will generally preclude HSA eligibility. However, exceptions apply for limited purpose FSAs and HRAs (those providing only certain benefits, e.g., dental and vision); suspended HRAs (where the employee elects to forgo reimbursements for the coverage period); FSAs and HRAs imposing annual deductibles, and HRAs providing benefits only after retirement. An otherwise eligible individual may be covered by an HRA which pays and reimburses expenses for (1) vision, dental and preventive care, and (2) premiums for coverage by an accident and health plan.[37] Coverage under a health FSA during the "grace period" (i.e., the period immediately following the end of a plan year during which unused benefits or contributions remaining may be paid or reimbursed to plan participants for qualified expenses) is disregarded coverage for HSA purposes if: (1) the balance in the health FSA at the end of the plan year is zero; or (2) the remaining balance in the health FSA at the end of the plan year is contributed to an HSA under the one-time rollover rule (see below). (Code Sec. 223(c)(1))

Limit on deductible contributions. The maximum annual HSA deductible contribution is the sum of the monthly contribution limits, based on eligibility and health plan coverage on the first day of the month. The monthly limit is 1/12 of the indexed amount for self-only coverage ($3,050 for 2010 and 2011) and for family coverage ($6,150 for 2010 and 2011). The

32. ¶H-1335.3; ¶2204.01; TD ¶288,101
33. ¶H-1335.3; ¶2204.01; TD ¶288,101
34. ¶H-1336.1 *et seq.*; ¶2204.01; TD ¶288,101

35. ¶H-1350.3 *et seq.*; ¶2204.01; TD ¶288,103
36. ¶H-1350.6; ¶2234.02; TD ¶289,106
37. ¶H-1350.4A

maximum HSA contribution is increased by an additional catch-up contribution amount (computed on a monthly basis) for individuals age 55 or older as of the last day of the calendar year who are not enrolled in Medicare. The catch-up contribution amount is $1,000 for 2010 and after. There is no requirement that the individual have earnings. (Code Sec. 223(b))[38] Contributions for a year can be made until the account holder's tax return due date (without extensions) for that year. Excess contributions are subject to a 6% penalty tax (on Form 5329). (Code Sec. 4973(a)(5), Code Sec. 223(f)(3))[39] Maximum annual HSA contributions are reduced by Archer MSA (¶1528) contributions for that year. (Code Sec. 223(b)(4))

For computing the annual HSA contribution, a taxpayer who is an eligible individual in the last month of a tax year is "deemed eligible" during every month of that year. (Code Sec. 223(b)(8)) Thus, he can make contributions for months before he was enrolled in a HDHP. But if he contributes under the "deemed eligible" rule and does not remain an eligible individual (except because of disability) during the testing period (from the last month of the tax year to the last day of the 12th month following that month), contributions for months in which he was "deemed eligible" are includible in gross income for the tax year of the first day during the testing period that the taxpayer is not an eligible individual and are subject to a 10% penalty tax. (Code Sec. 223(b)(8)(B))

HSA rollovers and carryover of HSA funds. Amounts in an HSA can be rolled over tax free from an HSA, or from an Archer MSA to an HSA. The rollover must be completed within 60 days after the date on which the account holder receives the amounts from the HSA or Archer MSA and is not taken into account in determining the annual contribution limits for the recipient HSA. Only one tax-free rollover into an HSA is permitted per one year period. (Code Sec. 223(f)(5), Code Sec. 220(f)(5))[40]

One-time rollovers from health FSAs or HRAs. After Dec. 20, 2006 and before Jan. 1, 2012, health FSA or HRA distributions may be rolled over via direct transfer to an HSA. (Code Sec. 106(e)) The amount transferred can't exceed the lesser of the balance in the health FSA or HRA: (1) as of Sept. 21, 2006; or (2) as of the date of the distribution. An individual is allowed only one rollover from each of his health FSAs or HRAs. (Code Sec. 106(e)(2)) Such rollovers are: excludable from income; not subject to employment tax; disregarded in applying the maximum deduction limit for other HSA contributions; and are not deductible. An employer allowing direct transfers from a health FSA or HRA to an HSA must on a nondiscriminatory basis permit all employees covered under its HDHP to make such transfers; a 35% excise tax applies for noncompliance. (Code Sec. 106(e)(5)(B)) A rollover can't be made for an individual who was not covered by a health FSA or HRA on Sept. 21, 2006.

For one-time rollovers from IRAs, see ¶4364.

Comparability rule for employer contributions. In general, employer contributions to employee HSAs must be the same amount or the same percentage of the HDHP deductible for all employees with the same category of HDHP coverage (self-only, or family coverage, i.e., any coverage other than self-only). But employers may make larger HSA contributions for nonhighly compensated employees than for highly compensated employees (as defined in Code Sec. 414(q), see ¶4326). (Code Sec. 4980G(d)) Employers that provide self + 1, self + 2 and self + 3 family coverage apply the comparability rules separately to each category. The comparability rules apply separately to full time, part-time, and former employees (except for former employees under COBRA continuation coverage). An employer that fails the comparability rule is subject to a 35% penalty tax. The comparability rules do not apply to HSA contributions made through a cafeteria plan. Instead, the Code Sec. 125 discrimination rules apply. (Code Sec. 4980G; Reg § 54.4980G-1 - Reg § 54.4980G-5)

---

38. ¶H-1350, H-1350.7; ¶2234.02; TD ¶289,107
39. ¶H-1350.20; ¶49,734; TD ¶289,118

40. ¶H-1350.9; ¶2234; TD ¶289,101

¶ 1530   Medicare Advantage Medical Savings Accounts.

Individuals eligible for Medicare can choose either the traditional Medicare program or a Medicare Advantage MSA, which is a medical savings account as defined in Code Sec. 220(d), (¶1528) but which is designated as a Medicare Advantage MSA by the individual account holder. (Code Sec. 138(b)(1)) A Medicare Advantage MSA is a tax-exempt trust (or a custodial account), similar to an IRA, created exclusively to pay qualified medical expenses of the account holder. The Health and Human Services Dept. makes contributions directly to the Medicare Advantage MSA designated by the account holder (the only other type of allowed contribution allowed is a trustee-to-trustee transfer from another Medicare Advantage MSA). Contributions and earnings on amounts held in a Medicare Advantage MSA aren't currently includible in income. (Code Sec. 138(a))

Distributions from a Medicare Advantage MSA for purposes other than qualified medical expenses of the account holder are included in income, and subject to a 50% penalty (except if made because of the account holder's disability or death). (Code Sec. 138(c)(2)) Distributions that are excludable from gross income can't be taken as a medical expense deduction. (Code Sec. 138(c)(1)) The 15% penalty on the amount includible in gross income for non-qualified distributions from regular Archer MSAs (¶1382) doesn't apply to any payment or distribution from a Medicare Advantage MSA. (Code Sec. 138(c)(2)(A))[41]

¶ 1531   Group-health plan continuation coverage (COBRA).

A group health plan (of or contributed to by an employer) must provide that each qualified beneficiary who would lose coverage under the plan because of a qualifying event may elect continuation coverage under the plan within a specified at-least-60-day election period. (Code Sec. 4980B(f)(1))[42]

"Qualified beneficiaries" are the covered employee, his spouse or dependent child, a deceased employee's surviving spouse in certain cases, and a child born to or placed for adoption with the covered employee during the COBRA coverage period. (Code Sec. 4980B(g)(1))[43]

"Qualifying events" include: death of the covered employee; termination or reduction of hours of his employment; divorce or legal separation from the covered employee; cessation of a child's dependency; and the employee's entitlement to certain Medicare benefits. (Code Sec. 4980B(f)(3))[44]

Continuation coverage must be identical to coverage provided under the plan to similarly situated beneficiaries who haven't had a qualifying event. (Code Sec. 4980B(f)(2)(A))[45] Coverage for a qualified beneficiary must begin on the date of the qualifying event and end not earlier than: a statutory maximum period, the end of the plan, the failure to pay a premium, or the eligibility for group health plan coverage or Medicare.[46] Coverage of the cost of pediatric vaccines can't be reduced below the coverage provided by the plan as of May 1, '93. (Code Sec. 4980B(f)(1))[47]

Employers (or for a multiemployer plan, the plan) and certain responsible persons are liable for an excise tax (Code Sec. 4980B(e))[48] if, with certain exceptions, a group health plan fails to provide the above coverage. (Code Sec. 4980B(a))[49]

COBRA subsidy. Workers who have been involuntarily terminated (i.e., assistance-eligible individuals or AEIs) between Sept. 1, 2008 and May 31, 2010 may receive a 65% subsidy on their COBRA continuation health insurance premiums for up to 15 months. The person providing the subsidy (e.g., an employer) receives a credit for the subsidy on the person's employment tax return. Most employers claim the credit on either their quarterly Form 941

---

41. ¶H-1348; ¶1384; TD ¶288,500
42. ¶H-1250 *et seq.*; ¶49,80B4
43. ¶H-1266; ¶49,80B4
44. ¶H-1303; ¶49,80B4
45. ¶H-1272; ¶49,80B4

46. ¶H-1294; ¶49,80B4
47. ¶H-1250 *et seq.*; ¶49,80B4
48. ¶H-1316; ¶49,80B4
49. ¶H-1315; ¶49,80B4

or annual Form 944. The subsidy period terminates when the AEI qualifies for other health care coverage or Medicare, or ceases to qualify for COBRA coverage. The subsidy isn't included in an individual's income when paid. (Code Sec. 139C) However, individuals whose modified adjusted gross income (MAGI, namely, AGI plus excluded foreign earned income and income from U.S. possessions or Puerto Rico) exceeds $125,000 ($250,000 for joint return filers) must increase their tax liability on their return for the year of the subsidy to repay part or all of the subsidy. A taxpayer who receives a COBRA premium subsidy for any month isn't eligible for the Health Coverage Tax Credit (HCTC) (¶2350) for that month, or the advance payment of the HCTC. (Code Sec. 35(g)(9))

¶ 1532 Group-health plan portability, access, renewability, and parity rules.

Group health plans must satisfy requirements regarding (1) portability, through limits on pre-existing condition exclusions (Code Sec. 9801; Reg § 54.9801-1), (2) prohibitions on excluding individuals from coverage based on factors such as health status, medical condition and history, genetic information, and claims experience (Code Sec. 9802; Reg § 54.9802-1, Reg § 54.9802-3T), (3) guaranteed renewability of health insurance coverage. (Code Sec. 9803)[50] and (4) subject to certain small employer and increased cost exceptions, parity between (a) medical and surgical benefits and (b) mental health and substance abuse benefits. (Code Sec. 9812, Reg § 54.9812-1T) A tax is imposed on any failure to meet these requirements, (Code Sec. 4980D)[1] Parity rules apply regarding: financial requirements and treatment limits, disclosure of information on medical necessity criteria and claim denials, and a plan's out-of-network provisions. (Code Sec. 9812, Reg § 54.9812-1T)

A group health plan can't terminate dependent child coverage due to a medically necessary leave of absence (LOA) from school before the earlier of: (1) the date that is 1 year after the first day of the medically necessary LOA; or (2) the date on which the coverage would otherwise terminate under the plan. (Code Sec. 9813(b)(1))[2] For the first plan year beginning on or after Sept. 23, 2010, subject to exceptions, group health plans and health insurance issuers that provide dependent coverage of children must continue to make such coverage available for an adult child until age 26. (Code Sec. 9815, Reg § 54.9815-2714T)

¶ 1533 Self-employed individual's health insurance deduction

A self-employed individual (or a partner or a more-than-2%-shareholder of an S corporation) can deduct as a business expense 100% of the amount paid during the tax year for medical insurance on himself, his spouse and his dependents. (Code Sec. 162(l)(1)(B)) Effective Mar. 30, 2010, the deduction also applies to any child of the taxpayer who has not attained age 27 as of the end of the year. (Code Sec. 162(l)(1)(D))

No deduction is allowed to the extent the deduction exceeds the individual's earned income as defined in Code Sec. 401(c) (net earnings from self-employment) derived from the trade or business for which the plan providing the coverage is established. (Code Sec. 162(l)(2)(A))[3] For purposes of applying the earned income limit to the deduction of a more-than-2% S corporation shareholder, that shareholder's wages from the S corporation are treated as his earned income. (Code Sec. 162(l)(5)(A))[4]

No individual who's eligible to participate in any subsidized health plan maintained by any employer of the individual *or of the individual's spouse* is entitled to the deduction. This test for eligibility is made for each calendar month. This rule is applied separately to (1) plans that provide coverage for qualified long-term care services (¶2145), or are qualified long-term care insurance contracts (¶2146) and (2) plans which don't include such coverage and aren't such contracts. (Code Sec. 162(l)(2)(B)) Thus, an individual eligible for employer-subsidized health insurance may still be able to deduct long-term care insurance premiums, so long as he

50. ¶H-1325 *et seq.*; ¶98,014 *et seq.*
1. ¶H-1325.34 *et seq.*; ¶98,014, ¶4980D4
2. ¶H-1325.22

3. ¶L-3510; ¶1624.403; TD ¶304,420
4. ¶L-3512; ¶1624.403; TD ¶304,421

isn't eligible for employer-subsidized long-term care insurance.[5]

¶ 1534   Contributions to funded welfare benefit plans.

An employer's contribution to a "welfare benefit fund" is deductible only for the tax year paid, and only to the extent the contribution doesn't exceed the "qualified cost" of the plan for its tax year that relates to (ends with or within) the employer's tax year. (Code Sec. 419(a), Code Sec. 419(b))[6] Contributions for independent contractors are also subject to this rule. (Code Sec. 419(g))[7] The rule, however, doesn't apply to a ten-or-more employer plan if no employer (or related employer) normally contributes more than 10% of total contributions, unless the plan uses experience ratings to determine each employer's contribution. (Code Sec. 419A(f)(6); Reg § 1.419A(f)(6)-1(b)(1))[8]

A welfare benefit fund is a fund that is part of an employer's plan through which the employer provides welfare benefits to employees or their beneficiaries, but doesn't include amounts held under certain kinds of insurance contracts. (Code Sec. 419(e); Reg § 1.419A(f)(6)-1(b)(4))[9]

¶ 1535   Death benefits to employee's beneficiaries.

Payments to the widow or other beneficiaries of a deceased employee, i.e., continuing the decedent's salary for a reasonable period, are deductible by the employer to the extent they qualify as a business expense. A benefit paid as a gift based on the beneficiary's need doesn't qualify as a business expense. (Reg § 1.404(a)-12(b)(2))[10]

¶ 1536   "Golden parachute" payments.

No deduction is allowed for an excess parachute payment. (Code Sec. 280G)[11] An excess parachute payment is the amount by which a parachute payment (below) exceeds the base amount (below) allocated to it. (Code Sec. 280G(b)(1)) If there's only one parachute payment the entire base amount is allocated to it.[12]

A parachute payment is any payment in the nature of compensation to (or for the benefit of) a disqualified individual (described below) *if*:

(1) the payment is contingent on a change (a) in the ownership or effective control of the corporation, *or* (b) in the ownership of a substantial part of the corporation's assets, *and*

(2) the aggregate present value of all such contingent compensation payments equals, or exceeds, three times the base amount. (Code Sec. 280G(b))[13] This base amount is the average annualized compensation income includible in a disqualified individual's gross income in the five-tax-year period preceding the tax year in which the change of ownership or control of the corporation occurs. (Code Sec. 280G(b), Code Sec. 280G(d))[14]

A disqualified individual is any individual who is: (1) an employee, independent contractor, or other person specified in regs to be issued who performs personal services for a corporation, *and* (2) is an officer, shareholder or highly compensated individual. (Code Sec. 280G(c); Reg § 1.280G-1, Q&As 15 to 20)[15] Highly compensated individual means a member of the highest paid 1% of employees or, if less, the highest paid 250 employees. (Code Sec. 280G(c))[16]

A parachute payment doesn't include an amount that the taxpayer can establish, by clear and convincing evidence, is reasonable compensation for services to be rendered on, or after, the date of change in ownership or control. (Code Sec. 280G(b)(4)(A)) The amount of an excess parachute payment can be reduced to the extent that the taxpayer can establish by clear and

---

5. ¶L-3510; ¶1624.403; TD ¶304,420
6. ¶s H-4101, H-4113 *et seq.*; ¶4194 *et seq.*; TD ¶278,001
7. ¶H-4104; ¶4194.01 *et seq.*
8. ¶H-4154; ¶419A4.02; TD ¶278,005
9. ¶H-4105 *et seq.*; ¶4194.02; TD ¶278,003
10. ¶H-4051 *et seq.*; ¶1624.277; TD ¶278,703

11. ¶H-3826; ¶280G4; TD ¶279,001
12. ¶H-3874; ¶280G4; TD ¶279,014
13. ¶H-3830; ¶280G4; TD ¶279,002
14. ¶H-3864; ¶280G4; TD ¶279,016
15. ¶H-3840; ¶280G4; TD ¶279,011
16. ¶H-3843; ¶280G4; TD ¶279,011

convincing evidence that the payment is reasonable compensation for personal services actually rendered before the date of change of ownership or control. (Code Sec. 280G(b)(4)(B))[17]

The parachute payment rules don't apply to a corporation (1) that was (immediately before the change in control or assets) a "small business corporation," without regard to whether it has a nonresident alien shareholder (¶3354) or (2) whose stock isn't readily tradeable if shareholder approval has been obtained. (Code Sec. 280G(b)(5)) A corporation that meets the requirements to elect to be treated as an S corporation, but does not elect S status, may nevertheless use the small business exemption. (Reg § 1.280G-1, Q&A 6(a)(1))[18]

Payments to or from a qualified pension or profit-sharing plan, Code Sec. 403(a) annuity, simplified employee pension or SIMPLE plan (¶4382 *et seq.*) aren't parachute payments. (Code Sec. 280G(b)(6); Reg § 1.280G-1, Q&A 8)[19]

For payments with respect to severances occurring within the "TARP authorities period" (Oct. 3, 2008 to Dec. 31, 2009, or to the extended period, which can't be later than Oct. 3, 2010), the golden parachute rules apply to any compensation to or for a covered executive (defined at ¶1519) on account of his severance from employment with an applicable employer (defined at ¶1519) because of an involuntary termination, or in connection with his employer's bankruptcy, liquidation, or receivership, if the aggregate present value of the payments equals or exceeds three times his base amount. Certain golden parachute rules (e.g., the reasonable compensation exception and small business corporation exception, see above) don't apply for the TARP-related severance pay rules. (Code Sec. 280G(e))

¶ 1537   Compensation payments as capital outlays.

Compensation payments that result in the acquisition of business property generally must be added to the property's basis.[20]

Payments otherwise designated as compensation may actually be payments for property. For example, where a partnership sells out to a corporation and the former partners agree to continue to work for the corporation, the salaries of the former partners may be in part payment for the transfer of their business. (Reg § 1.162-7(b)(1))[21]

¶ 1538   Year for deducting compensation.

An employer deducts compensation in the year allowed under its accounting method (¶2816 *et seq.*) with special rules for compensation in property and bargain sales (¶1216 *et seq.*), deferred compensation (¶1539), and contributions to employee benefit plans (¶4334).

If salary is paid or accrued in one year for services to be rendered in a later year, the deduction is allowed only over the period during which the services are rendered. This applies to both cash and accrual-basis employers.[22]

For limitations on accrual-basis taxpayers' deductions for compensation paid to related cash-basis taxpayers, see ¶2836.

¶ 1539   When to deduct deferred compensation.

An employer's contributions to a nonqualified deferred compensation plan are deductible in the tax year in which an amount attributable to the contribution is includible in the gross income of employees participating in the plan (Code Sec. 404(a)(5)), even if the employer is an accrual basis taxpayer.[23]

Benefits provided under a welfare benefit fund (Code Sec. 404(b)(2)(B)), and payments of bonuses or other amounts within 2½ months after the close of the tax year in which significant services required for payment have been performed (Reg § 1.404(b)-1T, Q&A-2(c)),

17. ¶H-3876; ¶280G4; TD ¶279,019
18. ¶H-3835; ¶280G4; TD ¶279,006
19. ¶H-3839; ¶280G4; TD ¶279,010
20. ¶H-3603; ¶1624.081; TD ¶276,006

21. ¶H-3604; ¶1624.205; TD ¶276,006
22. ¶H-3934; ¶1624.205; TD ¶279,520
23. ¶H-3677; ¶4044.16; TD ¶277,500

aren't treated as deferred compensation.[24]

To determine if compensation is deferred compensation, and when deferred compensation is paid, no amount is treated as paid or received until it's actually received by the employee. (Code Sec. 404(a)(11))[25]

If the all events test (¶2832) and recurring item exception (¶2833) are otherwise met, an accrual basis taxpayer may treat its payroll tax liability as incurred in Year 1, regardless of whether the compensation to which the liability relates is deferred compensation deductible under Code Sec. 404 in Year 2.[26]

¶ 1540 When to deduct bonuses paid to employees.

A cash basis employer deducts bonuses only for the year in which the bonuses are actually paid (¶1539).[27]

Bonuses by an accrual basis taxpayer are deductible in the tax year when all the events have occurred that establish the fact of liability to pay the bonus, the amount can be determined with reasonable accuracy, and economic performance has occurred for the liability (¶2833). (Reg § 1.461-1(a)(2)(i))[28]

To deduct a year-end bonus in the accrual year rather than the actual payment year an employer must pay the bonus within a brief period of time after the close of the employer's tax year. If an employer pays bonuses within 2 ½ months after the close of the tax year, then a deduction for the bonuses won't be subject to the deferred compensation rules (¶1539), which would bar the deduction until the bonus is included in the employee's income. (Reg § 1.404(b)-1T)[29] Payment after 2 ½ months is presumed to be deferred compensation, and that presumption can only be rebutted by showing that: (1) it was either administratively or economically impossible to avoid a later payment, and (2) as of the end of the employer's tax year, the impracticability was unforeseeable. (Reg § 1.404(b)-1T)[30]

For limitations on accrual-basis taxpayers' deductions for compensation paid to related cash-basis taxpayers, see ¶2836.

¶ 1541 When to deduct vacation pay.

Cash basis employers take a deduction when the vacation pay is paid (¶1539) in accordance with the general rules for cash basis employers.[31]

For an accrual basis employer, vacation pay earned during any tax year but not paid on or before 2½ months after the end of the tax year is deductible for the tax year of the employer in which it's paid. (Code Sec. 404(a)(5))[32]

¶ 1542 Travel Expenses.

The costs of away-from-home business travel can qualify as deductible expenses.

¶ 1543 Deduction for away-from-home travel costs.

Ordinary and necessary expenses incurred while traveling "away from home" in pursuit of a trade or business are deductible. Those expenses include amounts (other than amounts that are lavish or extravagant) paid for meals (subject to a percentage limit, see ¶1570) and lodging. (Code Sec. 162(a)(2))[33]

A taxpayer isn't away from home unless he is away *overnight,* or at least long enough to require rest or sleep.[34] He need not be away from his tax home for an entire 24-hour day or

24. ¶s H-3673, H-3674; TD ¶277,503
25. ¶H-3674; ¶4044.16
26. ¶H-3670; TD ¶279,504
27. ¶s H-3901, H-3916; ¶1624.218; TD ¶279,500
28. ¶H-3916; TD ¶279,503
29. ¶H-3919; TD ¶279,511
30. ¶H-3919; TD ¶279,512
31. ¶H-3922; ¶4614.01; TD ¶279,513
32. ¶H-3922; ¶4614.15; TD ¶279,513
33. ¶L-1701; ¶1624.114; TD ¶291,002
34. ¶L-1710; ¶1624.147

throughout the hours from dusk to dawn if his relief from duty is long enough to get necessary sleep. A layover sufficient only for a short rest and to get a meal isn't "overnight." [35]

Deductible business travel expenses include baggage charges, air, rail and bus fares, cost of transporting sample cases or display materials, expenses for sample rooms, cost of maintaining or operating a car, house trailer or airplane, telephone and telegraph expenses, laundry and dry cleaning costs, taxi fares, etc., from the airport or station to the hotel and back, from one customer to another, transportation from where meals and lodging are obtained to the temporary work assignment, and reasonable tips for any of these expenses. (Reg § 1.162-2(a))[36] Travel expenses don't include expenses of the taxpayer's own entertainment. [37]

¶ 1544 Home defined for travel expense purposes.

A taxpayer's home for travel expense purposes is his "tax home" —his principal place of business, employment station, or post of duty, regardless of where his family lives.[38]

Where an individual has no principal place of business or employment but continually changes work locations (e.g., a traveling salesperson), his regular residence is his tax "home." [39] If such a taxpayer has no regular place of abode in a real and substantial sense, he has no "home" and can't deduct travel expenses. [40]

If a taxpayer regularly works at two or more separate locations, his tax home is the general area where his *principal* employment or business is, determined on the facts of the particular case. Important factors are: (1) time spent, (2) business activity, and (3) financial return. Income is the most significant factor.[41] In rare situations, a taxpayer may have two tax homes.[42]

Costs of traveling to and from the minor place of employment, 50% of the cost of meals (but see ¶1570), and the cost of lodging at the minor post are deductible travel expenses.[43]

Certain state legislators may elect to treat their residence in their legislative district (instead of the state capitol) as their tax home. (Code Sec. 162(h), Reg § 1.162-24)[44]

¶ 1545 Temporary (one year or less) assignment away from home.

A temporary assignment away from home—an assignment whose termination can be foreseen within a fixed and reasonably short period—doesn't shift the "tax home." Therefore, a taxpayer may deduct the necessary traveling expenses in getting to his temporary assignment and also for the return trip to his tax home after the temporary assignment is completed, and his expenses for lodging and 50% of the cost of meals while he is in the place to which he is temporarily assigned.[45] If he returns home on his nonworking days, he may deduct his travel expenses to his home, but his travel expenses deduction is limited to the amount he would have spent to stay at his temporary location.[46]

A taxpayer isn't treated as being temporarily away from home if his period of employment exceeds one year (certain federal employees on crime investigations are exempt from this rule). (Code Sec. 162(a)) The one-year rule generally isn't triggered by short intermittent assignments that span more than one year.[47] Employment away from home at a single location for less than one year is treated as temporary, in the absence of facts and circumstances indicating otherwise. If employment away from home in a single location initially is realistically expected to last for one year or less, but later is realistically expected to exceed one year, then the employment will be treated as temporary (in the absence of facts and circumstances indicating otherwise) until the date that the taxpayer's realistic expectation changes (at which point the employment will no longer be "temporary"). [48]

35. ¶L-1710; ¶1624.147
36. ¶L-1705; ¶1624.114; TD ¶291,005
37. ¶L-1713; TD ¶291,007
38. ¶L-1801; ¶1624.125; TD ¶292,001
39. ¶L-1802; ¶1624.125; TD ¶292,002
40. ¶L-2025; ¶1624.125
41. ¶L-1807; ¶1624.141; TD ¶292,005
42. ¶L-1808
43. ¶s L-1805, L-2135; ¶1624.141; TD ¶292,005
44. ¶L-2026; ¶1624.141; TD ¶292,520
45. ¶s L-1810, L-2135; ¶1624.130; TD ¶292,009
46. ¶L-1813; TD ¶292,011
47. ¶L-1811; ¶1624.130
48. ¶L-1812; ¶1624.130; TD ¶292,009

¶ 1546   Indefinite assignment away from home.

An indefinite assignment away from home shifts the "tax home" and taxpayer can't deduct the expenses of travel, meals and lodging while in the location of the "indefinite" assignment.[49] Employment is indefinite if it lasts for more than one year, or there is no realistic expectation that the employment will last for one year or less.[50]

¶ 1547   Meals and lodging when not away from home.

The cost of a taxpayer's meals not incurred in traveling away from home isn't deductible unless allowed under Code Sec. 162 (business expenses) or Code Sec. 212 (expenses for production of income). Lodging costs not incurred in traveling away from home aren't deductible unless allowed under Code Sec. 217. (Reg § 1.262-1(b)(5)) IRS intends to amend these rules to provide that lodging costs not incurred in traveling away from home aren't deductible unless allowed under Code Sec. 162 or Code Sec. 217.

Pending additional guidance, IRS won't apply Reg § 1.262-1(b)(5) to an employee's non-away-from-home lodging his employer provides to him, or requires him to obtain, if: the lodging is on a temporary basis and is necessary for him to participate in or be available for a bona fide business meeting or function of the employer; and the expenses are otherwise deductible by the employee, or would be deductible if paid by him, under Code Sec. 162(a).[1]

¶ 1548   U.S. travel for both business and pleasure.

Transportation costs to and from the destination are deductible only if the trip is related primarily to the taxpayer's business. Expenses at the destination allocable to the taxpayer's business are deductible even if the round-trip travel expenses are disallowed because the trip was primarily for pleasure.[2] If the trip is primarily for business, but the taxpayer extends his stay for personal reasons, makes side trips, or engages in other nonbusiness activities, he may deduct only the expenses, such as lodging and 50% of the cost of meals, that he would have incurred if the trip had been totally for business. But no allocation is required for travel costs to and from the business destination. (Reg § 1.162-2(b)(1))[3]

¶ 1549   Foreign travel for both business and pleasure.

If travel is primarily for pleasure, the rules at ¶1548 apply, so that only the amount directly allocable to business is deductible. But under special rules for foreign travel, even where travel is primarily for business, a portion of the transportation cost is nondeductible if the travel has a pleasure element. The nondeductible part is computed on a time ratio, usually in the proportion of nonbusiness days to all travel days.

This allocation and denial of deduction isn't made if: (1) travel is for one week or less; or (2) less than 25% of the time is spent on nonbusiness activity; or (3) the individual traveling had no substantial control over the arranging of the trip; or (4) a personal vacation wasn't a major consideration in making the trip. (Code Sec. 274(c); Reg § 1.162-2(b), Reg § 1.274-4(f)(5))[4] For foreign conventions, see ¶1550.

¶ 1550   Convention expenses.

Travel expenses incurred in attending a domestic convention are subject to the regular business trip rules if attendance will benefit or advance the taxpayer's business or the employee's responsibilities as distinguished from serving some social, political, or other nonbusiness function. (Reg § 1.162-2(d))[5]

49. ¶L-1814; ¶1624.130; TD ¶292,012
50. ¶L-1811; ¶1624.130; TD ¶292,013
1. ¶L-1709; ¶1624.114; TD ¶291,000
2. ¶s L-1702, L-2135; ¶1624.119; TD ¶291,004

3. ¶L-1702; ¶1624.119; TD ¶291,004
4. ¶L-1726 *et seq.*; ¶2744.04; TD ¶291,507
5. ¶L-1716; ¶1624.119; TD ¶291,014

No business expense deduction is allowed for expenses allocable to a convention, seminar, or similar meeting held outside the North American area (defined below) unless the taxpayer establishes that the meeting is directly related to the active conduct of his trade or business, or to an activity relating to the production of income, and that after taking specified factors into account, it's as reasonable for the meeting to be held outside the North American area as within it. (Code Sec. 274(h)(1))

North American area means the U.S., its possessions, the Trust Territory of the Pacific Islands, Canada and Mexico. (Code Sec. 274(h)(3)(A)) U.S. possessions include Puerto Rico and the U.S. Virgin Islands.[6] "North American area" also includes Aruba, Antigua, Bahamas, Barbados, Barbuda, Bermuda, Costa Rica, Dominica, the Dominican Republic, Grenada, Guyana, Honduras, Jamaica, the Netherlands Antilles, Trinidad and Tobago.[7]

¶ 1551 Cruise ship convention—$2,000 deduction limit.

A deduction of up to $2,000 per individual per year is allowed for attending business conventions, etc., held aboard a cruise ship, but only if the ship is registered in the U.S. and all ports of call of the cruise ship are located in the U.S. or its possessions. (Code Sec. 274(h)(2)) A married couple filing a joint return can deduct $4,000 if each spent at least $2,000 for attending an otherwise deductible business-related cruise ship convention.[8] A taxpayer claiming the deduction must attach to his return two specified written substantiation statements (including one signed by the sponsor). (Code Sec. 274(h)(5))[9]

¶ 1552 Travel expense deduction for a companion.

No deduction is allowed (other than under Code Sec. 217, moving expenses) for travel expenses paid or incurred for a spouse, dependent, or other individual accompanying the taxpayer (or an officer or employee of the taxpayer) unless: (1) the spouse, etc., is an employee of the taxpayer; (2) the travel of the spouse, etc., is for a bona fide business purpose; and (3) the expenses would otherwise be deductible by the spouse, etc. (Code Sec. 274(m)(3))[10]

The limits on deductions for travel companions don't apply to a companion who (1) is a business associate (¶1563), (2) comes along for a bona-fide business purpose, and (3) could otherwise deduct the expense if he incurred it. (Reg § 1.274-2(g))

If a taxpayer is accompanied by a spouse on a business trip and the spouse's expenses aren't deductible, the deductible expense for transportation and lodging is the single rate cost of similar accommodations for the taxpayer. But the full rental for a car in which both spouses travel is deductible, since no part of the expense is attributable to the "extra" passenger.[11]

¶ 1553 Deduction for luxury water travel is limited.

The deduction allowed for travel by ocean liner, cruise ship, or other form of "luxury" water transportation is limited to twice the highest domestic per diem allowance of executive branch U.S. government employees (other than high-ranking executive personnel) multiplied by the number of days of luxury water travel. (Code Sec. 274(m)(1)(A)) If the cost includes separately stated amounts for meals and entertainment, these amounts must be reduced by 50% (¶1570). The per diem rule doesn't apply to expenses of a cruise-ship convention or seminar to which the rules at ¶1551 apply (Code Sec. 274(m)(1)(B)(i)), or to:

... expenses treated as compensation paid to an employee or otherwise included in the gross income of the recipient;

... reimbursed, accounted-for expenses of the taxpayer where the services are performed for someone else, and if performed for an employer, the reimbursement hasn't been treated

6. ¶s L-1744, L-1745; ¶2744.04; TD ¶291,515
7. ¶L-1746; ¶2744.04; TD ¶291,516
8. ¶L-1721; ¶2744.04; TD ¶291,018
9. ¶L-1722; ¶2744.04; TD ¶291,019
10. ¶L-1739; ¶2744.035; TD ¶291,023
11. ¶L-1740 *et seq.*; ¶1624.119

as compensation;

. . . expenses for recreational or social activities primarily for the benefit of employees;

. . . services and facilities made available by the taxpayer to the general public; and

. . . services and facilities sold to customers. (Code Sec. 274(m)(1)(B)(ii))[12]

¶ 1554   Above-the-line deduction for overnight travel of reservists.

A member of the Armed Forces reserves who travels over 100 miles from home for an overnight stay connected with the performance of services (e.g., to attend meetings), can deduct travel expenses as an above-the-line adjustment to gross income. The amount deductible is limited to the regular federal per diem rate for lodging, meals, and incidental expenses, and the standard mileage rate for car expenses plus parking fees and tolls. (Code Sec. 62(a)(2)(E)) Expenses in excess of these limits, or for overnight travel not over 100 miles from home, are miscellaneous itemized deductions subject to the 2%-of-AGI floor (¶3110).[13]

¶ 1555   Transportation Expenses.

Costs of local transportation (including the cost of operating and maintaining a car directly attributable to the conduct of a trade or business) can qualify as deductible expenses.

¶ 1556   Transportation expenses other than commuting expenses.

Transportation expenses (but not commuting expenses, see ¶1557) directly attributable to the conduct of the taxpayer's business are deductible even though he isn't away from home overnight. (Reg § 1.162-1(a)) These expenses (sometimes called local travel expenses) include air, train, bus and cab fares and costs of operating automobiles.[14] If a taxpayer works at two or more places each day, he can deduct the cost of getting from one to the other.[15]

¶ 1557   Expenses of daily transportation between home and work site.

Expenses of commuting between a taxpayer's residence and his regular business location, wherever situated, aren't deductible (Reg § 1.162-2(e), Reg § 1.162-2(f)).[16] But a taxpayer may deduct daily transportation expenses incurred in going between the taxpayer's residence and a temporary (¶1558) work location *outside* the metropolitan area where the taxpayer lives and normally works.[17]

Daily transportation expenses incurred in going between the taxpayer's residence and a temporary (¶1558) work location *within* the same metropolitan area is business transportation if: (1) the taxpayer has one or more regular work locations away from his residence; or (2) the taxpayer's residence is his principal place of business (¶1636 *et seq.*).[18]

¶ 1558   One-year temporary workplace rule.

A work location is "temporary" for purposes of deducting daily transportation costs (¶1557) if employment at the location is realistically expected to last (and in fact does last) for one year or less. If the employment initially is realistically expected to last for one year or less, but at some later date it is realistically expected to exceed one year, that employment is temporary (absent facts and circumstances indicating otherwise) until the date that the taxpayer's realistic expectation changes, and is treated as not temporary after that date.

Where an assignment at a work location is expected to last for more than one year, but the taxpayer is realistically expected to be present at that location *for no more than 35 workdays*

12. ¶L-1708; ¶2744.05; TD ¶291,009
13. ¶A-2611.4; ¶624.02; TD ¶560,706.3
14. ¶L-1601; ¶1624.150; TD ¶290,501
15. ¶L-1602; ¶1624.153; TD ¶290,504
16. ¶L-1608 *et seq.*; ¶1624.151; TD ¶290,512
17. ¶L-1605; ¶1624.130; TD ¶290,506
18. ¶L-1605; ¶1624.151; TD ¶290,505

(partial or complete) during each of the calendar years in that period, the location is temporary for a calendar year in which he actually works there for no more than 35 partial or complete workdays.

illustration: A taxpayer who normally works in an office building works at an offsite location on an assignment lasting 36 months, but he is at the offsite location for only 30 days each year. The offsite location is "temporary," and his round-trip transportation costs between home and that location are deductible.[19]

¶ 1559 Automobile expenses.

The expenses of operating and maintaining a car used for business purposes, such as gasoline, oil, repairs, insurance, depreciation, interest to buy the car, taxes, licenses, garage rent, parking, fees, tolls, etc., are deductible.[20] If a taxpayer makes both personal and business use of his car, he must apportion his expenses between business (deductible) and personal (nondeductible) transportation.[21] Report business auto expenses on Form 2106 or Form 2106-EZ (employees) or on Form 1040, Schedule C or Form 1040, Schedule C-EZ (self-employeds).[22]

caution: An employee who uses a car for his job is subject to the 2%-of-AGI floor on deducting the *un*reimbursed auto expenses he incurs, see ¶3104, and can't deduct interest on a car loan (¶1715).

¶ 1560 Transporting tools to work.

A taxpayer may deduct only *additional* expenses incurred because of the need to transport tools, etc., to work *and* only if the additional expenses can be determined accurately. The deduction is only for that portion of the cost of transporting the tools, etc., that exceeds the cost of commuting *by the same mode of transportation* without the tools, etc.[23]

¶ 1561 Business standard mileage rate.

Employees or self-employed individuals can use the optional business standard mileage rate in computing the deductible costs of operating passenger automobiles owned or leased by them (including vans and pickup or panel trucks) for business purposes.

For 2010, a taxpayer who uses this method multiplies the number of business miles by a rate of 50¢ per mile.[24]

A deduction using the standard mileage rate is in lieu of deducting operating and fixed costs. A taxpayer who uses the standard mileage rate forgoes deductions for depreciation (or leasing costs), maintenance and repairs, tires, gasoline (including taxes), oil, insurance, and registration fees. But deductions for parking fees and tolls are still available.[25]

Use of the standard mileage rate isn't available where taxpayer's auto is used for hire (e.g., as a taxi) or for five or more autos that are used simultaneously, such as in fleet operations, nor is it available for a purchased car if it has previously been depreciated using any method other than the straight-line method, or if Code Sec. 179 expensing or additional first-year depreciation has been claimed. The standard mileage rate may generally be used for a leased auto only if the taxpayer uses this method (or a fixed and variable rate (FAVR) allowance, see ¶1576) for the entire lease period (including renewals).[26]

Rural mail carriers receiving qualified reimbursements (equipment maintenance allowance) don't report them in income even if they exceed the amount of their expenses. (Code Sec. 162(o)(1)) However, if the expenses exceed the amount of the qualified reimbursement,

19. ¶L-1606; ¶1624.151; TD ¶290,507
20. ¶L-1902; ¶1624.150; TD ¶293,000
21. ¶L-1907; ¶1624.157; TD ¶293,014
22. ¶L-1901; ¶1624.157; TD ¶293,002

23. ¶L-1611; ¶1624.152; TD ¶290,515
24. ¶L-1903; ¶1624.157; TD ¶293,005
25. ¶L-1905; ¶1624.157; TD ¶293,009
26. ¶L-1903 *et seq.*; ¶1624.157; TD ¶293,006

the mail carrier can take the excess into account in computing miscellaneous itemized deductions under Code Sec. 67. (Code Sec. 162(o)(2))[27]

A taxpayer may use the optional business standard mileage rate in substantiating reimbursed expenses paid by another.[28] For consequences if the reimbursement is made under an accountable plan, or under a nonaccountable plan, see ¶3104.

¶ 1562 Entertainment Expenses.

Costs incurred for entertainment must meet strict tests in order to be deductible. A 50% rule also limits otherwise-allowable deductions for meals and entertainment.

Entertainment expenses, except as limited by the rules in ¶1570 (percentage limit) and ¶1572 (other restrictions), are deductible if they are ordinary and necessary expenses of carrying on a trade or business. (Code Sec. 274(a), Code Sec. 274(e); Reg § 1.162-1(a)) Strict substantiation requirements must be met (¶1580). But no deduction is allowed unless the taxpayer can show that the entertainment expenses are: (1) "directly related" to the active conduct of a trade or business (¶1565), or (2) "associated with" the active conduct of a trade or business (¶1566), or (3) covered by one of the exceptions at ¶1567. (Code Sec. 274(a))[29]

"Entertainment" includes any activity generally considered to be entertainment, amusement or recreation. This covers entertaining guests at night clubs, theaters, sporting events, and at entertainment facilities such as yachts, country clubs, hunting lodges, etc. If the expense involves the use of an entertainment facility, see ¶1568. (Reg § 1.274-2(b)(1)) It doesn't include: supper money furnished to an employee working overtime, a hotel room maintained by an employer and furnished to employees while traveling on business, or an auto used for business even though used for commuting to and from work.[30]

Expenses of entertaining customers or clients at the taxpayer's home may be ordinary and necessary. But only the *extra* expense incurred because they are present is deductible. Failure to show a business purpose for entertaining bars a deduction.[31]

¶ 1563 Who may be entertained?

A "business associate" who may be entertained is a person with whom the taxpayer could reasonably expect to engage or deal with in the active conduct of his trade or business. Examples are customers, suppliers, clients, employees, agents, partners, or professional advisors, *whether established or prospective*. (Reg § 1.274-2(b)(2)(iii))[32] For spouses, see ¶1564.

¶ 1564 Entertainment expenses allocable to spouse.

A taxpayer can deduct the cost of entertaining taxpayer's spouse or the spouse of a business customer if taxpayer can show a clear business purpose rather than a personal or social purpose for incurring the expenses. For example, a customer's spouse may join the party for the entertainment because it's impracticable, under the circumstances, to entertain the customer without the spouse. And if the taxpayer's spouse joins the party because the customer's spouse is present, the cost of the entertainment allocable to the taxpayer's spouse is also deductible. (Reg § 1.274-2(d)(2), Reg § 1.274-2(d)(4))[33]

¶ 1565 "Directly related" test for deducting costs of entertainment.

Amounts paid for entertainment are deductible if they are directly related to the active conduct of the taxpayer's trade or business. This test is met if the entertainment: (1) involved an active discussion aimed at getting immediate revenue; (2) occurred in a clear business setting such as a hospitality room; or (3) must be reported as compensation for services

---

27. ¶L-1911; ¶1624.157; TD ¶293,018
28. ¶L-4715; ¶2744.17; TD ¶293,011
29. ¶L-2101; ¶2744.01; TD ¶294,001
30. ¶L-2102; TD ¶294,003

31. ¶L-2108 *et seq.*; ¶2744.01; TD ¶294,009
32. ¶L-2103; ¶2744.10; TD ¶294,007
33. ¶L-2104 *et seq.*; ¶2744.01; TD ¶294,008

performed by an individual other than an employee. (Reg § 1.274-2(c)(1))[34] Costs generally aren't "directly related" if entertainment occurs where there's little or no possibility of engaging in the active conduct of business, e.g., at night clubs, theaters, or sporting events, but they may be deductible under the "associated with" rule (¶1566). (Reg § 1.274-2(c)(7))[35]

¶ 1566 "Associated with" test for deducting costs of entertainment.

Entertainment expenses that fail the directly related test but are associated with the active conduct of the taxpayer's business are deductible if the entertainment directly precedes or follows a substantial and bona fide business discussion. (Reg § 1.274-2(d)(1))[36] An entertainment expense is generally associated with the active conduct of a taxpayer's business if he can show a clear business purpose in incurring the expenditure. (Reg § 1.274-2(d)(2))[37]

The portion of an otherwise deductible expense allocable to the spouse of a person who engaged in the discussion is ordinarily considered associated with the active conduct of the business (Reg § 1.274-2(d)(4)),[38] see ¶1564.

Whether a business discussion is substantial depends on all the facts of each case. The taxpayer must show that he or his representative actively engaged in a discussion, meeting, negotiation, or other bona fide business transaction (other than entertainment) in order to get a specific business benefit. The meeting doesn't have to be for any specific length of time, but the business discussion must be substantial in relation to the entertainment. Nor does more time have to be devoted to business than entertainment. (Reg § 1.274-2(d)(3)(i))[39]

¶ 1567 Expenses to which "directly related" and "associated" tests don't apply.

Certain ordinary and necessary entertainment expenses are deductible even if they aren't "directly related" to or "associated with" the active conduct of the taxpayer's trade or business. But they are subject to the strict substantiation requirements (¶1580) that apply to other entertainment expenses. The exceptions are:

(1) Food and beverages furnished on the taxpayer's business premises primarily for the taxpayer's employees.[40]

(2) The expense (other than club dues, see ¶1569) of providing recreational, social, or similar activities primarily for the benefit of the taxpayer's employees, other than highly-compensated employees (defined at ¶4326).[41]

(3) Goods, services, and the use of a facility, if treated as compensation and as wages by the employer for withholding tax purposes.[42]

(4) Expenses connected with meetings of directors, shareholders, employees or trade associations.[43]

(5) Cost of providing entertainment or recreational facilities to the general public as a means of advertising or promoting good will in the community.[44]

(6) Expense of providing entertainment, goods, and services, or use of facilities, that are sold to the public in a bona fide transaction for adequate and full consideration.[45]

(7) Reimbursed and substantiated expenses or allowances of employees where the employer hasn't treated the expenses as wages subject to withholding, and reimbursed, accounted-for entertainment expenses of self-employeds reimbursed or covered with an allowance by the client or customer. (Code Sec. 274(e); Reg § 1.274-2(f)(2)) In these situations, the "directly related" and "associated with" tests apply to the payor. [46]

---

34. ¶L-2112; ¶2744.01; TD ¶294,013
35. ¶L-2116; ¶2744.01; TD ¶294,017
36. ¶L-2118; ¶2744.01; TD ¶294,019
37. ¶L-2118; ¶2744.01; TD ¶294,020
38. ¶L-2104; ¶2744.01; TD ¶294,008
39. ¶L-2119; ¶2744.01; TD ¶294,020
40. ¶L-2122; ¶2744.01; TD ¶294,025

41. ¶L-2125; ¶2744.01; TD ¶294,029
42. ¶L-2123; ¶2744.01; TD ¶294,026
43. ¶L-2129; ¶2744.01; TD ¶294,031
44. ¶L-2131; ¶2744.01; TD ¶294,033
45. ¶L-2132; ¶2744.01; TD ¶294,034
46. ¶L-2124; ¶2744.01; TD ¶294,028

¶ 1568   Entertainment facilities.

No deduction is allowed for any expense paid or incurred for an entertainment facility used in conjunction with any activity that is generally considered to be entertainment, amusement or recreation. (Code Sec. 274(a)(1)(B))[47] Entertainment facilities include yachts, hunting lodges, fishing camps, swimming pools, tennis courts, and bowling alleys. Facilities also may include airplanes, automobiles, hotel suites, apartments, and houses located in recreational areas (e.g., beach cottages and ski lodges). However, a facility isn't an entertainment facility unless it's actually used at least in part for entertainment. Expenses of an automobile or an airplane used on business trips are allowed. (Reg § 1.274-2(e)(2))[48]

The following expenditures aren't subject to the entertainment facility rules and are subject to the regular rules that apply to these items:

. . . Interest, taxes, and casualty losses on entertainment facilities.

. . . Out-of-pocket expenses for such items as food and beverages, or expenses for catering furnished during entertainment at a facility.

. . . Actual business (as opposed to entertainment) use of a facility, such as using a plane or car for business transportation or chartering a yacht to an unrelated person. (Reg § 1.274-2(e)(3)(iii), Reg § 1.274-6)[49]

¶ 1569   Club dues.

Deductions are generally barred for the cost of membership in any club organized for business, pleasure, recreation or other social purpose (Code Sec. 274(a)(3)), such as country clubs, golf and athletic clubs, airline clubs, hotel clubs, and business luncheon clubs. (Reg § 1.274-2(a)(2)(iii)(a)) However, a deduction is allowed to the extent dues are treated as compensation income to an employee. (Reg § 1.132-5(s)) Dues for membership in professional and trade associations and civic or public service organizations (e.g., Rotary, Kiwanis) are deductible. (Reg § 1.274-2(a)(2)(iii)(b))[50]

¶ 1570   Meal and entertainment deduction limits—the 50% rule.

The amount of an otherwise allowable deduction for meal or entertainment expenses (including meals while on business travel status, ¶1542) is reduced by 50%. This reduction applies to any expense for food or beverages, and any item for entertainment, amusement, or recreation, or for a facility used for such an activity. (Code Sec. 274(n)(1))

The 50% limit doesn't apply to:

. . . Expenses treated as compensation paid to an employee or otherwise included in the gross income of the recipient of the meal or entertainment. (Code Sec. 274(n)(2)(A))

. . . Meals and entertainment expenses that are reimbursed. (Code Sec. 274(n)(2)(A)) Instead, the percentage limit applies to the person making the reimbursement.

. . . Traditional recreational expenses for employees (other than those who are highly compensated, see ¶4326). (Code Sec. 274(n)(2)(A))

. . . Services and facilities made available by the taxpayer to the general public. (Code Sec. 274(n)(2)(A))

. . . Expenses of goods, services, or use of facilities, sold by the taxpayer in a bona fide transaction (entertainment sold to customers). (Code Sec. 274(n)(2)(A))

. . . Food or beverage expenses that are excludable from the gross income of the recipient under the de minimis fringe benefit rules. (Code Sec. 274(n)(2)(B))

. . . An expense that is part of a package that includes a ticket to attend certain charitable

---

47. ¶L-2149; ¶2744.02; TD ¶295,001
48. ¶L-2150; ¶2744.02; TD ¶295,002
49. ¶L-2152 *et seq.*; ¶2744.02; TD ¶295,004
50. ¶L-2181 *et seq.*; ¶2744.03; TD ¶295,201

sporting events. (Code Sec. 274(n)(2)(C)) The event must: (1) be organized for the primary purpose of benefiting a tax-exempt charitable organization, (2) contribute 100% of the net proceeds to the charity, and (3) use volunteers for substantially all work performed in carrying out the event. (Code Sec. 274(l)(1)(B))

... Food or beverage expenses of crews of certain drilling rigs and crews of certain commercial vessels (Code Sec. 274(n)(2)(E)), but not fishing vessels.[1]

Where an employee's deduction of unreimbursed employee business expenses is subject to the 2%-of-AGI floor discussed at ¶3110, the 50% limit is applied before the 2% floor.[2]

The deductible percentage of meals for certain transport workers (e.g., air transport employees, truck and bus drivers, railroad employees) while away from home during or incident to the period of duty subject to the hours of service limitations of the Dept. of Transportation is 80%. (Code Sec. 274(n)(3))[3]

¶ 1571 Limits on deductions for skyboxes.

Where a skybox or other private luxury box is leased for more than one sporting event, the amount allowable as a deduction for business-related entertainment use is limited to the face value of nonluxury box seat tickets for the seats in the box covered by the lease. (Code Sec. 274(l)(2)) This is reduced by 50% to determine the deduction. (Code Sec. 274(n))[4]

¶ 1572 Other restrictions on meal and entertainment deductions.

No deduction is allowed for any food or beverage expense unless—

(1) the expense isn't lavish or extravagant under the circumstances, and

(2) the taxpayer (or one of taxpayer's employees) is present when the food or beverages are furnished (Code Sec. 274(k)(1)), and

(3) the taxpayer establishes that the expenditure was directly related (¶1565) to the active conduct of taxpayer's business or, for an expenditure directly preceding or following a substantial and bona fide business discussion, was associated with the active conduct of the taxpayer's business (¶1566). (Code Sec. 274(a), Code Sec. 274(k))[5]

Neither the lavish or extravagant limit nor the presence test applies to any expense that is excepted from the percentage limit under ¶1570, above. (Code Sec. 274(k)(2))[6]

In determining the deduction for the cost of a ticket to an entertainment or recreation activity, the amount taken into account can't exceed the face value of the ticket (including any ticket tax). But the face value limit doesn't apply to a ticket to a charitable sporting event that's excepted from the percentage limit (¶1570). (Code Sec. 274(l)(1))[7]

¶ 1573 Deduction limit on entertainment expenses of officers, directors, and 10%-or-more owners.

For costs to provide entertainment-, amusement-, or recreation-related goods, services or facilities to "specified individuals" (e.g., an officer, director, or 10%-or-more owner of the entity, or a related entity) and their relatives or friends, an employer's deduction is limited to the amount of the costs which were treated by the employer as compensation on the employer's income tax return and as wages (or nonemployee compensation) to the qualified recipient. (Code Sec. 274(e)(2)(B), Code Sec. 274(e)(9); Prop Reg. § 1.274-9(b) ["Taxpayers may rely])[8]

Detailed rules apply for allocating plane costs between usage for entertainment of specified

---

1. ¶L-2138 *et seq.*; ¶2744.01; TD ¶294,507 *et seq.*
2. ¶L-2135; ¶2744.01; TD ¶294,506
3. ¶L-2145.1; ¶2744.01
4. ¶L-2146 *et seq.*; ¶2744.01; TD ¶294,519
5. ¶s L-2133 *et seq.*, L-2112, L-2118; ¶2744.01; TD ¶294,503 *et seq.*
6. ¶L-2134; ¶2744.12; TD ¶294,503 *et seq.*
7. ¶L-2145; ¶2744.01; TD ¶294,516
8. ¶L-2123; ¶2744.01; TD ¶294,026

individuals and expenses for all other users (but in making this allocation, expenses of bona fide charters to third parties aren't counted). The deduction limitation applies to all expenses of maintaining and operating a plane (e.g., fuel, crew's salaries, take-off, landing and hangar fees, insurance, depreciation or lease payments, and amounts expensed under Code Sec. 179).[9] Where a specified individual's flight includes a business segment and entertainment segment, the entertainment cost subject to the limitation is the excess of the total cost of the flights over the cost of the flights that would have been taken without the entertainment segment or segments.[10] The deduction limitation doesn't apply to business entertainment air travel or personal travel that can't be characterized as 'entertainment' (e.g., flight to attend family member's funeral). (Prop Reg. § 1.274-10(b) ['Taxpayers may rely']) [11]

¶ 1574   Expense Reimbursements.

An employee doesn't pay tax on an advance, reimbursement or other expense allowance received under an 'accountable plan.' The tax treatment of an advance or reimbursement to an independent contractor depends on whether he accounts to his principal for the expense.

An employee doesn't pay tax on an advance, reimbursement or other expense allowance received from his employer (or from a third party) under an 'accountable plan.' (Reg § 1.62-2(c)(4)) By contrast, an advance, etc., made under a 'nonaccountable plan,' is fully taxable to the employee and subject to FICA and income tax withholding. (Reg § 1.62-2(c)(5))[12]

An advance, etc., is treated as made under an 'accountable plan' if:

(1) the employee receives the advance, etc., for a deductible business expense that he paid or incurred while performing services as an employee of his employer (¶1575),

(2) the employee must adequately account to his employer for the expense within a reasonable period of time (¶1576), and

(3) the employee must return any excess reimbursement or allowance within a reasonable period of time (¶1577).

An advance, etc., that doesn't satisfy all three conditions is treated as paid under a nonaccountable plan—it is taxed to the employee and is subject to FICA and income tax withholding. (Code Sec. 62(c); Reg § 1.62-2(c)(5)) A per-hour or per-day reimbursement by pipeline industry employers for certain employee-provided equipment is made under a nonaccountable plan, but a limited amount of payments meeting safe harbor requirements are made under an accountable plan.[13] Similarly, auto mechanics' tool allowances relying on estimated actual expenses failed to qualify under the accountable plan rules. But IRS has set the criteria it would consider in allowing deemed-substantiation safe-harbors with industries that demonstrate they can't comply with the existing accountable plan rules.

If an employee does not timely return advances or reimbursements in excess of those that are substantiated, only the excess is treated as made under a nonaccountable plan. (Reg § 1.62-2(c)(3)(ii))[14]

An arrangement that would in part be an accountable plan and in part be a nonaccountable plan if both parts were viewed separately is treated as two expense allowance arrangements—one an accountable plan, and the other a nonaccountable plan.[15] But the entire reimbursement for business-travel meals and incidental expenses (M&IE) is deemed paid under a nonaccountable plan if an employer routinely doesn't track expenses and doesn't require employees either to substantiate actual expenses or pay back amounts exceeding the deemed substantiated amount (¶1576).[16]

---

9. ¶L-2123.2; TD ¶294,026.2
10. ¶L-2123.7
11. ¶L-2101.1; TD ¶294,001.1
12. ¶J-1050; TD ¶296,006.

13. ¶S-3672
14. ¶L-4703; TD ¶296,009
15. ¶L-4744; TD ¶296,007
16. ¶L-4704

¶ 1575   Business connection requirement for employee business expenses.

An arrangement satisfies the "business connection" requirement if it provides advances, allowances (including per diem or mileage allowances, or allowances for meals and incidental expenses only), or reimbursements only for business expenses that are allowable as deductions, and that are paid or incurred by the employee in connection with performing services as an employee. (Reg § 1.62-2(d))[17] For example, a reimbursement for an employee's meal eaten while he was away from home overnight on employer business (¶1543) satisfies the business connection requirement, but a reimbursement for an employee's (non-business-entertainment) meal eaten during a non-overnight trip (¶1543) on employer business wouldn't satisfy the requirement. An advance, reimbursement or allowance that would be treated as made partially under a nonaccountable plan solely because the expense is subject to the 50% deduction limit for business meals and entertainment (¶1570) is treated as made under an accountable plan. (Reg § 1.62-2(h)(1))[18]

¶ 1576   Accounting to employer for expenses.

To the extent an employee business expense such as travel or entertainment isn't deductible unless the substantiation requirements of Code Sec. 274(d) are met (¶1580 *et seq.*), the employee must meet those requirements within a reasonable period of time (¶1577), i.e., submit to the payor information sufficient to substantiate the requisite elements of each expense or use.

For all other business expenses, sufficient information must be submitted to enable the one making the reimbursement to identify the specific nature of each expense and to conclude that the expense is attributable to the employer's business activities. (Reg § 1.62-2(e)(3))

The following simplified substantiation rules apply to per diem or mileage allowances paid under an arrangement that otherwise qualifies as an accountable plan (¶1574):

. . . *Per diem allowance.* If a payor (i.e., the employer, its agent, or a third party) pays a per diem allowance in lieu of reimbursing actual expenses for lodging, meal and incidental expenses (M&IE) incurred or to be incurred by an employee for travel away from home, the amount of the expenses that is treated as substantiated for each calendar day (or part of that day) is the lesser of the per diem allowance or the amount computed at the federal per diem rate for the locality of travel for that day (or part of that day).[19] An employee who is "related" to his employer (¶1580) *isn't* considered to have accounted to his employer for the full federal per diem allowances for lodging and M&IE, and must substantiate any deductions he claims, but he may use the meals-only per diem (¶1582) and the business standard mileage rate (¶1561).[20]

. . . *Simplified (high-low) method for substantiating travel allowances.* A simplified method can be used for per diem amounts paid for lodging plus M&IE during travel within the continental U.S. If the regular federal per diem option isn't used, for post-Sept. 30, 2009 travel, he may reimburse up to $258 for high-cost localities ($193 for lodging and $65 for M&IE) and $163 for other localities ($111 for lodging and $52 for M&IE). For post-Sept. 30, 2010 travel, he may reimburse up to $233 for high-cost localities ($168 for lodging and $65 for M&IE) and $160 for other localities ($108 for lodging and $52 for M&IE). For travel outside the continental U.S., a separate lodging expense rate and M&IE rate is available for each locality outside the continental U.S.[21]

. . . *Mileage allowance.* An employee who receives a fixed mileage allowance of not more than the optional business standard mileage rate (¶1561) to cover transportation expenses while traveling away from home or for transportation expenses, is considered to have made an adequate accounting to his employer if the elements of time, place, and business purpose

17. ¶L-4703.1; TD ¶561,009
18. ¶L-4703.1; TD ¶532,004
19. ¶L-4717; ¶2744.18; TD ¶296,019
20. ¶L-4713; TD ¶296,014
21. ¶L-4718; ¶2744.18; TD ¶296,020

of the travel are substantiated. (Reg § 1.274-5T(f))[22]

...*Fixed and variable rate (FAVR) allowances for autos.* Where an employer provides a mileage allowance under a reimbursement or other expense allowance arrangement for an employee owned or leased car, the substantiation requirement is satisfied as to the amount if the employer reimburses in accordance with a fixed and variable rate (FAVR) allowance. A FAVR allowance is periodic fixed payments to cover fixed costs such as depreciation, coupled with periodic variable payments to cover operating costs such as gasoline. Among other things, a FAVR allowance may be paid only to an employee who substantiates at least 5,000 miles driven in connection with the performance of services as an employee, and at least five employees must be covered by the FAVR allowance.[23]

¶ 1577 Returning amounts in excess of expenses; when to substantiate.

Under an accountable plan, an employee must be required to return to the payor within a reasonable period of time any reimbursement in excess of substantiated business expenses. (Reg § 1.62-2(f)(1)) The definition of reasonable period of time depends on the facts and circumstances. However, under a safe-harbor rule, (1) an advance within 30 days of the time the employee has the expense, (2) an expense adequately accounted for within 60 days after it was paid or incurred, or (3) an amount returned to the employer within 120 days after the expense was paid or incurred will be treated as having occurred within a reasonable period of time. (Reg § 1.62-2(g)(2)(i)) If the employee is given a periodic statement (at least quarterly) that asks him to either return or adequately account for outstanding reimbursements and he complies within 120 days of the statement, the amount is adequately accounted for or returned within a reasonable period of time. (Reg § 1.62-2(g)(2))[24]

¶ 1578 Reporting reimbursed business expenses.

If an employee's expenses equal advances or reimbursements made under an accountable plan, he reports no income from the expenses and claims no deductions. However, if the employee's actual business expenses exceed nontaxable accountable-plan advances or reimbursements, and he wishes to deduct the excess, he can do so under the rules that follow for deductions under nonaccountable plan reimbursements.

An employee who pays for employment-related business expenses but receives a nonaccountable plan advance or reimbursement (e.g., he isn't required to account to the employer) reports the advance or reimbursement as income and claims otherwise allowable deductions on Form 2106 or Form 2106EZ, and on Form 1040, Schedule A as miscellaneous itemized deductions. The employee's meal and entertainment expenses are subject to the 50% limit (¶1570), and total miscellaneous itemized deductions are subject to the 2%-of-adjusted-gross-income limit (¶3110). The employee must be able to substantiate each element of his business expenditures. (Reg § 1.274-5T(f)(3))[25] For listed property, see ¶1584.

¶ 1579 Reimbursed expenses of a self-employed person.

Expenses of a self-employed person incurred on behalf of and reimbursed by a client or customer aren't included in the self-employed's gross income if the self-employed substantiates the expenses to his principal under the rules at ¶1580. But if he doesn't substantiate those reimbursed expenses to his principal, he must include the reimbursements in gross income and may deduct the expenses, subject to the usual limitations (e.g., 50% limit on business meals and entertainment), if he has kept the necessary records and receipts. (Reg § 1.274-5T(h)(1), Reg § 1.274-5T(h)(2))[26]

The client or customer must substantiate business travel or entertainment expenses (and is subject to the 50% limit) if a self-employed person accounts for those expenses to the client or

22. ¶L-4715; ¶2744.18; TD ¶296,016
23. ¶L-4725 *et seq.*; ¶2744.18; TD ¶296,029
24. ¶L-4746; TD ¶296,047
25. ¶L-4710; ¶2744.16; TD ¶296,012
26. ¶L-4757; ¶2744.16; TD ¶296,056

customer and is reimbursed. However, if the self-employed person doesn't account for the expenses, the client or customer doesn't have to substantiate reimbursed expenses (and isn't subject to the 50% limit). (Reg § 1.274-5T(h)(2), Reg § 1.274-5T(h)(4))[27]

A self-employed (or an employee) may adequately substantiate a meals and incidental expense to an initial payor that initially reimburses the expense, and the initial payor in connection with its performing services for a third party, may be reimbursed under a reimbursement or other expense allowance arrangement with the third party. Here, if the initial payor accounts to the third party in the same way that the self-employed (or employee) accounted for the expenses to the initial payor, then the third party bears the expenses and is subject to the percentage limit (¶1570) on the expenses.[28]

¶ 1580 Substantiating T&E and "Listed Property" Expenses. ▄▄▄▄▄▄▄▄

In order to deduct travel and entertainment (T&E) expenses, each expense must be substantiated. With respect to listed property, certain elements of each expenditure or business use must be proved.

Taxpayers must substantiate each element of every T&E expense for which a deduction is claimed. (Code Sec. 274(d)(1), Code Sec. 274(d)(2), Code Sec. 274(d)(3)) The elements of away from home travel expenses are explained at ¶1581; entertainment expenses, at ¶1583; and business gifts, at ¶1592.

Taxpayers can't claim deductions or credits for "listed property" unless they substantiate every element of each expenditure and use of the listed property (¶1584) for business or investment purposes. (Code Sec. 274(d)(4)) "Listed property" (¶1949) is passenger automobiles and other property used as a means of transportation (airplanes, trucks, boats, etc), certain computers, and property used for entertainment, recreation or amusement (but not cell phones for tax years beginning after 2009). For depreciation of "listed property," see ¶1948 *et seq.*

Generally, proper substantiation requires "adequate records" (¶1585 *et seq.*), or a taxpayer statement supported by sufficient corroborating evidence (¶1587), plus documentary evidence where required (¶1586). (Code Sec. 274(d))[29] Approximations or estimates aren't sufficient. (Reg § 1.274-5T(a))[30] However, statistical sampling may be used in some cases to establish the amount of meal and entertainment expenses that isn't subject to the 50% limit (¶1570).[31] All elements of an expenditure or use must be proved. Failure to prove any one will bar the deduction. (Reg § 1.274-5T(c)(1))[32]

In the usual instance, an employee who substantiates expenses to the employer need not account for them to the IRS. However, an employee who is "related" to his employer (certain close relatives of an individual employer, or a more than 10% shareholder of a corporate employer) may be asked by IRS to substantiate his expense accounts even though he has accounted to his employer. (Reg § 1.274-5T(f)(5)(ii))[33]

Simplified substantiation procedures apply to expenses of certain federal employees.[34]

¶ 1581 Proving travel and transportation expenses.

The taxpayer must prove all of the following elements by adequate records or by a sufficiently corroborated statement:

(1) The amount of each separate expenditure for traveling away from home, such as the cost of transportation or lodging. The daily cost of breakfast, lunch, and dinner and other incidental travel elements may be aggregated if they are set forth in reasonable categories, such as for meals, oil and gas, taxi fares, etc.

(2) The dates of the departure and return home for each trip, and the number of days spent

27. ¶L-4758; ¶2744.16; TD ¶296,057
28. ¶L-2138.1
29. ¶L-4600 *et seq.*; ¶2744.10; TD ¶295,301
30. ¶L-4601; ¶2744.10; TD ¶295,301

31. ¶L-4641; ¶2744.10
32. ¶s L-4644, L-4608; ¶2744.10; TD ¶295,302
33. ¶L-4713; ¶2744.16; TD ¶296,014
34. ¶L-4700; ¶624.02

on business away from home.

(3) The destinations or locality of the travel.

(4) The business reason for the travel or the nature of the business benefit derived or expected to be derived as a result of the travel. (Reg § 1.274-5T(b)(2))[35]

Incidental travel expenses, e.g., tips, aren't subject to these rules. Where records are incomplete and documentary proof is unavailable, the taxpayer may establish the amount of incidental travel expenses by reasonable approximations. (Reg § 1.162-17(d)(3))[36]

¶ 1582 Substantiation by use of optional meal or incidental expenses allowance.

Employees and self-employeds who are away from home on business travel may use standard per diem amounts to compute meal expense deductions (and in some instances to claim deductions for incidental expenses) instead of keeping records to substantiate the actual amount of the expense.[37]

Employees or self-employeds whose work directly involves moving people or goods (e.g., by plane, bus, truck, ship) and regularly involves travel to different localities with different meal and incidental expense (M&IE) rates may for post-Sept. 30, 2009 travel (and post-Sept. 30, 2010 travel) treat $59 as the federal M&IE (meals and incidental expenses) rate for any locality in the continental U.S. and $65 as the M&IE rate for any nonforeign locality outside the continental U.S. This method also can be used by payors of a per diem allowance only for M&IE away-from-home expenses to an employee in the transportation industry, if the payment qualifies as a regular meals-only allowance under the rules below.[38]

Employees and self-employed individuals who don't pay or incur meal expenses for a calendar day (or partial day) of travel away from home for post-Sept. 30, 2009 travel (and post-Sept. 30, 2010 travel) may deduct $5 per day as incidental expenses for each away-from-home calendar (or partial) day.[39]

If a payor (employer, its agent, or third party) pays a per diem allowance only for M&IE expenses in lieu of reimbursing these actual expenses incurred for travel away from home, the amount that's deemed substantiated is the lesser of the per diem allowance or the amount computed at the federal M&IE rate (¶1576) for the locality of travel for each calendar day (or part of a day) the employee is away from home.[40]

Using standard per diem amounts only releases the taxpayer from the duty of substantiating the actual amount. *Time, place and business purpose must still be substantiated.*

An employee who is out of pocket for M&IE or is reimbursed under a nonaccountable plan may deduct an amount computed under this method only as an itemized deduction (subject to the percentage limit on meal and entertainment expenses, ¶1570, and then to the 2%-of-AGI floor on miscellaneous itemized deductions, ¶3110). A self-employed individual deducts the amount in determining adjusted gross income. This deduction is subject to the percentage limit on meal and entertainment expenses.[41]

¶ 1583 Proving entertainment expenses.

For entertainment expenses, all these elements must be proved:

(1) The amount of each separate expenditure, except that incidental items like cab fares and telephone calls may be aggregated on a separate basis.

(2) The date the entertainment took place.

(3) The name (if any), address or location, and the type of entertainment, such as dinner or theater, if that information isn't clear from the location.

35. ¶L-4630; ¶2744.10; TD ¶295,324
36. ¶L-4633; TD ¶295,326
37. ¶L-4632; ¶2744.10; TD ¶294,502
38. ¶L-4721; ¶2744.17; TD ¶296,026
39. ¶L-4632.1; ¶2744.17; TD ¶295,325.1
40. ¶s L-4632, L-4717; ¶2744.10; TD ¶296,019
41. ¶L-4632; ¶2744.18; TD ¶294,502

(4) The reason for entertaining, or the nature of the business benefit derived or expected to be derived, and the nature of any business discussion or activity that took place. If deducting entertainment "associated with" the active conduct of business (¶1566), the date, duration, place and nature of the business discussion, the persons entertained who participated in the business discussion, and the business reason for the entertainment or the nature of business benefit derived or expected to be derived as the result of entertaining.

(5) The occupation or other information about the person or persons entertained, including name, title or other designation, sufficient to establish his business relationship to the taxpayer. (Reg § 1.274-5T(b)(4), Reg § 1.274-5T(b)(3))[42]

¶ 1584 Substantiating costs of listed property.

For listed property (¶1580), all the relevant elements from the following list must be proved for each expenditure or business use of the property:

(1) The amount and date of each separate expenditure (for example, the cost and date of acquisition or leasing, the cost and date of maintenance and repairs, etc.).

(2) The amount and date of each use of the item of listed property for business or investment, based on an appropriate measure (mileage for automobiles and other property used for transportation, time for other types of property, unless IRS approves an alternative method), and the total use of the item of listed property for the tax period.

(3) The business purpose for each expenditure or use with respect to the listed property. (Reg § 1.274-5T(b)(6))[43]

For optional business standard mileage rate, see ¶1561.

¶ 1585 Adequate records of T&E expenses and listed-property expenses.

Adequate records of T&E expenses and of listed property (¶1580) expenditures and uses consist of a currently maintained account book, diary, log, statement of expenses, trip sheet, or similar record and, where necessary (¶1586), documentary evidence such as receipts and paid bills, which together are sufficient to establish each element of every expenditure or use that must be substantiated. Information reflected on a receipt need not be duplicated in an account book or other record so long as the account book or other record and the receipt complement each other in an orderly fashion. (Reg § 1.274-5T(c)(2)(i))[44] Both written and computer records are adequate records. (Reg § 1.274-5T(c)(2)(ii)(C)(2))[45]

Where the business purpose of an expenditure is evident from the surrounding facts and circumstances, a written explanation isn't required. (Reg § 1.274-5T(c)(2)(ii)(B))[46]

¶ 1586 Adequate documentary evidence to support lodging expenditures and other expenditures of $75 or more.

Documentary evidence, such as receipts or bills marked paid is required to support all expenditures for (1) lodging while away from home and (2) for any other expenses of $75 or more (except for transportation charges for which documentary evidence is not readily available). (Reg § 1.274-5(c)(2)(iii))[47]

Documentary evidence (original documents, faxes, e-mail printouts)[48] must disclose the amount, date, place, and essential character of the expenditure. For example, a hotel receipt is sufficient to support expenditures for business travel if it contains the name and location of the hotel, the date or dates taxpayer stayed there, and separate amounts for charges such as for lodging, meals, and telephone. A restaurant receipt is sufficient to support an expenditure

---

42. ¶L-4635; ¶2744.10; TD ¶295,327
43. ¶L-4644; ¶2744.10; TD ¶295,333
44. ¶L-4616 *et seq.*; ¶2744.13; TD ¶295,311
45. ¶L-4616; ¶2744.13; TD ¶295,312

46. ¶L-4609; ¶2744.13; TD ¶295,307
47. ¶s L-4603, L-4619; ¶2744.13; TD ¶295,316
48. ¶L-4616; ¶2744.13; TD ¶295,316

for a business meal if it contains the name and location of the restaurant, the date and amount of the expenditure, and an indication that a charge (if any) is made for an item other than meals and beverages. A canceled check, together with a bill from the payee, ordinarily will establish the cost but may not alone show business purpose. (Reg § 1.274-5(c)(2)(iii))[49]

¶ 1587 Sufficiently corroborated statements used to substantiate expenses.

Taxpayers may substantiate the elements of their expenditures and uses not only by adequate records, but also by their own statements, written or oral, if those statements are supported by sufficient corroborating evidence. (Code Sec. 274(d))[50]

Corroborating evidence may be oral if from a disinterested, unrelated party who has knowledge of the expenditure or use in question. Written evidence has greater probative value, and its probative value increases if set down close to the time of the expenditure or use in question. (Reg § 1.274-5T(c)(1)) A taxpayer's written or oral statement must contain specific, detailed information about the element being substantiated, and the taxpayer must present other corroborative evidence sufficient to establish that element. (Reg § 1.274-5T(c)(3)(i))[1]

¶ 1588 Inadequate substantiation—remedies.

If a taxpayer hasn't fully substantiated a particular element of an expenditure or use, but does establish to IRS's satisfaction that he has substantially complied with the adequate records requirements, IRS may permit the taxpayer to establish the missing element by other evidence that it considers adequate. (Reg § 1.274-5T(c)(2)(v))

Where a taxpayer establishes that, by reason of "the inherent nature of the situation," he was unable to get either fully adequate records, or fully sufficient corroborating evidence in support of his own statement, he will be treated as satisfying the substantiation requirements if he presents other evidence that possesses the highest degree of probative value under the circumstances. (Reg § 1.274-5T(c)(4))[2]

Where a taxpayer establishes that he has maintained adequate records of an expenditure or use, but can't produce them because they have been lost through circumstances beyond his control (e.g., damage by fire, flood, etc.), he may prove his entitlement to a deduction by a reasonable reconstruction of the expenditure or use in question. (Reg § 1.274-5T(c)(5))[3] Destruction of records in marital disputes has been held to fall within this rule.[4]

¶ 1589 Business Gifts and Employee Awards. ▬▬▬▬▬▬▬▬▬▬▬▬▬▬

The costs of ordinary and necessary business gifts to individuals other than employees are deductible, subject to a $25 per-year per-person limit. Gifts to employees aren't deductible as gifts, but may be deductible as compensation. Certain noncash awards to employees are deductible.

¶ 1590 Business gifts.

The cost of ordinary and necessary business gifts may be deducted up to $25 a year to any one individual. Gift means any item excludable from gross income by the recipient under Code Sec. 102 (¶1213), but not excludable under any other Code income tax provision. (Code Sec. 274(b))[5] However, any item for general distribution having a cost of not more than $4 and on which the giver's name is clearly and permanently imprinted, and signs, display racks, or other promotional material donated to a retailer to be used on his business premises, aren't classified as gifts. (Code Sec. 274(b)(1); Reg § 1.274-3(b)(2))[6]

Since no amount transferred by or for an employer to or for the benefit of an employee is

49. ¶L-4619; ¶2744.13; TD ¶295,316
50. ¶L-4626 *et seq.*; ¶2744.14; TD ¶295,323
1. ¶L-4626; ¶2744.14; TD ¶295,323
2. ¶L-4628; ¶2744.15; TD ¶295,310

3. ¶L-4623; ¶2744.15; TD ¶295,320
4. ¶L-4624; TD ¶295,321
5. ¶L-2306; ¶2744.08; TD ¶303,005
6. ¶L-2306; ¶2744.08; TD ¶303,007

excludable as a gift (under Code Sec. 102) no such amount is deductible as a gift, though it may be deductible under other rules (e.g., as compensation).[7]

¶ 1591 Employee achievement awards.

An employer can deduct the cost of employee achievement awards (defined below). (Code Sec. 274(j)) The maximum deduction for awards made to one employee is $400 per year ($1,600 if the award is a qualified plan award, including the cost of awards that aren't qualified plan awards). (Code Sec. 274(j)(2)) The award must be given as part of a meaningful presentation under conditions and circumstances that don't create a likelihood that the payment is disguised compensation. (Code Sec. 274(j)(3))

An employee achievement award is an item of tangible personal property awarded to an employee because of length of service achievement, or safety achievement. (Code Sec. 274(j)(3))[8] Tangible personal property doesn't include cash or any gift certificate other than a nonnegotiable gift certificate conferring only the right to receive tangible personal property. (Reg § 1.274-3(b)(2)(iv))

A qualified plan award is an item awarded as part of a permanent, written, nondiscriminatory plan of the employer. (Code Sec. 274(j)(3)(B); Reg § 1.274-3(d))

A length-of-service award won't qualify for deduction under these rules if given during an employee's first five years of employment, or if a length-of-service award was given to the same employee during the same year or any of the earlier four years. (Code Sec. 274(j)(4)(B))

Safety achievement awards don't qualify if given to managerial, administrative, professional or clerical employees, or if such awards previously have been given to more than 10% of other employees during the year. (Code Sec. 274(j)(4)(C))[9]

No deduction is allowed for an employee achievement award (under the normal Code Sec. 162 ordinary and necessary rules or the Code Sec. 212 production of income rules) except under the above rules. (Code Sec. 274(j)(1))[10]

¶ 1592 Substantiating business gift expenses.

To substantiate business gift expenses adequate records or a sufficiently corroborated statement must show: (1) a description of the gift, (2) the taxpayer's cost, (3) when the gift was made, (4) the occupation or other information about the gift's recipient, including his name, title, or other designation sufficient to establish his business relationship to the taxpayer, and (5) the reason for making the gift or the nature of business benefit derived or expected. (Reg § 1.274-5T(b)(5))[11]

¶ 1593 Rent Expense.

Rent is deductible if paid for the use of property used in whole or in part in the taxpayer's trade, business, or profession, or for the production of income.

Rent for the use of real or personal property in the taxpayer's trade, business, or profession, is deductible. (Code Sec. 162(a)(3)) But rent for personal-use property isn't. (Code Sec. 262(a); Reg § 1.262-1(b)(3))[12]

Besides normal cash rent payable periodically, rent includes a lump sum paid as advance rental, bonus, etc.; a percentage of the tenant's receipts or profits; the tenant's payment of the expenses of maintaining the rented property (taxes, insurance, etc.), and payment in property other than money (deductible to the extent of the property's fair market value).[13]

---

7. ¶H-4009; ¶1624.363; TD ¶278,309
8. ¶L-2313; ¶2744.09; TD ¶303,012
9. ¶L-2315; ¶2744.09; TD ¶303,014
10. ¶L-2313 *et seq.*; ¶2744.09; TD ¶303,012

11. ¶L-4643; ¶2744.10; TD ¶295,332
12. ¶L-6604; ¶1624.285; TD ¶260,501
13. ¶L-6605 *et seq.*; ¶1624.285; TD ¶260,505

¶ 1594   Rent paid to related lessor.

Rentals paid between parties who are related either as members of a family or by stock ownership may not be deductible to the extent that they exceed the rent that would have been paid in an arm's-length transaction.

A corporation may deduct fair and reasonable rentals paid to corporate shareholders or their relatives. But excessive rentals can be treated as nondeductible dividends.[14] Reasonable rental payments by a shareholder for use of corporate property are deductible.[15]

¶ 1595   Rent under leaseback arrangements.

A transfer by sale or gift coupled with a leaseback may be more advantageous than a mortgage loan and can create tax benefits for the transferor. Tax advantages (including rent deduction) of a sale and leaseback arrangement may be lost if IRS treats it as a mortgage loan, a tax-free exchange, or a sham transaction.[16]

A gift in trust with a leaseback of the property to the grantor will generally be upheld as a valid rental or royalty arrangement by the courts if: (1) the transfer is complete and irrevocable, (2) the trustee is independent, and (3) the rental is reasonable. Reasonableness of rent and the independence of the trustee are questions of fact.[17]

¶ 1596   Rent or purchase; lease with purchase options.

A payment is deductible as rent only if the taxpayer-lessee hasn't taken or isn't taking title to the property and has no equity interest in it. (Code Sec. 162(a)(3)) Thus, payments made under conditional sales contracts aren't deductible as rent.[18]

A lease that contains an option permitting the lessee to buy the property may be construed as a sale so that none of the payments is deductible as rent. Whether the lease is considered to be a sale depends essentially upon the intent of the parties, as shown in the agreement, read in light of the facts and circumstances existing at the time the agreement was made.[19] Important factors indicating sale instead of lease include nominal option price, excessive rent, designating part of the payment as interest, rental plus option price equal to the property's value plus interest, and application of rent payments to the lessee's equity in the property.[20]

¶ 1597   Lease acquisition costs.

Payments made by a lessee to get a business lease aren't currently deductible but must be amortized over the period specified below. (Reg § 1.162-11(a)) This rule applies whether the tenant is on the cash or accrual basis and even though he has an option to buy the property.[21]

If the lease isn't renewable, lease acquisition costs are amortized over the unexpired term of the lease.[22] If the lease is renewable any renewal period must be taken into account in determining the amortization period, if less than 75% of the lease cost is attributable to the portion of the lease (exclusive of the renewal period) remaining on the date of acquisition of the lease.[23]

¶ 1598   Lessor's costs.

Costs incurred by a lessor in leasing his property, or by a lessee in subletting, aren't currently deductible but must be amortized ratably over the term of the lease.[24] For tax treatment of construction allowances, see ¶1346.

---

14. ¶L-6702; ¶1624.299; TD ¶260,522
15. ¶L-6710; ¶1624.299; TD ¶260,522
16. ¶L-6300 *et seq.*; ¶1624.299; TD ¶262,500
17. ¶L-6317; TD ¶262,510
18. ¶L-6209; ¶1624.284; TD ¶260,502
19. ¶L-6222 *et seq.*; ¶1624.305; TD ¶260,502

20. ¶L-6200 *et seq.*; ¶1624.305; TD ¶260,502
21. ¶L-6501; ¶1624.323; TD ¶261,501
22. ¶s L-6501, L-6504; ¶1624.323; TD ¶261,505
23. ¶L-6504 *et seq.*; ¶1624.323; TD ¶261,504
24. ¶L-6401; ¶1624.081; TD ¶262,001

The cost of MACRS improvements made by lessors are recoverable over the cost recovery period applicable to the leasehold improvements—regardless of the period of time the property is leased. (Code Sec. 168(i)(8))[25]

A lessor's payments for cancellation of a lease must be amortized and deducted over the remaining term of the *cancelled* lease,[26] except that if the payment is made in order to enter a lease with a new tenant, the payment must be amortized over the term of the *new* lease.[27]

¶ 1599   Year of deduction for rent.

The tax year in which the rent is paid by a cash basis taxpayer or incurred by an accrual basis taxpayer is generally the proper year for deduction.[28] But advance rentals must be apportioned and deducted over the term of the lease or other rental period.[29]

¶ 1600   Deferred payments for the use of property or services.

Rent and interest attributable to a deferred rental agreement must be both reported and deducted as if both parties are accrual basis taxpayers. This rule applies to leases of over $250,000 that require either: (1) at least one payment for the use of property to be paid after the close of the calendar year following the calendar year of the use of the property, or (2) increases (or decreases) in the amounts to be paid as rent. (Code Sec. 467)[30]

For lessees, the deductible rental amount for the tax year is the sum of:

(1) rent deemed accrued by allocating rents in accordance with the rental agreement, taking into account the present value of rent to be paid after the close of the period, and

(2) interest for the year on amounts taken into account for earlier tax years (under (1), above), but which are as yet unpaid. (Code Sec. 467(b)(1))[31]

Present value and interest are computed using a rate equal to 110% of the applicable federal rate (¶1116). (Code Sec. 467(e)(4))[32]

If the agreement is silent as to rent allocation or the agreement is a disqualified leaseback or long-term agreement, then constant rental accrual applies. (Code Sec. 467(b)(2), Code Sec. 467(b)(3)) The constant rental amount is an amount paid as of the close of each lease period which would result in a total present value equal to the present value of the total payments required under the lease. (Code Sec. 467(e)(1))[33]

A rental agreement is a disqualified leaseback or long-term agreement if:

(1) it is part of a leaseback transaction to any person who had an interest in the leased property within two years before the leaseback (Code Sec. 467(e)(2)), or the term of the agreement exceeds 75% of a prescribed recovery period (Code Sec. 467(b)(4)), *and*

(2) a principal purpose of the increased rents provided in the agreement is tax avoidance. (Code Sec. 467(b)(4))[34]

An agreement isn't a disqualified leaseback or long-term agreement if it qualifies for any of the various safe harbors, including the uneven rent test, which is met if the rent allocated to each calendar year does not vary from the average rent allocated to all calendar years by more than 10%. (Reg § 1.467-3(c))

Under regs to be issued, similar rules will apply to certain deferred payments for services. (Code Sec. 467(g))[35]

A reasonable rent holiday won't cause an agreement to be treated as a disqualified leaseback or long-term agreement. (Code Sec. 467(b)(5)) A rent holiday of 3 months or less at the

---

25. ¶L-6404; ¶1674.023; TD ¶262,004
26. ¶L-6405; ¶1624.081; TD ¶262,005
27. ¶L-6407; ¶1624.081; TD ¶262,006
28. ¶L-6616; ¶1624.285; TD ¶260,536
29. ¶L-6617; ¶s 1624.081, 1624.285; TD ¶260,537
30. ¶s L-6800, L-6801.13; ¶4674; TD ¶261,001

31. ¶L-6803; ¶4674; TD ¶261,035
32. ¶L-6804
33. ¶L-6805; ¶4674; TD ¶261,043
34. ¶L-6808; ¶4674; TD ¶261,050
35. ¶G-3451; ¶4674; TD ¶446,801

beginning of the lease term is disregarded in determining if the rental agreement has increasing or decreasing rent. (Reg § 1.467-1(c)(2)(i)(B)) A lessor's granting of an 11.5 month zero rent period in a 25-year lease was held to be a reasonable rent holiday in an area where such inducements were needed to attract lessees.[36]

¶ 1601　Research and Experimental Expenditures.

Taxpayers can choose whether to immediately deduct or to capitalize research and experimental (R&E) expenditures. In some cases, they also have the option of writing off the expenditures over several years.

¶ 1602　Deduct or capitalize research & experimental expenditures.

Taxpayers can choose whether to immediately deduct or to capitalize research and experimental (R&E) expenditures. (Code Sec. 174(a)(1)) If the taxpayer adopts current expense treatment, he must use it for all qualifying expenses for the year he adopts it and for all later years, unless he gets IRS permission to switch. (Code Sec. 174(a)(3))[37]

For R&E expenditures that aren't chargeable to depreciable or depletable property, instead of current deduction or capitalizing the taxpayer can elect (use Form 4562) to deduct the expenditures ratably over 60 months or longer, beginning with the month the taxpayer first realized benefits from the expenditures. (Code Sec. 174(b)(1); Reg § 1.174-4(b)(1))[38]

In general, expenditures that qualify as R&E costs are research and development costs in the experimental or laboratory sense. This includes all costs incident to the development or improvement of a product, including a pilot model, process, formula, invention, technique, patent or similar property. (Reg § 1.174-2(a))[39]

All taxpayers, including partners and S corporation shareholders, may elect to deduct all or any portion of these costs ratably over ten years. (Code Sec. 59(e)(1); Reg § 1.59-1)[40]

For limitations on deductions for R&E expenses that also qualify for the research credit or the orphan drug credit, see ¶ 2320 and ¶2330. For alternative minimum tax treatment of research and experimentation expenditures, see ¶ 3209.

¶ 1603　Legal and Accounting Expenses.

Legal expenses and accounting and related expenses may be deductible.

For expenses of determining or contesting tax liability, see ¶1513.

¶ 1604　Legal expenses.

Attorney's fees, court costs and other legal expenses can qualify as deductible business expenses. Legal expenses aren't deductible if they are either capital expenditures or a personal expense of the taxpayer. (Code Sec. 162, Code Sec. 262(a), Code Sec. 263)[41] Qualified legal expenses can include expenses incurred in litigation, for legal advice, and for the drafting of instruments,[42] but not to acquire, perfect or defend title to property. (Reg § 1.212-1(k))[43] A legal retainer must be capitalized if it is applied to legal expenses associated with the acquisition of a business.[44]

¶ 1605　Accounting and related expenses.

Fees for bookkeeping and accounting work incurred in the operation of the taxpayer's business are deductible.[45]

---

36. ¶L-6812; ¶4674; TD ¶261,053
37. ¶L-3117; ¶1744; TD ¶306,508
38. ¶L-3121 *et seq.*; ¶1744; TD ¶306,512
39. ¶L-3117; ¶1744; TD ¶306,505
40. ¶A-8194; ¶594; TD ¶695,503
41. ¶s L-2901, L-2969; ¶1624.040; TD ¶305,004
42. ¶L-2902; ¶1624.040; TD ¶305,004
43. ¶L-2908; ¶2634.01; TD ¶305,010
44. ¶L-2901.1; TD ¶305,002
45. ¶L-2959; TD ¶305,061

¶ 1606   Insurance Premiums. ■■■■■■■■■■■■■■■■■■■■■■■■■■■■■■■

Certain premiums that qualify as trade or business expenses, or as investment expenses, are deductible.

¶ 1607   Insurance premiums on nonlife policies.

Premiums for insurance against various types of risks, such as property damage, are generally deductible as business expenses (Code Sec. 162; Reg § 1.162-1(a)), but premiums on policies on taxpayer's residence, or for other personal use, aren't. (Code Sec. 262(a); Reg § 1.262-1(b))[46] Payments to an insurance company to assume capped costs certain to be incurred in the future isn't insurance for tax purposes.[47]

Self-insurance reserve funds aren't deductible even if taxpayer can't get business insurance coverage for certain business risks.[48] Neither are payments to "captive" insurance subsidiaries or other similar arrangements where there's no true risk-shifting.[49] But a limited deduction is allowed for certain payments made to a medical malpractice self-insurance pool.[50]

Premiums are nondeductible capital expenditures where paid for property insurance during construction. So are premiums for title insurance and for public liability and worker's compensation insurance paid in connection with the construction of a building.[1]

¶ 1608   Life insurance premiums.

Life insurance premiums aren't deductible if the taxpayer is directly or indirectly a beneficiary. (Code Sec. 264(a)(1); Reg § 1.264-1) See ¶1526. For example, the cost of a corporation's key person insurance isn't deductible.[2] Premiums paid by an individual for personal life insurance aren't deductible. (Reg § 1.262-1(b)(1))[3] For group-term premiums, see ¶1526.

¶ 1609   Time for deducting insurance premiums.

If a cash basis taxpayer pays an otherwise deductible premium for one year's coverage which applies in part to the following tax year, the entire premium is deductible in the year paid. But if premiums for several years are paid in advance, IRS and most courts require the premium to be amortized and deducted over the life of the policy, though one court has allowed a full deduction to a cash basis taxpayer in the year of payment where the taxpayer had consistently deducted premiums in the year of payment.

For an accrual basis taxpayer, deductibility of an accrued liability for insurance expense is determined under the economic performance rules—that is, when the premium is paid. But where prepaid premiums cover more than one year, an accrual basis taxpayer must prorate the premium paid in advance over the life of the policy.[4]

For the "12-month rule" exception to capitalization of certain intangibles, see ¶1671.

¶ 1610   Bribes, Kickbacks, Fines and Penalties. ■■■■■■■■■■■■■■■■■■

Certain illegal bribes, kickbacks, rebates and other payments aren't deductible. Nor are fines and penalties for violation of a law, including tax penalties.

Public policy isn't a ground for denying deduction. Unless a payment is nondeductible by law, it's deductible if ordinary and necessary. (Reg § 1.162-1)[5]

46. ¶L-3500 *et seq.*; ¶1624.032; TD ¶304,404
47. ¶L-3517
48. ¶L-3518; ¶1624.032; TD ¶304,423
49. ¶L-3520; ¶1624.032; TD ¶304,425
50. ¶L-3515; TD ¶304,413

1. ¶L-3530; TD ¶304,429
2. ¶L-3407; ¶2644; TD ¶304,006
3. ¶L-3401; ¶2644; TD ¶304,001
4. ¶L-3526 *et seq.*; ¶1624.081; TD ¶304,430 *et seq.*
5. ¶L-2609; ¶1624.377; TD ¶304,804

¶ 1611   Bribes and other illegal payments.

No deduction is allowed for any illegal bribe, kickback or other illegal payment under any law of the U.S., or of a state (if the state law is generally enforced), that subjects the payor to a criminal penalty or the loss of license or privilege to engage in business, whether or not that penalty or loss of license actually occurs. A kickback includes a payment in consideration of the referral of a client, patient, or customer. (Code Sec. 162(c)(2))[6]

No deduction is allowed for any kickback, rebate, or bribe made by any provider of services, supplier, physician, or other person who furnishes Medicare or Medicaid items or services, if made in connection with the furnishing of such items or services or the making or receiving of such payments. A kickback includes a payment for the referral of a client, patient, or customer. For these payments, deduction is denied regardless of legality. (Code Sec. 162(c)(3))[7]

No business expense deduction is allowed for any illegal bribe or kickback made directly or indirectly to any federal, state, or local public official or employee. If the payment is to an official or an employee of a foreign government, no deduction is allowed if the payment violates the U.S. Foreign Corrupt Practices Act. (Code Sec. 162(c)(1))[8]

Business kickbacks, fee-splitting, etc., that aren't specifically disallowed are deductible if they qualify as ordinary and necessary.[9]

¶ 1612   Illegal businesses and drug trafficking.

The ordinary and necessary expenses incurred in operating an illegal business are deductible, even though payment of the expense and the acts performed by the employees of the business are illegal (e.g., a bookmaker's expenses).[10] But there's no deduction or credit for amounts paid or incurred in illegal drug trafficking (Code Sec. 280E), although gross receipts may be adjusted for cost of goods sold.[11]

¶ 1613   Fines and penalties.

No business expense deduction is allowed for fines or similar penalties paid to a government for the violation of any law. (Code Sec. 162(f))[12] For example, state law penalties on public school teachers for striking aren't deductible. Similarly, penalties paid for violating federal environmental protection laws aren't deductible.[13]

Also, penalties paid in connection with federal, state, and local taxes are generally not deductible—for example, penalties for negligence, delinquency, or fraud relating to federal taxes (Reg § 1.162-21(b)), and for failure to withhold federal payroll taxes.[14]

¶ 1614   Domestic Production Activities Deduction. ■■■■■■■■■■■■■■■

Taxpayers are allowed a domestic production activities deduction (DPAD) under Code Sec. 199 equal to the specified percentage for the tax year of the taxpayer's qualified production activities income for the tax year, subject to certain limits.

¶ 1615   Deduction for manufacturing and production activities—Form 8903.

Taxpayers may claim a deduction on Form 8903 generally equal to 9% for tax years beginning in 2010 (and for later years) of the lesser of: (1) the taxpayer's "qualified production activities income" (¶1616) for the tax year or (2) taxable income (modified adjusted gross income, for individual taxpayers) without regard to this deduction, for the tax year. (Code Sec. 199(a); Reg § 1.199-1(a))

---

6. ¶L-2606; ¶1624.384; TD ¶304,801
7. ¶L-2608; ¶1624.384; TD ¶304,807
8. ¶L-2601; ¶1624.384; TD ¶304,801
9. ¶L-2601; ¶1624.384; TD ¶304,804
10. ¶L-2631; ¶1624.382; TD ¶304,815

11. ¶L-2632; ¶280E4; TD ¶304,815
12. ¶L-2701 *et seq.*; ¶1624.388; TD ¶302,501
13. ¶L-2701; ¶1624.388; TD ¶302,501
14. ¶L-2709; ¶1624.388; TD ¶302,507

The deduction as computed above is limited to 50% of the W-2 wages of the employer for the tax year. W-2 wages are the sum of the aggregate amounts that must be included on the employees' Forms W-2 under Code Sec. 6051(a)(3) (i.e., wages subject to withholding) and Code Sec. 6051(a)(8) (elective deferrals), that are made by the taxpayer during the calendar year that ends in the tax year. (Code Sec. 199(b); Reg § 1.199-1(a))[15] W-2 wages are the wages of employees including common-law employees and officers of a corporate employer which are properly included in a return filed with the Social Security Administration on or before the 60th day after the due date (including extensions) for that return. W-2 wages only include amounts that are properly allocable to domestic production gross receipts (DPGR) (¶1616). (Code Sec. 199(b)(2); Reg § 1.199-2(a)(1)) This allocation may be made using any reasonable method that satisfies IRS based on all facts and circumstances. Regs provide safe harbors for calculating W-2 wages. (Reg § 1.199-2(e)(2))[16]

The deduction is directly available to all taxpayers except pass-through entities (partnerships, S corporations, trusts and estates) and is available to owners of pass-through entities. (Code Sec. 199(d)) The deduction for partnerships and S corporations is determined at the partner or shareholder level. Partners or shareholders are treated as having W-2 wages equal to their allocable share of the entity's DPGR-related W-2 wages for the tax year. (Code Sec. 199(d)(1)(A); Reg § 1.199-5)

The otherwise allowable Code Sec. 199 deduction of a taxpayer with oil-related qualified production activities income is reduced by 3% of the least of (1) oil-related qualified production activities income for the tax year; (2) qualified production activities income for the tax year; or (3) taxable income (or for individuals, AGI), determined without regard to the domestic production activities deduction. (Code Sec. 199(d)(9)(A))

For treatment of the deduction for alternative minimum tax, see ¶3201.

¶ 1616 Qualified production activities income defined.

"Qualified production activities income" is equal to domestic production gross receipts (DPGR), reduced by the sum of: (1) the costs of goods sold that are allocable to the receipts; (2) other deductions, expenses, or losses that are allocable to these receipts; and (3) a ratable portion of other deductions, expenses, and losses that are not directly allocable to the receipts or to another class of income. (Code Sec. 199(c))[17]

DPGR is the taxpayer's gross receipts derived from:

... any lease, rental, license, sale, exchange or other disposition of qualifying production property—i.e., tangible personal property, many types of computer software and certain sound recordings (Code Sec. 199(c)(5))[18]—that was manufactured, produced, grown or extracted by the taxpayer in whole or in significant part within the U.S. (Code Sec. 199(c)(4)(A)(i)(I)),[19] Gross receipts from providing computer software to customers for their direct use while connected to the Internet may be treated as DPGR if certain conditions are met. (Reg § 1.199-3(i)(6)(iii))

... any lease, rental, license, sale, exchange or other disposition of qualified films produced by the taxpayer. (Code Sec. 199(c)(4)(A)(i)(II)) In general, the taxpayer's production of the qualified film must be substantial in nature, taking into account all the facts and circumstances. (Reg § 1.199-3(k)(6)) A qualified film (including any copyrights, trademarks, or other intangibles with respect to the film) is one for which 50% of the total compensation for production of the film is for services performed in the U.S. by actors, production personnel, directors and producers, and which does not depict certain sexually explicit conduct. (Code Sec. 199(c)(6))[20] A partner owning at least a 20% capital interest in the partnership is treated as having engaged directly in any film produced by the entity and a partnership is treated as having engaged directly in any film produced by any partner who owns at

---

15. ¶L-4325; ¶1994; TD ¶307,800
16. ¶L-4385.1; ¶1994.010; TD ¶307,803
17. ¶L-4367; ¶1994.084; TD ¶307,804

18. ¶L-4352; ¶1994.064; TD ¶307,805
19. ¶L-4327.1; ¶1994.036; TD ¶307,805
20. ¶L-4356; ¶1994.070; TD ¶307,805

least a 20% capital interest in the entity (similar rules apply to S corporations). (Code Sec. 199(d)(1)(A)(iv))

... any sale, exchange or other disposition of electricity, natural gas, or potable water produced by the taxpayer in the U.S. (Code Sec. 199(c)(4)(A)(i)(III))

... construction of real property performed in the U.S. by a taxpayer engaged in the active conduct of a construction trade or business in the ordinary course of that trade or business (Code Sec. 199(c)(4)(A)(ii)),[21] including construction and substantial renovation of residential and commercial buildings and infrastructure, such as roads, power lines, water systems, and communications facilities. A taxpayer qualifies for the deduction even if it doesn't own the property being constructed, and more than one taxpayer may qualify for the same construction project.[22] Gross receipts from the rental of real property that the taxpayer builds are not derived from construction and are not eligible for the deduction.[23] Generally, construction includes certain grading, demolition (including under Code Sec. 280B (¶1784)), clearing, excavating, and other activities that physically transform the land. (Reg § 1.199-3(m)(2)(iii), Reg § 1.199-3(m))

... engineering or architectural services with respect to the construction of real property in the U.S. performed in the U.S. by a taxpayer engaged in the active conduct of an engineering or architectural services trade or business in the ordinary course of that trade or business. (Code Sec. 199(c)(4)(A)(iii))[24]

Various de minimis rules are available for the computation of DPGR. (Reg § 1.199-1(d), Reg § 1.199-3)[25] Statistical sampling methods may be used if detailed conditions are met.[26] For a taxpayer's first four tax years beginning after 2005 and before 2010, Puerto Rico is included in the term "U.S." in determining DPGR.

Qualifying production property is treated as manufactured, produced, grown or extracted in whole or in significant part within the U.S. if, based on all of the facts and circumstances, the manufacturing, production, etc., activity performed in the U.S. is substantial in nature, or, under a safe harbor, if the direct labor and overhead costs incurred by the taxpayer in the U.S. for the manufacture, production, growth, or extraction of the property are at least 20% of the taxpayer's (1) total cost for the property, or (2) unadjusted basis in the property, in a transaction without cost of goods sold (e.g., a lease). (Reg § 1.199-3(g)(3)(i))[27]

DPGR does not include gross receipts derived from:

... the sale of food or beverages prepared by the taxpayer at a retail establishment (Code Sec. 199(c)(4)(B)(i)), i.e., tangible property used in the trade or business of selling food or beverages to the public if retail (rather than wholesale) sales occur at the facility. A facility won't be treated as a retail establishment if less than 5% of total gross receipts for the tax year derived from the sale of food or beverages prepared at the facility are for retail sales. If a facility is a retail establishment, but food or beverages are prepared there and sold at wholesale, the taxpayer may allocate its gross receipts.[28]

... the transmission or distribution of electricity, natural gas, or potable water. (Code Sec. 199(c)(4)(B)(ii))[29]

... the lease, rental, license, sale, exchange, or other disposition of land. (Code Sec. 199(c)(4)(B)(iii))[30]

... property leased, licensed, or rented by the taxpayer for use by any related person (defined in Code Sec. 199(c)(7)(B)). (Code Sec. 199(c)(7)(A))[31]

In computing qualified production activities income, taxpayers may allocate cost of goods sold, and other expenses, deductions, etc., between DPGR and other gross receipts under any

---

21. ¶L-4340; ¶1994.036; TD ¶307,805
22. ¶L-4335; ¶1994.036; TD ¶307,805
23. ¶L-4350; ¶1994.036; TD ¶307,805
24. ¶L-4338; ¶1994.036; TD ¶307,805
25. ¶L-4338; ¶1994.034; TD ¶307,853
26. ¶L-4336.4; ¶1994.129; TD ¶307,821.1

27. ¶L-4330; ¶1994.036; TD ¶307,805
28. ¶L-4330; ¶1994.036; TD ¶307,805
29. ¶L-4334; ¶1994.036; TD ¶307,805
30. ¶L-4350; ¶1994.074 *et seq.*; TD ¶307,805
31. ¶L-4346; ¶1994.038; TD ¶307,805

reasonable method. However, if the taxpayer has the necessary information readily available, and can do so without undue burden and expense, the taxpayer must make these allocations using a specific identification method under the regs. (Reg § 1.199-1(d)(2))[32]

¶ 1617 Miscellaneous Business Expenses.

Royalty payments, circulation costs, mine exploration and development costs, and other miscellaneous costs of carrying on a business are deductible subject to certain conditions and limits.

¶ 1618 Royalty payments.

Royalty payments made for the right to use patents, copyrights and similar rights are deductible.[33] Payments to acquire the property itself are capital expenditures.[34]

¶ 1619 Circulation costs.

Publishers of periodicals can deduct currently their expenditures to establish, maintain and increase circulation. (Code Sec. 173)[35] Or, instead, they may elect to capitalize those costs. (Reg § 1.173-1(c))[36] A taxpayer may elect (use Form 4562) to amortize circulation costs over three years beginning with the year the expenditure is made. (Code Sec. 59(e)(1); Reg § 1.59-1) For alternative minimum tax treatment of circulation costs, see ¶3210.

¶ 1620 Serial contingent payments for franchises, trademarks, or trade names.

In the case of a transfer of a franchise, trademark or trade name, a deduction is allowed to the transferee for serial payments contingent on the productivity, use, or disposition of the franchise, trademark or trade name transferred. (Code Sec. 1253(d)(1))[37]

¶ 1621 Stock reacquisition expenses.

No deduction is allowed for any amount paid or incurred by a corporation in connection with the reacquisition of its stock (e.g., greenmail) or of the stock of any related person as specially defined in Code Sec. 465(b)(3)(C). Amounts deductible as interest under Code Sec. 163 or as dividends paid under Code Sec. 561 are among expenses not subject to this rule. (Code Sec. 162(k)) The no-deduction rule doesn't apply to deductions for amounts properly allocable to indebtedness (e.g., loan commitment fees) and amortized over the term of the indebtedness. (Code Sec. 162(k)(2)(A)(ii))[38]

¶ 1622 Co-op housing maintenance and lease expenses.

Cooperative housing maintenance and lease expenses are deductible if the cooperative unit is used in a trade or business or for the production of income. However, no deduction is allowed to the co-op stockholder for any payment to the co-op (in excess of the stockholder's share of taxes and interest) to the extent the payment is properly allocable to amounts chargeable to the co-op's capital account. The basis of the stockholder's stock is increased by the amount of any deduction disallowed under this rule. (Code Sec. 216(d))[39]

---

32. ¶L-4367.1; ¶1994.084; TD ¶307,804
33. ¶L-3201; ¶1624.284; TD ¶307,501
34. ¶L-3203; ¶1624.284; TD ¶307,505
35. ¶L-2213; ¶1734.01; TD ¶300,515
36. ¶L-2215 *et seq.*; ¶1734; TD ¶300,516
37. ¶I-8415 *et seq.*; ¶12534.01
38. ¶s L-5305, L-5411; ¶1624.402; TD ¶301,033
39. ¶K-5900 *et seq.*; ¶2164.01; TD ¶213,014

¶ 1623   Mine exploration costs.

Domestic mine exploration costs incurred before a mine has reached the development stage are nondeductible capital expenditures. However, taxpayers may elect to deduct mining exploration expenditures for minerals (other than oil and gas) that qualify for percentage depletion (Code Sec. 617).[40]

Deducted exploration costs are subject to recapture when the mine reaches the producing stage, when taxpayer receives a bonus or royalty, or when he disposes of all or part of the property, whichever happens first (except where IRS allows recapture to be postponed on disposition of a *part* interest). (Code Sec. 617(b)(1), Code Sec. 1254(a)(1); Reg § 1.1254-1(b))[41]

All taxpayers, including partners and S corporation shareholders, may elect (use Form 4562) to deduct all or any portion of their deductible mine exploration costs ratably over ten years. (Code Sec. 59(e); Reg § 1.59-1)[42]

Corporations' deductions for exploration costs are cut back 30% if they elect to write off the costs in the year they are incurred. (Code Sec. 291(b)(1)) The amount cut back is amortized over 60 months. (Code Sec. 291(b))[43]

¶ 1624   Mine development costs.

A taxpayer who incurs expenditures to develop minerals other than oil or gas may: (1) deduct those expenditures in the year they were paid or incurred (Code Sec. 616(a));[44] (2) elect to treat them as deferred expenses and deduct them ratably as the units of produced minerals benefited by the expense are sold (Code Sec. 616(b); Reg § 1.616-2(a));[45] or (3) treat them as deferred expenses and elect (use Form 4562) to amortize them ratably over ten years. (Code Sec. 59(e); Reg § 1.59-1)[46]

Corporations' deductions for mine development costs are cut back 30% if the corporation elects to write off the costs in the year incurred. (Code Sec. 291(b)(1)(B)) The amount cut-back is amortized over 60 months. (Code Sec. 291(b))[47]

Deducted mine development costs are recaptured (on Form 4797) as ordinary income on disposition of the property. (Code Sec. 1254(a)(1); Reg § 1.1254-1(b))[48]

¶ 1625   Intangible oil and gas and geothermal well drilling and development costs.

Geological and geophysical costs incurred in exploring for oil and gas are capital expenditures.[49] Taxpayers, however, may capitalize, amortize (over 60 months) or expense the so-called intangible drilling and development costs (IDCs) of oil, gas and geothermal wells. (Code Sec. 59(e); Reg § 1.59-1; Code Sec. 263(c); Reg § 1.612-4, Reg § 1.612-5)[50] In general, such intangible costs include only those costs that in themselves don't have a salvage value, such as labor and fuel.[1] For alternative minimum tax treatment of IDCs, see ¶3208.

Deducted IDCs are recaptured (on Form 4797) as ordinary income on disposition of the oil or gas wells. (Code Sec. 1254(a)(1)(A); Reg § 1.1254-1(b))[2]

¶ 1626   Lobbying costs, influencing public on legislation.

Deductible business expenses don't include:

. . . any amount paid or incurred (1) in influencing legislation; (2) in connection with participation in or intervention in any political campaign or any attempt to influence the

---

40. ¶N-3103; ¶6174
41. ¶N-3601 *et seq.*; ¶6174.01
42. ¶N-3114; ¶594
43. ¶N-3104; ¶2914; TD ¶600,502
44. ¶N-3116; ¶6164; TD ¶213,512
45. ¶N-3123; ¶6164
46. ¶N-3124; ¶6164.04; TD ¶695,503

47. ¶N-3104; ¶2914
48. ¶N-3309 *et seq.*
49. ¶N-3201; ¶6124.001; TD ¶695,503
50. ¶N-3202 *et seq.*; ¶6124.008
1. ¶N-3206; ¶6124.009
2. ¶N-3406; ¶12,544 *et seq.*

general public with respect to elections, legislative matters, or referendums; or (3) in communicating directly with a covered executive branch official on official matters (Code Sec. 162(e)(1)),

... the portion of dues paid to a tax-exempt organization allocable to lobbying by the organization for which no deduction is allowed, if the organization informs taxpayer of the nondeductible portion. (Code Sec. 162(e)(3))

Taxpayers must allocate their costs between legislative-branch lobbying and executive-branch lobbying in determining the nondeductible amount by consistently using a reasonable method. (Reg § 1.162-28(a)(1), Reg § 1.162-29(c)(2))[3]

In-house expenditures of $2,000 or less per year aren't subject to these rules. (Code Sec. 162(e)(5)(B)(i))

The disallowance concerning influencing legislation, above, doesn't apply to legislation of a local government. (Code Sec. 162(e)(2)(A))[4]

¶ 1627   Civil damages.

Civil damages paid under judgments and out-of-court settlements arising out of normal business operations are deductible as business expenses[5] if the litigation is directly connected with the taxpayer's business.[6]

No deduction is allowed for two-thirds of treble damage or settlement payments to private parties where the taxpayer (payor) in a criminal proceeding for violation of federal anti-trust law is convicted or pleads guilty or no contest. (Code Sec. 162(g); Reg § 1.162-22)[7]

¶ 1628   Employee Business Expenses.

Employees are engaged in the trade or business of being employees and thus can deduct certain employment-connected business expenses, such as travel expenses, union dues, work clothes, etc., as described in the following paragraphs.

Unreimbursed employee business expenses are generally deductible only as miscellaneous itemized deductions subject to the 2%-of-AGI floor, see ¶3110. (Reg § 1.67-1T(a)(1)(i))[8] For unreimbursed moving expenses, see ¶1645 *et seq.* For travel expenses of reservists more than 100 miles from home, see ¶1554.

¶ 1629   Cost of seeking and securing employment.

An employee can deduct the expenses of seeking new employment in his same trade or business, whether or not he gets the new job. Any local transportation expenses and travel expenses away from home and costs such as printing and postage are deductible.

An employee can't deduct the cost of seeking employment in a different trade or business even if he gets the job. If an unemployed person is seeking a job and no substantial lack of continuity occurred between the time of the past employment and the seeking of the new employment, his trade or business is the services performed for his past employer. Where there's no continuity, or where a person looks for a job for the first time, the expenses aren't deductible, even if a job results.

If an individual travels to a destination where he both seeks new employment in his present trade or business and engages in personal activities, his round-trip travel expenses are deductible only if the trip is primarily related to seeking the new employment. Expenses allocable to seeking the job at the destination are deductible even if the travel expenses aren't.[9]

---

3. ¶L-2400 *et seq.*; ¶1624.395; TD ¶306,000 *et seq.*
4. ¶L-2401 *et seq.*; ¶1624.395; TD ¶306,012
5. ¶L-2500 *et seq.*; ¶1624.040; TD ¶303,500
6. ¶L-2502; ¶1624.040; TD ¶303,501
7. ¶L-2714; ¶1624.391; TD ¶303,511
8. ¶L-3900 *et seq.*; ¶1624.067; TD ¶561,603
9. ¶L-3850 *et seq.*; ¶1624.067; TD ¶351,503

¶ 1630   Labor union dues, fees, and assessments.

Deduction has been permitted for dues, fines paid to remain in the union, strike funds, compulsory payments for unemployment benefits, and a mandatory service charge paid to a union by a nonmember. Deductions were denied for noncompulsory unemployment benefit fund payments, assessments for sick, accident, or death benefits, and other payments in exchange for valuable benefits.[10]

¶ 1631   Uniforms and special work clothes.

Deduction for the cost and maintenance of clothing is allowed if: (1) the employee's occupation is one that specifically requires special apparel or equipment as a condition of employment; and (2) the special apparel or equipment isn't adaptable to general or continued usage so as to take the place of ordinary clothing.

Thus, protective clothing, such as safety shoes, helmets, fishermen's boots, work gloves, oil clothes, etc., are deductible if required for the job. But work clothing and standard work shoes aren't deductible even if the worker's union requires them.[11] Clothes ruined on the job aren't deductible unless the above tests are met.[12]

¶ 1632   Other deductible employee expenses.

These include:

. . . membership dues in professional or business societies,[13]

. . . small tools and supplies,[14]

. . . salesman's briefcase used in business,[15]

. . . salesman's commissions paid to a third party who made the sales,[16]

. . . expenses incurred by a securities analyst for a stock brokerage firm in seeking to get new business for the employer and by so doing increase his own salary,[17]

. . . expenses of business use of home, see ¶1635 *et seq.*, and

. . . qualifying education expenses, see ¶2229.

¶ 1633   Deductions for expenses of professional individuals.

Costs of entering a profession or securing the right to practice are nondeductible. (Reg § 1.212-1(f))[18]

Individuals can deduct the expenses of their business or profession, such as supplies, rent, transportation, business, travel, telephone, etc., if they are self-employed. But a professional who is an employee may deduct only expenses allowed to employees.

Professionals, whether or not employees, can also deduct expenses peculiar to their professions such as dues to professional organizations, continuing professional education, subscriptions to professional journals, malpractice insurance and payments to assistants. The cost of professional books, furniture, instruments and equipment are deductible if their useful lives are short. (Reg § 1.162-6) But expenses incurred by business or professional people to build up their reputations are capital expenditures to develop or enhance goodwill, unless the expenses can be tied directly to the production of added income.[19] The following material highlights the rules on deductions for professionals, etc.:

Accountants can't deduct costs of a CPA review course or the CPA exam.[20]

10. ¶s L-3908, L-3910; ¶1624.067; TD ¶351,508
11. ¶L-3801; ¶1624.067; TD ¶351,001
12. ¶L-3805; ¶1624.067; TD ¶351,005
13. ¶s L-3918, L-4100; ¶1624.195; TD ¶307,721
14. ¶L-3918; TD ¶351,517
15. ¶L-3918; TD ¶351,517
16. ¶L-4237
17. ¶L-4416
18. ¶L-4101; ¶1624.193; TD ¶307,702
19. ¶L-4100 *et seq.*; ¶1624.191; TD ¶307,702
20. ¶L-3719; ¶1624.193; TD ¶302,019

Lawyers have been allowed to deduct bar association dues, but not costs of securing admission to practice (including bar examination fees, expenses to be admitted to second state bar, travel) (Reg § 1.162-5, Reg § 1.212-1(f)) which must be amortized over taxpayer's remaining life expectancy. The cost of bar review courses can't be amortized.[21]

Doctors and dentists can't deduct costs of securing the right to practice, fees on their initial licensing, etc. (Reg § 1.212-1(f))[22] Fees paid to a hospital for staff privileges are amortizable over taxpayer's useful life, or the useful life of the hospital privilege if shorter.[23]

Teachers can deduct the cost of membership in professional societies, educational journals, and travel to teachers' conventions and similar events. Professors may deduct the costs of research, writing, or lecturing that the college or university expects, even though they receive no payment or extra compensation. Deductible costs may include travel and research costs.[24]

A financial analyst couldn't deduct the cost of a master's in management (equivalent of an MBA) because it was a minimum educational requirement to qualify for position of associate (investment banker) with her employer.[25]

¶ 1634 Impairment-related work expenses.

Impairment-related work expenses are deductible (on Form 2106 or Form 2106-EZ). They are ordinary and necessary expenses, including attendant care services (e.g., a blind taxpayer's use of a reader) at the place of employment, to enable an individual who has a handicap to work. (Code Sec. 67(d)) Impairment-related work expenses are itemized deductions but aren't subject to the 2%-of-AGI floor. (Code Sec. 67(b)(6))[26]

¶ 1635 Residence Used in Part for Business—Home Office Deduction. ▬▬▬▬

Employees and self-employed individuals may take office-at-home deductions if tough tests are met.

The general rule is that no deduction is allowed for the business use of a dwelling unit that's also used by the taxpayer as a residence during the tax year. But exceptions, discussed below, allow deductions under certain circumstances. (Code Sec. 280A(a)) The disallowance rule applies to individuals, trusts, estates, partnerships, and S corporations. However, disallowance doesn't apply to any deduction allowable without regard to its connection with either a business or income-producing activity. (Code Sec. 280A(b)) For example, the deductions allowed under Code Sec. 163 for interest, Code Sec. 164 for certain taxes, and Code Sec. 165 for casualty losses may be claimed without regard to their connection with the taxpayer's trade or business or income-producing activities. In effect, this means that the disallowance applies only to otherwise deductible business expenses (Code Sec. 162) and depreciation.[27]

The home office deduction isn't allowed for expenses of an income-producing activity, unless the activity is a trade or business.[28]

Allowable home-office expenses are deducted on Form 1040, Schedule A (employees), Form 1040, Schedule C (most self-employed persons, who must also attach Form 8829), and Form 1040, Schedule F (farmers).

In situations in the following paragraphs, otherwise allowable business expenses are deductible (subject to the limits discussed at ¶1641 and ¶1642) even though they are incurred in connection with the business use of a portion of a taxpayer's residence. In addition, the cost of capital improvements made to the entire residence may be recovered through depreciation to the extent allocable to the portion of the residence used for the taxpayer's business.[29]

An employee gets a deduction (subject to the 2%-of-AGI floor on miscellaneous itemized deductions, see ¶3110) only if the exclusive business use of a portion of his residence is for the

---

21. ¶L-4102; ¶s 1624.193, 1624.195; TD ¶256,202
22. ¶s L-4100, L-4101; ¶1624.193; TD ¶307,702
23. ¶L-4107; TD ¶307,705
24. ¶L-4108; ¶s 1624.191, 1624.195; TD ¶302,035
25. ¶L-3713

26. ¶L-3906 *et seq.*; ¶674; TD ¶351,506
27. ¶L-1301 *et seq.*; ¶280A4 *et seq.*; TD ¶258,001 *et seq.*
28. ¶L-1305; ¶280A4.013; TD ¶258,002
29. ¶L-1306 *et seq.*; ¶280A4.04; TD ¶258,039

convenience of his employer. (Code Sec. 280A(c)(1))[30]

Charges (including taxes) for basic local telephone services for the first telephone line for any residence are treated as personal expenses. (Code Sec. 262(b))[31]

¶ 1636   Residence used as principal place of business.

Deduction is allowed to the extent allocable to a portion of a residence *used exclusively* and *on a regular basis* (¶1641) as the taxpayer's principal place of business for *any* trade or business of the taxpayer. (Code Sec. 280A(c)(1)(A))[32]

Following are the two ways to meet the principal place of business requirement:

(1) Under the statutory administrative/management activities test, the principal place of business test is met if a portion of the home is used for the administrative or management activities of any trade or business of the taxpayer, but only if there is no other fixed location where the taxpayer conducts substantial administrative or management activities of that trade or business. (Code Sec. 280A(c)(1)) Examples of administrative or management activities are: billing customers, clients or patients; keeping books and records; ordering supplies; setting up appointments; and forwarding orders or writing reports. A taxpayer's administrative or management activities at sites that aren't fixed locations of the business (e.g., car or hotel room), don't count. Moreover, if a taxpayer conducts some administrative or management activities at a fixed location of the business outside the home, he can still claim a home-office deduction as long as those activities aren't substantial (e.g., the taxpayer occasionally does minimal paperwork at another fixed location of the business). A taxpayer's eligibility to claim a home office deduction under the above rules won't be affected by the fact that he conducts substantial non-administrative or non-management business activities at a fixed location outside the home (e.g., meeting with, or providing services to, customers, clients, or patients at a fixed location outside of his home).[33]

illustration: Most of a self-employed plumber's time is spent at customers' homes and offices installing and repairing plumbing. His sole office is in his home and he uses it exclusively and regularly for the administrative or management details of his business (phoning customers, ordering supplies, and keeping his books). The plumber's home office qualifies as a principal place of business.

(2) Under the comparative analysis test, set forth under the Supreme Court's *Soliman* decision, the determination of a taxpayer's principal place of business requires a comparative analysis of: (1) the relative importance of the activities performed at each business location, and (2) the time spent at each place, i.e., time spent at the home compared with time spent in each of the other places where business activities occur. If the nature of the trade or profession requires the taxpayer to meet or confer with clients or patients or to deliver goods or services to a customer, the place where that contact occurs, particularly where that place is a facility with unique or special characteristics, is often important.[34]

¶ 1637   Residence used to meet clients.

Deduction is allowed to the extent allocable to a portion of a residence that's *used exclusively* and *on a regular basis* (¶1641) as a place of business (even if not a principal place of business) that is used by patients, clients, or customers in meeting or dealing with the taxpayer in the normal course of his trade or business. (Code Sec. 280A(c)(1)(B)) This permits a doctor, lawyer, sales rep, insurance agent, claims adjuster, etc., to deduct office-at-home expenses even though he operates his business or profession primarily from an office away from his residence. Telephone conversations alone aren't enough; patients, customers, etc., must be physically present for deductions to be claimed under this rule.[35]

---

30. ¶L-1348 *et seq.*; ¶280A4.018; TD ¶258,021
31. ¶L-1307 *et seq.*; ¶2624; TD ¶258,035
32. ¶s L-1317, L-1324; ¶280A4.014; TD ¶s 258,005, 258,007

33. ¶L-1335; ¶280A4.014; TD ¶258,009
34. ¶L-1330 *et seq.*; ¶280A4.014; TD ¶258,010
35. ¶L-1344 *et seq.*; ¶280A4.016; TD ¶258,019

¶ 1638   Separate structure not attached to residence.

A deduction is allowed for costs allocable to a portion of a separate structure not attached to the residence if it's used *exclusively* and *on a regular basis* (¶1641) in connection with the taxpayer's business. (Code Sec. 280A(c)(1)(C)) For example, an artist's studio in a structure next to but not attached to his residence qualified under this rule.[36]

¶ 1639   Residence used by wholesaler or retailer for storage of inventory and product samples.

Deduction is allowed to the extent allocable to space within the residence that the taxpayer uses *on a regular basis* to store inventory and/or product samples in his business of selling products at retail or wholesale, if the residence is the sole fixed location of the trade or business. (Code Sec. 280A(c)(2)) The space in the residence doesn't have to be used *exclusively* for permissible storage purposes, but must be so used on a regular basis and must be a separately identifiable space suitable for storage.[37]

¶ 1640   Nonexclusive use of home as day-care facility.

A deduction is allowed if a residence is used to provide day-care services for compensation on a regular basis to children, physically or mentally handicapped individuals, or persons 65 or over. If there is only part-time use of a portion of the residence, allocation must be made first on the basis of the proportion of total space used to furnish services and then on the basis of the amount of time that space is used for those services compared to the total time the space is available for all uses. The deduction is allowed only if the day-care services aren't primarily educational and comply with any applicable state licensing, certification, or approval requirements. (Code Sec. 280A(c)(4))[38]

¶ 1641   "Exclusive" use on a "regular" basis.

For purposes of ¶1636 through ¶1640, a taxpayer is required to use a portion of his residence (or separate structure) for business on a regular basis; ¶1636 through ¶1638 require that portion to be used exclusively as a place of business.

Exclusive use means that the taxpayer must use a specific portion of a residence or detached structure for carrying on his business. For example, a taxpayer who uses a den to write legal briefs and prepare tax returns as well as for personal purposes doesn't meet the exclusive use test.[39] A portion of a room used exclusively for business can qualify for the deduction, even though the room isn't divided.[40] Expenses attributable to the exclusive but incidental or occasional trade or business use of a portion of a dwelling unit aren't deductible because the space isn't used on a regular basis.[41]

¶ 1642   Gross income limit on home office deduction.

The deduction is limited to the activity's gross income reduced by all other deductible expenses that are allowable regardless of qualified use and by the business deductions that aren't allocable to the use of the home itself. (Code Sec. 280A(c)(5)(A), Code Sec. 280A(c)(5)(B)) Expenses disallowed solely because they exceed business income can be carried forward (Code Sec. 280A(c)(5)), subject to the gross income limitation in the later year.[42]

36. ¶L-1347; ¶280A4.017; TD ¶258,020
37. ¶L-1355 *et seq.*; ¶280A4.02; TD ¶258,023
38. ¶L-1359; ¶280A4.03; TD ¶258,024 *et seq.*
39. ¶L-1317 *et seq.*; ¶280A4.011; TD ¶258,005
40. ¶L-1317; ¶280A4; TD ¶258,005
41. ¶L-1324; ¶280A4.012; TD ¶258,007
42. ¶L-1365 *et seq.*; ¶280A4.060; TD ¶258,027

¶ 1643   Allocation of home office expenses.

Allocation of expenses and depreciation on a house is generally based on a comparison of space used for business and personal purposes.[43]

¶ 1644   Rental by employer of space in employee's home.

No home-office deduction is allowed for expenses attributable to the rental by an employee of all or part of his home to his employer if the employee uses the rented portion to perform services as an employee of the employer. (Code Sec. 280A(c)(6))[44]

¶ 1645   Moving Expenses. ▬▬▬▬▬▬▬▬▬▬▬▬▬▬▬▬▬▬▬▬▬

An employee or self-employed individual may deduct certain expenses of moving to a new home if the move results from a change in the individual's principal place of work and if distance and time (working at the new location) tests are met. Exceptions apply to members of the armed forces.

¶ 1646   Claiming a moving expense deduction.

Form 3903 is filed by taxpayers, whether employed or self-employed, who claim moving expenses.[45] The deduction is ordinarily claimed on the return for the year in which the expenses were paid or incurred, see ¶1652. But in certain circumstances, taxpayers may elect to claim the deduction before satisfying the time tests, see ¶1649.

¶ 1647   Deductible above-the-line expenses.

An employee or self-employed individual who moves his residence because of a change in his principal place of work may deduct the reasonable expenses of (Code Sec. 217(b)(1)): (1) moving household goods and personal effects from the old residence to the new place of residence; and (2) traveling (including lodging but not meals) from the old residence to the new place of residence.[46]

If a taxpayer uses his auto to travel to the new home, he may deduct actual expenses (e.g., gas and oil) or for 2010, 16.5¢ per mile.[47]

Moving expenses are "above-the-line" deductions; that is, they are deductible from gross income in arriving at adjusted gross income. (Code Sec. 62(a)(15))[48]

In the case of any individual other than the taxpayer, the expenses above are deductible only if the individual has both the former residence and the new residence as his principal place of abode and is a member of the taxpayer's household. (Code Sec. 217(b)(2))[49]

🅡*observation:* There are no dollar limits on the amount of deductible moving expenses.

Moving expenses aren't deductible to the extent they are reimbursed by the employer and the reimbursements are excludable from the taxpayer's income (¶1250).

¶ 1648   50-mile distance test.

The new job site must be at least 50 miles farther from the taxpayer's old principal residence than was the old principal job site. If he didn't have a full-time job before the move, the new job site must be at least 50 miles from his old residence. (Code Sec. 217(c)(1))[50]

43. ¶L-1310 *et seq.*; ¶280A4.041; TD ¶258,041
44. ¶L-1354; ¶280A4.019; TD ¶258,003
45. ¶L-3601; TD ¶350,501
46. ¶L-3602 *et seq.*; ¶2174; TD ¶350,512
47. ¶L-3615; TD ¶350,515
48. ¶L-3602; ¶2174; TD ¶350,501
49. ¶L-3602; ¶2174; TD ¶350,502
50. ¶L-3619; ¶2174.01; TD ¶350,519

¶ 1649   39-week/78-week time tests.

A 39-week or 78-week test must be met: (Code Sec. 217(c)(2))

... 39-week test: An employee must be employed full-time in the general location of his new principal place of work for at least 39 weeks during the 12-month period immediately following his arrival in the new area. (Code Sec. 217(c)(2)(A))

... 78-week test: The taxpayer must be a "full time employee" or must "perform services as a self-employed individual on a full time basis" in the general location of his new principal place of work for at least 78 weeks during the 24-month period immediately following his arrival there. Thirty-nine of the 78 weeks must be during the 12-month period above. (Code Sec. 217(c)(2)(B))

Joint filers qualify for the deduction if either spouse satisfies the 39-week or 78-week test. But weeks worked by one spouse can't be added to weeks worked by the other. (Reg § 1.217-2(c)(4)(v), Reg § 1.217-1(c)(4))

Failure to meet the 39- or 78-week test doesn't bar deduction if the failure was caused by: (1) death or disability, or (2) involuntary separation from employment (other than for willful misconduct), or re-transfer for the benefit of the employer *(not* initiated by the employee), after getting full-time employment in which the taxpayer could reasonably have been expected to meet the test. (Code Sec. 217(d)(1))[1]

¶ 1650   Foreign moves (from the U.S.).

Expenses of moving from the U.S. or its possessions to a new principal place of work outside the U.S. or its possessions include the reasonable expenses (no dollar ceiling) of moving household goods and personal effects to and from storage, and of storing these items while the new place of work is the taxpayer's principal place of work. (Code Sec. 217(h))[2]

Moving expenses aren't deductible to the extent allocable to exempt foreign-source earned income. In the absence of evidence to the contrary, reimbursement of expenses to move to a foreign country is attributed to future services to be performed at the new place of work. (Reg § 1.911-3(e)(5)(i))[3]

¶ 1651   Moving to U.S. not connected with employment.

Moving expense deductions under special rules are allowed for persons who worked abroad and move to the U.S. (or its possessions) on retirement, and for the spouse or dependent who moves to the U.S. following the death of a person who worked abroad. (Code Sec. 217(i))[4]

¶ 1652   When to deduct moving expenses.

A taxpayer may:

• deduct moving expenses in the year the expenses were paid or incurred even though the 39- or 78-week condition isn't satisfied before the due date for filing (including extensions) (Code Sec. 217(d)(2); Reg § 1.217-2(a)(2)), or

• wait until the applicable condition is satisfied; then file an amended return claiming the deduction for the tax year the moving expense was paid or incurred. (Reg § 1.217-2(d))[5]

---

1. ¶L-3620 *et seq.*; ¶2174.01; TD ¶350,520 *et seq.*
2. ¶L-3610; ¶2174.03; TD ¶350,533
3. ¶L-3635; ¶9114.11; TD ¶350,535

4. ¶L-3632; ¶L-3633; ¶2174.03; TD ¶350,533
5. ¶L-3637; ¶2174; TD ¶350,537

¶ 1653   Moving expenses of members of the armed forces.

A move by an active duty member of the armed forces under a military order and incident to a permanent change of station can qualify for deduction regardless of the distance moved or the length of time worked at the new station. Cash reimbursements or allowances are excludable to the extent of moving and storage expenses actually paid or incurred, as are all in-kind moving and storage services provided by the military. This exclusion also applies to a spouse and dependents when they don't accompany an armed forces member and move to a location different from that *to* which he moves or different from that *from* which he moves. Where the military moves the member and family to or from separate locations and they incur unreimbursed expenses, their moves are treated as a single move to the member's new principal place of work. (Code Sec. 217(g)) No deduction is permitted for any moving or storage expense reimbursed by an excluded allowance. (Reg § 1.217-2(g)(6))[6]

¶ 1654   Capital Expenditures. ▬▬▬▬▬▬▬▬▬▬▬▬▬▬▬▬▬▬▬▬

Capital expenditures generally can't be deducted except through depreciation, expensing, depletion, or amortization deductions.

These rules apply only to the extent they don't conflict with the uniform capitalization rules (¶1660 *et seq.*). Taxpayers can elect to capitalize interest under Code Sec. 266 only after applying the uniform capitalization rules for interest under Code Sec. 263A (¶1662).

A capital expenditure differs from a deductible expense because the anticipated benefit of the capital expenditure extends beyond the tax year. Capital expenditures include amounts paid or incurred to add to the value, or to substantially extend the useful life, of property owned by the taxpayer. (Code Sec. 263; Reg § 1.263(a)-1)[7] (For repairs and maintenance of property, see ¶1668.)

Examples of capital expenditures include:

. . . Original cost of getting a business license that's good or renewable for an indefinite period.[8]

. . . Initiation fees or initial admission fees paid for business association, etc., memberships.[9]

. . . Costs incurred by a corporation related to the issuance, redemption and sale of its stock.[10]

. . . Installation costs of purchased machinery, equipment, etc., including labor, material and freight charges to the extent that these expenses don't conflict with the uniform capitalization rules (¶1660).[11] But costs of retiring and removing old depreciable assets in connection with the installation or production of replacement assets don't have to be capitalized.[12]

. . . Costs other than interest incurred to borrow funds and other finance costs are capital expenditures to be amortized over the life of the loan. (For capitalization of interest on produced property, see ¶1662.) This applies to commissions and other fees paid to get a loan, cost of issuing bonds, including legal fees and printing, costs and finder's fees and commissions paid by a lender to get borrowers.[13]

. . . Payments made to get the goodwill of a business, including payments for the use of an individual's name in a business bought from him; the cost of acquiring a dealer's franchise;[14] cost of acquiring customer lists.[15]

For amortization of "Code Sec. 197 intangibles," see ¶1975.

---

6. ¶L-3630; ¶2174.02; TD ¶350,530
7. ¶L-5601; ¶2634; TD ¶308,010
8. ¶L-4216; TD ¶307,717
9. ¶L-4230; TD ¶307,720
10. ¶L-5300 *et seq.*; TD ¶301,029

11. ¶L-5811; ¶2634.16; TD ¶308,010
12. ¶L-5811.1; TD ¶256,216
13. ¶L-6001 *et seq.*; ¶1624.081
14. ¶L-5711; ¶2634.10; TD ¶229,501
15. ¶L-5712; ¶2634.10

¶ 1655 Costs of acquisition, construction or erection of property.

Costs of acquisition, construction or erection of property are included in inventory if allocable to inventory, and capitalized if allocable to other property. (Code Sec. 263A(a))[16] These rules apply to real or tangible personal property that taxpayers produce and inventory that taxpayers acquire for resale. (Code Sec. 263A(b)(2)(A))[17] See ¶1660 *et seq.*

¶ 1656 Taxes, interest, and carrying charges—election to capitalize.

Some taxes and carrying charges that would normally be deducted currently or amortized may be capitalized if the taxpayer so elects.[18] For depreciable property this has the effect of deferring the deduction to later years as depreciation. For nondepreciable property, such as unimproved real estate, the capitalized expenses increase basis and reduce gain (or increase loss) on a later sale of the property. (Code Sec. 266; Reg § 1.212-1(n), Reg § 1.266-1)[19]

¶ 1657 Annual election for unimproved and unproductive real estate.

A taxpayer can elect to capitalize taxes, mortgage interest (subject to the interest capitalization rules at ¶1662) and deductible carrying charges on unimproved and unproductive real property. (Reg § 1.266-1(b))[20]

¶ 1658 Election for expenditures on real estate improvement project.

A taxpayer engaged in the development of real estate or the construction of an improvement to real estate can elect to capitalize the following items relating to the project:

. . . interest on loans,

. . . taxes measured by compensation paid to employees and taxes imposed on the purchase of materials, or on the storage, use, or other consumption of materials,

. . . other necessary charges, including fire insurance premiums. (Reg § 1.266-1(b)(1))[21]

¶ 1659 Capitalizing taxes, interest, etc., before installing or using personal property.

The election to capitalize deductible items also applies to interest on a loan to finance the purchase, transportation and installation of machinery and other assets, state and local taxes imposed on the taxpayer, transportation, storage, use or other consumption of the property, and state and local taxes, including sales and use taxes, and state and federal unemployment taxes and the taxpayer's share of federal social security taxes on the wages of employees engaged in transportation and installation of the assets. (Reg § 1.266-1)[22]

¶ 1660 Uniform capitalization rules.

A taxpayer must (1) include in inventory costs the "allocable costs" (defined below) of "property" (also defined below) that is inventory; (Code Sec. 263A(a)(1)(A)) and (2) capitalize the allocable costs of any other property. (Code Sec. 263A(a)(2)(B)) The *allocable costs* are:

. . . the direct costs of the property (Code Sec. 263A(a)(2)(A));

. . . the indirect costs, to the extent of the property's proper share of that part (or all) of the costs allocable to that property. (Code Sec. 263A(a)(2)(B))

Allocable costs include all depreciation deductions for the taxpayer's assets, and interest,

---

16. ¶G-5452; ¶263A4; TD ¶456,003
17. ¶s G-5461 *et seq.*, G-5476 *et seq.*; ¶263A4; TD ¶456,003
18. ¶L-5901; ¶2664; TD ¶256,221
19. ¶L-5901; ¶2664; TD ¶256,221
20. ¶L-5901; ¶2664; TD ¶256,223
21. ¶L-5904; ¶2664; TD ¶256,222
22. ¶s L-5901, L-5905; ¶2664; TD ¶256,224

but only where the underlying debt was incurred or continued to finance certain produced property, see ¶1662. Taxes are allocable indirect costs. (Code Sec. 263A(a)(2)(B)) Environmental remediation costs incurred by a manufacturer (e.g., to clean land it contaminated with hazardous waste) must be included in inventory costs under these rules.[23]

Allocable costs don't include:

. . . selling, marketing, advertising and distribution expenses (Reg § 1.263A-1(e)(3)(iii)(A));

. . . any amounts allowable as a deduction under Code Sec. 174 for research and experimental expenditures (Code Sec. 263A(c)(2));

. . . any cost to the extent allowable as a deduction under Code Sec. 263(c) (intangible drilling and development costs), Code Sec. 616(a) (mining development expenses) or Code Sec. 617(a) (mining exploration expenses) (Code Sec. 263A(c)(3));

. . . any qualified creative expense incurred by a "writer," "photographer" or "artist" that would otherwise be deductible. Expenses related to printing photographic plates, motion picture films, video tapes or similar items aren't qualified creative expenses (Code Sec. 263A(h));

. . . "deductible service costs." (Reg § 1.263A-1(e)(3)(iii)(K))

What is property? A taxpayer must include in inventory or capitalize the allocable costs for:

. . . real or tangible personal property (defined below) that the taxpayer *produced* (defined below) (Code Sec. 263A(b)(1));

. . . real or personal Code Sec. 1221(a)(1) property—inventory and property held primarily for sale to customers in the ordinary course of the taxpayer's trade or business—that the taxpayer acquired for resale. (Code Sec. 263A(b)(2)(A))

Tangible personal property includes a film, sound recording, video tape, book or similar property. (Code Sec. 263A(b))

A taxpayer "produces" tangible property if he constructs, builds, installs, manufactures, develops or improves it. (Code Sec. 263A(g)(1)) Where a taxpayer makes progress or advance payments to a contractor, the taxpayer is treated as producing any property the contractor produces for the taxpayer under the contract, to the extent of those payments (whether paid or incurred by the taxpayer under the contract or otherwise). (Code Sec. 263A(g)(2))

Property acquired for resale includes intangible as well as tangible property.

"Property" doesn't include (and so allocable costs don't have to be capitalized for):

. . . Any property produced by the taxpayer for use by the taxpayer other than in a trade or business or an activity conducted for profit. (Code Sec. 263A(c)(1))

. . . Any property produced by the taxpayer under a long-term contract (Code Sec. 263A(c)(4)) except for certain home construction contracts. (Code Sec. 460(e)(1))

. . . Timber and certain ornamental trees. (Code Sec. 263A(c)(5)(A))

. . . Personal property acquired for resale by certain taxpayers with average annual gross receipts of $10,000,000 or less. (Code Sec. 263A(b)(2)(B))[24]

Taxpayers who acquire and hold property for resale (such as retailers and wholesalers) may elect a simplified resale method to determine the additional costs properly allocable to the resale property. (Reg § 1.263A-3(d))[25]

For the application of the uniform capitalization rules to farmers and ranchers, see ¶4519.

---

23. ¶G-5500.1; ¶263A4 *et seq.*; TD ¶456,000 *et seq.*   TD ¶456,000
24. ¶G-5451 *et seq.*; ¶s 263A4 *et seq.*, 263A4.06 *et seq.*;   25. ¶G-5452 *et seq.*; ¶263A4.09; TD ¶456,011

¶ 1661 How to allocate costs to property.

Allocable costs (¶1660) must be allocated to inventory or capitalized as follows:

. . . Direct labor costs are generally allocated by using a specific identification ("tracing") method (Reg § 1.263A-1(g)(2)), but any reasonable method may be used. (Reg § 1.263A-1(f)(4))

. . . Indirect costs should be allocated to particular production, resale, etc., activities using either a specific identification ("tracing") method, the standard cost method, or a method using burden rates, such as ratios based on direct costs, hours, or other items, or similar formulas, so long as the method employed reasonably allocates indirect costs among production, resale, etc., activities. (Reg § 1.263A-1(g)(3)) Taxpayers may be able to use simplified methods such as the simplified production method (Reg § 1.263A-2) and the simplified resale method (Reg § 1.263A-3)[26]

¶ 1662 Interest capitalization rules.

A taxpayer must capitalize interest he pays or incurs during a production period that is allocable to property he produces if that property (1) has a long useful life (it is real property or property with a class life of 20 years or more); (2) has an estimated production period exceeding two years; or (3) has an estimated production period exceeding one year and a cost exceeding $1,000,000. (Code Sec. 263A(f)(1); Reg § 1.263A-8(b)(1))[27]

The taxpayer must also capitalize any interest on debt allocable to an asset needed to produce the above property. (Code Sec. 263A(f)(3); Reg § 1.263A-8(a)(2)) A taxpayer must capitalize interest whether he produces the property for his own use or for sale.

The "production period" begins on the date production of the property begins and ends on the date it is ready to be placed in service or is ready to be held for sale. (Code Sec. 263A(f)(4)(B))[28]

Interest isn't capitalized for real or personal property acquired solely for resale.

A taxpayer doesn't capitalize interest allocable to property that's not subject to the capitalization rules, such as property produced under a long-term contract (see the discussion of this and other exceptions at ¶1660). (Reg § 1.263A-8(d)(2)(v)(A)) Thus, a taxpayer who produces property under a long term contract capitalizes interest only to the extent he doesn't report income under the percentage of completion method.[29]

Allocating interest to produced property. Interest is allocable to property a taxpayer produces if the taxpayer incurred or continued the underlying debt to finance the construction or production of the property.

A taxpayer is treated as having incurred or continued debt to finance the production of income: (1) where the debt can be specifically traced to production expenditures, and (2) where the debt can't be so traced, but where production or construction expenditures exceed the debt that is directly traceable. (Reg § 1.263A-9(a)(2))

The interest on the debt incurred or continued to finance production is allocated to the property produced as follows:[30]

(1) interest (other than qualified residence interest) on a debt that is directly attributable to production expenditures for the produced property is assigned to that property; (Code Sec. 263A(f)(2)(A)(i); Reg § 1.263A-9(a)(2)(i)(A)), and

(2) interest on any other debt is assigned to the produced property to the extent that the taxpayer's interest costs could have been reduced if production expenditures (not attributable to the debt in (1), above) had not been incurred (Code Sec. 263A(f)(2)(A)(ii);

---

26. ¶G-5458; ¶263A4.06; TD ¶456,006
27. ¶L-5920; ¶263A4.11; TD ¶456,017 *et seq.*
28. ¶L-5932; ¶263A4.11; TD ¶456,023

29. ¶L-5918; ¶263A4.03; TD ¶456,017
30. ¶L-5926; ¶263A4.11; TD ¶456,021

Reg § 1.263A-9(a)(2)(i)(B)) (that is, had the expenditures that were incurred for construction been used instead to repay the debt).

Except as provided in regs, a flow-through entity applies the interest allocation rules at the entity level and then, to the extent the entity has insufficient debt to support the production or construction expenditures, at the beneficiary level. (Code Sec. 263A(f)(2)(C))[31]

¶ 1663   Computer software for own use.

A business buyer's treatment of software depends on how it is billed by the seller:

. . . If a charge for computer software is included in the price of the hardware (i.e., the computer) without a separate identification of the charge for software, then the buyer capitalizes and depreciates the cost along with the cost of the hardware. (Reg § 1.167(a)-14(b)(2))

. . . If the charge for the software is separately stated, it can be amortized over 36 months using the straight-line method. This rule *doesn't* apply to any software that's a Code Sec. 197 intangible. (Reg § 1.167(a)-14(b)(1))[32]

The cost of software licensed for a specific period of time (unless properly chargeable to capital account) is deducted over that term, in the same way that a business tenant may under Reg § 1.162-11 deduct the cost of acquiring a leasehold over the lease term. (Reg § 1.167(a)-14(b)(2))[33] Rental payments for leased software are deducted just like any other rentals.[34]

🅁ⓘ *caution:* Code Sec. 197 intangibles include software acquired in connection with the acquisition of a business. For 15-year amortization of such software, see ¶1977 *et seq.*

¶ 1664   Costs of developing computer software.

Costs of developing computer software (other than software that is a Code Sec. 197 intangible (¶1977)) can be either: (1) consistently expensed currently under Code Sec. 174(a), or (2) consistently treated as capital expenditures recoverable through deductions for ratable amortization over a period of 60 months from the date of completion of the development under Code Sec. 174(b) or over 36 months from the date the software is placed in service under Code Sec. 167(f)(1).[35] Costs of developing software may also qualify as research and experimental expenditures under Code Sec. 174[36] (for deductions under Code Sec. 174, see ¶1601). If costs for developing computer software that the taxpayer elected to treat as deferred expenses under Code Sec. 174(b) (¶1601) result in the development of property subject to depreciation, the 36 month amortization rule applies to the unrecovered costs. (Reg § 1.167(a)-14(b)(1))[37]

¶ 1665   Commissions paid upon transfer of property.

Commissions paid for the *purchase* of real estate or other property aren't deductible as expenses but must be capitalized and added to the cost of the property, whether or not the taxpayer is engaged in the real estate business.[38]

Commissions paid for the *sale* of real estate or other property by a taxpayer who is not engaged in the real estate business must be offset against the selling price to determine the gain or loss realized on the sale. If the seller is engaged in the real estate business, the commissions on property sales are deductible business expenses.[39]

---

31. ¶L-5928; TD ¶456,037
32. ¶L-7935; ¶1674.033; TD ¶265,434
33. ¶L-5621; ¶1674.033; TD ¶265,434
34. ¶L-5615 *et seq.*; ¶1674.033; TD ¶265,434
35. ¶L-5616; ¶1674.033; TD ¶256,236

36. ¶L-5615; ¶1674.033; TD ¶256,234
37. ¶L-7935; ¶1674.033; TD ¶265,434
38. ¶I-2536
39. ¶I-2537; ¶2634.05; TD ¶222,023

¶ 1666   Interest and carrying charges relating to straddles.

The interest and carrying charges properly allocable to personal property that is part of a straddle (¶2653) aren't deductible, but must be charged to the capital account of the property for which they were paid or incurred. (Code Sec. 263(g)(1)) However this requirement doesn't apply to any identified hedging transactions (¶2660). (Code Sec. 263(g)(3))[40]

"Interest and carrying charges" means the excess of:

. . . the sum of interest on indebtedness incurred or continued to buy or carry personal property that is part of a straddle, and amounts paid or incurred to insure, store, or transport that personal property, *over*

. . . the sum of: (1) the amount of interest income, including original issue discount, from the property includible in gross income for the taxable year, (2) any amount treated as ordinary income under Code Secs. 1271(a)(3)(A), 1281(a), (dealing with acquisition discount on short-term government and nongovernment obligations), or Code Sec. 1278 (dealing with market discount bonds), (3) the excess of any dividends includible in income over the dividends received deductions allowable for those dividends under Code Secs. 243, 244, 245, and (4) any payment for a security loan that's included in gross income for the tax year. (Code Sec. 263(g)(2)) Also, the term "interest" includes amounts paid or incurred in connection with personal property used in a short sale.[41]

¶ 1667   Architectural and transportation barrier removal expenses.

A taxpayer can elect to treat up to $15,000 of qualified architectural and transportation barrier removal expenses as a deduction rather than as a charge to capital account. (Code Sec. 190(a), Code Sec. 190(c)) To elect, claim the deduction as a separate item identified as such on the timely filed (including extension) return for the tax year for which the election is to apply. (Reg § 1.190-3(a))[42] For the credit for eligible access expenditures, see ¶2324.

¶ 1668   Repairs.

The cost of repairing business property of the taxpayer is deductible currently as a business expense, while an improvement that materially adds to the value or utility of the property or appreciably prolongs its useful life must be capitalized. (Reg § 1.162-4)[43]

Expenditures as part of a general plan of reconditioning, renovating, improving or altering property must be capitalized even though certain portions of the work standing alone might properly be classifiable as repairs.[44]

¶ 1669   Environmental cleanup costs; expensing election.

If a taxpayer acquires property in clean condition and contaminates it in the course of its everyday business operations, the cost of restoring the property to its approximate condition at the time of acquisition doesn't result in a permanent improvement that increases the property's value and the restoration costs are deductible. IRS has privately ruled that the cost a business incurs to remove mold from a building it owns and leases out is currently deductible. One court has held that the "restoration principle" doesn't apply to asbestos removal undertaken as part of a major remodeling project, and another court has allowed a current deduction for removing/encapsulating deteriorating asbestos taxpayer had installed because the work wasn't done to refurbish the building or prepare it for a new use and the cost represented only a small fraction of the building's value. The restoration principle

---

40. ¶L-5985; ¶2634; TD ¶228,715
41. ¶L-5985 *et seq.*; ¶2634
42. ¶L-3151 *et seq.*; ¶1904 *et seq.*; TD ¶256,219
43. ¶L-6101; ¶1624.171; TD ¶308,001
44. ¶L-6108; ¶1624.183; TD ¶308,010

doesn't apply where the taxpayer acquires already contaminated property. The cleanup expenses must be capitalized if the remediation results in permanent improvement or betterment of the property that increases its value, prolongs its useful life or adapts it to a new or different use. The cost of replacing a company's existing underground waste storage tanks (removing, cleaning, and discarding old tanks, and buying, installing, filling and monitoring new tanks) is currently deductible where new tanks, after being filled with waste and sealed, have no salvage value and no remaining useful life, and are used to facilitate permanent disposal of waste by-product.[45]

For expenses paid or incurred before 2010, taxpayers may elect to treat qualified environmental remediation expenses that would otherwise be chargeable to a capital account as deductible in the year paid or incurred. To be deductible currently, such expense has to be paid or incurred in connection with the abatement or control of hazardous substances (including petroleum products) at a qualified contaminated site. (Code Sec. 198) Special rules apply to expenses for depreciable property. (Code Sec. 198(b)(2)) Expensed qualified environmental remediation costs are subject to recapture upon the sale or other disposition of the property. (Code Sec. 198(e))[46]

(RIA) caution: Check http://ria.thomsonreuters.com/federaltaxhandbook to see if this provision has been extended.

¶ 1670 Capitalization rules for costs associated with intangible assets.

Taxpayers are required to capitalize amounts paid or incurred to (i) acquire or create an intangible asset, (ii) create or enhance a separate, distinct intangible asset, (iii) create or enhance a "future benefit" identified in published guidance as capitalizable, or (iv) "facilitate" the acquisition or creation of an intangible in (i) through (iii) (e.g., transaction costs). (Reg § 1.263(a)-4(b)(1)) Capitalizable costs cannot be deducted and are generally added to the basis of the intangible. (Reg § 1.263(a)-4)[47] These rules do not affect the treatment of amounts specifically provided for in a Code Section other than Code Sec. 162 or Code Sec. 212 (e.g., Code Sec. 174 research expenses). (Reg § 1.263(a)-4(b)(4))

(RIA) observation: Capitalized costs may be amortizable (e.g., payment to a departing employee for a 3-year noncompete covenant may be deducted ratably over the 3 years).

For the "12-month" and de minimis exceptions to these requirements, see ¶1671. For 15-year amortization of certain intangibles, see ¶1903.

¶ 1671 De minimis and 12-month rule exceptions to capitalization rules for intangibles.

The following are exceptions to the capitalization rules for intangibles discussed at ¶1670.

De minimis costs, — i.e., costs that don't exceed $5,000—paid to another party to create, originate, enter into, renew, or renegotiate an agreement (Reg § 1.263(a)-4(d)(6)(v)), or paid in the process of investigating a transaction (Reg § 1.263(a)-4(e)(4)(iii)) don't have to be capitalized even if they facilitate a capital transaction and otherwise would be subject to the capitalization rules. Payments made in the form of property are valued at fair market value at the time of payment. The de minimis rule applies on a transaction-by-transaction basis. If transaction costs (other than compensation and overhead) exceed $5,000, none of the costs are treated as de minimis. A pooling method may be used for de minimis transaction costs. Commissions paid to facilitate the acquisition of an intangible aren't treated as de minimis costs (and therefore must be capitalized).[48]

12-month rule. Capitalization is not required for amounts paid to create or facilitate the creation of any right or benefit that does not extend beyond the earlier of (1) 12 months after

45. ¶L-6154; TD ¶308,011
46. ¶L-6150.1; ¶1984

47. ¶L-5751; ¶2634; TD ¶256,300
48. ¶L-5757.1, ¶L-5760.2; ¶2634; TD ¶256,317

the first date on which the taxpayer realizes the right or benefit; or (2) the end of the tax year following the tax year in which the payment is made. (Reg § 1.263(a)-4(f)) Amounts paid to terminate an agreement before its expiration date create a benefit for the taxpayer that lasts for the unexpired term of the agreement immediately before the termination date. (Reg § 1.263(a)-4(f)(2)) The 12-month rule doesn't apply to amounts paid to create (or facilitate the creation of) financial interests or amortizable Code Sec. 197 intangibles or to amounts paid to create or enhance a right of indefinite duration. (Reg § 1.263(a)-4(f)(3), Reg § 1.263(a)-4(f)(4)) The 12-month rule does not affect the determination of whether a liability is incurred during the tax year, including the determination of whether economic performance has occurred. (Reg § 1.263(a)-4(f)(6))[49]

---

49. ¶L-5760.5 *et seq.*; ¶2634; TD ¶256,320

Chapter 4   Interest Expense—Taxes—Losses—Bad Debts

¶ 1700   Deduction for Interest. ▄▄▄▄▄▄▄▄▄▄▄▄▄▄

Generally, interest paid or accrued during the tax year is deductible whether or not it is incurred in a trade or business. It must be incurred with respect to a valid debt and be actually paid or accrued during the tax year.

To be deductible, interest must be paid or incurred with respect to a valid debt.[1] And the amount of interest must be definitely ascertainable.[2] But, to be deductible, interest need not be reasonable,[3] and may even be usurious.[4]

There's no deduction for interest incurred in most personal transactions and on certain kinds of debt (¶1715 *et seq.*). The amount of interest that's deductible on certain other kinds of debt is limited (for example, investment interest, see ¶1726 *et seq.*; qualified residence interest, see ¶1730 *et seq.*; interest incurred in a passive activity, see ¶1811 *et seq.*; and qualified education loan interest, see ¶2225 *et seq.*). For interest expenses that must be included in inventory or capitalized, see ¶1654 *et seq.*

¶ 1701   Interest is payment for the use or forbearance of money.

Interest includes the amount paid: (1) for the borrower's *use* of money during the term of a loan, or (2) for his *detention* of money after the due date for repayment. Merely designating a payment as "interest" won't make it deductible. [5] Nor does the fact that the payment is taxable interest to the lender make it deductible by the payor-borrower.[6]

These forms of "interest" are true interest for federal tax purposes:

. . . Interest and similar charges (¶1704) (including "points," ¶1703, but not fees for services) paid to lenders.[7]

. . . Bonuses and premiums the borrower is required to pay the lender to get the loan.[8]

. . . Discounts (including original issue discount (OID), see ¶1751)—i.e., where the borrower receives less than the face amount of the loan but is required to repay the full face amount, the difference is interest.[9]

. . . Foregone interest on below-market loans that the borrower is "deemed" to have paid to the lender (¶1308).[10]

. . . Interest paid by banks or other financial institutions on deposits, certificates or other evidences of indebtedness.[11] For amounts forfeited on premature withdrawal of a bank deposit, see ¶2171.

. . . Payments of redeemable ground rents. (Code Sec. 163(c))[12]

. . . Interest on deposits, down payments, etc., where the seller defers delivery of a purchased item[13] (for unstated interest, see ¶1707). For installment sale interest, see ¶1706.

. . . Interest on judgment debts.[14]

. . . Interest on declared but unpaid dividends.[15]

. . . Interest on deferred payments of legacies.[16]

---

1. ¶K-5060 *et seq.*; ¶1634; TD ¶311,502
2. ¶K-5024; ¶1634.025
3. ¶K-5001; ¶1634; TD ¶311,002
4. ¶K-5002; ¶1634.021; TD ¶311,002
5. ¶K-5020 *et seq.*; ¶1634; TD ¶311,501
6. ¶K-5020; ¶1634
7. ¶s K-5026, K-5030; ¶1634; TD ¶311,503, 311,526
8. ¶K-5028; ¶s 1634.001, 1634.005; TD ¶318,705
9. ¶K-5028; ¶s 1634.001, 1634.051; TD ¶311,503
10. ¶K-5039; ¶78,724 *et seq.*; TD ¶319,504
11. ¶E-3105, ¶E-3107; ¶4614.51
12. ¶K-5044; ¶1634; TD ¶311,523
13. ¶K-5045; TD ¶311,515
14. ¶K-5050; TD ¶311,518
15. ¶K-5051; ¶1635.014(75); TD ¶311,519
16. ¶K-5052; TD ¶311,520

References beginning with a single letter are to paragraphs in RIA's Federal Tax Coordinator 2d and RIA's Analysis of Federal Taxes: Income. Those beginning with numbers are to paragraphs in RIA's United States Tax Reporter. Those beginning with TD are to paragraphs in RIA's Tax Desk.

¶ 1702   Mortgage interest.

Interest on a mortgage on real property (including a condominium or co-op, ¶1714) generally is deductible. (Reg § 1.163-1(b))[17] For "points," see ¶1703. For prepayment penalties and late payment charges, see ¶1705. For who deducts mortgage interest, see ¶1713.

RIA *caution:* Interest on a home mortgage must be "qualified residence interest" (¶1730 *et seq.*) to be deductible.

¶ 1703   "Points."

"Points" (loan origination fees, loan processing fees, loan discount fees, etc., that are a specified percentage of the amount borrowed) a borrower pays, out of his own funds, to a lender to get a loan are deductible as interest *only* if they are *solely* for the use or forbearance of money and not a charge for services. This includes "points" on a VA or FHA home mortgage. But points paid for services of the lender *in lieu of* specific service charges (e.g., a one-point charge for appraisal, etc.) aren't deductible as interest. Nor is a "commitment fee" charged for the lender's agreement to make a future loan.[18]

Points paid by the *seller* aren't deductible as interest (except by certain cash basis buyers, see ¶1746). Rather, they are included in the seller's selling expenses, reducing the amount realized on sale. But a seller in the business of building and selling houses was allowed a *business* expense deduction for these payments.[19]

For when to deduct points, see ¶1745; home mortgage points, see ¶1746; and refinancing points, see ¶1747.

¶ 1704   Finance charges and credit card fees.

The amount of finance charges imposed on the unpaid balances of revolving charge accounts or budget charge accounts of retail stores, or on the unpaid balances of bank and oil company credit cards, is deductible as interest (subject to the bar on personal interest deductions, see ¶1715), as are credit card fees imposed for cash, check, or overdraft advances, but only to the extent the payment isn't a service charge, etc.[20]

¶ 1705   Prepayment penalties and late payment charges.

A penalty paid for prepaying a debt (including a mortgage) is deductible as interest,[21] as is a late payment charge (that isn't a service charge).[22]

¶ 1706   Interest and carrying charges on installment purchases and deferred tuition; 6% rule.

Interest on installment purchases that's separately stated or definitely determinable and provable is deductible as interest, subject to the rules for credit cards (¶1704).[23] For deduction of "unstated interest," see ¶1707.

If carrying charges (including finance charges, service charges, etc.) on an installment purchase of personal property or educational services are *separately stated* but the amount of *interest* included in the charges can't be ascertained, the installment payments are considered to include a 6% interest charge based on the average unpaid balance under the contract during the tax year. (Code Sec. 163(b); Reg § 1.163-2)[24]

---

17. ¶K-5043; ¶s 1634.050, 1634.052; TD ¶311,504
18. ¶K-5026; ¶1634.005; TD ¶311,506, 311,527
19. ¶I-2531, K-5027; TD ¶337,011
20. ¶K-5029, ¶K-5031; ¶1634.050; TD ¶311,507

21. ¶K-5034; ¶1634; TD ¶311,512
22. ¶s K-5032, K-5033; TD ¶311,510, 311,511
23. ¶K-5029 *et seq.*; ¶1634.050; TD ¶311,507
24. ¶K-5151; ¶1634.050; TD ¶319,502

¶ 1707   Unstated interest on deferred payment sales.

On certain deferred payment sales, part of each payment is treated as interest ("unstated interest") that's treated by the buyer as interest expense. The amount of this "unstated interest" attributed to the buyer is determined under the rules governing the unstated interest that's taxed to the seller (¶1309 *et seq.*). (Code Sec. 483(a); Reg § 1.483-1)[25]

These rules *don't apply* to buyers of: (1) personal use property (Code Sec. 1275(b)(1)); or (2) personal property on installment where payments include separately stated carrying charges otherwise treated as interest (¶1706). (Code Sec. 483(d)(3))[26]

¶ 1708   Interest on taxes.

Interest on delinquent tax payments may be deducted, to the extent it's otherwise deductible.[27] So, interest on sales, excise and similar taxes incurred in connection with taxpayer's business or investment activities may be deducted. But interest paid by an individual (or a trust, S corporation or other pass-through entity) on income tax underpayments, or on debt used to pay those taxes, is nondeductible personal interest (¶1715). (Reg § 1.163-9T(b)(2)) And interest on an income tax deficiency arising from an unincorporated business is also nondeductible personal interest that can't be deducted as a business expense.[28]

A corporation can't deduct interest paid on an understatement with respect to certain listed or reportable transactions that have a potential for tax avoidance or evasion, and that it didn't adequately disclose under Code Sec. 6664(d)(3)(A). (Code Sec. 163(m))[29]

¶ 1709   Corporate debt or equity; "thin" capitalization.

Corporations may favor heavy debt capitalization because interest paid on debt is deductible, while dividends paid on stock aren't. But a corporation's debt obligations may be treated as equity (stock), making the "interest" paid on them a nondeductible dividend. Also, repayment of a debt isn't taxable to the lender (corporation), while a stock redemption may be taxable, as a dividend, to the shareholders (¶3526 *et seq.*).[30] For disallowed deductions for interest on corporate debt payable in the issuer's stock, see ¶1710.

The corporate issuer's characterization (at issuance) of a corporate instrument (issued after 10/24/92) as stock or debt is binding on the issuer and all holders (unless the holder discloses inconsistent treatment on his return), but not on IRS. (Code Sec. 385(c))[31]

A number of key factors are relevant in whether purported corporate debt will be treated as debt for federal tax purposes. No single factor is controlling. They include:

- the right to enforce payment of principal and interest and the source of payments;
- whether there is subordination to or preference over any indebtedness of the corporation;
- whether there is a high ratio of debt to equity;
- whether there is convertibility into the stock of the corporation; and
- the relationship between holdings of stock in the corporation and holdings of the interest in question.[32]

¶ 1710   No deduction for interest on corporate debt payable in issuer's stock.

No deduction is allowed for interest paid or accrued on a disqualified debt instrument (Code Sec. 163(l)(1)), or OID (¶1751) on such an instrument.[33] A disqualified debt instrument

---

25. ¶K-5280 *et seq.*; ¶4834; TD ¶319,500 *et seq.*
26. ¶s K-5281, K-5282; ¶4834.01; TD ¶319,501
27. ¶K-5048; ¶1634.013; TD ¶311,509
28. ¶K-5513; TD ¶314,002
29. ¶K-5506.1; ¶1634.013; TD ¶311,509.1

30. ¶K-5790 *et seq.*; ¶3854 *et seq.*; TD ¶313,501
31. ¶K-5791 *et seq.*; ¶3854.01; TD ¶313,501
32. ¶K-5801 *et seq.*; ¶1634.057; TD ¶313,501
33. ¶K-5507; ¶1634.059; TD ¶313,502

is any corporate debt (or debt issued by a partnership to the extent of its corporate partners) that's payable in (1) equity (i.e., stock) of the issuer or a related party (under Code Sec. 267(b), see ¶2448, or Code Sec. 707(b), see ¶3731), and, (2) for debt instruments issued after Oct. 3, 2004, equity held by the issuer or any related party in any other person (basis in the equity is increased by the disallowed deduction). (Code Sec. 163(l)(2), Code Sec. 163(l)(6))[34] But it doesn't include certain debt issued by dealers in securities. (Code Sec. 163(l)(5))[35]

Debt is treated as payable in equity of the issuer or a related party only if:

(1) a substantial amount of the principal or interest is required to be paid or converted, or at the option of the issuer or related party, is payable in or convertible into, the equity,

(2) a substantial amount of the principal or interest is required to be, or at the option of the issuer or related party is, determined by reference to the value of the equity, or

(3) the debt is part of an arrangement that is reasonably expected to result in a transaction described in (1) or (2) (Code Sec. 163(l)(3)), such as in the case of certain issuances of a forward contract in connection with the issuance of debt, nonrecourse debt secured principally by stock, or certain debt instruments that are convertible at the holder's option when it's substantially certain that the right will be exercised.[36]

For these purposes, principal or interest is treated as required to be so paid, converted, or determined if it may be required at the option of the holder or a related party and there's a substantial certainty that the option will be exercised. (Code Sec. 163(l)(3))[37]

These rules deal only with the deduction by the issuer, generally for debt instruments issued after June 8, '97. They don't affect the treatment of a holder of an instrument.[38]

¶ 1711   Who may deduct interest?

With some exceptions (¶1712, ¶1713), a taxpayer's interest deduction is limited to interest he pays or accrues on his *own* indebtedness, and not for interest on debts of others.[39] But for joint obligors—i.e., persons who are jointly and severally liable for a debt—each obligor may deduct the amount of interest he actually pays on the debt.[40]

A person who is only secondarily liable for the debt, e.g., as endorser or guarantor, generally can't deduct interest on the debt. But if he actually pays all or part of the debt, he may be allowed to deduct the interest (or take a bad debt deduction, see ¶1851 *et seq.*).[41]

¶ 1712   Interest paid by another.

In certain cases where a person other than taxpayer pays or accrues the interest on taxpayer's debt, the payments are treated as made by taxpayer so he can deduct the interest. This occurs when the interest payor is acting (or is treated as acting) merely as taxpayer's agent (e.g., where a tenant pays the interest on his landlord's mortgage), or where taxpayer has given some consideration for the payor's payment.[42]

¶ 1713   Who deducts mortgage interest (and points).

A taxpayer who is personally liable for a mortgage debt may deduct the otherwise deductible mortgage interest (¶1702) (and points) he actually pays out of his own funds even if, when he makes the payments, he no longer owns the property subject to the mortgage (for points on seller-financed mortgages, see ¶1703; for co-ops, see ¶1714). But where a conveyance of mortgaged property would, under state law, automatically relieve the transferor of personal liability on the mortgage, he can't deduct the payments he makes after the transfer.[43]

---

34. ¶K-5508; ¶1634.059; TD ¶313,502
35. ¶K-5509; ¶1634.059; TD ¶313,502.2
36. ¶K-5507 *et seq.*; ¶1634.059; TD ¶313,502
37. ¶K-5507; ¶1634.059; TD ¶313,502
38. ¶K-5507; ¶1634.059; TD ¶313,502

39. ¶K-5120 *et seq.*; ¶1634.015; TD ¶318,401
40. ¶K-5130; ¶1634.015; TD ¶318,405
41. ¶K-5133; ¶1664.450; TD ¶318,407
42. ¶K-5129; ¶1634.018; TD ¶318,409
43. ¶K-5135, ¶K-5136; TD ¶318,601

A taxpayer who *isn't* personally liable for a mortgage debt may deduct the mortgage interest he actually pays *only* if he's the legal or equitable owner (solely or jointly with others) of the mortgaged property.[44] Home buyers whose occupancy of the residence gave them equitable (but not legal) title to it could deduct interest they paid on the builder's construction loan.[45]

Where the joint owners of mortgaged property are also jointly liable on the mortgage, each owner may deduct the mortgage interest he actually pays out of his own funds.[46]

⊘caution: Mortgage interest that's deductible *solely* because it's "qualified residence interest" may be deducted *only* by the person who owns the property, see ¶1730.

¶ 1714 Cooperative housing corporation's (co-op's) mortgage payments.

Tenant-stockholders of cooperative housing corporations (co-ops) deduct their share of the co-op's mortgage interest payments (subject to the "qualified residence interest" limits, see ¶1730). (Code Sec. 216)[47]

¶ 1715 No deduction for personal interest.

Noncorporate taxpayers can't deduct "personal interest." (Code Sec. 163(h)(1))[48] Personal interest is all interest *other than*: (1) interest properly allocable to trade or business debt (other than the trade or business of being an employee); (2) interest paid on qualified education loans (¶2225 *et seq.*); (3) qualified residence interest (¶1730 *et seq.*); (4) interest considered in computing income or loss from a passive activity (¶1811 *et seq.*); (5) investment interest (¶1728); (6) interest payable under Code Sec. 6601 on unpaid estate tax during the time there is a Code Sec. 6163 extension of time for paying the tax because of a remainder or reversionary interest (see ¶5035). (Code Sec. 163(h)(2))[49]

But no deduction is allowed for any interest payable under Code Sec. 6601 on any unpaid estate tax for the period when a Code Sec. 6166 payment extension (for estate tax attributable to certain closely held business interests) is in effect. (Code Sec. 163(k))[50]

¶ 1716 Net direct interest expense—market discount bonds.

Taxpayer's "net direct interest expense" with respect to any taxable market discount bond (¶1328) is deductible in a tax year only to the extent the expense exceeds the market discount allocable to the days during the year the bond was held by taxpayer. (Code Sec. 1277(a); Code Sec. 1278(a)(1)(C))[1] (For tax-exempt bonds, see ¶1723.)

"Net direct interest expense" is any excess of: (1) interest paid or accrued on debt incurred or continued to buy or carry a market discount bond, over (2) interest (including OID, ¶1316) includible in income for the tax year with respect to the bond. (Code Sec. 1277(c))[2]

The disallowed interest expenses are deductible in the year the bond is disposed of (Code Sec. 1277(b)(2)(A)) or, if taxpayer so elects (bond-by-bond), in an earlier year when (but only to the extent that) taxpayer has net interest income from the bond. (Code Sec. 1277(b)(1))[3]

¶ 1717 Net direct interest expense—short-term government obligations.

The "net direct interest expense" (¶1716) with respect to a short-term government obligation is deductible in a tax year only to the extent the expense exceeds the total of: (1) the daily portions of the acquisition discount for each day during the year that taxpayer held the obligation, plus (2) the amount of any other (stated) interest payable on the obligation that

---

44. ¶K-5136; ¶1634.015; TD ¶318,602
45. ¶K-5136; TD ¶318,602
46. ¶K-5138; TD ¶318,604
47. ¶K-5140; ¶K-5900 *et seq.*; ¶2164.01; TD ¶314,511
48. ¶K-5510; ¶1634.054; TD ¶314,000

49. ¶K-5511; ¶1634.054; TD ¶314,001
50. ¶K-5513; ¶1634.013; TD ¶314,002
1. ¶K-5341; ¶12,764.02; TD ¶316,501
2. ¶K-5342; ¶12,764.02; TD ¶316,502
3. ¶K-5343; ¶12,764.02; TD ¶316,503

accrues during the tax year while taxpayer held the obligation and that, because of taxpayer's accounting method, wasn't included in his gross income. (Code Sec. 1282(a))[4]

Deduction of disallowed interest expense generally is deferred until (as with market discount bonds, see ¶1716) taxpayer disposes of the obligation or makes the special election. (Code Sec. 1282(c))[5]

¶ 1718 Interest on business life insurance, annuity or endowment contract loans.

No deduction is allowed (for exception, see below) for any interest paid or accrued on any debt with respect to one or more life insurance policies owned by the taxpayer covering the life of any individual, or any annuity or endowment contract owned by the taxpayer covering any individual. (Code Sec. 264(a)(4))

For contracts issued before June 9, '97, the interest disallowance rule applies only if the covered individual is or was either an officer or employee of, or financially interested in, any trade or business currently or formerly carried on by the taxpayer. For policies purchased before June 21, '86, the disallowance rule generally didn't apply.[6]

A taxpayer *may* deduct a limited amount of interest (assuming it isn't barred by the rules at ¶1719 and ¶1720), subject to certain rate limitations, paid or accrued with respect to policies or contracts covering a "key person" (an officer or 20% owner) to the extent that the aggregate amount of the debt with respect to policies and contracts covering that person doesn't exceed $50,000. (Code Sec. 264(e)(1)) This exception applies only to a limited number of key persons (not more than the greater of: (1) 5 individuals, or (2) the lesser of 5% of total officers and employees, or 20 individuals). (Code Sec. 264(e)(3))[7]

¶ 1719 Single premium life insurance, endowment and annuity contracts.

No deduction is allowed for interest on debt incurred or continued to buy or carry single premium life insurance, endowment or annuity contracts. (Code Sec. 264(a)(2); Reg § 1.264-2) A contract is "single premium" if "substantially all" the premiums are paid within four years from the purchase date, or if an amount is deposited with the insurer for payment of a "substantial" number of future premiums on the contract. (Code Sec. 264(c); Reg § 1.264-3)[8]

¶ 1720 "Plan of purchase" borrowing against life insurance contracts.

No deduction is allowed for interest on debt incurred or continued to buy or carry a life insurance, endowment or annuity contract under a plan of purchase (borrowing for more than 3 years is presumed to be a plan (Reg § 1.264-4(d)(2))) contemplating systematic direct or indirect borrowing of part or all of the increases in the contract's cash value. The deduction is barred whether the lender is the insurer or another party (e.g., a bank). (Code Sec. 264(a)(3))[9]

There are exceptions to this rule, e.g., for borrowing incurred because of an unforeseen loss of income or substantial increase in financial obligations, or borrowing in connection with a taxpayer's trade or business. (Code Sec. 264(d); Reg § 1.264-4)[10]

¶ 1721 No deduction for interest allocable to unborrowed policy cash values ("inside buildup") on life insurance, annuity and endowment contracts.

Except as discussed below, no deduction is allowed for that portion of the taxpayer's interest expense that's allocable to unborrowed policy cash values — i.e., with respect to any life insurance policy, annuity, or endowment contract, the excess of (a) the cash surrender value of the policy or contract determined without regard to any surrender charge (or, if (a)

---

4. ¶K-5344; ¶12,814.02; TD ¶316,504
5. ¶K-5343; ¶12,814.02; TD ¶316,505
6. ¶K-5351; ¶2644; TD ¶316,801
7. ¶K-5352; ¶2644; TD ¶316,802

8. ¶K-5570 *et seq.*; ¶2644; TD ¶317,200 *et seq.*
9. ¶K-5584; ¶2644; TD ¶317,500
10. ¶K-5584 *et seq.*; ¶2644; TD ¶317,505

does not reasonably approximate the policy's, etc. actual value, a statutorily-defined amount), over (b) the amount of any loan with respect to the policy or contract. (Code Sec. 264(f))[11] This rule must be applied before the Code Sec. 263A uniform capitalization rules (¶1660). (Code Sec. 264(f)(6)(B))[12]

⊘ *observation:* Unless an exception (see below) applies, if a taxpayer owns a life insurance policy, etc., with "inside buildup" —i.e., the policy's cash surrender value exceeds the amount of any loans taken out with respect to it—the taxpayer will lose an allocable portion of any interest deduction to which he would otherwise be entitled.

The portion of the interest expense that's allocable to unborrowed policy cash values is an amount that bears the same ratio to that interest expense as (1) average unborrowed policy cash values of life insurance policies, and annuity and endowment contracts, issued after June 8, '97, bears to (2) the sum of: (i) for assets that are life insurance policies or annuity or endowment contracts, the average unborrowed policy cash values of the policies and contracts; and (ii) for assets that aren't described in (i), the average adjusted bases (under Code Sec. 1016) of those assets. (Code Sec. 264(f)(2))[13]

The disallowance rule doesn't apply to any of the following:

(1) Any policy or contract owned by an entity engaged in a trade or business if the policy or contract covers only one individual and if that individual is (at the time first covered by the policy or contract) a 20% owner of the entity, or an individual (who isn't a 20% owner) who is an officer, director, or employee of the trade or business. (Code Sec. 264(f)(4)(A))[14]

(2) Any annuity contract to which Code Sec. 72(u) applies (i.e., annuity contracts subject to the natural-person-as-holder requirement, ¶1360). (Code Sec. 264(f)(4)(B))[15]

(3) Any policy or contract held by a natural person. But, if a trade or business is directly or indirectly the beneficiary, the policy or contract is treated as held by the trade or business and not by a natural person, but this doesn't apply to any trade or business carried on as a sole proprietorship, or to any trade or business of performing services as an employee. (Code Sec. 264(f)(5)(A))[16]

(4) Certain insurance companies. (Code Sec. 264(f)(8)(B))[17]

(5) Any policy or contract issued before June 9, '97.[18]

For purposes of exception (1), above: (a) a policy or contract covering a 20% owner of an entity isn't treated as failing to meet the requirements because it covers the joint lives of the 20% owner and the owner's spouse (Code Sec. 264(f)(4)); and (b) if coverage for each insured individual under a master contract is treated as a separate contract for purposes of Code Sec. 817(h), Code Sec. 7702, and Code Sec. 7702A (technical insurance, annuity and modified endowment contract rules), then coverage for each such insured is treated as a separate contract. (Code Sec. 264(f)(4)(E)) A "master contract" doesn't include any group life insurance contract (as defined in Code Sec. 848(e)(2)).[19]

In applying the above rules, all members of a controlled group generally are treated as one taxpayer (Code Sec. 264(f)(8)(A)),[20] and in the case of partnerships and S corporations, the rules apply at the entity level. (Code Sec. 264(f)(5)(B))[21]

¶ 1722 Loans from qualified employer plans.

No deduction is allowed for interest on any loan from a qualified employer plan that isn't treated as a distribution, for the period: (1) on or after the first day the individual to whom the loan is made is a key employee (defined in Code Sec. 416(i)), or (2) during which the loan

11. ¶K-5601; ¶2644.01; TD ¶317,601
12. ¶K-5601; ¶2644.01; TD ¶317,601
13. ¶K-5604; ¶2644.01; TD ¶317,603
14. ¶K-5606; ¶2644.01; TD ¶317,605
15. ¶K-5606.1; ¶2644.01; TD ¶317,605
16. ¶K-5606.2; ¶2644.01; TD ¶317,605
17. ¶K-5606.3; ¶2644.01; TD ¶317,605
18. ¶K-5601; ¶2644.01; TD ¶317,601
19. ¶K-5606; ¶2644.01
20. ¶K-5602
21. ¶K-5603; ¶2644.01; TD ¶317,602

is secured by amounts attributable to elective deferrals under a Code Sec. 401(k) plan (¶4317) or a Code Sec. 403(b) annuity (¶4388 *et seq.*). (Code Sec. 72(p)(3))[22]

¶ 1723 Loans to buy or carry tax-exempt securities.

No deduction is allowed for interest on debt incurred or continued to buy or carry tax-exempt securities (e.g., state or local bonds, see ¶1333) (Code Sec. 265(a)(2)), or stock of a mutual fund ¶4201) distributing exempt interest. (Code Sec. 265(a)(4))[23]

¶ 1724 Registration-required obligations.

No deduction is allowed for interest on "registration-required obligations" (defined in Code Sec. 163(f)(2)) that aren't in registered form. (Code Sec. 163(f)(1))[24]

¶ 1725 Interest on corporate acquisition indebtedness.

The deduction allowed to a corporation for the interest it pays or accrues during a tax year on certain "corporate acquisition indebtedness" can't exceed $5,000,000. But all or part of the excess may not be subject to disallowance if specified tests (acquisition purpose, subordination, convertibility, and debt-equity) are met. (Code Sec. 279)[25]

¶ 1726 Investment Interest Deduction Limitations.

Noncorporate taxpayers can deduct investment interest only to the extent of net investment income.

¶ 1727 Investment interest deductions of noncorporate taxpayers—Form 4952.

The amount of investment interest (¶1728) that may be deducted in any tax year by a noncorporate taxpayer generally is limited to taxpayer's "net investment income" (¶1729) for the year. (Code Sec. 163(d)(1)) Form 4952 is used to compute the limitation.[26]

Interest that's disallowed because of this limit can be carried over and deducted in later years, subject to the later year's investment income limit. (Code Sec. 163(d)(2))[27]

¶ 1728 "Investment interest."

"Investment interest" is interest paid or accrued on indebtedness properly allocable to property held for investment. (Code Sec. 163(d)(3)(A))[28] But the deduction limit on investment interest (¶1727) doesn't apply to interest expense that must be capitalized (e.g., construction interest), or that's disallowed under Code Sec. 265 (¶1723).[29]

Property held for investment is: (1) any property that produces income properly allocable to portfolio income under the passive activity rules—e.g., interest, dividends (but stock is "held for investment" even if it doesn't pay dividends), royalties, annuities, see ¶1821; (Code Sec. 163(d)(5)(A)(i))[30] and (2) any interest in an activity involving a trade or business in which taxpayer doesn't materially participate, if that activity isn't "passive" under the passive activity rules (¶1823). (Code Sec. 163(d)(5)(A)(ii))[31]

Investment interest includes interest on a home mortgage (other than "qualified residence interest," see below) if its purpose is to acquire investment property. [32] It also includes any amount allowable as a deduction in connection with personal property used in a short sale. (Code Sec. 163(d)(3)(C))[33]

---

22. ¶K-5506, H-11065 *et seq.*; ¶724.23; TD ¶317,000
23. ¶K-5520 *et seq.*, ¶K-5546; ¶2654; TD ¶316,001
24. ¶K-5550 *et seq.*; ¶1634
25. ¶K-5405 *et seq.*; ¶s 1634, 2794
26. ¶K-5310 *et seq.*; ¶1634.053; TD ¶315,011
27. ¶K-5321; ¶1634.053; TD ¶315,021

28. ¶K-5312; ¶1634.053; TD ¶315,012
29. ¶K-5312; TD ¶315,012
30. ¶K-5322; ¶1634.053; TD ¶315,022
31. ¶K-5322; ¶1634.053; TD ¶315,018
32. ¶K-5313; TD ¶315,013
33. ¶K-5312; TD ¶315,012

Investment interest *doesn't include* interest on funds borrowed in connection with a trade or business, or any interest that is: (1) taken into account in determining taxpayer's income or loss from a passive activity, (2) qualified residence interest (¶1732) (Code Sec. 163(d)(3)(B)), or (3) properly allocable to a rental real estate activity in which, under the passive activity rules (¶1836), taxpayer actively participates.[34]

¶ 1729   "Net investment income" defined.

Taxpayer's "net investment income" for a tax year is the excess of "investment income" over "investment expenses" for the year. (Code Sec. 163(d)(4)(A))[35] (For the definition of net investment interest for alternative minimum tax purposes, see ¶3209.)

"Investment income" is the sum of: (1) gross income from property held for investment (¶1728); (2) any excess of *net gain* attributable to the disposition of investment property over *net capital gain* determined by only taking into account gains and losses from these dispositions; (3) so much of taxpayer's *net capital gain* (or *net gain,* if less) described in (2), as he elects (on Form 4952) to include in investment income (for the effect of such an election on net capital gain, see ¶2604); plus (4) before 2011, so much of taxpayer's qualified dividend income (dividends received from domestic and qualified foreign corporations that are taxable at net capital gains rates, see ¶1288 *et seq.*), as he elects (on Form 4952) to include in investment income. (For the effect of such an election on qualified dividend income, see ¶1290.) (Code Sec. 163(d)(4)(B); Reg § 1.163(d)-1)[36]

⚑*caution:* For sunset rule, see ¶1114.

"Investment expenses" are deductible expenses *other than interest* that are directly connected with the production of investment income (Code Sec. 163(d)(4)(C)), but limited to the amount allowed after the 2%-of-AGI floor (¶3110). Nonbusiness bad debts (¶1856) directly connected with the production of income are taken into account to the extent they are currently deductible.[37]

Investment income and expenses don't include any amounts taken into account in computing income or loss from a passive activity (¶1811 *et seq.*). (Code Sec. 163(d)(4)(D))[38]

¶ 1730   Qualified Residence Interest. ▬▬▬▬▬▬▬▬▬▬▬▬▬▬▬▬▬▬▬

Taxpayers may claim itemized deductions for "qualified residence interest" —i.e., interest on (1) up to $1,000,000 of acquisition debt and (2) up to $100,000 of home-equity debt. The debt must be secured by taxpayer's "qualified residence."

¶ 1731   Deduction of "qualified residence interest."

"Qualified residence interest" (¶1732) is not subject to these limits and special rules:

- personal interest deduction bar (¶1715) (Code Sec. 163(h)(2)(D); Reg § 1.163-10T(b));

⚑*observation:* In other words, qualified residence interest is not subject to the prohibition on the deduction of personal interest, and may be deducted under the general rule allowing the deduction of interest, discussed at ¶1700 *et seq.*

- investment interest limitations (¶1728) (Code Sec. 163(d)(3)(B)(i); Reg § 1.163-10T(b));
- passive activity interest limitations (¶1816) (Code Sec. 469(j)(7); Reg § 1.163-10T(b))
- uniform capitalization rules (¶1660). (Reg § 1.163-10T(b))[39]

But qualified residence interest is subject to the interest bars and limits in connection with: single premium insurance (¶1719); tax-exempt income (¶1723); related-party transactions

---

34. ¶K-5312 *et seq.*; ¶1634.053; TD ¶315,012
35. ¶K-5311; ¶1634.053; TD ¶315,015
36. ¶K-5315 *et seq.*; ¶1634.053; TD ¶315,015 *et seq.*

37. ¶K-5320; ¶1634.053; TD ¶315,020
38. ¶s K-5315, K-5320; ¶1634.053; TD ¶315,020
39. ¶K-5473; ¶1634.052; TD ¶314,501

(¶2836); the "at-risk" rules (¶1804 *et seq.*); accrued market discount (¶1716); and straddle interest (¶2653 *et seq.*). (Reg § 1.163-10T(b))[40]

For how the interest allocation rules apply to qualified residence interest, see ¶1741.

caution: For the treatment of residence interest for alternative minimum tax purposes, see ¶3209.

¶ 1732 What is "qualified residence interest"?

"Qualified residence interest" (see ¶1731) is any interest paid or accrued during the tax year on acquisition indebtedness (¶1733) or home equity indebtedness (¶1734) with respect to any property that, at the time the interest is accrued, is taxpayer's "qualified residence" (¶1735), but only to the extent the interest is paid or accrued while the debt is secured by the residence. (Code Sec. 163(h)(3)(A); Reg § 1.163-10T(j)(1)) For a cash basis taxpayer, it also includes certain "points" paid on debt incurred in connection with his principal residence. (Reg § 1.163-10T(j)(2)(i))[41] For treatment of certain mortgage insurance premiums as qualified residence interest, see ¶1736.

A debt may be part acquisition indebtedness and part home equity indebtedness.[42]

¶ 1733 Acquisition indebtedness.

Acquisition indebtedness (interest on which is deductible qualified residence interest, see ¶1731) is debt that: (1) meets the dollar limitation described below; (2) is incurred in acquiring, constructing or substantially improving taxpayer's "qualified residence" (¶1735) (or adjoining land) and (3) is secured by the residence. (Code Sec. 163(h)(3)(B)(i)) In general, acquisition debt must be an obligation of the taxpayer.[43] New debt a taxpayer incurs to refinance his acquisition indebtedness also qualifies, but only up to the amount of the refinanced debt. (Code Sec. 163(h)(3)(B)(i))[44] Debt is treated as incurred in acquiring, etc., a residence if the debt proceeds can be traced to payment of the costs of the acquisition, etc.[45]

The aggregate amount of debt that may be treated as acquisition indebtedness for any period can't exceed $1,000,000 ($500,000 for a married individual filing a separate return). (Code Sec. 163(h)(3)(B)(ii)) These dollar amounts are reduced (not below zero) by the aggregate amount of outstanding (including refinanced) "pre-Oct. 13, '87 indebtedness." (Code Sec. 163(h)(3)(D)) IRS says that where a single property is owned by more than one taxpayer, each owner doesn't get his own $1 million ceiling; rather a single acquisition debt ceiling applies to the property.[46] For where debt exceeds these limits, see ¶1741.

¶ 1734 Home equity indebtedness.

Home equity indebtedness (interest on which is deductible qualified residence interest, see ¶1731) is any debt (other than acquisition indebtedness, see ¶1733) secured by taxpayer's qualified residence (¶1735), to the extent the aggregate amount of the debt doesn't exceed the fair market value of the residence (as reduced by the amount of acquisition indebtedness on it). (Code Sec. 163(h)(3)(C)(i)) Unlike acquisition debt (¶1733), home equity debt generally may be used for any purpose without affecting its deductibility, see ¶1741. The aggregate amount treated as home equity indebtedness for any period may not exceed $100,000 ($50,000 for a married individual filing a separate return). (Code Sec. 163(h)(3)(C)(ii)) For debt that exceeds these limits, see ¶1741. IRS says that debt that isn't acquisition debt because it exceeds the $1 million dollar limit on that type of debt can qualify as home equity debt, but the Tax Court has previously held to the contrary.[47]

---

40. ¶K-5473 *et seq.*; TD ¶314,501
41. ¶K-5471; ¶1634.052; TD ¶314,502
42. ¶K-5491; TD ¶314,521
43. ¶K-5484; ¶1634.052; TD ¶314,515
44. ¶K-5488; ¶1634.052; TD ¶314,519
45. ¶K-5487; TD ¶318,001
46. ¶s K-5485, K-5489; ¶1634.052; TD ¶314,516
47. ¶K-5490; ¶1634.052; TD ¶314,520

¶ 1735   Qualified residence.

A qualified residence (see ¶1732) is: (1) taxpayer's principal residence (i.e., one that would qualify for exclusion of gain under Code Sec. 121 (¶2442) (Code Sec. 163(h)(4)(A)(i)(I)) and/or (2) any other residence (second residence) taxpayer properly elects to treat as qualified for the tax year, even if he didn't use it as a residence that year. But a second residence that taxpayer rents out to others during the year can't qualify unless he also uses it as a residence (i.e., uses it for personal purposes during the year for more than the greater of 14 days or 10% of the number of days it is rented out for a fair rental). (Code Sec. 163(h)(4)(A)(i)(II), Code Sec. 163(h)(4)(A)(iii); Reg § 1.163-10T(p)(3)(iii)) A taxpayer who has more than one residence that meets these tests may elect each year which to treat as the second (qualified) residence. (Code Sec. 163(h)(4)(A)(i); Reg § 1.163-10T(p)(3)(iv))[48]

A residence for this purpose includes a condominium or cooperative housing corporation (co-op). Any indebtedness secured by stock in a co-op is treated as secured by the house or apartment taxpayer is entitled to occupy. Even if local restrictions prohibit using the stock as security, it will be treated as securing the debt if taxpayer can show the debt was incurred to acquire the stock. (Code Sec. 163(h)(4)(B); Reg § 1.163-10T(p)(3))[49] A time-share can also qualify if it satisfies the above tests for rental property. (Reg § 1.163-10T(p)(6))[50]

A residence under construction may be treated as a qualified residence for a period of up to 24 months, but only if it otherwise qualifies as of the time it's ready for occupancy. (Reg § 1.163-10T(p)(5))[1]

For married taxpayers filing jointly, the second residence may be owned and/or used by either spouse. For spouses filing separately, each may have only one qualified residence (unless the other spouse gives written consent otherwise). (Code Sec. 163(h)(4)(A))[2]

¶ 1736   Mortgage insurance premiums paid or incurred in 2007 through 2010 for acquisition indebtedness on qualified residence treated as qualified residence interest.

Premiums paid or accrued by a taxpayer during the tax year for qualified mortgage insurance in connection with acquisition indebtedness (see ¶1733) with respect to a qualified residence of the taxpayer are treated as qualified residence interest (Code Sec. 163(h)(3)(E)(i)), subject to a phase-out based on the taxpayer's adjusted gross income (AGI) (below).[3]

> **observation:** To be deductible under the above rule, premiums for qualified mortgage insurance must be paid or accrued in connection with acquisition indebtedness. But, qualified mortgage insurance isn't a category of acquisition indebtedness, but rather a separate category of qualified residence interest. So, qualified mortgage insurance isn't subject to the amount limitations on acquisition indebtedness, and doesn't affect the amount of indebtedness that may qualify as acquisition indebtedness under those limitations, see ¶1733.

Qualified mortgage insurance means mortgage insurance provided by the Veterans Administration (VA), the Federal Housing Administration (FHA), or the Rural Housing Administration (RHA), and private mortgage insurance, as defined by Sec. 2 of the Homeowners Protection Act of '98 (12 U.S.C. 4901), as in effect on Dec. 20, 2006. (Code Sec. 163(h)(4)(E)(ii))

Except for amounts paid for qualified mortgage insurance provided by the VA or the RHA, any amounts paid by the taxpayer for qualified mortgage insurance that is properly allocable to any mortgage the payment of which extends to periods that are after the close of the tax year in which that amount is paid are chargeable to capital account and must be treated as

---

48. ¶K-5474 *et seq.*; ¶1634.052; TD ¶314,504
49. ¶K-5481; ¶1634.052; TD ¶314,511
50. ¶K-5482; TD ¶314,512

1. ¶K-5483; TD ¶314,513
2. ¶K-5480; ¶1634.052; TD ¶314,510
3. ¶K-5493.1; ¶1634.052; TD ¶314,519.1

paid in those periods to which they are allocated.

But, no deduction is allowed for the unamortized balance of premiums that have been capitalized if the mortgage is satisfied before the end of its term. (Code Sec. 163(h)(4)(F))

An individual may allocate prepaid qualified mortgage insurance premiums that are treated as qualified residence interest under Code Sec. 163(h)(3)(E) over the shorter of (1) the stated term of the mortgage, or (2) a period of 84 months. (Reg § 1.163-11T)[4]

The rules treating qualified mortgage insurance premiums as deductible qualified residence interest apply only if the amounts: (1) are paid or accrued before Jan. 1, 2011; (2) aren't properly allocable to any period after Dec. 31, 2010; and (3) are paid or accrued with respect to a mortgage insurance contract issued after Dec. 31, 2006. (Code Sec. 163(h)(3)(E))

The amount of mortgage insurance premiums otherwise treated as qualified residence interest under the rule above must be reduced (but not below zero) by: (a) for taxpayers other than married persons filing separately, 10% of the amount of qualified mortgage insurance for each $1,000 (or fraction thereof) that the taxpayer's AGI for the tax year exceeds $100,000, and (b) for married persons filing separately, 10% of the amount of qualified mortgage insurance for each $500 (or fraction thereof) that the taxpayer's AGI for the tax year exceeds $50,000. (Code Sec. 163(h)(3)(E)(ii))

☛*caution:* Check http://ria.thomsonreuters.com/federaltaxhandbook to see if this provision has been extended.

¶ 1737 Allocation Rules for Interest and Debt.

Debt proceeds may be used in ways that trigger more than one interest deduction limitations. To determine which limit applies (personal interest, ¶1715, investment interest, ¶1727, or passive activity interest, ¶1816), the interest and underlying debt must be properly allocated, generally by tracing the use of the borrowed money.

¶ 1738 Interest deduction limits require allocation of interest expense.

For certain taxpayers (see ¶1739), where the proceeds of a single debt are used for multiple purposes—e.g., to make investments *and* to buy "personal" items —the debt must be allocated among the various expenditures. (Reg § 1.163-8T)[5]

Interest expense is allocated the same way as the debt with respect to which the interest accrues, by tracing disbursements of the debt proceeds to specific expenditures. (Reg § 1.163-8T(a)(3), Reg § 1.163-8T(c)(1)) Except for qualified residence interest (¶1732), the nature of any property securing the debt isn't relevant. (Reg § 1.163-8T(c)(1))[6]

The interest, as allocated, is subject to the appropriate deduction limit, as follows:

. . . Interest allocated to a passive activity expenditure (current or former) is subject to the passive activity limitations (¶1816).

. . . Interest allocated to an investment expenditure is subject to the investment interest limitations (¶1727).

. . . Interest allocated to a personal expenditure is treated as personal interest (i.e., it's not deductible, see ¶1715).

. . . Interest allocated to a trade or business expenditure is treated as trade or business interest (i.e., it's not subject to the personal or investment interest limits). (Code Sec. 469(l)(4); Reg § 1.163-8T(a)(4)(i))[7]

The interest expense allocation rules don't control the allocation of interest for any purpose other than those listed above.[8]

---

4. ¶K-5493.1; ¶1634.052; TD ¶314,519.1
5. ¶K-5231 *et seq.*; ¶1634.055; TD ¶318,001
6. ¶K-5231; ¶1634.055; TD ¶318,001

7. ¶K-5232; ¶1634.055; TD ¶318,000 *et seq.*
8. ¶K-5234; TD ¶318,002

¶ 1739   Taxpayers who must allocate interest.

The interest expense allocation rules (¶1738) apply to all taxpayers *other than* widely-held C corporations. So, the rules apply to a pass-through entity (e.g., partnership or S corporation) that borrows money to make distributions to its owners (partners or shareholders), or whose debt is allocated to those distributions. Repayments of a pass-through entity's debt that is allocated partly to a distribution to its owners and partly to other expenditures are treated first as a repayment of the portion of the debt allocated to the distribution.[9]

¶ 1740   Time for allocation of debt and interest expense

Debt is allocated to an expenditure for the period: (1) beginning on the date the proceeds of the debt are used or treated as used to make the expenditure, and (2) ending on the date the debt is repaid or reallocated (¶1742), whichever is earlier. (Reg § 1.163-8T(c)(2)(i))[10]

Generally, interest expense that accrues on a debt is allocated in the same manner as the debt is allocated from time to time, regardless of when the interest is actually paid. (Reg § 1.163-8T(c)(2)(ii)(A))[11]

¶ 1741   Qualified residence interest as "allocable" interest.

Qualified residence interest (¶1730 *et seq.*) is deductible without regard to how that interest expense (or the underlying debt) is allocated. (Reg § 1.163-8T(m)(3))[12]

But, where the debt exceeds the qualified residence interest limits (¶1733, ¶1734), allocation is required for the "excess." (Reg § 1.163-10T(e))[13]

¶ 1742   Reallocation of interest

Where the use of debt proceeds, or of assets bought with debt proceeds, changes, the interest on the debt must be reallocated to the new use. The interest, as so reallocated, will be subject to any appropriate deduction limits (see ¶1738). (Reg § 1.163-8T(j)(1))[14]

¶ 1743   When Interest May Be Deducted. ▬▬▬▬▬▬▬▬▬▬▬▬▬▬▬▬

The proper time for deducting interest is generally determined by the taxpayer's method of accounting. Special rules govern when mortgage "points," unstated interest and original issue (OID) discount must be deducted.

¶ 1744   Cash method taxpayer's interest deduction.

A cash method taxpayer may deduct interest only if it is actually *paid* during the tax year. (Code Sec. 163(a)) (For accrual taxpayers, see ¶1748.) The payment can be with funds borrowed from another creditor, but not with funds borrowed from the same creditor, or by giving a note for the interest or adding the unpaid interest to principal.[15]

Contested interest (where the debtor claims he doesn't owe it) isn't deductible. But if a cash basis taxpayer transfers money or other property to provide for the satisfaction of the asserted (and otherwise deductible) interest, it's deductible in the year of the transfer. (Code Sec. 461(f))[16] For prepaid interest (including "points"), see ¶1745.

---

9. ¶K-5259 *et seq.*; ¶1634.056; TD ¶318,033
10. ¶K-5233; ¶1634.055; TD ¶318,008
11. ¶K-5233; ¶1634.055; TD ¶318,008
12. ¶K-5238; ¶1634.055; TD ¶318,005
13. ¶K-5499; TD ¶314,530
14. ¶K-5254 *et seq.*; ¶1634.055; TD ¶318,023
15. ¶K-5170 *et seq.*; ¶s 1634.030, 1634.031; TD ¶318,700 *et seq.*
16. ¶G-2442 *et seq.*; ¶4614.56 *et seq.*; TD ¶319,004, 319,005

¶ 1745 Prepaid interest (including "points").

Interest that is prepaid, including "points" (except certain home mortgage points, see ¶1746), is deductible only in the tax year to which, and to the extent that, the interest is allocable—i.e., as it accrues. (Code Sec. 461(g)(1)) Cash method taxpayers thus generally deduct points ratably over the term of the loan (for refinancings, see ¶1747).[17]

A taxpayer who "pays" points by receiving discounted loan proceeds gets no current deduction (except certain mortgage points, ¶1746).[18] Instead, the discount is treated as OID, deductible by the borrower under the OID rules (¶1751). Discounts *not* subject to the OID rules may be deducted ratably as the underlying debt is repaid.[19]

If the mortgage ends early, e.g., because of a prepayment, refinancing, foreclosure or similar event, taxpayer may deduct the remaining balance of points in the year it ends.[20]

¶ 1746 "Points" on a home mortgage—cash method taxpayer's deduction in year of payment.

A cash method taxpayer may (but doesn't have to) deduct points paid on indebtedness incurred in connection with the purchase or improvement of (and secured by) his principal residence, in the tax year of actual payment—i.e., in advance, not ratably (see ¶1745) (for refinancings, see ¶1747). The charging of points must reflect an established business practice in the geographical area where the loan is made, and the deduction allowed can't exceed the number of points generally charged there. (Code Sec. 461(g)(2)) For loans used to improve the residence, the points must be paid with funds other than those borrowed from the lender or mortgage broker.[21]

For loans used to acquire the residence, cash basis taxpayers may currently deduct amounts that meet the above tests *and* are: (1) clearly designated (on Form HUD-1) as points incurred in connection with the debt (including "points" on VA and FHA loans) —i.e., they aren't paid in lieu of nondeductible amounts that are ordinarily stated separately, e.g., appraisal fees; (2) computed as a percentage of the stated principal amount of the debt; *and* (3) paid directly by taxpayer to the lender (or mortgage broker). Condition (3) is met where taxpayer provides, from funds that haven't been borrowed for this purpose as part of the overall transaction, an amount at least equal to what is required to be applied as points at closing (even if the amount so provided is used for down payments, escrow deposits, etc., actually paid at closing).[22]

Points paid by (or charged to) the seller in connection with a loan to the buyer (taxpayer) also are deductible by the buyer if he subtracts them from the purchase price in computing the basis of the residence.[23]

¶ 1747 "Points" on refinancing.

Points paid to *refinance* an existing mortgage generally are deductible only ratably over the loan term (see ¶1745). But where the refinancing is incurred for home improvements, points paid from separate funds may be deducted currently.[24]

¶ 1748 Accrual method taxpayer's interest deduction.

Accrual method taxpayers deduct interest when all the events have occurred that fix the fact of the liability, the amount of the liability can be determined with reasonable accuracy,

---

17. ¶K-5177; ¶s 1634.005, 1634.032, 4614.75; TD ¶318,707
18. ¶K-5178; ¶4614.75; TD ¶319,201
19. ¶K-5176; ¶4614.75; TD ¶318,706
20. ¶K-5183; TD ¶319,206

21. ¶K-5178 *et seq.*; ¶s 1634.005, 4614.75; TD ¶319,201
22. ¶K-5179; ¶4614.75; TD ¶319,202
23. ¶K-5179; ¶4614.75; TD ¶318,606
24. ¶K-5180; ¶s 1634.005, 4614.75; TD ¶319,203

and economic performance (¶2832 *et seq.*) has occurred.[25] (For cash method, see ¶1744.)

The interest is deductible only in the year it accrues, without regard to when the (accrual basis) taxpayer pays it. For these purposes, interest (including prepaid interest) accrues ratably over the life of a loan. But interest that's contingent on events other than the creditor's demand for payment doesn't accrue until the contingency happens.[26]

Contested interest (where the debtor claims he doesn't owe it) isn't accruable or deductible. But if the accrual basis taxpayer transfers money or other property to provide for the satisfaction of the asserted interest, it's deductible in the year of the transfer. (Code Sec. 461(f))[27]

¶ 1749   Interest under the "Rule of 78s" method.

The Rule of 78s method can't be used to compute interest. Interest so computed must be recomputed under an economic accrual method for federal income tax purposes.[28]

¶ 1750   When to deduct "unstated interest."

The unstated interest allocated to a payment in a deferred payment sale (¶1707) is deducted by cash method buyers in the year the payment is made, and by accrual method buyers in the year the payment is due. (Reg § 1.483-2(a)(1)(ii))[29] But both cash and accrual taxpayers use the cash method rules to deduct interest on cash method debt instruments (¶1322). (Code Sec. 1274A(c)(1)(B))[30]

¶ 1751   Original issue discount (OID).

The issuer of a debt instrument issued with OID (see ¶1315 *et seq.*) may (with some exceptions, ¶1753) deduct part of the OID (¶1752) in each tax year the instrument is outstanding, even though the OID isn't paid until maturity. (Code Sec. 163(e)(1); Reg § 1.163-3(a)(1), Reg § 1.163-4(a)(1)) This current deduction rule applies regardless of the method of accounting used by the issuer.[31] But a cash method obligor of a short-term obligation can only deduct OID (and other interest) when it is paid. (Code Sec. 163(e)(2)(C))[32]

An issuer may deduct OID only to the extent the issuer is primarily liable on the debt instrument. (Reg § 1.163-7(a))[33]

OID for this purpose has the same meaning as for purposes of requiring the holder to include OID in gross income currently (see ¶1316) *except*:

. . . The de minimis exception doesn't apply. (Code Sec. 163(e)(2)(B))[34] But an issuer with de minimis OID may elect to deduct the OID at maturity. (Reg § 1.163-7(b)(2))[35]

. . . A nonpublicly traded debt instrument issued to a seller in exchange for personal use property isn't treated as issued with OID that the buyer (issuer) can deduct currently. (Code Sec. 1275(b)(1))[36]

¶ 1752   Amount of OID deductible currently.

The amount of OID the issuer of a debt instrument deducts currently (¶1751) is determined in the same way as the amount of OID the holder includes in gross income currently (using the constant yield method, see ¶1323), but without regard to (1) the reduction for any acquisition premium paid by the holder and (2) the treatment of stated interest as "qualified stated interest" where OID is de minimis. (Code Sec. 163(e)(2)(B); Reg § 1.163-7(a))[37]

---

25. ¶K-5200 *et seq.*; ¶1634.035 *et seq.*; TD ¶319,000 *et seq.*
26. ¶s K-5200, K-5201; ¶s 1634.035, 1634.036; TD ¶319,001
27. ¶G-2643*et seq.*; ¶4614.56 *et seq.*; TD ¶319,004, 319,005
28. ¶K-5153; ¶1634.030
29. ¶K-5283; ¶1634; TD ¶319,503
30. ¶K-5283; TD ¶319,503
31. ¶K-5700 *et seq.*; ¶1634.051; TD ¶319,701

32. ¶K-5712; ¶1634.032, 1634.051; TD ¶319,710
33. ¶K-5745; ¶1634.051; TD ¶319,714
34. ¶K-5727; ¶1634.051; TD ¶319,719
35. ¶K-5748; ¶1634.051; TD ¶319,725
36. ¶K-5724; TD ¶319,717
37. ¶K-5745 *et seq.*; ¶1634.051; TD ¶319,725 *et seq.*

¶ 1753 Limits on OID deduction for certain high yield OID obligations.

For certain applicable high yield discount obligations ("AHYDOs") (at least five percentage points over the applicable federal rate for month of issue) issued after July 10, '89, a C corporation can't deduct (or otherwise take into account) any part of the OID until actually paid. In some cases, the deduction may be barred for all or part of the OID, depending on the obligation's yield, maturity date and amount of OID. However, these rules are suspended for certain obligations issued in a debt-for-debt exchange, including an exchange resulting from a significant modification of a debt instrument, after Aug. 31, 2008 and before 2010 (before 2011 for certain obligations). (Code Sec. 163(e)(5))[38]

caution: Check http://ria.thomsonreuters.com/federaltaxhandbook to see if this exception has been extended.

¶ 1754 Deduction for Taxes.

Certain state, local, U.S. possessions and foreign taxes are deductible whether or not connected with a trade or business; so are some federal taxes (not income tax).

Only payments that are really taxes (regardless of what they are called) are deductible as taxes (see ¶1758). Taxes are charges imposed on persons or property by governmental authority to raise funds for the support of government or for public purposes. The mere fact that a levy is called a "tax" isn't conclusive. [39] Fees imposed primarily as charges for government services, e.g., fees for a driver's license or car inspection, or passport fees, aren't deductible as taxes.[40] Penalties paid to a government for violation of a law aren't taxes. (Code Sec. 162(f))[41]

¶ 1755 Which taxes are deductible?

Deductible *state, local and foreign taxes* are:

. . . state, local and foreign income, war profits and excess profits taxes (but a taxpayer can deduct state and local sales taxes instead of income taxes, see ¶1756);

. . . state, local and foreign real property taxes;

. . . state and local personal property taxes (see ¶1761);

. . . qualified motor vehicle taxes (see ¶1757) and

. . . other state, local and foreign taxes (e.g., occupational taxes) paid or accrued in business or for the production of income unless incurred in connection with an acquisition or disposition of property (e.g., sales taxes, see ¶1756). (Code Sec. 164(a)(1), Code Sec. 164(a)(3))[42]

For state unemployment and disability taxes, see ¶1759.

These *federal taxes* are deductible as taxes:

- Federal (and state) generation skipping transfer (GST) tax imposed on income distributions (¶5055 *et seq.*) (Code Sec. 164(a)(4), Code Sec. 164(b)(4));[43]
- Estate tax attributable to income in respect of a decedent (¶3971);
- Self-employment taxes (¶3140 *et seq.*) are one-half deductible. (Code Sec. 164(f))[44]

caution: For the deductibility of taxes for alternative minimum tax purposes, see ¶3209.

Taxes not included above (e.g., gasoline, diesel and other motor fuel taxes, Social Security (FICA) and unemployment (FUTA) taxes on employers, motor vehicle registration fees) aren't deductible as *taxes* (although some motor vehicle fees may qualify as personal property taxes), but may be deductible as *business expenses* or *expenses for the production of income* (¶1506

---

38. ¶K-5754 *et seq.*; ¶1634.051
39. ¶K-4003; ¶1644; TD ¶326,011
40. ¶K-4003 *et seq.*; ¶1644; TD ¶326,011
41. ¶K-4009; ¶1644; TD ¶326,008

42. ¶K-4001; ¶1644.03; TD ¶326,008
43. ¶K-4403 *et seq.*; ¶1644.06; TD ¶326,004
44. ¶K-4401; ¶1644.07; TD ¶326,002

et seq.). (Reg § 1.164-2(f))[45]

For deduction of taxes by individuals who don't itemize, see ¶1758.

These taxes aren't deductible as taxes, expenses or otherwise:

(1) Federal income taxes, including amounts withheld from wages, interest, etc.

(2) Alternative minimum tax.

(3) Social Security (FICA) tax on employees, and Railroad Retirement tax on employees and employee representatives. (Code Sec. 275(a)(1); Reg § 1.164-2(a))

(4) Federal war profits and excess profits taxes. (Code Sec. 275(a)(2); Reg § 1.164-2(b))

(5) Estate, inheritance, legacy, succession and gift taxes (Code Sec. 275(a)(3); Reg § 1.164-2(c)) except as noted above, whether state, federal or foreign.

(6) Income, war profits and excess profits taxes of any foreign country or U.S. possession if taxpayer takes the foreign tax credit for them (¶2375 *et seq.*). (Code Sec. 275(a)(4); Reg § 1.164-2(d)) But deduction is allowed for any tax that isn't allowable as a foreign tax credit because of Code Sec. 901(j) (which denies the credit for taxes paid to certain foreign countries, see ¶2377) (Code Sec. 901(j)(3)), or because of Code Sec. 901(k) (relating to minimum holding period requirements for certain taxes, see ¶2382).

(7) Excise taxes imposed on: charities' excess expenditures to influence legislation; private foundations; qualified pension, etc., plans; certain investment entities (REITs and RICs); excess golden parachute payments; greenmail (Code Sec. 275(a)(6)) and charitable split-dollar insurance transactions (¶2115). (Code Sec. 170(f)(10)(F)(iv))[46]

¶ 1756   Sales and use taxes.

Taxpayers may elect (on Schedule A of Form 1040) to deduct state and local *general sales and use* taxes instead of state and local *income* taxes, for tax years beginning before 2010. With limited exceptions, a sales or use tax is general if imposed at one rate with respect to the retail sale of a broad range of classes of items. (Code Sec. 164(b)(5); Reg § 1.164-3)[47]

Electing taxpayers may deduct either:

(1) the amount of state and local general sales taxes paid, by accumulating receipts; or

(2) the amount determined under IRS tables (see below), plus the actual amount of sales taxes paid on motor vehicles, boats and other IRS-specified items (e.g., aircraft, homes). (Code Sec. 164(b)(5)(H))[48]

The IRS tables (in IRS Pub. 600) provide an amount of sales taxes paid based on the taxpayer's state of residence, total available income, and number of exemptions. Taxpayers living in more than one state during the year must prorate the table amounts based on the number of days lived in each state. For married taxpayers (¶1763), use of the tables depends on whether they file jointly or separately, and whether they live in the same state.[49]

The elective sales tax deduction doesn't apply to sales taxes paid on items used in a taxpayer's trade or business.[50]

If the election is not made, state and local sales or use taxes are deductible only to the following extent: State or local sales or use taxes paid or incurred in connection with the acquisition or disposition of property, and taxes on the transfer of property (e.g., securities, real estate), aren't deductible (buyer treats them as part of the cost, seller as a reduction in the amount realized). Other sales taxes are deductible only if paid or incurred in a trade or business or for the production of income. (Code Sec. 164(a))[1]

45. ¶K-4000, L-2350*et seq.*; ¶1644; TD ¶327,001 *et seq.*
46. ¶L-2358; ¶1644; TD ¶327,003
47. ¶K-4510 *et seq.*; ¶1644.03; TD ¶326,019.1 *et seq.*
48. ¶K-4511; ¶1644.03; TD ¶326,019.2

49. ¶K-4511 *et seq.*; TD ¶326,019.2 *et seq.*
50. ¶K-4510 *et seq.*; ¶1644.03; TD ¶326,019.1 *et seq.*
1. ¶I-2502, ¶K-4500 *et seq.*, ¶L-2352.1, ¶P-1174.1; ¶1644.03, ¶1644.09; TD ¶326,006, TD ¶327,001

⚫*caution:* Check http://ria.thomsonreuters.com/federaltaxhandbook to see if this provision has been extended.

¶ 1757 Qualified motor vehicle taxes before 2010.

For purchases on or after Feb. 17, 2009 and before Jan. 1, 2010, a deduction was allowed for qualified motor vehicle taxes. The deduction generally was allowed to itemizers. (Code Sec. 164(a)(6)) It also was allowed to those claiming the standard deduction, see ¶1758.[2]

⚫*caution:* Check http://ria.thomsonreuters.com/federaltaxhandbook to see if this provision has been extended.

¶ 1758 Limitations on deduction for taxes if individual doesn't itemize.

An individual generally may deduct taxes only if he itemizes (on Schedule A of Form 1040). (Code Sec. 63(d))[3]

However, for tax years beginning in 2009, taxpayers could take an additional standard deduction amount for state and local real property taxes, up to a maximum of $500 ($1,000 for marrieds filing jointly). (Code Sec. 63(c)(1)(C))[4] Taxpayers could take an additional standard deduction amount for qualified motor vehicle taxes, see ¶1757.

⚫*caution:* Check http://ria.thomsonreuters.com/federaltaxhandbook to see if this provision has been extended.

For an individual who doesn't itemize, the deduction is limited to these taxes that are deductible "above the line" (i.e., from gross income in arriving at adjusted gross income, ¶3102): taxes attributable to a trade or business (including taxes on real property) (Code Sec. 62(a)(1)), or to property held for the production of rents or royalties (Code Sec. 62(a)(4)), and one-half of any self-employment taxes imposed on him. (Code Sec. 164(f))[5]

¶ 1759 State unemployment and disability taxes.

Employers' contributions to state unemployment insurance funds are deductible as taxes if the state so classifies them. Whether an employee's contributions to a state unemployment insurance fund or disability plan are deductible as taxes similarly is determined on a state-by-state basis.[6]

¶ 1760 Local benefit assessments.

Assessments that tend to increase the value of the assessed property (whether or not the value does increase) aren't deductible as taxes (but may be capitalized, see ¶1654 *et seq.*). But deduction *is* allowed, to the extent taxpayer shows the assessment is properly allocable to maintenance or interest charges. (Code Sec. 164(c)(1); Reg § 1.164-4(b)(1))[7]

¶ 1761 Personal property taxes.

Personal property taxes imposed by a state or local government are deductible. (Code Sec. 164(a)(2)) The tax must be imposed annually on personal property, on an ad valorem basis (i.e., based on the value of the personal property). (Code Sec. 164(b)(1))[8]

---

2. ¶K-4517; ¶1644.03; TD ¶326,019.7
3. ¶A-2701; ¶634; TD ¶561,201
4. ¶A-2810; ¶634
5. ¶L-2351; ¶624; TD ¶327,002

6. ¶K-4003 *et seq.*; ¶L-2353 *et seq.*; ¶1644.03; TD ¶327,006
7. ¶K-4600 *et seq.*; TD ¶326,020
8. ¶K-4502; ¶1644.03; TD ¶326,014

¶ 1762   Who deducts the tax?

Taxes generally are deductible only by the person on whom they are imposed. (Reg § 1.164-1(a))[9]

One who voluntarily pays a tax imposed on another isn't entitled to a deduction. So, a shareholder can't deduct his payment of the corporation's taxes, or vice versa. [10]

Property taxes are ordinarily imposed on, and so are deductible by, the property owner. (For the year of sale, see ¶1771.) A person who owns a beneficial interest in property may deduct property taxes he pays to protect that interest.[11]

Taxes on property that's leased are deductible by the landlord, even if it's the tenant who makes the payment (which tenant treats as additional rent expense, see ¶1593). (Reg § 1.162-11(a)) But a tenant deducts taxes paid on improvements the tenant makes where the useful life of the improvements will terminate before the end of the lease.[12]

¶ 1763   Married couple's deduction of taxes.

Spouses filing joint federal returns may deduct on that return all deductible taxes paid by either spouse, whether or not they file joint *state* returns.[13]

If the spouses file separate federal and separate state returns, each spouse may deduct only the state income taxes imposed on and actually paid by that spouse. If a joint state return was filed, then for federal tax purposes, that joint state tax is prorated according to each spouse's gross income, but not to exceed the amount actually paid by the spouse. [14]

¶ 1764   Property taxes on co-owned property.

An individual's deduction for taxes on property he owns with other persons as tenants-in-common may be limited to his pro rata part of the taxes, i.e., the amount attributable to his interest, even if he pays *all* the taxes on the property. This pro rata share limit applies where the tenant is only assessed for his share, where he has a right to contribution from the other tenants, or where his share won't be subject to sale on their default. [15]

Tenants by the entirety (i.e., spouses) and joint tenants with right of survivorship are entitled to deduct in full the taxes they pay on the jointly-owned property.[16]

¶ 1765   Cooperative and condominium housing realty taxes.

Tenant-stockholders of cooperative housing corporations (co-ops) deduct their share of the co-op's real property taxes. (Code Sec. 216)[17] Condominium owners deduct the real property taxes on their individual interests.[18]

¶ 1766   When cash basis taxpayers deduct taxes.

A cash basis taxpayer's taxes are deductible for the tax year he pays them. State and local taxes withheld from the taxpayer's wages are deductible in the year they are withheld.[19] (For accrual taxpayers, see ¶1768.) For prepaid taxes, see ¶1767.

The tax is deductible in the year of payment even if taxpayer contests the liability and seeks to recover the payment (see ¶1769).[20] For estimated tax payments, see ¶1767.

---

9. ¶K-4101 *et seq.*; ¶1644.01; TD ¶328,001
10. ¶K-4103, ¶K-4114; ¶1644.01; TD ¶328,021
11. ¶K-4103; ¶1644.01; TD ¶328,002
12. ¶K-4104; TD ¶328,004
13. ¶s K-4105, K-4107; ¶1644.01; TD ¶328,011
14. ¶s K-4106, K-4108; ¶1644.01; TD ¶328,010

15. ¶K-4112; ¶1644.01; TD ¶328,017
16. ¶K-4112; ¶1644.01; TD ¶328,016
17. ¶K-5900 *et seq.*; ¶2164.01.
18. ¶K-4103; TD ¶328,002
19. ¶K-4201 *et seq.*; ¶1644.02; TD ¶329,001
20. ¶K-4201; ¶4614.56; TD ¶329,001

¶ 1767   Prepaid taxes and estimated tax payments.

A cash basis taxpayer may deduct an advance payment of tax in the year of payment as long as it's an actual good faith payment and not a mere deposit. But the advance payment of state taxes that are later refunded won't be deductible unless taxpayer had a reasonable basis, at the time of payment, for believing he owed the taxes.[21]

Deduction in the year of payment also is allowed for advance estimated tax payments made under a pay-as-you-go tax collection system.[22]

¶ 1768   When accrual basis taxpayers deduct taxes.

An accrual basis taxpayer deducts a tax liability in his tax year in which all events have occurred which determine that he is liable for the tax and fix the amount of that liability, and economic performance (¶2833) has occurred—i.e., the tax is paid. (Code Sec. 461(h); Reg § 1.461-1(a)(2), Reg § 1.461-4(g)(6))[23] (For cash basis taxpayers, see ¶1766.) For ratable accrual of real property taxes, see ¶1770. For construction period taxes, see ¶1656.

An accrual basis taxpayer who pays an additional tax without protest or appeal deducts that additional tax in the year the tax was originally due, and not when it's later assessed or paid.[24] For contested tax, see ¶1769.

¶ 1769   When to deduct contested tax.

An accrual basis taxpayer who contests (through an overt act of protest or suit) an assessment can't deduct the contested portion of the tax until the contest is ended and the amount determined.[25]

A taxpayer (cash or accrual) who, by transferring sufficient cash or property, pays the contested liability without giving up the contest may deduct the tax in the year of payment, if otherwise deductible in that (or an earlier) year. But the contest must have existed at the time of transfer. (Code Sec. 461(f))[26] But foreign or U.S. possession income, war profits and excess profits tax can't be deducted until the contest is finally determined. (Code Sec. 461(f))[27]

¶ 1770   Election by accrual method taxpayers to accrue realty taxes ratably—Form 3115.

An accrual basis taxpayer may elect to accrue real property taxes that relate to a definite period of time ratably over that period. (Code Sec. 461(c)(1); Reg § 1.461-1(c)(1))[28]

IRS consent isn't required for an election made for the first tax year taxpayer incurs real property taxes. The election must be made by the return due date (with extensions) for that first year. In all other cases, the election may be made at any time, but requires IRS consent. (Code Sec. 461(c)(2)) Application for IRS's consent must be made in writing (on Form 3115) within 90 days (or 180 days, if taxpayer applies for an automatic extension) after the start of the first tax year to which the election applies.[29] The election is binding unless IRS consents to its revocation. (Reg § 1.461-1(c)(4))[30]

¶ 1771   Apportionment of real property taxes between seller and buyer.

For both cash and accrual taxpayers (Code Sec. 164(d)(2)), the real property tax on property that's sold during the tax year is considered to be imposed:

21. ¶K-4203; ¶1644.02; TD ¶329,005
22. ¶K-4204; ¶1644.02; TD ¶329,006
23. ¶G-2673, K-4300 *et seq.*; ¶4614.75; TD ¶329,007
24. ¶K-4320; TD ¶329,015
25. ¶K-4319 *et seq.*; ¶4614.56; TD ¶329,017

26. ¶s G-2445, G-2645; ¶s 1644.02, 4614.56; TD ¶329,017
27. ¶K-4322; TD ¶329,019
28. ¶K-4327 *et seq.*; ¶s 1644.02, 4614.45; TD ¶329,025
29. ¶s K-4329, K-4330; ¶4614.45; TD ¶329,026
30. ¶K-4334; ¶4614.45; TD ¶329,028

...on the seller to the extent properly allocable to that part of the real property tax year (period to which the tax relates) ending on the day before the date of sale; and

...on the buyer to the extent properly allocable to that part of the real property tax year beginning on the date of sale. (Code Sec. 164(d)(1); Reg § 1.164-6)[31]

For when the seller or buyer deducts the sale year realty tax, see ¶1772. For where seller took excessive deduction, see ¶1773.

¶ 1772   When seller or buyer deducts real property tax.

An *accrual basis* seller or buyer deducts his share of sale year realty tax (as apportioned, ¶1771) in his income tax year in which the accrual date (date of sale) falls. If an election to accrue realty taxes ratably (¶1770) is in effect for that year, his share of the tax is deductible in the year it accrues under the election. (Code Sec. 164(d)(2)(B); Reg § 1.164-6(d)(6))[32]

A *cash basis* seller or buyer deducts his portion of the sale year realty tax in the income tax year he pays it. But where the tax isn't payable until after the sale date, or where the buyer is liable for the tax under local law, the *seller* may, at his option, deduct the tax either in the year of sale (whether or not he actually paid it) or in the year of payment, if later. So, the seller can deduct a tax paid by the buyer. (Reg § 1.164-6(d)(1)(ii))[33]

¶ 1773   Excessive deduction of real property tax before sale.

If the seller (cash or accrual) deducted more than his share of realty taxes on property he sells in a later year, and that "excess" tax payment is allocable to and deductible by the buyer (see ¶1771), the seller is treated as receiving a recovery in the sale year. The seller must include this "recovery" in gross income for the sale year, to the extent he got a tax benefit (i.e., his excess deduction) in that earlier year (see ¶1205). (Reg § 1.164-6(d)(5))[34]

¶ 1774   Deduction for Losses. ■

Taxpayers may sustain a loss when their property is transferred, stolen, destroyed, confiscated, abandoned, taken by foreclosure or becomes worthless, and they receive less than adequate compensation for it. This loss may be deductible.

Subject to the limits discussed in the following paragraphs, the at-risk rules (¶1804 *et seq.*) and the passive loss rules (¶1811 *et seq.*), taxpayers may deduct losses they sustain that aren't compensated for by insurance or otherwise. (Code Sec. 165(a))[35]

For losses from a sale or exchange, see ¶ 2400 *et seq.*

¶ 1775   What is a deductible loss?

A deductible loss arises when a taxpayer loses or gives up money, property or rights, or when these items lose value as a result of an identifiable event. It must be shown that taxpayer sustained a loss of a type that's deductible and that the loss was sustained in the tax year; the amount of the loss also must be shown.[36]

To be deductible, a loss must be evidenced by a closed and completed transaction fixed by identifiable events (Reg § 1.165-1(b)), such as a sale, exchange, foreclosure, stock redemption, casualty, theft, abandonment, governmental condemnation or seizure. Mere fluctuations in an asset's value don't result in deductible losses.[37]

31. ¶K-4117; ¶1644.01; TD ¶328,005
32. ¶s K-4129, K-4130; ¶1644.01; TD ¶329,024
33. ¶K-4124 *et seq.*; ¶1644.01; TD ¶329,004
34. ¶K-4131; TD ¶328,009

35. ¶M-1000; ¶1654; TD ¶360,501
36. ¶M-1000 *et seq.*; ¶1654.020 *et seq.*; TD ¶360,500 *et seq.*
37. ¶M-1101, ¶M-1305 *et seq.*; ¶1654.020 *et seq.*; TD ¶361,001 *et seq.*

¶ 1776   How much loss is deductible?

The amount of a loss sustained on disposition of property is the adjusted basis of the property, minus the amount of any money and the fair market value of any property received in exchange. (Code Sec. 165(b); Reg § 1.165-1(c))[38] No loss is deductible to the extent taxpayer was reimbursed or compensated for it (¶1792, ¶1797). (Code Sec. 165(a))[39] Deduction isn't allowed to the extent that property has salvage value. (Reg § 1.165-1(c))[40] For limit on tax-exempt use losses, see ¶1783. For casualty and theft losses, see ¶1794 *et seq.* and ¶1800 *et seq.*

¶ 1777   Limits on losses of individuals.

Individuals may deduct losses only if they're from a trade or business (¶1778) (Code Sec. 165(c)(1)),[41] a transaction entered into for profit (¶1779) (Code Sec. 165(c)(2)),[42] or a casualty (¶1794) or theft (¶1800). (Code Sec. 165(c)(3))[43]

An individual's losses on personal transactions are deductible only if they qualify as casualty or theft losses. (Code Sec. 165(c)(3))[44] So, no loss deduction is allowed for a loss on taxpayer's residence or car (if used only for personal purposes) unless the loss is from casualty or theft. These rules also apply to losses of estates and trusts.[45]

Property that taxpayer holds partly for personal use and partly for business or income-producing use is treated as two properties: one personal, one business (or income-producing). Loss on the personal part (except by casualty or theft) isn't deductible.[46]

¶ 1778   What is a trade or business?

A trade or business is a pursuit or occupation carried on for profit (¶1779), whether or not profit actually results. An isolated transaction isn't a business. Taxpayer may engage in one business, in more than one business, or in no business.[47]

¶ 1779   Transactions for profit defined.

A transaction is entered into for profit if taxpayer intends to receive income from it overall. For a transaction involving property, taxpayer must intend to receive income from it or to profit from disposing of it.[48]

Profit must be the primary motive, not merely incidental. A loss deduction is possible where a secondary nonprofit motive exists, as long as the profit motive predominates.[49]

An activity is presumed to be engaged in for profit for a tax year if it shows a profit for any three or more out of five consecutive years ending in that tax year (or two out of seven years, for breeding, showing or racing of horses). (Code Sec. 183(d); Reg § 1.183-1(c))[50] A taxpayer who hasn't engaged in an activity for more than five years (seven, for horse breeding, etc.) can elect (on Form 5213) to postpone the determination as to whether these presumptions apply until the close of the fourth tax year (sixth, for horse breeding, etc.) after the tax year taxpayer first engages in the activity. (Code Sec. 183(e); Reg § 12.9)[1]

Whether the activities of an S corporation are "engaged in for profit" is determined at the entity level (Reg § 1.183-1(f)), as it is for partnerships.[2]

---

38. ¶M-1401; TD ¶363,001
39. ¶M-1408; ¶1654.304; TD ¶363,008
40. ¶M-1401; TD ¶363,001
41. ¶M-1501; ¶s 1654, 1654.060 *et seq.*; TD ¶421,000
42. ¶M-1510; ¶s 1654, 1654.060 *et seq.*; TD ¶421,000
43. ¶s M-1600, M-2100; ¶1654.300 *et seq.*, ¶1654.350 *et seq.*; TD ¶421,000
44. ¶M-1500; ¶1654; TD ¶361,508
45. ¶M-1524, C-2215, C-7214; TD ¶361,508
46. ¶M-1420; ¶s 1654.061, 1654.430; TD ¶363,020
47. ¶L-1100 *et seq.*; ¶1654.060 *et seq.*; TD ¶256,001
48. ¶M-1510; ¶1654.062; TD ¶422,005
49. ¶M-1512; ¶1654.062; TD ¶422,024
50. ¶M-5818; ¶1834.02; TD ¶422,017
1. ¶M-5821; ¶1834.02; TD ¶422,020
2. ¶M-5802; TD ¶422,002

¶ 1780 Hobby (not-for-profit) losses.

For individuals, partnerships, estates, trusts and S corporations, deductions attributable to an activity not engaged in for profit (¶1779) (Code Sec. 183(a); Reg § 1.183-1(a))[3] are allowed only as follows:

(1) The full amount of deductions (e.g., state and local property taxes) otherwise allowable for the tax year without regard to whether the activity is engaged in for profit (Code Sec. 183(b)(1); Reg § 1.183-1(b)(1)(i))—referred to as Category 1 deductions.

(2) Amounts allowable as deductions only if the activity were engaged in for profit, but only if the allowance *doesn't* result in a basis adjustment, *and only* to the extent the gross income from the activity exceeds the deductions in (1), above (Code Sec. 183(b)(2); Reg § 1.183-1(b)(1)(ii))—Category 2 deductions.

(3) Amounts allowable as deductions only if the activity were engaged in for profit, that if allowed *would* result in a basis adjustment (e.g., depreciation), *but only* to the extent the gross income from the activity exceeds deductions allowed or allowable under (1) and (2) (Code Sec. 183(b)(2); Reg § 1.183-1(b)(1)(iii), Reg § 1.183-1(b)(3))—Category 3 deductions.[4]

In other words, deductions attributable to the "not for profit" activity are allowed to the extent of income from it, or for the full amount of related deductions allowable regardless of profit-seeking, *whichever is larger.*[5]

But, the deductions allowable under these rules are subject to the 2%-of-AGI floor (¶3110) on miscellaneous itemized deductions. (Reg § 1.67-1T(a)(1)(iv))[6]

¶ 1781 Vacation home expenses.

Where an individual, trust, estate, partnership or S corporation owns a vacation home or a dwelling unit (below) and uses it for both personal and rental purposes, deduction of expenses is limited (Code Sec. 280A(a)),[7] except for those expenses which are deductible without regard to business use of the property—e.g., mortgage interest, property taxes and casualty losses. (Code Sec. 280A(b))[8]

The owner's personal use of the home (or portion of it) for even one day in the tax year triggers these "vacation home" limits. (Code Sec. 280A(e)(1))[9]

For any tax year in which the owner uses the (rented) vacation home or other dwelling unit for personal purposes, or rents it out for less than a fair rental, the owner's deduction for maintenance, utilities, depreciation, etc., can't exceed the percentage of those total expenses for the year "attributable" to the rental period. (Code Sec. 280A(e)(1))[10] If a taxpayer who rents out a dwelling unit also uses it as a residence (see below), the deductions attributable to rental use are *further* limited to no more than the gross income derived from rental use for that year, *minus* the sum of (1) the deductions allocable to rental use that are allowable whether or not the unit (or portion of it) was used for rental (e.g., interest and taxes), and (2) deductions allocable to the business or rental activity but which aren't allocable to the use of the home itself. Excess rental expenses may be carried forward to later years. (Code Sec. 280A(c)(5))[11]

The proper ratio for allocating interest and taxes to the rental period is: (1) number of days for which the property is rented, to (2) number of days of total use (according to IRS, but not according to some courts: they would use "number of days in the year").[12]

3. ¶M-5802; ¶1834 *et seq.*; TD ¶422,001
4. ¶M-5804 *et seq.*; ¶1834; TD ¶422,001 *et seq.*
5. ¶M-5804; ¶1834; TD ¶422,001
6. ¶A-2710; ¶674; TD ¶422,003
7. ¶M-6001 *et seq.*; ¶280A4; TD ¶423,001 *et seq.*
8. ¶M-6001; ¶280A4; TD ¶423,001
9. ¶M-6005; ¶280A4; TD ¶423,021
10. ¶M-6005, ¶M-6028 *et seq.*; ¶280A4.060 *et seq.*, ¶280A4.072; TD ¶423,008 *et seq.*, TD ¶423,021
11. ¶M-6018, M-6022; ¶280A4.060 *et seq.*; TD ¶423,023, 423,026
12. ¶M-6006; ¶280A4.065; TD ¶423,021

A home is used as a residence in any tax year in which the owner's use of the unit (or a portion of it) for personal purposes exceeds the longer of: (1) 14 days, or (2) 10% of the period of rental use. (Code Sec. 280A(d)(1))[13]

For purposes of applying the rules limiting rent-related deductions for a dwelling unit used as a residence, personal-use days don't include days the taxpayer used a dwelling unit as his principal residence (1) before or after a rental (or attempted rental) period of 12 or more consecutive months beginning or ending in the tax year, or (2) before a consecutive rental (or attempted rental) period of less than 12 months beginning in the tax year, at the end of which the residence is sold or exchanged. A fair rental rate must be charged. (Code Sec. 280A(d)(4))[14]

If a home is rented for less than 15 days a year, the owner can't deduct *any* of the rental expenses, but isn't taxed on any of the rental income. (Code Sec. 280A(g))[15]

¶ 1782 Worthless stock or securities.

A taxpayer may deduct a loss from worthlessness of stock or other securities (i.e., a bond, debenture, note, certificate or other evidence of indebtedness issued by a corporation or a government (or its political subdivision) with interest coupons or in registered form). (Code Sec. 165(a), Code Sec. 165(g)(1))[16]

Taxpayer must show that the security had value at the end of the year preceding the deduction year and that an identifiable event caused a loss in the deduction year.[17]

The amount of the loss is, to extent not compensated for (e.g., by insurance), the security's adjusted basis for determining loss on sale (¶ 2474). (Code Sec. 165(b); Reg § 1.165-1(c))[18]

The deduction is a capital loss if the security is a capital asset to taxpayer. (Code Sec. 165(g)(1)) Similarly, a loss from an abandoned security that is a capital asset is treated as a loss from the sale or exchange a capital asset on the last day of the tax year. (Reg § 1.165-5(i))[19]

An ordinary loss deduction is allowed if the security is:

. . . not a capital asset (Reg § 1.165-5(b));

. . . Code Sec. 1244 stock (¶ 2644 *et seq.*);

. . . for corporate taxpayers, stock in an "affiliated" corporation (at least 80%-owned by taxpayer), where more than 90% of the affiliate's gross receipts has been from sources other than passive income (royalties, dividends, etc.). (Code Sec. 165(g)(3))[20]

IRS says that a parent corporation is allowed an ordinary loss under these rules where its sub was an operating company (as opposed to an investment or holding company) that had no gross receipts during its existence.[21]

Certain losses by, or on stock of, small business investment companies also are ordinary losses. (Code Sec. 1242, Code Sec. 1243)[22]

Total worthlessness of the security is required for the deduction. No loss deduction is allowed for partial worthlessness or (except for dealers who inventory securities[23]) for mere decline in value. (Reg § 1.165-4, Reg § 1.165-5)[24]

A parent corporation can claim a worthless stock deduction on a merger of its subsidiary into the parent.[25]

No loss deduction is allowed on a shareholder's surrender of stock to the corporation,

---

13. ¶M-6024; ¶280A4.062, 280A4.064; TD ¶423,007
14. ¶M-6038; ¶280A4.067; TD ¶423,027
15. ¶M-6023; ¶280A4.064; TD ¶423,020
16. ¶M-3301; ¶1654.200 *et seq.*; TD ¶372,001
17. ¶M-3300 *et seq.*, ¶M-3400 *et seq.*; ¶1654.210; TD ¶372,010
18. ¶M-3305; ¶1654.205; TD ¶372,004
19. ¶M-3301; ¶1654.200; TD ¶372,001

20. ¶M-3310 *et seq.*; ¶1654.203; TD ¶372,021
21. ¶M-3313
22. ¶M-3308; ¶1654.203; TD ¶372,006
23. ¶G-5021; TD ¶228,718.1
24. ¶M-3304; ¶1654.200 *et seq.*; TD ¶372,009 *et seq.*
25. ¶M-3310

whether or not the surrender is pro rata. Instead, the shareholder's basis for stock surrendered is added to his basis for stock retained.[26]

¶ 1783 Limits on "tax-exempt use losses."

For leases entered into (and in the case of property treated as tax-exempt use property other than by reason of a lease, for property acquired) after Mar. 12, 2004,[27] a "tax-exempt-use loss" for any tax year isn't allowed. (Code Sec. 470(a)) (For exceptions, see below.)[28]

A tax-exempt use loss is the amount by which the total deductions allocable to a "tax-exempt use property" exceed the total income from the property, for the tax year. (Code Sec. 470(c)(1)) Tax-exempt use property is Code Sec. 168(h) property (generally, property subject to leases, or certain other arrangements, involving governments, tax-exempts, or foreign persons or entities), with certain modifications. However, property that would be treated as tax-exempt use property solely by reason of Code Sec. 168(h)(6) (dealing with property owned by partnerships and pass-through entities) is excepted from being tax-exempt use property. (Code Sec. 470(c)(2))[29]

A tax-exempt use loss in excess of gross income may be carried forward to the next tax year, subject to that year's limit. (Code Sec. 470(b)) A special loss carryforward limit applies for "former tax-exempt use property." (Code Sec. 470(e)(1))[30]

If, during the tax year, a taxpayer disposes of its entire interest in tax-exempt use property (or former tax-exempt use property), rules similar to the Code Sec. 469(g) disallowed passive activity loss and credit rules (¶1839) apply. (Code Sec. 470(e)(2))[31]

The limit on "tax-exempt use losses" doesn't apply to any lease (an "excepted lease") which meets the requirements of Code Sec. 470(d).[32]

¶ 1784 Demolition losses.

Except as noted below, no deduction is allowed to the owner or lessee of a building for any loss on demolition of the building, or for any of the demolition expenses. (Code Sec. 280B(1)) The loss or expenses must be capitalized and added to the basis of the land. (Code Sec. 280B(2))[33] However, taxpayers can deduct the cost of demolition of structures on business-related real property damaged or destroyed as a result of a federally declared disaster occurring after Dec. 31, 2007, and before Jan. 1, 2012. (Code Sec. 198A)[34] And the Tax Court held that a loss sustained before a building's demolition as a result of its abnormal retirement from a taxpayer's business because of a casualty to or an extraordinary obsolescence of the building isn't treated as sustained on account of the demolition.[35]

¶ 1785 Abandonment loss.

A loss deduction is allowed for loss of usefulness or for obsolescence of nondepreciable property, both tangible and intangible (e.g., land, a contract), if: (1) the loss is incurred in business or a transaction entered into for profit; (2) it arises from the sudden termination of usefulness in the business or transaction; and (3) the property is permanently discarded from use, or the business or transaction is discontinued. (Reg § 1.165-2) The taxpayer must be able to establish specifically which property has been abandoned.[36]

The loss is an ordinary loss not subject to capital loss limitations. (Reg § 1.165-2(b))[37] The loss can't exceed the adjusted basis of the property for determining loss on a disposition (¶

26. ¶M-3501; TD ¶373,001
27. ¶L-6901; ¶4704; TD ¶261,202
28. ¶L-6901 et seq.; ¶4704; TD ¶261,201 et seq.
29. ¶L-6901 et seq.; ¶4704; TD ¶261,201 et seq.
30. ¶L-6902, ¶L-6903; ¶4704; TD ¶261,202; 261,203
31. ¶L-6904; ¶4704; TD ¶261,204

32. ¶L-6906 et seq.; ¶4704; TD ¶261,206 et seq.
33. ¶M-2200 et seq.; ¶s 1654.180, 280B4; TD ¶376,019
34. ¶L-5801 et seq. ; ¶198A4.01; TD ¶256,213
35. ¶M-2201; ¶s 1654.180, 280B4; TD ¶376,019
36. ¶M-2301; ¶1654.150 et seq.; TD ¶376,001
37. ¶M-2353; TD ¶376,005

2474). (Reg § 1.165-1(c))[38] For the loss on an abandoned security, see ¶1782.

For losses on mortgaged property, see ¶1788 and ¶1789.

¶ 1786 Costs of unsuccessful investigation of proposed venture.

A corporation that pays or incurs expenses in *unsuccessfully* searching for or investigating a new venture may deduct those costs as a business loss, when it abandons the search or investigation (see ¶1504). But for a noncorporate taxpayer, these expenses are personal and nondeductible.[39] For expenses of a *successful* investigation, see ¶ 1500 *et seq.*

¶ 1787 Gambling losses.

A taxpayer may deduct gambling losses suffered in the tax year, but only to the extent of that year's gambling gains. (Code Sec. 165(d); Reg § 1.165-10) "Gains" include "comps" (complimentary goods and services taxpayer receives from a casino). Losses from one kind of gambling (e.g., horse bets) are deductible against gains from another kind (e.g., keno).[40] Individuals not engaged in the gambling business deduct gambling losses (to extent of gambling gains) only as miscellaneous itemized deductions (but not subject to the 2%-of-AGI floor),[41] and must report gambling gains even if they are exceeded by gambling losses.[42]

¶ 1788 Mortgagee's loss (or gain) on mortgaged property.

The mortgagee (mortgage lender) treats a loss on mortgaged property as follows:

A loss on *compromise or settlement* of the debt of an insolvent debtor is treated as a bad debt (¶1851 *et seq.*).[43]

A lender to whom mortgaged or pledged property is surrendered has a bad debt deduction if the fair market value (FMV) of the property received is less than the debt. (The mortgagee has a gain if the FMV of the surrendered property is greater than the debt's basis.)[44] For where the surrender is a repossession by the seller, see ¶ 2467.

A loss on a *mortgage foreclosure* is treated as a bad debt (see ¶1851) equal to the sum of: (1) the excess of the debt's basis over the net proceeds from the property foreclosure; (2) accrued interest previously reported as income; plus (3) legal and other expenses. This is true whether the price is paid by the mortgagee (by applying the debt to the price) or someone else. (Reg § 1.166-6(a))[45]

A mortgagee that bids on the property at the foreclosure sale *also* realizes a loss to the extent the debt applied to the bid exceeds the property's FMV. He realizes a taxable gain to the extent FMV exceeds the amount of the debt so applied. FMV is assumed to equal the bid price, absent convincing proof to the contrary. (Reg § 1.166-6(b))[46]

¶ 1789 Owner's loss on foreclosure, surrender or abandonment of mortgaged property.

The owner of mortgaged property, whether or not he's the mortgagor and whether or not he's personally liable for the mortgage debt, realizes a loss (occasionally a gain) on foreclosure of the mortgage or surrender of the property. The foreclosure (or surrender) is considered a sale or exchange.[47] The owner-borrower's gain or loss is the difference between adjusted basis of the transferred property and the amount realized. If the owner-borrower isn't personally liable for repaying the debt secured by the transferred property, the amount realized includes the full amount of the debt canceled by the transfer. If the borrower is personally liable, the

38. ¶M-2351; TD ¶376,004
39. ¶L-5018 *et seq.*; TD ¶301,013
40. ¶M-6100 *et seq.*; ¶s 1654.500, 1654.501; TD ¶424,001
41. ¶M-6105; TD ¶424,003
42. ¶J-1651; TD ¶197,001
43. ¶M-3709; ¶1664.350 *et seq.*; TD ¶371,021
44. ¶M-3710; ¶1664.353; TD ¶371,022
45. ¶M-3701; ¶1664.353 *et seq.*; TD ¶371,016
46. ¶M-3704; ¶1664.352; TD ¶371,019
47. ¶M-3801; ¶1654.451; TD ¶371,001

amount realized doesn't include any cancellation of debt income (¶1390) arising from the debt. But if the FMV of the property is less than the canceled debt, the amount realized includes canceled debt up to the FMV.[48]

Abandonment is generally treated as a sale or exchange.[49] For tax sales, see ¶1790.

¶ 1790   Loss on tax sale.

The tax treatment of an owner whose property is sold for delinquent taxes is similar to that for foreclosure (¶1789). The tax sale is a sale or exchange.[50]

¶ 1791   When to deduct loss.

A loss is deductible only for the tax year it's sustained. (Code Sec. 165(a)) This is the year the loss occurs, as evidenced by closed and completed transactions and as fixed by identifiable events in that year. (Reg § 1.165-1(d))[1] For casualty or theft losses, see ¶1798 and ¶1802.

¶ 1792   Deducting reimbursable losses.

If taxpayer has a claim for reimbursement on which there's a reasonable prospect of recovery, that "reimbursable" loss can't be deducted until it's reasonably certain the reimbursement will or won't be made. This may be ascertained by, among other things, settlement, adjudication or abandonment of the claim. (Code Sec. 165(a); Reg § 1.165-1(d))[2]

¶ 1793   Casualty, Disaster, and Theft Losses.

Losses from fire, storm, auto accident or other casualty, and losses from theft, are deductible, regardless of whether the loss is sustained in a business or for-profit transaction. An early deduction for disaster losses is available. An individual can elect to treat a loss on a frozen bank deposit as a casualty or theft loss.

¶ 1794   Casualty losses—Form 4684.

A deduction is allowed (report on Form 4684) for losses arising from a casualty (¶1795; for amount, see ¶1796) where taxpayer actually sustains a loss *and* the loss is on *property*. (Code Sec. 165(c)(3)) The property must suffer physical damage and not just a decline in value, even if that decline results from being in or near an area where casualties have occurred and might occur again.[3]

¶ 1795   "Casualty" defined.

A casualty is the complete or partial destruction of property resulting from an identifiable event of a sudden, unexpected or unusual nature such as a fire, storm, shipwreck, car crash, or similar event. Progressive deterioration from a steadily operating cause isn't a casualty.[4]

¶ 1796   Amount of casualty loss.

The amount treated as a loss from a casualty depends on whether taxpayer held the property for personal or for business purposes, as follows:

For property held for personal use, the amount of the casualty loss is the *lesser* of: (1) the property's adjusted basis (i.e., its basis for determining loss on disposition, see ¶2474), or (2) its decline in value (i.e., its fair market value (FMV) immediately before the casualty *minus* its FMV immediately afterward). This applies whether the property is totally destroyed or

48. ¶M-3803; TD ¶371,001, 371,006
49. ¶M-3808; ¶1654.155; TD ¶371,003
50. ¶M-3806; ¶1654.155, 1654.451; TD ¶371,001
1. ¶M-1301; ¶s 1654.090, 1654.111; TD ¶362,001

2. ¶M-2136; ¶1654.304; TD ¶362,001
3. ¶M-1601, ¶M-2132; ¶1654.300 *et seq.*; TD ¶366,000; 366,001
4. ¶M-1701; ¶1654.301; TD ¶366,008

merely damaged. (Reg § 1.165-7(b)) The loss is reduced for any salvage value, insurance or other compensation received (¶1797). (Reg § 1.165-1(c)(4))[5]

For property used in business or held for the production of income, the amount of the casualty loss is determined under the same rules as for personal-use property (above), except that if the property is *totally* destroyed, the amount of the loss is the property's adjusted basis in all cases. (Reg § 1.165-7(b)(1))[6]

The decline in a property's value should be ascertained by competent appraisal where possible.[7]

Costs of repairing, replacing, or cleaning up property after a casualty can be used to measure the amount of the loss (decline in value) if: the repair, etc., is necessary to restore the property to its pre-casualty condition; the amount spent isn't excessive; the repairs do no more than take care of the damage suffered; and the post-repair value is no greater than the pre-casualty value. (Reg § 1.165-7(a)(2))[8]

Except for individuals' casualty losses on personal-use property, the amount of a casualty loss, as determined above, is deductible in full. See ¶1775 *et seq.* A taxpayer may deduct a casualty loss on property not used in business or held for production of income only to the extent that: (1) the casualty loss exceeds $100 ("$100 floor"), and (2) all of taxpayer's casualty losses for the tax year exceed 10% of AGI for the year ("10%-of-AGI limit") (Code Sec. 165(h)),[9] as described below. For exceptions to the $100 floor and the 10%-of-AGI limit for losses incurred in a disaster, see below.

Corrosive drywall. For original and amended returns filed after Sept. 29, 2010, IRS is allowing individuals with corrosive drywall to apply a safe harbor formula to treat the costs of repairing the defective drywall as a casualty loss. In the case of any individual who pays to repair damage to his personal residence or household appliances that results from corrosive drywall, IRS won't challenge his treatment of damage resulting from corrosive drywall as a casualty loss if it is reported under the safe harbor rule. A taxpayer who does not have a pending claim for reimbursement may claim as a loss all unreimbursed amounts paid during the tax year to repair damage to his personal residence and household appliances resulting from corrosive drywall. A taxpayer who has a pending claim (or intends to pursue reimbursement) may claim a loss for 75% of the unreimbursed amount paid during the tax year to repair damage to the taxpayer's personal residence and household appliances that resulted from corrosive drywall.

$500/$100 floor. Each personal-use property casualty is subject to a separate $100 floor ($500 floor in 2009 only) to determine the extent it's deductible. But events closely related in origin give rise to a single casualty. Thus, one storm's damage to taxpayer's house and car is a single casualty, so only the total damage has to exceed $100 to be deductible. (Code Sec. 165(h)(1); Reg § 1.165-7(b)(4)(ii))[10] A single $100 floor applies where one casualty causes loss to joint filers, whether the loss is to property jointly or separately owned. But separate $100 floors apply to each spouse if they file separately, even if the property is jointly owned. (Code Sec. 165(h)(4)(B); Reg § 1.165-7(b)(4)(iii))[11]

10%-of-AGI floor. In addition to (and after applying) the $100 per casualty "floor" (above), personal-use property casualties are then subject to this other limit: If personal casualty losses for a tax year exceed personal casualty gains for that tax year, taxpayer may deduct those losses for that year, but only to the extent of the sum of:

(1) the amount of the personal casualty gains for the year, plus

(2) the amount by which (a) the excess of personal casualty losses over gains ((1) above), exceeds (b) 10% of taxpayer's adjusted gross income (AGI, ¶3102) (computed without regard

---

5. ¶M-1801 *et seq.*; ¶1654.304; TD ¶368,001
6. ¶M-1802; ¶1654.304; TD ¶368,001
7. ¶M-1809; ¶1654.304; TD ¶368,008
8. ¶M-1815; ¶1654.304; TD ¶368,013

9. ¶M-1900 *et seq.*; ¶1654.304; TD ¶368,501
10. ¶M-1901, ¶M-1902; ¶1654.304; TD ¶368,502; 368,503
11. ¶M-1904 *et seq.*; ¶1654.304; TD ¶368,506

to casualty gains). (Code Sec. 165(h)(2)(A))[12]

In determining a taxpayer's personal casualty gains and losses, the amount of any recognized loss is subject to the $100 floor (see above) before netting. (Code Sec. 165(h)(3)(B))[13]

If the personal casualty losses for a tax year exceed the personal casualty gains for that year, the deduction for personal casualty losses is allowable in computing AGI, to the extent of those gains. (Code Sec. 165(h)(4)(A))[14]

If the personal casualty gains for any tax year exceed the personal casualty losses for that year, all these gains and losses are treated as capital gains and losses (Code Sec. 165(h)(2)(B)) not subject to the 10% floor.[15]

Where property is held for both business (or profit) and personal purposes (e.g., a home office, ¶1635), these limits apply only to the personal part of the loss. (Reg § 1.165-7(b)(4)(iv))[16]

The 10%-of-AGI limit is waived for federally declared disasters for tax years beginning in 2009. (Code Sec. 165(h)(3)(A))[17] For a tax year in which an individual has a net disaster loss (with regard to disasters declared in tax years beginning after 2007), his losses are allowed to the extent of the sum of: (1) the amount of the personal casualty gains for the tax year, plus (2) the net disaster loss, plus (3) so much of the excess of personal casualty losses over personal casualty gains, reduced by the net disaster loss, as exceeds 10% of the individual's AGI. (Code Sec. 165(h)(3)(A)) The net disaster loss is the excess of the personal casualty losses attributable to a federally declared disaster occurring before Jan. 1, 2010 in a disaster area, over personal casualty gains. (Code Sec. 165(h)(3)(B))

caution: Check http://ria.thomsonreuters.com/federaltaxhandbook to see if the provisions discussed above have been extended.

¶ 1797   Insurance or other compensation for casualty loss.

The casualty loss deduction isn't allowed to the extent the loss is compensated by insurance or otherwise (see ¶1796). (Code Sec. 165(a)) But, costs incurred in collecting the compensation reduce the recovery so as to increase the loss deduction.[18]

Where an individual's casualty and theft losses aren't attributable to a business or for-profit transaction, a loss covered by insurance is taken into account only if taxpayer files a timely insurance claim. (Code Sec. 165(h)(5)(E)) But, this limit applies only to the extent the insurance policy would have provided reimbursement had the claim been filed.[19]

Compensation includes property insurance, damage recoveries, debt forgiveness, cash or property received from taxpayer's employer or from disaster relief agencies to rehabilitate the property (e.g., qualified disaster relief payments, see ¶1207), and condemnation awards. Compensation doesn't include disaster relief such as food, medical supplies, and other forms of assistance, unless they are replacements for lost or destroyed property. Nor does it include use and occupancy insurance reimbursements for lost business profits.[20]

A casualty loss to inventory is automatically reflected in cost of goods sold (¶2869). It isn't separately deducted as a loss unless adjustments are made to inventory.[21]

12. ¶M-1907, M-1911; ¶1654.304; TD ¶368,508
13. ¶M-1911; ¶1654.304; TD ¶368,512
14. ¶M-1908; TD ¶368,508
15. ¶M-1910; ¶1654.304; TD ¶368,509
16. ¶M-1906, M-1908.1; ¶1654.304, 280A4.044; TD ¶368,507, 368,511

17. ¶M-1907, M-1911; ¶1654.304; TD ¶368,508 *et seq.*
18. ¶M-1408, M-1421; ¶1654.304; TD ¶368,016, 363,019
19. ¶M-1914; ¶1654.304
20. ¶M-1411 *et seq.*; ¶1654.304; TD ¶363,011 *et seq.*
21. ¶M-1808; ¶s 1654.302, 4714.21; TD ¶368,007

¶ 1798 When to deduct casualty losses.

A casualty loss (like other losses, see ¶1782) is considered "sustained" (and deductible) only during the tax year the loss occurs, as fixed by identifiable events occurring in that year. (Code Sec. 165(a); Reg § 1.165-1(d)(1)) A loss may be sustained in the tax year even though repairs or replacements aren't made until a later year. And a loss may be sustained in a year *after* the casualty occurs, as when trees died a year after the year a blizzard damaged them.[22] For election to deduct disaster losses early, see ¶1799.

¶ 1799 Expensing of disaster losses and early deduction election for disaster losses.

A taxpayer may elect to currently deduct any qualified disaster expense (as defined in Code Sec. 198A(b)). A qualified disaster expense is any otherwise capitalizable expenditure paid or incurred in connection with a trade or business or with business-related property that, as a result of a federally declared disaster occurring after 2007 and before 2012, is: (1) for the abatement or control of hazardous substances that were released; (2) for the removal of debris from, or the demolition of structures on, damaged or destroyed real property; or (3) for the repair of damaged business-related property. (Code Sec. 198A(a))[23]

A taxpayer may *elect* to deduct a disaster loss (defined below) for the tax year *before* the year the loss occurred, instead of for the year the loss occurred (¶1798). (Code Sec. 165(i))[24]

> ✪*observation:* Claiming a disaster loss on the earlier year's return can save taxes immediately, without waiting until the end of the year the loss was sustained. In some cases, it may result in a net operating loss that will bring a refund through a carryback to an earlier year (¶4852). But deduction for the later loss year may save taxes where taxpayer expects to be in a higher bracket that year. Those weighing the value of an early disaster loss deduction also must consider the relative amounts of AGI they have or expect to have for the current and earlier tax years, and any other casualty losses incurred in those years.

Individuals who incur a disaster loss with respect to nonbusiness property are subject to the regular $100 floor, but the 10%-of-AGI limit was waived for federally declared disasters in 2009, see ¶1796. (Code Sec. 165(i))[25]

A disaster loss is a loss that's attributable to a disaster occurring in a disaster area and attributable to a federally declared disaster. (Code Sec. 165(i)(1))[26] Also, the loss must be *otherwise* deductible as a loss. (Reg § 1.165-11(b)(3)) A taxpayer whose residence is located in a disaster area may deduct any loss attributable to the disaster as a casualty loss if the residence is rendered unsafe by the disaster, and he is ordered (within 120 days after the disaster designation) by the state or local government to demolish or relocate the residence. (Code Sec. 165(k))[27] A non-casualty loss may be a disaster loss if incurred in the course of a trade or business or profit-seeking transaction. For example, a farmer might deduct a loss from a drought disaster, even though loss from drought is ordinarily not deductible as a casualty loss.[28]

The early deduction is elected on the return (original or amended) for the previous year, or on a refund claim. Elect by the later of: (1) the due date for the disaster year return (without regard to extensions), or (2) the due date for the previous year return *with* permitted extensions. Once made, the election becomes irrevocable after 90 days. (Reg § 1.165-11(e))[29]

For involuntary conversion of a principal residence damaged in a Federally-declared disaster, see ¶2433.

---

22. ¶M-1610; ¶1654.111; TD ¶366,066
23. ¶L-5801 *et seq.*; ¶198A4.01; TD ¶256,213
24. ¶M-2001; ¶1654.520; TD ¶369,002
25. ¶M-2009; ¶1654.304; TD ¶369,012

26. ¶M-2002; ¶1654.520; TD ¶369,001
27. ¶M-2010; ¶1654.302; TD ¶369,008
28. ¶M-2004; ¶1654.520; TD ¶369,009
29. ¶M-2011 *et seq.*; ¶1654.520; TD ¶369,003 *et seq.*

¶ 1800 Theft losses—Form 4684.

Theft losses (reported on Form 4684) are deductible (for amount, see ¶1801) under rules that closely follow those for casualty losses, including the $100/10%-of-AGI floors (¶1794 *et seq.*). (Code Sec. 165(a), Code Sec. 165(h)(1), Code Sec. 165(h)(2)) A theft is the unlawful taking and removing of money or property with the intent to deprive the owner of it, and includes larceny, robbery, embezzlement (Reg § 1.165-8(d)), burglary, extortion, kidnapping for ransom, blackmail and false representation.[30]

A theft loss deduction is not allowed for the decline in market value of stock purchased on the open market, where the decline is caused by the disclosure of accounting fraud or other illegal conduct on the part of officers or directors of the corporation that issued the stock.[31]

A taking by a person known to have a claim to the property (e.g., spouse, joint owner) isn't a theft unless there's evidence of criminal intent.[32]

Taxpayers who have lost money in Madoff-style schemes can claim the losses as ordinary losses.[33] They can treat net operating losses generated by those schemes as sole proprietorship losses potentially eligible to be carried back 3, 4, or 5 years.[34]

¶ 1801 Amount of theft loss.

For theft of business or investment property, the *deductible loss* is the adjusted basis of the property minus insurance or other compensation received or recoverable (¶1797). (Reg § 1.165-8(c))[35]

For theft of personal-use property, the *loss* is: (1) the lesser of the property's fair market value (FMV) immediately before theft or its adjusted basis, reduced by (2) insurance or other compensation received or recoverable. (Reg § 1.165-8(c)) The $100/10%-of-AGI floors (¶1796) are then applied to determine the amount of the loss that is *deductible*. (Code Sec. 165(c)(3))[36]

If stolen personal-use property is recovered in the deduction year, the loss is the lesser of: (1) the property's adjusted basis, or (2) the decline in its FMV between theft and recovery. If it's recovered after the deduction year, the excess of the earlier deduction over the loss determined as above is included in income (under the tax benefit rule, see ¶1205), to the extent the earlier loss deduction decreased taxpayer's tax.[37]

¶ 1802 When to deduct theft loss.

A theft loss (¶1800) is deductible in the year the loss is *discovered,* regardless of when the theft actually occurred. But the deduction is postponed to the extent taxpayer, in the year of discovery, had a reimbursement claim on which there was a reasonable prospect of recovery. (Code Sec. 165(e); Reg § 1.165-8(a))[38]

¶ 1803 Elections to treat frozen bank deposits as losses from casualty or from transaction entered into for profit.

If a "qualified individual" (other than the institution's officers, 1% owners, or those related to either)[39]) has a loss on a deposit in a bankrupt or insolvent qualified financial institution, and that loss may be reasonably estimated, the loss may be treated, at taxpayer's election: (10 as a casualty or theft loss (¶1794, ¶1800) instead of as a nonbusiness bad debt (¶1857) (Code Sec. 165(l)(1)),[40] or (2) as an ordinary loss incurred in a transaction entered into for

30. ¶M-2100 *et seq.*; ¶1654.351 *et seq.*; TD ¶367,001
31. ¶M-2111; ¶1654.351; TD ¶367,009
32. ¶M-2104; TD ¶367,003
33. ¶M-2108.1; ¶1654.350;TD ¶367,006.1
34. ¶M-4357; TD ¶356,025
35. ¶M-2125; ¶1654.370; TD ¶367,023
36. ¶M-2126; ¶1654.370; TD ¶367,025
37. ¶M-2129; TD ¶367,027
38. ¶M-2132; ¶1654.380; TD ¶367,036
39. ¶M-1762; ¶1654.530; TD ¶366,073
40. ¶M-1761; ¶1654.530; TD ¶366,071

profit, up to $20,000 ($10,000 for marrieds filing separately) of loss. (Code Sec. 165(l)(5))[41]

Elect by claiming the loss (casualty or ordinary) on the return (or timely amended return) for the tax year in which a reasonable estimate of the loss can be made.[42]

¶ 1804　At-Risk Limitations.

For certain taxpayers, deductions from specified leveraged investment activities are limited to the aggregate amount the taxpayer-investor has "at risk."

¶ 1805　Taxpayers subject to "at-risk" rules.

The at-risk rules (¶1807) apply to: (1) individuals, (2) C corporations but only if more than 50% in value of the corporation's stock is owned by not more than five individuals at any time during the last half of its tax year (Code Sec. 465(a)(1)),[43] and (3) estates and trusts.[44] But even if the stock ownership test is met, the at-risk rules *don't apply* to:

. . . certain active businesses ("qualifying businesses") carried on by a qualified C corporation (i.e., *not* a personal holding company, or personal service corporation determined by substituting 5% for 10% in Code Sec. 269A(b)(2)), (Code Sec. 465(c)(7))[45] or

. . . the activity of equipment leasing. (Code Sec. 465(c)(4))[46]

⬤ *observation:* Even though the at-risk rules don't apply to pass-through entities such as S corporations and partnerships, they *do* apply to determine whether a person with an interest in any of those entities may deduct items of loss, etc., passed through.

¶ 1806　"At-risk" activities.

The at-risk rules (¶1807) apply to:

. . . certain specified activities: (1) holding, producing or distributing motion pictures or video tapes, (2) farming, (3) equipment leasing, (4) exploring for, or exploiting, oil and gas resources, (5) exploring for, or exploiting, geothermal resources; (Code Sec. 465(c)(1)) and

. . . a "catch-all" group of activities that taxpayer engages in, in carrying on a trade or business or in the production of income, other than those above (Code Sec. 465(c)(3)),[47] e.g., real estate activities (see ¶1810).

In applying the at-risk rules to the specified activities, taxpayer's activity with respect to each property (e.g., each film in (1), above) is treated as a separate activity. (Code Sec. 465(c)(2)(A)) Activities in the "catch-all" group are treated as one activity ("aggregated") if either: (A) taxpayer actively participates in the management of the trade or business, or (B) the trade or business is carried on by a partnership or S corporation *and* 65% or more of the losses for the tax year is allocable to persons who actively participate in its management. (Code Sec. 465(c)(3)(B))[48]

¶ 1807　How the at-risk rules work—Form 6198.

For a taxpayer (¶1805) engaged in an at-risk activity (¶1806), any loss from the activity for the tax year is deductible in that year only to the extent that taxpayer is at risk (¶1808) with respect to the activity at the end of the year. (Code Sec. 465(a)) The losses so limited are the excess of the deductions allocable to the activity that otherwise would be allowed for the year, over the income (other than recapture, see ¶1809) received or accrued by taxpayer during the year from that same activity. (Code Sec. 465(d))[49]

---

41. ¶M-1765, M-1766; ¶1654.530; TD ¶366,076, 366,077
42. ¶M-1771; ¶1654.530; TD ¶366,072
43. ¶M-4511, M-4515; ¶4654; TD ¶402,001
44. ¶M-4512; TD ¶402,002
45. ¶M-4516 *et seq.*; ¶4654; TD ¶402,006 *et seq.*

46. ¶M-4529; ¶4654; TD ¶403,009
47. ¶M-4521; ¶4654; TD ¶403,001
48. ¶M-4522 *et seq.*; ¶4654; TD ¶403,002
49. ¶M-4502; ¶4654; TD ¶401,001

Any loss thus disallowed is treated as allocable to the same activity in the next tax year, and may be deducted in the later year subject to that year's at-risk limit for the activity. (Code Sec. 465(a)(2)) So, a current year's "loss" may include "suspended" loss accounts from earlier years. (Code Sec. 465(d))[50]

⚠️caution: In addition to the at-risk rules, losses and credits from an activity may also be subject to the passive activity rules, discussed at ¶1811 *et seq.*

Form 6198 is used to compute the deductible loss from an at-risk activity.[1]

For the at-risk rules otherwise applicable to real property, see ¶1810.

¶ 1808   Amounts considered "at risk."

A taxpayer is considered at risk for an activity to the extent of:

(1) the amount of money and the adjusted basis of other property taxpayer contributed to the activity (Code Sec. 465(b)(1)), plus

(2) amounts borrowed with respect to the activity to the extent taxpayer is personally liable for the repayment of or has pledged property, other than property used in the activity, as security for the borrowed amount. The borrowings can't exceed the fair market value of taxpayer's interest in the pledged property. No property is treated as security if it is directly or indirectly financed by indebtedness secured by property in (1), above. (Code Sec. 465(b)(1), Code Sec. 465(b)(2))[2]

Amounts borrowed "at risk" ((2) above) don't include borrowings from any person who has an interest in the activity other than as a creditor, or from a related person as specially defined. A corporation is at risk with respect to amounts it borrowed from a shareholder. (Code Sec. 465(b)(3))[3]

Any amounts, even equity capital contributed by taxpayer, aren't treated as at risk if the amounts are protected against loss through nonrecourse financing, guarantees, stop loss agreements or similar arrangements. (Code Sec. 465(b)(4))[4]

In determining the amount at risk for any tax year, the amount for that year is reduced by any losses allowed under these limitations in an earlier year. (Code Sec. 465(b)(5))[5]

¶ 1809   Recapture of losses where amount at-risk is less than zero.

If taxpayer's amount at risk (¶1808) is less than zero (e.g., by distributions to taxpayer or by debt changing from recourse to nonrecourse), taxpayer recognizes income to the extent of that negative amount. (Code Sec. 465(e)(1)(A)) But, the amount recaptured is limited to the excess of the losses previously allowed in that activity over any amounts previously recaptured. (Code Sec. 465(e)(2)) The amount added to income under this recapture rule is treated as a deduction allocable to the activity in the first succeeding year, and is allowed if and to the extent taxpayer's at-risk basis is increased. (Code Sec. 465(e)(1)(B))[6]

¶ 1810   At-risk rules for real property.

A taxpayer engaged in the activity of holding real property is subject to the at-risk rules, for losses on property placed in service after '86. The at-risk rules also apply to a taxpayer's losses from real estate attributable to an interest in a pass-through entity that is acquired after '86, regardless of when the entity acquired the real property.[7]

Taxpayer is considered at risk for his share of any "qualified nonrecourse financing"

---

50. ¶M-4502; ¶4564; TD ¶401,006
1. ¶M-4501; ¶4654; TD ¶401,001
2. ¶M-4541 *et seq.*; ¶4654; TD ¶404,001, 404,008
3. ¶M-4557 *et seq.*; ¶4654; TD ¶404,017, 404,018

4. ¶M-4568 *et seq.*; ¶4654; TD ¶404,028
5. ¶M-4507; ¶4654; TD ¶401,007
6. ¶M-4509; ¶4654; TD ¶401,009
7. ¶M-4533; TD ¶403,013

secured by the real property. (Code Sec. 465(b)(6); Reg § 1.465-27(b))[8]

¶ 1811 "Passive Activity" Losses and Credits.

Losses from passive activities—activities in which the taxpayer doesn't materially participate, and most rental activities—may only be used to offset passive activity income (which doesn't include portfolio income); thus they can't be used to offset income from, for example, compensation, interest or dividends. Any losses that are unused in a tax year because of this rule are carried forward to the following year(s) until used, or until the taxpayer disposes of the interest in the activity (or substantially all of the activity) in a taxable transaction. Passive activity credits may be used only to offset tax on income from passive activities, with a carryover of any unused credits. But, individuals who actively participate in rental real estate activities may use up to $25,000 of losses from those activities to offset nonpassive income; and those activities are not automatically passive for real estate professionals.

caution: For passive activity losses for alternative minimum tax purposes, see ¶3210.

¶ 1812 Disallowance of passive activity losses and credits—Form 8582; Form 8582-CR; Form 8810.

A taxpayer specified at ¶1813 may not deduct a passive activity loss (i.e., the excess of aggregate losses from passive activities over aggregate income from those activities, see ¶1815) (Code Sec. 469(a)(1)(A)) or use a passive activity credit (i.e, the excess of specified credits attributable to passive activities over the regular tax liability allocable to those activities) (Code Sec. 469(a)(1)(B)), except with respect to certain rental real estate activities (¶1833 *et seq.*). (Reg § 1.469-1T(a)(2))[9] For carryover of suspended losses and credits, see ¶1838. For deduction of suspended losses on disposition of the activity, see ¶1839.

A passive activity deduction disallowed for a tax year under these rules isn't taken into account as a deduction in computing taxable income (or self-employment income). (Reg § 1.469-1T(d)(3)) And a passive activity deduction that *is* allowed under these rules may still be disallowed under the Code Sec. 613A limit on percentage depletion of oil and gas wells, or the Code Sec. 1211 limit on capital losses. (Reg § 1.469-1(d)(2))[10]

Whether a loss is disallowed under these rules is determined *after* the application of the at-risk rules (¶1804 *et seq.*), and the interest deduction limitations (¶1726 *et seq.*), as well as other provisions measuring taxable income. (Reg § 1.469-2(d)(6), Reg § 1.469-1T(d))[11]

Where taxpayer's disallowed passive activity losses are derived from more than one activity, a ratable portion of the loss (if any) from each passive activity, in general, is disallowed. (Reg § 1.469-1T(f)(2)(i))[12] Any loss so disallowed is then generally allocated ratably among all passive activity deductions (¶1816) from the activity for the year. (Reg § 1.469-1T(f)(2)(ii))[13] If all or any portion of a passive activity credit is disallowed, a ratable portion of each credit from each passive activity, in general, is disallowed. (Reg § 1.469-1T(f)(3)(i))[14]

The passive activity limits are calculated on Form 8582 (individuals, estates, and trusts), Form 8582-CR (credits for individuals, estates, and trusts), or Form 8810 (closely held corporations and personal service corporations).[15]

---

8. ¶M-4534 *et seq.*; ¶4654; TD ¶403,014 *et seq.*
9. ¶M-4600 *et seq.*; ¶4694 *et seq.*; TD ¶411,001 *et seq.*
10. ¶M-4603; ¶4694.47; TD ¶411,002, 411,004
11. ¶M-4603 *et seq.*; ¶4694.30, 4694.31, 4694.47; TD ¶411,004 *et seq.*

12. ¶M-5501; ¶4694.40; TD ¶416,502
13. ¶M-5502; ¶4694.42; TD ¶416,503
14. ¶M-5604; ¶4694.44; TD ¶417,006
15. ¶M-5200; ¶4694, 4694.36; TD ¶411,001

¶ 1813   Who is subject to the passive activity rules?

The passive activity limits (¶1812) apply to any individual, estate, trust (Code Sec. 469(a)(2)(A)) (other than a trust, or portion of a trust, which is a grantor trust) (Reg § 1.469-1T(b)(2)), personal service corporation (PSC) as specially defined (Code Sec. 469(a)(2)(C), Code Sec. 469(j)(2)) and closely held C corporation (except as described at ¶1815 and ¶1816) as specially defined. (Code Sec. 469(a)(2)(B), Code Sec. 469(j)(1))[16] For pass-through entities, see ¶1814.

Spouses filing a joint return are treated as one taxpayer, with certain exceptions. (Reg § 1.469-1T(j)(1))[17]

The passive activity rules don't apply, except as regs may provide, to any corporation that isn't a PSC or a closely held corporation for the tax year. (Reg § 1.469-1T(g)(1))[18] But the rules *do* apply to any of the corporation's losses or credits that arose during a tax year when it *was* a PSC or closely held C corporation. (Code Sec. 469(f)(2))[19]

¶ 1814   Pass-through entities subject to the passive activity rules.

Partnerships (unless publicly traded, see below) and S corporations aren't subject to the passive activity rules (¶1812). (Code Sec. 469(a)(2)) But the rules *do* apply to the losses and credits passed through to the partners and shareholders.[20]

The passive activity rules apply to publicly traded partnerships (PTPs, defined below) that aren't treated as corporations (¶3302). The rules are applied separately with respect to items attributable to each PTP (except in certain situations involving the low-income housing and rehabilitation credits). (Code Sec. 469(k)(1)) A partner's net passive income for a tax year from a PTP can't be offset by losses from other passive activities.[21]

A PTP is a partnership the interests of which are traded on an established securities market (national or local exchange, or an over-the-counter market) or are readily tradable on a secondary market (or the substantial equivalent). (Code Sec. 469(k)(2); Reg § 1.469-10(b))[22]

¶ 1815   Passive activity loss defined.

A passive activity loss for a tax year is the amount, if any, by which the aggregate losses from all passive activities (¶1823) for the tax year exceed the aggregate income from all passive activities for that year—i.e., the excess of "passive activity deductions" (¶1816) over "passive activity gross income" (¶1818) for the year. (Code Sec. 469(d)(1); Reg § 1.469-2T(b)(1))[23]

For a closely held C corporation, the passive activity loss is the excess of passive activity deductions over the sum of passive activity gross income *plus* the corporation's net active (but not portfolio) income for the tax year. (Code Sec. 469(e)(2)(A); Reg § 1.469-1T(g)(4))[24]

For how passive loss characterization affects other Code provisions, see ¶1812.

¶ 1816   What is a passive activity deduction?

A deduction is a "passive activity deduction" for a tax year only if it: (1) arises in connection with the conduct of an activity that is a passive activity for that year (¶1823), or (2) is carried over as a passive activity deduction from an earlier tax year (¶1838). (Reg § 1.469-2T(d)(1))[25]

---

16. ¶M-4700 *et seq.*; ¶4694; TD ¶411,500 *et seq.*
17. ¶M-4702; ¶4694.70; TD ¶411,502
18. ¶M-4705; ¶4694; TD ¶411,504
19. ¶M-4705; TD ¶411,504
20. ¶s M-4709, M-5302; ¶4694.80; TD ¶411,508

21. ¶M-4710; ¶4694.85; TD ¶411,509
22. ¶M-4710; ¶4694.85; TD ¶411,510
23. ¶M-4601; ¶4694; TD ¶411,001
24. ¶M-5507 *et seq.*; ¶4694.36; TD ¶416,509
25. ¶M-5401; ¶4694.30; TD ¶416,001

The character (as a passive activity deduction) of an item allocated to taxpayer by a partnership or S corporation is determined, in any case in which participation is relevant, by taxpayer's participation in the activity that generated the item for the entity's tax year. (Reg § 1.469-2T(e))[26]

For when loss on the sale or other disposition of an interest in property is a passive activity deduction, see ¶1817.

Deductions in excess of a partner's (or shareholder's) basis, or in excess of the at-risk limits, aren't passive activity deductions for the tax year. (Reg § 1.469-2T(d)(6))[27]

¶ 1817 Loss on sale, exchange or other disposition as passive activity deduction.

Passive activity deductions (¶1816) include any loss recognized on the sale, exchange or other disposition of an interest in property used in an activity at the time of disposition, and any deduction allowed on account of the abandonment or worthlessness of the interest, *if and only if* the activity was a passive activity (¶1823) of taxpayer for the tax year of disposition (or other event giving rise to the deduction). (Reg § 1.469-2T(d)(5)(i))[28]

If the interest in property disposed of was used in more than one activity during the 12-month period ending on the date of disposition, the amount realized from the disposition (as well as the adjusted basis of the interest) must be allocated among the activities (with a de minimis exception) on a basis that reasonably reflects those uses. (Reg § 1.469-2(d)(5)(iii), Reg § 1.469-2T(d)(5)(i), Reg § 1.469-2T(d)(5)(ii))[29]

Passive activity deductions don't include: (1) a loss from the disposition of property that produces portfolio income (¶1821) (Reg § 1.469-2T(d)(2)(iv)), or (2) a deduction for a disposition of an entire interest in a passive activity if, under the rules for those dispositions (¶1839), the deduction isn't treated as a passive activity deduction. (Reg § 1.469-2T(d)(2)(v))[30]

¶ 1818 Passive activity gross income.

Passive activity gross income is, in general, gross income from a passive activity (¶1823). (Reg § 1.469-2T(c)(1))[31] The character (as passive activity gross income) of a partner's or S corporation shareholder's allocable items of gross income is determined, in general, by reference to the partner's or shareholder's participation in the activity(ies) that generated the items for the entity's tax year. (Reg § 1.469-2T(e)(1))[32] For when gain on disposition of a property interest is passive activity gross income, see ¶1819.

Passive activity gross income doesn't include portfolio income (¶1821), (Code Sec. 469(e)(1)(A)(i)(I); Reg § 1.469-2T(c)(3)(i)) compensation for personal services (as specially defined), (Code Sec. 469(e)(3); Reg § 1.469-2T(c)(4)) and certain other income, e.g., from intangible property (e.g., a patent) if a taxpayer's personal efforts contributed significantly to the property's creation; a tax refund; or, in some cases, reimbursement of a casualty or theft loss. (Code Sec. 469(c)(3)(B); Reg § 1.469-2(c)(6), Reg § 1.469-2(c)(7))[33]

¶ 1819 Gain on sale, exchange, or other disposition of interest in passive activity.

Gain recognized on the sale, exchange or other disposition of an interest in property generally is treated as passive activity gross income (¶1818) for the year the gain is recognized, if the activity in which the property was used was a passive activity (¶1823) for the year of disposition. (Reg § 1.469-2T(c)(2)(i)(A))[34] But gain from the disposition of an interest in property that is substantially appreciated (fair market value exceeds 120% of adjusted basis) is treated as not from a passive activity unless used in a passive activity for either 20%

---

26. ¶M-5402; ¶4694.80; TD ¶416,005
27. ¶M-4606; ¶4694.30; TD ¶411,007
28. ¶M-5406; ¶4694.32; TD ¶416,004
29. ¶M-5406; ¶4694.32; TD ¶416,004
30. ¶M-5421; ¶4694.31; TD ¶416,018

31. ¶M-5301; ¶4694.21; TD ¶415,001
32. ¶M-5302; ¶4694.80; TD ¶415,019
33. ¶M-5325, ¶M-5332 *et seq.*; ¶4694.22; ¶4694.66; TD ¶415,022,
    TD ¶415,028 *et seq.*
34. ¶M-5304; ¶4694.28; TD ¶415,002

of the period taxpayer held the interest or the entire 24-month period ending on the date of disposition. (Reg § 1.469-2(c)(2)(iii))[35]

For disposition of *entire* interest in (or substantially all of) a passive activity, see ¶1839.

¶ 1820 Disposition of interest in partnership or S corporation.

Where there's a disposition of a partnership interest or S corporation stock, a ratable portion of the net gain (or loss) is treated as gain (or loss) from the disposition of an interest in each trade or business, rental, or investment activity in which the entity owns an interest. (Reg § 1.469-2T(e)(3)(ii)(A))[36] But, gain attributable to certain substantially appreciated property (¶1819) isn't passive activity gross income (¶1818) if that gain exceeds 10% of the gain allocated to the activity. (Reg § 1.469-2T(e)(3)(iii))[37]

¶ 1821 Portfolio income.

Portfolio income (treated as not passive activity gross income, see ¶1818) includes all gross income, *other than* income derived in the ordinary course of a trade or business attributable to :

... interest;

... dividends from a C corporation or an S corporation's accumulated earnings and profits;

... annuities;

... royalties;

... net income from publicly traded partnerships (PTPs, ¶1814);

... income (including dividends) from a RIC (¶4201), REIT (¶4202), REMIC (¶4204), Code Sec. 1381(a) cooperative (¶4205), common trust fund (¶4208), controlled foreign corporation (¶4624) or qualified electing fund (¶4630);

... gain (loss) from the disposition of property that produces portfolio income;

... gain (loss) from the disposition of property held for investment (¶1728) (Code Sec. 469(e)(1)(A); Reg § 1.469-2T(c)(3)(i));

... income, gain or loss from investment of working capital.[38]

¶ 1822 Recharacterization of passive income as nonpassive income.

Certain income is treated as income that *isn't* from a passive activity, i.e., income from: significant participation activities (in which the taxpayer participates for more than 100 hours during the tax year, but doesn't materially participate); rental of nondepreciable property; net interest income from an equity-financed lending activity or certain rental property; and certain royalty income. (Reg § 1.469-2T(f)(1))[39]

¶ 1823 What is a passive activity?

A passive activity is any activity (¶1825) involving the conduct of any trade or business (¶1824) in which taxpayer doesn't materially participate (¶1827). (Code Sec. 469(c)(1)) For rental activities, see ¶1833.

¶ 1824 Trade or business activities under passive activity rules.

A trade or business that can be a passive activity (¶1823) includes any activity:

... in connection with a trade or business (under Code Sec. 162);

35. ¶M-5306; ¶4694.28; TD ¶415,004
36. ¶M-5708; ¶4694.82; TD ¶417,512
37. ¶M-5342; ¶4694.82; TD ¶415,045

38. ¶M-5325 *et seq.*; ¶4694.23; TD ¶415,023
39. ¶M-5335; ¶4694.25; TD ¶415,035

. . . with respect to which expenses are allowable as a deduction under Code Sec. 212 (for the production, etc., of income) (Code Sec. 469(c)(6));[40] and

. . . involving research or experimentation (under the Code Sec. 174 rules for deducting business-related research, etc., expenditures, see ¶1601). (Code Sec. 469(c)(5))[41]

For rules for grouping activities, see ¶1825.

Trade or business activities do not include rental activities (although rental activities generally are treated as passive activities, see ¶1833) or activities that are (under Reg § 1.469-1T(e)(3)(vi)(B)) incidental to an activity of holding property for investment. (Reg § 1.469-1(e)(2), Reg § 1.469-4(b)(1))[42]

¶ 1825 Rules for grouping "activities" for passive activity rule purposes.

A taxpayer may treat one or more trade or business activities (¶1824) or rental activities (¶1833) as a single activity if the activities are an appropriate economic unit for measuring gain or loss for Code Sec. 469 purposes (the "passive activity" rules) (Reg § 1.469-4(c)(1)), based on all the relevant facts and circumstances. (Reg § 1.469-4(c)(2))[43]

A rental activity (as defined in Reg § 1.469-1T(e)(3)) (Reg § 1.469-4(b)(2)) can't be grouped with a trade or business activity unless the activities being grouped together are an appropriate economic unit *and:*

. . . the rental activity is insubstantial in relation to the trade or business activity; or

. . . the trade or business activity is insubstantial in relation to the rental activity; or

. . . each owner of the trade or business activity has the same proportionate ownership interest in the rental activity. In that case the part of the rental activity that involves the rental of items of property for use in the trade or business may be grouped with the trade or business activity. (Reg § 1.469-4(d)(1))[44]

Real property rentals and personal property rentals (other than personal property rentals provided in connection with the real property, or vice versa) can't be grouped together. (Reg § 1.469-4(d)(2))[45]

Once the taxpayer has grouped activities, the taxpayer can't re-group them in later years. If a material change occurs that makes the original grouping clearly inappropriate, the taxpayer must regroup the activities. IRS may regroup activities to prevent tax avoidance. (Reg § 1.469-4(e), Reg § 1.469-4(f))[46] Taxpayers must report to IRS their groupings and regroupings of activities and the addition of specific activities within their existing groupings.[47]

In a year when there's a disposition of substantially all of an activity, taxpayer may under specified conditions treat the part disposed of as a separate activity. (Reg § 1.469-4(g))[48]

¶ 1826 Activities conducted through PSCs, closely-held corporations, S corporations and partnerships.

For purposes of the passive activity rules (¶1811 *et seq.*), a taxpayer's activities include those conducted through personal service corporations (PSCs), closely-held C corporations, S corporations, and partnerships. (Reg § 1.469-4(a))[49]

---

40. ¶M-4801 *et seq.*; ¶s 4694.01, 4694.02; TD ¶412,001 *et seq.*
41. ¶M-4802; ¶4694.02; TD ¶412,002
42. ¶M-4802; ¶4694.02; TD ¶412,002
43. ¶M-4803, M-4804; ¶4694.10; TD ¶412,003, 412,004
44. ¶M-4805; ¶4694.10; TD ¶412,005

45. ¶M-4806; ¶4694.10; TD ¶412,006
46. ¶M-4809; ¶4694.10; TD ¶412,013
47. ¶M-4808.1; TD ¶412,011
48. ¶M-5701.3; ¶4694.50; TD ¶412,001 *et seq.*
49. ¶M-4807.2; ¶4694.10; TD ¶412,009

¶ 1827 What is "material participation"?

A taxpayer materially participates in an activity only if he's involved in the activity's operations on a regular, continuous and substantial basis (¶1828 *et seq.*). (Code Sec. 469(h)) A trust materially participates in an activity if a fiduciary, in his capacity as such, so participates.[50] A closely held C corporation or personal service corporation materially participates, in general, only if one or more of its shareholders who own more than 50% of its stock (by value) themselves materially participate. (Code Sec. 469(h)(4)(A))[1]

¶ 1828 Material participation by individuals.

An individual materially participates in an activity for a tax year *if and only if* the individual meets at least *one* of the following tests:

(1) The individual participates (as defined at ¶1831) in it for more than 500 hours during the year. (Reg § 1.469-5T(a)(1))

(2) The individual's participation in the activity for the tax year is substantially all of the participation in it by all individuals (including nonowner individuals) for the year. (Reg § 1.469-5T(a)(2))

(3) The individual participates in the activity for more than 100 hours during the tax year and that isn't less than that of any other individual (including nonowners) for that year. (Reg § 1.469-5T(a)(3))

(4) The activity is a "significant participation activity" for the tax year, and the individual's aggregate participation in all significant participation activities that year exceeds 500 hours. A "significant participation activity" is a trade or business in which the individual significantly participates (for more than 100 hours), but in which he doesn't otherwise materially participate. (Reg § 1.469-5T(a)(4), Reg § 1.469-5T(c))

(5) The individual materially participated in the activity for any five tax years (consecutive or not) during the 10 immediately preceding tax years. (Reg § 1.469-5T(a)(5))

(6) The activity is a personal service activity, and the individual materially participated in the activity for any three tax years (consecutive or not) before the tax year. (Reg § 1.469-5T(a)(6), Reg § 1.469-5T(d))

(7) The individual meets a facts and circumstances test (¶1829). (Reg § 1.469-5T(a)(7))[2]

For participation by the individual's spouse, see ¶1832.

¶ 1829 Facts and circumstances test for material participation.

An individual materially participates (¶1828) in an activity if he participates on a regular, continuous and substantial basis during the year, based on all the facts and circumstances. (Reg § 1.469-5T(a)(7)) An individual who participates in the activity for 100 hours or less during the year doesn't meet this test. (Reg § 1.469-5T(b)(2)(iii))[3]

¶ 1830 Limited partner's material participation.

An individual limited partner is not treated as materially participating (¶1827) in any activity of a limited partnership with respect to his interest in that partnership (or to any gain or loss from the activity recognized on a sale or exchange of that interest) *unless* the individual would be treated as materially participating under the 500-hour, five-tax-years-out-of-ten, or three-year-personal-service-activity tests at ¶1828 (items (1), (5) or (6), respectively), if he weren't a limited partner. (Code Sec. 469(h)(2); Reg § 1.469-5T(e)(2))[4]

---

50. ¶M-5005; TD ¶413,024.
1. ¶M-4901 *et seq.*, ¶M-5006; ¶4694.06; TD ¶413,002 *et seq.*
2. ¶M-4901 *et seq.*; ¶4694.06; TD ¶413,002 *et seq.*

3. ¶M-4912; ¶4694.06; TD ¶413,012
4. ¶M-5003 *et seq.*; ¶4694.06; TD ¶413,022

An individual's partnership interest *isn't* treated as a limited partnership interest if the individual is a general partner in the partnership at all times during the partnership's tax year ending with or within the individual's tax year. (Reg § 1.469-5T(e)(3)(ii))[5]

Courts, including the Tax Court and Court of Federal Claims, have rejected IRS's view that an interest in a limited liability company (LLC) is treated as a limited partnership interest. IRS has acquiesced in the result in one of the Tax Court cases.[6]

¶ 1831 Participation defined.

Any work done by an individual (without regard to the capacity in which he does the work) in connection with the activity, where the individual owns (directly or indirectly) an interest in the activity at the time the work is done, is treated as participation by that individual in the activity, except as otherwise provided. (Reg § 1.469-5(f)(1))[7]

Work not of a type customarily done by an owner isn't treated as participation if one of its principal purposes is to avoid the passive loss rules. (Reg § 1.469-5T(f)(2)(i))[8]

An individual's work as an investor is not participation unless the individual is directly involved in day-to-day management or operations. (Reg § 1.469-5T(f)(2)(ii))[9]

¶ 1832 Spouse's material participation.

In determining whether a married taxpayer materially participates in an activity, the participation of taxpayer's spouse is taken into account (Code Sec. 469(h)(5)), without regard to whether the spouse owns an interest in the activity, or whether the spouses file a joint return for the year. (Reg § 1.469-5T(f)(3))[10]

¶ 1833 Rental activities as passive activities.

For purposes of the passive activity rules (¶1811 *et seq.*), all rental activities are treated as passive activities (Code Sec. 469(c)(2)), except for (a) individuals who actively participate in rental real estate activities (¶1834) and (b) certain real estate professionals (¶1837).[11]

A rental activity is any activity where payments are principally for the use of tangible property (Code Sec. 469(j)(8)), without regard to whether a lease, service contract, or other arrangement is involved. (Reg § 1.469-1T(e)(3)(i)(B)) But, a rental activity doesn't include an activity involving the use of tangible property if:

(1) The average period the customer uses the property is: 7 days or less (Reg § 1.469-1T(e)(3)(ii)(A)), or 30 days or less, and the owner (or someone on the owner's behalf) provides significant personal services (as defined in the regs). (Reg § 1.469-1T(e)(3)(ii)(B))

(2) The owner (or someone on the owner's behalf) provides extraordinary personal services (as defined in the regs), without regard to the average period the customer uses the property. (Reg § 1.469-1T(e)(3)(ii)(C))

(3) The rental of the tangible property is incidental to a nonrental activity of taxpayer (Reg § 1.469-1T(e)(3)(ii)(D)) (as measured by certain percentage and other tests). (Reg § 1.469-1T(e)(3)(vi))

(4) Taxpayer customarily makes the property available during defined business hours for nonexclusive use by various customers (Reg § 1.469-1T(e)(3)(ii)(E)) (e.g., a golf course).

(5) The property is provided for use in a nonrental activity of a partnership, joint venture, or S corporation in which taxpayer owns an interest, where taxpayer provided the property in his capacity as owner of that interest (Reg § 1.469-1T(e)(3)(ii)(F)) (not as a renter of the property to the partnership, etc.).[12]

---

5. ¶M-5003; ¶4694.06; TD ¶413,022
6. ¶M-5002; ¶4694.06; TD ¶413,021
7. ¶M-4902; ¶4694.06; TD ¶413,002
8. ¶M-4903; ¶4694.06; TD ¶413,003

9. ¶M-4903; ¶4694.06; TD ¶413,003
10. ¶M-4902; ¶4694.06; TD ¶413,002
11. ¶M-5100 *et seq.*; ¶s 4694.01, 4694.60, 4694.63; TD ¶413,501
12. ¶M-5101 *et seq.*; ¶4694.03; TD ¶413,502

¶ 1834   Individuals' active participation rental real estate losses up to $25,000 may be used against nonpassive income.

A natural person who: (1) has at least a 10% interest in any rental real estate activity (¶1835), and (2) otherwise "actively participates" in that activity (¶1836), may offset up to $25,000 of nonpassive income with that portion of the passive activity loss, or of the deduction equivalent of the passive activity credit, attributable to that activity. (Code Sec. 469(i)(1), Code Sec. 469(i)(2), Code Sec. 469(j)(5))[13]

For a married person filing a separate return, the allowance is $12,500 if he lives apart from his spouse at all times during the tax year (Code Sec. 469(i)(5)(A)(i)), and zero if he does not live apart from his spouse at all times during the tax year. (Code Sec. 469(i)(5)(B))[14]

The $25,000 allowance ($12,500 for marrieds filing separately) is reduced (but not below zero) by 50% of the amount by which taxpayer's adjusted gross income (AGI) as specially computed exceeds (1) $100,000 ($50,000 for marrieds filing separately), or (2) $200,000 ($100,000 for marrieds filing separately) in the case of rehabilitation investment credits (¶2308). There's no AGI-based phaseout of the $25,000 ($12,500) offset for low-income housing credits (¶2321) or the commercial revitalization deduction (¶1974). (Code Sec. 469(i)(3), Code Sec. 469(i)(5))[15]

¶ 1835   Who is a 10%-or-more owner entitled to rental real estate allowance?

An individual is a 10%-or-more owner (for the allowance at ¶1834) with respect to any interest in any rental real estate activity (¶1833) for any period only if *at all times* during that period (i.e., the tax year or shorter period the individual held the interest) his interest was at least 10% (by value) of all interests in that activity. The individual's interest includes any interest of his spouse. (Code Sec. 469(i)(6)(A))[16]

¶ 1836   What is "active participation"?

Taxpayer must participate (¶1831) in an activity in a significant and bona fide sense to actively participate in it. Taxpayer participates if he makes management decisions, e.g., approves new tenants, decides on rental terms, approves capital or repair expenditures or arranges for others to provide services (such as repairs). He need not have regular, continuous and substantial involvement in operations. But, a merely formal and nominal participation in management, without a genuine exercise of independent discretion and judgment, is insufficient.[17] The active participation test is less stringent than the material participation requirement (¶1827). Active participation isn't required to take low-income housing (¶2321) or rehabilitation investment credits (¶2308), or the commercial revitalization deduction (¶1974). (Code Sec. 469(i)(6)(B))[18]

In determining whether taxpayer actively participates, the participation of taxpayer's spouse is taken into account. (Code Sec. 469(i)(6)(D))[19]

A taxpayer isn't treated as actively participating (except as regs may provide) with respect to any interest as a limited partner. (Code Sec. 469(i)(6)(C))[20]

¶ 1837   Rental real estate activities of real estate professionals not treated as automatically passive.

For any tax year in which the taxpayer is a "qualifying taxpayer" (usually known as a real

---

13. ¶M-5131; ¶4694.60; TD ¶413,601
14. ¶M-5131; ¶4694.60; TD ¶413,601
15. ¶M-5142 *et seq.*; ¶4694.60; TD ¶413,612 *et seq.*
16. ¶M-5139; TD ¶413,609

17. ¶M-5138; ¶4694.60; TD ¶413,608
18. ¶M-5141; ¶4694.60; TD ¶413,611
19. ¶M-5138; ¶4694.70; TD ¶413,608
20. ¶M-5140; ¶4694.60; TD ¶413,610

estate professional), the rule treating all rental activities as passive activities (¶1833) doesn't apply to any rental real estate activity of the taxpayer. (Code Sec. 469(c)(7)(A)(i)) Instead, that activity is a passive activity unless the taxpayer materially participates (¶1827). (Reg § 1.469-9(e)(1))[21]

🔵 observation: So, real estate professionals who materially participate in a rental real estate activity may use losses or credits from the activity to offset other, non-passive income.

A taxpayer is a qualifying taxpayer (i.e., real estate professional) for a particular tax year if: (1) more than half of the personal services (see below) the taxpayer performs during that year are performed in real property trades or businesses (see below) in which the taxpayer materially participates (¶1827) (Code Sec. 469(c)(7)(B)(i)), and (2) the taxpayer performs more than 750 hours of services during that year in real property trades or businesses in which he materially participates. (Code Sec. 469(c)(7)(B)(ii))[22]

A taxpayer who owns at least one interest in rental real estate and who meets the above tests is a real estate professional. (Reg § 1.469-9(b)(6))[23]

In determining whether a taxpayer is a real estate professional, each of his interests in rental real estate is treated as a separate activity, unless he elects (by filing a specified statement with his original income tax return) to treat all interests in rental real estate as one activity. (Code Sec. 469(c)(7)(A); Reg § 1.469-9(g))[24] The election is binding for the tax year it's made and for all future years in which the taxpayer qualifies. Failure to elect in one year doesn't bar the election in a later year. (Reg § 1.469-9(g)(1)).[25]

Spouses filing a joint return qualify as real estate professionals only if one spouse separately satisfies the above tests (Code Sec. 469(c)(7)(B); Reg § 1.469-9(c)(4)), without regard to the other spouse's services.[26]

A closely-held C corporation qualifies as a real estate professional if more than 50% of its gross receipts for the tax year are derived from real property trades or businesses in which it materially participates. (Code Sec. 469(c)(7)(D)(i))[27]

A real property trade or business is any real property development, redevelopment, construction, reconstruction, acquisition, conversion, rental, operation, management, leasing or brokerage trade or business. (Code Sec. 469(c)(7)(C)) The determination of a taxpayer's real property trades or businesses is based on all relevant facts and circumstances. Once a taxpayer determines the real property trades or businesses in which personal services are provided, he can't redetermine them later unless the original determination was clearly erroneous or there's been a material change of facts and circumstances. (Reg § 1.469-9(d)(1))[28]

Personal services means any work performed by an individual in connection with a trade or business, but not as an investor. (Reg § 1.469-9(b)(4)) Services performed as an employee don't count, unless he is a more-than-5%-owner of the employer. (Code Sec. 469(c)(7)(D))[29]

¶ 1838 Carryover of suspended losses and credits.

Any deduction (or credit) from a passive activity (¶1823) that's disallowed under the passive loss rules (¶1811 *et seq.*) for a tax year is allocated among taxpayer's activities for the next tax year in a manner that reasonably reflects the extent each activity continues the business and rental operations that made up the loss activity. As so allocated, it is treated as a deduction (or credit) from that activity for that next year. (Code Sec. 469(b); Reg § 1.469-1(f)(4)(i))[30]

---

21. ¶M-5161; ¶4694.63; TD ¶413,801
22. ¶M-5168; ¶4694.63; TD ¶413,808
23. ¶M-5168; ¶4694.63; TD ¶413,808
24. ¶M-5163; ¶4694.63; TD ¶413,803, 413,804
25. ¶M-5163; ¶4694.63; TD ¶413,803

26. ¶M-5171; ¶4694.63; TD ¶413,811
27. ¶M-5172; ¶4694.63; TD ¶413,812
28. ¶M-5175; ¶4694.63; TD ¶413,815
29. ¶M-5169, M-5170 *et seq.*; ¶4694.63; TD ¶413,809, 413,810
30. ¶M-5504, ¶M-5604; ¶4694.45; TD ¶416,505, 417,006

¶ 1839 Disposition of taxpayer's entire interest in passive activity or substantially all of passive activity.

If a taxpayer disposes of his entire interest in a passive activity (or former passive activity), and all gain or loss realized on the disposition is recognized, the excess of: (1) any loss from the activity for the tax year of disposition (including losses carried over from earlier years, ¶1838), over (2) any net income or gain for that year from all other passive activities (including loss carryovers), is treated as loss *not* from a passive activity. (Code Sec. 469(g)(1)(A)) Loss from the activity under (1) is computed by taking into account all income, gain, and loss, including gain and loss recognized on the disposition.[31]

A taxpayer that disposes of *substantially all* of an activity may be able to treat the part disposed of as a separate activity. (Reg § 1.469-4(g)(2))[32]

Passive loss carryforwards ("suspended losses") are allowed against all the taxpayer's income (Code Sec. 469(g)(1)(A)), but carryforwards of passive activity credits ("suspended credits") aren't. [33]

Where the disposition is by installment sale, the amount treated as a nonpassive loss is the portion of the losses from each tax year that bears the same ratio to all these losses as the gain recognized on the sale bears to the gross profit from the sale. (Code Sec. 469(g)(3))[34]

Special rules apply where a disposition is to a related party (Code Sec. 469(g)(1)(B)), where the interest in the activity is transferred by reason of death (Code Sec. 469(g)(2)), or where the disposition is by gift. (Code Sec. 469(j)(6))[35]

¶ 1840 Net Operating Losses (NOLs).

An NOL sustained in one year may be used to reduce the taxable income for another year. It may be carried back to earlier years and yield tax refunds. If not exhausted in earlier years (or if taxpayer elects not to use the carryback), it may be carried forward to later years and reduce the tax for those years.

¶ 1841 NOL defined.

An NOL is the excess of business deductions (computed with certain modifications) over gross income in a particular tax year. A deduction is allowed for that loss, through an NOL carryback or carryover, in some other tax year(s) (see ¶1842) in which gross income exceeds business deductions. (Code Sec. 172(a); Reg § 1.172-1(a))[36]

An NOL deduction is allowed to individuals, corporations (Code Sec. 172), estates and trusts (Code Sec. 642(d)) (and charitable organizations with respect to the unrelated business income tax. (Code Sec. 512(b)(6))) IRS ruled that a taxpayer can carry back NOLs that accrue in years when it is not a closely held C corporation to offset portfolio income earned in years in which it was a closely held C corporation.[37]

An NOL deduction isn't allowed to partnerships (Code Sec. 703(a)(2)(D)), common trust funds (Code Sec. 584(g)) (but the deduction is allowed to the partners and beneficiaries), regulated investment companies (Code Sec. 852(b)(2)(B)), or S corporations (losses are passed through to shareholders). (Code Sec. 1366(a))[38]

¶ 1842 NOL carryover and carryback periods.

Except as noted below (or taxpayer elects to forgo carryback, ¶1845), a net operating loss (NOL) for any tax year may be carried back two years and forward 20 years (for NOLs for tax

---

31. ¶M-5701; ¶4694.50; TD ¶417,501
32. ¶s M-5701, M-5701.3; ¶4694.50; TD ¶417,504
33. ¶M-5701; ¶4694.50; TD ¶417,501
34. ¶M-5701.2; ¶4694.50; TD ¶417,503

35. ¶M-5704 *et seq.*; ¶4694.50; TD ¶417,507 *et seq.*
36. ¶M-4001 *et seq.*; ¶1724; TD ¶354,001
37. ¶M-5508; ¶4694; TD ¶416,510
38. ¶M-4003; ¶1724.02; TD ¶354,003

years beginning before Aug. 6, '97, carried back three years and forward 15 years). (Code Sec. 172(b)(1)(A))[39] A decedent's NOL can be carried back, but not forward.[40] For refunds based on NOL carrybacks, see ¶4852.

For the elective 3-, 4- or 5-year carryback period for 2008 and 2009 NOLs, see ¶1843.

A three-year carryback period applies to the following (other than farming losses, including certain GO Zone Act reforestation losses, for which a five-year carryback applies, see ¶4503):

... NOLs arising from property losses of individuals due to fire, storm, shipwreck, or other casualty, or from theft.

... For a small business, or a taxpayer engaged in the trade or business of farming, NOLs attributable to Federally declared disasters (¶1799). A small business is one whose average annual gross receipts (under Code Sec. 448(c)) are $5 million or less. (Code Sec. 172(b)(1)(F))[41]

An NOL attributable to a "specified liability loss" (SLL) —i.e., a product liability loss and/or losses attributable to certain deferred statutory liabilities—may be carried back 10 years. (Code Sec. 172(b)(1)(C), Code Sec. 172(f)) The carry*forward* is the usual 20 years (15 years for NOLs for tax years beginning before Aug. 6, '97). (Code Sec. 172(b)(1)(A)(ii)) (The 10-year carryback isn't precluded by making the election at ¶1845 to forgo the carryback.) (Reg § 1.172-13(c)(4)) To carry back the loss under the regular two-year/20-year (three-year/15-year for NOLs for tax years beginning before Aug. 6, '97) rules, taxpayer must so elect. (Code Sec. 172(f)(6))[42]

The SLL for a tax year can't exceed the amount of the NOL for that year. (Code Sec. 172(f)(2)) The Supreme Court has held that for consolidated groups, this "NOL limitation rule" applies at the group level (the single-entity approach); the product liability expenses of all members are combined and the resulting product liability loss is limited only by the amount of the group's consolidated net operating loss (CNOL).[43]

For the five-year carryback period for a qualified GO Zone loss, see ¶1844.

Other carryback or carryover periods apply to banks, small business investment companies, and REITs. (Code Sec. 172(b)(1))[44] Special rules limit the carryback of losses attributable to interest allocable to a corporate equity reduction transaction (CERT). (Code Sec. 172(b)(1)(E), Code Sec. 172(h))[45]

An NOL from the short tax year that results from an accounting year change generally can't be carried back unless it's: (a) $50,000 or less, or (b) less than the NOL for the 12-month period beginning with the first day of the short period. So, if the NOL is more than $50,000, the taxpayer must wait until the end of the 12-month period described in (b) to determine whether it can be carried back.[46]

Any portion of an NOL that is attributable to any of the following losses is considered to be a separate NOL and is applied as a carryover after the remainder of the NOL for that year is applied: (1) an SLL, (2) a CERT loss, (3) an individual's NOL attributable to a casualty or disaster, and an NOL of a farm or small business that's attributable to a Federally-declared disaster, or (4) a farming loss (¶4503). (Code Sec. 172(f)(5), Code Sec. 172(h)(4)(B), Code Sec. 172(b)(1)(F)(iv), Code Sec. 172(i)(2), Code Sec. 172(b)(1)(I)(iii))[47]

39. ¶M-4301; ¶1724.31; TD ¶356,001
40. ¶M-4004; ¶1724.02; TD ¶354,004
41. ¶M-4305.1, M-4305.2; ¶1724.434, 1724.436; TD ¶356,010, 356,011
42. ¶M-4322 *et seq.*; ¶1724.40; TD ¶356,006 *et seq.*
43. ¶E-9055.2, M-4322; TD ¶606,001
44. ¶M-4321 *et seq.*; ¶1724.38, 1724.39
45. ¶M-4306; ¶1724.35; TD ¶356,005
46. ¶G-1827 *et seq.*; ¶4424; TD ¶439,027 *et seq.*
47. ¶M-4333; ¶1724.49; TD ¶356,009

¶ 1843   Elective 3-, 4- or 5-year carryback period for 2008 and 2009 NOLs.

Taxpayers (except for certain taxpayers getting help from the Federal government under the Emergency Economic Stabilization Act of 2008) could have elected to increase the carryback period for an applicable NOL to 3, 4, or 5 years from 2 years. (Code Sec. 172(b)(1)(H)(i)(I)) An applicable NOL was the taxpayer's NOL for any tax year ending after Dec. 31, 2007, and beginning before Jan. 1, 2010. (Code Sec. 172(b)(1)(H)(ii)) Generally, an election could have been made for only one tax year, (Code Sec. 172(b)(1)(H)(iii)(I)) but an eligible small business (ESB, as defined in Code Sec. 172(b)(1)(H)(v)(II)) that made an election under Code Sec. 172(b)(1)(H), as in effect before enactment of P.L. 111-92, could have made an election for 2 tax years instead of just 1. (Code Sec. 172(b)(1)(H)(v)(I))

The amount of the NOL that could be carried back to the 5th tax year before the loss year could not be more than 50% of the taxpayer's taxable income for that 5th preceding tax year determined without taking into account any NOL for the loss year or for any tax year after the loss year. (Code Sec. 172(b)(1)(H)(iv)(I)) The amount of the NOL otherwise carried to tax years after the 5th preceding tax year was adjusted to take into account that the NOL could offset only 50% of the taxable income for that 5th preceding tax year. (Code Sec. 172(b)(1)(H)(iv)(II)) The 50% limitation didn't apply to the applicable 2008 NOL of an ESB with respect to which an election is made under Code Sec. 172(b)(1)(H), as in effect before enactment of P.L. 111-92. (Code Sec. 172(b)(1)(H)(iv)(III))

The extended carryback election had to be made by the due date (including extensions) for filing the taxpayer's last tax return for a tax year beginning in 2009. (Code Sec. 172(b)(1)(H)(iii)(II))

¶ 1844   Five-year carryback period for qualified disaster loss and qualified GO Zone loss.

A five-year carryback period applies for net operating losses (NOLs) to the extent of a qualified disaster loss. (Code Sec. 172(b)(1)(J)) A qualified disaster loss is the lesser of:

(1) the sum of:

(a) the losses allowable under Code Sec. 165 for the tax year attributable to a federally declared disaster occurring before Jan. 1, 2010 in a disaster area, and

(b) the deduction for the tax year for qualified disaster expenses that is allowable under Code Sec. 198A(a) (see ¶1799) or that would be allowable if not otherwise treated as an expense, or

(2) the taxpayer's NOL for the tax year. (Code Sec. 172(j)(1))[48]

See ¶3212 for discussion of the alternative tax net operating deduction (ATNOLD) rules for qualified disaster losses.

A five-year carryback period also applies for a qualified Gulf Opportunity (GO) Zone loss—which is the lesser of (1) the excess of the taxpayer's NOL for the tax year, over the specified liability loss for the tax year to which a 10-year carryback applies (¶1842), (Code Sec. 1400N(k)(2)(A)) or (2) the aggregate amount of the following deductions: (1) qualified GO Zone casualty losses (as defined in Code Sec. 1400N(k)(3)(A)); (2) certain moving and temporary housing expenses paid or incurred before Jan. 1, 2008; (3) depreciation or amortization deductions for qualified GO Zone property (¶1939) for the tax year the property is placed in service; and (4) deductions for certain repair expenses resulting from Hurricane Katrina paid or incurred before Jan. 1, 2008. (Code Sec. 1400N(k)(2)(B))[49]

The 5-year NOL carryback for casualty losses, and depreciation or amortization, doesn't

48. ¶M-4301 et seq.; ¶1724; TD ¶356,001 et seq.   49. ¶M-4342 et seq.; ¶14,00N4.06; TD ¶356,014 et seq.

254

apply to property ineligible under Code Sec. 1400N(p)(3) (i.e., property which is also ineligible for GO Zone bonus depreciation, see ¶1939). (Code Sec. 1400N(p)(1), Code Sec. 1400N(p)(2)) Among other limits, the amount of qualified GO Zone casualty loss is reduced by the amount of any gain recognized by the taxpayer from involuntary conversions of property located in the GO Zone caused by Hurricane Katrina. Electing taxpayers can't treat the loss as having occurred in any prior tax year under Code Sec. 165(i) (¶1799). (Code Sec. 1400N(k)(3))[50]

A taxpayer can irrevocably elect not to apply the 5-year loss carryback for any tax year. (Code Sec. 1400N(k)(4))

¶ 1845   Election to forgo NOL carryback.

A taxpayer may elect not to use the carryback period (¶1842) and instead only carry over the NOL for the allowed *carryforward* period. Once the election is made for any tax year (on a statement attached to the return or amended return), it's irrevocable for that year. (Code Sec. 172(b)(3); Reg § 301.9100-12T(d)) (The election also applies to alternative minimum tax NOLs (ATNOLs, see ¶3212.)[1]

¶ 1846   How the NOL deduction works.

Assume an NOL is sustained for a tax year beginning in 2010, and that the usual two-year carryback and 20-year carryover apply:

STEP (1). Compute the NOL. Note some deductions aren't allowed (¶1847 *et seq.*).

STEP (2). Find the earliest year to which this loss can be carried (here 2008).

STEP (3). Add this loss to all other NOLs carried to the year (2008), and deduct the total as an *NOL deduction*. Note that the 2010 loss is fully absorbed if 2008 taxable income (before NOL deduction) exceeds the sum of 2010 loss, plus pre-2010 losses, carried to 2008. File for refund if applicable.

STEP (4). To the extent the 2010 loss isn't deducted in 2008, it's carried to the next earliest year to which it may be carried (2009). Note that the amount carried to 2009 is reduced by "intervening years' modifications" (¶1850).

STEP (5). Repeat step (3)—that is, add the 2010 loss that may be carried to the next year (2009) to all other NOLs carried to that year, and deduct the total as an NOL deduction.

LATER STEPS. Repeat the process described in steps (3) and (4) for the first year after the loss year (2011 in our example) and then in order to each of the 19 following years or until the full amount of the NOL is absorbed, whichever happens first. If the loss is not absorbed by the 20th year succeeding the loss year, any further benefit is lost.[2]

¶ 1847   Computing the NOL for noncorporate taxpayers.

NOL for a noncorporate taxpayer (which may be carried to another year) is the deficit in taxable income for the year, with certain modifications: NOL carryback or carryover deduction from other years; personal exemptions; exclusion of gain from qualified small business stock (¶2648); and the Code Sec. 199 deduction for domestic production activities (¶1614) are not allowed; and deductions for capital losses and nonbusiness deductions are only allowed to a limited extent. (Code Sec. 172(d); Reg § 1.172-3(a))[3]

¶ 1848   Computing the NOL for corporate taxpayers.

A corporation's NOL is figured the same as its taxable income. But in computing the NOL for the year: (1) NOL carrybacks and carryovers from other years aren't deducted; (2) the

---

50. ¶M-4342 *et seq.*; ¶14,00N4.06; TD ¶356,014 *et seq.*
1. ¶M-4303; ¶1724.33; TD ¶356,003

2. ¶M-4402; ¶1724.10; TD ¶354,002
3. ¶M-4109 *et seq.*; ¶1724.12; TD ¶355,008 *et seq.*

deduction for dividends received is taken without limiting it by a percentage of the corporation's taxable income; (3) the deduction for dividends paid on certain preferred stock of public utilities is computed without limiting it to the year's taxable income; and (4) the Code Sec. 199 deduction for domestic production activities (¶1614) isn't allowed. (Code Sec. 172(d); Reg § 1.172-2(a))[4]

¶ 1849 Amount of NOL deduction.

The NOL deduction in any year is the sum of all NOL carrybacks and carryovers to that year. (Code Sec. 172(a))[5] For refunds based on NOL carrybacks, see ¶4852.

Where a husband and wife who make a joint return for the deduction year made a joint return for all other tax years involved in computing the NOL deduction, that deduction is computed on the basis of their joint NOLs and combined taxable incomes. (Reg § 1.172-7(c)) Special rules apply if they didn't make joint returns for all applicable years. (Reg § 1.172-7)[6]

✪ *caution:* For limits on the NOL deduction for alternative minimum tax purposes, see ¶3212.

¶ 1850 NOL exceeds income in year to which carried; "intervening year."

If the NOL carried to an earlier tax year exceeds the taxable income for that year, modifications must be made in that year's taxable income, in computing the unused portion of the NOL that can be carried to the next year. These "intervening year modifications" apply only in computing NOL carryovers, and don't affect taxable income for other purposes. (Code Sec. 172(b)(2); Reg § 1.172-5)[7] Deductions for intervening years which are based on, or limited to, a percentage of adjusted gross income (AGI, ¶3102) or taxable income must be recomputed, based on AGI or taxable income as modified. (Reg § 1.172-5(a)(2)(ii))[8]

¶ 1851 Deduction for Bad Debts.

Bad debts are deductible whether or not connected with taxpayer's business. Deduction is allowed for total worthlessness and, in some cases, for partial worthlessness.

Business bad debts are deductible as ordinary deductions. They are deductible if partially worthless as well as when wholly worthless. Nonbusiness bad debts are deducted only as short-term capital losses, and only when wholly worthless (¶1856).[9] An item can't be deductible both as a bad debt and as a loss. If it could be treated as either, it must be treated as a bad debt.[10]

But, a worthless debt that is evidenced by a security, and is owed by a corporation or a government, is a loss (see ¶1782), and not a bad debt, unless owed to a bank. (Code Sec. 165(g), Code Sec. 166(e), Code Sec. 582(a))[11]

¶ 1852 Bad debts of guarantors.

If taxpayer makes a guarantee agreement in the course of his trade or business, he's entitled to a business bad debt deduction for any payment he makes as guarantor, of principal or interest. (Reg § 1.166-9(a))[12]

If taxpayer makes a guarantee agreement in a transaction for profit (but not in the course of his business), and makes a payment of principal or interest, he's entitled to a nonbusiness bad debt deduction in the year his right of subrogation becomes totally worthless.

4. ¶M-4105 *et seq.*; ¶1724.11; TD ¶355,007
5. ¶M-4401; ¶1724.01; TD ¶354,001
6. ¶M-4405 *et seq.*; ¶1724.13; TD ¶354,006, 354,007
7. ¶M-4202 *et seq.*; ¶1724, 1724.20 *et seq.*; TD ¶357,002 *et seq.*
8. ¶M-4207; ¶1724.20 *et seq.*; TD ¶357,007

9. ¶M-2801 *et seq.*, ¶M-2901 *et seq.*; ¶1664; TD ¶320,501 *et seq.*, TD ¶323,001 *et seq.*
10. ¶M-2503; ¶1654.040; TD ¶320,508
11. ¶s M-3301, M-3309; ¶1664.160; TD ¶320,501, 372,001
12. ¶M-3207; ¶1664.450; TD ¶324,007

(Reg § 1.166-9(b), Reg § 1.166-9(e)(2))[13] For general timing rules, see ¶1853.

¶ 1853 Time for deducting worthless debt.

Deduction is allowed for the tax year the debt becomes wholly worthless. (Code Sec. 166(a)(1))[14] (For *partial* worthlessness of *business* debts, see ¶1855.) Taxpayer must show the debt had value at the beginning of the year and no value at the end, and that the worthlessness occurred in the particular tax year claimed.[15] Worthlessness is a question of fact requiring consideration of all pertinent evidence, including the debtor's financial condition and the value of any security. (Reg § 1.166-2(a))[16]

¶ 1854 Amount of bad debt deduction.

The amount deductible for a wholly worthless debt (¶1853) is its adjusted basis for determining loss on a sale or exchange (¶2400 *et seq.*), regardless of its face value. (Code Sec. 166(b); Reg § 1.166-1(d))[17] The adjustments used to figure adjusted basis are generally the debtor's payments on the debt. But a deduction allowed for a debt's partial worthlessness reduces the debt's basis to that extent, whether or not taxpayer got a tax benefit from the deduction.[18]

If the creditor (taxpayer) has no basis in the debt, there's no deduction.[19] So there's no deduction for wages, rents, alimony, etc., that were never received, unless these items were included in income. (Reg § 1.166-1(e))[20] Where taxpayer reports receivables at fair market value (FMV) rather than face, the deduction can't exceed FMV. (Reg § 1.166-1(d)(2))[21]

Where taxpayer fails to prove a debt's exact basis, it may be estimated by a court if taxpayer proves his right to *some* deduction.[22]

If a debt is compromised because of inability to pay the full amount, taxpayer deducts the debt's adjusted basis minus any cash and the value of any property received. If the debt is compromised for some other reason, taxpayer doesn't have a bad debt (but may have a loss).[23]

¶ 1855 Deduction for partially worthless business debts.

A deduction is allowed for partially worthless debts (Code Sec. 166(a)(2)) *only if*: (1) the debt is a business debt (see ¶1856); (2) IRS is satisfied that the specific debt is recoverable only in part; (3) the amount deducted was *charged off* on the books during the tax year; *and* (4) the debt is not evidenced by a security. (Code Sec. 166(d)(1), Code Sec. 166(e); Reg § 1.166-5(b))[24] (For deductibility of "worthless securities" as a loss, see ¶1782.)

Taxpayer may charge off and deduct a debt for partial worthlessness as it occurs. Or he can defer charge-off and deduction to a later year when partial worthlessness is greater, thus deducting several years' partial worthlessness in one year. Or he can defer deduction until total worthlessness (but not beyond the year of total worthlessness (Reg § 1.166-3(b)).[25]

¶ 1856 Effect of classification as business or nonbusiness bad debt.

The need to determine whether a debt is a business or nonbusiness debt (¶1857) arises only for noncorporate taxpayers. A corporation's debts are always business debts. (Code Sec. 166(d))[26]

---

13. ¶M-3210, M-3214; ¶1664.450; TD ¶324,011, 324,014
14. ¶M-2401; ¶1664; TD ¶320,501
15. ¶M-2701; ¶1664.220; TD ¶322,001
16. ¶M-2702; ¶1664.220; TD ¶322,002
17. ¶M-2402; ¶1664.210; TD ¶320,502
18. ¶s M-2406, M-2407; TD ¶320,504
19. ¶M-2404; ¶1664.210; TD ¶320,502

20. ¶M-2506; ¶1664.210; TD ¶320,503
21. ¶M-2402; TD ¶320,502
22. ¶M-2405; TD ¶320,502
23. ¶M-2408; TD ¶320,504
24. ¶M-2801 *et seq.*; ¶1664.270 *et seq.*; TD ¶322,501 *et seq.*
25. ¶M-2801; ¶1664.271; TD ¶322,502
26. ¶M-2800; ¶s 1664, 1664.300; TD ¶323,001

Business bad debts are fully deductible against income (Code Sec. 166(a)), while nonbusiness bad debts are short-term capital losses of limited deductibility. (Code Sec. 166(d)(1)(B))[27] Business and nonbusiness debts are deductible when wholly worthless (see ¶1853), but only business debts are deductible when partly worthless (see ¶1855). (Code Sec. 166(a), Code Sec. 166(d)(1)(A))[28]

¶ 1857   Business and nonbusiness debts defined.

A *business debt* is either: (1) a debt created or acquired in the course of taxpayer's trade or business (whether or not it was related to that business when it became worthless, see ¶1853); or (2) a debt the loss from whose worthlessness is incurred in taxpayer's trade or business. This applies if the loss is proximately related to taxpayer's business when the debt becomes worthless. A bad debt is proximately related to business if business is the dominant motivation for the debt. (Reg § 1.166-5(b))[29]

A *nonbusiness debt* (for noncorporate taxpayers, see ¶1856) is a debt other than a business debt. (Code Sec. 166(d)(2); Reg § 1.166-5(b), Reg § 1.166-5(d))[30]

¶ 1858   Shareholders' loans or guarantees for their corporations as business debts.

A shareholder in a corporation can't treat the corporation's business as his business even if he's the sole shareholder. So, an individual shareholder's loan to his corporation isn't a business debt (¶1857) unless he shows the debt is related to his own business.[31] Devoting one's time and energies to a corporation's affairs isn't of itself a trade or business. But a shareholder's loan to his corporation can be a business debt if he's in the business of promoting, financing, and selling corporations. He must be seeking other than a mere investor's return, since investing isn't a business.[32]

If the shareholder is also an officer or other employee of the corporation, he may claim his loan, guarantee, or indemnity was made to protect his job (i.e., his business of being an employee). Business debt status is allowed if his dominant motive (not just a significant motive) for the loan, etc., was to protect his job. Which motive is dominant is determined by several factors, especially the amount of salary as compared to the amount invested. These principles also apply to a shareholder-employee who claims that his loan or guarantee for another corporation (e.g., his corporation's customer) was to protect his job.[33]

---

27. ¶s M-2401, M-2901; ¶s 1664, 1664.300; TD ¶320,501
28. ¶s M-2401, M-2800; ¶s 1664.210, 1664.270, 1664.300; TD ¶322,501
29. ¶M-2902; ¶1664.301; TD ¶323,003

30. ¶M-2902; ¶1664.301; TD ¶323,003
31. ¶M-2904; ¶1664.303; TD ¶323,010
32. ¶M-2911; ¶1664.302; TD ¶323,006
33. ¶M-2914 *et seq.*; ¶1664.309; TD ¶323,011

Chapter 5 Depreciation, Amortization, Property Expensing and Depletion

¶ 1900   The Depreciation Allowance.

Generally, a taxpayer that buys business or income-producing property (not held for sale) with a useful life of more than one year can't deduct its full cost as an expense for that year. However, the Code allows an annual deduction of a portion of the cost of the property. This deduction may be a deduction for depreciation, amortization or depletion (cost recovery deductions).

For most tangible property, a depreciation deduction is provided under the Modified Accelerated Cost Recovery System (MACRS) (for non-transitional property placed in service after '86, see ¶1907, ¶1908), under pre-'87 ACRS (see below), or under useful-life depreciation (see ¶1962).

Under pre-'87 ACRS, virtually all tangible property placed in service after '80 and before '87 (and post-'86 transitional property) was depreciated by using a statutory rate and recovery period.[1]

For the depreciation or amortization of most intangibles, see ¶1903, ¶1961, ¶1964 and ¶1976 *et seq.*

For certain property, in lieu of all or part of the cost recovery deductions otherwise permitted, all or part of the cost can be deducted in the year in which it is placed in service ("expensed"), see ¶1941 *et seq.*, ¶1966 *et seq.*

¶ 1901   Claiming the depreciation deduction—Form 4562.

Form 4562 is used to claim the deduction for depreciation. Individuals and other noncorporate taxpayers (including S corporations) don't have to complete or attach Form 4562 if (1) the only depreciation (or amortization) claimed is for assets (other than listed property, see ¶1948) placed in service before the tax year, (2) no Code Sec. 179 expense deduction is claimed, and (3) deductions are not claimed for a vehicle reported on a form other than Schedule C or C-EZ.[2] For how employees, self-employeds and farmers claim depreciation on a car or truck, see ¶1956.

Failure to take a depreciation deduction in one year doesn't allow a taxpayer to take a larger deduction in later years (Reg § 1.167(a)-10(a)) unless the taxpayer treats the failure as an impermissible method of accounting, correctable by filing a Form 3115 and otherwise following the procedures for changing to a permissible method of accounting in a later year. For changes in computing depreciation or amortization as changes in method of accounting, see ¶2839. An amended return can be used to correct depreciation if the error (1) is a mathematical or posting error, or (2) involves property for which the taxpayer has used the improper method for one tax year, but not two tax years in a row.[3]

¶ 1902   What property is depreciable?

Most items of tangible property (Reg § 1.167(a)-2), and certain intangibles (Reg § 1.167(a)-3) (as explained at ¶1903) are depreciable if they meet the following requirements:

(1) they are used in a trade or business, or held for the production of income. (Code Sec. 167(a))[4]

(2) they have an exhaustible useful-life that can be determined with reasonable accuracy

---

1. ¶L-10900 *et seq.*, ¶L-10912 *et seq.*; ¶1684.05, ¶1688.400; TD ¶268,101, TD ¶268,102
2. ¶L-7501; ¶1674.001, ¶1684.025; TD ¶264,500
3. ¶G-2103, ¶G-2106.1, ¶G-2109, ¶G-2207.1; ¶4464.21, ¶4464.227,

¶4464.25; TD ¶442,402, TD ¶442,404, TD ¶442,407, TD ¶442,608
4. ¶L-7901; ¶1674.006; TD ¶265,401

References beginning with a single letter are to paragraphs in RIA's Federal Tax Coordinator 2d and RIA's Analysis of Federal Taxes: Income. Those beginning with numbers are to paragraphs in RIA's United States Tax Reporter. Those beginning with TD are to paragraphs in RIA's Tax Desk.

(Reg § 1.167(a)-1(a)), (Reg § 1.167(a)-1(b)), (Reg § 1.167(a)-2), (Reg § 1.167(a)-3);[5] however, the mere fact that property diminishes in value doesn't mean that it's depreciable, if the decrease isn't the result of exhaustion, wear and tear, or obsolescence. (Reg § 1.167(a)-1(a))[6]

(3) they aren't inventory or stock in trade. (Reg § 1.167(a)-2) Thus, IRS ruled that property held primarily for sale isn't held depreciable even if it is sometimes rented to others before sale.[7]

Land (as distinct from buildings and other real property improvements) isn't depreciable.[8] However, a taxpayer holding a life estate or other term interest in land can amortize the cost of the interest over the term if (1) the interest is acquired by purchase, (2) the interest isn't created by the taxpayer's division of a larger interest and (3) the remainder interest isn't held by a person related to the taxpayer.[9]

Some courts have held that property can be depreciated under MACRS or ACRS even if it doesn't have a determinable useful life, but IRS disagrees.[10]

Natural resources such as oil, gas, other minerals in the ground and timber qualify for *depletion* (¶1979 et seq.), not depreciation. (Reg § 1.167(a)-2)[11]

Property used solely for personal purposes isn't depreciable. (Reg § 1.167(a)-2) Property used both for personal and for business or income-producing purposes is depreciable to the extent of nonpersonal usage.[12]

¶ 1903   When intangible assets are depreciable.

An intangible asset is depreciable (but not under MACRS, see ¶1908, or under pre-'87 ACRS, see ¶1900) if it's used in a trade or business or production of income, has a limited, ascertainable useful life, and the taxpayer can show the cost of that asset. (Reg § 1.167(a)-3(a))

caution: Some intangibles (for example, goodwill) can be depreciated or amortized, even though they don't have a limited, ascertainable useful life. For how to depreciate or amortize most depreciable intangibles, see ¶1961, ¶1964 and ¶1976 et seq.

¶ 1904   Who is entitled to depreciation deductions?

Ordinarily the owner of depreciable property is the person entitled to deduct depreciation.[13] This is the person that has the benefits and burdens of ownership and not necessarily the owner of legal title.[14]

A *lessor* (landlord) deducts depreciation on property that is already on the leased premises when he leases out the property and on any improvements he constructs during the term of the lease. (Reg § 1.167(a)-4) But he can't deduct depreciation where the lease requires the lessee to replace property at the lessee's expense. In that case, the lessor suffers no "depreciable" loss, i.e., wear and tear, etc.[15] For the rules that apply to lessor-financed construction allowances on retail property, see ¶1346 and ¶1923.

A *lessee* (tenant) ordinarily depreciates the cost of improvements he makes,[16] see ¶1922, but the costs of acquiring a lease are amortizable, not depreciable, see ¶1597.

If a life tenancy is in depreciable property, the life tenant deducts depreciation as if he were the absolute owner of the property. (Code Sec. 167(d)) After the life tenant's death, the depreciation deduction, if any, is allowed to the remainderman. (Reg § 1.167(h)-1)[17]

5. ¶L-7901; ¶1674.006; TD ¶265,407
6. ¶L-7501; TD ¶264,501
7. ¶L-7905; ¶1674.006; TD ¶265,401
8. ¶L-7901; ¶1674.006; TD ¶265,401
9. ¶L-7831 et seq.; ¶1674.120 ; ¶2734; TD ¶265,023 et seq.
10. ¶L-8201, ¶L-10901.1; TD ¶266,001, TD ¶268,103
11. ¶s L-7929, N-2250 et seq.; ¶6114 et seq.; TD ¶265,430

12. ¶L-7908; ¶1674.006; TD ¶265,409
13. ¶L-7802; ¶1674.002; TD ¶265,001
14. ¶L-7803 et seq.; ¶1674.002; TD ¶265,002
15. ¶L-7808, ¶L-7809; ¶1674.023; TD ¶265,007, TD ¶265,008
16. ¶L-7809; ¶1674.023; TD ¶267,020
17. ¶L-7830; ¶1674.117; TD ¶265,022

Various rules limit the depreciation or amortization of life estates and other limited interests in non-depreciable property.[18]

A tenant-stockholder of a cooperative housing corporation who uses his proprietary lease in a trade or business or for the production of income, can, subject to an adjusted basis limitation and a carryover rule, depreciate the portion of the cost of his stock allocable to depreciable property. (Code Sec. 216(c))[19]

¶ 1905   When depreciation begins and ends.

The depreciation period generally begins when an asset is placed in service (Reg § 1.167(a)-10(b)), namely when it's in a condition or state of readiness and availability for a specifically defined function.[20] The depreciation period ends when the asset is retired from service, or its cost or other basis is fully recovered, or it's sold or disposed of—whichever occurs first. (Code Sec. 167, Code Sec. 168(d); Reg § 1.167(a)-10(b), Reg § 1.167(b)-0(a))

For MACRS property (¶1906 *et seq.*), the rules for the beginning and end of depreciation are subject to depreciation conventions (see ¶1927). For useful-life depreciable property (¶1962 *et seq.*), a proportionate part of a year's depreciation is allowed for the part of the year during which an asset is placed in service, but only if no depreciation convention is adopted for the asset. (Reg § 1.167(a)-10(b))

No depreciation deduction is allowed for MACRS property placed in service and disposed of in the same year. (Reg § 1.168(d)-1(b)(3)(ii))

¶ 1906   The Modified Accelerated Cost Recovery System (MACRS). ▬▬▬▬▬

MACRS depreciation is determined under one of two systems: (1) the general depreciation system (GDS) or (2) the alternative depreciation system (ADS), which is mandatory for some MACRS property (and elective for all other MACRS property, see ¶1930 *et seq.*). For "bonus depreciation," see ¶1933 *et seq.*

In both systems, the depreciation deduction is determined by applying the depreciation method (¶1925) to the depreciable basis (¶1921) of the property (¶1907, ¶1908), over the applicable recovery period (¶1924), and subject to the applicable placed-in-service conventions (¶1927).[21] For use of optional depreciation tables (reproduced at ¶1117), see ¶1911.

¶ 1907   MACRS property.

Subject to the exceptions discussed in ¶1908 (and the expensing and amortization rules discussed at ¶1941 *et seq.* and ¶1966 *et seq.*), most tangible depreciable property (as described at ¶1902) must be depreciated under MACRS. (Code Sec. 168(a))[22]

¶ 1908   Property excluded from MACRS.

The following property isn't depreciable under MACRS: intangible property, see ¶1903 (Code Sec. 168(a)); property ineligible for MACRS under "anti-churning" rules; property which the taxpayer elects to depreciate under a method not expressed in a term of years, e.g., the income-forecast method (¶1961)); public utility property for which the taxpayer doesn't use the MACRS normalization method of accounting; motion picture films or video tapes, including videocassettes; and master sound recordings.[23] (Code Sec. 168(f))

¶ 1909   General asset and vintage accounts for property under MACRS.

Taxpayers can elect to maintain one or more general asset (i.e., "vintage") accounts for eligible MACRS property. (Code Sec. 168(i)(4)) The election is made (on Form 4562) on a

---

18. ¶L-7831 *et seq.*; ¶1674.120 *et seq.*, ¶2734; TD ¶265,023 *et seq.*
19. ¶K-5921 *et seq.*, ¶L-7828; ¶2164.01; TD ¶265,019
20. ¶L-7602; ¶1674.085; TD ¶264,506

21. ¶L-8100 *et seq.*; ¶1684 *et seq.*; TD ¶266,001
22. ¶L-8201; ¶1684; TD ¶266,008
23. ¶L-8201; ¶1684; TD ¶266,008

timely filed return (including extensions) for the tax year in which the assets are placed in service. For partnerships and S corporations, the election is made at the entity level. (Reg § 1.168(i)-1(k))[24]

A general asset account (GAA) can include assets that are placed in service in the same tax year and have the same applicable depreciation method, recovery period, asset class (see ¶1912) and convention. However, vehicles that are subject to the depreciation caps for passenger autos (¶1953) may be grouped only in their own GAA. (Reg § 1.168(i)-1(c)(2)) Assets either used in a personal activity (Reg § 1.168(i)-1(c)(1), Reg § 1.168(i)-1(h)(1)) or for which a credit or deduction recapture event has occurred (Reg § 1.168(i)-1(j)) can't be included in a GAA.[25] The depreciation allowance for each GAA, determined by using the applicable depreciation method, recovery period, and convention for the assets in the GAA, is recorded in a depreciation reserve account for each GAA. (Reg § 1.168(i)-1(d)(1))

For a disposition of an asset from a GAA (Reg § 1.168(i)-1(e)(2)):

(1) The amount realized is recognized as ordinary income to the extent of the excess of (a) the unadjusted depreciable basis (i.e., generally cost) of the GAA plus any expensed costs for assets in the GAA, over (b) any amounts recognized as ordinary income on previous asset dispositions. Any remaining amount is recognized as income under other applicable Code sections, other than the Code Sec. 1245 and Code Sec. 1250 depreciation recapture rules. (Code Sec. 168(i)(4); Reg § 1.168(i)-1(b)(4), Reg § 1.168(i)-1(e)(2))

If an asset disposition is a "qualifying disposition" (i.e., is of less than all assets in the GAA and occurs due to a casualty, charitable contribution, cessation of business, etc.) and the taxpayer wants to end GAA treatment for the asset(s) as of the first day of the tax year in which the disposition occurs, the gain, loss, or other deduction for the asset(s) takes into account the adjusted basis (i.e., unadjusted depreciable basis of the asset or assets, less depreciation allowed or allowable). (Reg § 1.168(i)-1(e)(3))

(2) Except for a "qualifying disposition," the unadjusted depreciable basis of the GAA and the depreciation reserve of the GAA aren't affected (i.e., reduced). (Reg § 1.168(i)-1(e)(2))

(3) Except when a GAA ends, no loss is realized upon the disposition of an asset, since the asset is treated as having an adjusted basis of zero. (Reg § 1.168(i)-1(e)(2)(i)) On a disposition of all remaining assets, the taxpayer at his option may treat the GAA as ended (by reporting the gain, loss or other deduction on the timely filed, including extensions, return for the disposition year) or as not ended. (Reg § 1.168(i)-1(e)(3))[26]

¶ 1910   "Step into the shoes" rule for certain carryover-basis property.

If property is acquired in certain nontaxable transfers (such as transactions described in Code Sec. 332 (¶3577), Code Sec. 351 (¶3510) or Code Sec. 361 (¶3562)) the transferee "steps into the shoes" of the transferor for the depreciation period and method of the transferred property. This applies to the extent that the transferee's basis in the property equals the transferor's adjusted basis. (Code Sec. 168(i)(7)(B), Code Sec. 168(i)(7)(C))[27]

¶ 1911   IRS optional MACRS rate tables.

Instead of making the MACRS computations described at ¶1906 for either the general or alternate depreciation systems, a taxpayer can, with no notice to IRS, instead rely on tables provided by IRS (reproduced at ¶1117), subject to the following rules:

(1) All the tables' rates (accelerated or straight-line) are applied to the property's *unadjusted depreciable basis*. For that purpose, unadjusted depreciable basis is the basis for determining gain or loss, not reduced by prior depreciation, and reflecting reductions in basis for: (a) personal-use percentage of the asset for the tax year; (b) any portion of the

---

24. ¶L-8931; TD ¶266,215
25. ¶L-8922, ¶L-8925.1; TD ¶266,215

26. ¶L-8923 *et seq.*; TD ¶266,215
27. ¶L-10401; ¶1684.04; TD ¶266,508

asset that is expensed under Code Sec. 179 (¶1941); and (c) other initial basis adjustments—e.g., for the Code Sec. 44 disabled-access credit (¶2324), or, unless the taxpayer "elected out," for bonus depreciation ¶1933 *et seq.*). (Reg § 1.168(b)-1(a)(3))

(2) The taxpayer must use the tables to compute the annual depreciation allowances for the entire recovery period of the property. However, a taxpayer may not continue to use the tables if there are any adjustments to the basis of the property for reasons other than: (a) depreciation allowed or allowable, or (b) an addition or an improvement to such property that is subject to depreciation as a separate item of property.

(3) Use of the tables is denied for a short tax year and for later tax years with respect to MACRS personal property not fully depreciated by the end of the short tax year (¶1926).[28]

illustration: T bought an item of used 7-year property for $10,000 and placed it in service on Aug. 11, Year 1. T used the item exclusively in his business. Also, T didn't expense the item under Code Sec. 179, and no other Code provisions requiring initial basis adjustments applied to the item. The unadjusted depreciable basis of the property is $10,000. The percentages for 7-year property using the 200% declining balance method and the half-year convention are found in Table 1, see ¶1117. Each year of the recovery period, multiply $10,000 by the percentages for 7-year property in Table 1. The depreciation deduction each year of the recovery period is as follows:[29]

Year	Basis	Percentage	Deduction
1	$10,000	14.29%	$1,429
2	10,000	24.49%	2,449
3	10,000	17.49%	1,749
4	10,000	12.49%	1,249
5	10,000	8.93%	893
6	10,000	8.92%	892
7	10,000	8.93%	893
8	10,000	4.46%	446

¶ 1912 Determining the MACRS recovery class for an asset.

The assignment of MACRS property to a recovery class is generally made by reference to that property's class life as of Jan. 1, '86. (Code Sec. 168(i)(1)) The class life of many types of assets is carried in Rev Proc 87-56, 1987-2 CB 674. The assignment to a MACRS recovery class is determined as follows (Code Sec. 168(e)(1)):

MACRS Recovery Class	Property With a Class Life (in Years) of:
3-Year	4 or less
5-Year	More than 4 but less than 10
7-Year	10 or more but less than 16
10-Year	16 or more but less than 20
15-Year	20 or more but less than 25
20-Year	25 or more

In addition, MACRS assigns certain property specific classes as follows (and as described at ¶1913 *et seq.*): certain water utility property is in the 25-year class; residential rental property is in the 27.5-year class; nonresidential real property placed in service before May 13, '93 is in the 31.5-year class; nonresidential real property placed in service after May 12, '93 is in the 39-year class; and any railroad grading and tunnel bore is in the 50-year class. (Code

---

28. ¶L-8602, ¶L-8904 *et seq.*; ¶1684; TD ¶267,008   29. ¶L-8910

Sec. 168(c))[30]

¶ 1913   The three-year MACRS class.

This class includes:

... Depreciable personal property with a class life of four years or less (Code Sec. 168(e)(1)), such as: tractor units for use over-the-road; breeding hogs; special handling devices used in the manufacture of food and beverages; and special tools used in the manufacture of rubber products, finished plastic products, and motor vehicles.

... All racehorses placed in service after 2008 and before 2014, racehorses more than two years old when placed in service after 2013, and other horses more than 12 when placed in service. (Code Sec. 168(e)(3)(A))

... Qualified rent-to-own (RTO) property (certain consumer durables held for rent). (Code Sec. 168(e)(3)(A)(iii), Code Sec. 168(i)(14))[31]

¶ 1914   The five-year MACRS class.

This class includes:

... Depreciable personal property with a class life of more than four years and less than ten years (Code Sec. 168(e)(1)), such as: information systems (computers); heavy general purpose trucks; trailers and trailer-mounted containers; breeding or dairy cattle; ; certain assets used in the drilling of oil and gas wells, construction, the manufacture of textile yarns, apparel, and other finished goods, and the cutting of timber. Also, IRS ruled that support vessels used in offshore oil and gas operations (whether or not used in connection with drilling) are five-year property.[32]

... Any automobiles or light-general purpose trucks (Code Sec. 168(e)(3)(B)(i));

... Semiconductor manufacturing equipment (Code Sec. 168(e)(3)(B)(ii)) in ADR class 36.0;

... Computer-based telephone central office switching equipment (Code Sec. 168(e)(3)(B)(iii));

... Qualified technological equipment (Code Sec. 168(e)(3)(B)(iv));

... Code Sec. 1245 property used in connection with research and experimentation (Code Sec. 168(e)(3)(B)(v));

... Gas station pump canopies (but not the concrete footings used to anchor the canopies);[33]

... Certain energy-related property. (Code Sec. 168(e)(3)(B)(vi), Code Sec. 48(a)(3)(A));

... Most farming equipment and machinery (other than grain bins, cotton ginning assets, fences, or other land improvements), the original use of which commences with the taxpayer after Dec. 31, 2008, and which is placed in service before Jan. 1, 2010. (Code Sec. 168(e)(3)(B)(vii))[34]

caution: Check http://ria.thomsonreuters.com/federaltaxhandbook to see if the above provision has been extended.

... Qualified New York Liberty Zone leasehold improvement property (unless the taxpayer elects out of 5-year MACRS). This is certain property located in the Liberty Zone and placed in service after Sept. 10, 2001 and before 2007. Such property is depreciated via straight line only. (Code Sec. 1400L(c))

Consumer durable property (such as tangible personal property used in a home) subject to rent-to-own contracts is also 5-year property if it isn't qualified rent-to-own property (see ¶1913).[35]

---

30. ¶L-8202; ¶1684; TD ¶266,202
31. ¶L-8204; ¶1684.01; TD ¶266,203
32. ¶L-8205; ¶1684.01; TD ¶266,205

33. ¶L-8205; TD ¶266,205
34. ¶L-8205; ¶1684.01; TD ¶266,205
35. ¶L-8205; ¶1684.01; TD ¶266,205

¶ 1915   The seven-year MACRS class.

This class includes:

. . . Property with a class life of 10 years or more, but less than 16 years (Code Sec. 168(e)(1)), such as: office furniture, fixtures, and equipment; machinery and equipment used in agriculture (including vineyard trellising); certain assets (except helicopters) used in air transport; certain assets used in exploration for and production of petroleum and natural gas products, the manufacture of wood products and furniture, and theme and amusement parks and recreation facilities (e.g., bowling alleys).

. . . Property that doesn't have a class life and isn't specifically assigned to any other MACRS class. (Code Sec. 168(e)(3)(C)(v)) Under this rule, the Tax Court held that street light assets of an electric utility are seven-year property.

. . . Any horse not assigned to the three-year class (see ¶1913).

. . . Railroad tracks. (Code Sec. 168(e)(3)(C)(i))[36]

. . . Motorsports entertainment complexes, as defined in Code Sec. 168(i)(15), placed in service before 2010. (Code Sec. 168(e)(3)(C)(ii))[37]

caution: Check http://ria.thomsonreuters.com/federaltaxhandbook to see if the above provision has been extended.

. . . Alaska natural gas pipeline property placed in service after calendar year 2013, or treated, by election, as placed in service after 2013 if placed in service after 2004 and before 2013. (Code Sec. 168(e)(3)(C)(iii))[38]

. . . Effective for property placed in service after Apr. 11, 2005, "natural gas gathering lines" the original use of which begins with the taxpayer. (Code Sec. 168(e)(3)(C)(iv)) Property won't qualify if the taxpayer or a related person (1) entered into a binding contract for the property's construction before Apr. 12, 2005 or (2) began to construct the property before Apr. 12, 2005. There is no AMT depreciation adjustment (¶3207) for the entire recovery period of natural gas gathering lines. (Code Sec. 56(a)(1)(B))[39]

¶ 1916   The ten-year MACRS class.

This class includes:

. . . Property with a class life of 16 years or more but less than 20 (Code Sec. 168(e)(1)), such as: water transport equipment not used in marine construction; assets used in petroleum refining, manufacture of grain and grain mill products, sugar and sugar products, and vegetable oils and vegetable oil products.[40]

. . . A single purpose agricultural or horticultural structure (Code Sec. 168(e)(3)(D)(i)).

. . . Any tree or vine bearing fruit or nuts (Code Sec. 168(e)(3)(D)(ii)).

. . . Qualified smart electric meters or qualified smart electric grid systems placed in service after Oct. 3, 2008. (Code Sec. 168(e)(3)(D), Code Sec. 168(i)(18), Code Sec. 168(i)(19))[41]

¶ 1917   The 15-year MACRS class.

This class includes:

(1) Property with a class life of 20 years or more but less than 25 years (Code Sec. 168(e)(1)), such as: land improvements (e.g., sidewalks and roads) that aren't explicitly included in another class and aren't buildings or structural improvements; "modern" golf-course greens; assets such as service-station and car-wash buildings; and concrete footings used to anchor gas station pump canopies.

36. ¶L-8206; ¶1684.01; TD ¶266,206
37. ¶L-8206.3; ¶1684.01; TD ¶266,206
38. ¶L-8206.2; ¶1684.01

39. ¶L-8206.1; ¶1684.01; TD ¶266,206
40. ¶L-8207; ¶1684.01; TD ¶266,207
41. ¶L-8207; ¶1684.01; TD ¶266,207

(2) Municipal wastewater treatment plants (Code Sec. 168(e)(3)(E)(i));

(3) Telephone distribution plants and comparable equipment used for two-way exchange of voice and data communications. (Code Sec. 168(e)(3)(E)(ii))

(4) Any Code Sec. 1250 property (generally, depreciable real property) which is a retail motor fuels outlet (many gas stations qualify). (Code Sec. 168(e)(3)(E)(iii))[42]

(5) Qualified leasehold improvement property, qualified restaurant property and qualified retail improvement property. With certain modifications, qualified leasehold improvement property is defined as it is for bonus first-year depreciation (¶1934) and must be placed in service before 2010. Qualified restaurant property is (1) a building improvement placed in service before 2010 if (a) the improvement is placed in service more than three years after the date the building was first placed in service and (b) more than 50% of the building's square footage is devoted to the preparation of, and seating for, on-premises consumption of prepared meals (the more-than-50% test) or (2) a building placed in service during calendar year 2009 that passes the more-than-50% test. Qualified retail improvement property must be placed in service during calendar year 2009 and includes certain interior improvements to retail space that are placed in service more than 3 years after the date the building was first placed in service and that meet other requirements. (Code Sec. 168(e)(3)(E), Code Sec. 168(e)(6), Code Sec. 168(e)(7), Code Sec. 168(e)(8))[43]

⚠ caution: Check http://ria.thomsonreuters.com/federaltaxhandbook to see if the above provisions have been extended.

(6) Initial clearing and grading land improvements relating to gas utility property. (Code Sec. 168(e)(3)(E)(vi))[44]

(7) Certain new electrical transmission property, generally placed in service after Apr. 11, 2005 (and not disqualified under certain transition rules), (Code Sec. 168(e)(3)(E)(vii)), and certain new "natural gas distribution lines," generally placed in service after Apr. 11, 2005 (and not disqualified under certain transition rules) and before Jan. 1, 2011. (Code Sec. 168(e)(3)(E)(viii))[45]

⚠ caution: Check http://ria.thomsonreuters.com/federaltaxhandbook to see if the above provisions have been extended.

¶ 1918   The 20-year MACRS class.

This class includes property with a class life of 25 years or more (Code Sec. 168(e)(1)), such as farm buildings (other than single purpose agricultural or horticultural structures) and gas utility distribution facilities.[46]

¶ 1919   Residential and nonresidential buildings under MACRS.

A 27.5-year class is specifically assigned to residential rental property. (Code Sec. 168(c)) Residential real property is defined as a building or structure for which 80% or more of the gross rental income is from dwelling units (Code Sec. 168(e)(2)(A)). In applying the 80% test, multiple structures that are located on the same tract or parcel (or contiguous tracts or parcels) and operated as a single integrated unit are treated as a single building or structure.[47] Otherwise-qualifying residential rental property can include manufactured homes, and, if permanently anchored, mobile homes.[48] A 39-year class life is specifically assigned to nonresidential real property (Code Sec. 168(c)), which is a classification that includes, generally, buildings or structures that aren't residential rental property. (Code Sec. 168(e)(2)(B)[49] Nonresidential real property placed in service before May 13, '93, had a 31.5-year class.[50] Whether an asset is part of a building or structure—and, thus, depreciated over a longer

42. ¶L-8208, ¶L-8804.1; ¶1684.02; TD ¶266,213
43. ¶L-8208.1, ¶L-8208.2; ¶L-8208.5; ¶1684.02; TD ¶266,208.1, TD ¶266,208.2
44. ¶L-8208; ¶1684.01
45. ¶L-8208.3, ¶L-8208.4; ¶1684.01

46. ¶L-8209; ¶1684.01; TD ¶266,209
47. ¶L-8211.1; TD ¶266,211
48. ¶L-8211; TD ¶266,211
49. ¶L-8210; ¶1684.02; TD ¶266,211
50. ¶L-8210.1; ¶1684.02; TD ¶266,211

period than if it were treated as a separate asset—may depend on whether the asset would not have qualified as tangible personal property for purposes of prior law's investment tax credit. Elevators and escalators are treated as part of a building or structure.[1]

¶ 1920 Additions or improvements to real property.

The depreciation for any additions to, or improvement of, any real property (whether or not recovery property) is determined in the same manner as the depreciation deduction for the real property would be determined if the real property were placed in service at the same time as the addition or improvement. (Code Sec. 168(i)(6)(A))[2]

¶ 1921 Basis of recovery property for computing MACRS depreciation deductions.

If the taxpayer doesn't choose to apply the optional IRS depreciation tables (¶1911), MACRS depreciation deductions are computed on the property's adjusted basis (also referred to by IRS as the "unrecovered basis"), except that salvage value is considered to be zero, i.e., disregarded. (Code Sec. 168(b)(4)) This "unrecovered basis" is adjusted (i.e., ordinarily reduced) by depreciation previously allowed or allowable.[3] For the basis used if the optional IRS depreciation tables are applied, see ¶1911. For mixed-use property, see ¶1902.

¶ 1922 Depreciation of leasehold improvements by lessees.

Lessees are treated as any other owner-taxpayer for purposes of determining MACRS deductions for lessees' improvements subject to MACRS rules. Thus, a lessee's deductions for the property are determined without regard to the lease term. (Code Sec. 168(i)(8))

Where the lease ends or terminates before the end of the MACRS recovery period of the lessee's improvement, and the lessee doesn't retain the improvement, the lessee has a gain or loss for the remaining unrecovered basis of the property.[4]

observation: A gain would arise if, for example, the tenant is paid to terminate the lease and the payment exceeds the basis of the leasehold improvements (and lease acquisition costs, if any).

For amortization of lease acquisition costs, see ¶1597.

¶ 1923 Leasehold improvements by lessor.

A lessor is entitled to recover the cost of depreciable leasehold improvements that it makes. If such improvements are made for the lessee (e.g., to customize the space for the lessee) and are irrevocably disposed of or abandoned by the lessor at the termination of the lease by the lessee, then for purposes of determining gain or loss, the improvement is treated as disposed of by the lessor at that time. (Code Sec. 168(i)(8)(B))[5]

A lessor may advance construction funds to the lessee to help the lessee pay for retail leasehold improvements. If, under the rules explained at ¶1346, a lessee excludes the funds from income, the lessor treats the improvements as its own nonresidential real property, including for purposes of the disposition-of-improvements rule (see above). (Code Sec. 110(b))[6]

¶ 1924 MACRS depreciation periods.

For the 3-year, 5-year, 7-year, 10-year, 15-year and 20-year MACRS classes, the depreciation period is the same as the name of the class (e.g., 5 years for 5-year property). The depreciation period is 25 years for the water utility property class, 27.5 years for the residential rental property class, 39 years for the nonresidential real property class (but 31.5 years if

---

1. ¶L-8210; TD ¶266,211
2. ¶L-9105; TD ¶266,006
3. ¶L-8601; ¶1684; TD ¶266,003

4. ¶L-9106; ¶1684.02; TD ¶267,020
5. ¶L-9106; ¶1684.02; TD ¶267,020
6. ¶J-2265; ¶1104; TD ¶123,005

the property is placed in service before May 13, '93) and 50 years for the railroad grading or tunnel bore class. (Code Sec. 168(c))[7]

Where the 150% declining balance method is elected for MACRS property eligible for the 200% declining balance method, the applicable recovery period is as follows (Code Sec. 168(b)(2)): for property placed in service before '99, the recovery period provided under the "Alternative Depreciation System" (ADS) discussed at ¶1930 *et seq.*; for property placed in service after '98, the regular MACRS recovery periods described above.[8]

Shorter depreciation periods apply for "qualified Indian reservation property" placed in service after '93 and before 2010. (Code Sec. 168(j))[9]

✏️caution: Check http://ria.thomsonreuters.com/federaltaxhandbook to see if the above provision has been extended.

¶ 1925   MACRS depreciation methods.

There are three depreciation methods used for MACRS property: the 200% and 150% declining balance methods with an appropriate switch to straight-line to maximize deductions, and the straight-line method. (Code Sec. 168(b)) Under the declining balance methods, the depreciation rate (in percentage terms) generally is determined by dividing the declining balance percentage (200% or 150%) by the applicable recovery period. For example, the 200% declining balance method applied to property with a 5-year recovery period results in a depreciation rate of 40% (i.e., 200% ÷ 5). This 40% rate remains constant for each tax year in which the 200% declining balance method is used.[10]

The 200% declining balance method can be used for MACRS property in the three-, five-, seven-, and ten-year recovery classes except for any property that must be depreciated on either of the methods discussed below. (Code Sec. 168(b)(1))

The 150% declining balance method must used for MACRS property in the 15-year class (except for qualified leasehold improvements, qualified restaurant property, and qualified retail improvement property, see ¶1917) and the 20-year class (Code Sec. 168(b)(2)(A)), any property (placed in service after '88) used in a farming business (Code Sec. 168(b)(2)(B)), qualified smart electric meters or qualified smart electric grid systems (unless described in Code Sec. 168(b)(3)) (Code Sec. 168(b)(2)(C)), and, if the taxpayer elects (as discussed below), any other property (other than that for which straight-line must be used). (Code Sec. 168(b)(2)(D))

The straight-line method must be used for: residential rental property; nonresidential real property; qualified leasehold improvements; qualified restaurant property; qualified retail improvement property; qualified Liberty Zone leasehold improvement property; any railroad grading or tunnel bore; any tree or vine bearing fruit or nuts; and water utility property. (Code Sec. 168(b)(3))[11]

For property not required to use the straight-line method, a taxpayer can elect (as discussed below) the straight-line method over the recovery period (¶1924) that applies to the property. (Code Sec. 168(b)(3))[12]

The elections discussed above to use the 150% declining balance method or the straight-line method are made on a class-by-class basis and are irrevocable. (Code Sec. 168(b)(5))

✏️observation: Also, an alternative depreciation system election changes the depreciation method from accelerated to straight-line, see ¶1930 *et seq.*, as does an election to forego accelerated depreciation and bonus depreciation in exchange for the present allowance of certain otherwise-deferred tax credits, see ¶1933.

For computing depreciation under IRS optional MACRS rate tables, see ¶1911.

---

7. ¶L-8802; ¶s 1684.01, 1684.02; TD ¶267,004
8. ¶L-8103; ¶1684.01; TD ¶267,017
9. ¶L-8806; ¶1684.01; TD ¶267,007

10. ¶L-8902 *et seq.*; ¶1684.01; TD ¶266,004
11. ¶L-8917; ¶s 1684.01, 1684.02; TD ¶267,018
12. ¶L-8920 *et seq.*; ¶1684.01; TD ¶267,018

For the depreciation methods that must be used for alternative minimum tax purposes, see ¶3207 *et seq.*

¶ 1926   Effect of short tax years on MACRS depreciation.

The depreciation allowance for MACRS personal property placed in service or disposed of in a short year can't be determined by using the IRS optional MACRS rate tables. The depreciation allowance for the short tax year is instead determined by: (1) multiplying the property's depreciable basis by the applicable depreciation rate, and (2) multiplying the product obtained in step (1) by a fraction, the numerator of which is the number of months (including fractions of months) the property is deemed in service during the short year under the applicable convention, and the denominator is 12.[13] The depreciation allowance for any tax year following the short tax year is determined by consistently using either the "allocation method" or the "simplified method" described in a revenue procedure. [14]

Rules are provided for how the half-year and mid-quarter conventions for MACRS personal property apply where property is placed in service or disposed of in a short tax year.[15]

When a taxpayer has a short tax year other than the first year in the recovery period, the MACRS depreciation allowance for that short year must account for the difference between recovery years and tax years.[16]

MACRS depreciation deductions for real property for the year it is placed in service, or disposed of, is based on the mid-month convention and on the number of months the property is in service, see ¶1927, regardless of the length of the taxpayer's tax year. [17]

¶ 1927   MACRS depreciation conventions.

The mid-month depreciation convention applies in determining MACRS depreciation deductions for the year that the following property is placed in service or disposed of: property in the 27.5–year class (residential rental property), property in the 39-year class (31.5-year class if placed in service before May 13, '93) (nonresidential real property), railroad gradings and tunnel bores. Under this rule, property placed in service (or disposed of) during any month is treated as placed in service (or disposed of) at the mid-point of that month in computing MACRS depreciation deductions for the acquisition and disposition years. (Code Sec. 168(d)(2), Code Sec. 168(d)(4)(B))[18]

In the case of all other MACRS property (referred to below as MACRS personal property), the half-year depreciation convention generally applies. The half-year convention treats all MACRS personal property placed in service or disposed of during a tax year as placed in service or disposed of on the mid-point of that tax year. (Code Sec. 168(d)(1), Code Sec. 168(d)(4)(A))

Except as noted below, the mid-quarter convention applies to all MACRS personal property placed in service during a tax year if more than 40% of the total basis of all of that property placed in service during the year is placed in service during the year's last three months. (Code Sec. 168(d)(3))[19] Under the mid-quarter convention, property is treated as placed in service or disposed of on the mid-point of the applicable quarter. (Code Sec. 168(d)(4)(C))

When determining if the mid-quarter convention applies, the taxpayer excludes:

. . . That portion of the basis of property that is expensed under Code Sec. 179; see ¶1941. (Reg § 1.168(d)-1(b)(4)(i))

. . . Nonresidential real property, residential rental property, and any railroad grading or tunnel bore. (Code Sec. 168(d)(3)(B)(i))

. . . Property placed in service and disposed of in the same tax year. (Code

---

13. ¶L-9002; ¶1684.01; TD ¶267,301
14. ¶L-9003 *et seq.*; ¶1684.01; TD ¶267,302
15. ¶L-8705, ¶L-8712; ¶1684.01; TD ¶266,705, TD ¶266,712
16. ¶L-9007; ¶1684.01; TD ¶267,301

17. ¶L-9104; ¶1684.01; TD ¶267,301
18. ¶L-8713; ¶1684.01, ¶1684.02; TD ¶266,713
19. ¶L-8103; ¶1684.01; TD ¶266,707

Sec. 168(d)(3)(B)(ii))

. . . Property excluded from MACRS under Code Sec. 168(f) (Reg § 1.168(d)-1(b)(1)), such as films, videotapes and sound recordings.

. . . The basis of a business car, if the taxpayer elects for the placed-in-service year to claim deductions using the standard mileage allowance method (¶1561).

. . . That portion of basis attributable to the personal-use portion of mixed-use assets (e.g., a self-employed's car used for both business and personal use). (Reg § 1.168(d)-1(b)(4)(iii))

¶ 1928   MACRS deductions for property after use change.

Effective generally for changes in the use of MACRS property in the hands of its owner in a tax year ending after June 16, 2004, the following rules apply.

Personal-use property converted to business or income-producing use (e.g., personal residence converted to rental property) is treated as placed in service on the conversion date, and is subject to the Code Sec. 168 depreciation method, recovery period, and placed-in-service convention applicable to the property beginning in the tax year of the conversion. The property's depreciable basis in the change year is the lesser of its fair market value or adjusted depreciable basis when it is converted. This rule doesn't apply when other rules (e.g., listed property rules under Code Sec. 280F(b)(2)(A)) prescribe the depreciation treatment for a change to business use. (Reg § 1.168(i)-4(b))

MACRS property converted from business or income-producing use to personal use generally is treated as a disposition, with depreciation for the conversion year computed by applying the applicable convention (¶1927). However, the conversion doesn't result in gain, loss, or depreciation recapture. (Reg § 1.168(i)-4(c))

For use changes after placed-in-service year, where the asset continues to be MACRS property in the taxpayer's hands (e.g., commercial property converted to residential rental property), MACRS depreciation for the change year is determined as though the change occurred on the first day of that year. (Reg § 1.168(i)-4(d)(2)(iii))

If a use-change results in:

. . . A shorter recovery period and/or a faster depreciation method, adjusted depreciable basis as of the beginning of the change year is depreciated over the shorter recovery period and/or by the faster method beginning with the year of change as though the property were first placed in service in that year. (Reg § 1.168(i)-4(d)(3)) Taxpayers may elect to continue to depreciate the property as though the change in use had not occurred. (Reg § 1.168(i)-4(d)(3)(ii))

. . . A longer recovery period and/or slower depreciation method, adjusted depreciable basis is depreciated over the longer recovery period and/or by the slower method beginning with the year of change as if the property had been originally placed in service with the longer recovery period and/or slower depreciation method. (Reg § 1.168(i)-4(d)(4))

Where use changes during placed-in-service year, the depreciation allowance generally is established by the primary use of the property during that tax year, determined in a consistently applied and reasonable manner. In determining whether property is used within or outside the U.S. during the placed-in-service year, the predominant use of the property governs. (Reg § 1.168(i)-4(e))

General asset accounts. A change in use doesn't cause or permit the revocation of a general asset account election (¶1909), but the property generally is removed from its existing general asset account and placed in a separate general asset account. (Reg § 1.168(i)-1(h)(2))[20]

20. ¶L-8108; TD ¶266,010

¶ 1929 Depreciating MACRS property acquired in a like-kind exchange or involuntary conversion.

MACRS property may be acquired (1) in exchange for MACRS property in a Code Sec. 1031 like-kind property exchange (¶2418 *et seq.*) or (2) to replace involuntarily converted MACRS property in a Code Sec. 1033 involuntary conversion (¶2430 *et seq.*). (Reg § 1.168(i)-6(c)(1)) The replacement property is for depreciation purposes divided into the depreciable exchanged basis (i.e., remaining basis of the relinquished property carried over to the replacement property), and the depreciable excess basis (i.e., additional consideration to acquire the replacement property). Where the properties share the same recovery class and depreciation method, the depreciable exchanged basis is written off over what's left of the relinquished property's recovery period; and the depreciable excess basis is in effect treated as a separate property with a recovery period that begins anew. (Reg § 1.168(i)-6(c)(3)(ii))[21]

illustration: In 2008, ABX Corp. bought a refrigerator truck (5-year MACRS property, ¶1914) for $100,000 and placed it in service that year. In 2010, ABX acquires a used truck in exchange for the truck bought in 2008 by trading in the truck bought in 2008 and paying $50,000 cash. ABX uses the optional rate tables (¶1911) to compute depreciation and is subject to the half-year convention (¶1927) in 2008 and 2010. ABC claimed $20,000 of depreciation in 2008 (20%), and $32,000 in 2009 (32%). For 2010, ABX may claim a depreciation deduction of $9,600 for the relinquished truck ($100,000 × .192 [recovery year 3 table percentage for 5-year property] × 6/12 [half-year convention applies]). The remaining depreciable basis of the relinquished truck (i.e., the depreciable exchanged basis) is $38,400 ($100,000 cost − $20,000 − $32,000 − $9,600), which is depreciated over 2010—2013 (what's left of the original recovery period). ABX's depreciable excess basis in the replacement truck is $50,000, the cash it pays to acquire it. Per the table percentages, the depreciation allowance for this excess basis is $10,000 for 2010 (20%), $16,000 for 2011 (32%), $9,600 for 2012 (19.2%), $5,760 for 2013 and 2014 (11.52%), and $2,880 (5.76%) for 2015.

If ABX's replacement truck were new instead of used, and it were eligible for bonus depreciation (see ¶1933 *et seq.*), ABX could claim a bonus depreciation allowance on both the remaining basis of the old truck and the cash paid to acquire the new truck. (Reg § 1.168(k)-1(f)(5)(iii)(A)) But if qualifying property is placed in service and disposed of in an exchange or involuntary conversion in the same tax year, the remaining basis of the exchanged or involuntarily converted property isn't eligible for bonus depreciation. (Reg § 1.168(k)-1(f)(5)(iii)(B))[22]

Complex rules apply if the exchanged properties aren't depreciated with the same period and/or method. (Reg § 1.168(i)-6(c)(3)(iii), Reg § 1.168(i)-6(c)(4))[23]

Election out. A taxpayer may elect not to apply the above "split basis" approach to the exchanged properties, and, instead, treat the exchanged basis and excess basis, if any, in the replacement property as placed in service at the time of replacement and the adjusted depreciable basis of the relinquished MACRS property as being disposed of. (Reg § 1.168(i)-6(i))[24]

¶ 1930 The straight-line "alternative depreciation system" (ADS) of MACRS.

The alternative depreciation system (ADS) is a straight-line depreciation system, with generally longer depreciation periods than under the general depreciation system. (Code Sec. 168(g)(2)(C), Code Sec. 168(g)(3)(B)) ADS uses the same depreciation conventions as MACRS (Code Sec. 168(g)(2)(B)), see ¶1927, and like MACRS, disregards salvage value. (Code Sec. 168(g)(2)(A))

Depreciation deductions must be computed under ADS only for certain specified properties, see ¶1931. However, ADS must be used for all properties including properties depreciated under MACRS for purpose of computing earnings and profits of corporations (Code

21. ¶L-10600 *et seq.*; TD ¶269,400 *et seq.*
22. ¶L-10602; ¶1684.048; TD ¶269,416
23. ¶L-10601.2A; TD ¶269,403
24. ¶L-10601.8; TD ¶269,413

Sec. 312(k)(3)(A)). ADS also applies for purposes of computing the depreciation tax preference under the alternative minimum tax, under the rules explained at ¶3207.[25] ADS may be elected for all other properties—on a class by class basis for personal property and on an individual basis for residential rental and nonresidential real properties. (Code Sec. 168(g)(7)(A))

An ADS election is an irrevocable year-by-year election. (Code Sec. 168(g)(7)(B)) This election is in addition to the straight-line MACRS election (¶1925).

Property excluded from MACRS because a depreciation method not measured in term of years is elected (¶1908) is also excluded from ADS. (Code Sec. 168(f)(1))

¶ 1931 MACRS property required to be depreciated under ADS.

The following MACRS property must be depreciated under ADS:

. . . "Luxury" automobiles and other "listed" (i.e., mixed-use) property used 50% or more for personal purposes, see ¶1950. (Code Sec. 280F(b)(1))

. . . Properties used predominantly outside the U.S.[26] (Code Sec. 168(g)(1)(A)), except certain properties listed in the Code.[27] (Code Sec. 168(g)(4))

. . . Tax-exempt use property (generally, certain property leased to tax-exempt organizations, governmental units or foreign persons or entities, see Code Sec. 168(h)(3)).[28] (Code Sec. 168(g)(1)(B))

. . . Tax-exempt bond financed property.[29] (Code Sec. 168(g)(1)(C))

. . . Imported business equipment from countries that discriminate against U.S. goods from the date the equipment is placed on a restricted list by Presidential Executive Order. (Code Sec. 168(g)(6))[30]

. . . Pre-production costs of farming property excluded from the inventory-capitalization rule of Code Sec. 263A (discussed in ¶1660 *et seq.*).[31]

. . . Intermodal cargo containers not used predominantly in the direct transportation of property to or from the U.S.[32]

¶ 1932 ADS depreciation periods.

The prescribed ADS straight-line periods are:

. . . except as discussed below, the property's "class-life" (¶1912). (Code Sec. 168(g)(3)(B))

. . . four years—for qualified rent-to-own property (¶1913). (Code Sec. 168(g)(3)(B))[33]

. . . five years—for automobiles, light-purpose trucks (Code Sec. 168(g)(3)(D)) and qualified technological equipment.[34] (Code Sec. 168(g)(3)(C))

. . . nine years—for qualified Liberty Zone leasehold improvement property (¶1914). (Code Sec. 1400L(c))

. . . 10 years—for most new farming equipment and machinery placed in service during calendar year 2009. (Code Sec. 168(g)(3)(B))

caution: Check http://ria.thomsonreuters.com/federaltaxhandbook to see if the above provision has been extended.

. . . 12 years—for personal property with no class life and not governed by any other rule discussed in this list. (Code Sec. 168(g)(2)(C))

. . . 14 years—for property treated as natural gas gathering lines under the timing rules and other rules discussed at ¶1915. (Code Sec. 168(g)(3)(B))

25. ¶A-8220; ¶s 564.01, 1684.03; TD ¶267,501
26. ¶L-9406; ¶s 280F4, 1684.03; TD ¶267,502
27. ¶L-9406; ¶1684.03; TD ¶267,504
28. ¶L-9600 *et seq.*; ¶s 1684.03, 1684.06; TD ¶267,502
29. ¶L-9500 *et seq.*; ¶1684.03; TD ¶267,502
30. ¶L-9405; ¶1684.03; TD ¶267,502
31. ¶L-9402; ¶s 263A4, 263A4.15, 1684.03; TD ¶267,502
32. ¶s L-9402, L-9407; TD ¶267,502
33. ¶L-9403; ¶1684; TD ¶267,503
34. ¶L-9403 *et seq.*; ¶1684.03; TD ¶267,503

... 20 years—for any Code Sec. 1250 property (generally depreciable real property) which is a retail motor fuels outlet and, for property placed in service after Oct. 22, 2004, initial clearing and grading land improvements relating to gas utility property (¶1917). (Code Sec. 168(g)(3)(B))

... 22 years—for Alaska natural gas pipeline property placed in service after 2004 (¶1915). (Code Sec. 168(g)(3)(B))

... 30 years—property treated as electrical transmission property under the timing and other rules discussed at ¶1917. (Code Sec. 168(g)(3)(B))

... 35 years—property treated as natural gas distribution lines under the timing and other rules discussed at ¶1917. (Code Sec. 168(g)(3)(B))

... 39 years—for (1) qualified leasehold improvement property, and building improvements that are qualified restaurant property, placed in service before 2010 and (2) qualified retail improvement property, and buildings that are qualified restaurant property, placed in service during calendar year 2009 (¶1917). (Code Sec. 168(g)(3)(B))

caution: Check http://ria.thomsonreuters.com/federaltaxhandbook to see if the above provision has been extended.

... 40 years—for nonresidential real property and for residential rental property other than low or moderate income housing qualifying for the 27.5-year period (Code Sec. 168(g)(2)(C)) and any Code Sec. 1245 real property with no class life. (Code Sec. 168(g)(3)(E))

Also, the ADS depreciation period is 5 years for semiconductor manufacturing equipment, 9.5 years for computer-based telephone central office switching equipment, 10 years for railroad tracks, 15 years for single-purpose agricultural or horticultural structures, 20 years for trees or vines bearing fruit or nuts, 24 years for a municipal wastewater treatment plant or for telephone distribution plant equipment and 50 years for railroad gradings, tunnel bores, or water utility property. (Code Sec. 168(g)(2)(C), Code Sec. 168(g)(3)(B))[35]

For "tax-exempt use property" (¶1931) subject to a lease, the above depreciation periods can't be less than 125% of the lease term. (Code Sec. 168(g)(1)(B), Code Sec. 168(g)(3)(A))[36]

¶ 1933   50% bonus first-year depreciation allowance.

A bonus first-year depreciation allowance applies to "qualified property" (¶1934). The allowance, which is claimed in the first year that the property is placed in service by the taxpayer for use in its trade or business or for the production of income, is equal to 50% of the unadjusted depreciable basis (see ¶1911) of property acquired, generally, after Dec. 31, 2007 and before Jan. 1, 2011. (Code Sec. 168(k); Reg § 1.168(k)-1(d)(1))

caution: Check http://ria.thomsonreuters.com/federaltaxhandbook to see if the above provision has been extended.

The adjusted basis of the property is reduced by the bonus depreciation before computing the amount otherwise allowable as a depreciation deduction for the tax year and any later tax year. (Code Sec. 168(k)(1)(B)) There is no AMT depreciation adjustment (¶3207) for the entire recovery period of qualified property. (Code Sec. 168(k)(2)(G); Reg § 1.168(k)-1(d)(2)(ii))[37]

For property placed in service after Oct. 3, 2008 and before 2013, 50% bonus first-year depreciation is available for qualified cellulosic biofuel plant property. (Code Sec. 168(l)) For property purchased after Dec. 20, 2006 and placed in service before Oct. 4, 2008, 50% bonus first-year depreciation was available for qualified cellulosic biomass ethanol plant property.[38]

Additionally, 50% bonus first-year depreciation applies to "qualified reuse and recycling property." This is reuse and recycling property that is purchased new by the taxpayer after

---

35. ¶L-9403; ¶1684.03; TD ¶267,503
36. ¶L-9602; ¶1684.06

37. ¶L-9310 *et seq.*; ¶1684.025 *et seq.*; TD ¶269,340 *et seq.*
38. ¶L-9356; ¶1684.08; TD ¶696,514

Aug. 31, 2008 and meets other detailed requirements. (Code Sec. 168(m))[39]

A 30% bonus first-year depreciation allowance applies to "qualified New York Liberty Zone property"—i.e., certain property used in the New York Liberty Zone (an area of southernmost Manhattan described in Code Sec. 1400L(h)).[40] One of the requirements for being qualified New York Liberty Zone property is that the property be placed in service before Jan 1, 2007 (before Jan 1, 2010 for certain qualifying nonresidential real property and certain residential rental property).[41]

⚫️ *caution:* Check http://ria.thomsonreuters.com/federaltaxhandbook to see if the above provision has been extended.

For the bonus depreciation available for "qualified GO Zone property," see ¶1939, and for "qualified disaster assistance property," see ¶1940.

For "eligible qualified property" (generally, "qualified property," see ¶1934, that is originally used and acquired after Mar. 31, 2008 and placed in service before Jan. 1, 2010 (Jan. 1, 2011 for certain long-production period property and certain aircraft), corporations can elect to forego bonus depreciation and accelerated depreciation (see ¶1925) in exchange for the present allowance, as refundable tax credits, of the following otherwise-deferred (under the rules at ¶2303) "pre-2006 credits": (1) research credits (¶2320) from tax years beginning before 2006 and (2) credits against regular tax for AMT paid (¶2373), to the extent the AMT is attributable to tax years before 2006. Otherwise applicable credit limits are increased by 20% of the difference between depreciation allowed for eligible qualified property if bonus depreciation is claimed less depreciation allowed if bonus depreciation isn't claimed. Cumulatively, the total increase in credit limitations can't exceed the lesser of $30 million or 6% of the pre-2006 credits. (Code Sec. 168(k)(4)) A corporation can choose to exclude from the election "extension property" (eligible qualified property placed in service after 2008 (after 2009 for certain long-production period property and certain aircraft)). (Code Sec. 168(k)(4)(H)(i)(I)) If a corporation doesn't choose to exclude extension property from the election, the election is computed separately for extension property and property that isn't extension property. (Code Sec. 168(k)(4)(H)(i)(II)) The election could be made beginning with the first tax year ending after Mar. 31, 2008 or the first tax year ending after Dec. 31, 2008. (Code Sec. 168(k)(4)(H)(ii)))[42]

⚫️ *caution:* Check http://ria.thomsonreuters.com/federaltaxhandbook to see if the above provision has been extended.

50% bonus depreciation also applied for certain qualified property acquired after May 5, 2003 and before Jan. 1, 2005, and 30% bonus depreciation applied for certain qualified property acquired after Sept. 10, 2001, and before May 6, 2003.[43]

¶ 1934 "Qualified property" eligible for the bonus first-year depreciation allowance.

"Qualified property" eligible for bonus first-year depreciation (¶1933) includes most tangible personal property, "qualified leasehold improvement property" (i.e. certain interior improvements to nonresidential buildings), and most computer software. (Code Sec. 168(k)(2)(A)(i))[44] In addition to being of a qualifying type, the property must meet original use (¶1935), timely acquisition (¶1936), and timely placed-in-service (¶1937) requirements. (Reg § 1.168(k)-1(b)(1))

Property is ineligible for a bonus first-year depreciation allowance if it must be depreciated under the alternative depreciation system, see ¶1931, ¶1950, or is qualified New York Liberty Zone leasehold improvement property, see ¶1914. (Code Sec. 168(k)(2)(D)) If placed in service

39. ¶L-9361; ¶1684.09
40. ¶L-9340 *et seq.*; ¶1400L4.05 *et seq.*; TD ¶267,700 *et seq.*
41. ¶L-9342; ¶14,00N4.06; TD ¶267,702
42. ¶L-15213 *et seq.*; ¶1684.0293; TD ¶380,511 *et seq.*

43. ¶L-9311 *et seq.*, ¶L-9321 *et seq.*; ¶1684.025 *et seq.*; TD ¶269,340 *et seq.*, TD ¶269,351 *et seq.*
44. ¶L-9312; ¶1684.026; TD ¶269,342

after Dec. 31, 2008 and before Jan. 1, 2010, "qualified retail improvement property," see ¶1917 (Code Sec. 168(e)(8)(D), Code Sec. 168(e)(3)(E)(ix)), and "qualified restaurant property," see ¶1917, are also ineligible. (Code Sec. 168(e)(7)(B), Code Sec. 168(e)(7)(A)(i))[45]

caution: Check http://ria.thomsonreuters.com/federaltaxhandbook to see if the above provision has been extended.

¶ 1935 Original-use requirement for the bonus first-year depreciation allowance for "qualified property."

The original use of qualified property must begin with the taxpayer after Dec. 31, 2007. (Code Sec. 168(k)(2)(A)(ii))

"Original use" is the first use, whether or not that use is *by the taxpayer*. (Code Sec. 168(k)(2)(A)(ii); Reg § 1.168(k)-1(b)(3)(i)) New property first used by a taxpayer for personal use or as inventory and later used by the taxpayer in a trade or business meets the original-use requirement. (Reg § 1.168(k)-1(b)(3)(ii)) There are special rules for reconditioned or rebuilt property, sale-leasebacks, syndication transactions and fractional interests. (Code Sec. 168(k)(2)(E)(ii), Code Sec. 168(k)(2)(E)(iii); Reg § 1.168(k)-1(b)(3))[46]

¶ 1936 Acquisition requirement for the bonus first-year depreciation allowance for "qualified property."

To be "qualified property" for purposes of the 50% bonus first-year depreciation allowance (¶1933), otherwise eligible property must be:

(A) acquired by the taxpayer after Dec. 31, 2007, and before Jan. 1, 2011, but only if no written binding contract for the acquisition was in effect before Jan. 1, 2008, or

(B) acquired by the taxpayer under a written binding contract which was entered into after Dec. 31, 2007, and before Jan. 1, 2011. (Code Sec. 168(k)(2)(A)(iii))

caution: Check http://ria.thomsonreuters.com/federaltaxhandbook to see if the above provision has been extended.

Special rules apply to property manufactured, constructed or produced by or for the taxpayer, and to certain property purchased under a contract entered into by, or certain property constructed for or by, (1) users of the property and (2) persons related to the taxpayer or to users of the property. (Code Sec. 168(k)(2)(E); Reg § 1.168(k)-1(b)(4))[47]

¶ 1937 Placed-in-service requirement for the bonus first-year depreciation allowance for "qualified property."

To be "qualified property" for purposes of the bonus first-year depreciation allowance (¶1933), otherwise eligible property generally must be placed in service by the taxpayer before Jan. 1, 2011 (Jan. 1, 2012 for certain aircraft and certain property with a long production period). (Code Sec. 168(k)(2)(A)(iv))[48]

caution: Check http://ria.thomsonreuters.com/federaltaxhandbook to see if the above provision has been extended.

Also, there are special rules for sale-leasebacks, syndication transactions and certain partnership terminations and non-recognition transactions. (Reg § 1.168(k)-1(b)(5))[49]

45. ¶L-9313; ¶1684.026; TD ¶269,343
46. ¶L-9314 *et seq.*; ¶1684.026; TD ¶269,344 *et seq.*
47. ¶L-9315 *et seq.*, ¶1684.026; TD ¶269,345 *et seq.*
48. ¶L-9316 *et seq.*; ¶1684.027; TD ¶269,346 *et seq.*
49. ¶L-9316 *et seq.*; ¶1684.027; TD ¶269,346 *et seq.*

¶ 1938 Election not to claim bonus first-year depreciation allowance for "qualified property."

For "qualified property" eligible for 50% bonus first-year depreciation (¶1933), the taxpayer may elect not to claim bonus first-year depreciation. This election-out may be made for any class of property for any tax year. (Code Sec. 168(k)(2)(D)(iii)) A taxpayer that elects to claim no bonus depreciation also loses its exemption (discussed at ¶1933) from AMT depreciation adjustments for the elected-for property. (Reg § 1.168(k)-1(e)(6))

Rules are provided for the time and manner of making the above elections. (Reg § 1.168(k)-1(e)(3)) An election-out can be revoked only with IRS consent, except that if the election was made on a timely filed return, the taxpayer can revoke the election by filing an amended return within 6 months of the original return's due date. (Reg § 1.168(k)-1(e)(7))[50]

¶ 1939 50% bonus first-year depreciation allowance for qualified GO Zone property.

Taxpayers can claim a bonus first-year depreciation allowance equal to 50% of the adjusted basis of qualified Gulf Opportunity Zone (GO Zone) property. If claimed, the property's adjusted basis is reduced by the amount of that deduction before computing otherwise allowable depreciation for the tax year and any later tax year. (Code Sec. 1400N(d)(1))[1] Generally, qualified GO Zone property must be property described at ¶1934 or a building, must meet detailed use requirements and must be placed in service by the taxpayer before 2008 (before 2009 for nonresidential real property or residential rental property). But under an exception for specified GO Zone extension property—property in IRS-identified areas in which 2005 hurricanes damaged more than 60% (in the aggregate) of the occupied housing units—nonresidential real property or residential rental property can be placed in service before 2011 (but bonus depreciation is limited to the adjusted basis attributable to manufacture, construction or production before 2010) and certain property in those buildings can be placed in service 90 days after that. (Code Sec. 1400N(d)(2)(A), (Code Sec. 1400N(d)(6))[2]

caution: Check http://ria.thomsonreuters.com/federaltaxhandbook to see if the above provision has been extended.

Taxpayers may elect out of bonus first-year depreciation for any class of GO Zone property for any tax year. (Code Sec. 1400N(d)(2)(B)(iv))[3]

Recapture rules apply similar to those under Code Sec. 179(d)(10), see ¶1947. (Code Sec. 1400N(d)(5)) Thus, under detailed guidance issued by IRS, taxpayers must give back the benefit of bonus depreciation for an asset when the asset ceases to be qualified GO Zone property.[4] Also, there is no AMT depreciation adjustment for qualified GO Zone property. (Code Sec. 1400N(d)(4))[5]

¶ 1940 50% bonus first-year depreciation allowance for qualified disaster assistance property.

The 50% first-year bonus depreciation and exemption from AMT depreciation adjustments (and election to decline those tax benefits) that apply to "qualified property" (¶1933 *et seq.*) also apply to "qualified disaster assistance property." (Code Sec. 168(n)(1), Code Sec. 168(n)(2)(D))

In general, qualified disaster assistance property is property that meets the following requirements: (1) the property is described at ¶1934 or is nonresidential real property or residential rental property, (2) substantially all of the use of the property must be in a trade

50. ¶L-9318 *et seq.*; ¶1684.0291; TD ¶269,348.1 *et seq.*
1. ¶L-9336 *et seq.*; ¶14,00N4.02 *et seq.*; TD ¶269,331 *et seq.*
2. ¶L-9337 *et seq.*; ¶14,00N4.021; TD ¶269,332 *et seq.*
3. ¶L-9338, ¶14,00N4.023; TD ¶269,334
4. ¶L-9339; ¶14,00N4.024; TD ¶269,335
5. ¶A-8221.1; ¶14,00N4.02; TD ¶696,514

276

or business of the taxpayer and in a "disaster area" with respect to a "federally declared disaster" declared after Dec. 31, 2007 and occurring before Jan. 1, 2010, (3) the property must rehabilitate or replace property destroyed or condemned as a result of the disaster and be similar in nature to and located in the same county as the property being rehabilitated or replaced, (4) the original use of the property must begin with an "eligible taxpayer" on or after the "applicable disaster date," (5) the property must be acquired by the taxpayer on or after the "applicable disaster date" by "purchase" and no written binding contract for the acquisition can be in effect before the "applicable disaster date", and (6) the property must be placed in service by the "eligible taxpayer" by the end of the third calendar year (fourth calendar year for nonresidential real property and residential rental property) following the "applicable disaster date." (Code Sec. 168(n)(2)(A), Code Sec. 168(n)(2)(C))

✐/caution: Check http://ria.thomsonreuters.com/federaltaxhandbook to see if the above provision has been extended.

Certain types of property (including property to which bonus depreciation under Code Sec. 168(k) applies, see ¶1933) are excluded from being "qualified disaster assistance property" even if they satisfy the requirements discussed above. (Code Sec. 168(n)(2)(B))

Recapture rules apply similar to those under Code Sec. 179(d)(10), see ¶1947. (Code Sec. 168(n)(4))[6]

¶ 1941 Sec. 179 Expense Election—Form 4562. ▬▬▬▬▬▬▬▬▬▬

Many taxpayers are eligible to deduct (in lieu of depreciation) the cost (subject to dollar limits) of most tangible personal property, and certain other property, used in the active conduct of a trade or business.

Taxpayers, except trusts, estates and certain noncorporate lessors (Code Sec. 179(d)(4), Code Sec. 179(d)(5)), can elect on Form 4562 to expense (deduct in lieu of depreciation) the cost (subject to the dollar limits discussed below) of "section 179 property" (see ¶1946). (Code Sec. 179(a), Code Sec. 179(b)(1))

The maximum amount for tax years beginning in 2010 and 2011 is $500,000, and, for tax years beginning in 2008 or 2009, $250,000. For tax years beginning after 2011, the maximum amount is $25,000. (Code Sec. 179(b)(1)) For special dollar limits for certain types of property, see ¶1942 *et seq.*

For tax years beginning in 2010 and 2011, the maximum annual expensing amount generally is reduced dollar-for-dollar by the amount of section 179 property placed in service during the tax year in excess of $2,000,000 (the investment ceiling). For tax years beginning in 2008 and 2009 the investment ceiling is $800,000. For tax years beginning after 2011, the investment ceiling is $200,000. (Code Sec. 179(b)(2)) For special investment ceiling rules for certain types of property, see ¶1942 *et seq.*

The amount of deduction is further limited to the amount of taxable income from any of taxpayer's active trades or businesses. Taxable income, for this purpose, is computed without regard to the cost of any qualified expense property, the deduction for one-half of self-employment tax, any net operating loss carryback or carryforward, and any deductions suspended under other Code sections (Code Sec. 179(b)(3); Reg § 1.179-2(c)(1)), e.g., the passive activity rules. Employees are considered to be engaged in the active conduct of the trade or business of their employment. (Reg § 1.179-2(c)(6)(iv))

An amount that can't be deducted because of the taxable income limit is carried over indefinitely until it can be deducted. (Code Sec. 179(b)(3)(B)), except that amounts attributable to "qualified real property" (see ¶1946) can't be carried forward beyond tax years beginning in 2011 (and are instead included in the depreciable basis of the property under special rules). (Code Sec. 179(f)(4))[7]

Where an expense election deduction is allocated to a taxpayer from a partnership or an S

---

6. ¶L-9365 *et seq.*; ¶1684.085 *et seq.*; TD ¶267,755 *et seq.*   7. ¶L-9900 *et seq.*; ¶1794 *et seq.*; TD ¶268,400 *et seq.*

corporation, the deduction limitation, the investment limitation, and the "taxable income" limitation are applied at both the partnership (or S corporation) level and the taxpayer level. (Code Sec. 179(d)(8); Reg § 1.179-2(c)) However, for purposes of the investment limitation, the cost of qualifying property that the partnership or S corporation placed in service isn't attributed and allocated to the partner or shareholder. (Reg § 1.179-2(b)(3))[8]

Rules are provided for applying the annual dollar limitation to a controlled group of corporations. (Code Sec. 179(d)(7); Reg § 1.179-2(b)(1))[9]

Married taxpayers filing jointly are treated as one taxpayer in applying the expense deduction limit. (Reg § 1.179-2(b)(5)) Married taxpayers filing separately may elect other than a 50-50 allocation of the expense deduction. Absent the election, the 50-50 allocation applies. (Code Sec. 179(b)(4); Reg § 1.179-2(b)(6))[10]

For tax years beginning before 2012, an expensing election or specification of property to be expensed may be revoked without IRS's consent, but, if revoked, can't be re-elected. (Code Sec. 179(c)(2)) A taxpayer may make or revoke an expensing election on an amended return filed within the time prescribed by law for filing an amended return for the tax year for which the election is made. (Reg § 1.179-5(c)(1)) A taxpayer that elected to expense only part of the cost basis of property for a particular tax year (or didn't make any expensing election) may file an amended return and expense any part of the cost basis of property that was not expensed under a prior Code Sec. 179 election. (Reg § 1.179-5(c)(2))[11]

For a limit on the expensing election for SUVs, see ¶1945.

For prohibition of the expensing election for passenger autos and other "listed property" not predominantly used in business, see ¶1950.

For a dollar cap on the expensing election for passenger autos, see ¶1953.

¶ 1942   Increase in expense amount for enterprise zone property and renewal property.

The applicable maximum regular Code Sec. 179 expense election amount (described at ¶1941) is increased by $35,000 for:

. . . "qualified zone property," placed in service, generally, before 2010, of an enterprise zone business; and (Code Sec. 1397A(a)(1), Code Sec. 1400(a), Code Sec. 1400(f))[12]

. . . "qualified renewal property" acquired by purchase, generally, before 2010, in a renewal community. (Code Sec. 1400J)[13]

caution: Check http://ria.thomsonreuters.com/federaltaxhandbook to see if the above provisions have been extended.

Only 50% of expensing-eligible enterprise zone and qualified renewal property is taken into account before subtracting the applicable Code Sec. 179 phaseout amount (described at ¶1941). (Code Sec. 1397A(a)(2), Code Sec. 1400J(a))[14] Recapture (¶1947) applies if the above types of property cease to qualify during their normal recovery periods. (Code Sec. 1397A(b), Code Sec. 1400J(a))[15]

Qualified zone property or qualified renewal property must meet the following tests:

(1) it is purchased (with the Code Sec. 179(d)(2) exceptions noted at ¶1946) by the taxpayer after the empowerment zone or renewal community designation took effect,

(2) the original use of the property in an empowerment zone or renewal community commences with the taxpayer, and

(3) 85% or more of the use of the property is in an empowerment zone (certain designated

8. ¶L-9909 et seq.; ¶1794.01; TD ¶268,414
9. ¶L-9908; ¶1794.01; TD ¶268,411
10. ¶L-9907; ¶1794.01; TD ¶268,412
11. ¶L-9933; ¶1794.04; TD ¶268,409
12. ¶L-9951, ¶J-3396.4; ¶1397A4; ¶14,004.01; TD ¶268,402

13. ¶L-9985; ¶14,00J4; TD ¶268,701
14. ¶L-9952, ¶L-9988.1; ¶1397A4; ¶14,00J4; TD ¶268,413, TD ¶268,704
15. ¶L-9964, ¶L-9989; ¶1397A4, ¶14,00J4; TD ¶268,428; TD ¶268,705

distressed areas) or renewal community (i.e., communities designated as such by HUD) and in the active conduct of a qualified business by the taxpayer in the empowerment zone or renewal community. (Code Sec. 1397D(a)(1), Code Sec. 1400J(a))[16]

Certain substantial renovation projects are treated as satisfying requirements (1) and (2). (Code Sec. 1397D(a)(2), Code Sec. 1400J(b)) There's no expensing election increase for qualified zone property substantially all the use of which is in certain parcels described in Code Sec. 1391(g)(3)(A)(iii). (Code Sec. 1397A(c))[17]

¶ 1943 Increased expensing election for qualified section 179 disaster assistance property.

For property placed in service after Dec. 31, 2007 for disasters declared after Dec. 31, 2007, the maximum regular Code Sec. 179 expensing allowance (¶1941) is increased by the lesser of (1) $100,000, or (2) the cost of "qualified section 179 disaster assistance property" (see below) placed in service during the tax year. In addition, the regular phaseout level for the amount of expensing-eligible property placed in service during the year (¶1941) is increased by the lesser of (1) $600,000, or (2) the cost of qualified section 179 disaster assistance property placed in service during the tax year. (Code Sec. 179(e)(1))

"Qualified section 179 disaster assistance property" means section 179 property (see ¶1946) which is "qualified disaster assistance property." (Code Sec. 179(e)(1)) For the requirements, including time limitations, for "qualified disaster assistance property," see ¶1940.

For purposes of the special Code Sec. 179 expensing rules that apply to qualified zone property and qualified renewal property (see ¶1942), "qualified section 179 disaster assistance property" isn't treated as qualified zone property or qualified renewal property unless the taxpayer elects not to claim the additional expensing available for "qualified section 179 disaster assistance property." (Code Sec. 179(e)(3))

Recapture rules similar to the recapture rules under Code Sec. 179(d)(10) (see ¶1947) apply with respect to any "qualified section 179 disaster assistance property." (Code Sec. 179(e)(4))[18]

¶ 1944 Increased expensing election for qualified Code Sec. 179 GO Zone property.

The maximum regular Code Sec. 179 expensing allowance (¶1941) is increased by the lesser of (1) $100,000, or (2) the cost of qualified Code Sec. 179 Gulf Opportunity (GO) Zone property placed in service during the tax year. In addition, the regular phaseout level for the amount of expensing-eligible property placed in service during the year (¶1941) is increased by the lesser of (1) $600,000 or (2) the cost of qualified Code Sec. 179 GO Zone property placed in service during the tax year. (Code Sec. 1400N(e)(1))[19]

Among the requirements for qualified Code Sec. 179 GO Zone property is that the property be placed in service by Dec. 31, 2007 (see ¶1939), except that qualified Code Sec. 179 GO Zone property that is placed in service in "specified portions of the GO Zone" (i.e., certain highly damaged portions of the GO Zone) includes property placed in service before calendar year 2009. (Code Sec. 1400N(e)(2))[20]

¶ 1945 Restricted expensing deduction for heavy SUVs.

No more than $25,000 of the cost of a heavy SUV (sport utility vehicle) may be expensed under Code Sec. 179. (Code Sec. 179(b)(5)) The $25,000 expensing limit applies to any 4-

---

16. ¶L-9953, ¶L-9985; ¶1397A4, ¶14,00J4; TD ¶268,430, TD ¶268,701
17. ¶L-9953, ¶L-9985; ¶1397A4, ¶14,00J4; TD ¶268,430, TD ¶268,701
18. ¶L-9907.3; ¶1794.06; TD ¶268,411.2
19. ¶L-9996, ¶L-9996.1; ¶14,00N4.025; TD ¶268,601, TD ¶268,602
20. ¶L-9997, ¶L-9997.1; ¶14,00N4.025; TD ¶268,601, TD ¶268,601.1

wheeled vehicle which (1) is primarily designed (or can be used) to carry passengers on public streets, roads and highways (except for rail vehicles), and (2) has a GVWR (gross, or loaded, vehicle weight rating) of more than 6,000 pounds but not more than 14,000 pounds. (Code Sec. 179(b)(5)(B)(i))

observation: Amounts in excess of the $25,000 limit can be depreciated over the 5-year MACRS recovery period (¶1914) *without regard to* the depreciation dollar caps for luxury autos (¶1953).

A vehicle is *not* subject to the $25,000 expensing limit if it (1) is designed for more than nine individuals in seating rearward of the driver's seat; (2) is equipped with an open cargo area, or a covered box not readily accessible from the passenger compartment, of at least six feet in interior length; or (3) has an integral enclosure, fully enclosing the driver compartment and load carrying device, does not have seating rearward of the drivers seat, and has no body section protruding more than 30 inches ahead of the leading edge of the windshield. (Code Sec. 179(b)(5)(B)(ii))[21]

For prohibition of the expensing election for passenger autos and other "listed property" not predominantly used in business, see ¶1950.

For dollar caps on the expensing election for passenger autos, see ¶1953.

¶ 1946   Property eligible and ineligible for expense election.

Subject to the overall maximum dollar amount and investment ceiling discussed at ¶1941, property eligible for the expense election consists of the following assets, if "purchased" for use in the active trade or business of the taxpayer:

. . . tangible recovery property that's Code Sec. 1245 property (most depreciable property other than buildings and other land improvements),

. . . if placed in service in a tax year beginning before 2012, off-the-shelf computer software, (Code Sec. 179(d)(1)) and,

. . . if placed in service in a tax year beginning in 2010 or 2011, up to $250,000 per year of qualified real property. (Code Sec. 179(f)(1), Code Sec. 179(f)(3)) Qualified real property is required to be one of the following types of property (defined as discussed at ¶1917, but without regard to otherwise-applicable Jan. 1, 2010 placed-in-service deadlines): (1) qualified leasehold improvement property, (2) qualified restaurant property or (3) qualified retail improvement property. (Code Sec. 179(f)(2))

Code Sec. 179 property *does not include* property used in the production of income (Code Sec. 212 property), air conditioning and heating units, property used for lodging, property used outside the U.S., property used by certain tax-exempt organizations, property used by governmental units or foreign persons or entities. (Code Sec. 179(d)(1)) The election isn't available for the portion of the property's basis that's determined by reference to the basis of other property held at any time by the purchaser (e.g., trade-ins).[22]

Purchase is any acquisition of property *except* property (1) acquired from certain individuals or entities related to the taxpayer (or from a decedent) or (2) whose basis is determined by reference to the adjusted basis of the person from whom acquired (e.g., gifts).[23]

For prohibition of the expensing election for passenger autos and other "listed property" not predominantly used in business, see ¶1950.

¶ 1947   Recapture of amount expensed under Code Sec. 179—Form 4797.

A Code Sec. 179 recapture is triggered when the business use of property placed in service in an earlier year is reduced to 50% or less during the recapture period.

21. ¶L-9907.2; ¶1794.015; TD ¶268,411.1   23. ¶L-9925; ¶1794.02; TD ¶268,427
22. ¶L-9903, L-9922; ¶1794.02; TD ¶268,424, 268.424.1

The recapture period of the expense election is the entire recovery period of the qualifying Section 179 property. (Code Sec. 179(d)(10))

The recapture amount (report on Form 4797) equals the expense deduction taken minus the MACRS depreciation amount that would have been allowed on the expensed amount from the time the property was placed in service up to and including the year of recapture. (Reg § 1.179-1(e)(1))[24] For depreciation recapture, see ¶2692 *et seq.*

¶ 1948 "Luxury" Automobiles and "Listed Property." ▀▀▀▀▀▀▀▀▀▀

MACRS depreciation deductions and the Code Sec. 179 expense election are limited for "luxury" business autos and other "listed property." Lessees of such property are subject to special rules.

The following restrictions on depreciation (and the Code Sec. 179 expense election) apply to listed property (defined at ¶1949):

. . . Depreciation is under the straight-line method, and, generally, over longer recovery periods (and is ineligible for bonus depreciation, see ¶1934, and elective expensing, see ¶1941), if it is used no more than 50% for business, see ¶1950 *et seq.*

. . . Depreciation of passenger autos ("luxury autos") is subject to maximum ceiling limitations, see ¶1953.

. . . An employee may depreciate listed property only if its use is for the convenience of his employer and as a condition of employment, see ¶1957 *et seq.*

. . . A taxpayer who leases a "luxury" auto for business must add into income an "inclusion amount," see ¶1958 *et seq.*

. . . A taxpayer who leases listed property, other than a luxury auto, must take into income an "inclusion amount" when the property is no longer used more than 50% for business, see ¶1960.

. . . Specific recapture rules apply to listed property, see ¶2700.

. . . Strict substantiation rules apply to listed property expenses, see ¶1580 and ¶1584.

Lessors of listed property who are regularly engaged in the business of leasing that property aren't subject to the limitations applicable to owners for any listed property they lease or hold for leasing. (Code Sec. 280F(c)(1))[25]

¶ 1949 "Listed property" defined.

"Listed property" consists of:

. . . passenger autos (defined as discussed at ¶1953);

. . . any other property used as a means of transportation (e.g., trucks, buses, trains, boats, airplanes), except for "qualified nonpersonal use vehicles" (defined below);

. . . any property of a type generally used for entertainment, recreation or amusement, including photographic, phonographic, communication and video recording equipment, except if that property is used either exclusively at the taxpayer's regular business establishment, or in connection with the taxpayer's principal trade or business;

. . . any computer or peripheral equipment except those owned or leased by the taxpayer, and used exclusively at the taxpayer's regular business establishment;

. . . any other property specified by regs; and

. . . for tax years beginning before Jan. 1, 2010, any cellular telephone or other similar telecommunications equipment. (Code Sec. 280F(d)(4); Reg § 1.280F-6(b))[26]

For purposes of the above rules, "qualified nonpersonal use vehicles" (QNPUVs) are vehicles (1) that by reason of their nature, aren't likely to be used more than a de minimis amount

---

24. ¶L-9935; ¶1794.03; TD ¶268,428
25. ¶L-10201; ¶280F4; TD ¶267,630

26. ¶L-10002; ¶280F4; TD ¶267,616

for personal purposes (Code Sec. 274(i)) and (2) that, subject to transition rules, are placed in service after July 6, 2003 (Reg § 1.280F-6(f)). Regs list many types of QNPUVs, including, but not limited to, clearly marked police and fire vehicles. (Reg § 1.274-5(k)) For uses occurring after May 19, 2010 (Reg § 1.274-5(m)), clearly marked public safety officer vehicles were added to the list. (Reg § 1.274-5(k))[27]

¶ 1950 Depreciation and expensing restrictions for listed property used no more than 50% for business.

If, for the year listed property (¶1949) is placed in service, it is used 50% or less in a qualified business use (i.e., it isn't used predominantly on an annual basis in a qualified business use), the listed property: (1) doesn't qualify for the expense election (¶1941) (Reg § 1.280F-3T(c)(1)), (2) is depreciable only under straight-line and the "ADS" recovery periods (¶1932), and (3) is ineligible for the bonus first-year depreciation allowance (¶1933). (Code Sec. 168(k)(2)(D)(i), Code Sec. 280F(b)(1))[28]

🅡️observation: Under Code Sec. 280F(b)(1), if qualified business use for listed property starts out by being 50% or less of total use, the straight-line ADS deduction method is required for that property for that year and for all later years.

The actual deduction amount, however, is computed by using the "business/investment use" percentage (defined at ¶1952) and not by the qualified business use percentage. (Reg § 1.280F-6(d)(3)(i))[29]

The disallowed MACRS depreciation and Code Sec. 179 expense election deduction (if any) for the current and earlier years allocable to personal use is lost for all later years. (Code Sec. 280F(d)(2); Reg § 1.280F-4T(a)(1))[30]

If the more-than-50% requirement isn't met in a post-acquisition year (during the property's normal recovery period), the listed property becomes, retroactively to acquisition, straight-line ADS property. (Reg § 1.280F-3T(c)(2))[31] Depreciation previously taken in excess of straight-line (including amounts expensed, ¶1941, and bonus depreciation, ¶1933) is recaptured (on Form 4797). (Code Sec. 280F(b)(2)(A); Reg § 1.280F-3T(b)(2), Reg § 1.280F-3T(d)(2))[32]

¶ 1951 "Qualified business use" for listed property defined.

For purposes of the depreciation and expensing restrictions discussed at ¶1950 and the income inclusion discussed at ¶1960, "qualified business use" generally is any use in a trade or business of the taxpayer. (Code Sec. 280F(d)(6)(B))[33]

"Qualified business use doesn't include:

. . . Code Sec. 212 production-of-income use. (Reg § 1.280F-6(d)(2))

. . . Leasing property to any 5% owner of the taxpayer or to any person related to the taxpayer. Leasing aircraft to such persons, however, is qualified business use if business use, without counting the lease use, is at least 25% of the aircraft's total use.

. . . The use of listed property as compensation for services by a 5% owner or a related person.

. . . The use of listed property as compensation for services by any person other than a 5% owner or a related person, unless the provider of the property includes the value of the compensation in the recipient's gross income, properly reports it and, where necessary, treats it as wages subject to withholding. (Code Sec. 280F(d)(6)(C))[34]

---

27. ¶L-10002, ¶L-4658 *et seq.*; ¶280F4, ¶2744.10; TD ¶267,616, TD ¶295,346 *et seq.*
28. ¶L-10018; ¶280F4; TD ¶267,615
29. ¶L-10029; ¶280F4; TD ¶267,622
30. ¶L-10019; ¶280F4; TD ¶267,617

31. ¶L-10021; ¶280F4; TD ¶267,625
32. ¶s L-10021, L-10032; ¶280F4; TD ¶267,625
33. ¶L-10025 *et seq.*; ¶280F4; TD ¶267,621
34. ¶s L-10025, L-10027; ¶280F4; TD ¶267,621

¶ 1952   "Business/investment use" for listed property defined.

"Business/investment use" (see ¶1950 and ¶1959) is the total of business use and investment use of any listed property for the tax year. For example, if an item of listed property is used 70% in a trade or business and 20% for the production of income, the taxpayer may claim, if the property otherwise qualifies, accelerated depreciation deductions (including the expense election deduction) based on 90% business/investment use. Business or investment use (with an exception concerning automobiles, see below) is determined under the normal rules of Code Sec. 162 and Code Sec. 212. (Reg § 1.280F-6(d)(3)(i)) (Reg § 1.280F-6(d)(5), Ex 2)[35]

The use of a taxpayer's automobile by another person (even if that other person is a 5% owner or a related person) is treated as business/investment use of the taxpayer if:

(1) its use is directly connected with the taxpayer's business,

(2) the value of that use is properly reported by the taxpayer as income to the other person, and where required, tax is withheld on that income, or

(3) the use of the taxpayer's automobile by that other person results in payment of fair market rent. (Reg § 1.280F-6(d)(3)(iv))

¶ 1953   Depreciation and expensing of business automobiles—"luxury" auto dollar caps.

Autos used in a trade or business normally are depreciated as 5-year MACRS property. (Code Sec. 168(b)(1), Code Sec. 168(e)(3)(B)) However, the deduction normally obtained for an auto by applying the MACRS 5-year property rules, the bonus depreciation allowance (¶1933), and the Code Sec. 179 expensing rules (¶1941), is limited by the so-called "luxury auto" dollar caps. (Code Sec. 280F(a)(1), Code Sec. 280F(d)(1)). The dollar caps are adjusted for inflation, based on the placed-in-service year. (Code Sec. 280F(d)(7))

The dollar caps apply to passenger autos, i.e., four-wheeled vehicles manufactured primarily for use on public streets, roads, and highways, and rated at an unloaded gross vehicle weight of 6,000 pounds or less. For a truck or van, the 6,000-pound test is applied to the truck's or van's gross (loaded) vehicle weight. (Code Sec. 280F(d)(5)(A); Reg § 1.280F-6(c)) Excepted from the dollar caps are ambulances or hearses used directly in a trade or business, taxis and other vehicles used directly in the trade or business of transporting people or property for pay, and trucks or vans specified by IRS regs. (Code Sec. 280F(d)(5)(B)) Thus, under regs, qualified nonpersonal use vehicles (discussed at ¶1949) are excepted (but, generally, only if placed in service after July 6, 2003). (Reg § 1.280F-6(c)(3)(iii), Reg § 1.280F-6(f))[36]

🄫observation: Sport-utility vehicles (SUVs) are trucks. Thus, SUVs rated at more than 6,000 pounds gross (loaded) vehicle weight are exempt from dollar caps because they fall outside of the Code Sec. 280F(d)(5) definition of a passenger auto.

For the restricted expensing deduction for heavy SUVs, see ¶1945. For the luxury-auto dollar cap amounts, see ¶1954 and ¶1955.

For qualified clean fuel vehicle property (certain property that enables cars to burn clean fuel) placed in service before 2006, the luxury auto dollar caps didn't apply. (Code Sec. 280F(a)(1)(C)(i), Code Sec. 179A(c)(1)(A), Code Sec. 179A(f))[37]

For purpose-built passenger vehicles (certain electric cars) placed in service before 2007, the luxury auto dollar caps were approximately tripled. (Code Sec. 280F(a)(1)(C)(ii))[38]

---

35. ¶L-10029; ¶280F4; TD ¶267,622
36. ¶L-10003; ¶280F4; TD ¶267,603
37. ¶L-10003.1; ¶179A4, ¶280F4; TD ¶267,604
38. ¶L-10004.1; ¶280F4; TD ¶267,602

¶ 1954   Regular "luxury" auto depreciation and expensing dollar cap amounts.

The regular luxury auto dollar caps (i.e., limits on regular maximum depreciation and expensing allowances, see ¶1953) apply to passenger autos that are ineligible for bonus first-year depreciation (see ¶1934). For example, a passenger auto is ineligible if it was previously owned (see ¶1935) or if the taxpayer "elects out" of the bonus depreciation allowance under the rules explained at ¶1938. For the increased first-year cap that applies to passenger autos that are eligible for bonus first-year depreciation, see ¶1955.

The annual depreciation dollar caps for (1) autos, and (2) trucks or vans (passenger autos built on a truck chassis, including minivans and sport-utility vehicles (SUVs) built on a truck chassis) first placed in service in 2010, are subject to the luxury auto dollar limits, and are used 100% for business are as follows:[39]

. . . for the placed-in-service year, $3,060 for autos, $3,160 for trucks and vans;

. . . for the second tax year, $4,900 for autos, $5,100 for trucks and vans;

. . . for the third tax year, $2,950 for autos and $3,050 for trucks and vans; and

. . . for each succeeding year, $1,775 for autos and $1,875 for trucks and vans.

observation: For rented (i.e., leased) automobiles and other listed property, income "inclusion amounts" apply instead of the above deduction limits, see ¶1958 *et seq.*

Where the "business/investment use percentage" (defined at ¶1952) is less than 100%, the caps are reduced proportionally to correspond to the taxpayer's business/investment use percentage. (Code Sec. 280F(a)(2))[40] Moreover, depreciation after the normal 5-year recovery period (actually six years because of the operation of the applicable convention) is based on unrecovered basis, i.e., adjusted basis determined as if the auto had been used 100% for business, so that the disallowed MACRS depreciation for the earlier years allocable to personal use is lost forever. (Code Sec. 280F(a)(1)(B), Code Sec. 280F(d)(8))

illustration: In June of 2010 a calendar year taxpayer bought and placed in service a $20,000 previously owned passenger car. The car is used 100% for business for 2010 and 2011, and 80% for all later years. Here are the MACRS depreciation deductions for each of the first four tax years assuming that the taxpayer uses regular 200% declining balance depreciation, doesn't make a Code Sec. 179 expense election for the car, and uses the half-year depreciation convention (¶1927) for 2008.

Year	MACRS Deductions
2010 (20% of $20,000 is $4,000 but limited to 100% of $3,060)	$ 3,060
2011 (32% of $20,000 is $6,400 but limited to 100% of $4,900)	4,900
2012 (19.20% of $20,000 is $3,840 but limited to 80% of $2,950)	2,360
2013 (11.52% of $20,000 is $2,304 but limited to 80% of $1,775)	1,420
Total 2010 through 2013 MACRS deductions	$11,740

If the vehicle purchased in the above illustration is a truck or van subject to the auto dollar limits, the dollar limits would be higher. For example, the deduction would be $3,160 for 2009 and $5,100 for 2010.

Where a vehicle isn't "predominantly used in a qualified business use" (as defined at ¶1951) only straight-line depreciation is available and neither the bonus first-year depreciation allowance nor the Code Sec. 179 expense election can be claimed for it, as explained at ¶1950.

A taxpayer that uses the IRS standard mileage allowance method (discussed at ¶1561) for a

39. ¶L-10004, ¶L-10004.4; ¶280F4; TD ¶267,601, TD ¶267,602.3   40. ¶L-10004; ¶280F4; TD ¶267,601

tax year isn't subject to the above limitations for that year.[41]

For vehicles placed in service in 2009, the dollar caps for cars were: for the 1st tax year, $2,960 for autos, $3,060 for trucks and vans; for the 2d tax year, $4,800 for autos, $4,900 for trucks and vans; for the 3rd tax year, $2,850 for autos and $2,950 for trucks and vans; and for each succeeding year, $1,775 for autos and $1,775 for trucks and vans.[42]

¶ 1955   Enhanced first-year "luxury auto" depreciation and expensing dollar cap for passenger autos eligible for bonus first-year depreciation.

For passenger autos that are eligible for bonus first-year depreciation (¶1933) (i.e., generally, new passenger autos acquired and placed in service in calendar year 2008, 2009 or 2010, see ¶1934 *et seq.*), the regular first-year dollar cap on depreciation and Code Sec. 179 expensing is increased by $8,000. (Code Sec. 168(k)(2)(F))

🅡*caution:* Check http://ria.thomsonreuters.com/federaltaxhandbook to see if the above provisions have been extended.

Thus, for example, unless the taxpayer elects-out of bonus depreciation, the enhanced first-year dollar caps for eligible passenger autos placed in service in 2010—including those trucks and vans that are treated as passenger autos for purposes of the dollar-cap rules (see ¶1953, and ¶1954)—are $11,060 for autos and $11,160 for the trucks and vans.[43]

🅡*observation:* The enhanced first-year depreciation dollar cap does not affect the dollar caps for years after the placed-in-service year.

For vehicles eligible for the bonus depreciation that was available, as discussed at ¶1933, under prior law, the first-year dollar caps were increased by $7,650 for property eligible for prior law 50% bonus depreciation and $4,600 for property eligible for prior law 30% bonus depreciation.[44]

¶ 1956   Claiming auto depreciation (Form 2106, Form 2106-EZ, Form 4562, etc.).

Self-employeds and sole proprietors report their vehicle expenses on Form 1040, Schedule C (Form 1040, Schedule C-EZ for certain small businesses) or if they are farmers on Form 1040, Schedule F with Form 4562 attached. Employees deduct employee business expenses (including depreciation) on Form 2106. But if an employee is reimbursed for business related car expenses under an accountable plan (¶1574) and the expenses don't exceed the reimbursements, Form 2106 doesn't have to be filed. Form 2106-EZ can be used by an employee if (1) he isn't reimbursed by his employer for any expenses (amounts included in Box 1 of Form W-2 aren't considered reimbursements), and (2) if he claims vehicle expenses, he is using the standard mileage rate (and if he owns the vehicle, also used the standard mileage rate in the year the auto was first placed in service).[45] Otherwise, depreciation is reported on Form 4562, see ¶1901.

¶ 1957   Requirements for "listed property" deductions by employees.

Listed property that an individual owns and uses in connection with his employment is eligible for MACRS deductions only if the property is required for the convenience of the employer and as a condition of employment. "Convenience of the employer," and "condition of employment" are defined as used in determining the exclusion from gross income for lodging furnished to an employee, see ¶1269 *et seq.*

To satisfy the condition-of-employment requirement, the property must be required for the employee to properly perform the duties of his or her employment. This requirement isn't satisfied merely by an employer's statement that the property is required as a condition of

---

41. ¶L-10013 *et seq.*; ¶280F4; TD ¶267,612
42. ¶L-10004, ¶L-10004.4; ¶280F4; TD ¶267,601, TD ¶267,602.3,
43. ¶L-10004.1A; ¶280F4; TD ¶267,602.2
44. ¶L-10004.2, ¶L-10004.3; ¶1684.0281; TD ¶267,602.1, TD ¶267,602.2A
45. ¶L-10004; TD ¶267,601

employment. (Code Sec. 280F(d)(3))[46]

A computer at home, even if used exclusively for the employer's work, is listed property if the taxpayer-employee doesn't qualify under the "office-at-home" requirements of Code Sec. 280A(c)(1), discussed in ¶1635 *et seq.*[47] If a home computer is listed property, the employee gets no depreciation or other deduction, unless he proves the computer is: (1) for the convenience of the employer, and (2) required as a condition of employment. (Reg § 1.280F-6(a))[48]

¶ 1958 Lessees' limitations on listed property.

Lessees of business autos and other listed property under leases of 30 days or more are subject to the MACRS limitations discussed in the preceding paragraphs, although indirectly. (Code Sec. 280F(c)(2), Code Sec. 280F(c)(3))[49]

Deductions for rental payments aren't limited. Instead, during every lease year, lessees of "luxury" autos must include in gross income an "inclusion amount," figured from IRS's tables, as discussed at ¶1959 *et seq.*

The "inclusion amount" for a business auto is based on the fair market value of the auto and the lessee's business/investment use. An amount must be included in the lessee's gross income for each year the auto is leased, whether or not it's used 100% for business/investment purposes. (Reg § 1.280F-5T(d), Reg § 1.280F-5T(e)) (Reg § 1.280F-5T(h)(2))[50]

For listed property other than business autos, there's no annual "inclusion amount." The lessee must, however, take an "inclusion amount" into income for the first year the property ceases to be used predominantly in a qualified business use (see ¶1960). (Reg § 1.280F-5T(f))[1]

¶ 1959 "Inclusion amount" for leased business autos, trucks, and vans.

For passenger autos, trucks, and vans that are subject to the luxury auto limits (¶1953) and are first leased in 2010, the inclusion amount (see ¶1958) for each tax year of the lease is computed as follows: (Reg § 1.280F-7(a)(2))[2]

(1) Find the line from the appropriate table at ¶1118, which includes the fair market value of the leased auto, truck or van.

(2) Prorate the dollar amount for the number of days in the lease term included in the tax year at issue.

(3) Multiply the prorated dollar amount by the "business/investment use" (see ¶1952) percentage for the auto, truck or van for that tax year. The resulting amount is the inclusion amount.

For the last tax year of the lease, the dollar amount for the preceding year is used.

illustration: On Apr. 1, 2010, a calendar year taxpayer leased and placed in service an auto (not a truck or van) with a FMV of $31,500. The lease is for three years and the business/investment use is 100% in each year. The taxpayer must include the following "inclusion amounts" (from Table at ¶1118) in gross income: for 2010, $24.11 ($32 inclusion amount × 275/365); for 2011, $70 (full inclusion amount); for 2012, $104 (full inclusion amount); and for 2013, $31.16 ($125 inclusion amount × 91/365). (Reg § 1.280F-7(a)(2)(i))

For vehicles first leased in 2010, there's no inclusion amount unless the fair market value of the vehicle exceeds $16,700.[3]

Income inclusion amounts for business autos leased before 2010 are carried in earlier (pre-2010) issues of the RIA Federal Tax Handbook.

46. ¶L-10022; ¶280F4; TD ¶267,618
47. ¶L-10023; TD ¶267,619
48. ¶L-10023; ¶280F4; TD ¶267,619
49. ¶L-10200 *et seq.*; ¶280F4; TD ¶267,629

50. ¶L-10202, ¶L-10203; ¶280F4; TD ¶267,631, TD ¶267,632
1. ¶L-10205; ¶280F4; TD ¶267,631
2. ¶L-10204, ¶L-10204.2; ¶280F4; TD ¶267,632, TD ¶267,633
3. ¶L-10204, ¶L-10204.2; ¶280F4; TD ¶267,632, TD ¶267,633

¶ 1960 Inclusion amount for MACRS leased listed property other than automobiles.

A lessee of listed property other than automobiles must include in gross income an inclusion amount in the first tax year in which the leased property isn't used predominantly — i.e., more than 50% — in a qualified business use, see ¶1951. (Reg § 1.280F-5T(f)(1))

The inclusion amount for MACRS listed property other than automobiles is the sum of the amount computed under Step (1) and Step (2), below. (Reg § 1.280F-7(b)(2))

STEP (1): Multiply the following three items: (a) the fair market value of the property, (b) the business/investment use of the property for the year that use is 50% or less, and (c) the applicable percentage from Table II reproduced at ¶1117. (Reg § 1.280F-7(b)(2)(i))

STEP (2): Multiply the following three items: (a) the fair market value of the property, (b) the average of the business/investment use for all tax years (in which the property is leased) that precede the year the business/investment use is 50% or less, and (c) the applicable percentage from Table I reproduced at ¶1117. (Reg § 1.280F-7(b)(2)(ii))

Special computation rules apply when a lease term for listed property begins within nine months of the end of the lessee's tax year, or when the lease term is less than one year. (Reg § 1.280F-5T(g))[4]

¶ 1961 Depreciation Deduction Under the Income Forecast Method.

Depreciation deductions under the income forecast method are figured by multiplying the cost of the property (but only amounts that satisfy the Code Sec. 461(h) economic performance standard, ¶2833) less estimated salvage value, by a fraction, the numerator of which is the year's income generated by the property, and the denominator of which is all income earned before the close of the tenth tax year following the year in which the property was placed in service.

Under the income forecast method, the depreciation deduction for the tenth tax year after the tax year in which the property was placed in service is equal to the taxpayer's entire remaining basis in the property. (Code Sec. 167(g)(1)(C)) Taxpayers using the income forecast method pay (or receive) interest in recomputation years (generally in the third and tenth years after the property was placed in service, unless income earned by the property is within 10% of original estimates; use Form 8866 to compute) based on the recalculation of depreciation under a look-back method (but there's no look-back for property that had a cost basis of $100,000 or less). (Code Sec. 167(g))[5] (For 15-year amortization for films, sound recordings, video tapes, etc., see ¶1977.)

For property placed in service after Aug. 5, '97, the income forecast method (or any similar method) can be used only for: (1) Motion picture films, video tapes, and sound recordings; (2) copyrights; (3) books; (4) patents; and (5) any other property to be specified in regulations. The income forecast method or any similar method cannot be used to depreciate amortizable section 197 intangibles (see ¶1976). (Code Sec. 167(g)(6))[6]

For property placed in service after Oct. 22, 2004, rules specifically address the effect on the calculation of depreciation under the income forecast method of "participations and residuals" (costs that, by contract, vary with the amount of income earned from property). (Code Sec. 167(g)(5)(E), Code Sec. 167(g)(7))[7]

¶ 1962 Depreciation Deduction Under the "Useful-Life" Rules.

Property not depreciable under MACRS (¶1900, ¶1906 through ¶1908) or under ACRS (¶1900) (including, but not limited to, all depreciable property placed in service before '81) is usually depreciable under the useful-life rules. Under the useful-life rules, a depreciable asset

4. ¶L-10206 *et seq.*; ¶280F4; TD ¶267,634
5. ¶L-10704; ¶1674.100; TD ¶268,004
6. ¶L-10704A; ¶1674.100; TD ¶268,004
7. ¶L-10705, ¶L-10707, ¶L-10707.1, ¶L-10707.1A; ¶1674.100

is depreciated over the period during which a depreciable asset, or group of similar assets, may reasonably be expected to be useful to the taxpayer in his trade or business or in income production.[8] Under the useful-life rules, a permissible method of depreciation is either one that is (1) prescribed by Code Sec. 167, or, (2) where a method isn't prescribed by Code Sec. 167, a method that results in a reasonable allowance. (Code Sec. 167(a); Reg § 1.167(b)-0)[9] Useful-life property generally can't be depreciated below salvage value. (Reg § 1.167(a)-1(c), Reg § 1.167(b)-2(a))[10]

¶ 1963 Basis for depreciation.

Under the useful life rules (¶1962), the basis on which depreciation is taken is the adjusted basis under Code Sec. 1011 for the purpose of gain or loss on a sale or other disposition. (Code Sec. 167(c)(1)) For property acquired after Aug. 10, '93, if property is acquired subject to a lease, no portion of the adjusted basis can be allocated to the leasehold interest, and the entire adjusted basis is taken into account in determining any depreciation for the property subject to the lease. (Code Sec. 167(c)(2)) The no-allocation rule also applies to leases that terminate immediately after the acquisition.[11]

¶ 1964 Certain intangibles excluded from 15-year amortization.

For property acquired after Aug. 10, '93, certain property excluded from Code Sec. 197 (15-year amortization of many intangibles, see ¶1976 *et seq.*) is depreciated as follows:

(1) Computer software, in those situations in which it is excluded from 15-year amortization (see ¶1978), generally is depreciated using the straight-line method with a useful life of 36 months, beginning on the first day of the month that it is placed in service; see ¶1663 for exceptions. (Code Sec. 167(f)(1); Reg § 1.167(a)-14(b)(1))

(2) Rights to service debts secured by residential realty are depreciated using the straight-line method with a useful life of 108 months. (Code Sec. 167(f)(3); Reg § 1.167(a)-14(d)(1))

(3) Amortization of a right (other than one acquired as part of the purchase of a trade or business) to receive a fixed amount of tangible property or services under a contract or from a governmental unit is found by dividing its basis by a fraction (amount of tangible property or services received during the year divided by total amount of tangible property or services received or to be received). The cost or other basis of a right to receive an unspecified amount of tangible property or services over a fixed period is amortized ratably over the period of the right. The basis of a right to an unspecified amount over a fixed duration of less than 15 years is amortized over the term of the right. (Code Sec. 167(f)(2); Reg § 1.167(a)-14(c))

(4) If the purchase price of an interest in a patent or copyright (other than one acquired as part of a purchase of a trade or business) is payable at least annually either as a fixed amount per use or as a fixed percentage of revenue derived, the depreciation deduction is equal to the amount of the purchase price paid or incurred during the year. Otherwise, basis is depreciated either ratably over its remaining useful life or under the income forecast method (¶1961). (Code Sec. 167(f)(2); Reg § 1.167(a)-14(c)(4))

Effective for leases entered into after Mar. 12, 2004, the useful life of property described at items (1), (3) or (4) on the above list that, if it were tangible property, would be "tax-exempt use property" (see ¶1931), can't be less than 125% of the lease term. (Code Sec. 167(f)(1)(C), Code Sec. 167(f)(2))[12]

Effective for intangible assets created on or after Dec. 31, 2003 (Reg § 1.167(a)-3(b)(4)), taxpayers may treat an intangible asset as having a useful life of 15 years unless:

. . . an amortization period or useful life for the intangible asset is specifically prescribed or

8. ¶L-11800 *et seq.*; ¶1674.040 *et seq.*; TD ¶268,122
9. ¶L-11901; ¶1674.100; TD ¶268,001
10. ¶L-11711; ¶1674.044; TD ¶268,123

11. ¶L-7911.1; ¶1784; TD ¶265,413
12. ¶L-7935, ¶L-8018, ¶L-8025, ¶L-8030; ¶1674.013, ¶1674.025, ¶1674.033; TD ¶265,434, TD ¶269,025, TD ¶269,026

prohibited by other rules (e.g., 15-year amortization under Code Sec. 197, see ¶1976);

. . . the intangible asset is described in Reg § 1.263(a)-4(c) (intangibles acquired from another person in a purchase or similar transaction) or Reg § 1.263(a)-4(d)(2) (relating to created financial interests);

. . . the useful life of the intangible asset can be estimated with reasonable accuracy; or

. . . the intangible asset is described in Reg § 1.263(a)-4(d)(8) (relating to certain benefits arising from the provision, production, or improvement of realty), in which case the taxpayer may treat the intangible asset as having a useful life equal to 25 years solely for purposes of Reg § 1.167(a)-3(a). (Reg § 1.167(a)-3(b)(1))

The above useful life safe harbor doesn't apply to amounts that must be capitalized by Reg § 1.263(a)-5 (amounts paid to facilitate an acquisition of a trade or business, a change in the capital structure of a business entity, and certain other transactions). (Reg § 1.167(a)-3(b)(2)) Under the safe harbor, the basis of the intangible (determined without regard to salvage value) is amortized ratably over 15 or 25 years beginning on the first day of the month in which the intangible asset is placed in service by the taxpayer. The intangible asset is not eligible for amortization in the month of disposition. (Reg § 1.167(a)-3(b)(3))[13]

¶ 1965 Specialized "useful-life" depreciation methods.

These include:

. . . operating day method used for equipment affected chiefly by wear and tear rather than obsolescence, such as rotary oil drills;[14]

. . . sinking fund method (Reg § 1.167(b)-4(a));[15]

. . . unit-of-production method used for property, the usefulness of which is closely related to its use in production or to a source of supply or similar factor. (Reg § 1.167(b)-0(b), Reg § 1.611-5(a), Reg § 1.611-5(b)(2))[16]

¶ 1966 Special Expensing and Amortization Provisions. ▮▮▮▮▮▮▮

Instead of being subject to the ordinary depreciation or expensing rules, certain property is expensed or amortized as described below or at ¶1967 through ¶1978.

For example, taxpayers can elect to expense 50% of the cost of qualified advanced mine safety equipment property placed in service after Dec. 20, 2006 and before 2010. (Code Sec. 179E)

⚫*caution:* Check http://ria.thomsonreuters.com/federaltaxhandbook to see if the above provision has been extended.

Research and experimental expenditures connected with a trade or business may be amortized over a 60-month period (¶1601). Also, start-up expenditures (¶1501), organization costs of a corporation (¶3520) and organization costs of a partnership (¶3707) may be amortized over a 180-month period. Bond premium or discount (¶2172 *et seq.*) and lease acquisition costs are also amortized (¶1597).

¶ 1967 Expensing election for costs of film and TV production

For qualified film and television (TV) productions commencing before Jan. 1, 2010, taxpayers may elect to deduct production costs in the year the costs are incurred (i.e., to expense them) instead of capitalizing the costs and recovering them through depreciation allowances. (Code Sec. 181(a)(1))[17] In general, expensing doesn't apply to the portion of the cost of any qualifying film or TV production that exceeds $15 million for each qualifying production. The limit is $20 million if production expenses are "significantly incurred" in areas (1) eligible for

---

13. ¶L-8001; ¶1674.013; TD ¶269,001
14. ¶L-10709; ¶1674.100; TD ¶268,015
15. ¶L-10711

16. ¶L-10702; ¶1674.100; TD ¶268,001
17. ¶L-3140 *et seq.*; ¶1814 *et seq.*; TD ¶269,451 *et seq.*

designation as a low-income community or (2) eligible for designation by the Delta Regional Authority (a federal-state partnership covering parts of certain states) as a low-income community or isolated area of distress. For productions beginning before Jan. 1, 2008, exceeding the respective $15 million and $20 million ceilings meant that none of the costs qualify. (Code Sec. 181(a)(2))[18]

⚫*caution:* Check http://ria.thomsonreuters.com/federaltaxhandbook to see if the above provision has been extended.

A qualified film or TV production generally is any production of a motion picture or video tape if at least 75% of the total compensation expended on the production is "qualified compensation." Qualified compensation (but not participations and residuals, as defined by Code Sec. 167(g)(7)(B)) is compensation for services performed in the U.S. by actors, directors, producers, and other relevant production personnel. For property which is one or more episodes in a television series, only the first 44 episodes qualify. Sexually explicit productions, as defined by section 2257 of title 18 of the U.S. Code, do not qualify. (Code Sec. 181(d))[19]

Temporary regs explain how and when to make the election, including special rules for making the election if it was not made, or not properly made, on a return filed before Mar 12, 2007. (Reg § 1.181-2T) The election can be revoked only with prior consent of IRS (Code Sec. 181(c)(2))[20]

Recapture of the benefits of the expensing is required if a production no longer qualifies for expensing in tax years after the year for which the expensing election is made. (Reg § 1.181-4T(a))[21]

¶ 1968   Expensing elections for refining costs.

Under Code Sec. 179B, small business refiners may elect to expense 75% of "qualified capital costs" paid or incurred after 2002 to comply with certain EPA diesel fuel sulfur control requirements. Among the requirements for being qualified capital costs is that the costs be incurred no later than the earlier of (1) Dec. 31, 2009 or (2) the date one year after the date that the taxpayer must comply with the sulfur control requirements.[22]

⚫*caution:* Check http://ria.thomsonreuters.com/federaltaxhandbook to see if the above provision has been extended.

Under Code Sec. 179C, refiners (even if they aren't small business refiners) can elect to expense 50% of the costs of "qualified refinery property" placed in service after Aug. 8, 2005. Among the requirements for "qualified refinery property" are that (1) the property be part of a qualified refinery (see below) (2) no written binding contract for construction of the property be in effect before June 15, 2005 and (3) the property be placed in service before either (a) Jan. 1, 2010, or (b) Jan. 1, 2014 and be either (i) subject to a written binding construction contract entered into before Jan. 1, 2010 or (ii) if self-constructed, be property the construction of which began before Jan. 1, 2010 and after June 14, 2005. For property placed in service before Oct. 4, 2008, the Jan. 1, 2010 dates in the preceding rule were, instead, Jan. 1, 2008. The election can be revoked only with IRS consent.[23]

⚫*caution:* Check http://ria.thomsonreuters.com/federaltaxhandbook to see if the above provision has been extended.

A qualified refinery must be located in the U.S. and be designed, primarily, to process liquid fuels from crude oil or qualified fuels (as defined in Code Sec. 45K(c)), or directly from shale or tar sands. (Code Sec. 179C(d)) A dry mill process used to produce ethanol from corn is a qualifying process.[24]

18. ¶L-3144 *et seq.*; ¶1814.01; TD ¶269,453 *et seq.*
19. ¶L-3142 *et seq.*; ¶1814.07 *et seq.*; TD ¶269,452
20. ¶L-3146 *et seq.*; ¶1814.05, ¶1814.13; TD ¶269,455
21. ¶L-3147; ¶1814.15

22. ¶L-3161 *et seq.*; ¶179B4; TD ¶307,101 *et seq.*
23. ¶L-3156 *et seq.*; ¶179C4; TD ¶269,371 *et seq.*
24. ¶L-3157.1; ¶179C4; TD ¶269,372

¶ 1969   Expensing for costs of making commercial buildings energy efficient.

Taxpayers may expense the cost of "energy efficient commercial building property" placed in service in calendar years 2006 through 2013. (Code Sec. 179D(a)) The deduction for any building for any tax year can't be more than the excess (if any) of (1) $1.80 × the square footage of the building over (2) the deductions allowed under Code Sec. 179D(a) for earlier years. (Code Sec. 179D(b))

"Energy efficient commercial building property" is property that is (1) depreciable or amortizable), (2) installed on or in a building located in the U.S. and (3) certified as being installed as part of a plan that will meet a 50% energy use reduction test described in Code Sec. 179D(c). In some situations in which the 50% test isn't satisfied, a partial deduction is permitted. (Code Sec. 179D(d)(1))

For property installed on government property, the person primarily responsible for designing the property is treated as the taxpayer. (Code Sec. 179D(d)(4))[25]

¶ 1970   Amortization elections for pollution control facilities.

A taxpayer may elect to amortize, over 60 months, part or all of the cost of new identifiable pollution control treatment facilities used in connection with a plant or other property in operation before '76. (Code Sec. 169(a), Code Sec. 169(d)) MACRS depreciation can be taken on any portion that doesn't qualify. (Code Sec. 169(g)) Also, a taxpayer may elect to amortize over an 84-month period *air* pollution control facilities used in connection with an electric generation plant or other property that is primarily coal fired. That election is available only for facilities that are both (1) placed in service in connection with a plant or other property placed in operation after Dec. 31, '75 and (2) placed in service after Apr. 11, 2005. (Code Sec. 169(d)(5)) For both 60 month amortization and 84 month amortization, certain limits apply. (Code Sec. 169(f), Code Sec. 291(a)(4), Code Sec. 1363(b)(4))[26]

¶ 1971   Amortization election for expenses for creating or acquiring music.

For any tax year beginning after Dec. 31, 2005 and before Jan. 1, 2011, a taxpayer may elect to amortize over a 5-year period expenses that are both (1) paid or incurred to create or acquire a musical composition (including words), or a copyright to such property, and (2) otherwise properly capitalizable. The 5-year period begins with the month in which the composition or copyright is placed in service. The election doesn't apply to expenses that are Code Sec. 263A(h) qualified creative expenses (¶1660), subject to a specified simplified amortization procedure, amortizable section 197 intangibles (¶1977) or not otherwise allowable as a deduction. (Code Sec. 167(g)(8))[27]

caution: Check http://ria.thomsonreuters.com/federaltaxhandbook to see if the above provision has been extended.

¶ 1972   Expensing and amortization of reforestation expenditures—Form 4562.

Effective for expenses paid or incurred after Oct. 22, 2004, taxpayers other than trusts may elect to deduct up to $10,000 ($5,000 if married filing separately) of reforestation costs, and taxpayers (including estates and trusts) may elect to amortize the balance of reforestation costs over 84 months. (Code Sec. 194) Use Form 4562.

For expenses paid or incurred before Oct. 23, 2004, taxpayers other than trusts may elect to amortize, over a seven-year period, up to $10,000 of reforestation expenditures in connection with qualified timber property.[28]

An individual needn't itemize to claim deductions under Code Sec. 194. (Code

---

25. ¶L-3170 *et seq.*; ¶179D4; TD ¶308,100 *et seq.*
26. ¶L-12600 *et seq.*; ¶1694, ¶2914

27. ¶L-10707.19; ¶1674.027; TD ¶268,017
28. ¶N-6301 *et seq.*; ¶1944 *et seq.*; TD ¶272,001 *et seq.*

Sec. 62(a)(11))[29] Costs expensed or amortized under Code Sec. 194 are recaptured as ordinary income (to the extent of gain) if there's a disposition of the timber property within ten years. (Code Sec. 1245(a)(2)(C))[30]

Taxpayers making either election must create and maintain separate accounts for each qualified timber property. Any property subject to either election may not be included in any other timber account (e.g., a depletion block) for which depletion is allowed under Code Sec. 611 (¶1979 *et seq.*). And, at no time may an amortizable timber account become part of a depletable account for purposes of deduction under Code Sec. 165(a).[31]

IRS consent to revoke the election is granted only in rare and unusual circumstances.[32]

For certain periods ending before 2008, additional timber expensing benefits were available to certain taxpayers with small timber operations located in the GO Zone, Rita GO Zone or Wilma GO Zone (¶2308, ¶2309). (Code Sec. 1400N(i))[33]

¶ 1973   24-month amortization for certain oil or gas costs; 7-year amortization for major integrated oil companies.

Except for expenses of major integrated oil companies (see below), geological and geophysical ("G and G") expenses paid or incurred in connection with exploring or developing oil or gas within the U.S (as defined in Code Sec. 638) are amortized over the 24-month period beginning on the date that the expenses are paid or incurred. In calculating the amortization deductions, a half-year convention applies. (Code Sec. 167(h)(1), Code Sec. 167(h)(2))

observation: Thus, 25% of the expenditures are deducted in the year paid or incurred (Year 1), 50% in Year 2, and 25% in Year 3.

"G and G" expenses of a major integrated oil company are amortizable over a 7-year period (a 5-year period for expenses paid or incurred after May 17, 2006 and before Dec. 20, 2007). (Code Sec. 167(h)(5))

Amortization continues over the full 24-month period (5- or 7-year period for a major integrated oil company) even if the underlying property is abandoned or retired. (Code Sec. 167(h)(4), Code Sec. 167(h)(5))[34]

¶ 1974   50% expensing or 120-month amortization for qualified commercial revitalization expenditures.

A taxpayer that places into service a qualified revitalization building in a renewal community (communities designated as such by HUD) after 2001 but before 2010 may elect to write off qualified revitalization expenses by either (1) deducting *one-half* of qualified revitalization expenses for any qualified revitalization building for the tax year in which the building is placed in service or (2) amortizing *all* such expenses *over a 120-month period* beginning with the month in which the building is placed in service. (Code Sec. 1400I(a))

caution: Check http://ria.thomsonreuters.com/federaltaxhandbook to see if the above provision has been extended.

The total amount of eligible expenses per building can't exceed the lesser of $10,000,000, or the commercial revitalization expense amount allocated to the building by the commercial revitalization agency for the state in which the building is located. (Code Sec. 1400I(c)(2))

¶ 1975   Amortization of Intangibles.

The cost of most acquired intangible assets, including goodwill and going concern value, is amortized ratably over a 15-year period.

---

29. ¶A-2601; ¶N-6301; ¶624.04; TD ¶560,702
30. ¶N-3704; ¶12,454.03; TD ¶299,026
31. ¶N-6301; ¶N-6310; ¶1944; TD ¶272,001, TD ¶272,009

32. ¶N-6301; ¶1944; TD ¶272,001
33. ¶N-6304.1; ¶14,00N4.045; TD ¶272,001
34. ¶N-3201; ¶1674.126, TD ¶271,701

¶ 1976 Fifteen-year amortization of intangibles—Form 4562.

The cost of most acquired intangible assets, including goodwill and going concern value, is amortized ratably over a 15-year period. Specifically, taxpayers claim deductions on Form 4562 for "amortizable section 197 intangibles" (¶1977) by amortizing the adjusted basis (for purposes of determining gain) of that intangible ratably over a 15-year period beginning on the *later* of: the first day of the month in which the intangible is acquired, or, for property held in connection with the conduct of a trade or business or a production-of-income activity, the first day of the month in which the conduct of the trade or business or the activity begins. (Code Sec. 197(a); Reg § 1.197-2(f)(1)(i)))[35]

No loss deduction is permitted on the disposition of an amortizable section 197 intangible if the taxpayer retains one or more other intangibles acquired in the same transaction or series of related transactions along with the intangible disposed of. (Code Sec. 197(f)(1)(A)) On the disposition of the intangible, the bases of the other intangibles acquired in the same transaction or series of related transactions are increased, under a formula, by the amount of the loss barred. (Code Sec. 197(f)(1)(A)(ii))[36]

Anti-churning rules keep taxpayers from converting existing intangibles for which a depreciation or amortization deduction isn't allowable under prior law into amortizable section 197 intangibles. (Code Sec. 197(f)(9))[37]

Effective for leases entered into after Mar. 12, 2004, the amortization period of Code Sec. 197 property that, if it were tangible property, would be "tax-exempt use property" (see ¶1931), can't be less than 125% of the lease term. (Code Sec. 197(f)(10))[38]

If, after Aug. 8, 2005, more than one amortizable section 197 intangible is disposed of in one transaction, or a series of related transactions, all of the amortizable section 197 intangibles in the transaction (or transactions)—except for any amortizable section 197 intangible with an adjusted basis greater than its fair market value—are treated as a single asset for Code Sec. 1245 recapture purposes (see ¶2695). (Code Sec. 1245(b)(8))[39]

For depreciation of intangibles generally and of many intangibles that aren't section 197 intangibles, see ¶1903, ¶1961 and ¶1964.

For property acquired before Aug. 11, '93, (except for certain elections), the 15-year amortization provisions discussed above didn't apply.[40]

¶ 1977 Amortizable section 197 intangible.

An amortizable section 197 intangible is any section 197 intangible acquired (after Aug. 10, '93) and held in connection with the conduct of a trade or business or a Code Sec. 212 production-of-income activity. (Code Sec. 197(c)(1)) An acquisition may be made in the form of a stock acquisition or redemption.[41] Amortizable section 197 intangibles include:[42]

. . . goodwill (Code Sec. 197(d)(1)(A); Reg § 1.197-2(b)(1)),[43]

. . . going concern value (Code Sec. 197(d)(1)(B); Reg § 1.197-2(b)(2)),[44]

. . . workforce in place (Code Sec. 197(d)(1)(C)(i); Reg § 1.197-2(b)(3)),[45]

. . . business books and records, operating systems, or any other information base (including lists or other information with respect to current or prospective customers) (Code Sec. 197(d)(1)(C)(ii); Reg § 1.197-2(b)(4)),[46]

. . . any patent (but see the caution below), copyright (but see the caution below), process, design, pattern, know-how, format or similar item (Code Sec. 197(d)(1)(C)(iii); Reg § 1.197-

35. ¶L-7951; ¶1974; TD ¶269,002
36. ¶L-7977; ¶1974; TD ¶269,015
37. ¶L-7983 *et seq.*; ¶1974; TD ¶269,010
38. ¶L-7951; ¶1974; TD ¶269,002
39. ¶I-10219.1; ¶12,454.05
40. ¶L-7951; ¶1974; TD ¶269,002

41. ¶L-7966; ¶1974; TD ¶269,002
42. ¶L-7952 *et seq.*; ¶1974; TD ¶269,002
43. ¶L-7953; ¶1974; TD ¶269,004
44. ¶L-7953; ¶1974; TD ¶269,004
45. ¶L-7954; ¶1974; TD ¶269,004
46. ¶L-7955; ¶1974; TD ¶269,004

2(b)(5)),[47]

... customer-based intangibles (Code Sec. 197(d)(1)(C)(iv); Reg § 1.197-2(b)(6)), including the deposit base and any similar asset of a financial institution. (Code Sec. 197(d)(2)(B)) Customer based intangibles are the composition of market, share, and any other value resulting from the future provision of goods or services out of relationships with customers (contractual or otherwise) in the ordinary course of business (Code Sec. 197(d)(2)(A)),[48]

... supplier-based intangibles. (Code Sec. 197(d)(1)(C)(v)) Supplier-based intangibles are the value resulting from the future acquisitions of goods or services out of relationships (contractual or otherwise) in the ordinary course of business with suppliers of goods or services to be used or sold by the taxpayer (Code Sec. 197(d)(3); Reg § 1.197-2(b)(7)),[49]

... government granted licenses, permits or other rights (but see the caution below) (Code Sec. 197(d)(1)(D); Reg § 1.197-2(b)(8)),[50] and

... franchises, trademarks and trade names. (Code Sec. 197(d)(1)(F); Reg § 1.197-2(b)(10))[1]

caution: Certain patents, copyrights, and government granted rights (above) qualify only if acquired with the acquisition of a business, see below.

Section 197 intangibles also include any other item that is similar to workforce in place, information base, know-how, customer-based intangibles or supplier-based intangibles. (Code Sec. 197(d)(1)(C)(vi))[2]

The following intangibles are treated as section 197 intangibles only if acquired in connection with the acquisition of assets constituting a trade or business or a substantial portion thereof:[3]

... Computer software. (Code Sec. 197(e)(3)) (For the exclusion of "off-the-shelf" computer software from 15-year amortization, see ¶1978. For software developed by the taxpayer, see ¶1664.)

... Films, sound recordings, video tapes and books. (Code Sec. 197(e)(4)(A); Reg § 1.197-2(c)(4))[4]

... Copyrights and patents. (Code Sec. 197(e)(4)(C))

... Rights to receive tangible property or services under a contract granted by the government. (Code Sec. 197(e)(4)(B))

... Contract rights and government grants if the right has a fixed duration of less than 15 years, or is fixed in amount and, without regard to Code Sec. 197 would be recoverable under a method similar to the unit of production method. (Code Sec. 197(e)(4)(D); Reg § 1.197-2(c)(13))[5]

Covenants not to compete or similar arrangements are section 197 intangibles if entered into in connection with the acquisition of an interest in a trade or business or a substantial portion thereof. (Code Sec. 197(d)(1)(E); Reg § 1.197-2(b)(9)) The Tax Court held that a covenant not to compete agreed to by the seller in connection with a corporation's repurchase of 23 % of its stock was a section 197 intangible because (1) an acquisition of an interest in a trade or business (as distinct from an acquisition of the trade or business's assets) isn't subject to the substantial portion requirement, and (2) alternatively, the 23% portion was substantial.[6]

¶ 1978   Intangibles excluded from section 197 intangibles.

The following are never treated as section 197 intangibles regardless of how acquired:[7]

... interests in corporations, partnerships, trusts and estates. (Code Sec. 197(e)(1)(A))

47. ¶L-7957; ¶1974; TD ¶269,004
48. ¶L-7961; ¶1974; TD ¶269,004
49. ¶L-7964; ¶1974; TD ¶269,004
50. ¶L-7967; ¶1974; TD ¶269,004
1. ¶L-7968; ¶1974; TD ¶269,004
2. ¶L-7952; ¶1974; TD ¶269,004

3. ¶L-7952; ¶1974; TD ¶269,004
4. ¶L-7958.3; ¶1974; TD ¶269,014
5. ¶L-7967; ¶1974; TD ¶269,004
6. ¶L-7966; ¶1974; TD ¶269,004
7. ¶L-7952.1, L-7968 *et seq.*; ¶1974; TD ¶269,010

... computer software that's readily available for purchase by the general public, is subject to a non-exclusive license, and hasn't been substantially modified. (Code Sec. 197(e)(3)(A)) For 36-month straight line depreciation see ¶1964.

... futures, foreign currency contracts and notional principal contracts. (Code Sec. 197(e)(1)(B))

... land. (Code Sec. 197(e)(2)) But the right to use an American viticultural area (AVA) designation isn't an interest in land, and, thus, *is* a section 197 intangible as a government-granted license, permit or other right (see ¶1977).[8]

... leases of tangible property. (Code Sec. 197(e)(5)(A))

... debt instruments, except for deposit bases and similar items. (Code Sec. 197(e)(5)(B))

... mortgage servicing rights secured by residential real property. (Code Sec. 197(e)(6))

... sports franchises, if acquired before Oct. 23, 2004.[9]

... any fees for professional services or transaction costs incurred by parties to a transaction with respect to which any part of the gain or loss isn't recognized under the rules in Code Secs. 351 through 368 that govern corporate organizations and reorganizations. (Code Sec. 197(e)(7))

... accounts receivable. (Reg § 1.197-2(b)(6))

Also, intangibles created by the taxpayer (or for the taxpayer by contract) aren't subject to 15-year amortization if they are (1) not (a) certain rights granted by a governmental unit, (b) covenants not to compete made in connection with acquisition of an interest in a trade or business, or (c) franchises, trademarks and trade names, and (2) not created in connection with a transaction (or a series of related transactions) that involves the acquisition of assets which constitute all, or a substantial portion of, a trade or business. (Code Sec. 197(c)(2); Reg § 1.197-2(d)(2)) Thus, the costs of creating, as opposed to acquiring, customer relationships aren't subject to 15-year amortization.[10]

¶ 1979 Depletion Deduction.

All exhaustible natural deposits and timber qualify for deduction of a reasonable allowance for depletion based on the taxpayer's cost or other basis of the resources — cost depletion. For mines and certain interests in oil or gas wells, the depletion deductions may be computed as a specified percentage of gross income if that is greater than cost depletion.

A taxpayer can claim percentage depletion on one property and cost depletion on another, or claim, on the same property, cost depletion for one year and percentage for another.[11]

Where the property is entitled to either cost or percentage depletion, the allowable deduction is the greater of the two (Code Sec. 613)[12] Percentage depletion for oil and gas wells (except for gas from certain domestic geothermal deposits or geopressured brine) is limited to "independent producers and royalty owners," see ¶1982. The allowable deduction is never less than cost depletion. (Code Sec. 611, Code Sec. 612, Code Sec. 613) There's no official form for computing depletion, but Form T must be attached to the income tax return if a deduction for depletion of timber is taken.[13] The basis of the property must be reduced by the depletion deduction allowed or allowable, whichever is larger.[14]

A taxpayer may take a depletion deduction only if he owns an "economic interest" in the mineral deposit or the timber. (Reg § 1.611-1(b))[15]

8. ¶L-7972; ¶1974
9. ¶L-7968.1; ¶1974; TD ¶269,010
10. ¶L-7975; ¶1974; TD ¶269,013
11. ¶N-2004, N-2250 *et seq.*; ¶6114; TD ¶270,501
12. ¶N-2004; ¶6114; TD ¶270,501
13. ¶N-3101 *et seq.*, ¶N-6107; ¶6114.027; TD ¶270,503
14. ¶N-3009; ¶6124.001; TD ¶214,000
15. ¶N-2055, ¶N-2056, ¶N-2058 *et seq.*; ¶6114 *et seq.*; TD ¶270,504, TD ¶270,506

¶ 1980   Cost depletion.

This deduction is based on the property's adjusted basis, the number of recoverable units of mineral at the beginning of the year and the number of units sold or for which payment is received during the year. (Reg § 1.611-2(a)) An elective safe harbor may be used to determine recoverable oil and gas reserves.[16] Taxpayer's total cost depletion deductions can't exceed his basis for the mineral property.[17]

Basis for cost depletion and gain or loss is its cost or other basis plus or minus basis adjustments. (Code Sec. 612) It doesn't include the basis of nonmineral property, such as amounts recoverable through depreciation, or the residual value of land and improvements at the end of operations. (Reg § 1.612-1(b)(1))[18] Additional basis adjustments also apply to natural resources. (Code Sec. 1016(a))

¶ 1981   Percentage depletion.

This is a specified percentage of the "gross income from the property" for the tax year. It can never exceed 50% (100% for oil and gas properties) of taxable income from the property before deducting depletion. (Code Sec. 613(a)) For this purpose, taxable income from the property is the excess of gross income from the property over the allowable deductions (exclusive of depletion) attributable to the mining processes (including mining transportation) on which depletion is claimed. (Reg § 1.613-5(a))[19]

The 100%-of-taxable-income limit doesn't apply to so much of the depletion allowance as is determined under the rules relating to oil and gas produced from marginal properties (¶1982) for any tax year beginning before calendar year 2010, except for tax years beginning in calendar year 2008. (Code Sec. 613A(c)(6)(H))

Ⓡⓘⓐ*caution:* Check http://ria.thomsonreuters.com/federaltaxhandbook to see if the above provision has been extended.

Percentage depletion, like cost depletion, reduces basis. But percentage depletion continues to be deductible as long as there is gross income from the property even after taxpayer's basis for the property has been reduced to zero. Cost depletion is to be used where higher than percentage depletion. (Code Sec. 613(a))[20]

A corporation's deductible depletion allowance for iron ore or coal (including lignite) is cut back by 20% of the otherwise allowable percentage depletion deduction in excess of the adjusted basis of the property at the close of the tax year (determined without regard to the depletion deduction for the tax year). (Code Sec. 291(a)(2))

The minerals listed below qualify for percentage depletion at the rates shown. (Code Sec. 613(b); Reg § 1.613-2(b))[21]

	Rate (%)
Oil and gas	(See ¶1982)
Sulphur and uranium	22
U.S. deposits of: anorthosite, clay, laterite, and nephelite syenite (to the extent that alumina and aluminum compounds are extracted therefrom), asbestos, bauxite, celestite, chromite, corundum, fluorspar, graphite, ilmenite, kyanite, mica, olivine, quartz crystals (radio grade), rutile, block steatite talc and zircon	22

16. ¶N-2255.2; TD ¶270,701
17. ¶N-2250 *et seq.*; ¶6114.020 *et seq.*; TD ¶270,701
18. ¶N-3000 *et seq.*; ¶s 6124, 6124.001; TD ¶270,703
19. ¶N-2702; ¶6134.009 *et seq.*; TD ¶271,013
20. ¶N-2300 *et seq.*; ¶6114; TD ¶271,000 *et seq.*
21. ¶N-2311; ¶s 2914, 6134 *et seq.*; TD ¶271,002

U.S. deposits of ores of antimony, beryllium, bismuth, cadmium, cobalt, columbium, lead, lithium, manganese, mercury, molybdenum, nickel, platinum and platinum group metals, tantalum, thorium, tin, titanium, tungsten, vanadium and zinc	22
U.S. deposits of: gold, silver, copper, and iron ore and oil shale	15
Geothermal deposits in U.S. or its possessions	15
Metal mines that don't qualify for 22% or 15% rate, above	14
Rock asphalt and vermiculite	14
Ball clay, bentonite, china clay, sagger clay, and refractory clay exclusive of clay entitled to the 22% rate, above, or to 7½% or 5% rates	14
Asbestos (not entitled to 22% rate above), brucite, coal, lignite, perlite, sodium chloride and wollastonite	10
Natural gas from geopressurized brine from U.S. wells drilled after Sept. '78 and before '84	10
Clay and shale used or sold for use in the manufacture of sewer pipe or brick, and clay, shale, and slate used or sold for use as sintered or burned lightweight aggregates	7½
Clay used or sold for use, in the manufacture of drainage and roofing tile, flower pots and kindred products	5
Gravel, peat, pumice, sand, scoria, shale (other than shale entitled to 15% or 7½% rates, above) and stone (other than dimension and ornamental stone)	5
Bromine, calcium chloride and magnesium chloride (if from brine wells)	5
Other minerals: 14%, except generally 5% if used or sold as rip rap, ballast, road material, rubble, concrete aggregates or for similar purposes.	

Natural resources that don't qualify for percentage depletion include timber (Reg § 1.611-1(a)), minerals from sea water and other inexhaustible sources. (Code Sec. 613(b)(7)) Coal or iron ore disposed of with a retained economic interest that qualifies for capital gain-ordinary loss treatment doesn't qualify for percentage depletion. (Reg § 1.611-1(b)(2))[22] For the treatment of percentage depletion for alternative minimum tax purposes, see ¶3208.

¶ 1982　Oil, gas and geothermal deposits percentage depletion.

Percentage depletion applies to oil and gas only in the following cases:[23]

• *Crude oil and natural gas production of independent producers and royalty owners.* 15% depletion is allowed a taxpayer who isn't a retailer or refiner for so much of his "average daily production" of domestic crude oil and domestic natural gas as doesn't exceed his "depletable oil quantity" or "depletable natural gas quantity." "Marginal production" may qualify for a higher percentage depletion rate (not to exceed 25%; for 2009, the percentage is 15%)[24] if the price of domestic crude oil is below $20 for the calendar year preceding the calendar year in which the tax year in question begins. (Code Sec. 613A(c)(6))

22. ¶N-2314; ¶s 6114.023, 6314.04; TD ¶271,003
23. ¶N-2400 *et seq.*; ¶613A4; TD ¶271,014
24. ¶N-2425; ¶613A4; TD ¶271,018

The maximum depletable amount is 1,000 barrels of oil or 6,000,000 cubic feet of gas per day. A taxpayer who has both crude oil and natural gas production allocates the maximum depletable amount between oil and gas at the rate of 6,000 cubic feet of gas per barrel of oil. Over-ceiling production isn't entitled to any depletion. (Code Sec. 613(d), Code Sec. 613A)

The deduction can't exceed 65% of the taxpayer's taxable income from all sources. (Code Sec. 613A(d)) Also, the deduction for any costs for which taxpayer claims the 15% enhanced oil recovery credit (¶2323) must be reduced by that credit amount. (Code Sec. 43(d)(1))

• *Production of natural heat from geothermal deposits and natural gas production from geopressured brine* located in the U.S. or its possession. (Code Sec. 613(e), Code Sec. 613A(b)(2))[25]

Percentage depletion isn't available with respect to any lease bonus, advance royalty or other amount payable without regard to production from any oil, gas or geothermal property. (Code Sec. 613(e)(3), Code Sec. 613A(d)(5))[26] The restriction on the use of percentage depletion applies only to oil and natural gas; other minerals from oil and gas wells can qualify.[27]

¶ 1983   Related and commonly controlled producers.

The depletable ceiling amounts applicable to oil or gas production of independent producers or royalty owners who are related or are under common control is allocated among them. Allocation is required among corporations that are part of a controlled group; corporations, trusts and estates owned by the same or related persons; and an individual and his spouse and minor children. (Code Sec. 613A(c)(8))[28]

¶ 1984   Aggregation and division of depletable property.

Cost or percentage depletion must be computed separately for each property. (Code Sec. 612, Code Sec. 613)[29] A "property" is each separate interest owned by the taxpayer in each separate tract or parcel of land. (Code Sec. 614(a)) "Interest" means economic interest. It includes working or operating interests, royalties, overriding royalties and net profits interests. It also includes production payments to the extent they aren't treated as loans. (Reg § 1.614-1(a)(2)) Separate properties may be aggregated and treated as a single property. (Code Sec. 614(b), Code Sec. 614(c), Code Sec. 614(e)) A single interest in a "mine" may be treated as two or more separate properties, at the taxpayer's election. (Code Sec. 614(c)(2); Reg § 1.614-3(b))

25. ¶N-2316; ¶s 6134.001, 613A4; TD ¶271,014
26. ¶N-2105 *et seq.*; ¶613A4.02; TD ¶271,010
27. ¶N-2400 *et seq.*; TD ¶271,014

28. ¶N-2420; ¶613A4; TD ¶271,026
29. ¶N-2901; ¶6114 *et seq.*; TD ¶271,027

Chapter 6 Charitable Contributions—Medical Expenses— Alimony—Other Nonbusiness Deductions

¶ 2100   Charitable Contribution Deduction.

An individual who itemizes can deduct charitable contributions up to 50%, 30% or 20% of his adjusted gross income, depending on the type of property contributed and the type of donee. A corporation generally can deduct charitable contributions up to 10% of its taxable income. Amounts that exceed the ceilings can be carried forward for five years. The deduction allowed for property contributions is usually the property's fair market value, but the deduction is reduced for gifts of certain types of property.

For individuals, charitable contributions are deductible only as an itemized deduction on Schedule A (Form 1040). (Reg § 1.170A-1(a))[1]

💡*caution:* For years before 2010, the itemized deduction for charitable contributions is subject to reduction if adjusted gross income exceeds specified amounts, see ¶3114.

For the charity's requirement to disclose the deductibility of contributions to it, see ¶4118.

¶ 2101   What is a deductible charitable contribution?

A deductible charitable contribution generally is one that:

. . . is to or for the use of a qualified charitable organization (¶2102) (Code Sec. 170(c));

. . . is paid within the taxpayer's tax year, regardless of the taxpayer's accounting method (¶2133) (except for certain accrual basis corporations, see ¶2134) (Code Sec. 170(a));

. . . is within the applicable statutory ceilings for individuals (¶2124 *et seq.*), and corporations (¶2132) (Code Sec. 170(b)); *and*

. . . meets certain substantiation requirements (¶2135 *et seq.*). (Reg § 1.170A-13)[2]

¶ 2102   Qualified charitable organizations.

A qualified charitable organization is one that fits into one of the categories specified in the law *and* which IRS has ruled (or the donor establishes) is eligible to receive deductible charitable contributions.[3] IRS Pub. No. 78, "Cumulative List of Organizations described in Section 170(c)," lists qualified charitable organizations, but isn't exhaustive.[4]

Qualified charitable organizations include:

. . . a corporation, trust, community chest, fund or foundation (including a private foundation) that is organized *and* operated exclusively for charitable, religious, educational, scientific or literary purposes, or for the prevention of cruelty to children or animals, or to foster and conduct national or international amateur sports competition (but only if none of the activities involves providing athletic facilities or equipment); *and* that is organized or created in the U.S. or its possessions, or under their laws; *and* none of whose net earnings inures to the benefit of any private shareholder or individual. Corporate contributions to noncorporate donees must be used in the U.S. or its possessions (Code Sec. 170(c)(2));[5]

. . . U.S. states or possessions, their political subdivisions, the U.S., and the District of Columbia, *but only* if the gift is exclusively for public purposes (Code Sec. 170(c)(1));[6]

---

1. ¶A-2701; ¶1704.01; TD ¶330,201
2. ¶K-2803; ¶1704 *et seq.*; TD ¶330,202
3. ¶K-2850 *et seq.*; ¶1704.20; TD ¶330,265

4. ¶K-2945; ¶1704.21; TD ¶330,279
5. ¶K-2862 *et seq.*; ¶1704.20 *et seq.*; TD ¶330,269
6. ¶K-2899; ¶1704.25; TD ¶330,274

References beginning with a single letter are to paragraphs in RIA's Federal Tax Coordinator 2d and RIA's Analysis of Federal Taxes: Income. Those beginning with numbers are to paragraphs in RIA's United States Tax Reporter. Those beginning with TD are to paragraphs in RIA's Tax Desk.

... certain war veterans' organizations, (Code Sec. 170(c)(3));[7] certain domestic fraternal societies, orders or associations, (Code Sec. 170(c)(4))[8]; and certain nonprofit cemetery companies. (Code Sec. 170(c)(5))[9]

¶ 2103   Charitable deductions barred for certain contributions.

No charitable deduction is allowed for the following types of contributions:

... A contribution to a charity that conducts lobbying activities on matters of direct financial interest to the donor's trade or business, if a principal purpose of the contribution was to avoid federal income tax by getting a charitable deduction for lobbying expenses for which a business expense deduction would be disallowed (¶1626) if the donor had conducted the activities directly. (Code Sec. 170(f)(9))[10]

... A contribution to an organization which is disqualified from tax exemption because a substantial part of its activities is lobbying, or if it participates in any political campaign. (Reg § 1.170A-1(j)(5))[11]

... A contribution made to or for an individual (except for certain students, see ¶2123), unless made to the individual as an agent for a qualified organization (¶2102).[12]

... Contributions by church members earmarked to cover the minister s medical expenses. The church does not have control over the use of the funds.[13]

... A transfer to charity to the extent the donor derives an economic benefit (for exception, see (¶2104). Thus, no charitable deduction is allowed for: tuition (or required "donation" of excess "tuition" payment) even for parochial school; or [14] a payment in connection with a person's admission to an old age or retirement home operated by a charity, to the extent allocable to care to be given (may be partly a *medical* expense, see ¶2147) or the privilege of being admitted.[15]

... vacation, sick, or personal leave given up by an employee in exchange for his employer's contributions of amounts to a charity under a leave-sharing program.[16]

... Contributions of clothing and household items that are not in good used condition or better (but deduction may be allowed if amount claimed for the item exceeds $500 and the taxpayer includes a qualified appraisal of the item with his return). Household items include furniture, furnishings, electronics, appliances, linens, and similar items, but don't include food, paintings, antiques, and other art objects, jewelry, gems, or collections. IRS may also deny a deduction for any contribution of clothing or a household item with minimal monetary value, such as used socks or undergarments. IRS says the price a buyer actually pays for a used item in a store such as a thrift shop is an indication of value, but dismissed as inaccurate "standard value listings" supplied by organizations like the Salvation Army. It also says valuation under a fixed formula or method (e.g., percentage of replacement cost), doesn't work well for used clothing. (Code Sec. 170(f)(16))[17]

¶ 2104   Fundraising events, entertainment, etc., for charity.

Where amounts are paid in connection with admission to fundraising events for charity (e.g., shows, lotteries and athletic events), the receipt of tickets or other privileges raises a presumption that the payment isn't a gift. Taxpayer must show that a clearly identifiable part of the payment is a gift. Only the part made with the intention of making a gift *and* for which taxpayer receives no consideration qualifies as a contribution.[18] The charity must show

7. ¶K-2915; ¶1704.27; TD ¶330,275
8. ¶K-2921; ¶1704.26; TD ¶330,276
9. ¶K-2925; ¶1704.28; TD ¶330,277
10. ¶K-2804; ¶1624.395; TD ¶330,204
11. ¶K-2871; ¶1704.30; TD ¶332,613
12. ¶K-2953; ¶1704.20; TD ¶330,203
13. ¶K-2970; ¶1705.22(65); TD ¶330,203.
14. ¶K-3110, K-3111; ¶1704.38; TD ¶330,242
15. ¶K-3047; ¶1704.38; TD ¶330,231
16. ¶H-1013; TD ¶130,507
17. ¶K-3177.6; ¶1704.41.
18. ¶K-3089; ¶1704.38; TD ¶330,245

(in its solicitation, tickets, receipts or other related documents) the value (or reasonable estimate) of the event, and how much of the contribution is deductible.[19] For an organization's fundraising disclosure requirements, see ¶4119.

However, the donor may deduct a contribution in full if the benefit is inconsequential or insubstantial. This applies if the charity informs patrons how much is deductible *and* any of these tests is met: (1) the fair market value (FMV) of all benefits received in connection with the payment is not more than 2% of the payment, or the following dollar figures: $96 for 2010 ($97 for 2011), if less; or (2) the payment is at least $48 for 2010 ($48.50 for 2011) and in connection with it the donor receives only token benefits (bookmarks, calendars, mugs, posters, tee shirts, etc.) generally costing less than $9.60 for 2010 ($9.70 for 2011), or (3) the charity mails or otherwise distributes free, unordered items to patrons.[20]

A taxpayer may rely on either a contemporaneous written acknowledgment (for contributions of $250 or more, see ¶2137) or a written disclosure statement (for quid pro quo contributions of more than $75, see ¶4119) for the FMV of any goods or services he receives from the charity. The taxpayer can't treat an estimate as the FMV where he knows, or has reason to know, it's unreasonable. (Reg § 1.170A-1(h)(4))[21] Payment to a college or university where the donor receives a *right to buy* seating at an athletic event (even in a skybox) is 80% deductible as a contribution. No amount paid for the tickets themselves is deductible. (Code Sec. 170(l))[22] Taxpayer's failure to use the ticket, etc., doesn't increase the amount of the deduction.[23]

Amounts paid for raffle tickets, to play bingo, etc., aren't contributions[24] (for deduction as a gambling loss, see ¶1787).

¶ 2105 Charitable contribution v. business expense.

Transfers to a charity that are directly related to a taxpayer's business and are made with a "reasonable expectation of financial return commensurate with" the amount transferred may be deductible as business expenses, and not as charitable contributions. But no business expense deduction is allowed for the transfer if *any* part of it is deductible as a charitable contribution. (Reg § 1.162-15(a)(2))[25]

☑️ observation: Business expense treatment may be preferable where the "contribution" exceeds the charitable deduction ceiling, ¶2124 *et seq.*

¶ 2106 Gift of property.

A gift of property to a qualified charitable donee (¶2102) is a charitable contribution to the extent of the property's fair market value (FMV) at the time of the gift, whether or not it has appreciated (Reg § 1.170A-1(c)), except for gifts of ordinary income-type property (¶2107), and certain gifts of tangible personal property or capital gain property (¶2110).[26] For substantiation requirements, see ¶2136.

The property's FMV is reduced for restrictions placed by the donor on marketability or use (e.g., 3-year bar on transfer or license of donated patent).[27]

No gain is realized on a charitable contribution of appreciated property (except for certain bargain sales, see ¶2112).[28]

☑️ observation: This means the taxpayer can deduct his basis in the property plus his paper profit, which he isn't taxable on.

---

19. ¶K-3105; ¶1704.38; TD ¶330,257
20. ¶K-3106; ¶1704.38; TD ¶330,262
21. ¶K-3087.2; ¶1704.38; TD ¶334,016
22. ¶K-3100; ¶1704.38; TD ¶330,256
23. ¶K-3094; TD ¶330,250

24. ¶K-3090; ¶1704.38; TD ¶330,246
25. ¶K-3068 *et seq.*; ¶1624.363; TD ¶334,700 *et seq.*
26. ¶K-3150 *et seq.*; ¶1704.40 *et seq.*; TD ¶331,601
27. ¶K-3151; TD ¶331,601
28. ¶K-3208 *et seq.*, ¶K-3179 *et seq.*; ¶1704.43; TD ¶331,679

Taxpayer's charitable deduction for the gift can't exceed the property's FMV (at contribution), even if it's less than his basis.[29] Nor is taxpayer allowed a loss deduction on the difference between the property's basis and FMV.[30]

Where taxpayer arranged for his credit card rebate (1% of purchases) to be paid to charity, the rebate amounts were treated as excludable from taxpayer's gross income and as charitable donations made by taxpayer.[31]

Special rules apply to gifts of patents[32] and taxidermy property.[33]

¶ 2107   Gift of ordinary income-type appreciated property—deduction reduced.

For charitable gifts of ordinary income-type property (below), the amount contributed (property's fair market value (FMV), ¶2106) must be reduced by the amount which would have been recognized as gain other than long-term capital gain if the property had been sold by the donor for its then FMV. (Code Sec. 170(e)(1))[34] For exceptions, see ¶2108 *et seq.*

Ordinary income-type property is property which, if sold by taxpayer (donor) at its FMV on the date it was contributed, would have resulted in *some* amount of gain other than long-term capital gain. (Code Sec. 170(e)(1)) This includes: inventory or other property held for sale to customers; Code Sec. 306 stock (¶3535 *et seq.*); capital assets held for less than the long-term holding period as of the date contributed; property subject to depreciation, etc., recapture; property used in taxpayer's trade or business; and art works, letters, memoranda and similar property created by or for taxpayer. (Reg § 1.170A-4(b))[35]

For contributions before Jan. 1, 2010, taxpayers that aren't C corporations and donate "apparently wholesome food" inventory to eligible charities are entitled to the same enhanced deduction available to C corporations (see ¶2108), except that the deduction can't exceed 10% of net income as specially calculated. (Code Sec. 170(e)(3)(C)(i)(I))[36]

⚠ *caution:* Check http://ria.thomsonreuters.com/federaltaxhandbook to see if the above provision has been extended.

¶ 2108   Enhanced deductions for C corporation gifts of property for specific purposes.

A C corporation may claim an enhanced deduction equal to the lesser of (a) basis plus half of the property's appreciation, or (b) twice the property's basis, for:

(1) Contributions of inventory, property held primarily for sale to customers in the ordinary course of its trade or business, or depreciable or real property used in its trade or business, if the contribution is to an exempt Code Sec. 501(c)(3) organization (other than certain private foundations) that uses the property solely for the care of the ill, the needy or infants, and that meets other specified requirements. (Code Sec. 170(e)(3)(A))[37]

(2) Certain contributions of scientific equipment or apparatus constructed by the taxpayer to a higher education institution or a tax-exempt organization (but not a private foundation) organized and operated primarily to conduct scientific research. (Code Sec. 170(e)(4))[38]

(3) Contributions before Jan. 1, 2010, of (a) food inventory (it must be apparently wholesome food, i.e., meant for human consumption and meet certain quality and labeling standards); and (b) qualified contributions of book inventory to certain public schools if donee certification requirements are met. (Code Sec. 170(e)(3)(C), Code Sec. 170(e)(3)(D))[39]

29. ¶K-3151; ¶1704.41; TD ¶331,601
30. ¶M-1015; TD ¶331,679
31. ¶K-2800; ¶1704; TD ¶330,200
32. ¶K-3177.1; ¶1704.42; TD ¶331,616.2
33. ¶K-3171.1
34. ¶K-3158 *et seq.*; ¶1704.42; TD ¶331,609

35. ¶K-3161; ¶1704.42; TD ¶331,610
36. ¶K-3201.1; ¶1704.42; TD ¶331,702
37. ¶K-3201 *et seq.*; ¶1704.42; TD ¶331,701 *et seq.*
38. ¶K-3221 *et seq.*; ¶1704.42; TD ¶331,721 *et seq.*
39. ¶K-3201 *et seq.*; ¶1704.42; TD ¶331,701 *et seq.*

(4) For tax years beginning before 2010, certain contributions of computer technology or equipment (software, computer or peripheral equipment, and fiber optic cable) to schools or libraries for use in the U.S. for educational purposes that is related to the donee's purpose or function. (Code Sec. 170(e)(6))[40]

🅡🅘🅐️*caution:* Check http://ria.thomsonreuters.com/federaltaxhandbook to see if the above pre-2010 provisions have been extended.

¶ 2109   Property contribution where taxpayer realizes income on gift.

If a taxpayer realizes income (ordinary income or capital gain) on his gift of property, his charitable deduction isn't subject to the reduction described at ¶2107. Thus, he may deduct the full fair market value of donated installment obligations, obligations issued at a discount, or other receivables. (Reg § 1.170A-4(a))[41]

¶ 2110   Limits on contributions of tangible personal property; gifts to certain private foundations.

For certain gifts, the amount treated as contributed and deductible (subject to deduction ceilings, see ¶2124 *et seq.*) is the property's fair market value (FMV) *reduced* by the total amount of the gain that would have been long-term capital gain (determined without regard to Code Sec. 1221(b)(3), see ¶2622) if the property were sold for its then FMV. (Code Sec. 170(e)(1)(B))[42] The donor's charitable deduction is thus limited to his basis for these contributions:

. . . tangible personal property that's unrelated to the donee's exempt function (e.g., art to a church that then sells it) (Code Sec. 170(e)(1)(B)(i)); and

. . . any capital gain property except for publicly traded stock (limited to aggregate contributions of not more than 10% of the value of a corporation's outstanding stock by a donor and his family) given to a private foundation that isn't an operating foundation or community foundation and that doesn't make timely qualifying distributions. (Code Sec. 170(e)(1)(B)(ii), Code Sec. 170(e)(5)).[43]

Contributions of tangible personal property for which a FMV deduction is claimed, but which is not used for exempt purposes, if the donee sells or disposes of tangible personal property with a claimed value of at least $5,000: (1) in the year of contribution, the deduction is limited to the taxpayer's basis; or (2) after the year of contribution but within the 3 year period beginning on the contribution date, the donor includes in income the amount of the claimed deduction in excess of his basis in the property. These rules do not apply if the organization makes a proper certification to IRS. A $10,000 penalty applies for fraudulent identifications of property (i.e., stating it is exempt use property while knowing it was not intended for such use). (Code Sec. 170(e)(1)(B)(i)(II), Code Sec. 170(e)(7), Code Sec. 6720B)[44]

¶ 2111   Liabilities transferred as part of contribution.

The donor's charitable contribution must be reduced by any liability that's assumed (e.g., by the donee) in connection with the gift. (Reg § 1.170A-3(d)) Where the donor transfers property subject to a liability, the amount of that debt is treated as an amount realized for purposes of the bargain sale rules, see ¶2112 (but not for the rule at ¶2109).[45]

A reduction also must be made for the amount of any interest on the liability attributable

---

40. ¶K-3241 *et seq.*; ¶1704.42; TD ¶331,741 *et seq.*
41. ¶K-3178 *et seq.*; TD ¶331,618
42. ¶K-3167 *et seq.*; ¶1704.42; TD ¶331,615

43. ¶K-3167 *et seq.*; ¶1704.42; TD ¶331,615
44. ¶K-3167; ¶V-2704.1; ¶1704.42.
45. ¶K-3155, K-3198; ¶1704.44; TD ¶331,605

to any period after the contribution was made. (Code Sec. 170(f)(5))[46]

¶ 2112 Bargain sale to charity.

A taxpayer who sells property to (or exchanges it with) a charity and receives less than its fair market value (FMV) may treat the "bargain" element as a charitable contribution. (Code Sec. 1011(b); Reg § 1.170A-4(c)(2)) In computing the deduction, the amount considered contributed (excess of FMV over selling price) must be reduced by the amount of any required adjustment for ordinary income-type appreciated property (¶2107) for the contribution portion. (Reg § 1.170A-4(c), Reg § 1.1011-2(a))[47]

But the donor generally also realizes taxable gain on the sale. His basis for measuring gain is only the portion of his total cost or other basis for the property that the bargain selling price (amount realized) bears to its FMV. (Code Sec. 1011(b); Reg § 1.1011-2) This is basis times the selling price, divided by FMV. (Reg § 1.170A-4(c)(2)(i))[48]

illustration: J owns long-term stock that cost $12,000 and is worth $20,000 when he sells it to charity for $12,000. A contribution deduction of $8,000 ($20,000 – $12,000) is allowable. J's basis for the stock is reduced to $7,200 ($12,000 cost × $12,000 selling price ÷ $20,000 FMV) against his $12,000 selling price, giving J a $4,800 taxable gain.

¶ 2113 Gift of stock to charity followed by redemption ("charitable bail-out").

Owners of closely held corporations may in effect withdraw earnings from their firms tax-free by making a charitable contribution of their corporate stock, which the corporation then redeems. As long as the charity has no legal obligation to sell back the stock, the donor is allowed a charitable deduction even if the redemption was preplanned.[49] However, a contribution of stock which is then redeemed from a private foundation may be subject to self-dealing penalty excise taxes (¶4127).

¶ 2114 Contributions of partial interests in property.

For transfers in trust, a contribution of a partial interest in property (e.g., where the donor transfers only his right to use the property, ¶2120, or his income interest in it) qualifies for a charitable deduction if the interest is:

• a remainder interest transferred to a charitable remainder trust (CRT, ¶2116), or a pooled income fund (¶2117), (Code Sec. 170(f)(2)(A)); or

• an income interest in a charitable lead trust (¶2119). (Code Sec. 170(f)(2)(B))[50]

For transfers not in trust, no charitable deduction is allowed for a contribution of less than the donor's entire interest in the donated property except to the extent the deduction would have been allowed had the transfer been in trust. (Code Sec. 170(f)(3)(A))[1] However, this bar doesn't apply to contributions of:

• A remainder interest in a personal residence or a farm. (Code Sec. 170(f)(3)(B)(i));[2]

• An undivided portion of taxpayer's entire interest (even if partial) in property (Code Sec. 170(f)(3)(B)(ii)), such as a remainder or income interest.[3] No deduction is allowed for a contribution of an undivided portion of a taxpayer's entire interest in tangible personal property unless, immediately before the contribution, all interests in the property are held by the taxpayer or the taxpayer and the donee. Additionally, the FMV of any additional contribution of a fractional interest in property is the lesser of: (1) its FMV at the time of

---

46. ¶K-3157; ¶1704.44; TD ¶331,607
47. ¶K-3190; ¶1704.43; TD ¶331,690
48. ¶K-3194; ¶1704.43; TD ¶331,690
49. ¶K-3186; TD ¶331,686

50. ¶K-3250 *et seq.*; ¶1704.46; TD ¶331,619 *et seq.*
1. ¶K-3250 *et seq.*; ¶1704.45; TD ¶331,619 *et seq.*
2. ¶K-3440 *et seq.*; ¶1704.45; TD ¶331,619
3. ¶K-3451 *et seq.*; ¶1704.45; TD ¶331,621

the initial fractional contribution, or (2) its FMV at the time of the additional contribution. (Code Sec. 170(o)(1)(A), Code Sec. 170(o)(2)) The deduction is recaptured under certain circumstances. (Code Sec. 170(o)(3)(A), Code Sec. 2522(e)(2)(A))

• A partial interest in property where *all* of taxpayer's interests in the property are given to one or more charities (e.g., income interest to one charity and remainder interest to another charity). (Reg § 1.170A-6(a));[4]

• A partial interest in real property (including remainders and perpetual restrictions) exclusively for "conservation purposes," including qualifying facade easements. (Code Sec. 170(f)(3)(B)(iii), Code Sec. 170(h))[5] A facade easement must, among other things: preserve the building's entire exterior and prohibit any change inconsistent with its historical character; donee and donor must enter into a written agreement certifying that donee is able and committed to manage and enforce the restriction; and a donor must include with the tax return an appraisal, pictures of the property, description of the restriction, and pay a $500 fee for deductions exceeding $10,000. The deduction is reduced to reflect any rehabilitation credits claimed for the property during the preceding five years. (Code Sec. 170(f)(13), Code Sec. 170(h))[6]

¶ 2115 No charitable deduction for "personal benefit contract" (charitable split-dollar insurance) transactions.

No charitable deduction is allowed for a transfer to or for the use of a charity if the charity directly or indirectly pays or paid any premium on any personal benefit contract (e.g., split-dollar life insurance, see ¶1268) for the transferor. Also, no deduction is allowed if there is an understanding or expectation that any person will directly or indirectly pay any premium on any such contract for the transferor. A charity must pay an excise tax (use Form 8870) if it or any such person pays such premiums. (Code Sec. 170(f)(10))[7]

¶ 2116 Charitable remainder trusts (CRTs)—CRATs and CRUTs.

A charitable remainder trust (CRT) is a trust formed to make current distributions to one or more noncharitable income beneficiaries and to pay the entire remainder to charity or use it for a charitable purpose, that is *either* a "charitable remainder annuity trust" (CRAT) or a "charitable remainder unitrust" (CRUT). (Code Sec. 664(d); Reg § 1.664-1)[8]

¶ 2117 Pooled income funds.

A pooled income fund is a trust formed to pay income to one or more noncharitable beneficiaries and the remainder to charity. It must be maintained by the donee charity (no donor or income beneficiary may be a trustee) and meet certain other requirements. (Code Sec. 642(c)(5); Reg § 1.642(c)-5)[9]

¶ 2118 Contributions to donor advised funds.

Donor advised funds (DAFs) are charitable accounts set up and sponsored by an organization to which donors contribute and provide advice on the account's distributions and investments, although the sponsoring organization must have final say on the actual distributions and investments. Contributions to DAFs are deductible only if: (1) the sponsoring organization is not one listed in Code Sec. 170(f)(18)(A) (e.g., a war veteran's organization or domestic fraternal lodge); and (2) the donor obtains contemporaneous written acknowledgment from the sponsoring organization certifying it has legal control over the contribution. (Code

4. ¶K-3473; ¶1704.45; TD ¶331,621
5. ¶K-3473 *et seq.*; ¶1704.45; TD ¶331,625
6. ¶K-3473 *et seq.*; ¶1704.45; TD ¶331,625

7. ¶K-3661, K-3667; ¶1704.305; TD ¶331,622
8. ¶K-3261 *et seq.*, ¶K-3291 *et seq.*; TD ¶331,629
9. ¶K-3363 *et seq.*; ¶s 1704.46, 6424.03; TD ¶331,632

Sec. 170(f)(18)(A))[10]

¶ 2119   Contribution of income interest in trust—charitable lead trusts.

A charitable deduction is allowed for a contribution of an income interest in trust (remainder to a noncharity) *only* if: (1) the donor is taxable on the trust income, and (2) the donated income interest is either a "guaranteed annuity" or a "unitrust interest." (Code Sec. 170(f)(2)(B); Reg § 1.170A-6) This type of trust is a "charitable lead trust." [11]

¶ 2120   Contributing use of property.

A taxpayer who gives a charity the *right to use* property (e.g., rent-free use of office space), while retaining the property itself, can't take a charitable deduction for the rental or other value of this right (under the partial-interest gift rules, ¶2114). (Code Sec. 170(f)(3)(A))[12]

¶ 2121   Performing services for charity and related deductible transportation expenses.

No charitable deduction is allowed for the value of services a taxpayer renders to charity. (Reg § 1.170A-1(g))[13]

However, the taxpayer is allowed a charitable deduction for his unreimbursed out-of-pocket expenses (for travel expenses, see ¶2122) necessarily incurred in performing services (other than lobbying) free for a charity. (Code Sec. 170(f)(6); Reg § 1.170A-1(g))[14]

A taxpayer who uses his car in performing these services may deduct 14¢ per mile as a contribution (Code Sec. 170(i)) or his actual (unreimbursed) expenses for gas and oil. Parking fees and tolls are deductible in either case, as are deductions otherwise allowable for interest or taxes connected with the car, but not depreciation, insurance and repairs.[15]

¶ 2122   Charitable travel expenses.

No charitable deduction is allowed for taxpayer's travel expenses (including meals and lodging), whether or not reimbursed, while away from home unless there's no significant element of personal pleasure, recreation or vacation in the travel. (Code Sec. 170(j)) Even then, deduction is limited to amounts necessarily incurred for meals and lodging while away from home overnight in rendering these services.[16]

¶ 2123   Maintaining student in taxpayer's home.

A charitable deduction is allowed to a taxpayer who, under a written agreement with a charity and without compensation, maintains an elementary or high school student (who isn't his dependent or relative) in his home. (Code Sec. 170(g); Reg § 1.170A-2)[17] The charitable contribution in any year is the amount so contributed, but not more than $50 times the number of full calendar months (15 days or more is a "month") during the year for which the individual was a member of taxpayer's household and a full-time student. (Code Sec. 170(g); Reg § 1.170A-2(b))[18]

---

10. ¶K-3987; ¶1704.285; TD ¶331,200
11. ¶K-3345 *et seq.*; ¶1704.46; TD ¶331,633
12. ¶K-3440.2; ¶1704.45; TD ¶331,626
13. ¶K-3551; ¶1704.36; TD ¶332,301
14. ¶K-3601 *et seq.*; ¶1704.37; TD ¶332,301 *et seq.*

15. ¶K-3614 *et seq.*; ¶1704.37; TD ¶332,614 *et seq.*
16. ¶K-3620 *et seq.*; ¶s 1704.37, 2744.01; TD ¶332,620 *et seq.*
17. ¶K-3650 *et seq.*; ¶1704.33; TD ¶332,650 *et seq.*
18. ¶K-3651; ¶1704.33; TD ¶332,651

¶ 2124   Charitable deduction ceilings for individuals.

There's a ceiling on the amount an individual may deduct each year as a charitable contribution, based both on the type of property contributed and the type of charity to which the contribution is made. The ceilings (below) for any tax year are a percentage of taxpayer's "contribution base" (below) for the year, subject to an overall 50% ceiling for all charitable gifts. (Code Sec. 170(b)(1))[19] For carryover of excess contributions, see ¶2130.

If the contributions are all to "50% charities" (listed at ¶2125), the year's ceiling is 50% of taxpayer's contribution base for the year, except for contributions of appreciated capital gain property (¶2127). (Code Sec. 170(b)(1)(A))[20]

If the contributions are all to "30% charities" (¶2126), or are "for the use" of *any* charities, the ceiling is 30% of taxpayer's contribution base (except for contributions of appreciated capital gain property, see ¶2127) or, if less, 50% of his contribution base minus his contributions to 50% charities. (Code Sec. 170(b)(1)(B); Reg § 1.170A-8(c))[21]

An individual's "contribution base" for a year is his adjusted gross income (AGI, see ¶3102) for the year, but without deducting any NOL carryback to that year. (Code Sec. 170(b)(1)(G))[22]

For spouses filing joint returns, these ceilings apply to the couple's combined contributions and their combined contribution base. (Reg § 1.170A-2(a)(1), Reg § 1.170A-8(a)(1))[23]

For qualified conservation contributions (i.e., contribution of a qualified real property interest to a qualified organization exclusively for conservation) made in tax years beginning before 2010, the 30% limit is 50% of the contribution base less all other charitable contributions, and the carryforward period (¶2130) is 15 years. For qualified farmers and ranchers (more than 50% of gross income from farming as defined at Code Sec. 2032A(e)), this limit is 100% of the contribution base less all other charitable contributions. For property in agriculture or livestock production to be eligible for the 100% limit, the qualified real property interest must include a restriction that the property remain generally available for such production. (Code Sec. 170(b)(1)(E), Code Sec. 170(b)(2)) In a tax year in which an individual has made a qualified conservation contribution and one or more contributions subject to the limitations in Code Sec. 170(b)(1), the qualified conservation contribution may be taken into account only after taking into account contributions subject to the limitations in Code Sec. 170(b)(1).[24]

Ⓡ*caution:* Check http://ria.thomsonreuters.com/federaltaxhandbook to see if the above provision has been extended.

¶ 2125   50% charities.

For purposes of the deduction ceilings for individuals (¶2124), "50% charities" are:

(1) churches (or church conventions or associations);

(2) tax-exempt educational organizations;

(3) tax-exempt hospitals and certain medical research organizations;

(4) certain organizations holding property for state and local colleges and universities;

(5) a U.S. state or possession, or any political subdivision of any of these, or the U.S. or the District of Columbia, if the contribution is for exclusively public purposes;

(6) organizations organized and operated exclusively for charitable, religious, educational, scientific or literary purposes, or for the prevention of cruelty to children or animals, or to

---

19. ¶K-3670; ¶1704.05; TD ¶333,001
20. ¶K-3671; ¶1704.05; TD ¶333,004
21. ¶s K-3671, K-3674, K-3684 *et seq.*; ¶s 1704.05, 1704.10 *et seq.*; TD ¶333,009

22. ¶K-3672; ¶1704.05; TD ¶333,002
23. ¶K-3673; ¶1704.06; TD ¶333,003
24. ¶K-3694.1 *et seq.*; ¶1704.11 *et seq.*

foster national or international amateur sports competition if they normally get a substantial part of their support from the government or general public;

(7) certain private foundations;

(8) certain membership organizations more than one-third of whose support comes from the public. (Code Sec. 170(b)(1)(A))[25]

¶ 2126   30% charities.

For purposes of the ceilings on an individual's charitable deduction (¶2124), "30% charities" are qualifying charitable organizations (¶2102), that aren't 50% charities (¶2125), e.g., war veterans' organizations, fraternal orders, cemetery companies, and certain private non-operating foundations. (Code Sec. 170(b)(1)(B); Reg § 1.170A-8(c))[26]

¶ 2127   Gifts of appreciated capital gain property to 50% charities—30% ceiling.

An individual's deduction ceiling in the tax year for gifts of certain appreciated capital gain property (below) to 50% charities is 30% of his contribution base (¶2124), unless he makes an election to reduce the amount of his contribution (in which case the 50% ceiling applies, see ¶2128). (Code Sec. 170(b)(1)(C))[27] For ceiling on gifts to 30% charities, see ¶2129.

This rule applies to any capital asset which, if sold for fair market value at contribution, would have given rise to long-term capital gain, *other than* property subject to the reduction at ¶2110. (Code Sec. 170(b)(1)(C))[28]

¶ 2128   Individual's election of 50% ceiling for appreciated property contributions.

An individual donor whose gift of capital gain property to a 50% charity is otherwise subject to the 30% ceiling (¶2127) may elect the 50% ceiling for the gift *but only* if he reduces the amount of his contribution (as described at ¶2107)—i.e., his contribution is limited to his basis in the property. (Code Sec. 170(b)(1)(C)(iii))[29]

recommendation: Elect where the appreciation is small (value of increased current deduction is greater than loss of eventual deduction of appreciation) or where the 30% limit will prevent deduction of the appreciation even over the carryover period (¶2130).

Once made, the election applies to all gifts of capital gain property (¶2127) to 50% charities made by the donor in the tax year. In computing carryovers to this year, contributions of this property in an earlier year for which the election was *not* made are reduced as if they were subject to the reduction when made. (Code Sec. 170(b)(1)(C)(iii); Reg § 1.170A-8(d)(2))[30]

Elect by attaching a statement specified in the regs, to the original income tax return for the election year. (Reg § 1.170A-8(d)(2)(iii))[31]

¶ 2129   Gifts of appreciated capital gain property to 30% charities—20% ceiling.

An individual's deduction ceiling for gifts of appreciated long-term capital gain property to 30% charities is 20% of his contribution base (¶2124) (and there's no election like the one for gifts to 50% charities, see ¶2128). (Code Sec. 170(b)(1)(D))[32]

---

25. ¶K-3720 *et seq.*; ¶1704.08; TD ¶333,005
26. ¶K-3684 *et seq.*; ¶1704.10 *et seq.*; TD ¶333,010
27. ¶K-3686, K-3687; ¶1704.11; TD ¶333,013, 333,014
28. ¶K-3687; ¶1704.05; TD ¶333,014

29. ¶K-3689; ¶1704.11; TD ¶333,018
30. ¶K-3689 *et seq.*; ¶1704.11; TD ¶333,018
31. ¶K-3690; TD ¶333,019
32. ¶K-3694; ¶1704.11; TD ¶333,017

¶ 2130 Carryover of excess charitable contributions by individuals.

If an individual's charitable gifts for a tax year exceed the percentage ceilings for the year (¶2124), the excess may generally be carried forward and deducted for up to five years (subject to the later year's ceiling). (Code Sec. 170(d)(1)) A statement must be filed with the return for the year the carryover is deducted. The carryforward is available even if the individual didn't itemize his deductions in the contribution year. (Reg § 1.170A-10(a)(2))[33]

For a 15-year carryforward period for pre-2010 qualified conservation contributions, see ¶2124.

Contributions are deductible in the following order, up to 50% of the contribution base:

(1) Contributions qualifying for the 50% charity limit (¶2125).

(2) Contributions qualifying for the 30% charity limit (¶2126) up to the lesser of:

... 30% of the contribution base, or

... (a) 50% of the contribution base minus (b) contributions to 50% limit organizations. For this purpose, (b) includes contributions of capital gain property subject to the 30% limit (¶2127).

(3) Contributions of capital gain property subject to the 30% limit (up to the lesser of 30% of the contribution base or 50% of the contribution base minus other contributions to 50% organizations).

(4) Contributions qualifying for the 20% limit (¶2129) up to the lesser of:

... 20% of the contribution base,

... 30% of the contribution base minus contributions subject to the 30% limit,

... 30% of the contribution base minus contributions of capital gain property subject to the special 30% limit, or

... 50% of the contribution base minus the total of contributions to 50% and 30% limit organizations. (Code Sec. 170(b)(1))[34]

Where charitable contributions in more than one limitation category are carried over, the ordering rules are applied to determine the deduction limits for each category of contribution. Starting with the first (50% limitation) category, the allowable deduction limit is determined. Current contributions in that category are deducted first. Next, within that category, amounts carried over are deducted, up to the limitation amount for the category. Then, the same process is applied to the next limitation category according to the ordering rules. (Reg § 1.170A-10(b), Reg § 1.170A-10(c)) If there are carryovers from two or more years in any category, the carryover from the earlier year is considered first.[35]

¶ 2131 Excess charitable contributions on decedent's final return.

If an individual dies, any charitable contribution that can't be used on the decedent's final return (under the normal ceilings, see ¶2124) is lost. (Reg § 1.170A-10(d)(4)(iii))[36]

¶ 2132 Corporation's 10% charitable deduction ceiling and five-year carryover.

A corporation's charitable deduction for a tax year can't exceed 10% of its taxable income for the year. Taxable income for this purpose is computed without deductions for charitable

---

33. ¶K-3701 *et seq.*, ¶K-3711; ¶1704.13; TD ¶333,301, 333,310
34. ¶K-3701 *et seq.*; ¶s 1704.05, 1704.13; TD ¶333,302
35. ¶K-3701 *et seq.*; ¶1704.05; TD ¶333,307
36. ¶K-3710; ¶1704.13; TD ¶333,306

contributions or dividends received, or net operating loss carrybacks or capital loss carrybacks to the year. (Code Sec. 170(b)(2); Reg § 1.170A-11(a))[37] To the extent contributions in any year exceed this limit, the excess can be carried forward and deducted for five years. (Code Sec. 170(d)(2))[38]

For certain farm-related qualified conservation contributions made in tax years beginning before Jan. 1, 2010 by nonpublicly traded corporations that are qualified farmers, the limit is 100% of taxable income less all other charitable contributions, see ¶2124. (Code Sec. 170(b)(2)(B)(i)(II))

caution: Check http://ria.thomsonreuters.com/federaltaxhandbook to see if the above provision has been extended.

¶ 2133   When to deduct charitable contributions.

A charitable contribution is deductible in the tax year it's paid (subject to percentage ceilings, see ¶2124, ¶2132) (Code Sec. 170(a)), regardless of the donor's accounting method (except for accrual method corporations, see ¶2134) or when the gift was pledged. (Reg § 1.170A-1(a))[39]

A contribution is "paid" when it's unconditionally delivered to the donee. A contribution by check that's delivered unconditionally is paid when delivered, if it clears in due course. If the check is mailed unconditionally and clears in due course, the contribution is paid when mailed. (Reg § 1.170A-1(b))[40]

A contribution charged on a credit card is deductible by a cash basis donor in the year the charge is made, *not* in any later year when the credit card company is paid.[41]

Special rule for Haiti earthquake relief. Taxpayers could elect to claim a charitable contribution deduction in tax year 2009 (rather than under the usual rules, in 2010) for cash donations made after Jan. 11, 2010 and before Mar. 1, 2010, specifically for the relief of victims in areas affected by the Jan. 12, 2010 earthquake in Haiti. Cash contributions include contributions made by text message, check, credit card or debit card. For a cash contribution the Code Sec. 170(f)(17) (¶2136) recordkeeping requirement could be satisfied by a telephone bill if it showed the name of the donee organization, the date of the contribution, and the amount of the contribution. Thus, for example, in the case of a charitable contribution made by text message and chargeable to a telephone or wireless account, a bill from the telecommunications company containing the relevant information satisfied the recordkeeping requirement. For cash contributions made by other means, taxpayers should keep a bank record, such as a cancelled check, or a receipt from the charity showing the name of the charity and the date and amount of the contribution. (P.L. 111-126, 1/22/2010)[42]

¶ 2134   Accrual method corporation's election to deduct contribution paid 2-1/2 months after year-end.

An accrual method corporation whose board of directors has authorized a charitable contribution during the tax year may elect to deduct all or part of the contribution in that (authorization) year, if the contribution is paid by the 15th day of the third month following the close of the year. (Code Sec. 170(a)(2))[43]

Elect by reporting the contribution in the return and attaching a declaration signed by a principal officer together with a copy of the directors' resolution authorizing the contribution. (Code Sec. 170(a)(2); Reg § 1.170A-11(b))[44]

---

37. ¶K-3830 *et seq.*; ¶1704.14; TD ¶333,022
38. ¶K-3830 *et seq.*; ¶1704.14; TD ¶333,315
39. ¶K-3851; ¶s 1704.02, 1704.03; TD ¶333,701
40. ¶K-3858 *et seq.*; ¶1704.02; TD ¶333,706

41. ¶K-3861; ¶1704.02; TD ¶333,707
42. ¶K-3855.2; ¶1704.02; TD ¶333,705.1
43. ¶K-3882 *et seq.*; ¶1704.03; TD ¶333,718
44. ¶K-3883; ¶1704.03; TD ¶333,718

¶ 2135 **Specialized Rules for Claiming Charitable Contributions—$250, $500 and $5,000 Rules.** ▰▰▰▰▰▰▰

Taxpayers (donors) must substantiate their charitable deductions, and supply appraisals and other information for certain property contributions. No charitable deduction is allowed for a contribution of $250 or more unless taxpayer substantiates it by a contemporaneous written acknowledgement from the donee. Special rules apply for contributions of cars, boats, and planes.

¶ 2136 **Charitable contributions must be substantiated; donor's receipt.**

A charitable deduction isn't allowed unless the taxpayer can prove his right to it. (Code Sec. 170(a)(1))[45] For *donee's* information return requirement, see ¶4745.

For cash contributions, the taxpayer must keep either a cancelled check, receipt or other reliable evidence. (Reg § 1.170A-13(a)(1))[46] A taxpayer can't deduct *any* contribution of a cash, check, or other monetary gift unless he maintains as a record of the contribution a bank record or a written communication from the donee organization showing its name, plus the date and amount of the contribution. (Code Sec. 170(f)(17)) For contributions of property (other than cash), the taxpayer must have a receipt from the donee and keep records showing the donee's name and describing the gift. (Reg § 1.170A-13(b)(1))[47]

For contributions made via payroll deductions, the taxpayer must retain a pay stub, Form W-2, or other employer document showing the amount withheld for the purpose of payment to the donee plus a pledge card or similar donee document showing the donee's name.[48]

For contributions made through the Combined Federal Campaign (CFC) or a similar program (e.g., a United Way Campaign), the organization receiving the donation (e.g., the United Way) may be treated as the donee for substantiation purposes even if it distributes the funds to another organization. However, the written communication must contain the name of the ultimate recipient.[49]

Additional substantiation is required for: contributions of $250 or more (¶2137); noncash contributions exceeding $500 (¶2138); and contributions of cars, boats and planes (¶2139).

¶ 2137 **Substantiation requirement for contributions of $250 or more.**

No charitable deduction is allowed for any (cash or property) contribution of $250 or more unless taxpayer substantiates it by a contemporaneous written acknowledgement (not just a cancelled check) from the donee (or its agent). (Code Sec. 170(f)(8)(A); Reg § 1.170A-13(f)(1))[50]

In general, the written acknowledgment must state: (1) the amount of cash and a description (but not the value) of any property other than cash contributed; (2) whether the donee provided any goods or services in consideration for the contribution; (3) a description and good-faith estimate of the value of those goods or services; and (4) if the goods or services consist entirely of intangible religious benefits (e.g., admission to a religious ceremony, but not religious school tuition or fees), a statement to that effect. (Code Sec. 170(f)(8)(B)(i); Reg § 1.170A-13(f)(2)) Special requirements apply for gifts to a pooled income fund (¶2117). (Reg § 1.170A-13(f)(13))[1]

The written acknowledgement requirement doesn't apply:

. . . if the donee files a substantiating return (under regs to be issued), (Code Sec. 170(f)(8)(D));[2] or

---

45. ¶K-3901 *et seq.*; ¶1704.50, TD ¶334,001
46. ¶K-3919; ¶1704.50; TD ¶334,007
47. ¶s K-3926, K-3927; ¶1704.50; TD ¶334,011
48. ¶K-3939

49. ¶K-3941; TD ¶334,023
50. ¶K-3933; ¶1704.50; TD ¶334,015
1. ¶K-3933 *et seq.*; ¶1704.50; TD ¶334,015 *et seq.*
2. ¶K-3938

... to transfers to a charitable lead trust (¶2119), charitable remainder annuity trust or charitable remainder unitrust (¶2116). (Reg § 1.170A-13(f)(13))[3]

Goods or services that have insubstantial value (¶2104), and certain annual membership benefits the charity provides to the taxpayer, the taxpayer's employees, or the partners of a partnership donor, in exchange for the contribution are disregarded in determining the $250 threshold. (Reg § 1.170A-13(f)(8)(i), Reg § 1.170A-13(f)(9)(i))[4]

Separate payments are generally treated as separate contributions and aren't aggregated (Reg § 1.170A-13(f)(1)).[5]

An employer's payment to a charity of $250 or more withheld from taxpayer's paycheck (the amount withheld from each single paycheck treated as a separate contribution), may be substantiated by a combination of (1) a pay stub, Form W-2, or other employer provided document showing the amount withheld for this purpose, and (2) a pledge card or other donee document which states it doesn't provide any consideration for the payroll contributions. (Reg § 1.170A-13(f)(11))[6]

¶ 2138 Proving noncash contributions exceeding $500.

For noncash contributions that are:

(1) more than $500 but not more than $5,000, the donor must attach to its return a description of the contributed property. This requirement doesn't apply to a C corporation. (Code Sec. 170(f)(11)(B))

(2) more than $5,000 but not more than $500,000, the donor must obtain a "qualified appraisal" (one meeting specified IRS requirements) and attach to its return information about the property and appraisal (i.e., appraisal summary) as required by IRS. (Code Sec. 170(f)(11)(C))

(3) more than $500,000, the donor must attached a qualified appraisal to its return. (Code Sec. 170(f)(11)(D))

The above requirements in (2) and (3) don't apply to: patents, copyrights, etc. as described in Code Sec. 170(e)(1)(B)(iii) (¶2106); property described in Code Sec. 1221(a)(1) (e.g., stock in trade, inventory); publicly traded securities; and "qualified vehicle donations" (¶2139). (Code Sec. 170(f)(11)(A)(ii)(I))

IRS will disallow a deduction for property contributed if the above reporting requirements aren't met unless the failure was due to reasonable cause. (Code Sec. 170(f)(11)(A))[7]

¶ 2139 Charitable contributions of cars, boats and planes.

Special rules apply for charitable contributions of motor vehicles, boats and airplanes that aren't in taxpayer's inventory or held for sale in the ordinary course of his business ("qualified vehicle donations"), if the donation's claimed value exceeds $500. (Code Sec. 170(f)(12)) The donor's charitable deduction can't exceed the gross proceeds from the charity's sale proceeds unless:

(1) there's a "significant intervening use" of the vehicle by the charity (actual, significant use to substantially further the charity's regularly conducted activities) prior to its sale;

(2) the charity materially improves the vehicle (significantly increases its value) prior to its sale (minor repairs or routine maintenance aren't enough); or

(3) the charity sells it at a price significantly below FMV (or gives it away) to a needy

3. ¶K-3940.3; ¶1704.50
4. ¶K-3934; ¶1704.38; TD ¶334,016
5. ¶K-3934; ¶1704.50; TD ¶334,017
6. ¶K-3940; ¶1704.50; TD ¶334,020
7. ¶K-3942; ¶1704.50; TD ¶334,024

individual, in direct furtherance of its charitable purpose of relieving the poor and distressed or the underprivileged who need vehicles.

If (1), (2), or (3) apply, the donor may claim a deduction for the vehicle's FMV, using the "blue book" value for a similar vehicle (until regs are issued, private party sale amount may be used).

A deduction for donated vehicles whose claimed value exceeds $500 isn't allowed unless the taxpayer substantiates the contribution by a contemporaneous written acknowledgement from the donee (on Form 1098-C). (Code Sec. 170(f)(12)(A)) It must:

... contain the donor's name and taxpayer identification number (TIN), the vehicle identification number (or similar number), and if exceptions (1), (2), or (3) in the list above apply, supporting details;

... indicate whether the donee provided goods or services in consideration of the vehicle (and, if so, describe them and estimate their value, or, if they consist solely of intangible religious benefits, a statement to that effect);

... generally be made within 30 days after the vehicle's sale (within 30 days of the contribution if exceptions (1), (2) or (3) apply); and

... if the charity sells the vehicle and none of the three above exceptions apply, state that the vehicle was sold in an arm's length transaction between unrelated parties, show the gross proceeds, and declare that the deductible amount can't exceed the gross proceeds.[8]

¶ 2140 IRS "Statement of Value" for gifts of art appraised at $50,000 or more.

At the taxpayer's request, IRS will issue a Statement of Value that taxpayer may rely on to substantiate the value of an item of art (paintings, sculpture, antique furniture, carpets, rare manuscripts, historical memorabilia and similar objects) that has been appraised at $50,000 or more and transferred as a charitable gift. The taxpayer must request the statement before filing the return that first reports the gift, and must attach a copy of the statement (or of the request, if the statement hasn't been received yet) to that return.[9]

¶ 2141 Medical Expenses.

An individual who itemizes can deduct the amount by which certain unreimbursed medical and dental expenses paid during the year for himself, his spouse and his dependents exceed 7.5% of his adjusted gross income (for tax years beginning after 2012, see ¶101.1).

¶ 2142 How much is deductible—7.5%-of-adjusted-gross-income floor.

The amount of medical expenses (¶2145) an individual may deduct (on Schedule A, Form 1040) in a tax year is the amount by which his unreimbursed payments for those expenses exceed 7.5% of his adjusted gross income (AGI, ¶3102), for the year. (There's no ceiling on the deduction.) For taxpayers under age 65, the "floor" rises to 10% of AGI for tax years starting after 2012. (Code Sec. 213(a))[10] But any expense allowed as a Code Sec. 21 dependent care credit (¶2354), Code Sec. 35 credit for health insurance costs (¶2350), or Code Sec. 162(l) self-employed medical insurance deduction (¶1533) can't be treated as a medical expense. (Code Sec. 213(e), Code Sec. 35(g)(2), Code Sec. 162(l)(3))[11]

observation: The deduction is lost to the extent the medical expenses don't exceed 7.5% of AGI. There's no carryover.

8. ¶K-3948.1; ¶1704.41; TD ¶334,028.1
9. ¶T-10080 *et seq.*; ¶1704.50; TD ¶526,012

10. ¶K-2000 *et seq.*; ¶2134 *et seq.*; TD ¶346,001
11. ¶K-2003; ¶s 2134, 2134.04; TD ¶346,002

caution: For the percentage floor on deductible medical expenses for purposes of the alternative minimum tax, see ¶3209.

¶ 2143   Whose medical expenses may taxpayer deduct?

A taxpayer may deduct his own medical expenses, and those of his spouse and dependents if the status as spouse, etc., exists either when the medical care was rendered or when the expenses were paid. (Code Sec. 213(a); Reg § 1.213-1(e)(3)) For this purpose, "dependent" is defined in Code Sec. 152 (see ¶3119), determined without the gross income test for qualifying relatives, the rule that a joint return filer can't be a dependent, and the rule that a dependent is ineligible to have dependents (Code Sec. 213(a); Reg § 1.213-1(a)(3)(i)) A child of divorced parents is considered a dependent of both if Code Sec. 152(e) applies (see ¶3126), so that each parent may deduct the medical expenses he or she pays for the child). (Code Sec. 213(d)(5))[12] An organ donor's medical expenses are deductible by the payor, whether donor or recipient.[13]

¶ 2144   Decedent's medical expenses.

Expenses for a decedent's medical care that are paid out of his estate are treated as paid by him (and may be deducted) in the year incurred if: (1) they're paid within one year after his death, (2) they aren't deducted for federal estate tax purposes, and (3) a statement is filed with the income tax return (or amended return) showing that the expenses weren't allowed for estate tax purposes and that the estate tax deduction is waived. (Code Sec. 213(c))[14]

observation: The choice of an income tax or estate tax deduction depends primarily on the extent to which the expense is deductible for income tax purposes, the decedent's top income tax rate, and the top effective estate tax rate.

¶ 2145   What kinds of medical expenses are deductible?

Deductible medical expenses are amounts paid for the diagnosis, mitigation, treatment, prevention of disease or for the purpose of affecting the body's structure or function (Code Sec. 213(d)(1))[15] and the costs of nursing services (Reg § 1.213-1(e)(1)(ii))[16] (and related insurance payments, ¶2146, and transportation, ¶2149).

The cost of the following is deductible as medical expenses:

. . . Eyeglasses, artificial teeth or limbs (Reg § 1.213-1(e)(1)(ii)), hearing aids, and similar items.[17]

. . . Discretionary medical procedures affecting the body's structure or function, including legal abortions and procedures to prevent or facilitate pregnancy (e.g., egg donor fees; but in vitro fertilization costs for a taxpayer who wasn t infertile weren't deductible).[18]

. . . Eye surgery to correct defective vision, including laser procedures (e.g., LASIK).[19]

. . . Smoking cessation programs[20] and prescribed drugs designed to alleviate nicotine withdrawal, but not non-prescription nicotine gum and nicotine patches.[21]

. . . Attending a medical conference on a chronic disease suffered by an individual, his spouse, or dependent (but not meal and lodging costs, ¶2150).[22]

. . . Legally procured prescription drugs (e.g., not aspirin) and insulin. (Code Sec. 213(b), Code Sec. 213(d)(3)) A controlled substance (such as marijuana) obtained for medical purposes, in violation of the federal Controlled Substances Act, isn't legally procured and is

---

12. ¶K-2300 *et seq.*; ¶s 2134.01, 2134.02; TD ¶346,011
13. ¶K-2159; TD ¶346,008
14. ¶K-2405, C-9556; ¶2134.03; TD ¶346,020
15. ¶K-2100 *et seq.*; ¶s 2134.04, 2134.08; TD ¶346,003
16. ¶K-2111; ¶2134.04; TD ¶346,506
17. ¶K-2162; ¶2134.04; TD ¶348,012

18. ¶K-2110; ¶2134.04; TD ¶346,505
19. ¶K-2162
20. ¶K-2117; ¶2134.04; TD ¶346,508
21. ¶K-2137; ¶2134.04; TD ¶346,505
22. ¶K-2161; ¶2134.04; TD ¶346,010

nondeductible even if state law permits its doctor-prescribed use.[23]

. . . Weight-loss program for treatment of a specific disease (e.g., obesity, hypertension), but not the cost of diet food.[24]

. . . Diagnostic tests aiding in the detection of heart attack, diabetes, cancer, and other diseases (but not the collection and storage of DNA, absent a showing of how the DNA will be used for medical diagnosis). These include pregnancy tests, tests on healthy individuals, and tests taken not at the direction of a physician. Such a test will not fail to qualify due to high cost or if a less expensive alternative may be available.[25]

. . . Sex-change costs (except for breast augmentation undertaken to improve appearance).[26]

. . . Service animals used in mental health therapy.[27]

Expenses that aren't deductible as medical care include:

. . . Expenses merely beneficial to the individual's general health. (Reg § 1.213-1(e)(1)(ii))[28]

. . . Costs of cosmetic surgery or similar procedure (e.g., teeth whitening), unless necessary to ameliorate a deformity arising from, or directly related to, a congenital abnormality, a personal injury resulting from an accident or trauma or a disfiguring disease (Code Sec. 213(d)(9))—e.g., breast reconstruction surgery after cancer mastectomy.[29]

. . . Payments for illegal operations or treatments. (Reg § 1.213-1(e)(1)(ii))[30]

Qualified long-term care services are treated as medical care (Code Sec. 213(d)(1)(C)) (unless provided by a relative who isn't a licensed professional, or by a related corporation or partnership. (Code Sec. 213(d)(11))) These services include necessary diagnostic, preventive, therapeutic, curing, treating, mitigating, and rehabilitative services, and maintenance or personal care services, which are required by a chronically ill individual and provided under a plan of care prescribed by a licensed health care practitioner. (Code Sec. 7702B(c)(1))[31]

¶ 2146 Accident and health insurance; Medicare.

The cost of insurance that's deductible as a medical expense is limited to amounts paid for insurance that covers *medical care* as defined at ¶2145. (Code Sec. 213(d)(1)(D))[32]

Amounts paid as *voluntary* premiums under Part B of Medicare (supplementary medical insurance benefits for the aged and disabled) are deductible as medical care, as are voluntary premiums under Medicare Part A (basic Medicare) (Code Sec. 213(d)(1)(D)), but not the *mandatory* employment or self-employment taxes paid for basic coverage under Medicare A. (Reg § 1.213-1(e)(4)(i)(a))[33]

When an insurance contract covers both medical care and other items (e.g., loss of income), no amount is treated as for medical care *unless:* the charge for medical insurance is separately stated, the amount treated as paid for medical insurance doesn't exceed the separately-stated charge, *and* the charge isn't unreasonably large in relation to the total premium for the contract. (Code Sec. 213(d)(6))[34]

Medical expenses include premiums paid for a qualified long-term care insurance contract, up to annual limits. For an individual whose attained age before the close of the tax year is:

. . . 40 or less, the limit is $330 for 2010 ($340 for 2011);

. . . more than 40, but not more than 50, the limit is $620 for 2010 ($640 for 2011);

. . . more than 50, but not more than 60, the limit is $1,230 for 2010 ($1,270 for 2011);

23. ¶K-2137 *et seq.*; ¶2134.04, 2134.06; TD ¶347,003
24. ¶K-2116
25. ¶K-2105.1; TD ¶346,502.5
26. ¶K-2101
27. ¶K-2162
28. ¶K-2103; ¶2134.04; TD ¶347,003

29. ¶K-2109; ¶2134.04; TD ¶346,505
30. ¶K-2106; ¶2134.04; TD ¶346,503
31. ¶s K-2100, K-2122.1; ¶2134.03; TD ¶346,005
32. ¶K-2140 *et seq.*; ¶2134.08; TD ¶346,301
33. ¶K-2140; ¶2134.08; TD ¶346,301
34. ¶K-2141; ¶2134.08; TD ¶346,302

. . . more than 60, but not more than 70, the limit is \$3,290 for 2010 (\$3,390 for 2011);

. . . more than 70, the limit is \$4,110 for 2010 (\$4,240 for 2011). (Code Sec. 213(d)(10))[35]

Qualified long-term care insurance contracts must provide only coverage of qualified long-term care services, must not pay or reimburse expenses to the extent the expenses are reimbursable under Medicare (or would be but for a deductible or coinsurance amount), must be guaranteed renewable, and must meet other detailed requirements. (Code Sec. 7702B(b))[36]

¶ 2147   Deductible costs of care at hospitals and other institutions.

The cost of in-patient care (including meals and lodging, see ¶2150) furnished by a hospital is a deductible medical expense. (Reg § 1.213-1(e)(1)(v))[37]

The cost of in-patient care (including meals and lodging) at a medical-care institution that is *not* a hospital qualifies if the individual is there primarily for the availability of medical care (as defined at ¶2145), and the meals and lodging are a necessary incident to that care. If this test isn't met, only that part of the cost attributable to medical care qualifies. Medical care status depends on the patient's condition and the nature of the services he receives—not on the nature of the institution, which may be federal, state, local or private. Where this test is met, a medical deduction is allowed for:

. . . costs (including tuition, meals and lodging) of a mentally or physically handicapped person at a special school (Reg § 1.213-1(e)(1)(v)), e.g., a school for children with learning disabilities like dyslexia. Costs allocable to medical care at a regular school qualify if the school supplies a cost breakdown;[38]

. . . costs of a nursing home or home for the aged. But if the person isn't there principally for medical reasons, only the cost of medical care qualifies. (Reg § 1.213-1(e)(1)(v))[39]

¶ 2148   "Medical" capital expenses for equipment or improvements.

Amounts incurred for elevators, swimming pools and other permanent improvements to taxpayer's property (including capital expenditures to accommodate a residence to a physically handicapped individual) may be deductible medical expenses (¶2145) if the primary purpose is for the medical care of taxpayer, his spouse or dependents. But the medical deduction is limited to that portion of the expenses that exceeds the amount by which the improvement increases the value of taxpayer's property. (Reg § 1.213-1(e)(1)(iii))[40]

illustration: On his doctor's advice, J installs an elevator in his two-story, single family home to avoid climbing stairs and to alleviate his heart condition. The cost of installing it is \$5,000 and it decreases the value of J's home by \$3,000 (because buyers don't want a single family home with an elevator). The full \$5,000 is a medical expense.

Some expenses incurred by or for a physically handicapped individual to remove structural barriers in his residence to accommodate his physical condition (e.g., constructing access ramps, widening doorways, installing support bars) are presumed not to increase the value of the residence and may be deductible in full. (Reg § 1.213-1(e)(1)(iii))[41]

Capital expenditures that are related only to the sick person and are detachable from the property aren't permanent improvements, so their full cost can be a medical expense, e.g., detachable inclinators and air conditioners. (Reg § 1.213-1(e)(1)(iii))[42]

All the costs of operating or maintaining a medical capital asset are deductible, even if none

35. ¶K-2141.1; ¶2134.075; TD ¶346,303
36. ¶K-2141.1 et seq.; ¶77,02B4; TD ¶346,304
37. ¶K-2142; ¶2134.04; TD ¶347,501
38. ¶K-2143 et seq.; ¶s 2134.10, 2134.11; TD ¶347,502
39. ¶K-2147; ¶2134.11; TD ¶347,504
40. ¶K-2180 et seq.; ¶2134.13; TD ¶348,009
41. ¶K-2181; ¶2134.13; TD ¶348,010
42. ¶K-2192; ¶s 2134.04, 2134.12; TD ¶348,012

or only a portion of the cost of the asset itself qualifies. (Reg § 1.213-1(e)(1)(iii))[43]

¶ 2149   Transportation expenses for medical care.

The costs of transportation primarily for and essential to medical care (¶2145) qualify as medical expenses. (Code Sec. 213(d)(1)(B)) This includes food and lodging expense (¶2150) while en route to the place of medical treatment (Reg § 1.213-1(e)(1)(iv)), as well as taxi, train, plane and bus fares and the cost of ambulance services.[44]

Deductible medical expenses also include certain out-of-pocket car expenses, e.g., for gas, oil, parking fees and tolls, but not depreciation, repair, insurance or maintenance. Instead of claiming the actual costs of gas and oil, in 2010, a taxpayer may deduct a flat 16.5¢ for each mile he uses the car for qualified medical transportation.[45]

However, no medical expense deduction is permitted for the cost of commuting to and from work even if taxpayer's illness or disability requires a special method of transportation.[46]

¶ 2150   "Away from home" expenses (meals and lodging)—$50 per night rule.

Expenses for meals and lodging away from home aren't medical expenses unless they're part of the cost of care in a hospital or other institution (¶2147) or medical travel (¶2149).[47]

Taxpayer may deduct as a medical expense amounts paid for lodging (not food) while away from home, that is primarily for and essential to medical care in a hospital or equivalent, up to $50 per night for each individual. (Code Sec. 213(d)(2))[48]

No deduction is allowed for lavish or extravagant lodging or where the travel has any significant element of personal pleasure, recreation or vacation. (Code Sec. 213(d)(2)(B))[49]

¶ 2151   When to deduct medical expenses; prepaid insurance.

Only medical expenses actually paid during the tax year are deductible. (Code Sec. 213(a)) Deduction is thus allowed for payments in the year even though the expenses were incurred in an earlier year. (Reg § 1.213-1(a)(1)) If the payment is made by credit card, the amount is deductible in the year the charge is made regardless of when the credit card bill is paid.[50]

Advance payment of anticipated medical expenses doesn't qualify for a current deduction unless there is a contractual obligation to pay in the current year.[1]

Certain insurance premiums paid by a taxpayer who is under 65 during the payment year, for medical care for himself, his spouse and dependents for the period *after* he reaches 65 are deductible in the year paid. (Reg § 1.213-1(e)(4)(i)(b))[2]

¶ 2152   Medical expenses compensated for by insurance or otherwise.

Medical expenses aren't deductible if they have been compensated for by insurance or otherwise. (Code Sec. 213(a)) Taxpayer must reduce his medical expenses by amounts so compensated before applying the 7.5%-of-AGI floor (¶2142). But no reduction is required for amounts received as compensation for loss of earnings or as damages for personal injuries.[3]

If reimbursements in a tax year exceed medical expenses in that year, no medical deduction

43. ¶K-2182; ¶2134.13; TD ¶348,011
44. ¶K-2200 *et seq.*; ¶s 2134.04, 2134.09; TD ¶348,500
45. ¶K-2214 *et seq.*; ¶s 2134.04, 2134.09; TD ¶348,514 *et seq.*
46. ¶K-2202; ¶2134.09; TD ¶348,502
47. ¶K-2217; TD ¶348,517
48. ¶K-2218; ¶s 2134.04, 2134.09; TD ¶348,518

49. ¶K-2218; ¶s 2134.04, 2134.09; TD ¶348,518
50. ¶K-2401; ¶2134.03; TD ¶346,016
1. ¶K-2403; ¶2134.03; TD ¶346,018
2. ¶K-2404; ¶2134.03; TD ¶346,019
3. ¶K-2601 *et seq.*; ¶s 2134.14, 2134.15; TD ¶346,021

is allowed.[4] Any part of the excess that's attributable to an employer's contribution is taxable; the rest is tax-free.[5] For reimbursement in later year, see ¶2153.

¶ 2153   Reimbursement in year after medical expenses are paid.

If a taxpayer is reimbursed for medical expenses in a year after he paid (and deducted) them, he must report the reimbursement as income to the extent attributable to the earlier deduction (Reg § 1.213-1(g))—i.e., to the extent he got a "tax benefit," see ¶1205.[6]

¶ 2154   Alimony or Separate Maintenance.

Payments of alimony or separate maintenance made under a divorce or separation instrument are deductible by the payor spouse and taxable to the payee spouse. Alimony must be paid in cash and must not continue beyond the death of the payee spouse. A payment that's fixed as child support isn't alimony.

¶ 2155   Tax treatment of alimony or separate maintenance payments.

Alimony or separate maintenance (¶2156) payments are taxable to the payee spouse, in the year received. (Code Sec. 71(a); Reg § 1.71-1(b)(5))[7]

The payments are deductible by the payor spouse in the year paid, as a deduction from gross income. (Code Sec. 62(a)(10), Code Sec. 215(a)) The payor doesn't have to itemize to be allowed the deduction.[8]

These rules don't apply if the spouses file a joint return with each other. (Code Sec. 71(e))[9] For requirement that the spouses live apart, see ¶2158.

¶ 2156   Alimony requirements.

To qualify as alimony, a payment must be made in cash, under a divorce or separation instrument (¶2157). (Code Sec. 71(b)(1)) A transfer of property other than cash can't be alimony[10] (for "nonalimony" designation of a cash transfer, see ¶2162).

There must be no requirement that payments continue beyond the death of the payee spouse (e.g., to the estate) or that any substitute payment (in cash or property) be made after the death of the payee spouse—i.e., the payments must end at the payee spouse's death. (Code Sec. 71(b)(1)(D)) If this rule isn't satisfied, *none* of the payments (even those made during the payee spouse's life) is alimony. (Reg § 1.71-1T(b), Q&A-10) If it isn't clear from the divorce or separation agreement whether payments cease at the payee spouse's death, local law controls.[11]

recommendation: To make sure of alimony treatment, the divorce or separation instrument should specify that otherwise qualifying payments will cease at the death of the recipient. Where alimony treatment isn't desired, the instrument should specify that payments aren't to be treated as alimony (see ¶2162).

¶ 2157   Payments must be under a divorce or separation instrument.

To be alimony, a payment must be made under a divorce or separation instrument. (Code Sec. 71(b)(1)(A)).[12] This means a:

(1) decree of divorce or separate maintenance or a written instrument issued incident to

4. ¶K-2605; TD ¶346,025
5. ¶H-1114; ¶2134.15; TD ¶133,012
6. ¶K-2604; ¶2134.15; TD ¶346,024
7. ¶J-1413, K-6001; ¶714 *et seq.*, ¶2154; TD ¶198,502, 341,001
8. ¶A-2621, K-6002; ¶714.10, 2154 *et seq.*; TD ¶341,502, 560,720

9. ¶K-6001; ¶714.03; TD ¶341,501
10. ¶K-6005; ¶714.01; TD ¶341,505
11. ¶K-6036 *et seq.*; ¶714.01; TD ¶341,536 *et seq.*
12. ¶K-6013; ¶714; TD ¶341,513

the decree,

(2) written separation agreement, or

(3) decree not described in (1) e.g., a temporary support order. (Code Sec. 71(b)(2))[13]

If made under a decree of divorce or separate maintenance (or a written instrument incident to the decree), the payment must be made after the decree. (Reg § 1.71-1(b)(1)(i))[14] If made under a separation agreement, the payment must be made after the execution of that agreement. (Reg § 1.71-1(b)(2))[15]

¶ 2158 Separate household requirement for alimony.

Spouses who are legally separated (but not divorced) under a divorce or separate maintenance decree must not live in the same household when the payment is made, or it won't be alimony (¶2156). (Code Sec. 71(b)(1)(C)) But if the spouses aren't legally separated, a payment under a written separation agreement or temporary support order may be alimony even if they are members of the same household. (Reg § 1.71-1T(b), Q&A 9)[16]

The spouses aren't treated as members of the same household if one spouse is preparing to leave it, and does leave within one month after the payment.[17]

¶ 2159 "Alimony" payments to a third party.

Payments made in cash by the payor spouse to a third party on behalf of the payee spouse under the terms of the divorce or separation instrument can be alimony (¶2156). (Code Sec. 71(b)(1)(A)) Payments are on behalf of the payee spouse if they satisfy an obligation to that spouse. Thus, cash payments of the payee spouse's rent, mortgage, tax or tuition liabilities that the payor spouse makes as required by the instrument can qualify as alimony, as can payments made to a third party (e.g., a charity) at the payee spouse's written request if the spouses intend them to be alimony.[18]

But payments made to maintain property *owned by the payor spouse* but used by the payee spouse (including mortgage payments, realty taxes, and insurance premiums) are *not* payments on behalf of the payee spouse (i.e., not alimony) even if made under the terms of the divorce or separation instrument. (Reg § 1.71-1T(b))[19]

A payor spouse who is required by the divorce or separation instrument to pay the mortgage on a home he owns jointly with the payee spouse may deduct one-half of those payments as alimony, if they otherwise qualify (the rest may be deductible as qualified residence interest if paid on a qualified home, see ¶1730 *et seq.*).[20]

¶ 2160 Life insurance contracts as alimony.

Premiums that one spouse pays for insurance on his life as required by the divorce or separation instrument are alimony if the other (payee) spouse owns the policy.[21]

¶ 2161 Support payments for the payor's children aren't alimony.

A payment under a divorce or separation instrument that's "fixed" (or treated as fixed) as support for a child of the payor spouse *isn't* alimony. (Code Sec. 71(c)(1))[22] This applies if the instrument designates a specified amount of money or a part of a payment to be child

13. ¶K-6013; ¶714.01; TD ¶341,513
14. ¶K-6018; ¶714.06; TD ¶341,518
15. ¶K-6018; ¶714.06; TD ¶341,518
16. ¶K-6035; ¶s 714.01, 714.06; TD ¶341,535
17. ¶K-6035; ¶714.01; TD ¶341,535

18. ¶K-6006; ¶714.01; TD ¶341,506
19. ¶K-6007; TD ¶341,507
20. ¶K-6008; TD ¶341,508
21. ¶K-6010; ¶714.01; TD ¶341,510
22. ¶K-6046; ¶714.02; TD ¶342,001

support. The actual amount may fluctuate. (Reg § 1.71-1T(c))[23]

A portion of a payment may be *treated* as fixed if the payment is to be reduced on the happening of a specified contingency relating to the child (Code Sec. 71(c)(2)), e.g., on the child's 18th birthday, or when he dies, marries or leaves school.[24] A payment may also be treated as fixed if it ends or is reduced at a time that can clearly be associated with the contingency. (Reg § 1.71-1T(c))[25]

If a divorce or separation instrument provides a specified amount for alimony and a specified amount for child support, and the payor spouse pays the payee spouse less than the amount designated for child support, then the *entire* payment is treated as child support and no part is treated as alimony. (Code Sec. 71(c)(3))[26]

¶ 2162 Designating that payments aren't to be treated as alimony.

If a divorce or separation instrument designates a payment that would otherwise qualify as alimony as *not* to be treated as alimony (e.g., as a property settlement), the payment won't qualify as alimony. (Code Sec. 71(b)(1)(B); Reg § 1.71-1T, Q&A 8)[27]

¶ 2163 Alimony trusts.

A payor spouse can't deduct payments the payee spouse receives from an alimony trust which aren't includable in the payor's income under the Code Sec. 682 trust rules. (Code Sec. 215(d))[28] Under those rules, a wife who's divorced or legally separated, or separated under a written separation agreement, includes in her gross income her share of trust income that (without this rule) would be includible in her husband's income. This shifts the liability for tax on the income from the husband to the wife. But amounts payable for support of the husband's minor children are taxable to the husband. (Code Sec. 682(a))[29]

¶ 2164 Recapture rules—excess front-loading of alimony.

If there are "excess" alimony payments ("front-loading"), the payor spouse must "recapture" the "excess" by including it in his gross income for the third post-separation year (below) (Code Sec. 71(f)(1)(A)) (on Form 1040, line 11, cross out "received" and write "recapture").[30] The same amount is deducted by the payee spouse in computing adjusted gross income for *the payee's* third post-separation year (on Form 1040, line 31a; cross out "paid" and write "recapture"). (Code Sec. 71(f)(1)(B))[31]

The "recapture" amount is the sum of:

(1) the excess of (a) the alimony or separate maintenance payments in the second post-separation year, over (b) the sum of the payments in the third year plus $15,000 (Code Sec. 71(f)(2)(B)); *plus*

(2) the excess of (a) the payments in the first post-separation year, over (b) the sum of the average of the payments in the second year (minus any excess payment in (1), above) and third year, plus $15,000. (Code Sec. 71(f)(2)(A))[32]

illustration: H makes alimony payments of $50,000 in the first post-separation year, $20,000 in the second year, and nothing in the third year. H must recapture $32,500: $5,000 from the second year ($20,000 − ($0 + $15,000)) and $27,500 from the first year ($50,000 − ($7,500 + $15,000)), where the $7,500 equals $15,000 ($20,000 − $5,000) ÷ 2, i.e., the average of the second and third year payments after reduction of the second year

23. ¶K-6047; TD ¶342,002
24. ¶K-6049; ¶714.02; TD ¶342,004
25. ¶K-6049; ¶714.02; TD ¶342,002
26. ¶K-6048; ¶714.02; TD ¶342,003
27. ¶K-6033; ¶714.01; TD ¶341,533

28. ¶K-6009; ¶2154.02; TD ¶341,509
29. ¶K-5432 *et seq.*; ¶6824; TD ¶657,039
30. ¶K-6043, K-6044; ¶714.03; TD ¶341,543, 341,544
31. ¶K-6044; ¶714.03; TD ¶341,544
32. ¶K-6044; ¶714.03; TD ¶341,544

payments by the $5,000 recaptured from the second year.[33]

observation: The payor spouse is in effect allowed to pay up to $15,000 of excess alimony in each of the first two post-separation years without recapturing the excess.

The first post-separation year is the first calendar year in which the payor spouse paid alimony, etc., to the payee spouse. The second and third post-separation years are the succeeding calendar years. (Code Sec. 71(f)(6))[34]

There's no recapture if payments cease because either spouse dies or the payee spouse remarries before the close of the third post-separation year. Nor does recapture apply to temporary support payments or payments that fluctuate because of a continuing liability to pay, for at least three years, a fixed portion of income from business, property or services (including self-employment). (Code Sec. 71(f)(5))[35]

¶ 2165 Pre-'85 instruments—alimony rules.

The alimony rules discussed at ¶2154 *et seq.*, don't apply to a pre-'85 instrument unless it is: (1) modified after '84 to expressly provide that those (post-'84) rules are to apply, or (2) incorporated into a post-'84 divorce decree that changes the terms of the payments.[36]

To be alimony under a pre-'85 instrument, payments must be "periodic;" see Reg § 1.71-1(d).[37]

Any part of a periodic payment that the decree, instrument or agreement *specifically fixed* as for support of the payor's minor children isn't alimony. (Reg § 1.71-1(c))[38]

¶ 2166 "Nonbusiness" Expenses.

Individuals may deduct most ordinary and necessary expenses that, though not connected with their trade or business, are paid or incurred for the collection or production of income; the management, conservation or maintenance of property held for the production of income; or the determination, collection or refund of any tax.

But a *personal expense* or a *capital expenditure* for which deductions are barred can't be deducted as a nonbusiness expense. (Code Sec. 262(a), Code Sec. 263; Reg § 1.212-1(e))[39]

For 2%-of-adjusted gross income (AGI) floor on nonbusiness deductions, see ¶3110. For reduction in itemized deductions if AGI exceeds specified amounts in pre-2010 years, see ¶3114.

caution: For nonbusiness expenses under the alternative minimum tax, see ¶3209.

¶ 2167 "Nonbusiness" (investment) expenses.

Taxpayer may deduct a wide variety of expenses related to his investments (not amounting to a business) if they are ordinary and necessary for the production or collection of income, or for the management, conservation or maintenance of property held for the production of income. (Code Sec. 212(1), Code Sec. 212(2))[40]

Home office expenses allocable to "nonbusiness" investment activities aren't deductible (but this doesn't affect deductions for interest, taxes or casualty losses). (Code Sec. 280A)[41]

Expenses of a convention, seminar, or similar meeting (e.g., day-trading courses) aren't

33. ¶K-6044; ¶714.03; TD ¶341,545
34. ¶K-6045; ¶714.03; TD ¶341,546
35. ¶K-6043; ¶714.03; TD ¶341,547
36. ¶K-6100 *et seq.*; ¶714; TD ¶343,007
37. ¶K-6138 *et seq.*; ¶714.13; TD ¶343,005
38. ¶K-6192 *et seq.*; ¶714.16
39. ¶s L-1400, L-1415, L-5601; ¶s 2124 *et seq.*, 2624, 2634; TD ¶255,507, 256,201
40. ¶L-1401 *et seq.*; ¶2124 *et seq.*; TD ¶336,001
41. ¶L-1305; ¶280A4; TD ¶258,002

deductible as nonbusiness (investment) expenses. (Code Sec. 274(h)(7))[42]

¶ 2168   Tax determination costs.

Individuals may deduct all the ordinary and necessary expenses incurred in connection with the determination, collection, or refund of any tax (for legal fees, see ¶2169). (Code Sec. 212(3)) This applies to income, estate, gift, property and any other tax imposed by federal, state, municipal or foreign authorities. Included are the costs of: preparing tax returns, determining the extent of liability, contesting tax liability (including transferee liability[43]), getting tax counsel, protesting assessments, prosecuting refunds, compromising liability (Reg § 1.212-1(e)), a tax text used by an individual to prepare his own tax return,[44] tax advice[45] (including divorce and estate planning[46]), property appraisal to substantiate a claimed deduction,[47] and contesting civil penalties, whether taxpayer is successful or not.[48]

¶ 2169   "Nonbusiness" legal expenses.

An individual may deduct nonbusiness legal fees, e.g., attorney's fees, court costs, etc., if incurred to produce income, preserve income-producing property, etc. (Reg § 1.212-1(k))[49], as a miscellaneous itemized deduction (see ¶3110).[50]

Nonbusiness legal expenses incurred to acquire, perfect, or defend title to property are *not* deductible, but any of those costs that are allocable to collecting accrued rents on the property may be deducted. (Reg § 1.212-1(k))[1]

Legal expenses in connection with divorce, separation or a support decree are personal expenses which cannot be deducted by either spouse (Reg § 1.262-1(b)(7))[2] *except that*:

. . . the part of legal fees attributable to the production or collection of taxable alimony is deductible by the payee spouse (Reg § 1.262-1)[3] and

. . . taxpayer can deduct fees paid to his attorney for tax research and advice relating to a divorce and property settlement if the fee for the tax work is segregated, *but not* legal fees he pays to his spouse's attorney for tax advice given to the spouse.[4]

¶ 2170   Tax-exempt income expenses.

A taxpayer may not deduct costs incurred in the production of tax-exempt income (Code Sec. 265(a)(1))[5] (such as interest on indebtedness incurred or continued to buy or carry tax-exempt securities, see ¶1723). If expenses are attributable to both taxable and tax-exempt income, and can't be specifically identified, they must be prorated. (Reg § 1.265-1(c))[6]

¶ 2171   Premature withdrawal penalties.

An individual may deduct any interest or principal he forfeits to a bank or other financial institution as a penalty for premature withdrawal from a time savings account, certificate of deposit or similar deposit. The penalty is deductible from gross income in computing adjusted gross income (AGI, ¶3102), (Code Sec. 62(a)(9)) and[7] not as an interest expense (so it can't be netted against interest income, and taxpayer doesn't have to itemize).[8]

42. ¶L-1724; ¶s 2124.01, 2744.07; TD ¶291,021
43. ¶L-3015; TD ¶307,205
44. ¶L-3001 *et seq.*; ¶2124.14; TD ¶307,206
45. ¶L-3007; ¶2124.14; TD ¶307,210
46. ¶L-3010, L-3009; ¶2124.14; TD ¶307,208, 307,209
47. ¶L-3005; TD ¶307,206
48. ¶L-3006; ¶2124.14; TD ¶307,206
49. ¶L-2902 *et seq.*; ¶2124.12; TD ¶305,005
50. ¶L-2903; ¶674; TD ¶305,002

1. ¶L-2908 *et seq.*; ¶2124.12; TD ¶305,018
2. ¶L-2962; ¶s 2124.13, 2624; TD ¶305,064
3. ¶L-2965; ¶s 2124.13, 2624; TD ¶305,067
4. ¶L-3010; ¶2124.13; TD ¶307,208
5. ¶K-9000 *et seq.*; ¶2654; TD ¶653,017
6. ¶K-9002; ¶2654; TD ¶653,017
7. ¶K-5880; ¶624; TD ¶560,719
8. TD ¶560,719

¶ **2172** **Bond Premium Amortization.** ▬▬▬▬▬▬▬▬▬▬▬▬▬▬▬▬▬

Any premium on tax-exempt bonds must be amortized. A premium on taxable bonds may be amortized at the holder's election. The amortized amount reduces basis and, for taxable bonds, is treated as an offset to the interest received.

Premium on tax-exempt bonds *must* be amortized. (Code Sec. 171(a)(2); Reg § 1.171-1(c)(1)) Premium on taxable bonds *may* be amortized at the holder's option (see ¶2173). (Code Sec. 171(a)(1), Code Sec. 171(c); Reg § 1.171-1(c)(2))[9] For securities dealers, see ¶2176.

"Bonds" include a bond, debenture, note, or certificate or other evidence of indebtedness. (Code Sec. 171(d); Reg § 1.171-1(d)(1)) But the bond premium amortization rules don't apply to certain specified debt obligations. (Reg § 1.171-1(b)(2))[10]

Bond premium generally arises when the stated interest rate on the bond is higher than the market yield for the bond at the time of purchase. The amount of premium on a bond is the excess of the holder's basis in the bond immediately after its acquisition over the sum of all amounts payable on the bond after the acquisition date (other than payments of qualified stated interest, ¶1317). (Reg § 1.171-1(d)(1))[11] Basis for this purpose is the holder's basis for determining loss on sale. (Code Sec. 171(b)(1)(A); Reg § 1.171-1(e)(1)(i))[12]

If a convertible bond is purchased at a premium, any amount attributable to the conversion feature of the bond is excluded from amortizable bond premium. (Code Sec. 171(b)(1))[13] Regs provide special rules for variable rate debt instruments, inflation-indexed debt instruments, and bonds subject to contingencies. (Reg § 1.171-3)[14] For amortization of callable bonds, see ¶2174.

The regs discussed above don't apply for bonds acquired before Mar. 2, '98, unless an election is made. (Reg § 1.171-5(a)(1))[15]

¶ **2173** **Amortization deduction, basis reduction.**

For *tax-exempt* bonds, no deduction is allowed for the amortizable bond premium for a tax year. (Code Sec. 171(a)(2))[16] The basis of the bond is reduced by the amortizable bond premium barred as a deduction. (Code Sec. 1016(a)(5)); Reg § 1.1016-5(b)(3))[17]

For *taxable* bonds, a deduction *is* allowed for the amortizable bond premium (Code Sec. 171(a)(1)) if the election at ¶2175 is made. The bond premium (computed under a constant-yield method based on yield to maturity (Code Sec. 171(b)(3)(A); Reg § 1.171-1(a)(1)) allocable to an accrual period is deducted as an offset to the qualified stated interest (¶1317) allocable to the period. (Code Sec. 171(e); Reg § 1.171-2(a)(1))[18] The holder's basis in the bond is reduced by the offset amount. (Code Sec. 1016(a)(5))[19]

🅡🅘🅐*observation:* If the holder of a taxable bond doesn't elect to amortize bond premium, the premium will be recovered when the bond is redeemed or sold.

¶ **2174** **Amortization of callable bonds.**

The holder of a taxable bond generally amortizes bond premium by reference to the bond's stated maturity date (see ¶2173) even if the bond is likely to be called. (Code Sec. 171(b)(1)(B)(ii); Reg § 1.171-3(c)(4)(ii)(A), Reg § 1.171-3(e), Ex. 2)[20]

If the issuer calls the bond, the holder can deduct the unamortized bond premium (excess of

9. ¶K-5611; ¶s 1714.01, 10,164; TD ¶318,201
10. ¶K-5614; ¶1714.01; TD ¶318,204
11. ¶K-5616; ¶1714; TD ¶318,206
12. ¶K-5611; ¶1714.02; TD ¶318,201
13. ¶K-5622; ¶1714.035; TD ¶318,212
14. ¶K-5624 *et seq.*; ¶1714.036 *et seq.*; TD ¶318,214 *et seq.*

15. ¶K-5633; ¶1714.01; TD ¶318,223
16. ¶K-5611; ¶1714; TD ¶318,201
17. ¶P-5043; ¶10,164; TD ¶216,026
18. ¶K-5611; ¶1714.03; TD ¶318,201
19. ¶P-5043; ¶10,164; TD ¶216,026
20. ¶K-5627; ¶1714.03; TD ¶318,217

the bond's adjusted basis as of the start of the year over the greater of (a) the amount received on early redemption or (b) the amount due on maturity). (Code Sec. 171(b)(2); Reg § 1.171-3(c)(5)(ii), Reg § 1.171-3(e), Ex. 2)[21]

¶ 2175   Making the election to amortize bond premium.

The election to amortize bond premium on taxable bonds (¶2172) is made by (a) offsetting interest income with bond premium in the holder's timely filed return for the first tax year to which the election applies and (b) attaching an election statement to the return. (Code Sec. 171(c)(2); Reg § 1.171-4(a)(1)) IRS consent to make the election isn't needed. (Reg § 1.171-5(c)(1))[22]

A holder who has elected to treat all interest on the bond as original issue discount (OID, ¶1316) is treated as having elected to amortize bond premium. (Reg § 1.171-4(a)(2))[23]

Once made, the election (unless revoked with IRS consent) is binding for the year made and later years. It applies to all taxable bonds held by the taxpayer at the beginning of the first tax year to which the election applies, and also to all taxable bonds thereafter acquired by the taxpayer. (Code Sec. 171(c)(2); Reg § 1.171-4(b))[24]

recommendation: Generally, the election should be made because it provides a current interest income offset which is preferable to a future capital loss deduction.

¶ 2176   Dealers in securities—bond premium amortization.

Taxable bonds that are the holder's stock in trade, or held primarily for sale to customers in the ordinary course of the holder's trade or business, or of a kind that would be included in inventory if on hand at the end of the tax year, aren't subject to the bond amortization rules. (Code Sec. 171(d); Reg § 1.171-1(b)(2)(iv)) Thus, dealers can't amortize the bond premium.[25]

Tax-exempt bonds held primarily for sale to customers in the ordinary course of the holder's trade or business must be adjusted for amortizable bond premium. (Code Sec. 75(a))[26]

---

21. ¶K-5628; ¶1714.03; TD ¶318,218
22. ¶K-5633; ¶1714.04; TD ¶318,223
23. ¶K-5633; ¶1714.04; TD ¶318,223

24. ¶K-5633; ¶1714.04; TD ¶318,223
25. ¶K-5651; ¶1714.01; TD ¶318,213
26. ¶K-5651; ¶754; TD ¶318,251

Chapter 7   Education—Tax Credits, Exclusions, Deductions

¶ 2200   Education—Tax Credits, Exclusions, Deductions. ▬▬▬▬▬▬▬▬▬

There are a number of tax breaks designed specifically to help defray the costs of saving and paying for higher education, and one (the Coverdell education savings account, or CESA) that helps with pre-college costs as well.

There are three main categories of tax breaks for education:

(1) Tax credits, see ¶2201 *et seq.*,

(2) Exclusions, see ¶2205 *et seq.*, and

(3) Deductions, see ¶2222 *et seq.*

Other tax breaks. Pre-age-59 ½ distributions from traditional IRAs and Roth IRAs are excepted from the 10% premature distribution penalty tax to the extent they don't exceed qualified higher education expenses for the distribution year; see ¶4344 and ¶4357. Additionally, there's an unlimited gift-tax exclusion for gifts made on behalf of another individual directly to a qualifying educational organization; see ¶5040.

¶ 2201   Tax Credits for Higher Education ▬▬▬▬▬▬▬▬▬▬▬▬▬

An individual taxpayer may claim an income tax credit for the Hope scholarship tax credit (renamed the American opportunity tax credit (AOTC) for 2010, ¶2202) and the Lifetime Learning credit (¶2203) for higher education expenses at accredited post-secondary educational institutions paid for themselves, their spouses, and their dependents. The American opportunity tax credit is available in 2010 for qualified expenses of the first four years of undergraduate education; the Lifetime Learning credit is available for qualified expenses of any post-high school education at "eligible educational institutions." Both credits can't be claimed in the same tax year for expenses of any one student (see ¶2203), and phase out for higher-income taxpayers (see ¶2202, ¶2203).

¶ 2202   American opportunity tax credit (Hope scholarship credit)—Form 8863.

For tax years beginning in 2010, individuals may elect (on Form 8863, attached to an original or amended return filed by the limitations period for filing a claim for credit or refund for the year the credit is claimed) a personal, partially refundable tax credit equal to 100% of up to $2,000 of qualified higher-education tuition and related expenses (¶2204) plus 25% of the next $2,000 of expenses paid for education furnished to an eligible student in an academic period. Thus, the maximum American opportunity tax credit (AOTC)/Hope scholarship credit is $2,500 a year for *each* eligible student. (Code Sec. 25A(a)(1), Code Sec. 25A(i)(1))

For 2010, the availability of the credit phases out ratably for taxpayers with modified AGI (AGI increased by foreign, possessions, and Puerto Rico income exclusions) of $80,000 to $90,000 ($160,000 to $180,000 for joint filers). (Code Sec. 25A(i)(4)) Married taxpayers must file jointly to claim the credit. (Code Sec. 25A(g)(6)) The student's name and TIN must be included on the return of the taxpayer claiming the credit. (Code Sec. 25A(g)(1)) The AOTC/Hope (or Lifetime Learning credit, ¶2203) and tax-free CESA distributions (¶2205) are allowed for the same student for the same year, as long as the credit isn't claimed for education expenses used to generate the tax-free CESA distribution. (Code Sec. 530(d)(2)(C)(i))

The AOTC/Hope credit may be elected for a student's expenses for 4 tax years, and only for students who have not completed the first 4 years of post-secondary education as of the beginning of the tax year. (Code Sec. 25A(b)(2), Code Sec. 25A(i)(2); Reg § 1.25A-3(d)(1)(iii))

References beginning with a single letter are to paragraphs in RIA's Federal Tax Coordinator 2d and RIA's Analysis of Federal Taxes: Income. Those beginning with numbers are to paragraphs in RIA's United States Tax Reporter. Those beginning with TD are to paragraphs in RIA's Tax Desk.

325

Additionally, for at least one academic period during the year, the student must be enrolled for at least half of the normal full-time workload for his course of study. (Code Sec. 25A(b)(3)(B); Reg § 1.25A-3(d)(1)(ii))

If a dependency deduction for an individual is allowed to another taxpayer, the dependent can't claim the AOTC/Hope credit, and qualified tuition and expenses paid by the dependent during the tax year are treated as paid by the taxpayer who is allowed the dependency deduction. (Code Sec. 25A(g)(3)) If a third party (not the taxpayer, spouse, or dependent) pays a student's qualified expenses directly to an educational institution, the student is treated as receiving the payment from the third party and, in turn, paying the expenses. If the student in such a case is claimed as a dependent on another's return, the expenses deemed to be paid by the student would be treated as expenses of the taxpayer claiming the student as a dependent. (Reg § 1.25A-5(a), Reg § 1.25A-5(b)) If a taxpayer is eligible to but does not claim a student as a dependent, only the student can claim the education credit for the student's qualified tuition and related expenses. (Reg § 1.25A-1(f))

observation: It may pay for a parent not to claim the student as a dependent if (1) the parent can't claim education credits because of high modified AGI, and (2) the student pays or is deemed to pay the expense and has sufficient tax liability to claim the credit.

If qualified tuition and expenses are paid during one tax year for an academic period that begins during the first 3 months of the next tax year, the academic period is treated for AOTC/Hope credit purposes as beginning in the earlier year. (Code Sec. 25A(g)(4)) Thus, the credit is allowed only in the tax year in which the expenses are paid. (Reg § 1.25A-3(e)) Special rules apply for tuition refunds and excludable tuition assistance received after the tax year in which qualified tuition and related expenses are paid. (Reg § 1.25A-5(c), Reg § 1.25A-5(f)) An AOTC/Hope credit isn't allowed for a student convicted (as of the end of the tax year for which the credit is claimed) of a felony offense for possessing or distributing a controlled substance, or by a nonresident alien for any part of the tax year (unless treated as a resident alien under a Code Sec. 6013(g) or Code Sec. 6013(h) election) (Code Sec. 25A(b)(2)(D), Code Sec. 25A(g)(7))[1]

Subject to an exception, 40% of a taxpayer's otherwise allowable AOTC/Hope credit for 2010 is refundable. No portion of the credit is refundable if the taxpayer claiming the credit is a child subject to the kiddie tax under Code Sec. 1(g) or a resident of a U.S. possessions (who instead claim the credit where they reside). (Code Sec. 25A(i)(6))

If 2010 is a tax year to which the Code Sec. 26(a)(2) limitation (¶2372) doesn't apply, the credit can't exceed the excess of: (1) the sum of: the regular tax liability, plus alternative minimum tax (AMT) liability, over (2) the sum of the credits under Code Sec. 21 through Code Sec. 26—other than the adoption credit, the residential energy efficiency property credit, and the Code Sec. 30D new qualified plug-in electric drive motor vehicle credit—plus the foreign tax credit. (Code Sec. 25A(i)(5))

For tax years beginning in 2011, the nonrefundable Hope tax credit equals 100% of up to $1,200 of qualified higher-education tuition and related expenses (¶2204) plus 50% of the next $1,200 of expenses. (Code Sec. 25A(b)(1)) The credit is available for an individual student for 2 years, if he hasn't completed the first 2 years of post-secondary education before the beginning of the second tax year. (Code Sec. 25A(b)(2)) The credit phases out ratably at the same modified AGI ranges as for the Lifetime Learning credit at ¶2203. (Code Sec. 25A(d))

caution: Check http://ria.thomsonreuters.com/federaltaxhandbook to see if the American opportunity tax credit has been extended (in lieu of the Hope credit).

---

1. ¶A-4500 *et seq.*; ¶25A4; TD ¶568,923

¶ 2203 Lifetime Learning credit—Form 8863.

Taxpayers may elect (use Form 8863) a Lifetime Learning credit equal to 20% of up to $10,000 of qualified tuition and related expenses paid (defined at ¶2204) during the tax year. The maximum credit is $2,000. (Code Sec. 25A(a)(2), Code Sec. 25A(c)(1))

Unlike the American opportunity tax credit (AOTC)/Hope credit (¶2202), which is available for the qualifying expenses of each qualifying student, the Lifetime Learning credit is available only per taxpayer. So, for example, a joint filing couple with two children could claim no more than a $2,000 Lifetime Learning credit, even if each family member is a qualifying student with qualifying expenses. The credit is phased out ratably for taxpayers with modified AGI (¶2202) from $50,000 to $60,000 ($100,000 to $120,000 for marrieds filing jointly) for 2010.

The same treatment of expenses paid by dependent, adjustment for tax-free scholarships, etc., treatment of certain prepayments, denial of double benefit, denial of credit to marrieds not filing jointly, and nonresident alien bar that apply for AOTC/Hope credit purposes (¶2202) also apply to the Lifetime Learning credit. (Code Sec. 25A(d), Code Sec. 25A(e), Code Sec. 25A(f), Code Sec. 25A(g), Code Sec. 25A(h))

Expenses for a student for whom an AOTC/Hope scholarship credit (¶2202) is allowed for the tax year don't qualify for the Lifetime Learning credit. (Code Sec. 25A(c)(2))[2]

¶ 2204 Qualified tuition and related expenses for education credit purposes

Qualified tuition and related expenses for the American opportunity tax credit (AOTC)/Hope credit (¶2202) and Lifetime Learning credit (¶2203) purposes means tuition and fees required for the enrollment or attendance of the taxpayer, his spouse, or tax dependent, at a post-secondary educational institution eligible to participate in the federal student loan program. For the AOTC/Hope credit in tax years beginning in 2010, it also includes course materials.[3]

Room and board, insurance, transportation, or other similar personal, living, or family expenses, don't qualify for the AOTC/Hope or Lifetime Learning credit, whether or not paid to an educational institution. Student activity fees and fees for course-related books, supplies, and equipment qualify for the AOTC/Hope or Lifetime Learning credit only if they must be paid directly to the educational institution as a requirement for the enrollment or attendance of the student.(Code Sec. 25A(f); Reg § 1.25A-2(d)(2), Reg § 1.25A-2(d)(3))

The cost of any course of instruction at an eligible institution taken to acquire or improve job skills qualifies for the Lifetime Learning credit, but not the Hope credit, even if it involves sports, games, hobbies, or is a noncredit course. (Code Sec. 25A(c)(2)(B); Reg § 1.25A-2(d)(5))

Qualified tuition and related expenses must be reduced by scholarship amounts excludable from income under Code Sec. 117 (¶2216), educational assistance under chapter 30 through 35 of title 38 U.S. Code or under chapter 1606 of title 10 U.S. Code, and other tax-free payments. However, qualified amounts are not reduced by amounts paid by gift, bequest, devise, or inheritance. (Code Sec. 25A(g)(2)) No credit is allowed for any expense for which an income tax deduction is allowed. (Code Sec. 25A(g)(5)) Special rules apply for tuition refunds and excludable tuition assistance received after the tax year in which qualified tuition and related expenses are paid. (Reg § 1.25A-2(d)(2))

¶ 2205 Coverdell Education Savings Accounts (CESAs) ▬▬▬▬▬▬

Taxpayers can contribute up to $2,000 per year to Coverdell Education Savings

---

2. ¶A-4500 *et seq.*; ¶25A4; TD ¶568,933   3. ¶A-4474 *et seq.*; ¶25A4.07; TD ¶568,937

Accounts (CESAs) in 2010, formerly called education IRAs, for beneficiaries under age 18 (and, in 2010, special needs beneficiaries of any age). The account is exempt from income tax, and distributions of earnings from CESAs are tax-free if used for qualified education expenses.

caution: For EGTRRA sunset rules, see ¶1114.

¶ 2206 Coverdell Education Savings Accounts (CESAs)—Form 5305-E and 5305-EA.

A CESA is a trust (Form 5305-E) or custodial account (Form 5305-EA) created exclusively for the purpose of paying an individual beneficiary's qualified education expenses. (Code Sec. 530(b)(1), Code Sec. 530(g)) These accounts are exempt from tax except for the unrelated business income tax. (Code Sec. 530(a)) Allowable annual contributions to CESAs (no more than $2,000 per beneficiary to all accounts in 2010) aren't deductible (and aren't taxable when withdrawn), but distributions of earnings from CESAs for qualified education expenses are tax-free (¶2208).

CESAs can't invest in life insurance contracts, and, except for common trust or investment funds, trust assets can't be commingled. The account balance must be distributed to the beneficiary within 30 days after he turns age 30 (unless, in 2010, he has special needs), or, if sooner, to the beneficiary's estate within 30 days after the beneficiary's death (Code Sec. 530(b)(1), Code Sec. 530(d)(8)),[4] unless transferred to a family member's CESA. see ¶2208.

caution: For EGTRRA sunset rules, see ¶1114.

¶ 2207 Contributions to CESAs.

Annual contributions to CESAs for any beneficiary can't exceed $2,000 in 2010, must be made in cash, and can't be made after the beneficiary turns age 18 (unless, in 2010, the beneficiary has special needs). (Code Sec. 530(b)(1)(A)) CESA contributions for a year may be made as late as the unextended tax return due date for that year. (Code Sec. 530(b)(4))[5]

If the contributor is an individual, the $2,000 limit phases out ratably between $95,000 and $110,000 ($190,000 and $220,000 for joint filers in 2010) of modified AGI (AGI plus income excluded under Code Sec. 911, Code Sec. 931, and Code Sec. 933) (Code Sec. 530(c))[6]

observation: Thus, in 2010, a corporation may contribute to a CESA that has an employee's child as beneficiary. The contribution would, however, be taxed to the employee.

caution: For EGTRRA sunset rules, see ¶1114.

An individual who has received a military death gratuity or Servicemembers' Group Life Insurance (SGLI) payment can roll it over (contribute it) to one or more CESAs, without regard to the above annual contribution limit. (Code Sec. 530(d)(9)(A)) or the AGI phase-out limit. The contribution must be made before the end of the one-year period beginning on the date on which the contributor received the payment. (Code Sec. 530(d)(9)(A)) The rule allowing only one rollover contribution to a CESA during any 12-month period (¶2208) doesn't apply to this rollover. (Code Sec. 530(d)(9)(B))[7]

Excess contributions are subject to a 6% excise tax in the contribution year and each year that an excess amount is in the account (report on Form 5329, Part V). However, the excise tax doesn't apply to rollover contributions, or contributions (with net earnings attributable to

---

4. ¶A-4615; ¶5304; TD ¶147,215
5. ¶A-4606; ¶5304

6. ¶A-4604; ¶5304; TD ¶147,204
7. ¶A-4619.1; ¶5304.01; TD ¶147,219.1

the excess contributions) returned before June 1 of the year following the contribution year. (Code Sec. 4973(e))[8]

For the gift tax treatment of CESAs, see ¶5040.

¶ 2208 Distributions from CESAs.

A distribution from a CESA is included in the gross income of the distributee generally as provided under the annuity rules of Code Sec. 72. (Code Sec. 530(d)(1)) Thus, distributions consist of a pro-rata share of principal (recovered tax-free) and accumulated earnings (which *may* be excludable under the CESA rules). Distributions from a CESA are entirely excluded if qualified education expenses of the beneficiary equal or exceed total CESA distributions for the year. (Code Sec. 530(d)(2)(A))

Qualified education expenses are:

... Higher education tuition, fees, books, and supplies, and, for half-time or greater students, certain room and board charges. (Code Sec. 530(b)(2)(A))

... In 2010, elementary and secondary (K through 12) public, private or religious school tuition and expenses, including tutoring, room and board, transportation, uniforms, and extended day programs. (Code Sec. 530(b)(4))

... In 2010, special needs services for special needs beneficiaries enrolled in any of the above types of schools. (Code Sec. 530(b)(2)(A), Code Sec. 530(b)(3)(B))

... The purchase of any computer technology or equipment or expenses for Internet access and related services for use by the beneficiary and his family during any of the years that the beneficiary is in school, but not expenses for computer software designed for sports, games or hobbies unless it is predominantly educational in nature. (Code Sec. 530(b)(4))

... Contributions to a qualified tuition program (QTP, see ¶2209) on behalf of a designated beneficiary, (Code Sec. 530(b)(2)(B))[9] but in applying the Code Sec. 72 annuity rules to a CESA distribution that's contributed to a qualified tuition program (¶2210) for a designated beneficiary, any part of the contribution which is not includible in gross income (because it doesn't exceed the beneficiary's qualified education expenses) won't result in an increase in the investment in the contract. (Code Sec. 530(b)(2)(B))

☝caution: For EGTRRA sunset rules, see ¶1114.

Qualified education expenses are reduced by the same tax-free scholarships and similar payments that reduce qualified tuition and related expenses for education credit purposes (¶2204) (Code Sec. 530(d)(2)(C)(i)(I)), and by the expenses taken into account in determining the education credit (¶2201).[10]

Distributions aren't taxed if rolled over within 60 days (but not more than once in a 12-month period) into a CESA for the same beneficiary or a member of the beneficiary's family (as defined at ¶2212) who is under age 30. (Code Sec. 530(d)(5), Code Sec. 530(d)(6))[11] A CESA transfer to a beneficiary's family member under a divorce decree or after the beneficiary's death also isn't taxable. (Code Sec. 530(d)(7))

If CESA distributions exceed qualified tuition expenses in a year, the excludable part of the distributions is the earnings portion of the distributions times a fraction having as its numerator the year's qualified education expenses and as its denominator the year's total distributions. (Code Sec. 530(d)(2)(B))[12] The balance of the earnings portion of the distribution is taxable. Any savings bond redemption proceeds transferred to a CESA in a tax-free transfer under Code Sec. 135 (see ¶2221) do *not* increase the investment in the contract in applying

8. ¶A-4607; ¶49,734; TD ¶147,205
9. ¶A-4610; ¶5304; TD ¶147,210
10. ¶A-4612; ¶5304; TD ¶147,212

11. ¶A-4619; ¶5304; TD ¶147,219
12. ¶A-4609; ¶5304; TD ¶147,209

the Code Sec. 72 rules to the taxation of CESA distributions. (Code Sec. 135(c)(2)(C))

Any taxable amount also is subject to a 10% additional tax, but not (1) if made on or after the beneficiary's death or disability, (2) to the extent the taxable amount doesn't exceed (a) the amount of a tax-free scholarship received by the beneficiary, or (b) the "advanced education costs" received by the beneficiary at a U.S. service academy (e.g., U.S. Military Academy), (3) if the distribution is taxable solely because of the rule (explained above) reducing the total amount of qualified education expenses by the expenses taken into account in determining the education credit for the year, or (4) if the tax is attributable to income on a contribution withdrawn (along with associated income) before June 1 of the year following the contribution year. (Code Sec. 530(d)(4))[13]

If aggregate distributions from CESAs and qualified tuition programs (¶2209) in a year exceed an individual's qualified education expenses, the expenses must be allocated among the distributions. (Code Sec. 530(d)(2)(D)) No deduction, credit, or exclusion is allowed under any other Code provision for an education expense taken into account in determining the CESA exclusion. (Code Sec. 530(d)(2)(D))[14]

¶ 2209   Qualified Tuition Programs (QTPs) —529 Plans. ▰▰▰▰▰▰

Distributions from a qualified tuition program (QTP, also known as a 529 plan) are excludable to the extent used to pay for qualified higher education expenses.

¶ 2210   Qualified tuition programs (QTPs).

A person can make nondeductible cash contributions to a qualified tuition program (QTP, or 529 plan) on behalf of a designated beneficiary. The earnings on the contributions build up tax-free and distributions from a QTP are excludable to the extent used to pay for qualified higher education expenses. A QTP is a tax-exempt program established and maintained by a state (including a state agency or instrumentality), or one or more eligible educational institutions (including private ones) under which a taxpayer may:

(1) buy tuition credits or certificates on behalf of a designated beneficiary (¶2212) which entitle the beneficiary to a waiver or payment of qualified higher education expenses (¶2211)—i.e., a prepaid educational services account, or

(2) make contributions to an account set up to meet the designated beneficiary's qualified higher education expenses—i.e., an educational savings account. This option is available only for state (or state agency or instrumentality) programs. (Code Sec. 529(b)(1)(A); Prop Reg. § 1.529-2(c) ["Taxpayer may rely,"] [15]

🅡 *observation:* Prepaid educational services accounts allow credits or certificates to be purchased at the current tuition rate, even though they won't be used for some time.

A QTP must require all purchases or contributions to be made in cash (there is no dollar limit on contributions), provide separate accounting for each designated beneficiary, prohibit the contributor and designated beneficiary from directing, indirectly or directly, the investment of contributions or earnings (but a change in investment strategy is allowed once per calendar year), prohibit pledging an interest in the program as security, and provide adequate safeguards to prevent contributions in excess of amounts necessary for the beneficiary's qualified higher education expenses. (Code Sec. 529(b))[16] A QTP maintained by a private educational institution generally must get a ruling that it meets applicable requirements. (Code Sec. 529(b)(1))[17]

For the gift-tax treatment of contributions to a QTP, see ¶5040.

---

13. ¶H-12254.1
14. ¶A-4609 *et seq.*; ¶5304 *et seq.*; TD ¶147,214
15. ¶A-4727; ¶5294; TD ¶672,302

16. ¶A-4727; ¶5294; TD ¶672,302
17. ¶A-4729; ¶5294; TD ¶672,302

¶ 2211 Tax treatment of distributions from qualified tuition programs.

Distributions from a qualified tuition program (QTP) are includible in the distributee's income under the Code Sec. 72 annuity rules, to the extent not excluded under any other Code provision. (Code Sec. 529(c)(3)(A))[18]

In-kind distributions (e.g., tuition credits or waivers, payment vouchers) from state-sponsored QTPs aren't includible in gross income if the benefit, if paid for by the distributee, would have been a payment of a qualified higher education expense. (Code Sec. 529(c)(3)(B); Prop Reg. § 1.529-1(c), ["Taxpayer may rely,"]) [19]

Cash distributions are fully excludable if they don't exceed qualified higher education expenses, reduced by expenses for which in-kind distributions were received. If cash distributions exceed qualified expenses, the amount otherwise includible under the Code Sec. 72 annuity rules is reduced by the ratio of qualified expenses to distributions. (Code Sec. 529(c)(3)(B)(ii))[20]

Qualified higher education expenses for QTP purposes are: (1) tuition, fees, books, supplies, equipment required for the enrollment or attendance of a designated beneficiary (¶2212) at an eligible educational institution, and expenses for special needs services; (2) room and board costs (subject to a limit) for students who are at least half-time; and (3) subject to conditions, expenses paid or incurred in 2010 for the purchase of any computer technology or equipment, or Internet access and related services. (Code Sec. 529(e)(3))[21]

🅡🆃🅰 *caution:* Check http://ria.thomsonreuters.com/federaltaxhandbook to see if the rule in (3), above has been extended.

For QTP exclusion purposes, total annual qualified higher education expenses are reduced by excludable scholarships or educational assistance received, and by any qualified higher education expenses taken into account in determining the AOTC/HOPE and Lifetime Learning credits (¶2201 *et seq.*) allowed to the taxpayer or any other person. (Code Sec. 529(c)(3)(B)(v))[22]

Distributions from a QTP aren't taxed if transferred (rolled over) within 60 days (but not more than once in 12 months) to another QTP for the same designated beneficiary or to a QTP for a member of the designated beneficiary's family (¶2212). (Code Sec. 529(c)(3)(C)(iii))[23] A change in the designated beneficiary isn't a distribution if the new beneficiary is a member of the old beneficiary's family; see ¶2212. (Code Sec. 529(c)(3)(C)(ii))[24]

A 10% additional tax applies to QTP distributions includible in gross income, in the same way, and with the same exceptions, as for CESA distributions (see ¶2217). (Code Sec. 529(c)(6))[25]

If total distributions from a QTP and from a CESA (see ¶2205 *et seq.*) exceed qualified higher education expenses otherwise taken into account under the QTP rules (after the above reductions), the taxpayer must allocate the expenses among the distributions for purposes of determining the QTP exclusion. (Code Sec. 529(c)(3)(B)(vi))[26]

¶ 2212 Designated beneficiary of a qualified tuition program.

The designated beneficiary of a qualified tuition program (QTP, see ¶2210) is:

(1) the individual so designated at the start of participation in the QTP; (Code

18. ¶A-4709 *et seq.*; ¶5294.02; TD ¶147,101 *et seq.*
19. ¶A-4709; ¶5294.02; TD ¶147,101
20. ¶A-4709; ¶5294.02; TD ¶147,101
21. ¶A-4711; ¶5294; TD ¶672,310
22. ¶A-4709; ¶5294.02; TD ¶147,101

23. ¶A-4721; ¶5294.02; TD ¶147,105
24. ¶A-4722; ¶5294.02; TD ¶147,107
25. ¶A-4720; ¶5294.02; TD ¶147,109
26. ¶A-4716; ¶5294.02; TD ¶147,101

Sec. 529(e)(1)(A))

(2) where beneficiaries are changed and the new one is a member of the same family (spouses, individuals meeting the relationship tests at ¶3119, spouses of these individuals, and first cousins of the beneficiary), the individual who is the new beneficiary; and (Code Sec. 529(e)(1)(B), Code Sec. 529(e)(2))

(3) in the case of an interest in a QTP purchased by a state or eligible educational institution as part of a scholarship program it operates, the individual receiving the interest as a scholarship. (Code Sec. 529(e)(1)(C))[27]

¶ 2213 Employer-Provided Educational Benefits; Scholarships and Fellowships. ■■■■

An employee may exclude the value of educational benefits provided by an employer if the benefit qualifies as a working condition fringe or is provided under an educational assistance program. Qualified tuition reductions for employees of educational institutions and qualifying scholarships and fellowships also are excludable.

¶ 2214 When education benefits are excluded as working condition fringes.

Employer-provided educational expenses are excludable from an employee's income as a working condition fringe benefit to the extent that if the employee paid for the benefit, the amount paid could have qualified as a deductible employee business expense. For the criteria that apply in determining if education is a deductible employee business expense, see ¶2229. (Reg § 1.132-1(f), Reg § 1.132-5(a)(2))[28] No business expense deduction is allowed for expenses incurred to meet minimum job qualifications, or qualify for a new trade or business.

¶ 2215 Exclusion for employer-provided educational assistance under a qualified program.

For 2010, an employee may exclude educational assistance provided under an employer's qualified educational assistance program, up to an annual maximum of $5,250. (Code Sec. 127(a)(1)) The education received need not be job-related. (Code Sec. 127(a)(2))

RIA/caution: For EGTRRA sunset rules, see ¶1114.

Expenses paid by an employer for education or training provided to the employee that aren't excludable under this provision can only be excluded from income if they qualify as a working condition fringe benefit (¶2214). (Code Sec. 132(j)(8))

"Educational assistance" means the employer's payment for or provision of tuition, fees, books, supplies and equipment under an educational assistance program, including amounts for graduate-level courses. It doesn't include meals, lodging, transportation, or tools or supplies (other than textbooks) that may be retained after the course ends. (Code Sec. 127(c)(1); Reg § 1.127-2(c)(3))[29]

Eligibility requirements can't discriminate in favor of "highly compensated employees" (see ¶4326). (Code Sec. 127(b)(2); Reg § 1.127-2(e)(1))[30] No deduction or credit can be taken by the employee for any amount excluded from income. (Code Sec. 127(c)(7))[31]

¶ 2216 Exclusion for qualifying scholarships and fellowships.

A scholarship or fellowship isn't taxable, to the extent it's a "qualified scholarship" granted to a degree candidate at an educational organization and isn't a stipend (¶2218). (Code Sec. 117(a), Code Sec. 117(c))[32] A "qualified scholarship" is any amount received as a

---

27. ¶A-4701; ¶5294; TD ¶672,309
28. ¶H-2052; ¶1324.05; TD ¶136,516
29. ¶H-2065; ¶1274.01; TD ¶136,525

30. ¶H-2069; ¶1274.01; TD ¶136,526
31. ¶H-2064; ¶1274.01; TD ¶136,525
32. ¶J-1230; ¶1174.01; TD ¶193,501

scholarship and used for tuition and fees required for enrollment at an educational organization, and for required fees, books, supplies and equipment. (Code Sec. 117(b)(2))[33] An "educational organization" is one that normally maintains a regular faculty, curriculum and regularly enrolled student body in attendance. (Code Sec. 117(b)(2)(A))[34]

¶ 2217 Exclusion for qualified tuition reductions for school employees.

Qualified tuition reductions for employees of educational institutions are excluded from the recipient's gross income. (Code Sec. 117(d)) A "qualified tuition reduction" is the amount of tuition reduction provided to an employee of an educational organization for below-graduate-level education (not services, see ¶2218) at that or a similar institution, for the employee (whether active, retired, or disabled), or the employee's spouse or dependent children. (Code Sec. 117(d)(2)) But a tuition reduction for a graduate student engaged in teaching or research can be tax-free. (Code Sec. 117(d)(5))[35]

A qualified tuition reduction provided with respect to a highly compensated employee (¶4326) is excludable only if it's available to all employees on a nondiscriminatory basis. (Code Sec. 117(d)(3))[36]

¶ 2218 Payments for teaching or research.

For 2010, the exclusions for qualified scholarships (¶2216) and qualified tuition reductions (¶2217) don't apply to any amount received that represents payment for teaching, research or other services performed by the student as a condition for receiving the qualified benefit. (Code Sec. 117(c)(1))[37] This no-payment-for-services rule doesn't apply to amounts received under certain health professions scholarship programs. (Code Sec. 117(c)(2)).[38]

⊘*caution:* For EGTRRA sunset rules, see ¶1114.

¶ 2219 Higher Education Exclusion for Savings Bond Income. ▬▬▬▬▬▬▬

Qualified U.S. savings bond income is excluded if redemption proceeds don't exceed qualified higher education expenses. The exclusion phases out at higher levels of modified adjusted gross income.

¶ 2220 Exclusion of savings bond income—Form 8815.

An individual who pays qualified higher education expenses (¶2221) during a tax year excludes from that year's gross income any amount of income from the redemption, that year, of any "qualified U.S. savings bond" (Series EE bond issued after '89, or Series I bond). (Code Sec. 135(a), Code Sec. 135(c)(1))[39] Use Form 8815 to compute the exclusion. Form 8818 (one per bond) may be used to keep a record of the redemptions.[40]

If taxpayer's aggregate redemption proceeds (principal plus interest) for a tax year exceed the qualified higher education expenses paid that year, the excluded interest is limited to the otherwise excludable amount times this fraction: the qualified expenses paid that year, divided by the year's aggregate redemption proceeds. (Code Sec. 135(b)(1))[41]

Illustration: Taxpayer redeems $8,000 of qualified U.S. savings bonds ($4,000 interest, $4000 principal) and pays qualified higher education expenses of $6,000. The exclusion ratio is 75% ($6,000 ÷ $8,000), so $3,000 of the interest (75% × $4,000) (and the $4,000 principal) is excludable.[42]

---

33. ¶J-1232; ¶1174.01; TD ¶193,502
34. ¶J-1244; ¶1174.01; TD ¶193,507
35. ¶J-1252 *et seq.*; ¶1174.02; TD ¶193,512
36. ¶J-1255; ¶1174.02; TD ¶193,514
37. ¶J-1258; ¶1174.01; TD ¶193,517

38. ¶J-1258.1; ¶1174.05; TD ¶193,517
39. ¶J-3051; ¶1354 *et seq.*; TD ¶157,001
40. ¶J-3051; ¶1354.02; TD ¶157,001
41. ¶J-3052; ¶1354.02; TD ¶157,002
42. ¶J-3052; ¶1354.02; TD ¶157,002

The individual must have bought the bond(s) after having reached age 24 (Code Sec. 135(c)(1)(B)) and must be the sole owner (or joint owner with his spouse). The exclusion isn't available to the owner of a bond that was bought by another individual (other than a spouse). Nor is it available to a parent who buys the bonds and puts them in the name of a child or other dependent. But the owner may designate an individual (including a child) as the beneficiary for amounts payable at death without losing the exclusion.[43] A married individual must file a joint return to get the exclusion. (Code Sec. 135(d)(2))[44]

For 2010, the exclusion phases out for a taxpayer whose modified adjusted gross income (modified AGI, see below) for the year exceeds $70,100 ($105,100 on a joint return). For 2011, the phaseout amount is $71,100 ($106,650 on a joint return). The amount of the reduction in the exclusion (but not below zero) equals the amount otherwise excludable (*but for* this phaseout) times this fraction: the excess of modified AGI over the appropriate phaseout amount, divided by $15,000 ($30,000 for a joint return). (Code Sec. 135(b)(2)) Thus, the exclusion is not available in 2010 when modified AGI reaches $85,100, or $135,100 for a joint return ($86,100, or $136,650 for a joint return for 2011).[45]

The exclusion generally applies only if the owner redeems the bonds, i.e., not if he transfers them to the educational institution (see ¶2221 for exceptions).[46]

Modified AGI is AGI determined without the Code Sec. 221 deduction for interest on a qualified education loan (¶2225), the Code Sec. 222 deduction for higher education expenses (¶2223), the Code Sec. 199 U.S. production activities deduction (¶1614), the savings bond interest exclusion, itself, or the Code Sec. 911, Code Sec. 931, and Code Sec. 933 exclusions for income earned abroad or the Code Sec. 137 exclusion for employer-provided adoption assistance (¶1256). (Code Sec. 135(c)(4))[47]

¶ 2221   Qualified higher education expenses for savings bond exclusion.

For purposes of the savings bond exclusion (¶2220), qualified higher education expenses are tuition and fees required for the enrollment or attendance of taxpayer, taxpayer's spouse or any dependent for whom taxpayer is allowed a dependency exemption (¶3119), at an eligible educational institution, (Code Sec. 135(c)(2)(A)) e.g., most colleges, junior colleges, nursing schools and vocational schools. (Code Sec. 135(c)(3)) Expenses for any course or other education involving sports, games or hobbies, other than as part of a degree program, don't count. (Code Sec. 135(c)(2)(B))[48] The transfer of redemption proceeds to a QTP (¶2209) or to a CESA (see ¶2214) for the taxpayer (or his spouse or dependent) also is a qualified higher education expense. (Code Sec. 135(c)(2)(C))[49]

Expenses otherwise taken into account must be reduced by amounts received for excludable qualified scholarships (¶2216), certain educational assistance allowances and other tax-exempt payments (other than gifts, bequests, devises or inheritances), and a payment, waiver, or reimbursement of qualified higher education expenses under a qualified tuition program. (Code Sec. 135(d)(1))[50] The amount of qualified higher education expenses also must be reduced by the amount of such expenses taken into account in figuring the exclusions for distributions from CESA (¶2214) and qualified tuition programs (¶2209), and by expenses taken into account in determining the education credits (¶2201) allowed to the taxpayer or any other person with respect to those expenses. This reduction is made before applying the rules reducing the excluded amount where redemption proceeds exceed higher education expenses and where taxpayer's modified AGI exceeds specified dollar amounts) (see ¶2220). (Code Sec. 135(d)(2))[1]

---

43. ¶s J-3055, J-3056; ¶1354.01; TD ¶s 157,005, 157,006
44. ¶J-3051; ¶1354; TD ¶157,001
45. ¶J-3053; ¶1354.03; TD ¶157,003
46. ¶J-3051; ¶1354.02; TD ¶157,001
47. ¶J-3054; ¶1354.03; TD ¶157,004

48. ¶s J-3057, J-3061; ¶1354.02; TD ¶s 157,007, 157,011
49. ¶J-3059; ¶1354; TD ¶157,009
50. ¶J-3060; ¶1354.02; TD ¶157,010
1. ¶J-3060; ¶1354; TD ¶157,010

¶ **2222** **Above-the-Line Deduction for Higher-Education Expenses (before 2010)** ▬▬▬

For tax years beginning before 2010, eligible individuals could claim an above-the-line deduction for higher education expenses.

⬤*caution:* Check http://ria.thomsonreuters.com/federaltaxhandbook to see if this provision has been extended.

¶ **2223** **Above-the-line deduction for higher-education expenses before 2010 — Form 8917.**

For tax years beginning before 2010, eligible individuals could deduct (on Form 8917) higher education expenses (¶2224)—i.e., "qualified tuition and related expenses" of the taxpayer, his spouse, or dependents—as an adjustment to gross income to arrive at adjusted gross income. (Code Sec. 222(a)) The higher education deduction couldn't exceed:

... $4,000 for taxpayers whose modified AGI for the tax year doesn't exceed $65,000 ($130,000 for a joint return);

... $2,000 for taxpayers whose modified AGI exceeds $65,000 ($130,000 for a joint return), but doesn't exceed $80,000 ($160,000 for a joint return); and

... zero for other taxpayers. (Code Sec. 222(b)(2)(B))

⬤*caution:* Check http://ria.thomsonreuters.com/federaltaxhandbook to see if this provision has been extended.

Modified AGI is AGI determined without regard to the higher-education expense, the U.S. production activities deduction (¶1614) or the exclusions for foreign, possessions, and Puerto Rico income. (Code Sec. 222(b)(2))

The deduction for higher-education expenses was allowed for any tax year only to the extent the qualified tuition and related expenses are for enrollment at a higher education institution during that year, except that the deduction was allowed for expenses paid during a tax year if the expenses are in connection with an academic term beginning during that year or during the first 3 months of the next year. (Code Sec. 222(d)(3))

The higher-education expense deduction wasn't allowed:

... unless the taxpayer included on his tax return for the relevant year the name and TIN of the individual for whom the higher education expenses were paid, (Code Sec. 222(d)(2))

... for any expense for which a deduction was allowed to the taxpayer under any other provision of Chapter 1 of the Code, (Code Sec. 222(c)(1))

... for a tax year with respect to an individual's qualified tuition and related expenses if he or any other person elected to claim a Hope credit or Lifetime Learning credit (see ¶2201 *et seq.*) with respect to that individual for that year. (Code Sec. 222(c)(2)(A))

Higher-education expense deductions could not be claimed by a taxpayer who: files separately for the tax year (Code Sec. 222(d)(4)); may be claimed as a dependent (¶3119) on another's return (Code Sec. 222(c)(3)); or is a nonresident alien for any part of the tax year, unless treated as a resident alien under a Code Sec. 6013(g) or Code Sec. 6013(h) election (to treat a spouse as a resident alien) by a U.S. citizen or resident with a nonresident alien spouse. (Code Sec. 222(d)(5))[2]

---

2. ¶A-4471; ¶2224; TD ¶352,001

¶ 2224   Higher-education expenses for the pre-2010 above-the-line deduction.

For purposes of the above-the line deduction for higher-education expenses (¶2223), higher education expenses consist of qualified tuition and related expenses, defined the same way as for the American opportunity tax credit/Hope and Lifetime Learning Credit purposes (¶2201), but reduced by the amount of the expenses that are taken into account in determining amounts excluded under: Code Sec. 135 (interest on bonds used to pay for higher education expenses, ¶2219), Code Sec. 529(c)(1) (distributions from qualified tuition plans, but limited to the excludible earnings from such plans, ¶2209) and Code Sec. 530(d)(1) (full amount of distributions from CESAs, ¶2205). Qualified tuition and related expenses also are reduced by certain excludible scholarships and other payments. (Code Sec. 222(c)(2)(B), Code Sec. 222(d)(1))[3]

¶ 2225   Deduction for Interest Paid on Qualified Education Loans. ■■■■■■■■■

Qualifying individuals may claim an above-the-line deduction for up to $2,500 of interest paid on a qualified higher education loan.

¶ 2226   Up to $2,500 of qualified education loan interest deductible above-the-line.

Student loan interest generally is treated as personal interest and thus isn't deductible. However, individuals may deduct a maximum of $2,500 annually for interest paid on qualified higher education loans. (Code Sec. 221)[4] The deduction is claimed as an adjustment to gross income to arrive at adjusted gross income. (Code Sec. 62(a)(17))[5] There's no deduction for any amount for which a deduction is allowable under any other Code provision (e.g., home equity loan; see ¶1734). (Code Sec. 221(e)(1))[6]

For 2010, the deduction phases out ratably for taxpayers with modified AGI between $60,000 and $75,000 ($120,000 and $150,000 for joint returns). (Code Sec. 221(b)(2)(B)) Modified AGI is AGI figured without regard to the deduction for qualified education loan interest, the deduction for qualified higher education expenses (¶2222), the Code Sec. 199 U.S. production activities deduction (¶1614), and without regard to the exclusions for foreign, possession, and Puerto Rico income. (Code Sec. 221(b)(2)(C)(i))[7]

✐caution: For EGTRRA sunset rules, see ¶1114.

A person who is claimed as a dependent on another's return can't claim the education interest deduction. (Code Sec. 221(c))[8] The deduction may be claimed only by a person legally obligated to make the interest payments. (Reg § 1.221-1(b))[9] Married couples must file joint returns to take the deduction. (Code Sec. 221(e)(3))[10]

For information reporting requirements for interest payments received on qualified education loans, see ¶4745.

¶ 2227   Qualified education loan defined.

A qualified higher education loan is any debt incurred by the taxpayer solely to pay qualified higher education expenses that are: (1) incurred on behalf of the taxpayer, the taxpayer's spouse, or any dependent of the taxpayer as of the time the debt was incurred; (2) paid or incurred within a reasonable period of time before or after the debt is incurred; and (3) attributable to education furnished during a period when the recipient was an eligible student (as defined for the American opportunity tax credit/Hope credit purposes, i.e., at least

3. ¶A-4474; ¶2224
4. ¶K-5500 et seq.; ¶2214; TD ¶314,100 et seq.
5. ¶K-5501; ¶2214
6. ¶K-5503.2; ¶2214.02; TD ¶314,109

7. ¶K-5502; ¶2214.01; TD ¶314,106
8. ¶K-5503
9. ¶K-5501.1
10. ¶K-5501

a half-time student, see ¶2202). (Code Sec. 221(d)(1))

Revolving lines of credit generally aren't qualified education loans unless the borrower agreed to use the line of credit to pay only qualifying higher education expenses. A qualified education loan includes debt used to refinance debt that qualifies as a qualified education loan, but doesn't include certain debt owed to a related person or a loan under a qualified employer plan. (Code Sec. 221(e)(1))[11]

Qualified higher education expenses include tuition, fees, room and board, and related expenses, but must be reduced by the amount excluded by reason of such expenses under the rules for: employer-provided educational assistance benefits (¶2215), income from U.S. Savings Bonds used to pay higher education expenses (¶2219), CESAs (¶2205), qualified tuition plans (¶2209), and scholarship or fellowship grants (¶2216). (Code Sec. 221(d)(2)) They also must be reduced by veterans' and armed forces' educational assistance allowances and any other educational assistance excludable from the student's gross income (other than as a gift, bequest, devise or inheritance). (Reg § 1.221-1(f)(2))[12]

¶ 2228   Education Expenses Related to Business or Employment. ▬▬▬▬

A taxpayer can deduct costs incurred to maintain or improve skills required in his business or employment, but not costs incurred to meet minimum requirements for a trade or profession or to qualify for a new trade or profession.

¶ 2229   When business- or employment-related expenses are deductible.

Education expenses are deductible if made by a taxpayer either to maintain or improve skills required in his business or employment or to meet the express requirements of his employer, or the requirements of law or regs, imposed as a condition to retaining his salary, status or employment. (Reg § 1.162-5)[13]

A lawyer who has actually practiced law may generally deduct the expenses of any further legal education on the grounds that it maintains or improves required skills even though the education qualifies him to practice as a specialist.[14] A non-lawyer employed in allied fields where a legal education is helpful or customary can't deduct legal education costs. (Reg § 1.162-5(b)(3))[15]

Deductions aren't allowed if the education:

. . . is needed to meet the minimum requirements for taxpayer's present or intended employment, trade, business or profession (Reg § 1.162-5(b)(2))[16] or

. . . is undertaken to fulfill general education aspirations or for other personal reasons,[17] or

. . . is part of a program of study that will lead to qualifying the individual in a new trade or business. (Reg § 1.162-5(b)(3)(i))[18]

Expenses that are otherwise deductible won't be disallowed because the course of studies leads to a degree. (Reg § 1.162-5(a))[19]

Self-employed taxpayers claim education deductions on Schedule C, C-EZ, or F of Form 1040; employees claim unreimbursed education expenses as miscellaneous itemized deductions on Schedule A, Form 1040.

---

11. ¶K-5504; ¶2214.02; TD ¶314,110
12. ¶K-5504.3
13. ¶L-3701; ¶1624.185; TD ¶302,001
14. ¶s L-3724, L-3722; ¶1624.185; TD ¶302,020
15. ¶L-3720 *et seq.*; TD ¶302,020 *et seq.*

16. ¶L-3713; ¶1624.185; TD ¶302,020
17. ¶L-3704; ¶1624.193; TD ¶302,001
18. ¶L-3715; ¶1624.185; TD ¶302,015
19. ¶L-3701; ¶1624.185; TD ¶302,001

¶ 2230   Travel and transportation expenses of education.

The expenses of travel as a form of education aren't deductible. (Code Sec. 274(m)(2))[20] However, travel expenses that are a necessary adjunct to other deductible education expenses may be deductible.[21]

Local transportation expenses for deductible education are deductible. These are expenses incurred in going directly from work to school, and, if the taxpayer is regularly employed and goes to school on a strictly temporary basis, the costs of returning from school to home, or the round-trip costs of going from home to school and back. In general, attendance at school is temporary if it is realistically expected to last (and does in fact last) for one year or less.[22]

Costs of seminar cruises or tours are disallowed if taken primarily for personal purposes even though part of the time is devoted to qualifying professional education.[23] Even if not for personal purposes, the deduction is limited under the rules at ¶1550 and ¶1551.

¶ 2231   Teachers' education expenses.

If the minimum teaching requirements have *already* been met, a teacher may deduct the expense of any education required to retain his or her position, salary or status, even if the education will qualify the teacher to teach a new or different subject. (Reg § 1.162-5) Costs of courses to renew a provisional teaching certificate, or that lead to a *permanent* certificate are deductible if necessary to continue teaching.[24] The cost of education to maintain or improve skills is deductible even if it leads to an advanced degree (Reg § 1.162-5(c)) or qualifies the teacher for a change of duties. (Reg § 1.162-5(b))[25] Education to meet minimum requirements isn't deductible. (Reg § 1.162-5(b)(2))[26]

¶ 2232   Limited above-the-line deduction for educator expenses—before 2010.

For tax years beginning before 2010, an eligible educator—a grade K through 12 teacher, instructor, counselor, principal, or aide in a school for at least 900 hours during a school year (Code Sec. 62(d)(1))—could claim an "above the line deduction" (i.e., an adjustment to gross income to arrive at adjusted gross income) for up to $250 of trade or business expenses paid or incurred for books, supplies (other than nonathletic supplies for courses of instruction in health or physical education), computer equipment (including related software and services) and other equipment, and supplementary materials used in the classroom. (Code Sec. 62(a)(2)(D)) A deduction was allowed only to the extent the amount of expenses exceeded the amount excludable from income under Code Sec. 135 (education savings bonds), Code Sec. 529(c)(1) (qualified tuition programs), or Code Sec. 530(d)(2) (Coverdell education savings accounts). (Code Sec. 62(d)(2))

caution: Check http://ria.thomsonreuters.com/federaltaxhandbook to see if this provision has been extended.

---

20. ¶L-3734; ¶1624.185; TD ¶302,034
21. ¶L-3734; ¶1624.185; TD ¶302,034
22. ¶L-3730; ¶1624.185; TD ¶302,030
23. ¶L-3733; ¶2744.04; TD ¶302,033

24. ¶L-3703; ¶1624.185; TD ¶302,003
25. ¶L-3705; ¶1624.185; TD ¶302,025
26. ¶L-3714; ¶1624.185; TD ¶302,005

Chapter 8   Tax Credits

¶ 2300   **Tax Credits.** ▬▬▬▬▬▬▬▬▬▬▬▬▬▬▬▬▬▬▬▬▬▬▬▬▬▬

Tax credits are either business credits intended to provide special incentives for the achievement of certain economic objectives, or personal credits, which provide tax benefits to certain taxpayers (e.g., the elderly or disabled, etc.). The foreign tax credit, however, may apply to both business and nonbusiness taxpayers.

The three main categories of tax credits are:

(1) The business incentive credits, see ¶2301 *et seq.*

(2) The personal (refundable and nonrefundable) credits, see ¶2342 *et seq.*

(3) The foreign tax credit, see ¶2375 *et seq.*

For credit for alternative minimum tax (AMT), see ¶2373.

For tax credits attributable to certain "passive" activities, see   ¶1811 *et seq.*

¶ 2301   **Business Incentive Credits.** ▬▬▬▬▬▬▬▬▬▬▬▬▬▬▬▬▬▬▬▬▬▬

Certain business incentive credits are combined into one general business credit (GBC) for purposes of determining each credit's allowance limitation for the tax year.

¶ 2302   **General business credit (GBC)—Form 3800.**

The GBC is made up of the:

. . . investment credit (Code Sec. 38(b)(1)) (¶2307 *et seq.*) (which includes the rehabilitation credit (¶2308), the energy credit (¶2311), the qualifying advanced coal and gasification project credits (¶2312), the qualifying advanced energy project credit (¶2313), and the pre-2011 qualifying therapeutic discovery project credit (¶2314));

. . . pre-Sept. 2011 work opportunity credit (Code Sec. 38(b)(2)), see ¶2318 *et seq.*;

. . . pre-2011 alcohol fuels credit (Code Sec. 38(b)(3)), see ¶2319;

. . . pre-2010 research credit (Code Sec. 38(b)(4)), see ¶2320;

. . . low-income housing credit (Code Sec. 38(b)(5)), see ¶2321 *et seq.*;

. . . enhanced oil recovery (EOR) credit (Code Sec. 38(b)(6)), see ¶2323;

. . . disabled access credit (DAC) (Code Sec. 38(b)(7)), see ¶2324;

. . . renewable electricity production credit (Code Sec. 38(b)(8)), see ¶2325;

. . . pre-2010 empowerment and D.C. zone employment credit (Code Sec. 38(b)(9)), see ¶2326;

. . . pre-2010 Indian employment credit (Code Sec. 38(b)(10)), see ¶2328;

. . . FICA tip credit (Code Sec. 38(b)(11)), see ¶2329;

. . . orphan drug credit (Code Sec. 38(b)(12)), see ¶2330;

. . . pre-2010 new markets credit (Code Sec. 38(b)(13)), see ¶2331;

. . . small employer pension plan startup credit (Code Sec. 38(b)(14)), see ¶2333;

. . . pre-2011 employer-provided child care credit (Code Sec. 38(b)(15)), see ¶2332;

. . . railroad track maintenance credit for tax years beginning before 2010 (Code Sec. 38(b)(16), Code Sec. 45G);

. . . pre-2010 biodiesel fuel credit (Code Sec. 38(b)(17)), see ¶2335;

. . . the pre-2010 low sulfur diesel fuel production credit (Code Sec. 38(b)(18)), see ¶2336;

. . . marginal oil and gas well production credit (Code Sec. 38(b)(19), Code Sec. 45I);

References beginning with a single letter are to paragraphs in RIA's Federal Tax Coordinator 2d and RIA's Analysis of Federal Taxes: Income. Those beginning with numbers are to paragraphs in RIA's United States Tax Reporter. Those beginning with TD are to paragraphs in RIA's Tax Desk.

339

. . . distilled spirits credit (Code Sec. 38(b)(20), Code Sec. 5011(a));

. . . advanced nuclear power facility production credit (Code Sec. 38(b)(21)), Code Sec. 45J(a)) for facilities placed in service before 2021;

. . . nonconventional source production credit (Code Sec. 38(b)(22)), see ¶2341;

. . . pre-2010 new energy efficient home credit (Code Sec. 38(b)(23)), see ¶2337;

. . . pre-2011 energy efficient appliance credit (Code Sec. 38(b)(24)), see ¶2338;

. . . applicable portion (attributable to depreciable property) of the alternative motor vehicle credit (Code Sec. 38(b)(25)), see ¶2365;

. . . applicable portion (that attributable to depreciable property) of the pre-2011 alternative fuel vehicle refueling property credit (Code Sec. 38(b)(26)), see ¶2366;

. . . mine rescue training credit for tax years beginning before 2010 (Code Sec. 38(b)(31), Code Sec. 45N);

. . . agricultural chemicals security tax credit (Code Sec. 38(b)(32)), see ¶2340;

. . . pre-2010 differential wage payment credit (Code Sec. 38(b)(33)), see ¶2339;

. . . carbon dioxide sequestration credit (Code Sec. 38(b)(34)), see ¶2316;

. . . applicable portion (attributable to depreciable property) of the new qualified plug-in electric drive motor vehicles credit (Code Sec. 38(b)(35)), see ¶2369; and

. . . small employer health insurance credit (Code Sec. 38(b)(36)), see ¶2369.

caution: Check http://ria.thomsonreuters.com/federaltaxhandbook to see if any expiring credits have been extended.

The retention credit for hiring qualified individuals in 2010 (¶2317), credit for excise tax payments to the Trans-Alaska Pipeline Liability Fund (Code Sec. 4612(e)(1)), the pre-2010 renewal community employment credit (Code Sec. 1400H(a), see ¶2327), and the community development corporation credit for pre-July '99 contributions[1] aren't included in the above Code Sec. 38(b) list, but are also part of the current year business credit.

¶ 2303 Limitation on general business credits (GBCs) based on tax liability.

A GBC is allowed against income tax for a particular tax year equal to the sum of: (1) the business credit carry*forwards* carried to the tax year, (2) the *current year* GBC, plus (3) the business credit carry*backs* carried to the tax year. (Code Sec. 38(a))[2]

The GBC allowed for any tax year (except for the empowerment zone employment credit, the New York Liberty Zone business employee credit, and "specified credits," see below) is limited to the excess of taxpayer's "net income tax" over the greater of: (1) the tentative minimum tax for the tax year, or (2) 25% of the amount of the taxpayer's "net regular tax" that exceeds $25,000. (Code Sec. 38(c)(1))[3] Spouses who file separate returns are each limited to $12,500 instead of $25,000, but if the taxpayer's spouse has no carryforward, carryback or current year GBC in the tax year that ends within or with the taxpayer's tax year, the taxpayer gets the full amount of $25,000. (Code Sec. 38(c)(6)(A))[4]

For estates and trusts, the $25,000 amount is reduced to an amount equal to $25,000 multiplied by a fraction (numerator is the estate's or trust's total income not allocated to beneficiaries, denominator is the estate's or trust's total income). (Code Sec. 38(c)(6)(D))[5]

Net income tax is the sum of the regular tax liability and the alternative minimum tax (AMT), ¶3200), reduced by the credits listed below. Net regular tax is the regular tax liability reduced by the sum of the following credits (Code Sec. 38(c)(1)): (1) household and dependent

---

1. ¶L-15650 *et seq.*; ¶384.01; TD ¶384,031
2. ¶L-15200; ¶384.01; ¶384.03; TD ¶380,500
3. ¶L-15202; ¶384.02; TD ¶380,502
4. ¶L-15204; ¶384.02; TD ¶380,505
5. ¶L-15207; ¶384.02; TD ¶380,507

care credit (Code Sec. 21); (2) credit for the elderly and disabled (Code Sec. 22); (3) child tax credit (Code Sec. 24); (4) mortgage credit (Code Sec. 25); (5) American opportunity (Hope) and Lifetime Learning credits (Code Sec. 25A); (6) saver's credit for elective deferrals and IRA contributions (Code Sec. 25B); (7) nonbusiness energy property credit (Code Sec. 25C); (9) residential energy efficient property (Code Sec. 25D); (8) foreign tax and possessions tax credit (for American Samoa) (Code Sec. 27, Code Sec. 936); (9) Puerto Rico economic activity credit (Code Sec. 30A; (10) alternative motor vehicle credit (Code Sec. 30B); (11) qualified alternative fuel vehicle refueling property credit (Code Sec. 30C); (12) pre-2010 D.C. homebuyer credit (Code Sec. 1400C); (13) new qualified plug-in electric drive motor vehicles credit (attributable to non-depreciable property); (Code Sec. 30D); and (14) qualified plug-in electric drive motor vehicles (QPEVs) (attributable to non-depreciable property) (Code Sec. 30(c)(2)(A)).[6]

The pre-2010 empowerment zone employment credit (¶2326) is limited to the excess of the taxpayer's net income tax over the greater of: (1) 75% of his tentative minimum tax, or (2) 25% of so much of its net regular tax liability as exceeds $25,000. This limitation is reduced by the general credits (not including the empowerment zone employment credit, New York Liberty Zone business employee credit, eligible small business (ESB) credits, and other specified credits, see below) allowed for the tax year. (Code Sec. 38(c)(2)) The effect is that the empowerment zone employment credit may be used to offset up to 25% of a taxpayer's AMT.[7]

"Specified credits" may offset 100% of a taxpayer's AMT. (Code Sec. 38(c)(4)) Specified credits include: (Code Sec. 38(c)(4)(B)) (1) pre-2011 alcohol fuel credit (¶2319); (2) the low-income housing credit for buildings placed in service after 2007 (¶2321); (3) credits determined under Code Sec. 45 (¶2325) to the extent attributable to electricity or refined coal produced at a facility which is originally placed in service after Oct. 22, 2004 and during the 4-year period beginning on the date the facility was originally placed in service; (4) the FICA tip credit (¶2329); (5) for tax years beginning after 2007 but before Jan. 1, 2010, the Code Sec. 45G railroad maintenance credit; (6) the small employer health insurance credit (¶2334); (7) the rehabilitation investment credit for qualified rehabilitation expenditures properly taken into account after 2007 (¶2308); (8) the credits determined under Code Sec. 46 to the extent attributable to the energy credit under Code Sec. 48 (¶2311); and (9) pre-Sept. 2011 work opportunity tax credit (¶2318). Indian coal production credit during the 4-year period the property is first placed in service (¶2325)— is also a specified credit. (Code Sec. 45(e)(10))[8]

ESB credits determined in tax years beginning in 2010 may offset 100% of a taxpayer's AMT. (Code Sec. 38(c)(5)(A)) ESB credits are the sum of the credits listed in Code Sec. 38(b) (¶2301) that are determined for the tax year with respect to an ESB (defined below). The ESB credits can't be taken into account under Code Sec. 38(c)(2), Code Sec. 38(c)(3), Code Sec. 38(c)(4) (see above). (Code Sec. 38(c)(5)(B)) An ESB is, with respect to any tax year, a corporation the stock of which is not publicly traded, a partnership, or a sole proprietorship, if the average annual gross receipts of the corporation, partnership, or sole proprietorship for the three-tax-year period preceding the tax year does not exceed $50,000,000. Rules similar to the rules of Code Sec. 448(c)(2) and Code Sec. 448(c)(3) apply.(Code Sec. 38(c)(5)(C)) Credits determined with respect to a partnership or S corporation are *not* treated as ESB credits by any partner or shareholder unless the partner or shareholder meets the $50 million average annual gross receipts test for the tax year in which the credits are treated as current year business credits. (Code Sec. 38(c)(5)(D))[9] For five-year carryback for ESB credits, see ¶2304.

¶ 2304   Carryback or carryforward of general business credit (GBC)–Form 3800.

There's a one-year carryback (5-year carryback for the marginal well production credit under Code Sec. 39(a)(3); and a 5-year carryback for eligible small business—ESB, see

---

6. ¶L-15202; ¶384.02, 384.03; TD ¶380,502
7. ¶L-15202.1; ¶384.02; TD ¶380,503
8. ¶L-15202.3; ¶384.02; TD ¶380,503.1
9. ¶L-15202.4; ¶384.01

¶2303—credits for credits determined in tax years beginning in 2010) and 20-year carryforward (on Form 3800). (Code Sec. 39(a); Code Sec. 39(a)(4)) No part of any unused current GBC attributable to a component credit may be carried back to tax years before the first tax year that the component credit was allowable. (Code Sec. 39(d))[10]

¶ 2305　Deduction for unused qualified business credits after the carryover period.

If any portion of a qualified business credit (investment credit, pre-Sept. 2011 work opportunity credit (¶2318), pre-2011 alcohol fuels credit (¶2319), pre-2010 research credit (¶2320), enhanced oil recovery credit, pre-2010 empowerment zone employment credit (¶2326), FICA tip credit (¶2329), pre-2010 new markets tax credit (¶2331), small employer pension plan startup credit (¶2333), pre-2010 Indian employment credit (¶2328), pre-2010 biodiesel fuels credit (¶2335), pre-2010 low sulfur diesel fuel production credit (¶2336), pre-2010 new energy efficient home credit (¶2337), and small employer health insurance credit (¶2334), Code Sec. 196(c)) hasn't been allowed after the carryover period expires, the taxpayer can deduct the unused portion in the first tax year after the last tax year of the carryover period (or in the tax year of the taxpayer's death or cessation if earlier). (Code Sec. 196(a), Code Sec. 196(b)) But, for the research credit for a tax year beginning before '90 and for the investment tax credit (other than the rehabilitation credit), the deduction is 50% of the unused amount. (Code Sec. 196(d))[11]

¶ 2306　Ordering rules for the general business credits (GBCs).

The order in which the component credits of the GBC are used in a tax year or as a carryback or carryforward is determined on the basis of the order they are listed in Code Sec. 38(b) (¶2302) as of the close of the tax year in which the credit is used. (Code Sec. 38(d)(1)) The order in which the component credits of the business investment credit are used is determined on the basis of the order they are listed in Code Sec. 46 as of the close of the tax year in which the credit is used. (Code Sec. 38(d)(2)) Carryovers of pre-'91 regular investment credits are used before the rehabilitation credit. (Code Sec. 38(d)(3)(B)(ii))[12]

¶ 2307　The investment tax credits—Form 3468.

The Code Sec. 46 investment tax credit (claimed on Form 3468) consists of: (1) the rehabilitation investment credit (Code Sec. 47), see ¶2308 *et seq.*; (2) the energy credit (Code Sec. 48(a)), see ¶2311;[13] (3) the qualifying advanced coal project credit (Code Sec. 48A), see ¶2312;[14] (4) the qualifying gasification project credit; (Code Sec. 48B(e)), see ¶2312;[15] (5) the qualifying energy project credit (Code Sec. 48C), see ¶2313[16]; and (6) the qualifying therapeutic discovery project credit (Code Sec. 48C), see ¶2314.[17]

Property qualifying for the rehabilitation credit (depreciable or amortizable property) is treated as investment credit property. (Code Sec. 50(a)(5)) But certain otherwise qualified property is denied the applicable credit if it's property used:

. . . predominantly outside the U.S., except for property listed in Code Sec. 168(g)(4)—dealing with rolling stock, spacecraft, satellites, etc. (Code Sec. 50(b)(1))

. . . predominantly to furnish, or in connection with the furnishing of, permanent lodging, except for certain nonlodging commercial facilities, lodging facilities used by transients, certified historic structures, and energy property. (Code Sec. 50(b)(2))

. . . by certain tax-exempt organizations. (Code Sec. 50(b)(3)) If property is leased to a partnership or other pass-through entity, a proportionate share of the property is treated as

10. ¶L-15209; ¶384.01, ¶384.03; TD ¶380,509
11. ¶L-15212; ¶1964.01; TD ¶380,510
12. ¶L-15208; ¶384.01; TD ¶380,508
13. ¶L-16500; ¶s 474, 484; TD ¶381,400

14. ¶L-16450; ¶s 48A4; TD ¶381,400
15. ¶L-16470; ¶s 48B4; TD ¶381,401
16. ¶L-16461 *et seq.*; ¶48C4; TD ¶381,421 *et seq.*
17. ¶L-15625 *et seq.*; ¶48D4

leased to each tax-exempt entity partner (under the rules of Code Sec. 168(h)(5) and (6)) in determining whether any portion of the property is tax-exempt use property. (Code Sec. 50(b)(4))

... by the U.S. or other governmental units, except for short-lease property. (Code Sec. 50(b)(4))[18]

A *lessee* of new investment credit property can take the investment credit on the property if the lessor elects to pass it to him. (Code Sec. 50(d); Reg § 1.48-4) The election statement is described in the regs. (Reg § 1.48-4(f), Reg § 1.48-4(g)) The effect is to treat the lessee as having acquired the property for its FMV, but the lessor's basis is used instead when lessor and lessee are members of a controlled group. The lessee uses the same investment credit life for the property as the lessor.[19] But a lessor's election to pass the credit from property with an over 14-year ADR depreciation "class life" to his lessee results in only a partial transfer of the credit if the lease is for a period that is less than 80% of the property's "class life" and isn't a "net lease." (Reg § 1.48-4(a)(2))[20]

If there is a net decrease in the amount of nonqualified nonrecourse financing (under the *at-risk* rules, ¶1804 *et seq.*) as of the close of a tax year following that in which property was placed in service, the net decrease is treated as an increase in the credit base for the property. Thus, an increase in the taxpayer's at-risk amount for an investment credit property is additional qualified investment. (Code Sec. 49(a)(2))[21]

¶ 2308 Rehabilitation investment credits–Form 3468.

The rehabilitation credit (claimed on Form 3468) for a building is 10% (20% for a certified historic structure) of the qualified rehabilitation expenditure. (Code Sec. 47(a))[22]

For eligible buildings located in the Gulf Opportunity (GO) Zone (as defined in Code Sec. 1400M) paid or incurred before Jan. 1, 2010, the credit was 13% (26% for a certified historic structure) of the qualified rehabilitation expenditures. (Code Sec. 1400N(h))[23]

A qualified rehabilitation expenditure is any amount charged to capital account and incurred in connection with the rehabilitation (including reconstruction, or an addition or improvement) of a qualified rehabilitated building (¶2309) that's depreciable under Code Sec. 168, and is nonresidential real property, residential rental property, or real property with a class life of more than 12.5 years. Expenditures for which straight-line depreciation isn't used are not qualified expenditures. (Code Sec. 47(c)(2))[24] If bonus first-year depreciation (¶1933) is claimed for the building, the credit may be claimed only if the taxpayer depreciates the remaining adjusted depreciable basis of rehabilitation expenses using the straight line method. (Reg § 1.168(k)-1(f)(10)), Reg § 1.1400L(b)-1(f)(9))[25]

Also excluded are expenditures in connection with the rehabilitation of a building that are allocable to that portion of the building that is (or that is reasonably expected to be) tax-exempt-use property. (Code Sec. 47(c)(2)(B)(v))[26]

In addition to owner-taxpayers of qualified property, the rehabilitation credits are available to lessees for qualified expenditures incurred by them, but only if, on the rehabilitation's completion date, the remaining term of the lease (without regard to renewal) is at least the recovery period under Code Sec. 168(c). (Code Sec. 47(c)(2)(B)(vi))[27]

18. ¶L-16501; ¶504.01; TD ¶381,401
19. ¶s L-16506, L-17010 *et seq.*; ¶484.10; TD ¶381,403
20. ¶L-17015; ¶484.10
21. ¶L-16505; ¶494; TD ¶381,402
22. ¶L-16103; ¶484.13; TD ¶381,503
23. ¶L-16120; ¶14,00N4.04; TD ¶381,518.1
24. ¶L-16102; ¶474; TD ¶381,502
25. ¶L-16102.1; ¶1684.025, ¶14,00L4.05; TD ¶381,502
26. ¶L-16115; ¶474; TD ¶381,516
27. ¶L-16102; ¶474; TD ¶381,501

¶ 2309   Which buildings qualify for the rehabilitation credit?

A "qualified rehabilitated building" is any building (and its structural components) that satisfies all of the following requirements:

(1) Except for certified historic structures, the building was first placed in service before '36. (Code Sec. 47(c)(1)(B))

(2) The building has been substantially rehabilitated. A substantial rehabilitation is one in which the qualified rehabilitation expenditures during the 24-month period selected by the taxpayer (as prescribed in regs) and ending with or within the year exceed the greater of: (a) $5,000; or (b) the adjusted basis of the building and its structural components as of the first day of the 24-month period, or of the holding period (without regard to reconstruction), whichever is later. (Code Sec. 47(c)(1)(C)(i)) Rehabilitation includes reconstruction. (Code Sec. 47(c)(1)(D))[28]

(3) The building was placed in service before the beginning of the rehabilitation.

(4) For any building other than a certified historic structure, the building retains in place (a) at least 75% of the external walls (including at least 50% as external walls), and (b) at least 75% of its internal structural framework.

(5) The building must be depreciable or amortizable. (Code Sec. 47(c)(1)(A))[29]

For any rehabilitation that may reasonably be expected to be completed in phases set forth in architectural plans and specifications completed before the rehabilitation begins, a 60-month (instead of 24-month) period applies. For certain buildings located in the GO Zone (¶2308), Rita Gulf Opportunity (GO) Zone, or Wilma GO Zone (as defined in Code Sec. 1400M) on which rehabilitation had begun, the 24-month or 60-month is tolled for 12 months. (Code Sec. 47(c)(1)(C)(ii))[30]

¶ 2310   Progress expenditure rehabilitation credit—Form 3468.

If any building being rehabilitated by or for the taxpayer has a normal rehabilitation period of 2 years or more, and it's reasonable to expect the building to be a qualified rehabilitated building (¶2309) in the taxpayer's hands when placed in service (Code Sec. 47(d)(2)), the taxpayer may irrevocably elect (on Form 3468) to account for qualified rehabilitation expenditures made for that property as follows:

(1) where it's reasonable to believe that more than half these expenditures will be made *directly* by the taxpayer, any qualified rehabilitation expenditure is taken into account for the tax year it's properly chargeable to capital account (i.e., includible in computing the property's basis), and

(2) where it's reasonable to believe that *no* more than half the qualified expenditure will be made directly by the taxpayer, any qualified rehabilitation expenditure is taken into account in the tax year it's paid. (Code Sec. 47(d)(1); Reg § 1.46-5(g)(1))[31]

¶ 2311   Energy credit—Form 3468.

A taxpayer can claim (on Form 3468) the following energy credits (in each case, the percentage applies to the basis of eligible energy property placed in service during the year):

(1) 30% for qualified fuel cell property, (Code Sec. 48(a)(2)(A)(i)(I)) i.e., a fuel cell power plant with a nameplate capacity of at least 0.5 kilowatt (kW) of electricity using an electrochemical process, and an electricity only generation efficiency of greater than 30%. The

28. ¶L-16106; ¶474; TD ¶381,506
29. ¶L-16101, L-16103; ¶474; TD ¶381,503
30. ¶L-16113; ¶474; TD ¶381,514
31. ¶L-16200; ¶474; TD ¶381,519

credit can't exceed an amount equal to $1,500 for each 0.5 kW of capacity. The credit isn't available after 2016. (Code Sec. 48(c))

(2) 30% for solar energy property, (Code Sec. 48(a)(2)(A)(i)(II)) i.e., equipment that uses solar energy to generate electricity, to heat or cool (or provide hot water for) a structure, or to provide solar process heat (but not for heating a swimming pool). (Code Sec. 48(a)(3)(A)(i)) The 30% credit is available only for periods ending before 2017. (Code Sec. 48(a)(2)(A)(i)(II)) After 2016, the credit will be 10%. (Code Sec. 48(a)(2)(A)(ii))

(3) 30% for solar energy to illuminate the inside of a structure using fiber optic distributed sunlight, for periods ending before 2017. (Code Sec. 48(a)(2)(A)(i)(III), Code Sec. 48(a)(3)(A)(ii))

(4) 10% for equipment used to produce, distribute, or use energy derived from a geothermal deposit. (Code Sec. 48(a)(2)(A)(ii), Code Sec. 48(a)(3)(A)(iii))

(5) 10% for qualified microturbine property, (Code Sec. 48(a)(2)(A)(ii), Code Sec. 48(a)(3)(A)(iv)) i.e., a stationary microturbine powerplant with a nameplate capacity of less than 2,000 kWs, and has an electricity only generation efficiency of not less than 26% at International Standard Organization conditions. The credit can't exceed $200 for each kW of the property's capacity and isn't available after 2016. (Code Sec. 48(c)(2))

(6) 10% for combined heat and power system property, (Code Sec. 48(a)(3)(A)(v)) i.e., property which uses the same energy source to simultaneously or sequentially produce electrical power, mechanical shaft power, or both (at least 20% of total useful energy), while generating steam or other forms of useful thermal energy, including heating or cooling applications (at least 20% of total useful energy); and has a greater than 60% energy efficiency percentage. The property must be placed in service before 2017. (Code Sec. 48(c)(3)(A))

(7) 30% for qualified small wind energy property, (Code Sec. 48(a)(3)(A)(vi)) i.e., property that uses a qualifying small wind turbine (with a nameplate capacity of not more than 100 kWs) to generate electricity. This doesn't include any property after 2016. (Code Sec. 48(c)(4))

(8) 10% for geothermal heat pump systems equipment, i.e. equipment that uses the ground or ground water as a thermal energy source to heat a structure or as a thermal energy sink to cool a structure, but only for a period ending before 2017. (Code Sec. 48(a)(3)(A)(vii))

No credit is allowed for property unless it's depreciable or amortizable; its construction, reconstruction or erection is completed by the taxpayer or, if acquired by the taxpayer, its original use begins with the taxpayer; and it meets the official quality and performance standards in effect at the time of acquisition. (Code Sec. 48(a)(3)) The credit is allowed for public utility property. (Code Sec. 48(a)(3))[32] There is no reduction in basis for purposes of determining the energy credit if property is financed in whole or in part by subsidized financing or tax-exempt private activity bonds. (Code Sec. 48(a)(4))[33]

A taxpayer can receive a grant in lieu of the energy credit. The basis of the property is reduced by 50% of the amount of the grant. (Code Sec. 48(d))[34]

¶ 2312 Credits for qualifying advanced coal projects and gasification projects.

A credit can be claimed for investments in qualifying advanced coal projects. The credit is 20% of the qualified investment for the tax year in integrated gasification combined cycle projects, 15% of the qualified investment for the tax year in projects that use other advanced coal-based generation technologies; and 30% of the qualified investment for advanced coal-based generation technology projects. The application period for the 2010-2011 allocation

---

32. ¶L-16501; ¶484; TD ¶381,601   34. ¶L-16440; ¶484.02; TD ¶381,608
33. ¶L-16415; ¶484; TD ¶381,603

round began on Mar. 2, 2010, and ends on Mar. 1, 2011. The applications have to be submitted to DOE before Nov. 1, 2010 and to IRS before Mar. 3, 2011. (Code Sec. 48A(a))[35] A separate investment credit can also be claimed for qualified investment in qualifying gasification projects. The credit is 20% or 30% of the qualified investment for the tax year. (Code Sec. 48B(a)) The total credit amount has been allocated so IRS won't conduct an allocation round in 2010-2011. The Code Sec. 48B credit is not allowed for any qualified investment for which the Code Sec. 48A credit is allowed. (Code Sec. 48B(e))[36]

¶ 2313   New qualified advanced energy manufacturing project (QAEMP) credit.

A taxpayer can claim a 30% credit for investment in qualified property used in a QAEMP, (Code Sec. 48C) i.e., a project that re-equips, expands, or establishes a manufacturing facility for the production of property designed to: (1) be used to produce energy from the sun, wind, or geothermal deposits or other renewable resources; (2) manufacture fuel cells, microturbines, or an energy storage system for use with electric or hybrid-electric motor vehicles; (3) manufacture electric grids to support the transmission of intermittent sources of renewable energy, including storage of that energy; (4) manufacture equipment for use for carbon capture or sequestration; or (5) refine or blend renewable fuels (but not fossil fuels), to produce energy conservation technologies (including energy-conserving lighting technologies and smart grid technologies). It also includes a facility for the production of new qualified plug-in electric drive motor vehicles (¶2367); qualified plug-in electric vehicles (¶2367); components designed specifically for these vehicles; or other advanced energy property designed to reduce greenhouse gas emissions. (Code Sec. 48C(c)(1))[37] Qualified property must be depreciable (tangible) property used in a QAEMP (Code Sec. 48C(b)(1)) and doesn't include property designed to manufacture equipment for use in the refining or blending of any transportation fuel (other than renewable fuels). (Code Sec. 48C(c)(1)(B)) The property's basis is reduced by the amount of credit received.[38]

¶ 2314   Pre-2011 Qualifying therapeutic discovery project (QTDP) credit—Form 8942.

Eligible taxpayers (those employing 250 or fewer workers) may claim a 50% investment credit for qualified investments made in a tax year beginning in 2009 or 2010 for QTDP. IRS, in consultation with the HHS Secretary, will award certifications for qualified investments, but not in excess of $1 billion for the 2009-2010 period. (Code Sec. 48D))

caution: Check http://ria.thomsonreuters.com/federaltaxhandbook to see if the credit has been extended.

Qualified investments are costs for expenses necessary for and directly related to the conduct of a QTDP. The costs must satisfy certain certification (on Form 8942) and timing requirements and can't be excluded costs as defined by Code Sec. 48D(b)(3) (e.g., interest expense, facility maintenance expenses). A QTDP is one designed to develop a product, process, or therapy to diagnose, treat, or prevent diseases and afflictions by: (1) conducting preclinical activities, clinical trials and studies, and research protocols, or (2) by developing technology or products designed to diagnose diseases and conditions, including molecular and companion drugs and diagnostics, or to further the delivery or administration of therapeutics. (Code Sec. 48D(c)(1))

QTDP expenditures don't qualify for the research or orphan drug credits, or bonus depreciation, and if a credit is allowed for an expense related to depreciable property, its basis is reduced by the credit amount. Additionally, expenses taken into account in determining the

---

35. ¶L-16450; ¶s 48A4; TD ¶381,413   37. ¶L-16463; ¶48C4; TD ¶381,423
36. ¶L-16470; ¶s 48B4; TD ¶381,414   38. ¶L-16461 *et seq.*; ¶48C4; TD ¶381,421 *et seq.*

credit are nondeductible to the extent of the credit claimed attributable to the expenses. (Code Sec. 48D(e)) A taxpayer can receive a grant in lieu of the credit. (Code Sec. 48D(f))

¶ 2315 Recapture of investment credits—Form 4255.

If investment credit property is disposed of or ceases to be investment credit property for the taxpayer before the end of the recapture period, the credit taken for all earlier years is recaptured on Form 4255 (i.e., added to the tax liability for the recapture year). (Code Sec. 50(a)(1)) The recapture percentage is 100% during the first full year after the property is placed in service. This percentage decreases by 20 percentage points every succeeding full year. There's no recapture after the fifth full year. (Code Sec. 50(a)(1)) Recapture applies only to credit used to reduce tax liability. If any part of it isn't used, carrybacks and carryovers of the credit must be appropriately adjusted. (Code Sec. 50(a)(3))

No recapture applies to a transfer by reason of death (Code Sec. 50(a)(4)(A)), a mere change in form of doing business (Code Sec. 50(a)(4)(B)), or a transfer between spouses or incident to divorce (under the rules of Code Sec. 1041(a)). (Code Sec. 50(a)(5)(B))[39]

Different recapture computation methods apply to progress expenditures credit (¶2310) depending on whether the recapture year occurs before or after the progress expenditure property is placed in service. (Code Sec. 50(a)(2))[40]

If the amount of nonqualified nonrecourse financing (¶1810) for at-risk property increases as of the close of the tax year, then the tax for the tax year is increased by the total decrease in credits allowed in earlier tax years that would result if the credit base for the earlier credits had been reduced by the amount of the increase in the nonqualified nonrecourse financing. For purposes of computing recapture, the increase in nonqualified nonrecourse financing is treated as reducing the credit base and correspondingly reducing the qualified investment in the year the property was placed in service. (Code Sec. 49(b)(1)) The transfer of (or an agreement to transfer) any evidence of indebtedness won't be treated as an increase in nonqualified nonrecourse financing, if the transfer occurs (or the agreement is entered into) more than one year after the indebtedness was incurred. (Code Sec. 49(b)(2))[41]

If a taxpayer fails to pay the principal on a level payment nonqualified nonrecourse loan (¶1810) used for qualified energy property, the taxpayer is treated as increasing the amount of nonqualified nonrecourse financing to the extent of the recapture. (Code Sec. 49(b)(3))[42]

¶ 2316 Carbon dioxide sequestration credit—Form 8933.

A carbon dioxide sequestration credit is allowed for carbon dioxide captured. (Code Sec. 45Q) The credit for any tax year is an amount equal to the sum of: (1) $20 per metric ton of qualified carbon dioxide which is captured by the taxpayer at a qualified facility and disposed of by the taxpayer in secure geological storage; and (2) $10 per metric ton of qualified carbon dioxide which is captured by the taxpayer at a qualified facility and used by the taxpayer as a tertiary injectant in a qualified enhanced oil or natural gas recovery project. (Code Sec. 45Q(a)(2)) These amounts are inflation adjusted in any tax year beginning in a calendar year after 2009. (Code Sec. 45Q(d)(7)) Qualified carbon dioxide is carbon dioxide captured from an industrial source that would otherwise be released into the atmosphere as industrial emission of greenhouse gas, and is measured at the source of capture and verified at the point of disposal or injection. (Code Sec. 45Q(b)(1))

To claim the credit (on Form 8933), a person must: (1) own an industrial facility at which carbon capture equipment is placed in service, (2) capture not less than 500,000 metric tons of qualified carbon dioxide there during the tax year, and (3) physically or contractually ensure

---

39. ¶L-17301; ¶504.02; TD ¶381,405
40. ¶L-17314; ¶504.02; TD ¶381,407

41. ¶L-17307; ¶494; TD ¶381,408
42. ¶L-16419; ¶494; TD ¶381,607

that the qualified carbon dioxide is securely stored in a geologic formation (for carbon dioxide used as a tertiary injectant in an enhanced oil recovery project, this requirement applies only to carbon dioxide captured after Feb. 17, 2009).[43]

¶ 2317 Up-to-$1,000 retention credit for "retained workers" in 2011.

For any tax year ending after Mar. 18, 2010, the Hiring Incentives to Restore Employment Act (HIRE Act, PL 111–147, 3/18/2010) §102 provides an up-to-$1,000 increase (retention credit) to the general business credit (GBC) for "retained workers." A retained worker is any qualified individual (as defined under the 2010 payroll tax holiday and who makes the certification on Form W-11, see ¶3024):

(1) who was employed by the taxpayer on any date during the tax year,

(2) who was employed by the taxpayer for a period of not less than 52 consecutive weeks, *and*

(3) whose wages (as defined for income tax withholding in Code Sec. 3401(a), see ¶3004) for that employment during the last 26 weeks of the period (described in item (2) above) equaled at least 80% of the wages for the first 26 weeks of that period. (HIRE Act §102(b))[44]

The amount of the retention credit is for each retained worker (above) with respect to which the 52-consecutive-week requirement in (2), above, is *first* satisfied during the tax year, the *lesser* of: (a) $1,000; or (b) 6.2% of the wages (as defined in Code Sec. 3401(a)) paid by the taxpayer to the retained worker during the 52-consecutive-week-period. (HIRE Act §102(a))

⊘ observation: If a retained worker's wages during the 52-consecutive-week-period exceed $16,129.03, the retention credit for that retained worker is $1,000.

⊘ observation: Since the retention credit applies in the tax year in which the 52-consecutive-week test is *first* satisfied, the retention credit for each retained employee only applies in one tax year (i.e., the year in which an employee first satisfies the 52-consecutive-week test).

⊘ observation: For an employer using the calendar year as its tax year, the retention credit is claimed on the employer's 2011 tax return. But, certain fiscal year taxpayers may have to claim the credit on returns for two tax years on an employee-by-employee basis.

An employer can qualify for the retention credit and the payroll tax holiday (or the work opportunity credit) for the same employee.[45] No portion of the unused GBC under Code Sec. 38 for any tax year that is attributable to the retention credit can be carried to a tax year *beginning* before Mar. 18, 2010. (HIRE Act §102(c)) The retention credit applies to employers in U.S. possessions (including Puerto Rico and the Northern Mariana Islands). (HIRE Act §102(d))

¶ 2318 Work opportunity tax credit (WOTC) before Sept. 2011—Forms 5884, 8850.

The WOTC allows employers who hire members of certain targeted groups before Sept. 2011 to get a credit against income tax (use Form 5884) of a percentage of first-year wages up to $6,000 per employee ($12,000 for qualified veterans; and $3,000 for qualified summer youth employees). Where the employee is a long-term family assistance (LTFA) recipient, the WOTC is a percentage of first *and* second year wages, up to $10,000 per employee. (Code Sec. 51)

Generally, the percentage of qualifying wages is 40% of first-year wages, for a maximum

43. ¶L-18401 *et seq.*; ¶45Q4
44. ¶L-15218; ¶384.05; TD ¶380,522

45. ¶L-15217; ¶384.05; TD ¶380,521

WOTC of $2,400 (.4 × $6,000) (Code Sec. 51(a)); it's 25% for employees who have completed at least 120 hours, but less than 400 hours of service for the employer. (Code Sec. 51(i)) However, for LTFA recipients, it includes an additional 50% of qualified-second year wages for a maximum credit of $9,000 [(.4 × $10,000) + (.5 × $10,000)]. (Code Sec. 51(e))[46]

The WOTC reduces the employer's wage deduction dollar-for-dollar. (Code Sec. 280C(a); Reg § 1.280C-1)[47] But the taxpayer can elect not to take the WOTC. (Code Sec. 51(j))[48]

Wages paid (1) for federally funded on-the-job training, (Code Sec. 51(c)(2)(A))[49] and (2) to an individual who performs the same or substantially similar services as those of employees participating in or affected by a strike or lockout at the employer's plant don't qualify for the credit. (Code Sec. 51(c)(3))[50] Creditable wages are reduced by any supplementation payments made to the employer for an employee under Social Security Act §482(e). (Code Sec. 51(c)(2)(B))[1]

The targeted groups are: Qualified IV-A recipients (qualified recipients of aid to families with dependent children or successor program); qualified veterans; qualified ex-felons; designated community residents (i.e., the former "high-risk youths" targeted group but with the maximum age requirement raised and the residency requirement expanded to include rural renewal residents); vocational rehabilitation referrals; qualified summer youth employees; qualified food stamp recipients; qualified SSI recipients; long-term family assistance recipients, i.e., members of a family that receives or received assistance under a IV-A program for a minimum period of time; and unemployed veterans and disconnected youths who begin work for an employer after 2008 and before 2011. (Code Sec. 51(d))[2]

To be eligible for the WOTC, a new employee must be certified as a member of a targeted group by a State Employment Security Agency (SESA). The employer can either get the certification by the day the prospective employee begins work or complete a pre-screening notice (use Form 8850) for the employee by the day he is offered employment, and submit it to the SESA (not to IRS) as part of a request for certification within 28 days after the employee begins work. (Code Sec. 51(d)(13)) No WOTC is allowed for employees who are related to the employer or to certain owners of the employer. (Code Sec. 51(i))[3]

¶ 2319   Alcohol fuels credit generally before 2011—Form 6478; refundable fuel excise tax credits

For sales or uses before 2011 (except for periods during which the removal-at-terminal excise tax on gasoline, diesel fuel and kerosene drops to 4.3¢ a gallon) (Code Sec. 40(e)(1)) (see ¶1115) (Code Sec. 4081(d)(1)), an *alcohol fuels* credit (computed on Form 6478) is allowed for alcohol (other than that produced from petroleum, natural gas, coal or peat, or with a proof less than 150) (Code Sec. 40(d)(1)) used as a fuel. The credit equals the sum of: (1) the alcohol mixture credit, (2) the alcohol credit, (3) the small ethanol producer credit, and (4) the cellulosic biofuel producer credit. (Code Sec. 40(a))

⚡*caution:* Check http://ria.thomsonreuters.com/federaltaxhandbook to see if the credit has been extended.

The credit can't be carried over to any tax year beginning after the three-tax year period beginning with the tax year in which the credit ceases to apply. (Code Sec. 40(e)(2)) The fuel credit will be reduced to take into account excise tax exemptions. (Code Sec. 40(c))

The alcohol mixture credit is 60¢ for each 190-or-greater-proof gallon of alcohol used by the taxpayer in the production of a qualified mixture. A "qualified mixture" is a mixture of

46. ¶L-17775 *et seq.*; ¶514; TD ¶380,700
47. ¶L-17780; ¶514; TD ¶380,703
48. ¶L-17781; ¶514; TD ¶380,704
49. ¶L-17784.2; ¶514; TD ¶380,707

50. ¶L-17783.3; ¶514; TD ¶380,707
1. ¶L-17783; ¶514
2. ¶L-17776 *et seq.*; ¶514; TD ¶380,701
3. ¶L-17784.2; ¶514; TD ¶380,709

alcohol and gasoline or of alcohol and a special fuel that is either sold by the taxpayer producing the mixture to any person for use as a fuel or used as a fuel by the taxpayer producing the mixture. (Code Sec. 40(b)(1), Code Sec. 40(h)(1))

The alcohol credit is 60¢ per gallon of 190-or-greater proof alcohol that during the tax year is either: (a) used by the taxpayer as a fuel in a trade or business, or (b) sold by the taxpayer at retail to a person and placed in the fuel tank of that person's vehicle. (Code Sec. 40(b)(2)(A), Code Sec. 40(h)(1)(A)) A taxpayer gets no credit as a user (under (a) above) for any alcohol that was sold in a retail sale described in (b), above. (Code Sec. 40(b)(2)(B))

If the alcohol has a proof of at least 150 but less than 190, the alcohol mixture credit and the alcohol credit is 45¢ per gallon. (Code Sec. 40(b)(3), Code Sec. 40(h)(1)(B))

A tax of 60¢ per gallon (reported on Form 720) applies if a credit was taken and the mixture or alcohol is used other than as a fuel, the mixture is separated, or the alcohol is mixed. For alcohol with a proof less than 190 the tax is 45¢ per gallon. (Code Sec. 40(d)(3), Code Sec. 40(h)(1)(C))

A small ethanol producer is eligible for a credit of 10¢ per gallon of qualified ethanol fuel production. (Code Sec. 40(b)(4)) A small producer is one whose productive capacity for alcohol does not exceed 60 million gallons at any time during the tax year. "Alcohol" is defined as methanol or ethanol, without regard to proof or source restrictions. (Code Sec. 40(g))

The cellulosic biofuel producer credit is an income tax credit for each gallon of qualified cellulosic fuel production of the producer for the tax year. (For fuels sold or used on or after Jan. 1, 2010, the credit excludes fuels with significant water, sediment, or ash content, such as "black liquor.") In general, the amount of the credit per gallon is $1.01. However, for cellulosic biofuel that is alcohol, the $1.01 credit amount is reduced by (1) the credit amount applicable for such alcohol under the alcohol mixture credit as in effect at the time cellulosic biofuel is produced; and (2) in the case of cellulosic biofuel that is ethanol, the credit amount for small ethanol producers as in effect at the time the cellulosic biofuel fuel is produced. The credit terminates on Dec. 31, 2012. (Code Sec. 40(b)(6))

A recapture tax of 10¢ per gallon is imposed on alcohol not used as fuel and reported on Form 720.[4] (Code Sec. 40(d)(3)(C)) A cooperative can elect to pass through the small ethanol producer credit to its patrons. (Code Sec. 40(g)(6)) A taxpayer can elect out of the alcohol fuel credit (Code Sec. 40(f)(1)) by not taking the credit. (Reg § 301.9100-6T(e))[5] The credit doesn't apply to fuel produced outside the U.S. for use outside the U.S. (Code Sec. 40(d)(7))

¶ 2320   Research credit before 2010—Form 6765.

For amounts paid or incurred before 2010 (Code Sec. 41(h)(1)), the research credit (claimed on Form 6765) equals the sum of:

(1) 20% of the excess (if any) of the qualified research expenses for the tax year over a base amount, (unless the taxpayer elects the alternative simplified research credit, which would then replace this item (1)).

(2) The university basic research credit, i.e., 20% of the basic research payments determined under Code Sec. 41(e)(1)(A).

(3) 20% of the taxpayer's expenditures on qualified energy research undertaken by an energy research consortium. (Code Sec. 41(a))[6]

caution: Check http://ria.thomsonreuters.com/federaltaxhandbook to see if the credit has been extended.

---

4. ¶L-17507; TD ¶382,207
5. ¶L-17504; ¶404.04; TD ¶382,208

6. ¶L-15300 *et seq.*; ¶414 *et seq.*; TD ¶384,002

The base amount is a fixed-base percentage of taxpayer's average annual gross receipts from a U.S. trade or business (including any foreign sub's gross receipts), net of returns and allowances, for the 4 tax years before the credit year, and can't be less than 50% of the year's qualified research expenses. The fixed base percentage for a non-startup company is the percentage (not exceeding 16%) that taxpayer's total qualified research expenses is of total gross receipts for tax years beginning after '83 and before '89. (Code Sec. 42(c))[7]

Except when a taxpayer elects the alternative simplified research credit, described below, the Code assigns a fixed-base percentage of 3% in making the base amount computation for each of its first 5 tax years in which a "startup company" has qualified research expenses. (Code Sec. 41(c)(3)(B)(ii)(I)) For the second 5 tax years, the fixed-base percentage is a specified amount of the ratio or percentage—increased annually during this second 5 year period—determined by dividing qualified research expenses by gross receipts.[8]

To qualify for the research credit, research must be conducted within the U.S. (including Puerto Rico and U.S. possessions). (Code Sec. 41(d), Code Sec. 41(f)) An expense must:

(a) qualify as a research and experimental expenditure under Code Sec. 174;

(b) relate to research undertaken for the purpose of discovering information that is technological in nature and the application of which is intended to be useful in developing a new or improved business component of the taxpayer; and

(c) be for research in which substantially all of the activities are elements of a process of experimentation that relates to a new or improved function, performance, reliability or quality. (Code Sec. 41(d)(1); Reg § 1.41-4(a)(5))

Additional tests apply to research costs of software developed for the taxpayer's internal use. (Code Sec. 41(d)(4)(E)) Certain activities (e.g., marketing, surveys, duplication of existing business components, post-commercial-production activities) aren't qualified expenses. (Code Sec. 41(d)(4)) To pass test (b), above, research must be intended to eliminate uncertainty about the development or improvement of a business component, and the process of experimentation must fundamentally rely on principles of the physical or biological sciences, engineering, or computer science. A taxpayer may use existing technologies and may rely on existing principles of these sciences. Courts generally have applied these tests strictly.[9] The issuance of certain patents is conclusive evidence that a taxpayer has discovered technological-in-nature information that is intended to eliminate uncertainty about the development or improvement of a business component. (Reg § 1.41-4(a)(3)(iii))

Qualified research expenses (QREs) are amounts the taxpayer pays or incurs during the tax year "in carrying on any trade or business" (including certain start-up costs) of the taxpayer for: in-house research expenses, which consist of certain wages and supplies, and contract research expenses, i.e., 65% of amounts paid to certain nonemployees, and 100% of the taxpayer's expenditures to eligible small businesses, universities, and federal laboratories for qualified energy research. (Code Sec. 41(b); Reg § 1.41-2)[10]

Any expense taken into account in computing the orphan drug credit (¶2330) for a tax year can't be taken into account in computing the credit. (Code Sec. 45C(c)(1)) But, any orphan drug expenses for any tax year which are QREs can be taken into account in determining base period research expenses in later tax years. (Code Sec. 45C(c)(2))[11]

No deduction is allowed for that portion of the otherwise deductible QREs or basic research expenses that equals the credit for the tax year. (Code Sec. 280C(c)(1)) If a taxpayer capitalizes rather than deducts expenses, the amount of the expenses capitalized during the year is

7. ¶L-15309.1
8. ¶L-15309 *et seq.*; ¶414 *et seq.*; TD ¶384,015
9. ¶L-15412
10. ¶L-15401 *et seq.*; ¶414.01; TD ¶384,008
11. ¶L-15606; ¶414.04

reduced by the excess of the credit over the amount allowable (without regard to that disallowance) as a deduction for the tax year. (Code Sec. 280C(c)(2))[12] But a taxpayer may avoid the reduction for any tax year by claiming a reduced credit for the year. The election limits the taxpayer to a credit in the amount of the research credit before any reduction less the product of that credit amount times the maximum corporate tax rate. (Code Sec. 280C(c)(3))[13]

A taxpayer can elect an *alternative simplified research* credit equal to 14% of the excess of the QREs for the tax year over 50% of the average QREs for the three tax years preceding the tax year for which the credit is being determined. (Code Sec. 41(c)(5)(A), Reg § 1.41-9T(a)) If a taxpayer has no QREs in any one of the three preceding tax years, the alternative simplified research credit is 6% of the QREs for the tax year for which the credit is being determined. (Code Sec. 41(c)(5)(B)) The election applies to the tax year for which it is made and all following tax years unless revoked with IRS's consent. It can't be made or revoked on an amended return. (Code Sec. 41(c)(5)(C); Reg § 1.41-9T(b))[14]

The 20% *university basic research credit* component applies to 100% of cash expenditures by corporations (except S corporations, personal holding companies, or service organizations) for basic research over the sum of: (1) the minimum basic research amount, plus (2) the maintenance-of-effort amount. (Code Sec. 41(e); Reg § 1.41-7)[15] The minimum basic research amount (Code Sec. 41(e)(4); Reg § 1.41-7) is the greatest of: (1) 1% of the average amount paid for in-house and contract research expenses during the base period (the three tax years before the first tax year beginning after '83); (Code Sec. 41(e)(7)(B)) (2) the contract research expense for the base period; or (3) 50% of the basic research payments if taxpayer wasn't in existence for a full year in the base period.[16] The maintenance-of-effort amount is: (1) the average charitable contribution to all educational institutions during the base period (see above) multiplied by the cost-of-living adjustment, *minus* (2) the charitable contributions to educational institutions for the year. (Code Sec. 41(e)(5)(A))[17]

¶ 2321   Low-income housing credit for qualified buildings—Forms 8609, 8586.

The low-income housing credit is allowed annually over a ten-year credit period beginning with the tax year the qualified building is placed in service, or, under an irrevocable election (on Form 8609), the next tax year. (Code Sec. 42(f)(1)) The credit period for an existing building can't begin before the first tax year of the tax period for rehabilitation expenses for the building. (Code Sec. 42(f)(5)(A))[18]

The credit equals the qualified building's qualified basis times the applicable percentage (see below) (Code Sec. 42(a)) prescribed by IRS for the month placed in service or elected in agreement with the housing credit agency. (Code Sec. 42(b)(2)(A)) The building owner can't claim a credit amount in excess of the allocation received from the state or housing credit agency for that year. (Reg § 1.42-1T(e)(1))[19]

IRS prescribes percentages that will yield, over a ten-year period, credit amounts that will have a present value equal to 70% of the qualified basis of new buildings (not federally subsidized) and 30% of the qualified basis of existing buildings and federally subsidized new buildings, see following table. For any new building that is placed in service *after* July 30, 2008 and *before* Dec. 31, 2013 that is not federally subsidized for the tax year the applicable percentage won't be less than 9% (notwithstanding an irrevocable election by the taxpayer on or before July 30, 2008 to apply lesser applicable percentage). (Code Sec. 42(b))[20]

---

12. ¶L-3131; ¶s 280C4, 414.04; TD ¶306,508
13. ¶L-15308; ¶s 280C4, 414.04; TD ¶384,019
14. ¶L-15302.2; ¶414.0107; TD ¶384,003.1
15. ¶L-15501 *et seq.*; ¶s 414.01, 414.02; TD ¶384,018
16. ¶s L-15508, L-15507; ¶414.02

17. ¶L-15509; ¶414.02
18. ¶L-15700 *et seq.*; ¶424.10, 424.55; TD ¶383,001
19. ¶L-15702; ¶424.10; TD ¶383,001
20. ¶L-15718; ¶424.10; TD ¶383,001

Month	Year	70% present value credit	30% present value credit
Nov.	2010	7.57%	3.24%
Oct.	2010	7.58%	3.25%
Sept.	2010	7.65%	3.28%
Aug.	2010	7.69%	3.30%
July	2010	7.73%	3.31%
June	2010	7.81%	3.35%
May	2010	7.85%	3.36%
Apr.	2010	7.82%	3.35%
Mar.	2010	7.81%	3.35%
Feb.	2010	7.84%	3.36%
Jan.	2010	7.76%	3.32%
Dec.	2009	7.79%	3.34%

A credit for rehabilitation expenditures (treated as a separate building (Code Sec. 42(e)(1))) is allowed only if during any 24-month period they are the greater of: 10% of the building's adjusted basis or $3,000 per low-income unit. (Code Sec. 42(e)(3)(A))

To claim the credit, taxpayers must file Form 8586 for each tax year in the ten-year credit period. (Code Sec. 42(g)(4))[21] Form 8609 is filed once with the taxpayer's tax return.[22]

A qualified low-income building is a building that at all times during the "compliance period" of 15 tax years beginning with the first tax year of the credit period, is part of a qualified low-income housing project. (Code Sec. 42(c)(2), Code Sec. 42(i)(1), Code Sec. 42(g)) In addition, no credit is allowed unless an extended low income housing commitment (for an additional 15-year period) between the taxpayer and the housing credit agency is in effect at the end of the tax year. (Code Sec. 42(h)(6))[23]

¶ 2322 Recapture of low-income housing credit—Form 8611.

If, at the close of any year in the compliance period (¶2321), the building's qualified basis is less than it was at the close of the earlier tax year, the taxpayer's tax for the year is increased (Code Sec. 42(j)(1), Code Sec. 42(j)(4)(B)) by the sum of:

(1) the total decrease in taxpayer's general business credits for all earlier tax years that would have resulted if the accelerated portion of the credit (below) allowable for the earlier tax years wasn't allowed for all earlier tax years for the decrease in qualified basis, plus

(2) an amount of nondeductible interest on (1), above, computed at the rate charged for overpayment of tax, see ¶4855. (Code Sec. 42(j)(2))

The accelerated portion of the credit for the earlier tax years is the excess of the total credit allowed for the earlier tax years over the total credit that would have been allowable for those years if the total credit that would have been allowable for the entire compliance period were allowable ratably over 15 years. (Code Sec. 42(j)(3))[24]

The disposition of a building (or interest in it) won't result in an increase in tax from credit recapture if it's reasonably expected that the building will continue to be operated as a qualified low-income building for the remaining compliance period for that building. The otherwise applicable statute of limitations is extended until three years after IRS is notified of noncompliance with the low-income housing tax credit rules. (Code Sec. 42(j)(6))[25]

21. ¶S-3456; ¶424.50; TD ¶383,002
22. ¶S-3451; ¶424.50; TD ¶383,002
23. ¶L-15719 *et seq.*; ¶424.60; TD ¶383,004
24. ¶L-16050 *et seq.*; ¶424.85; TD ¶383,014
25. ¶L-16050 *et seq.*; ¶424.85; TD ¶383,014

¶ 2323   Enhanced oil recovery (EOR) credit—Form 8830.

The EOR credit (claimed on Form 8830) for any tax year is 15% of the taxpayer's qualified EOR costs for the tax year. (Code Sec. 43(a)) These are amounts paid or incurred for: (1) qualifying tangible property that's depreciable or amortizable; (2) qualifying tertiary injectant acquisition and use costs that qualify for a deduction under Code Sec. 193; (3) qualifying intangible drilling and development costs (IDCs) that are eligible for the Code Sec. 263(c) expensing election; and (4) Alaska gas treatment plant construction costs. (Code Sec. 43(c)(1)) The credit is phased out as the average per barrel wellhead price of domestic crude oil (reference price) for the last calendar year that ended before the tax year in question exceeds $28 (adjusted for inflation). (Code Sec. 43(b)) No credit applies for 2010.[26]

¶ 2324   Disabled access credit (DAC)—Form 8826.

An "eligible small business" (ESB) may elect (on Form 8826) to apply the DAC against income tax of 50% of the amount of "eligible access expenditures" for the tax year that's over $250 and not more than $10,250. (Code Sec. 44(a))

🅡🅘🅐 *observation:* For any tax year, the credit can't exceed $5,000 [50% of ($10,250 – $250)].

For partnerships and S corporations, the limitation applies at the entity and the individual partner or shareholder levels. (Code Sec. 44(d)(3))

An ESB for any tax year is any person who either: (1) has gross receipts of $1 million for the past tax year, net of returns and allowances, or (2) employed 30 or less full-time employees in the past tax year; an employee who is employed at least 30 hours a week for 20 or more calendar weeks in the tax year is full-time. (Code Sec. 44(b), Code Sec. 44(d)(5))

Eligible access expenditures are amounts paid or incurred so a business can comply with Americans With Disabilities Act of '90 (ADA, as in effect on Nov. 5, '90). (Code Sec. 44(c)(1)) These expenses include *only* expenses that are necessary to comply with ADA, that are paid or incurred: (1) for the purpose of removing architectural, communication, physical or transportation barriers in connection with any facility first placed in service before Nov. 6, '90, which prevent a business from being accessible to, or usable by, disabled individuals; (2) to provide qualified interpreters or other effective methods of making aurally delivered materials available to hearing impaired individuals; (3) to provide qualified readers, taped texts and other effective methods of making visually delivered materials available to visually impaired individuals; (4) to acquire or modify equipment or devices for disabled individuals; or (5) to provide other similar services, modifications, materials or equipment. (Code Sec. 44(c))[27] DAC didn't apply to software expenses to improve access to a business website.[28]

¶ 2325   Credit for producing electricity from renewable resources—Form 8835.

A renewable electricity production credit (claimed on Form 8835) is allowed for electricity produced by taxpayers from: (1) wind, (2) closed-loop biomass (see Code Sec. 45(c)(2)), (3) open-loop biomass (see Code Sec. 45(c)(3)), (4) geothermal energy, (5) small irrigation power, (6) municipal solid waste, (7) qualified hydropower production, (8) marine and hydrokinetic renewables (e.g., waves and tides), and (9) solar. Qualified facilities for (1) have to be originally placed in service before 2013. Qualified facilities for (2) through (6) must be originally placed in service before 2014. Qualified facilities for marine and hydrokinetic renewable energy must be placed in service after Oct. 2, 2008 and before 2012; small irrigation power facilities placed in service after Oct. 2, 2008 qualify as marine and hydrokinetic renewable

---

26. ¶L-17615; ¶434.01; TD ¶384,050   28. ¶L-17902; TD ¶382,502
27. ¶L-17900 *et seq.*; ¶444; TD ¶382,500 *et seq.*

energy facilities. Qualified facilities for solar energy had to be placed in service before 2006. (Code Sec. 45(a), Code Sec. 45(c), Code Sec. 45(d))[29] The electricity production credit is generally available for a 10-year period beginning on the placed-in-service date of the qualifying facility for electricity produced during that period. (Code Sec. 45(a)(2)(A)) The 10-year credit period for a qualified hydropower facility begins on the date that the qualifying efficiency improvements or additions to capacity are placed in service. (Code Sec. 45(d)(9)(C)) For open-loop biomass, geothermal and solar energy, small irrigation power, and municipal solid waste facilities placed in service before Aug. 8, 2005, a 5-year credit period applied. (Code Sec. 45(b)(4)(B))

For 2010, the credit is 2.2¢ per kilowatt hour (kW-h). (Code Sec. 45(a)) But, for electricity produced and sold at any qualifying facility using open-loop biomass, small irrigation power, landfill gas, trash, or hydropower the amount of the credit (before it's indexed for inflation for the calendar year), is reduced by 1.1¢ per kW-h. (Code Sec. 45(b)(4)) The credit is allowed for qualified electricity sold to an unrelated person (Code Sec. 45(a)(2)(B))[30] and produced from U.S. (or U.S. possession) facilities (see above). The credit is allocated to a taxpayer in proportion to his ownership interest in the gross sales from the qualifying facility. (Code Sec. 45(e))[31]

The credit is proportionately phased out when the national average price of electricity produced from the applicable renewable resource exceeds a specified, inflation-adjusted threshold price per kW-h. (Code Sec. 45(b)(1)) There is no phaseout for 2010.[32]

A credit applies for the domestic production of refined coal from a qualified facility placed in service after Oct. 22, 2004 and before 2010 or, for a facility producing steel industry fuel placed in service before 2010. (Code Sec. 45(c)(7), Code Sec. 45(d)(8)) The refined coal credit is equal to $6.27 for 2010 (as indexed for inflation) per ton of qualified refined coal and phases out as the market price of refined coal exceeds certain threshold levels. (Code Sec. 45(d)(8)) No phaseout applies for 2010.[33] A credit of $2 per barrel-of-oil equivalent amount (indexed for inflation) is allowed for "steel industry fuel" produced and sold after Sept. 30, 2009. (Code Sec. 45(d)(8))

For Indian coal sold before Jan. 1, 2013, from a qualified facility placed in service before 2009, an inflation-adjusted Indian coal production credit is allowed ($2.2 per ton for 2010). (Code Sec. 45(e)(10))[34]

Taxpayers can elect to have qualified property of certain qualified facilities treated as energy property eligible for a 30% investment credit under Code Sec. 48 (¶2311). These facilities are wind facilities placed in service in 2009 through 2012; and the other Code Sec. 45(d) facilities (other than refined or Indian coal facilities or solar facilities) placed in service in 2009 through 2013 that are otherwise eligible for the Code Sec. 45 credit, for which no such credit has been allowed. Qualified property is tangible property or other tangible property (not including a building or its structural components) for which depreciation (or amortization) is allowable but only if the property is used as an integral part of the qualified facility. (Code Sec. 48(a)(5)) The irrevocable election (on Form 3468) is made on a timely filed return (including extensions) for the tax year in which the facility is placed in service.[35]

No Code Sec. 45 credit is allowed for energy property for which a grant is made by the Energy Secretary; if the credit is allowed, recapture applies. The basis of the property is reduced by 50% of the amount of the grant. (Code Sec. 48(d), ARRA § 1603)[36]

29. ¶L-17751 *et seq.*; ¶454; TD ¶384,054
30. ¶L-17754; ¶454; TD ¶384,054
31. ¶L-17755; ¶454; TD ¶384,055
32. ¶L-17760 *et seq.*; ¶454; TD ¶384,056
33. ¶L-17771.7B; ¶454.16; TD ¶384,054.1
34. ¶L-17771.8; ¶454.17; TD ¶384,054.1
35. ¶L-16401.1; ¶484.01; TD ¶381,601.1
36. ¶L-17773; ¶454.19; TD ¶384,058.1

¶ 2326   Pre-2010 empowerment zone employment credit—Form 8844.

Before 2010, employers can claim (on Form 8844) an empowerment zone employment credit for any tax year equal to 20% of the qualified zone wages paid or incurred during the calendar year that ends with or within that tax year. (Code Sec. 1396(a), Code Sec. 1400(d)) The amount of qualified zone wages taken into account for each employee can't exceed $15,000 for a calendar year (Code Sec. 1396(c)(2)) Thus, the credit can't exceed $3,000 per qualified employee.[37] Qualified zone wages don't include wages taken into account for the work opportunity tax credit (WOTC, ¶2315), and the $15,000 maximum amount above is reduced by the amount of wages taken into account for the WOTC. (Code Sec. 1396(c)(3))[38] The credit reduces an employer's wage deduction for the year. (Code Sec. 280C(a))[39]

For periods ending before 2010 (Code Sec. 1400(f)), qualified employers can claim a DC Zone wage credit equal to 20% of qualified wages (up to $15,000 per year) paid to employees residing in the District of Columbia and employed in the DC Enterprise Zone. (Code Sec. 1400(d))[40]

✔caution: Check http://ria.thomsonreuters.com/federaltaxhandbook to see if the credits have been extended.

¶ 2327   Pre-2010 renewal community employment credit—Form 8844.

For wages paid or incurred before 2010, a "renewal community" (as designated under Code Sec. 1400E) is treated, subject to modifications, as an "empowerment zone" for purposes of Code Sec. 1396 (which provides an employment credit for certain wages paid by employers in empowerment zones, see ¶2326). (Code Sec. 1400H(a))

In applying Code Sec. 1396 to renewal communities, (1) the credit is 15% of qualified wages, and (2) the maximum amount of qualified wages that can be used to figure the credit is $10,000 per employee per year. (Code Sec. 1400H(b)) Qualified wages for purposes of the renewal community employment credit don't include amounts taken into account in figuring the work opportunity credit, and the $10,000 of maximum wages per qualified employee is reduced by the amount of wages used to figure either credit.[41]

✔caution: Check http://ria.thomsonreuters.com/federaltaxhandbook to see if the credit has been extended.

¶ 2328   Pre-2010 Indian employment credit—Form 8845.

For tax years beginning before 2010 (Code Sec. 45A(f)),[42] the Indian employment credit (claimed on Form 8845) is 20% of the excess, if any, of the sum of qualified wages and qualified employee health insurance costs (not in excess of $20,000 per employee) paid or incurred (other than paid under salary reduction arrangements) to qualified employees (enrolled Indian tribe members and their spouses who meet certain requirements) during the tax year (Code Sec. 45A(a)(1), Code Sec. 45A(b)(2)) over the sum of these same costs paid or incurred in calendar year '93—determined as if the Indian employment credit had been in effect in '93. (Code Sec. 45A(a)(2); Code Sec. 45A(c)) Tax credits claimed for certain terminated employees are recaptured. (Code Sec. 45A(d)) Deductions for wages and health insurance costs are reduced by the credit. (Code Sec. 280C(a))

✔caution: Check http://ria.thomsonreuters.com/federaltaxhandbook to see if the credit has been extended.

---

37. ¶L-15630 *et seq.*; ¶13,964; TD ¶384,021
38. ¶L-15632; ¶13,964; TD ¶384,024
39. ¶L-15639.2; ¶13,964; TD ¶384,030

40. ¶L-15640; ¶14,004.01
41. ¶L-15661; ¶14,00H4; TD ¶384,601
42. ¶L-15670 *et seq.*; ¶45A4; TD ¶384,039

¶ 2329   FICA tip credit—Form 8846.

A food and beverage establishment is allowed a credit (on Form 8846) for the amount of the employer's FICA tax obligation (7.65%) attributable to employee tips received for providing, delivering, or serving food or beverages (whether or not the tips are reported as required by Code Sec. 6053). However, no credit is given for tips used to meet the federal minimum wage rate. (Code Sec. 45B) Employers determine their Code Sec. 45B credit using the minimum wage in effect on Jan. 1, 2007 (Code Sec. 45B(b)(1)) (i.e., $5.15).[43] No deduction is allowed for any amount taken into account in determining the FICA tip credit. (Code Sec. 45B(c)) A taxpayer can elect out of the credit for any tax year. (Code Sec. 45B(d))[44]

¶ 2330   Qualified clinical testing expense ("orphan drug") credit—Form 8820.

A taxpayer that incurs qualified clinical testing expenses (QCTEs) for drugs for rare diseases may claim (on Form 8820) a credit equal to 50% of those expenses for the tax year. (Code Sec. 45C)[45] QCTEs are amounts which, with certain modifications, would qualify as qualified research expenses for the research credit (¶2320). (Code Sec. 45C(b)(1))

¶ 2331   Pre-2010 new markets tax credit—Form 8874.

Before 2010, a "new markets tax credit" applies for qualified equity investments to acquire stock in a community development entity (CDE). Nationally, the maximum annual amount of qualifying equity investments was capped at $5 billion for 2009. (Code Sec. 45D) A CDE is any domestic corporation or partnership (1) whose primary mission is serving or providing investment capital for low-income communities or low-income persons, (2) that maintains accountability to residents of low-income communities through representation on governing or advisory boards of the CDE, and (3) is certified by Treasury as an eligible CDE. A qualified equity investment is stock or a similar equity interest acquired directly from a CDE for cash. Substantially all (at least 85%, reduced to 75% for the final year of the 7-year credit period) of the cash must be used by the CDE to make investments in, or loans to, qualified active businesses located in low-income communities or certain financial services to businesses and residents in low-income communities. A qualified equity investment made by an LLC (classified as a partnership) can include cash from a nonrecourse loan or a recourse loan to the LLC that the LLC invests as equity in a qualified CDE, where the loan is indebtedness for federal income tax purposes. (Code Sec. 45D; Reg § 1.45D-1(c)(5))[46]

The new markets tax credit (claimed on Form 8874) is: (a) 5% for the year in which the equity interest is purchased from the CDE and for the first two anniversary dates after the purchase (for a total credit of 15%), *plus* (b) 6% on each anniversary date thereafter for the following 4 years (for a total of 24%).[47] The credit is recaptured if the entity fails to continue to be a CDE or the interest is redeemed within seven years, unless it is permitted to correct its failure, and does so. (Code Sec. 45D(g); Reg § 1.45D-1(e))[48]

caution: Check http://ria.thomsonreuters.com/federaltaxhandbook to see if the credit has been extended.

¶ 2332   Pre-2011 credit for employer-provided child care—Form 8882.

A tax credit for 'employer-provided child care' (Code Sec. 45F(a)) applies for 2010. It is equal to the sum of the following expenses (up to $150,000) for the tax year: Code

43. ¶L-17860 *et seq.*; ¶45B4; TD ¶382,000 *et seq.*
44. ¶L-17860 *et seq.*; ¶45B4; TD ¶382,005
45. ¶L-15615 *et seq.*; ¶45C4

46. ¶L-17920 *et seq.*; ¶L-17924; ¶45D4 *et seq.*; TD ¶384,700 *et seq.*
47. ¶L-17922; ¶45D4; TD ¶384,702
48. ¶L-17928; ¶45D4.10; TD ¶384,713

Sec. 45F(b))[49]

(1) 25% of qualified child care expenses, which are expenses to buy, build, rehabilitate, or expand property to be used as part of an employer's qualified child care facility, for which a deduction for depreciation (or amortization) is allowable, and which isn't part of the taxpayer's (or an employee's) principal residence. Qualifying child care expenses also include operating costs of a taxpayer's qualified child care facility (including costs related to employee training, scholarship programs, and to providing increased compensation to employees with higher levels of child care training), and amounts paid under a contract with a qualified child care facility to provide child care services to the taxpayer's employees. (Code Sec. 45F(c)(1)(A)) Qualified child care expenses don't include expenses in excess of the FMV of the care. (Code Sec. 45F(c)(1)(B))

(2) 10% of qualified child care resource and referral expenses (i.e., amounts paid or incurred under a contract to provide child care resource and referral services to an employee).[50]

Generally, for purposes of (1), above, a qualified child care facility is one principally used to provide child care assistance, and which meets the requirements of the state or local government in which it is located, including its licensing as a child care facility. (Code Sec. 45F(c)(2)(A)) The facility must be open to the taxpayer's employees during the tax year, and, if it is the taxpayer's principal trade or business, at least 30% of its enrollees must be the dependents of the taxpayer's employees.[1]

caution: For EGTRRA sunset rules, see ¶1114.

The provision of child care resource and referral services or facilities can't discriminate in favor of highly compensated employees (within the meaning of Code Sec. 414(q)) (see ¶4326). (Code Sec. 45F(c)(2)(B), Code Sec. 45F(c)(3))[2]

A taxpayer claiming a Code Sec. 45F credit for acquiring, constructing, rehabilitating, or expanding a qualified child care facility must reduce its basis in the facility by the amount of the credit. (Code Sec. 45F(f)(1)(A))[3] No deduction or credit is allowed for any amount taken into account in determining Code Sec. 45F credit. (Code Sec. 45F(f)(2))[4]

Recapture rules apply for the first 10 years after the facility is placed in service. (Code Sec. 45F(d))[5]

For purposes of the credit, all persons treated as one employer under Code Sec. 52(a) or Code Sec. 52(b) are treated as one taxpayer. Regs are to address credit allocations between an estate or trust and its beneficiaries, and among partners of a partnership. (Code Sec. 45F(e))[67]

¶ 2333 Small employer pension plan startup credit—Form 8881.

Eligible small employers that adopt a new qualified defined benefit or defined contribution plan (including a Code Sec. 401(k) plan, SIMPLE plan, or SEP) may claim a credit. The credit equals 50% of administrative and retirement-related education expenses for the plan for each of the first three plan years, with a maximum credit of $500 for each year. The first credit year is the tax year that includes the date the plan becomes effective, or, electively, the preceding tax year. (Code Sec. 45E(a), Code Sec. 45E(b), Code Sec. 45E(d)(3))[8]

The pension plan startup credit is available only to businesses that did not employ, in the preceding year, more than 100 employees with compensation of at least $5,000. But, an employer isn't an eligible employer if, during the three-tax year period immediately preceding the first tax year for which the credit is otherwise allowable, it or any member of any

49. ¶L-17872; ¶45F4; TD ¶382,102
50. ¶L-17870 *et seq.*; ¶45F4; TD ¶382,100 *et seq.*
1. ¶L-17874; ¶45F4; TD ¶382,104
2. ¶L-17875; ¶45F4; TD ¶382,105
3. ¶L-17876; ¶45F4; TD ¶382,106
4. ¶L-17877; ¶45F4; TD ¶382,107
5. ¶L-17878; ¶45F4.01; TD ¶382,108
6. ¶L-17879; TD ¶382,109
7. ¶L-17870; ¶45F4; TD ¶382,100
8. ¶L-15690 *et seq.*; ¶45E4; TD ¶384,060 *et seq.*

controlled group including the employer (or any predecessor of either) established or maintained a qualified employer plan to which contributions were made, or benefits were accrued, for substantially the same employees that are in the qualified employer plan. (Code Sec. 45E(c)(2))[9] For purposes of Code Sec. 45E, all persons treated as a single employer under Code Sec. 52(a) or Code Sec. 52(b) or Code Sec. 414(m) or Code Sec. 414(o) are treated as one taxpayer. (Code Sec. 45E(e)(1))[10] To be eligible for the credit, the plan must cover at least one nonhighly compensated employee. If the credit is for the cost of a payroll-deduction IRA plan, it must be made available to all employees who have worked with the employer for at least three months. (Code Sec. 45E(d)(1))[11]

No deduction is allowed for that portion of the qualified startup costs paid or incurred for the tax year which is equal to the credit. (Code Sec. 45E(e)(2))[12] An eligible employer may elect not to have the credit apply for any tax year. (Code Sec. 45E(e)(3))[13]

¶ 2334   Small employer health insurance credit–Forms 8941; 990-T.

Subject to a phaseout (see below), an eligible small employer (ESE) may claim a credit (on Form 8941) equal to a percentage (35% in the initial phase—tax years beginning in 2010 to 2013; 50% in tax years beginning after 2013) of nonelective contributions for health insurance for its employees. (Code Sec. 45R) An ESE is generally an employer with no more than 25 full-time equivalent employees (FTEs) employed during its tax year, and whose employees have average annual wages of no more than $50,000. (Code Sec. 45R(d))

The FTEs of an ESE are determined by dividing the total hours of service (up to 2,080 hours of service determined by an employee's actual hours of service, a days-worked equivalency method, or a weeks-worked equivalency method) by 2,080. (Code Sec. 45R(d)) Average annual wages are determined by dividing (a) total wages (as defined for FICA purposes, without regard to the wage base limitation) paid to employees during the ESE's tax year by (b) the number of the FTEs for the year. The result is rounded down to the nearest $1,000 (if not otherwise a multiple of $1,000). (Code Sec. 45R(d)(3)(A), Code Sec. 45R(e)(4)) Aggregation rules apply in determining ESE status. (Code Sec. 45R(b))[14]

Self-employed individuals, including partners and sole proprietors, 2% S corporation shareholders, and 5% owners of the employer (within the meaning of Code Sec. 416(i)(1)(B)(i)): (1) aren't treated as employees; (2) their wages or hours are not counted in determining either the number of FTEs or the amount of average annual wages; and (3) premiums paid on their behalf are not counted in determining the credit. (Code Sec. 45R(e))

In the initial phase, an ESE has to contribute at least 50% of the cost of an employee's insurance premiums under a contribution arrangement. But, for a tax year beginning in 2010, an employer that pays an amount equal to at least 50% of the premium for single (employee-only) coverage for each employee enrolled in coverage is deemed to satisfy the uniformity requirement (under Code Sec. 45R(d)(4)) for a qualifying arrangement, even if the employer doesn't pay the same percentage of the premium for each employee.[15]

In the initial phase, the credit equals the lesser of the following two amounts multiplied by the percentage (described above):

(1) total nonelective contributions the ESE made on behalf of the FTEs during the tax year for qualifying health coverage. (Code Sec. 45R(b)) Qualifying health insurance for claiming the credit in the initial phase is health insurance coverage within the meaning of Code Sec. 9832(b)(1) (generally health insurance coverage bought from a state licensed insurance company). (Code Sec. 45R(g)(2))

9. ¶L-15692; ¶45E4; TD ¶384,202
10. ¶L-15699.1; TD ¶384,202
11. ¶L-15694; TD ¶384,202
12. ¶L-15698; ¶45E4; TD ¶384,208

13. ¶L-15699; ¶45E4; TD ¶384,209
14. ¶L-15682 *et seq.*; ¶45R4.02; TD ¶384,302
15. ¶L-15689.5 *et seq.*; ¶45R4.02; TD ¶384,302

(2) total nonelective contributions the ESE would have paid if each employee were enrolled in a plan with a premium equal to the average premium for the small group market in the state (or in an area in the state) in which the employer is offering health insurance coverage.[16] (Code Sec. 45R(b))

In tax years beginning after 2013, an ESE has to offer insurance through an exchange and an ESE can only claim the credit for two consecutive tax years. (Code Sec. 45R(d)(4); Code Sec. 45R(e)(2))

Generally, state tax credits and payments to an ESE do not reduce the credit, and state direct payments to an insurance company are treated as paid on an ESE's behalf. But, in no event can the amount of the credit exceed the amount of an ESE's net premium payments.[17]

The applicable percentage for *tax-exempt ESEs* is 25% for 2010 to 2013 and 35% after 2013. For tax-exempt ESEs, the credit is a refundable tax credit (claimed on Form 990-T) limited to the amount of the employer's payroll taxes (income tax and Medicare tax withheld from employees' wages and the employer share of Medicare tax on employees' wages) during the calendar year in which the tax year begins. (Code Sec. 45R(b); Code Sec. 45R(f))

The credit reduces the ESE's Code Sec. 162 deduction. (Code Sec. 45R(e)(5))[18]

¶ 2335 Pre-2010 biodiesel fuel credit—Form 8864.

For fuels produced and sold or used before 2010 (Code Sec. 40A(g)), a taxpayer can claim a credit (on Form 8864) equal to the sum of: (1) a biodiesel mixture credit of $1 per gallon of biodiesel used in the production of a qualified biodiesel mixture; (2) a biodiesel credit of $1 per gallon of biodiesel, not in a mixture, that's used as a fuel in the taxpayer's trade or business, or sold at retail and placed in a vehicle fuel tank; and (3) for an eligible small agri-biodiesel producer, a small agri-biodiesel producer credit of 10¢ per gallon of agri-biodiesel (up to a 15,000,000 gallon maximum) that is: (a) used by the producer or sold by the producer for use, in the production of a qualified biodiesel mixture in a trade or business or as fuel in a trade or business, or (b) sold at retail and placed in a vehicle fuel tank by the producer or a person buying from the producer. (Code Sec. 40A(a), Code Sec. 40A(b))[19] The credit is inapplicable to fuel produced outside the U.S. for use outside the U.S. (Code Sec. 40A(d)(5)) Renewable diesel is treated like biodiesel. (Code Sec. 40A(f))[20]

⚠️*caution:* Check http://ria.thomsonreuters.com/federaltaxhandbook to see if the credit has been extended.

¶ 2336 Pre-2010 low sulfur diesel fuel production credit—Form 8896.

For qualified costs paid or incurred during the applicable period (i.e., before 2010) (Code Sec. 45H(c)(4)), small business refiners can claim (on Form 8896) a credit of 5¢ per gallon of low sulfur diesel fuel (diesel fuel with sulfur content of 15 parts per million) or less (Code Sec. 45H(c)(5)), to a maximum of 25% of the refiner's qualified capital costs, reduced by the facility's aggregate low sulfur diesel fuel credits for all earlier tax years. (Code Sec. 45H(a), Code Sec. 45H(b)(1)) For a small business refiner with average daily domestic refinery runs for the 1-year period ending on Dec. 31, 2002 of more than 155,000 barrels, the 25% is reduced (not below zero) by the product of the above percentage (before application of this rule) and the ratio of the excess over 155,000 barrels to 50,000 barrels. (Code Sec. 45H(b)(2))[21]

⚠️*caution:* Check http://ria.thomsonreuters.com/federaltaxhandbook to see if the credit has been extended.

---

16. ¶L-15689.8A; ¶45R4.06
17. ¶L-15689.6B; ¶45R4.06
18. ¶L-15681; ¶45R4; TD ¶384,301

19. ¶L-17570; ¶40A4; TD ¶382,400
20. ¶L-17585; ¶40A4.05; TD ¶382,409
21. ¶L-17550; ¶45H4; TD ¶382,300

¶ 2337   Pre-2010 new energy efficient home credit—Form 8908.

For homes acquired before 2010, eligible contractors (including manufacturers of manufactured homes) that construct new energy-efficient homes can qualify for a $2,000 or $1,000 credit (claimed on Form 8908) per qualifying home. (Code Sec. 45L(a), Code Sec. 45L(g))[22] A structure qualifies for the credit if it meets specific energy saving requirements, and its construction, which includes substantial reconstruction and rehabilitation, is substantially completed after Aug. 8, 2005. It must be located in the U.S. (Code Sec. 45L(a), Code Sec. 45L(b)(2))[23] A property's basis is reduced by the amount of credit. (Code Sec. 45L(e))[24]

⚠️*caution:* Check http://ria.thomsonreuters.com/federaltaxhandbook to see if the credit has been extended.

A home (including a manufactured one) qualifies for the $2,000 credit if it is certified to have a projected 50% reduction in the level of annual heating and cooling energy consumption, compared to comparable dwellings, and at least ⅕ of the 50% reduction is from building envelope component improvements—insulation materials or systems specifically and primarily designed to reduce heat loss or gain, exterior windows (including skylights), doors, and any duct sealing and infiltration reduction measures. (Code Sec. 45L(a)(2), Code Sec. 45L(c))[25]

A manufactured home qualifies for a $1,000 credit if it is either (1) certified to have a projected 30% reduction in the level of annual heating and cooling energy consumption, compared to comparable dwellings, and its building envelope component improvements account for at least one-third of the 30% reduction, or (2) it meets the requirements under the Energy Star Labeled Homes program. (Code Sec. 45L(a)(2), Code Sec. 45L(c)(3))[26]

¶ 2338   Pre-2011 energy efficient appliance credit—Form 8909.

Manufacturers can qualify for a credit for producing energy efficient dishwashers, clothes washers, and refrigerators produced by the taxpayer during the calendar year in the U.S. The credit (claimed on Form 8909) depends on the type of appliance and how much energy it saves (for dishwashers: $75 for 2009 through 2010; for clothes washers: $150 to $250 for 2009 through 2010 (commercial); and for refrigerators: $100 to $200 for 2009 through 2010) (Code Sec. 45M(b)) The aggregate credit amount allowed to a taxpayer for all tax years beginning after 2007 isn't allowed to exceed $75 million, with an exception for the refrigerator credit and the clothes washer credit. (Code Sec. 45M(e))[27]

⚠️*caution:* Check http://ria.thomsonreuters.com/federaltaxhandbook to see if the credit has been extended.

¶ 2339   Pre-2010 differential wage payment credit—Form 8932.

For payments made before 2010 (Code Sec. 45P(f)), eligible small business employers (ESBEs) that pay differential wages (¶3004) to a qualified employee can claim a credit (on Form 8932) equal to 20% of up to $20,000 of differential pay made to a qualified employee during the tax year. (Code Sec. 45P) A qualified employee is one who was an employee for the 91-day period immediately before the period for which any differential wage payment is made. (Code Sec. 45P(b)(2)) An ESBE is one that: (1) employed on average less than 50 employees on business days during the tax year; and (2) under a written plan, provides eligible differential wage payments to each of its qualified employees. Taxpayers under common control are aggregated when determining if a taxpayer is an ESBE. (Code Sec. 45P(b)(3))

---

22. ¶L-17940; ¶45L4; TD ¶569,570
23. ¶L-17944; ¶45L4; TD ¶569,574
24. ¶L-17949.3; ¶45L4; TD ¶569,579.1

25. ¶L-17947; ¶45L4; TD ¶569,575
26. ¶L-17949; ¶45L4; TD ¶569,577
27. ¶L-17950; ¶45M4; TD ¶569,580

The credit can't be claimed by a taxpayer that has failed to comply with the employment and reemployment rights of members of the uniformed services (as provided under Chapter 43 of Title 38 of the United States Code). (Code Sec. 45P(d)) No deduction may be taken for that part of compensation which is equal to the credit, and the amount of any otherwise allowable income tax credit for compensation paid to an employee must be reduced by the differential wage payment credit allowed for the employee. (Code Sec. 280C(a))[28]

caution: Check http://ria.thomsonreuters.com/federaltaxhandbook to see if the credit has been extended.

¶ 2340 Agricultural chemicals security tax credit—Form 8931.

For expenses paid or incurred before Jan. 1, 2013, a taxpayer can claim (on Form 8931) a 30% credit for qualified chemical security expenditures for the tax year with respect to eligible agricultural businesses. The credit is limited to $100,000 per facility reduced by the aggregate amount of the credits allowed for the facility in the prior 5 years. In addition, each taxpayer's annual credit is limited to $2,000,000. Any deduction for the security expenditure is reduced by the amount of the credit claimed. (Code Sec. 45O)[29]

¶ 2341 Alternate (nonconventional source) fuel production credit–Form 8907.

A credit of $3 (adjusted for inflation), multiplied by the barrel of oil equivalent (BOE) of certain qualified fuels, is allowed (claimed on Form 8907), subject to a phaseout, for producing fuel from a nonconventional source. Qualified fuels include certain gas from biomass or liquid, gaseous or solid synthetic fuels from coal (including lignite) produced by a facility placed in service before July 1, '98, and sold before Jan. 1, 2008. (Code Sec. 45K(a))[30] For 2009, there is also $3.40 (indexed for inflation) per BOE allowed for certain coke and coke gas (other than that produced from petroleum based products) produced and sold after Dec. 31, 2005 at a facility placed in service before Jan. 1, '93 or after June 30, '98 and before Jan. 1, 2010. The credit for coke and coke gas isn't subject to a phaseout. The amount of credit-eligible coke produced can't exceed an average BOE of 4,000 barrels a day. (Code Sec. 45K(g))[31]

¶ 2342 Personal (Refundable and Nonrefundable) Credits.

Taxpayers, whether or not in business, may qualify for one or more personal credits. Some credits are refundable—i.e., the excess of the credit over tax liability is refunded to the taxpayer, some are partly refundable, and some are nonrefundable.

The *refundable* credits are:

... Making Work Pay Credit (MWPC) for 2010, see ¶2343;

... Earned income credit (EIC), see ¶2344 *et seq.*;

... Health coverage tax credit for displaced workers and PBGC pensionees, see ¶2350;

... Credit for income tax withheld, see ¶2351;

... Credit for excess social security tax withheld, see ¶2352;

... Credit for adoption expenses, see ¶2359;

... Child tax credit (partly refundable), see ¶2361;

... First-time homebuyer credit for purchases before Oct. 1, 2010, see ¶2369;

... Alternative minimum tax (AMT) refundable credit for individuals, see ¶2373;

... American opportunity tax credit (AOTC)/Hope credit (partly refundable), see ¶2202;

... Credit for capital gain tax paid by an RIC, see ¶4201; and

28. ¶L-15676; ¶45P4
29. ¶L-18300; ¶45O4; TD ¶384,064
30. ¶L-17700 *et seq.*; ¶45K4; TD ¶396,001
31. ¶L-17706.1; ¶45K4; TD ¶396,001

. . . Credit for excise tax on certain nontaxable uses of fuels. (Code Sec. 6420, Code Sec. 6421, Code Sec. 6427)

The *nonrefundable* credits are:

- Credit for the elderly and the permanently and totally disabled, see ¶2353;
- Credit for child and dependent care expenses, see ¶2354 *et seq.*;
- Child tax credit (but see above), see ¶2360;
- Credit for certain home mortgage interest, see ¶2362;
- AOTC/Hope credit (but see above) and Lifetime Learning credit, see ¶2201 *et seq.*;
- Nonbusiness energy property credit, see ¶2363;
- Residential energy efficient property credit, see ¶2364;
- Alternative motor vehicle credit, see ¶2365;
- Credit for alternative fuel vehicle refueling property, see ¶2366;
- New qualified plug-in electric drive motor vehicles (NQPEDMV) credit, see ¶2367;
- Qualified plug-in electric vehicle (QPEV) credit, see ¶2367;
- First-time DC homebuyer credit (before 2010), see ¶2368;
- "Saver's" credit for elective deferrals and IRA contributions, see ¶2371;
- AMT credit, see ¶2373;
- Credit for qualified tax credit bonds (QTCBs) (refundable option), see ¶2374; and
- Credit for Build America Bonds (refundable option), see ¶2374.

For the limit on the combined amount of certain personal nonrefundable credits, see ¶2372.

¶ 2343 Making Work Pay Credit (MWPC) for 2010—Schedule M.

For tax years beginning in 2010, eligible individuals are allowed a refundable MWPC equal to the *lesser* of (1) 6.2% of earned income (below) or (2) $400 ($800 for a joint return). (Code Sec. 36A(a)) An eligible individual is any individual who isn't a nonresident alien (or an estate or trust) and can't be claimed as a dependent by another. (Code Sec. 36A(d)(1)(A))[32]

Earned income (as defined at ¶2345) doesn't include net earnings from self-employment that aren't included in computing taxable income, but does include nontaxable combat pay (under Code Sec. 112, see ¶1225). (Code Sec. 36A(d)(2))[33]

The credit phases out at a rate of 2% of modified AGI (AGI increased by excluded foreign, possession, and Puerto Rico income) above $75,000 ($150,000 for joint returns). (Code Sec. 36A(b))[34]

⊘*observation:* The credit is zero at modified AGI of $95,000 ($190,000 for joint returns).

Most workers receive the credit during the year through reduced income tax withholding (under the IRS Pub No. 15-T tables).[35] But the credit still must be claimed on Schedule M, attached to Form 1040 or Form 1040A. The social security number of the taxpayer (of at least one spouse, for joint returns) must be included. (Code Sec. 36A(d)(1)(B))[36]

¶ 2344 Earned income credit—overview—Schedule EIC.

An eligible individual (¶2346) is allowed an earned income credit (EIC) equal to the credit percentage of earned income (up to an "earned income amount") for the tax year. (Code Sec. 32(a)(1)) The EIC for a tax year (determined under IRS tables) can't be more than the

---

32. ¶A-4290 *et seq.*; ¶36A4; TD ¶568,870 *et seq.*
33. ¶A-4291; ¶36A4; TD ¶568,871
34. ¶A-4293; ¶36A4; TD ¶568,873

35. ¶A-4294; ¶36A4; TD ¶568,874
36. ¶A-4291; ¶36A4; TD ¶568,871

excess (if any) of (1) the credit percentage of the earned income amount, over (2) the phaseout percentage of AGI (or earned income, if greater) over a phaseout amount. (Code Sec. 32(a)(2)) For 2010, these amounts are (but see below for joint return phaseouts):[37]

Qualifying Children:	The Credit % is:	The Earned Income Amount is:	The Phaseout % is:	The Phaseout Amount is:
FOR 2010				
No qualifying children	7.65%	$ 5,980	7.65%	$ 7,480
1 qualifying child	34%	$ 8,970	15.98%	$16,450
2 qualifying children	40%	$12,590	21.06%	$16,450
3 or more qualifying children	45%	$12,590	21.06%	$16,450

The higher credit percentage for 3 or more qualifying children applies for 2010. (Code Sec. 32(b)(3)(A))[38]

The joint return phaseout amounts for 2010 are $5,000 above the thresholds for other taxpayers (and increased for inflation) Code Sec. 32(b)(3)(B)—i.e., $12,490 for no qualifying children, and $21,460 for one or more qualifying children.[39]

🅡 *caution:* For EGTRRA sunset rules, see ¶1114.

The maximum EIC for 2010 is $457 (no qualifying children), $3,059 (one qualifying child), $5,036 (two qualifying children), or $5,666 (three or more qualifying children.[40] It's completely phased out at the following amounts of earned income (or AGI, if greater):

. . . no qualifying children, $13,460 ($18,470 for joint filers),

. . . one qualifying child, $35,535 ($40,545 for joint filers), and

. . . two qualifying children, $40,363 ($45,373 for joint filers).

. . . three or more qualifying children, $43,352 ($48,362 for joint filers).[41]

Taxpayers claiming the credit must file Form 1040 or Form 1040A (or Form 1040EZ if no qualifying child) and attach Schedule EIC.[42] No EIC is allowed if the taxpayer has excess disqualified income, see ¶2347.

The EIC is refundable.[43] For advance payment before 2011, see ¶2349.

No EIC is allowed for 10 years after a year in which the credit was claimed fraudulently (2 years for erroneously claimed credit due to reckless or intentional disregard of the rules). If the EIC is denied under deficiency procedures, including administrative procedures (but not mathematical or clerical errors), no credit is allowed for any later tax year unless the taxpayer provides information IRS requires to demonstrate eligibility (Code Sec. 32(k); Reg § 1.32-3(b)) (use Form 8862). (Reg § 1.32-3(c))[44] For due diligence requirements for return preparers, see ¶4889.

¶ 2345   Earned income defined for EIC purposes.

Earned income for EIC purposes includes wages, salaries, tips, and other employee compensation, but only if those amounts are includible in gross income for the tax year; plus net earnings from self-employment less the Code Sec. 164(f) deduction for half of self-employment tax (¶1755), for the year. (Code Sec. 32(c)(2)(A)) Taxpayers may elect to treat nontaxable combat pay (¶1225) as earned income. (Code Sec. 32(c)(2)(B)(vi))[45]

37. ¶A-4201 *et seq.*; ¶324 *et seq.*; TD ¶569,001 *et seq.*
38. ¶A-4201; ¶324.01; TD ¶569,001
39. ¶A-4202; ¶324.01; TD ¶569,002
40. ¶A-4201; ¶324.01; TD ¶569,001
41. ¶A-4202

42. ¶A-4201; ¶324.01; TD ¶569,001
43. ¶A-4201; ¶324.01; TD ¶569,001
44. ¶A-4205 *et seq.*; ¶324.02; TD ¶569,007
45. ¶A-4222 *et seq.*; ¶324.05; TD ¶569,023 *et seq.*

Earned income is reduced by any net loss in earnings from self-employment (Reg § 1.32-2(c)(2)) and *doesn't* include any amount received as a pension or an annuity (including social security or VA benefits), any amount subject to the 30% withholding tax on U.S. income (not connected with U.S. business) of nonresident alien individuals (Code Sec. 32(c)(2)(B)), unemployment or worker's compensation (Reg § 1.32-2(c)(2)), amounts earned while an inmate in a penal institution, or amounts received for "workfare" services to the extent subsidized by a state program. (Code Sec. 32(c)(2)(B)(iv)) Earned income is determined without regard to community property laws. (Code Sec. 32(c)(2))[46]

¶ 2346 Eligible individual defined for EIC purposes.

An individual who has a "qualifying child" (¶2348) for the tax year is an eligible individual. (Code Sec. 32(c)(1)(A)(i)) An individual who doesn't have a qualifying child for the tax year is an eligible individual *if*:

. . . his principal place of abode is in the U.S. for more than half the tax year (U.S. Armed Forces personnel are considered to have a U.S. abode while they're stationed outside the U.S. on extended active duty (Code Sec. 32(c)(4))),

. . . either he or his spouse (if any) is older than 24 but younger than 65 before the end of the tax year, *and*

. . . he can't be claimed as another's dependent for a tax year beginning in the same calendar year as his tax year. (Code Sec. 32(c)(1)(A)(ii))[47]

An individual can't be an eligible individual for a tax year if he: is another's qualifying child (¶2348) (Code Sec. 32(c)(1)(B)); elects to exclude foreign earned income (¶4612) (Code Sec. 32(c)(1)(C)); or is a nonresident alien unless he elects under Code Sec. 6013(g) or Code Sec. 6013(h) to be treated as a U.S. resident. (Code Sec. 32(c)(1)(D))[48]

Married individuals are eligible for only one EIC on their combined earned income and must file a joint return to claim the credit. (Code Sec. 32(d))[49]

Except for short-period returns due to an individual's death, only individuals filing a return for a full 12-month year can claim the credit. (Code Sec. 32(e))[50]

A person can't be an eligible individual unless he includes his (and his spouse's) taxpayer identification number (TIN, social security number, not an individual taxpayer identification number (ITIN) or adoption taxpayer identification number (ATIN)) and the name, age, and TIN (not ITIN or ATIN) of any qualifying child on the return for the tax year. (Code Sec. 32(m), Code Sec. 32(c)(1)(E), Code Sec. 32(c)(1)(F), Code Sec. 32(c)(3)(D))[1]

¶ 2347 No EIC where disqualified income is more than $3,100 in 2010.

A taxpayer with "disqualified income" over $3,100 in 2010 can't claim the earned income credit (EIC). (Code Sec. 32(i)(1))[2] Disqualified income means:

(1) interest or dividends to the extent includible in gross income for the year (Code Sec. 32(i)(2)(A));

(2) tax-exempt interest (as defined for return disclosure rules) received or accrued in the year (Code Sec. 32(i)(2)(B));

(3) the excess (if any) of (a) gross income from nonbusiness rents or royalties, over (b) the sum of noninterest deductions clearly and directly allocable to that gross income plus properly allocable interest deductions (Code Sec. 32(i)(2)(C));

---

46. ¶A-4222 *et seq.*; ¶324.05; TD ¶569,023 *et seq.*
47. ¶A-4209, A-4217; ¶324.02; TD ¶569,009, 569,017
48. ¶A-4209; ¶324.02; TD ¶569,009
49. ¶A-4221; ¶324.02; TD ¶569,022

50. ¶A-4209; ¶324.02; TD ¶569,009
1. ¶A-4219; ¶324.02; TD ¶569,020
2. ¶A-4205; ¶324.02; TD ¶569,004

(4) capital gain net income for the year (but not gain treated as long-term capital gain under Code Sec. 1231(a)(1), ¶2684) (Code Sec. 32(i)(2)(D)); and

(5) the excess, if any, of total income from all passive activities for the year (without regard to amounts otherwise included in earned income, or other disqualified income) over total losses from all passive activities for the year (as so determined). (Code Sec. 32(i)(2)(E))[3]

¶ 2348   Qualifying child defined for EIC purposes.

A "qualifying child" for EIC purposes means a qualifying child of the taxpayer, as defined for the dependency exemption in Code Sec. 152(c) (¶3120) but without the requirement that the child not have provided more than half his own support, and without regard to a custodial parent's release of the dependency exemption (¶3126). (Code Sec. 32(c)(3)(A))[4]

¶ 2349   Advance payment of EIC before 2011—Form W-5.

For tax years beginning before Jan. 1, 2011, an employee who is eligible for the EIC and has a qualifying child (¶2348) may receive advance payment of the credit, by providing the employer with a Form W-5. (Code Sec. 3507(b); Reg § 31.3507-2) The advance payment amount (from IRS tables), added to the employee's paycheck (but reflected separately on the Form W-2Code Sec. 6051(a)(7)),[5] depends on his earnings in the pay period (Code Sec. 3507(c)(1))[6] He still must file a return to claim the credit. (Code Sec. 6012(a)(8))[7] Advance payments over the allowed EIC are recaptured. (Code Sec. 32(g))[8]

¶ 2350   Refundable credit for health insurance costs of trade-displaced workers and PBGC pension recipients—Form 8885.

An "eligible individual" may claim (file Form 8885 with Form 1040) a refundable health coverage tax credit (HCTC) equal to 80% (65% for "coverage months" beginning after 2010) of the amount paid by the taxpayer for coverage of the taxpayer and qualifying family members (spouse and dependents (Code Sec. 35(d))) under qualified health insurance as defined in Code Sec. 35(e) (i.e., COBRA continuation coverage and certain state-based coverage options) for eligible coverage months beginning in the tax year. (Code Sec. 35(a))[9] Qualifying family members may continue claiming the HCTC for up to 24 months (but not past Dec. 31, 2010) after the eligible individual enrolls in Medicare, divorces, or dies. (Code Sec. 35(g)(9))[10]

Eligibility is determined on a monthly basis. An "eligible individual" is an (1) "eligible TAA recipient" as defined in Code Sec. 35(c)(2),[11] (2) "eligible alternative TAA recipient" as defined in Code Sec. 35(c)(3),[12] or (3) "eligible PBGC pension recipient" (i.e., an individual who has reached age 55 as of the first day of the month (but isn't entitled to Medicare), and is receiving a benefit for the month that is, in any part, paid by the Pension Benefit Guaranty Corporation (PBGC) under title IV of the Employee Retirement Income Security Act of '74, dealing with plan terminations (Code Sec. 35(c)(4))). (Code Sec. 32(c)(1))[13]

A month is an eligible coverage month if on the first day of the month the taxpayer is an "eligible individual," is covered by qualified health insurance for which he paid the premium, doesn't have other specified subsidized coverage (defined in Code Sec. 35(f)), and isn't imprisoned under federal, state, or local authority. (Code Sec. 35(b))[14] An individual can't claim the HCTC for any month he receives a COBRA premium subsidy under 2009 ARRA Sec. 3001

3. ¶A-4204; ¶324.02; TD ¶569,005
4. ¶A-4210 *et seq.*; ¶324.02; TD ¶569,010 *et seq.*
5. ¶S-3152; ¶60,514; TD ¶812,002
6. ¶H-4855 *et seq.*; ¶324.03; TD ¶569,028
7. ¶S-1710; TD ¶570,209
8. ¶H-4855.1; ¶324.03; TD ¶569,028

9. ¶A-4231 *et seq.*; ¶354; TD ¶569,401 *et seq.*
10. ¶A-4235.3; ¶354; TD ¶569,404.1
11. ¶A-4232; ¶354; TD ¶569,402
12. ¶A-4233; ¶354; TD ¶569,402
13. ¶A-4234; ¶354; TD ¶569,402
14. ¶A-4231; ¶354; TD ¶569,401

(¶1531). (Code Sec. 35(g)(9))[15]

Married taxpayers filing separate returns may claim the credit. For joint returns, the eligibility requirements are considered met for any month if one spouse meets them.[16]

An individual can't claim the HCTC if he can be claimed as a dependent on another's tax return. (Code Sec. 35(g)(4))[17]

Individuals can get the credit in advance by registering with IRS's HCTC advance payment program. (Code Sec. 7527)[18]

¶ 2351 Credit for income tax withheld.

The recipient of wages, pensions, annuities, gambling winnings, etc., is allowed a credit for the amount of income tax withhold from those amounts in a calendar year, for the last tax year beginning in that calendar year. (Code Sec. 31(a); Reg § 1.31-1(a))[19] For amounts withheld under the backup withholding rules (¶3045 *et seq.*), the credit is allowed for the tax year in which the income is received. (Code Sec. 31(c))[20]

If spouses file separate returns, each must claim credit for the actual amount of tax withheld from his or her salary or wages. In a community property state, each spouse may claim a credit for half the tax withheld on community wages. (Code Sec. 31(a); Reg § 1.31-1(a))[21]

¶ 2352 Credit for excess social security tax withheld.

If more than the maximum social security tax (¶1107) is withheld from an employee's wages for a calendar year because he worked for two or more employers, the excess is a credit against income tax on the employee's return for the year. (Code Sec. 31(b)(1), Code Sec. 6413(c)(1); Reg § 1.31-2(a)(2), Reg § 31.6413(c)-1) If a husband and wife both work, the ceiling is applied separately to each. If more than the maximum was withheld by one employer, the employee can't claim the credit; the employer must refund the over-collection.[22]

¶ 2353 Credit for the elderly and permanently and totally disabled—Schedule R.

The credit is available to a "qualified individual" —i.e., one who: (1) is 65 or older at the end of the tax year, or (2) is under 65 at the end of the tax year, retired on permanent and total disability, received taxable disability income during the tax year, and hadn't reached mandatory retirement age on the first day of the tax year. (Code Sec. 22(b))[23]

Permanently and totally disabled means the individual is unable to engage in any substantial gainful activity because of a medically determinable physical or mental impairment that can be expected to result in death, or that has lasted or can be expected to last for a continuous period of at least 12 months. (Code Sec. 22(e)(3))[24] IRS requires a physician's statement (part of Schedule R of Form 1040 or Form 1040A) certifying the disability to be kept as part of taxpayer's records (but not filed). For joint returns, the statement is required for each spouse under 65 who is retired on permanent and total disability.[25]

Disability income is gross income from amounts received as (or in lieu of) wages while out of work due to a permanent and total disability. (Code Sec. 22(c)(2))[26]

Married individuals must file a joint return to claim the credit unless they qualify as married living apart, ¶3133. (Code Sec. 22(e)(1)) A nonresident alien isn't eligible for the credit (Code Sec. 22(f)), unless he has a U.S. spouse and elects under Code Sec. 6013(g) or

15. ¶H-1324.10; ¶354; TD ¶569,408
16. ¶A-4231; ¶354; TD ¶569,401
17. ¶A-4231; ¶354; TD ¶569,401
18. ¶H-4870 *et seq.*; ¶75,274; TD ¶569,406
19. ¶A-4005 *et seq.*; ¶314.01; TD ¶568,502
20. ¶J-9009; ¶s 314.01, 34,064; TD ¶568,504
21. ¶A-4006; ¶314.01; TD ¶568,503
22. ¶A-4002; ¶314.02; TD ¶568,506
23. ¶A-4101; ¶224; TD ¶568,702
24. ¶A-4102; ¶224.02; TD ¶568,705
25. ¶A-4102; TD ¶568,706
26. ¶A-4103; ¶224.02; TD ¶568,708

Code Sec. 6013(h) to be treated as a U.S. resident. (Reg § 1.37-1(d))[27]

The credit is 15% of an "initial amount" (Step 1 below), reduced by amounts based on the taxpayer's AGI (Step 2) and on the taxpayer's income from tax-free pensions and annuities (Step 3) (use Form 1040, Schedule R, or Form 1040A, Schedule 3):

Step (1): The "initial amount" is:

. . . $5,000 for a single person, 65 or over;

. . . $5,000 for spouses filing jointly, one spouse is a qualified individual, 65 or over;

. . . $7,500 for spouses filing jointly, both spouses are qualified individuals, 65 or over;

. . . $3,750 for a married person, 65 or over, filing separately. (Code Sec. 22(c)(2)(A))

For *individuals under 65*, the "initial amount" is the *lesser* of the above initial amount, or:

• single persons/married filing separately: taxpayer's disability income for the year;

• joint returns, both spouses under 65 and disabled: spouses' combined disability incomes;

• joint returns, one spouse under 65 and disabled, other spouse 65 or older: sum of $5,000 plus disabled spouse's disability income;

• joint returns, both spouses under 65, one spouse disabled: disabled spouse's disability income. (Code Sec. 22(c)(2)(B))

Step (2): If AGI exceeds a threshold amount ($7,500 for single persons; $10,000 for joint returns; $5,000 for married filing separately), the "initial amount" must be reduced by one-half of the excess. (Code Sec. 22(d)) The reduction applies regardless of the taxpayer's age.

observation: Step (2) eliminates the credit for joint filers at AGI of $25,000 (both spouse 65 or over) or $20,000 (if one is), and for a single person at AGI of $17,500.

Step (3): The initial amount as adjusted under Step (2) must be further reduced by the sum of the amounts received by the individual (for a joint return, by either spouse) as a pension or annuity or as a disability benefit that's: (a) excluded from gross income and payable under title II of the Social Security Act, the Railroad Retirement Act of '74, or a law administered by the VA; or (b) excluded from gross income under any non-Code provision of law. (Code Sec. 22(c)(3)(A))[28] Social security benefits (under Code Sec. 86, ¶1281) (Code Sec. 86(f)(1)) and worker's compensation that reduces such benefits (Code Sec. 22(c)(3)(B)) are received as a pension or annuity.[29]

¶ 2354   Credit for household and dependent care expenses.

The credit may be claimed by an individual who: (1) has one or more qualifying individuals (¶2355) and (2) incurs employment-related expenses (¶2356) enabling him to be gainfully employed. (Code Sec. 21(a)(1); Reg § 1.21-1(a))[30]

The credit for 2010 is 35% of employment-related expenses, for taxpayers with AGI of $15,000 or less. The percentage decreases by 1% for each $2,000 (or fraction) of AGI over $15,000, but not below 20%. (Code Sec. 21(a)(1), Code Sec. 21(a)(2); Reg § 1.21-1(a))[31]

The maximum amount of employment-related expenses that may be used to compute the credit for 2010 is $3,000 for one qualifying individual, or $6,000 for two or more qualifying individuals. (Code Sec. 21(c); Reg § 1.21-2(a)(1)) These maximums must be reduced, dollar-for-dollar, by the total amount excludable from gross income under Code Sec. 129 (dependent care assistance exclusion, ¶1272). (Code Sec. 21(c); Reg § 1.21-2(a))[32]

27. ¶A-4101; TD ¶568,702
28. ¶A-4105, A-4106; ¶224.02; TD ¶568,703, 568,704
29. ¶A-4107; ¶224.02; TD ¶568,709

30. ¶A-4301 *et seq.*; ¶214; TD ¶569,301 *et seq.*
31. ¶A-4301; ¶214; TD ¶569,301
32. ¶A-4302, A-4303; ¶214.04; TD ¶569,303

💧*caution:* For EGTRRA sunset rules, see ¶1114.

An otherwise eligible taxpayer may claim the credit for a qualifying individual who lives him for more than half the year, even if he doesn't provide more than half the household maintenance costs. (Code Sec. 21(a); Reg § 1.21-1(b))[33]

¶ 2355   Qualifying individual defined for the dependent care credit.

Qualifying individuals for a taxpayer's dependent care credit (¶2354) are:

. . . a taxpayer's under-age-13 dependent (as defined in Code Sec. 152(a)(1) for the dependency exemption, ¶3120) (Code Sec. 21(b)(1)(A), Reg § 1.21-1(b)(1));

. . . a taxpayer's dependent who is physically or mentally incapable of self care and who has the same principal place of abode as the taxpayer for more than half the tax year. For this purpose, "dependent" is defined in Code Sec. 152 (¶3119), but without the gross income test for qualifying relatives, the rule that a joint filer can't be a dependent, and the rule that a dependent can't have dependents (Code Sec. 21(b)(1)(B); Reg § 1.21-1(b)(1)); or

. . . the taxpayer's spouse, if the spouse is physically or mentally incapable of self care and has the same principal place of abode as the taxpayer for more than half the tax year. (Code Sec. 21(b)(1)(C); Reg § 1.21-1(b)(1))[34]

¶ 2356   Employment-related expenses for the dependent care credit.

Employment-related expenses qualifying for the credit are expenses for household services or for the care of qualifying individuals (¶2355) that are incurred to enable the taxpayer to be gainfully employed (for earned income limit, see ¶2357). Costs of a housekeeper, maid, baby-sitter, or cook ordinarily qualify. (Code Sec. 21(b)(2)(B); Reg § 1.21-1(d))[35]

Payments for services provided outside taxpayer's household count only if incurred for a qualifying individual who either is a dependent under age 13, or regularly spends at least 8 hours each day in taxpayer's household. (Code Sec. 21(b)(2)(B); Reg § 1.21-1(e)(1))[36] Also, for services performed by a *dependent care center*, the center must comply with all applicable state or local laws and regulations. (Code Sec. 21(b)(2)(C); Reg § 1.21-1(e)(2))[37]

💧*observation:* The credit isn't available for expenses of full institutional care unless incurred for a dependent under age 13.

Payments to taxpayer's relatives or household members don't qualify if the person paid is: a dependent (under Code Sec. 151(c)) of the taxpayer or his spouse, a child of the taxpayer (under Code Sec. 151(f)(1)) under 19 at the end of the tax year, taxpayer's spouse, or the parent of taxpayer's child who's a qualifying individual. (Code Sec. 21(e)(6); Reg § 1.21-4(a))[38]

¶ 2357   Earned income limit on employment-related expenses.

The amount of employment-related expenses (¶2356) that may be taken into account can't exceed: (1) for an individual who isn't married at the end of the tax year, his earned income, or (2) for an individual who is married at the end of the tax year, the lesser of his, or his spouse's, earned income for the year (even if married for only part of the year). (Code Sec. 21(d)(1); Reg § 1.21-2(b))[39]

A spouse who is a full-time student or who is a qualifying individual because incapable of

---

33. ¶A-4301; ¶214.03; TD ¶569,301
34. ¶A-4312; ¶214.02; TD ¶569,312
35. ¶A-4319 *et seq.*; ¶214.03; TD ¶569,319 *et seq.*
36. ¶A-4325; ¶214.03; TD ¶569,325

37. ¶A-4327; ¶214.03; TD ¶569,327
38. ¶A-4331; ¶214.01; TD ¶569,331
39. ¶A-4304, A-4305; ¶214.05; TD ¶569,304, 569,305

self-care is deemed to have earned income of $250 per month if there's one qualifying individual in the household, and $500 a month if there are two or more qualifying individuals. But this deemed earned income rule applies to only one spouse for any given month. (Code Sec. 21(d)(2); Reg § 1.21-2(b)(4))[40]

¶ 2358   Claiming the dependent care credit—Form 2441, Form 1040A Schedule 2.

The credit is claimed on Form 2441 (Form 1040) or Form 1040A, Schedule 2.[41]

The credit is available to married couples only on a joint return. (Code Sec. 21(e)(2); Reg § 1.21-3(a))[42] A married individual living apart from his spouse may claim the credit on a separate return if he maintains a household for which he furnishes over half the maintenance costs for the tax year, the household is a qualifying individual's principal place of abode for more than half the tax year, and the other spouse is absent for the last six months of the tax year. (Code Sec. 21(e)(4), Reg § 1.21-3(b))[43]

Divorced or legally separated parents claim the credit for a child under who is under age 13 or physically or mentally incapable of self-care as follows: if the child receives more than half his support during the year from his parents, and is in the custody of one or both of the parents for more than half the calendar year, he's a qualifying individual for the parent having longer custody. That parent may claim the credit even if he can't claim the child as a dependent and even if he released the dependency exemption (¶3126) to the other parent. (Code Sec. 21(e)(5); Reg § 1.21-1(b)(5))[44]

The care provider's name, address, and taxpayer identification number (TIN) must be included on taxpayer's return. The TIN isn't required for tax-exempt care providers (write "tax-exempt" instead). (Code Sec. 21(e)(9)) The care provider should give this information and certify the TIN on Form W-10. If the care provider doesn't comply with a request, the taxpayer should furnish whatever information is available, and include a statement that the other required information was requested but wasn't given. (Code Sec. 21(e)(9))[45]

No credit is permitted for a qualifying individual unless his TIN is included on the return claiming the credit. (Code Sec. 21(e)(10))[46]

¶ 2359   Adoption expense credit—Form 8839.

An individual may claim a credit (use Form 8839 with Form 1040) for qualified adoption expenses (Code Sec. 36C(a)(1)), which are reasonable and necessary adoption fees, court costs, attorney fees, and other expenses that are directly related to and the principal purpose of which is for the taxpayer's legal adoption of an eligible child (an individual under age 18, or physically or mentally incapable of self-care (Code Sec. 36C(d)(2)(A))). The credit is refundable, and is allowed against income tax and alternative minimum tax. (Code Sec. 36C(d)(1)(A)) The total amount that may be taken as a credit for all tax years for the adoption of a child is $13,170 for 2010 ($13,360 for 2011). (Code Sec. 36C(b)(1))[47]

The credit begins to phase out for taxpayers with AGI (as specially modified) over $182,520 for 2010 ($185,210 for 2011) and is fully eliminated at $222,520 for 2010 ($225,210 for 2011) of modified AGI. (Code Sec. 36C(b)(2))[48]

If the expenses are paid or incurred before the tax year the adoption becomes final, the credit is allowed for the year after the year when they're paid or incurred. For expenses paid or incurred during or after the tax year the adoption becomes final, the credit is allowed for

---

40. ¶A-4306; ¶214.06; TD ¶569,306
41. ¶A-4301; ¶214.08; TD ¶569,301
42. ¶ A-4310; ¶214.07; TD ¶569,310
43. ¶A-4311; ¶214.07; TD ¶569,311
44. ¶A-4314; ¶214.07; TD ¶569,314

45. ¶A-4334; ¶214.09; TD ¶569,328
46. ¶A-4333; ¶214TD ¶569,333
47. ¶A-4401, A-4407, A-4410; ¶36C4; TD ¶569,501, 569,507, 569,510
48. ¶A-4404; ¶36C4; TD ¶569,504

the year they're paid or incurred. (Code Sec. 36C(a)(2))[49]

For an adoption of a child with special needs (defined in Code Sec. 36C(d)(3)), the taxpayer is treated as having paid the maximum credit amount (i.e., $13,170 for 2010; $13,360 for 2011) less the total qualified adoption expenses actually paid or incurred in all tax years for the adoption, in the tax year the adoption becomes final. (Code Sec. 36C(a)(3))[50]

The credit's not allowed for a foreign adoption unless it becomes final. Expenses paid or incurred in the tax year the adoption is finalized or in earlier years are allowed in the year finalized. Expenses paid or incurred after that year are taken into account when paid or incurred. (Code Sec. 36C(e)) Taxpayers may treat certain adoptions as final if the competent authority enters a decree of adoption or a home state enters a decree of re-adoption.[1]

No adoption expense credit is allowed if a deduction or credit (or exclusion, ¶1256) is otherwise allowed, or government funds are received, for the expense. (Code Sec. 36C(b)(3)).[2]

To get the credit, married individuals must file jointly (unless legally separated or living apart). (Code Sec. 36C(f)(1))[3] The taxpayer's return must include (if known) the name, age and taxpayer identification number (TIN) of the child. (Code Sec. 36C(f)(2))[4]

Taxpayer with unused credits from pre-2010 tax years (i.e., when the credit was nonrefundable and subject to a tax liability limit plus 5-year carryover) may still claim those carryovers in 2010 (to as late as 2014, if from 2009) as permitted under the rules then in effect.[5]

¶ 2360   Child tax credit.

For 2010, individuals may claim (on Form 1040 or Form 1040A) a maximum $1,000 child tax credit for each qualifying child (¶3120) the taxpayer can claim as a dependent. (Code Sec. 24(a))[6] The child must be under 17, and a U.S. citizen or resident alien. (Code Sec. 24(c))[7]

The amount of the allowable credit is reduced (not below zero) by $50 for each $1,000 (or fraction thereof) of modified AGI (AGI increased by excluded foreign, possession, and Puerto Rico income) above: $110,000 for joint filers, $75,000 for unmarried individuals, and $55,000 for marrieds filing separately. (Code Sec. 24(b))[8]

For 2010, the child tax credit can't exceed the excess of: (1) the sum of: regular tax liability (¶2372) plus alternative minimum tax (AMT) liability, over (2) the sum of the credits under Code Sec. 21 – Code Sec. 26—other than the child tax credit, the "saver's" credit, the residential energy efficient property credit, the new qualified plug-in electric drive motor vehicle credit, the American Opportunity tax credit, the alternative motor vehicle credit, and the qualified plug-in electric vehicle credit—plus the foreign tax credit. (Code Sec. 24(b)(3)) This means the credit can offset both AMT.[9] For refundability of excess, see ¶2361.

caution: For EGTRRA sunset rules, see ¶1114.

No child credit is allowed for a child for a tax year unless the taxpayer's return includes the child's name and taxpayer identification number (TIN). (Code Sec. 24(e))[10]

No credit is allowed for a short tax year unless due to taxpayer's death. (Code Sec. 24(f))[11]

---

49. ¶A-4402; ¶36C4; TD ¶569,502
50. ¶A-4401; ¶36C4; TD ¶569,501
1. ¶A-4402, A-4403; ¶36C4; TD ¶569,502, 509,503
2. ¶A-4409; ¶36C4; TD ¶569,509
3. ¶A-4412, A-4413; ¶36C4; TD ¶569,512, 569,513
4. ¶A-4414; ¶36C4; TD ¶569,514
5. ¶A-4406; ¶36C4; TD ¶569,506

6. ¶A-4051; ¶244; TD ¶569,101
7. ¶A-4053; ¶244; TD ¶569,103
8. ¶A-4052; ¶244; TD ¶569,102
9. ¶A-4054; ¶244.01; TD ¶569,104
10. ¶A-4059; ¶244; TD ¶569,109
11. ¶A-4051; ¶244; TD ¶569,101

¶ 2361   When child tax credit is refundable—Form 8812.

The child tax credit is refundable, but only to the extent of the *greater of*: (1) 15% of taxable earned income above $3,000 for 2010, or (2) for a taxpayer with three or more qualifying children, the excess of his social security taxes for the tax year over his earned income credit (¶2344) for the year. (Code Sec. 24(d)) IRS calls the amount of the child tax credit that's refundable (on Form 8812) the "additional child tax credit."[12]

Earned income is defined in Code Sec. 32 (¶2345), and includes amounts excluded from gross income under Code Sec. 112 (combat zone pay, see ¶1225). (Code Sec. 24(d)(1))[13]

⊘observation: While a certain level of earned income is needed for the child tax credit to be refundable, earned income isn't required for the credit to be claimed against tax liability.

⊘caution: For EGTRRA sunset rules, see ¶1114.

¶ 2362   Credit for mortgage interest under QMCC program—Form 8396, Form 8828.

Under a state or local government qualified mortgage credit certificate (MCC) program, certificate holders claim a credit (on Form 8396) (Code Sec. 25) equal to the MCC rate multiplied by the interest paid or accrued by the taxpayer during the tax year on a mortgage. (Code Sec. 25(a)(1)) If the MCC rate exceeds 20%, the credit is limited to $2,000. (Code Sec. 25(a)(2)) A three-year carryover is allowed for certain excess amounts. (Code Sec. 25(e))[14] The credit is subject to recapture on Form 8828 if the taxpayer sells or otherwise disposes of any interest in the residence within nine years after the mortgage was provided. (Code Sec. 143(m))[15]

¶ 2363   Nonbusiness energy property credit for 2010—Form 5695.

For property placed in service in 2010 (Code Sec. 25C(g)), a taxpayer can claim (on Form 5695) a credit equal to 30% of the cost of: (1) qualified energy efficiency improvements to his home, and (2) residential energy property expenditures; up to a total $1,500 credit for 2010. (Code Sec. 25C(a), Code Sec. 25C(b)) The expenses must be made on or in connection with a dwelling unit located in the U.S. owned and used by taxpayer as his principal residence (under Code Sec. 121) at the time of installation. (Code Sec. 25C(c), Code Sec. 25C(d))[16]

Qualified energy efficiency improvements are energy efficient building envelope components such as insulation materials or systems specifically and primarily designed to reduce heat loss/gain; exterior windows, skylights or doors; and certain metal or asphalt roofs installed on a dwelling unit with pigmented coatings or cooling granules to reduce heat gain, that meet criteria established by the 2000 International Energy Conservation Code (or Energy Star program requirements, for a metal or asphalt roof). (Code Sec. 25C(c)) Taxpayers can rely on an appropriate manufacturer's certification that a component meets energy requirements, unless IRS withdraws it before taxpayer's purchase. Also, the component must be expected to last for at least five years. (Code Sec. 25C(c)(1)(C)) This requirement is met if the manufacturer offers a two-year warranty to repair or replace at no extra charge.[17]

Residential energy property expenses are expenses for qualified energy property (including labor costs for onsite preparation, assembly, or original installation) that meet specific standards set forth in Code Sec. 25C(d)(2)(B) and Code Sec. 25C(d)(2)(C). This property includes:

. . . energy-efficient building property (electric heat pump water heater, electric heat pump;

---

12. ¶A-4055; ¶244.02; TD ¶569,105
13. ¶A-4055; ¶244.02; TD ¶569,105
14. ¶A-4008 *et seq.*; ¶254 *et seq.*; TD ¶568,507 *et seq.*

15. ¶I-4901 *et seq.*; ¶1434.02
16. ¶A-4751; ¶25C4; TD ¶569,551
17. ¶A-4752 *et seq.*; ¶25C4; TD ¶569,552 *et seq.*

central air conditioner; natural gas, propane or oil water heater; or a stove burning biomass fuel to heat or provide hot water to a taxpayer's residence in the U.S.) that meets specific energy efficiency standards;

... a qualified natural gas, propane, or oil furnace; or qualified natural gas, propane, or oil hot water boiler; or

... an advanced main air circulating fan. (Code Sec. 25C(d))[18]

An expense won't fail to qualify just because it was made for two or more dwelling units; the credit is computed separately for the expenses for each dwelling unit. (Code Sec. 25C(e)(2)(B))[19] If the credit is allowed for an expense for a property, the increase in the property's basis that would otherwise result is reduced by the credit allowed (¶2478). (Code Sec. 25C(f), Code Sec. 1016(a)(33))[20]

caution: Check http://ria.thomsonreuters.com/federaltaxhandbook for the credit's extension.

¶ 2364 Residential energy efficient property credit—Form 5695.

For property placed in service before 2017 (Code Sec. 25D(g)), an individual is allowed an annual credit (on Form 5695) for the purchase of residential energy efficient property equal to the sum of 30% of the amount paid for:

... qualified solar energy property (i.e., property that uses solar power to generate electricity in a home);

... qualified solar water heating property;

... qualified fuel cell property, up to a maximum $500 credit for each 0.5 kilowatt (kw) of capacity);

... qualified small wind energy property; and

... qualified geothermal heat pump property. (Code Sec. 25D(a), Code Sec. 25D(b)(1), Code Sec. 25D(d))[21]

The equipment must be installed in a dwelling unit that's located in the U.S. and used as the taxpayer's residence (Code Sec. 25D(d)), and can't be used to heat a swimming pool or hot tub. (Code Sec. 25D(e)(3)) For fuel cell expenses, the dwelling unit must be the taxpayer's principal residence (as defined in Code Sec. 121) (Code Sec. 25D(d)(3)) and special dollar limits apply for joint occupancy. (Code Sec. 25D(e)(4))[22]

Taxpayers can rely on an appropriate manufacturer's certification that a component meets energy requirements, unless IRS withdraws it before taxpayer's purchase.[23]

The credit covers installation and hardware costs. (Code Sec. 25D(e)(1)) An expense is treated as made when the original installation is completed, except an expense for the construction or reconstruction of a structure is treated as made when the taxpayer's original use of the constructed or reconstructed structure begins. (Code Sec. 25D(e)(8))[24] If the equipment is used less than 80% for nonbusiness purposes, only the expenses properly allocable to nonbusiness use are taken into account. (Code Sec. 25D(e)(7))[25]

For tax years beginning after 2009 (when Code Sec. 26(a)(2) doesn't apply, ¶2372), the credit can't exceed the excess of (a) the sum of regular tax liability plus alternative minimum tax (AMT), over (b) the sum of the credits under Code Sec. 21 – Code Sec. 26 (except this credit) plus the foreign tax credit for the tax year. (Thus, the credit is allowed against AMT).

18. ¶A-4753; ¶25C4; TD ¶569,553
19. ¶A-4755; ¶25C4; TD ¶569,555
20. ¶A-4757; ¶25C4; TD ¶569,557
21. ¶A-4781, A-4782; ¶25D4; TD ¶569,561, 569,562

22. ¶A-4782, A-4785; ¶25D4; TD ¶569,562, 569,565
23. ¶A-4782.1; TD ¶569,562.1
24. ¶A-4783; ¶25D4; TD ¶569,563
25. ¶A-4784; ¶25D4; TD ¶569,564

If the credit exceeds this limit, the excess is carried to the next tax year. (Code Sec. 25D(c))[26]

If the credit is allowed for an expense for a property, the basis increase is reduced by the credit allowed (¶2478). (Code Sec. 25D(f), Code Sec. 1016(a)(34))[27]

¶ 2365   Alternative motor vehicle credit—Form 8910.

Taxpayers can claim (on Form 8910) an alternative motor vehicle credit (AMVC) for qualifying vehicles (five types, see below) placed in service during the tax year. (Code Sec. 30B(a)) The credit is allowed to the vehicle's owner (or lessor) (Code Sec. 30B(b)) or, for vehicles sold to and used by certain tax-exempt entities, the seller. (Code Sec. 30B(h)(6))[28]

Any part of the credit attributable to depreciable property is treated as part of the general business credit (¶2302). (Code Sec. 30B(g)(1))[29] The remaining portion is a nonrefundable personal credit that, for tax years beginning after 2009 (when Code Sec. 26(a)(2) doesn't apply, ¶2372), can't exceed the excess of: (1) the sum of regular tax liability plus alternative minimum tax (AMT), over (2) the sum of the credits under Code Sec. 21 – Code Sec. 26 (other than the AMVC, residential energy efficient property credit, qualified plug-in electric vehicle credit, and new qualified plug-in electric drive motor vehicle credit) plus the foreign tax credit, for the year. (Code Sec. 30B(g)(2)) Thus, the credit is allowed against AMT.[30] But it can't be carried to other tax years.[31]

To qualify for the AMVC, a motor vehicle (defined in Code Sec. 30B(h)(1)) must comply with the applicable provisions of the Clean Air Act, and applicable motor vehicle safety provisions (Code Sec. 30B(h)(10)), and must be used predominantly in the U.S. (Code Sec. 30B(h)(7))[32]

No AMVC is allowable for any part of the cost taken into account under Code Sec. 179. (Code Sec. 30B(h)(7)) The vehicle's basis must be reduced by the AMCV allowed. (Code Sec. 30B(h)(4)) But a taxpayer may elect not to claim the AMVC for a vehicle. (Code Sec. 30B(h)(9))[33]

The AMVC is the sum of the following five credits: (Code Sec. 30B)

(1) New qualified fuel cell motor vehicle credit for the purchase (before 2015 (Code Sec. 30B(k)(1))) of a fuel cell vehicle. The credit equals a base credit amount that depends upon the vehicle's weight class and, for passenger cars or light trucks (vehicles weighing 8,500 pounds or less), plus an amount that depends upon the vehicle's rated fuel economy compared to a base fuel economy. A qualifying fuel cell vehicle must be propelled by power derived from one or more cells that convert chemical energy directly into electricity by combining oxygen with hydrogen fuel stored on board the vehicle. (Code Sec. 30B(b))[34]

(2) New advance lean-burn technology motor vehicle credit for the purchase (before 2011 (Code Sec. 30B(k)(2))) of an advanced lean burn technology motor vehicle. The credit equals: (a) a fuel economy credit amount that varies with the vehicle's rated fuel economy compared to a 2002 model year standard, plus (b) a conservation credit amount based on the vehicle's estimated lifetime fuel savings compared to a comparable 2002 model year vehicle. A qualifying advanced lean-burn technology motor vehicle is a passenger car or light truck with an internal combustion engine that's designed to operate primarily using more air than is necessary for complete combustion of the fuel, incorporates direct injection, and achieves at least 125% of the 2002 model year city fuel economy. (Code Sec. 30B(c))[35] For phaseout, see below.

(3) New qualified hybrid motor vehicle credit for the purchase (before 2011 Code Sec. 30B(k)) of an auto or light truck. The credit amount varies with the vehicle's rated fuel economy compared to the 2002 model year. A new qualified hybrid motor vehicle is a motor

---

26. ¶A-4781.1; ¶25D4; TD ¶569,561.1
27. ¶A-4788; ¶25D4; TD ¶569,568
28. ¶L-18021; ¶30B4; TD ¶397,101
29. ¶ L-18022; ¶30B4; TD ¶397,102
30. ¶ L-18022.1; ¶30B4; TD ¶397,102.1

31. ¶L-18023; ¶30B4; TD ¶397,103
32. ¶L-18021; ¶30B4; TD ¶397,101
33. ¶L-18023; ¶30B4; TD ¶397,103
34. ¶L-18024; ¶30B4.01; TD ¶397,104
35. ¶L-18025; ¶30B4.02; TD ¶397,105

vehicle that draws propulsion energy from onboard sources of stored energy that include both an internal combustion engine or heat engine using combustible fuel and a rechargeable energy storage system (e.g., batteries). (Code Sec. 30B(d))[36] For phaseout, see below.

(4) New qualified alternative fuel motor vehicle credit (for property purchased before 2011 (Code Sec. 39B(k)(4))). The credit equals 50% of a vehicle's incremental cost, plus an additional 30% if the vehicle meets certain emissions standards, but not more than between $4,000 and $32,000 depending upon the weight of the vehicle. A reduced credit applies to certain "mixed-fuel" vehicles. A new qualified alternative fuel motor vehicle is a motor vehicle that's only capable of operating on an alternative fuel, compressed natural gas, liquefied natural gas, liquefied petroleum gas, hydrogen, and any liquid fuel that is at least 85% methanol. (Code Sec. 30B(e))[37]

(5) Plug-in electric vehicle conversion credit for any motor vehicle that's converted (before 2012) into a Code Sec. 30D qualified plug-in electric drive motor vehicle (¶2367). The credit is 10% of the cost of converting the vehicle, with a $4,000 credit maximum. (Code Sec. 30B(i))[38]

A credit is also available for certain new qualified "heavy" hybrid vehicles weighing in excess of 8,500 pounds, including heavy trucks, buses, industrial, agricultural or military vehicles. (Code Sec. 30B(d)(2)(B))

Phaseout. The credit for advanced lean burn technology and hybrid motor vehicles phases out beginning in the second calendar quarter following that in which a manufacturer sells its 60,000th qualified vehicle for use in the U.S. (50% credit reduction in second and third quarter; 75% in fourth and fifth quarter; 0 credit allowed thereafter). (Code Sec. 30B(f)) The credit is completely phased out for Toyota and Honda cars. The credit was reduced for Fords as of Apr. 1, 2009 (with no credit after Mar. 31, 2010), and as of July 1, 2010 (no credit after Dec. 31, 2010 because credit expires) for Volkswagens.[39]

For a list of qualifying vehicles and AMVC amounts, see http://www.irs.gov/businesses/corporations, under "Alternative Motor Vehicle Credit."

¶ 2366   Credit for alternative fuel vehicle refueling property—Form 8911.

For property placed in service before 2011 (2015 for property relating to hydrogen) (Code Sec. 30C(g)), a taxpayer can claim (on Form 8911) a credit equal to 50% (30% for hydrogen property) of the cost of qualified alternative fuel vehicle refueling (QAFVR) property placed in service by the taxpayer during the tax year. (Code Sec. 30C(a), Code Sec. 30C(e)(6)(A)(i))[40]

QAFVR property—i.e., certain property for the storage or dispensing of a clean-burning fuel or electricity into the fuel tank or battery of a motor vehicle—is defined in Code Sec. 179A(d) (dealing with clean-fuel vehicles and certain refueling property) but with certain modifications, e.g., property installed on property used as the taxpayer's principal residence (under Code Sec. 121) doesn't need to be depreciable. Property used outside the U.S. doesn't qualify. (Code Sec. 30C(c), Code Sec. 30C(e)(3))[41]

For tax years beginning in 2010, the maximum credit for all QAFVR property placed in service at a location is: (a) $50,000 ($200,000 for hydrogen property) for depreciable QAFVR property used in a trade or business, and (b) $2,000 ($1,000 for hydrogen property) for nonbusiness QAFVR property. For tax years beginning after 2010, the maximum credit is $30,000 for depreciable QAFVR property and $1,000 for nonbusiness QAFVR property. (Code Sec. 30C(b), Code Sec. 30C(e)(6))[42]

Any portion of the QAFVR property credit attributable to depreciable property is treated as

36. ¶L-18026, L-18029; ¶30B4.03; TD ¶397,106, 397,109
37. ¶L-18029.1; ¶30B4.06; TD ¶397,109.1
38. ¶l-18029.3; ¶30B4.08; TD ¶397,109.3
39. ¶L-18028; ¶30B4.04; TD ¶397,108

40. ¶L-18041; ¶30C4; TD ¶397,201
41. ¶L-18043; ¶30C4.02; TD ¶397,203, 397,205
42. ¶L-18041, L-18041.1; ¶30C4; TD ¶397,201, 397,201.1

a part of the general business credit (¶2302). (Code Sec. 30C(d)(1)) The remaining portion, a personal credit, can't exceed the excess of (1) regular tax liability (defined in Code Sec. 26(b)) for the tax year reduced by the sum of allowable nonrefundable personal credits plus the foreign tax credit, over (2) tentative minimum tax for the tax year. (Code Sec. 30C(d)(2))[43]

No QAFVR property credit is allowable for the portion of the cost that's taken into account under Code Sec. 179 expensing. (Code Sec. 30C(e)(3))[44] Recapture rules apply. (Code Sec. 30C(e)(5))[45] The basis of the property must be reduced by the amount of the credit allowed. (Code Sec. 30C(e)(1), Code Sec. 1016(a)(36))[46] But a taxpayer may elect not to claim the credit. (Code Sec. 30C(e)(4))[47]

¶ 2367   Electric vehicle credits—Form 8936, Form 8834.

New qualified plug-in electric drive motor vehicle credit. A taxpayer can claim (on Form 8936) a credit for each new qualified plug-in electric drive motor vehicle (NQPEDMV) placed in service during the tax year. (Code Sec. 30D(a))[48] For a conversion credit, see ¶2365.

To qualify for the credit, a vehicle must be treated as a motor vehicle for purposes of title II of the Clean Air Act (effectively barring low-speed motor vehicles from the credit); have a gross vehicle weight (GVWR) of less than 14,000 pounds; and be propelled to a significant extent by an electric motor that draws electricity from a battery that has a capacity of at least 4 kilowatt hours, and be capable of being recharged from an external source of electricity. The taxpayer must be the original user of the vehicle (which must be used predominantly in the U.S. (Code Sec. 30C(f)(4)), and must have acquired it for use or lease and not for resale. (Code Sec. 30D(d)(1))[49] The credit is available to the owner or lessor.[50]

The amount of the NQPEDMV credit is the sum of: (1) $2,500; plus (2) for a vehicle that draws propulsion energy from a battery with not less than five kilowatt (kw) hours of capacity, $417 for each kw hour of capacity in excess of five kw hours, but not in excess of $5,000. Thus, the maximum credit is $7,500, regardless of weight. (Code Sec. 30D(b))[1]

The credit (as computed above) phases out beginning in the second calendar quarter following that in which a manufacturer sells its 200,000th plug-in electric drive motor vehicle for use in the U.S. after 2009 (50% credit reduction in second and third quarter; 75% in fourth and fifth quarter; 0 credit allowed thereafter). (Code Sec. 30D(e))[2]

Any portion of the credit attributable to depreciable property is treated as part of the general business credit (¶2302). (Code Sec. 30D(c)(1)) The remaining portion is a nonrefundable personal credit. For tax years beginning after 2009 (when Code Sec. 26(a)(2) doesn't apply (¶2372), the personal credit can't exceed the excess of: (a) the sum of regular tax liability and alternative minimum tax (AMT), over (b) the sum of the credits under Code Sec. 21 – Code Sec. 26 (other than this credit and the residential energy efficient property credit) and the foreign tax credit for the tax year. (Code Sec. 30D(c)(2))[3]

observation: Thus, the NQPEDMV credit can be claimed against AMT.

The vehicle's basis, and any other allowable deduction or credit, must be reduced by the amount of the NQPEDMV credit allowed. (Code Sec. 30D(f)(1), Code Sec. 30D(f)(2))[4] But a taxpayer may elect not to claim the credit. (Code Sec. 30D(f)(6))[5]

Plug-in electric vehicle credit. For vehicles acquired before 2012 (Code Sec. 30(f)), a

43. ¶L-18042; ¶30C4.01; TD ¶397,202
44. ¶L-18045; ¶30C4; TD ¶397,205
45. ¶L-18045; ¶30C4; TD ¶397,205
46. ¶L-18041.1; ¶30C4; TD ¶397,201.1
47. ¶L-18044; ¶30C4; TD ¶397,204
48. ¶L-18031; ¶30D4; TD ¶397,131
49. ¶L-18032.3; ¶30D4.04; TD ¶s 397,134.1, 397,136

50. ¶L-18033; ¶30D4.05; TD ¶397,138
1. ¶L-18031.2; ¶30D4.015; TD ¶397,132.1
2. ¶L-18031.4; ¶30D4.02; TD ¶397,133.1
3. ¶L-18034, L-18034.1; ¶30D4.07; TD ¶397,132, 397,133
4. ¶L-18033.2, L-18033.3; ¶30D4.06; TD ¶397,140, 397,141
5. ¶L-18034.2; ¶30D4; TD ¶397,144

taxpayer can claim (on Form 8834) a credit equal to 10% of the cost of each qualified plug-in electric vehicle (QPEV) placed in service during the tax year. (Code Sec. 30(a)) The maximum credit for a vehicle is $2,500. (Code Sec. 30(b))[6]

A QPEV is an electric drive low-speed vehicle, motorcycle, or 3-wheeled vehicle if its original use begins with the taxpayer; it's acquired for use or lease; it's manufactured primarily for use on public streets, roads and highways (e.g., not golf courses); its GVWR is less than 14,000 pounds; and it's propelled to a significant extent by an electric motor that draws electricity from a battery with a capacity of at least 4 kw hours (at least 2.5 kw hours for a 2- or 3-wheeled vehicle) and is capable of being recharged from an external source of electricity. (Code Sec. 30(d))[7] The vehicle can't be used predominantly outside the U.S. (Code Sec. 30(e)(4)[8] Taxpayers can rely on certain manufacturer certifications.[9]

Any portion of the QPEV credit attributable to depreciable property is treated as part of the general business credit (¶2302). (Code Sec. 30(c)(1)) The remaining portion is a nonrefundable personal credit that, for tax years beginning after 2009 (when Code Sec. 26(a)(2) doesn't apply, ¶2372), can't exceed the excess of: the sum of regular tax liability plus AMT, over the sum of the credits under Code Sec. 21 – Code Sec. 26 (other than this credit, the residential energy efficiency credit, and the NQPEDMV credit) and the foreign tax credit for the tax year. (Code Sec. 30(c)(2))[10]

The vehicle's basis (Code Sec. 30(e)(1)) and any other allowable deduction or credit (Code Sec. 30(e)(2)) must be reduced by the amount of the credit allowed. (Code Sec. 30(e)(1))[11] But the taxpayer can elect not to claim the credit. (Code Sec. 30(e)(6))[12]

¶ 2368 Credit for first-time homebuyers in D.C. before 2010—Form 8859.

An individual who (or whose spouse, if married) hasn't had an ownership interest in a principal residence in the District of Columbia (D.C.) in the one-year period before acquiring a principal residence in D.C. is allowed a one-time-only nonrefundable personal credit (use Form 8859) of up to $5,000 of the residence's purchase price (Code Sec. 1400C(a), Code Sec. 1400C(c), Code Sec. 1400C(g)), for purchases before 2010. (Code Sec. 1400C(i)) The credit phases out ratably between modified AGI (AGI increased by the foreign earned income, possessions, and Puerto Rico exclusions) of $70,000 and $90,000 ($110,000 and $130,000 for joint filers). (Code Sec. 1400C(b)) The maximum credit for a married individual filing separately is $2,500. The basis of the residence is reduced by the amount of the credit claimed. (Code Sec. 1400C(h))[13] No D.C. homebuyer credit is allowable for the purchase if the taxpayer or his spouse can claim the first-time homebuyer credit (¶2369) for it. (Code Sec. 1400C(e))[14]

 caution: Check http://ria.thomsonreuters.com/federaltaxhandbook for the credit's extension.

¶ 2369 First-time homebuyer credit for purchases before Oct. 1, 2010—Form 5405.

A refundable first-time homebuyer credit (FTHBC, claimed on Form 5405) is available to first-time homebuyers (and long-term residents) for qualifying 2010 purchases of a principal residence in the U.S. (Code Sec. 36(a)) The credit applies to residences purchased (1) before May 1, 2010; or (2) before Oct. 1, 2010 by a taxpayer who entered into a written binding contract before May 1, 2010, to close on the purchase before July 1, 2010. (Code Sec. 36(h)).[15] For eased rules for qualifying service members, see ¶2370.

A 'principal residence' is as defined for the Code Sec. 121 homesale exclusion. (Code

6. ¶L-18036; ¶304; TD ¶397,171
7. ¶L-18037; ¶304.01; TD ¶397,172
8. ¶L-18038; ¶304.02; TD ¶397,173
9. ¶L-18039.3; ¶304; TD ¶397,182
10. ¶L-18039, L-18039.1; ¶304.06; TD ¶397,179, 397,180

11. ¶L-18038.1, L-18038.2; ¶304; TD ¶397,177, 397,178
12. ¶L-18039.2; ¶304; TD ¶397,181
13. ¶A-4250 *et seq.*; ¶1400C4; TD ¶568,800 *et seq.*
14. ¶A-4261.1; ¶14,00C4; TD ¶568,805.1
15. ¶A-4271; ¶364; TD ¶568,851

Sec. 36(c)(2)) It can be a house, houseboat, mobile home, co-op, or condo.[16] But the credit isn't allowed if the purchase price exceeds $800,000. (Code Sec. 36(b)(3))[17]

'First-time homebuyers.' The credit is equal to the lesser of 10% of the purchase price (defined in Code Sec. 36(c)(4)) or $8,000 ($4,000 for married individuals filing separately). (Code Sec. 36(a), Code Sec. 36(b)(1)(A), Code Sec. 36(b)(1)(B))[18] For AGI phaseout, see below.

A taxpayer is a first-time homebuyer if he (and his spouse, if married) had no present ownership interest in a principal residence in the U.S. during the 3-year period before the purchase of the home to which the credit applies. (Code Sec. 36(c)(1)) IRS says that a taxpayer who owns property that formerly was his principal residence, but that's been rented out for the past three years, can qualify for the credit. Eligibility for the credit is determined on the date of purchase.[19]

'Long-term residents.' If an individual (and, if married, his spouse) has had the same principal residence for any 5-consecutive year period during the 8-year period ending on the date of the purchase of a later principal residence, he is treated as a first-time homebuyer of the later residence for FTHTC purposes. The individual is allowed an FTHTC equal to the lesser of: (1) 10% of the purchase price; or (2) $6,500 ($3,250 for a married individual filing separately). (Code Sec. 36(c)(6), Code Sec. 36(b)(1)(D))[20]

If two or more unmarried individuals buy a principal residence, the maximum $8,000 (or $6,500) credit is shared among them. (Code Sec. 36(b)(1)(C)) Any reasonable allocation method can be used, including one based on the taxpayers' contributions to the purchase price as either tenants in common or joint tenants, or on their ownership interests as tenants in common. But the amount allocated to an individual can't be more than what he's allowed (e.g., $6,500 for a long-term resident). IRS explains how the full credit may apply even if one buyer doesn't qualify for any credit because of the phaseout rules.[21]

Purchase means any acquisition, but only if: (i) the property isn't acquired from a person related (under Code Sec. 36(c)(5)) to the buyer or, if married, the buyer's spouse; and (ii) the property's basis in the buyer's hands isn't determined either by reference to its adjusted basis in the hands of the person from whom acquired, or under Code Sec. 1014(a) (property acquired from a decedent). A residence constructed by the taxpayer is treated as purchased by him on the date he first occupies it. (Code Sec. 36(c)(3))[22]

Limitations. The FTHBC isn't allowed unless the taxpayer (or his spouse, if married) has attained 18 years of age as of the date of purchase. (Code Sec. 36(b)(4)) No FTHBC is allowed if the taxpayer: (a) is a nonresident alien, (b) disposes of the home (or it ceases to be his (or his spouse's) principal residence) before the end of the tax year, or (c) can be claimed as a dependent by another taxpayer for the tax year of purchase. (Code Sec. 36(d))[23]

No FTHBC is allowed unless a properly executed copy of the settlement statement used to complete the purchase is attached to the tax return. (Code Sec. 36(d)(4))[24]

Phaseout. The FTHBC phases out for individuals with modified adjusted gross income (MAGI) between $125,000 and $145,000 ($225,000 and $245,000 for joint filers) for the tax year of purchase. MAGI is AGI for the tax year increased by the foreign earned income, possessions, and Puerto Rico exclusions. (Code Sec. 36(b)(2))[25]

Election to accelerate credit into previous year. Eligible first-time homebuyers may elect to treat a principal residence purchase as made on Dec. 31 of the year before the purchase, to claim the FTHBC for the earlier year. For example, a taxpayer eligible for the FTHBC because of a home purchased in 2010 may treat the purchase as occurring on Dec. 31, 2009

---

16. ¶A-4275; ¶364; TD ¶568,855
17. ¶A-4277.1; ¶364; TD ¶568,857.1
18. ¶A-4271; ¶364; TD ¶568,851
19. ¶A-4274; ¶364; TD ¶568,854
20. ¶A-4274.1; ¶364; TD ¶568,854.1

21. ¶A-4271.1; ¶364; TD ¶568,851.1
22. ¶A-4276; ¶364; TD ¶568,856
23. ¶A-4277.2 *et seq.*; ¶364; TD ¶568,857.2 *et seq.*
24. ¶A-4286; ¶364; TD ¶568,866
25. ¶A-4273; ¶364; TD ¶568,853

(and file an amended return for 2009 to claim a refund of the FTHBC).(Code Sec. 36(g))[26]

Recapture. For principal residences purchased after 2008, an FTHCB claimed for the purchase must be recaptured (i.e., repaid) only if, during the 36-month period beginning on the purchase date, the taxpayer disposes of the residence or it stops being his (and his spouse's) principal residence (Code Sec. 36(f)(4)(D))—e.g., it becomes a vacation home or business or rental property.[27]

✔️*illustration (1):* Bob, a first-time homebuyer, purchases a home for $100,000 in 2010 and claims a $8,000 FTHBC. In 2011, he sells his home for $120,000. He has no adjustments to basis. He must pay an additional tax of $8,000 for 2011.

If the sale is to an unrelated person, the recapture tax can't exceed the gain from the sale (taking into account basis adjustments for the FTHBC allowed). (Code Sec. 36(f)(3))[28]

✔️*illustration (2):* Assume that Bob in *Illustration (1)* sold his home to an unrelated person for $98,000 in 2011. He has no adjustments to basis. To determine the amount of gain for recapture purposes, his $100,000 basis is reduced to $92,000 by the $8,000 credit. His gain is $6,000 ($98,000 amount realized – $92,000 basis). He must pay an additional tax of $6,000 for 2011. The remaining $2,000 of unrecaptured credit is never recaptured.

No amount is recaptured after a taxpayer's death (Code Sec. 36(f)(4)(B)), or if the home is involuntarily converted (e.g., destroyed in a storm) and the taxpayer buys a new principal residence within two years. The 36-month recapture rule applies to the replacement principal residence during the recapture period in the same way as if it were the converted residence. (Code Sec. 36(f)(4)) There is no recapture on the transfer of a residence to a spouse or to a former spouse incident to divorce, but the recapture rules then apply to the transferee spouse. (Code Sec. 36(f)(4)(C))[29]

For homes bought before 2009, recapture is generally required. The FTHBC must be repaid in 15 equal installments over a 15-year period beginning with tax year 2010. Recapture is accelerated if a taxpayer disposes of his residence or it ceases to be his and his spouse's principal residence before the end of the 15-year recapture period.[30]

¶ 2370   Eased FTHBC rules for qualifying service members.

Eased first-time homebuyer credit (FTHBC, see ¶2369) rules apply for individuals on qualified official extended duty (generally, active duty service as a member of the uniformed services or the U.S. Foreign Service, or as an intelligence community employee that's (i) on a duty station at least 50 miles from the individual's principal residence or under orders compelling residence in government furnished quarters, and (ii) under a call or order to duty for a period over 90 days or for an indefinite period). (Code Sec. 36(f)(4)(E); Code Sec. 36(h)(3))

- For an individual (and, if married, his spouse) who serves on qualified official extended duty service outside the U.S. for at least 90 days during the period Jan. 1, 2009 – Apr. 30, 2010, the FTHBC expiration date is extended for one year, through Apr. 30, 2011 (June 30, 2011, for an individual who enters into a written binding contract before May 1, 2011, to close on the purchase of a principal residence before July 1, 2011). (Code Sec. 36(h)(3))[31]

- No recapture applies on disposition of a principal residence (or a use cessation that otherwise would cause recapture) by an individual in connection with Government orders received by him (or his spouse) for qualified official extended duty service (Code Sec. 36(f)(4)(E)), and any 15-year recapture with respect to a home acquired before Jan. 1, 2009, ceases to apply in the tax year of the disposition.[32]

26. ¶A-4272; ¶364; TD ¶568,852
27. ¶A-4281; ¶364.01; TD ¶568,861
28. ¶A-4281; ¶364.01; TD ¶568,861
29. ¶A-4281; ¶364.01; TD ¶568,861

30. ¶A-4280; ¶364.01; TD ¶568,860
31. ¶A-4271; ¶364; TD ¶568,851
32. ¶A-4281.1; ¶364.01; TD ¶568,861.1

¶ 2371   "Saver's" credit for elective deferrals and IRA contributions—Form 8880.

An eligible lower-income taxpayer can claim a nonrefundable credit (use Form 8880 with Form 1040 or Form 1040A) for a percentage of up to $2,000 of his qualified retirement savings contributions—"the saver's credit." (Code Sec. 25B(a)) The applicable percentage (50%, 20%, or 10%) depends on filing status and AGI. For tax years beginning in 2010, the amounts (as adjusted for inflation) (Code Sec. 25B(b)) are:

. . . Joint filers: $0 to $33,500, 50%; $33,500 to $36,000, 20%; and $36,000 to $55,500, 10% (no credit if AGI is above $55,500).

. . . Heads of households: $0 to $25,125, 50%; $25,125 to $27,000, 20%; and $27,000 to $41,625, 10% (no credit if AGI is above $41,625).

. . . All other filers: $0 to $16,750, 50%; $16,750 to $18,000, 20%; and $18,000 to $27,750, 10% (no credit if AGI is above $27,750).

For tax years beginning in 2011, the amounts are:

. . . Joint filers: $0 to $34,000, 50%; $34,000 to $36,500, 20%; and $36,500 to $56,500, 10% (no credit if AGI is above $56,500).

. . . Heads of households: $0 to $25,500, 50%; $25,500 to $27,375, 20%; and $27,375 to $42,375, 10% (no credit if AGI is above $42,375).

. . . All other filers: $0 to $17,000, 50%; $17,000 to $18,250, 20%; and $18,250 to $28,250, 10% (no credit if AGI is above $28,250).[33]

The taxpayer's AGI is determined without regard to the foreign, possessions, and Puerto Rico income exclusions. (Code Sec. 25B(e))[34]

An individual is eligible for the credit if he has reached age 18 by the end of the tax year. But he isn't eligible if he's a full-time student or another claims him as a dependent for the tax year beginning in the calendar year his tax year begins. (Code Sec. 25B(c))[35]

The credit is available for elective contributions to a Code Sec. 401(k) plan (including a SIMPLE 401(k)), Code Sec. 403(b) annuity, Code Sec. 457 plan, SIMPLE IRA plan, or salary reduction SEP; contributions to a traditional or Roth IRA; and voluntary after-tax employee contributions to a qualified retirement plan or Code Sec. 403(b) annuity. (Code Sec. 25B(d)(1))[36] The credit is in addition to any otherwise applicable deduction or exclusion.[37][38]

The amount of any credit-eligible contribution is reduced (not below zero) by the distributions received by the individual (and by his spouse, for joint returns) from any of the above savings arrangements during a testing period to the extent they're either taxable or are Roth IRA distributions that aren't rolled over. The testing period consists of the tax year for which the credit is claimed, the two preceding tax years, and the period after the end of the tax year and before the due date (including extensions) for filing the taxpayer's return for that year. (Code Sec. 25B(d)(2)) Distributions listed in Code Sec. 25B(d)(2)(C), such as qualified plan loans not treated as distributions, don't reduce a credit-eligible contribution.[39]

For tax years beginning after 2009 (when Code Sec. 26(a)(2) doesn't apply, ¶2372), the credit is limited to the excess of: (1) the sum of regular tax liability plus alternative minimum tax (AMT), over (2) the sum of the credits under Code Sec. 21 – Code Sec. 26 (other than this credit, the residential energy efficient property credit, the new qualified plug-in electric drive motor vehicle credit, the American Opportunity tax credit (for 2010 only), the alternative

33. ¶A-4451; ¶25B4; TD ¶569,201
34. ¶A-4451; ¶25B4; TD ¶569,201
35. ¶A-4452; ¶25B4; TD ¶569,202
36. ¶A-4453; ¶25B4; TD ¶569,203
37. ¶A-4451
38. ¶A-4451; ¶25B4; TD ¶569,201
39. ¶A-4454; ¶25B4; TD ¶569,204

motor vehicle credit, and the qualified plug-in electric vehicle credit) plus the foreign tax credit for the tax year. (Code Sec. 25B(g)) Thus, the credit is allowed against AMT.[40]

¶ 2372 Limit on combined amount of certain nonrefundable personal credits.

For tax years beginning after 2009 (i.e., when Code Sec. 26(a)(2) doesn't apply), the dependent care credit (¶2354), credit for the elderly and permanently and totally disabled (¶2353), mortgage credit (¶2362), Hope credit (¶2202) (after 2010), Lifetime Learning credit (¶2203), saver's credit (¶2371), nonbusiness energy property credit (¶2364), and alternative fuel vehicle refueling property credit (¶2366) are allowed only to the extent that the total amount doesn't exceed the excess of: (a) the taxpayer's regular tax liability for the tax year, over (b) his tentative minimum tax, determined without the alternative minimum tax foreign tax credit (AMTFTC) for the year. (Code Sec. 26(a)(1))[41]

> **◉ observation:** The Code Sec. 26(a)(1) limitation effectively prevents taxpayers from using the above-listed credits to offset AMT. The other nonrefundable personal credits—the child tax credit (¶2360), American Opportunity tax credit (for 2010 only) (¶2202), residential energy efficient property credit (¶2364), qualified plug-in electric vehicle credit (¶2366), alternative motor vehicle credit (¶2365), and new qualified plug-in electric motor vehicle credit (¶2365) are each subject to separate limitations that allow them to offset AMT.

Regular tax liability means the tax imposed by Chapter 1 *except for*: (Code Sec. 26(b))

(1) The AMT. (Code Sec. 55)

(2) Penalty taxes on certain premature distributions. (Code Sec. 72(m)(5)(B), Code Sec. 72(q), Code Sec. 72(t), Code Sec. 72(v))

(3) Tax on nonqualified withdrawals from capital construction funds. (Code Sec. 7518(g)(6))

(4) Accumulated earnings tax. (Code Sec. 531)

(5) Personal holding company tax. (Code Sec. 541)

(6) Certain recoveries of foreign expropriation losses. (Code Sec. 1351(d)(1))

(7) Tax on certain built-in gains of S corporations. (Code Sec. 1374)

(8) Tax imposed when passive investment income of an S corporation having Subchapter C earnings and profits exceeds 25% of gross receipts. (Code Sec. 1375)

(9) Tax on transfers of high-yield interest to disqualified holders of FASITs. (Former Code Sec. 860K)

(10) The 30% tax on U.S. source income earned by nonresident aliens and foreign corporations. (Code Sec. 871(a), Code Sec. 881)

(11) The interest paid as additional income on tax deferred by installment sales of timeshares and residential lots. (Code Sec. 453(l)(3), Code Sec. 453A(c))

(12) Recapture of federal subsidy from use of mortgage bonds and mortgage credit certificates. (Code Sec. 143(m))

(13) Tax on transfers of residual interests in a REMIC to a disqualified organization. (Former Code Sec. 860E(e))

(14) The branch profits tax. (Code Sec. 884)

(15) Additional tax on Archer MSA distributions and health savings account (HSA) distributions not used for medical expenses. (Code Sec. 220(f)(4), Code Sec. 223(f)(4))

(16) Additional tax on distributions from Coverdell education savings accounts not used for higher education expenses. (Code Sec. 530(d)(4))

(17) Penalty tax for certain distributions from Medicare Advantage MSA not used for qualified medical expenses. (Code Sec. 138(c)(2))

---

40. ¶A-4455; ¶25B4; TD ¶569,205

41. ¶A-4901, A-4902; ¶264; TD ¶569,601, 569,602

(18) Recapture of the first-time homebuyer credit. (Code Sec. 36(f))

(19) Interest and tax for violations of Code Sec. 409A nonqualified deferred compensation (NQDC) rules and tax on NQDC from certain tax-indifferent entities. (Code Sec. 409A(a)(1)(B), Code Sec. 409A(b), Code Sec. 457A(c)(1)(B)), (Code Sec. 26(b)(2))[42]

For tax years to which Code Sec. 26(a)(2) applies (i.e., tax years beginning before 2010), the combined total of the above credits was limited to the sum of: (1) the taxpayer's regular tax liability for the tax year reduced by the foreign tax credit (¶2375), plus (2) the AMT for the year. (Code Sec. 26(a)(2)) Thus, the credits could offset both regular tax and AMT[43]

🅡*caution:* Check http://ria.thomsonreuters.com/federaltaxhandbook to see if the Code Sec. 26(a)(2) limitation has been extended.

¶ 2373   Credit for alternative minimum tax (AMT)—Form 8801; Form 8827.

The minimum tax credit (MTC or AMT credit) is equal to (compute on Form 8801, Form 8827 for corporations) the adjusted net minimum tax (ANMT) the taxpayer paid in all earlier tax years for "deferral preferences" (for a corporation, also "exclusion preferences"), less the allowable MTCs for those years. (Code Sec. 53(a), Code Sec. 53(b)) The allowable credit for a tax year is limited (subject to the rule below for individuals and at ¶1933) to the excess of: (1) taxpayer's regular tax liability (¶2372) reduced by the sum of allowable nonrefundable credits *over* (2) the tentative minimum tax (¶3201), for the year. (Code Sec. 53(c))[44]

For a small corporation exempt from AMT for a tax year (¶3205), the regular tax liability otherwise used in computing the year's credit limitation is reduced by 25% of the amount over $25,000. (Code Sec. 55(e)(5))[45]

A *noncorporate taxpayer's* ANMT for a tax year equals: (a) the AMT for the year, *less* (b) the amount of AMT that would have arisen if the only applicable AMT preferences and adjustments were "exclusion preferences." (Code Sec. 53(d)(1)(B))[46]

A *corporation's* ANMT for a tax year equals item (a), above. (Code Sec. 53(d)(1)(B))[47]

"Deferral preferences" are all the AMT preferences and adjustments except those for: (i) depletion, (ii) tax-exempt interest, (iii) itemized deductions of noncorporate taxpayers, (iv) the standard deduction, (v) personal exemptions, and (vi) the exclusion of gain from qualified small business stock. (Code Sec. 53(d)(1)(B)(ii)) "Exclusion preferences" are the AMT preferences/adjustments that aren't deferral preferences.[48]

Refundable AMT credit for individuals. For tax years beginning before 2013, if an individual has a "long-term unused MTC," his MTC for the year can't be less than the AMT refundable credit amount for the year (Code Sec. 53(e)(1)), and the "extra" amount so allowed is refundable. (Code Sec. 53(e)(4)) An individual's "long-term unused MTC" for a tax year is the portion of his MTC (determined under Code Sec. 53(b), above) attributable to ANMT for tax years before the third tax year immediately preceding the tax year. (Code Sec. 53(e)(3)(A)) For this purpose, credits are treated as allowed under Code Sec. 53(a) on a first-in, first-out (FIFO) basis. (Code Sec. 53(e)(3)(B))[49]

The AMT refundable credit for a tax year is the amount (not in excess of the long-term unused MTC for the year) equal to the greater of:

(1) 50% of the long-term unused MTC for the tax year, or

(2) the amount (if any) of the AMT refundable credit amount determined under Code Sec. 53(e) for the taxpayer's preceding tax year (but not including any increase under Code

---

42. ¶A-4905; ¶264, 264.01; TD ¶569,605
43. ¶A-4901; ¶264; TD ¶569,601
44. ¶A-8801; ¶534; TD ¶691,501
45. ¶A-8807; ¶534; TD ¶691,507

46. ¶A-8802; ¶534; TD ¶691,502
47. ¶A-8802; ¶534; TD ¶691,502
48. ¶A-8804; ¶534; TD ¶691,504
49. ¶A-8808, A-8811; ¶534.01; TD ¶691,508, 691,511

Sec. 53(f)(2), below). (Code Sec. 53(e)(2)) Thus, long-term unused MTCs may be claimed over a two-year period.[50]

The AMT refundable credit amount, and the MTC determined under Code Sec. 53(b), for the first two tax years beginning after 2007 are each increased by 50% of the total amount of interest and penalties attributable to the AMT ISO adjustment (¶3209) that were paid by the taxpayer before Oct. 3, 2008 and that (but for the payment) would have been abated. (Code Sec. 53(f)(2))[1] For abatement, see ¶3209.

¶ 2374 Qualified tax credit bonds; Build America Bonds—Form 8038-CP.

Taxpayers holding qualified tax credit bonds (QTCBs) on specified "credit allowance date" during the tax year are entitled to a nonrefundable credit (rather than interest payments) against regular income tax and alternative minimum tax (AMT) liability. The credit accrues quarterly and is includible in gross income as interest paid on the bond. The amount of the credit is determined by multiplying the bond's credit rate by its face amount. The credit rate is determined by IRS and is a rate that allows the bonds to be issued without discount and interest cost to the issuer. A QTCB is a specified type of bond that is part of an issue that meets requirements relating to expenditures, reporting, arbitrage, maturity, and financial conflicts of interest. (Code Sec. 54A)[2] These bonds can be QTCBs:

. . . *Qualified forestry conservation bonds (QFCBs)* issued after May 22, 2008, QFCBs can be issued by qualified issuers (states and Code Sec. 501(c)(3) organizations) to finance qualified forestry conservation projects. (Code Sec. 54A(d)(1)(A), Code Sec. 54B)[3]

. . . *New clean renewable energy bonds (new CREBs)* issued for capital expenditures incurred by government bodies, public power providers, or cooperative electric companies to finance qualified renewable energy facilities. (Code Sec. 54A(d)(1)(B), Code Sec. 54C)[4] Before new CREBs were added to the Code as qualified tax credit bonds, "old" CREBs, which could be issued through Dec. 31, 2009, were available under Code Sec. 54.[5]

. . . *Qualified energy conservation bonds (QECBs)* issued by a state or local government for qualified conservation purposes. (Code Sec. 54A(d)(1)(C), Code Sec. 54D)[6]

. . . *Qualified zone academy bonds (QZABs)* issued through 2010 by a state or local government for repairing and renovating schools as well as for school equipment and teacher training. Code Sec. 54A(d)(1)(D), Code Sec. 54E)[7]

. . . *Qualified school construction bonds (QSCBs)* issued after Feb. 17, 2009 by a state or local government for constructing, rehabilitating, or repairing a public school facility, or for acquiring land where a facility is to be constructed. (Code Sec. 54A(d)(1)(E); Code Sec. 54F)[8]

Build America Bonds. For 2009 and 2010, state and local government issuers can elect to treat otherwise tax-exempt bonds issued to finance capital projects, as taxable Build American Bonds (BABs). A taxpayer that holds a BAB on an interest payment date in the tax year is allowed a nonrefundable credit equal to 35% of the interest payable by the issuer on that date. The credit is allowed against regular tax and AMT, and is treated as taxable interest. (Code Sec. 54AA(a))[9] For certain "qualified" BABs, in lieu of the holder's credit, the issuer can elect (on Form 8038-CP) a "direct payment" option and claim a refundable credit from IRS equal to 35% (45%, for Recovery Zone Economic Development Bond (RZEDB) BABs (Code Sec. 1400U-2(a))[10]) of each interest payment made under the bond. (Code Sec. 6431(a))[11]

Direct Pay Tax Credit Bonds. For new CREBs, QECBs, QZABs, or QSCBs originally issued

50. ¶A-8809; ¶534.01; TD ¶691,509
1. ¶A-8812; ¶534.01; TD ¶691,512
2. ¶L-15530 *et seq.*; ¶54A4; TD ¶568,521
3. ¶L-15550 *et seq.*; ¶54B4
4. ¶L-15560 *et seq.*; ¶54C4
5. ¶L-16480 *et seq.*; ¶544; TD ¶384,800

6. ¶L-15570 *et seq.*; ¶54D4; TD ¶384,800
7. ¶L-15580 *et seq. et seq.*; ¶1397E4
8. ¶L-15590 *et seq.*; ¶54F4; TD ¶384,130
9. ¶L-15600 *et seq.*; ¶54AA4
10. ¶J-3339; ¶1400U-24
11. ¶L-15607; ¶64,314.01

after Mar. 18, 2010, the issuer may make an irrevocable election (on Form 8038-CP) for the bond to be treated as a "Direct Pay Tax Credit Bond" under Code Sec. 6431, entitling the issuer to receive a direct payment from IRS of an amount based on a market-determined interest rate, on the bond's interest payment dates. Special limits apply to new CREBs or QECBs. If the issuer elects the direct payment option, the holder can't claim any otherwise available QTCB credit for the bond, and is taxed on any bond interest paid to him. Any income tax deduction otherwise allowed to the issuer is reduced by the amount of the payment made under Code Sec. 6431 for the interest. (Code Sec. 6431(f))[12]

¶ 2375 Foreign Tax Credit.

Most U.S. taxpayers who pay income taxes to foreign governments may deduct them for U.S. tax purposes or may credit them dollar-for-dollar against their U.S. tax liability on their worldwide income.

Taxpayers may elect to take a foreign tax credit against U.S. income tax for income tax paid to a foreign country (or province, state, city, etc., thereof) or U.S. possession, or deduct them. (Code Sec. 901, Code Sec. 27, Code Sec. 164(a)(3); Reg § 1.901-1(a))[13] Foreign income taxes may not, however, be deducted in the same year that a credit is claimed for any foreign income tax and excess eligible foreign taxes eligible for carryover cannot be claimed in a year in which a deduction for current foreign taxes is taken. The deduction of other foreign taxes doesn't effect the creditability of foreign income taxes. (Code Sec. 164(a), Code Sec. 275(a)(4), Code Sec. 904(c); Reg § 1.901-1(c), Reg § 1.901-1(h)(2))[14]

The credit for foreign taxes paid or accrued is allowed to U.S. citizens, domestic corporations, and electing possessions corporations for compulsory payments of taxes to foreign countries and U.S. possessions, (Code Sec. 901(b)(1), Code Sec. 901(g)) except to the extent attributable to income eligible for a dividends received deduction.[15]) Aliens residing in the U.S. or residing in Puerto Rico during the entire tax year may credit taxes paid to foreign countries (Code Sec. 901(b)(3)). Nonresident aliens and foreign corporations can claim the credit for foreign or possessions tax only on certain income effectively connected with a U.S. business.[16] (Code Sec. 901(b)(4), Code Sec. 906)

A U.S. person who is a member of a partnership, a beneficiary of an estate or trust or a shareholder of an electing regulated investment company (RIC) may credit his share of foreign tax paid or accrued by the partnership, estate, trust or RIC. (Code Sec. 901(b)(5), Code Sec. 853(a)) Tax credits of a partnership, however, must be allocated in accordance with the partners' interests in the partnership, or, in the case of special allocations, in accordance with the items to which the credit relates. Allocations to claim foreign tax credits that do not track associated income may be reallocated. (Reg § 1.704-1)[17] Taxes imposed on a trust or estate on distributions to a beneficiary, including taxes on trust income imposed on a settlor or other person would be treated as owner but for Code Sec. 672(f), are creditable. (Code Sec. 642(a), Code Sec. 665(d)(2)) On a joint return, the credit is based on total taxes paid by both spouses. (Reg § 1.902-1(e))[18] The Code Sec. 936 possessions tax credit has been generally phased out, but remained effective for American Samoa for the first four tax years beginning after 2005 and before 2010. (Act Sec. 309(a), Div. C, P.L. 110-343, 10/3/2008)[19]

caution: Check *http://ria.thomsonreuters.com/federaltaxhandbook* for whether this provision has been extended.

A foreign tax is only creditable by the taxpayer upon whom foreign law imposes legal liability for the tax, even if another person pays the tax. (Reg § 1.901-2(f)) In addition, foreign

12. ¶L-15547 *et seq.*; ¶64,314.02; TD ¶568,521
13. ¶O-4002; ¶9014.04; TD ¶391,013
14. ¶O-4002; ¶K-4701; ¶2754; TD ¶326,025
15. ¶D-2226; TD ¶605,603
16. ¶O-4101, ¶O-4108; ¶O-1085;¶O-15111; ¶9014.01; TD ¶392,001
17. ¶B-2903.1 *et seq.*; ¶7044.07.
18. ¶O-4103; ¶O-4410; ¶9014 *et seq.*; TD ¶392,001 *et seq.*
19. ¶O-1500.1; ¶9314.06; TD ¶394,500.1

tax credits may be suspended when certain related persons account for the associated income in another tax period (known as a tax credit splitting event) (Code Sec. 909(d)).[20]

¶ 2376 When and how to claim foreign tax credit—Form 1116; Form 1118.

The credit is claimed on Form 1116 by an individual, trust or estate, and on Form 1118 by a corporation. (Reg § 1.905-2(a)(1))[21] A cash basis taxpayer may elect to credit *all* qualified foreign taxes on an accrual basis, but the election is binding with respect to all taxes for that year, whenever paid. (Code Sec. 905(a); Reg § 1.905-1(a))[22]

¶ 2377 What taxes qualify for a foreign tax credit?

Income taxes, war profits taxes and excess profits taxes paid or accrued during the tax year to a foreign country or a U.S. possession qualify for the foreign tax credit. (Code Sec. 901) However, a tax conditioned on its eligibility for the credit (a soak up tax), or used by the foreign country to provide a subsidy, does not qualify. A payment qualifies only if it is for a tax based on income or a so-called *in lieu* of tax. (Code Sec. 903) Taxes on wages, dividends, interest and royalties generally qualify. (Reg § 1.901-2)[23] In the case of certain elections and transactions (e.g., qualified stock purchases, acquisitions of partnership interests with a Code Sec. 754 election in place) that create additional asset basis for cost recovery in the U.S., a portion of the foreign income tax paid on the income or gain attributable to the underlying foreign assets will be disqualified. (Code Sec. 901(m))[24]

Taxes imposed by and paid to blacklisted countries may not be credited, but may be taken as itemized deductions. (Code Sec. 901(j))[25] The credit is generally denied to international boycott participants (see ¶4633).

¶ 2378 Limitations on the foreign tax credit.

The total credit for foreign taxes for a year is limited to the amount of U.S. tax that would be imposed on the taxpayer's foreign source income (Code Sec. 904(a))[26] and separate calculations are required for different categories of income (see ¶2379).

For tax years in which Code Sec. 26(a)(2) does not apply, the U.S. tax against which an individual may credit foreign income taxes is reduced by his allowable nonrefundable personal credits (see ¶2372) except certain specified personal credits, i.e., the child tax credit (¶2360), the modified Hope credit/American Opportunity tax credit in effect for 2009 and 2010 (¶2201), the saver's credit (¶2371), the alternative motor vehicle credit (¶2365), the credit for qualified plug-in electric vehicles, and the credit for new qualified plug-in electric drive motor vehicles allowable for the year (¶2367). (Code Sec. 904(i))

⚫*caution:* Check *http://ria.thomsonreuters.com/federaltaxhandbook* to see if the modified Hope credit/American Opportunity tax credit has been extended.

An individual may elect an exemption from the limitation (by not filing the Form 1116) on *de minimis* amounts if he has $300 or less ($600 in the case of joint filers) of creditable foreign taxes and no foreign source income other than qualified passive income, so long as the amounts are shown on Form 1099 or other statement. However, there is no carryover of excess foreign taxes to or from a tax year for which the election is made. (Code Sec. 904(k)(2); Reg § 1.904(j)-1)[27]

A special loss-netting rule requires a taxpayer to reduce foreign source capital gain by U.S.

20. ¶O-4102.2 *et seq.*; ¶9094.
21. ¶O-5501; ¶9054.02; TD ¶391,013
22. ¶O-5504; ¶9054.01; TD ¶391,014
23. ¶O-4200 *et seq.*; ¶9014.02; TD ¶391,005
24. ¶O-4211.1; ¶9014
25. ¶O-4007 *et seq.*; ¶K-4701; ¶9014.07; TD ¶391,012
26. ¶O-4401 *et seq.*; ¶9044.01; TD ¶393,001
27. ¶O-4413, ¶O-5500 *et seq.*; ¶9054.03

capital losses (Code Sec. 904(b)(2) and (3); Reg § 1.904(b)-1(c) and (d), Reg § 1.904(b)-1(e)(1)) and the limitation is reduced to take into account any preferential rates for capital gain and qualifying dividends (¶1290). (Code Sec. 904(b)(2); Reg § 1.904(b)-1(c) and (d), Reg § 1.904(b)-1(e)(1)) Certain noncorporate taxpayers with foreign source net capital gain of less than $20,000 may elect not to apply these adjustments. (Reg § 1.904(b)-1(b)(3), Reg § 1.904(b)-1(a)(1), Reg § 1.904(b)-1(f)(4))[28]

If foreign income taxes paid or accrued exceed the amount that may be credited for the tax year, the excess may be carried back 1 year and forward 10 years, using the current year's credits first. (Code Sec. 904(c)) Taxes are treated as carried over to the extent of any unused limitation in a year in which the taxpayer does not elect the credit, which generates no tax benefit, but a taxpayer may file an amended return within 10 years from the return due date for the year of the deduction to claim the foreign tax credit. (Reg § 1.904-2)[29] Special rules apply to carryovers of oil and gas extraction taxes. (Code Sec. 907(f))[30]

¶ 2379   Separate limitations on separate income categories.

The credit limitation is computed separately for two categories of income, i.e., the passive category income and the general category income, and is the lesser of: (1) the amount of foreign taxes paid or accrued with respect to that category, or (2) the U.S. tax on the foreign income in that category. General limitation income includes high-taxed income that otherwise would be treated as passive. (Code Sec. 901(b), Code Sec. 904(a), Code Sec. 904(d)(2)(B)(iii)) Expenses are allocated and apportioned to gross foreign source income in each category to determine foreign source taxable income (TI) in each category. (Reg § 1.861-8 – 17) The maximum credit for each category is equal to the (total foreign source TI in the category ÷ total TI) × U.S. income tax rate.[31] Additional limitations apply to foreign taxes on foreign mineral income (Reg § 1.901-3(a))[32] and foreign oil and gas extraction income. (Code Sec. 907; Reg § 1.907(a)-1, Reg § 1.907(b)-1, Reg § 1.907(c)-1, Reg § 1.907(d)-1, Reg § 1.907(f)-1)[33]

Dividends, interest, rents, and royalties received from a CFC are characterized according to the source of the income to the CFC and are subject to separate limitations only to the extent that the limitations would apply to the CFC's income. Look through treatment extends to dividends from 10% - 50% U.S. owned foreign corporations (also called noncontrolled Section 902 corporations) (¶2382). Subpart F inclusions are subject to a separate limitation based on the character of the income triggering the inclusions. (Code Sec. 904(d)(3)); Reg § 1.904-4, Reg § 1.904-5)[34]

The credit is denied for foreign withholding tax if the underlying property wasn't held for a minimum holding period, or to the extent that the recipient is obligated to make related payments with respect to positions in substantially similar or related property. (Code Sec. 901(l)) Transactions with brief asset holding period may be reportable transactions (see ¶4893).[35]

For treatment of certain foreign source income as domestic income, see ¶2380.

¶ 2380   Source rules and recapture of foreign source losses.

In applying the credit limitation (¶2378), certain includible Subpart F income (¶4625), i.e., interest, dividends, or income from a qualifying electing fund (QEF) (¶4630), is treated as U.S. source (¶4648) (Code Sec. 904(h)) notwithstanding a contrary treaty obligation, unless there is an express treaty override.[36]

28. ¶O-4404 *et seq.*; ¶9044.01; TD ¶393,005
29. ¶O-4601 *et seq.*, ¶O-5109; ¶9044.02, ¶9074.04; TD ¶394,001
30. ¶O-5200 *et seq.*, ¶O-5109, ¶O-5230; ¶9044.02, ¶9074.04 ; TD ¶394,001
31. ¶O-4401, ¶O-11001 *et seq.*; ¶9044 *et seq.*; TD ¶393,001
32. ¶O-5100 *et seq.*; ¶9014.02; TD ¶393,006
33. ¶O-5200 *et seq.*
34. ¶O-4300 *et seq.*; ¶9044.01; TD ¶393,006
35. ¶O-4011.1; ¶9041.08; TD ¶391,101.1
36. ¶O-4368.1, ¶O-4501 *et seq.*, ¶O-4511; ¶9044.01

Up to 50% (or more if the taxpayer elects) of foreign source income in any year is recharacterized as U.S. source income (which reduces the credit limitation) to the extent of any existing overall foreign loss (OFL), i.e., an excess of deductions properly allocable against foreign source income, until the OFL is completely offset. If a foreign loss offsets income in a different limitation category, income in a later year will be recharacterized as income in that other category up to the amount of the offset. (Code Sec. 904(f)) Corporations track these amounts on Form 1118, Schedule J.[37] Special overall foreign loss recapture rules apply generally to disposition of controlled foreign corporation (CFC) (¶4624) stock. (Code Sec. 904(f)(3)(D))

If a taxpayer has an overall domestic loss (ODL), that portion of U.S. source income in each later year equal to the lesser of (i) the full amount of the unrecharacterized loss not carried back, or (ii) 50% of U.S. source income for the later tax year, is recharacterized as foreign source. (Code Sec. 904(g); Reg § 1.904(g)-1T)[38]

¶ 2381 Determining amount of foreign tax payments.

A cash-basis taxpayer uses the currency exchange rate in effect on a payment date. An accrual taxpayer translates foreign taxes at the average exchange rate for the year to which the taxes relate unless the taxes are paid more than two years after, or any time before, the tax year to which they relate, or if the taxes are denominated in an inflationary currency. A taxpayer may elect to use the spot rate for foreign taxes paid in any currency other than the taxpayer's functional currency. (Code Sec. 986(a)(1); Reg § 1.905-3T(b))[39]

¶ 2382 Credit for foreign tax paid or accrued by a foreign affiliate.

A U.S. corporate shareholder may also be entitled to deemed-paid credits for a portion of foreign taxes paid by a foreign subsidiary in which it holds at least 10% of the voting stock (1st tier corporation), including taxes on earnings distributed or included in gross income of a U.S. corporate shareholder under Subpart F. A deemed paid credit may also arise for taxes paid or accrued by a 2nd- through 6th-tier foreign corporation, except that foreign taxes deemed paid on Code Sec. 956 increased investments in U.S. property cannot exceed the amount that would be deemed-paid if the inclusion were distributed up the chain of foreign corporations to the U.S. shareholder in cash. (Code Sec. 902; Reg § 1.902-1)[40] The corporation claims a credit (subject to the general limitations, ¶2378) against dividend income from the affiliate, treating a portion of the foreign tax as dividend income. (Code Sec. 78, Code Sec. 902; Reg § 1.78-1(a))

A holding period requirement must be satisfied to credit taxes on dividends and deemed paid taxes for stock (except in the case of securities dealers or brokers in the active conduct of a foreign securities dealer business); otherwise the credit is disallowed and neither the deduction disallowance (¶1755) nor the gross-up applies. (Code Sec. 901(k))

37. ¶O-4700 *et seq.*; ¶9044.01; TD ¶393,020 *et seq.*
38. ¶O-4720.1; ¶9044.01; TD ¶393,024

39. ¶O-5300; ¶9864.01
40. ¶O-4904; ¶O-4800 *et seq.*; ¶9024.01; ¶9604.03

Chapter 9 Sales and Exchanges—Tax Free Exchanges— Basis

¶ 2400 Gain or Loss on Sales or Exchanges. ▰▰▰▰▰▰▰▰▰▰▰▰▰

When a taxpayer sells or exchanges property at a price higher than his cost or tax basis, he realizes a gain. If he sells at less than his basis, he realizes a loss. He doesn't realize gain or loss when property merely goes up or down in value.

¶ 2401 Computing gain or loss on a sale or exchange.

Taxpayers have gain to the extent the amount realized from a sale or exchange exceeds their adjusted basis (usually cost, increased for improvements and decreased for depreciation or amortization). If the adjusted basis of the property disposed of exceeds the amount realized, the difference is a loss. (Code Sec. 1001(a))[1]

observation: Whether gain or loss is recognized in the year of sale depends on whether it was realized in a taxable or tax-deferred transaction.

¶ 2402 Amount realized.

The amount realized on a sale or other disposition of property is the amount of money plus the fair market value (FMV) of any property received by the seller. (Code Sec. 1001(b))[2] Where the buyer of property assumes a debt of the seller, or pays one (e.g., pays seller's taxes or legal fees), the amount of the debt is added to the amount realized by the seller. (Reg § 1.1001-2(a))[3] FMV is the price at which the property would change hands between a willing buyer and a willing seller, neither being under any compulsion to buy or sell and both having reasonable knowledge of relevant facts. (Reg § 1.170A-1(c)(2), Reg § 1.412(c)(2)-1(c)(1), Reg § 1.1445-1(g)(7))[4]

If a taxpayer sells a capital asset, his selling expenses (such as brokers' commissions) ordinarily reduce the amount realized, thus reducing the gain or increasing the loss realized on the sale.[5]

For the effect of unstated interest on a deferred payment sale or installment sale of property, see ¶1309.

¶ 2403 Amount realized on sale of property subject to a debt.

If property is sold subject to a mortgage or other debt, the amount of the mortgage is included in the sales price whether or not the seller is personally liable on the mortgage debt. This is so whether or not the buyer assumes the mortgage.[6]

In determining the gain or loss on property, its fair market value is treated as being not less than the amount of the nonrecourse debt to which it's subject. (Code Sec. 7701(g))[7]

¶ 2404 Open sales.

When a seller receives payment in the form of a property right or obligation whose value depends on future events, if the seller can prove that the right or obligation has no ascertainable value, he reports gain only when the proceeds from the obligation exceed his basis, and

---

1. ¶I-2501; ¶10,014; TD ¶222,001
2. ¶I-2502; ¶10,014; TD ¶222,002
3. ¶I-2517; ¶10,014.03; TD ¶222,011
4. ¶P-6002; ¶10,114.25; TD ¶481,001
5. ¶I-2531 *et seq.*; ¶10,014; TD ¶222,023
6. ¶I-2517; ¶10,014.03; TD ¶222,011
7. ¶I-2522; TD ¶222,019

References beginning with a single letter are to paragraphs in RIA's Federal Tax Coordinator 2d and RIA's Analysis of Federal Taxes: Income. Those beginning with numbers are to paragraphs in RIA's United States Tax Reporter. Those beginning with TD are to paragraphs in RIA's Tax Desk.

loss is fixed only when further payments can't reasonably be expected.[8] For contingent payment sales and open sales under the installment sale rules, see ¶ 2455.

¶ 2405 Repossession of mortgaged real estate.

When real property is sold and the sale gives rise to a debt to the seller secured by the real property (a purchase-money mortgage or similar lien), and the seller later repossesses the property (through voluntary transfer or foreclosure) because of actual or imminent default by the buyer, then (1) no loss results to the seller from the repossession or reacquisition, nor does the mortgage debt become worthless; and (2) the seller's gain on repossession is limited to the money and the value of other property (except the repossessed property) received by the seller with respect to the original sale to the extent these amounts haven't already been reported as income. The resulting gain can't exceed the gain on the original sale. (Code Sec. 1038)[9]

If a homeseller's gain isn't recognized under the exclusion rules explained at ¶ 2442 and he repossesses the home and then resells it within one year after the date of the repossession, the above rules don't apply; the resale of the home is treated as part of the transaction constituting the original sale of the property. (Code Sec. 1038(e))[10]

⊘observation: If the resale isn't made within one year, the regular repossession rules above apply.

¶ 2406 Personal property repossessed.

Gain or loss to the seller on repossession of personal property sold in a deferred payment transaction not on the installment method is the difference between the fair market value of the property when repossessed and the basis of the defaulted obligation (decreased by amounts paid on the note and increased for costs incurred in connection with the repossession). Gain or loss is reported in the year of repossession.[11]

¶ 2407 When cash basis taxpayers report gain or loss.

A cash basis seller reports gain on a sale or exchange in the year the sales proceeds are received, actually or constructively. A loss is reported in the year the transaction is completed by a fixed, identifiable event.[12]

¶ 2408 When accrual basis taxpayers report gain or loss.

An accrual basis seller reports gain or loss in the year the sale is completed and an unqualified right to the purchase price arises—usually when title passes to the buyer.[13] For securities sales, see ¶2410.

¶ 2409 Delivery of deed or title in escrow.

Where both the deed (or other evidence of title) and the purchase price are placed in escrow pending examination and approval of the title by the buyer, a sale isn't completed (and gain or loss isn't realized) until the buyer signifies approval. Until then, the seller doesn't have an unqualified right to payment. Once the buyer approves title, the seller can't postpone reporting gain by directing the escrow agent to hold the payment.[14]

But if the deed is delivered in escrow as security for the performance of an unconditional obligation of the buyer (usually payment of the purchase price), the sale is completed when the deed is delivered and the buyer enters into possession of the property.[15]

8. ¶G-6567 *et seq.*; ¶4534.49; TD ¶467,015
9. ¶G-6851 *et seq.*; ¶10,384; TD ¶471,001
10. ¶G-6877 *et seq.*; ¶10,384; TD ¶471,013
11. ¶G-6801; TD ¶471,020

12. ¶I-2601; ¶4514.001; TD ¶222,401
13. ¶I-2602; ¶4464.07; TD ¶222,402
14. ¶I-1112; ¶4514.087; TD ¶220,608
15. ¶I-1124; ¶4514.101; TD ¶222,030

¶ 2410　Sales and exchanges of securities.

Gain or loss on the sale of securities arises when the seller has sold or committed himself to sell specific shares.[16] Gain or loss on the exchange of securities arises when the taxpayer acquires a right to specific securities.[17]

In stock exchange transactions, cash and accrual basis taxpayers realize gain or loss on the trade date, and not on the later settlement date.[18] For short sales, see ¶ 2639.

No gain or loss is recognized by owners of securities when they loan the securities in return for the contractual obligation of the borrower to return identical securities. (Code Sec. 1058(a))[19] But there wasn't such a securities lending arrangement where an agreement underlying a securities transaction reduced the transferor's opportunity for gain on the securities transferred.[20]

Gain or loss isn't recognized if the lender of the securities timely purchases replacement securities with collateral furnished by the borrower, after the borrower has defaulted on the agreement due to bankruptcy.[21]

Transactions structured to appear to be loans are sometimes found to be sales where they have the practical effect of sales, e.g., certain forward share and/or lending agreements where the taxpayer no longer has any substantial risk of loss.[22]

¶ 2411　Sales of load mutual funds with reinvestment right.

A load charge incurred in buying mutual fund shares is disregarded (in whole or in part) in computing gain or loss on the disposition of those shares within 90 days, if the buyer was given a reinvestment right under which shares in the same (or another) mutual fund could be bought at less than the usual load charge. The load charge is disregarded to the extent of the reduction in the load charge on the later purchase. (Code Sec. 852(f))[23]

¶ 2412　Significant modification of debt instrument treated as exchange.

A significant modification of a debt instrument results in an exchange of the original debt instrument for a modified instrument that differs materially either in kind or in extent. (Reg § 1.1001-3(b))[24]

🅡 *observation:* The like-kind exchange rules (¶2418 *et seq.*) don't apply to exchanges of bonds, notes or other evidences of indebtedness. Exchanges of corporate bonds, but not of government bonds, may be tax-free under the reorganization provisions of the Code, but only to the extent the principal amount isn't increased. Thus, in most cases, an exchange (or modification, which is considered an exchange for tax purposes) results in the holder's recognizing gain or loss. For example, if a modification of a debt instrument results in a reduction of the debt, the debtor will have cancellation of debt income. (¶1390)

Examples of significant modifications in the terms of a debt instrument include:

. . . A change in the yield of a debt instrument, if the yield varies from the annual yield on the unmodified instrument (determined as of the date of the modification) by more than the greater of: 1/4 of 1% (25 basis points), or 5% of the annual yield of the unmodified instrument (.05 × annual yield). (Reg § 1.1001-3(e)(2)(ii))

. . . A modification that changes the timing of payments (including any resulting change in the amount of payments), if it results in the material deferral of scheduled payments.

16. ¶I-2615; ¶12,234.07; TD ¶222,601
17. ¶I-2616; ¶12,234.07, 4514.112; TD ¶222,603
18. ¶I-2615.1; ¶4514.112; TD ¶222,602
19. ¶I-1311, I-3802; ¶10,584; TD ¶221,007
20. ¶I-1311; TD ¶221,007, TD ¶221,007

21. ¶I-1311
22. ¶I-3111 *et seq.*; TD ¶221,000 *et seq.*
23. ¶P-5038 *et seq.*; ¶8524.02; TD ¶216,021
24. ¶I-1050 *et seq.*; ¶10,014.83; TD ¶220,400 *et seq.*

(Reg § 1.1001-3(e)(3)(i))

In some situations, a modification of a debt instrument may cause it to be recharacterized as an instrument or property right that is not debt, but usually a deterioration in the debtor's financial condition is not taken into account in making that determination.[25]

Qualifying taxpayers may elect to treat a substitution of certain publicly traded debt instruments for new ones as a realization event even if the substitution doesn't result in a significant modification of the terms of the old debt instrument, and therefore is not an exchange for tax purposes. Electing taxpayers do not recognize any realized gain or loss on the date of the substitution. Instead, gain or loss generally is taken into account as income or deductions over the term of the new debt instruments.[26]

¶ 2413 Nontaxable Exchanges.

A taxpayer doesn't recognize gain or loss on exchanges of common or preferred stock for other common or preferred stock of the same corporation. A corporation doesn't recognize gain or loss when it sells or exchanges its own stock for property or services. Certain U.S. obligations can be exchanged tax-free. Additionally, Code Sec. 1043 allows deferral of gain for conflict of interest sales by certain federal employees and related persons.

¶ 2414 Stock for stock of same corporation.

No gain or loss is recognized on the exchange of common stock for other common, or preferred stock for other preferred, of the same corporation. (Code Sec. 1036(a)) It's tax-free whether between a shareholder and the corporation or between two shareholders.[27]

Nonqualified preferred stock (¶3514) is treated as property other than stock for purposes of the rule allowing tax-deferred exchanges of preferred stock in the same corporation. (Code Sec. 1036(b))[28]

An exchange between individual shareholders, of common for preferred stock in the same corporation, isn't tax-free. (Reg § 1.1036-1(a))[29] However, reorganization exchanges of stock for stock or stock and securities of the same or different corporations may be tax-free, see ¶3541 *et seq.*

¶ 2415 Corporation's sale or exchange of its own stock for property or services.

A corporation doesn't recognize gain or loss on the sale or exchange of its stock (including treasury stock) for money, other property or services. (Code Sec. 1032(a); Reg § 1.1032-1)[30] And it doesn't recognize gain or loss on the lapse of an option (warrant) to buy or sell its stock (including treasury stock). (Code Sec. 1032(a); Reg § 1.1032-3(d))[31]

¶ 2416 Tax-free exchanges of U.S. obligations.

IRS regs may provide for the tax-free exchange of one U.S. obligation (bond, note, etc.) for another. (Code Sec. 1037(a)) The Treasury designates the specific obligations it will exchange for the previously issued obligations without recognition of gain or loss.[32]

¶ 2417 Tax-free exchanges of insurance policies and annuities.

No gain or loss is recognized upon the exchange of a life insurance contract for another or for an endowment or annuity contract, an endowment contract for an annuity or endowment

---

25. ¶I-1075.1; ¶10,014.83
26. ¶I-1081.8; ¶10,014.83; TD ¶220,411
27. ¶I-3301; ¶10,364; TD ¶225,501
28. ¶I-3301.1; ¶10,364; TD ¶225,501

29. ¶I-3301; TD ¶225,501
30. ¶I-3201, I-3208; ¶10,324; TD ¶233,401
31. ¶I-6517; ¶10,324; TD ¶252,010
32. ¶I-3400 *et seq.*; ¶10,374; TD ¶227,301

contract providing for regular payments beginning at a date not later than the beginning date under the old contract, or an annuity contract for another. To qualify for tax-free exchange treatment, the insured or annuitant must remain the same. (Code Sec. 1035) The direct transfer of a portion of funds from one annuity contract to another annuity contract qualifies as a nontaxable exchange under Code Sec. 1035. Thus, the direct exchange of part of the cash surrender value of an annuity contract for a new annuity contract issued by a second insurance company is tax-free even though the original annuity contract continued to exist.[33]

To the extent provided in regs, the rules allowing a tax-free exchange of insurance policies and annuities don't apply to any exchange having the effect of transferring property to a non-U.S. person. (Code Sec. 1035(c))[34]

No gain or loss is recognized on the exchange of a life insurance contract or an annuity contract for a qualified long-term care contract. (Code Sec. 1035(a))[35]

¶ 2418   "Like-Kind" (Code Sec. 1031) Exchanges.

No gain or loss is recognized where business or investment property is exchanged solely for like-kind property. Multi-party exchanges may qualify. However, gain, but not loss, is recognized if boot is also received.

This nonrecognition provision doesn't apply to: stock in trade (inventory) and other property held primarily for sale; stocks, bonds, and notes; choices in action; interests in a partnership; certificates of trust or beneficial interest; or other securities or evidences of indebtedness or interest. (Code Sec. 1031(a))[36]

The rule barring exchanges of stocks from nonrecognition treatment does not apply to certain shares in a mutual ditch, reservoir, or irrigation company. (Code Sec. 1031(i))[37]

Nonrecognition under Code Sec. 1031 is mandatory if the conditions are met.[38]

Report on Form 8824, in addition to Form 1040, Schedule D, Form 4797, or Form 6252 (whichever applies).[39]

¶ 2419   Like-kind defined.

"Like-kind" refers to the nature, character, or class of the property, not to its grade or quality. Thus, an exchange of real estate for real estate is an exchange of "like-kind" property. It doesn't matter where the real estate is located (but foreign and U.S. real property can't be like-kind) or whether it's improved or not. (Code Sec. 1031(h); Reg § 1.1031(a)-1(b))[40]

Personal property used predominantly in the U.S. and personal property used predominantly outside the U.S. aren't like-kind. (Code Sec. 1031(h)(2)(A)) In general, predominant use of relinquished property is determined based on the 2-year period that ends when the property is relinquished, and predominant use of the replacement property is determined based on the 2-year period beginning on the acquisition date. (Code Sec. 1031(h)(2)(B))[41]

Depreciable tangible personal property is exchanged for property of a "like kind" if it is exchanged for property of a like kind or like class. It is of a like class to other depreciable tangible personal property if the exchanged properties are either within the same General Asset Class or within the same Product Class. (Reg § 1.1031(a)-2(b)(1)) General asset classes are set forth by Revenue Procedure (Reg § 1.1031(a)-2(b)(2)); product classes are in Sectors 31, 32, and 33 (pertaining to manufacturing industries) of the North American Industry Classification System (NAICS) Manual. (Reg § 1.1031(a)-2(b)(3))[42]

IRS has ruled that cars, light general-purpose trucks, crossovers, sport-utility vehicles

---

33. ¶J-5302.2 *et seq.*; ¶10,354; TD ¶146,617
34. ¶J-5306.1; ¶10,354; TD ¶146,623
35. ¶J-5301; ¶10,354; TD ¶146,616
36. ¶I-3050 *et seq.*; ¶10,314 *et seq.*; TD ¶223,601 *et seq.*
37. ¶I-3091.1; ¶10,314.04

38. ¶I-3052; TD ¶223,603
39. ¶I-3051; TD ¶223,602
40. ¶I-3059; ¶10,314.02; TD ¶223,701
41. ¶I-3064.1; ¶10,314.04; TD ¶223,706
42. ¶I-3060 *et seq.*; ¶10,314.02; TD ¶223,703 *et seq.*

(SUVs), minivans, and cargo vans are all like-kind for purposes of Code Sec. 1031.[43]

No like classes are provided for nondepreciable or intangible personal property (e.g., a patent or copyright); an exchange of such property qualifies for nonrecognition only if the exchanged properties are of a like kind. (Reg § 1.1031(a)-2(c)(1)) The goodwill or going concern value of a business can't be like-kind property. (Reg § 1.1031(a)-2(c)(2)) Reversing a long-held position, IRS has determined that intangible assets such as trademarks, tradenames, mastheads, and customer-based intangibles, that can be valued separately and apart from goodwill, can qualify as like-kind property, as can emissions credits.[44]

An exchange of real property for a 30-year leasehold on real property is a like-kind exchange. (Reg § 1.1031(a)-1(c))[45] An exchange of real property for an interest in a Delaware statutory trust (DST) that owned real property was like-kind since the DST was a grantor trust (¶3956) and the taxpayers (who received DST interests as replacement property) were treated as owning undivided fractional shares of the real property held by the DST.[46] Also, an undivided fractional interest in real property may qualify as like-kind replacement property for other real property.[47] Development rights that a corporation intended to acquire as replacement property were like-kind to a fee interest in relinquished property.[48]

Trade-ins are a common type of nontaxable exchange. Whether the taxpayer pays money or not, the trade-in is still a nontaxable exchange. (Reg § 1.1031(a)-1(c))[49]

IRS won't challenge whether a dwelling unit (e.g., a vacation home) qualifies as property held for productive use in a trade or business or for investment purposes if the unit (whether relinquished property or replacement property) meets certain ownership, rental, and personal use tests.[50]

¶ 2420   Multi-party (including deferred) nontaxable exchanges.

If a taxpayer wants to (or will only) exchange his property for like-kind property, but the party who wants taxpayer's property doesn't own the like-kind property, the taxpayer can still set up a nontaxable exchange if the other party acquires the like-kind property and taxpayer then exchanges his property for that like-kind property.

illustration: A holds Whiteacre for investment. He doesn't want to sell it if that would result in tax, but he would exchange it for Blackacre. B wants Whiteacre. C owns Blackacre and is willing to sell, but doesn't want Whiteacre. B buys Blackacre from C for cash. A transfers Whiteacre to B for Blackacre. The exchange is nontaxable to A.

The exchange is nontaxable (if the time limits at ¶2423 are met) even where the taxpayer transfers property in exchange for a written promise by the transferee to deliver like-kind property to the taxpayer in the future, i.e., a deferred or nonsimultaneous exchange.

A multiparty nontaxable exchange can be set up by using a qualified intermediary (QI) (someone other than the taxpayer or a "disqualified person," e.g., taxpayer's agent) to facilitate the transaction. (Reg § 1.1031(k)-1(g)(4))[1] Reverse exchanges (replacement property is acquired before the relinquished property is transferred) may be implemented using qualified exchange accommodation arrangements under IRS-approved safe-harbor rules. However, the safe-harbor rules do not apply to replacement property owned by the taxpayer within the 180-day period ending on the date of transfer of ownership of the property to an exchange accommodation titleholder. IRS recognizes, however, that under case law, some reverse exchanges may still qualify even if they do not meet the safe-harbor requirements.[2]

IRS Office of Chief Counsel said that a taxpayer may engage in a "reverse" like-kind exchange (in which replacement property is parked with an accommodation titleholder before

---

43.   ¶I-3066; TD ¶223,708
44.   ¶I-3065; ¶10,314.02; TD ¶223,707
45.   ¶I-3076; ¶10,314.03; TD ¶223,716
46.   ¶I-3074
47.   ¶I-3092.1; TD ¶224,003.1

48.   ¶I-3073
49.   ¶I-3057; ¶10,314.15; TD ¶223,708
50.   ¶I-3083.2 *et seq.*; ¶10,314.01; TD ¶224,001
1.   ¶I-3119, I-3120; ¶10,314.10; TD ¶224,230
2.   ¶I-3095 *et seq.*; ¶10,314.10; TD ¶224,800 *et seq.*

the relinquished property's transfer), and a deferred "forward" like-kind exchange, using the same relinquished property in both exchanges.[3]

Where property or cash is set aside in a qualified escrow account, qualified trust, or similar account ("exchange funds") pending completion of a deferred like-kind exchange, the exchange funds are generally treated as an exchange facilitator loan, i.e., a demand loan from the taxpayer to the exchange facilitator (i.e., the QI, transferee, escrow holder, trustee, or other party holding exchange funds for the taxpayer in the deferred exchange), and all items of income, deduction, and credit (including capital gains and losses) attributable to the exchange funds are taken into account by the exchange facilitator. (Reg § 1.468B-6(c)(1), Reg § 1.468B-6(f)(1))[4] Exchange facilitator loans are subject to imputed-interest rules, but exemptions are available (e.g., if $2 million or less is treated as loaned and the funds are held for six months or less). (Reg § 1.7872-16(c), Reg § 1.7872-16(d), Reg § 1.7872-16(f), Reg § 1.7872-16(g))[5] If all earnings attributable to the exchange funds are paid to the taxpayer under the terms of the agreement, then the taxpayer takes all items of income, deduction, and credit into account. (Reg § 1.468B-6(c)(2))[6]

¶ 2421 Taxing "boot" in otherwise nontaxable exchange.

If a taxpayer receives boot—money or any other property that doesn't qualify for nonrecognition of gain—in an otherwise nontaxable exchange of stock (¶2414), insurance policies (¶2417), like-kind property (¶2418), or U.S. obligations (¶2416), then gain to the taxpayer is recognized (is taxable) in an amount not exceeding the value of the boot received (Code Sec. 1031(b)), but loss to the taxpayer isn't recognized (isn't deductible) to any extent. (Code Sec. 1031(c))[7]

⚫illustration: Taxpayer exchanges business real estate worth $50,000 and having an adjusted basis of $30,000 for business real estate worth $40,000 plus $10,000 cash. His total gain is $20,000 ($40,000 + $10,000 – $30,000 basis), but the amount recognized is limited to the boot—$10,000. The tax on the remaining $10,000 gain is deferred because the transaction qualifies as a like-kind exchange.

Where the taxpayer gives money in the nontaxable exchange, no gain is recognized. But if the boot given is property other than money, gain or loss may be recognized. Thus, where stock that has depreciated in value is given in connection with a nontaxable exchange of real estate, loss on the stock is recognized to the extent the stock's adjusted basis exceeds its fair market value. (Reg § 1.1031(d)-1(e))[8]

¶ 2422 Assumption of liabilities.

Liabilities assumed are treated as a cash equivalent (boot). Whether a liability is "assumed" for this purpose is determined under Code Sec. 357(d) (see ¶3516). (Code Sec. 1031(d)) The taxpayer who assumes the liability is the one giving the boot, while the taxpayer whose liability is assumed *receives* the boot.[9] If each party assumes a liability of the other, only the net liability is boot given or received. (Reg § 1.1031(b)-1(c))

In determining the basis of the property received in a nontaxable exchange, liabilities assumed by the other party are treated as money (boot) received by the taxpayer. (Reg § 1.1031(d)-2)

---

3. ¶I-3098.6
4. ¶J-1379.1 *et seq.*; ¶468B4.2
5. ¶J-1379.1A *et seq.*; ¶78,724.14
6. ¶J-1379.1J *et seq.*; ¶468B4.2

7. ¶I-3160; ¶10,314.11; TD ¶225,001
8. ¶I-3163; ¶10,314.11; TD ¶225,001
9. ¶I-3165; ¶10,314.12; TD ¶225,005

¶ 2423   Time limits on like-kind exchanges.

Like-kind treatment is barred if the property to be received is not identified (e.g., by being specified in the contract) on or before 45 days after the transfer, or isn't received within 180 days after the transfer or by the due date (with extensions) of the return for the year of transfer if earlier. (Code Sec. 1031(a)(3))[10] There's no good faith exception to these deadlines,[11] but the deadlines may be extended for like-kind exchanges affected by disasters.[12] There is also a safe harbor method of reporting gain or loss for certain taxpayers who initiate deferred like-kind exchanges but fail to complete the exchange because a qualified intermediary defaults on its obligation to acquire and transfer replacement property to the taxpayer.[13]

¶ 2424   Related-party exchanges.

Where a taxpayer exchanges like-kind property with a related taxpayer under Code Sec. 267(b) (see ¶2448), or Code Sec. 707(b)(1) (see ¶3731) and, within two years of the date of the last transfer that was part of the exchange, either party disposes of the property received in the exchange, then gain or loss not recognized in the exchange is recognized on the date the later disposition occurs. A disposition includes indirect transfers. Exceptions are made for death, certain involuntary conversions, and non-tax-avoidance transactions. (Code Sec. 1031(f))[14] Form 8824 must be filed for the year of the exchange and also for the two years following the exchange.[15]

A qualified intermediary (QI) (¶2420) can't be used to circumvent the limitations that would have applied to a direct exchange between related parties. For example, an exchange was part of a transaction to avoid the related party rules (and didn't qualify for nonrecognition treatment) where: (1) a taxpayer (T) transferred appreciated property to a QI, which (2) sold it to an unrelated party and used the proceeds to purchase like-kind property from a party related to T, then (3) transferred that property to T.[16]

¶ 2425   Exchanges of multiple properties.

These are exchanges in which more than one "exchange group" (see below) is created, or exchanges in which only one exchange group is created but there is more than one property being transferred or received within that exchange group. To compute gain, (1) separate the properties transferred into "exchange groups," (2) offset all liabilities assumed by the taxpayer as part of the exchange by all liabilities of which the taxpayer is relieved as part of the exchange, with the excess liabilities assumed or relieved allocated among the exchange groups, and (3) apply the rules of Code Sec. 1031 and the regs separately to each exchange group to determine the amount of gain recognized in the exchange and the basis of the properties received in the exchange. (Reg § 1.1031(j)-1(a)(2)(i))[17]

Each "exchange group" consists of the properties transferred and received in the exchange, all of which are of a like kind or like class. (Reg § 1.1031(j)-1(b)(2)(i))[18]

¶ 2426   Rollover of Gain From Certain Sales.

Eligible taxpayers may elect to roll over gain from (1) the sale of publicly traded securities tax-free into an investment in a Specialized Small Business Investment Company (SSBIC) (¶2427), (2) the sale of qualified empowerment zone assets (¶2428), and (3) the sale of qualified small business stock (¶2429), if certain holding period and reinvestment requirements are met.

---

10. ¶I-3099; ¶10,314.08; TD ¶224,209
11. ¶I-3101; TD ¶224,209
12. ¶S-8012; TD ¶904,003
13. ¶I-3120.2 *et seq.*; TD ¶224,244 *et seq.*
14. ¶I-3132 *et seq.*; ¶10,314.07; TD ¶224,701

15. ¶I-3132; TD ¶224,701
16. ¶I-3137
17. ¶I-3187; TD ¶225,402
18. ¶I-3138 *et seq.*; ¶10,314.10; TD ¶225,408

¶ 2427   Rollover of securities sale gain into SSBICs.

An individual and a C corporation may elect to limit the amount of capital gain they recognize on the sale of "publicly traded securities" (securities traded on an open market) to the excess of the amount realized on the sale, over (1) the cost of any common stock or partnership interest in a specialized small business investment company (SSBIC) bought during the 60-day period beginning on the sale date, reduced by (2) any part of that cost previously taken into account under this rule. (Code Sec. 1044(a), Code Sec. 1044(c)(1))[19]

An SSBIC is any partnership or corporation licensed by the Small Business Administration under Sec. 301(d) of the Small Business Investment Act of '58 as in effect on May 13, '93. (Code Sec. 1044(c)(3))[20]

The gain an individual may roll over under the SSBIC rules for any tax year may not exceed the lesser of: $50,000, or $500,000 reduced by any gain excluded (rolled over) under this rule in all preceding years. (Code Sec. 1044(b)(1)) For married persons filing separately, the limits are $25,000 and $250,000, respectively. (Code Sec. 1044(b)(3))[21]

A C corporation's rollover for any tax year may not exceed the lesser of $250,000 or $1,000,000 reduced by any gain excluded under this rule in all preceding years. (Code Sec. 1044(b)(2)) This includes exclusions by members of the corporation's controlled group, or by its predecessor. (Code Sec. 1044(b)(4))[22]

Elect by reporting the entire gain from the sale of the publicly traded securities on Schedule D of the return on or before the due date (including extensions) for the year the publicly traded securities are sold and by attaching a statement to Schedule D showing (1) how the nonrecognized gain was calculated; (2) the SSBIC in which common stock or a partnership interest was purchased and the date the stock or interest was purchased; and (3) the basis of the SSBIC stock or interest. (Reg § 1.1044(a)-1(b))[23]

For the effect of gain not recognized under the SSBIC rules upon taxpayer's basis in an SSBIC investment, see ¶2505.

¶ 2428   Election to roll over gain from qualified empowerment zone assets.

A taxpayer can elect to defer recognition of capital gain on the sale of a qualified empowerment zone asset held for more than one year where replacement empowerment zone assets are purchased within 60 days. (Code Sec. 1397B(a), Code Sec. 1391(d)(1)(A)(i)) DC Enterprise Zone assets aren't eligible for the tax-free rollover treatment. (Code Sec. 1397B(b)(1)(B))

The rollover rules do not apply to any gain treated as ordinary income or any gain attributable to real property, or an intangible asset, which is not an integral part of an enterprise zone business. (Code Sec. 1397B(b)(2))

If the rollover is elected, capital gain from the sale of a qualified empowerment zone asset is recognized only to the extent that the amount realized from the sale exceeds the cost of any qualified empowerment zone asset (with respect to the same zone as the asset sold) purchased during the 60-day period beginning on the sale date, reduced by any part of the cost previously taken into account under this rollover rule. (Code Sec. 1397B(a))

The basis of the replacement zone asset is reduced by gain not recognized on the rollover, but this rule doesn't apply for purposes of Code Sec. 1202 (exclusion for gain on the sale of small business stock; see ¶2648). (Code Sec. 1397B(b)(4))

The holding period of the replacement zone asset includes the holding period of the original zone asset, except that the replacement asset must actually be held for more than one year to

19. ¶I-3791; ¶10,444; TD ¶225,503
20. ¶I-3794; ¶10,444; TD ¶225,503
21. ¶I-3792; ¶10,444; TD ¶225,504

22. ¶I-3793; ¶10,444; TD ¶225,504
23. ¶I-3795; ¶10,444; TD ¶225,505

qualify for another tax-free rollover. (Code Sec. 1223(13), Code Sec. 1397B(b)(5)(A))[24]

¶ 2429   Election to roll over capital gain from sale of QSBS.

Taxpayers other than corporations may elect to roll over capital gain from the sale of qualified small business stock (QSBS) (defined at ¶2649) held for more than six months, so that gain is recognized only to the extent that the amount realized exceeds (1) the cost of QSBS bought during the 60-day period beginning on the sale date, reduced by (2) any part of the cost previously taken into account under the rule. (Code Sec. 1045(a))

Rules similar to the rules that, under Code Sec. 1202(g) (¶2648), determine which holders of interests in pass-through entities are eligible for the 50% exclusion of gain from the sale of QSBS, apply to the rollover of gain from the sale of QSBS by a pass-through entity. (Code Sec. 1045(b)(5))[25]

The holding period of the replacement stock includes the holding period of the stock sold, but not for purposes of determining whether the 6-month holding period required for rollovers is met. To qualify as small business stock, the issuing corporation must meet an active business test during substantially all of the taxpayer's holding period for the stock. For purposes of the rollover provision, the replacement stock must meet this active business requirement for the six-month period following the purchase. (Code Sec. 1045(b)(4))[26]

For adjustments to basis of the replacement QSBS, see ¶2506.

¶ 2430   Involuntary Conversions. ▉▉▉▉▉▉▉▉▉▉▉▉▉▉▉▉▉▉▉▉▉▉▉

No gain is recognized when property is compulsorily or involuntarily converted into property similar or related in service or use. Where property is involuntarily converted into money or into property that isn't similar or related in service or use, a taxpayer can avoid tax on any gain, if he so elects and he buys property that's similar or related in service or use or if he acquires control of a corporation that owns such property (or acquires the property within a specified time). The cost of the replacement property must be equal to or more than the net proceeds from the converted property. And the replacement must generally be made within two years after the close of the first tax year in which any part of the gain is realized. (Code Sec. 1033) A loss on an involuntary conversion is recognized or not recognized without regard to the involuntary conversion rules. (Reg § 1.1033(a)-1(a))[27] Individuals use Form 1040 Schedule D, to report gain or loss from an involuntary conversion. Form 4797 is used to report an involuntary conversion of assets used in a trade or business.[28]

¶ 2431   Nonrecognition of gain on involuntary conversions.

Where property is involuntarily converted into other property similar or related in service or use to the converted property, no gain is recognized. (Code Sec. 1033(a)(1)) However, where the taxpayer receives dissimilar property or cash when his property is involuntarily converted, he must, within a specified time, buy "replacement" property, see ¶2438,[29] or must buy 80% control of a corporation owning or, within the specified time, acquiring replacement property.[30] Gain is recognized only to the extent the amount realized on the conversion exceeds the cost of the replacement property. (Code Sec. 1033(a)(2)(A))[31]

If a principal residence is involuntarily converted and gain is excluded under Code Sec. 121 (¶2442), then the amount realized for purposes of the involuntary conversion provisions is the amount realized less the excluded gain. (Code Sec. 121(d)(5)(B))[32]

---

24. ¶I-3430 *et seq.*; ¶13,97B4; TD ¶227,350 *et seq.*
25. ¶I-9201; ¶10,454; TD ¶247,201
26. ¶I-9204; ¶10,454; TD ¶247,204
27. ¶I-3701; ¶10,334; TD ¶229,701
28. ¶I-3773; ¶10,334.26; TD ¶229,702

29. ¶I-3700 *et seq.*; ¶10,334 *et seq.*; TD ¶229,701
30. ¶I-3743; ¶10,334.23; TD ¶229,736
31. ¶I-3701; ¶10,334.31; TD ¶229,743
32. ¶I-4565; ¶1214.14; TD ¶225,745

A business that realized gain from a state disaster relief grant to reimburse it for disaster-related damage to real and personal property may elect to defer the gain to the extent that an amount equal to the grant proceeds is used to timely purchase property similar or related in service or use to the destroyed or damaged property.[33]

¶ 2432 Involuntary conversion defined.

An involuntary conversion is the compulsory or involuntary conversion of taxpayer's property into similar property, dissimilar property or money as a result of the property's destruction, theft, seizure, requisition or condemnation (actual or threatened). (Code Sec. 1033(a))

Involuntary conversion includes certain sales—sales in actual or threatened condemnation (¶2435), certain sales (or the destruction) of livestock due to disease (Code Sec. 1033(d)), and the sale or exchange of livestock (in excess of the number taxpayer would sell if he followed his usual business practices) solely on account of drought, flood, or other weather-related conditions. (Code Sec. 1033(e)(1))[34]

If property is sold or otherwise transferred to the federal government, a state or local government, or an Indian tribal government to implement hazard mitigation under the Robert T. Stafford Disaster Relief and Emergency Assistance Act (as in effect on Apr. 15, 2005) or the National Flood Insurance Act (as in effect on that date), the sale or transfer is treated as an involuntary conversion. (Code Sec. 1033(k))[35] The sale of publicly traded stock under a state escheat law has also been ruled an involuntary conversion.[36]

¶ 2433 Principal residence or contents converted as result of federally declared disaster.

If the taxpayer's principal residence, or any of its contents, is located in a disaster area and is compulsorily or involuntarily converted because of a "federally declared disaster" declared in a tax year beginning after 2007 and occurring before 2010, any gain resulting from the receipt of insurance proceeds for personal property that was part of the contents of the residence and wasn't "scheduled property" for insurance purposes, isn't recognized, regardless of the use to which the taxpayer puts those proceeds. (Code Sec. 1033(h)(1))[37] "Federally declared disaster" and "disaster area" are defined in Code Sec. 165(h)(3)(C)(i). (Code Sec. 1033(h)(3)) Insurance proceeds received for the home or its "separately scheduled" contents are treated as received for a single item of property, and any property which is similar or related in service or use to the residence so converted (or its contents) is treated for purposes of the involuntary conversion rules as property similar or related in service or use to that single item of property.[38]

⊘ caution: Check http://ria.thomsonreuters.com/federaltaxhandbook to see if this provision has been extended.

For the extended replacement period that applies, see ¶2441.

¶ 2434 Insurance that compensates for the loss of the right to use property.

Insurance proceeds that compensate for the loss of the right to use the property due to loss or destruction may qualify for nonrecognition as involuntary conversion proceeds, but the proceeds of a use and occupancy insurance contract that expressly insures against actual lost profits don't qualify and are treated as taxable income. (Reg § 1.1033(a)-2(c)(8))[39]

---

33. ¶I-3702; TD ¶229,713
34. ¶N-1216 *et seq.*; ¶10,334.01; TD ¶229,713.1
35. ¶I-3716.1; ¶10,334.01; TD ¶193,606
36. ¶I-3709

37. ¶I-3772.1 *et seq.*; ¶10,334.40; TD ¶229,750
38. ¶I-3772.2; ¶10,334.40; TD ¶229,750
39. ¶I-3724; ¶10,334.12; TD ¶229,749

¶ 2435   Condemnations—actual or threatened.

A disposition under the threat or imminence of condemnation is treated as an involuntary conversion. (Code Sec. 1033(a)(2)(E)(ii))

Threat or imminence of condemnation exists (1) when taxpayer is informed, orally or in writing, by a representative of a governmental body or an authorized public official, that the body or official has decided to acquire the property, and taxpayer has reasonable grounds to believe that condemnation proceedings will be initiated if he doesn't voluntarily sell, and (2) where the taxpayer gets information as to a decision to acquire the property for public use through a report in the news media, if a representative of the governmental body or public official involved confirms the published report and taxpayer has reasonable grounds to believe that the necessary steps to condemn will be taken if he doesn't sell.[40] Sales to third parties (as distinguished from the condemning agency) also qualify as involuntary conversions if made under the threat or imminence of condemnation.[41] IRS has provided guidance stating that equipment replacements mandated by the Federal Communications Commission also constitute involuntary conversions.

¶ 2436   Amount of condemnation awards.

Condemnation proceeds cannot be greater than the amount specifically awarded for the requisitioned property. It may, however, be less if there are any legal or other expenses or special assessments which must be deducted. But sums withheld from the award to pay liens on the property don't reduce the amount realized.[42]

¶ 2437   Severance damages.

Where only part of the property is condemned, the owner may be paid severance damages as compensation for a loss of value in the part of the property retained. Severance damages may be paid, for example, because of impairment of access to the property retained.[43] Payments are considered severance damages only if specifically agreed to in the condemnation proceeding; otherwise, the entire award is considered made for the condemned property.[44] Where severance damage proceeds are used to acquire replacement property, the taxpayer may elect nonrecognition under the involuntary conversion rules with respect to any gain from receipt of the severance damages.[45]

¶ 2438   Replacement property.

The replacement property must be similar or related in service or use to the property replaced. (Code Sec. 1033(a)(1)) "Similar or related in service or use" means the use of the replacement property must be substantially similar to the use of the replaced property.[46]

As an alternative to direct replacement of the converted property, the taxpayer may acquire control of a corporation owning property similar to that converted. (Code Sec. 1033(a)(2)(A)) Where this method is used, however, the special "like-kind" replacement rule (¶2440) isn't available. The replacement property must qualify under the "similar use" rule. (Code Sec. 1033(g)(2))[47]

This test as applied to an owner-lessor of property looks to the use of the replacement property from the lessor's viewpoint, not the lessee's. If the replacement property involves similar business risks, management and landlord services, etc., it will qualify even though

---

40. ¶I-3703; ¶10,334.02; TD ¶229,713
41. ¶I-3706; TD ¶229,714
42. ¶I-3764; ¶10,334.31; TD ¶229,745
43. ¶I-3768; ¶10,334.14; TD ¶229,747

44. ¶I-3770; ¶10,334.14; TD ¶229,747
45. ¶I-3768; ¶10,334.14; TD ¶229,747
46. ¶I-3725; ¶10,334.22; TD ¶229,727
47. ¶I-3743; ¶10,334.22; TD ¶229,736

the lessee's use of the new property differs from the lessee's use of the old. [48]

Tangible property acquired and held for productive use in a trade or business is treated as similar or related in service or use to property that (a) was held for investment or for productive use on a trade or business, and (b) was involuntarily converted as a result of a federally declared disaster (see ¶2433) declared in a tax year beginning after 2007 and occurring before 2010. (Code Sec. 1033(h)(2))[49]

⊙illustration: If a business loses its delivery truck in a federally declared disaster, it can avoid current tax on the gain realized by timely (see ¶2441) reinvesting the insurance proceeds in a production machine.

If, because of drought, flood, or other weather-related conditions or soil contamination or other environmental contamination, it is not feasible for the taxpayer to reinvest the proceeds from compulsorily or involuntarily converted livestock (see ¶2432) in property similar or related in use to the old livestock, he may reinvest the proceeds in other property used for farming purposes. In the case of soil contamination or other environmental contamination, "other property used for farming purposes" includes real property. (Code Sec. 1033(f))[50]

¶ 2439 Related-person exception to nonrecognition rule.

Nonrecognition treatment for gain in an involuntary conversion isn't permitted if a taxpayer described below acquires replacement property or stock from a related party (under Code Sec. 267(b) (¶2448), or Code Sec. 707(b)(1) (¶3731):

. . . C corporations.

. . . A partnership if one or more C corporations own, directly or indirectly under Code Sec. 707(b)(3) (¶3733) more than 50% of the capital interest or the profits interest of the partnership at the time of the involuntary conversion.

. . . Any other taxpayer (including an individual) if, with respect to property which is involuntarily converted during the tax year, the aggregate realized gain on property on which there is realized gain exceeds $100,000. (Code Sec. 1033(i)(2))[1]

However, nonrecognition does apply to the extent the related party acquired the replacement property or stock from an unrelated party, within the period allowed for the acquisition of replacement property or stock. (Code Sec. 1033(i)(1))[2]

In the case of a partnership (or S corporation), this denial of nonrecognition rule applies to a partnership (or S corporation) and to each partner (or S shareholder). Thus, the annual $100,000 limit applies to both the entity and each partner (or S corporation shareholder).[3]

¶ 2440 Replacement of condemned real estate.

A replacement of condemned real estate held for productive business use or for rental or investment qualifies for nonrecognition treatment if the replacement property is property of a like-kind. (Code Sec. 1033(g)(1)) Determination of whether replacement property is of like-kind is made under the rules at ¶2418, rather than the "similar use" rule. For example, improved realty isn't similar in use to unimproved realty (Reg § 1.1033(a)-2(c)(9)(i)), but the two properties are of like-kind.[4]

The like-kind rule doesn't apply to real estate held primarily for sale (Code Sec. 1033(g)(1)) or where control of a corporation owning replacement property is acquired. (Code Sec. 1033(g)(2))[5]

---

48. ¶I-3730; TD ¶229,730
49. ¶I-3772.6; ¶10,334.2205; TD ¶229,752
50. ¶N-1220; ¶10,334.08; TD ¶118,003
1. ¶I-3733.1, I-3733.2, I-3734; ¶10,334.221; TD ¶229,722

2. ¶I-3733.1; ¶10,334.221; TD ¶229,722
3. ¶I-3733.2; ¶10,334.221; TD ¶229,723
4. ¶I-3727; ¶10,334.22 *et seq.*; TD ¶229,728
5. ¶I-3727; ¶10,334.22, 10,334.23; TD ¶229,728

¶ 2441   Replacement period.

Converted property must be replaced within a period:

(1) beginning with (a) the date the property was destroyed, stolen, condemned, etc., or (b) the date condemnation or requisition was first threatened or became imminent, whichever is earlier (Code Sec. 1033(a)(2)(B)), and

(2) ending (a) two years after the close of the first tax year in which any part of the gain is realized (three years in the case of condemnation or threat of condemnation of real property described at ¶2440; four years for principal residences converted due to federally declared disasters, see ¶2433), or (b) at a later date allowed by IRS upon application by the taxpayer. (Code Sec. 1033(a)(2)(B), Code Sec. 1033(g)(4), Code Sec. 1033(h)(1)(B)) The replacement period is extended to five years for property involuntarily converted in the Hurricane Katrina disaster area and compulsorily or involuntarily converted after Aug. 24, 2005, by reason of Hurricane Katrina, if substantially all of the use of the replacement property is within the Hurricane Katrina disaster area.[6] A similar five-year replacement period applies to property involuntarily converted due to storms and tornados on after May 3, 2007 in the 24-county Kansas disaster area[7] and to property involuntarily converted by reason of a Midwestern disaster on or after the "applicable disaster date"[8] in the Midwestern disaster area.[9]

If a taxpayer sells livestock on account of drought, flood, or other weather-related conditions (see ¶2438) which result in the area being designated as eligible for assistance by the federal government, the replacement period is extended to four years. This four-year period may be extended further by IRS on a regional basis if the weather-related conditions continue for more than three years. (Code Sec. 1033(e)(2)) For persistent droughts, IRS has extended the replacement period until the end of taxpayers' first tax year ending after the first drought-free year (as specially defined) for applicable regions.[10]

¶ 2442   Exclusion of Gain on Principal Residence. ▬▬▬▬▬▬▬▬▬▬

A taxpayer can exclude from income up to $250,000 of gain ($500,000 for joint filers meeting certain conditions) from the sale of a home owned and used by the taxpayer as a principal residence for at least 2 of the 5 years before the sale. (Code Sec. 121(a))

The exclusion doesn't apply if, within the 2-year period ending on the sale date, the exclusion applied to another home sale by the taxpayer. (Code Sec. 121(b)(3))[11]

Married taxpayers filing jointly for the year of sale may exclude up to $500,000 of home-sale gain if (1) either spouse owned the home for at least 2 of the 5 years before the sale, (2) both spouses used the home as a principal residence for at least 2 of the 5 years before the sale, and (3) neither spouse is ineligible for the full exclusion because of the once-every-2-year limit. (Code Sec. 121(b)(2)(A))[12] A surviving spouse qualifies for the up-to-$500,000 exclusion if the sale occurs not later than 2 years after the spouse's death, if the requirements for the $500,000 exclusion were met immediately before the spouse's death and the survivor hasn't remarried as of the date of the sale. (Code Sec. 121(b)(4))[13]

For the excludable amount where married taxpayers aren't eligible for the full $500,000 exclusion, see ¶2444.

Gain from the sale or exchange of property that is attributable to periods of "nonqualified use" is not eligible for the exclusion. (Code Sec. 121(b)(4)(A) [sic Code Sec. 121(b)(5)(A)])[14]

"Nonqualified use" refers to any period after 2008 during which the property is not used as

6. ¶I-3772.8; ¶10,334.42; TD ¶229,754.2
7. ¶I-3772.9; ¶10,334.44; TD ¶229,754.3
8. ¶S-8567; ¶14,00R4.06; TD ¶570,462
9. ¶I-3772.10; ¶10,334.45; TD ¶229,754.4
10. ¶N-1216.2 *et seq.*; ¶10,334.08; TD ¶229,713.2 *et seq.*

11. ¶I-4520 *et seq.*; ¶1214; TD ¶225,700 *et seq.*
12. ¶I-4536; ¶1214.02; TD ¶225,716
13. ¶I-4538.1; ¶1214.02; TD ¶225,718.1
14. ¶I-4568.1; ¶1214.07; TD ¶225,748.1

the principal residence of the taxpayer, or his spouse or former spouse. (Code Sec. 121(b)(4)(C)(i) [sic Code Sec. 121(b)(5)(C)(i)])[15]

The gain allocated to periods of nonqualified use is the total amount of gain, multiplied by a fraction (1) the numerator of which is the aggregate periods of nonqualified use during the period the taxpayer owned the property, and (2) the denominator of which is the period the taxpayer owned the property. (Code Sec. 121(b)(4)(B) [sic Code Sec. 121(b)(5)(B)])[16]

The exclusion also does not apply to gain attributable to post-May 6, '97 depreciation, and that gain is not taken into account in determining the amount of gain allocated to qualified use. (Code Sec. 121(b)(4)(D) [sic Code Sec. 121(b)(5)(D)])[17]

Exceptions to the definition of "period of nonqualified use" include (1) use occurring in the five-year testing period after the date the residence was last used as a principal residence, (2) temporary absence (not to exceed an aggregate period of two years), and (3) any period during which the taxpayer or his spouse is serving on qualified official extended duty (not to exceed an aggregate period of ten years), see ¶2445. (Code Sec. 121(b)(4)(C)(ii) [sic Code Sec. 121(b)(5)(C)(ii)])[18]

The exchange or involuntary conversion (destruction (but only if the residence is totally destroyed), as well as condemnation) of a principal residence is treated as a sale for purposes of the home-sale exclusion. (Code Sec. 121(d)(5)(A))[19] A taxpayer may elect not to apply the exclusion to the sale or exchange of a principal residence. (Code Sec. 121(f))[20]

The exclusion doesn't apply to gain attributable to post-May 6, '97 depreciation claimed for rental or business use of a principal residence. (Code Sec. 121(d)(6))[21]

If property is used for both residential and business (or investment) purposes, no allocation of gain is required if both the residential and non-residential portions of the property are within the same dwelling unit, but gain isn't excludable to the extent of any post-May 6, '97, depreciation. However, gain is allocated if the part of the home for which the use requirement isn't met is separate from the dwelling unit. (Reg § 1.121-1(e)(1))[22]

The exclusion isn't available to individuals subject to the expatriate tax rules (see ¶4653). (Code Sec. 121(e))[23]

For a taxpayer who acquired a home in a like-kind exchange (¶2418 *et seq.*) in which any gain wasn't recognized, or a donee of such a taxpayer, the exclusion doesn't apply for the 5-year period beginning with the date of the acquisition. (Code Sec. 121(d)(10))[24]

If home-sale gain is entirely excluded under Code Sec. 121, the transaction is not reported on the return at all. However, Schedule D entries are necessary if there is taxable gain on the home sale (e.g., realized gain exceeds the excludable amount).[25]

¶ 2443   Reduced exclusion for partially qualifying principal residence sales.

A reduced maximum exclusion may apply to taxpayers who sell their principal residence but (1) fail to qualify for the 2-out-of-5-year ownership and use rule, or (2) previously sold another home within the two-year period ending on the sale date of the current home in a transaction to which the exclusion applied (¶2442). If the taxpayer's failure to meet either rule occurs because he must sell the home due to a change of place of employment, health or, to the extent provided by regs, other unforeseen circumstances, then he may be entitled to a reduced maximum exclusion. Under these circumstances, the maximum gain that can be excluded is equal to the full $250,000 or $500,000 exclusion times a fraction having as its numerator the shorter of (a) aggregate periods of ownership and use of the home by the

15. ¶I-4568.3; ¶1214.07; TD ¶225,748.3
16. ¶I-4568.2; ¶1214.07; TD ¶225,748.2
17. ¶I-4568.7; ¶1214.07; TD ¶225,748.7
18. ¶I-4568.4; ¶1214.07; TD ¶225,748.4
19. ¶I-4565; ¶1214.14; TD ¶225,745
20. ¶I-4570; ¶1214.20; TD ¶225,753

21. ¶I-4568; ¶1214.06; TD ¶225,748
22. ¶I-4532 *et seq.*; ¶1214.06; TD ¶225,712 *et seq.*
23. ¶I-4569; ¶1214.18; TD ¶225,749
24. ¶I-4561.1; ¶1214.14; TD ¶225,741.1
25. ¶I-4521; ¶1214; TD ¶225,701

taxpayer as a principal residence during the 5 years ending on the sale date, or (b) the period of time after the last sale to which the exclusion applied, and before the date of the current sale, and having 2 years (or its equivalent in months) as its denominator. (Code Sec. 121(c)(2))[26]

RIA *illustration:* S, a single taxpayer, sells her principal residence because she has a new job in another city. On the sale date, she has owned the home and used it as her principal residence for the last 18 months. She has never excluded gain from another home sale. Since S fails to meet the use and ownership requirements for the exclusion because of a change in place of employment, the amount of gain excluded by her can't exceed $187,500 ($250,000 times 1.5 years of ownership and use divided by 2 years). Thus, if S realized a gain of $50,000 on her home sale, all of it would be excludable.

The up-to-ten-year suspension for qualifying military services or Foreign Service members or intelligence community employees explained at ¶2445 may be elected to determine the amount of the reduced exclusion. (Code Sec. 121(d)(9)(A))[27]

To claim a reduced maximum exclusion, the sale or exchange must be made because of a change of place of employment, health, or unforeseen circumstances. If a safe harbor in the regs applies, a sale is deemed to be made by reason of a change in place of employment, health, or unforeseen circumstances. If a safe harbor does not apply, a sale or exchange is by reason of a change in place of employment, health, or unforeseen circumstances only if the primary reason for the sale or exchange is one of those reasons. (Reg § 1.121-3(b))[28]

A sale or exchange is because of a change in place of employment, if, in the case of a qualified individual (taxpayer, spouse, co-owner of the residence, or a person whose principal place of abode is in the same household as the taxpayer), the primary reason for the sale or exchange is a change in the location of the individual's employment (including self-employment). Under a safe harbor, this condition is treated as met if (1) the new place of employment is at least 50 miles farther from the residence sold or exchanged than was the former place of employment (for the formerly unemployed, 50 miles between the new place of employment and the residence sold or exchanged), and (2) the change in place of employment occurs during the taxpayer's ownership and use of the home as his principal residence. (Reg § 1.121-3(c))[29]

The health condition is met if the primary reason for the sale is to (1) obtain, provide, or facilitate the diagnosis, cure, mitigation, or treatment of disease, illness, or injury of a qualified individual, or (2) obtain or provide medical or personal care for a qualified individual suffering from a disease, illness, or injury. A qualified individual includes those listed above under change of employment, plus (a) the taxpayer's family members listed in Code Sec. 152(a) (other than paragraph (9)), even if they aren't his dependents; and (b) descendants of the taxpayer's grandparent (e.g., first cousins). A sale or exchange doesn't qualify for the health condition if it is merely beneficial to the general health or well-being of the individual. Under a safe harbor, the health condition is treated as met if a doctor recommends a change of residence for the health reasons listed above in (1) or (2). (Reg § 1.121-3(d))[30]

A sale or exchange is caused by unforeseen circumstances if the primary reason for the sale or exchange is an event that the taxpayer could not reasonably have anticipated before purchasing and occupying the residence. A sale or exchange by reason of unforeseen circumstances (other than a circumstance covered by one of the safe harbors listed in regs, such as an involuntary conversion, or death of a qualified individual, or designated by IRS as an unforeseen circumstance in published guidance or in a ruling issued to a specific taxpayer) does not qualify for the reduced maximum exclusion if the primary reason for the sale or exchange is a preference for a different residence or an improvement in financial circumstances. (Reg § 1.121-3(e))[31]

26. ¶I-4557; ¶1214.08; TD ¶225,737
27. ¶I-4563.1; ¶1214; TD ¶225,708.1
28. ¶I-4541; ¶1214.08; TD ¶225,721

29. ¶I-4542 *et seq.*; ¶1214.08; TD ¶225,722 *et seq.*
30. ¶I-4545 *et seq.*; ¶1214.08; TD ¶225,725 *et seq.*
31. ¶I-4547 *et seq.*; ¶1214.08; TD ¶225,727 *et seq.*

¶ 2444   Amount excludable if married taxpayers ineligible for full exclusion.

If married taxpayers filing a joint return aren't eligible for the $500,000 maximum exclusion under the rules explained at ¶2442, the amount of the exclusion that they may claim is the sum of each spouse's maximum exclusion determined on a separate basis as if they had not been married. However, for purposes of this rule, each spouse is treated as owning the property during the period that either spouse owned the property. (Code Sec. 121(b)(2)(B))[32]

¶ 2445   Ownership and use tests to qualify for home-sale exclusion.

In general, the full home-sale exclusion applies only if the taxpayer owned the home and used it as a principal residence for at least 2 of the 5 years ending on the date that it is sold. (Code Sec. 121(a))

A taxpayer is treated as the owner and seller of the residence held by a trust during the period that he is treated as the owner of the trust or the portion of the trust that includes the residence under the rules of Code Sec. 671 through Code Sec. 679 (grantors and others treated as substantial owners), see ¶3956 *et seq.* Similar treatment applies to certain single-owner entities. (Reg § 1.121-1(c)(3))[33]

Each unmarried taxpayer who jointly owns a principal residence may be eligible to exclude from gross income up to $250,000 of gain that is attributable to that taxpayer's interest in the property. (Reg § 1.121-2(a)(2))[34]

Gain from the sale or exchange of partial interests (other than interests remaining after the sale or exchange of a remainder interest) in the taxpayer's principal residence is excludable if the interest sold or exchanged includes an interest in the dwelling unit. Only one maximum limitation amount of $250,000 ($500,000 for certain joint returns) applies to the combined sales or exchanges of partial interests. (Reg § 1.121-4(e))[35]

The bankruptcy estate of an individual in a chapter 7 or 11 bankruptcy case under title 11 of the United States Code succeeds to and takes into account his home-sale exclusion if the individual otherwise satisfies the requirements. (Reg § 1.1398-3)[36]

Under the following circumstances, a taxpayer may "tack on" someone else's ownership and/or use period to his or her own ownership and/or use period.

. . . An unmarried individual whose spouse was deceased on the home-sale date may tack on the decedent's ownership and use period to his or her own ownership and use period. (Code Sec. 121(d)(2))[37]

. . . An individual who receives a home in a Code Sec. 1041(a) transaction (¶2447), such as a tax-free transfer from one spouse to another, may tack on the transferor's ownership period to his or her own ownership period. (Code Sec. 121(d)(3)(A))[38]

. . . An individual is treated as using a home as his or her principal residence during any period of ownership that the individual's spouse or former spouse is granted use of the property under a divorce or separation instrument. (Code Sec. 121(d)(3)(B))[39]

However, if a taxpayer voluntarily demolishes his principal residence and builds a new principal residence on the same land, the period he owned and used the demolished principal residence is not taken into account in determining whether he qualifies for the exclusion on the sale of the new principal residence.[40]

A relief provision applies to a taxpayer who becomes physically or mentally incapable of

32. ¶I-4537; ¶1214.02; TD ¶225,717
33. ¶I-4529 *et seq.*; ¶1214.12; TD ¶225,709 *et seq.*
34. ¶I-4535; ¶1214.02; TD ¶225,715
35. ¶I-4567; ¶1214.16; TD ¶225,747
36. ¶C-9718.01; ¶13,984.01; TD ¶225,742

37. ¶I-4559; ¶1214.10; TD ¶225,739
38. ¶I-4558; ¶1214.10; TD ¶225,738
39. ¶I-4558; ¶1214.10; TD ¶225,738
40. ¶I-4527; TD ¶225,707

self-care and, during the 5-year period ending on the home's sale date, owns and uses the home as a principal residence for periods aggregating at least 1 year. Here, the taxpayer is treated as having used the home as a principal residence during any time in the 5-year period in which he owns the home and lives in a facility (including a nursing home) licensed by a state or political subdivision to care for someone in the taxpayer's condition. (Code Sec. 121(d)(7))[41] The up-to-ten-year suspension for qualifying military services, Foreign Services members, or employees of an intelligence community (discussed below) also may be elected for this relief provision. (Code Sec. 121(d)(9)(A))

A member of the uniformed services or the Foreign Service, an employee of the intelligence community for sales or exchanges after Dec. 20, 2006, and a Peace Corps Volunteer serving outside the U.S. for tax years beginning after 2007, can elect to suspend the 5-year period for measuring ownership and use during any period that he or his spouse is serving on extended duty at least 50 miles from the residence or while residing under orders in Government quarters. (Code Sec. 121(d)(9)(A), Code Sec. 121(d)(12)) For sales or exchanges before June 18, 2008, the extended duty for an employee of the intelligence community had to be at a duty station located outside the U.S. (Code Sec. 121(d)(9)(C)) The 5-year period can't be extended by more than 10 years. (Code Sec. 121(d)(9)(B))[42]

Effective for individuals dying in 2010, the home-sale exclusion will be extended to decedents' estates, heirs, and trusts that were qualified revocable trusts immediately before such an individual's death, so that they will be allowed to take into account the decedent's ownership and use of the home while alive. (Code Sec. 121(d)(11))[43] For sunset rule for this provision with respect to decedent's estates, etc., see ¶1114.

¶ 2446 Sales and Exchanges Between Related Taxpayers. ▃▃▃▃▃▃▃

No gain or loss is recognized on a transfer of property between spouses (or former spouses incident to divorce). No deduction is allowed for any loss from the sale or exchange of property between specified related taxpayers. A loss from a transfer between members of the same controlled group is generally deferred until the property is transferred outside the group.

¶ 2447 Gain or loss on transfer to spouse.

No gain or loss is recognized on a transfer of property to (or in trust for the benefit of) the transferor's spouse, or to a former spouse incident to a divorce. (Code Sec. 1041(a))[44] Certain transfers to third parties on behalf of (i.e., in satisfaction of an obligation or liability of) the spouse or former spouse qualify for nonrecognition. (Reg § 1.1041-1T(c), Q&A-9)[45] However, the no-gain-or-loss rule doesn't apply to transfers in trust where liability exceeds basis (Code Sec. 1041(e)),[46] to transfers in trust of installment obligations (Code Sec. 453B(g)),[47] or where the transferee spouse is a nonresident alien. (Code Sec. 1041(d))[48]

A transfer of property is incident to divorce if it occurs within one year after the date the marriage ceases (Code Sec. 1041(c)(1)) or the transfer is related to the cessation of the marriage. (Code Sec. 1041(c)(2)) A transfer is related to the cessation if the transfer is under a divorce or separation instrument and the transfer occurs not more than six years after the date the marriage ceases. For later transfers, there's a presumption that the transfer isn't related to the cessation. (Reg § 1.1041-1T(b), Q&A-7)[49]

41. ¶I-4563; ¶1214.14; TD ¶225,743
42. ¶I-4528.1; ¶1214.14; TD ¶225,708.1
43. ¶I-4560; ¶1214.14; TD ¶225,740
44. ¶s I-3609, I-3601; ¶10,414; TD ¶228,201
45. ¶I-3604; ¶10,414; TD ¶228,205

46. ¶I-3605; ¶10,414; TD ¶228,206
47. ¶I-3606; ¶10,414; TD ¶228,207
48. ¶I-3608; ¶10,414
49. ¶I-3610; ¶10,414; TD ¶228,302

¶ 2448   Losses from sales and exchanges between related taxpayers.

No deduction is allowed for losses from sales or exchanges between certain related taxpayers. (Code Sec. 267(a)) The following are related taxpayers:

Members of the seller's family, but only brothers and sisters (whole or half blood), spouse, ancestors, and lineal descendants. (Code Sec. 267(a), Code Sec. 267(b)(1), Code Sec. 267(c)(4))[50] In-laws aren't members of the seller's family. [1]

Controlled corporations. A taxpayer and his controlled corporation, and a fiduciary and a corporation controlled by the trust or grantor. "Control" is direct or indirect ownership of more than 50% in value of the outstanding stock. (Code Sec. 267(b)(2), Code Sec. 267(b)(8))[2]

Controlled group member. Corporations that are members of the same controlled group of corporations. (Code Sec. 267(b)(3))[3] Loss from a sale or exchange between members of a controlled group is deferred, as explained at ¶2450.

A corporation and a partnership if the same persons own more than 50% in value of the outstanding stock of the corporation, and more than 50% of the capital interest, or the profits interest, in the partnership. (Code Sec. 267(b)(10))[4]

An S corporation and another S corporation if the same persons own more than 50% in value of the outstanding stock of each corporation. (Code Sec. 267(b)(11))[5]

An S corporation and a C corporation if the same persons own more than 50% in value of the outstanding stock of each corporation. (Code Sec. 267(b)(12))[6]

An estate and a beneficiary of that estate, except in the case of a sale or exchange in satisfaction of a pecuniary bequest. (Code Sec. 267(b)(13))[7]

Trustees, grantors, and beneficiaries, that is, the grantor and the fiduciary of a trust; the fiduciary and the beneficiary of a trust; the fiduciaries of two different trusts with the same grantor; a fiduciary of one trust and the beneficiary of another trust with the same grantor; and a trust fiduciary and a corporation more than 50% in value of the outstanding stock of which is owned directly or indirectly by or for the trust or its grantor. (Code Sec. 267(b)(4), Code Sec. 267(b)(5), Code Sec. 267(b)(6), Code Sec. 267(b)(7), Code Sec. 267(b)(8))[8]

Exempt organizations. A person and an exempt organization controlled, directly or indirectly, by that person or the members of his family. (Code Sec. 267(b)(9))[9]

In applying the related taxpayer rules, ownership of stock is attributed to the taxpayer as follows:

(1) A stockholder is considered to own a proportionate share of the stock owned by the corporation.

(2) A partner is considered to own a proportionate share of the stock owned by the partnership.

(3) If an individual owns some stock in a corporation, he's considered the owner of stock owned by his partner.

(4) A beneficiary is considered to own a proportionate share of the stock owned by the trust or estate.

(5) An individual is considered to own stock owned by members of his family, as defined above, whether or not he's the actual owner of stock in the same corporation. (Code Sec. 267(c); Reg § 1.267(c)-1)[10]

---

50. ¶I-3512; ¶2674.03, 2674.04; TD ¶227,905
1. ¶I-3515; ¶2674.03; TD ¶227,907
2. ¶I-3519; ¶2674.03; TD ¶227,908
3. ¶I-3522; ¶2674.05; TD ¶227,910
4. ¶I-3532; ¶s 2674.03, 2674.04; TD ¶227,921
5. ¶I-3531; ¶2674.03; TD ¶227,920

6. ¶I-3531; ¶2674.05; TD ¶227,920
7. ¶I-3533; ¶2674.03; TD ¶227,922
8. ¶I-3527; ¶2674.03; TD ¶227,917
9. ¶I-3530; ¶2674.03; TD ¶227,904
10. ¶I-3516; ¶2674.04; TD ¶227,913

¶ 2449 Later sale by related buyer.

A related buyer is allowed to reduce his gain on property he resells at a gain by the loss disallowed to his seller if these conditions are met: (1) a loss deduction was barred under the rules on related taxpayers (¶2448), (2) the resale or exchange is at a gain, and the property is either the property on which the loss was disallowed or property the basis of which is determined by reference to the basis of that property, and (3) the loss deduction on the original sale to the taxpayer wasn't barred under the wash sale rules (¶2461). (Code Sec. 267(d); Reg § 1.267(d)-1)[11]

Illustration: H sells to his wife, B, for $5,500, farmland, with an adjusted basis for determining loss to him of $8,000. The loss of $2,500 is not allowable to H. B exchanges the farmland, held for investment purposes, with an unrelated individual, for two city lots, also held for investment purposes. The basis of the city lots in the hands of B ($5,500) is a substituted basis determined by reference to the basis of the farmland. Later, B sells the city lots for $10,000. Although her realized gain is $4,500 ($10,000 minus $5,500), her recognized gain is only $2,000, the excess of the realized gain of $4,500 over the loss of $2,500 not allowable to H. (Reg § 1.267(d)-1(a)(4), Ex (4))

¶ 2450 Loss between members of controlled group.

With some exceptions, a loss from a transfer between members of the same controlled group is deferred (rather than denied). The loss is recognized when the property is transferred outside the group if the loss would be recognized under consolidated return principles. (Code Sec. 267(f)(2))[12]

For purposes of any Code section other than Code Sec. 267 which refers to a relationship which would result in a disallowance of losses under Code Sec. 267, deferral under Code Sec. 267(f)(2) is treated as a disallowance. (Code Sec. 267(f)(4))[13]

¶ 2451 Gain on sale of employer stock to ESOP or EWOC.

A taxpayer (but not a C corporation) or taxpayer's executor who sells qualified securities (certain common stock) to an employee stock ownership plan (ESOP) or eligible worker-owned cooperative (EWOC) that holds specified percentages of the securities, may elect nonrecognition of gain if the seller buys "qualified replacement property" (securities of another corporation that doesn't exceed certain passive income limits) within a specified period of time. The seller's gain is recognized only to the extent the proceeds of sale exceed his cost for the replacement property. Nonrecognition treatment applies only if the gain on the sale of the stock would otherwise have been long-term capital gain. (Code Sec. 1042)[14] However, with some exceptions (e.g., for gifts), gain not recognized on the sale to the ESOP is recognized on the disposition of the replacement property. (Code Sec. 1042(e))[15]

The Third and Eighth Circuits have ruled that a corporation cannot deduct payments to redeem stock held in its ESOP under Code Sec. 404(k), while the Ninth Circuit has held to the contrary.[16]

The deferral of gain under Code Sec. 1042 also applies to the sale of stock of a qualified refiner or processor to an eligible farmers' cooperative. (Code Sec. 1042(g)(1))

¶ 2452 Installment Sales and Other Deferred Payment Sales. ▬▬▬▬▬▬

Under the installment method, a nondealer (unless he elects out) reports gain on a sale as payments are received, instead of reporting all the gain in the year of sale.

11. ¶I-3541; ¶2674; TD ¶227,927
12. ¶s E-8250, I-3524 *et seq.*; ¶2674.05; TD ¶227,912
13. ¶I-3524 *et seq.*; TD ¶227,912
14. ¶H-12103 *et seq.*; ¶10,424
15. ¶H-1211.1; ¶10,424
16. ¶H-12117.5A

For unstated interest on installment (and other deferred payment) sales, see ¶1309 *et seq.*

¶ 2453 Reporting gain under the installment sale rules—Form 6252.

The installment sale rules must be used to report gain on the disposition of non-dealer property where at least one payment is to be received after the close of the tax year in which the disposition occurs (Code Sec. 453(b)(1)) unless the taxpayer elects not to use the installment method (see ¶2456) or the transaction is one for which the installment method can't be used (see ¶2454).[17] The amount of a payment that's income to the taxpayer is that portion of the installment payments received in the year that the gross profit realized or to be realized bears to the total contract price (the "gross profit ratio"). (Code Sec. 453(c); Reg § 15A.453-1(b)(2)(i))[18]

illustration: Taxpayer sells personal-use property for a gross profit of $2,000 at a contract price of $8,000. The gross profit ratio is 25% ($2,000 ÷ $8,000). Therefore, 25% of each payment collected on the sale (including the down payment) is gain and is included in gross income for the tax year it's collected. The ratio remains constant for all installment payments received on the sale.

Payments include:

(a) amounts actually received by the seller, e.g., cash, other property, foreign currency, marketable securities, or evidences of indebtedness of persons other than the buyer. (Reg § 15A.453-1(b)(3)(i))[19] Evidences of indebtedness of the buyer are treated as payment if they are payable on demand or readily tradable. (Code Sec. 453(f)(4))[20]

(b) the buyer's payments of the seller's selling expenses,[21] and

(c) the amount by which qualifying debt assumed or taken subject to by the buyer exceeds the seller's basis. (Reg § 15A.453-1(b)(3)(i))[22]

Gross profit is the selling price less the property's adjusted basis (as increased by selling expenses). (Reg § 15A.453-1(b)(2)(v))[23] The selling price is the gross selling price without reduction to reflect any existing mortgage or other encumbrance on the property (whether assumed or taken subject to by the buyer) and without reduction to reflect any selling expenses. Neither interest (whether stated or unstated) nor original issue discount is part of the selling price. (Reg § 15A.453-1(b)(2)(ii))

Gain recaptured under Code Sec. 1245 (¶2695) or Code Sec. 1250 (¶2696), including gain attributable to the Code Sec. 179 expense election (¶1941 *et seq.*), or so much of the unrealized receivables under Code Sec. 751 (¶3756) as relates to Code Sec. 1245 or Code Sec. 1250, is fully taxed as ordinary income in the year of sale. Only gain that isn't recapture income is taken into account under the installment method. (Code Sec. 453(i))[24] The recaptured amount is added to the adjusted basis of the property for purposes of determining basis recovered and gain recognized from each installment.[25]

While gain on the sale of a partnership interest qualifies for installment reporting, gain attributable to inventories and unrealized receivables held by the partnership does not.[26]

The total contract price is the selling price, reduced by debt on the property that the buyer assumes (or takes subject to), but only to the extent of the seller's basis in the property. (Reg § 15A.453-1(b)(2)(iii))[27]

---

17. ¶G-6000 *et seq.*; ¶4534.01; TD ¶461,000 *et seq.*
18. ¶G-6052 *et seq.*; ¶4534.21; TD ¶462,003
19. ¶G-6151; ¶4534.22 *et seq.*; TD ¶462,501 *et seq.*
20. ¶G-6163; ¶4534.23; TD ¶462,509
21. TD ¶462,503
22. ¶G-6155; ¶4534.27; TD ¶462,504

23. ¶G-6053; ¶4534.21; TD ¶462,004
24. ¶G-6097 *et seq.*; ¶4534.05; TD ¶462,018
25. ¶G-6097; ¶4534.05; TD ¶462,018
26. ¶G-6010; ¶4534.05; TD ¶461,005
27. ¶G-6060; ¶4534.21; TD ¶462,013

¶ 2454 Where installment method can't be used.

The installment method cannot be used by dealers in property, real or personal. (Code Sec. 453(b)(2))[28] However, the installment method may be used for:

- dispositions by farmers (not merchants) of any property used or produced in the trade or business of farming (Code Sec. 453(l)(2)(A)); and
- dispositions to an individual in the ordinary course of a taxpayer's trade or business of the following, but only if interest is paid on the tax deferred when the installment method is used: (Code Sec. 453(l)(2)(B))

... a timeshare right to use, or a timeshare right to an ownership interest in, residential real property for not more than six weeks per year, or a right to use specified camp-grounds for recreational purposes (timeshare rights or ownership interests held by the spouse, children, grandchildren or parents of an individual are treated as held by the individual), or

... any residential lots, but only if the taxpayer (or any related person) isn't to make any improvements with respect to the lots.[29]

The installment method can't be used for:

... Sales of stock or securities traded on an established securities market (Code Sec. 453(k)(2)(A)), but it can be used for unregistered restricted stock sold in a private placement.[30]

... Sales at a loss.[31]

... Sales of depreciable property between persons related within the Code Sec. 1239(b) rules (¶2691), and between controlled partnerships as defined in Code Sec. 707(b)(1)(B) ¶3731 *et seq.*),[32] unless it's established to IRS's satisfaction that the sale didn't have as one of its principal purposes the avoidance of federal tax. (Code Sec. 453(g))[33]

¶ 2455 Contingent payment sales.

The installment method is used to report contingent payment sales (sales or other disposi-tions of property in a tax year in which the total selling price can't be determined at the close of that tax year), unless the taxpayer elects not to use the installment method. (Reg § 15A.453-1(c)(1)) In general, basis is allocated to payments received and to be received by treating the stated maximum selling price as the selling price. (Reg § 15A.453-1(c)(2)(i)) However:

... If the maximum selling price can't be determined, but the maximum period over which payments may be received is fixed, the seller's basis is allocated to the tax years in which payments may be received in equal annual increments. (Reg § 15A.453-1(c)(3)(i))

... If the agreement neither specifies a maximum selling price nor limits payments to a fixed period, the transaction may be a sale or payments under the agreement may be rent or royalty income. If the transaction is a sale, basis (including selling expenses) generally is recovered in equal annual increments over a period of 15 years starting with the date of sale. (Reg § 15A.453-1(c)(4))[34]

A seller may (if IRS grants permission) use an alternative basis recovery method if it's able to demonstrate that applying the normal basis recovery rule would substantially and inappro-priately defer recovery of basis and the alternative method would likely result in basis

28. ¶G-6601, G-6014.1; ¶4534.01, 4534.03; TD ¶466,001, 461,008
29. ¶G-6600 *et seq.*; ¶4534.01; TD ¶466,003 *et seq.*
30. ¶G-6016 *et seq.*; ¶4534.01; TD ¶461,012
31. ¶G-6015; ¶4534.01; TD ¶461,011
32. ¶G-6208; ¶4534.17; TD ¶463,503
33. ¶G-6201; ¶4534.17; TD ¶463,501
34. ¶G-6250 *et seq.*; ¶4534.30; TD ¶463,000 *et seq.*

recovery at a rate at least twice as fast. (Reg § 15A.453-1(c)(7))[35]

¶ 2456 Electing out of the installment method.

An election not to have the installment method apply to a sale is made by reporting an amount realized equal to the selling price (including the full face amount of any installment obligation) on the tax return filed for the year the sale occurs. (Reg § 15A.453-1(d)(3)(i))[36]

The election out must be made on or before the due date (including extensions) for filing the return for the year of sale. (Code Sec. 453(d)(2))[37] A late election is allowed only if IRS concludes taxpayer had good cause for the failure to timely elect. (Reg § 15A.453-1(d)(3)(ii))[38]

An election out may be revoked only with IRS consent. (Code Sec. 453(d)(3))[39]

observation: Consider electing out of the installment method if the seller will be in a much higher tax bracket in post-sale years than in the sale year, or if he is selling a property with large suspended passive activity losses so these losses can be used immediately to offset nonpassive income, see ¶1839).

A taxpayer who elects not to report a deferred-payment sale on the installment method recognizes gain on the sale according to his method of accounting. The amount realized attributable to a debt instrument received is the debt instrument's issue price as determined under the OID rules discussed at ¶1319. (Reg § 1.1001-1(g))[40]

¶ 2457 Character of installment gain where depreciable realty is sold.

When depreciable real property is sold by a noncorporate taxpayer, the gain may be partially 25%-rate gain (unrecaptured section 1250 gain subject to a maximum tax of 25%, see ¶2605), and partially adjusted net capital gain (taxed at a maximum rate of 15%, see ¶2604). If there are both types of gain, the 25%-rate gain is taken into account as payments are received before any adjusted net capital gain is included. (Reg § 1.453-12(a)) See ¶2600 *et seq.* for the taxation of capital gains.[41]

illustration: T sells depreciable real property for a total price of $150,000. He has a total gain of $30,000, $20,000 of which is 25%-rate gain, and $10,000 of which is adjusted net capital gain. The sales price is payable in five equal annual installments of $30,000, with the first installment due in the year of sale. T takes $6,000 of gain into account as each installment is paid. The entire gain of $6,000 on the receipt of the first three installments, and $2,000 of the gain on the receipt of the fourth installment, is taxed as 25%-rate gain. The remaining $4,000 of gain on the fourth installment and the entire $6,000 of gain on the fifth installment is taxed at a maximum rate of 15%.

Net Code Sec. 1231 gain that would otherwise be taxed as long-term capital gain, is taxed as ordinary income to the extent of non-recaptured net Code Sec. 1231 losses for the preceding five years (¶2685). If net Code Sec. 1231 gain for a tax year consists of both 25%-rate gain and adjusted net capital gain, the 25%-rate gain is recharacterized as ordinary income first. This rule also applies to installment payments. (Reg § 1.453-12(d), Ex. 3)[42]

¶ 2458 Sale, exchange, or satisfaction of installment obligations.

For installment obligations satisfied at face value, gain or loss is computed under the general rules (¶2453) for computing income on the installment method.[43]

If an installment obligation is satisfied at other than face or is sold or exchanged, gain or

35. ¶G-6279, G-6280; ¶4534.30; TD ¶463,020
36. ¶G-6360; ¶4534.08; TD ¶461,503
37. ¶G-6352; ¶4534.08; TD ¶461,502
38. ¶G-6353; ¶4534.08; TD ¶461,502
39. ¶G-6362; ¶4534.08; TD ¶461,509
40. ¶G-6351, G-6550 *et seq.*; ¶4534.45 *et seq.*; TD ¶467,001
41. ¶G-6102; ¶4634.57; TD ¶462,023
42. ¶G-6105; ¶4534.58; TD ¶462,025
43. ¶G-6052; ¶4534.22; TD ¶465,002

loss is the difference between the basis of the obligation and the amount realized. If it's distributed, transmitted, or disposed of other than by sale or exchange, gain or loss is the difference between its basis and its fair market value (FMV) (Code Sec. 453B(a)),[44] except that if it's distributed in a complete liquidation of a subsidiary to which Code Sec. 337(a) applies (¶3577), no gain or loss is recognized. (Code Sec. 453B(d))[45] If there's a repossession by the seller of the personal property sold following the buyer's default (i.e., a disposition of the installment obligation by the seller),[46] the seller's gain or loss is: (1) the FMV of the property, plus anything received from the buyer in addition to the repossessed property; minus (2) the seller's basis in the installment obligation, plus any expense in connection with the repossession.[47] Transmission of an installment obligation at death doesn't result in gain or loss to the decedent. (Code Sec. 453B(c); Reg § 1.451-1(b)(2))[48]

The basis of an obligation is the excess of its face value over the amount equal to the income that would be returnable if the obligation were fully satisfied. (Code Sec. 453B(b))[49]

⊘ *observation:* This means the basis is the unrecovered cost.

¶ 2459   Sale to related person who then resells.

If a person disposes of property in an installment sale (first disposition) to a related person (see below) who then disposes of the property (second disposition) within two years of the first disposition, and before all payments are made on the first disposition, the amount the related person (the buyer in the first disposition) realizes as a result of the second disposition is treated as being received by the original seller at the time of the second disposition. (Code Sec. 453(e)(1), Code Sec. 453(e)(2))

The amount treated as received by the person making the first disposition because of the second disposition can't be more than:

. . . the lesser of the total amount realized on any second disposition of the property occurring in the tax year, or the total contract price for the first disposition; minus

. . . the sum of the aggregate amount of payments received with respect to the first disposition before the close of the tax year in which the second disposition occurs, and the aggregate amount treated as received with respect to the first disposition because of earlier dispositions of installment obligations by related persons. (Code Sec. 453(e)(3))[50]

For purposes of these rules, if the second disposition isn't a sale or exchange, the property's fair market value is treated as the amount realized. (Code Sec. 453(e)(4))[1]

A "related person" is someone whose stock would be attributed to the initial seller under Code Sec. 318(a) (¶3534), other than under the option attribution rules, or a person who bears a relationship to the initial seller under Code Sec. 267(b) (¶2448) for purposes of the rules disallowing the deduction of losses on sales between related persons. (Code Sec. 453(f)(1))[2]

Exceptions exist for involuntary conversions, deaths, corporations' reacquisition of their own stock, and where IRS rules out tax avoidance. (Code Sec. 453(e)(6), Code Sec. 453(e)(7))[3]

The two-year period stops running when puts, options, or short sales, etc., are involved. (Code Sec. 453(e)(2)(B))[4] For marketable securities, there's no two-year limit. (Code Sec. 453(e)(2)(A))[5]

---

44. ¶G-6454 *et seq.*; ¶453B4.05; TD ¶465,004
45. ¶G-6489; ¶453B4.11; TD ¶465,037
46. ¶G-6476; ¶453B4.07; TD ¶465,044
47. ¶G-6481; ¶453B4.07; TD ¶465,048
48. ¶G-6507; ¶453B4.13; TD ¶465,019
49. ¶G-6456; ¶453B4.07; TD ¶465,006

50. ¶G-6401 *et seq.*; ¶4534.18; TD ¶464,500 *et seq.*
1. ¶G-6403; ¶4534.18; TD ¶464,506
2. ¶G-6416; ¶4534.18; TD ¶464,503
3. ¶G-6411; ¶4534.18; TD ¶464,512
4. ¶G-6409; ¶4534.18; TD ¶464,510
5. ¶G-6408; ¶4534.18; TD ¶464,510

¶ 2460   Sales of certain property for more than $150,000—"pledge and interest" rule.

The following rules apply to an installment sale of "any" property (except personal use or farm property, and dealer sales of timeshares or residential lots) where the selling price is over $150,000: (Code Sec. 453A)[6]

(1) If an installment obligation from the sale plus all other installment obligations that arose from dispositions during the tax year and are still outstanding at the close of the tax year total over $5,000,000, the seller must pay, as additional tax, interest at the underpayment rate (¶4867) on the deferred tax attributable to those installment obligations.

(2) If an installment obligation from the sale becomes security for any indebtedness, the net proceeds of the indebtedness are treated as a payment of the obligation as of the later of the time the indebtedness becomes secured or the proceeds of the indebtedness are received by the seller. (Code Sec. 453A(d)(1)) Payment of indebtedness is treated as secured by an interest in an installment obligation to the extent that an arrangement allows the taxpayer to satisfy all or part of the debt with the installment obligation (i.e., gives him the *right* to repay the loan by transferring the installment note to his creditor). (Code Sec. 453A(d)(4))

¶ 2461   Wash Sales. ▬▬▬▬▬▬▬▬▬▬▬▬▬▬▬▬▬▬▬▬▬▬

No loss deduction is allowed for any loss from any sale or other disposition of stock or securities (including contracts or options to acquire or sell stock or securities) if within a period beginning 30 days before and ending 30 days after the sale the taxpayer acquires, or has entered into a contract or option to acquire, substantially identical stock or securities.

¶ 2462   Wash sale loss disallowance rule.

Losses on the sale of (or on a contract or option to sell) stock or securities are not deductible if, within a period beginning 30 days before the date of the sale and ending 30 days after the date of the sale, the taxpayer acquires or has entered into a contract or option to acquire stock or securities that are substantially identical. (Code Sec. 1091(a); Reg § 1.1091-1(a))[7]

illustration: June 1: T buys 100 shares of Corp A stock for $15 per share. Dec. 1: T buys 100 shares of Corp A stock for $10 per share. Dec. 31: T sells the 100 shares of Corp A stock bought on June 1 for $10 per share realizing a $500 loss. No loss deduction is allowed because substantially identical stock was purchased within 30 days before the sale. The same result would occur if the second purchase had been made on the following Jan. 30.

caution: This rule can ensnare investors (e.g., investors in mutual funds) who participate in automatic dividend reinvestment plans since the automatic reinvestment of dividends within the prohibited period is a purchase of substantially identical securities.

Loss is also disallowed where the repurchase is made either by an individual retirement account (IRA) as defined by Code Sec. 408 (¶4352) or by a Roth IRA as defined by Code Sec. 408A (¶4368), established for the exclusive benefit of the original purchasing taxpayer or his beneficiaries.[8]

"Substantially identical securities" requires something less than precise correspondence. Stock or securities of different issuers or obligors are not substantially identical. Stock or securities of the same issuer are substantially identical if they are substantially the same in all important particulars.[9]

observation: It is often possible to recognize losses by selling a particular security and

---

6. ¶G-6300 *et seq.*; ¶453A4; TD ¶464,001   8. ¶I-3906, P-5019; TD ¶227,014
7. ¶I-3901; ¶10,914; TD ¶227,001   9. ¶I-3914 *et seq.*; ¶10,914; TD ¶227,019

investing the proceeds in a similar but not substantially identical security (e.g., sell common stock in one drug company and buy stock in another drug company, or sell stock in one exchange-traded fund and buy stock in another exchange-traded fund that invests in the same types of securities).

The wash sale rule also disallows a loss on the closing of a short sale of stock or securities, or the sale, exchange, or termination of a securities futures contract to sell, if, within the period beginning 30 days before the date the short sale is closed and ending 30 days after that date: (1) substantially identical stock or securities are sold, or (2) another short sale of (or securities futures contracts to sell) substantially identical stock or securities is entered. (Code Sec. 1091(e))[10]

Special wash sale rules apply to residual interests in real estate mortgage investment conduits (REMICs) (Code Sec. 860F(d))[11] and to tax straddles. (Reg § 1.1092(b)-1T, Reg § 1.1092(b)-5T)[12]

The wash sale rule doesn't apply to a dealer in stocks or securities if the loss is sustained in a transaction made in the ordinary course of that business. (Code Sec. 1091(a))[13]

For the basis of the acquired stock, see ¶2500. For the holding period, see ¶2667 *et seq.*

¶ 2463 Basis of Property.

Basis is the amount of investment in property for tax purposes. It is the point of departure for determining gain or loss on the disposition of the property, for computing annual deductions for depreciation, amortization, depletion, casualty losses, bad debts, and losses from "at-risk" activities, and for many other tax computations. A taxpayer's basis for property acquired in a taxable exchange is usually its cost, subject to certain adjustments.

In general, basis for computing loss and gain is the same, whatever the transaction may be. But the basis for computing loss differs from the basis for computing gain for (1) property converted from personal use to business or income-producing use (¶2473), and (2) property acquired by gift (¶2508).

For determining basis in corporate transactions and in nontaxable exchanges, see ¶2482 *et seq.*

For basis of property acquired by gift, or from a decedent or a spouse, see ¶2507 *et seq.*

¶ 2464 Cost as basis.

The original basis for property is its cost to the taxpayer, except where otherwise specifically provided (Code Sec. 1012) (see ¶2496 *et seq.*) or where the transaction is not made at arm's length (see below). Cost is the amount paid in cash or other property, and liabilities incurred (¶2465). (Reg § 1.1012-1(a))[14] Payments made in connection with the acquisition of property, e.g., commissions and legal fees, are included in basis as part of the property's cost.[15]

IRS and most courts say that the cost basis of property received in an arm's-length taxable exchange is the fair market value (FMV) of the property *received* in the exchange, at the time of the exchange, unless the FMV of the property received cannot be determined with a fair degree of certainty. Then, the FMV of the property given up will be used as a way of valuing the property received. However, a substantial minority of courts say the cost basis of property received in an arm's-length taxable exchange is the FMV of the property given up, not the property received.[16]

10. ¶I-3905; ¶10,914; TD ¶227,006
11. ¶I-3902, I-3903; ¶860A4; TD ¶227,011 *et seq.*
12. ¶I-7528; ¶10,924; TD ¶228,418
13. ¶I-3917; ¶10,914; TD ¶227,020

14. ¶P-1119; ¶10,124 *et seq.*; TD ¶211,100
15. ¶P-1102; ¶10,124.03
16. ¶P-1114; ¶10,124.46; TD ¶211,106

When property isn't bought in an arm's-length deal, its basis is its FMV. This can occur in sham transactions, or where the buyer, for personal reasons, pays more than what the property is worth (e.g., to help out a friend).[17]

¶ 2465 Mortgages and other liabilities as part of basis.

Taxpayer's cost of property includes the amount of a mortgage or other liability that he assumes in connection with the purchase, plus the amount of any liabilities that the purchased property is subject to (whether or not the taxpayer assumes the liabilities).[18] Redeemable ground rents are treated as mortgages. (Code Sec. 1055)[19]

illustration: J buys a building by paying $20,000 cash and giving an $80,000 mortgage. J's basis is $100,000. It would also be $100,000 if instead J assumed an existing $80,000 mortgage. And it would be $100,000 if, in addition to paying $20,000 cash, J acquired the building subject to the mortgage without assuming it, or if J agreed to pay $80,000 but no mortgage was involved, or if J agreed to pay his seller's debt of $80,000.

Mortgages or other liabilities aren't part of the cost if they are contingent *and* there's a clear indication they might never have to be paid or that taxpayer doesn't intend to pay.[20]

¶ 2466 Effect of OID and unstated interest on basis.

If the original issue discount (OID) rules (¶1751 *et seq.*) or the unstated interest rules (¶1707), apply so that a part of a debt included in the buyer's cost for the property is treated as OID or unstated interest, the buyer's basis doesn't include the OID or unstated interest part. (Reg § 1.483-2(a)(2))[21]

For adjustments to the basis of OID instruments, see ¶2470.

¶ 2467 Basis of repossessed mortgaged real estate.

A seller's basis in repossessed property is equal to the adjusted basis of the mortgage debt (determined under Code Sec. 453 and Code Sec. 1011) to the seller (as of the date of repossession), *plus* the sum of: (1) the repossession gain, and (2) the amount of money and the fair market value of other property (other than the buyer's obligations) which the seller transfers in connection with the repossession.

If the mortgage debt isn't discharged on repossession, the seller's basis in the mortgage debt is zero. (Code Sec. 1038(c))[22]

¶ 2468 Satisfaction of debt or claim with property.

The cost basis of property received in whole or partial satisfaction of a debt or claim is the amount of the debt or claim satisfied, but not more than the property's fair market value.[23]

¶ 2469 Property acquired through exercise of options.

The basis of property acquired by exercising an option or warrant other than an option granted for services is (a) the basis of the option, plus (b) the option price.[24]

¶ 2470 Holder's basis in certain debt instruments acquired at a discount.

The holder's basis in a debt instrument issued with original issue discount (OID) is increased by the OID currently included in gross income under the rules discussed at ¶1315

17. ¶P-1108; ¶10,124.22; TD ¶211,104
18. ¶P-1104 *et seq.*; ¶10,124.04; TD ¶211,118
19. ¶P-1175; ¶10,554; TD ¶211,138
20. ¶P-1134; ¶10,124.04; TD ¶211,104

21. ¶s P-1138, P-1139; TD ¶211,120, 211,121
22. ¶G-6872 *et seq.*; ¶10,384; TD ¶471,009
23. ¶P-1116; ¶10,384; TD ¶211,107
24. ¶P-1165 *et seq.*; ¶10,124.13; TD ¶211,133

et seq. (Code Sec. 1272(d)(2))[25] This rule also applies for inflation-indexed debt instruments (¶1335), whose basis must be reduced for deflation adjustments.[26]

Short-term debt instruments. If the holder includes the daily portions of acquisition discount (or OID) in gross income, that holder increases his basis in the debt instrument by the amount so included. (Code Sec. 1283(d)(1))[27]

Tax-exempt obligations issued with OID. A holder's basis is increased by the amount of OID that the holder would have had to include in gross income currently if the obligation had not been tax-exempt. (Code Sec. 1288(a)(2), Code Sec. 1288(b)(3))[28]

Market-discount bonds. Where an election is made to include accrued market discount in income currently (see ¶1329), the basis of the bond is increased by the amount of income so included. (Code Sec. 1278(b)(4))[29]

For determining cost of, and original basis in, property received in exchange for an OID debt instrument, see ¶2466.

¶ 2471 Cost of intangible assets.

The basis of goodwill, a patent, a copyright, or a covenant not to compete is the amount taxpayer paid for it.[30]

Where a patent is obtained from the government, the basis is the cost of development, such as research and experimental expenditures (but not if deducted currently), drawings, attorneys' and governmental fees, etc. The value of any time spent on an invention isn't part of an inventor's basis. The basis of a copyright acquired from the government is the cost of securing the copyright from the government, including the cost of producing the work covered by the copyright, but not including the value of the author's time.[31]

Accounts receivable in the hands of a cash basis taxpayer have a zero basis.[32]

¶ 2472 Basis allocation, including "applicable asset acquisitions."

If a single transaction involves a number of separate properties, the total cost is allocated to establish the cost of the individual properties. The total basis is allocated to each item in proportion to the fair market value (FMV) of each item at the time of acquisition.[33]

However, for an applicable asset acquisition (defined below), the residual method must be used to allocate the purchase price. Under the residual method, the purchase price is reduced first by the amount of cash, demand deposits, and similar accounts. The amount remaining is allocated among the following assets in proportion to (but not in excess of) their FMV on the purchase date, in the following order: (1) certificates of deposit, U.S. Government securities, readily marketable stock or securities, foreign currency, and other items designated by IRS; (2) all assets other than those in the other categories; (3) all Code Sec. 197 intangibles (¶1977) except those in the nature of goodwill and going concern value; and (4) Code Sec. 197 intangibles in the nature of goodwill and going concern value.

The parties to an applicable asset acquisition may agree in writing to an allocation of consideration for, or a determination of the FMV of, any asset (including covenants not to compete) in the acquisition. The parties are bound by the allocation or valuation unless IRS determines that it's not appropriate. (Code Sec. 1060(a); Reg § 1.1060-1(c)(4), Reg § 1.1060-1(e))[34]

An applicable asset acquisition is any direct or indirect transfer of a group of assets that is a trade or business in the hands of either the seller or buyer if (except for certain like-kind

25. ¶P-5044; ¶12,714.01; TD ¶216,028
26. ¶G-5044.1
27. ¶P-5047; ¶12,814.01; TD ¶216,028
28. ¶P-5048; ¶12,884; TD ¶216,028
29. ¶J-4573 *et seq.*; ¶12,764.02; TD ¶154,005

30. ¶P-1178, P-1179, P-1180; ¶10,124.38; TD ¶212,511, 212,514
31. ¶P-1178; ¶1674.025; TD ¶211,111
32. ¶P-1121; TD ¶211,108
33. ¶P-1300 *et seq.*; ¶10,124.55; TD ¶212,500
34. ¶P-1400 *et seq.*; ¶10,604; TD ¶212,001 *et seq.*

exchanges) the buyer's basis in the transferred assets is determined wholly by reference to the buyer's consideration. (Code Sec. 1060(c); Reg § 1.1060-1(b)(1))[35]

The buyer and seller have to provide IRS with specified information about the assets (use Form 8594). (Code Sec. 1060(b); Reg § 1.1060-1(e)(1))[36]

¶ 2473 Personal use property converted to business use.

When a residence or other nonbusiness property is converted from personal use to business or income-producing use, for purposes of calculating losses or depreciation (but not for purposes of calculating gain), the basis for the property on the date of its conversion is the lower of its adjusted basis or fair market value on that date. This basis must thereafter be adjusted for depreciation, etc., after conversion. (Reg § 1.167(g)-1)[37]

¶ 2474 Adjusted basis.

Basis must be increased or decreased to reflect certain events, such as capital improvements or depreciation, whether the original basis was cost or something else.[38]

The basis of property is adjusted (increased) to include the amount of the capital expenditures with respect to the property. (Code Sec. 1016(a)(1))[39] A lessee's basis for his leasehold is increased by his capital expenditures.[40] However, a lessee's capital improvements don't increase or diminish the lessor's basis of the leased property. (Code Sec. 1019)[41]

Basis can be increased for items that are ordinarily deductible as expenses if the taxpayer has capitalized those items, e.g., taxes and carrying charges, see ¶1656.

For adjusted basis for alternative minimum tax purposes, see ¶3213.

¶ 2475 Contributions and returns of capital.

A stockholder's contribution of property to his corporation will increase his basis for his corporate stock.[42] A partner's contribution of cash to his partnership increases his basis in his partnership interest. See ¶3738 *et seq.*

Basis must be reduced for receipts representing a return of capital (Code Sec. 1016(a)(1); Reg § 1.1016-2(a)), such as damages taxpayer received for injury to property.[43]

¶ 2476 Depreciation, amortization, and other deductions.

Basis must be reduced for depreciation, cost recovery, amounts expensed under Code Sec. 179, amounts claimed under the Code Sec. 1400I commercial revitalization deduction, or amortization deductions with respect to the property. The amount of the reduction is the larger of (1) the amount of the depreciation, cost recovery, amortization, or depletion deductions *allowable* under the law, or (2) the amount that was actually *allowed* and resulted in a reduction of tax. (Code Sec. 1016(a)(2))

Basis must also be reduced for the Code Sec. 179D energy efficient commercial building property deduction for property placed in service after 2005 and before 2014. (Code Sec. 1016(a)(31))[44]

Allowable depreciation (or cost recovery) is the amount the taxpayer was entitled to deduct under the law, whether or not he actually took more or less and whether or not a tax benefit results. Where a taxpayer didn't adopt a depreciation method under Code Sec. 167, the

35. ¶P-1402 *et seq.*; ¶10,604; TD ¶212,002
36. ¶S-4301; ¶10,604; TD ¶212,012
37. ¶P-1908; ¶1674.037; TD ¶213,017
38. ¶P-1700 *et seq.*; ¶s 10,114, 10,164.01; TD ¶213,000 *et seq.*
39. ¶P-1801; ¶10,164.01; TD ¶213,501
40. ¶L-6510; ¶10,164
41. ¶P-1809; ¶10,194; TD ¶213,504
42. ¶F-1916; ¶10,164.02
43. ¶P-1821; ¶10,164.03; TD ¶213,515
44. ¶L-3176; ¶10,164; TD ¶308,106

amount allowable is figured under the straight-line method. (Code Sec. 1016(a))[45]

The depreciation (or cost recovery) *allowed* is the amount claimed on a tax return and allowed by IRS.[46]

In the case of business autos for which the optional business standard mileage rate, see ¶1561, is used, depreciation is considered to have been allowed at the rate of 17¢ for 2006, 19¢ for 2007, 21¢ for 2008 and 2009, and 23¢ for 2010.[47]

¶ 2477 Partial losses due to casualty or theft.

If property is partly lost or destroyed through casualty or theft, the basis is reduced by (1) the amount of insurance or other reimbursement received, and (2) the amount of deductible loss. But if a loss is *not* deductible under the rules discussed at ¶1793 *et seq.*, no basis reduction is required.

Expenditures with respect to such property, e.g., to remove debris and to restore the property to pre-casualty condition, increase the basis, unless they are deducted as repairs.[48]

¶ 2478 Basis of credit property reduced by certain credits earned.

The basis of investment credit property (¶2307), for purposes of computing depreciation or cost recovery deductions and gain or loss, must be reduced by 100% of the amount of the credit for which the property qualifies. (Code Sec. 50(c)(1))[49] The basis of energy credit property (¶2311) must be reduced by 50% of the allowed credit. (Code Sec. 50(c)(3)(A))[50]

If a pre-2007 credit is taken for the cost of a qualified electric vehicle, the basis of the property is reduced by the amount of the credit. (Code Sec. 30(e)(1))[1]

The basis of property also must be reduced for certain other credits, such as: the Code Sec. 25C nonbusiness energy property credit for property placed in service before 2008 or in 2009 or 2010 (¶2363) (Code Sec. 1016(a)(33))[2]; the Code Sec. 25D residential energy efficient property credit for property placed in service before 2017 (¶2364) (Code Sec. 1016(a)(34))[3]; the Code Sec. 30B alternative motor vehicle credit (¶2365) (Code Sec. 1016(a)(35))[4]; the Code Sec. 30D credit for new qualified plug-in electric drive motor vehicles allowed for tax years beginning after 2008 for property purchased before 2015 (¶2367) (Code Sec. 1016(a)(37))[5]; the Code Sec. 45F credit for employer-provided child care (¶2332) (Code Sec. 1016(a)(28))[6]; and the Code Sec. 45L energy efficient homes credit for homes acquired before 2010 (¶2337). (Code Sec. 1016(a)(32))[7]

¶ 2479 Recaptured tax credits.

Where certain tax credits are recaptured, a percentage of the recapture amount is added back to basis immediately before the event causing the recapture. The term "recapture amount" means any increase in tax (or adjustment in carrybacks or carryovers) due to the credit recapture provision. (Code Sec. 50(c)(2), Code Sec. 50(c)(3)(B))[8]

¶ 2480 Special lessor-lessee rule doesn't require basis-reduction adjustment.

A lessor of certain credit property who elects to pass the credit for the leased property to the lessee is not required to make the basis-reduction adjustment (¶2478). (Code Sec. 50(d)(5))[9]

45. ¶P-1902; ¶1674.085; TD ¶214,002
46. ¶P-1903; ¶s 1674, 1684; TD ¶214,003
47. ¶P-1909; ¶1624.157; TD ¶214,007
48. ¶P-1811; ¶1654.304; TD ¶213,503
49. ¶P-2000 *et seq.*; ¶504.03; TD ¶213,006
50. ¶P-2005; ¶504.03; TD ¶213,006
1. ¶L-18015; ¶304; TD ¶397,007
2. ¶P-1710.4; ¶10,164; TD ¶569,557

3. ¶P-1710.5; ¶10,164; TD ¶569,568
4. ¶L-18023; ¶10,164; TD ¶397,103
5. ¶P-1710.6; ¶10,164; TD ¶213,011.4
6. ¶P-1710.1; ¶10,164; TD ¶213,011.5
7. ¶P-1710.01; ¶10,164; TD ¶213,011.3
8. ¶P-2007; ¶504.03; TD ¶213,006
9. ¶P-2008; TD ¶213,007

¶ 2481   Basis in partnership or S corporation.

The basis of a partner's interest in a partnership or of a shareholder's stock in an S corporation is adjusted to reflect a partner's or shareholder's share of the required adjustments to the basis of partnership or S corporation property when credits are either allowed or recaptured. (Code Sec. 50(c)(5))[10]

¶ 2482   Property Acquired in Nontaxable Exchanges. ▬▬▬▬▬▬▬▬▬▬▬

The basis of property received in a nontaxable exchange, depending on the type of transaction, generally will be the same as its basis in the hands of the transferor or will be the same as the basis of the property transferred by the recipient in the exchange. If gain is recognized in part on the transaction, the basis of the property received may have to be adjusted.

¶ 2483   Basis of property received by corporation in tax-free transfer.

The basis of property received by a controlled corporation in a tax-free transfer, whether upon the incorporation of the corporation or otherwise, see ¶3510 *et seq.,* is equal to the basis of the property in the transferor's hands increased by any gain recognized by the transferor on the transfer. (Code Sec. 362(a)(1))[11]

The basis to a corporation of property acquired from a shareholder as a contribution to capital equals the basis of that property in the hands of the shareholder increased by the gain (if any) recognized by the shareholder on the transfer. (Code Sec. 362(a)(2))[12]

For limitations on an increase in basis due to the assumption of a liability and/or a built-in loss, see ¶2485.

¶ 2484   Acquirer's basis in property received in reorganization.

The basis of property received by the acquiring corporation in a tax-free reorganization (¶3541), is the transferor's (target's) basis increased by any gain recognized to the target. However, if the property consists of stock or securities of the target, this rule applies only if the property was acquired in exchange for stock or securities of the acquirer or the acquirer's parent corporation. (Code Sec. 362(b))[13]

For when an acquirer must reduce basis in assets received in a tax-free reorganization if the transferor has cancellation of debt income in connection with the transfer, see ¶1394.

For limitations on basis increase due to the assumption of a liability, see ¶2485.

¶ 2485   Limits on basis increase due to assumption of liability and/or built-in loss.

For purposes of the basis increase in the case of a tax-free transfer to a controlled corporation (¶2483) or in a reorganization exchange (see ¶2484), the property's basis can't be increased above its fair market value (FMV) on account of gain recognized by the transferor as a result of a liability assumed by the transferee. For this purpose, FMV is determined without regard to Code Sec. 7701(g) (which generally provides that a property's FMV is not less than the amount of nonrecourse debt to which it is subject). (Code Sec. 362(d)(1))[14]

Also, if property transferred was not taxable in the hands of the transferor but is taxable in the hands of the transferee corporation, and the total basis for the property in the hands of the transferee would otherwise (if not for this basis limitation rule) exceed its FMV, then the basis for each property in the hands of the transferee is its FMV. (Code Sec. 362(e)(1)) If this

---

10. ¶P-2009; TD ¶213,008
11. ¶F-1851; ¶3624.01; TD ¶232,001
12. ¶F-1851; ¶3624.05; TD ¶232,309

13. ¶F-4305; ¶3624.04; TD ¶233,501
14. ¶F-1852; ¶3624.01; TD ¶232,002

rule doesn't apply, a second carryover basis limitation rule (not limited to property as to which the transferor would not have recognized gain or loss) limits the total basis for property transferred by any transferor to its FMV. (Code Sec. 362(e)(2)) However, the transferor and transferee can jointly elect to reduce the basis of the stock received by the transferor instead of the basis of the assets transferred in the hands of the transferee. (Code Sec. 362(e)(2)(C)) IRS has prescribed how to make the election.[15]

¶ 2486 Target's basis in property received in reorganization.

The basis of property (other than stock and securities of another corporation that is a party to the reorganization, see ¶3555 *et seq.*) received under a plan of reorganization by the target equals the fair market value of the property. (Code Sec. 358(a)(2), Code Sec. 358(f))[16]

¶ 2487 Taxable acquisition of property by corporation for its stocks or bonds.

In cases other than tax-free contributions or reorganizations, the basis of property a corporation acquires in exchange for its stock is the fair market value of the stock at the time of the exchange.[17] The cost to a corporation of property it acquires in exchange for its bonds is the face amount of the bonds.[18] For bonds with original issue discount or unstated interest, see ¶2466.

¶ 2488 Basis of property to distributee shareholders or security holders.

For purposes of determining basis, property received by a distributee in connection with a transfer to a controlled corporation, a reorganization, or a corporate division (¶3510 *et seq.*), is classified as either nonrecognition property or other property. "Nonrecognition property" is property received without recognition of gain or loss to the recipient (stock in the transferee corporation in the case of a transfer to a controlled corporation, and stock or securities in the distributing corporation in tax-free reorganizations and corporate divisions). (Code Sec. 358(a)(1)) "Other property" is anything except "nonrecognition property" and money.

The basis of "nonrecognition property" is the same as the basis of the property given up in the exchange, except that this amount is (1) decreased by any money received, by the fair market value of any "other property" received, and by the loss, if any, recognized by the distributee on the exchange; and (2) increased by any part of the distribution that is treated as a dividend, and by any other gain recognized by the distributee on the exchange. (Code Sec. 358(a)(1))[19] The basis must be allocated among the nonrecognition property received in the transaction without recognition of gain or loss. (Reg § 1.358-2(a)(2))[20]

Where, as part of the consideration for the transfer of the distributee corporation's property to the acquirer, another party to the deal assumes a liability of the distributee, the assumption of that liability is treated as though it were money received by the distributee on the reorganization exchange (for basis purposes only). (Code Sec. 358(d)(1))[21]

✪ observation: Thus, the basis of the nonrecognition property received by the distributee on the exchange is reduced by an amount equal to the liabilities assumed.

IRS may provide adjustments for divisive reorganization transactions (¶3559) among affiliated group members. (Code Sec. 358(g))

IRS has issued regs for determining the basis of stock or securities received in connection with a corporate reorganization or a corporate division. (Reg § 1.358-1, Reg § 1.358-2)[22]

15. ¶F-1871 *et seq.*; ¶3624.02, 3624.03; TD ¶232,001
16. ¶F-4304; ¶3584.02; TD ¶233,301
17. ¶P-1158; ¶10,124.47; TD ¶211,130
18. ¶P-1160; TD ¶211,130
19. ¶F-4034; ¶3584.02; TD ¶232,541 *et seq.*
20. ¶F-4036; ¶3584.03; TD ¶232,544
21. ¶F-4035; ¶3584.02; TD ¶232,543
22. ¶F-1802 *et seq.*, F-4036 *et seq.*; ¶3584 *et seq.*

¶ 2489 Basis of other property received in tax-free transfer or reorganization.

The basis of property, other than stock or securities, received by a shareholder upon a tax-free transfer to a controlled corporation, a reorganization, or a corporate division (¶3510 *et seq.*) is its fair market value. (Code Sec. 358(a)(2))[23]

¶ 2490 Basis of property received in complete liquidation of corporation.

If property is received in a complete liquidation and any gain or loss is recognized on the receipt of the property, its basis in the hands of the shareholder-distributee is its fair market value at the time of the distribution. (Code Sec. 334(a))[24]

¶ 2491 Basis after partnership incorporates.

If a partnership incorporates, the basis of the corporation in the partnership's property and the basis of the former partners in their stock in the corporation depends on the method used to incorporate.

If the partnership transfers all of its assets subject to its liabilities to a newly formed corporation in return for all its stock, then distributes the stock to the partners, the corporation's basis in the partnership's assets is equal to the partnership's basis in the assets before the transaction and each partner's basis in the stock of the corporation is equal to the adjusted basis of that partner's interest in the partnership.

If the partnership distributes all of its assets subject to liabilities to the partners, who in turn transfer them to the new corporation for its stock, the corporation's basis in its assets is the same as the partners' basis in the assets prior to their contribution to the corporation and the partners' basis in the stock of the corporation is the same as their basis in the assets distributed in liquidation reduced by liabilities assumed by the corporation.

If the partners transfer their interests in the partnership to the new corporation in exchange for its stock and the corporation then liquidates the partnership, the corporation's basis in its assets is equal to the partners' basis in their partnership interests before the transaction and the partners' basis in their stock is equal to their basis in their partnership interests reduced by the liabilities assumed by the corporation.[25]

¶ 2492 Property received as a dividend.

The basis for property received as a dividend, including stock or stock rights received as a taxable stock dividend, is its fair market value on the date of distribution. (Code Sec. 301(d))[26]

¶ 2493 Basis allocation for nontaxable stock dividend.

If a shareholder gets a nontaxable dividend of stock or stock rights, the (adjusted) basis of the old stock (that is, of the stock on which the dividend was distributed) is allocated between the old and new stock (or rights) in proportion to the fair market value (FMV) of each on the date of distribution. (Code Sec. 307(a)) Where only part of the stock dividend is nontaxable, the basis of the old stock is allocated between the old stock and that part of the new stock (or rights) which isn't taxable, in proportion to the FMV of each on the date of distribution. The date of distribution is, in both cases, the date on which the new stock (or the stock rights) was distributed, not the record date.[27]

illustration: S bought one share of voting common for $45. The corporation distributed two new shares of voting common for each share held. This gave S three shares of voting

---

23. ¶F-1804, F-4034, F-4304, F-5014; ¶3584.02; TD ¶231,912, 232,542, 233,304
24. ¶F-13119; ¶3344.01; TD ¶245,427
25. ¶s F-1011, F-1805; TD ¶231,015
26. ¶P-5400 *et seq.*; ¶3014.03; TD ¶217,501 *et seq.*
27. ¶P-5301; ¶3074.01 *et seq.*; TD ¶217,001

common with a basis of $15 each. If he had owned two shares before the distribution, one purchased for $30 and the other for $45, he would have six shares: three with a basis of $10 each, and three with a basis of $15 each.

If the FMV of stock rights at the time of distribution is less than 15% of the FMV of the stock on which they were distributed, the basis for the rights received is zero unless the taxpayer elects to allocate basis to the rights. (Code Sec. 307(b)(1))[28]

¶ 2494   Basis of stock acquired through dividend reinvestment plans (DRP).

If a corporation allows shareholders to receive dividends in either cash or stock, then, depending on the situation, the receipt of stock is treated either as the receipt of a taxable stock dividend, because the shareholder has the choice of receiving either cash or stock, or as the receipt of a cash dividend which the shareholder used to buy stock (in some cases, at a discount). If the transaction is treated as a stock dividend, the shareholder's basis is equal to the value of the shares received at the time of the receipt. On the other hand, if the transaction is treated as a cash dividend, the shareholder's basis in the shares is equal to the amount of cash he could have received.[29] The basis of stock acquired after 2010 in connection with a DRP, while held as part of the DRP, will be determined using one of the methods which can be used used for determining the basis of stock in a mutual fund. (Code Sec. 1012(d)(1)) Thus, the average basis method for mutual fund shareholders (see ¶2498) also is available for shares of stock acquired after 2010 in connection with a DRP, but only if the shares are identical (i.e., have the same CUSIP number, or other acceptable security identifier number). (Reg § 1.1012-1(e)(1))[30]

¶ 2495   Effect of extraordinary dividends on corporate shareholder's basis.

If a corporation receives an extraordinary dividend with respect to a share of stock that it hasn't held for more than 2 years before the dividend announcement date, the basis of the stock is reduced (but not below zero) by the non-taxed portion (i.e., the excess (if any) of: (a) the distribution amount over (b) the portion of the dividend that is included in gross income, reduced by the amount of any dividend received deduction allowable under Code Sec. 243, Code Sec. 244, or Code Sec. 245). (Code Sec. 1059) Where a redemption is treated as an extraordinary dividend, the basis in the nonredeemed shares is also reduced if the redemption is part of a partial liquidation of the redeeming corporation, or isn't pro rata as to all shareholders, but not if the redemption wouldn't have been treated (in whole or in part) as a dividend if an option hadn't been taken into account under the Code Sec. 318(a)(4) option attribution rules or the Code Sec. 304(a) related-party stock purchase rules.[31]

¶ 2496   Identifying shares transferred.

Where taxpayer can adequately identify which shares of stock are transferred, the basis used is the basis of that stock or those bonds (specific identification). Shares of stock or bonds are adequately identified where it can be shown that the shares or bonds that were delivered to the transferee are from a lot acquired on a certain date or for a certain price. (Reg § 1.1012-1(c)(1); Reg § 1.1012-1(c)(2))[32]

If a number of lots were acquired and the ones sold can't be adequately identified, a first-in, first-out (FIFO) rule applies. If the earliest lot purchased or acquired is held in a stock certificate that represents multiple lots of stock, and the taxpayer does not adequately identify the lot from which the stock is sold or transferred, the stock sold or transferred is charged against the earliest lot included in the certificate. (Reg § 1.1012-1(c)(1)(i)) Where shares are held in more than one account, the FIFO rule applies only to the particular account from

---

28. ¶P-5303; ¶3074.03; TD ¶217,002
29. ¶P-5402; TD ¶174,008
30. ¶P-5201.4; ¶10,124.7701; TD ¶218,001.4

31. ¶P-5100 *et seq.*; ¶10,594; TD ¶216,022
32. ¶P-5202; ¶10,124.78; TD ¶218,002 *et seq.*

which the shares were transferred.[33]

¶ 2497 Adequate identification v. wrong delivery.

In certain situations, if a taxpayer specifically identifies certain shares of stock or bonds as the ones to be transferred, and certain other conditions are met, these will be treated as the ones transferred even though some other lot is actually delivered. This rule applies (1) for sales of stock or bonds held by a broker or agent (Reg § 1.1012-1(c)(3)(i)), (2) where a single certificate represents different lots of stock (Reg § 1.1012-1(c)(3)(ii)), and (3) for certain transfers by a trustee, executor or administrator. (Reg § 1.1012-1(c)(4))[34]

¶ 2498 Methods for determining basis of mutual fund shares.

A taxpayer who sells mutual fund shares held by a custodian or agent in an account may elect to determine the basis of the shares sold by determining the average basis using the "single-category method." (Reg § 1.1012-1(e)(7)(i)) A taxpayer who had been using a "double-category method" for stock acquired before Apr. 1, 2011 could continue to use that method for sales before that date. (Reg § 1.1012-1(e)(7)(iii)) Generally, the single-category method groups in one category all shares regardless of holding period (but treats shares sold as sold on a first-in-first-out (FIFO) basis so that shares that qualify for long-term capital gain or loss treatment are treated as sold before shares that would get short-term treatment); the double-category method divides all shares by their holding period. The basis is then averaged over all the shares in their respective category. (Reg § 1.1012-1(e)(7)) A shareholder who doesn't elect the average-basis method must use the normal first-in, first-out (FIFO) method for determining which shares were sold, see ¶2496.

An election to use the average basis method for shares of stock that the taxpayer sells before 2012 applies to all identical shares of stock the taxpayer holds in any account. (Reg § 1.1012-1(e)(10)(ii)) However, unless a single-account election is in effect, a taxpayer may not average together the basis of identical stock held in separate accounts that the taxpayer sells, exchanges, or otherwise disposes of after 2011. (Reg § 1.1012-1(e)(7)(i))[35]

¶ 2499 Determining basis for certain securities held in brokerage accounts.

In the case of a sale, exchange or other disposition on or after the "applicable date" (defined below), the broker reported basis in a "specified security" (defined below) is determined under the conventions prescribed in existing regulations and applied to each separate account, on an account-by-account basis. (Code Sec. 1012(c)(1)) Reported basis is computed using a FIFO method, the specific-identification method, or the average-basis convention (Reg § 1.1012-1) (see ¶2496 and ¶2498).[36]

A "specified security" is stocks, notes, and other debt, certain commodity contracts and derivatives, and other securities deemed appropriate by the IRS. (Code Sec. 6045(g)) The applicable date is Jan. 1, 2012 for "average basis" stock, Jan. 1, 2011 for other stock, and Jan. 1, 2013 for other specified securities. (Code Sec. 6045(g))[37]

¶ 2500 Basis of stock acquired in wash sale.

Where a loss is disallowed under the wash sale rule (¶2461), the basis of the acquired stock takes account of the unrecognized loss in the following manner: (Code Sec. 1091(d))

(1) If the sales price is less than the repurchase price, the basis of the new stock is the basis of the stock sold plus the difference between the repurchase and the sales prices.

Illustration: T owns 100 shares of X company common which cost $100 per share. On May 1,

---

33. ¶P-5212 *et seq.*; ¶10,124.83; TD ¶218,011 *et seq.*
34. ¶P-5200 *et seq.*; ¶10,124.78; TD ¶218,002 *et seq.*
35. ¶P-5214 *et seq.*; ¶10,124.7801; TD ¶218,013 *et seq.*

36. ¶P-5201.1; ¶10,124.7701; TD ¶218,001.1
37. ¶P-5201.3; ¶60,45A4 *et seq.*; TD ¶814,401 *et seq.*

T sells the 100 shares at $80 per share. On May 20, T buys 100 shares of X common at $90 per share. No loss is allowed on the May 1 sale. The basis of each share acquired May 20 is $110, i.e., the basis of the shares sold ($100) plus the $10 difference between the repurchase and sale prices ($90 – $80). (Reg § 1.1091-2(a))

(2) If the sales price is more than the repurchase price, the basis of the new stock is the basis of the stock sold minus the difference between the sale and the repurchase prices.[38]

Illustration: If, in the above illustration, the May 1 sale price had been $90 per share and the May 20 repurchase price was $80 per share, the basis of each share acquired May 20 would be $90, i.e., the basis of shares sold ($100) minus the difference between the sale and repurchase prices ($90 – $80). (Reg § 1.1091-2(a))

¶ 2501 Basis of properties after nontaxable exchange.

The basis of property received in a like-kind exchange and nontaxable exchanges of stock in the same corporation (¶2414), U.S. obligations (¶2416), and life insurance and annuity contracts (¶2417) where no part of the gain is recognized is the adjusted basis of the property traded away. (Code Sec. 1031(d))

If money is received as part of the exchange and some gain is recognized, basis in the property received is decreased by the money received and increased by the gain recognized. Reg § 1.1031(d)-1(b)) If money is paid, basis is increased by the amount paid. (Reg § 1.1031(d)-1(a))

If other property (boot) is received and some gain is recognized, basis must be allocated (according to fair market value) to all the properties received. (Reg § 1.1031(d)-1(c))

If boot is given as part of the exchange, and gain or loss is recognized on transfer of the boot, the basis of the nonrecognition property received is the total basis of all the properties given, increased by any recognized gain on the boot, or decreased by any recognized loss on the boot. (Reg § 1.1031(d)-1(e))[39]

¶ 2502 Basis after exchange of multiple properties.

In an exchange of multiple properties qualifying for nonrecognition of gain or loss (see ¶2425), the aggregate basis of properties received in each of the "exchange groups" is determined under regs. (Reg § 1.1031(j)-1(c))[40]

¶ 2503 Basis of replacement property after involuntary conversion.

If property is involuntarily converted directly into similar property and gain on the conversion isn't recognized under Code Sec. 1033(a)(1) (see ¶2431), the basis of the property received is the basis of the converted property (1) decreased by the amount of any money received that wasn't spent in acquiring similar property, and (2) increased by the amount of gain recognized, or decreased by the amount of loss recognized. (Code Sec. 1033(b)(1)) Where the taxpayer's property is involuntarily converted into money or other property that isn't similar or related in use to the converted property (¶2431) and, within the prescribed period (¶2441), the taxpayer purchases other property that is similar or related in service or use to the converted property, and elects not to recognize any part of the gain, the basis of the replacement property is its cost, reduced by the amount of gain that isn't recognized. If more than one piece of property is bought as replacement, the basis (cost less nonrecognized gain) is allocated to each piece in proportion to its respective cost. (Code Sec. 1033(b)(2))[41] Where a taxpayer satisfies the replacement property requirement by buying a controlling stock interest in a corporation (¶2431), the corporation reduces its basis in its assets by the amount by

38. ¶P-5019; ¶10,914; TD ¶216,007
39. ¶I-3176 *et seq.*; ¶10,314.13; TD ¶225,200 *et seq.*
40. ¶I-3193; ¶10,314.14; TD ¶225,409
41. ¶P-1154; ¶10,334.33; TD ¶211,128

which the taxpayer reduces its basis in the stock. (Code Sec. 1033(b)(3))[42]

¶ 2504 Basis of replacement for stock sold to ESOP or EWOC.

If the seller of qualified securities to an employee stock ownership plan (ESOP) or eligible worker-owned cooperative (EWOC) reinvests in qualified replacement property and elects gain nonrecognition (¶2451), basis is reduced by the gain not recognized. If more than one item of replacement property is bought, basis reduction is allocated among each such item (as the cost of that item bears to the cost of all items). (Code Sec. 1042(d))[43]

¶ 2505 Basis for SSBIC rollovers.

Any gain not recognized under the specialized small business investment company (SSBIC) rollover rules (¶2427), reduces taxpayer's basis in any SSBIC investment made during the 60-day rollover period. If taxpayer makes more than one SSBIC investment during this period, the bases of those other investments are reduced in the order they were acquired. (Code Sec. 1044(d))[44]

¶ 2506 Basis for QSBS rollovers.

Gain from the sale of qualified small business stock (QSBS) that isn't recognized because of the Code Sec. 1045(a) rollover election (see ¶2429) reduces (in the order acquired) the basis for determining gain or loss of any QSBS that's purchased by the taxpayer within the 60-day rollover period beginning on the sale date. (Code Sec. 1045(b)(3))[45]

¶ 2507 Property Acquired by Gift, from a Decedent, or from a Spouse. ▬▬▬▬

Special rules apply to determine the basis of property acquired by gift, from a decedent, or from a spouse.

For the basis of property acquired by a gift or transfer in trust during the life of the transferor, see ¶2508 *et seq.*

For the basis of property acquired from a decedent, see ¶2512 *et seq.*

For basis of property acquired from a decedent dying in 2010, see ¶2523.

For the basis of property acquired from a spouse (or former spouse), see ¶2524.

¶ 2508 Basis of property acquired by gift or transfer in trust.

A donee's original or unadjusted basis (that is, the basis before adjustments made while the donee owned it) for property the donee acquires by gift is the same as the property's adjusted basis in the hands of the donor, or in the hands of the last preceding owner who didn't acquire the property by gift. (Code Sec. 1015(a))[46] But if the property's fair market value (FMV) at the date of the gift is lower than that adjusted basis, then the property's basis for determining *loss* is its fair market value on that date. (Code Sec. 1015(a))[47]

Since two different methods determine basis of property acquired as a gift, it's possible that neither gain nor loss determined in reference to basis will be realized when the donee sells or exchanges the property. (Reg § 1.1015-1(a)(2))[48]

> **⊘ illustration:** Taxpayer acquires by gift income-producing property with an adjusted basis of $100,000 at the date of gift. The FMV on the date of gift is $90,000. Taxpayer later sells the property for $95,000. Taxpayer has neither gain nor loss, since the basis for determining gain is $100,000 and the basis for determining loss is $90,000.

---

42. ¶P-1154.1; ¶10,334.231; TD ¶211,129
43. ¶H-12110; ¶10,424
44. ¶I-3791; ¶10,444; TD ¶225,503
45. ¶I-9206; ¶10,454; TD ¶247,208

46. ¶P-3103; ¶10,154.01; TD ¶215,002
47. ¶P-3104; ¶10,154.01; TD ¶215,002
48. ¶P-3105; TD ¶215,002

If a transfer in trust is made for consideration (whether full and adequate, or less), the basis is the same as it would be in the hands of the grantor, increased by the amount of gain or decreased by the amount of loss recognized to the grantor upon the transfer under the law applicable to the year in which the transfer was made. (Code Sec. 1015(b))[49]

For part sales and part gifts, see ¶2509.

¶ 2509 Basis after transfer that is part purchase, part gift.

Where a transfer of property is in part a purchase and in part a gift, the transferee's basis is the greater of cost or the transferor's adjusted basis for the property at the time of the transfer.[50] However, for determining loss, the basis can't exceed the property's fair market value at the time of transfer. (Reg § 1.1015-4) In either event, basis is increased to the extent of any gift tax paid (¶2511).

¶ 2510 Basis rules for donees of partial interests.

If two or more donees receive partial interests in the same property, the basis to each is his or her proportionate part of the donor's basis. To determine the part of total basis allowable to life tenants and remaindermen, apply the rules at ¶2522. (Reg § 1.1015-1(b))[1]

¶ 2511 Increase in basis for gift tax paid.

If the property's fair market value at the date of the gift is greater than the donor's adjusted basis, the donee's basis (donor's adjusted basis) is increased by the part of the gift tax paid that is attributable to the net appreciation in value of the gift. This portion is determined by multiplying the gift tax paid by a fraction whose numerator is the net appreciation in value of the gift and whose denominator is the amount of the gift. (Code Sec. 1015(d)(6))

If a gift consists of more than one item of property, the gift tax paid with respect to each item is computed by allocating to each item a proportionate part of the gift tax paid with respect to the gift. If more than one gift was made during the calendar year (or preceding calendar period), the total tax paid must be apportioned to each gift to determine the amount paid on each gift. (Code Sec. 1015(d)(2))

The gift tax paid on a husband-wife split gift is the sum of the taxes, computed separately, paid with respect to each half of the gift. (Code Sec. 1015(d)(3); Reg § 1.1015-5(b)(3))[2]

¶ 2512 Property acquired from a decedent.

The rules set out below applied for decedents dying before 2010, and will apply again for decedents dying after 2010 under the EGTRRA sunset provisions discussed at ¶1111.

The basis of property acquired from a decedent by inheritance, bequest, devise, etc. (see ¶2515), that hasn't been sold, exchanged, or otherwise disposed of before the decedent's death, is generally equal to its fair market value (FMV) at the date of the decedent's death. (Code Sec. 1014(a)(1)) However, if:

(1) the fiduciary elects for estate tax purposes to value the decedent's gross estate at the alternate valuation date (¶5027), the basis of the property is its FMV at that date (Code Sec. 1014(a)(2));

(2) the fiduciary elects for estate tax purposes the special use valuation method of valuing farm or other closely held business real property included in the decedent's gross estate (¶5028), the basis of the real property is its value determined for purposes of the special use

---

49. ¶P-3112; ¶10,154.16; TD ¶215,018
50. ¶P-1113; ¶10,154; TD ¶215,006

1. ¶P-3131; ¶10,154.06; TD ¶215,016
2. ¶P-3107 *et seq.*; ¶10,154.01; TD ¶215,004 *et seq.*

valuation election (rather than its FMV). (Code Sec. 1014(a)(3))[3]

(3) land acquired at death is subject to a qualified conservation easement, it is excluded from the decedent's gross estate under the rules explained at ¶5027, and its basis (to the extent that it's subject to the easement) is the basis in the hands of the decedent. (Code Sec. 1014(a)(4))[4]

FMV on the date of the decedent's death (or the alternate valuation date, if applicable) doesn't apply to determine the basis of property:

... that's appreciated property reacquired by the donor within one year of transfer to decedent, see ¶2514;

... included in the decedent's estate but disposed of by the taxpayer before the decedent's death, see ¶2516;

... that's stock in a domestic international sales corporation (DISC) or former DISC (Code Sec. 1014(d)), or of certain foreign entities; or

... that is a right to receive income in respect of a decedent (Code Sec. 1014(c)), see ¶3967.[5]

For the basis of property acquired from a decedent dying in 2010, see ¶2523.

¶ 2513   When estate tax value is also income tax basis.

The fair market value (FMV) of property at the decedent's death or at the alternate valuation date as appraised for federal estate tax purposes (or, if no federal estate tax return is required to be filed, the FMV of the property appraised as of the date of death for purposes of state inheritance taxes) is considered also to be the FMV for purposes of determining the income tax basis of property acquired from a decedent. (Reg § 1.1014-3(a))[6] But the value for estate tax purposes is only presumptively correct for basis purposes. Except where facts have been misrepresented, neither taxpayer nor IRS is barred from using a value for basis purposes that differs from the value accepted for estate tax purposes. However, where a discount is allowed in valuing property (e.g., artwork) for estate tax purposes, full value generally will not be allowed in valuing the same property for estate tax purposes.[7]

¶ 2514   Appreciated property reacquired by donor.

If: (1) appreciated property was acquired by the decedent by gift during the one-year period ending at death, and (2) that property is acquired from the decedent by (or passes from the decedent to) the donor of the property (or the donor's spouse), the basis of the property in the hands of the donor (or spouse) is the adjusted basis of the property in the decedent's hands immediately before his death. (Code Sec. 1014(e)(1))[8]

¶ 2515   When is property considered acquired from a decedent?

Property is acquired from a decedent if it is acquired by bequest, devise, or inheritance, or by the decedent's estate from the decedent. (Code Sec. 1014(b)(1))[9] Property acquired from a decedent includes certain pre-death transfers and other classes of property (see ¶2519 *et seq.*). Qualified terminable interest property (QTIP) includible in a surviving spouse's estate (¶5009) is treated as passing from that surviving spouse for purposes of determining the remaindermen's basis. (Code Sec. 1014(b)(10))[10] Property acquired from a decedent excludes:

... Property the fiduciary acquires after the decedent's death, the basis of which to the fiduciary (or a distributee, if it's distributed) is its cost or other basis with appropriate

---

3. ¶P-4001; ¶s 10,144, 10,144.05; TD ¶215,501
4. ¶P-4021.1; ¶10,144.055; TD ¶215,517
5. ¶P-4001; ¶10,144.02; TD ¶215,518 *et seq.*
6. ¶P-4022; ¶10,144.03; TD ¶215,506

7. ¶s P-4023, P-4024; ¶10,144.03; TD ¶215,506
8. ¶P-4002; ¶10,144.02; TD ¶215,522
9. ¶P-4102; ¶10,144.01; TD ¶215,507
10. ¶P-4104; ¶10,144.01; TD ¶215,507

adjustments. (Reg § 1.1014-3(c))[11]

... Property bought from a decedent's estate. Its basis to the buyer is its cost or other basis with appropriate adjustments.[12]

... Income in respect of a decedent (IRD, see ¶3967). (Code Sec. 1014(c)) Its basis is equal to the decedent's basis (if any).[13]

... Property transferred by the executor, administrator or trustee to a beneficiary in discharge of a specific pecuniary bequest. The beneficiary's basis is the fair market value of the property on the date of the transfer. (Reg § 1.1014-4(a)(3))[14]

¶ 2516   Property acquired from decedent and included in decedent's gross estate.

Property is considered to have been acquired from a decedent if it was acquired from a decedent by reason of: death, form of ownership, or other conditions and the property is required to be included in determining the value of the decedent's gross estate whether or not an estate tax return is required or an estate tax is payable. Acquisitions covered by this rule include acquisitions as surviving joint tenant or tenant by the entirety (see ¶2517), acquisitions through exercise of a general power of appointment (¶2520), and gifts within three years of death (if includible in the gross estate for estate tax purposes, see ¶5003). (Reg § 1.1014-2(b))[15] If property is acquired before the death of the decedent, this basis must be reduced by the amount actually allowed to the taxpayer as deductions for depreciation, obsolescence, amortization, and depletion for the period before the decedent's death. (Code Sec. 1014(b)(9))[16] If property received as a gift (including a gift in trust) is disposed of by the donee before the donor's death, the property isn't treated as acquired from a decedent and the donee's basis is determined under the rules for gifts, see ¶2508. But property received in exchange for such gift property, or property acquired through reinvesting proceeds of sale of such gift property (or property acquired in further exchange or reinvestments), is treated as acquired from a decedent if it is includible in the decedent's gross estate. (Reg § 1.1014-3(d))[17]

¶ 2517   Tenants by the entirety and joint tenants.

Property that a person acquires as the surviving tenant by the entirety or as a surviving joint tenant is property acquired from a decedent to the extent the property is includible in the decedent's gross estate, see ¶5011 *et seq.* The part of the property that's treated as acquired from the decedent gets a stepped-up basis.[18] The reduction in basis for depreciation and similar deductions is required only for depreciation, etc., allowed to the surviving joint owner, whose new basis is at issue. (Code Sec. 1014(b)(9)) Local law applies to determine how depreciation is allocated to a husband and wife who file joint returns. (Reg § 1.1014-6(a)(2))[19]

¶ 2518   Community property.

Where a spouse dies owning community property and at least one-half of the entire community interest is includible in the deceased spouse's gross estate (whether or not an estate tax return is required or an estate tax is payable), the surviving spouse's interest is treated as property acquired from a decedent. (Code Sec. 1014(b)(6))[20]

⊘observation: Under the above rule, the surviving spouse's share of the community property plus the decedent's share (included in the decedent's estate) is treated as property acquired from the decedent. Thus, both shares get a stepped-up basis.

---

11. ¶P-4054; ¶10,144.02; TD ¶215,511
12. ¶P-4118; TD ¶215,511
13. ¶P-4003; ¶10,144.02; TD ¶215,523
14. ¶P-4055; TD ¶215,511
15. ¶P-4103; ¶10,144.01; TD ¶215,011

16. ¶P-4027; ¶10,144.01; TD ¶215,013
17. ¶P-3124; ¶10,144.02; TD ¶215,012
18. ¶P-4115; ¶10,144.01; TD ¶215,502
19. ¶P-4028 *et seq.*; ¶10,144.01; TD ¶215,502
20. ¶P-4112; ¶10,144.01; TD ¶215,510

¶ 2519   Inter vivos trust with power to revoke, alter, etc.

Property acquired from a decedent includes property that the decedent during his lifetime transferred in trust to pay the trust income to, or on the order of, the decedent, where the decedent also reserved to himself at all times before his death the right to (1) revoke the trust (Code Sec. 1014(b)(2)), or (2) make any change in the enjoyment of the trust through the exercise of a power to alter, amend, or terminate the trust (whether alone or with the consent of another not having an interest adverse to his). (Code Sec. 1014(b)(3))[21]

¶ 2520   Power to appoint property.

Property acquired from a decedent includes property passing without full and adequate consideration under a general power of appointment exercised by the decedent in his will. (Code Sec. 1014(b)(4))[22]

¶ 2521   Basis of postponed or contingent remainder interests.

Taxpayer's basis for property acquired from a decedent is determined on the date of the decedent's death under the rules at ¶2512 *et seq.*, whether or not, at the decedent's death, the taxpayer's interest was conditional or contingent, and whether or not the taxpayer can immediately possess and enjoy the property. (Reg § 1.1014-4(a)(2))[23]

¶ 2522   Multiple interests in one property.

Where more than one person has an interest in property acquired from a decedent, the basis in the property is determined and adjusted without regard to the multiple interests. Therefore, a life tenant makes basis adjustments for depreciation as if he were the absolute owner. His basis adjustments are an adjustment in the hands of every person who receives an interest by reason of the decedent's death. (Reg § 1.1014-4(b))[24]

¶ 2523   Basis of property acquired from a decedent dying in 2010.

Effective for individuals dying in 2010, estate and generation-skipping transfer taxes are completely repealed (see ¶5000), and the basis of property acquired from a decedent, in the hands of the person acquiring or receiving it, generally is the lower of the fair market value (FMV) on the date of the decedent's death or the adjusted basis of the property immediately before the death of the decedent. (Code Sec. 1022(a)) However, each estate receives $1.3 million of basis to be added to the carryover basis of any one or more of the assets held at death. (Code Sec. 1022(b)(2)(B)) Also, an estate generally receives additional basis equal to the sum of (a) the decedent's unused capital loss carryforwards, (b) the decedent's unused net operating loss carryforwards, and (c) the amount of losses that would have been allowable under Code Sec. 165 if the property acquired from the decedent had been sold at FMV immediately before death. (Code Sec. 1022(b)(2)(C)) Also, estates are allowed an additional $3 million of basis, to be allocated among the assets passing to a surviving spouse. (Code Sec. 1022(c)) However, no addition to basis may increase the new basis of any asset above its FMV on the date of death. (Code Sec. 1022(d)(2))[25] For post-2010 sunset provisions, see ¶1114.

✔*caution:* Check http://ria.thomsonreuters.com/federaltaxhandbook to see if the repeal of the estate and generation skipping taxes will remain in effect.

---

21. ¶P-4109; ¶10,154.17; TD ¶215,508
22. ¶P-4110; ¶10,144.01; TD ¶215,509
23. ¶P-4018; TD ¶215,503

24. ¶P-4014 *et seq.*; ¶10,144.06; TD ¶215,505
25. ¶P-4060; ¶10,224.02

¶ 2524 Basis of property transferred between spouses or incident to a divorce.

The transferee is treated as acquiring the property by gift; the transferee's basis in the property received is the transferor's adjusted basis in the property. (Code Sec. 1041(b)) This rule applies even where the transaction is a sale between the spouses or where the transferee-spouse pays the transferor-spouse (as required under the divorce settlement) for the transfer of title to the property to the transferee-spouse. (Reg § 1.1041-1T(a), Q&A-2) This carryover basis rule applies whether the adjusted basis of the transferred property is less than, equal to, or greater than its fair market value at the time of transfer and applies for purposes of determining loss as well as gain, upon later sale by the transferee. (Reg § 1.1041-1T(d), Q&A-11)[26] Exceptions apply to certain transfers in trust (where liabilities assumed by the trust exceed the transferor's adjusted basis) (Code Sec. 1041(e)), and to transfers of installment obligations into a trust (Code Sec. 453B(g)).[27] The transferor must, at the time of the transfer, give the transferee records sufficient to determine the adjusted basis and holding period of the property at the date of transfer. (Reg § 1.1041-1T(e), Q&A-14)[28]

---

26. ¶P-1146; ¶10,414; TD ¶211,124
27. ¶P-1147; ¶10,414; TD ¶211,125

28. ¶P-1153; ¶10,414; TD ¶211,127

Chapter 10 Capital Gains and Losses—Section 1231—Depreciation Recapture

¶ 2600 Capital Gains and Losses. ▄▄▄▄▄▄▄▄▄▄▄▄▄▄▄▄▄▄▄▄▄▄▄▄▄▄▄

The tax treatment of capital gains and losses depends on whether the gains and losses are long-term or short-term and on whether the taxpayer is a corporation or not. For noncorporate taxpayers, the maximum tax rate on net long-term capital gains is lower than the top rate on ordinary income. The maximum tax rate on long-term capital gains depends on the type of capital asset sold, and the taxpayer's marginal tax rate (the top rate of tax on the person's ordinary income). The long-term capital gains of corporations, and the short-term gains of corporations and of noncorporate taxpayers, are taxable at the same rates as their ordinary income. The deduction for capital losses is limited, but unused capital losses of noncorporate taxpayers may be carried over indefinitely (¶2612) and unused capital losses of corporate taxpayers can generally be carried back for three years and carried over for five years, see ¶2615.

The main features of the income tax treatment of capital gains and losses are:

. . . Short-term capital gains and losses are netted, long-term capital gains and losses are netted, and then long- and short-term are netted with each other (¶2602 *et seq.*). Further netting may be required if a noncorporate taxpayer has capital losses as well as long-term capital gain subject to differing maximum rates of tax. (¶2609)

. . . A net capital gain (excess of net long-term capital gain over net short-term capital loss) of a noncorporate taxpayer is generally taxed more favorably than ordinary income. The maximum tax rate depends on whether the net capital gain is adjusted net capital gain (¶2603), collectibles gain (¶2607) or section 1202 gain (¶2608), or unrecaptured section 1250 gain (¶2605).

. . . Section 1231 nets gains and losses to arrive at a net of long-term capital gain or ordinary loss (¶2610 and ¶2684 *et seq.*).

. . . Recapture provisions restrict the possibility of converting ordinary income into capital gains via cost recovery or depreciation (¶2692 *et seq.*).

Capital gains and losses are the gains and losses from sales or exchanges (¶2676) of capital assets (¶2617). But capital gain treatment also applies to gains in certain transactions involving assets that aren't capital assets (such as depreciable property used in business, ¶2686).[1]

⚫*observation:* Not all losses (capital or ordinary) are deductible. An individual can only deduct losses incurred in business or transactions for profit, or resulting from a casualty or theft. Thus, a loss on a sale of a personal residence is a nondeductible capital loss.

Report capital gains and losses on Schedule D of the applicable return (e.g., for individuals, Form 1040). Taxpayers may report the total of their capital gains and losses transactions on Schedule D and provide details on attachments such as brokers' statements. Individuals whose only capital gains are capital gains distributions (other than unreported section 1250 gain or collectibles gain) reported on Form 1099-DIV do not have to file a Schedule D. They enter capital gains on Form 1040 or 1040A and complete a capital gain tax worksheet in the instructions.

For the deduction when stock or securities become worthless, see ¶1782.

---

1. ¶I-5100 *et seq.*; ¶12,214 *et seq.*; TD ¶223,300 *et seq.*

References beginning with a single letter are to paragraphs in RIA's Federal Tax Coordinator 2d and RIA's Analysis of Federal Taxes: Income. Those beginning with numbers are to paragraphs in RIA's United States Tax Reporter. Those beginning with TD are to paragraphs in RIA's Tax Desk.

¶ 2601   Tax effect of capital asset sales and exchanges.

If a capital asset is held for not more than the short-term holding period (¶2667), the gain or loss from its sale or exchange is short-term. If held for more than the short-term holding period, gain or loss is long-term. (Code Sec. 1222)[2]

Short-term capital gains and losses are netted to get net short-term capital gain or net short-term capital loss. (Code Sec. 1222(5), Code Sec. 1222(6))

Long-term capital gains and losses are netted to get net long-term capital gain or net long-term capital loss. (Code Sec. 1222(7), Code Sec. 1222(8))

There's a further netting if one group shows a loss and the other a gain:

If there's a net short-term gain, it's taxable (both for noncorporate and corporate taxpayers) at the same rate as ordinary income.[3]

If capital losses exceed capital gains, see ¶2611 *et seq.* (noncorporate) or ¶2615 (corporate).

If net long-term capital gains exceed net short-term capital losses, the excess is net capital gain, taxed under the rules at ¶2603 to ¶2611 (individuals and other noncorporate taxpayers) or ¶2613 *et seq.* (corporate taxpayers). (Code Sec. 1222(11))

¶ 2602   Capital gain net income defined.

A taxpayer who has an excess of capital gains over capital losses (whether long-term or short-term) for the tax year, has "capital gain net income" (Code Sec. 1222(9)), which is included in gross income.[4]

¶ 2603   Noncorporate taxpayers' tax on net capital gain.

A noncorporate taxpayer's net capital gain is taxed as follows:

. . . Net capital gain that is adjusted net capital gain (¶2604) is taxed at a maximum rate of 15%. If the adjusted net capital gain would otherwise be taxed at a rate below 25% if it were ordinary income, it is taxed at a zero percent rate. (Code Sec. 1(h)(1)(B), Code Sec. 1(h)(1)(C))

. . . That part of net capital gain attributable to unrecaptured section 1250 gain (¶2605) is taxed at a maximum rate of 25%. (Code Sec. 1(h)(1)(D))

. . . Net capital gain attributable to collectibles gain (¶2607), and section 1202 gain (¶2608) is taxed at a maximum rate of 28%. (Code Sec. 1(h)(1)(E), Code Sec. 1(h)(4))[5]

IRS is authorized to issue regs applying the applicable rates for long-term capital gain to sales by passthrough entities and sales of interests in those entities. (Code Sec. 1(h)(9))[6]

Sellers of interests in S corporations, partnerships, and trusts held for more than one year recognize collectibles gain if the entity owns such appreciated assets at the time of sale. (Code Sec. 1(h)(5)(B)) Regs explain how to figure the seller's deemed collectibles gain and his residual long-term gain or loss and use the same approach for sales of interests in various entities. (Reg § 1.1(h)-1) See ¶3765 for the regs' approach in the context of sales of partnership interests, which also may cause a partner to recognize unrecaptured section 1250 gain. However, sales of interests in S corporations and trusts don't trigger unrecaptured section 1250 gain—only collectibles gain and residual long-term capital gain or loss.[7]

For netting rules where the noncorporate taxpayer has capital losses, see ¶2609.

---

2. ¶s I-5103, I-5102; ¶s 12,224.01, 12,224.02; TD ¶223,501
3. ¶s I-5111, I-5116; ¶12,224.01; TD ¶223,326
4. ¶I-5111; ¶12,224.03; TD ¶223,306

5. ¶I-5110; ¶14.08; TD ¶223,309
6. ¶I-5110.14; ¶14.08; TD ¶223,324
7. ¶I-5110.14; ¶14.08; TD ¶223,324

For tax years beginning after 2010, a "sunset" provision provides that amendments made by Sec. 301 of the Jobs and Growth Tax Relief Reconciliation Act of 2003 (PL 108-27, 5/28/2003) won't apply(see ¶1114). Instead, the rules in effect for capital gains taken into account before May 6, 2003 will apply. Under those rules, after 2010, long-term capital gains of noncorporate taxpayers now taxed at a rate of 0% will be taxed at a rate of 10% (8% for assets held over five years), and long-term capital gains now taxed at a rate of 15% will be taxed at a rate of 20% (18% for assets held over five years).[8]

caution: Check http://ria.thomsonreuters.com/federaltaxhandbook for new law updates that could affect the rate at which long-term capital gains are taxed in 2011 and later years.

¶ 2604   Adjusted net capital gain defined.

Adjusted net capital gain is net capital gain (¶2601) determined without taking qualified dividend income (see ¶1290) into account less the amount that the taxpayer takes into account as investment income under Code Sec. 163(d)(4)(B)(iii) (see ¶1729), reduced (but not below zero) by the sum of:

... unrecaptured section 1250 gain (¶2605), and

... 28% rate gain (as defined at ¶2606), and increased by

the amount of qualified dividend income. (Code Sec. 1(h)(3))[9]

observation: Effectively, adjusted net capital gain is the sum of that part of a taxpayer's net capital gain that is eligible to be taxed at a maximum rate below 25% (see ¶2603), plus the amount of qualified dividend income.

¶ 2605   Noncorporate taxpayer's unrecaptured section 1250 gain taxed at a maximum rate of 25%.

Unrecaptured section 1250 gain, taxed at a maximum rate of 25%, is the excess (if any) of:

(1) the amount of long-term capital gain (¶2601) which is not otherwise treated as ordinary income, and which would be treated as ordinary income if Code Sec. 1250(b)(1) recapture applied to all depreciation (rather than only to depreciation in excess of straight line), and the applicable percentage under Code Sec. 1250(a) (¶2696) were 100%, over

(2) the excess (if any) of the amount of losses taken into account in computing 28% rate gain (¶2606) over the amount of gains taken into account in computing 28% rate gain. (Code Sec. 1(h)(6))[10]

The amount in (1), above, from sales exchanges and conversions described in Code Sec. 1231(a)(3)(A) (i.e., section 1231 gain, see ¶2684) for any tax year can't exceed the net section 1231 gain (see ¶2685) for that tax year. (Code Sec. 1(h)(6)(B))

observation: Under MACRS, real property must be depreciated using the straight-line method (¶1925). Thus, any gain on the sale or exchange of such property that's attributable to depreciation will be unrecaptured section 1250 gain if held for more than one year.

illustration: Y, an individual, sells nonresidential real property on Aug. 15 for $200,000, realizing a gain of $50,000. This is Y's only transaction involving a capital asset for the year. Y has held the property for more than one year. He depreciated the property using MACRS, and claimed $25,000 of depreciation during his ownership. There is no depreciation recapture under Code Sec. 1250(b)(1) because Y didn't claim accelerated depreciation.

---

8. ¶T-11062; ¶79,006.87; TD ¶880,014   10. ¶I-5110.8; ¶14.08; TD ¶223,317
9. ¶I-5110.10; ¶14.08; TD ¶223,320

However, $25,000 of Y's gain, representing depreciation deductions claimed by Y, is unrecaptured section 1250 gain.

For how to handle unrecaptured section 1250 gain where a sale of real property is reported on the installment method, see ¶2457.

For how unrecaptured section 1250 gain can arise on sale of a partnership interest, see ¶3765.

¶ 2606   Noncorporate taxpayer's 28% rate gain.

The term 28% rate gain means the sum of collectibles (¶2607) gain and losses and section 1202 gain (¶2608), less the sum of collectibles loss, the net short-term capital loss for the tax year, and the long-term capital loss carryover to the tax year. (Code Sec. 1(h)(4))[11]

observation: As a result of the way 28% rate gain is defined, a long-term capital loss carryover from an earlier tax year will always be used first to offset 28% rate gain, see ¶2609.

¶ 2607   Noncorporate taxpayer's collectibles gain or loss.

Collectibles gain or loss is gain or loss from the sale or exchange of a collectible which is a capital asset held for more than one year, but only to the extent such gain or loss is taken into account in computing gross income. (Code Sec. 1(h)(5)) Any work of art, rug or antique, metal or gem, stamp or coin, alcoholic beverage, or any other tangible personal property specified by IRS for this purpose is a collectible.[12]

For how collectibles gain can arise on the sale of interests in a partnership, S corporation, or trust, see ¶2603.

¶ 2608   Noncorporate taxpayers' section 1202 gain.

Section 1202 gain is the excess of (1) the gain that would be excluded from gross income on the sale of certain qualified small business stock under Code Sec. 1202, if the percentage limitations of Code Sec. 1202(a) (see ¶2648) didn't apply, less (2) the gain actually excluded under Code Sec. 1202. (Code Sec. 1(h)(7))[13]

observation: If 50% of the gain on the disposition of qualifying small business stock is excluded from gross income, the 50% includible in gross income is taxed at a maximum rate of 28% (since it's excluded from adjusted net capital gain). This makes the maximum effective rate on the gain from the sale of qualified small business stock 14%.

See ¶3209 for AMT treatment of section 1202 gain.

¶ 2609   Netting rules where taxpayer has capital losses.

The following netting and ordering rules apply where the taxpayer has capital losses:

(1) Short-term capital losses are applied first to reduce short-term capital gains, if any, otherwise taxable at ordinary income rates. If there's a net short-term capital loss, it reduces any net long-term gain from the 28% group, then gain from the 25% group, and finally reduces adjusted net capital gain (15% or lower group).

(2) Long-term capital losses are handled as follows:

. . . A net loss from the 28% group (including long-term capital loss carryovers from prior years) is used first to reduce gain from the 25% group, then to reduce adjusted net capital

---

11. ¶I-5110.11; ¶14.08; TD ¶223,321
12. ¶I-5110.12; ¶14.08; TD ¶223,322

13. ¶I-5110.13; ¶14.08; TD ¶223,323

gain (15% or lower group).

... A net loss from the 15% or lower group is used first to reduce net gain from the 28% group, then to reduce gain from the 25% group.[14]

illustration: T, in the 33% bracket, has a 28%-group loss of $40,000 from the sale of collectibles. T has unrecaptured section 1250 gain of $25,000, and adjusted net capital gain of $25,000. T's net capital gain is $10,000 (total gain of $50,000 less $40,000 loss). T's 28% group loss completely offsets the unrecaptured section 1250 gain of $25,000, and $15,000 of adjusted net capital gain, leaving him with adjusted net capital gain of $10,000.

¶ 2610 Noncorporate taxpayer's nonrecaptured net section 1231 losses.

For 2010, if any Section 1231 gain is treated as ordinary income under Code Sec. 1231(c) (relating to Section 1231 gain being treated as ordinary income to the extent of nonrecaptured Section 1231 losses, see ¶2685), the amount to be treated as ordinary income is allocated first to any net section 1231 gain in the 28% group, then to any section 1231 gain in the 25% group, and then to any net section 1231 gain in the 0%/15% group.[15]

¶ 2611 Capital losses of noncorporate taxpayers.

A noncorporate taxpayer may deduct capital losses only to the extent of capital gains plus (if the losses exceed the gains) the lower of:

(1) $3,000 ($1,500 for married individuals filing separate returns), or

(2) the excess of the losses over the gains. (Code Sec. 1211(b))[16]

illustration: B has a short-term capital loss of $100 and a long-term capital loss of $3,600 for his tax year. His total capital loss for the tax year is $3,700. This capital loss is deductible from ordinary income up to a maximum of $3,000. See ¶2612 for carrying over the excess capital loss.

A noncorporate taxpayer's capital losses for a tax year consist of the capital losses sustained during the year plus the total of all capital losses sustained in other years that are carried to that tax year (¶2612). (Code Sec. 1212(b); Reg § 1.1211-1(b)(1))[17]

¶ 2612 Noncorporate capital loss carryovers.

If an individual, trust or estate sustains a net capital loss that exceeds the maximum deductible in the current year (¶2611), the excess is carried forward to later years indefinitely until it's absorbed. (Code Sec. 1212(b)) Carry*backs* aren't allowed.[18] A decedent's unused capital loss is lost; it can't be carried over.[19] For the use in tax years beginning in 2010 of a decedent's unused capital losses to increase his estate's basis in his capital assets, see ¶2523.

The capital loss keeps its original character as long- or short-term when carried over. (Code Sec. 1212(b)(1))[20]

For purposes of determining the amount of excess long-term or short-term capital loss that is carried over, that excess is reduced by assuming the existence of a short-term capital gain equal in amount to the lesser of: (1) $3,000 ($1,500 for marrieds filing separately), (2) the excess of allowed losses over gains (¶2611), or (3) "adjusted taxable income." Adjusted taxable income is taxable income increased by (a) the lesser of the amounts computed in (1) and (2), above (which is the amount described in ¶2611), and (b) the personal exemption. For this

14. ¶I-5107; ¶14.08; TD ¶223,307
15. ¶I-9003.1
16. ¶I-5112; ¶12,114; TD ¶223,327
17. ¶I-5113; ¶12,124 *et seq.*; TD ¶223,337

18. ¶I-5122; ¶12,124.01; TD ¶223,336
19. ¶I-5133; TD ¶223,344
20. ¶I-5123; ¶12,124.01; TD ¶223,337

purpose, any excess of deductions allowed over gross income is taken into account as negative taxable income. (Code Sec. 1212(b)(2))[21]

✔️*observation:* This means that short-term capital loss is used to offset ordinary income before long-term capital loss is used,

¶ 2613 Capital gains of corporate taxpayers.

Corporate taxpayers must include capital gains in full in gross income but only to the extent that they exceed capital losses.[22]

¶ 2614 Corporation's alternative tax on capital gains.

A corporation with an excess of net long-term capital gain over net short-term capital loss ("net capital gain") (Code Sec. 1222(11)) pays an alternative tax instead of the regular corporate tax if the alternative tax is smaller. The alternative tax applies a tax rate of 35% to the corporation's net capital gain, but only if the top regular corporate tax rate for the year (see ¶1112) is higher than 35% (determined without regard to the additional tax on (1) the corporation's taxable income over $100,000, and (2) the corporation's taxable income over $15,000,000). (Code Sec. 1201(a))[23]

✔️*observation:* Thus, the above alternative tax doesn't apply for 2010, since the top corporate rate is 35%.

¶ 2615 Corporation's capital losses.

Corporations may deduct capital losses only to the extent of their capital gains. Excess capital losses can't be deducted from a corporation's ordinary income. (Code Sec. 1211(a))[24]

A corporation's capital losses in excess of its capital gains for the current year are carried back three years, but only to the extent the loss isn't attributable to a foreign expropriation capital loss and to the extent that the carryback doesn't increase or produce a net operating loss for the tax year to which it's carried back. (Code Sec. 1212(a)(1)(A)) A net capital loss can't be carried back to a tax year in which the corporation is either a regulated investment company or a real estate investment trust. (Code Sec. 1212(a)(3))

The carryforward period is five years (eight years for regulated investment companies; ten years for foreign expropriation capital losses). (Code Sec. 1212(a)(1)(B), Code Sec. 1212(a)(1)(C))[25]

A capital loss carryback or carryover is treated as a short-term capital loss whether or not it was short-term when sustained. (Code Sec. 1212(a)(1)) A carryover from one year can't be included in computing a new net capital loss for another year. (Code Sec. 1222(10))[26]

¶ 2616 Assets to Which Capital Gain and Loss Rules Apply. ▬▬▬▬▬▬

The capital gain or loss rules apply to assets that are capital in nature. An asset's character depends upon what it is and what use it has in taxpayer's hands.

¶ 2617 Capital assets defined.

Capital assets include all assets held by the taxpayer except:

(1) Stock in trade of the taxpayer or other property of a kind that would properly be included in the inventory of the taxpayer if on hand at the close of the tax year.

21. ¶I-5123; ¶12,124.01; TD ¶223,337
22. ¶I-5116; ¶12,114; TD ¶223,331
23. ¶I-5117; ¶12,014; TD ¶223,332

24. ¶I-5121; ¶12,114; TD ¶223,335
25. ¶I-5125 *et seq.*; ¶12,124.04; TD ¶223,339
26. ¶I-5125; ¶12,124.04; TD ¶223,341

(2) Property held by the taxpayer primarily for sale to customers in the ordinary course of his trade or business.

(3) Accounts or notes receivable acquired in the ordinary course of a trade or business for services rendered or from the sale of any properties described in (1) or (2), above.

(4) Depreciable property, amortizable Code Sec. 197 intangibles, and real property used in the taxpayer's trade or business.

(5) Certain copyrights, literary, artistic, or musical works (unless, for musical works or copyrights in them, the election discussed at ¶2622 is made), and certain letters, memoranda, or similar property, see ¶2622.

(6) U.S. government publications (e.g., Congressional Record) received from the government without charge or below the price sold to the public, in the hands of the recipient and carryover-basis transferees.

(7) Commodities derivative financial instruments held by a commodities derivatives dealer (except for certain instruments not connected to the dealing activity).

(8) Any hedging transaction (e.g., to manage risk of price changes or currency fluctuations) clearly identified as such before the close of the day on which it was acquired, originated, or entered.

(9) Supplies of a type regularly used or consumed by the taxpayer in the ordinary course of the taxpayer's trade or business. (Code Sec. 1221(a))[27]

Property held for personal use is a capital asset, as is property used for the production of income (even if depreciable). (Reg § 1.1221-1(b)) Examples of capital assets include stock and securities held for investment,[28] including tax-exempt bonds[29] (discussed at ¶2636). The right to receive future lottery payments is not a capital asset (a payment received in exchange for that right is ordinary income, not capital gain).[30]

¶ 2618   Hedging transactions.

The term capital asset doesn't include property that's part of a hedging transaction. (Reg § 1.1221-2(a)) A hedging transaction is a transaction that a taxpayer enters into in the normal course of the taxpayer's trade or business, primarily to reduce the risk of price changes or currency fluctuations with respect to ordinary property, or to reduce the risk of interest rate or price changes or currency fluctuations with respect to borrowings or ordinary obligations. (Reg § 1.1221-2(b)(1)) Property is ordinary property if its sale or exchange by the taxpayer couldn't produce capital gain or loss regardless of the holding period. An obligation is an ordinary obligation if performance or termination of the obligation by the taxpayer could not produce capital gain or loss. (Reg § 1.1221-2(c)(2))[31] Thus, hedging in corn futures (to stabilize the cost of corn inventory) as an integral part of a taxpayer's inventory-purchase system produces ordinary income and loss.[32]

A taxpayer must identify a transaction (including recycling an existing hedge) as a hedging transaction before the close of the day he enters it. (Reg § 1.1221-2(f)(1))[33]

The accounting method used for a hedging transaction must clearly reflect income and reasonably match the timing of the transaction with the timing of the item(s) being hedged. Special rules detail the accounting methods for various transactions. (Reg § 1.446-4)[34]

---

27. ¶I-6001; ¶12,214; TD ¶249,001
28. ¶I-6201; ¶12,214.21; TD ¶250,001
29. ¶I-7801
30. ¶I-6824.1; TD ¶223,014

31. ¶I-6231 *et seq.*; ¶12,214.80; TD ¶250,006
32. ¶I-6268; TD ¶250,009
33. ¶I-6250; ¶12,214.80; TD ¶250,007
34. ¶G-2519 *et seq.*; ¶4464.01; TD ¶447,501 *et seq.*

¶ 2619 Options to buy or sell.

Gain or loss from the sale or exchange of a noncompensatory option to buy or sell property is considered a gain or loss from the sale or exchange of a capital asset if the optioned property is (or would be if acquired) a capital asset in the taxpayer's hands. (Code Sec. 1234(a)(1); Reg § 1.1234-1(a))[35] If the holder of an option incurs a loss because he fails to exercise the option, the option is considered to have been sold or exchanged on the date it expires. (Code Sec. 1234(a)(2); Reg § 1.1234-1(b))[36]

A dealer in options is considered a dealer in the property subject to the option, and any gain or loss received from sale or exchange of the option is ordinary. (Reg § 1.1234-1(d))[37]

¶ 2620 "Put" and "call" options; straddles.

There are no tax consequences to the buyer or writer of an option until the option is exercised, otherwise closed out or lapses. The holder treats the premium paid as a nondeductible capital expenditure at the time of payment. The premium isn't included in income of the writer at the time of receipt.[38] The premium received by the writer for granting a "put" or "call" option that's not exercised ("lapses"), so that the writer simply keeps the money, is generally treated as ordinary income, and gain or loss to the writer on repurchase of an option ("closing transaction") is also generally ordinary. (Reg § 1.1234-1(b)) However, gain or loss to a nondealer from a lapse or closing transaction involving options in stocks, securities, commodities or commodity futures is treated as short-term capital gain or loss. (Code Sec. 1234(b); Reg § 1.1234-3)[39]

Where a put is exercised, the premium received by the writer for granting the option is deducted from the option price for the property in determining the net basis to the writer of the property purchased. The holder deducts the premium from the amount received from the writer, in computing the gain or loss realized on the sale. Where a call is exercised, the premium received by the writer (i.e., seller) for granting the option is added to the sale proceeds received. This is included in the holder's (buyer's) basis for the property.[40]

illustration: A bought a 180-day put from B for $5,000 that gave A the right to sell 1,000 shares of stock to B for $50,000. The stock originally cost A $25,000. The put was timely exercised. A has a gain of $20,000 on the sale ($50,000, less $30,000 ($5,000 paid for put and $25,000 original cost of stock). B's basis in the stock is $45,000 ($50,000 paid to A on the exercise of the put, less $5,000 received by B from A for the put).

When the put or call is bought from the original holder (or his assignee), the buyer is treated as a holder, and the amount paid by him to the original holder is likewise treated as a premium. However, the original holder is not treated as a writer, and must include that premium in his amount realized upon disposition of the option, see ¶2619.[41]

observation: Thus, if a holder (other than a dealer) of a put or call option on publicly traded stock closes out a position by selling the option on an exchange, the gain or loss is a capital gain or loss.

A "straddle" option combines a put and a call. (Reg § 1.1234-3(b)(4))[42] The allocation of a premium received for a straddle or multiple option between or among the component options is made on the basis of the relative market value of the component options at the time of their issuance or on any other reasonable and consistently applied basis which is acceptable to IRS.

35. ¶I-6504; ¶12,344; TD ¶252,002
36. ¶I-6510; ¶12,344; TD ¶252,003
37. ¶I-6509; ¶12,344.03
38. ¶s I-6521, I-6522; ¶12,344 *et seq.* TD ¶252,001, 252,005
39. ¶I-6515; ¶12,344 *et seq.*; TD ¶252,006
40. ¶s I-6530, I-6531; ¶s 12,344.03, 12,344.04; TD ¶252,008, 252,009
41. ¶I-6523; ¶s 12,344.03, 12,344.04; TD ¶252,002
42. ¶I-6528; ¶12,344.06

(Reg § 1.1234-3(e))[43]

¶ 2621 Patents.

If an individual inventor or his financial backer transfers (other than by gift, inheritance or devise) all substantial rights to a patent, or an undivided interest (e.g., a half, a third) in those rights, the transfer is considered a sale or exchange of a long-term capital asset even though the transferor hasn't held the patent property for the period required for long-term treatment (see ¶2667), and even though the payments to the seller are: (1) made periodically during the buyer's use of the property, or (2) contingent on the productivity, use or disposition of the buyer's rights in the property (i.e., are like royalties). (Code Sec. 1235(a))[44]

It's not necessary that the patent or patent application be in existence at the time of that transfer for long-term capital gain treatment to apply. (Reg § 1.1235-2(a))[45]

This treatment doesn't apply to a transfer by the inventor's employer. (Code Sec. 1235(b)(2)(A))[46] Nor does it apply to transfers made (directly or indirectly) to or by certain persons related to the inventor. (Code Sec. 1235(b)(2)(B); Reg § 1.1235-2(f))[47]

Transferors that don't qualify for this special long-term capital gain treatment nevertheless qualify for capital gain or loss treatment if they can establish that the patent is a capital asset or a Section 1231 asset. (Reg § 1.1235-1(b))[48]

The long-term capital gain rule doesn't apply unless all substantial rights (or an undivided interest in those rights) are transferred. (Reg § 1.1235-2(b))[49]

¶ 2622 Copyrights, literary, musical, artistic composition, etc.

Copyrights, literary, artistic, and (except as noted below) musical compositions, etc., aren't capital assets or Section 1231 assets if the taxpayer is either (1) the author or creator of property through his own personal efforts, or (2) the donee of the author or creator, or one who otherwise has a basis for the property determined in whole or in part by reference to the basis in the hands of that donor.

A letter, memorandum or similar property prepared or produced for a taxpayer isn't a capital asset to him (or his donee or other carryover-basis transferee). (Code Sec. 1221(a)(3))[50]

A taxpayer may elect to treat a sale or exchange of musical compositions or copyrights in musical works created by the taxpayer's personal efforts (or having a basis determined by reference to the basis in the hands of a taxpayer whose personal efforts created them) as the sale or exchange of a capital asset. (Code Sec. 1221(b)(3)) A taxpayer must make the election on Schedule D, Capital Gains and Losses, of the appropriate tax return on or before the due date (including extensions) of his return for the tax year of the sale or exchange. (Reg § 1.1221-3T(b)) The election is revocable with IRS consent. IRS automatically grants taxpayers a six-month extension from the due date of the taxpayer's income tax return (excluding extensions) to revoke an election, if the taxpayer timely filed his income tax return and, within the 6-month extension period, files an amended return that treats the sale or exchange as the sale or exchange of property that is not a capital asset. (Reg § 1.1221-3T(c))[1]

Where a taxpayer inherits creative property (such as a copyright, composition or similar property) from a decedent dying in 2010, and the taxpayer's basis for figuring gain from a sale or exchange is determined in whole or in part by reference to the basis of certain earlier holders of the property under the modified-carryover-basis-at-death rules of Code Sec. 1022

43. ¶I-6528
44. ¶I-8301; ¶12,354; TD ¶229,101
45. ¶I-8307
46. ¶I-8322; ¶12,354.04; TD ¶229,102
47. ¶s I-8301, I-8325; ¶12,354.06; TD ¶229,112
48. ¶I-6700; ¶12,354.01; TD ¶229,101
49. ¶I-8301; ¶12,354.09; TD ¶229,106
50. ¶I-6601 *et seq.*; ¶12,214; TD ¶252,501
1. ¶I-6601; ¶12,214.45; TD ¶252,501

(¶2523), the property is a capital asset. (Code Sec. 1221(a)(3)(C))[2]

¶ 2623   Real property.

Real property held primarily for sale in the ordinary course of the taxpayer's trade or business doesn't qualify as a capital asset. Whether particular real estate sold is a capital asset is decided on a case by case basis taking into consideration many factors including number and taxpayer's frequency of sales, subdividing and promotional activities. For example, where a husband and wife purchased a parcel of property containing a number of lots to build a home and then sold the property they didn't need, those excess lots were held for investment purposes and the proceeds of their sale resulted in capital gains and losses.[3]

¶ 2624   Five-year land subdivision rule for noncorporate taxpayers.

A taxpayer other than a C corporation (e.g., an individual, trust, estate or S corporation) won't be treated as holding land primarily for sale to customers merely because the taxpayer subdivided a tract of land into lots or parcels and engaged in advertising, promotion, selling activities or the use of sales agents in selling lots in the subdivision, if the taxpayer:

... hasn't previously held any part of the same land primarily for sale to customers in the ordinary course of business, and, in the year of sale doesn't hold any other real estate for sale to customers;

... doesn't (while he holds the land or as part of a contract of sale with the buyer) make "substantial improvements" on the land that substantially increase the value of the lot sold (except, if elected, improvements needed to make marketable land that has been held for ten years or more); and

... either has owned the land for five years or more, or acquired it by inheritance or devise. (Code Sec. 1237(a); Reg § 1.1237-1(a)(2), Reg § 1.1237-1(a)(5), Reg § 1.1237-1(b)(1))[4]

However, if more than five lots or parcels in the same tract are sold or exchanged, gain from any sale or exchange (which occurs in or after the tax year in which the sixth lot or parcel is sold or exchanged) of any lot or parcel covered by the above 5-year rule will be treated as ordinary income to the extent of 5% of the selling price. (Code Sec. 1237(b)(1); Reg § 1.1237-1(e)(2))[5]

The sale or exchange of qualifying subdivided land that's business property can result in an ordinary loss, see ¶2684. (Reg § 1.1237-1(f))[6]

¶ 2625   Sale of a sole proprietorship.

When a sole proprietorship is sold, there isn't a sale of just one asset (the business). Rather, there's a sale of the individual assets that comprise the business. Thus, gain or loss on some assets will be ordinary while on others it will be capital.[7]

¶ 2626   Allocation of selling price on sale of business.

If assets of a going business are sold, the selling price must be allocated among the assets (including goodwill) for purposes of determining gain or loss (and the type of gain or loss, e.g., capital gain or ordinary income) separately for each. Allocation is made under the rules for determining the buyer's basis in each of them, see ¶2472.[8]

---

2. ¶I-6601.2; ¶12,214.45
3. ¶I-6300 *et seq.*; ¶12,214; TD ¶250,502
4. ¶I-6400 *et seq.*; ¶12,374.01; TD ¶251,501
5. ¶I-6420; ¶12,374.05; TD ¶251,502

6. ¶I-6424; ¶12,374.01; TD ¶251,512
7. ¶I-8501; ¶12,214.53; TD ¶229,401
8. ¶I-8506 *et seq.*; ¶12,214.51; TD ¶212,000

¶ 2627 Goodwill and covenants not to compete.

Goodwill is a capital asset, unless it is treated as an amortizable section 197 intangible under the rules explained at ¶1975 *et seq.* To the extent that the Code Sec. 197 rules don't apply, proceeds from the sale of a business that are allocable (¶2626) to goodwill are taxed under the capital gain and loss rules,[9] and payments for a covenant not to compete that is severable from the sale of goodwill results in ordinary income.[10]

¶ 2628 Investments by dealer in securities.

A securities dealer who buys securities for resale to customers may also hold securities purchased as investments for the dealer's own account. But gain from the sale or exchange of those securities won't be capital gain unless (1) the security is clearly identified in the dealer's records as a security held for investment on the day it is acquired, and (2) the security is not held by the dealer primarily for sale to customers in the ordinary course of a trade or business at any time after the acquisition date. (Code Sec. 1236(a))[11]

A loss is a capital loss if the security has ever been clearly identified in the dealer's records as held for investment, even though held primarily for sale at the time of its disposition. (Code Sec. 1236(b); Reg § 1.1236-1(b))[12]

¶ 2629 Franchise, trademark or trade name transfers.

The transfer of a franchise, trademark or trade name isn't a sale or exchange of a capital asset if the transferor retains any significant power, right or continuing interest (such as the right to terminate at will, prescribe standards of quality or require the transferee to sell only the transferor's products). (Code Sec. 1253(a), Code Sec. 1253(b)(2))[13] In any case, ordinary income treatment applies to payments received by a transferor that are contingent on production, use, or disposition of a franchise, trademark or trade name. (Code Sec. 1253(c))[14]

For deduction of these payments, see ¶1620; for amortization of payments made for the transfer of a franchise, trademark, or trade name, see ¶1977.

¶ 2630 Life estates, term of years, etc.

A life tenant, a tenant for a term of years, or an income beneficiary of a trust is generally entitled to capital gain on the sale of that interest.[15] However, where the interest was acquired by gift, from a decedent, by a transfer in trust or by a transfer from a spouse (or a former spouse incident to divorce), that part of the basis that's determined under the Code rules for those types of acquisitions (e.g., fair market value basis where acquired from a decedent dying before 2010, see ¶2516) isn't taken into account in computing gain or loss on the sale or exchange of the interest, unless the entire interest in the underlying property is transferred in the same transaction. (Code Sec. 1001(e); Reg § 1.1001-1(f))[16]

¶ 2631 Small business investment company (SBIC) stock.

Losses from the sale, exchange or worthlessness of SBIC stock are deductible by a shareholder as an ordinary loss attributable to the shareholder's business. (Code Sec. 1242; Reg § 1.1242-1) Gains on the sale or exchange of SBIC stock are capital gains.[17]

9. ¶I-8601; ¶12,214.55; TD ¶229,501
10. ¶I-8603; ¶12,214.56; TD ¶229,502
11. ¶I-6209; ¶12,364.01; TD ¶250,004
12. ¶I-6215; ¶12,364.01
13. ¶s I-8401; ¶12,534 *et seq.*; TD ¶229,301

14. ¶I-8412; ¶12,534.01; TD ¶229,306
15. ¶I-7014; ¶12,214.66
16. ¶P-3129; ¶10,144.07; TD ¶215,015
17. ¶I-9543; ¶12,424 *et seq.*; TD ¶355,011, TD ¶372,006

¶ 2632   Regulated investment company stock.

A loss realized on the sale or exchange of stock in a regulated investment company is a long-term capital loss to the extent of any long-term capital gain realized via a distribution made with respect to the stock, if the taxpayer held the stock for six months or less. Similarly, the loss of a shareholder who receives an exempt-interest dividend on stock which is held for six months or less is disallowed to the extent of the exempt interest dividend received by the shareholder. Rules for periodic liquidations differ. (Code Sec. 852(b)(4))[18]

¶ 2633   Sale or exchange of debt instruments issued with original issue discount.

If a debt instrument is issued with original issue discount (OID) as defined at ¶1316, and if at the time of original issue there was an intention to call the debt instrument before maturity, any gain realized on the sale or exchange of the instrument is treated as ordinary income to the extent the gain doesn't exceed the OID reduced by the part of the OID previously included in the income of any holder. For purposes of this rule, any part of the OID that would have been included in the income of the holder had there been no acquisition premium is treated as if it had been included. (Code Sec. 1271(a)(2)(A))

The above rule doesn't apply to tax-exempt obligations or to the sale or exchange by a holder who purchased the debt instrument at a premium. (Code Sec. 1271(a)(2)(B))[19]

¶ 2634   Sale or exchange of short-term government obligations.

On the sale or exchange of any short-term government obligation, any gain realized that doesn't exceed an amount equal to the ratable share of the acquisition discount is treated as ordinary income (Code Sec. 1271(a)(3)(A)) unless the seller was required to include the acquisition discount in gross income currently under the rules at ¶1330. (Code Sec. 1283(d)(3))[20]

¶ 2635   Sale or exchange of short-term nongovernment obligations.

On the sale or exchange of any short-term nongovernment obligation, any gain realized that doesn't exceed an amount equal to the ratable share of OID is treated as ordinary income (Code Sec. 1271(a)(4)(A)) unless the seller was required to include the acquisition discount in gross income currently under the rules at ¶1330. (Code Sec. 1283(d)(3))[21]

¶ 2636   Sale or exchange of tax-free bonds.

The sale or exchange of tax-exempt obligations is a taxable event even if the interest on the bonds is exempt. The seller has gain to the extent that the amount realized exceeds his adjusted basis (see ¶2474) in the bonds. The seller's basis for this purpose means the price he paid, whether or not he bought the bonds at a discount. However, the holder of a tax-exempt bond issued with original issue discount (OID) can increase his adjusted basis of the bond by the amount of OID accrued during the period the bond is held.[22]

¶ 2637   Constructive Sales of Appreciated Financial Positions. ▮▮▮▮▮▮

The constructive sale rules restrict a taxpayer's ability to defer recognition of gain on appreciated property he owns even though he locks in his gain and limits risk of loss through the use of short-sales-against-the-box and similar transactions. In general, the taxpayer is treated as constructively selling property he owns if he borrows and

---

18. ¶E-6162; ¶8524.02
19. ¶I-8001; ¶12,714; TD ¶227,601
20. ¶I-8004; ¶12,714.05; TD ¶227,602
21. ¶I-8005; ¶12,714.05; ¶12,814; TD ¶227,603
22. ¶I-4001 *et seq.*; TD ¶227,401 *et seq.*

sells the same or substantially identical property.

A taxpayer must recognize gain upon entering into a constructive sale of any appreciated financial position in stock, a partnership interest, or certain debt instruments. (Code Sec. 1259) In general, an appreciated financial position is any position with respect to any stock, debt instrument, or partnership interest if there would be gain if the position were sold, assigned, or otherwise terminated at its fair market value. (Code Sec. 1259(b)(1)) Except as provided at ¶2638, a constructive sale of an appreciated position occurs when the taxpayer (or a related person):

(1)   enters into a short sale of the same or substantially identical property,

(2)   enters into an offsetting notional principal contract with respect to the same or substantially identical property,

(3)   enters into a futures or forward contract to deliver the same or substantially identical property,

(4)   in the case of an appreciated financial position that's a short sale or a contract described in (2) or (3) above with respect to any property, the taxpayer acquires the same or substantially identical property, or

(5)   to the extent prescribed in regs, enters into one or more other transactions (or acquires one or more positions) that have substantially the same effect as a transaction described in (1), (2), (3), or (4) above. (Code Sec. 1259(c)(1))[23]

Persons are "related" with respect to a transaction if their relationship is described in Code Sec. 267(b) (¶2448) or Code Sec. 707(b) (¶3731), and the transaction is entered into with a view toward avoiding the purposes of the constructive sale rules. (Code Sec. 1259(c)(4))[24]

The constructive sale rules don't apply to a short sale of stock that the seller borrows if he doesn't hold substantially identical property at the time of the sale. However, if he acquires the same stock that he borrowed and sold, and has a gain, the constructive sale rules apply on the acquisition date even if the acquired stock isn't delivered to the lender.[25]

As a result of a constructive sale,

. . . the taxpayer recognizes gain as if the position were sold, assigned, or otherwise terminated at its FMV value on the constructive sale date (Code Sec. 1259(a)(1)), and

. . . for purposes of applying the Code for periods after the constructive sale, (1) an appropriate adjustment is made in the amount of gain or loss later realized on the position for the gain taken into account because of the constructive sale rule, and (2) a new holding period for the position begins as if the taxpayer had acquired the position on the date of the constructive sale. (Code Sec. 1259(a)(2))[26]

illustration: On May 1, 2010, S bought 100 shares of ABC stock for $10,000. On Sept. 3, 2010, S sold short 100 shares of ABC stock for $16,000. He made no other transactions involving ABC stock for the rest of 2010 and the first 30 days of 2011. S's short sale is treated as a constructive sale of an appreciated financial position because a sale of the ABC stock on the date of the short sale would have resulted in a gain. S recognizes a $6,000 short-term capital gain from the constructive sale and he has a new holding period in his ABC stock that begins on Sept. 3, 2010.

The term "appreciated financial position" does *not* include (1) certain positions with respect to nonconvertible debt if certain specified conditions with respect to principal and interest are met (Code Sec. 1259(b)(2)(A)); (2) any hedge with respect to a position described in (1), above (Code Sec. 1259(b)(2)(B)); and (3) any position which is marked to market under

---

23. ¶I-7732; ¶12,594; TD ¶228,602
24. ¶I-7733; ¶12,594; TD ¶228,603

25. ¶I-7732; ¶12,594; TD ¶228,602
26. ¶I-7731; ¶12,594; TD ¶228,601

any Code section or the regs under those Code sections. (Code Sec. 1259(b)(2)(C))[27]

¶ 2638 Exceptions to constructive sale rules.

A taxpayer is not treated as having made a constructive sale solely because the taxpayer enters a contract for the sale of any stock, debt instrument, or partnership interest which isn't a marketable security if the contract settles within one year after the date the contract is entered. (Code Sec. 1259(c)(2))[28] In addition, any transaction which would otherwise cause a constructive sale during the tax year is disregarded if:

(1) it's closed on or before the 30th day after the close of the tax year it was entered,

(2) the taxpayer holds the appreciated financial position to which the transaction relates (e.g., the stock where the transaction is a short sale) throughout the 60-day period beginning on the date the transaction is closed, and

(3) at no time during that 60-day period is the taxpayer's risk of loss reduced with respect to the position (applying the principles of Code Sec. 246(c)(4), relating to suspension of the holding period where the risk of loss is diminished for purposes of the dividends received deduction, see ¶3312). (Code Sec. 1259(c)(3)(A))[29]

observation: If a taxpayer meets the above requirements, a "short sale against the box" is not a constructive sale as long as he remains at risk with respect to the appreciated financial position for sixty days after the closing.

If a transaction which would otherwise cause a constructive sale of an appreciated financial position, is closed during the tax year or during the 30 days after the close of the tax year, the third requirement above isn't violated if the taxpayer enters another transaction during that 60-day period if that transaction:

. . . also would otherwise be treated as a constructive sale of that appreciated financial position,

. . . is closed on or before the 30th day after the close of the tax year in which the transaction (described in (1) above) occurs,

. . . the appreciated financial position is held throughout the 60-day period beginning on the date the transaction is closed, and

. . . at no time during that 60-day period is the taxpayer's risk of loss with respect to the position reduced by reason of a circumstance which would be described in Code Sec. 246(c)(4). (Code Sec. 1259(c)(3)(B))[30]

¶ 2639 Short Sales.

In a short sale, an investor sells a security for delivery in the future. The short seller may meet his obligation to deliver by buying the security on the delivery ("closing") date. If the security has declined in value by the time he closes or covers the sale, he has a gain equal to the price at which he sold minus his cost; if the value has increased, his purchase price is higher than the sale price, and the short seller has a loss. The nature of the gain or loss on a short sale depends upon the nature of the property used to close the short transaction.

If the property used to close the short sale is a capital asset in the hands of the short seller, the gain or loss on the transaction is capital gain or loss. (Code Sec. 1233(a); Reg § 1.1233-1(a)(2))[31] Where the property used to close the short sale is a capital asset, the period the taxpayer held the property determines whether the gain or loss is long or short term, unless

---

27. ¶I-7739 *et seq.*; ¶12,594; TD ¶228,609 *et seq.*
28. ¶I-7736; ¶12,594; TD ¶228,606
29. ¶I-7737; ¶12,594; TD ¶228,607

30. ¶I-7738; ¶12,594; TD ¶228,608
31. ¶I-7704; ¶12,334.01; TD ¶228,901

the limits at ¶2640 *et seq.* apply. (Reg § 1.1233-1(a)(3))[32]

⚡caution: Entering into certain short sales may result in a taxpayer recognizing gain under the constructive sale rules (¶2637 *et seq.*).

Entering into a securities futures contract (¶2661) to sell is treated as a short sale and the settlement of the contract is treated as the closing of the short sale for determining whether gain or loss is long- or short-term and for the holding period rules at ¶2670. (Code Sec. 1233(e)(2)(E))[33]

For the effect of the wash sale rules on short sales, see ¶2462.

¶ 2640   Capital gain limits on short sales.

Capital gain realized in a short sale is short-term, regardless of the actual holding period, where the seller either: (1) as of the date of the short sale, has owned for not more than one year (determined without regard to the effect of the short sale on the holding period, see ¶2670) property that's "substantially identical" (¶2462) to that which he used to close the sale, or (2) after the short sale and on or before its closing, he acquires substantially identical property. (Code Sec. 1233(b); Reg § 1.1233-1(c)(2)) This doesn't apply to any capital gain on property in excess of the amount of substantially identical property. This keeps the taxpayer from turning what would normally be a short-term capital gain into a long-term capital gain.[34]

The above rule applies only to stocks, securities and commodity futures. (Code Sec. 1233(e)(2)(A))[35]

¶ 2641   Capital loss limits on short sales.

If property "substantially identical" (¶2462) to that sold short was held by the taxpayer for more than one year as of the sale date, any loss on closing of the short sale is long-term capital loss, regardless of how long he held the property used to close the sale. (Code Sec. 1233(d)) This doesn't apply to any capital loss on property used to close the short sale in excess of the amount of substantially identical property. (Code Sec. 1233(e)(1))[36] This rule applies only to stocks, securities and commodity futures. (Code Sec. 1233(e)(2)(A))[37]

¶ 2642   Commodity futures and hedging transactions.

Commodity transactions are generally subject to the same rules for short sales as stocks and securities. A commodity future is a contract to buy some fixed amount of a commodity at a future date at a fixed price. Gain or loss from the short sale of a commodity future is capital gain or loss if the future used to close the short sale is a capital asset to the taxpayer. However, the short sale rules don't apply where the sale of the commodity future is a bona fide hedging transaction, see ¶2660. (Code Sec. 1233(g); Reg § 1.1233-1(b))[38] A transaction is a bona fide hedging transaction if the commodity future purchased is directly related to the taxpayer's business, e.g., flour millers buying and selling wheat futures.[39]

¶ 2643   Gain recognition required when property sold short becomes worthless.

If a taxpayer enters into a short sale of property, and that property becomes substantially worthless, the taxpayer recognizes gain in the same manner as if the short sale were closed when the property becomes substantially worthless. (Code Sec. 1233(h)(1))[40] To the extent

32. ¶I-7708; ¶12,334.01; TD ¶228,905
33. ¶I-7712.2; ¶12,334.09; TD ¶228,911.1
34. ¶I-7710; ¶s 12,334.03, 12,334.06; TD ¶228,907
35. ¶I-7709; ¶12,334.03; TD ¶228,905
36. ¶I-7714; TD ¶228,913
37. ¶I-7709; ¶12,334.03; TD ¶228,905
38. ¶I-7724; ¶12,334.14; TD ¶228,901
39. ¶I-7724; ¶s 12,214.80, 12,334.12
40. ¶I-7707.1; ¶12,334.02; TD ¶228,917

provided in regs, this rule will also apply for any option with respect to property, any offsetting notional principal contract with respect to property, any futures or forward contract to
deliver any property, and any other similar transaction. (Code Sec. 1233(h)(1))[41]

Where property becomes substantially worthless during a tax year and any short sale of the
property remains open at that time, then the statutory period for the assessment of any
deficiency attributable to any part of the gain on the transaction doesn't expire before the
earlier of: (1) the date which is three years after the date IRS is notified by the taxpayer (in a
manner that IRS may prescribe by regs) of the substantial worthlessness of the property, or
(2) the date which is six years after the date the return for the tax year during which the
position became substantially worthless is filed. In addition, the deficiency may be assessed
before the expiration of the assessment period described above in spite of any other law or
rule of law which would otherwise prevent the assessment. (Code Sec. 1233(h)(2))[42]

¶ 2644   Section 1244 ("Small Business Corporation") Stock.

Loss on the sale, exchange or worthlessness of Section 1244 stock is deductible,
within limits, as an ordinary loss, even though gain on the stock is capital gain. This
ordinary deduction is available only to an individual to whom the stock was issued by
a small business corporation, or an individual who was a partner in a partnership at
the time the stock was issued to a partnership by a small business corporation.
Transferees of these original purchasers don't qualify. (Code Sec. 1244(a))[43]

The aggregate amount of the ordinary loss is limited to $50,000 on separate returns and
$100,000 on joint returns each year. Spouses may deduct the $100,000 maximum in a joint
return even if only one spouse owned the stock. (Code Sec. 1244(b))[44]

A loss on qualifying Section 1244 stock is deductible as an ordinary loss attributable to the
shareholder's business. As such, the loss is deductible in full from gross income and may give
rise to a net operating loss. Losses exceeding the limits must be treated as regular capital
losses. (Reg § 1.1244(b)-1(a))[45]

¶ 2645   Qualifying for Section 1244 ordinary loss treatment.

To qualify as Section 1244 stock, all of the following tests must be met: (Code
Sec. 1244(c))[46]

. . . The stock must be stock of a domestic corporation. It may be common or preferred,
voting or nonvoting). (Reg § 1.1244(c)-1(b))[47]

. . . The stock must have been issued for money or property (other than stock and securities). But stock issued for the cancellation of corporate debt (not evidenced by a security or
issued for services) does qualify. Stock issued for services rendered or to be rendered to, or
for the benefit of, the issuing corporation, does not qualify. (Reg § 1.1244(c)-1(d)(1))[48]

. . . The issuing corporation must have met a test in which it shows that over 50% of its
receipts were from business operations.[49]

. . . The stock had to be issued by a domestic "small business" corporation, see ¶2647.[50]

¶ 2646   How to claim the Section 1244 ordinary loss—Form 4797.

Claim the ordinary loss on Form 4797 (attached to Form 1040). No information statement
is required to be filed with the return but records must be maintained to establish a loss and

41. ¶I-2616.1; ¶12,334.02; TD ¶228,615
42. ¶T-4221.2; ¶12,334.02; TD ¶228,917
43. ¶I-9503; ¶12,444.02; TD ¶247,301
44. ¶I-9505; ¶12,444.01; TD ¶247,359
45. ¶I-9502; ¶12,444; TD ¶247,362

46. ¶I-9508 *et seq.*; ¶12,444.03; TD ¶247,302
47. ¶I-9508 *et seq.*; ¶12,444.03; TD ¶247,302 *et seq.*
48. ¶I-9511, I-9512; ¶12,444.03; TD ¶247,309 *et seq.*
49. ¶I-9524 *et seq.*; ¶12,444.03; TD ¶247,336
50. ¶I-9517; ¶12444.03; TD ¶247,325 *et seq.*

whether the stock qualifies as Section 1244 stock. (Reg § 1.1244(e)-1(b))[1]

¶ 2647   Small business corporation (SBC) defined.

A corporation is an SBC if at the time the stock is issued its capital receipts don't exceed $1,000,000. (Special designation rules must be met for stock issued in a year capital receipts do exceed $1,000,000.)[2] Capital receipts means the aggregate amount of money and other property received by the corporation for stock, as a contribution to capital, and as paid-in surplus. This includes amounts received for the Section 1244 stock and for all stock issued previously. (Code Sec. 1244(c)(3)(A))[3]

¶ 2648   Exclusion of Gain from Qualified Small Business Stock (QSBS). ▬▬▬▬

Under the rules described below, a taxpayer (other than a corporation) may exclude part (or, in some cases, all) of the gain realized on the disposition of QSBS (defined at ¶2649) held for more than five years. (Code Sec. 1202(a)(1))

For QSBS acquired after Sep. 27, 2010 and before 2011, noncorporate taxpayers may exclude all of the gain on the disposition of QSBS stock. For QSBS acquired after Feb. 17, 2009 and before Sep. 28, 2010, noncorporate taxpayers can exclude 75% of any gain realized on the disposition of QSBS. For QSBS acquired before Feb. 18, 2009 (or after 2010), noncorporate taxpayers may exclude 50% of the gain on the disposition of QSBS. (Code Sec. 1202(a))[4]

The exclusion is 60%, rather than 50%, for periods that the 75% or 100% exclusion doesn't apply, for gain on the sale of empowerment zone stock (but not District of Columbia Enterprise Zone stock) acquired after Dec. 21, 2000, held for more than five years, and not attributable to periods after 2014. The empowerment zone stock must be in a corporation that qualifies as an enterprise zone business under Code Sec. 1397C(b) during substantially all of the taxpayer's holding period. (Code Sec. 1202(a)(2))[5]

However, a taxpayer (or a related party) who takes an offsetting short position before the required five-year holding period is completed cannot exclude gain from the disposition of QSBS. (Code Sec. 1202(j))[6]

For each corporation in which the taxpayer invests, the total amount of gain eligible for the partial exclusion for a tax year may not exceed the greater of:

. . . $10,000,000 ($5,000,000 for marrieds filing separately) (Code Sec. 1202(b)(1)(A), Code Sec. 1202(b)(3)(A)) reduced by taxpayer's total gain on dispositions of the corporation's stock that he took into account in earlier years. (Code Sec. 1202(b)(1)(A)) The amount of eligible gain is allocated equally between spouses who file jointly, to apply this limit to later years (Code Sec. 1202(b)(3)(B)); or

. . . ten times the aggregate adjusted bases of any of the corporation's QSBS that taxpayer disposed of during the year. (Code Sec. 1202(b)(1)(B)) For this purpose, the adjusted basis of any stock doesn't include any additions to basis after the date it was originally issued (Code Sec. 1202(b)(1)), or any reductions for SSBIC rollovers (¶2505). (Code Sec. 1044(d))[7]

The exclusion is denied where the corporation redeems stock from the taxpayer or a related person during certain periods, or buys its own stock in excess of certain amounts during specified periods. (Code Sec. 1202(c)(3))[8]

Additional rules apply where passthrough entities hold the stock. (Code Sec. 1202(g))[9]

For the rollover of gain from QSBS to other QSBS, see ¶2429.

---

1. ¶I-9537, I-9538; ¶12,444.05; TD ¶247,363, 247,365
2. ¶I-9518 *et seq.*; ¶12,444.04; TD ¶247,326
3. ¶I-9518; ¶12,444.04; TD ¶247,327
4. ¶I-9100 *et seq.*; ¶12,024; TD ¶246,600 *et seq.*
5. ¶I-9100.1B; ¶12,024; TD ¶246,602
6. ¶I-9115; ¶12,024.03; TD ¶246,610
7. ¶I-9112 *et seq.*; ¶12,024.01; TD ¶246,603 *et seq.*
8. ¶I-9102; ¶12,024; TD ¶246,637
9. ¶I-9116; ¶s 12,024, 12,024.03; TD ¶246,612

For alternative minimum tax treatment of the exclusion, see ¶3209.

¶ 2649 Qualified small business stock (QSBS) defined.

Qualified small business stock (QSBS) is any stock in a C corporation which is originally issued after Aug. 10, '93 if:

. . . as of the date of issuance, the corporation is a qualified small business. (Code Sec. 1202(c)(1)(A)) This means a domestic C corporation whose total gross assets (treating all members of the same parent-subsidiary controlled group as one corporation) at all times after Aug. 10, '93 and before the issuance, and immediately after the issuance (taking into account amounts received in the issuance), don't exceed $50,000,000, and that meets certain reporting requirements (Code Sec. 1202(d));

. . . the taxpayer claiming the exclusion acquired the stock at its original issuance for money or other property (not stock) or as compensation for services provided to the corporation (other than services performed as an underwriter) (Code Sec. 1202(c)(1)(B)); *and*

. . . during substantially all of taxpayer's holding period for the stock, the corporation is a C corporation (other than certain excluded corporations) *and* meets an active business test. (Code Sec. 1202(c)(2)(A), Code Sec. 1202(e)) An SSBIC (¶2427) meets the active business test.[10]

¶ 2650 Tax- Free Capital Gains for Investment in Renewal Communities and DC Zone Assets. ████████████████████████

Taxpayers will be able to exclude all capital gains realized from the sale of certain qualifying community renewal or DC Zone assets held for more than 5 years.

¶ 2651 Tax-free capital gains from sale of qualifying community renewal assets held for more than 5 years.

Taxpayers will be able to exclude 100% of their "qualified capital gain" recognized on the sale or exchange of a "qualified community asset" if the asset is (1) acquired after 2001 and before 2010 and (2) held for more than 5 years. (Code Sec. 1400F(a), Code Sec. 1400F(b)(2)(A)(i), Code Sec. 1400F(b)(3)(A), Code Sec. 1400F(b)(4)(A)(i))

"Qualified capital gain" is gain recognized on the sale or exchange of a capital asset, or property used in a trade or business, as defined in Code Sec. 1231(b), see ¶2686. (Code Sec. 1400F(c)(1)) It doesn't include (1) any gain attributable to periods before 2002 or after 2014 (Code Sec. 1400F(c)(2)), (2) gain recaptured under Code Sec. 1245 (¶2695) or under Code Sec. 1250 (¶2696) (including gain that would be recaptured if Code Sec. 1250 applied to all depreciation rather than just to additional depreciation) (Code Sec. 1400F(c)(3), Code Sec. 1400B(e)(3)), (3) gain attributable to real property, or an intangible asset, that isn't integral to a "renewal community business" (as defined in Code Sec. 1400G) (Code Sec. 1400F(c)(3), Code Sec. 1400B(e)(4)), and (4) gain attributable in whole or in part to certain related-party transactions. (Code Sec. 1400F(c)(3), Code Sec. 1400B(e)(5))

A "qualified community asset" is qualifying stock in a U.S. corporation (defined in Code Sec. 1400F(b)(2)), a qualifying capital or a profits interest in a U.S. partnership (defined in Code Sec. 1400F(b)(3)), or qualifying community business property (defined in Code Sec. 1400F(b)(4)).

Special rules apply for subsequent holders of qualifying property (Code Sec. 1400F(d)), and where qualifying community assets cease to qualify as a renewal community business (or property ceases to be used in such a business) after the 5-year period beginning after the date

---

10.   ¶I-9101 *et seq.*; ¶12,024.02; TD ¶246,639 *et seq.*

the taxpayer acquired the assets. (Code Sec. 1400F(d))[11]

¶ 2652   Tax-free gain from the sale or exchange of qualifying D.C. Zone assets.

Gross income doesn't include qualified capital gain from the sale or exchange of any DC Zone asset held for more than five years. Qualified capital gain is any gain recognized on the sale or exchange of: a capital asset, or property used in the trade or business. (Code Sec. 1400B(a), Code Sec. 1400B(e)(1))

Qualified capital gain does *not* include any gain (1) attributable to periods before '98 or after 2014 (Code Sec. 1400B(e)(2)), (2) which would be treated as ordinary income under the recapture rules of Code Sec. 1245 (¶2695) or Code Sec. 1250 (¶2696) if Code Sec. 1250 applied to all depreciation rather than the additional depreciation (Code Sec. 1400B(e)(3)), (3) which is attributable to real property, or an intangible asset, that is not an integral part of a DC Zone business (Code Sec. 1400B(e)(4)), or (4) is attributable, directly or indirectly, in whole or in part, to a transaction with a related person (under Code Sec. 267(b) or Code Sec. 707(b)(1)). (Code Sec. 1400B(e)(5))

In general, a DC Zone asset is qualifying DC Zone business stock, DC Zone partnership interests, and DC Zone business property, acquired before 2010. (Code Sec. 1400B(b)(1))[12]

caution: Check http://www.ria.thomsonreuters.com/federaltaxhandbook to see if this provision has been extended.

¶ 2653   Tax Straddles and Section 1256 Contracts ████████████████████

Losses on certain unregulated straddles are deferred, to the extent taxpayer has an offsetting unrecognized gain. Related interest and carrying charges must be capitalized. Regulated futures contracts are subject to the "mark-to-market" rule which treats the unrealized capital gain (or loss) from the contract for the year as 60% long-term and 40% short-term. Hedging transactions are excepted from these rules.

There are a number of rules provided to restrict tax avoidance opportunities in commodity futures straddles and to curb certain tax shelters involving tax straddles.[13]

Under the constructive sale rules (¶2637), a taxpayer must recognize gain (but not loss) upon entering into a constructive sale of any appreciated financial position in stock, a partnership interest, or certain debt instruments. (Code Sec. 1259). The constructive sale rules generally are intended to apply to transactions that are identified as hedging or straddle transactions under other Code provisions such as Code Sec. 1092(a)(2) (dealing with a special rule for straddles that are identified as straddles at the close of a tax year), Code Sec. 1092(b)(2) (dealing with regs with respect to identified mixed straddles, ¶2658), Code Sec. 1092(e) (dealing with an exception for hedging transactions), and Code Sec. 1256(e) (dealing with the nonapplication of the mark-to-market rules to hedging transactions, ¶2660).[14]

¶ 2654   Straddle defined.

A straddle is "offsetting positions" with respect to personal property. (Code Sec. 1092(c)(1)) A "position" is an interest, including a futures or forward contract or option, in personal property. (Code Sec. 1092(d)(2)) In general, personal property does not include stock (but it does include stock options and contracts to buy stock). (Code Sec. 1092(d)(3)(A)) However, stock is included in the definition of personal property for straddle purposes if (1) the stock is part of a straddle in which at least one of the offsetting positions is either an option to buy or sell the stock or substantially identical stock or securities, or a position on substantially similar or related property (other than stock); or (2) the stock is in a corporation formed or

---

11. ¶I-8801 *et seq.*; ¶14,00F4; TD ¶229,952 *et seq.*
12. ¶I-8750 *et seq.*; ¶14,00B4; TD ¶246,550 *et seq.*

13. ¶I-7500 *et seq.*; ¶10,924; TD ¶228,401
14. ¶I-7746

availed of to take positions in personal property that offset positions taken by any share-holder. (Code Sec. 1092(d)(3)(B))

A taxpayer holds "offsetting positions" if he has reduced his risk of loss from holding the property by holding one (or more) other positions, whether or not the items of personal property involved in the different positions are the same kind. (Code Sec. 1092(c)(2)(A))[15]

¶ 2655 Recognition of losses postponed on certain nonregulated futures straddles (loss deferral rule).

Loss deductions on nonregulated straddles, that is, those straddle positions not on the "mark-to-market" system (see ¶2656), are limited to the amount by which the losses exceed "unrecognized gains" on any offsetting straddle positions. Losses in excess of the limitation (deferred losses) are carried forward to the next year and are subject to the deferral rules in that year. (Code Sec. 1092(a)(1))[16]

¶ 2656 Regulated futures contracts, etc. (Section 1256 contracts), under "mark-to-market" system.

Taxpayers must report (on Form 6781) gains and losses from regulated futures contracts and other "Section 1256 contracts" (¶2657) on an annual basis under the "mark-to-market" rule. All Section 1256 contracts must be marked to market at year end. Each Section 1256 contract held by a taxpayer is treated as if it were sold for fair market value on the last business day of the year. (Code Sec. 1256(a)(1)) If a taxpayer holds Section 1256 contracts at the beginning of a tax year, any gain or loss later realized on the contracts must be adjusted to reflect any gain or loss taken into account with respect to the contracts in an earlier year. (Code Sec. 1256(a)(2))

Any capital gain or loss on a Section 1256 futures contract that is marked-to-market is treated as if 40% of the gain or loss is short-term capital gain or loss, and as if 60% of the gain or loss is long-term capital gain or loss. (Code Sec. 1256(a)(3))[17]

The wash sale rules (¶2462) don't apply to losses taken into account when a Section 1256 contract is marked to market. (Code Sec. 1256(f)(5))[18]

¶ 2657 Section 1256 contracts defined.

Section 1256 contracts include: regulated futures contracts, foreign currency contracts, nonequity options, dealer equity options, and dealer securities futures contracts (¶2663) (Code Sec. 1256(b))[19] For a partnership that's a qualified fund, Section 1256 contracts include bank forward contracts, foreign currency futures contracts, and similar instruments prescribed by IRS regs. (Code Sec. 988(c)(1)(E)(iv)(I))[20] However, a foreign currency call option isn't a foreign currency transaction that is treated as a Section 1256 contract.[21]

Section 1256 contracts do not include any securities futures contract, or option on a securities futures contract, unless the contract or option is a dealer securities futures contract, or for tax years beginning after July 1, 2010, any interest rate swap, currency swap, basis swap, interest rate cap, interest rate floor, commodity swap, equity swap, equity index swap, credit default swap, or similar agreement. (Code Sec. 1256(b)(2))[22]

---

15. ¶I-7503 *et seq.*; ¶10,924; TD ¶228,406
16. ¶I-7523; ¶10,924; TD ¶228,403
17. ¶I-7602, ¶I-7603.3; ¶12,564 *et seq.*; TD ¶228,700 *et seq.*
18. ¶I-7602; ¶12,564.02; TD ¶228,701

19. ¶I-7604; ¶12,564.01; TD ¶228,704
20. ¶I-7607; ¶9884.01
21. ¶I-7611
22. ¶I-7604; ¶12,564.01

¶ 2658   Election for mixed straddles.

If straddles are composed of at least one position in a Section 1256 contract (¶2657) and one or more positions in interests in property that aren't Section 1256 contracts, a taxpayer may elect on Form 6781 to exclude all positions in the mixed straddle, including Section 1256 contracts, from the mark-to-market rules in which case they will be subject to the loss deferral, wash sale, and short sale rules, and the straddle won't be a mixed straddle. (Code Sec. 1256(d))[23] If that election isn't made, so that the straddle is a mixed straddle, a taxpayer may elect to offset gains and losses in the mixed straddle by either separately identifying the positions of the mixed straddle, or establishing a mixed straddle account. (Reg § 1.1092(b)-4T)[24]

¶ 2659   Carryback election for losses from Section 1256 contracts—Form 6781.

Noncorporate taxpayers can elect (on Form 6781) to have net commodity futures capital losses carried back three years and applied against net commodities futures capital gains during that period. (Code Sec. 1212(c)) The carryback applies only if, after netting Section 1256 contracts with capital gains and losses from other sources, there's a net capital loss for the tax year that, but for the election, would be a capital loss carryforward under the normal rules (¶2612). The lesser of the net capital loss or the net loss resulting from the application of the mark-to-market rule is a "net Section 1256 contracts loss" which may be carried back. (Code Sec. 1212(c)(4)) Capital losses carried back must be treated as if 40% of the losses are short-term capital losses and 60% are long-term capital losses. (Code Sec. 1212(c)(1)) The losses must be absorbed in the earliest year to which they may be carried back. Any remainder is then carried forward to the next year. The losses may be applied in the carryback year against the lesser of "net Section 1256 contracts gain" or capital gain net income for that year. (Code Sec. 1212(c)(5))

Capital losses that are carried forward, to the extent they were determined under the mark-to-market rule, continue to be treated as losses from Section 1256 contracts in the year to which they are carried. (Code Sec. 1212(c)(6))[25]

¶ 2660   Hedging transactions not covered by the mark-to-market rules.

The "mark-to-market" rules don't apply to "hedging transactions" as defined in Code Sec. 1256(e)(2). (Code Sec. 1256(e)(1))[26]

¶ 2661   Securities Futures Contracts ▬▬▬▬▬▬▬▬▬▬

Gain or loss from a securities futures contract generally has the same character as gain or loss from transactions in the underlying security. A dealer securities futures contract is treated as a section 1256 contract.

¶ 2662   Gain or loss from nondealer securities futures contracts.

Gain or loss on the sale, exchange, or termination of a securities futures contract (as defined in Code Sec. 1234B(c)) generally has the same character as gain or loss from transactions in the underlying security. (Code Sec. 1234B(a)(1)) For example, if the underlying asset would be a capital asset in the hands of the taxpayer, gain or loss from the sale of the contract is capital gain or loss. This rule does not apply to securities futures contracts that are not capital assets because they are Code Sec. 1221(a)(1) inventory assets, are identified as Code Sec. 1221(a)(7) hedging transactions, or any income derived in connection with a contract

---

23. ¶I-7616; ¶12,564.03; TD ¶228,714
24. ¶I-7571 *et seq.*; ¶10,924

25. ¶I-7606; ¶12,124.02; TD ¶228,706
26. ¶I-7620; ¶12,564.05; TD ¶228,715

which would otherwise not be capital gain. (Code Sec. 1234B(a)(2))[27]

Except as provided in regs to Code Sec. 1092(b) or Code Sec. 1234B, or in Code Sec. 1233, capital gain or loss from the sale, exchange, or termination of a securities futures contract to sell property is treated as short-term capital gain or loss. (Code Sec. 1234B(b))

If the security to which a securities futures contract (that is not a Code Sec. 1256 contract (see ¶2663)) is acquired in satisfaction of that contract, the taxpayer's holding period for the security includes the period for which the taxpayer held the contract if the contract was a capital asset in the taxpayer's hands. (Code Sec. 1223(14))[28]

¶ 2663 Dealer securities futures contracts are section 1256 contracts.

Dealer securities futures contracts are treated as Code Sec. 1256 contracts (see ¶2656). (Code Sec. 1256(b)(1)(E)) A dealer securities futures contract is any securities futures contract (see ¶2662) and any option to enter into such a contract that (1) is entered into by the dealer (or, in the case of an option, is purchased or granted by the dealer) in the normal course of his activity of dealing in such contracts or options, as the case may be, and (2) is traded on a qualified board or exchange. (Code Sec. 1256(g)(9)(A))[29]

¶ 2664 Conversion and Constructive Ownership Transactions ■■■■■■■■

Capital gain on the disposition of property that was part of a conversion transaction (i.e., functionally equivalent to a loan) is treated as ordinary income. Certain gains from derivative contracts (constructive ownership transactions) with respect to financial assets are recharacterized as ordinary income.

¶ 2665 Gain recharacterized on conversion transactions similar to loans.

Gain recognized on the disposition or other termination of any position held as part of a conversion transaction (defined below), that would otherwise be treated as capital gain, is treated as ordinary income, to the extent it doesn't exceed the applicable imputed income amount. (Code Sec. 1258(a))[30] The applicable imputed income amount equals the excess of (1) taxpayer's net investment in the transaction multiplied by 120% of (a) the applicable federal rate (¶1116), compounded semiannually, for the period covered by the transaction, if the transaction has a definite term, or of (b) the federal short-term rates (compounded daily) in effect under Code Sec. 6621(b) for the period of the conversion transaction, if the term of the transaction is indefinite, over (2) the amount already so treated with respect to the same transaction. (Code Sec. 1258(b), Code Sec. 1258(d)(2))[31]

When a taxpayer disposes or terminates all positions of an identified (as part of the same transaction, on taxpayer's books and records) netting transaction within a 14-day period in a single tax year, all gains and losses on those positions realized within that period are netted to determine the amount of gain treated as ordinary income. (Reg § 1.1258-1(b))[32]

A conversion transaction is any transaction where substantially all of taxpayer's expected net return is attributable to the time value of his net investment, and which is:

... the holding of any property (whether or not actively traded) and substantially contemporaneous making of a contract to sell that or substantially identical property at a price determined in accordance with the contract (Code Sec. 1258(c)(2)(A));

... a straddle (¶2654) of actively traded personal property (Code Sec. 1258(c)(2)(B));

... any other transaction that is marketed or sold as producing capital gains, and substantially all of the expected return from that transaction is attributable to the time value of

---

27. ¶I-6280 *et seq.*; ¶12,34B4; TD ¶250,200 *et seq.*
28. ¶I-8924.1; ¶12,234.27; TD ¶223,521
29. ¶I-7615.1; ¶12,564.01; TD ¶228,712

30. ¶I-8200 *et seq.*; ¶12,584; TD ¶227,801
31. ¶I-8208; ¶12,584; TD ¶227,806
32. ¶I-8209.1 *et seq.*; ¶12,584; TD ¶227,802

the taxpayer's net investment in the transaction (Code Sec. 1258(c)(2)(C)); or

. . . a conversion transaction as specified in regs to be issued. (Code Sec. 1258(c)(2)(D))[33]

Conversion transactions don't include transactions of options dealers and commodities traders in the normal course of their trade or business. (Code Sec. 1258(d)(5)(A))[34]

¶ 2666   Certain long-term capital gains from constructive ownership transactions are recharacterized as ordinary income.

The amount of long-term capital gain a taxpayer can recognize from certain derivative contracts (constructive ownership transactions (defined in Code Sec. 1260(d))) with respect to certain financial assets is limited, and an interest charge is imposed on the tax underpayment for each year that the constructive ownership transaction was open. (Code Sec. 1260) If a taxpayer has gain from a constructive ownership transaction with respect to any financial asset and that gain would otherwise be treated as a long-term capital gain, then (1) the gain is treated as ordinary income to the extent it exceeds the net underlying long-term capital gain, and (2) to the extent gain is treated as long-term capital gain, the determination of the capital gain rate (or rates) applicable to the gain under Code Sec. 1(h) (i.e., the individual capital gains rates) is determined on the basis of the respective rate (or rates) that would have applied to the net underlying long-term capital gain. (Code Sec. 1260(a))[35]

¶ 2667   Holding Period.

The length of time that a capital asset is held before its sale or exchange determines whether the proceeds from the sale or exchange are taxable as long-term capital gain or loss or as short-term capital gain or loss.

The length of time an asset is held is also crucial in qualifying for Section 1231 (capital gain/ordinary loss) treatment, see ¶2686.

Holding a capital asset for the short-term holding period (one year or less) results in short-term capital gain or loss on the sale or exchange of that asset. (Code Sec. 1222(1), Code Sec. 1222(2)) Holding a capital asset for the long-term holding period (more than one year) results in long-term capital gain or loss on the sale or exchange of that asset. (Code Sec. 1222(3), Code Sec. 1222(4))[36]

The long-term holding period is more than six months for futures transactions in any commodity subject to the rules of a board of trade or commodity exchange. (Code Sec. 1222)[37]

¶ 2668   How to measure the holding period.

The holding period is computed in terms of calendar months, not days.[38] It begins on the day after the day of acquisition and ends on the day of sale, exchange or other disposition. Thus, the taxpayer excludes the day of acquisition but includes the date of disposition.[39]

illustration: A capital asset is acquired on Feb. 15. To meet the long-term holding period, it must be held until Feb. 16 of the following year. To meet the more-than-six-month long-term holding period for a commodity future (¶2667), it must be held until Aug. 16 of the year in which it was bought. If the asset were acquired on Jan. 31, it would have to be held until Feb. 1 of the following year to meet the more-than-one-year holding period, or until Aug. 1 of the year in which it was bought to meet the more-than-six-month period.

33. ¶I-8205; ¶12,584; TD ¶227,805
34. ¶I-8210 *et seq.*; ¶12,584
35. ¶I-8251; ¶12,604; TD ¶229,551
36. ¶I-8901; ¶12,234; TD ¶223,501

37. ¶I-8971; ¶12,234.27; TD ¶223,550
38. ¶I-8904; ¶12,234.01; TD ¶223,504
39. ¶s I-8904, I-8906; ¶12,234.01; TD ¶223,502

¶ 2669 Holding period of partnership interest.

A partner doesn't have a divided holding period in his partnership interest unless he acquired portions of it at different times or in exchange for property transferred at the same time but resulting in different holding periods. (Reg § 1.1223-3(a)) The holding period of a portion of a partnership interest is determined based on a fraction equal to the fair market value (FMV) of the portion of the partnership interest received in the transaction to which the holding period relates over the FMV of the entire partnership interest (determined immediately after the transaction). (Reg § 1.1223-3(b))[40]

✅illustration: A contributes $5,000 and a nondepreciable capital asset that he's held for two years to a partnership for a 50% interest in it. His basis in the capital asset is $5,000, and its FMV is $10,000. After the exchange, A's basis in his interest in the partnership is $10,000, and the FMV of the interest is $15,000. A's holding period in one-third of the interest received for cash begins on the day after the contribution. Under Code Sec. 1223(1), A has a two-year holding period in two-thirds of the interest received in the partnership for the capital asset.

¶ 2670 Holding period for stocks and securities.

The holding period for stocks and securities acquired by purchase, whether on a registered securities exchange or in the "over-the-counter" market, is determined by reference to the "trade date" on which the stock or security is acquired and the "trade date" on which it is sold. The "settlement dates" aren't considered. [41]

The holding period for stock or securities acquired from a corporation by the exercise of rights begins on and includes the day the rights are exercised. (Code Sec. 1223(5); Reg § 1.1223-1(f))[42]

The holding period for property "substantially identical" to that sold short in a transaction to which the rule at ¶2640 applies is considered to begin on the day the short sale is closed or, if earlier, on the date the property is sold, given away or otherwise disposed of. (Code Sec. 1233(b)(2); Reg § 1.1233-1(c)(2))[43]

The holding period for stock, stock rights or other property received as a taxable dividend begins on the date the distribution is actually or constructively received.[44] If the distribution is tax-free, the holding period for the stock, etc., includes the period that the underlying stock was held. (Code Sec. 1223(4); Reg § 1.1223-1(e))[45]

The holding period for restricted stock (or property) begins after it is substantially vested, unless an election (¶1220) is made to include the property in income in the year of transfer, in which case it begins just after the transfer. (Code Sec. 83(f); Reg § 1.83-4(a))[46]

Where the loss on a sale of stock or securities is disallowed under the "wash sale" rules (¶2461), the holding period for the new similar stock includes the holding period for the old stock that was sold. (Code Sec. 1223(3))[47]

The holding period for U.S. Treasury bonds and notes is measured from the acquisition date; for those sold at auction, this is the date the Treasury gives notice of acceptance to bidders; for those sold in a subscription offering at a specified interest rate, it's the date the buyer submits an offer.[48]

If an individual elects to roll over gain from qualified small business stock (QSBS) by way

40. ¶I-8934.1; ¶12,234.29; TD ¶223,556
41. ¶I-8914 *et seq.*; ¶12,234.07; TD ¶223,513
42. ¶I-8924; ¶12,234.25; TD ¶223,520
43. ¶I-7720; ¶12,334.03; TD ¶228,919
44. ¶I-8918; TD ¶223,517

45. ¶I-8921; ¶12,234.25; TD ¶223,518
46. ¶I-8916; ¶834 *et seq.*; TD ¶223,515
47. ¶I-8929; ¶12,234.25; TD ¶223,525
48. ¶I-8915; TD ¶223,514

of the timely acquisition of other QSBS stock (¶2429) the holding period for the acquired QSBS stock includes the holding period for the sold QSBS stock. (Code Sec. 1223(13))[49]

¶ 2671   Property acquired through options.

The holding period for property acquired through the exercise of an option begins the day after the option is exercised.[50]

¶ 2672   Holding period for property inherited from a decedent.

The holding period of property acquired from a decedent starts with the date of death.[1] However, property acquired from a decedent which is sold within the short-term capital gain holding period after the decedent's death is considered to be held for the *long*-term capital gain holding period if the person selling the property has a basis that is determined under Code Sec. 1014 (by reference to the property's fair market value on date of death or alternate valuation date). (Code Sec. 1223(9))[2]

The long-term holding period is also met where special use valuation property (¶5028) is acquired by a "qualified heir" from the decedent's estate, and is sold within the short-term holding period to another "qualified heir." (Code Sec. 1223(10))[3]

The holding period of the surviving spouse's share of community property that vested at the time of the acquisition by the community (as opposed to the share inherited from the deceased spouse) starts from the date of acquisition.[4]

¶ 2673   Holding period for gifts.

The holding period for property acquired by gift includes the donor's holding period if the property has the same basis for gain or loss (see ¶2463 *et seq.*) in whole or in part in the hands of the donee as it would have in the donor's hands. (Code Sec. 1223(2); Reg § 1.1223-1(b)) But if the property is sold by the donee at a loss based on its market value on the date of the gift (and not the donor's basis), the holding period starts from the date of the gift.[5]

¶ 2674   Tax-free exchange property.

The holding period for property received in a partially or wholly tax-free exchange (¶2413), includes the holding period for the property surrendered. This "tacking on" applies where the new property has the same basis, in whole or in part, as the old property (Code Sec. 1223(1)), e.g., like-kind exchanges, tax-free stock distributions (¶2670), involuntary conversions (¶2675), or incorporations and tax-free corporate reorganizations (¶3510 *et seq.*).[6]

¶ 2675   Replacements for property lost or damaged in an involuntary conversion.

The holding period of the original property is tacked on to that of property acquired to replace property lost or damaged in an involuntary conversion (¶2430 *et seq.*), where gain isn't recognized.[7]

¶ 2676   Sales and Exchanges.

Unless a transaction involving a capital asset is treated as a sale or exchange, any resulting gain or loss doesn't qualify as capital gain or loss.

---

49. ¶I-9207; ¶12,234.24; TD ¶247,211
50. ¶I-8949; ¶12,234.10; TD ¶223,542
1. ¶I-8944; ¶12,234.21; TD ¶223,537
2. ¶I-8942; ¶12,234.21; TD ¶223,535
3. ¶I-8943; ¶12,234.21; TD ¶223,536

4. ¶I-8945; ¶12,234.21; TD ¶223,538
5. ¶I-8966; ¶12,234.22; TD ¶223,511
6. ¶I-8960 *et seq.*; ¶12,234.18; TD ¶223,507
7. ¶I-8963; ¶12,234.18; TD ¶223,507

A sale is a transfer of property for an amount of money or a money equivalent that is fixed or determinable. An exchange is a transfer of property for property other than money or a cash equivalent. (Reg § 1.1002-1(d))[8]

To qualify as a sale or exchange, the transaction must be complete, and bona fide in all respects. If it's real in substance as well as form, it qualifies as a sale or exchange even though it was designed to reduce taxes.[9] However, it may be treated as a sham for tax purposes if (a) there is no business motive for the transaction other than getting tax benefits, and (b) the transaction has no economic substance.[10]

Where shareholders deal with their corporation, or family members sell or exchange property among themselves, IRS scrutinizes the deal closely. If a sale or exchange is a sham, IRS can disallow any of the sought-after tax consequences.[11]

¶ 2677 Gain or loss from certain terminations treated as capital gain or loss.

Gain or loss attributable to the cancellation, lapse, expiration, or other termination of the following is treated as gain or loss from the sale of a capital asset:

(1) a right or obligation (other than a securities futures contract under Code Sec. 1234B) with respect to property which is (or on acquisition would be) a capital asset in the hands of the taxpayer (Code Sec. 1234A(1)), or

(2) a section 1256 contract (¶2657) not described in (1) above which is a capital asset in the hands of the taxpayer. (Code Sec. 1234A(2))

These rules don't apply to the retirement of any debt instrument (whether or not through a trust or other participation arrangement). (Code Sec. 1234A)[12]

observation: It's not clear whether the rule discussed in (1), above, would change the rule discussed at ¶1342 that amounts received by a lessor for the cancellation of a lease are rent taxable as ordinary income.

¶ 2678 Retirement of debt instruments.

In general, amounts received by a holder on retirement of a debt instrument are treated as received in exchange for the debt instrument. (Code Sec. 1271(a)(1))[13]

¶ 2679 Payment with property as a sale.

A debtor realizes gain or loss when he transfers property to his creditor in complete or partial satisfaction of his debt. The transfer is treated as a sale or exchange of the property by the debtor. Gain or loss is the difference between the amount of debt satisfied and the basis of the transferred property.[14]

¶ 2680 Cancellation of lease or distribution agreement as sale or exchange.

Amounts received by a lessee or tenant for the cancellation of a lease, or by a distributor of goods for the cancellation of a distributorship agreement, are considered amounts received *in exchange* for the lease or agreement. (Code Sec. 1241)[15] Thus, Section 1231 treatment (see ¶2684) is available for gain or loss from the cancellation of a business lease or distributorship held long-term. If the lease was for the tenant's home, a gain would be taxed as a capital gain, but any loss wouldn't be deductible.[16]

8. ¶I-1002, I-1104; ¶12,224.07; TD ¶220,201
9. ¶I-1212 *et seq.*; ¶12,224.07; TD ¶220,600 *et seq.*
10. ¶M-5901
11. ¶I-1201 *et seq.*; TD ¶220,801
12. ¶I-7619; ¶12,34A4; TD ¶221,208

13. ¶I-1901; ¶12,714; TD ¶221,501
14. ¶I-1501 *et seq.*; ¶10,014.17; TD ¶221,401
15. ¶I-1400 *et seq.*; ¶12,414; TD ¶221,201
16. ¶M-1500; ¶12,414

¶ 2681   Convertible bonds.

No gain or loss is realized upon the conversion of bonds into stock of the *same* corporation under a conversion privilege set forth in the terms of the bond.[17]

¶ 2682   Sale with leaseback, reservations or restrictions.

The fact that a sale of property is accompanied by a leaseback doesn't bar recognizing the sale as closed for tax purposes.[18] But a leaseback of realty (including renewal options) extending for 30 years or more may be considered an exchange of like-kind property in which gain or loss isn't recognized.[19] A sale restricting the buyer's use of the property may be recognized as a completed sale, as where stock is sold subject to security-device restrictions,[20] but if the rights retained are significant enough, the seller may be considered as selling only a partial interest or as granting a license to use.[21]

¶ 2683   Part gift, part sale; conditional gifts.

If an owner combines a gift with a sale (e.g., to a family member) gain is realized to the extent the price received exceeds the owner's adjusted basis. However, no loss is recognized if the amount received is less than the owner's basis.Reg § 1.1001-1(e))[22]

If a donor gives appreciated property to a donee on condition the donee pay the donor's gift tax, there's a sale by the donor for the amount of the gift tax. To the extent the gift tax paid by the donee exceeds the donor's basis, the donor has income.[23]

¶ 2684   Capital Gain-Ordinary Loss Rule. ■■■■■■■■■■■■■■■■■■■■■■■■■■■■

Under Code Sec. 1231, if there's a net gain for the tax year from sales, exchanges, and involuntary or compulsory conversions of certain assets, it's treated as long-term capital gain. A net loss is treated as an ordinary loss.

¶ 2685   Applying the Section 1231 rules—Form 4797.

If the recognized gains are greater than the recognized losses on sales, exchanges and involuntary conversions of Section 1231 assets, the net amount is treated as a long-term capital gain, except as discussed below. But, if those losses are greater than those gains, the net amount is treated as an ordinary loss. (Code Sec. 1231(a); Reg § 1.1231-1(b))[24] Section 1231 gains and losses are reported and netted on Form 4797.

A net Section 1231 gain is treated as ordinary income to the extent of nonrecaptured net Section 1231 losses. (Code Sec. 1231(c)(1))

A nonrecaptured net Section 1231 loss is the net Section 1231 loss for the five most recent preceding tax years that hasn't been offset by a net Section 1231 gain in an intervening tax year. (Code Sec. 1231(c)(2)) Net Section 1231 gain means the excess of the Section 1231 gains over the Section 1231 losses. Net Section 1231 loss means the excess of the Section 1231 losses over the Section 1231 gains. (Code Sec. 1231(c)(3), Code Sec. 1231(c)(4))[25]

illustration: X Corp., a calendar year taxpayer, had a net Section 1231 loss of $1,000,000 in 2006 that was offset against ordinary income. X Corp. had no net Section 1231 gain in 2007, 2008, or 2009, but has a net Section 1231 gain of $1,400,000 (consisting of a $2,000,000 gain on condemnation of land, and a $600,000 loss on the sale of machinery) in

17. ¶I-1909; ¶10,014.42; TD ¶221,600
18. ¶I-1122; TD ¶220,620
19. ¶I-3077; TD ¶223,717
20. ¶I-1125
21. ¶I-1602 *et seq.*

22. ¶I-1006; ¶10,014.06; TD ¶220,205
23. ¶I-1007; TD ¶222,411
24. ¶I-9001; ¶12,314; TD ¶223,201
25. ¶I-9003; ¶12,314.15; TD ¶223,205

2010. $1,000,000 of the net Section 1231 gain for 2010 is treated as ordinary income, and the remaining $400,000 is treated as long-term capital gain.

If the recognized losses from involuntary conversions arising from fire, storm, shipwreck or other casualty, or from theft, exceed the recognized gain, they aren't included in the Section 1231 computations. (Code Sec. 1231(a)(4)(C), Code Sec. 1231(c)(5))[26]

Capital gain treatment under Section 1231 is also barred to the extent that the depreciation recapture rules apply, see ¶2692 *et seq.*

¶ 2686 Section 1231 assets defined.

Section 1231 assets are certain assets used in taxpayer's trade or business that were held for more than one year at the time of disposition. Except as explained below, these assets include depreciable tangible and intangible personal property, and real property, whether or not depreciable. They include timber, certain livestock (other than poultry), and unharvested crops that are transferred with land. (Code Sec. 1231(b))

They don't include: (1) inventory, (2) property held primarily for sale to customers in the ordinary course of the taxpayer's business, (3) copyrights, artistic, literary, or musical compositions (unless, for musical compositions or copyrights in them, the election discussed at ¶2622 is made), letters or memoranda, or similar property, in the hands of the creator or other taxpayer described in Code Sec. 1221(a)(3), and (4) U.S. government publications obtained without charge or below the price sold to the general public. (Code Sec. 1231(b)(1); Reg § 1.1231-1(c))[27]

Property held for rent usually is treated as property used in business, but IRS (with the support of some, but not all, courts) denies this status where rental activity is slight.[28]

¶ 2687 Timber cutting treated as sale or exchange—Form T.

A taxpayer may elect to treat the cutting of timber as a sale or exchange qualifying for Section 1231 capital gain-ordinary loss treatment. (Code Sec. 631(a), Code Sec. 1231(b)(2))[29] Taxpayers who elect must file Form T with their returns.[30]

The taxpayer must have owned the timber, or held a contract right to cut it, for more than one year before the timber is cut. (Code Sec. 631(a); Reg § 1.631-1(b)(1)) The timber must be cut for sale or for use in the taxpayer's business. (Reg § 1.631-1)[31]

Once made, the election can be revoked only with IRS's consent (Code Sec. 631(a)) unless it was made for a tax year ending before Oct. 23, 2004 in which case it can be revoked for any later tax year without IRS's consent.[32]

¶ 2688 Timber, coal or U.S. iron ore sold with a retained economic Interest.

A disposition of timber, coal or U.S. iron ore held more than 1-year qualifies for Section 1231 treatment if disposed of under a contract in which the taxpayer retains an economic interest. (Code Sec. 631(b), Code Sec. 631(c), Code Sec. 1231(b)(2); Reg § 1.631-2(a)(1), Reg § 1.631-3(a)(1))[33] For sales of timber, Section 1231 treatment also applies if the owner makes an outright sale of the timber even if no economic interest is retained. (Code Sec. 631(b))[34]

When the disposition qualifies for Section 1231 treatment, no cost depletion deduction

---

26. ¶I-9004; ¶s 12,314.09, 12,314.15; TD ¶223,206
27. ¶I-9007 *et seq.*; ¶12,314 *et seq.*; TD ¶223,208 *et seq.*
28. ¶I-9013; ¶12,314.02 *et seq.*; TD ¶223,213
29. ¶N-6201; ¶12,314; TD ¶271,603
30. ¶N-6213; TD ¶271,604

31. ¶N-6208; ¶6314.01 *et seq.*; TD ¶271,603
32. ¶N-6212.1; ¶6314.02; TD ¶271,604
33. ¶N-7001 *et seq.*; ¶6314; TD ¶223,208
34. ¶N-7001; ¶6314

(¶1980) is allowed. (Reg § 1.611-1(b)(2)) And, for dispositions of coal and iron ore, no percentage depletion deduction is allowed if the maximum tax rate for the year on net capital gain is less than the maximum rate for ordinary income. (Code Sec. 631(c); Reg § 1.611-1(b)(2))[35]

¶ 2689   Advance payments for timber, coal or domestic iron ore.

Advance or minimum royalty payments or other amounts received or accrued before cutting of timber or before the mining of coal or iron ore (disposed of with a retained economic interest) are treated as realized from a sale subject to Section 1231 if the contract of disposal provides that they are to be applied as payment for timber cut later or coal or iron ore mined later. (Reg § 1.631-2(d)(1), Reg § 1.631-3(c)(1)) But if the right to cut or to mine ends or is abandoned before the timber, coal or iron ore that has been paid for is cut or mined, the advance payments for them are ordinary income. (Reg § 1.631-2(d)(2), Reg § 1.631-3(c)(2))

If the taxpayer elects to treat the date of payment as the date of disposal of timber (Code Sec. 631(b); Reg § 1.631-2(b)(1)), Section 1231 applies only if the timber is held for the required period at the time of the advance payment. (Reg § 1.631-2(c)(2)) If the election isn't made, the required holding period is measured as of the time it's cut. (Reg § 1.631-2(d)(1))[36] This election is made by attaching a specified statement to the return (filed not later than the due date, including extensions) for the year payment is received. (Reg § 1.631-2(c))[37]

¶ 2690   Sale of Depreciable Property to Related Parties. ▬▬▬▬▬▬▬▬▬▬▬

Any recognized gain on the sale or exchange of depreciable property is ordinary income if it's made directly or indirectly between related persons.

¶ 2691   Capital gain bar on sales or exchanges of depreciable property.

In a direct or indirect sale or exchange of property between related persons, any gain recognized is treated as ordinary income if that property is, in the hands of the transferee, subject to the Code Sec. 167 allowance for depreciation, or an amortizable Code Sec. 197 intangible asset. (Code Sec. 197(f)(7), Code Sec. 1239(a)) It also applies to property that would be subject to depreciation except that the buyer has elected amortization instead of depreciation (Reg § 1.1239-1(a)), and to patent applications. (Code Sec. 1239(e))[38]

Related persons are:

(1) a person and all entities that are controlled entities with respect to that person (see below) (Code Sec. 1239(b)(1));

(2) a taxpayer and any trust in which the taxpayer or his spouse is a beneficiary (unless the interest is a remote contingent interest) (Code Sec. 1239(b)(2));

(3) an executor of an estate and a beneficiary of the estate (except in the case of a sale or exchange in satisfaction of a pecuniary bequest). (Code Sec. 1239(b)(3))

(4) an employer and any person related to the employer (within the meaning of (1) through (3) above) (Code Sec. 1239(d)(1)); and

(5) a welfare benefit fund controlled directly or indirectly by anyone in (3), above (Code Sec. 1239(d)(2)).[39]

A controlled entity ((l), above) means, with respect to any person:

. . . a corporation more than 50% of the value of the stock of which is owned (directly or indirectly) by or for the person (Code Sec. 1239(c)(1)(A)),

. . . a partnership more than 50% of the capital interest or profits interest in which is owned

---

35. ¶N-7021; ¶6114.013; TD ¶2711,605
36. ¶N-7025 *et seq.*; ¶6314 *et seq.*
37. ¶N-7026

38. ¶I-8702; ¶12,394; TD ¶229,601
39. ¶I-8703 *et seq.*; ¶12,394; TD ¶229,602

(directly or indirectly) by or for the person (Code Sec. 1239(c)(1)(B)), or

... any entity that is a related person to the person under Code Sec. 267(b)(3) (controlled group of corporations), Code Sec. 267(b)(10) (certain related corporations and partnerships), Code Sec. 267(b)(11) (S corporations controlled by the same person) or Code Sec. 267(b)(12) (S corporations and C corporations controlled by the same person). (Code Sec. 1239(c)(1)(C))

And, under Code Sec. 267(c), there is attribution for stock owned by children, grandchildren, ancestors and siblings, as well as by the spouse. (Code Sec. 1239(c)(2))[40]

¶ 2692 Depreciation Recapture.

Two provisions restrict the possibility of converting ordinary income into capital gains by use of depreciation or amortization deductions.

One applies to personal property that is Section 1245 property; the other, to real property that is Section 1250 property. (Code Sec. 1245(a)(3), Code Sec. 1250(c)) Recapture applies only to the extent of gain on a sale or other "disposition" (¶2699) of property. (Code Sec. 1245(a)(1), Code Sec. 1250(a)) Compute recapture on Form 4797.

¶ 2693 What is Section 1245 property?

Section 1245 property includes:

(1) all MACRS property other than residential real property (27.5-year class) and nonresidential real property (39-year class; 31.5-year class if placed in service before May 13, '93);

(2) all ACRS property other than 19-year, 18-year or 15-year real property: (a) that is residential rental property, (b) that is foreign-held realty, (c) with respect to which an optional (straight-line) cost recovery period was elected, or (d) that includes any one of certain categories of subsidized low-income rental housing;

(3) other property subject to the depreciation rules of Code Sec. 167 or the amortization rules of Code Sec. 197 (¶1977) that's personal property, certain real property (not including buildings) and real property to the extent of certain amortization (or Code Sec. 179) deductions taken.[41]

Section 1245 property includes property, other than a building or its structural components, used as an integral part of manufacturing, production or extraction, or for furnishing transportation, communication or other public utility services, and research or storage facilities used in connection with any of these activities. It also includes single purpose agricultural or horticultural structures, and storage facilities (except buildings and their structural components) used in distributing petroleum or any primary product of petroleum. (Code Sec. 1245(a)(3); Reg § 1.1245-3)[42]

Property for which a qualified disaster expense would have been capitalized but for the rules of Code Sec. 198A (see ¶1784) is treated as Section 1245 property for purposes of depreciation recapture. (Code Sec. 198A(d))[43]

¶ 2694 What is Section 1250 property?

All real property subject to depreciation that isn't Section 1245 property is Section 1250 property. (Code Sec. 1250(c)) Thus, Section 1250 property includes:

(1) MACRS residential real property (in the 27.5-year class) and nonresidential real property (in the 39-year class; 31.5-year class if placed in service before May 13, '93).

(2) The types of ACRS real property that aren't Section 1245 property, see ¶2693.

---

40. ¶I-8708; ¶12,394; TD ¶229,605
41. ¶I-10101 *et seq.*; ¶12,454.01; TD ¶223,105

42. ¶I-10101; ¶12,454.01; TD ¶223,105
43. ¶L-5816; ¶198A4.01

(3) The following real property placed in service before '81: (a) depreciable intangible real property, such as a leasehold interest in land, (b) all depreciable buildings and their structural components, and (c) other depreciable real property excluded from the definition of Section 1245 property (¶2693). (Reg § 1.1250-1(e)(3))[44]

¶ 2695   Recapture rules for Section 1245 property.

A gain on the disposition (¶2699) of Section 1245 property is treated as ordinary income to the extent of depreciation or amortization allowed or allowable on the property. (Code Sec. 1245(a))[45] The following deductions are treated as amortization for purposes of the Section 1245 recapture rules: the expense deduction under Code Sec. 179 (¶1941 *et seq.*); the deduction for clean fuel vehicles placed in service before 2006 under Code Sec. 179A; the deductions for refining costs under Code Sec. 179B and Code Sec. 179C (¶1968); the deduction for the cost of energy efficient commercial buildings under Code Sec. 179D (¶1969); the deduction for the costs incurred before 2010 of qualified film and TV productions under Code Sec. 181 (¶1967); qualified architectural and transportation barrier removal expenses under Code Sec. 190 (¶1667); and reforestation expenses under Code Sec. 194 (¶1972). (Code Sec. 1245(a)(2)(C))[46]

The environmental remediation expensing deduction (¶1669) (Code Sec. 198(e)),[47] the commercial revitalization deduction (¶1974) (Code Sec. 1400I(f)(2)),[48] and the amortization of a Section 197 intangible (¶1977) (Code Sec. 197(f)(7)) also are subject to recapture under Code Sec. 1245.[49]

The amount of gain treated as ordinary income on the disposition is limited to the lower of:

(1) the recomputed basis of the property minus the adjusted basis of the property. (Code Sec. 1245(a)(1)(A)) Recomputed basis is the adjusted basis of the property increased by the recapturable depreciation and amortization deductions reflected in the adjusted basis (Code Sec. 1245(a)(2)); or

(2) in the case of a sale, exchange or involuntary conversion, the amount realized minus the adjusted basis of the property; or in the case of any other disposition, the fair market value of the property minus the adjusted basis of the property. (Code Sec. 1245(a)(1)(B))[50]

If a taxpayer disposes of more than one amortizable Code Sec. 197 intangible (¶1977) in a transaction or a series of related transactions, all of the amortizable intangibles are treated as one Code Sec. 1245 property for purposes of the recapture rules. However, this rule does not apply to any such intangible if its adjusted basis exceeds its fair market value. (Code Sec. 1245(b)(8))[1]

¶ 2696   Recapture rules for Section 1250 property.

Part or all of the gain on the sale or other disposition (¶2699) of Section 1250 property may be treated as ordinary income. (Code Sec. 1250(a))[2] But where property was held more than one year, there's no depreciation recapture if it was depreciated via straight line. (Code Sec. 1250(b)) Thus, Section 1250 recapture doesn't apply to residential rental or nonresidential real property depreciated under MACRS. For Section 1250 property held more than one year, the amount of gain treated as ordinary income is the lower of (1) the "applicable percentage" of the portion of the "additional depreciation" (see below) attributable to periods after '75, or (2) in the case of a sale, exchange or involuntary conversion, the excess of the

44. ¶I-10112 *et seq.*; ¶12,504.01; TD ¶223,109
45. ¶I-10200 *et seq.*; ¶12,454; TD ¶223,102
46. ¶I-10204; ¶12,454.05; TD ¶223,103
47. ¶L-6150.3; ¶1984
48. ¶L-12709; ¶14,00I4; TD ¶269,308

49. ¶L-7981.2; ¶1974; TD ¶223,103
50. ¶I-10200; ¶12,454.05; TD ¶223,102
1. ¶I-10219.1; ¶12,454.05; TD ¶223,106.1
2. ¶I-10400 *et seq.*; ¶12,504; TD ¶223,107

amount realized over the adjusted basis, or in the case of any other disposition, the fair market value of the property over its adjusted basis. (Code Sec. 1250(a)(1))[3]

Special rules apply to determine the amount to be recaptured as ordinary income for (a) additional depreciation attributable to periods after '69 and before '76 to determine the amount to be recaptured as ordinary income (Code Sec. 1250(a)(2)), and (b) additional depreciation attributable to periods before '70. (Code Sec. 1250(a)(3))[4]

Additional depreciation is the excess of actual post-'63 depreciation deductions over the amount that would have resulted during the same period had the straight-line method been used for the entire period the property was held. (Code Sec. 1250(b)(1), Code Sec. 1250(b)(3))[5] For additional amounts for corporations, see ¶2697.

The applicable percentage differs depending upon various factors, including whether the property is nonresidential real property, residential real property or low income housing.[6]

For the tax treatment of a noncorporate taxpayer's unrecaptured Code Sec. 1250 gain, see ¶2605.

¶ 2697   Additional 20% recapture on disposition of realty by corporations.

For sales or other dispositions (of both residential and nonresidential property), 20% of the amount by which the gain recapturable if Section 1245 rules applied exceeds the gain recaptured under Section 1250 is treated as ordinary income (to the extent of gain) to a corporation. (Code Sec. 291(a))[7] This rule applies to an S corporation only if it was formerly a C corporation for any of the three immediately preceding tax years. (Code Sec. 1363(b)(4))[8]

¶ 2698   Treatment of basis reduction for investment credit.

In determining the recapturable amount, the reduction of basis for the investment credit is treated as a deduction allowed for depreciation. (Code Sec. 50(c)(4)(A))[9] However, this basis reduction is disregarded in computing straight-line depreciation for purposes of determining "additional depreciation" subject to recapture for Section 1250 property. (Code Sec. 50(c)(4)(B))[10]

¶ 2699   Transactions and events that trigger or escape depreciation recapture.

The following is a list of transactions and events that either trigger or escape depreciation recapture:

* A sale in a sale and leaseback transaction, a sale under a conditional sales contract, and a transfer of title back to the seller, creditor, or new purchaser upon foreclosure of a security interest, triggers recapture, but not a transfer of legal title to a creditor upon creation of a security interest, or a transfer of legal title to a debtor upon termination of a security interest. (Reg § 1.1245-1(a)(3), Reg § 1.1250-1(a)(2)(i))

* Trade-ins, exchanges and involuntary conversions. Section 1245 depreciation not recaptured unless gain is recognized or non-Section 1245 property is acquired. (Code Sec. 1245(b)(4); Reg § 1.1245-4(d)) Section 1250 depreciation not recaptured except where gain is recognized, stock is bought to acquire control of a corporation owning replacement property, or non-Section 1250 property is acquired. (Code Sec. 1250(d)(4); Reg § 1.1250-3(d))

* Conversion to personal use (except for Code Sec. 179 property, see ¶1947) doesn't trigger recapture, but a later sale will.

3. ¶I-10400 *et seq.*; ¶12,504.06; TD ¶223,110
4. ¶I-10402; ¶12,504.06; TD ¶223,110
5. ¶I-10403; ¶12,504.06; TD ¶223,110
6. ¶I-10417 *et seq.*; ¶s 12,394, 12,504.06; TD ¶223,111
7. ¶I-10422 *et seq.*; ¶2914; TD ¶223,108
8. ¶I-10422; ¶2914, 13634.01; TD ¶614,503,
9. ¶I-10204; TD ¶223,103
10. ¶I-10507

- Lease termination or disposition where depreciation was taken by lessee (or sublessee). Generally recaptured. (Reg § 1.1245-2(a)(3)(i))

- Incorporation of a business. Not recaptured except to the extent that gain is otherwise recognized. (Code Sec. 1245(b)(3), Code Sec. 1250(d)(3); Reg § 1.1245-4(c), Reg § 1.1250-3(c))

- Corporate distributions in kind including liquidating distributions. Generally recaptured except in tax-free complete liquidation of a subsidiary with carryover basis (recaptured on disposition by parent-transferee). (Code Sec. 1245(b)(3), Code Sec. 1250(d)(3); Reg § 1.1245-4(c), Reg § 1.1250-3(c))

- Corporate split-ups and reorganizations. Generally not recaptured except to extent that gain is otherwise recognized on transfer of the property. (Code Sec. 1245(b)(3), Code Sec. 1250(d)(3); Reg § 1.1245-4(c), Reg § 1.1250-3(c))

- S corporations. Not recaptured on election or termination of status.

- Partnerships. Recaptured on sale of partnership interest. Not recaptured on contribution to a partnership but may be if property is subject to a liability. (Code Sec. 1245(a), Code Sec. 1245(b)(3), Code Sec. 1250(a), Code Sec. 1250(d)(3); Reg § 1.1245-4(c), Reg § 1.1250-3(c))

- Gifts. Not recaptured, but recapturable depreciation carried over to donee. (Code Sec. 1245(b)(1), Code Sec. 1250(d)(1); Reg § 1.1245-4(a), Reg § 1.1250-3(a))

- Death of owner. Neither recaptured nor carried over (except as provided under the Code Sec. 691 rules (income in respect of a decedent). (Code Sec. 1245(b)(2), Code Sec. 1250(d)(2); Reg § 1.1245-4(b), Reg § 1.1250-3(b))[11]

- Gain realized by an estate or trust from distribution of depreciable property in satisfaction of a fixed dollar bequest or from a distribution in kind where gain or loss is realized by election is recapturable. (Reg § 1.1245-4(b), Reg § 1.1250-3(b))[12]

For the effect of depreciation recapture on installment sales, see ¶2453.

¶ 2700 Special recapture rules for listed property.

A reduction of business use of listed property (¶1948 *et seq.*) from more-than-50% to 50% or less triggers recapture of excess depreciation previously taken. (Code Sec. 280F(b)(2)(A)) "Excess depreciation" means depreciation allowable for years before the first year in which the property wasn't predominantly used in a qualified business use, over the amount of depreciation which would have been allowable for those years if the property hadn't been predominantly used in a qualified business use for the year it was acquired and there had been no Section 179 expense election for the property. (Code Sec. 280F(b)(2)(B))[13]

---

11. ¶I-10002, I-10301 *et seq.*; ¶s 12,454.03, 12,504.01; TD ¶223,114   13. ¶L-10032; ¶280F4; TD ¶267,625
12. ¶C-7154; ¶s 12,454.03, 12,504.01; TD ¶223,114

Chapter 11   Tax Accounting—Inventories

¶ 2800   Accounting Periods.

Each taxpayer must compute taxable income and file a return on the basis of an accounting period called a tax year. An S corporation generally has to use a calendar year as its tax year unless it specially elects to use a fiscal year. So does a personal service corporation. A partnership generally has to use a "majority interest tax year" unless it makes the fiscal year election.

¶ 2801   Tax year.

Taxpayers must compute their taxable income on the basis of their tax year. (Code Sec. 441(a); Reg § 1.441-1(a)) "Tax year" is the taxpayer's annual accounting period (the annual period on the basis of which the taxpayer regularly computes his income in keeping his books) (Code Sec. 441(c)), but only if that's the calendar year or a fiscal year. (Code Sec. 441(b)(1))[1]

The calendar year is the 12-month period ending on Dec. 31. (Code Sec. 441(d)) A taxpayer must use the calendar year, if the taxpayer keeps no books (unless it gets IRS consent to use a fiscal year (Reg § 1.441-1(c)(2))), or has no annual accounting period, or has an annual accounting period that doesn't qualify as a fiscal year (Code Sec. 441(b)(2), Code Sec. 441(g)), or if the taxpayer hasn't established a fiscal year. (Reg § 1.441-1(b)(1)(iv))[2]

A fiscal year is any 12-month period ending on the last day of a month other than December, or the 52-53 week tax year described at ¶2802. (Code Sec. 441(e))[3]

If a return is properly made for a period of less than 12 months (see ¶2804), the tax year is the short tax year for which the return is made. (Code Sec. 441(b)(3))[4]

Certain taxpayers must use a required tax year. (Code Sec. 441(f)(3), Code Sec. 441(f)(4); Reg § 1.441-1(b)(2))

¶ 2802   Tax year of 52-53 weeks.

A 52-53 week tax year varies from 52 to 53 weeks and always ends on the same day of the week. The day chosen must be either the day of the week that last occurs in a calendar month or the day that falls nearest to the end of the calendar month (in which case the last day of the tax year may fall in the next month). (Code Sec. 441(f)(1); Reg § 1.441-2(a)(1)) A taxpayer may elect a 52-53 week tax year if it otherwise satisfies Code Sec. 441 and its regs. (Reg § 1.441-2(a)(3))[5]

Wherever the applicability of any provision of the Code, or filing date, is expressed in terms of tax years beginning, including, or ending with reference to a specified date that's the first or last day of the month, the actual opening and closing dates of 52-53 week years are disregarded. The year is considered to begin on the first day of the calendar month beginning nearest to the first day of that tax year, and to end on the last day of the calendar month ending nearest to the last day of that tax year. (Code Sec. 441(f)(2)(A))[6]

If a pass-through entity or an pass-through owner, or both, use a 52-53-week tax year and the tax years of both end with reference to the same calendar month, then, for purposes of determining the tax year in which pass-through items are taken into account by its owner, the owner's tax is deemed to end on the last day of the pass-through's tax year. (Reg § 1.441-2(e)(1)) Similarly, if the tax year of a personal service corporation (PSC) and an employee-

1. ¶G-1000 *et seq.*; ¶4414; TD ¶431,001
2. ¶s G-1001, G-1003; ¶4414; TD ¶431,001
3. ¶G-1004; ¶4414; TD ¶431,006
4. ¶s G-1001; ¶4414; TD ¶431,001
5. ¶G-1101; ¶4414; TD ¶432,501
6. ¶G-1103; ¶4414; TD ¶432,503

References beginning with a single letter are to paragraphs in RIA's Federal Tax Coordinator 2d and RIA's Analysis of Federal Taxes: Income. Those beginning with numbers are to paragraphs in RIA's United States Tax Reporter. Those beginning with TD are to paragraphs in RIA's Tax Desk.

owner end with reference to the same calendar month, then for purposes of determining the tax year in which an employee-owner takes into account items that are deductible by the PSC and includible in the income of the employee-owner, the employee-owner's tax year is deemed to end on the last day of the PSC's tax year. (Reg § 1.441-2(e)(2))

¶ 2803 Establishing a tax year.

A new taxpayer generally may adopt any tax year that satisfies Code Sec. 441 and its regs, without IRS approval, by filing its first federal income tax return using that tax year. (Reg § 1.441-1(c)(1)) However, a newly formed partnership, S corporation, or personal service corporation that wants to adopt a tax year other than its required tax year, a tax year elected under Code Sec. 444 (¶2813), or a 52-53 week tax year (¶2802) that ends with reference to its required tax year or one elected under Code Sec. 444 must establish a business purpose and get IRS approval. (Reg § 1.441-1(c)(2)) Use Form 1128 following IRS procedures.[7]

If taxpayer's "annual accounting period" (¶2801), as established by the basis on which taxpayer keeps his books, is the calendar year or a fiscal year, his tax year is that annual accounting period. (Code Sec. 441(b)(1), Code Sec. 441(c)) Otherwise, the taxpayer must use the calendar year as his tax year. (Code Sec. 441(b)(2), Code Sec. 441(g))[8]

A new taxpayer using a 52-53 week tax year (¶2802) must file a statement (specified in the regs) with the return for its first 52-53 week tax year. (Reg § 1.441-2(b)(1)(ii))[9]

¶ 2804 Short tax years.

A taxpayer must use a tax "year" of less than 12 months if: (1) the taxpayer isn't in existence for what would otherwise be his full tax year (Code Sec. 443(a)(2));[10] or (2) the taxpayer properly changes his annual accounting period (¶2814). (Code Sec. 443(a)(1))[11] But if the short year arises because of the taxpayer's death, his last return may be filed and the tax paid as if he had lived to the end of his last tax year. (Reg § 1.443-1(a)(2))[12]

For filing requirements for short years, see ¶ 4716 and ¶ 4724.

¶ 2805 Computing tax for a short year.

If the short year results from a change of the taxpayer's annual accounting period, the short period's taxable income must be annualized. (Code Sec. 443(b))

Under the general method of annualization, gross income for the short period (less allowable deductions for the short period and, for individuals, the ratable amount of personal exemptions) is multiplied by 12 (months) and divided by the number of months in the short period. The result is the annualized taxable income on which the tentative tax is computed. The tax due is arrived at by multiplying the tentative tax by the number of months in the short period and dividing by 12. (Code Sec. 443(b)(1); Reg § 1.443-1(b)(1)(i))[13] Special annualization rules apply to the alternative minimum tax. (Code Sec. 443(d))[14]

There are exceptions to the annualization requirements for self-employment tax, accumulated earnings tax, personal holding company tax, undistributed foreign personal holding company income and income of regulated investment companies.[15]

The net operating loss (NOL) deduction can reduce actual income for the short period before computing short period income on an annual basis. Therefore, if the NOL deduction wipes out short period actual income there would be nothing to annualize and therefore no short period taxable income.[16]

---

7. ¶4414; TD ¶432,001
8. ¶G-1051; ¶4414; TD ¶432,001
9. ¶s G-1054, G-1753; ¶4414; TD ¶432,004
10. ¶G-1153; ¶4434; TD ¶431,011
11. ¶G-1155; ¶4434; TD ¶431,011

12. ¶G-1154; ¶4434; TD ¶431,011
13. ¶G-1166; ¶4434; TD ¶431,012
14. ¶A-8119; ¶4434; TD ¶691,018
15. ¶G-1163; ¶4434
16. ¶G-1166; ¶4434; TD ¶431,012

The income is *not* annualized if the short year is caused by the taxpayer not being in existence for a full tax year. (Code Sec. 443(b)) In this case, tax is computed as if the short period were a full year, and individuals need not prorate their personal exemptions. (Reg § 1.443-1(a)(2))[17]

If a taxpayer changes to or from a 52-53 week year, income for the short period must be annualized, with this exception: if the short period is 359 days or more, it is treated as a full tax year, while if it is six days or less it is added to the following tax year. (Reg § 1.443-1(b)(1)(ii))[18]

¶ 2806 Optional look-back method of computing tax for the short period.

The annualizing method at ¶2805 may create a tax hardship for taxpayers who have a disproportionately large amount of taxable income in the short period. To avoid this, taxpayers may use an optional method that computes the tax for the full 12 months starting at the beginning of the short year and prorates the tax according to the amount of income earned in the short period. (Code Sec. 443(b)(2))

The optional method is available only on a claim for credit or refund, filed no later than the due date (including extensions) of taxpayer's return for the first tax year that ends on or after the day that is 12 months after the first day of the short period. (Reg § 1.443-1(b)(2)(v)(a))[19]

¶ 2807 Tax year of sole proprietorship.

A sole proprietorship must use the same tax year as the proprietor. Thus, a calendar year employee who later operates as a sole proprietorship must use the calendar year for the proprietorship unless he gets IRS consent to use a fiscal year.[20]

¶ 2808 Tax years of trusts and estates.

Trusts must use the calendar year, except for trusts exempt from tax under Code Sec. 501(a), wholly charitable trusts described in Code Sec. 4947(a)(1) (Code Sec. 644)[21] and grantor trusts.[22] Estates may adopt either a calendar year or a fiscal year.[23]

¶ 2809 Tax years of foreign sales corporations and DISCs.

Foreign Sales Corporations (FSCs) and Domestic International Sales Corporations (DISCs) must use the tax year of the shareholder (or group of shareholders with the same 12-month tax year) with the highest percentage of voting power. (Code Sec. 441(h)(1))[24]

¶ 2810 Tax year of S corporation.

An S corporation (unless it makes the election at ¶2813, or elects a 52-53 week tax year (¶2802) ending with reference to its required year) must have a "required year," i.e., a calendar year or any other accounting year for which it shows a business purpose satisfactory to IRS; use Form 2553. (Code Sec. 1378; Reg § 1.441-1(b)(2)(i)(L), Reg § 1.441-1(b)(2)(ii)(B), Reg § 1.1378-1(a))[25]

¶ 2811 Tax year of personal service corporation.

The tax year of a personal service corporation (PSC) must be a calendar year unless the corporation makes the election at ¶2813, elects a 52-53 week tax year ending with reference

17. ¶G-1162; ¶4434; TD ¶431,012
18. ¶G-1108; ¶4434
19. ¶G-1170 *et seq.*; ¶4434; TD ¶431,013
20. ¶G-1062; ¶4414; TD ¶432,006
21. ¶G-1400; ¶6454; TD ¶651,009
22. ¶G-1401; ¶6454; TD ¶651,009
23. ¶C-7008; ¶4414; TD ¶661,008
24. ¶O-1726; ¶4414
25. ¶G-1250; ¶13,784; TD ¶433,201

to the calendar year or the year elected under the rules at ¶2813, or can satisfy IRS that there's a business purpose for a different tax year. (Code Sec. 441(i)(1); Reg § 1.441-1(b)(2)(i)(B), Reg § 1.441-3(a))[26]

A PSC is, as defined under the rules permitting IRS to reallocate PSC income and deductions (¶2859), any corporation whose principal activity is the performance of personal services that are substantially performed by employee-owners. But for this purpose PSC doesn't include S corporations, and the term "owner-employee" includes all employees with *any* stock ownership in the corporation. In determining ownership, attribution from a corporation (under Code Sec. 318(a)(2)(C)) is applied if *any* stock is owned by the shareholder in that corporation. (Code Sec. 441(i)(2))[27] Certain independent contractors who own stock in the corporation and perform personal services for or on behalf of it are treated as employees. (Reg § 1.441-3(g)(2))[28]

The performance of personal services is considered the corporation's principal activity if the corporation's compensation cost for a testing period for activities that are considered the performance of personal services exceeds 50% of its total compensation cost for the period. (Reg § 1.441-3(e)(1)) The testing period is the preceding tax year (or, for a corporation's first tax year, the period beginning the first day of the first tax year and ending the last day of that tax year or, if earlier, the last day of the calendar year in which that tax year began). (Reg § 1.441-3(c)(2)) Personal services are substantially performed by employee-owners if during the testing period more than 20% of the corporation's compensation cost (excluding qualified plan or SEP contributions) attributable to the performance of personal services is attributable to personal services performed by employee-owners. (Reg § 1.441-3(f)), Reg § 1.441-3(e)(2)(ii))[29]

¶ 2812   Tax year of partnership—"majority interest tax year."

Unless the partnership makes the election at ¶2813, or can satisfy IRS that there's a business purpose for a different tax year (Code Sec. 706(b)(1)(C))[30] a partnership must adopt:

(1) the "majority interest tax year" (Code Sec. 706(b)(1)(B)(i))—the tax year of one or more of the partners having an aggregate interest in partnership profits and capital of more than 50% on each testing day (the first day of the partnership's tax year as otherwise determined, or days prescribed by IRS) (Code Sec. 706(b)(4)(A));

(2) the tax year of all its principal (5%-or-more) partners, if there's no majority interest tax year (Code Sec. 706(b)(1)(B)(ii));

(3) the "least-aggregate-deferral" year, if there's no majority interest tax year and the principal partners don't have the same tax year. (Code Sec. 706(b)(1)(B)(iii); Reg § 1.706-1(b)(2)(i)(C))[31]

A partnership may have a tax year other than its required year if it makes an election under Code Sec. 444 (¶2813), elects to use a 52-53-week tax year (¶2802) that ends with reference to its required year or a tax year elected under Code Sec. 444, or establishes a business purpose for it and gets IRS approval. (Reg § 1.706-1(b)(2)(ii))

A partnership that's required to change to a majority-interest tax year isn't required to change to another tax year for either of the two tax years following the year of change. (Code Sec. 706(b)(4)(B))[32]

A partnership tax year ends as dictated by the accounting period selected or required, except that it closes earlier: (1) for a partner who sells his entire interest or whose interest is completely liquidated (Code Sec. 706(c); (Reg § 1.706-1(c)(2)(i)), and (2) with respect to all its partners on the date the partnership terminates for tax purposes. (Reg § 1.706-1(c)(1))[33]

---

26. ¶G-1300; ¶4414; TD ¶433,401
27. ¶G-1302; ¶4414; TD ¶433,403
28. ¶G-1306; ¶4414
29. ¶G-1303; ¶4414

30. ¶G-1200 *et seq.*; ¶7064.01; TD ¶433,002
31. ¶G-1200 *et seq.*; ¶7064.01; TD ¶433,001
32. ¶G-1201; ¶7064.01
33. ¶G-1224, G-1225; ¶7064.02; TD ¶433,024

¶ 2813   Section 444 election of tax year other than required tax year—Form 8716; Form 8752; Form 1120, Schedule H.

An S corporation, personal service corporation (PSC), or partnership may elect (on Form 8716) to have a tax year other than the required tax year (Code Sec. 444(a)), but only if the deferral period (number of months between beginning of elected fiscal tax year and following Dec. 31) for the tax year elected isn't longer than three months. (Code Sec. 444(b)(1); Reg § 1.444-1T(b))[34]

A partnership or S corporation that elects has to make a "required payment" (report on Form 8752) that approximates the tax the partners or S corporation shareholders would have paid on short-period income if the election hadn't been made. (Code Sec. 7519; Reg § 1.444-3T)[35]

A PSC that elects a fiscal tax year but doesn't make required minimum distributions to its employee-owners before the end of the calendar year must postpone part or all of its corresponding deduction to its next fiscal tax year. (Code Sec. 280H) To figure the required minimum distribution and maximum deductible amount, use Form 1120, Schedule H.[36]

¶ 2814   How to change accounting periods—Form 1128.

A taxpayer must get prior IRS approval to change accounting periods unless the change is authorized by the Code or one of those listed at ¶2815. (Reg § 1.441-1(e), Reg § 1.442-1(a))[37]

IRS will approve a request for a change in tax years only if the taxpayer establishes a substantial business purpose for the change,[38] and agrees to any terms, conditions or adjustments required to effect the change, including any that IRS feels are necessary to avoid a substantial distortion of the taxpayer's income as a result of the change. (Reg § 1.442-1(b)(1))[39]

To request IRS approval, file Form 1128 within the time and in the manner as provided in IRS administrative procedures. (Reg § 1.442-1(b)(1), Reg § 1.442-1(b)(3))[40] Fiscal year individuals must follow an exclusive procedure to change to a calendar year.[41]

If a taxpayer changed its annual accounting period within 48 months before the last month of the requested tax year, a copy of the application for the previous change, the ruling letter, and any other related correspondence from IRS, must be attached to the application.[42]

Limitations apply to the carryback of certain NOLs and capital losses generated in the short period necessary to effect a change of tax year.[43]

¶ 2815   "No prior approval needed" changes of accounting period.

A taxpayer that has adopted a tax year generally must continue to use it unless it obtains IRS approval to change or is otherwise authorized to change without the IRS approval under the Code (e.g., Code Sec. 444, ¶2813) or regs. (Reg § 1.442-1(a))[44] A taxpayer may change his annual accounting period without IRS approval, or with "automatic" IRS approval, where the taxpayer:

... changes to a 52-53 week tax year that ends with reference to the same calendar month as the month ending his previous tax year (Reg § 1.441-2(b)(2));[45]

... is an individual who marries a person with a different tax year (Reg § 1.442-1(d)(1));[46]

34. ¶G-1500 *et seq.*; ¶4444; TD ¶434,003
35. ¶s G-1500, G-1550; ¶75,194; TD ¶434,012
36. ¶G-1600; ¶280H4; TD ¶434,014
37. ¶G-1800; ¶4424; TD ¶435,000
38. ¶G-1803 *et seq.*; ¶4424; TD ¶435,015
39. ¶G-1812 *et seq.*; ¶4424
40. ¶G-1701.1; ¶4424; TD ¶435,002
41. ¶G-1726; ¶4424; TD ¶436,001
42. ¶G-1882
43. ¶G-1827 *et seq.*; ¶4424; TD ¶439,027
44. ¶G-1701; ¶s 4424, 7064.01; TD ¶435,001
45. ¶G-1101; ¶4414; TD ¶432,501
46. ¶G-1708; ¶4424; TD ¶435,013

. . . is an individual with a fiscal year tax year who changes to a calendar year tax year;[47]

. . . is a partnership changing its tax year to meet the tests described at ¶2812;[48]

. . . is a C corporation that meets certain tests;[49]

. . . is an S corporation changing its tax year to meet the tests described at ¶2810;[50]

. . . is a personal service corporation changing to a calendar year or a 52-53 week tax year ending with reference to a calendar year; (Reg § 1.441-3(b)(2))[1]

. . . is a subsidiary corporation required to change its tax year to that of members of its affiliated group that file a consolidated return. (Reg § 1.442-1(c))

¶ 2816   Accounting Methods. ▀▀▀▀▀▀▀▀▀▀▀▀▀▀▀▀▀▀▀▀▀▀▀▀▀▀▀

Methods of tax accounting are the methods and systems by which taxpayers determine the amount of their income, gains, losses, deductions and credits, as well as the time when those items must be realized and recognized. Various methods of tax accounting are permissible, but each must be used consistently, and each must clearly reflect income.

¶ 2817   Establishing a method of accounting.

Because a taxpayer's book accounting method determines his accounting method, a taxpayer establishes a tax accounting method by setting up books, keeping accounts, and preparing income tax returns under any of the permissible methods. The method first used in accounting for business income and deductions in connection with each trade or business, as evidenced in the taxpayer's income tax return in which the income or deductions are first reported, must be followed consistently after that. (Reg § 1.446-1(d)(1))[2] The requirement to maintain books and records can be met by using certain electronic storage systems.[3]

A taxpayer may use one method of accounting to keep personal books and another to keep the books for his trade or business. But the two must be strictly separated. (Reg § 1.446-1(c)(1)(iv)(b))

A taxpayer whose only income is wages doesn't have to keep formal books in order to establish an accounting method, but may establish a method of accounting by means of tax returns (or copies) or other records. (Reg § 1.446-1(b)(2))[4]

A new taxpayer may adopt a method of accounting in connection with filing the first income tax return. An existing taxpayer entering into a business that's separate and distinct from any trade or business that the taxpayer previously carried on may adopt a method of accounting for the separate and distinct business in connection with filing the first tax return reporting income from the business. (Reg § 1.446-1(e)(1))[5]

Use of different accounting methods isn't permitted if there's a creation or shifting of profits or losses between the taxpayer's various trades or businesses (e.g., by using inventory adjustments, sales, purchases or expenses, and this results in a distortion of the taxpayer's income). (Reg § 1.446-1(d)(3))[6]

Taxpayers may use any combination of the cash, accrual, and specifically permitted special methods of accounting if the combination clearly reflects income and is consistently used. (Reg § 1.446-1(c)(1)(iv))[7]

---

47. ¶G-1725; ¶4424; TD ¶436,001
48. ¶G-1222; ¶4424; TD ¶433,020
49. ¶G-1800 *et seq.*; ¶4424; TD ¶435,008
50. ¶G-1250.1; ¶13,784; TD ¶433,201
1. ¶G-1301; ¶4424; TD ¶433,402
2. ¶G-2051; ¶4464.01; TD ¶440,518

3. ¶G-2019; ¶60,014; TD ¶440,509 *et seq.*
4. ¶G-2051; TD ¶440,518
5. ¶G-2051; ¶4464.01; TD ¶440,518
6. ¶G-2052; ¶4464.01; TD ¶440,803
7. ¶G-2003; ¶4464.09; TD ¶440,802

¶ 2818   Limits on choice of accounting methods.

The accrual method is mandatory for purchases and sales (unless IRS consents to a change) where inventories must be used. (Reg § 1.446-1(c)(2)(i)) Inventories must be used where the production, purchase or sale of merchandise is an income-producing factor. (Reg § 1.446-1(a)(4)(i))[8] However, exceptions apply for certain small businesses:

- *$1 million or less average gross receipts.* Taxpayers (other than tax shelters) with 3-year average annual gross receipts of $1 million or less do not have to account for inventories or use an accrual method of accounting. Instead they may treat merchandise inventory in the same way that cash method taxpayers must treat material or supplies that are not incidental (under Reg § 1.162-3). Generally, a taxpayer has average annual gross receipts of $1 million or less if for each earlier tax year, its (or its predecessor's) average annual gross receipts for the 3-tax-year period ending with the applicable prior tax year does not exceed $1 million (using the method of accounting actually used for federal tax purposes).[9]

- *More than $1 million but not more than $10 million average gross receipts.* Qualifying small businesses with 3-year average annual gross receipts of more than $1,000,000 but not more than $10,000,000 that are not prohibited from using the cash method under Code Sec. 448 (see below) and otherwise would have to keep inventories and use accrual accounting may, instead, use the cash method for an eligible trade or business. Generally, a taxpayer has average annual gross receipts of $10 million or less if, for each prior tax year ending after Dec. 30, 2000, its average annual gross receipts for the 3-tax-year period ending with the applicable prior tax year does not exceed $10 million. Qualifying small businesses that may use the cash method for all of their trades and businesses are: (1) businesses whose principal business activity for the immediately preceding tax year is other than mining, manufacturing, wholesale trade, retail trade, or information industries; (2) service providers, including those providing property incident to those services; and (3) fabricators or modifiers of tangible personal property on demand in accordance with customer design or specifications.[10]

C corporations (other than qualified personal service corporations), and partnerships with a C corporation (other than a qualified personal service corporation) as a partner, with average annual gross receipts of more than $5 million for any prior 3-tax-year period (or the period of its existence, if less) can't use the cash method. Tax shelters can't use the cash method in any event. (Code Sec. 448(a))[11] The limitation on the cash method doesn't apply to farming businesses (except tax shelters) (Code Sec. 448(b)(1)), but for special farm accounting rules, see ¶4505 *et seq.*[12] For purposes of these restrictions, an accounting method that records some but not all items on the cash method (i.e., a hybrid method) is treated as the cash method of accounting. (Reg § 1.448-1T(a)(4))[13] Tax-exempt trusts are treated as C corporations with respect to unrelated trade or business income. (Code Sec. 448(d)(6))[14]

¶ 2819   The Cash Method of Accounting. ▬▬▬▬▬▬▬▬▬▬▬▬▬

Under the cash method, gross income includes cash or property actually or constructively received during the tax year. Deductions are usually taken in the year cash or property is actually paid or transferred. It doesn't matter when the income was earned, or when the expense was incurred.

---

8. ¶G-5000; ¶4464.07; TD ¶440,827
9. ¶G-5005A, ¶G-5005.3; ¶4714.10; TD ¶450,508
10. ¶G-5005.4; ¶4714.15
11. ¶G-2054; ¶4484; TD ¶440,806

12. ¶G-2057; ¶s 614.053, 4474; TD ¶440,814
13. ¶G-2054; ¶4484; TD ¶440,806
14. ¶G-2055; ¶4484; TD ¶440,806

¶ 2820   Cash basis accounting.

Under the cash basis method of accounting, income is reported when cash or property is actually or constructively received (¶2822), and deductions are taken in the year cash or property is paid or transferred.[15]

For income a taxpayer receives under a claim of right, see ¶1204. For restrictions on use of the cash method by certain taxpayers, see ¶2818; for exceptions to those restrictions for small businesses, see ¶2818.

¶ 2821   When is a check income?

A check issued by a solvent payor is income when received by a cash basis payee, unless there's a restriction on the payee's right to cash the check.[16] Receipt of a check by an agent is considered receipt by the principal.[17]

¶ 2822   Constructive receipt of income.

Income not actually received is constructively received and reportable if it's within the taxpayer's control. Cash basis taxpayers must report money unconditionally subject to their demand as income, even if they haven't received it.[18] There's no constructive receipt if the amount is available only on surrender of a valuable right,[19] or if there are substantial limits on the right to receive it. (Reg § 1.451-2(a))[20]

¶ 2823   Timing of deductions under the cash method.

Cash method taxpayers generally take deductions (if otherwise allowable) in the year the items are paid. (Reg § 1.461-1(a)(1))[21] There's no constructive payment doctrine.[22]

Where an expense (e.g., rent or an insurance premium) relates to a period covering more than 12 months, IRS and most courts agree that the deduction must be spread over the period to which the expense applies.[23] For an exception for points paid on a home mortgage, see ¶1746. For deduction of prepaid taxes, see ¶1767.

A check is payment when delivered, not when cashed, if it's honored when it's first presented for payment.[24]

¶ 2824   The Accrual Method of Accounting. ▄▄▄▄▄▄▄▄▄▄▄▄

Under the accrual method, income is reported in the tax year in which the right to the income becomes fixed and the amount of the income can be determined with reasonable accuracy. Deductions are claimed in the period in which all events have occurred that determine the fact of the liability and the amount of the liability can be determined with reasonable accuracy.

¶ 2825   Accrual basis accounting.

Income accrues and must be reported in the year all events have occurred that determine taxpayer's right to receive it (¶2832), and the amount can be determined with reasonable accuracy (Reg § 1.451-1(a)), even if it's received in a later year. That is, the right to receive the income must not be contingent on a future event; the amount must be reasonably susceptible of accurate estimate; and there must be a reasonable expectation that it will be received

---

15. ¶G-2410 *et seq.*; ¶s 4464.05, 4514.003; TD ¶441,001
16. ¶G-2415; ¶s 4514.003, 4514.004; TD ¶441,003
17. ¶G-2419; TD ¶441,002
18. ¶G-2424; ¶4514.036 *et seq.*; TD ¶441,005
19. ¶G-2426; ¶4514.036; TD ¶441,007

20. ¶G-2425; ¶4514.036; TD ¶441,006
21. ¶G-2436 *et seq.*; ¶4614.01; TD ¶441,401
22. ¶G-2443; TD ¶441,409
23. ¶s L-3526 *et seq.*, L-6616 *et seq.*; ¶1624.081; TD ¶441,410
24. ¶G-2438; ¶4614.02; TD ¶441,404

in due course.[25]

Accrual basis taxpayers do not need to accrue income from the performance of services that, based on their experience, will not be collected if, among other things, interest isn't charged on the debt and there is no penalty for late payment. This "nonaccrual experience method" is available only for: (1) amounts owing for services in the fields of health, law, engineering, architecture, accounting, actuarial science, performing arts, or consulting, or (2) other services, if the taxpayer's three-year average annual gross receipts doesn't exceed $5 million. Uncollectible amounts may be determined using specified safe-harbor methods. (Code Sec. 448(d)(5)) A taxpayer's nonaccrual experience method must be tested against actual experience unless he has adopted one of the five safe harbor methods in the regs. (Reg § 1.448-2(d))[26]

¶ 2826 Contingent rights to income.

Where the right to income is contingent on a future event, an accrual basis taxpayer doesn't have to recognize the income until that event occurs.[27]

Advance payments to a retailer under which it agreed to purchase specified amounts from its supplier were held by a court to be income on receipt. But another court found similar cash advances by a wholesaler to a retailer in exchange for a volume purchase commitment not includible on receipt; they were contingent on the purchases being made. Generally adopting the latter approach, IRS allows taxpayers to adopt an advance trade discount method of accounting in which advance trade discounts, aren't recognized as income on receipt by accrual method taxpayers with inventories but instead are taken into account in the amount and manner that the taxpayer accounts for the discount in its financial statements.[28]

Where litigation is involved and liability to the taxpayer is admitted, the income must be recognized if the taxpayer can accurately estimate the amount of recovery.[29] But if liability isn't admitted, the income accrues when the litigation is concluded or settlement reached, whichever is earlier.[30] An offer in compromise is income when the dispute is settled or the offer is unconditionally accepted.[31]

¶ 2827 Income accrual for disputed liability for goods.

If an accrual method taxpayer overbills a customer due to clerical error and the customer discovers the error and, in the following year, disputes its liability, gross income accrues in the year of sale for the correct amount. An accrual method taxpayer does not accrue income in the year of sale if, during that year, the customer disputes its liability because incorrect goods were shipped. However, income does accrue in the year of sale if excess quantities of goods are shipped and the customer agrees to pay for them.[32]

¶ 2828 Dealers' reserves.

Dealers commonly discount customers' notes with a finance company that keeps a portion of the amount due the dealer as security against possible default by the customer. A dealer that uses the accrual method must include the full amount of the discount price, undiminished by the portion retained by the finance company—the "dealer reserve," in income as soon as the notes are sold to the finance company. This is so even if the dealer assigned the notes to the finance company "without recourse." [33]

---

25. ¶G-2471; ¶4514.012; TD ¶441,701
26. ¶G-2501 *et seq.*; ¶4514.023 *et seq.*; TD ¶441,707
27. ¶s G-2484, G-2485; ¶s 4514.011, 4514.012; TD ¶441,703
28. ¶G-2483
29. ¶G-2506; ¶s 4514.021, 4514.055; TD ¶441,704

30. ¶G-2506; ¶4514.055; TD ¶441,704
31. ¶s G-2506, G-2507; ¶4514.058
32. ¶G-2511.1
33. ¶G-2513; ¶4514.017; TD ¶441,702

¶ 2829   Deferral method for certain advance payments.

Under the deferral method of accounting for advance payments, accrual basis taxpayers can defer to the next succeeding tax year the inclusion in gross income of specified advance payments to the extent the advance payments are not recognized in revenues (or, in certain cases, are not earned) in the tax year of receipt. Except for certain short tax years of less than 93 days, deferral to a tax year later than the next succeeding tax year isn't allowed. Alternately, taxpayer, under the full inclusion method of accounting for advance payments, can include the full amount of advance payments in gross income in the tax year of receipt, whether or not the taxpayer earns the full amount of advance payments in that tax year.[34]

An advance payment is eligible for the deferral method if:

(A) including the payment in income for the tax year of receipt generally is a permitted method of accounting for tax purposes (without regard to the revenue procedure authorizing the deferral method));

(B) taxpayer recognizes the payment (partially or completely) in revenues in its applicable financial statement for a later tax year (or, if doesn't have one, it earns the payment, partially or completely, in a later tax year); and

(C) the payment is for: services; sale of goods (other than goods for which the taxpayer uses the deferral method of Reg § 1.451-5(b)(1)(ii), see ¶2830); use (including by license or lease) of intellectual property; occupancy or use of property ancillary to the provision of services; sale, lease, or license of computer software; guaranty or warranty contracts ancillary to the preceding items; subscriptions (other than those for which an election under Code Sec. 455 is in effect), whether or not provided in a tangible or intangible format; organization membership (other than those for which an election under Code Sec. 456 is in effect); or any combination of the preceding items.

illustration: Accrual method, calendar year C Corp sells and repairs TVs. On July 1, 2010, C receives an advance payment for a 2-year contract under which it will repair or replace broken parts in a customer's TV. In its applicable financial statement, C recognizes ¼ of the payment in revenues for 2010, ½ in revenues for 2011, and ¼ in revenues for 2012. Under the deferral method, C includes ¼ of the payment in gross income for 2010 and the remaining ¾ of the payment in gross income for 2011.

observation: Given the deferral possibilities outlined above, cash-basis service providers who bill in advance should consider switching to the accrual method. The benefits of deferring reporting a portion of cash receipts for one year (on an ongoing basis, if applicable), should be compared with the costs and effort of making the accounting method change.

Payments ineligible for the deferral method include rent (unless it's for the use of intellectual property, occupancy or use of property ancillary to the provision of services, or software) and payments for financial instruments (e.g., debt instruments, letters of credit). (Rev Proc 2004-34, 2004-1 CB 991, as modified)[35]

¶ 2830   Advance payments received for merchandise or construction.

Advance merchandise payments and advance payments under long-term construction contracts are reported by accrual method taxpayers when the income is properly accruable under their method of accounting.[36] But that method must be used for all tax reporting and for credit purposes. (Reg § 1.451-5(b))[37]

An accrual basis taxpayer or a taxpayer using one of the long-term contract methods (¶2848 *et seq.*) can defer reporting an advance payment received under an agreement for the sale or

34. ¶G-2548; ¶4514.191; TD ¶441,712
35. ¶G-2548; ¶4514.191; TD ¶441,712
36. ¶G-2592 *et seq.*; ¶s 4514.121 *et seq.*, 4514.191; TD ¶441,715
37. ¶G-2595; TD ¶441,715

other disposition in a future tax year of goods held primarily for sale to customers, or for the building, installing, constructing or manufacturing of items, where the work isn't completed in the year the advance payment is received. (Reg § 1.451-5(a)(1)) Deferral also applies to advance payments for services to be performed under the agreement as an integral part of the above activities, and for gift certificates. (Reg § 1.451-5(a)(2))[38] Amounts due and payable under the contract are treated as advance payments received. (Reg § 1.451-5(a))[39]

There's a limited deferral for certain inventoriable goods. Where a payment for goods is received several years before they are delivered, taxpayer can postpone reporting the advance payments for one year past the year total advance payments first equal or exceed the anticipated cost of the goods. Thereafter, all prepayments received are reported and actual or expected costs deducted. (Reg § 1.451-5(c))[40] A taxpayer who defers reporting advance payments for merchandise must attach an annual information schedule to its tax return for each year. (Reg § 1.451-5(d))[41]

Use Form 3115 (¶2840) to get IRS consent to switch to deferral. (Reg § 1.451-5(e))[42]

¶ 2831 Advance payments or security deposits.

Amounts received as security aren't taxable until used. A deposit that guarantees the customer's payment of amounts owed to the creditor isn't a deposit but an advance payment includible in income (unless deferred, see ¶2829 and ¶2830), while a deposit securing someone's property is a true security deposit and not an advance payment.[43]

¶ 2832 Timing of expense deductions—all-events test.

Expenses are deductible under the accrual method in the period in which: (1) all events have occurred that determine the fact of the liability; (2) the amount of the liability can be determined with reasonable accuracy; and (3) economic performance (¶2833) has occurred. (Code Sec. 461(h)(4); Reg § 1.461-1(a)(2)) The fact of a liability—generally, the earlier of the event fixing the liability (e.g., the required performance) or when payment is due—isn't established by executing a contract for services to be provided in the future. A reasonable estimate of the liability must be accrued for the tax year in which it was incurred. If there is a difference between the estimate and the amount finally determined, the difference must be added to or deducted from income when the final determination is made.[44] But an automobile company couldn't deduct its anticipated warranty costs under the accrual method based on estimates; until a claim had been filed under the warranty, liability for it remained contingent.[45]

Where the accrual doesn't involve a current expense, but results in the creation of an asset having a useful life extending substantially beyond the end of the tax year, the deduction must be taken as depreciation, amortization or similar deduction. (Reg § 1.461-1(a)(2))[46]

An accrual basis taxpayer may deduct a properly accrued expense, regardless of whether he has actually paid that expense.[47]

¶ 2833 Economic performance.

Accrual basis taxpayers won't be considered to have met the all-events test (¶2832), until economic performance has occurred. (Code Sec. 461(h))[48] Economic performance occurs when the property or service to which the accrual relates is actually provided or used. (Code Sec. 461(h)(2)(A))[49] A taxpayer is allowed to treat property or services as provided when he

---

38. ¶s G-2592, G-2594; TD ¶441,715
39. ¶G-2599; ¶4514.121 *et seq.*; TD ¶441,715
40. ¶G-2596; ¶4514.166; TD ¶441,717
41. ¶G-2597; TD ¶441,718
42. ¶G-2598; TD ¶441,719
43. ¶J-1435 *et seq.*; ¶s 4514.193, 4514.194; TD ¶441,711

44. ¶G-2620 *et seq.*; ¶4614.15; TD ¶442,000
45. ¶G-2620 *et seq.*; ¶4614.15; TD ¶442,000
46. ¶G-2620; ¶4614.15; TD ¶442,001
47. ¶G-2620; ¶4614.15; TD ¶442,000
48. ¶G-2653; ¶4614.15; TD ¶442,012
49. ¶G-2656; ¶4614.15; TD ¶442,013

pays for them, but only if he can reasonably expect the property or services to be provided by the other person within 3 ½ months after the payment is made. (Reg § 1.461-4(d)(6)(ii))[50]

Certain "recurring" expenditures may be treated as incurred in the year the all events test is otherwise met, even though economic performance doesn't occur until the following year. This applies if:

(1) economic performance occurs on or before the date taxpayer files a timely (including extensions) return for the tax year the expense is accrued or, if shorter, 8 ½ months after the close of that year; and

(2) the item is recurring and taxpayer consistently treats items of that kind as incurred in the tax year the all-events test (not including the economic performance test) is met; and

(3) the item is either not a material item or its accrual in the year before economic performance results in a more proper match against income than would be achieved by accruing it in the year of economic performance. (Code Sec. 461(h)(3)(A); Reg § 1.461-5(b))[1]

The recurring item exception is allowed for payroll taxes on compensation and, under a safe harbor, for bonuses and vacation pay.[2] A taxpayer can adopt the recurring item exception as part of its method of accounting for any type of income for the first tax year that type of item is incurred. (Reg § 1.461-5(d)(1)) Tax shelters can't use the recurring item exception. (Code Sec. 461(i)(1); Reg § 1.461-5(c))[3]

The above 3 ½ month rule and 8 ½ month recurring item exception apply only to property or services completely provided within that period; a prorated deduction isn't allowed where all services to be performed aren't provided within that period.

¶ 2834   Accruing contested liability.

An otherwise deductible expense isn't allowable, as long as the taxpayer denies and contests the liability, until the contest is resolved by agreement or final court decision.[4] However, a deduction is allowed in the year of transfer (payment) where:

(1) the taxpayer contests an asserted liability;

(2) the taxpayer transfers money or other property to satisfy the liability;

(3) the contest with respect to the asserted liability exists after the transfer; and

(4) but for the contest, a deduction would be allowed for the tax year of the transfer (or an earlier year). (Code Sec. 461(f)) The contest need not involve court proceedings.[5]

Except as provided under Code Sec. 468B (¶2835), economic performance does not occur when a taxpayer transfers money or property to a trust, escrow account, or court to provide for the satisfaction of a contested workers compensation, tort, or a liability that arises out of a breach of contract or violation of law and requires a payment or a series of payments to another person unless the trust, escrow account, or court is the claimant, or the taxpayer's payment discharges the taxpayer's liability to the claimant. (Reg § 1.461-2(e)(2)(ii))[6]

¶ 2835   Accrual basis taxpayer's payments for tort liabilities.

If the liability of a taxpayer requires a payment to another person that arises out of a tort, "economic performance" (¶2833) occurs as the payments are made. (Code Sec. 461(h)(2)(C))[7] A qualified payment to a court-ordered or designated settlement fund that extinguishes a taxpayer's tort liability is economic performance for the liability as the payment is made. The present or future claims against the taxpayer must arise out of personal injury, death or

---

50. ¶G-2656; ¶4614.15; TD ¶442,014
1. ¶G-2686; ¶4614.15; TD ¶442,035
2. ¶K-4302.1; ¶4614.17; TD ¶442,606
3. ¶G-2458; ¶4614.15; TD ¶442,035

4. ¶G-2643; ¶s 4614.56, 4614.59; TD ¶442,006
5. ¶G-2645; ¶s 4614.56, 4614.59; TD ¶442,007
6. ¶G-2645; ¶4614.56; TD ¶442,007
7. ¶G-2736; ¶4614.15; TD ¶442,019

property damage. (Code Sec. 468B)[8]

¶ 2836 Accrual basis taxpayer's payables to related cash basis taxpayer.

An accrual basis taxpayer can deduct expenses and interest owed to a related cash basis person only when payment is made and the amount involved is includible in the gross income of the cash basis payee. (Code Sec. 267(a)(2)) That is, an accrual basis taxpayer is treated as on the cash method for purposes of deducting amounts owed to a related cash basis person.[9]

The rule applies in general to all deductible expenses if the timing of the deduction depends on the taxpayer's method of accounting or on electing to expense the item. But it doesn't apply to defer the deduction of otherwise deductible original issue discount or below-market loan interest. (Reg § 1.267(a)-2T(b), Q&A-2) Nor does it apply to defer the deduction of otherwise deductible depreciation, or amortization, except as to amounts owed to a related person for interest, rent or for the performance or nonperformance of services (which amount the payor capitalized or treated as a deferred expense). (Reg § 1.267(a)-2T(b), Q&A-4)[10]

The above rule barring an accrual method corporation from deducting unpaid accrued interest on a loan made to the company from its cash-basis owner, continues to apply after the loan is sold by the owner to an unrelated third-party. Interest that accrued in years before the sale cannot be deducted by the corporation until the unrelated party includes it in income. However, interest that accrues in the year of the sale can be deducted before it is paid.[11]

¶ 2837 Changes of Accounting Methods. ▬▬▬▬▬▬▬▬▬▬▬▬▬▬

Usually, taxpayers may change their methods of accounting only with IRS consent, and only on IRS-imposed terms. However, automatic consent is available in certain circumstances where IRS-prescribed procedures are followed.

¶ 2838 IRS permission to change method of accounting.

Generally, once a taxpayer has adopted an accounting method, he must continue to use it until: IRS requires him to change the method, or he requests, and gets, IRS permission to change. (Code Sec. 446(e); Reg § 1.446-1(e)(2)) This is so even if the taxpayer has been using an incorrect method, or a method that doesn't clearly reflect income.[12] Taxpayers can't, without IRS consent, retroactively change from an erroneous to a permissible accounting method by filing amended returns, even if the time for amending the return for the first year in which the erroneous method was used hasn't expired.[13]

Taxpayers under examination[14] or before an appeals office[15] or federal court[16] may request prospective accounting method changes in certain circumstances.

For automatic consent procedures for certain accounting method changes, see ¶2845.

For changes to inventory methods, see ¶2881.

¶ 2839 What is a change in accounting method?

A change in accounting method is a change of the taxpayer's overall method of accounting or a change in the treatment of a material item of income or expense. Changes in overall methods of accounting include changes:

... from the cash to accrual basis, or vice-versa;

... from the long-term contract method to the cash or accrual method, or vice-versa;

... from one basis of inventory valuation to another;

8. ¶G-2788 et seq.; ¶468B4; TD ¶442,025
9. ¶G-2700 et seq.; ¶2674; TD ¶442,027
10. ¶G-2701 et seq.; ¶2674; TD ¶442,028
11. ¶G-2701
12. ¶G-2201; ¶4464; TD ¶442,601

13. ¶G-2201; ¶s 4464.21, 4464.22; TD ¶442,601
14. ¶G-2237; ¶4464.22; TD ¶442,605
15. ¶G-2256.1; ¶4464.22; TD ¶442,605
16. ¶G-2257.1; ¶4464.22; TD ¶442,605

. . . to or from a specialized basis, e.g., the crop basis. (Reg § 1.446-1(e)(2)(ii))[17]

A material item is any item that involves the proper time for the inclusion of the item in income or the taking of a deduction. It doesn't include corrections of mathematical or posting errors, or errors in computing tax liability. (Reg § 1.446-1(e)(2)(ii))[18]

Depreciation changes that aren't accounting method changes include: adjustments in the useful life of a depreciable or amortizable asset for which depreciation is determined under Code Sec. 167 (other than under current (or former) Code Sec. 168, Code Sec. 1400I, and Code Sec. 1400L); changes in computing depreciation or amortization allowances in the tax year in which the use of an asset changes in the hands of the same taxpayer; changes in depreciation caused by certain revocations of elections and late elections; and changes in the placed-in service date. (Reg § 1.446-1(e)(2)(ii), Reg § 1.167(e)-1(a)(2))

However, most changes in computing depreciation (or amortization) are treated as accounting method changes. Changes that are accounting method changes include changes: in depreciation or amortization methods, recovery periods or conventions, e.g., half-year to midquarter (but a switch from 200% or 150% declining balance to straight line is allowable without IRS's consent in the first tax year in which it produces a higher allowance); from regular MACRS to the alternative depreciation system; in claiming bonus first-year depreciation without electing; from treating property as nondepreciable or nonamortizable to depreciable or amortizable (or vice versa); and from depreciating or amortizing an item to deducting it as an expense (or vice versa). (Reg § 1.167(e)-1(a)(1), Reg § 1.446-1(e)(2)(ii))[19]

¶ 2840 Applying for a change in accounting method—Form 3115.

An application for change generally must be filed with IRS on the latest version of Form 3115 by the end of the tax year of the change. (Under transition rules, IRS also accepted pre-revised Form 3115 (i.e., pre-Dec. 2009 version) before May 31, 2010, unless IRS guidance specified the new version.) (Reg § 1.446-1(e)(3)(i))[20] However, automatic consent accounting method change requests (¶2845), may be made on Form 3115:

(1) with a timely filed (including extensions) original income tax return for the change year (file a copy with the IRS National Office), or

(2) within six months of the original tax return due date (excluding extensions) for the change year, if the taxpayer (a) timely filed (including extensions) its return for the change year; (b) files an amended return within the six-month extension period; (c) attaches the original Form 3115 to the amended return; (d) files a copy with the national office at the same time or sooner; and (e) writes "FILED PURSUANT TO Reg § 301.9100-2" at the top of the application.[21]

Extensions won't be granted except in unusual and compelling circumstances. The taxpayer must include all information required by the form, and state that he agrees to the conditions set by IRS and will take into account any required adjustments (¶2841).[22]

¶ 2841 Adjustments required on change—Code Sec. 481(a) adjustments.

In any year in which taxpayer uses a different tax accounting method from the method used in the preceding year, Code Sec. 481(a) adjustments must be made to prevent items of income or expense from being duplicated or entirely omitted. (Reg § 1.446-1(e)(3)(i))[23] The adjustments must take into account inventories, accounts receivable, accounts payable, and any other necessary items. (Reg § 1.481-1(b))[24] The adjustments can be positive (increasing taxable income), or negative (decreasing taxable income). (Reg § 1.481-1(c))[25]

17. ¶G-2103; ¶4464.21; ¶4464.24; TD ¶442,403
18. ¶G-2104; ¶4464.24; TD ¶442,404
19. ¶G-2106.1; ¶4464.25; TD ¶442,407
20. ¶G-2225; ¶4464.22; TD ¶442,601
21. ¶G-2203.9; ¶4464.225
22. ¶G-2220 *et seq.*; ¶4464.22
23. ¶G-2215; ¶4464.21; TD ¶443,301
24. ¶G-2290 *et seq.*; ¶4814; TD ¶443,301
25. ¶G-2304; ¶4814; TD ¶443,302

¶ 2842 When Code Sec. 481(a) adjustments are taken into account.

Except as noted below or where the Code or another federal statute provides otherwise, the Code Sec. 481(a) adjustment required as a result of an accounting method change (¶2841), must be taken into account in the year of change—i.e., the first tax year in which the taxpayer's method of accounting is different from that used in the previous tax year. (Code Sec. 481(a); Reg § 1.481-1(a)(1)) This applies to both positive and negative adjustments. (Reg § 1.481-1(c))[26]

Instead of taking the Code Sec. 481(a) adjustment into account in the year of change, taxpayer may take it into account over an appropriate period agreed to (in writing) by IRS. (Code Sec. 481(c); Reg § 1.481-4(a), Reg § 1.481-4(b)) The adjustment must be taken into account ratably over the years included in the adjustment inclusion period (¶2843).[27]

¶ 2843 Adjustment inclusion periods prescribed by IRS—four-year/one-year rules.

The Code Sec. 481(a) adjustment period for voluntary accounting method changes, including automatic consent changes (¶2845) is one tax year for negative adjustments and four tax years for positive adjustments beginning with the year of change.[28] However, taxpayers may elect to account for a positive adjustment in the year of change if it's less than $25,000. Cooperatives generally must take the adjustment into account for the year of change. Taxpayers that terminate their existence or cease to engage in a trade or business must take any remaining balance into account in the year of the cessation or termination. Except for LIFO discontinuance, acceleration of a Code Sec. 481(a) adjustment isn't required on conversion from C to S corporation status, or vice versa.[29]

If an accounting method issue (an issue regarding whether the taxpayer's accounting treatment of an item is proper, but only if changing the taxpayer's treatment of that item could constitute a change in accounting method) results from an examination, any resulting positive Code Sec. 481(a) adjustment is made in the earliest tax year under examination, with a one-year Code Sec. 481(a) adjustment period.[30]

Situations with a different "adjustment inclusion period" are explained at the place in this Handbook where the item subject to the accounting rule is discussed.

¶ 2844 Relief for high-impact adjustments.

Where Code Sec. 481(a) adjustments increase taxable income of the change-over year by more than $3,000, the taxpayer can compute his tax for that year using whichever of these two methods produces the lower tax:

(1) *Three-year allocation*—The tax that would have resulted if one-third of the increase had been included in taxable income in each of the two preceding years and in the change-over year. (Code Sec. 481(b)(1); Reg § 1.481 2(a))

(2) *Allocation of specific years under new method of accounting*—Where the taxpayer establishes his taxable income under the new method of accounting for one or more tax years consecutively preceding the year of change (in which the old method was actually used), the tax is reduced to the amount that would have been paid if:

(a) the tax for the preceding years was figured under the new method, and

(b) the then remaining adjustments were allocated to the change-over year. (Code Sec. 481(b)(2); Reg § 1.481-2(b))[31]

In making the above computations, the entire Code Sec. 481(a) adjustment required as a

---

26. ¶G-2360; ¶4814; TD ¶440,817
27. ¶G-2309; ¶4814; TD ¶443,304
28. ¶G-2311; ¶4814; TD ¶443,303

29. ¶G-2308; ¶4814; TD ¶443,303
30. ¶G-2308; ¶4464.21; TD ¶442,555
31. ¶G-2401; ¶4814; TD ¶443,304

result of the accounting method change is taken into account. (Reg § 1.481-1(d))[32]

¶ 2845 Automatic consent procedures for certain accounting method changes

IRS provides automatic procedures for obtaining IRS consent to make some accounting method changes. Guidance on these are contained in *Rev Proc 2008-52,* 2008-36 IRB 587, which for changes within its scope is the exclusive means of obtaining an accounting method change.[33] Some of the more commonly applicable "automatic consent" items are those involving: permissible to permissible accounting method for depreciation; uniform capitalization methods of small resellers; cash or hybrid method to accrual method; series E or EE U.S. savings bonds; timing of incurring liabilities for employee compensation, workers' compensation, and payroll taxes; change from LIFO; retail safe harbor method (and certain other methods) for estimating inventory shrinkage; and capitalizing costs incurred in acquiring or creating intangible assets. There is generally no user fees for automatic-consent accounting method change requests.[34] For applying for an automatic consent accounting method change, see ¶2840.

¶ 2846 Reserves for Expenses.

Taxpayers often maintain accounting reserves for various future liabilities. Generally, no deduction is allowed for additions to these reserves.

¶ 2847 Reserves for estimated expenses and contingent liabilities.

Deduction or exclusion from income isn't allowed for additions to reserves for estimated expenses or contingent liabilities, even if reserves are required by state law or by contract, unless the reserve is expressly authorized by the Code (e.g., depreciation)[35] or is a reserve for trading stamps or coupons (Reg § 1.451-4(a))[36] or for container deposits. However, the use of this method for container deposits applies only where the containers are leased or loaned (*not* sold). Thus, no reserve is permitted for refundable deposits on empty beverage containers under states' environmental and conservation laws. The deposits are includible in income when received and refunds are deductible when paid.[37]

¶ 2848 Long-Term Contracts.

Long-term contracts generally must be accounted for by the percentage-of-completion method. For how to account for long-term contracts for alternative minimum tax purposes, see ¶3208.

¶ 2849 Accounting for long-term contracts.

Taxpayers must account for long-term contracts (except for certain home and other real property construction contracts, see ¶2850) under the percentage-of-completion method (¶2852), subject to an election to use a modified percentage-of-completion method ("10% method," see ¶2853). (Code Sec. 460)[38]

A long-term contract is any contract for the manufacture, building, installation, or construction of property, if not completed in the tax year in which entered into. (Code Sec. 460(f)(1); Reg § 1.460-1(b)(1)) Whether the taxpayer reasonably expected that the contract would be completed within the tax year is not relevant.[39] But a manufacturing contract isn't long-term unless it involves manufacture of a unique item (of a type not normally included in inventory), or an item that normally requires more than 12 months to complete.[40] (Code Sec. 460(f)(2))

---

32. ¶G-2401; ¶4814; TD ¶443,304
33. ¶G-2203 *et seq.*; ¶4464; TD ¶442,606 *et seq.*
34. ¶G-2203.13
35. ¶s G-2733, G-2737; ¶4514.017; TD ¶442,036
36. ¶G-2742; ¶s 4514.161, 4514.163; TD ¶442,037

37. ¶G-2740; TD ¶442,039
38. ¶s G-3100, G-3229; ¶4514.125; TD ¶445,001
39. ¶G-3103; ¶4604; TD ¶445,027
40. ¶s G-3102, G-3106; ¶4604; TD ¶445,029

¶ 2850 Exception for small construction contracts.

Home construction contracts (specially defined) aren't limited to the percentage-of-completion method. Nor are any other real property construction contracts if originally estimated to be completed within two years of the contract start date, and if the taxpayer's average annual gross receipts for the three previous tax years don't exceed $10 million (including receipts of certain related businesses). (Code Sec. 460(e); Reg § 1.460-3(b)) Regs provide reporting methods for exempt contracts. (Reg § 1.460-4(c))[41]

¶ 2851 Allocation of costs to long-term contracts.

All costs that directly benefit, or are incurred by reason of, a long-term contract (including research and experimental costs) must be allocated to the contract in the same manner as costs were allocated to extended-period long-term contracts entered into before Mar. 1, '86, under Code Sec. 451 and former Reg. § 1.451-3(d) except that past service pension costs must be allocated to the contract. Also, in the case of a cost-plus contract or a federal long-term contract or subcontract, any other costs (e.g., general and administrative expenses) must be allocated to the contract if identified by the taxpayer (or a related person) as being attributable to it under the contract, or under federal, state, or local law or regulation. (Code Sec. 460(c)(1), Code Sec. 460(c)(2))[42] Interest costs are allocated to long-term contracts in a way that's similar to the way interest costs are allocated under the uniform capitalization rules (Code Sec. 263A(f)) (¶1660) that apply to property produced by a taxpayer. (Code Sec. 460(c)(3); Reg § 1.460-5(b)(2)(v))[43]

The allocation rules don't apply to any expenses for unsuccessful bids and proposals; marketing, selling, and advertising expenses; or independent research and development expenses (IR&D). IR&D expenses don't include expenses directly attributable to a long-term contract in existence when the expenses are incurred, or expenses under an agreement to perform research and development. (Code Sec. 460(c)(4), Code Sec. 460(c)(5))[44] Costs of a guaranty, warranty, or maintenance agreement aren't treated as part of a long-term contract. (Reg § 1.460-1(d)(2))

Alternatively, a taxpayer may elect to use the simplified cost-to-cost allocation method, under which a contract's completion factor is determined based upon only direct material costs; direct labor costs; and depreciation, amortization, and cost recovery allowances on equipment and facilities directly used to manufacture or construct the subject matter of the contract. Material or labor costs associated with a subcontractor's activities must be allocated to the contract. A taxpayer electing this method must use it to apply the look-back method (¶2854) and to determine alternative minimum taxable income. Elect the simplified cost-to-cost method for all long-term contracts entered into during the tax year by using it on the original federal income tax return for the election year. The election isn't available if the percentage-of-completion method (¶2852) is not used for all long-term contracts or if the 10% method (¶2853) is used. (Code Sec. 460(b)(3)(A); Reg § 1.460-5(c))[45]

Home construction contracts and real property construction contracts not subject to long-term contract accounting restrictions (¶2849) are exempt from the above cost allocation rules other than the interest allocation rules. (Code Sec. 460(e))[46]

¶ 2852 Percentage-of-completion method.

Under this method, a long-term contract's percentage of completion must be determined by comparing costs allocated to the contract and incurred before the close of the tax year, with estimated total contract costs. (Code Sec. 460(b)(1)(A)) For qualified property placed in service

41. ¶G-3209; ¶4604; TD ¶445,033
42. ¶G-3143 *et seq.*; ¶s 4514.132, 4604; TD ¶445,016
43. ¶G-3150; ¶s 4514.132, 4604; TD ¶445,019
44. ¶G-3154 *et seq.*; ¶4604; TD ¶445,021
45. ¶G-3138; ¶4604; TD ¶445,023
46. ¶G-3209 *et seq.*; ¶4604; TD ¶445,033

in 2010 (as well as 2011 for certain property with a long production period), 50% bonus depreciation (¶1933) isn't a taken into account in applying the percentage of completion method. (Code Sec. 460(c)(6)) Events that occur after the end of the tax year that are reasonably subject to estimate as of the last day of the tax year are taken into account.[47]

Gross income recognized in a particular year under the percentage-of-completion method equals total revenue expected from the contract times the cumulative percentage of the contract completed as of the end of the tax year, less the total cumulative amount of contract revenue required to be included in gross income in all preceding tax years. (This can result in a deductible loss for a year if total estimated contract costs increase.) (Reg § 1.460-4(b)(2))[48]

If the total contract price has not been included in gross income by the completion year, the taxpayer must include the remaining portion of the total contract price in gross income for the following tax year. (Reg § 1.460-4(b)(3))

When the contract is completed (or, for amounts received or accrued after completion, when those amounts are received or accrued), the taxpayer must either pay or is entitled to receive interest computed under the look-back method discussed at ¶2854. (Code Sec. 460(b)(1)(B))[49]

¶ 2853   Modified percentage-of-completion method—"the 10% method."

For purposes of the percentage-of-completion method (¶2852), a taxpayer may elect not to recognize income under the contract and not to take into account any costs allocable to the long-term contract for any tax year if, as of the end of the tax year, less than 10% of the estimated total contract costs have been incurred. (Code Sec. 460(b)(5)) Elect by using the 10% method for all long-term contracts entered into during the tax year on the original federal income tax return for the election year. If elected, the method is used to apply the look-back method (¶2854) and to determine alternative minimum taxable income. It can't be used if the simplified cost-to-cost method (¶2851) is used. (Reg § 1.460-4(b)(6)(ii))[50]

¶ 2854   Look-back method for interest on tax—Form 8697.

In the tax year a long-term contract (with exceptions, below) is completed, the taxpayer must compare the amount of taxes paid in previous years under the percentage method with the tax that would have been owed if actual, rather than anticipated, costs and contract price had been used to compute gross income. Interest at the "adjusted overpayment rate" (overpayment rate (¶4855) for the calendar quarter in which the "interest accrual period" begins) for any "interest accrual period" (period beginning the day after the return due date, without extensions, and ending on the return due date of the following tax year) is owed by or payable to the taxpayer (use Form 8697) if there is, respectively, an underpayment or overpayment for any tax year. (Code Sec. 460(b)(2), Code Sec. 460(b)(7))[1] For pass-through entities, see ¶2855.

Taxpayers may elect (for all contracts completed in the election year and all future years, revocable only with IRS consent) not to apply the look-back method if at the close of each contract year before the tax year in which the look-back method would otherwise have to be applied, the cumulative taxable income (or loss) under the contract (using estimated contract price and costs) is within 10% of the cumulative look-back income or loss under the contract. (Code Sec. 460(b)(6)) Elect by attaching a statement to a timely filed (including extensions) original return for the election year. (Reg § 1.460-6(j))[2]

The look-back method doesn't apply to any contract whose gross price (at completion) doesn't exceed the lesser of $1,000,000 or 1% of taxpayer's average annual gross receipts for the three tax years preceding the tax year the contract was completed if the contract is

---

47. ¶s G-3123; ¶4604; TD ¶445,002
48. ¶G-3126 *et seq.*; ¶4604; TD ¶445,002
49. ¶G-3156; ¶4604; TD ¶445,044

50. ¶G-3229 *et seq.*; ¶4604; TD ¶445,088
1. ¶G-3161 *et seq.*; ¶4604; TD ¶445,054
2. ¶G-3203.1; ¶4604; TD ¶445,049

completed within two years of its start date. (Code Sec. 460(b)(3)(B))[3] Nor does it apply to home construction contracts or others described at ¶2850. (Reg § 1.460-6(b)(2))[4]

¶ 2855 Simplified look-back marginal-impact method for pass-through entities.

For partnerships, S corporations and trusts (that aren't 50% or more held directly or indirectly by five or fewer persons), a simplified look-back marginal-impact method is applied at the entity level if substantially all the income from the contract is U.S.-source. The amount of taxes treated as overpaid or underpaid under a contract in any year is found by multiplying the amount of contract income over- or under-reported for the year by the top marginal tax rate applicable for the year. (Code Sec. 460(b)(4); Reg § 1.460-6(d)(1))[5] Individuals, C corporations and owners of closely-held pass-through entities may elect to use this method. Also, widely-held pass-through entities may use it for foreign contracts. (Reg § 1.460-6(d)(4))[6]

¶ 2856 Long-term contract following mid-contract change.

The tax treatment following a mid-contract change in taxpayer of a long-term contract depends on whether the change is a "constructive completion transaction" or a "step-in-the-shoes transaction." In a constructive completion transaction, the old taxpayer is treated as completing the contract and the new taxpayer as entering into a new contract on the transaction date. This approach applies to any transaction not subject to the step-in-the-shoes approach. (Reg § 1.460-4(k)(2)) In general, with a step-in-the-shoes transaction, the old taxpayer's obligation to account for the contract terminates on the transaction date and is assumed by the new taxpayer. The new taxpayer assumes the old taxpayer's methods of accounting for the contract, with both the contract price and allocable contract costs based on amounts taken into account by both parties. Special rules apply to the treatment of certain partnership transactions. (Reg § 1.460-4(k), Reg § 1.460-6(g))[7]

¶ 2857 Reconstruction of Income by IRS. ████████████████

Where taxpayer's records are inadequate, IRS can reconstruct taxpayer's income by whatever method will in its opinion most clearly reflect income.

The methods most often used are:

The net worth method. Here, IRS attempts to establish an opening net worth or total value of the taxpayer's assets at the beginning of a given year. It then proves increases in the taxpayer's net worth for each later year during the period under examination and calculates the difference between the adjusted net values of the taxpayer's assets at the beginning and end of each of the years involved. The taxpayer's nondeductible expenditures, including living expenses, are added to these increases. If the resulting figure for any year is substantially greater than the taxable income reported by the taxpayer for that year, IRS treats the excess as unreported taxable income.[8]

Bank deposit method. The bank deposit method assumes that all deposits represent income unless the taxpayer can show otherwise.[9]

Percentage markup method. IRS determines taxpayer's net income by applying certain percentages, e.g., gross profit to sales, or net income to gross income, or net income to sales, derived from other taxpayers in the same kind of business.[10]

¶ 2858 Reallocations of Income by IRS. ████████████████

IRS is authorized (under Code Sec. 482) to distribute, apportion, or allocate gross income, deductions, credits or allowances among two or more organizations, trades,

---

3. ¶G-3158; ¶4604; TD ¶445,050 *et seq.*
4. ¶G-3159; TD ¶445,051
5. ¶G-3195 *et seq.*; ¶4604; TD ¶445,074
6. ¶G-3201; ¶4604; TD ¶445,074

7. ¶G-3246; ¶4604.04
8. ¶G-2912; ¶s 4464.41, 4464.42; TD ¶444,010
9. ¶G-2941; ¶s 4464.41, 4464.67; TD ¶444,027
10. ¶G-2948; ¶s 4464.41, 4464.76; TD ¶444,031

or businesses owned or controlled by the same interests in order to prevent tax evasion or to reflect the true taxable income of any of those entities. A similar rule also allows IRS to reallocate tax items (under Code Sec. 269A) for a personal service corporation.

IRS can reallocate income under Code Sec. 482 regardless of the entities' *motives* for shifting it, and can reallocate even if the shift was unintentional. (Reg § 1.482-1(c))[11]

If an allocation is made for a transaction between controlled taxpayers, IRS will also take into account the effect of any other non-arm's length transaction between the same controlled taxpayers in the same tax year which will result in a setoff against the original allocation. (Reg § 1.482-1(g)(4)(i)) Procedures have been issued for notifying IRS of a proposed setoff.[12]

The tax treatment of services transactions ensures that valuable intangibles cannot be transferred outside the U.S. for less than arm's length consideration, and update guidance on the transfer pricing methods to determine the arm's-length price in services transactions. (Reg § 1.482-9)[13]

Under advance pricing agreements (APAs) with IRS, taxpayers can prospectively determine and apply transfer pricing methodologies to international transactions by related foreign or domestic taxpayers (and resolve other related issues).[14] APAs and related background information can't be released to the public. (Code Sec. 6103(b), Code Sec. 6110(b))

¶ 2859 Reallocation of personal service corporation income.

To prevent tax avoidance or evasion or to clearly reflect income, IRS may allocate all income, deductions, credits, exclusions and other allowances between a personal service corporation (PSC) and its employee-owner who owns more than 10% of the PSC stock (on any day in the tax year) if: substantially all of its services are performed by or for one other corporation, partnership, or entity (including related parties) and are availed of principally to avoid federal income tax by securing for any employee-owner significant tax benefits that he wouldn't otherwise have. (Code Sec. 269A(a))[15] A PSC is one whose principal activity is the performance of personal services, substantially all of which are performed by employee-owners for one other corporation, partnership, or entity (including related parties). The Code Sec. 318 attribution rules apply for purposes of the 10% test, except that for purposes of applying the Code Sec. 318(a)(2)(C) rules, attribution is triggered by 5% rather than 50% stock ownership. (Code Sec. 269A(b)(2))[16]

¶ 2860 Previously Reported Income Repayments. ▆▆▆▆▆▆▆▆

Taxpayers who must repay amounts they previously reported as income may deduct the repayments in the year the repayments are made. If the amount repaid exceeds $3,000, the taxpayer may recover the tax paid on that amount in the year he reported it, if that gives him the greater tax benefit.

¶ 2861 Deducting the repayment of previously reported income.

A taxpayer who must repay previously-reported income is entitled to deduct the amount repaid.[17] For relief where the repayment exceeds $3,000, see ¶2862.

For a cash basis taxpayer, the year of the deduction, and accordingly the year that the special computation might be available, is the year the income previously reported was repaid. If the taxpayer reported the income as constructively received, the year of deduction is the year he had to relinquish his claim to the income. (Reg § 1.1341-1(e))[18]

11. ¶G-4018; ¶4824
12. ¶G-4108; ¶4824.08
13. ¶G-4200; ¶G-4500; ¶4824.04, ¶4824.06
14. ¶G-4700 *et seq.*; ¶4824.07

15. ¶G-4751; ¶269A4
16. ¶G-4756; ¶269A4
17. ¶G-3001; ¶13,414; TD ¶203,015
18. ¶G-3027; ¶13,414.01; TD ¶444,520

For an accrual basis taxpayer, the year of deduction is the year liability for repayment becomes fixed. Where the taxpayer received the income reported, the year of deduction is the year it's finally established the taxpayer had no unrestricted right to it. (Reg § 1.1341-1(e))[19]

¶ 2862   Repayments that exceed $3,000.

If the amount of the deduction allowed for a tax year (¶2861) with respect to an item reported as income in an earlier tax year is more than $3,000, and:

... that item was included in gross income in the earlier year because it appeared that the taxpayer had an unrestricted right to it then; and

... the deduction is allowed because it was shown after the close of the earlier year that taxpayer did *not* have an unrestricted right to all or part of that item, then the tax for the year in which the deduction is allowed is the lesser of:

(1) the tax for that year computed with the deduction,

(2) the tax for that year computed *without the deduction,* minus the decrease in tax for the earlier year that would result solely from excluding the deductible repayment. (Code Sec. 1341(a))

This relief for repayments exceeding $3,000 doesn't apply:

... where repayment is required because of a liability that arose later, as distinguished from absence of an unrestricted right to the income previously reported;[20]

... where an item was originally included in gross income by reason of the sale or other disposition of stock-in-trade, or other property includible in inventory if on hand at close of the earlier tax year, or property held primarily for sale to customers in the ordinary course of business—i.e., it doesn't apply to sales returns and allowances and similar items (Code Sec. 1341(b)(2); Reg § 1.1341-1(f));

... to deductions attributable to bad debts or to legal fees and other expenses incurred in contesting the repayment of income previously included. (Reg § 1.1341-1(g), Reg § 1.1341-1(h))[21]

¶ 2863   Inventories. ▆▆▆▆▆▆▆▆▆▆▆▆▆▆▆▆▆▆▆▆▆▆▆▆▆▆▆▆▆▆▆▆

Where producing, buying or selling merchandise is an income-producing factor, inventories are needed to determine the correct cost of goods sold.

Inventories serve to allocate the expense of buying merchandise to the year in which that merchandise is sold.[22]

Inventories must be used whenever IRS finds their use is needed to clearly determine a taxpayer's income. (Code Sec. 471) Generally, this is the case where the "production, purchase or sale of merchandise" is an income producing factor. (Reg § 1.471-1)[23] A taxpayer that must use inventories also must use the accrual method of accounting for its purchases and sales. (Reg § 1.446-1)[24] However, IRS has excepted non-tax-shelters with average annual gross receipts of $1 million or less from having to account for inventories and certain taxpayers with not more than $10 million average annual gross receipts, see ¶2818. Also, pending the release of further guidance IRS will not assert that construction contractors must maintain inventory accounts for the supplies used in their businesses.[25]

⚫*caution:* Under the uniform inventory inclusion and capitalization rules (¶1660 *et seq.*), certain direct and indirect costs are either included in inventory or capitalized.

---

19. ¶G-3028; ¶13,414.01; TD ¶444,520
20. ¶G-2308; ¶13,414; TD ¶444,511
21. ¶s G-3032, G-3034, G-3035; ¶13,414.01; TD ¶444,523
22. ¶G-5000 *et seq.*; ¶4714; TD ¶450,500

23. ¶G-5001; ¶4714; TD ¶450,501
24. ¶G-2089; ¶4464.07; TD ¶450,506
25. ¶G-5001

¶ 2864   What goods are included in inventory?

Inventories include all merchandise that is held for sale in the ordinary course of business or that is to become a physical part of merchandise intended for sale. Inventories generally cover finished or partly finished goods as well as raw materials and supplies acquired for sale or that will physically become a part of merchandise intended for sale. For items to be included in inventory, taxpayer must have title. (Reg § 1.471-1)[26] Prescription drugs and similar items administered by healthcare providers are not merchandise.[27]

Merchandise shipped on approval or sold on sample is kept in the seller's inventory until its acceptance. Consigned goods or goods in the hands of others for processing (e.g., dyeing) and returnable in kind are kept in the consignor's inventory. A seller's inventory includes goods he has contracted to sell but not yet segregated and applied to the contract, while a buyer's inventory includes merchandise in transit to him or that for other reasons hasn't been reduced to possession but to which he has title. But a buyer does *not* include in inventory goods ordered for future delivery.[28]

Containers that are to be *sold* with the merchandise they contain should be included in the seller's inventory, regardless of whether they are returnable. If the containers are merely leased or loaned with a deposit received to guarantee the return, they aren't included in inventory since they aren't part of the merchandise held for sale. In that case they can be inventoried at cost the same as supplies, considered as fixed assets and depreciated, or, if they have a useful life of less than a year, currently deducted.[29]

Under an IRS accounting method safe harbor, rotable spare parts (parts that can be reserviced or repaired and used repeatedly) can be capitalized and depreciated, rather than included in inventory.[30]

¶ 2865   Valuing inventory.

The two most commonly recognized bases of valuing inventories are: (1) cost, and (2) cost or market, whichever is lower. (Reg § 1.471-2(c))[31] Farmers may use other valuation methods, see ¶4513 *et seq.* For inventories of dealers in securities, see ¶2879.

Consistency from year to year in whatever inventory procedure is adopted is of first importance. (Reg § 1.471-2(b))[32]

¶ 2866   Valuation of unsalable, slow-moving and traded-in goods.

Any goods in inventory that are unsalable at normal prices or in the normal way because of damage, imperfections, style changes, etc., can at the taxpayer's option be written down — that is, valued at selling prices less direct costs of disposition, whether the cost or the lower of cost or market method is used. If the goods consist of raw materials or partly finished goods held for use or consumption, they must be valued upon a reasonable basis, considering the usability and condition of the goods, but in no case at less than scrap value. (Reg § 1.471-2(c))[33] Selling price means the actual price at which goods are offered for sale during a period ending not later than 30 days after the date of inventory. (Reg § 1.472-2(c))[34]

Normal but slow-moving inventory (i.e., goods in excess of current demand) can't be written down based on arbitrary cut-off time periods.[35]

---

26. ¶G-5006 *et seq.*; ¶4714; TD ¶450,509 *et seq.*
27. ¶G-5001
28. ¶G-5009; ¶4714; TD ¶450,517
29. ¶G-5010; ¶4714; TD ¶450,513
30. ¶G-5006.1; TD ¶265,444

31. ¶G-5101; ¶s 4714.21, 4714.41, 4714.51; TD ¶451,001
32. ¶G-5002; ¶4714.21; TD ¶450,502
33. ¶G-5159; ¶4714.35; TD ¶451,510
34. ¶G-5161; ¶4714.35; TD ¶451,511
35. ¶G-5164; TD ¶451,514

¶ 2867 Prohibited valuation methods and practices.

The following aren't permitted:

(1) Deducting from inventory a reserve for price changes or an estimated depreciation in the value of inventory (but for permissible estimates of inventory shrinkage, see ¶2868).

(2) Valuing work in process, or other parts of the inventory, at a nominal price or at less than its proper value.

(3) Omitting portions of the stock on hand.

(4) Using a constant price or nominal value for so-called normal quantity of material or goods in stock.

(5) Segregating indirect production costs into fixed and variable classifications and allocating only the variable costs to the cost of goods produced while treating fixed costs as currently deductible (the "direct cost" method).

(6) Treating all or substantially all indirect production costs (whether classified as fixed or variable) as currently deductible (the "prime cost" method). (Reg § 1.471-2(f))[36]

¶ 2868 Estimates of inventory shrinkage.

A method of determining inventories doesn't fail to clearly reflect income solely because it uses estimates of inventory shrinkage that are confirmed by a physical count only after the last day of the tax year if the taxpayer: (1) normally does a physical count at each location on a regular and consistent basis, and (2) makes proper adjustments to inventories and to its estimating methods if estimates are greater or less than actual shrinkage. (Code Sec. 471(b)) Use the automatic consent procedure (¶2845), with some modifications, to change to the retail safe harbor method of estimating inventory shrinkage (using a historical ratio of shrinkage-to-sales to estimate shrinkage occurring between the last physical inventory and the end of the tax year), or to a method that clearly reflects income other than the retail safe harbor method if the method being changed from didn't estimate inventory shrinkage.[37]

¶ 2869 What is cost?

The cost of goods on hand at the start of an accounting period is the amount at which they were valued in the closing inventory of the period before. (Reg § 1.471-3(a))[38]

The cost of the goods purchased ordinarily is the invoice price reduced by trade or other discounts. Strictly cash discounts approximating a fair interest rate may be deducted at the option of the taxpayer if the method is consistently followed. (Reg § 1.471-3(b))[39] To this net invoice price should be added transportation or other necessary charges incurred in acquiring possession of the goods. (Reg § 1.471-3(b))[40]

The costs of goods produced by the taxpayer include, in addition to the opening inventory, cost of raw materials and supplies entering into or consumed in manufacture, regular and overtime direct labor costs, and the indirect costs required to be included under the "full absorption" method. (Reg § 1.471-3(c))[41]

For the uniform capitalization rules for including costs in inventory, see ¶1660 *et seq.*

¶ 2870 Valuing inventory using the lower of cost or market method.

Under this method, market value on the inventory date is compared with the cost of each item. The lower of the two is the inventory value of the item. Total inventory is the aggregate

---

36. ¶G-5124; ¶4714.21; TD ¶451,020
37. ¶G-5120.1; ¶4714.38; TD ¶451,014
38. ¶G-5102; ¶4714.41; TD ¶451,002

39. ¶G-5107, G-5108; ¶4714.41; TD ¶451,003
40. ¶G-5103, G-5110; ¶4714.41; TD ¶451,006
41. ¶s G-5102 *et seq.*, G-5402; ¶4714.41

of the inventory values so computed for each item in the inventory. It is *not* the lower of the total cost or total market value of all items. (Reg § 1.471-4(c))[42]

¶ 2871 Market value defined.

Market value normally means the current bid price prevailing at the inventory date for the particular merchandise in the volume usually purchased by the taxpayer. Market price is applied to: (1) goods purchased and on hand, and (2) the basic elements of cost (materials, labor and overhead) of goods in process of manufacture and of finished goods on hand. (Reg § 1.471-4(a))[43]

Market price may not be applied to goods on hand or in process if the merchandise is covered by a firm sales contract at fixed prices (i.e., not legally subject to cancellation by either buyer or seller). If, under the contract, the taxpayer is protected against actual loss, the goods must be inventoried at cost with no deduction for inventory decline. (Reg § 1.471-4(a)) Moreover, goods covered by firm sales contracts at the end of the year must be valued at cost even though the contracts are cancelled after the close of the year at the customer's request.[44] If the contract gives the seller an almost certain loss, IRS says the seller isn't allowed to write the inventory down but must value it at cost, thus taking the loss when actually realized (Reg § 1.471-4(a)), but some courts disagree.[45]

A taxpayer may write down inventory below market if in the regular course of business he has offered the merchandise for sale at below-market prices. (Reg § 1.471-4(b))

If no market exists, or if quotations are nominal because of an inactive market, the taxpayer must use whatever evidence of a fair market price at the date or dates nearest his inventory date as may be available, e.g., specific purchases and sales made by the taxpayer or others in reasonable volume and in good faith, or compensation paid for cancellation of contracts for purchase commitments. (Reg § 1.471-4(b))[46]

¶ 2872 Inventory cost identification methods.

Under the specific identification method, goods are matched with their invoices (less appropriate discounts) to find the cost of each item.[47]

Where it isn't possible or practicable to identify each item of inventory with its cost, an assumption must be made to determine which items were sold and which remain in inventory. Although only two methods of costing intermingled merchandise are specifically approved (the "first-in, first-out" (FIFO) and the "last-in, first-out" (LIFO) methods, ¶2873), any method that comes within the best accounting practice of the particular business and clearly reflects income is acceptable. Two permissible cost identification methods are averaging the cost of each type or grade of goods in the inventory (¶2875), and mainly relying on the taxpayer's accounting records to arrive at the correct inventory value (¶2877). The base stock method (the assumption that a certain portion of inventory will be maintained from year to year and therefore need not be revalued) isn't permitted.[48]

The inventory price index computation (IPIC) method, under which inventory price indexes are computed with reference to consumer or producer price indexes published by the U.S. Bureau of Labor Statistics (BLS) (Code Sec. 472(f); Reg § 1.472-8(e)(3)) is intended to simplify the use of the dollar-value LIFO method (¶2875).[49]

---

42. ¶G-5150; ¶4714.51; TD ¶451,501
43. ¶G-5151; ¶4714.51; TD ¶451,502
44. ¶G-5154 *et seq.*; ¶4714.51; TD ¶451,505
45. ¶G-5154 *et seq.*; ¶4714.51; TD ¶451,503

46. ¶G-5157; ¶4714.51; TD ¶451,508
47. ¶s G-5121, G-5265; ¶4714.41; TD ¶452,020
48. ¶G-5125 *et seq.*; ¶4714.41
49. ¶G-5253; ¶4724; TD ¶452,055

¶ 2873   FIFO (first-in, first-out) and LIFO (last-in, first-out).

Under the FIFO method, the cost of goods that are so intermingled they cannot be identified with specific invoices is considered to be the cost of goods most recently purchased or produced. (Reg § 1.471-2(d))[50]

Under the "last-in, first-out" method of inventory valuation, the most recently purchased merchandise is treated as the first sold. (Code Sec. 472(b)(1))[1] LIFO may generally be used only where inventory is valued at cost. (Reg § 1.472-2(b))[2] If a taxpayer had written down inventory to a lower market value, the difference between that value and cost must be restored to income ratably over a three-year period (beginning with the year of the election to LIFO). (Code Sec. 472(d))[3]

In order to use LIFO for tax purposes, the enterprise must also use LIFO in its reports to partners, stockholders, etc., and for credit purposes. (Code Sec. 472(c))[4]

Qualifying heavy equipment dealers using LIFO or FIFO may, like auto dealers, use replacement cost to determine the cost of their heavy parts inventory under safe harbor rules.[5]

¶ 2874   Electing LIFO—Form 970.

File Form 970 (or other acceptable statement) with the return for the tax year as of the close of which LIFO is first to be used (Reg § 1.472-3)[6] or re-elected in the fifth or later tax year after changing from LIFO (otherwise IRS permission is needed for the change, see ¶2838 *et seq.*) Once made, the election applies to all later years unless IRS grants permission to change. (Reg § 1.472-5)[7] Automatic consent procedures (¶2845) apply to adoption of certain specialized LIFO methods and to changes from LIFO.

¶ 2875   Dollar value LIFO and simplified dollar value LIFO.

Under this method a taxpayer who deals in a large variety of products may value inventory by the use of the dollar value rather than natural units. The assumption is that items in the inventory are homogeneous. The taxpayer is therefore required to break up the inventory into a series of "pools" —the natural business unit pool or multiple pools. (Reg § 1.472-8)[8] Any taxpayer electing to use the dollar-value LIFO method can elect to compute an inventory price index in accordance with the Inventory Price Index Computation method (Reg § 1.472-8(e)(3)(ii), see ¶2872.

An eligible small business may elect to use a simplified dollar-value method of pricing inventories for purposes of the LIFO method. Under this method, the cost of each grade of goods is averaged. (Code Sec. 474(a)) An eligible small business is a taxpayer whose average annual gross receipts don't exceed $5,000,000 for the three-tax-year period ending immediately before the tax year. (Code Sec. 474(c))[9]

¶ 2876   Retailers' inventory.

Retailers can value each item of merchandise in stock at the end of the year at its retail selling price but adjusted to approximate cost by eliminating the average percent of markup. (Reg § 1.471-8(a))[10] This retail inventory method may be used in conjunction with FIFO and specific identification methods, as well as LIFO, if the taxpayer adjusts his selling price for both markups and markdowns. (Reg § 1.471-8(g))[11] Price change adjustments are determined

---

50. ¶G-5121; ¶4714.41; TD ¶451,017
1. ¶G-5200; ¶4724; TD ¶452,001
2. ¶G-5212; ¶4724; TD ¶452,001
3. ¶G-5208; ¶4724; TD ¶452,009
4. ¶G-5307; ¶4724; TD ¶452,076
5. ¶G-5248.4

6. ¶G-5202; ¶4724; TD ¶452,003
7. ¶G-5201; ¶4724; TD ¶452,002
8. ¶G-5245 *et seq.*; ¶4724; TD ¶452,046
9. ¶G-5302 *et seq.*; ¶4744; TD ¶452,070
10. ¶G-5351; ¶4724.06; TD ¶453,001
11. ¶G-5357; ¶4724.06; TD ¶453,006

by reference generally to U.S. Bureau of Labor Statistics price indexes. (Reg § 1.472-1(k))[12]

¶ 2877 Book (perpetual) inventory method.

Under this method inventory accounts are charged with the actual cost of goods purchased or produced, and credited with the cost of goods used, transferred or sold. The net amount is considered to be the cost of the goods on hand, if the balances shown on the books are adjusted at reasonable intervals to conform to physical inventories. (Reg § 1.471-2(d))[13]

¶ 2878 Miners' and manufacturers' inventory.

Miners and manufacturers who use a single process or uniform series of processes, and derive a product of two or more kinds, sizes or grades with a unit cost substantially alike, may allocate a share of total cost to each kind, size or grade as a basis for pricing inventories. (Reg § 1.471-7)[14]

¶ 2879 Securities and commodities dealers' inventories—mark-to-market rules.

Any security that's inventory in the hands of a securities dealer must be included in inventory at its fair market value. (Code Sec. 475(a)(1)) In the case of a non-inventory security that's held at the close of a tax year, the dealer must recognize gain or loss as if the security were sold for its fair market value on the last business day of that year, and any gain or loss must be taken into account for that tax year, generally as ordinary income or loss. (Code Sec. 475(a)(2), Code Sec. 475(d)(3))[15] A "security" doesn't include any security held for investment, certain other securities, and hedges of those securities (but only if the hedge is clearly identified as a hedge in the dealer's records before the close of the business day on which it was acquired, originated or entered into). (Code Sec. 475(b))[16] A security also doesn't include nonfinancial customer paper arising from the sale of nonfinancial goods or services by sellers or providers of those goods or services which are held by them (or related parties) at all times since issue. (Code Sec. 475(c)(4))[17] Commodities dealers may elect (under interim procedures[18]) to apply the mark-to-market rules to commodities held by them in the same way that the rules apply to securities held by securities dealers. (Code Sec. 475(e)(1)) Once made, the election may be revoked only with IRS consent. (Code Sec. 475(e)(3))[19] Where the Code Sec. 475 rules don't apply, a securities dealer inventories securities at: (1) cost, (2) lower of cost or market, or (3) market value. (Reg § 1.471-5)[20]

A dealer is one who regularly buys and sells securities to customers (or enters into or terminates positions in securities with customers) in the ordinary course of business. (Code Sec. 475(c)(1))[21] If one's sole business is trading in securities he's not a dealer[22] (but for the mark-to-market election by traders, see ¶2880).

¶ 2880 Mark-to-market election for securities and commodities traders.

A person engaged in the trade or business of securities trader or commodities trader may elect (under interim procedures[23]) to have the following mark-to-market rules apply to the trade or business: (1) gain or loss is recognized on any security (or commodity) held in connection with the trade or business at the close of any tax year as if the security (or commodity) were sold for its fair market value on the last business day of the tax year, and (2) gain or loss is taken into account for the tax year (Code Sec. 475(f)(1)(A), Code Sec. 475(f)(2)) as ordinary income or loss. Once made, the election may be revoked only with

12. ¶G-5362; ¶4724.06; TD ¶453,011
13. ¶G-5119; ¶4714.21; TD ¶451,013
14. ¶G-5020; ¶4714.85; TD ¶450,520
15. ¶I-7652; ¶4754
16. ¶I-7657 *et seq.*; ¶4754
17. ¶I-7657.1; ¶4754

18. ¶I-7669; ¶4754.02
19. ¶I-7667 *et seq.*; ¶4754.01
20. ¶G-5021; ¶s 4754, 4714.67
21. ¶G-5023; ¶4754
22. ¶I-7656.1; ¶4754
23. ¶I-7675; ¶4754.02

IRS consent. (Code Sec. 475(f)(3)) These elective mark-to-market rules don't apply to securities or commodities that have no connection to the electing person's trading activities if they are clearly identified as such before the close of the day acquired. (Code Sec. 475(f)(1)(B)) Securities and commodities subject to this election aren't subject to the constructive sale rules of Code Sec. 1259 (¶2637). (Code Sec. 475(f)(1)(C))[24]

¶ 2881 Changing inventory method—Form 3115.

A change in the method of valuing inventory, with the exception of a change to LIFO (¶2874) and to certain specialized LIFO methods (¶2845), requires IRS approval. This includes adoption of either: (1) cost, or (2) cost or market, whichever is lower, where the taxpayer has been on a different basis, and changes to and from the various methods of determining inventory costs. Use Form 3115, under the rules at ¶2840. (Reg § 1.446-1(e))[25] An automatic consent procedure also applies for certain taxpayers changing *from* LIFO (¶2845).[26]

---

24. ¶I-7670 *et seq.*; ¶4754.01
25. ¶s G-2101 *et seq.*, G-5201 *et seq.*; ¶4464.21; TD ¶451,022

26. ¶G-5217 *et seq.*; ¶s 263A4.10, 4464.21, 4724; TD ¶452,018

Chapter 12 Withholding Tax on Wages and Other Income Payments

¶ 3000   Withholding on Wages. ▰▰▰▰▰▰▰▰▰▰

Employers must withhold income tax from wages paid to employees, but not from amounts paid to independent contractors. "Wages" includes most forms of taxable compensation. Employees are entitled to minimum, and sometimes additional, withholding exemptions or allowances. Withheld tax must be paid through tax deposits or electronic funds transfers.

For withholding on certain federal payments (e.g., social security payments), see ¶3009. For other nonpayroll withholding (backup withholding, withholding for pension, annuities, and gambling winnings, etc.), see ¶3032. For withholding from U.S. source amounts paid to non-resident aliens and foreign corporations, see ¶4662.

¶ 3001   Withholding by employers.

Employers must withhold. (Code Sec. 3402(a)(1); Reg § 31.3402(a)-1(b))[1] An employer is any person or organization for whom an individual performs any service as an employee. (Code Sec. 3401(d)) An employer includes any person paying wages to a former employee, (Reg § 31.3401(d)-1(b)) and includes tax-exempt organizations. (Reg § 31.3401(d)-1(d))[2] Employers who outsource some or all of their payroll responsibilities remain liable for all taxes, penalties and interest due.[3]

If the actual employer doesn't have control over the payment of wages, the person who does have control must withhold. (Code Sec. 3401(d)(1)) A lender, surety or other person is personally liable for the employee income tax required to be withheld if he: (1) directly pays wages to another's employees (Code Sec. 3505(a)), or (2) supplies funds specifically for the payment of the wages of another's employees knowing the employer can't or doesn't intend to pay payroll taxes. In the case of (2), liability is limited to 25% of the amount supplied (inclusive of interest). (Code Sec. 3505(b); Reg § 31.3505-1(b))

A disregarded single-owner entity is treated as a separate entity (i.e., as a corporation) for purposes of employment taxes and related reporting requirements. (Reg § 1.1361-4(a)(7), Reg § 301.7701-2(c)(2)) An owner of a disregarded entity treated as a sole proprietorship is subject to self-employment taxes. (Reg § 301.7701-2(c)(2))[4]

If a person pays wages on behalf of a nonresident employer not engaged in trade or business in the U.S., that person must withhold. (Code Sec. 3401(d)(2))[5]

¶ 3002   Employees defined.

Every individual who performs services subject to the will and control of an employer both as to what is to be done and how it's to be done, is an employee for withholding purposes. It doesn't matter that the employee has considerable discretion and freedom of action, so long as the employer has the *legal right* to control both the method and the result of the services. (Reg § 31.3401(c)-1(b)) For how IRS determines whether a worker is an employee or independent contractor, see ¶3003.

It doesn't matter that the employee is designated a partner, agent or independent contractor, or how payments are measured or paid or what they're called. (Reg § 31.3401(c)-1(e))[6]

No distinction is made between classes of employees. Managers and other supervisory personnel are employees. An officer of a corporation is an employee (Code Sec. 3401(c)), but a

---

1. ¶H-4222; ¶34,024; TD ¶531,001
2. ¶H-4226; ¶34,014.60; TD ¶534,001
3. ¶V-1664
4. ¶H-4223; TD ¶534,002
5. ¶s H-4229, H-4236, H-4374; ¶34,014.60; TD ¶532,038
6. ¶H-4251; ¶34,014.37; TD ¶535,001

References beginning with a single letter are to paragraphs in RIA's Federal Tax Coordinator 2d and RIA's Analysis of Federal Taxes: Income. Those beginning with numbers are to paragraphs in RIA's United States Tax Reporter. Those beginning with TD are to paragraphs in RIA's Tax Desk.

director in his capacity as director isn't an employee. (Reg § 31.3401(c)-1(f))[7]

Persons in business for themselves aren't employees. For example, self-employed physicians, lawyers, dentists, veterinarians, construction contractors and others who offer their services to the public aren't employees. (Reg § 31.3401(c)-1(c))[8]

Qualified real estate agents and direct sellers are treated as independent contractors, not employees. (Code Sec. 3508(a))[9]

Statutory employees, such as certain drivers, life insurance salespersons, home workers, and other salespersons, who are treated as employees for FICA purposes (Code Sec. 3121(d)(3)) but aren't common law employees, aren't employees for income tax purposes.[10]

Crew leaders who pay agricultural laborers that they provide to another person are employers unless a written contract designates them as employees of that person. (Code Sec. 3401(g))[11]

observation: A person not treated as an employee for income tax purposes can't be covered under employee plans, e.g., medical reimbursement and group-term life insurance plans.

If payment is made for services rendered and the payor isn't sure whether the payee is an employee or independent contractor, the payor may get an IRS ruling by filing Form SS-8. (Reg § 31.3401(d)-1(d))[12] Adverse rulings can be reviewed by the Tax Court (Code Sec. 7436) after IRS sends an adverse notice of determination.[13]

Employees who have been misclassified as independent contractors by an employer use Form 8919 to figure and report the employee's share of uncollected Social Security and Medicare taxes due on their compensation. The worker performing the services must meet one of several criteria supporting his belief that he is an employee, e.g., receipt of an SS-8 determination letter.[14]

¶ 3003 How IRS determines employee or independent contractor status.

To determine whether a worker is an independent contractor or an employee, IRS examines the relationship between the worker and the business, and considers all evidence of control and independence. The facts that provide this evidence fall into the following three categories:

(1) *Behavioral control* covers facts that show whether the business has a right to direct and control how the work is done through instructions, training, or other means. Employees are generally given instructions on when and where to work, what tools to use, where to purchase supplies, what order to follow, etc.

(2) *Financial control* covers facts that show whether the business has a right to control the financial and business aspects of the worker's job. This includes the extent to which the worker has unreimbursed business expenses; the extent of his investment in the facilities being used; the extent to which he makes his services available to the relevant market; how he is paid; and the extent to which he can realize a profit or incur a loss.

(3) *Type of relationship* includes written contracts describing the relationship the parties intended to create; the extent to which the worker is available to perform services for other, similar businesses; whether the business provides the worker with employee-type benefits, such as insurance, a pension plan, vacation pay, or sick pay; the permanency of the relationship; and the extent to which services performed by the worker are a key aspect of the company's regular business.

7. ¶H-4252; ¶s 34,014.39, 34,014.40; TD ¶535,003
8. ¶H-4258; ¶34,014.47, 34,014.48, 34,014.50, 34,014.61; TD ¶535,001
9. ¶H-4283; ¶34,014.37; TD ¶535,032
10. ¶H-4300; ¶624.03; TD ¶542,007
11. ¶H-4227; ¶34,014.18
12. ¶H-4282; ¶34,014.37; TD ¶535,008
13. ¶U-2143; ¶74,364; TD ¶806,067
14. ¶S-1709.1; TD ¶570,208.1

IRS's three-category approach essentially distills the 20-factor test IRS had used to determine whether a worker was an employee or an independent contractor.[15]

In certain cases in which a taxpayer has a reasonable basis for treating an individual as a nonemployee (e.g., judicial precedent, IRS ruling, past audit allowance), a special statutory rule (section 530 of the '78 Revenue Act) may allow nonemployee treatment regardless of the above factors.[16]

¶ 3004   Wages subject to withholding.

"Wages" cover all types of employee compensation, including salaries, fees, bonuses, commissions and fringe benefits. It's immaterial whether payments are based on the hour, day, week, month, year or on a piecework or percentage plan, or whether they're called wages, salaries, fees, etc. (Code Sec. 3401(a); Reg § 31.3401(a)-1(a)(2), Reg § 31.3401(a)-1(a)(3))[17] Bonuses received for signing employment contracts are wages, as are payments received for canceling employment contracts.[18] Wages also include amounts includible in an employee's gross income for failure to comply with the Code Sec. 409A deferred compensation rules (¶1277). (Code Sec. 3401(a)) For withholding purposes they are treated as paid in the year they are includable in gross income.[19]

Noncash wages are the fair market value of the goods, lodging, meals or other consideration given for services. (Reg § 31.3401(a)-1(a)(4))[20]

Vacation allowances[21] and back pay, including retroactive wage increases, are wages. (Reg § 31.3401(a)-1(b)(3))[22] Amounts received as "front pay" are wages subject to withholding, according to IRS, but some courts have disagreed. Front pay is an amount paid to an individual for pay he would have received after a settlement date or court award but for the employer's wrongful conduct and the circumstances—e.g., extreme animosity between the parties—that make it impractical to place the employee in the position.[23]

Supplemental unemployment compensation benefits are treated as wages for income tax purposes (Code Sec. 3402(o)(1)(A), Code Sec. 3402(o)(2)),[24] but they aren't subject to FICA if certain conditions are met.[25] Differential wage payments are also wages for income tax purposes and are treated as supplemental wage payments (¶3011). These are payments to employees for periods that they are called to active duty with the U.S. uniformed services (for more than 30 days) that represent all or part of the wages that they would otherwise received from the employer. (Code Sec. 3401(h)) They are not subject to FICA and FUTA withholding.[26]

Withholding is computed on gross wages before any deductions by the employer for social security tax, pensions, union dues, insurance, etc. (Reg § 31.3401(a)-1(b)(5))[27]

¶ 3005   Tips.

Wages includes tips. (Code Sec. 3401(f)) However, withholding isn't required on cash tips of less than $20 a month received by an employee, or for tips paid in any medium other than cash (such as passes, tickets or other goods or commodities). (Code Sec. 3401(a)(16); Reg § 31.3401(a)(16)-1) But if cash tips amount to $20 or more in a month, none of the cash tips are exempt. The $20 test is applied separately with respect to cash tips received by the employee for his services to each employer. (Reg § 31.3401(a)(16)-1[28] (For the business tax credit for employer FICA tax paid on tips for food and beverage service, see ¶2329.)

---

15. ¶H-4259; TD ¶535,009
16. ¶H-4303 *et seq.*; ¶34,014.375; TD ¶537,003
17. ¶H-4326; ¶s 34,014.02, 34,014.09; TD ¶532,001
18. ¶H-4360.2, ¶H-4361.1
19. ¶H-4326, ¶H-4333.1; ¶34,014.025; TD ¶532,046
20. ¶H-4327; ¶34,014.09; TD ¶532,001
21. ¶H-4364; ¶34,014.04; TD ¶532,029

22. ¶H-4355; ¶34,014.09; TD ¶532,024
23. ¶H-4360.1
24. ¶H-4351
25. ¶H-4664
26. ¶H-4372; ¶34,014.11; TD ¶532,036
27. ¶H-4331; TD ¶532,001
28. ¶H-4341; ¶34,014.31; TD ¶532,011

¶ 3006 Exempt "wages"—fringes, reimbursed expenses, domestic service, etc.

The following aren't wages subject to income tax withholding:

... Fringe benefits if it's reasonable to believe that the employee will be able to exclude them from income as a qualified scholarship, a no-additional-cost service, a qualified employee discount, a working condition fringe, a de minimis fringe, a qualified transportation fringe, a qualified moving expense reimbursement, an on-premises athletic facility, or an employee achievement award. (Code Sec. 3401(a)(19))[29] (For the employer's election not to withhold on a vehicle fringe benefit, see ¶3007.)

... Amounts specifically advanced or reimbursed to employees for traveling or other ordinary and necessary expenses incurred or reasonably expected to be incurred in the employer's business. But they must be either paid separately, or specifically identified if combined with wages in a single payment. (Reg § 31.3401(a)-4(a)) If a reimbursement or other expense allowance arrangement meets the requirements of Code Sec. 62(c) (¶3104, i.e., an "accountable plan"), payments that don't exceed the substantiated expenses aren't wages and aren't subject to withholding. Payments that aren't substantiated within a reasonable period of time or are in excess of substantiated expenses are wages and subject to withholding. Per diem or mileage allowances at a rate in excess of the deemed substantiated amount are subject to withholding. If the arrangement doesn't meet the Code Sec. 62(c) requirements (i.e., a "nonaccountable plan"), all amounts paid are wages and subject to withholding. (Reg § 31.3401(a)-4(a), Reg § 31.3401(a)-4(b), Reg § 1.62-2(h)(1), Reg § 1.62-2(h)(2))[30]

... Moving expense reimbursements, if a corresponding deduction is allowable under the normal Code Sec. 217 rules, see ¶1645, (determined without regard to the Code Sec. 274(n) percentage limit on meal expenses). (Code Sec. 3401(a)(15))[31]

... Tips, under the circumstances at ¶3005.

... Benefits paid by a labor union to workers unemployed because of a strike or lockout.[32]

... Payments for agricultural labor except if during the year: (1) cash payments to an employee are $150 or more, or (2) the employer pays all such employees $2,500 or more (unless the employee is a hand harvest laborer who is paid on a customary basis, commutes daily to the farm from his permanent residence and was employed in agriculture less than 13 weeks during the prior year). (Code Sec. 3401(a)(2), Code Sec. 3121(a)(8))[33]

... Payments for domestic service in a private home, local college club or fraternity or sorority chapter. (Code Sec. 3401(a)(3))[34]

... Certain payments for services by a U.S. citizen for an employer outside the U.S. (Code Sec. 3401(a)(8)(A)(i))[35]

... Premiums paid by an employer for group term insurance on an employee's life. (Code Sec. 3401(a)(14))[36]

... Payments to or on behalf of an employee or his beneficiary to or from a qualified plan (except payments for services rendered by an employee of the plan) (Code Sec. 3401(a)(12)(A)); to or under a qualified annuity plan (Code Sec. 3401(a)(12)(B)); under a SIMPLE retirement account (Code Sec. 3401(a)(12)(D)); to or under a governmental section 457 plan (Code Sec. 3401(a)(12)(E)); or, if it's reasonable to believe the employee will be entitled to exclude the payment, for contributions to a simplified employee pension for an employee. (Code Sec. 3401(a)(12)(C))[37]

... Payments made under educational assistance or dependent care programs if it's reasonable to believe that the employee can exclude them. (Code Sec. 3401(a)(18))[38]

29. ¶H-4400 *et seq.*; ¶s 34,014.09, 34,024; TD ¶533,001
30. ¶H-4340; ¶34,014.03; TD ¶532,004
31. ¶H-4418; ¶34,014.30; TD ¶533,014
32. ¶H-4354; ¶34,014.10; TD ¶532,023
33. ¶H-4426; ¶34,014.18; TD ¶536,023

34. ¶H-4450 *et seq.*; ¶34,014.19; TD ¶536,006
35. ¶s H-4442, H-4443; ¶34,014.23; TD ¶536,013
36. ¶H-1518 *et seq.*, ¶H-4400 *et seq.*; ¶34,014.29
37. ¶H-10500 *et seq.*; ¶34,014.27; TD ¶553,237
38. ¶H-4401; ¶34,014.05; TD ¶533,001

. . . Payment of deceased employee's accrued wages to his estate or beneficiaries.[39]

. . . Combat zone compensation excludible under Code Sec. 112. (Code Sec. 3401(a)(1))[40]

. . . Employer contributions to medical savings accounts. (Code Sec. 3401(a)(21), Code Sec. 3401(a)(22))[41]

. . . Qualified adoption expenses paid under an employer's adoption assistance program.[42]

. . . Disqualifying dispositions of stock acquired through the exercise of an incentive stock option (ISO) or an option under an employee stock purchase plan (ESPP) (Code Sec. 421(b)) or with respect to any amount treated as compensation as a result of the ESPP discount option rule which treats a part of the gain on a disposition of stock acquired through the exercise of an option under an ESPP as compensation income if the option price at which the stock was acquired was between 85% and 100% of its fair market value at the time the option was granted. (Code Sec. 423(c))[43]

¶ 3007   Employer's election not to withhold on vehicle fringe benefit.

Employers may elect not to withhold on an employee's use of an employer-provided vehicle where that use is wages to the employee. The employer must notify the employee of the election and include the amount of the benefit on a timely furnished Form W-2. (Code Sec. 3402(s))[44]

¶ 3008   Withholding on sick pay—Form W-4S.

If the recipient of sick pay that isn't wages requests the payor (on Form W-4S) to withhold a specified amount of at least $20 from each payment, the payor must withhold that amount. (Code Sec. 3402(o)(1)(C); Reg § 31.3402(o)-3(b)) An employee doesn't have to request withholding if his employer makes the sick payments since employers are required to withhold income tax from sick pay.[45]

¶ 3009   Voluntary withholding agreements—Form W-4 and Form W-4V.

Household, and other employees who aren't subject to income tax withholding may elect to have tax withheld, if their employers agree. (Code Sec. 3402(p)) Other employees can also have their withholding increased voluntarily. (Code Sec. 3402(i))

The rules generally applicable to mandatory withholding, including withholding rates and tables, apply to the voluntary withholding. An employee requests voluntary withholding by filing a Form W-4 with his employer—unless he wants the voluntary withholding to apply for a *limited period of time*. In that case, he must also give the employer a statement that includes the date the voluntary withholding is to terminate.

A voluntary withholding agreement may be terminated by employer or employee by giving advance notice to the other in accordance with the regs. (Reg § 31.3402(p)-1)[46]

A taxpayer can request voluntary withholding at a rate of 7%, 10%, 15%, or 25% on certain federal payments, including Social Security benefits, crop disaster payments, and Commodity Credit Corporation loans (Code Sec. 3402(p)(1)), and at a 10% rate on unemployment compensation payments (¶1283). (Code Sec. 3402(p)(2)) Use Form W-4V.[47]

¶ 3010   Fringe benefits.

Fringe benefits must be treated as paid at least annually. Except for transfers of either personal property of a kind normally held for investment or real property (which must be

---

39. ¶H-4350; ¶34,014.07; TD ¶532,019
40. ¶H-4447; ¶34,014.17; TD ¶536,004
41. ¶H-4326; ¶34,014.67; TD ¶533,001
42. ¶H-4401; TD ¶533,001
43. ¶H-4448.2; TD ¶532,035.1

44. ¶s H-4411, H-4412; ¶34,024.27; TD ¶533,010
45. ¶H-4337; ¶H-4481 *et seq.*; ¶34,024.25; TD ¶532,015
46. ¶H-4477 *et seq.*; ¶34,024.19; TD ¶538,049 *et seq.*
47. ¶H-4483 *et seq.*; ¶34,024.25; TD ¶538,053 *et seq.*

reported when they are actually paid), an employer may elect to treat fringe benefits as paid quarterly, semiannually, annually, or on another basis. An employer may also treat a fringe benefit as paid in installments, even if the entire benefit is paid at one time. Benefits provided in a calendar year must be treated as paid by Dec. 31 of that year.[48]

Employers may treat fringe benefits as part of regular wages for the payroll period and compute withholding on the total, or instead withhold 25% of the value of the benefit from regular wages. (Reg § 31.3501(a)-1T, Q&A-10) Any noncash fringe benefit provided in a calendar quarter may be treated as provided on the last day of that quarter. (Reg § 31.3501(a)-1T, Q&A-1)[49]

For when withholding isn't required on a presumptively tax-free fringe benefit, see ¶3006. For the election to not withhold on the value of a vehicle fringe benefit provided to the employee, see ¶3007.

¶ 3011   Supplemental wage payments.

Withholding on bonuses, commissions, overtime pay or other supplemental wages paid:

... *with regular wages*, should be determined as if the total supplemental and regular wages were a single payment for the regular payroll period; (Reg § 31.3402(g)-1(a))

... *at a different time*, can be determined by adding the supplemental wages either to the regular wages for the current payroll period or to the last preceding payroll period within the same calendar year; (Reg § 31.3402(g)-1(a))

... *where tax has been withheld on regular wages*, generally can be determined by using a flat rate of not less than 25% in 2010 without allowance for exemptions and without reference to any regular wage payment. (Reg § 31.3402(g)-1(a)) Where tax has been withheld on regular wages (during the calendar year of the payment or the preceding one), withholding generally can be determined (at the employer's option) by using a flat rate of 25% in 2010 without allowance for exemptions and without reference to any regular wage payment, if the supplemental wages are either paid at a different time than the regular wages or are separately stated on the employer's payroll records. (Reg § 31.3402(g)-1(a))[50]

🅡🅘🅐 *caution:* For EGTRRA sunset rules, see ¶1114.

However, for supplemental wage payments totalling more than $1 million for a calendar year, the withholding rate is increased to the maximum tax rate under Code Sec. 1 (35% for 2010).[1] The employer has the option of treating either the entire supplemental payment or just that which brings the total payment over $1 million as subject to this mandatory withholding. (Reg § 31.3402(g)-1(a)(4)(iv))[2]

Where tax isn't withheld from regular wages for employees who receive both regular wages and supplemental wages (e.g., tips), the flat supplemental withholding rate can't be used; the tips are added to the current or preceding regular wage payment and withholding is computed at the regular graduated rates.[3] A payment qualifies as supplemental wages even if no regular wages have been paid to the employee.

Extra pay for working during a vacation period is treated as a supplemental wage payment. (Reg § 31.3402(g)-1(c))[4] Employers have the option to treat tips and overtime pay as either regular or supplemental wages. (Reg § 31.3402(g)-1(a))[5]

IRS has issued guidance on withholding on supplemental wages in a variety of situations.[6]

---

48. ¶H-4403; ¶34,024; TD ¶533,002 *et seq.*
49. ¶H-4404 *et seq.*; ¶s 34,024, 34,024.27; TD ¶533,003
50. ¶s H-4509, H-4510, H-4511; ¶34,024.13; TD ¶538,516
1. ¶H-4542; ¶34,024.13; TD ¶538,519
2. ¶H-4505 *et seq.*; ¶34,024.13; TD ¶538,520

3. ¶H-4507
4. ¶H-4508; ¶34,024.13; TD ¶538,514
5. ¶H-4505 *et seq.*; ¶34,024.13; TD ¶538,503
6. ¶H-4540

¶ 3012   Computing the amount withheld—percentage and wage bracket methods.

There are two principal systems of withholding: (1) the percentage or exact method, and (2) the wage bracket method. IRS provides tables to use for each.[7] Whichever method is used, the employer applies the withholding allowances and marital status indicated by the employee, see ¶3014 *et seq.* For variations of these two methods, see ¶3013.

If an employer fails to withhold income tax and the employee's portion of FICA taxes because the employer failed to treat the payee as an employee, for prior years the withholding rate is generally reduced to 1.5% of wages for income tax withholding, and only 20% of the regular amount to be withheld for FICA will generally have to be withheld. Certain exceptions apply. (Code Sec. 3509)[8]

¶ 3013   Alternative withholding methods.

IRS also authorizes withholding on the basis of: (1) annualized wages, (2) cumulative wages, (3) part-year employment, (4) average estimated wages, and (5) any other method that results in substantially the same amount of withholding as the percentage method. (Methods (2) and (3) are at the employee's request.) (Code Sec. 3402(h))[9]

¶ 3014   Employee's withholding allowance certificate—Form W-4.

An employer should ask each new employee to fill out a Form W-4 withholding allowance certificate before employment begins. (Code Sec. 3402(f)(2)(A)) Employers must take into account the marital status and exemptions and allowances of each employee on the basis of that Form W-4. A certificate filed by a new employee is effective on the first payment of wages. (Code Sec. 3402(f)(3)) If an employee fails to furnish a certificate, the employer must withhold tax as if the employee were a single person with no withholding exemptions or allowances. (Code Sec. 3401(e); Reg § 31.3402(f)(2)-1(e))[10]

An employer can establish a system for its employees to file Form W-4 electronically. (Reg § 31.3402(f)(5)-1(c))[11]

¶ 3015   Withholding exemptions.

An employee is allowed: (1) a regular exemption for himself, unless he's claimed as another's dependent; (2) a regular exemption for his spouse, unless the spouse is employed and claims a regular exemption; (3) an exemption for each dependent he may claim on his tax return; (Code Sec. 3402(f)(1); Reg § 31.3402(f)(1)-1)[12] and (4) additional withholding allowances, ¶3016.

A taxpayer working for more than one employer must allocate his allowances on separate Forms W-4 filed with each employer. (Code Sec. 3402(f)(7); Reg § 31.3402(m)-1(f)(2))[13]

The withholding exemption allowance is the same amount as allowed for a personal exemption, ¶3115. (Code Sec. 3402(a)(2))[14]

¶ 3016   Additional withholding allowances.

Employees may claim (on Form W-4) additional withholding allowances for: estimated tax credits like those shown on Form 1040, except for any earned income credit if the employee is receiving advance payment of it (¶2349); and estimated itemized deductions and other deductions including the additional standard deduction for the aged and blind, but only if his spouse doesn't have in effect a Form W-4 claiming the same allowances. (Code Sec. 3402(m);

7. ¶H-4493 *et seq.*; ¶34,024.02 *et seq.*; TD ¶538,004 *et seq.*
8. ¶H-4225; ¶35,094; TD ¶531,004
9. ¶H-4492; ¶34,024.18; TD ¶538,006 *et seq.*
10. ¶H-4523 *et seq.*; ¶34,024.09 *et seq.*; TD ¶538,031

11. ¶H-4523.1 *et seq.*; ¶34,024.11; TD ¶538,039
12. ¶H-4512; ¶34,024.10; TD ¶538,020
13. ¶H-4516; ¶34,024.10; TD ¶538,024
14. ¶H-4512; ¶34,024.10; TD ¶538,020

Reg § 31.3402(m)-1)[15]

RIA/caution: A taxpayer who has too little tax withheld because he has claimed too many withholding allowances may have to pay a penalty for underpayment of estimated tax, see ¶3159.

An additional withholding allowance (called a "standard deduction allowance") can be claimed by an employee who is single and has only one job; is married and has only one job, if his spouse does not work; or if his wages from a second job or his spouse's wages (or the total of both) are $1,000 or less. (Code Sec. 3402(f)(1)(E); Reg § 31.3402(f)(1)-1(e))[16]

¶ 3017   Employees with no tax liability.

Employees with no tax liability can be exempt from income tax withholding. To qualify, the employee certifies on Form W-4 to his employer that he expects to have no federal income tax liability for the current year, *and* he had no federal income tax liability in the preceding year. (Code Sec. 3402(n); Reg § 31.3402(n)-1)[17]

An employee who can be claimed as a dependent on someone else's tax return (whether or not actually claimed) cannot claim exemption from withholding for 2010 (and 2011) if his income exceeds $950 and includes more than $300 of unearned income, such as interest and dividends. Special calculations have to be made by an employee who is 65 or older and/or blind.[18]

¶ 3018   Amending withholding certificate.

The employee *must* amend his Form W-4, reducing the number of allowances, within ten days: (Code Sec. 3402(f)(2)(B); Reg § 31.3402(f)(2)-1(b))

. . . when the spouse he has been claiming is divorced or legally separated from him, or claims her own allowance on a separate W-4;

. . . when he loses the right to exemption for a claimed dependent;

. . . when he loses the right to the number of withholding allowances he has claimed.[19] The employer must give effect to an amended W-4 no later than the beginning of the first payroll period ending (or the first payment of wages made without regard to a payroll period) on or after the 30th day after the day the amended W-4 is furnished. (Code Sec. 3402(f)(3)(B)(i))[20]

An amended Form W-4 must be filed by Dec. 1 if the number of allowances is expected to *decrease* for next year. If the change resulting in the decrease occurs in December, the amended Form must be furnished within ten days of the date of the change. The number of allowances drops if a spouse or dependent died during the year or an individual will no longer qualify as a dependent.[21]

If the number of allowances is expected to increase next year, the employee can amend his W-4 by Dec. 1. If the change arises in December, the amended W-4 may be filed on or after the date of the change. (Code Sec. 3402(f)(2)(C); Reg § 31.3402(f)(2)-1(c)) This W-4 doesn't take effect and isn't to be made effective with respect to any payment of wages in the calendar year it's furnished. (Code Sec. 3402(f)(3)(B)(iii))[22]

¶ 3019   Employer withholding tax return—Form 941.

Every employer (except household employers, see ¶3030) must file with IRS a quarterly return reporting withheld income taxes on Form 941. (Reg § 31.6011(a)-1, Reg § 31.6011(a)-4) Employers must submit copies of W-4S to IRS only when directed to do so by written notice

---

15. ¶H-4518 *et seq.*; ¶s 34,024.10, 34,024.23; TD ¶538,026
16. ¶H-4513; ¶34,024.10; TD ¶538,021
17. ¶H-4526; ¶34,024.24; TD ¶538,034
18. ¶H-4519; ¶34,024.24; TD ¶538,034

19. ¶H-4531; ¶34,024.11; TD ¶538,040
20. ¶H-4534; ¶34,024.11; TD ¶538,041.1
21. ¶H-4532; ¶34,024.11; TD ¶538,041
22. ¶H-4532; ¶34,024.11; TD ¶538,041

or as directed in published guidance. (Reg § 31.3402(f)(2)-1(g)(1)) Where a serious underwithholding problem is found to exist for a particular employee, IRS will notify the employer to withhold income tax from that employee at a more appropriate rate (i.e., issue a "lock-in letter"). (Reg § 31.3402(f)(2)-1(g)(2))[23]

In certain cases (e.g., for taxpayers who must separately account, see ¶3026) IRS can require monthly wage withholding returns. (Reg § 31.6011(a)-5(a)(1))[24]

Form 941 must be filed by Apr. 30, July 31, Oct. 31 and Jan. 31 for the calendar quarters ending Mar. 31, June 30, Sept. 30 and Dec. 31, respectively, unless monthly filing is required. But the returns may be filed ten days later if timely deposits in full payment of the tax are made. (Reg § 31.6071(a)-1(a))[25]

Form 941, Schedule D, can be used to explain reporting discrepancies after (1) statutory mergers and consolidations, and (2) acquisitions satisfying the requirements for predecessor-successor status (here, discrepancies may arise between amounts reported to the Social Security Administration on Form W-2 and amounts reported to IRS on Form 941).[26]

Employers with annual employment tax liabilities of $1,000 or less who have received written notification from IRS that they qualify for the program can file Form 944 annually, instead of Form 941. (Reg § 31.6011(a)-4T(a)(4))[27]

For nonpayroll withholding (backup withholding, withholding for pension, annuities, and gambling winnings, etc.), see ¶3032.

¶ 3020   Errors in withholding and payment of tax.

Where underwithholding of FICA and income tax is ascertained before the return is filed, the employer must report and pay the correct amount of tax by the due date of the return. (Reg § 31.6151-1, Reg § 31.6205-1(b)(1), Reg § 31.6205-1(c)(1))[28]

Rules are provided for making corrections (in some cases on an interest-free basis) after the return is filed.[29] Form 941-X is used to correct errors in a previously filed Form 941.

¶ 3021   Wage and tax statement—Form W-2.

Along with other information, Form W-2 includes the amount of wages paid by the employer to the employee and the taxes withheld from the wages during the calendar year. (Code Sec. 6051(a)) For tax years beginning after Dec. 31, 2010, an employer must show the value of the employee's health insurance coverage sponsored by the employer (Code Sec. 6051(a)(14)); however, IRS has provided that such reporting is optional for 2011.[30]

An employer in business must give each employee copies of Form W-2, on or before Jan. 31 of the year after the calendar year for which the wages were paid. If an employee leaves the job before the end of the calendar year and isn't expected to return within the calendar year, Form W-2 must be given to him not later than 30 days after the employer receives a written request for it from the employee, if that 30-day period ends before Jan. 31. (Code Sec. 6051; Reg § 31.6051-1(d))[31]

¶ 3022   Nonreceipt of Form W-2 by employee—Form 4852.

If an employee doesn't receive a Form W-2, he should ask his employer for it. If the employer doesn't provide the form, the taxpayer should telephone IRS toll-free at the number listed in the income tax return instructions; IRS will ask the employer to send a copy or duplicate form. If the employee hasn't received a Form W-2 in time to file his tax return, he should file a return estimating wages and the income tax withheld on Form 4852.[32]

23. ¶S-2603; ¶s 34,034, 35,014.002; TD ¶557,001
24. ¶S-2604; ¶60,114.011; TD ¶557,004
25. ¶S-4918; ¶60,114.011; TD ¶557,002
26. ¶S-3195.1
27. ¶S-4918

28. ¶S-5525; ¶35,014.005; TD ¶559,516
29. ¶S-5526; ¶35,014.005; TD ¶559,516
30. ¶S-3152; ¶60,514; TD ¶812,002
31. ¶S-4930; ¶60,514
32. ¶S-3193; TD ¶812,025

¶ 3023   Earned income credit notice to employees with no tax withheld—Notice 797.

An employer must notify any employee who has not had any tax withheld from his wages (other than an employee who certifies, see ¶3017, that he has no tax liability) that the employee may be eligible for a refund because of the earned income credit (¶2344 *et seq.*). IRS Notice 797 or a written statement containing an exact reproduction of the wording in Notice 797 must be used and must be furnished within one week (before or after) the date the employee should receive a timely Form W-2 or, if none is required, before Feb. 8th of the following calendar year. (Reg § 31.6051-1(h))[33]

¶ 3024   Payroll taxes.

The Federal Insurance Contributions Act (FICA) imposes two taxes, the Old Age, Survivors and Disability Insurance (OASDI) tax and the Medicare Hospital Insurance (HI) tax. These taxes are imposed on employers for wages paid with respect to employment and on employees for wages received with respect to employment. The OASDI tax rate is 6.2% on wages up to an annually-adjusted "wage base" (see ¶1107).

The HI tax rate generally is 1.45% on all wages, regardless of amount. For tax years beginning after 2012, an additional 0.9% HI tax applies to certain high wage earners; see ¶1107.

¶ 3025   Payroll tax holiday in 2010 for hiring unemployed workers—Form W-11.

The OASDI tax on employers doesn't apply to wages paid by a qualified employer with respect to employment during the period beginning on Mar. 19, 2010 and ending on Dec. 31, 2010, of any qualified individual for services performed:

. . . in a trade or business of the qualified employer; or

. . . for a qualified employer that is tax-exempt under Code Sec. 501(a), in furtherance of the activities related to the purpose or function on which the employer's exemption is based. (Code Sec. 3111(d)(1))

💡*observation:* The payroll tax holiday applies only to the 6.2% OASDI portion of the employer's tax. It doesn't apply to the 1.45% Medicare (HI) portion of the employer's tax, nor to any part of the employee's tax. It also doesn't affect the self-employment tax paid by self-employed individuals.

💡*caution:* Check http://ria.thomsonreuters.com/federaltaxhandbook to see if the above provision has been extended.

A qualified employer is any employer other than the U.S., a state, or a political subdivision of a state (i.e., a local government, or an instrumentality). (Code Sec. 3111(d)(2)(A)) However, a public institution of higher education is a qualified employer even though it is a government instrumentality. (Code Sec. 3111(d)(2)(B))

A qualified individual is anyone who:

(1) Begins employment with a qualified employer after Feb. 3, 2010, and before Jan. 1, 2011.

(2) Certifies by signed affidavit, under penalties of perjury (use Form W-11), that he hasn't been employed for more than 40 hours during the 60-day period ending on the date the individual begins employment with the qualified employer.

(3) Isn't employed to replace another employee of the qualified employer unless that other employee separated from employment voluntarily or for cause.

---

33. ¶H-4851 *et seq.*; ¶s 324.04, 60,514; TD ¶569,027

(4) Isn't related to the qualified employer in a way that would disqualify him for the work opportunity tax credit (WOTC) under Code Sec. 51(i)(1). (Code Sec. 3111(d)(3))

An employer may qualify for the payroll tax holiday if it hires an otherwise qualified individual to replace one who was terminated for cause or due to other facts and circumstances (e.g., a factory is closed due to lack of demand). When the factory reopens, the payroll tax holiday can be claimed both for rehiring old workers and hiring new workers. The holiday will also be available for employees hired after the employer downsizes.[34]

Special rule for first calendar quarter of 2010. The payroll tax holiday doesn't apply for wages paid during the first calendar quarter of 2010. Instead, the amount by which the qualified employer's OASDI tax for wages paid during the first calendar quarter of 2010 would have been reduced if the payroll tax holiday had been in effect for that quarter is treated as a payment against the qualified employer's OASDI tax for the second calendar quarter of 2010. (Code Sec. 3111(d)(5)(B)) The payment is treated as made on the date when the employer's second-quarter OASDI tax is due.[35] Although a qualified employee who begins work after Feb. 3, 2010 can be eligible for the payroll tax holiday, only the employer's portion of OASDI on his wages paid with respect to employment after Mar. 18, 2010 is forgiven (see above).

Election out; coordination of payroll holiday with WOTC. A qualified employer may elect, in the manner that IRS requires, not to have the payroll tax holiday apply. (Code Sec. 3111(d)(4)) Unless the employer elects out of the payroll holiday, wages paid or incurred to a qualified individual won't qualify for the WOTC (see ¶2318) during the one-year period beginning on the date that the qualified employer hired the individual. (Code Sec. 51(c)(5)) The election can be made on an employee-by-employee basis.[36]

Railroad retirement tax holiday. Effective for compensation paid after Mar. 18, 2010, there's a railroad retirement tax holiday that is similar in many respects to the OASDI tax holiday. (Code Sec. 3221(c), as amended by Act Sec. 101(d))[37]

For the up-to-$1,000 tax credit for retaining qualified individuals, see ¶2317.

Form 941 (¶3019) has been revised in light of the above. Additionally, an employer reports the wages and tips paid to the qualified employee for which it claims the payroll tax exemption (or credit) in Box 12 of revised Form W-2, using new code CC. On revised Form W-3, the total of such amounts for all eligible employees is entered on new Line 12b (HIRE exempt wages and tips).[38]

¶ 3026   Separate accounting for employment tax.

IRS can require an employer who fails to collect, account for, deposit, etc., income or related employment taxes or make timely deposits or file returns to make deposits in a special trust account. (Code Sec. 7512; Reg § 301.7512-1(b))[39]

¶ 3027   Deposit of employment taxes.

An employer is either a monthly or semi-weekly depositor. (Reg § 31.6302-1(a))

An employer is a monthly depositor for the entire calendar year if the aggregate amount of employment taxes reported for the lookback period (i.e., the 12-month period ended the preceding June 30) is $50,000 or less. (Reg § 31.6302-1(b)(2)(i), Reg § 31.6302-1(b)(4)) These employers must deposit taxes on or before the 15th day of the following month. (Reg § 31.6302-1(c)(1))[40]

An employer is a semi-weekly depositor for the entire calendar year if the aggregate amount of employment taxes reported for the lookback period (i.e., the 12-month period ended

34. ¶H-4687.1; ¶31,114; TD ¶541,002.1
35. ¶H-4687.5; ¶31,114; TD ¶541,002.1
36. ¶H-4687.6; ¶31,114; TD ¶541,002.1
37. ¶H-4687.1

38. ¶H-4687.7
39. ¶S-5541 *et seq.*; ¶75,124; TD ¶531,002
40. ¶S-5503; ¶63,014; TD ¶559,503

the preceding June 30) exceeds $50,000. (Reg § 31.6302-1(b)(3), Reg § 31.6302-1(b)(4)) The employer must deposit taxes on or before the following dates. (Reg § 31.6302-1(c)(2))[41]

If the wage payment date is:

. . . Wednesday, Thursday, and/or Friday, the deposit date is on or before the following Wednesday.

. . . Saturday, Sunday, Monday, and/or Tuesday, the deposit date is on or before the following Friday.

If a return period (quarterly or annual) ends during a semi-weekly period, the employer must designate on his deposit coupon the proper return period for which the deposits relates (the period in which the payment is made). If the return period ends during a semi-weekly period during which the employer has two or more payment dates, two deposit obligations may exist. (Reg § 31.6302-1(c)(2)(ii))[42]

Notwithstanding the above rules, under the "one-day rule," if on any day an employer has $100,000 or more of employment taxes accumulated, these taxes must be deposited by the close of the next banking day. (Reg § 31.6302-1(c)(3)) The day after a monthly depositor becomes subject to the one-day rule it becomes a semi-weekly depositor for the remainder of that calendar year and for the following calendar year. (Reg § 31.6302-1(b)(2)(ii))[43]

If a tax deposit day isn't a banking day, deposits are timely if made on the next day that is a banking day. (Reg § 31.6302-1(c)(4)) In addition, if one of the three weekdays following the close of a semi-weekly period is a bank holiday, the employer has an extra banking day to deposit taxes. (Reg § 31.6302-1(c)(2)(iii))[44]

Deposits are considered timely if mailed (postmarked, or date marked by a designated delivery service, see ¶4754) at least two days before the due date if the deposit is actually received by the bank. (Code Sec. 7502(e)) But a deposit of $20,000 or more by a person who is required to make a deposit more than once a month must be actually received by the due date. (Code Sec. 7502(e)(3))[45]

Some taxpayers must deposit taxes by electronic funds transfer (¶3029).

¶ 3028   Deposit safe harbor and de minimis rules.

Under the single deposit safe harbor, an employer will be considered to have satisfied his deposit obligations if:

(1) the amount of any shortfall (the excess of the amount required to be deposited over the amount deposited for the applicable period—monthly, semi-weekly or daily) doesn't exceed the greater of $100 or 2% of the amount of employment taxes required to be deposited (Reg § 31.6302-1(f)(1)(i), Reg § 31.6302-1(f)(2)), and

(2) the employer deposits the shortfall on or before the shortfall make-up date. (Reg § 31.6302-1(f)(1)(ii)) For a monthly depositor this is no later than the due date for the quarterly return. For a semi-weekly or a one-day depositor this is on or before the first Wednesday or Friday (whichever is earlier) falling on or after the 15th day of the month following the month the deposit was required to be made. (Reg § 31.6302-1(f)(3))[46]

Under a de minimis rule, an employer with accumulated employment taxes of less than $2,500 for a return period (quarterly or annual) doesn't have to make deposits and can instead remit his full liability with a timely filed return for the period. (Reg § 31.6302-1(f)(4))[47]

---

41. ¶S-5506; ¶63,014; TD ¶559,504
42. ¶S-5507; ¶63,014; TD ¶559,505
43. ¶S-5510; ¶63,014; TD ¶559,507
44. ¶S-5512; ¶63,014; TD ¶559,508

45. ¶T-10777 *et seq.*; ¶63,014, 75,024
46. ¶S-5513 *et seq.*; ¶63,014; TD ¶559,509
47. ¶S-5516; ¶63,014; TD ¶559,510

¶ 3029   Tax deposits by electronic funds transfer.

Unless exempted, taxpayers whose aggregate annual deposits of certain taxes exceeded $200,000 in a tax year must deposit taxes by electronic funds transfer. (Code Sec. 6302(h); Reg § 31.6302-1(h)(2)(i)(A)) Once taxpayers exceed the $200,000 threshold, they have a one-year grace period before being required to use EFT. They must then use EFT in all later years even if their deposits fall below the threshold. (Reg § 31.6302-1(h)(2)(ii)) The EFT rules apply to return periods beginning after Dec. 31 of the year following the year in which the threshold is exceeded. (Reg § 31.6302-1(h)(2)(i))[48]

A taxpayer required to deposit by EFT must use the Electronic Federal Tax Payment System (EFTPS) to make federal tax deposits.[49] Taxpayers must enroll in EFTPS before they can make EFT deposits. Enroll on-line at www.eftps.com.[50] EFTPS deposits may be initiated directly via EFTPS-Online, EFTPS-PC Software supplied by IRS, or EFTPS-Phone, or through a financial institution using an Automated Clearing House (ACH) credit transaction. Under this system, payments can be made weekly, monthly, or quarterly, and businesses can schedule payments up to 120 days in advance of the due date. Scheduled payments can be changed or cancelled up to two business days in advance of the scheduled date. Tax practitioners and payroll companies can use EFTPS to make payments on behalf of their clients without having to register for EFTPS (although their clients must do so).[1]

Federal income taxes (including estimated taxes) (Reg § 1.6302-4), estate (Reg § 20.6302-1) and gift taxes (Reg § 25.6302-1), employment taxes (Reg § 31.6302-1(h)(2)(iii)), and various excise taxes (Reg § 40.6302(a)-1) may be made voluntarily by EFT.[2]

A taxpayer required to deposit taxes by EFT that (without reasonable cause) deposits by other means is subject to the Code Sec. 6656 failure to deposit penalty.[3]

To induce employers who are not required to use the EFT system to use it, IRS is offering a refund of a previously paid federal tax deposit penalty with interest. To qualify, the employer must use EFT for one year (four consecutive quarters), make all Form 941 payments on time, and have previously fully paid the penalty. IRS automatically determines which employers have achieved the four quarters of EFT compliance and reverses the most recent full-paid FTD penalty minus any outstanding taxes.[4]

⚡/caution: Proposed regs would eliminate paper coupons after 2010, expanding the use of the electronic payment system. However, some businesses paying a minimal amount of tax could continue making payments with the related tax return.

¶ 3030   Payment of Domestic Service Employment Tax ("Nanny tax") ■■■■■■■

Domestic service employment taxes (income tax, FICA, and FUTA) can be paid in a lump sum when the employer's income tax return is filed.

¶ 3031   "Nanny tax"—Form 1040, Schedule H.

Employers of domestic service employees must file annual returns of domestic service employment taxes on a calendar-year basis (Code Sec. 3510(a)(1)) on or before the 15th day of the fourth month following the close of the employer's tax year. (Code Sec. 3510(a)(2)) Household employers report withheld income and FICA tax for their household employees on their individual income tax return (Form 1040, Schedule H) and need employer identification numbers (EINs, apply on Form SS-4).[5]

Annual Form 940 (FUTA) doesn't have to be filed for domestic employees. There is no requirement to make deposits of domestic service employment taxes, or to pay installments of

48. ¶S-5620 *et seq.*; ¶63,014; TD ¶559,850 *et seq.*
49. ¶S-5621; TD ¶559,857
50. ¶S-5630; TD ¶559,857
1. ¶S-5631 *et seq.*; TD ¶559,851 *et seq.*

2. ¶S-5629; TD ¶559,863 *et seq.*
3. ¶V-1658; TD ¶559,853
4. ¶S-5629
5. ¶S-2608; ¶35,104; TD ¶557,007

these taxes under Code Sec. 6157 (Code Sec. 3510(a)(3)), dealing with quarterly payment of FUTA tax.

"Domestic service employment taxes" are: (1) any FICA and FUTA taxes on remuneration paid for domestic service in a private home of the employer (for dollar threshold see below), and (2) and any income tax on these payments that is withheld under the Code Sec. 3402(p) voluntary withholding agreement rules (¶3009) (for the otherwise applicable exemption from income tax withholding on domestic service employment, see ¶3006). (Code Sec. 3510(c))[6]

Domestic service is service of a household nature performed in and about the private home of the person for whom the services are performed. (Reg § 31.3121(a)(7)-1(a), Reg § 31.3401(a)(3)-1(a))[7]

Noncash payments for domestic services in an employer's private home are excluded from FICA wages. Cash remuneration paid by an employer for domestic service in the employer's private home isn't FICA wages if the cash remuneration paid during the year is less than the "applicable dollar threshold" —$1,700 in 2010 and 2011. (Code Sec. 3121(a)(7), Code Sec. 3121(x))[8]

⊙ observation: The dollar threshold applies separately to each domestic employee. Thus, for example, if an employer pays $1,650 each to a babysitter and a housekeeper in 2010, no FICA tax is due for either.

Domestic service performed in the private home of the employer in any year by an individual under the age of 18 during any portion of the year is excepted from employment for FICA if the service isn't the principal occupation of the employee. (Code Sec. 3121(b)(21))[9]

Form W-2. An employer must furnish Form W-2 to household employees whose wages are subject to Social Security taxes even if they aren't subject to income tax withholding. (Reg § 31.6051-1(b)(1)) Use a Form W-3 transmittal to file even one Form W-2.[10]

¶ 3032   Nonpayroll Withheld Taxes. ■■■■■■■■■■■■■■■■■■■■■■■■■■■■■

Income tax on gambling winnings, payments subject to backup withholding, retirement plan payments, IRAs, annuities and certain other deferred compensation are withheld under "nonpayroll withheld taxes" rules.

The employment tax deposit rules of ¶3027 *et seq.* apply to determine the time and manner of making deposits of nonpayroll withheld taxes. (Reg § 31.6302-4(a))[11] Whether a taxpayer is a monthly or a semi-weekly depositor for a calendar year is based on an annual determination and generally depends on the aggregate amount of nonpayroll withheld taxes reported by the taxpayer for the "lookback period" —i.e., the second calendar year preceding the current calendar year. Thus, the lookback period for calendar year 2010 is calendar year 2008. A new taxpayer is treated as having nonpayroll withheld taxes of zero for any calendar year in which the taxpayer didn't exist. (Reg § 31.6302-4(c)(2)(iv))[12]

A taxpayer is a monthly depositor of nonpayroll withheld taxes for a calendar year if the amount of nonpayroll withheld taxes accumulated in the lookback period is $50,000 or less. A taxpayer ceases to be a monthly depositor of nonpayroll withheld taxes on the first day after the taxpayer is subject to the "one-day rule" (¶3027) with respect to nonpayroll withheld taxes. At that time, the taxpayer immediately becomes a semi-weekly depositor of nonpayroll withheld taxes for the remainder of the calendar year and the succeeding calendar year. (Reg § 31.6302-4(c)(2)(ii))

A taxpayer is a semi-weekly depositor of nonpayroll withheld taxes for a calendar year if the amount of nonpayroll withheld taxes accumulated in the lookback period exceeds $50,000. (Reg § 31.6302-4(c)(2)(iii))

6. ¶S-2608.3; ¶35,104
7. ¶H-4654; TD ¶536,006
8. ¶H-4653 *et seq.*; ¶35,104; TD ¶544,009
9. ¶H-4611.1
10. ¶S-3159; TD ¶812,004
11. ¶S-5584 *et seq.*; ¶63,014
12. ¶S-5585; ¶63,014; TD ¶559,005

Nonpayroll withheld taxes are income taxes withheld from: gambling winnings (¶3034) (Reg § 31.6302-4(b)(1)); retirement pay for services in the Armed Forces under Code Sec. 3402 (Reg § 31.6302-4(b)(2); retirement plan payments, IRAs, annuities and certain other deferred compensation (¶3035) (Reg § 31.6302-4(b)(3)); certain payments by governmental entities made after 2011 (Code Sec. 3402(t)); and under the backup withholding rules (¶3045). (Reg § 31.6302-4(b)(5))[13]

For the requirement that some taxpayers deposit nonpayroll withheld taxes by electronic funds transfer (EFT), see ¶3029.

¶ 3033   Annual nonpayroll tax return—Form 945.

Taxpayers who withhold income tax from nonpayroll payments must report the withholding annually on Form 945. The return must be filed on or before Jan. 31 following the calendar year. However, if timely deposits of tax have been made, the return may be filed by Feb. 10. (Reg § 31.6071(a)-1(a)(1))[14]

¶ 3034   Withholding on gambling winnings—Form W-2G and Form 5754.

In 2010, payors must withhold 25% on proceeds of more than $5,000 (Code Sec. 3402(q)(1)) from:

(1) a wagering transaction in a parimutuel pool with respect to horse races, dog races or jai alai if the amount of the proceeds is at least 300 times as large as the amount wagered; (Code Sec. 3402(q)(3)(C)(ii))

(2) a wager placed in a state-conducted lottery; (Code Sec. 3402(q)(3)(B))

(3) a sweepstakes, wagering pool or lottery (other than a state-conducted lottery); or (Code Sec. 3402(q)(3)(C)(i))

(4) all other wagering transactions if the amount of the proceeds is at least 300 times as large as the amount wagered. (Code Sec. 3402(q)(3)(A))[15]

caution: For EGTRRA sunset rules, see ¶1114.

"Proceeds" means amount received from the wager reduced by the amount of the wager. (Code Sec. 3402(q)(4)(A))[16] Amounts paid with respect to identical wagers are treated as paid with respect to a single wager. (Reg § 31.3402(q)-1(c)(1)(ii))[17]

A person who receives gambling winnings subject to withholding must provide certain information on Form W-2G or Form 5754 and give it to the payor. (Code Sec. 3402(q)(6); Reg § 31.3402(q)-1(e))[18]

The above withholding rules don't apply to slot machines, keno and bingo winnings. (Code Sec. 3402(q)(5)) However, backup withholding (¶3045) may apply.[19] And a payor must file Form a W-2G for every person the payor pays $1,200 or more in winnings from slot machines or bingo, or $1,500 or more from Keno (after deducting the cost of the winning Keno game). (Reg § 7.6041-1)[20]

Casinos and other sponsors of poker tournaments must report tournament winnings of more than $5,000. Sponsors who comply with the reporting requirement will not need to withhold federal income tax. However, if the reporting requirement is not met, IRS will enforce it and also require the sponsor to pay any tax that should have been withheld.[21]

Withholding on Indian casino profits. Withholding equal to a payment's proportionate share of annualized tax is required under tables provided by IRS (Reg § 31.3402(r)-1(a)(2)) on payments to Indian tribal members from the net revenue of most gambling activities of the

13. ¶S-5581; ¶63,014
14. ¶S-2609.1 *et seq.*, S-4918; TD ¶559,000 *et seq.*
15. ¶J-8603; ¶34,024.26; TD ¶554,001 *et seq.*
16. ¶J-8606 *et seq.*; ¶34,024.26; TD ¶554,002
17. ¶J-8610; ¶34,024.26; TD ¶554,006
18. ¶J-8614; ¶34,024.26; TD ¶554,010
19. ¶J-8604; ¶34,024.26; TD ¶554,002
20. ¶S-3697; ¶60,414; TD ¶816,025
21. ¶J-8603; ¶34,024.26; TD ¶554,002

tribe (i.e., class II and III gaming activities). (Code Sec. 3402(r))[22]

¶ 3035 Pension, Annuity and Other Withholding. ▬▬▬▬▬▬▬

Withholding of 20% is required on any designated distribution that's an eligible rollover distribution, unless there's a direct trustee-to-trustee transfer. Withholding is required on periodic and lump-sum payments from certain employee plans and certain annuities. However, certain recipients may elect not to have tax withheld.

¶ 3036 Mandatory 20% withholding on eligible rollover distributions.

Unless a distributee elects to have the distribution paid directly to an eligible retirement plan under the Code Sec. 401(a)(31)(A) trustee-to-trustee rules (¶4319), a payor must withhold 20% of any designated distribution that's an "eligible rollover distribution" as defined by Code Sec. 402(f)(2)(A). The Code Sec. 3405(a) and Code Sec. 3405(b) elective withholding rules (¶3037 *et seq.*) don't apply to an eligible rollover distribution. (Code Sec. 3405(c); Reg § 31.3405(c)-1, Q&A-1)[23]

An eligible rollover distribution (reported by the payor on Form 1099-R) (Reg § 31.3405(c)-1, Q&A-16) is any distribution to an employee from a qualified trust (not from an IRA, SEP, or SIMPLE plan) *other than:*

. . . a required distribution under Code Sec. 401(a)(9);

. . . any distribution that is one of a series of substantially equal periodic payments made (a) not less frequently than annually for the life (or life expectancy) of the employee (or joint lives or expectancies of the employee and his designated beneficiary), or (b) for a specified period of ten years or more; or

. . . a hardship distribution from a 401(k) or 403(b) plan. (Code Sec. 3405(c)(3), Code Sec. 402(c)(4), Code Sec. 402(f)(2)(A), Code Sec. 403(b)(8)(B); Reg § 1.402(c)-2, Q&A-3[24]

No withholding is required: (1) if the total distribution paid to the distributee under the plan within one tax year is expected to be less than $200; or (Reg § 31.3405(c)-1, Q&A-14[25] (2) for qualified hurricane distributions, see ¶4344. (Code Sec. 1400Q(a))[26]

¶ 3037 Required withholding for designated distributions.

Withholding is required for designated distributions (Code Sec. 3405(d)(1)),[27] but the recipient generally may elect out, see ¶3039, unless the distribution is an eligible rollover distribution, see ¶3036. Designated distributions are periodic as well as nonperiodic (including lump-sum) payments from pension, profit sharing, stock bonus or other employer deferred compensation plans, as well as from IRAs (other than Roth IRAs) and commercial annuities, whether or not the contract was purchased under an employer's plan for employees. (Code Sec. 3405(e)) Annuity payments and other distributions under a state or local government deferred compensation plan, other than a Code Sec. 457 plan, including the Civil Service Retirement System are subject to income tax withholding as well. (Reg § 35.3405-1T, Q&A-22 and 23)[28]

The payor of a designated distribution must withhold and is liable for the payment of the tax (unless the payee elects out). But in the case of a qualified pension, profit sharing, stock bonus, annuity, or 457 governmental plan, the plan administrator has the responsibility, unless he directs the payor to withhold and provides the payor with the information set out in the regs. In that case, the responsibility reverts to the payor. (Code Sec. 3405(d); Reg § 35.3405-1T, Q&A E-3)[29]

22. ¶J-8616.1; ¶34,024.261; TD ¶554,013
23. ¶J-8577 *et seq.*; ¶34,054; TD ¶553,244 *et seq.*
24. ¶J-8586; ¶4024.04; TD ¶553,246
25. ¶s J-8584; ¶4014.22; TD ¶553,247

26. ¶H-11006.1; ¶14,00Q4; TD ¶553,244
27. ¶J-8501 *et seq.*; ¶34,054; TD ¶553,204
28. ¶J-8504 *et seq.*; ¶34,054; TD ¶553,203
29. ¶J-8518 *et seq.*; ¶34,054; TD ¶553,205

¶ 3038   Withholding from periodic payments.

Tax must be withheld in accordance with a recipient's withholding certificate or, if none, by treating the payee as a married individual claiming three withholding exemptions (Code Sec. 3405(a)(4))[30] even if the payor is aware the payee is single. (Reg § 35.3405-1T, Q&A B-4) The amount to be withheld is calculated separately from any amounts that actually are wages to the payee for the same period. (Reg § 35.3405-1T, Q&A B-1)

To prevent underwithholding due to reduced withholding in connection with the Making Work Pay Credit (¶2343) in 2009 and 2010, IRS has provided optional procedures for pension payors allowing for increased withholding.[31]

¶ 3039   Election out of withholding on periodic payments—Form W-4P.

A recipient of periodic payments (except for certain U.S. citizens and expatriates living abroad, see ¶3043) may elect not to have any tax withheld. The election remains in effect until revoked. (Code Sec. 3405(a)(2))[32] Elect (or revoke) on Form W-4P.[33]

If the recipient doesn't furnish his taxpayer identification number (TIN) to the payor or if IRS has notified the payor that the TIN furnished is incorrect, an election out of withholding isn't effective. (Code Sec. 3405(e)(12))[34]

For periodic payments that are "eligible rollover distributions," see ¶3036.

¶ 3040   Withholding from nonperiodic distributions.

The payor of any nonperiodic distribution that is not an eligible rollover distribution subject to 20% mandatory withholding (¶3036) must withhold an amount equal to 10% of that distribution (Code Sec. 3405(b)(1)),[35] unless the recipient elects out of withholding (¶3041).

¶ 3041   Electing out of withholding on nonperiodic distributions—Form W-4P.

A payee (except for recipients of eligible rollover distributions (¶3036), and certain U.S. citizens and expatriates living abroad (¶3043)) may elect exemption from withholding for any nonperiodic distribution. The election is made on Form W-4P on a distribution-by-distribution basis. (Code Sec. 3405(b)(2)(A), Code Sec. 3405(b)(2)(B))[36]

If the recipient doesn't furnish his taxpayer identification number (TIN) to the payor or if IRS has notified the payor that the TIN furnished is incorrect, an election out of withholding isn't effective. (Code Sec. 3405(e)(12))[37]

¶ 3042   Payor must notify payee of right to elect to have no tax withheld.

For periodic payments, the notice to make, renew, or revoke the election out of withholding is required no earlier than six months before and no later than the date of the first payment. For nonperiodic payments the notice should be given not earlier than six months before the distribution and not later than the time that will give the payee reasonable time to elect out. (Code Sec. 3405(e)(10)(B); Reg § 35.3405-1T, Q&A D-4 and D-9)[38] The notice must state that withholding will apply unless the payee elects otherwise, and if he elects no withholding, estimated tax may apply. A sample statement is in the regs. (Reg § 35.3405-1T, Q&A D-21 and D-25)[39]

30. ¶J-8525; ¶34,054; TD ¶553,220
31. ¶J-8501 *et seq.*
32. ¶J-8526; ¶34,054; TD ¶553,221
33. ¶J-8528; ¶34,054; TD ¶553,221
34. ¶J-8513; TD ¶553,212

35. ¶J-8533; ¶34,054; TD ¶553,227
36. ¶J-8539; ¶34,054; TD ¶553,230
37. ¶J-8513; ¶34,054; TD ¶553,212
38. ¶J-8528 *et seq.*, ¶J-8539 *et seq.*; ¶34,054; TD ¶553,223
39. ¶J-8541, J-8543; ¶34,054; TD ¶553,223

¶ 3043 Electing out of withholding where payment is delivered outside the U.S.

An election out of withholding can't be made for any periodic or nonperiodic payment that is to be delivered outside the U.S. and its possessions (Code Sec. 3405(e)(13)(A)) *unless* the recipient certifies to the payor that the recipient is neither a U.S. citizen, a resident alien, nor a nonresident alien who in the last ten years has lost his U.S. citizenship in order to avoid U.S. taxes and is therefore subject to Code Sec. 877. (Code Sec. 3405(e)(13)(B))[40]

¶ 3044 Backup Withholding.

A payor of any reportable payment must withhold a specified percentage of the payment.

¶ 3045 When backup withholding is required.

In 2010, a payor of any reportable payment (¶3046) must withhold 28% of the payment if:

(1) The payee has failed to furnish his taxpayer identification number (TIN) to the payor (Code Sec. 3406(a)(1)(A)) or furnishes an "obviously incorrect number," (Code Sec. 3406(h)(1)) i.e., one without nine digits or which includes letters of the alphabet. (Reg § 31.3406(h)-1(b))

(2) IRS or a broker has notified (the "B-notice") the payor that the TIN furnished by the payee is incorrect. (Code Sec. 3406(a)(1), Code Sec. 3406(d)(2))

(3) There has been a notified payee underreporting with respect to interest and dividends. (Code Sec. 3406(a)(1)(C))

(4) The payee has failed to make the exemption certification (on Form W-9) with respect to interest and dividends. (Code Sec. 3406(a)(1)(D))[41]

caution: For EGTRRA sunset rules, see ¶1114.

Backup withholding doesn't apply to any payment made to an organization exempt from tax under Code Sec. 501(a) (with certain exceptions); the U.S., a state, the District of Columbia, a U.S. possession, or their political subdivisions; a foreign government or its political subdivisions; an international organization; any wholly-owned agency or instrumentality of any of the above political entities; or any other person specified in regs. (Code Sec. 3406(g)(1)) Payments to a fiduciary or nominee account, or to an exempt recipient (Reg § 31.3406(d)-5(b)) aren't subject to backup withholding.[42]

¶ 3046 Reportable payments.

Reportable payments include most payments for which information returns are required, such as an interest or dividend payment. (Code Sec. 3406(b)(1))[43] Original issue discount (OID) is treated as a payment of interest for backup withholding purposes, but the amount withheld is limited to the cash paid. (Reg § 31.3406(b)(2)-2(a))[44] For amounts paid after 2011, reportable credit card transactions (¶4745) are reportable payments. (Code Sec. 3406(b)(3))

Reportable payments are treated as if they were wages. Amounts deducted and withheld are treated as if they were deducted and withheld from wages. (Code Sec. 3406(h)(10))[45]

¶ 3047 How to stop backup withholding.

A payee can stop backup withholding once it has started, by showing that there was no underreporting, correcting any underreporting, showing that backup withholding will cause undue hardship and that it's unlikely he will underreport again, or showing that a bona fide

---

40. ¶J-8554; ¶34,054
41. ¶J-9001; ¶34,064; TD ¶554,501
42. ¶J-9109; ¶34,064; TD ¶554,502

43. ¶J-9101; ¶34,064; TD ¶554,503
44. ¶J-9111; ¶34,064
45. ¶J-9009; TD ¶554,501

dispute exists as to whether there has been any underreporting. (Reg § 35a.3406-2(g)(1), Reg § 31.3406(c)-1(g)) If IRS determines that backup withholding should stop, it will give the payee a written certification to that effect and notify payors and brokers to stop withholding. (Reg § 35a.3406-2(h)(1), Reg § 35a.3406-2(d)(1), Reg § 31.3406(c)-1(g)(1))

Withholding must stop as of the close of the day before the "stop date" (generally 30 days after receipt of the stop notice from IRS or a copy of the certification IRS gave the payee, whichever is earlier). (Code Sec. 3406(e)(3)(C)) The payor may elect to shorten or eliminate the 30-day period. (Code Sec. 3406(e)(5)(C); Reg § 35a.3406-2(e)(2)(iii), Reg § 31.3406(c)-1(e)(2)(i)(B)).[46]

---

46. ¶J-9607; ¶34,064; TD ¶554,513

Chapter 13 Individual's Tax Computation—Kiddie Tax— Self-Employment Tax—Estimated Tax

¶ 3100 How Income Tax on Individuals is Computed. ▮▮▮▮▮▮▮▮▮▮▮▮▮▮▮▮

An individual's annual income tax liability on taxable income is computed using either the tax rate schedules or (if taxable income is less than $100,000) the tax tables, see ¶1101 *et seq.* This tax liability may be increased by other taxes, e.g., self-employment tax or alternative minimum tax, and is reduced by certain credits.

For taxation of unearned income of children subject to the kiddie tax, see ¶3135 *et seq.*

For the threshold amounts of gross income that must be reached before a tax return must be filed, see ¶4701.

¶ 3101 Steps in computing taxable income.

An individual taxpayer first computes gross income—generally all income from all sources (Code Sec. 61), see ¶1200 *et seq.*

From gross income, taxpayer subtracts the deductions specified at ¶3102 to reach adjusted gross income (AGI). (Code Sec. 62)

Finally, taxpayers who itemize reduce AGI by allowable deductions and personal exemptions (¶3115) (Code Sec. 63(a)), see ¶3109 *et seq.* Nonitemizers reduce AGI by the standard deduction (¶3112) and personal exemptions. (Code Sec. 63(b))[1]

¶ 3102 Deductions taken "above the line" to reach adjusted gross income (AGI).

Subtract the following deductions from gross income to reach AGI: (Code Sec. 62)[2]

. . . Trade or business expenses (¶1508) (other than unreimbursed employee business expenses, see ¶3104). For business-related deductions of "statutory employees," see ¶3103.

. . . Self-employed medical insurance premiums, ¶1533.

. . . Moving expenses, ¶1645 *et seq.*

. . . 50% of self-employment tax, ¶1755.

. . . Amortization of reforestation expenditures, ¶1972.

. . . Amounts forfeited to a bank or savings institution for premature withdrawal of funds from a deposit account, ¶2171.

. . . Alimony and separate maintenance payments, ¶2154 *et seq.*

. . . Employee expenses that are reimbursed by the employer or a third party, ¶3104.

. . . Employee business expenses of certain performing artists (¶3105) and of state and local government employees compensated on a fee basis, ¶3106.

. . . Jury duty pay remitted to an employer, ¶3107.

. . . Contributions to tax-favored retirement plans for the self-employed, ¶4327.

. . . Contributions to individual retirement accounts (IRAs) or annuities, ¶4351.

. . . The "total taxable amount" of a retirement plan lump-sum distribution with respect to a participant born before '36, to the extent included in recipient's gross income, ¶4339.

. . . Deductions for property held for production of rents or royalties. (Code Sec. 62(a)(4))

. . . Depreciation and depletion deductions of a life tenant or an income beneficiary of a trust, or of an heir, legatee or devisee of an estate, ¶3927.

. . . Losses from the sale or exchange of property, ¶2400.

. . . Repayments of supplemental unemployment compensation. (Code Sec. 62(a)(12))

---

1. ¶A-2500 *et seq.*; ¶634; TD ¶560,500 *et seq.*   2. ¶A-2601; ¶624; TD ¶560,702

References beginning with a single letter are to paragraphs in RIA's Federal Tax Coordinator 2d and RIA's Analysis of Federal Taxes: Income. Those beginning with numbers are to paragraphs in RIA's United States Tax Reporter. Those beginning with TD are to paragraphs in RIA's Tax Desk.

509

... Certain foreign housing costs of individuals having income earned abroad, ¶4614.

... Contributions to an Archer medical savings account (Archer MSA, see ¶1528).

... Contributions to a health savings account (HSA, see ¶1529).

... Deduction for interest on qualified education loans, ¶2225 *et seq.*

... Payments for deductible higher education expenses before 2010, ¶2222 *et seq.*

... Up to $250 of qualifying expenses of educators before 2010, ¶2232.

... Certain unreimbursed travel expenses of National Guard and Reserve members, ¶1554.

... Attorney fees and court costs of civil rights suits and whistleblower awards, ¶3108.

caution: Check http://ria.thomsonreuters.com/federaltaxhandbook to see if the education expense deductions have been extended.

¶ 3103   Business-related expenses of "statutory employees."

For purposes of computing adjusted gross income, the allowable deductions attributable to the services rendered by a statutory employee (drivers, life insurance salespersons, home workers and other salespersons meeting certain conditions) are treated as trade or business expenses (deductible on Schedule C, rather than as itemized deductions).[3]

¶ 3104   Reimbursed and unreimbursed employee expenses.

In computing AGI, an employee can deduct from gross income employee expenses for which the employee is reimbursed by the employer, its agent, or third party (for whom the employee performs services as an employee of the employer) under an express agreement for reimbursement or other expense allowance under an accountable plan. (But there's no normal "deduction," since the reimbursement is excluded from the employee's gross income —i.e., no deduction for the expense to the extent there's no inclusion of the reimbursement.) (Code Sec. 62(a)(2)(A); Reg § 1.62-2(c)(4))[4] The expense must be otherwise allowable as a deduction (i.e., not a personal expense).[5]

If the reimbursement is for less than the total expenses paid or incurred by the employee, the unreimbursed expenses are deductible from *adjusted* gross income (not gross income), as an itemized deduction, subject to, for example, the 2%-of-AGI floor (¶3110), and the percentage limit on meal and entertainment expenses (¶1570). (Reg § 1.62-1T(e)(3))[6]

A reimbursement or other expense allowance arrangement under an accountable plan is one that meets tests for (1) business connection, (2) substantiation, and (3) return of amounts in excess of expenses. (Reg § 1.62-2(c)(2)) See ¶1574 *et seq.* for details.

A payor can have more than one arrangement as to one employee. (Reg § 1.62-2(c)(1))[7]

¶ 3105   Expenses of certain performing artists.

Expenses of certain performing artists are deductible (use Form 2106 or Form 2106-EZ) in arriving at adjusted gross income (AGI) (despite the disallowance of unreimbursed employee business expenses as above-the-line deductions). (Code Sec. 62(a)(2)(B)) To qualify, the taxpayer must have earned at least $200 as a performing artist from each of at least two employers during the tax year. (Code Sec. 62(b)(1)(A), Code Sec. 62(b)(2)) Also, the allowable expenses must exceed 10% of gross income from the services, and AGI for the year (before deducting these expenses) can't exceed $16,000. (Code Sec. 62(b)(1)(B), Code Sec. 62(b)(1)(C)) A married performing artist who lives with his spouse at any time during the year must file a joint return to deduct these expenses to reach AGI. (Code Sec. 62(b)(3)(A)) The two-employer requirement and 10%-of-gross-income test are applied separately to each spouse, but the

3. ¶A-2603; ¶624.03; TD ¶560,704
4. ¶A-2604; ¶624.02; TD ¶561,001
5. ¶A-2602; ¶624.02; TD ¶561,001

6. ¶A-2605; ¶624.02; TD ¶561,003
7. ¶L-4703.2; TD ¶561,006

$16,000 test is applied to their combined income. (Code Sec. 62(b)(3)(B))[8]

¶ 3106 Business expenses of state and local officials paid on a fee basis.

Employee business expenses relating to service as an official of a state or local government (or a political subdivision thereof) are deductible in computing AGI, if the official is compensated on a fee basis. (Code Sec. 62(a)(2)(C))[9]

¶ 3107 Jury duty pay remitted to an employer.

An individual may deduct jury pay from gross income if the individual is required to remit any of the jury pay to his employer in exchange for compensation for the period the individual was performing jury duty. (Code Sec. 62(a)(13))[10]

¶ 3108 Attorney fees & court costs of civil rights suits and whistleblower awards.

Any deduction allowable under Chapter 1 for attorney fees and court costs paid by, or on behalf of, the taxpayer in connection with the following is deductible from gross income:

. . . an action involving a claim (1) of unlawful discrimination (defined in Code Sec. 62(e)), (2) of a violation of subchapter III of chapter 37 of title 31, United States Code (Claims Against the U.S. Government), or (3) made under Sec. 1862(b)(3)(A) of the Social Security Act (42 U.S.C. 1395y(b)(3)(A)) (private cause of action under the Medicare Secondary Payer statute), but only up to the amount includible in taxpayer's gross income for the tax year on account of the judgment or settlement. (Code Sec. 62(a)(20))[11]

. . . any Code Sec. 7623(b) whistleblower award, but only up to the amount includible in taxpayer's gross income for the tax year on account of the award. (Code Sec. 62(a)(21))[12]

¶ 3109 Itemized deductions.

Itemized deductions are all the allowable Chapter 1 deductions *other than* the deductions taken from gross income to reach adjusted gross income (¶3102) and the deductions for personal exemptions. (Code Sec. 63(d))[13]

caution: For itemized deductions under the alternative minimum tax, see ¶3209.

¶ 3110 Miscellaneous itemized deductions—2%-of-AGI floor.

Miscellaneous itemized deductions are allowed only to the extent that they, in the aggregate, exceed 2% of adjusted gross income (AGI). (Code Sec. 67(a))[14] To the extent any other limit or restriction is placed on a miscellaneous itemized deduction, that other limit applies before the 2% floor. For example, the 2% floor is applied after the percentage limit for business meals and entertainment (¶1570). (Reg § 1.67-1T(a)(2))[15]

observation: Miscellaneous itemized deductions that don't exceed 2% of AGI are lost. There's no carryover.

Miscellaneous itemized deductions are itemized deductions *other than* deductions for medical expenses; taxes; interest; charitable contributions; casualty and theft losses; gambling losses (non-professional gamblers); impairment-related work expenses; estate tax on income in respect of a decedent; personal property used in a short sale; restored amounts held under claim of right; annuity payments ending before investment is recovered; amortizable bond premium; tenant-stockholder share of co-op housing corp expenses. (Code Sec. 67(b))[16]

8. ¶A-2611; ¶624.02; TD ¶560,705
9. ¶A-2611.1; ¶624.02; TD ¶560,706
10. ¶A-2623; ¶624.04; TD ¶560,723
11. ¶A-2628; ¶624.04; TD ¶560,715.2
12. ¶A-2629; ¶624.04; TD ¶560,702

13. ¶A-2700 *et seq.*; ¶634; TD ¶561,201
14. ¶A-2711 *et seq.*; ¶674; TD ¶561,601
15. ¶A-2711; ¶674; TD ¶561,601
16. ¶A-2721 *et seq.*; ¶674; TD ¶561,603

Miscellaneous itemized deductions *include* unreimbursed employee business expenses, including union and professional dues and home office expenses; expenses related to investment income or property, e.g., investment counsel or advisory fees; allowable losses from traditional IRAs (¶4357) or Roth IRAs (¶4373); tax return preparation costs and related expenses, including credit/debit card convenience fees charged for paying federal individual income taxes (for deduction of tax determination costs as business expenses, see ¶1513); tax counsel and appraisal fees paid to determine the amount of a casualty loss or charitable contribution of property; and hobby expenses to the extent of hobby income. (Reg § 1.67-1T(a)(1))[17]

If an expense relates to both a trade or business activity (not subject to the 2% floor) and a production of income or tax preparation activity (subject to the 2% floor) the taxpayer must allocate it between the activities on a reasonable basis. (Reg § 1.67-1T(c))[18]

¶ 3111   2% floor applied to partnerships, S corporations, and other pass-through entities.

A partner or S corporation shareholder must take into account separately his distributive or pro rata share of the partnership's or S corporation's miscellaneous itemized deductions. Similarly, the 2% floor applies to the grantor (or other person treated as the owner) of a grantor trust with respect to items treated as miscellaneous itemized deductions of the grantor (or other owner). (Reg § 1.67-2T(b)(1))[19] Similar rules apply to affected investors in common trust funds (Reg § 1.67-2T(d)(1)(ii)),[20] nonpublicly offered regulated investment companies (RICs), (Reg § 1.67-2T(e)(1)(ii))[21] and REMICs. (Reg § 1.67-3T(b)(1))[22]

The above rules don't apply to publicly offered RICs (Code Sec. 67(c)(2)), cooperatives, and REITs. (Code Sec. 67(c)(3))[23] For estates and trusts, see ¶3921.

¶ 3112   Standard deduction.

The standard deduction is the sum of the basic standard deduction, and the additional standard deduction, as adjusted each year for inflation. (Code Sec. 63(c)(1))[24] The basic standard deduction amounts for 2010 are:[25]

Basic Standard Deduction

Filing Status	2010
Joint filers and surviving spouses	$11,400
Heads of household	8,400
Singles	5,700
Marrieds filing separately	5,700

For 2010, the basic standard deduction of individuals who can be claimed as dependents by another taxpayer can't exceed the greater of (a) $950 or (b) $300 plus the individual's earned income. But the basic standard deduction can't be more than the regular basic standard deduction amount shown above ($5,700 for 2010). (Code Sec. 63(c)(5))[26]

The standard deduction is zero for: a married individual filing separately whose spouse itemizes deductions; a nonresident alien individual; and an individual filing a short-year return due to an accounting period change. (Code Sec. 63(c)(6))[27]

Elderly and blind taxpayers get additional standard deductions. (Code Sec. 63(c)(3)) A taxpayer who is 65 before the end of his tax year, or blind at the end of his tax year, is entitled to an additional standard deduction. For 2010, the additional standard deduction amounts are:

17. ¶A-2722 *et seq.*; ¶674; TD ¶561,603
18. ¶A-2725, A-2726 *et seq.*; ¶674; TD ¶561,603
19. ¶A-2715; ¶674; TD ¶561,610
20. ¶A-2716; ¶674; TD ¶561,611
21. ¶A-2717; ¶674; TD ¶561,612
22. ¶A-2713; ¶674; TD ¶561,608
23. ¶A-2713; ¶674; TD ¶561,601
24. ¶A-2801; ¶634; TD ¶562,001
25. ¶A-2803; ¶634; TD ¶562,003
26. ¶A-2806; ¶634; TD ¶562,003
27. ¶A-2802; ¶634; TD ¶562,002

(Code Sec. 63(f)(1), Code Sec. 63(f)(2), Code Sec. 63(f)(3), Code Sec. 63(c)(4))[28]

Additional Standard Deduction

Filing Status	2010
Marrieds and surviving spouses	$1,100
Heads of household	1,400
Singles	1,400

caution: For EGTRRA sunset rules, see ¶1114.

One who's elderly *and* blind gets each additional standard deduction. (Code Sec. 63(c)(3))[29]

A married individual who files a separate return can claim a spouse's additional standard deduction if the spouse has no gross income and isn't the dependent of another taxpayer. (Code Sec. 63(f)(1)(B), Code Sec. 63(f)(2)(B), Code Sec. 151(b))[30]

An individual claiming an additional standard deduction for blindness must get (and keep, but not file) a certification from an eye doctor or registered optometrist. If blindness is certified as irreversible, certification is necessary only once.[31]

On a decedent's final return, the fiduciary may claim the full amount of the appropriate standard deduction regardless of the date of death.[32]

caution: For the standard deduction under the alternative minimum tax, see ¶3209.

caution: Check http://ria.thomsonreuters.com/federaltaxhandbook to see if components of the standard deduction that applied before 2010 have been extended.

¶ 3113 Election to itemize deductions in computing taxable income.

No itemized deductions are allowed unless an election to itemize is made on the return. (Code Sec. 63(e)(1), Code Sec. 63(e)(2)) A taxpayer who elected to itemize and wants to switch to the standard deduction, or vice versa, can. But the change isn't allowed unless his separately filing spouse makes a consistent change, and both spouses consent in writing to assessment of any deficiency resulting from the change. (Code Sec. 63(e)(3); Reg § 1.63-1)[33]

¶ 3114 Reduction in itemized deductions (3%/80% rule) before 2010.

For tax years beginning in 2010, individuals aren't subject to the Code Sec. 68 reduction in itemized deductions that otherwise applies if AGI exceeds certain amounts. (Code Sec. 68(g))[34]

Under Code Sec. 68, if an individual's AGI exceeds an inflation-adjusted "applicable amount" (for 2009: $166,800 ($83,400 for married filing separately), certain otherwise allowable itemized deductions are reduced by the *lesser* of: (1) 3% of the excess of AGI over the applicable amount, or (2) 80% of the itemized deductions otherwise allowable for the tax year. (Code Sec. 68(a), Code Sec. 68(b))[35]

The reduction is determined after the application of any other limits on an itemized deduction (Code Sec. 68(d))[36] and doesn't apply to the deductions for medical expenses, investment interest, nonbusiness casualty and theft losses, and gambling losses. (Code Sec. 68(c))[37]

caution: For EGTRRA sunset rules, see ¶1114.

28. ¶A-2806, A-2807; ¶634; TD ¶562,004, 562,005
29. ¶A-2804; ¶634; TD ¶562,004
30. ¶A-2804; TD ¶562,004
31. ¶A-2808; TD ¶562,006
32. ¶C-9603; ¶60,124.04; TD ¶579,507
33. ¶A-2702; ¶634; TD ¶561,202
34. ¶A-2731; ¶684; TD ¶561,801
35. ¶A-2731; ¶684; TD ¶561,801
36. ¶A-2731; ¶684; TD ¶561,803
37. ¶A-2731; ¶684; TD ¶561,802

¶ 3115   Deduction for personal exemptions.

Each taxpayer may be entitled to an exemption for himself and his spouse (¶3118), and may qualify for an additional exemption for each dependent (¶3119 *et seq.*).

For 2010, the exemption amount is $3,650. (Code Sec. 151(d))[38]

But an individual (e.g., a child) who can be claimed as a dependent by another (e.g., the child's parent) (without regard to the pre-2010 personal exemption phase-outs, ¶3117 (Code Sec. 151(d)(3)(D))), can't claim a personal exemption for himself. (Code Sec. 151(d)(2))[39]

⊘caution: The child can't claim a personal exemption even if the parent doesn't take the dependency exemption.

⊘caution: For EGTRRA sunset rules, see ¶1114.

Resident aliens can claim exemptions under the same rules as U.S. citizens. (Code Sec. 6013(g); Reg § 1.6013-1(b))[40]

⊘caution: For personal exemptions under the alternative minimum tax, see ¶3209.

No exemption is allowed for any individual unless his taxpayer identification number (TIN) is included on the return claiming the exemption. (Code Sec. 151(e))[41]

¶ 3116   Effect of death on personal exemptions.

The deduction for personal exemptions on a decedent's final return isn't reduced or pro-rated because the return is for a short year. (Reg § 1.443-1(a)(2)) However, if the decedent could be claimed as a dependent by another taxpayer (e.g., a parent), the decedent's personal exemption isn't allowed on the final return.[42]

If one spouse dies during the tax year, the survivor can claim the deceased spouse's exemption on a joint return, unless the survivor remarries in that year.[43] A surviving spouse who has no gross income for the calendar year his spouse died can be claimed as an exemption on the decedent's final separate return.[44]

¶ 3117   Phase-out of personal exemptions before 2010.

For tax years beginning after 2009, the rule phasing out personal exemptions for individuals whose AGI exceeds certain amounts doesn't apply. (Code Sec. 151(d)(3)(E))[45]

Under the pre-2010 phase-out, the personal exemption amount of a taxpayer whose AGI exceeds an inflation-adjusted threshold amount is reduced by an "applicable percentage." (Code Sec. 151(d)(3)(A)) The applicable percentage is 2% for each $2,500 (or fraction thereof) by which AGI exceeds the threshold amount, except that for married persons filing separately, the applicable percentage is 2% for each $1,250 (or fraction thereof) by which AGI exceeds the threshold amount. The applicable percentage can't exceed 100%. (Code Sec. 151(d)(3)(B))[46]

⊘caution: For EGTRRA sunset rules, see ¶1114.

¶ 3118   Exemptions for spouse.

If a married couple files a joint return, each spouse is allowed one personal exemption, whether or not a spouse has gross income or is a dependent of another taxpayer (but the *other* taxpayer will be denied an exemption, see ¶3119). (Reg § 1.151-1(b))[47]

---

38. ¶A-3500.1; ¶1514; TD ¶562,201
39. ¶A-3501, A-3502; ¶1514; TD ¶562,203, 564,401
40. ¶A-3507; ¶1514; TD ¶562,205
41. ¶A-3501.1, A-3603; ¶s 1514, 61,094; TD ¶562,404
42. ¶C-9602; ¶4434; TD ¶579,508

43. ¶A-3504; ¶1514.01; TD ¶562,204
44. ¶A-3504; ¶1514.01; TD ¶562,204
45. ¶A-3502; ¶1514; TD ¶564,401
46. ¶A-3502; ¶1514; TD ¶564,401
47. ¶A-3501; ¶1514.01; TD ¶562,203

⊘*illustration:* A son and his wife file a joint return, but the son's mother supports him for the entire tax year while he's in college. The son (and his wife) can claim a personal exemption for himself. But even if all other dependency tests are met, the mother can't claim a dependency exemption for the son.

On a separate return, a taxpayer may claim an exemption for a spouse only if, for the calendar year in which the taxpayer's tax year begins, the spouse has no gross income *and* isn't the dependent of another. (Code Sec. 151(b))[48]

⊘*observation:* If the son's wife (above) filed a separate return, she couldn't claim an exemption for her husband, since he's a dependent of his mother.

¶ 3119   Exemption for dependents.

A taxpayer is entitled to a deduction equal to the exemption amount (¶3115) for each person who qualifies as his "dependent" for the tax year. (Code Sec. 151(c))[49]

A person qualifies as a taxpayer's dependent if he is the taxpayer's qualifying child (¶3120) or qualifying relative (¶3122). (Code Sec. 152(a))[50] But an individual who is a taxpayer's dependent for a tax year is treated as having no dependents for his tax year beginning in the calendar year when the taxpayer's tax year begins. (Code Sec. 152(b)(1))[1] Also, an individual can't be a taxpayer's dependent if he has made a joint return with his spouse for the tax year beginning in the calendar year when the taxpayer's tax year begins. (Code Sec. 152(b)(2))[2]

A dependent must be a U.S. citizen, national, or resident, or a resident of a contiguous country (i.e., Canada or Mexico) at some time in the calendar year in which the taxpayer's tax year begins. (Code Sec. 152(b)(3)(A))[3] But a nonresident alien child who is legally adopted by the taxpayer (or lawfully placed with taxpayer for legal adoption by him) can be the taxpayer's dependent if he has the same principal place of abode as taxpayer and is a member of taxpayer's household for the entire tax year, and taxpayer is a U.S. citizen or national. (Code Sec. 152(b)(3))[4]

¶ 3120   Qualifying child.

A taxpayer's "qualifying child" (¶3119) for a tax year is an individual who: (1) bears a relationship to the taxpayer specified below; (2) has the same principal place of abode as the taxpayer for more than half the tax year; (3) hasn't reached a specified age (see below); and (4) hasn't provided over half his own support for the calendar year in which the taxpayer's tax year begins. (Code Sec. 152(c)(1), Code Sec. 152(c)(2))[5] For tie-breaking rules, see ¶3121.

The following relationships of an individual to the taxpayer meet requirement (1), above:

. . . a child (defined below) of the taxpayer, or a child's descendant (Code Sec. 152(c)(2)(A)), or

. . . a brother, sister, stepbrother, stepsister, half-brother, or half-sister of the taxpayer or a descendant of these relatives. (Code Sec. 152(c)(2)(B), Code Sec. 152(f)(4))[6]

For this purpose, the term "child" means an individual who is:

• a son, daughter, stepson, or stepdaughter of the taxpayer (Code Sec. 152(f)(1)(A)(i)) , or
• an eligible foster child of the taxpayer (Code Sec. 152(f)(1)(A)(ii)), i.e., an individual who is placed with the taxpayer by an authorized placement agency or by judgment, decree, or other order of any court of competent jurisdiction. (Code Sec. 152(f)(1)(C))[7]

In determining if an individual is taxpayer's son, daughter, stepson, stepdaughter, brother,

48. ¶A-3501; ¶1514.01; TD ¶562,203
49. ¶A-3601; ¶1524; TD ¶562,401
50. ¶A-3601; ¶1524; TD ¶562,401
1. ¶A-3626; ¶1524; TD ¶562,431
2. ¶A-3622; ¶1524; TD ¶562,427

3. ¶A-3623; ¶1524; TD ¶562,428
4. ¶A-3624; ¶1524; TD ¶562,429
5. ¶F-3605.2; ¶1524; TD ¶568,408
6. ¶F-3605.3; ¶1524; TD ¶562,409
7. ¶F-3605.3; ¶1524; TD ¶568,409

or sister, one who's legally adopted by an individual, or lawfully placed with one for legal adoption by him, is treated as a child of that individual by blood. (Code Sec. 152(f)(1)(B))[8]

An individual meets the age requirement in (3), above, if he:

. . . is younger than the taxpayer and hasn't reached age 19 as of the end of the calendar year in which the taxpayer's tax year begins;

. . . is younger than the taxpayer and is a student who hasn't reached age 24 as of the end of that calendar year (Code Sec. 152(c)(3)(A)); or

. . . is permanently and totally disabled, as defined in Code Sec. 22(e)(3) (¶2353), at any time during that calendar year. (Code Sec. 152(c)(3)(B))[9]

❂ observation: If a child of the taxpayer doesn't meet the definition of a "qualifying child," for example, because he doesn't meet the age test, he may still qualify as a dependent under the "qualifying relative" test, ¶3122.

An individual who is married and files a joint return (unless the return is filed only to claim a refund) for the tax year beginning in the calendar year in which the taxpayer's tax year begins can't be a qualifying child. (Code Sec. 152(c)(1)(E))[10]

¶ 3121 Tie-breaking rules where two or more taxpayers claim a qualifying child.

If an individual may be and is claimed as a qualifying child by two or more taxpayers for a tax year beginning in the same calendar year, the following tie-breaking rules apply (generally uniformly to all provisions relying on the same definition, according to IRS):

(1) If two or more taxpayers may claim an individual as a qualifying child for a tax year beginning in the same calendar year, the individual is treated as the qualifying child of the taxpayer who is: (a) a parent of the individual, or (b) if item (a) doesn't apply, the taxpayer with the highest adjusted gross income (AGI) for that tax year. (Code Sec. 152(c)(4)(A))

(2) If the parents don't file a joint return together, the child is treated as the qualifying child of: (a) the parent with whom the child resided for the longest period of time during the tax year, or (b) if the child resided with both parents for the same amount of time during the tax year, the parent with the highest AGI. (Code Sec. 152(c)(4)(B))

(3) If an individual's parents may claim him as a qualifying child but no parent does, another taxpayer may claim him as a qualifying child, but only if that taxpayer's AGI is higher than the highest AGI of any parent of the individual. (Code Sec. 152(c)(4)(C))[11]

¶ 3122 Qualifying relative.

A "qualifying relative" (¶3119) for a tax year is an individual:

(1) who bears a specified relationship to the taxpayer;

(2) whose gross income for the calendar year in which that tax year begins is less than the exemption amount (¶3115);

(3) with respect to whom taxpayer provides over half his support (¶3124) for the calendar year in which that tax year begins (for multiple support agreements, see ¶3123); and

(4) who isn't a qualifying child (¶3120) of that taxpayer or of any other taxpayer for any tax year that begins in the calendar year in which that tax year begins. (Code Sec. 152(d)(1)) Under an administrative exception, an individual is not a qualifying child of any other taxpayer if the individual's parent (or other person with respect to whom the individual is defined as a qualifying child) isn't required by Code Sec. 6012 to file an income tax return and (i) does not file one, or (ii) files one solely to get a refund of withheld tax.[12]

8. ¶F-3612; ¶1524; TD ¶562,420
9. ¶F-3605.4; ¶1524; TD ¶562,410
10. ¶F-3605.2; ¶1524; TD ¶562,408

11. ¶A-3605.5; ¶1524; TD ¶562,411
12. ¶A-3605.6; ¶1524; TD ¶562,412

The following relationships of an individual to the taxpayer meet the relationship test (item (1), above): a child or a descendant of a child, including foster and adopted children who qualify under the rules in ¶3120; a brother, sister, half-brother, half-sister, stepbrother, or stepsister; the father or mother, or an ancestor of either; stepfather or stepmother; a nephew or niece; an uncle or aunt; a son-in-law, daughter-in-law, father-in-law, mother-in-law, brother-in-law, or sister-in-law; and an individual (other than one who, at any time in the tax year, was the taxpayer's spouse, determined without regard to Code Sec. 7703) whose principal place of abode is the taxpayer's home and who is a member of the taxpayer's household, for the taxpayer's tax year. (Code Sec. 152(d)(2), Code Sec. 152(f)(4))[13]

¶ 3123 Multiple support agreement—Form 2120.

For purposes of the support test for qualifying relatives (¶3122), over one-half of an individual's support for a calendar year is treated as received from the taxpayer if:

(1) no one person contributed over half of that support;

(2) over half of that support was received from 2 or more persons each of whom, but for the fact that he alone didn't contribute over half of that support, would have been entitled to claim the individual as a dependent for a tax year beginning in that calendar year;

(3) the taxpayer contributed over 10% of that support; *and*

(4) each person described in (2), other than the taxpayer, who contributed over 10% of that support agrees not to claim the individual as a dependent for that year, by giving the taxpayer a signed statement to that effect (waiver declaration). The waiver(s) needn't be filed with IRS, but must be kept in taxpayer's records. A Form 2120 showing that the taxpayer has waivers from the other eligible persons, with their names, addresses and social security numbers, must be attached to Form 1040 or Form 1040A. (Code Sec. 152(d)(3); Reg § 1.152-3(c))[14]

¶ 3124 "Support" defined.

Support includes:[15]

. . . food, school lunches, toilet articles and haircuts;

. . . clothing;

. . . recreation, including toys, summer camp, horseback riding, entertainment, vacations;

. . . medical and dental care, including premiums on accident and health insurance;

. . . child care expenses, even though a credit is also allowed for these expenses;

. . . allowances, gifts;

. . . son's or daughter's wedding costs;

. . . lodging—when furnished in kind, it's measured by its fair market value rather than actual cost (Reg § 1.152-1(a)(2));[16]

. . . education—these costs include board, uniforms at military schools, and tuition, even where free schooling is available. Scholarship payments received by a dependent are treated as support furnished by someone other than the taxpayer. However, scholarships aren't counted in determining if the taxpayer furnished more than half the dependent's support if the dependent is the taxpayer's child (including stepchild, foster child, or child adopted or placed for adoption) who's a full-time student at an educational institution (Code Sec. 152(f)(5), Reg § 1.152-1(c)).[17]

Social security benefits received by a child and used for his support are considered provided by the child (Reg § 1.152-1(a)(2)(ii));[18]

---

13. ¶A-3606; ¶1524; TD ¶562,413
14. ¶A-3731; ¶1524; TD ¶563,801
15. ¶A-3711 *et seq.*; ¶1524.06; TD ¶563,302 *et seq.*

16. ¶A-3701, A-3714 *et seq.*; ¶1524.09; TD ¶563,309
17. ¶A-3721; ¶1524.07; TD ¶563,316
18. ¶A-3712; TD ¶563,306

Armed Forces dependency allotments—the amount contributed by the government *and* the amount withheld from the pay of the member of the Armed Forces are treated as contributed by the member.[19]

¶ 3125　Allocating support of several contributors to several dependents.

Where more than one member of a household contributes towards expenses that are equally applicable to all members of the household, the contributors are presumed (absent contrary evidence) to have pooled their contributions towards the support of all members. The total contributed is divided equally among the members as amounts paid for their support, unless there is proof of how much was actually spent for particular members.[20]

¶ 3126　Release of dependency exemption by custodial parent—Form 8332

A child is treated as being the "qualifying child" (¶3120) or "qualifying relative" (¶3122) of the noncustodial parent for a calendar year if:

(1) the child receives over half of his support during the calendar year from his parents;

(2) the child's parents: (a) are divorced or legally separated under a decree of divorce or separate maintenance; (b) are separated under a written separation agreement; or (c) live apart at all times during the last six months of the calendar year, whether or not they are or were married;

(3) the child's in the custody of one or both parents for over half the calendar year;

(4) the custodial parent releases his claim to the exemption for the child by signing a written declaration (on Form 8332) stating that he won't claim that child as a dependent for the tax year beginning in that calendar year, *and*

(5) the noncustodial parent attaches that written declaration to the noncustodial parent's return for the tax year beginning during that calendar year. (Code Sec. 152(e)(1), Code Sec. 152(e)(2); Reg § 1.152-4(b))[21]

A child also is treated as a qualifying child or qualifying relative of the noncustodial parent for a calendar year if a "qualified pre-'85 instrument" executed between the parents allows the noncustodial parent to claim the child as a dependent and that parent provides at least $600 for the child's support during the year. (Code Sec. 152(e)(3)(A))[22]

The custodial parent is the parent with whom the child resides for the greater number of nights during the calendar year. (Code Sec. 152(e)(4)(A); Reg § 1.152-4(d))[23]

The above rules apply despite: the Code Sec. 152(c)(1)(B) requirement that a qualifying child have the same principal place of abode as the taxpayer for more than half the year, ¶3120; the Code Sec. 152(c)(4) tie-breaking rules, ¶3121; or the Code Sec. 152(d)(1)(C) support test for qualifying relatives, ¶3122. (Code Sec. 152(e)(1); Reg § 1.152-4(a))[24]

In certain cases, IRS will treat a child of parents who are divorced, separated, or living apart as the dependent of both parents for purposes of Code Sec. 105(b) (employer-provided medical expense reimbursements, ¶1257), Code Sec. 132(h)(2)(B) (excludable fringe benefits, ¶1244), Code Sec. 213(d)(5) (deductible medical expenses, ¶2143), Code Sec. 220(d)(2) (Archer Medical Savings Accounts (MSAs), ¶1528), and Code Sec. 223(d)(2) (Health Saving Accounts (HSAs), ¶1529) when the custodial parent hasn't released the claim to the exemption for the child under Code Sec. 152(e)(2).[25]

The above rules don't apply where, under the Code Sec. 152(d)(3) rules for multiple support agreements (¶3123), more than half the child's support is treated as having been received from a taxpayer. (Code Sec. 152(e)(5))[26]

19. ¶A-3711; ¶1524.09; TD ¶563,305
20. ¶A-3708; TD ¶563,325
21. ¶A-3851; ¶1524.10; TD ¶564,051
22. ¶A-3815; ¶1524.10; TD ¶564,015

23. ¶A-3858; ¶1524.10; TD ¶564,058
24. ¶A-3851; ¶1524.10; TD ¶564,051
25. ¶A-3860; ¶1524.10; TD ¶564,051
26. ¶A-3851; ¶1524.10; TD ¶564,051

For purposes of these rules, if a parent remarries, support of a child received from this remarried parent's spouse is treated as received from the parent. (Code Sec. 152(e)(6))[27]

¶ 3127 Dependents of married couples.

On a joint return, the married couple can claim exemptions for all persons who are dependents of either or both spouses. On a separate return, however, a spouse can claim exemptions only for his own dependents.[28]

If a husband and wife in a community property state file separate returns, they can divide the total of their exemptions for dependents between them, but they can't divide an exemption for any one dependent.[29]

¶ 3128 Effect of birth, death, and divorce on exemption for dependent.

If a taxpayer's child is born alive at any time during the year, and the dependency tests (¶3119) are met, the taxpayer is allowed a full exemption for the child.[30]

If a dependent died during the year, and the dependency tests were met for the part of the year he lived, the taxpayer can claim a full exemption for him.[31]

In determining relationships qualifying for a dependency exemption (¶3120, ¶3122), death or divorce doesn't end relationships established by marriage. Thus, the relationship of son-in-law and father-in-law survives the spouse's death. (Reg § 1.152-2(d))[32]

¶ 3129 Exemption and other tax breaks for kidnapped children.

Solely for the purposes listed below, a taxpayer's child who is presumed by law enforcement authorities to have been kidnapped by a non-family member, and who had, for the tax year in which the kidnapping occurred, the same principal place of abode as the taxpayer for more than half of the portion of that year before the kidnapping date, is treated as meeting the requirement that a qualifying child (¶3120) have the same principal place of abode as the taxpayer for more than half the tax year for all tax years ending during the period that the individual is kidnapped. (Code Sec. 152(f)(6)(A)) This rule applies for purposes of the dependency deduction; the child tax credit; surviving spouse or a head of a household status; and the earned income credit. (Code Sec. 152(f)(6)(B)) Comparable treatment applies to certain qualifying relatives (¶3120). (Code Sec. 152(f)(6)(C))[33]

¶ 3130 Tax rate schedules for individuals.

There's a tax rate schedule for:

(1) Single persons (not married at year's end), including certain marrieds living apart (¶3133), see ¶1102. These rates are more favorable than those for marrieds filing separate returns, but less favorable than head of household and (generally) joint return rates.

(2) Married couples filing joint returns, and certain widows and widowers who qualify as "surviving spouses" (¶3132), see ¶1103. These are often the most favorable rates.

(3) Heads of household, see ¶1105—more favorable rates than those for single persons.

(4) Married persons filing separately, see ¶1104—least favorable rates. (Code Sec. 1)[34]

For 2010, there are 6 tax brackets at rates of 10%, 15%, 25%, 28%, 33% and 35%. (Code Sec. 1)[35]

caution: For EGTRRA sunset rules, see ¶1114.

27. ¶A-3851; ¶1524.10; TD ¶564,051
28. ¶A-3607; ¶1524.03
29. ¶A-3605.1; TD ¶562,407
30. ¶A-3602; ¶1524.03; TD ¶562,403
31. ¶A-3602; ¶1524.03; TD ¶562,403
32. ¶A-3607; ¶1524.03; TD ¶562,414
33. ¶A-3601.1; ¶1514.02; TD ¶562,402
34. ¶A-1003 *et seq.*; ¶14.08; TD ¶560,504
35. ¶A-1100; ¶14.08; TD ¶568,201

¶ 3131 Tax tables.

IRS has drawn up tax tables, based on the tax rates. (Code Sec. 3(a)(1))[36] The 2010 table for Form 1040, Form 1040A or Form 1040EZ filers with taxable income less than $100,000 is reproduced at ¶1110. However, the tables aren't used by those who file a short period return because they changed their accounting period. (Code Sec. 3(b)(1))[37]

¶ 3132 When surviving spouse (qualifying widow/er) gets lower joint return rates.

A surviving spouse (qualifying widow/er) whose spouse died during either of the surviving spouse's two tax years immediately preceding the tax year (Code Sec. 2(a)(1)) is taxed at joint return rates (Code Sec. 1(a)(2)) if the surviving spouse:

. . . hasn't remarried at any time before the end of the tax year (Code Sec. 2(a)(2)(A)),

. . . "maintains" (pays over 50% of the costs of) a household as his home that's the "principal place of abode" of a dependent (a) who is taxpayer's son or daughter (including adopted children, but not foster children), stepson ,or stepdaughter, and (b) for whom taxpayer is entitled to a dependency deduction for the tax year (Code Sec. 2(a)(1)), and

. . . could file a joint return with the deceased for the year of death. (Code Sec. 2(a)(2)(B))[38]

observation: The surviving spouse rules *don't* apply for the year the spouse died. For when a joint return can be filed (and joint return rates used) in such year, see ¶4707.

A special rule applies for spouses of individuals in "missing status" as a result of "combat zone" or "qualified hazardous duty area" service. If an MIA or POW is officially determined to be dead, and so is removed from the missing status rolls, surviving spouse status doesn't depend on the actual date of death. The relevant date is the date of the official determination, or, if earlier, two years after the date of official termination of combat activities in that zone. If a later actual death is established, that date will control. (Code Sec. 2(a)(3))[39]

¶ 3133 Certain married individuals living apart treated as unmarried.

A married taxpayer is considered single for tax purposes if the taxpayer meets all of the following tests (Code Sec. 7703(b); Reg § 1.7703-1(b)):

(1) Files a separate return.

(2) Maintains as his home a household that for more than half the tax year is the principal place of abode of a child (defined in Code Sec. 152(f)(1), ¶3120) for whom he's entitled to a dependency deduction for the year, or would be so entitled if the taxpayer hadn't released the exemption to the noncustodial parent (¶3126). (Code Sec. 7703(b)(1))

(3) Furnishes over half the cost of maintaining the household. (Code Sec. 7703(b)(2))

(4) Spouse doesn't live with him during last 6 months of the tax year. (Code Sec. 7703(b)(3))[40]

observation: Individuals treated as unmarried under this "abandoned spouse" rule can use the single or head of household rates.

Either or both spouses can qualify as "unmarried" by meeting the tests. If only one spouse qualifies, the other spouse must use married-filing-separately rates.[41]

A taxpayer who doesn't meet the above rules is considered married even though living apart from his spouse, unless legally separated under a decree of divorce or separate maintenance. (Reg § 1.7703-1(a))[42]

---

36. ¶A-1100; ¶34 *et seq.*; TD ¶568,251
37. ¶A-1181; ¶34.02; TD ¶568,251
38. ¶A-1700 *et seq.*; ¶24.02; TD ¶567,002
39. ¶A-1703; ¶24.02; TD ¶567,003
40. ¶A-1610 *et seq.*; ¶77,034.01; TD ¶566,511
41. ¶A-1403; ¶77,034.01; TD ¶566,511
42. ¶A-1611; ¶77,034.01; TD ¶566,511

¶ 3134   Head of household status.

To qualify as a head of household for a tax year, a taxpayer must: (1) be unmarried (or treated as unmarried, ¶3133) at the end of the year; (2) not be a surviving spouse; (3) not be a nonresident alien at any time that year; *and* (4) maintains a household:

(a) that's his home, and for more than half of the tax year, the principal place of abode of (i) the taxpayer's qualifying child (below) or (ii) an individual for whom the taxpayer may claim a dependency deduction. (Code Sec. 2(b)(1)(A)), or

(b) (not necessarily his own) that for the tax year is the principal place of abode for either the taxpayer's father or mother, if the taxpayer's entitled to a dependency deduction for that parent. (Code Sec. 2(b)(1)(B))[43]

A qualifying child for this purpose is defined in Code Sec. 152(c) (¶3120), but without regard to Code Sec. 152(e) (custodial parent's release of exemption, ¶3126). But a taxpayer isn't eligible for head of household status if the child is married at the end of taxpayer's tax year and isn't taxpayer's dependent because he filed a joint return and/or isn't a U.S. citizen or resident. (Code Sec. 2(b)(1)(A)(i))[44]

¶ 3135   Tax on Unearned Income of Children—Kiddie Tax ▬▬▬▬▬

Under the "kiddie tax" rules, certain children (¶3137) are taxed at their parents' highest tax rate on the child's unearned income over $1,900 for 2010 (and 2011) if that tax is higher than what the child would otherwise pay on it. The parents can instead elect to include the child's gross income over $1,900 on their own return.

¶ 3136   Computing the kiddie tax—Form 8615.

A child subject to the kiddie tax (¶3137) pays a tax (computed on Form 8615, attached to the child's Form 1040 or 1040A) equal to the *greater* of:

(1) the sum of (a) the tax that would be imposed if the child's taxable income for the tax year were reduced by the child's net unearned income (¶3138), plus (b) the child's share of the allocable parental tax (below) (Code Sec. 1(g)(1)(B)), or

(2) the tax imposed on the child without regard to (1), above (Code Sec. 1(g)(1)(A))—i.e., the tax imposed on the child as a single person.[45]

The "child's share" of the allocable parental tax ((1), above) equals the amount that bears the same ratio to the total allocable parental tax (below) as the child's net unearned income bears to the total net unearned income of all children of that parent to whom these rules apply. (Code Sec. 1(g)(3)(B); Reg § 1.1(i)-1T, Q&A5)[46]

The "allocable parental tax" is the excess of: (1) the tax that would be imposed on the parent's taxable income if that income included the net unearned income of all that parent's children subject to these rules, over (2) the tax imposed on the parent without regard to these rules. (Code Sec. 1(g)(3)(A); Reg § 1.1(i)-1T, Q&A4)[47]

Parents of a child subject to the kiddie tax must give the child their taxpayer identification number (TIN) so it can be included on the child's return. (Code Sec. 1(g)(6))[48] If a child can't get the required information from his parent, he (or his legal representative) may request the necessary information from IRS. (Code Sec. 6103(e)(1)(A)(iii); Reg § 1.1(i)-1T, Q&A22)[49]

caution: For the child's alternative minimum tax, see ¶3204.

---

43. ¶A-1401.1 *et seq.*; ¶24.03; TD ¶565,501.1 *et seq.*
44. ¶A-1406*et seq.*; ¶24.03; TD ¶565,506 *et seq.*
45. ¶A-1301 *et seq.*; ¶14.09; TD ¶568,301
46. ¶A-1310; ¶14.09; TD ¶568,310

47. ¶A-1311; ¶14.09; TD ¶568,311
48. ¶S-1544; ¶14.09; TD ¶568,303
49. ¶S-6403; ¶61,034.04; TD ¶568,303

¶ 3137   Child subject to kiddie tax.

A child is subject to the kiddie tax if: (1) the child either (a) is under age 18 at the end of the tax year, or (b) is age 18, or 19-23 if a full-time student, at the end of the tax year *and* his earned income doesn't exceed one-half of his support; (2) either parent is alive at the end of the tax year; (3) the child doesn't file a joint return for the tax year; *and* (4) the child's unearned income is more than $1,900 for 2010 (and 2011). (Code Sec. 1(g)(2))[50]

¶ 3138   "Net unearned income" for kiddie tax purposes.

"Net unearned income" is the portion of the child's "AGI not attributable to earned income" (i.e., investment income), reduced by the sum of the following amounts (Code Sec. 1(g)(4)(A); Reg § 1.1(i)-1T, Q&A6):

(1) the amount in effect for the tax year under Code Sec. 63(c)(5)(A) (Code Sec. 1(g)(4)(A)(ii)(I); Reg § 1.1(i)-1T, Q&A6) (relating to one component of the standard deduction for a child who can be claimed as a dependent—i.e., $950 for 2010 and 2011, ¶3112);

(2) the greater of (a) the amount in (1), or (b) the amount of the itemized deductions directly connected with the production of the unearned income if the child itemizes deductions (Code Sec. 1(g)(4)(A)(ii)(II); Reg § 1.1(i)-1T, Q&A6);

(3) adjustments to income attributable to the unearned income, such as the penalty on early withdrawal of savings.[1]

But a child's net unearned income can't exceed his taxable income. (Code Sec. 1(g)(4)(B))[2]

Thus, for 2010 (and 2011), the child's first $950 of unearned income isn't taxed at all, the next $950 of unearned income is taxed at the child's tax rate, and the child's "excess" unearned income is taxed at the parent's marginal rate.[3]

Earned income means earned income as defined in Code Sec. 911(d)(2)—i.e., income attributable to wages, salaries, or other amounts received as compensation for personal services. (Code Sec. 1(g)(4)(A)(i); Reg § 1.1(i)-1T, Q&A6) Distributions from certain qualified disability trusts are treated as earned income. (Code Sec. 1(g)(4)(C))) But the taxable part of social security or pension benefits paid to the child are unearned income. (Reg § 1.1(i)-1T, Q&A9) Unearned income also includes taxable interest, dividends, capital gains (including capital gain distributions), rents, royalties, etc.[4]

¶ 3139   Parents' election to be taxed on child's unearned income—Form 8814.

A parent can irrevocably elect (on Form 8814) to include in the parent's gross income for the tax year, the child's gross income in excess of $1,900 for 2010 (and 2011). (Code Sec. 1(g)(7)(B)(i); Reg § 301.9100-8(a)(4)(i)) The child is then treated as having no gross income for the year and isn't required to file a return. (Code Sec. 1(g)(7)(A))[5]

The election applies only if the child's gross income is only from interest, dividends, and capital gain distribution; it's more than $950 and less than $9,500 for 2010 (and 2011); the child made no estimated tax payments for, and didn't apply any overpayments to, the year; and backup withholding didn't apply. (Code Sec. 1(g)(7)(A))[6]

The electing parent's tax equals the sum of: (1) the tax on the parent's taxable income after taking into account the child's gross income over $1,900, plus (2) 10% of the lesser of (a) $950 or (b) the excess of the child's income over $950. (Code Sec. 1(g)(7)(B)(ii))[7] Any interest income that is a tax preference item of the child is treated as that of the electing parent.

---

50. ¶A-1301; ¶14.09; TD ¶568,301
1. ¶A-1305; ¶14.09; TD ¶568,305
2. ¶A-1305; ¶14.09; TD ¶568,305
3. ¶A-1304 *et seq.*; ¶14.09; TD ¶568,305

4. ¶A-1301.1, A-1307; ¶14.09; TD ¶568,301.1, 568,307
5. ¶A-1326; ¶14.11; TD ¶568,401
6. ¶A-1327; ¶14.11; TD ¶568,402
7. ¶A-1330; ¶14.11; TD ¶568,405

(Code Sec. 1(g)(7)(B)(iii))[8]

⊘illustration: S, age 6, received $2,400 in interest income in 2010. He has no other income, no itemized deductions, and isn't subject to backup withholding. No estimated tax payments were made with his name or social security number. His parents elect to include S's income on their tax return instead of filing a return for him. They include $500 of S's gross income on their tax return ($2,400 − $1,900). They also must pay an additional tax of $95 (10% of $950). If the parents are in the 28% bracket, the total tax cost to them of the election is $235 ($95 + $140 (28% of $500)).

⊘caution: The election could increase total family taxes, because the income picked up from the child could lower various tax breaks of the parent that are geared to AGI.

¶ 3140 Self-Employment Tax

Self-employed persons pay social security and Medicare taxes as part of their income tax. This self-employment (SE) tax is based on net earnings from self-employment, not on taxable income.

¶ 3141 Self-employment tax imposed—Schedule SE.

The self-employment (SE) tax consists of: (1) a social security (OASDI) tax, and (2) a Medicare (hospital insurance) tax. These taxes are imposed (compute on Form 1040, Schedule SE) on self-employment income (¶3142). (Code Sec. 1401(a), Code Sec. 1401(b)).[9] For contribution bases and rates for the SE tax, see ¶1108. For who is subject to the SE tax, see ¶3146.

¶ 3142 Self-employment income subject to self-employment (SE) tax.

Self-employment (SE) income consists of net earnings from self-employment (¶3143). But in computing an individual's SE tax (¶3141), the maximum amount of SE income subject to OASDI tax for a tax year (whether 12 months or less) is the contribution base (¶1108) for the calendar year in which the tax year begins, minus the amount of any wages received by the individual in the same tax year. If net earnings from self-employment are less than $400 ($100 for a church employee (Code Sec. 1402(j)(2)(B))), SE income for that year is zero. (Code Sec. 1402(b); Reg § 1.1402(b)-1)[10]

⊘observation: Since a 7.65% deduction (¶3143) is allowed from net profits (i.e., net earnings from self-employment before that deduction), an individual can have actual net profits of up to $433.13 (92.35% of $433.13 = $400) without triggering SE tax.

A mitigation provision can come into play where wages were erroneously reported as self-employment income or vice versa. (Code Sec. 6521)[11]

¶ 3143 Net earnings from self-employment.

This is gross income, under the individual's income tax accounting method, from a trade or business carried on by him, less allowable deductions for that business, plus his distributive share of partnership taxable income (whether or not distributed) or loss from a partnership of which he's a member. (Code Sec. 1402(a); Reg § 1.1402(a)-1)[12] A deduction is allowed for an amount equal to 7.65% of his net earnings from self-employment for the tax year (determined without this deduction). (Code Sec. 1402(a)(12))[13]

An individual with more than one business must combine the net earnings from each to determine self-employment income. The gains and loss from the businesses are netted, so a loss in one reduces a gain in another. (Reg § 1.1402(a)-2(c))[14] If an individual has a part-time

8. ¶A-1331; ¶14.11; TD ¶568,406
9. ¶A-6001; ¶14,024; TD ¶575,501
10. ¶A-6031 *et seq.*; ¶14,024.02; TD ¶576,001 *et seq.*
11. ¶T-3634; ¶14,024.18, 65,214.01; TD ¶836,007

12. ¶A-6100 *et seq.*; ¶14,024.07; TD ¶576,012
13. ¶A-6114; ¶14,024; TD ¶576,025
14. ¶A-6103; ¶14,024; TD ¶576,011

business and a regular job as an employee, only the income from the part-time business is included in determining net earnings.[15]

In computing net earnings from self-employment, the following deductions *aren't* allowed:

. . . deduction for personal exemptions (Code Sec. 1402(a)(7));

. . . deduction for half of SE taxes (Code Sec. 1402(a)(12));

. . . deduction for net operating losses (Code Sec. 1402(a)(4));

. . . domestic production activities deduction (Code Sec. 1402(a)(16));

. . . nonbusiness deductions;[16]

. . . other than for a tax year beginning in 2010, a deduction for a self-employed individual's health insurance costs. (Code Sec. 162(l)(4));[17]

Net earnings from self-employment *don't include*:

• certain income received by a retired partner under a written plan of the partnership (Code Sec. 1402(a)(10));[18]

• dividends or interest on investments (Code Sec. 1402(a)(2));[19]

• gains (or losses) from disposition of a capital asset or other property that's not inventory or held for sale to customers (Code Sec. 1402(a)(3));[20] but options and commodities dealers must include gains and losses derived from dealing or trading in options and regulated futures subject to mark-to-market rules in SE net earnings (Code Sec. 1402(i));[21]

• gain or loss of a securities or commodities trader that is treated as ordinary solely by reason of the election of mark-to-market treatment (Code Sec. 475(f)(1)(D));[22]

• qualified disaster relief (or mitigation) payments (Code Sec. 139(d));[23]

• rents from real estate (and personal property leased with it) held for investment. (Code Sec. 1402(a)(1)) But rents are included in net earnings if received by real estate dealers in the normal course of business (Reg § 1.1402(a)-4(a)),[24] or if the rent is for living quarters where *services* (e.g., maid service) are also rendered primarily for the occupant's convenience (Reg § 1.1402(a)-4(c)(2)), such as in hotels, boarding houses, tourist camps or homes, parking lots, warehouses and storage garages;[25]

• rents paid in crop shares unless paid under an arrangement where the landowner (or tenant) materially participates in crop production or controls and directs the farming operation and pays the farmer at a fixed rate as his employee (Reg § 1.1402(a)-4(b));[26]

• certain termination payments received by former insurance salesmen (Code Sec. 1402(k));[27]

• a shareholder's share of an S corporation's income (whether distributed or not) or loss. [28]

A passive activity loss that's disallowed for income tax purposes isn't taken into account in computing net earnings from self-employment. (Reg § 1.469-1T(d)(3))[29]

Holding public office isn't an SE trade or business, except for certain state or local officials paid solely on a fee basis (¶3146). (Code Sec. 1402(c)(1))[30]

¶ 3144   Partner's self-employment tax.

A partner's net earnings from self-employment are, generally, his distributive share of the partnership's taxable income arising out of the trade or business of the partnership plus his guaranteed payments. (Code Sec. 1402(a); Reg § 1.1402(a)-1(a)(2), Reg § 1.1402(a)-1(b))[31]

---

15. ¶A-6083; ¶14,024; TD ¶576,036
16. ¶A-6113; ¶14,024; TD ¶576,023
17. ¶A-6113; ¶1624.403; TD ¶576,023
18. ¶A-6166; ¶14,024.16; TD ¶576,211
19. ¶A-6108; ¶14,024.05; TD ¶576,021
20. ¶A-6109; ¶14,024.06; TD ¶576,022
21. ¶A-6112; ¶14,024.06; TD ¶576,017
22. ¶A-6112.1; ¶4754.01; TD ¶576,017
23. ¶A-6105; ¶1394; TD ¶576,018

24. ¶A-6105, A-6106; ¶14,024.04; TD ¶576,018
25. ¶A-6107; ¶14,024.04; TD ¶576,020
26. ¶A-6202 *et seq.*; ¶14,024.04; TD ¶576,018
27. ¶A-6032.1; ¶14,024.155; TD ¶576,009
28. ¶A-6084; TD ¶576,037
29. ¶M-4603; ¶4694.47; TD ¶411,002
30. ¶A-6095; ¶14,024.13; TD ¶576,051
31. ¶A-6150 *et seq.*; ¶14,024.16; TD ¶576,200 *et seq.*

The distributive share of any item of income or loss of a limited partner is excluded. But this exclusion doesn't apply to guaranteed payments to that partner for services actually rendered to or on behalf of the partnership, to the extent the payments are shown to be remuneration for those services. (Code Sec. 1402(a)(13))[32]

¶ 3145 Married couple's self-employment (SE) tax.

SE tax is computed on the separate self-employment income of each spouse, whether or not they file joint returns. But the spouses are jointly and severally liable for SE tax due on a joint return. (Code Sec. 6017; Reg § 1.6017-1(b))[33]

¶ 3146 Who is subject to self-employment (SE) tax?

The SE tax is a tax on self-employed individuals (U.S. citizens and resident aliens). (Code Sec. 1401, Code Sec. 1402(b)) Income earned as an employee isn't subject to SE tax (Code Sec. 1402(c)(2)),[34] with these exceptions:

... Members of the clergy, see ¶3147.

... Persons 18 or older employed to sell magazines and newspapers to the public at a fixed price, whose pay is the excess of the fixed price over their cost. (Code Sec. 1402(c)(2)(A))[35]

... U.S. citizens employed by a foreign government, its wholly owned instrumentality, or an international organization (e.g., the U.N.). (Code Sec. 1402(c)(2)(C))[36]

... Fishing boat crewmen who work on a boat that normally has fewer than 10 crew members and who get no fixed remuneration other than a share of the catch and certain small cash payments. (Code Sec. 1402(c)(2)(F))[37]

... Sharecroppers whose earnings depend on production.[38]

... State or local government official whose pay is *solely* fees, unless his services are covered by social security under a federal-state agreement. (Code Sec. 1402(c)(2)(E))[39]

Statutory employees (¶3103) don't pay SE tax (they pay FICA instead) even if treated as self-employed for income tax purposes. (Code Sec. 1402(d), Code Sec. 3121(d)(3))[40]

Members of certain religious sects who are conscientiously opposed to social security and file a benefits exemption (on Form 4029) are exempt from SE tax. (Code Sec. 1402(g); Reg § 1.1402(h)-1)[41]

¶ 3147 Members of the clergy.

Members of the clergy, members of religious orders, and Christian Science practitioners are subject to self-employment tax on services performed in the exercise of their ministry (Code Sec. 1402(c)(4), Code Sec. 1402(c)(5)) *unless* they have taken a vow of poverty (Code Sec. 1402(c))[42] or irrevocably elect (on Form 4361) *not* to be covered. (Code Sec. 1402(e))[43]

¶ 3148 Farmers' self-employment (SE) tax.

Self-employed persons must pay SE tax on the income from their farming operations. (Code Sec. 1402(a)) Conservation reserve program (CRP) payments are treated as includible farm income unless received by an individual who is getting social security retirement or disability payments. (Code Sec. 1402(a)(1)) Since a farmer has an optional method of computing SE tax on farm income (¶3149), he may have to distinguish farm income from other self-employment income. Farm income comes from an operation on a farm in which more than half the time is

32. ¶A-6157; ¶14,024.16; TD ¶576,207
33. ¶S-1812; ¶60,174; TD ¶570,607
34. ¶A-6092; ¶14,024.09; TD ¶576,049
35. ¶A-6087.1; ¶14,024.09; TD ¶576,049
36. ¶A-6097; ¶14,024.09; TD ¶576,053
37. ¶A-6090; ¶14,024.14; TD ¶576,047

38. ¶A-6202; ¶14,024.04; TD ¶576,066
39. ¶A-6092; ¶14,024.13; TD ¶576,051
40. ¶A-6093; ¶14,024.09; TD ¶576,050
41. ¶A-6327 *et seq.*; ¶14,024.15; TD ¶576,092
42. ¶A-6301; ¶14,024.10; TD ¶576,075
43. ¶A-6321; ¶14,024.10; TD ¶576,085

devoted to farming activities. (Reg § 1.1402(a)-13)[44]

¶ 3149　Optional methods for computing self-employment earnings.

The optional method—referred to as the "nonfarm optional method" for nonfarming businesses and the "farm optional method" for farming businesses—is as follows: For 2010 and 2011, if an individual's gross income from the business is not more than $6,720, he may elect to treat 66⅔% of that gross income as his SE net earnings from the business. If it's more than $6,720 and his net profits from the business are less than $4,851, he may elect to treat $4,480 as SE net earnings from the business. But if net profits are at least $4,851, he must use the net profits. (Code Sec. 1402(a), Code Sec. 1402(l); Reg § 1.1402-15(a)(1))[45]

The optional nonfarm method may be used for 2010 and 2011 only if: net profits from the nonfarming business are less than $4,851 *and* less than 72.189% of gross nonfarm income, SE net earnings were at least $400 in 2 of the prior 3 years, *and* taxpayer's used this method for fewer than 5 years (consecutive or not). (Code Sec. 1402(a), Code Sec. 1402(h))[46]

An individual may use the optional farm method for 2010 and 2011 if gross farm income is not more than $6,720, or net farm profits are less than $4,851. (Code Sec. 1402(a), Code Sec. 1402(h))[47]

An individual with both farm and nonfarm incomes may use both methods (if otherwise allowed): the farm optional method for the farm income and the nonfarm optional method for the nonfarm income. For 2010 and 2011, if both methods are used, the combined total SE net earnings can't be more than $4,480. (Code Sec. 1402(a); Reg § 1.1402(a)-15)[48]

Elect the optional method by computing (on Schedule SE, Form 1040) SE net earnings under that method. The election may be made or revoked after the return is filed, on an amended return. (Code Sec. 1402(a); Reg § 1.1402(a)-16)[49]

¶ 3150　Individual Estimated Tax

An individual must make four quarterly installment payments of estimated tax based on the amount of his "required annual payment" to avoid an underpayment penalty. The required annual payment is the lower of 90% of the tax shown on the current year return or 100% (110%, for high income individuals) of the tax shown on the prior year return. There's no penalty if the tax shown on the return (after withholding) is less than $1,000, or if other specified exceptions or waivers apply.

To avoid the penalty, an individual must: (1) pay each "required installment" (¶3153) by its due date (¶3156), (2) meet an exception (¶3160), *or* (3) get a waiver (¶3161).[50]

¶ 3151　How to pay estimated tax—Form 1040-ES.

Make estimated tax payments by check or money order using payment-voucher Form 1040-ES (Form 1040-ES(NR) for nonresident aliens); by phone or online using a credit (MasterCard, VISA, American Express, or Discover) or debit card: call 1-888-729-1040 or 1-800-272-9829, or go to www.PAY1040.com,, www.officialpayments.com, or www.payUSAtax.com; by EFTPS using the Internet or phone; or by EFW if filing electronically. (Reg § 301.6311-2)[1]

Estimated tax liability is computed as the expected taxes on expected taxable income for the year, minus the tax withheld (or to be withheld) from the year's wages and the expected tax credits (Code Sec. 6654(f), Code Sec. 6654(g); Reg § 1.6654-5(a)), taking into account the taxes, credits, and other amounts listed in Reg § 1.6654-1(a)(4). (Reg § 1.6654-5(b))[2]

---

44. ¶A-6201 *et seq.*; ¶614.051; TD ¶576,064
45. ¶A-6117; ¶14,024.20; TD ¶576,028
46. ¶A-6121; ¶14,024.20; TD ¶576,028
47. ¶A-6122; ¶14,024.20; TD ¶576,030
48. ¶A-6119; ¶14,024.20; TD ¶576,032

49. ¶A-6125; ¶14,024.20; TD ¶576,029, 576,031
50. ¶S-5200; ¶66,544 *et seq.*; TD ¶571,300
1. ¶S-5253; ¶63,114; TD ¶571,341
2. ¶A-5201; ¶66,544.01; TD ¶571,301

¶ 3152 Married individuals' estimated tax.

A married person determines estimated tax liability based on his separate income. Spouses making joint estimated tax payments apply the rules on a joint basis. Joint estimated tax payments don't affect the choice of joint or separate income tax returns.[3] Joint payments can be apportioned between the spouses' separate returns. (Reg § 1.6654-2(e)(5))[4]

¶ 3153 Amount of required installment.

Unless the annualized income method (¶3154) is used, the amount of each required installment is 25% of the "required annual payment." For most individuals, the required annual payment is the lower of: (1) 90% of the tax shown on the current year's return (or, if no return is filed, 90% of the current year tax), or (2) 100% of the tax shown on the previous year's return, if that tax year was a 12-month year and the taxpayer filed a return (even a late one) for that year. (Code Sec. 6654(d)(1))[5]

Different rules apply to high income individuals. If an individual's previous year's return showed adjusted gross income exceeding $150,000 ($75,000 for marrieds filing separately), the required annual payment is the lower of (1), above, or 110% of the tax shown on the previous year's return. (Code Sec. 6654(d)(1)(C))[6]

¶ 3154 Annualized income method.

For any installment for which the taxpayer establishes that the "annualized income installment" (below) is less than the required installment determined under the rules at ¶3153, the annualized income installment becomes the required installment. (Code Sec. 6654(d)(2)(A)(i)) The annualized income installment is the excess (if any) of:

(1) an amount equal to the "applicable percentage" (below) of the annualized tax (computed by placing taxable income, alternative minimum taxable income (AMTI), and adjusted self-employment income (below) on an annualized basis) for the months in the tax year ending before the due date for the installment, over

(2) the sum of any earlier required installments for the tax year. (Code Sec. 6654(d)(2)(B))[7]

The applicable percentages are 22.5%, 45%, 67.5% and 90%, respectively, for the first, second, third and fourth required installments. (Code Sec. 6654(d)(2)(C)(ii))[8]

Adjusted self-employment income means self-employment income (¶3142) except that wages for calendar months ending before the installment due date must be annualized as in (2), above. (Code Sec. 6654(d)(2)(C)(iii))[9]

If, for an installment, the annualized income installment is the required installment because it's less than the installment determined under the rules at ¶3153, the excess must be recaptured—i.e, added to the next required installment that isn't an annualized income installment. (Code Sec. 6654(d)(2)(A)(ii))[10]

¶ 3155 Withholding as payment of estimated tax.

Any withholding is treated as a payment of estimated tax. An equal part of the withheld tax is considered paid on each installment date unless the individual establishes the dates the amounts were actually withheld. (Code Sec. 6654(g)(1))[11]

♥ *recommendation:* An individual who underpays an early required installment can avoid or reduce the underpayment penalty by increasing withholding for the rest of the year.

3. ¶A-5254; ¶66,544.01; TD ¶571,347
4. ¶A-5255; ¶66,544.01; TD ¶571,347
5. ¶S-5204; ¶66,544.03; TD ¶571,304
6. ¶S-5204.1; ¶66,544.03; TD ¶571,305
7. ¶S-5219 *et seq.*; ¶66,544.04; TD ¶571,312 *et seq.*

8. ¶S-5235; ¶66,544.04; TD ¶571,330
9. ¶S-5225; ¶66,544.04; TD ¶571,318
10. ¶S-5229; ¶66,544.04; TD ¶571,324
11. ¶S-5248; ¶66,544.02; TD ¶571,342

¶ 3156　Time for paying installments.

Calendar year individuals (not farmers and fishermen (¶3157) or nonresident aliens (¶3158)) must pay estimated taxes in four installments, due Apr. 15, June 15, Sept. 15 of the current year, and Jan. 15 of the next year. (Code Sec. 6654(c)) But individuals who first have income subject to the tax after Mar. 31 make the first payment by the due date for the period in which he has the income.[12] The last installment, ordinarily due on Jan. 15, needn't be paid if he files his return and pays the tax shown on it by Jan. 31. (Code Sec. 6654(h))[13]

For fiscal year taxpayers, the due dates are the 15th day of the 4th, 6th, and 9th month of the fiscal year and the 15th day of the first month of the next tax year. (Code Sec. 6654(k))[14]

¶ 3157　Farmers and fishermen.

A farmer or fisherman doesn't have to pay estimated tax for a year if he files his return and pays the tax shown on it by Mar. 1 of the next year. Otherwise, he must make one estimated tax payment for the year, due Jan. 15 of the next year.[15] The required installment calculation (¶3153) uses 66⅔% (not 90%) of the current year tax. (Code Sec. 6654(i)(1))[16]

An individual is a farmer or fisherman if at least 66⅔% of his gross income for the current or preceding tax year is from farming or fishing. (Code Sec. 6654(i)(2))[17]

¶ 3158　Nonresident aliens—Form 1040-ES(NR).

Nonresident aliens required to file U.S. income tax returns (¶4657) must pay three required installments for the year, due on June 15, Sept. 15, and Jan. 15 of the next year. (Code Sec. 6654(j)(2))[18] The required installments (compute on Form 1040-ES(NR)) are 50%, 25%, and 25%, respectively, of the required annual payment (¶3153). (Code Sec. 6654(j)(3)(A)) The applicable percentages under the annualized income method (¶3154) are 45%, 67.5%, and 90%, respectively. (Code Sec. 6654(j)(3)(B))[19]

¶ 3159　Penalty for underpayment of estimated tax—Form 2210, Form 2210F.

The penalty for underpayment equals the product of the interest rate (using simple interest) (Code Sec. 6622(b)) on deficiencies (¶4867), times the amount of the underpayment (below), for the period of the underpayment (below). (Code Sec. 6654(a))[20]

The *amount of the underpayment* is the excess of the "required installment" (¶3153) over any amount paid on or before the due date of the installment. (Code Sec. 6654(b)(1))[21] It's adjusted to reflect only the number of days the underpayment is outstanding.[22]

The *period of underpayment* runs from that due date to the earlier of: (1) Apr. 15 following the end of the tax year, or (2) the date the underpayment is paid. (Code Sec. 6654(b)(2)) For these purposes, a payment is credited against unpaid installments in the order the installments are required to be paid. (Code Sec. 6654(b)(3))[23]

Form 2210 (Form 2210F for farmers and fishermen) may be used to compute the penalty,[24] or IRS will compute it and send a bill.[25] For exceptions, see ¶3160. For waivers, see ¶3161.

12. ¶S-5241, S-5241; ¶66,544.02; TD ¶571,335, 571,336
13. ¶S-5268; ¶66,544.02; TD ¶571,362
14. ¶S-5243; ¶66,544.02; TD ¶571,337
15. ¶S-5247; ¶66,544.06; TD ¶571,340
16. ¶S-5237; ¶66,544.06; TD ¶571,332
17. ¶S-5238; ¶66,544.06; TD ¶571,332
18. ¶S-5246; ¶66,544.07

19. ¶S-5236; ¶66,544.07
20. ¶S-5260; ¶66,544.02; TD ¶571,353
21. ¶S-5261, S-5262; ¶66,544.02; TD ¶571,355, 571,356
22. ¶S-5260; ¶66,544.02; TD ¶571,353
23. ¶S-5262 *et seq.*; ¶66,544.02; TD ¶571,357
24. ¶S-5265; TD ¶571,359
25. ¶S-5260; ; TD ¶571,353

¶ 3160   Exceptions to underpayment penalty.

The underpayment penalty (¶3160) doesn't apply:

(1) if the tax shown on the return (or the tax due if no return is filed) is less than $1,000 after reduction for withholding tax paid (Code Sec. 6654(e)(1)),[26] or

(2) if the individual was a U.S. citizen or resident for the entire preceding tax year, he had no tax liability for that year, and that year was a 12-month year (Code Sec. 6654(e)(2)),[27] or

(3) for the 4th installment, if the individual (not a farmer or fisherman, ¶3157) files his return by the end of the 1st month after the tax year (Jan. 31 for calendar year taxpayers), and pays in full the tax computed on the return (Code Sec. 6654(h)),[28] or

(4) in certain cases while a Title 11 bankruptcy case is pending. (Code Sec. 6658(a))[29]

¶ 3161   Waiver of penalty.

The underpayment penalty (¶3160) may be waived by IRS if:

(1) failure to pay was due to casualty, disaster, or other unusual circumstances where penalty would be inequitable or against good conscience (Code Sec. 6654(e)(3)(A)),[30] or

(2) underpayment was due to reasonable cause (not willful neglect), and the taxpayer retired (after reaching age 62) or became disabled during the year for which the payments in question were required or in the preceding tax year. (Code Sec. 6654(e)(3)(B))[31]

---

26. ¶S-5266; TD ¶571,360
27. ¶S-5267; ¶66,544.05; TD ¶571,361
28. ¶S-5268; ¶66,544.02; TD ¶571,362

29. ¶V-7378; ¶66,584; TD ¶571,363
30. ¶S-5270; ¶66,544.05; TD ¶571,364
31. ¶S-5272.1; ¶66,544.05; TD ¶571,365

Chapter 14   Alternative Minimum Tax

¶ 3200   Alternative Minimum Tax. ▬▬▬▬▬▬▬▬▬▬▬▬▬▬▬▬▬▬▬▬▬▬▬▬▬

The alternative minimum tax (AMT) equals the excess (if any) of the tentative minimum tax over the regular tax.

The AMT was designed to prevent a taxpayer from avoiding all tax liability by using exclusions, deductions, and credits. It's paid only if and to the extent it exceeds the taxpayer's regular tax. (Code Sec. 55(a)) Taxpayers who are subject to the regular tax generally are subject to the AMT. (Code Sec. 55(a), Code Sec. 55(b)) Thus, partnerships (Code Sec. 701) and S corporations (Code Sec. 1363(a)) aren't subject to AMT but their partners and shareholders are. Foreign corporations are subject only as to taxable income effectively connected with conduct of a U.S. trade or business. (Code Sec. 882(a)(1))[1] For a "small corporation" exemption, see ¶3205.

For the AMT credit (against regular tax), see ¶2373.

For the AMT refundable credit available to individuals, see ¶2373.

¶ 3201   Computing the AMT—Form 6251; Form 4626.

The alternative minimum tax (AMT) equals the excess (if any) of the tentative minimum tax (see below) for the tax year, over the regular tax (see below) for the tax year. (Code Sec. 55(a)) AMT is computed on Form 6251 for individuals, Schedule I, Form 1041, for fiduciaries (estates and trusts), or Form 4626 for C corporations.[2]

For a noncorporate taxpayer (other than a married person filing separately), the tentative minimum tax for the tax year equals 26% of the "taxable excess" (defined below) that doesn't exceed $175,000, plus 28% of the taxable excess above $175,000, reduced by the AMT foreign tax credit (AMTFTC, ¶3214) for the year. (Code Sec. 55(b)(1)(A)(i)) For marrieds filing separately, substitute $87,500 for $175,000. (Code Sec. 55(b)(1)(A)(iii)) But for 2010, tentative minimum tax on net capital gain and qualified dividend income is computed using the long-term capital gain rates that apply for regular tax purposes (Code Sec. 55(b)(3)), see ¶2603. "Taxable excess" is the excess of alternative minimum taxable income (AMTI, ¶3202) for the tax year over the "exemption amount" (¶3203). (Code Sec. 55(b)(1)(A)(ii))[3]

✔**caution:** For sunset rule, see ¶1114.

For a corporation (other than a small corporation, ¶3205), the tentative minimum tax (Code Sec. 55(b)(1)) for the tax year is 20% of AMTI (15% for qualified timber gain for tax years beginning before May 23, 2009, ¶2614 (Code Sec. 55(b)(4))[4]) for the year in excess of the exemption amount, reduced by the AMTFTC for the year. (Code Sec. 55(b)(1)(B))[5]

✔**caution:** Check http://ria.thomsonreuters.com/federaltaxhandbook to see if the 15% qualified timber gain rate has been extended.

The regular tax is the regular tax liability used for determining the limitation on various nonrefundable credits (¶2372), reduced by the regular (i.e., not the AMT) foreign tax credit (¶2375) and the possessions tax credit, and without including any investment credit recapture (¶2315), low-income housing credit recapture (¶2322), or Code Sec. 45(e)(11)(C) income tax increase for cooperatives from electricity production credits passed through to patrons. (Code Sec. 55(c)(1))[6]

---

1. ¶A-8130 *et seq.*; ¶554; TD ¶691,000 *et seq.*
2. ¶A-8101; ¶554.01; TD ¶691,001
3. ¶A-8101, ¶A-8102; ¶554.01; TD ¶691,001, TD ¶691,002
4. ¶A-8103.1; ¶554.02TD ¶691,003.1
5. ¶A-8103; ¶554.01; TD ¶691,003
6. ¶A-8105; ¶554.01; TD ¶691,005

References beginning with a single letter are to paragraphs in RIA's Federal Tax Coordinator 2d and RIA's Analysis of Federal Taxes: Income. Those beginning with numbers are to paragraphs in RIA's United States Tax Reporter. Those beginning with TD are to paragraphs in RIA's Tax Desk.

In computing regular tax liability for AMT purposes, income averaging for farmers and fishermen is not taken into account. (Code Sec. 55(c)(2))[7]

⊘*observation:* This means that the "regular tax" used to determine if the farmer or fisherman is subject to AMT is computed as if income averaging had not been used. Thus, the use of three-year income averaging does not trigger or increase AMT liability.

The Code Sec. 291 "cutback" rules generally apply before the AMT rules. (Code Sec. 59(f))[8]

¶ 3202 Alternative minimum taxable income (AMTI).

AMTI is taxable income, with various "adjustments," plus tax preferences, see ¶3206 *et seq.* (Code Sec. 55(b)(2))[9] The AMT can apply if a taxpayer has only adjustments. A taxpayer without preferences must still compute AMTI with the adjustments.[10]

All Code provisions that apply in determining regular taxable income also apply in determining AMTI. (Reg § 1.55-1(a)) For example, the limitations on the use of capital losses by noncorporate (¶2611, ¶2612) and corporate (¶2615) taxpayers also apply for AMTI purposes. Thus, an individual who exercised incentive stock options (ISOs) in Year 1 to buy company stock couldn't use the AMT capital losses he realized in Year 2 when the company went bankrupt and his stock became worthless to reduce his Year 1 AMTI, since a noncorporate taxpayer's capital losses can only be carried forward and not back.[11]

A noncorporate taxpayer's net capital gain and qualified dividend income for 2010 are included in AMTI (but taxed as long-term capital gains, see ¶3201).[12]

⊘*caution:* For sunset rule, see ¶1114.

The at-risk rules (¶1804), and the partnership (¶3735) and S corporation (¶3372) loss limitation rules, are applied with the AMT adjustments and preferences. (Code Sec. 59(h))[13]

In taking the Code Sec. 199 domestic production activity deduction (¶1614) into account for AMTI purposes: (1) qualified production activities income (¶1616) is determined without any adjustments under Code Sec. 56 – Code Sec. 59; and (2) for a corporation, the taxable income limit (¶1615) on the deduction is applied by substituting "AMTI" for "taxable income." (Code Sec. 199(d)(6); Reg § 1.199-8(d))[14]

If a taxpayer's regular tax is determined by reference to an amount other than taxable income (e.g., unrelated business taxable income of an exempt organization, ¶4122), that amount is treated as taxable income in determining AMTI. (Code Sec. 55(b)(2))[15]

There are rules for the apportionment of items that are treated differently for AMT purposes among holders of interests in regulated investment companies (RICs), real estate investment trusts (REITs), and common trust funds. (Code Sec. 59(d))[16]

¶ 3203 AMT exemption amount.

For tax years beginning in 2010 (and in 2011), the exempt portion of an individual's alternative minimum taxable income (AMTI, ¶3202)—the AMT exemption amount—is:

. . . *Married individuals filing jointly and surviving spouses:* $45,000, less 25% of AMTI exceeding $150,000 (zero exemption when AMTI is $330,000);

. . . *Unmarried individuals:* $33,750, less 25% of AMTI exceeding $112,500 (zero exemption when AMTI is $247,500) (but for a child subject to the kiddie tax, see ¶3204); and

7. ¶A-8105; ¶554.01; TD ¶691,005
8. ¶A-8203.3; ¶594
9. ¶A-8101; ¶554.01; TD ¶691,001
10. ¶A-8109; TD ¶691,008
11. ¶A-8108; ¶554.01; TD ¶691,007

12. ¶A-8101; TD ¶691,001
13. ¶A-8115 *et seq.*; ¶594; TD ¶691,014 *et seq.*
14. ¶A-8103.2; ¶1994.130; TD ¶691,003.2
15. ¶A-8107; ¶554.01; TD ¶691,006
16. ¶A-8111; ¶594; TD ¶691,010

. . . *Married individuals filing separately:* $22,500, less 25% of AMTI exceeding $75,000 (zero exemption when AMTI is $165,000). (Code Sec. 55(d)(1), Code Sec. 55(d)(3)) But AMTI is increased by the lesser of $22,500 or 25% of the excess of AMTI (without the exemption reduction) over $165,000. (Code Sec. 55(d))[17]

⊘*caution:* Check http://ria.thomsonreuters.com/federaltaxhandbook to see if the 2010 individual AMT exemption amounts have been increased.

For estates and trusts, the AMT exemption amount is $22,500, less 25% of AMTI exceeding $75,000 (zero exemption when AMTI is $165,000).[18]

For corporations, the AMT exemption amount is $40,000, less 25% of AMTI exceeding $150,000 (zero exemption when AMTI is $310,000).[19] For "small corporations," see ¶3205.

In no case can the AMT exemption amount be less than zero. (Code Sec. 55(d))[20]

¶ 3204   AMT exemption amount of a child subject to the kiddie tax.

The AMT exemption amount for a child subject to the kiddie tax (¶3137) can't exceed the child's earned income (under Code Sec. 911(d)(2)) for the tax year plus $6,700 for 2010 ($6,800 for 2011). (Code Sec. 59(j)) But this exemption amount can't be more than the child's regular AMT exemption (i.e., the unmarried individual's $33,750 [before phaseout] exemption amount for 2010 [and 2011], ¶3203).[21]

¶ 3205   AMT exemption for "small corporations."

A corporation's tentative minimum tax (¶3201) is zero (making the corporation exempt from AMT) for a tax year if its average annual gross receipts (determined by applying Code Sec. 448(c)(2) and Code Sec. 448(c)(3), ¶2818) (Code Sec. 55(e)(1)(D)) for all three-tax-year periods beginning after '93 and ending before the tax year don't exceed $7,500,000. (Code Sec. 55(e)(1)(A)) Substitute $5,000,000 for $7,500,000 for the first three-tax-year period (or portion thereof) taken into account under the test. (Code Sec. 55(e)(1)(B))[22]

Notwithstanding the above tests, a corporation is exempt from AMT for its first tax year (Code Sec. 55(e)(1)(C)) unless it fails the gross receipts test because its gross receipts are aggregated with an existing corporation's (under Code Sec. 448(c)(2)) or it's treated as having a predecessor corporation (under Code Sec. 448(c)(3)(D)).[23]

A corporation that has been exempt from AMT and that ceases to meet the gross receipts test becomes subject to AMT prospectively from the first day of the first tax year for which the gross receipts test isn't met, except that the Code Sec. 56(g)(4)(A) ACE depreciation adjustment (¶3211) doesn't apply. (Code Sec. 55(e)(2)) However, prospective-only application doesn't apply to certain items carried over in Code Sec. 381 transactions (¶3564) or to other property with a basis carried over from a transferor. (Code Sec. 55(e)(3))[24]

For a limitation on the AMT credit for corporations exempt from AMT, see ¶2373.

¶ 3206   AMT adjustments and preferences.

Adjustments differ from preferences, in computing alternative minimum taxable income (AMTI, ¶3202). Adjustments involve *substituting* AMT treatment of an item for the regular tax treatment. Preferences involve *adding* the difference between the AMT treatment and the regular tax treatment. Some (but not all) adjustments can be negative amounts—i.e., they

17. ¶A-8162; ¶554.01; TD ¶691,302
18. ¶A-8164; ¶554.01; TD ¶691,304
19. ¶A-8161; ¶554.01; TD ¶691,301
20. ¶A-8161 *et seq.*; ¶554.01; TD ¶691,301 *et seq.*

21. ¶A-8163; ¶594; TD ¶691,303
22. ¶A-8141, ¶A-8142; ¶554; TD ¶691,201
23. ¶A-8140 *et seq.*; ¶554; TD ¶691,201
24. ¶A-8141, ¶A-8143; ¶554; TD ¶691,201, TD ¶691,202

may result in AMTI that's less than taxable income. Preferences can't be negative amounts.[25]

A taxpayer can avoid preference/adjustment treatment for certain costs by electing amortization (use Form 4562), rather than a current deduction. (Code Sec. 59(e); Reg § 1.59-1)[26]

¶ 3207 Depreciation adjustment.

Except as provided below, the following rules apply to all taxpayers subject to the AMT, for depreciable property placed in service after '86 (and after July 31, '86 and before '87, for which the taxpayer elected to have the MACRS rules, ¶1906 *et seq.*, apply):

(1) For property placed in service before '99, AMT depreciation for Code Sec. 1250 property (¶2694) and property depreciated under the straight-line method for regular tax purposes is computed using the Alternative Depreciation System (ADS, ¶1930). For property subject to accelerated depreciation for regular tax purposes, AMT depreciation is computed using ADS recovery periods and the 150% declining balance method (switching to straight-line in the year that method yields a higher allowance).

(2) For property placed in service after '98, AMT depreciation is computed using the 150% declining balance method (switching to straight-line in the year that method yields a higher allowance), except straight-line is used for Code Sec. 1250 property and other property for which straight-line is used for regular tax purposes. (Code Sec. 56(a)(1)(A), Code Sec. 56(a)(1)(C)(ii)) The recovery period is the same as for regular tax purposes.[27]

The AMT adjustment (i.e., the amount to be added or subtracted in computing alternative minimum taxable income [AMTI, ¶3202]) generated by the above calculations is determined by subtracting the amount of AMT depreciation for all property covered by the above rule from the MACRS depreciation for that property.[28]

The above rules don't apply to: (a) certain property to which the MACRS rules don't apply; (b) natural gas gathering lines placed in service after Apr. 11, 2005 (Code Sec. 56(a)(1)(B), Code Sec. 56(a)(1)(C));[29] (c) qualified property under Code Sec. 168(m) (qualified reuse and recycling property, ¶1933) or Code Sec. 168(n) (qualified disaster assistance property, ¶1940) (Code Sec. 168(m)(2)(D), Code Sec. 168(n)(2)(D));[30] (d) for bonus first-year depreciation—qualified property under Code Sec. 168(k) (¶1933), under Code Sec. 1400L(b) (qualified New York Liberty Zone property, ¶1940), under Code Sec. 1400N(d) (GO Zone property, ¶1939), or under Code Sec. 168(l) (qualified cellulosic biomass ethanol plant property, ¶1933); (Code Sec. 168(k)(2)(G), Code Sec. 1400L(b)(2)(E), Code Sec. 1400N(d)(4), Code Sec. 168(l)(6));[31] and (e) qualified Indian reservation property placed in service after '93. (Code Sec. 168(j)(3))[32]

¶ 3208 Other AMT preferences and adjustments applicable to all taxpayers.

(1) Tax-exempt interest on certain private activity bonds (not certain housing bonds or bonds issued in 2009 or 2010), less related expenses that aren't deductible for regular tax purposes, is a preference item. (Code Sec. 57(a)(5))[33]

caution: Check http://ria.thomsonreuters.com/federaltaxhandbook to see if the exception for bonds issued in 2009-2010 has been extended.

(2) Except for independent oil and gas producers and royalty owners, the excess of percentage depletion (¶1981) over the property's adjusted basis (disregarding the current year's depletion) at the end of the year is a preference item. (Code Sec. 57(a)(1))[34]

---

25. ¶A-8191; ¶564, ¶574; TD ¶695,501
26. ¶A-8194 *et seq.*; ¶594; TD ¶695,503
27. ¶A-8220; ¶564.01; TD ¶696,513
28. ¶A-8220; ¶564.01; TD ¶696,513
29. ¶A-8221 *et seq.*; ¶564.01; TD ¶695,500 *et seq.*
30. ¶A-8221 *et seq.*; ¶1684.029, ¶1400L4.07, ¶1684.08;

TD ¶696,514
31. ¶A-8221 *et seq.*; ¶1400L4.07, ¶1684.08; TD ¶696,514
32. ¶L-8806; ¶1684.01
33. ¶A-8201, ¶A-8202; ¶574; TD ¶696,501, TD ¶696,501.1
34. ¶A-8233; ¶574; TD ¶696,518

(3) Excess intangible drilling costs (IDCs) are a preference. This is the excess of the allowable Code Sec. 263(c) IDC deduction for the tax year for oil, gas, and geothermal wells (¶1625), over the amount that would have been allowable had the costs been capitalized and amortized ratably over 120 months. For integrated oil companies, the preference equals this excess, reduced by 65% of the net income received from all oil, gas, and geothermal properties. For other taxpayers, the preference applies only to the extent that, had it applied fully, it would have increased alternative minimum taxable income (AMTI, ¶3202) by more than 40% of the AMTI for the tax year (without the IDC preference or the alternative tax NOL deduction, ¶3212). Compute the preference separately for oil and gas properties, and for geothermal properties. (Code Sec. 57(a)(2), Code Sec. 57(b), Code Sec. 59(e)(6))[35]

(4) The deduction for amortization of pollution control facilities (under Code Sec. 169, ¶1970) (adjustment) is computed for AMT purposes without the Code Sec. 291(a)(4) 20% cutback that applies for regular tax purposes. For facilities placed in service after '86 and before '99, the AMT deduction is the amount allowable under the Alternative Depreciation System (ADS, ¶1930). For facilities placed in service after '98, the AMT deduction is determined under Code Sec. 168 using straight-line depreciation. (Code Sec. 56(a)(5))[36]

(5) Mine exploration and development costs are adjusted. The AMT deduction is the amount that results from capitalizing the costs allowed under Code Sec. 616(a) or Code Sec. 617(a) for the tax year without the Code Sec. 291(b)(1) 30% cutback (¶1623, ¶1624), and amortizing them ratably over 10 years. (Code Sec. 56(a)(2)(A), Code Sec. 59(e)(6))[37]

(6) For long-term contracts (except home construction contracts) (adjustment), AMTI is computed using the percentage-of-completion method of accounting (¶2852). For small construction contracts (under Code Sec. 460(e)(1), ¶2850), use the Code Sec. 460(b)(3) simplified cost allocation method (¶2855) to find the percentage of contract completed. (Code Sec. 56(a)(3); Reg § 1.460-4(f))[38]

(7) The alcohol fuel credit amount that's included in gross income (¶1206) isn't included in AMTI (adjustment). (Code Sec. 56(a)(7))[39]

¶ 3209　AMT preferences and adjustments for noncorporate taxpayers only.

(1) *Itemized deductions adjustment.* Itemized deductions for AMT purposes are computed the same as for regular tax purposes, *except:*

(a) Medical expenses are deductible only to the extent they exceed 10% (rather than 7.5%) of the taxpayer's adjusted gross income (AGI). (Code Sec. 56(b)(1)(B))[40]

(b) Property, income, and state and local general sales taxes generally aren't deductible if not allowed in computing AGI (¶1758). (Code Sec. 56(b)(1)(A)(ii), Code Sec. 56(b)(1)(E))[41]

(c) Qualified housing interest (rather than qualified residence interest [QRI]) is deductible. (Code Sec. 56(b)(1)(C), Code Sec. 56(e)) Thus, home equity indebtedness isn't allowed for AMT purposes unless it's used to buy, build, or substantially improve the taxpayer's principal residence or one other qualified residence.[42]

(d) Net investment income (the limit on deduction of investment interest) is generally computed the same as for regular tax (¶1729), but excluding qualified housing interest (not QRI) and taking into account AMT adjustments and preferences. Tax-exempt bond interest that's an AMT preference (¶3208) is included. (Code Sec. 56(b)(1)(C))[43]

(e) Miscellaneous itemized deductions (¶3110) aren't allowed. (Code Sec. 56(b)(1)(A)(i))[44]

35. ¶A-8238 *et seq.*; ¶574; TD ¶696,532 *et seq.*
36. ¶A-8237; ¶564.01; TD ¶696,531
37. ¶A-8235; ¶564.01; TD ¶696,529
38. ¶A-8202 *et seq.*; ¶564.01; TD ¶696,502 *et seq.*
39. ¶A-8247; ¶564.01; TD ¶696,540
40. ¶A-8307; ¶564.02; TD ¶697,007
41. ¶A-8308; ¶564.02;TD ¶697,008;
42. ¶A-8310 *et seq.*; ¶564.02; TD ¶697,010 *et seq.*
43. ¶A-8313; ¶564.02; TD ¶697,013
44. ¶A-8315; ¶564.02; TD ¶697,014

(f) The Code Sec. 68 overall itemized deduction limit (not in effect for 2010, ¶3114) doesn't apply. (Code Sec. 56(b)(1)(F))[45]

(2) *Standard deduction and personal exemptions adjustments.* The standard deduction (including the pre-2010 real property tax deduction component) *isn't* allowed, but the pre-2010 disaster loss standard deduction *is* allowed (¶3112). The deduction for personal exemptions (including those of trusts and estates) (¶3115) *isn't* allowed. (Code Sec. 56(b)(1)(E))[46]

(3) *State, etc., tax recoveries adjustment.* If an itemized deduction for state, etc., taxes paid is permitted for regular tax purposes but denied for AMT purposes ((1)(b), above), and any portion of that tax is refunded, the refund isn't included in AMTI. (Code Sec. 56(b)(1)(D))[47]

(4) *Research and experimental (R&E) expenditures adjustment.* The deduction allowed is the amount that results from capitalizing Code Sec. 174(a) R&E expenditures (¶1602) and amortizing them on a straight-line basis over 10 years. (Code Sec. 56(b)(2)(A)(ii), Code Sec. 59(e)(6)) This doesn't apply to expenses incurred in an activity in which the taxpayer materially participates under Code Sec. 469(h) (¶1827). (Code Sec. 56(b)(2)(D))[48]

(5) *Incentive stock option (ISO) adjustment.* The Code Sec. 83 restricted property rules (¶1219) (not the favorable Code Sec. 421 rules that apply for regular tax purposes, ¶1223) apply in determining AMTI, unless the stock is acquired and disposed of in the same tax year. (Code Sec. 56(b)(3))[49] The amount included in AMTI (but not regular income) equals the excess of the stock's fair market value (FMV) on the exercise date over the exercise (strike) price. This applies to vested stock, and to nonvested stock for which the taxpayer makes a Code Sec. 83(b) election (¶1220).[50] But certain underpayments of tax (and interest or penalty) attributable to pre-2008 ISO adjustments are abated. (Code Sec. 53(f)(1))[1]

(6) *Qualified small business stock (QSBS) exclusion preference.* For tax years beginning in 2010, 7% of the amount excluded from gross income on the disposition of QSBS (¶2648 *et seq.*) is an AMT preference. (Code Sec. 57(a)(7))[2]

RIA *caution:* For sunset rule, see ¶1114.

¶ 3210 Preferences and adjustments applicable to all noncorporate taxpayers and to certain corporations.

(1) *Farm losses.* No loss is permitted from any "tax shelter farm activity" of a noncorporate taxpayer or personal service corporation, except to the extent the taxpayer is insolvent at the end of the tax year. A tax shelter farm activity is (a) a farming syndicate (under Code Sec. 464(c), ¶4511), or (b) any other "passive activity" (¶1823) consisting of farming unless the taxpayer materially participates in it. (Code Sec. 58(a), Code Sec. 58(c)(1))[3]

(2) *Passive losses.* The rules limiting the regular tax deduction of losses from passive activities (¶1811 *et seq.*) apply for AMT purposes *except that:*

. . . AMT preferences and adjustments are taken into account;

. . . qualified housing interest (¶3209) (rather than qualified residence interest) is omitted from the passive loss calculation (Code Sec. 58(b)); and

. . . the amount of losses disallowed under the regular tax limitation is reduced by the amount, if any, by which the taxpayer is insolvent at year end. (Code Sec. 58(c)(1))[4]

---

45. ¶A-8306; ¶564.02; TD ¶697,006
46. ¶A-8305, ¶A-8315; ¶564.02; TD ¶697,005, TD ¶697,015
47. ¶A-8309; ¶564.02; TD ¶697,009
48. ¶A-8316; ¶564.02; TD ¶697,016
49. ¶A-8302, ¶A-8303; ¶564.02; TD ¶697,002

50. ¶A-8302, ¶H-2508.2; TD ¶697,002, TD ¶697,003
1. ¶T-3925, ¶T-9638; ¶64,044; TD ¶837,518, TD ¶842,038
2. ¶A-8304, ¶A-8304.1; ¶574; TD ¶697,004, TD ¶697,004.1
3. ¶A-8242; ¶584; TD ¶699,001
4. ¶A-8244; ¶584; TD ¶699,003

(3) *Circulation expenditures.* Under an adjustment only for individuals and personal holding companies, the AMT circulation expenditures deduction is the amount that results from capitalizing the costs and amortizing them over three years (¶1619). (Code Sec. 56(b)(2))[5]

¶ 3211   Earnings and profits adjustments applicable only to corporations

A corporations's alternative minimum taxable income (AMTI, ¶3202) is *increased* by 75% of the excess of its adjusted current earnings (ACE, defined below) over its pre-adjustment AMTI (i.e., AMTI before this adjustment or the alternative tax net operating loss deduction [ATNOLD, ¶3212]). (Code Sec. 56(c)(1), Code Sec. 56(g)(1)) If pre-adjustment AMTI exceeds the ACE amount, AMTI is *reduced* by 75% of the difference, but this reduction is limited to the total amount of AMTI increases under this rule in earlier years. (Code Sec. 56(g)(2)) The ACE adjustment doesn't apply to S corporations, regulated investment companies, real estate investment trusts, or real estate mortgage investment conduits. (Code Sec. 56(g)(6))[6]

ACE equals pre-adjustment AMTI plus those items (and related deductions) that, although included in earnings and profits (E&P) as computed for Subchapter C purposes, never enter into the calculation of regular income or AMTI. But interest on certain tax-exempt housing bonds or bonds issued in 2009 or 2010, certain cancellation of debt income (¶1391), and the "inside buildup" on life insurance contracts (¶1721), aren't included. No deduction is allowed for items that won't ever be deductible for E&P purposes. But an adjusted dividends received deduction (¶3306) and the Code Sec. 199 production activities deduction (¶1614) are allowed. There are additional adjustments, such as: requiring a special depreciation method for property placed in service before '94, including "excess" percentage depletion deductions (¶3208) taken for mines placed in service before '90, disallowing the installment method, and certain E&P adjustments, Also, in computing ACE, the adjusted basis of property to which an ACE adjustment applies generally takes that adjustment into account. (Code Sec. 56(g)(3), Code Sec. 56(g)(4), Code Sec. 56(g)(5); Reg § 1.56(g)-1)[7]

Special adjustments apply for Blue Cross, Blue Shield and similar organizations (Code Sec. 56(c)(3))[8] and for merchant marine capital construction funds. (Code Sec. 56(c)(2))[9]

¶ 3212   Alternative tax net operating loss deduction.

For AMT purposes, an alternative tax net operating loss deduction (ATNOLD or ATNOL deduction) is allowed instead of the regular tax net operating loss (NOL) deduction (RNOLD, see ¶1840 *et seq.*). (Code Sec. 56(a)(4))[10]

In general, the ATNOLD is the same as the RNOLD *except that:*

(1) the amount of the ATNOLD is limited to 90% of alternative minimum taxable income (AMTI, ¶3202) determined without regard to the ATNOLD and the Code Sec. 199 production activities deduction (¶1614). But the 90%-of-AMTI limitation doesn't apply to carrybacks and carryovers of amounts attributable to: 2008 or 2009 NOLs for which an extended carryback period is elected under Code Sec. 172(b)(1)(H) (¶1843), pre-2010 qualified disaster losses, or certain other disaster losses such as qualified GO Zone losses (¶1844) (Code Sec. 56(d)(1)(A), Code Sec. 56(d)(3), Code Sec. 1400N(k)(1)(B)), which can offset up to 100% of AMTI;[11] and

(2) the ATNOL is determined with AMT adjustments and reduced by AMT preferences (but only to the extent the preference increased the NOL for the year). (Code Sec. 56(d)(2))[12]

caution: Check http://ria.thomsonreuters.com/federaltaxhandbook to see if the qualified

---

5. ¶A-8245; ¶564.02; TD ¶699,004

6. ¶A-8401 *et seq.*; ¶564.03; TD ¶698,001 *et seq.*

7. ¶A-8404 *et seq.*; ¶564.03; TD ¶698,004 *et seq.*

8. ¶A-8197; ¶564.03

9. ¶A-8198; ¶564.03

10. ¶A-8210 *et seq.*; ¶564.01; TD ¶696,000 *et seq.*

11. ¶A-8212, ¶A-8213; ¶564.01; TD ¶696,508, TD ¶696,509

12. ¶A-8211; ¶564.01; TD ¶696,503

disaster loss deduction has been extended.

An election to forgo the regular NOL carryback period (¶1845) also applies for ATNOLD purposes. (The election must be made for regular tax purposes to get it for AMT purposes.)[13]

The difference between the regular tax basis and AMT basis (¶3213) of stock acquired under an incentive stock option (ISO) isn't an adjustment and doesn't result in an ATNOL.[14]

¶ 3213 Different AMT adjusted basis for some property.

For AMT purposes, the adjusted bases of the following types of property are computed by taking into consideration the AMT preference or adjustment listed below with the property:

(1) Depreciable property subject to the Code Sec. 56(a)(1) depreciation adjustment, ¶3207.

(2) Property subject to the Code Sec. 56(b)(2) adjustment for circulation or research and experimental expenditures (¶3209, ¶3210) paid or incurred after '86.

(3) Property subject to the Code Sec. 56(a)(2) adjustment for mine exploration or development expenditures (¶3208) paid or incurred after '86.

(4) Pollution control facilities subject to the Code Sec. 56(a)(5) adjustment (¶3208), if placed in service after '86. (Code Sec. 56(a)(6))

(5) Stock acquired under an incentive stock option (ISO) (¶3209). Generally, the basis of the stock is determined under the Code Sec. 83 rules rather than the Code Sec. 421 rules. (Code Sec. 56(b)(3)) Thus, the taxpayer gets a cost basis in the ISO stock for regular tax purposes, and a fair market value basis in the stock for AMT purposes (¶1223).[15]

¶ 3214 AMT foreign tax credit.

The AMT foreign tax credit (AMTFTC) is available to both corporate and noncorporate taxpayers. (Code Sec. 55(b)(1)(A)(i), Code Sec. 55(b)(1)(B)(ii))[16]

The AMTFTC is computed the same as the regular foreign tax credit (¶2375), except that in applying the Code Sec. 904 limitation on the amount of the credit: (1) alternative minimum taxable income (AMTI, ¶3202) is substituted for taxable income (but see below); (2) the "pre-credit tentative minimum tax" is substituted for "the tax against which the foreign tax credit is taken"; (3) items included in AMTI by reason of the ACE adjustment (¶3211) are sourced on an item-by-item basis; and (4) the AMT rate (¶3201) is used in determining "high-taxed" income. (Code Sec. 59(a)(1), Code Sec. 59(a)(2); Reg § 1.904-4(k))[17]

If a taxpayer so elects for the first tax year for which he claims an AMTFTC (Code Sec. 59(a)(3)(B)(i)), the AMTFTC limitation is figured in a simplified way, based on the proportion that regular taxable income from sources outside the U.S. (but not in excess of the taxpayer's entire AMTI) bears to the entire AMTI for the tax year. (Code Sec. 59(a)(3)(A)) Letting taxpayers use foreign source regular taxable income to compute the limitation eliminates the need to reallocate and reapportion every deduction.[18] Once made, the election applies to all tax years and can be revoked only with IRS consent. (Code Sec. 59(a)(3)(B)(ii))[19]

13. ¶A-8216; ¶564.01; TD ¶696,006
14. ¶A-8211; TD ¶696,507
15. ¶A-8193; ¶564.01 *et seq.*; TD ¶695,502
16. ¶A-8181;¶594; TD ¶691,401
17. ¶A-8181; ¶594; TD ¶691,401
18. ¶A-8183; ¶594; TD ¶691,403
19. ¶A-8183; ¶594; TD ¶691,403

Chapter 15 Corporations—Accumulated Earnings Tax—Personal Holding Companies—Consolidated Returns—Estimated Tax—S Corporations

¶ 3300 Taxation of Corporations.

A corporation is an entity distinct from its shareholders. How a corporation is taxed depends on whether it is a C corporation or an S corporation.

¶ 3301 What is a corporation for tax purposes—Form 8832?

Under regs that set forth a "check-the-box" system of classifying entities for federal tax purposes, the following business entities are mandatorily classified as corporations:

. . . A business entity organized under a federal or state statute, or under a statute of a federally recognized Indian tribe, if the statute describes or refers to the entity as incorporated or as a corporation, body corporate, or body politic.

. . . An association as determined under Reg § 301.7701-3.

. . . A business entity organized under a state statute, if the statute describes or refers to the entity as a joint-stock company or joint-stock association.

. . . An insurance company.

. . . A state-chartered business entity conducting banking activities, if any of its deposits are insured under the Federal Deposit Insurance Act.

. . . A business entity wholly owned by a state or any of its political subdivisions.

. . . A business entity that's taxable as a corporation under a provision of the Code other than Code Sec. 7701(a)(3), such as a publicly traded partnership.

. . . Certain foreign business entities ("per se" corporations) (Reg § 301.7701-2(b)(8)), and the business entities formed under the laws of U.S. territories and possessions. (Reg § 301.7701-2(b))[1]

Under the "check-the-box" regs, if a joint undertaking is an entity separate from its owners for federal tax purposes, the entity is a business entity and not a trust, and the business entity is an "eligible entity" (i.e., not mandatorily classified as a corporation), it may elect its classification for federal tax purposes. An eligible entity with at least two members may elect to be classified as a partnership or as an association (i.e., a corporation). An eligible entity with a single owner may elect to be classified as an association or to be disregarded as an entity separate from its owner.[2] An eligible entity that wishes to elect a classification other than its default classification, or any eligible entity that wishes to change its classification does so by filing Form 8832 with the IRS Center designated on the form.[3]

An entity organized in more than one jurisdiction is treated as a corporation for federal tax purposes if it is so treated in any of those jurisdictions. (Reg § 301.7701-2(b)(9))[4]

¶ 3302 Publicly traded partnerships (PTPs) as corporations.

A publicly traded partnership (PTP) is taxable as a corporation. (Code Sec. 7704(a))[5] A partnership is a PTP if interests in the partnership either: (1) are traded on an established securities market (including, a national exchange, a regional or local exchange, certain foreign exchanges, and an interdealer quotation system), or (2) are readily tradable on a secondary market or its substantial equivalent. (Code Sec. 7704(b); Reg § 1.7704-1)[6]

However, a PTP won't be treated as a corporation if at least 90% of its gross income for the

1. ¶D-1101 et seq.; ¶77,014.14; TD ¶600,202
2. ¶D-1151; ¶77,014.15; TD ¶580,501
3. ¶D-1158; ¶77,014.15; TD ¶580,511
4. ¶D-1101.1; ¶77,014.13; TD ¶600,202
5. ¶D-1321; ¶77,044; TD ¶600,300
6. ¶D-1343; ¶77,044.03; TD ¶600,302

References beginning with a single letter are to paragraphs in RIA's Federal Tax Coordinator 2d and RIA's Analysis of Federal Taxes: Income. Those beginning with numbers are to paragraphs in RIA's United States Tax Reporter. Those beginning with TD are to paragraphs in RIA's Tax Desk.

tax year is specified passive-type income, and certain other requirements are met. (Code Sec. 7704(c))[7]

For how C corporations are taxed, see ¶3303 *et seq.*

¶ 3303 How C Corporations Are Taxed. ▬▬▬▬▬▬▬▬▬▬▬▬

C corporations generally are subject to tax at graduated rates on their taxable income. The benefits of the graduated rates phase out after taxable income reaches a specified amount.

For the rates at which a C corporation's income is taxed, and for the amount at which the graduated rates are phased out, see ¶1112. For limits on the use of graduated rates and other tax benefits by members of a controlled group of corporations, see ¶3341.

C corporations that are qualified personal service corporations (PSCs, see ¶3333) are taxed at a flat 35% rate. (Code Sec. 11(b)(2))[8]

Some C corporations are also subject to an alternative minimum tax (¶3200 *et seq.*).

For penalty taxes imposed on corporations with unreasonable earnings accumulations, see ¶3316 *et seq.*

For personal holding company tax, see ¶3323 *et seq.*

For taxation of corporations making certain outbound transfers, see ¶3588.

For corporate income tax returns generally, see ¶4724.

¶ 3304 C corporation's taxable income.

A C corporation's taxable income equals its gross income less the deductions allowed by the Code. (Code Sec. 63)[9] Generally a C corporation's gross income doesn't include contributions to its capital. (Code Sec. 118) While governmental payments designed to subsidize business operations may constitute income rather than a capital contribution, a governmental economic development grant may constitute a capital contribution.[10] For a C corporation's gain or loss from distributing property to its shareholders, see ¶3538.

¶ 3305 Computing a C corporation's tax.

A C corporation's tax is computed by applying the Code Sec. 11 rates in effect for its tax year (¶1112) to its taxable income (¶3304) for that year, and then subtracting any available tax credits (¶2300 *et seq.*).[11]

Special rules apply for computing the tax for years that straddle a rate change (Code Sec. 15(a))[12] and for short tax years, see ¶2805.

For reporting and paying the tax, see ¶4724 *et seq.*

¶ 3306 Dividends-Received Deduction. ▬▬▬▬▬▬▬▬▬▬▬▬

Corporate shareholders are allowed a deduction for dividends received.

¶ 3307 Deduction for dividends from domestic corporations—70%, 80%, and 100% deductions.

Subject to specific disallowances, reductions, and limitations (¶3311 *et seq.*), a C corporation may deduct 70% of the dividends received or accrued from domestic corporations. (Code Sec. 243(a)(1))[13] The deduction is 80% for dividends received or accrued from a corporation at least 20% of the stock of which (not counting preferred stock described in Code Sec.

---

7. ¶D-1363 *et seq.*; ¶77,044; TD ¶600,303
8. ¶D-1006; ¶s 114.01, 114.02; TD ¶600,901
9. ¶D-1001; ¶634; TD ¶600,501
10. ¶F-1901; ¶1184; TD ¶600,501

11. ¶D-1001 *et seq.*; ¶114.01; TD ¶600,501
12. ¶D-1009 *et seq.*; ¶154.01; TD ¶600,506
13. ¶D-2201; ¶2434.01; TD ¶600,509

1504(a)(4)) is owned, by vote and value, by the corporate shareholder. (Code Sec. 243(c))[14]

Members of an affiliated group (as specially defined) that file separate returns may deduct 100% of the dividends received from other group members if certain requirements are met. (Code Sec. 243(a)(3), Code Sec. 243(b))[15]

For a small business investment company's dividends-received deduction, see ¶4205.

The deduction applies to taxable dividends (¶1287 *et seq.*) (Code Sec. 243(a)), "boot" dividends (¶3556), consent dividends (¶3338)[16] and the "dividend equivalent" portion of high yield OID obligations (¶1753). (Code Sec. 163(e)(5)(B))[17] For dividends that aren't deductible, see ¶3315.

¶ 3308   Dividends from regulated investment companies (RICs)—mutual fund dividends.

A corporate shareholder that receives a properly designated dividend (other than capital gain or exempt-interest dividends) from a RIC (a mutual fund) is eligible for the dividends-received deduction to the extent the RIC would have been allowed to deduct the amount as a dividends-received deduction if it were taxed as a regular corporation. (Code Sec. 243(d)(2), Code Sec. 854(b)(4))[18]

¶ 3309   Dividends on certain public utility preferred stock.

Dividends received from a public utility are eligible for the dividends-received deduction, but the deduction is reduced if the utility was entitled to a dividends-*paid* deduction (¶3334) on those dividends. (Code Sec. 244(a))[19]

¶ 3310   Dividends from foreign corporations and possession corporations.

A U.S. corporation that owns at least 10% (by vote and value) of the stock of a foreign corporation (other than a foreign passive investment company) may deduct the applicable percentage (70% or 80%, see ¶3307) of the U.S.-source portion of the dividends it receives from that foreign corporation. (Code Sec. 245(a)(1), Code Sec. 245(a)(2))[20]

The U.S.-source portion of any dividend is the amount that bears the same ratio to the dividend that the payor's post-'86 undistributed U.S. earnings bears to its total post-'86 undistributed earnings. (Code Sec. 245(a)(3), Code Sec. 245(a)(4), Code Sec. 245(a)(5))[21] Special rules apply for dividends paid out of pre-'87 earnings.[22]

A 100% dividends-received deduction is allowed (instead of the above percentage deductions) if all the foreign corporation's gross income is effectively connected with its U.S. business in the year the dividends are earned, and all its outstanding stock is owned by the U.S. payee both in that year and in the payee's tax year in which the dividends are received. (Code Sec. 245(b))[23]

For DISC dividends, see ¶3315.

¶ 3311   Taxable income limit on dividends-received deduction.

In the case of dividends that are subject to the 70% or 80% (but not the 100%) rule (¶3307), the dividends received deduction (DRD) may not exceed 70% or 80% of the corporation's taxable income. Net operating loss (NOL) deductions, capital loss carrybacks, and the DRD itself are not taken into account when computing taxable income for this limitation. (Code Sec. 246(b)(1)) A corporation is not subject to this limitation where it has an NOL for the tax

14. ¶D-2205 *et seq.*; ¶2434.01; TD ¶600,509
15. ¶D-2223 *et seq.*; ¶2434.01; TD ¶600,509
16. ¶D-2209 *et seq.*; ¶2434.01; TD ¶602,019
17. ¶D-2221; ¶1634.051; TD ¶600,512
18. ¶D-2216, ¶E-6163; ¶8524.02; TD ¶600,512
19. ¶D-2222; ¶2434.02; TD ¶600,512
20. ¶D-2244; ¶2434.03; TD ¶600,509
21. ¶s D-2244, D-2246; ¶2434.03
22. ¶D-2246; ¶2434.03
23. ¶D-2247; ¶2434.03; TD ¶600,509

year. (Code Sec. 246(b)(2))[24]

If a taxpayer receives both 80% and 70% dividends, this limitation is applied in two stages. First, the 80% deduction for dividends from 20%–owned corporations is restricted to 80% of taxable income. Second, for dividends qualifying for the 70% deduction, the limitation is 70% of the taxable income reduced by dividends from 20% or greater owned corporations. (Code Sec. 246(b)(3))[25]

For this purpose, taxable income is computed without regard to the deductions for capital loss carrybacks, NOLs, dividends received, and the deduction for income attributable to domestic production activities (¶1616), and without regard to any basis reduction for extraordinary dividends (¶2495). (Code Sec. 246(b)(1))[26]

¶ 3312 Holding period requirements.

No dividends-received deduction is allowed for any dividend on any share of stock that's held by the taxpayer for 45 days or less during the 91-day period beginning on the date that is 45 days before the date on which the stock becomes ex-dividend with respect to the dividend (90 days or less out of the relevant 181-day period for any preferred stock with respect to which the taxpayer gets dividends that are attributable to a period or periods aggregating in excess of 366 days). (Code Sec. 246(c)) In other words, a dividends received deduction is allowed only if the taxpayer's holding period for the dividend paying stock is satisfied over a period immediately before or immediately after the taxpayer becomes entitled to receive the dividend.[27]

In determining how long the shareholder has held the stock, the day of disposition but not the day of acquisition is taken into account. (Code Sec. 246(c)(3)(A))[28]

The shareholder's holding period for the stock is reduced for any period during which the shareholder:

(1) has an option to sell, is under a contractual obligation to sell, has made (and not closed) a short sale of, or is the grantor of an option to buy, substantially identical stock or securities (as defined under the "wash sale" rules, see ¶2461). (Code Sec. 246(c)(4)(A), Code Sec. 246(c)(4)(B); Reg § 1.246-3(c)(2))[29]

(2) has diminished its risk of loss by holding one or more other positions with respect to substantially similar or related property (i.e., the fair market values (FMV) of the stock and the property primarily reflect a single firm or enterprise and changes in the stock's FMV are reasonably expected to approximate (directly or indirectly) changes in the property's FMV), where changes in the FMVs of the stock and the positions are reasonably expected to vary inversely. (Code Sec. 246(c)(4)(C); Reg § 1.246-5)[30]

¶ 3313 No dividends-received deduction where shareholder is obligated to make certain payments.

A corporate shareholder gets no dividends-received deduction for any dividends received on any stock acquired after July 18, '84 to the extent the shareholder is under an obligation (by a short sale or otherwise) to make related payments with respect to positions in substantially similar or related property (as defined at ¶3312). (Code Sec. 246(c)(1)(B))[31]

¶ 3314 Deduction reduced for dividends on debt-financed portfolio stock.

The 70% and 80% dividends-received deduction (but not the 100% deduction) (¶3307) is reduced for dividends on debt-financed portfolio stock with a holding period that began after July 18, '84. As reduced, the applicable percentage for deducting these dividends equals: (1)

24. ¶s D-2251, D-2252; ¶2434.04; TD ¶600,518
25. ¶D-2253; ¶2434.04; TD ¶600,518
26. ¶D-2251; ¶2434.04; TD ¶600,518
27. ¶D-2263; ¶2434.04; TD ¶600,516

28. ¶D-2263; ¶2434.04
29. ¶s D-2264, D-2266; ¶2434.04; TD ¶600,517
30. ¶D-2268 *et seq.*; ¶2434.04; TD ¶600,517
31. ¶D-2261; ¶2434.04; TD ¶600,515

70% (80% for dividends from 20%-owned corporations), multiplied by (2) 100% minus the "average indebtedness percentage." (Code Sec. 246A(a), Code Sec. 246A(b)) The reduction for any dividend may not exceed the interest deduction (including short sale expense) allocable to that dividend. (Code Sec. 246A(e))[32]

¶ 3315   Dividends from certain corporations aren't deductible.

No dividends-received deduction is allowed for dividends from:

. . . a corporation that's exempt from tax as a charitable organization under Code Sec. 501 or as a farmer's cooperative under Code Sec. 521. (Code Sec. 246(a)(1))[33]

. . . a DISC (¶4622) or former DISC to the extent paid out of accumulated DISC income or previously taxed income, or amounts considered distributed in the year of qualification as a DISC. (Code Sec. 246(d))[34]

. . . a REIT. (Code Sec. 243(d)(3))[35]

. . . a mutual savings bank, savings and loan associations and other banks allowed a deduction under Code Sec. 591. (Code Sec. 243(d)(1))[36] However, certain dividends from federal home loan banks qualify to the extent set out in a specific formula. (Code Sec. 246(a)(2))[37]

¶ 3316   Accumulated Earnings Tax. ▬▬▬▬▬▬▬

Every corporation, unless specifically exempt, that accumulates earnings and profits (rather than distributes them) in order to avoid the imposition of income tax on its shareholders is subject to an annual accumulated earnings (penalty) tax, equal to 15% (for tax years beginning after 2002 and before 2011) of its "accumulated taxable income" for the year. The tax is in addition to the regular corporate tax.

¶ 3317   Purpose to avoid tax versus "reasonable needs" of the business.

The accumulated earnings penalty tax is only imposed on a corporation whose earnings and profits (E&P) were accumulated with the purpose of avoiding income tax on its shareholders. (Code Sec. 532(a))[38] A corporation that accumulates E&P beyond the reasonable needs of its business is considered to have done so to avoid tax on its shareholders *unless* it proves the contrary by the preponderance of the evidence. (Code Sec. 533(a))[39]

An accumulation is in excess of the reasonable needs of a business if it exceeds the amount that a prudent business person would consider appropriate for the present purposes of the business and for its reasonably anticipated future needs. (Code Sec. 537; Reg § 1.537-1(a), Reg § 1.537-1(b)(1))[40] The reasonable needs of a corporation's business include the Code Sec. 303 death tax redemption needs of the business (Code Sec. 537(a)(2)[41] and the excess business holdings redemption needs of the business. (Code Sec. 537(a)(3))[42]

Corporations facing an accumulated earnings tax may use a formula to compute the amount reasonably needed for working capital, to test their liability for the penalty. The Tax Court in Bardahl Manufacturing Corp held that necessary working capital should be determined by: (1) calculating a corporation's operating cycle percentage (the period of time, expressed as a percent of a year, needed to convert cash to inventory, inventory to sales and accounts receivable, and accounts receivable to cash), and then (2) multiplying that percentage times the corporation's total operating expenses for the year (cost of goods sold and other expenses). The result of this two-step Bardahl formula is the amount of liquid assets necessary to meet the ordinary operating expenses for one complete operating cycle.[43]

32. ¶D-2255; ¶2434.05; TD ¶600,520
33. ¶D-2213; ¶2434.04; TD ¶600,513
34. ¶D-2212; ¶2434.04; TD ¶600,513
35. ¶D-2215; ¶2434.01; TD ¶600,513
36. ¶D-2211; ¶2434.01; TD ¶600,513
37. ¶s D-2214, D-2219; ¶2434.04; TD ¶600,512

38. ¶D-2601; ¶5324.01; TD ¶601,001
39. ¶D-2704; ¶s 5324.01, 5374; TD ¶601,014
40. ¶D-2779, D-2783, D-2792; ¶s 5314, 5374; TD ¶601,019
41. ¶D-2828;¶5374; TD ¶601,030
42. ¶D-2830; ¶5374; TD ¶601,030
43. ¶D-2848; ¶5374; TD ¶601,032

A corporation with a history of paying dividends isn't likely to be hit with the penalty.[44]

¶ 3318 Application of the accumulated earnings tax.

The tax applies to every corporation (unless specifically exempt, see ¶3319), regardless of the number of shareholders (Code Sec. 532(a), Code Sec. 532(c))—i.e., even if it's widely held.[45]

The tax applies to foreign corporations on their U.S.-source income if *any* of their shareholders is subject to U.S. income tax on distributions. (Reg § 1.532-1(c))[46]

The accumulated earnings tax is in addition to other income taxes imposed on the corporation, and is assessed and paid with those taxes. (Code Sec. 531; Reg § 1.531-1)[47]

For permissible accumulations, see ¶3322.

¶ 3319 Corporations exempt from the accumulated earnings tax.

The accumulated earnings tax *doesn't apply* to:

... personal holding companies (subject to their own penalty tax, see ¶3323) (Code Sec. 532(b)(1));

... tax-exempt corporations (Code Sec. 532(b)(2));

... passive foreign investment companies (¶4629) (Code Sec. 532(b)(3));

... S corporations (¶3353 *et seq.*). (Code Sec. 1363(a))[48]

¶ 3320 Accumulated earnings tax rate.

For tax years beginning after 2002 and before 2011, the accumulated earnings tax is 15% of accumulated taxable income (¶3321). (Code Sec. 531)[49]

caution: For the effect of the sunset rules in tax years beginning after Dec. 31, 2010 , see ¶1114.

¶ 3321 Accumulated taxable income.

A corporation's accumulated taxable income is its taxable income, adjusted as described below, *minus:* (1) the dividends-paid deduction (¶3334), and (2) the accumulated earnings credit (¶3322). (Code Sec. 535(a))[50]

The corporation's taxable income is *reduced* by:

... federal income and excess profits taxes accrued during the tax year (not the accumulated earnings tax or the personal holding company tax) (Code Sec. 535(b)(1));

... taxes of foreign countries and U.S. possessions accrued or deemed paid by a domestic corporation and included in the foreign tax credit (¶2375 *et seq.*) (Code Sec. 535(h)(1));[1]

... charitable contributions in excess of the deduction ceiling (¶2132) (Code Sec. 535(b)(2));[2]

... net capital gains (less attributable taxes). (Code Sec. 535(b)(6)(A)) A mere holding or investment company deducts net *short*-term capital gain (less attributable taxes) to the extent it doesn't exceed capital loss carryover to the year (Code Sec. 535(b)(8)(B)); other corporations must reduce their net capital gain deduction by net capital losses from any earlier year (Code Sec. 535(b)(7)(A), Code Sec. 535(b)(8)(B));[3]

... net capital losses. (Code Sec. 535(b)(5)(A)) A mere holding or investment company gets no net capital loss deduction (Code Sec. 535(b)(8)(A)); any other corporation must reduce its

44. ¶D-2715; ¶5374; TD ¶601,016
45. ¶s D-2602, D-2603; ¶5324; TD ¶601,002
46. ¶D-2607; ¶5324; TD ¶601,003
47. ¶D-2601, V-2053; ¶5314; TD ¶601,001
48. ¶D-2602; ¶5324; TD ¶601,002

49. ¶D-2601, ¶T-11051; ¶s 5324.01, 5354; TD ¶601,001
50. ¶D-2901; ¶5354.01; TD ¶601,009
1. ¶D-2913; ¶5354.01; TD ¶601,009
2. ¶D-2906; ¶5354.01; TD ¶601,009
3. ¶D-2908; ¶5354.01; TD ¶601,009

net capital loss deduction by the lesser of: (1) its nonrecaptured capital gain deduction, or (2) its accumulated E&P as of the close of the preceding tax year. (Code Sec. 535(b)(5))[4]

Taxable income is *increased* by:

. . . special corporate deductions (e.g., for dividends received (¶3306 *et seq.*), but not for organizational expenditures) (Code Sec. 535(b)(3));

. . . net operating loss deduction (¶1840 *et seq.*) (Code Sec. 535(b)(4));

. . . capital loss carryback or carryover (¶2615). (Code Sec. 535(b)(7)(B))[5]

¶ 3322   Accumulated earnings credit.

For corporations, other than a mere holding or investment company, the accumulated earnings credit equals the *greater* of:

(1) $250,000 ($150,000 for a corporation whose principal function is the performance of health, legal, engineering, accounting, or certain other services) *plus* dividends paid during the first 2½ months of the tax year *minus* accumulated earnings and profits (E&P) at the end of the preceding tax year (Code Sec. 535(c)(2), Code Sec. 535(c)(4)); or

(2) an amount equal to that part of the E&P for the tax year that is retained for the reasonable needs of the business *minus* the net capital gain deduction, if any, allowed in adjusting the corporation's taxable income (¶3321). (Code Sec. 535(c)(1)) The E&P "retained" for a tax year is the amount in excess of dividends-paid deduction (¶3335). (Code Sec. 535(c)(4))[6]

A mere holding or investment company's accumulated earnings credit is the amount, if any, by which $250,000 plus dividends paid in the first 2½ months of the tax year exceeds accumulated E&P at the close of the preceding year. (Code Sec. 535(c)(3), Code Sec. 535(c)(4))[7]

⊘ *observation:* A mere holding or investment company gets no credit for reasonable needs.

¶ 3323   Personal Holding Company Tax. ▬▬▬▬▬▬▬

A closely held corporation whose income is largely of investment character may be a personal holding company (PHC). For any year in which a corporation is a PHC (see ¶3325) it is liable for a 15% (for tax years beginning after 2002 and before 2011) penalty tax on its undistributed PHC income, in addition to "regular" income tax. (Code Sec. 541)[8] The tax is reported on Form 1120, Schedule PH. (Reg § 1.6012-2(b))[9]

The foreign tax credit isn't allowed against the PHC tax. (Reg § 1.545-2(a)(3))[10]

⊘ *caution:* For the effect of the EGTRRA sunset rules in tax years beginning after Dec. 31, 2010, see ¶1114.

¶ 3324   Undistributed PHC income subject to the PHC penalty tax.

A corporation's undistributed PHC income that is subject to the PHC tax is its taxable income (Code Sec. 545(a))[11] adjusted as described below.

. . . The following amounts are *subtracted* from taxable income:

. . . Federal income tax accrued during the year, and U.S. possession and foreign income taxes not deductible in computing taxable income. (Code Sec. 545(b)(1))[12]

. . . Excess charitable contributions, i.e., amounts over the *corporate* ceiling up to the

---

4. ¶D-2911; ¶5354.01; TD ¶601,009
5. ¶D-2907; ¶5354.01; TD ¶601,009
6. ¶D-2915; ¶5354.01; TD ¶601,012
7. ¶D-2915; ¶5354.01; TD ¶601,013
8. ¶D-3202; ¶5414; TD ¶601,501

9. ¶D-3601; ¶5454.02; TD ¶609,805
10. ¶D-3619; ¶9014
11. ¶D-3603; ¶5454; TD ¶601,516
12. ¶D-3606; ¶5454; TD ¶601,516

amount allowed under the *individual* ceiling (¶2124 *et seq.*). (Code Sec. 545(b)(2))[13]

... Net capital gain (i.e., excess of net long-term capital gain over net short-term capital loss), minus income taxes attributable to that excess. (Code Sec. 545(b)(5))[14]

... The preceding tax year's net operating loss (NOL) carryforward. (Code Sec. 545(b)(4))[15]

... Dividends-paid deduction (¶3334 *et seq.*). (Code Sec. 545(a))[16]

... The following amounts are *added* to taxable income:

... Special corporate deductions, e.g., for dividends received (¶3306 *et seq.*). (Code Sec. 545(b)(3))[17]

... NOL deduction. (Code Sec. 545(b)(4))[18]

... Expenses and depreciation exceeding income from property (unless income was highest obtainable). (Code Sec. 545(b)(6))[19]

¶ 3325   What is a personal holding company (PHC)?

Any corporation (unless specifically exempt, see ¶3326) is a personal holding company (PHC) if, for the tax year:

... at any time during the last half of the year more than 50% in value of its outstanding stock is owned, directly or indirectly, by or for not more than five individuals ("stock ownership test," see ¶3327); *and*

... at least 60% of its adjusted ordinary gross income is PHC income (see ¶3329). (Code Sec. 542(a))[20]

¶ 3326   Corporations exempt from PHC classification.

The following entities cannot be PHCs:

... S corporations (¶3353 *et seq.*); (Code Sec. 1363(a))

... tax-exempt corporations; (Code Sec. 542(c)(1))

... banks or domestic building and loan associations; (Code Sec. 542(c)(2))

... life insurance companies; (Code Sec. 542(c)(3))

... surety companies; (Code Sec. 542(c)(4))

... certain active lending or finance companies; (Code Sec. 542(c)(6), Code Sec. 542(d))

... small business investment companies (¶2631), if no shareholders own, directly or indirectly, a 5%-or-more interest in a small business concern to which the investment company provides funds; (Code Sec. 542(c)(7))

... corporations subject to the jurisdiction of a court in a bankruptcy case or in a receivership, foreclosure or similar proceeding in a federal or state court if the proceedings aren't primarily to avoid the PHC tax; (Code Sec. 542(c)(8)) and

... foreign corporations. (Code Sec. 542(c)(5))[21]

¶ 3327   Determining stock ownership.

For purposes of the PHC tests (¶3325), an individual is the owner of any stock he owns directly or indirectly (Code Sec. 542(a)(2)), or constructively under these rules:

(1) Stock owned by or for a corporation, partnership, estate or trust is considered owned

---

13. ¶D-3609; ¶5454; TD ¶601,516
14. ¶D-3610; ¶5454; TD ¶601,516
15. ¶D-3614; ¶5454; TD ¶601,516
16. ¶D-3800; ¶5454; TD ¶601,516
17. ¶D-3613; ¶5454; TD ¶601,516

18. ¶D-3614; ¶5454; TD ¶601,516
19. ¶D-3615; ¶5454; TD ¶601,516
20. ¶D-3203; ¶5424; TD ¶601,502
21. ¶D-3301; ¶5424.02; TD ¶601,503

proportionately by its shareholders, partners or beneficiaries. (Code Sec. 544(a)(1))[22]

(2) Stock owned by or for an individual's family or partner is considered owned by the individual. An individual's family includes only his brothers and sisters (whether by the whole or half blood), spouse, ancestors and lineal descendants. (Code Sec. 544(a)(2))[23]

(3) If any person has an option to acquire stock, the stock subject to the option is considered owned by that person. An option to acquire the option, and each one of a series of these options, is considered an option to acquire the stock. (Code Sec. 544(a)(3))[24]

Stock that may be considered owned by an individual under either rule (2) or rule (3) is considered owned by him under rule (3). (Code Sec. 544(a)(6))[25]

Rules (2) and (3) apply only if the result is to make the corporation a PHC or to make income PHC income (¶3329). (Code Sec. 544(a)(4))[26]

Stock *constructively* owned by a person under rule (1) or rule (3) is considered *actually* owned by that person for purposes of again applying rule (1), or applying rule (2), to make *another* person the *constructive* owner of the same stock. (Code Sec. 544(a)(5))[27]

Only outstanding stock (i.e., not Treasury stock) is counted. (Reg § 1.542-3(b))[28] Outstanding securities convertible into stock are considered outstanding stock *but only if* converting them would make the corporation a PHC or the income PHC income (except where there are differing conversion dates). (Code Sec. 544(b))[29]

¶ 3328   Adjusted ordinary gross income used in PHC test.

For purposes of the PHC tests (¶3325), *adjusted ordinary gross income* is ordinary gross income (below) minus certain interest income, with these adjustments: for each of the separate categories of rents, mineral, oil and gas royalties, working interests in an oil or gas well and property produced by the taxpayer, gross income from the category is reduced (but not below zero) by certain expenses allocated to each category. (Code Sec. 543(b)(2))[30]

Ordinary gross income is gross income minus all gains from the sale or other disposition of capital assets (including unstated interest) and of Code Sec. 1231(b) assets. (Code Sec. 543(b)(1))[31]

¶ 3329   Personal holding company (PHC) income used in PHC test.

For purposes of the PHC tests (¶3325), PHC income is the portion of adjusted ordinary gross income (¶3328), that consists of: dividends; interest; annuities; rents (¶3330); mineral, oil and gas royalties; copyright, patent, etc., royalties (but not certain "active business computer software royalties"); produced film rents; compensation for more-than-25% shareholder's use of corporate property (¶3331); amounts received under personal service contracts (¶3332); and amounts received from estates and trusts. (Code Sec. 543(a))[32]

¶ 3330   Rents.

The adjusted income from rents is PHC income (¶3329), unless *both* these tests are met:

(1) adjusted income from rents is 50% or more of adjusted ordinary gross income (¶3328); *and*

(2) certain other *undistributed* "PHC income" (as specially defined) is 10% or less of ordinary gross income (¶3328). This "PHC income" *includes* copyright royalties and adjusted income from mineral, oil and gas royalties but *excludes* rents and compensation for a 25%-or-more shareholder's use of corporate property. The 10% test is met if the total of (a)

---

22. ¶D-3406; ¶5444.01; TD ¶601,512
23. ¶D-3408; ¶5444.01; TD ¶601,512
24. ¶D-3410; ¶5444.01; TD ¶601,512
25. ¶D-3411; ¶5444.01 *et seq.*; TD ¶601,512
26. ¶s D-3408, D-3410; ¶5444.01; TD ¶601,512
27. ¶D-3411; ¶5444.01; TD ¶601,512

28. ¶D-3402; ¶5424.04; TD ¶601,510
29. ¶D-3412; ¶5444.01 *et seq.*; TD ¶601,513
30. ¶D-3506; ¶5424.03; TD ¶601,504
31. ¶D-3505; ¶5424.03; TD ¶601,504
32. ¶D-3507; ¶5434 *et seq.*; TD ¶601,505

dividends paid during the tax year, plus (b) late-paid dividends (¶3336), plus (c) consent dividends (¶3338), equals or exceeds the amount, if any, by which "PHC income" exceeds 10% of ordinary gross income. (Code Sec. 543(a)(2))[33]

Rents are compensation (however designated) for the use of, or the right to use, property (Code Sec. 543(a)(1)(A), Code Sec. 543(b)(3)), *except* for: compensation for a shareholder's use of corporate property that is PHC income (¶3331), copyright royalties, produced film rents, or compensation for the right to use any tangible personal property manufactured or produced by the corporation, if during the tax year it's engaged in substantial manufacturing or production of property of the same type. (Code Sec. 543(b)(3))[34]

¶ 3331   Compensation for use of corporate property by a 25%-or-more shareholder.

Amounts received by the corporation from a shareholder as compensation for the use of, or right to use, tangible property of the corporation is included in the corporation's PHC income (¶3329), if, during the tax year, 25% or more in value of the corporation's outstanding stock is owned by or for an individual entitled to use that property (directly or through a sublease). (Code Sec. 543(a)(6)(A)) But this doesn't apply if the corporation's PHC income doesn't exceed 10% of its ordinary gross income (¶3328). This specially defined PHC income is computed by *excluding* adjusted income from rents and compensation for a 25%-or-more shareholder's use of tangible corporate property, and by *including* copyright royalties and adjusted income from mineral, oil and gas royalties. (Code Sec. 543(a)(6))[35]

¶ 3332   Receipts under personal service contract.

PHC income (¶3329) includes amounts received under a contract under which the corporation furnishes personal services, and amounts received from the sale or other disposition of the contract, if:

(1) some person other than the corporation has the right to designate (by name or description) the individual who performs the services, or if the individual who is to perform the services is so designated in the contract, *and*

(2) at some time during the tax year 25% or more in value of the corporation's outstanding stock is owned, directly or indirectly, by or for that individual. (Code Sec. 543(a)(7); Reg § 1.543-1(b)(8)(i))[36]

¶ 3333   Qualified Personal Service Corporations

Qualified personal service corporations (PSCs) are subject to special rules, e.g., they are subject to a flat 35% tax rate and are required to use the cash method for accounting purposes. A corporation is a PSC if it meets two tests:

(1) Substantially all of its activities involve the performance of services in the fields of health, law, engineering, architecture, accounting, actuarial science, performing arts, or consulting. "Substantially all" means that 95% or more of the time spent by the corporation's employees, serving in their capacity as employees, is devoted to performing such services. Brokerage services, including commission-based financial services, are excepted from consulting services.

(2) Substantially all (95% or more) of the stock by value (not including treasury shares) is held directly or indirectly by: employees performing the services or retired employees who had performed such services; or the estates of such employees, or any other person who, during the two-year period starting with the date that such an employee died, acquired that individual's stock because his death. (Code Sec. 448(d)(2); Reg § 1.448-1T(e)(4))[37]

---

33. ¶D-3522; ¶5434.07; TD ¶601,506
34. ¶D-3524; ¶s 5434.06, 5434.07, 5434.09; TD ¶601,506
35. ¶D-3527; ¶5434.06; TD ¶601,514

36. ¶D-3531; ¶5434.05; TD ¶601,515
37. ¶G-2058 *et seq.*; ¶4484; TD ¶440,809

For the tax rate applicable to qualified PSCs, see ¶3303. For the rules on allowable accounting methods, see ¶2818. For the tax year of personal service corporations, see ¶2811.

¶ 3334   Dividend Distributions to Cut Special Taxes on Corporations. ▬▬▬▬▬

A deduction for dividends paid is allowed in computing the accumulated earnings penalty tax (¶3316) and personal holding company penalty tax (¶3323), and in determining a corporation's qualification as a regulated investment company (e.g., mutual fund) (¶4201) or real estate investment trust (REIT) (¶4202). A deduction is also allowed in some cases for undistributed amounts shareholders consent to report as dividends.

Depending on the entity involved, the dividends-paid deduction may consist of:

(1) dividends paid during the tax year (¶3335),

(2) "late paid" dividends (¶3336),

(3) liquidating dividends (¶3337),

(4) consent dividends (¶3338),

(5) dividend carryover—only for personal holding companies (PHCs) (¶3339), and

(6) deficiency dividends (¶3340)—only for PHCs. (Code Sec. 561 *et seq.*; Reg § 1.561-1)[38]

¶ 3335   Dividends paid during the tax year.

The dividends-paid deduction includes dividends (¶1289) paid during the tax year. (Code Sec. 561(a)(1)) But the dividend must actually be paid,[39] and must actually be received by the shareholder in the year for which the deduction is claimed. (Reg § 1.561-2(a)(1))[40]

No deduction is allowed if the dividend is preferential, i.e., it must be pro rata. (Code Sec. 562(c); Reg § 1.562-2(a))[41]

The amount of "dividends" paid is the amount by which the distribution reduces the corporation's earnings and profits (E&P). (Code Sec. 316(a), Code Sec. 562(a))[42]

A PHC's (¶3323 *et seq.*) dividends-paid deduction may equal its undistributed PHC income even if this exceeds its E&P. (Code Sec. 316(b)(2), Code Sec. 562(a))[43]

IRS will treat an optional stock distribution by a RIC or REIT declared before Jan. 1, 2013 for a tax year ending before Jan. 1, 2012 as a property distribution equal to the amount of cash that would have been received if the shareholder elected to receive cash instead of stock.[44]

¶ 3336   Deduction for "late paid" dividends.

A corporation may treat dividends paid after the close of the tax year but within the first 2½ months of the next year ("late paid dividends") as paid on the last day of the earlier year for purposes of the accumulated earnings tax (¶3316 *et seq.*) and, if elected (on the earlier year return), PHC tax (¶3323 *et seq.*). (Code Sec. 563(a), Code Sec. 563(b))[45]

¶ 3337   Liquidating distributions.

Corporations (including mutual funds and REITs) other than PHCs may include liquidating distributions in their dividends-paid deduction, to the extent the distribution is properly chargeable to E&P. (Code Sec. 562(b)(1)(A))[46] Where there's a deficit in E&P at the start of the tax year of distribution, no dividends-paid deduction is allowed if current E&P for that year doesn't exceed the deficit. (Reg § 1.562-1(b)(1))[47] A liquidation for this purpose includes

38. ¶D-3800; ¶5614; TD ¶602,000 *et seq.*
39. ¶D-3806; ¶5614.01; TD ¶602,003
40. ¶D-3810; ¶5614.01
41. ¶D-3819 *et seq.*; ¶5624.06; TD ¶602,003
42. ¶D-3807; ¶s 3164 *et seq.*, 5614, 5624; TD ¶602,004
43. ¶D-3807; ¶s 3164.03, 5614; TD ¶602,005
44. ¶J-2506
45. ¶D-3825 *et seq.*; ¶5634; TD ¶602,007
46. ¶D-3828; ¶5624.02; TD ¶602,010
47. ¶D-3835; ¶5624.02; TD ¶602,013

a redemption of stock to which Code Sec. 302 applies (¶3526 *et seq.*), other than a redemption by a mere investment or holding company. (Code Sec. 562(b)(1))[48]

If a *complete* liquidation of a corporation other than a PHC occurs within 24 months after the plan of liquidation is adopted, any distribution under the plan within the 24-month period is treated as a dividend for this purpose, to the extent of the corporation's E&P for the tax year of the distribution, computed without regard to capital losses. (Code Sec. 562(b)(1)(B)) Thus, the dividends-paid deduction is allowed for the amount of the distribution up to the amount of current E&P even if there's an E&P deficit at the start of the year. (Reg § 1.562-1(b)(1))[49]

For PHCs only distributions made within 24 months after the plan of liquidation is adopted qualify for the dividends-paid deduction.[50] Distributions (in this period) to *corporate* shareholders qualify to the extent the undistributed PHC income for the tax year of the distribution is allocable to corporate shareholders. (Code Sec. 562(b)(2))[1] Distributions to *noncorporate* shareholders qualify if the corporation designates the amount distributed as a dividend and notifies the shareholders that it must be reported as a dividend. (Code Sec. 316(b)(2)(B), Code Sec. 562(b)(2))[2]

¶ 3338 Consent dividends—Form 972 and Form 973.

A corporation may claim a dividends-paid deduction for amounts with respect to "consent" stock (below) it doesn't actually pay out as dividends, if those who are shareholders on the last day of its tax year consent (on Form 972) to report these hypothetical amounts as dividend income on their tax returns. (Code Sec. 565(a); Reg § 1.565-1(a), Reg § 1.565-1(b))[3]

This amount is treated for all tax purposes as if it had been distributed in money to the consenting shareholder on the last day of the corporation's tax year, and contributed to the corporation's capital by the shareholder on the same day. (Code Sec. 565(c))[4]

Consent stock includes common stock, and preferred stock with unlimited participation rights. (Code Sec. 565(c); Reg § 1.565-6(a)(1))[5]

The corporation must file the Form 972 duly executed by each consenting shareholder, and a return on Form 973, with its income tax return not later than the due date (with extensions) of the return. (Reg § 1.565-1(b)(3))

¶ 3339 Dividend carryover for PHC.

A PHC may increase its dividends-paid deduction for the tax year by the excess of: (1) dividends paid in the two preceding tax years, over (2) its undistributed PHC income for those years. (Code Sec. 564; Reg § 1.564-1)[6]

¶ 3340 PHC deficiency dividend deduction—Form 976.

If a corporation is "determined" to be liable for a deficiency in PHC tax (¶3323 *et seq.*) for any tax year, it may reduce or eliminate the deficiency (or get a refund of part or all of any deficiency paid) by making a "deficiency dividend" distribution and then claiming a deduction (on Form 976) for it. This deduction is allowed only for purposes of determining the *PHC tax* for that year (but not any interest, additional amounts or assessable penalties computed with respect to the PHC tax). (Code Sec. 547(a))[7]

The deduction isn't allowed if the determination finds that any part of the deficiency is due to fraud or willful failure to file a timely income tax return. (Code Sec. 547(g))[8]

48. ¶D-3829; ¶s 5624.02, 5624.05; TD ¶602,010
49. ¶D-3836; ¶5624.02; TD ¶602,014
50. ¶D-3837; ¶s 3164.03, 5624.02; TD ¶602,015
1. ¶D-3844 *et seq.*; ¶5624.02; TD ¶602,018
2. ¶D-3838 *et seq.*; ¶s 3164.03, 5624.02; TD ¶602,016
3. ¶s D-3851, D-3854, D-3861; ¶5654; TD ¶602,019

4. ¶D-3853; ¶5654; TD ¶602,021
5. ¶s D-3859, D-3861; ¶5654; TD ¶602,024
6. ¶D-3869; ¶5644; TD ¶602,030
7. ¶s D-3703, D-3716; ¶5474; TD ¶601,519
8. ¶D-3719; ¶5474; TD ¶601,517

A "determination" is a final court decision, a closing agreement, or a signed agreement with IRS relating to PHC tax liability. (Code Sec. 547(c))[9]

¶ 3341   Limitation on Tax Benefits for Members of "Controlled Groups."

If two or more corporations constitute a controlled group of corporations, the corporate tax rate schedule (¶1112) is applied to the group as one, and the group is allowed only one credit and exemption in computing the accumulated earnings (¶3322) and alternative minimum taxes (¶3203).[10] However, under final regs, a group member that incurs a loss for a tax year may not apply that loss to reduce the amount of the combined taxable income (or combined alternative minimum taxable income) of the controlled group for purposes of determining the amount of the additional tax or the reduction in the exemption amount. (Reg § 1.1561-2(a)(ii)(A), Reg § 1.1561-2(b)(1))

A controlled group of corporations is a group of two or more corporations connected through stock ownership and may consist of a parent-subsidiary group, a brother-sister group or a combined group (a combined parent-sub/brother-sister group).

A *parent-subsidiary controlled group* consists of one or more chains of corporations connected through stock ownership with a common parent where:

. . . the common parent owns stock having at least 80% of the total combined voting power of all classes of stock entitled to vote or at least 80% of the total value of shares of all classes of stock, of at least one other corporation in the chain; *and*

. . . at least 80% of the stock (combined voting power or value) of each corporation in the chain (other than the parent) is owned by one or more of the other corporations in the chain. (Code Sec. 1563(a)(1); Reg § 1.1563-1(a)(2))[11]

A *brother-sister controlled group* consists of two or more corporations if (a) more than 50% of the total combined voting power of all classes of stock, or (b) more than 50% of the value of all shares of stock, of each corporation is owned by five or fewer persons who are individuals, estates, or trusts, taking into account the stock ownership of each person only to the extent the stock ownership is identical for each corporation. (Code Sec. 1563(a)(2), Code Sec. 1563(f)(5); Reg § 1.1563-1(a)(3))[12]

Specific constructive ownership rules apply in determining whether these stock ownership tests are met. (Code Sec. 1563(d))[13]

¶ 3342   Consolidated Returns by Affiliated Groups.

An affiliated group (defined at ¶3343) can elect to file a single consolidated return instead of each group member filing a separate return.

Any affiliated group of one or more chains of "includible" corporations (¶3343) connected through the requisite stock ownership with a common parent may file a consolidated return in place of separate returns by each member (Code Sec. 1501, Code Sec. 1502, Code Sec. 1503, Code Sec. 1504, Code Sec. 1505)[14] Generally, once this election to file a consolidated return is made, the group must continue to file a consolidated return. (Reg § 1.1502-75(a)(2))[15]

Tax saving considerations usually determine whether to file a consolidated return. Advantages of consolidated returns include:

. . . operating losses of one group member offset operating profits of other members.[16]

. . . capital losses of one group member offset capital gains of other members.[17]

. . . deferral of income on intercompany distributions.[18]

. . . group's ability to use of foreign taxes paid by a member in excess of its limitation on

9. ¶D-3705; ¶5474; TD ¶601,517
10. ¶E-10301; ¶15,614; TD ¶607,301; TD ¶607,401 *et seq.*
11. ¶E-10601; ¶15,634; TD ¶607,501
12. ¶E-10613, ¶15,634; TD ¶607,509
13. ¶E-10700 *et seq.*; ¶15,634; TD ¶607,702 *et seq.*
14. ¶E-7500 *et seq.*; ¶15,014 *et seq.*; TD ¶603,601
15. ¶E-10000; ¶15,024.16; TD ¶606,801
16. ¶E-7503; ¶15,024; TD ¶603,203
17. ¶E-7503; ¶15,024; TD ¶603,203
18. ¶E-9050 *et seq.*; ¶15,024; TD ¶603,203

foreign tax credits.[19]

... the 70% or 80% dividends-received deduction for dividends received from unrelated corporations, that may not be fully usable on a separate return basis because of the income limitation rule, may be fully used in a consolidated return. (¶3307)[20]

Regs prescribe detailed rules for treating items of income, gain, deduction and loss of members from intercompany transactions. The rules are designed to clearly reflect the group's taxable income (and tax liability) as a whole by preventing intercompany transactions from creating, accelerating, avoiding, or deferring consolidated taxable income or consolidated tax liability. (Reg § 1.1502-13)[21] Regs also provide a special rule that applies to intercompany obligations which creates a deemed satisfaction and reissuance model that must be applied to intercompany obligations upon various events. (Reg § 1.1502-13(g))[22]

When a member of a consolidated group claims a loss on the disposition or worthlessness of a share of another member's stock, the unified loss rules determine what portion of that loss is allowable. The unified loss rules apply when a consolidated group member transfers stock of a subsidiary, and after taking into account all applicable rules, the share is a loss share (i.e., is a share of stock with a basis exceeding its value). In such a case: (1) the members' bases in the transferred subsidiary stock (S) is redetermined to reduce any disparity between the members' bases in the S stock. These rules only reallocate investment adjustments previously applied to members' bases in shares of S stock. (2) If the transferred share is still a loss share after the basis redetermination under (1), the transferor members' basis in the transferred loss share is reduced. (3) If the transferred share is still a loss share after the basis reductions under (1) and (2), attributes of S and of its lower-tier subsidiaries are reduced. Thus, the selling group is now entitled to claim its stock loss, but the departing member must reduce its tax attributes immediately after it leaves the group, thereby denying that member (or the consolidated group it joins) from enjoying a second tax benefit. (Reg § 1.1502-36) The unified loss rules applies to "transfers" or worthlessness events on or after Sept. 17, 2008, except that the former loss disallowance rules will apply if there is a "binding contract" that was in effect before Sept. 17, 2008 and at all times thereafter. (Reg § 1.337(d)-2).[23] Different rules applied with respect to the deduction of losses on the disposition of subsidiary stock before Sep. 17, 2008.[24]

Special anti-avoidance rules under Reg § 1.1502-35 bar the circumvention of the basis redetermination and loss suspension rules,[25] including rules aimed at preventing groups from avoiding the loss suspension rule by "reimporting" losses to the group. (Reg § 1.1502-35(g)(3))[26]

Special rules apply when assets are distributed to multiple group members from a liquidating member in a Code Sec. 332 liquidation. (Reg § 1.1502-80)[27]

¶ 3343   "Affiliated group" defined.

In order to qualify as an affiliated group:

(1) the common parent must directly own at least 80% of the total voting power and 80% of the total value of the stock in at least one other "includible" corporation; *and*

(2) one or more of the other includible corporations must directly own at least 80% of the stock (by vote or value) in each of the remaining includible corporations (i.e., not the parent). (Code Sec. 1504(a))[28]

All corporations connected through these stock ownership requirements are "includible" corporations *except*:

---

19. ¶E-9050 *et seq.*; ¶15,024; TD ¶603,203
20. ¶E-8905; ¶2434.01; TD ¶605,604
21. ¶E-8250 *et seq.*; ¶15,024; TD ¶604,500 *et seq.*
22. ¶E-8401; ¶15,024.03; TD ¶604,701
23. ¶E-8574 *et seq.*; ¶3374.025.

24. ¶E-8640*et seq.*; ¶3374.025; TD ¶605,251
25. ¶E-8566; ¶3374.025
26. ¶E-8569; ¶3374.025
27. ¶E-7552.2 ; ¶15,024.03
28. ¶E-7601; ¶s 15,024.16, 15,024.17; TD ¶603,300

. . . tax-exempt organizations;

. . . life insurance companies, except (under certain conditions) where two or more insurance companies are themselves an affiliated group;

. . . RICs (mutual funds) and REITs (¶4201 *et seq.*);

. . . foreign corporations, except for certain Mexican or Canadian subs of a U.S. parent;

. . . corporations that have a Code Sec. 936 election (possessions tax credit) in effect for the tax year;

. . . DISCs (¶4622);

. . . S corporations. (Code Sec. 1504(b), Code Sec. 1504(c))[29]

¶ 3344 Forms for consolidated reporting—Form 851, Form 1120, and Form 1122.

A consolidated return is made by the common parent on Form 1120 with an attached Form 851 (affiliation schedule), and a Form 1122 (consent) signed by each sub unless a consolidated return was filed (or required) for the preceding tax year. (Reg § 1.1502-75(b), Reg § 1.1502-75(h))[30]

¶ 3345 Dual Consolidated Losses

A corporation that is subject to tax on its worldwide income in the U.S. and a foreign jurisdiction (e.g. a company incorporated in the U.S. but managed and controlled in another country) is referred to as a "dual resident corporation" (DRC). If a DRC is a resident of a foreign country that permits its losses to offset the income of other commonly controlled foreign corporate residents, then the DRC could use a single loss to offset both foreign and U.S. taxable income.[31] The use of a dual consolidate loss to offset the income of a domestic affiliate is permitted only if the loss does not offset the income of a foreign corporation under foreign law. (Reg § 1.1503(d)-8)[32]

¶ 3346 Corporate Estimated Tax.

Corporations (including S corporations) owing $500 or more in income tax for the tax year must make estimated tax payments, or be subject to a penalty. (Code Sec. 6655(f))

For quick refund where a corporation pays *too much* in estimated tax, see ¶4853.

¶ 3347 The required annual payment.

A corporation must make installment payments (¶3349) of its "required annual payment," which equals the *lesser* of:

(1) 100% of the tax shown on its return for the year (or if no return is filed, 100% of its tax for that year); or

(2) 100% of the tax shown on its return for the preceding tax year (except as noted below). (Code Sec. 6655(d)(1)(B))[33]

A corporation's required annual payment can't be based on the preceding year's tax if:

. . . it didn't file a return for the preceding tax year showing a liability for tax (Code Sec. 6655(d)(1)) (a return showing zero tax, e.g., because of a net operating loss (NOL), isn't a return showing a liability for tax);

. . . the preceding tax year was less than 12 months (Code Sec. 6655(d)(1)); or

. . . it's a "large corporation." (Code Sec. 6655(d)(2)(A)) However, a large corporation may use its last year's tax to determine the amount of its first required installment for any tax year, but it must recapture any resulting reduction in that first installment, by increasing

---

29. ¶E-7646; ¶s 15,024, 15,024.17; TD ¶603,301
30. ¶E-7754 *et seq.*; ¶15,024.16; TD ¶603,603
31. ¶E-9200 *et seq.*; ¶15,024.005; TD ¶606,008
32. ¶E-9201 *et seq.*; ¶15,024.005
33. ¶s S-5327, S-5328; ¶66,554; TD ¶609,216 *et seq.*

its next required installment by the amount of the reduction. (Code Sec. 6655(d)(2)(B))[34]

A corporation is "large" in any tax year if it (or any predecessor corporation) had taxable income of $1,000,000 or more for any of the three immediately preceding tax years. For this purpose, taxable income doesn't include carryback or carryover of NOLs or capital losses. Special rules apply to controlled groups. (Code Sec. 6655(g)(2))[35]

¶ 3348 What is "tax" for estimated tax purposes?

A corporation's "tax" for estimated tax purposes is the excess of: (1) the sum of its regular corporate (income) tax, the alternative minimum tax, and (for foreign corporations) the tax on gross transportation income (¶4646), over (2) the sum of its tax credits. (Code Sec. 6655(g)(1))[36]

For S corporations, regular corporate taxes also include: built-in gains tax (¶3365) or tax on net capital gains for certain S corporations (¶3364), tax on excess passive income (¶3368), and tax on recapture of pre-S election investment credit (Code Sec. 6655(g)(4)(A)), but not the LIFO recapture tax (¶3367).[37]

Special rules apply for foreign corporations, insurance companies and tax-exempt organizations (for unrelated business income tax). (Code Sec. 6655(g)(1), Code Sec. 6655(g)(3))[38]

¶ 3349 "Required installments" of corporate estimated tax—Form 8109.

Generally, a corporation pays its estimated tax electronically, if required (see ¶3029), otherwise on Form 8109 in four equal installments ("required installments") of its "required annual payment" (¶3347) (assuming that those days do not fall on a Saturday, Sunday, or legal holiday).[39] (Code Sec. 6655(c)(1), Code Sec. 6655(d)(1)(A)) For a calendar year corporation, the installments are due as follows: first, Apr. 15; second, June 15; third, Sept. 15; fourth, Dec. 15. (Code Sec. 6655(c)(2)) For a fiscal year corporation, they are due on the 15th day of the corresponding months of the tax year (Code Sec. 6655(i)(1)) (i.e., the fourth, sixth, ninth and twelfth months).[40]

Congress revises the estimated payment amount from time to time for certain corporations.[41]

For lower installments in certain situations, see ¶3350 and ¶3351.

¶ 3350 Lower "annualized income installment" as required installment—Form 8842.

A corporation may use an "annualized income installment" as its estimated tax installment, if that's less than the "required installment" (¶3349). (Code Sec. 6655(e)(1)(A))[42]

The annualized income installment is the excess (if any) of:

(1) the applicable percentage of the full year's tax computed by placing on an annualized basis (as provided by regs) the taxable income, alternative minimum taxable income, and modified alternative minimum taxable income for the months to which the installment applies, *over*

(2) the sum of any earlier required installments for the tax year. (Code Sec. 6655(e)(2)(A), Code Sec. 6655(e)(2)(B); Reg § 1.6655-2)[43]

Alternatively, a corporation may elect on Form 8842, by the due date of the first installment (Reg § 1.6655(e)-1(b)) to determine its annualized income based on its income for *either:*

---

34. ¶S-5328 *et seq.*; ¶66,554; TD ¶609,218
35. ¶S-5331 *et seq.*; ¶66,554; TD ¶609,221
36. ¶S-5322; ¶66,554; TD ¶609,205
37. ¶S-5401; ¶66,554; TD ¶628,501
38. ¶S-5321 *et seq.*, S-5421; ¶66,554

39. ¶T-10796; ¶75,034; TD ¶570,240
40. ¶S-5324.1; ¶66,554; TD ¶609,201
41. ¶S-5324.1; ¶66,554 ; TD ¶609,201
42. ¶S-5326; ¶66,554; TD ¶609,216
43. ¶S-5338 *et seq.*; ¶66,554; TD ¶609,223

(1) the first two months (first installment), first four months (second), first seven months (third) and first ten months (fourth); *or* (2) the first three months (first), first five months (second), first eight months (third), and first eleven months (fourth). (Code Sec. 6655(e)(2)(C))[44]

Any reduction in an installment resulting from using the annualization method must be made up (recaptured). This is done by increasing the amount of the next required installment that *isn't* determined under the annualization method, by the amount of the reduction. (Code Sec. 6655(e)(1)(B))[45]

¶ 3351   Use of lower "adjusted seasonal installment" as required installment.

A corporation may use an "adjusted seasonal installment" as its estimated tax installment if it's less than the required installment (¶3349) or the annualized income installment (Code Sec. 6655(e)(1)(A)), but only if the corporation's "base period percentage" (below) for any six consecutive months of the tax year is at least 70%. (Code Sec. 6655(e)(3)(B); Reg § 1.6655-3)[46]

A corporation computes its adjusted seasonal installment by: (1) computing the taxable income for all months during the tax year before the filing month (i.e., the month the installment is required to be paid), (2) dividing this amount by the base period percentage for those preceding months, (3) determining the tax on the result, (4) multiplying that tax by the base period percentage for the filing month and all preceding months in the tax year (Code Sec. 6655(e)(3)(C), Code Sec. 6655(e)(3)(D)(ii)), and subtracting the aggregate of all earlier required installments. (Code Sec. 6655(e)(3)(A); Reg § 1.6655-3(c))[47]

The "base period percentage" for any specific period of months is the average percent that the corporation's taxable income for the corresponding months in each of the three preceding tax years bears to its taxable income for those three years. (Code Sec. 6655(e)(3)(D)(i); Reg § 1.6655-3(d))[48]

Any reduction in an installment resulting from the adjusted seasonal method must be made up (recaptured), by increasing the amount of the next required installment that *isn't* determined under the adjusted seasonal method, by the amount of the reduction. (Code Sec. 6655(e)(1)(B))[49]

¶ 3352   Penalty for failure to pay estimated tax—Form 2220.

A corporation that underpays its estimated tax must add to its income tax an amount equal to the underpayment interest rate (¶4867) times the amount of the underpayment, for the period of the underpayment. (Code Sec. 6655(a)) Compute on Form 2220.[50]

The amount of the underpayment is the excess of the required installment (¶3349) over the amount (if any) of the installment paid on or before the due date for the installment. (Code Sec. 6655(b)(1))[1]

The period of the underpayment runs from the due date for the installment to the earlier of: (1) the 15th day of the third month after the close of the tax year, or (2) with respect to any portion of the underpayment, the date the portion is paid. (Code Sec. 6655(b)(2)) For this purpose, a payment of estimated tax is credited against unpaid required installments in the order those installments were due. (Code Sec. 6655(b)(3))[2]

No estimated tax penalty is imposed for any tax year if the tax shown on the return for that year (or if no return is filed, the tax liability) is less than $500. (Code Sec. 6655(f))[3] Nor is the penalty imposed for a period in which the failure to pay the required installment(s) results from a pending Title 11 bankruptcy case. (Code Sec. 6658(a))[4]

44. ¶S-5342 *et seq.*; ¶66,554; TD ¶609,226
45. ¶S-5347; ¶66,554; TD ¶609,232
46. ¶S-5344; ¶66,554; TD ¶609,233
47. ¶S-5345 *et seq.*; ¶66,554; TD ¶609,234
48. ¶S-5346; ¶66,554; TD ¶609,235
49. ¶S-5348; ¶66,554; TD ¶609,236

50. ¶S-5358; ¶66,554; TD ¶609,208
1. ¶S-5359; ¶66,554; TD ¶609,209
2. ¶S-5324; ¶66,554; TD ¶609,210
3. ¶S-5359; ¶66,554; TD ¶609,213
4. ¶V-7378; TD ¶571,363

¶ 3353 S Corporations. ▬▬▬▬▬▬▬▬▬▬▬▬▬▬▬▬▬▬▬▬▬▬▬▬

An eligible corporation may elect to be taxed as an S corporation which, with limited exceptions, isn't taxed at the corporate level. Instead, its items of income, loss, deduction and credit are passed through to, and taken into account by, its shareholders in computing their individual tax liabilities.

¶ 3354 S election eligibility.

An S corporation is a corporation for which an election to be taxed under Subchapter S of the Code is in effect. (Code Sec. 1361(a)(1))[5] Only a small business corporation may elect to be an S corporation. (Code Sec. 1362(a)(1)) A corporation (or an unincorporated entity that's taxable as a corporation) qualifies as a small business corporation if it meets all of the following requirements:[6]

(1) It must be a domestic corporation (created under the law of the U.S. or of any state). (Code Sec. 1361(b)(1))[7]

(2) It must not be *ineligible.* (Code Sec. 1361(b)(1); Reg § 1.1361-1(d))

A corporation is ineligible if it is:

... a financial institution that uses a reserve method of accounting for bad debts,

... taxable as an insurance company (with certain exceptions),

... a DISC or former DISC (¶4622) (Code Sec. 1361(b)(2)), or

... a taxable mortgage pool. (Reg § 301.7701(i)-4(c)(1))[8]

(3) It can't have more than 100 shareholders, see ¶3356. (Code Sec. 1361(b)(1)(A); Reg § 1.1361-1(e))[9]

(4) All shareholders must be individuals, decedents' estates, bankruptcy estates, trusts described at ¶3357, or tax-exempt Code Sec. 501(c)(3) charitable organizations (Code Sec. 1361(b)(1)(B); Reg § 1.1361-1(f)), except that an otherwise eligible S corporation can be wholly owned by another S corporation, see ¶3355. A partnership can hold S corporation stock as a nominee for an eligible shareholder. (Reg § 1.1361-1(e)(1))[10] With a very limited exception for certain banks that are S corporations, Individual Retirement Accounts (including one designated as a Roth IRA) may not be shareholders in an S corporation. (Reg § 1.1361-1(h)(1)(vii), Reg § 1.1361-1(h)(3)(i)(G))

(5) No shareholder may be a nonresident alien (Code Sec. 1361(b)(1)(C)), or be married to a nonresident alien who has a current ownership interest in his stock under local law (unless the spouses elect under Code Sec. 6013(g) to be taxed as U.S. residents (¶3115)). (Reg § 1.1361-1(g)(1))[11]

(6) It must have only one class of stock, see ¶3358. (Code Sec. 1361(b)(1)(D); Reg § 1.1361-1(b)(1))[12]

¶ 3355 S corporation subsidiaries—Form 8869.

S corporations may have 80%-or-more owned C ("regular") corporation subsidiaries and wholly-owned S corporation subsidiaries. (Code Sec. 1361(b))

A C corporation subsidiary is treated as a separate taxpayer. If it operates profitably, it pays tax on its income. If it operates at a loss, it cannot pass the loss through to the S corporation. A C corporation subsidiary may file a consolidated return with other C corporations with which it is affiliated. The S corporation cannot be included in this return (¶3343).

5. ¶D-1421; ¶13,614 *et seq.*; TD ¶611,001
6. ¶D-1431; ¶13,614; TD ¶611,001
7. ¶D-1432; ¶13,614.01; TD ¶611,001
8. ¶D-1434 *et seq.*; ¶ 77,014.32; TD ¶611,002

9. ¶D-1441; ¶13,614.02; TD ¶611,003
10. ¶D-1445; ¶13,614.03; TD ¶611,005
11. ¶D-1457; ¶13,614.03; TD ¶611,001
12. ¶D-1496; ¶13,614.04; TD ¶611,043

An S corporation cannot have a corporate shareholder. (Code Sec. 1361(b)(1)(B); Reg § 1.1361-1(f)) This rule ordinarily prevents a subsidiary from being an S corporation. However, an S corporation can have an S corporation subsidiary if it owns 100% of the subsidiary's stock, the sub is not an ineligible corporation, and the S corporation parent elects (on Form 8869)[13] to treat the subsidiary as a qualified subchapter S subsidiary (QSub). (Code Sec. 1361(b)(3)(B); Reg § 1.1361-2, Reg § 1.1361-3)[14]

A QSub isn't treated as a separate corporation for federal tax purposes; rather, its assets, liabilities, and items of income, deduction, and credit are treated as those of the parent S corporation. (Code Sec. 1361(b)(3)(A); Reg § 1.1361-4)[15] However, except to the extent otherwise provided by IRS, QSubs are treated as separate entities for purposes of making information returns. (Code Sec. 1361(b)(3)(E))[16]

If a QSub loses its qualification, the QSub is treated as if it sold an undivided interest in its assets (based on a percentage of the stock sold) and transferred the remaining assets to itself in a tax-free incorporation. Thus, an S corporation sells 21% of the stock of its QSub to an unrelated party, it will recognize 21% of the gain on the QSub's assets and will not recognize the remaining gain. (Code Sec. 1361(b)(3)(C); Reg § 1.1361-5)[17] If QSub status terminates, the corporation or its successor may not elect QSub status or S corporation status before its fifth year beginning after the first tax year for which the termination was effective, without IRS consent. (Code Sec. 1361(b)(3)(D); Reg § 1.1361-5(c))[18] For elections and terminations after 2004, IRS may waive inadvertent or invalid QSub elections and terminations of elections. (Code Sec. 1362(f))[19]

A QSub uses the parent S corporation's EIN. If the election terminates, the sub must get an EIN; but if the entity either had an EIN before becoming a QSub or got an EIN while it was a QSub, it must use that EIN. (Reg § 301.6109-1(i))[20] However, where an S corporation undergoes a type F reorganization in which the operating S corporation becomes a QSub of a new holding corporation, the holding company must obtain a new EIN and the existing S corporation (now the QSub) must retain its EIN.[21]

¶ 3356   Number of shareholders.

In applying the 100-shareholder limit (¶3354), everyone who owns stock is counted separately, even if the stock is owned jointly with someone else (e.g., joint tenant, tenant in common), except as follows:

(1) A husband and wife (and their estates) are treated as one shareholder, no matter how the stock is held (separately, jointly, etc.). (Code Sec. 1361(c)(1)(A)(i); Reg § 1.1361-1(e)(2))[22]

(2) Where stock is owned by a grantor trust and also by the grantor directly, they are treated as one shareholder.[23]

(3) All members of a family and their estates are treated as one shareholder. Family members include the common ancestor, lineal descendants of the common ancestor, and the spouses (or former spouses) of the lineal descendants or common ancestor. But, an individual isn't considered a common ancestor if, on the applicable date, the individual was more than six generations removed from the youngest generation of shareholders who would (but for this limitation) be family members. For this purpose, a spouse (or former spouse) is treated as being of the same generation as the individual to which such spouse is (or was) married. Adopted children are treated as children if they are (i) legally adopted children, (ii) children who are lawfully placed with an individual for legal adoption and (iii) eligible foster children (defined under Code Sec. 152(f)(1)(C), ¶3120) (Code Sec. 1361(c)(1)) The applicable date is the latest of: the date the S election was made; the earliest date that a

---

13. ¶D-1539; ¶13,614.05; TD ¶611,006
14. ¶D-1540; ¶13,614.05; TD ¶611,006
15. ¶D-1531; ¶13,614.05; TD ¶611,006
16. ¶D-1532; ¶13,614.05; TD ¶611,007
17. ¶D-1536; ¶13,614.05; TD ¶611,006
18. ¶D-1538; ¶13,614.05; TD ¶611,006

19. ¶D-1564.1; ¶13,624.03; TD ¶623,018
20. ¶D-1532; ¶13,614.05; TD ¶611,007
21. ¶D-1532; ¶13,614.05; TD ¶611,010
22. ¶D-1447; ¶s 13,614.02, 13,614.03; TD ¶611,003
23. ¶D-1461; ¶s 13,614.02, 13,614.03; TD ¶611,003

family member holds stock in the S corporation; or Oct. 22, 2004. (Code Sec. 1361(c)(1)(B)(ii))[24]

Each potential current beneficiary (i.e., one who may receive a discretionary distribution of income or principal during the relevant period) of an electing small business trust is treated as a shareholder in applying the limit. The trust is treated as the shareholder for periods when there's no potential current beneficiary. (Code Sec. 1361(c)(2)(B)(v); Reg § 1.1361-1(m)(4)) However, unexercised powers of appointment are not taken into account in determining potential current beneficiaries. In addition, a person who first becomes a potential current beneficiary during the one-year period ending with the date of the trust's disposition of all of its stock in an S corporation, isn't a potential current beneficiary of that corporation. (Code Sec. 1361(e)(2))[25]

¶ 3357 Trusts as shareholders.

Only the following trusts may be S corporation shareholders:

(1) Grantor trusts—domestic trusts that are treated as being owned by an individual ("grantor") who is a U.S. citizen or resident, during the period the trust holds the S corporation stock. The grantor, not the trust, is treated as the shareholder. (Code Sec. 1361(c)(2)(A)(i), Code Sec. 1361(c)(2)(B)(i); Reg § 1.1361-1(h)(1)(i), Reg § 1.1361-1(h)(3)(i)(A)) But after the grantor dies, the trust may continue as the shareholder for two years. (Code Sec. 1361(c)(2)(A)(ii))[26]

(2) Code Sec. 678 trusts—where a person other than the grantor is treated as the substantial owner of the trust, during the period the trust holds the S corporation stock. The deemed owner, who must be a U.S. citizen or resident, is treated as the shareholder. (Code Sec. 1361(c)(2)(A)(i), Code Sec. 1361(c)(2)(B)(i); Reg § 1.1361-1(h)(1)(i), Reg § 1.1361-1(h)(3)(i)(A))[27]

(3) Voting trusts, but each beneficiary is counted as a separate shareholder. (Code Sec. 1361(c)(2)(A)(iv), Code Sec. 1361(c)(2)(B)(iv); Reg § 1.1361-1(h)(1)(v), Reg § 1.1361-1(h)(3)(i)(E))[28]

(4) Testamentary trusts, for 2-years beginning with the day when stock was transferred to the trust under the testator's will. (Code Sec. 1361(c)(2)(A)(iii); Reg § 1.1361-1(h)(1)(iv))[29]

(5) "Qualified Subchapter S trusts" (QSSTs), if the beneficiary elects (on Form 2553, in certain circumstances) to be treated as the owner of the trust so that it is eligible to hold the S stock (as in (1), above), and is treated as the shareholder. (Code Sec. 1361(d); Reg § 1.1361-1(j)) For purposes of applying the passive activity loss rules (¶1811 *et seq.*) and the at-risk rules (¶1804 *et seq.*) to a beneficiary of a QSST, a disposition of S corporation stock by a QSST is treated as a disposition by that beneficiary. (Code Sec. 1361(d)(1)(C))[30]

A QSST can be converted to an electing small business trust if certain conditions are met.[31]

(6) "Electing small business trusts (ESBTs)." (Code Sec. 1361(c)(2)(A)(v), Code Sec. 1361(e); Reg § 1.1361-1(m)) These trusts are subject to fewer restrictions than QSSTs but carry a heavy tax cost, see ¶3910. To elect, the trustee must sign and file a specified statement with the service center with which the corporation files its income tax return. In the case of a newly electing S corporation, the trustee can attach the ESBT's consent to the Form 2553.[32] An ESBT can be converted to a QSST if certain conditions are met.[33]

(7) Tax exempt Code Sec. 401(a) qualified plan trusts. (Code Sec. 1361(c)(6))[34]

---

24. ¶D-1447.1; ¶13,614.02; TD ¶611,003.1
25. ¶D-1484 *et seq.*; ¶13,614.03; TD ¶611,037
26. ¶s D-1460, D-1461; ¶13,614.03; TD ¶611,018
27. ¶D-1461; ¶13,614.03; TD ¶611,018
28. ¶D-1492; ¶13,614.03; TD ¶611,017
29. ¶D-1491; ¶13,614.03; TD ¶611,017

30. ¶D-1465 *et seq.*; ¶13,614.03; TD ¶611,020 *et seq.*
31. ¶D-1489; ¶13,614.03; TD ¶611,041
32. ¶D-1482; ¶13,614.03; TD ¶611,034
33. ¶D-1490; ¶13,614.03; TD ¶611,042
34. ¶D-1493; ¶13,614.03

¶ 3358   One class of stock.

A corporation is treated as having only one class of stock (¶3354), if:

. . . all outstanding shares of its stock confer identical rights to distribution and liquidation proceeds, based on certain governing provisions (i.e., corporate charter, by-laws, state law, etc.) (Reg § 1.1361-1(l)(1), Reg § 1.1361-1(l)(2)(i)); and

. . . it hasn't issued any instrument or obligation or entered into any arrangement that's treated as a second class of stock. (Reg § 1.1361-1(l)(4))[35]

The one-class-of-stock rule isn't violated *solely* because of differences in voting rights. Thus, voting and nonvoting common can be issued. (Code Sec. 1361(c)(4))[36]

Buy-sell agreements among shareholders, redemption agreements and agreements restricting the transferability of stock generally won't violate the one-class-of-stock rule *unless:* (1) a principal purpose of the agreement is to circumvent the rule, and (2) it establishes a purchase price for the stock that's significantly above or below its fair market value (FMV). (Reg § 1.1361-1(l)(2)(iii))[37]

A call option, warrant or similar instrument is, with certain exceptions, treated as a second class of stock if it's substantially certain to be exercised and has a strike price substantially below the stock's FMV on the date it's issued, transferred to an ineligible shareholder, or materially modified. (Reg § 1.1361-1(l)(4)(iii)(A))[38]

Straight debt isn't treated as a second class of stock if specified safe harbor rules are met. (Code Sec. 1361(c)(5)(A), Code Sec. 1361(c)(5)(B))[39] However, any instrument, obligation or arrangement is, with certain exceptions, treated as a second class of stock if: (1) it constitutes equity or otherwise results in the holder being treated as the owner of stock under general tax law, and (2) its principal purpose is to circumvent these rules. (Reg § 1.1361-1(l)(4))[40] Restricted bank director stock is not taken into account for the one class of stock requirement. (Code Sec. 1361(f)(1))[41]

¶ 3359   How to elect S corporation status—Form 2553.

The S election is made by the corporation (Code Sec. 1362(a)(1)) by filing a Form 2553 signed by its authorized officer, with the required shareholder consents (¶3360) (and IRS user fee), at the IRS Service Center designated on the form. (Reg § 1.1362-6(a)(2))[42]

An S election for a tax year may be made during the preceding tax year, or by the 15th day of the third month of the tax year for which it's to be effective. (Code Sec. 1362(b)(1)) If this first tax year is less than two months and 15 days, the election must be made no later than two months and 15 days after the first day of that year. (Code Sec. 1362(b)(4))[43]

An S election will be effective retroactively to the first day of a tax year *only if:*

. . . on all days in the tax year before the day the election is made, the corporation would have been eligible to elect (Code Sec. 1362(b)(2)(B)(i)), *and*

. . . all persons who were shareholders at any time during the tax year before the day of the election, but who aren't shareholders on that date, consent (along with persons who *are* shareholders, see ¶3360). (Code Sec. 1362(b)(2)(B)(ii))[44]

If either of the above conditions isn't met, the election is treated as made for the next tax year. (Code Sec. 1362(b)(2))[45]

A partnership that converts to a corporation under check-the-box rules (¶3301) or under a

---

35. ¶D-1496 *et seq.*; ¶13,614.04; TD ¶611,043
36. ¶D-1499; ¶13,614.04; TD ¶611,043
37. ¶D-1507 *et seq.*; ¶13,614.04; TD ¶611,045
38. ¶D-1523; ¶13,614.04; TD ¶611,046
39. ¶D-1517; ¶13,614.04; TD ¶611,046
40. ¶D-1512 *et seq.*; ¶13,614.04; TD ¶611,046
41. ¶D-1444.1; ¶13,614.02
42. ¶D-1552, ¶T-10004; ¶s 13,624, 13,624.01; TD ¶612,001
43. ¶s D-1565, D-1568; ¶13,624.01; TD ¶612,008, 612,011
44. ¶D-1566; ¶13,624.01; TD ¶612,009
45. ¶D-1566; ¶13,624.01; TD ¶612,009

state law conversion statute may make an S election effective for the corporation's first tax year.[46]

IRS may waive invalid elections (e.g., because of an inadvertent failure to get all the necessary consents, ¶3360, or to qualify to elect S status). (Code Sec. 1362(f))[47] For IRS's authority to treat late elections or nonexistent elections as timely, see ¶3361.

¶ 3360 Shareholder consents.

All shareholders owning stock in the corporation on the day it elects S status must consent to the election. (Code Sec. 1362(a)(2); Reg § 1.1362-6(b)(2)(i))[48]

The consents may be given on Form 2553 (¶3359), or on separate statements attached to the Form 2553. (Reg § 1.1362-6(b))[49]

A shareholder's failure to file a timely consent won't invalidate an otherwise valid timely filed election if consents are filed within an extended period of time as granted by IRS, and IRS is satisfied that: (1) there was reasonable cause for the failure; (2) the extension was requested within a reasonable time; and (3) its interests won't be jeopardized by treating the election as valid. (Reg § 1.1362-6(b)(3)(iii)(A))[50]

¶ 3361 Relief for late or nonexistent S elections

If an S election is made after the date (specified at ¶3359) for making it, or if no election is made, and IRS determines there was reasonable cause for the failure to timely elect, IRS can treat the election as timely made. (Code Sec. 1362(b)(5)) Generally the relief is obtained through the issuance of a private letter ruling.[1]

IRS has provided procedures for requesting relief for a failure to make a timely valid S corporation election without asking for a private letter ruling (e.g., automatic relief) where the entity fails to qualify for its intended status as an S corporation, electing small business trust (ESBT), qualified Subchapter S trust (QSST), or qualified Subchapter S subsidiary (QSub) on the intended effective status date solely because of the failure to file the appropriate election in a timely fashion.[2]

Special rules apply for requests for automatic relief when a community property spouse fails to timely consent to an S corporation election.[3]

¶ 3362 "Taxable income" of an S corporation.

An S corporation's taxable income is computed in the same manner as an individual's taxable income *except that*: (Code Sec. 1363(b))[4]

(1) Items of income (including tax-exempt interest), loss, deduction or credit must be separately stated if their separate treatment by a shareholder could affect his tax liability. (Code Sec. 1363(b)(1))

(2) The corporation can't take the following deductions allowed to individuals: personal exemptions; foreign taxes; charitable contributions; net operating loss (NOL) deduction; additional itemized deductions; and oil and gas depletion. (Code Sec. 1363(b)(2))

(3) A deduction is allowed for the amortization of the corporation's organization expenditures under Code Sec. 248 (¶3520). (Code Sec. 1363(b)(3))[5]

(4) The Code Sec. 291 rules that reduce certain corporate tax benefits apply to an S corporation (or any predecessor) that was a C corporation for any of the 3 immediately preceding tax years. (Code Sec. 1363(b)(4))[6]

46. ¶D-1456; TD ¶580,512
47. ¶D-1564.1; ¶13,614.03; TD ¶612,006
48. ¶D-1554; ¶13,624.01; TD ¶612,002
49. ¶D-1555; ¶13,624.01; TD ¶612,001
50. ¶D-1564.2; ¶13,624.03; TD ¶612,004
1. ¶D-1572.1; ¶13,624.01; TD ¶612,014

2. ¶D-1572.2 *et seq.*; ¶13,624.03; TD ¶612,014 *et seq.*
3. ¶D-1572.3; ¶13,624.03; TD ¶612,016; TD ¶612,006.5
4. ¶D-1591; ¶13,634.01; TD ¶614,501
5. ¶D-1594; ¶13,634.01; TD ¶614,501
6. ¶D-1595; ¶13,634.01; TD ¶614,503

Except as otherwise provided in the Code, or to the extent inconsistent with the Subchapter S rules, the Subchapter C rules (transfers to related corporations, redemptions, reorganizations, liquidations, etc., see ¶3510 *et seq.*) apply to an S corporation and its shareholders. (Code Sec. 1371(a))[7] But there are these modifications:

. . . With respect to liquidating distributions, no gain or loss is recognized on distributions of installment obligations where the shareholders' receipt of them (as part of a 12-month complete liquidation) isn't treated as payment for their stock by reason of Code Sec. 453(h)(1). (Code Sec. 453B(h)(1))[8]

. . . Except for the organization expenditures deduction (above), Code provisions governing the computation of taxable income which apply only to corporations (e.g., dividends-received deduction, ¶3306) don't apply to S corporations. (Code Sec. 1363(b))[9]

. . . Limitations on the amount allowed for: (1) expensing certain depreciable assets (Code Sec. 179(d)(8)), and (2) writing off reforestation expenses (Code Sec. 194(b)(2)(B)) are determined at both the corporate and shareholder level.[10]

. . . Generally. an item (e.g., an NOL) cannot be carried over from a year the corporation was a C corporation to a year the corporation was an S corporation (except in computing the built-in gains tax, see ¶3365). (Code Sec. 1371(b)(1))[11]

¶ 3363   Deductions for fringe benefits—Form W2.

In applying the Code's fringe benefit rules, an S corporation is treated as a partnership and its more-than-2% shareholders are treated as partners. (Code Sec. 1372) Fringe benefits furnished by an S corporation to its more-than-2% shareholder-employees are treated like partnership guaranteed payments.[12]

observation: An S corporation is entitled to deduct the cost of fringe benefits for its more-than-2% shareholder-employees, who are required to include the value of those benefits in income.

S corporation fringe benefits are reported on Form W-2.[13]

¶ 3364   Taxation of S corporations.

An S corporation is generally exempt from federal income taxes. (Code Sec. 1363(a))[14] Instead, the corporation's income is passed through, and taxed, to its shareholders (¶3370). But some S corporations may be subject to one or more of these corporate-level taxes: the tax on recognized built-in gains (¶3365); the tax on excess net passive income (¶3368); the tax on LIFO recapture (¶3367); the tax on capital gains attributable to certain substituted basis property, if S election was made before '87;[15] the tax on recapture of investment credit.[16] For an S corporation's liability to make estimated tax payments, see ¶3346 *et seq.*

¶ 3365   Built-in gains tax—Form 1120S, Schedule D.

An S corporation is subject to a corporate-level built-in gains tax in any tax year beginning in the recognition period (below) in which it has a "net recognized built-in gain" (¶3366). (Code Sec. 1374(a)) But the tax is imposed only on S corporations that were formerly C corporations. (Code Sec. 1374(c)(1))[17]

In addition, the built-in gains tax may be imposed where an S corporation acquires property and its basis in the property is determined by reference to the basis that the property had in the hands of a C corporation. (Code Sec. 1374(d)(8)(A); Reg § 1.1374-1(e))[18]

7. ¶D-1602; ¶13,714; TD ¶614,511
8. ¶s D-1600, D-1601; ¶453B4.11; TD ¶614,509
9. ¶D-1595; ¶13,634.01; TD ¶614,503
10. ¶D-1596; ¶1794.01; TD ¶614,504
11. ¶D-1603; ¶13,714.01; TD ¶614,510
12. ¶D-1621; ¶13,724; TD ¶614,505

13. ¶S-3178; TD ¶812,019
14. ¶D-1641; ¶13,634; TD ¶615,001
15. ¶D-1674 *et seq.*; ¶13,744.02; TD ¶615,002
16. ¶s D-1640, D-1685; ¶13,714.03; TD ¶615,029
17. ¶D-1643; ¶13,744.01; TD ¶615,002
18. ¶D-1650; ¶13,744.01; TD ¶615,002

The built-in gains tax (computed on Form 1120S, Schedule D) equals the highest corporate rate (¶1112) times the net recognized built-in gain. (Code Sec. 1374(b)(1))[19]

In this computation, net recognized built-in gains are taken into account only to the extent of the excess of the net *unrealized* built-in gain over net recognized built-in gains for earlier tax years in the recognition period. (Code Sec. 1374(c)(2); Reg § 1.1374-2(a))[20] Net unrealized built-in gain means the excess (if any) of: (1) the fair market value of the S corporation's assets (including inventory) over (2) the aggregate adjusted basis of the assets, at the start of its first tax year as an S corporation ("S tax year"). (Code Sec. 1374(d)(1))[21]

The recognition period is the ten-year period beginning on the first day of the corporation's first S tax year. For tax years beginning in 2009 and 2010, the recognition period is reduced to seven years; for property acquired from C corporations in carryover basis transactions, the recognition period is reduced to seven years from the date the property was acquired. (Code Sec. 1374(d)(7))[22]

⚡*caution:* Check http://ria.thomsonreuters.com/federaltaxhandbook to see if the seven year recognition period has been extended to 2011.

The built-in gains tax applies to transactions occurring after Dec. 26, '94, regardless of the date of the S corporation's election. (Reg § 1.1374-8(a))[23]

Regs prevent gain or loss from being counted twice for the built-in gains tax when a C corp converting to S status owns stock in a subsidiary that's later liquidated. (Reg § 1.1374-3)[24]

¶ 3366 Net recognized built-in gain defined.

The *net recognized built-in gain* for any tax year in the recognition period (¶3365) is the *lesser of:* (1) the amount that would be the S corporation's taxable income for that year if only recognized built-in gains (below) and recognized built-in losses are taken into account, or (2) the taxable income for that year determined without taking into account NOL carryovers or special corporate deductions, e.g., for dividends received. (Code Sec. 1374(d)(2)(A))[25] However, if (1) is more than (2), the excess is treated as recognized built-in gain in the next tax year, but only if the S election was made after Mar. 31, '88. (Code Sec. 1374(d)(2)(B); Reg § 1.1374-2(c))[26]

Recognized built-in gain means any gain recognized (and certain related amounts taken into account) during the recognition period on the disposition of any asset held on the first day of the corporation's first S tax year (¶3365), but only to the extent the gain doesn't exceed the excess (if any) of the asset's fair market value over its adjusted basis, on that first day. (Code Sec. 1374(d)(3); Reg § 1.1374-4)[27]

Special rules apply to determine an S corporation's recognized built-in gain on the disposition of transferred-basis and exchanged-basis property acquired after it became an S corporation. (Code Sec. 1374(d)(8); Reg § 1.1374-8)[28]

¶ 3367 LIFO recapture.

A C corporation that maintained its inventory using the last-in first-out (LIFO) method for its last tax year before the S corporation election is effective must include a "LIFO recapture amount" in its income for that last C corporation year. (Code Sec. 1363(d)(1))[29] In addition, a C corp that transfers LIFO inventory to an S corp must include a LIFO recapture amount in income the year of the transfer. (Reg § 1.1363-2(a))[30]

The "LIFO recapture amount" is the excess (if any) of the inventory amount under FIFO

19. ¶D-1657; ¶13,744.01; TD ¶615,004
20. ¶D-1657; ¶13,744.01; TD ¶615,003
21. ¶D-1658; ¶13,744.01; TD ¶615,015
22. ¶D-1655; ¶13,744.01; TD ¶615,014
23. ¶D-1666; ¶13,744.03; TD ¶615,020
24. ¶D-1650.1; ¶13,744.01

25. ¶D-1644; ¶13,744.01; TD ¶615,003
26. ¶D-1645; ¶13,744.01; TD ¶615,005
27. ¶D-1646 *et seq.*; ¶13,744.01; TD ¶615,007
28. ¶D-1650 *et seq.*; ¶13,744.01; TD ¶615,011, 615,012
29. ¶D-1581; ¶13,634.02; TD ¶613,001
30. ¶D-1583; ¶13,634.02; TD ¶613,003

over the inventory amount under LIFO, at the close of the last C corporation tax year. (Code Sec. 1363(d)(3))[31]

Any resulting increase in tax is payable in four equal installments over four tax years. The first installment must be paid on or before the due date (without regard to extensions) for the tax return for the last year for which the corporation was a C corporation. The other three installments must be paid on or before the due date for the corporation's return for the three succeeding tax years. (Code Sec. 1363(d)(2))[32]

A C corporation holding LIFO inventory indirectly through a partnership must recognize a lookthrough LIFO recapture amount if it either elects to be an S corporation or transfers its partnership interest to an S corporation in a nonrecognition transaction. (Reg § 1.1363-2(b))[33]

¶ 3368   Tax on excess net passive income.

A corporate-level tax is imposed on an S corporation's "excess net passive income" (below) for any tax year in which it has: (1) accumulated earnings and profits (i.e., E&P from a year it was taxed as a C corporation) at the close of the tax year, and (2) passive investment income (¶3369) that exceeds 25% of gross receipts (¶3369). This tax is imposed at the highest regular corporate rate (¶1112). (Code Sec. 1375(a))[34]

IRS can waive the tax if the S corporation shows that its determination of no year-end C corporation E&P was made in good faith, and that within a reasonable time after it was determined otherwise, those E&P were distributed. (Code Sec. 1375(d))[35]

Net passive income is passive investment income reduced by deductions directly connected with the production of that income. (Code Sec. 1375(b)(2)) A deduction item that is attributable partly to passive investment income and partly to other income is allocated on a reasonable basis. (Reg § 1.1375-1(b)(3)(ii))[36] But passive investment income may not be reduced by the NOL deduction or any of the special corporate deductions (e.g., for dividends received). (Code Sec. 1375(b)(2))[37]

Excess net passive income means that amount that bears the same ratio to the total net passive income for the year as: (1) the amount by which the passive investment income for the tax year exceeds 25% of gross receipts for the year ("excess passive investment income"), bears to (2) the total passive investment income for the tax year. However, an S corporation's excess net passive income for the year can't exceed its taxable income for the year computed as though it were a C corporation but without any NOL deduction or any of the special corporate deductions described above. (Code Sec. 1375(b)(1))[38]

¶ 3369   "Passive investment income" and "gross receipts" defined.

For purposes of the tax on excess net passive income (¶3368), and involuntary terminations (¶3379), passive investment income means gross receipts derived from royalties, rents, dividends, interest, annuities, and, for tax years beginning before May 26, 2007, (to the extent of gains) sales or exchanges of stock or securities. (Code Sec. 1362(d)(3)(C), Code Sec. 1375(b)(3))[39]

However, in the case of a bank, a bank holding company, a financial holding company, or a depository institution holding company, passive investment income does not include (1) interest income earned by the bank or company or (2) dividends on assets that must be held by the bank or company. (Code Sec. 1362(d)(3)(C)(v)(I))[40]

Gross receipts are the total amount received or accrued under the S corporation's accounting method before reduction for returns, allowances, cost, or deductions. But gross receipts don't include amounts received in nontaxable sales or exchanges except to the extent gain is

31. ¶D-1582; ¶13,634.02; TD ¶613,002
32. ¶D-1585; ¶13,634.02; TD ¶613,007
33. ¶D-1582.1; ¶13,634.02
34. ¶D-1690 *et seq.*; ¶13,754; TD ¶615,021
35. ¶D-1696; ¶13,754.01; TD ¶615,026

36. ¶D-1693 *et seq.*; TD ¶615,023
37. ¶D-1693; ¶13,754; TD ¶615,023
38. ¶D-1692; ¶13,754; TD ¶615,025
39. ¶D-1713 *et seq.*; ¶s 13,624.02, 13,754; TD ¶615,022
40. ¶D-1737.1; ¶13,624.02

recognized by the corporation. (Code Sec. 1362(d)(3), Code Sec. 1375(b)(3))[41]

Special rules apply to determine gross receipts from the sale of capital assets.[42]

¶ 3370   Taxation of S corporation's shareholders.

An S corporation's income is taxed directly to its shareholders by allocating the corporation's items of income, loss, deduction and credit for each day in its tax year pro rata among the persons who were shareholders on that day. (Code Sec. 1366(a)(1); Reg § 1.1366-1(a); Code Sec. 1377(a)(1))[43]

Items of income, loss, deduction and credit are separately allocated to each shareholder whenever separate treatment could affect the tax liability of a shareholder. (Code Sec. 1366(a)(1)(A); Reg § 1.1366-1(a)) Under regs, the following S corporation items must be taken into account separately:

. . . The combined net amount of gains and losses from sales or exchanges of capital assets grouped by applicable holding periods, Code Sec. 1(h) tax rates, and by any other classification that may be relevant in determining the shareholder's tax liability.

. . . The combined net amount of gains and losses from sales or exchanges of Code Sec. 1231 property grouped by applicable holding periods, Code Sec. 1(h) tax rates, and by any other classification that may be relevant in determining the shareholder's tax liability.

. . . The charitable contributions, grouped by the Code Sec. 170(b) percentage limitations (see ¶2124 *et seq.*), paid by the corporation within its tax year.

. . . The foreign taxes paid (or accrued) by the corporation.

. . . Each of separate items involved in determining credits, except credits for certain uses of gasoline and special fuels.

. . . Each of these separate items: Code Sec. 165(d) gains and losses from wagering transactions; Code Sec. 175 soil and water conservation expenditures, Code Sec. 179 expense election deductions; Code Sec. 213 medical, dental, etc., additional itemized deductions for individuals under Code Sec. 212 *et seq.*; and any other deductions subject to the Code Sec. 67 or Code Sec. 68 limitations on itemized deductions.

. . . Any of the corporation's items of portfolio income or loss, and related expenses, as defined in the regulations under Code Sec. 469.

. . . The corporation's tax-exempt income, i.e., income that is permanently excludible from gross income.

. . . The corporation's alternative minimum tax adjustments described in Code Sec. 56, and Code Sec. 58 and tax preference items described in Code Sec. 57; and

. . . Any item identified in IRS guidance (including forms and instructions) as an item required to be separately stated. (Reg § 1.1366-1(a)(2))[44]

The character of any item in the shareholder's hands is determined as if the item had been realized directly from the source from which the corporation realized it, or as if it had been incurred in the same manner as incurred by the corporation. (Code Sec. 1366(b); Reg § 1.1366-1(b))[45]

A shareholder's share of an S corporation's items is taken into account in his tax year that includes the last day of the corporation's tax year (¶2810). (Code Sec. 1366(a)(1); Reg § 1.1366-1(a)(1))[46]

When shareholders perform services for an S corporation but don't draw a salary, any dividends paid to the shareholders in lieu of reasonable compensation for these services are treated as wages subject to employment taxes. Even where an S corporation pays a salary to shareholders for services together with dividends, IRS can recharacterize all or part of the

41. ¶s D-1702, D-1703; ¶13,624.02; TD ¶615,022
42. ¶D-1701 *et seq.*; ¶13,624; TD ¶615,503
43. ¶D-1761 *et seq.*; ¶13,664; TD ¶614,701
44. ¶D-1765; ¶13,664; TD ¶614,701
45. ¶D-1762; ¶13,664; TD ¶614,703
46. ¶D-1764; ¶13,774; TD ¶614,702

dividends as additional compensation subject to employment taxes.[47]

If a shareholder sells all of his S corporation stock during the corporation's tax year and if all affected shareholders (all terminating shareholders and their transferees) consent (by attaching a specified statement to Form 1120S for the tax year during which the shareholder's entire interest is terminated), the corporation's tax year can be split into two tax years, the first of which ends on the date the seller's interest in the S corporation is terminated. Items will be allocated between those tax years according to its normal method of accounting. (Code Sec. 1377(a)(2); Reg § 1.1377-1(b))[48] This also applies where the S corporation elects to terminate its tax year because of a "qualifying disposition." (Reg § 1.1368-1(g))[49]

If a shareholder dies (or a trust terminates) before the end of an S corporation tax year, his (or its) pro rata part of the corporation's items is reported on his (its) final return. (Code Sec. 1366(a)(1))[50]

¶ 3371 Amount passed through to shareholders reduced for corporate-level taxes.

The amount of any corporate-level built-in gains tax (¶3365) that's imposed on an S corporation is treated as a loss sustained by the corporation during the tax year. The character of the loss is determined by allocating it proportionately among the recognized built-in gains giving rise to the tax. (Code Sec. 1366(f)(2); Reg § 1.1366-4(b)) If a corporate-level tax is imposed on an S corporation's excess net passive income (¶3368), each item of passive investment income that's passed through to a shareholder is reduced by a pro rata part of that tax. (Code Sec. 1366(f)(3); Reg § 1.1366-4(c))[1]

¶ 3372 Shareholders' deductions and losses limited to basis.

All deductions and losses of an S corporation (e.g., capital losses and NOLs) are passed through to and (except as otherwise limited by the Code) deductible by shareholders. However, a shareholder may deduct his pro rata share of these passed-through items only to the extent of his adjusted basis (¶3374) in his S corporation stock, determined by taking into account the increases in basis for his share of the S corporation income during the year, and the decreases in basis for nondividend distributions for the year, plus any debt owed to him by the corporation. A shareholder gets no basis increase for debts of the corporation that he guaranties. (Code Sec. 1366(d)(1); Reg § 1.1366-2)[2]

Any deduction or loss that can't be deducted (for lack of basis) is suspended and may be carried over to be used whenever the shareholder has basis to apply against all or part of the amount the shareholder carried over. The loss is personal to the shareholder to whom it is disallowed and suspended, and cannot be transferred in any manner. However, where there is a post-2004 tax-free transfer of S corporation stock to a spouse or to a former spouse incident to divorce (¶2447), any disallowed losses or deductions are carried over to the spouse or former spouse. (Code Sec. 1366(d)(2); Reg § 1.1366-2(a)(2))[3] Special rules apply where the S corporation is in bankruptcy or is insolvent. (Code Sec. 108(d)(7)(B))[4]

If an S corporation's stock, or the debt it owes to a shareholder, becomes worthless in any tax year of the corporation or shareholder, the corporate items for that year will be taken into account by the shareholders and the adjustments to basis of stock or debt will be made, before the worthlessness is taken into account. (Code Sec. 1367(b)(3))[5]

---

47. ¶H-4329; TD ¶532,002
48. ¶D-1769; ¶13,774; TD ¶614,707
49. ¶D-1771; ¶13,684.09; TD ¶614,711
50. ¶D-1774; ¶13,664; TD ¶614,715
1. ¶D-1767; ¶13,664.02; TD ¶614,705

2. ¶D-1775; ¶13,664; TD ¶614,716
3. ¶D-1785; ¶13,664; TD ¶614,718
4. ¶D-1786; ¶1084.03; TD ¶614,718
5. ¶D-1789; ¶13,674; TD ¶614,722

¶ 3373 Consistent treatment on shareholder's return and S corporation's return— Form 8082.

A shareholder must on his own return treat a Subchapter S item in a manner that is consistent with the treatment of that item on the corporation's return (Form 1120S). A shareholder that treats a Subchapter S item differently must notify IRS of the inconsistency (Code Sec. 6037) on Form 8082.[6]

¶ 3374 Shareholder's basis in S corporation's stock or debt.

A shareholder's basis in the stock of an S corporation is *increased* by his share of the corporation's income items that are passed through to him—i.e., its separately and non-separately computed income items (including tax-exempt income) and the excess of the deduction for depletion over the basis of depletable property. (Code Sec. 1367(a)(1); Reg § 1.1367-1(b)) Debt discharge income of an S corporation that is excluded from its income is not income to a shareholder, and, thus, does not increase shareholder basis in the S corporation's stock.[7] Basis in stock is *decreased* (but not below zero) by: the shareholder's share of the corporation's items of deduction, loss and nondeductible expenses (except those chargeable to capital account); the shareholder's depletion deduction for oil and gas property; and distributions to the shareholder that aren't taxable as dividends. (Code Sec. 1367(a)(2); Reg § 1.1367-1(c))[8]

In any tax year of an S corporation when the total of the amount of items (other than distributions) that reduce a shareholder's basis in stock exceeds the amount that would reduce that basis to zero, the balance is applied to reduce the basis (but not below zero) of any shareholder debt in the S corporation. (Code Sec. 1367(b)(2)(A); Reg § 1.1367-2(b))[9]

If the shareholder's basis in S corporation debt in any tax year is reduced below his original basis in it, that basis must be increased to (but not above) its original amount, before the shareholder's basis in *stock* is increased. (Code Sec. 1367(b)(2)(B); Reg § 1.1367-2(b)) Thus, to the extent that, in any later year, the total amount of items that increase basis exceed the total amount of items that decrease basis, the net increase is applied first to increase the basis of debt to its original level before it is applied to increase the basis of stock.[10] For purposes of the basis adjustment rules, shareholder advances aggregating less than $25,000 and not evidenced by separate written instruments and repayments on the advances are treated as a single indebtedness. (Reg § 1.1367-2(a)(2))[11]

For contributions made in tax years beginning after 2005 and before 2010, the decrease in a shareholder's basis in his S corporation stock by reason of a charitable contribution made by the S corporation equals the shareholder's pro rata share of the adjusted basis of the contributed property. (Code Sec. 1367(a)(2)) Where this rule applies to limit the decrease in the basis resulting from the contribution, the rule that limits the aggregate amount of losses and deductions that may be taken by the S corporation shareholder to his basis in the S corporation's stock and debt does not apply to the extent of the excess (if any) of: ... the shareholder's pro rata share of the charitable contribution, over ... the shareholder's pro rata share of the adjusted basis of such property. (Code Sec. 1366(d)(4))[12]

✔*caution:* Check http://ria.thomsonreuters.com/federaltaxhandbook to see if the basis adjustment to stock of S corporations making charitable contributions under Code Sec. 1367(a)(2) has been extended to 2011.

---

6. ¶D-1801; ¶60,374; TD ¶614,724
7. ¶D-1863; ¶13,674; TD ¶617,001
8. ¶D-1865; ¶13,674; TD ¶617,001
9. ¶D-1877; ¶13,674; TD ¶617,007

10. ¶D-1881; ¶13,674; TD ¶617,009
11. ¶D-1878;¶13,674.10; TD ¶617,007
12. ¶D-1775; ¶13,674; TD ¶617,001

¶ 3375   Tax treatment of S corporation distributions.

The amount of a distribution from an S corporation to a shareholder equals the amount of cash distributed plus the fair market value (at distribution) of any other property distributed. (Code Sec. 301(c), Code Sec. 1368(a))[13]

If an S corporation has no accumulated earnings and profits (E&P), the amount distributed reduces the shareholder's basis in his stock (¶3374). If the amount exceeds basis, the excess is treated as payment in exchange for stock, i.e., as capital gain. (Code Sec. 1368(b)(2))[14]

If an S corporation has accumulated E&P, its distributions are treated as follows: (Code Sec. 1368(c))[15]

(1) The portion of the distribution that doesn't exceed the accumulated adjustments account (AAA, see ¶3377) is taxed the same as a distribution from an S corporation with no accumulated E&P (above). If more than one distribution is made in a tax year, and the total amount distributed exceeds the amount in the AAA at the end of that year, the balance in that account is allocated among the distributions in proportion to the size of each distribution. (Code Sec. 1368(c)(1))[16]

(2) The portion of the distribution that remains after applying (1) is treated as a dividend to the extent it doesn't exceed the S corporation's accumulated E&P. (Code Sec. 1368(c)(2))

(3) Any portion of the distribution remaining after applying (2) is treated the same as a distribution by an S corporation with no accumulated E&P. (Code Sec. 1368(c)(3))[17]

The tax effects of an S corporation's distributions to shareholders with respect to stock are determined only after taking into account:

(1) adjustments that increase the basis of the shareholder's stock and

(2) adjustments to the accumulated adjustments account (AAA), other than for distributions to shareholders and without regard to any net negative adjustments, for the S corporation's tax year. (Code Sec. 1368(d); Reg § 1.1368-1(e)(2))[18]

observation: The effect of taking the basis increases, but not the decreases, into account is that the shareholder may receive more nontaxable distributions, at the cost of a decrease in the amount of loss that he may deduct.

An S corporation may elect, with the consent of all affected shareholders (i.e., those to whom distributions are made), to treat distributions as made out of accumulated E&P *before* being made out of the AAA. (Code Sec. 1368(e)(3); Reg § 1.1368-1(f)(2))[19]

¶ 3376   S corporation's earnings and profits.

An S corporation, unlike a C corporation, generally does not generate earnings and profits (E&P).[20] Any E&P carried over from prior C corporation years, or acquired from a C corporation in a reorganization remain unadjusted while the corporation retains S corporation status, except as follows: (Code Sec. 1371(c)(1))

... E&P are reduced to reflect distributions that are taxable to the shareholders as dividends. (Code Sec. 1371(c)(3))

... E&P are adjusted (up or down) to reflect the effect of redemptions, liquidations, tax-free reorganizations and corporate divisions. (Code Sec. 1371(c)(2))

... E&P are reduced to reflect any tax paid by an S corporation because of the recapture of a pre-S election investment credit. (Code Sec. 1371(d)(3))[21]

---

13. ¶D-1813; ¶13,684; TD ¶616,501
14. ¶D-1815; ¶s 13,684, 13,684.07; TD ¶616,502
15. ¶s D-1817, D-1816; ¶13,684.01; TD ¶616,502
16. ¶D-1816, D-1819; ¶13,684.01; TD ¶616,502
17. ¶s D-1817, D-1816; ¶13,684.01; TD ¶616,502

18. ¶D-1818
19. ¶D-1835; ¶13,684.03; TD ¶616,509
20. ¶D-1631; ¶13,684.01 *et seq.*; TD ¶616,507
21. ¶D-1633; ¶13,714.03; TD ¶616,507

... E&P are adjusted for LIFO recapture tax. (¶3367) (Code Sec. 1363(d)(5))[22]

For purposes of determining the S corporations accumulated E&P, all pre–'86 S corporation generated E&P has been eliminated for tax years beginning after May 25, 2007.[23]

¶ 3377 Accumulated adjustments account (AAA)

The accumulated adjustment account (AAA) is a corporate account consisting of the corporation's income that was previously taxed to its shareholders and not distributed. An S corporation's AAA[24] is increased each tax year by:

(1) Separately computed items of income (other than income that is exempt from tax).

(2) Nonseparately computed income.

(3) The excess of deductions for depletion over the basis of property subject to depletion. (Code Sec. 1368(e)(1); Reg § 1.1368-2(a)(2))[25]

The AAA is decreased each tax year by:

(a) Items of separately computed loss and deduction.

(b) Nonseparately computed loss.

(c) Nondeductible expenses (other than expenses chargeable to capital account) unless related to tax-exempt income.

(d) The amount of the shareholder's deduction for depletion under Code Sec. 611 with respect to oil and gas wells.

(e) Distributions from an S corporation that has no E&P and distributions that are made out of the AAA.

(f) The amount that was treated as paid out of the AAA on redemptions that were treated as payments in exchange for stock under Code Sec. 302(a) or Code Sec. 303(a). That amount is the same percentage of the amount in the account before the redemption, that the number of redeemed shares was of the total number of outstanding shares before the redemption. (Code Sec. 1368(e)(1); Reg § 1.1368-2(a)(3))[26]

Special ordering rules apply with regard to the above mentioned increases and decreases. (Reg § 1.1368-2(a)(5))[27]

Where there is a net negative adjustment for the tax year, any net loss for the year is disregarded in adjusting the AAA for purposes of distributions made during the tax year. (Code Sec. 1368(e)(1)(C))[28]

The balance in an S corporation's AAA at the end of a tax year may be reduced below zero if the items that reduce the AAA exceed the sum of the AAA plus the items that increase the AAA (items (1) – (3), above). (Code Sec. 1368(e)(1)(A)) Income in a later year will cause the AAA to become positive only after the negative balance has been restored as illustrated in regs. (Reg § 1.1368-3)[29]

The AAA isn't to be adjusted (i.e., reduced) for federal taxes attributable to any tax year when the S corporation was a C corporation. (Code Sec. 1368(e)(1))[30]

If distributions made during the year exceed the AAA at the close of the tax year, then the AAA is allocated pro rata among each of the distributions (Code Sec. 1368(c); Reg § 1.1368-2(b)(1))[31]

Special rules apply to distributions after the S election is terminated. (Code Sec. 1371(e))[32]

---

22. ¶D-1581; TD ¶616,507
23. ¶D-1632; ¶13,684.07
24. ¶D-1823; ¶13,684.02; TD ¶616,506
25. ¶D-1824; ¶13,684.02; TD ¶616,506
26. ¶D-1825, D-1827; ¶13,684.02; TD ¶616,506
27. ¶D-1829; ¶13,684.02; TD ¶616,506

28. ¶D-1826.1; TD ¶616,506
29. ¶D-1830; ¶13,684.02; TD ¶616,506
30. ¶D-1823; ¶13,684.02; TD ¶616,506
31. ¶D-1819; ¶13,684.02; TD ¶616,505
32. ¶D-1846 *et seq.*; ¶13,714.04; TD ¶616,516

¶ 3378   Voluntary revocation of the S election; rescission.

A corporation's S election may be revoked with the consent of holders of a majority of the corporation's issued and outstanding stock (including non-voting stock). (Code Sec. 1362(d)(1); Reg § 1.1362-2(a)(1))[33]

If no effective date is specified, a revocation is effective for the tax year in which made, if made by the 15th day of the third month of that year. Otherwise, it will be effective as of the first day of the next tax year. (Code Sec. 1362(d)(1)(C))[34] However, if the revocation specifies that it is to be effective on a date that is on or after the date it's made, it will be effective on that date even if it causes the corporation's tax year to be split. (Code Sec. 1362(d)(1)(D))[35]

A corporation may *rescind* the revocation at any time before it becomes effective. A rescission may be made only with the consent of each person who consented to the revocation and of each person who became a shareholder during the period from the day after the date the revocation was made through the date the rescission is made. (Reg § 1.1362-2(a)(4))[36]

¶ 3379   Involuntary termination of S election.

A corporation's S election is terminated if either:

(1) The corporation ceases to meet any of the S corporation eligibility requirements discussed at ¶3354. (Code Sec. 1362(d)(2)(A)) The termination is effective as of the day the eligibility requirement is no longer met (Code Sec. 1362(d)(2)(B));[37] or

(2) The S corporation's passive investment income (¶3369) exceeds 25% of its gross receipts for three consecutive tax years and at the end of each of those years, the corporation had accumulated E&P (¶3368). The termination is effective as of the first day of the first tax year beginning after the third of these years. (Code Sec. 1362(d)(3)(A))[38]

IRS can waive inadvertent terminations if certain conditions are met. (Code Sec. 1362(f)) Regs explain how to request relief. (Reg § 1.1362-4(c))[39] IRS has waived terminations where, for example, the S corporation temporarily had an ineligible shareholder such as a nonresident alien, an ineligible trust or another corporation, or where the S corporation had an ineligible subsidiary.[40]

QSubs are eligible for the same relief (as discussed above) for an inadvertently invalid QSub election or inadvertent termination. (Reg § 1.1362-4)

A corporation's filing a voluntary bankruptcy petition does not terminate its S corporation election.[41]

¶ 3380   When new S election can be made after termination or revocation.

After a revocation or termination of its S election, a corporation must wait five years before making a new S election unless IRS consents to an earlier election. (Code Sec. 1362(g))[42]

33. ¶D-1901; ¶13,624.02; TD ¶623,001
34. ¶D-1903; ¶13,624.02; TD ¶623,003
35. ¶D-1905; ¶13,624.02; TD ¶623,003
36. ¶D-1907 *et seq.*; ¶13,624.02; TD ¶623,005
37. ¶D-1911; ¶13,624.02; TD ¶623,006
38. ¶D-1914; ¶13,624.02; TD ¶623,008
39. ¶D-1928; ¶13,624.03; TD ¶623,018
40. ¶D-1937 *et seq.*; TD ¶623,025
41. ¶D-1911
42. ¶s D-1951, D-1953; ¶13,624.02; TD ¶623,023

Chapter 16 Corporate Transactions—Organization–Distributions—Reorganization—Acquisitions—Liquidations

¶ 3510 Incorporations and Transfers to Controlled Corporations-Code Sec. 351. ▬▬

Incorporating a business or transferring property to a controlled corporation can be partly or wholly tax-free if technical requirements are satisfied. But an intentional failure to satisfy the requirements may not result in the recognition of gain or loss in every case.[1]

No gain or loss is recognized if property (¶3511) is transferred to a corporation solely in exchange for stock (¶3512) of that corporation, if, immediately after the transfer, the transferor or transferors are in control (¶3513) of the corporation. (Code Sec. 351(a))[2]

For exceptions, see ¶3517 and ¶3518.

For transfers to foreign corporations, see ¶3588.

For basis of property received in the exchange, see ¶2482 *et seq.*

¶ 3511 Property.

Property that may be transferred tax-free under Code Sec. 351 includes cash, tangible property and intangible personal property, e.g., stock, partnership interests, patent rights, and working interests in oil and gas properties.[3]

Property doesn't include: (i) services to the transferee corporation (Code Sec. 351(d)(1));[4] (ii) transferee corporation debt not evidenced by a security (Code Sec. 351(d)(2));[5] or (iii) unpaid interest on transferee corporation debt accrued during the transferor's holding period for the debt. (Code Sec. 351(d)(3))[6]

¶ 3512 Stock.

Property must be transferred *solely in exchange for stock*, which does not include (1) stock rights, options or warrants (Reg § 1.351-1(a)), or (2) nonqualified preferred stock (Code Sec. 351(g)) (¶3556)[7]

Shares in an association, joint stock company or insurance company are treated as stock. (Code Sec. 7701(a)(7))[8] A transferee can be treated as receiving stock even if no stock certificate is issued.[9]

¶ 3513 Control.

Control means at least 80% of the transferee's combined voting power and at least 80% of all other classes of the transferee's stock, see ¶3553. (Code Sec. 368(c))[10] The transferor group must hold at least 80% of the voting power immediately after the transfer; but not every transferor must hold voting stock.[11]

---

1. ¶F-1014; TD ¶231,014
2. ¶F-1001; ¶3514.01; TD ¶231,001
3. ¶F-1101 *et seq.*; ¶3514.03; TD ¶231,004
4. ¶F-1104; ¶3514.03; TD ¶231,004
5. ¶F-1102; TD ¶231,004
6. ¶F-1103; TD ¶231,004

7. ¶F-1004; ¶3514.04; TD ¶231,005
8. ¶F-1004; ¶3514.04; TD ¶231,005
9. ¶F-1004 *et seq.*; ¶3514.05; TD ¶231,005
10. ¶s F-1200 *et seq.*, F-5501 *et seq.*; ¶3514.05; TD ¶231,701
11. ¶F-1202; TD ¶231,702

References beginning with a single letter are to paragraphs in RIA's Federal Tax Coordinator 2d and RIA's Analysis of Federal Taxes: Income. Those beginning with numbers are to paragraphs in RIA's United States Tax Reporter. Those beginning with TD are to paragraphs in RIA's Tax Desk.

¶ 3514   Gain on receipt of cash or property ("boot").

If transferors receive *boot* (defined at ¶3556) as well as stock in an otherwise qualifying Code Sec. 351 transfer, nonrecognition is limited and the transferor (i) recognizes gain up to the amount or fair market value of the boot, and (ii) does not recognize any losses. (Code Sec. 351(b))[12]

¶ 3515   Assumption of liabilities.

When a corporation assumes liabilities (¶3516) in connection with an otherwise tax-free exchange, the transfer is still tax-free (Code Sec. 357(a))[13] subject to the following exceptions.

• *Tax avoidance rule.* If the principal purpose for the assumption of liabilities is tax avoidance or isn't a bona fide business purpose, the full amount of *all assumed liabilities are treated as cash received* (even those assumed for nontax avoidance or valid business purposes) and taxed as boot (¶3514). (Code Sec. 357(b)(1))[14]

• *Excess liabilities rule.* If the total liabilities assumed exceed the transferor's adjusted basis in the transferred property, gain is recognized to the extent of the excess. (Code Sec. 357(c)(1))[15]

Where both anti-abuse rules apply, tax avoidance takes precedence and all liabilities are treated as boot. (Code Sec. 357(c)(2)(A))[16]

The excess liabilities rule does not apply to any liability (i) that would give rise to a deduction when paid by the transferor, or (ii) would be a liquidating payment to a partner described in Code Sec. 736(a), see ¶3769. (Code Sec. 357(c)(3)(A))[17]

The excess liabilities rule applies to transfers in a divisive Type D reorganization under Code Sec. 361.[18] It does not apply, however, to acquisitive reorganizations in which the transferor corporation goes out of existence (and cannot benefit from the transferee's assumption of liabilities), i.e., Code Sec. 351 transfers that also qualify as either (1) a Type A or Type C reorganization, or (2) a nondivisive Type D or Type G reorganization that meets the requirements of Code Sec. 354(b)(1) (discussed at ¶3544 *et seq.*).[19]

The amount of a liability assumed in a Code Sec. 351 exchange reduces the transferor's basis in the stock received, regardless of whether the transferor recognizes any gain or loss on the exchange. (Code Sec. 358(a), Code Sec. 358(d)(1)) However, the transferor's basis in the stock will not be reduced by the assumption of any liability described in Code Sec. 357(c)(3) that would have been deductible by the transferor had it not been assumed. (Code Sec. 358(d)(2))[20]

If a transferor's basis in stock received in a Code Sec. 351 exchange exceeds the fair market value (FMV) of the stock, the basis is reduced (but not below FMV) by the amount of any liability that (i) is assumed in exchange for the stock, and (ii) did not otherwise reduce the transferor's basis in the stock by reason of the assumption. However, basis is not reduced if (1) the trade or business with which the liability is associated is transferred as part of the exchange to the person assuming the liability, or (2) substantially all of the assets with which the liability is associated are transferred as part of the exchange to the person assuming the liability. (Code Sec. 358(h); Reg § 1.358-5)[21]

---

12. ¶F-1501; ¶3514.10; TD ¶231,302
13. ¶F-1509; ¶3574.01; TD ¶231,501
14. ¶F-1511 *et seq.*; ¶3574.02; TD ¶231,504
15. ¶F-1515 *et seq.*; ¶3574.03; TD ¶231,507
16. ¶F-1519; TD ¶231,510

17. ¶F-1521; ¶3574; TD ¶231,512
18. ¶F-4203; TD ¶233,010
19. ¶F-4204; TD ¶235,008
20. ¶F-1803; ¶F-1521; ¶3584.04; TD ¶232,543; TD ¶233,302
21. ¶F-1803.1; TD ¶231,905

¶ 3516 When a liability is treated as assumed.

Except as provided in regs,

(1) A recourse liability is treated as having been assumed by the transferee if, based on all the facts and circumstances, the transferee has agreed to, and is expected to, satisfy it, regardless of whether the transferor has been relieved of the liability. (Code Sec. 357(d)(1)(A))

(2) A nonrecourse liability is treated as having been assumed by the transferee of any asset subject to the liability, except that the amount so treated is reduced by the lesser of:

(i) the amount of the liability that the owner of other, untransferred assets subject to the same liability, has agreed with the transferee to, and is expected to, satisfy, or

(ii) the FMV of other, untransferred assets, determined without regard to Code Sec. 7701(g) (providing generally that the FMV of property subject to nonrecourse debt is not less than the debt). (Code Sec. 357(d)(2))[22]

🖉*observation:* If the owner of untransferred assets securing nonrecourse debt doesn't agree to pay any of it, the amount of the liability treated as assumed by the transferee isn't reduced at all, in which case liabilities may exceed basis and trigger gain recognition.

For the limit on basis increase for assumption of liabilities, see ¶2485.

¶ 3517 Transfers to investment companies (swap funds).

Gain or loss is recognized on the transfer of property to an investment company in exchange for its stock when the transfer diversifies a transferor's interests, i.e., a significant portion of the assets transferred by two or more transferors are nonidentical, (Reg § 1.351-1(c)(5))[23] except in cases where each transferor transfers a portfolio of already diversified assets, (Reg § 1.351-1(c)(6))[24] Gain or loss is also recognized when a transfer to an investment company results in the transferred property being held by a regulated investment company (RIC), a real estate investment trust (REIT), or a corporation more than 80% of the value of whose total investment assets are marketable securities, interests in mutual funds or REITS, or stocks and securities (including specified types of property, such as money, that are treated as stocks or securities under Code Sec. 351(e)(1).[25] (Reg § 1.351-1(c)(1))[26]

¶ 3518 Transfer of debtor's property in a bankruptcy or similar proceeding.

The Code Sec. 351 nonrecognition rule does not apply to transfers in a bankruptcy, receivership, foreclosure or similar proceeding (including agency receivership proceedings involving banks). Gain or loss is recognized to the extent the stock received by the debtor in exchange for assets is used to satisfy the debtor's indebtedness. (Code Sec. 351(e)(2))[27]

¶ 3519 Gain or loss to corporation on issuance of stock.

A corporation does not recognize gain or loss on the exchange of its stock (including treasury stock) for property or money. (Code Sec. 1032(a))[28] Similarly, no gain or loss is recognized in otherwise taxable transactions where a corporation acquires stock directly or indirectly from the issuing corporation in what otherwise would be a transferred basis transaction and immediately transfers the stock to acquire money or other property (including services), and no party receiving the issuing corporation stock receives a substituted basis in

---

22. ¶F-1509.2; ¶3574.01; TD ¶231,502
23. ¶F-1307; ¶3514.06; TD ¶232,103
24. ¶F-1307.1; ¶3514.06; TD ¶232,103
25. ¶F-1303; ¶3514.06; TD ¶232,101

26. ¶F-1302; ¶3514.06; TD ¶232,102
27. ¶F-1308; ¶3514.07; TD ¶231,018
28. ¶I-3201; ¶10,324; TD ¶233,401

the stock of the issuing corporation. (Reg § 1.1032-3(b), Reg § 1.1032-3(c))[29] For stock issued to a creditor in satisfaction of a corporation's debt, see ¶1400.

¶ 3520   Deductibility of costs of organizing a corporation.

A corporation is deemed to have made an election to deduct up to $5,000 of its organizational expenditures in the tax year in which it begins business (and there is no requirement for a separate election statement). (Reg § 1.248-1T(c)) The $5,000 amount is reduced (but not below zero) by the amount, if any, by which its total organization expenditures exceeds $50,000. Remaining organizational expenditures are deductible ratably over the 180-month period beginning with the month in which it begins business. (Code Sec. 248(a))[30]

A corporation may irrevocably forgo the deemed election by clearly electing to capitalize *all* organizational expenditures on a timely filed Federal income tax return (including extensions) for the tax year in which it begins business. (Reg § 1.248-1T(c))

Qualifying expenses include outlays for legal services, incorporation fees, temporary directors' fees and organizational meeting costs. Costs relating to capital structure, e.g., of issuing stock, can't be deducted or otherwise recovered. (Code Sec. 248(b); Reg § 1.248-1(b))[31]

¶ 3521   Corporate Distributions; Earnings and Profits (E&P).

A distribution of property (i.e., money, securities, and any other property except stock of the distributing corporation) by a corporation to its shareholders is taxable to the shareholders as a dividend to the extent it is made out of current or accumulated earnings and profits (E&P) (¶1287 *et seq.*).[32] The amount of a distribution is reduced by an associated liability only if it is assumed by the shareholder within the meaning of Code Sec. 357(d) (¶3516). (Reg § 1.301-1(g))[33]

¶ 3522   Earnings and profits (E&P).

A distribution of money or other property by a corporation to its shareholders is treated as a dividend and is taxable as ordinary income to the extent it is made out of current and accumulated earnings and profits (E&P) (¶1287 *et seq.*). The portion of the distribution in excess of E&P is treated as a return of capital to the extent of the shareholder's basis in the stock of the distributing corporation (his cost or net capital investment). (Code Sec. 301(c)) The remainder of the distribution, if any, is generally taxed as capital gain.[34]

For tax treatment of the distributing corporation, see ¶3538 *et seq.*

For increases in E&P for alternative minimum tax purposes, see ¶3211.

¶ 3523   How distributions affect E&P.

With certain exceptions discussed below, distributions of property by a corporation with respect to its stock reduce E&P by the following amounts:

(1) The amount of money distributed. (Code Sec. 312(a)(1))[35]

(2) The principal (face) amount of the corporation's obligations (i.e., its own notes, bonds, etc.) distributed without original issue discount (OID) (¶1315 *et seq.*). (Code Sec. 312(a)(2))[36]

(3) The aggregate issue price of the corporation's obligations distributed with OID. (Code Sec. 312(a)(2))[37]

(4) The adjusted basis of other distributed property (Code Sec. 312(a)(3), Code Sec. 312(b))[38]

29. ¶I-3213; ¶10,324
30. ¶L-5202 ; TD ¶301,023
31. ¶L-5204; ¶2484; TD ¶301,028
32. ¶J-2351; ¶3014.01
33. ¶J-2352.1; ¶3014.02; TD ¶172,002
34. ¶J-2352 *et seq.*; ¶3014; TD ¶172,001
35. ¶F-10502; ¶3124.02; TD ¶171,008
36. ¶F-10503; ¶3124.02; TD ¶171,008
37. ¶F-10504; ¶3124.02; TD ¶171,008
38. ¶F-10505; ¶3124.02; TD ¶171,008

as determined for purposes of computing E&P. (Code Sec. 312(b)(1))[39]

E&P is *not* reduced in the case of the following types of distributions.

(1) Distributions of appreciated property (other than the corporation's own obligations) increase E&P to the extent of any gain realized (FMV over adjusted basis) by the distributing corporation on the distribution. (Code Sec. 312(b)(1))[40] This decreases the reduction to E&P for the distribution of property by the amount of any liability assumed by the shareholder in connection with the distribution or to which the distributed property is subject. (Code Sec. 312(c); Reg § 1.312-3)[41]

(2) Redemption distributions that are treated as payment in exchange for stock (¶3526) reduce E&P by an amount not in excess of the ratable share of the distributing corporation's E&P attributable to the redeemed stock. (Code Sec. 312(n)(7))[42]

(3) Reorganizations and other tax-free distributions don't reduce E&P if the distributee does not recognize any gain. (Code Sec. 312(d)(1)(A); Reg § 1.312-11(b), Reg § 1.312-11(c))[43]

(4) Tax-free distributions of a corporation's own stock (stock dividends under Code Sec. 305(a)) don't reduce E&P. (Code Sec. 312(d)(1)(B); Reg § 1.312-1(d)) If a distribution of stock is *taxable* to the shareholders (see ¶1298), E&P is reduced by the FMV of the taxable portion of the stock or rights. (Reg § 1.312-1(d))[44]

(5) Distributions to 20% corporate shareholders may require adjustments to E&P solely for purposes of determining the distributee's income and stock basis. (Code Sec. 301(e))[45]

Basis can be different for E&P and taxable income (TI) purposes because the corporation may use different depreciation or cost recovery methods for E&P and TI purposes. (¶3524).[46]

¶ 3524 Effect of depreciation on E&P.

Depreciation deductions for E&P purposes are often lower than the corresponding deductions for purposes of computing taxable income (¶1900 *et seq.*). For MACRS property (other than property expensed under Code Sec. 179 and Code Sec. 179A), the E&P deduction is computed under the alternative depreciation system (ADS), even if a different system is used in computing taxable income. (Code Sec. 312(k)(3)(A))[47] For ACRS property placed in service before '87, the E&P deduction is computed by using the straight-line method over the regular or alternative ACRS recovery periods, which may be longer than those used in computing taxable income.[48] The E&P deduction for depreciable property placed in service before '81 is computed by using the straight-line or similar method (e.g., units of production) even if an accelerated method is used in computing taxable income.[49] For expensed property, i.e., Code Sec. 179 and Code Sec. 179A property, the cost is deducted from E&P ratably over five tax years. (Code Sec. 312(k)(3)(B))[50]

observation: Additional first-year depreciation deduction under Code Sec. 168(k) (¶1933 *et seq.*) is not allowed for purposes of computing E&P.

¶ 3525 Other adjustments to E&P reflecting economic gain or loss.

Other common adjustments are made to E&P to reflect economic gain or loss.

. . . Circulation expenses must be capitalized and treated as part of the basis of the asset to which they relate even if they are deducted currently in computing taxable income. (Code Sec. 312(n)(3))[1]

39. ¶F-10505; ¶s 3124.02, 3124.04; TD ¶171,008
40. ¶F-10506; ¶3124.02; TD ¶171,011
41. ¶F-10508; ¶3124.02; TD ¶171,011
42. ¶F-10701; ¶3124.07; TD ¶171,034
43. ¶F-10801; ¶3124.02; TD ¶171,034
44. ¶F-10509 *et seq.*; ¶3124.02; TD ¶171,015
45. ¶F-10601 *et seq.*; ¶3014; TD ¶171,008
46. ¶F-10300 *et seq.*; ¶3124.01 *et seq.*; TD ¶171,008
47. ¶F-10303; ¶3124.04; TD ¶171,022
48. ¶F-10307; ¶3124.04; TD ¶171,022
49. ¶F-10309; ¶3124.04; TD ¶171,022
50. ¶F-10304; ¶3124.04; TD ¶171,023
1. ¶F-10206; ¶3124.07; TD ¶171,019

. . . Completed contract method of accounting can't be used for E&P purposes. The percentage of completion method must be used instead. (Code Sec. 312(n)(6))[2]

. . . Construction period carrying charges (interest, property taxes, etc.) must be capitalized as part of the assets to which they are allocable. (Code Sec. 312(n)(1)(A)) The capitalized amounts must be written off for E&P purposes, as is the asset itself.[3]

. . . Depletion is taken into account on a *cost,* not percentage, basis. (Reg § 1.312-6(c)(1))[4]

. . . Estimated tax payments by a cash method taxpayer reduce E&P in the year paid.[5]

. . . Exempt income (e.g., state or local bond interest) increases E&P. (Reg § 1.312-6(b))[6]

. . . Installment sales are accounted for without regard to the installment method, i.e., principal amounts must be treated as received in the year of sale. (Code Sec. 312(n)(5))[7]

. . . Intangible drilling and development costs that are deductible when paid or incurred for taxable income purposes (other than costs incurred in connection with a nonproductive well) must be capitalized and deducted ratably over a 60-month period for E&P purposes. (Code Sec. 312(n)(2)(A))[8]

. . . Income tax liabilities reduce E&P as of the close of the tax year, for an accrual basis corporation, and according to some courts, a cash basis corporation. (IRS and other courts say a cash basis corporation reduces E&P only when the tax is *paid.*)[9]

. . . Life insurance proceeds increase E&P if the corporation is the beneficiary even if not includible in taxable income.[10]

. . . LIFO recapture amount increases and decreases at the close of each tax year increase or decrease E&P by the same amount. (Code Sec. 312(n)(4))[11]

. . . Losses that are recognized but not allowed as a deduction decrease E&P by the disallowed amount.[12]

. . . Mineral exploration and development costs that are deductible for taxable income purposes must be capitalized and deducted ratably over a 120-month period for E&P purposes. (Code Sec. 312(n)(2)(B))[13]

. . . Loss carryovers and carrybacks don't reduce E&P of the year to which they are carried and reductions of loss carryovers do not increase E&P in a later carryover year.[14]

. . . Organizational expenses must be capitalized and treated as part of the basis of the asset to which they relate even if they are amortized in computing taxable income (as described at ¶3520). (Code Sec. 312(n)(3))[15]

. . . Premiums paid for life insurance on corporate officers reduce E&P even if they are not deductible in computing taxable income.[16]

¶ 3526   Stock Redemptions. ▬▬▬▬▬▬▬▬▬▬▬▬

The acquisition by a corporation of its own stock from a shareholder in exchange for cash or property is treated as a taxable dividend distribution to the shareholder (¶1287 *et seq.*) unless the redemption qualifies for sale or exchange treatment, in which case it is treated as a sale or exchange for which capital gain treatment is allowed (if the stock is a capital asset in the hands of the taxpayer) whether or not the stock acquired is cancelled, retired, or held as treasury stock. (Code Sec. 317(b))[17] A redemption will be treated as a sale or exchange of stock if it qualifies under any of the following exceptions:

(1) The redemption is *substantially disproportionate* (¶3527).

---

2. ¶F-10008; ¶3124.07; TD ¶171,021
3. ¶F-10208; ¶3124.07; TD ¶171,025
4. ¶F-10314; ¶3124.04; TD ¶171,024
5. ¶F-10224; ¶3124.03; TD ¶171,009
6. ¶F-10101; ¶s 3124.01, 3124.07; TD ¶171,012
7. ¶F-10405; ¶3124.07; TD ¶171,021
8. ¶F-10221; ¶3124.07; TD ¶171,026
9. ¶F-10223, F-10225; ¶3124.03; TD ¶171,009

10. ¶F-10102; ¶3124.07; TD ¶171,012
11. ¶F-10212; ¶3124.07; TD ¶171,021
12. ¶F-10403; ¶3124.05
13. ¶F-10220; ¶3124.07; TD ¶171,026
14. ¶F-10012; ¶3124.03; TD ¶171,032
15. ¶F-10204; ¶3124.07; TD ¶171,028
16. ¶F-10234; TD ¶175,042
17. ¶F-11001; ¶3174.01; TD ¶241,002

(2) The distribution is in *complete redemption* of a shareholder's interest (¶3528).

(3) The redemption is *not essentially equivalent to a dividend* (¶3530).

(4) The redemption is in partial liquidation of a noncorporate shareholder (¶3531).

(5) The distribution is in redemption of a decedent's stock to pay death taxes (¶3532). (Code Sec. 302(a))[18]

For constructive ownership rules applicable to redemptions, see ¶3534.

¶ 3527 Substantially disproportionate redemptions.

A redemption is *substantially disproportionate* if it satisfies both of the following tests:

(1) *80% test.* Immediately after the redemption, the ratio of the shareholder's voting stock to the corporation's total outstanding voting stock is less than 80% of that ratio immediately before the redemption. The same 80% test must also be met with regard to the corporation's *common stock,* voting and nonvoting, based on the FMV of the aggregate shares of each class of common stock. (Code Sec. 302(b)(2)(C))

(2) *50% test.* Immediately after the redemption, the shareholder owns less than 50%, by vote, of the corporation's total voting stock. (Code Sec. 302(b)(2)(B))[19]

A redemption solely of nonvoting stock doesn't qualify as substantially disproportionate. However, if voting stock is redeemed at the same time in a redemption that qualifies as substantially disproportionate, the redemption of the nonvoting stock (other than Section 306 stock) will also be substantially disproportionate. (Reg § 1.302-3(a))[20]

¶ 3528 Complete redemptions—termination of a shareholder's interest in the corporation.

To qualify as a complete redemption, all stock in the corporation that is owned, or treated as owned under the constructive ownership rules (¶3534) (unless waived (¶3529)) by the shareholder must be redeemed. (Code Sec. 302(b)(3)) Accordingly, if a shareholder owns both common and preferred stock, the redemption of all the shares of only one class of stock will not qualify as a complete redemption.[21]

A redemption on the installment basis can qualify as a complete redemption if the corporation and the shareholder are bound by a purchase agreement to complete the redemption by a certain date and for a maximum price.[22]

¶ 3529 Family attribution rules waived on complete terminations.

An individual who receives a distribution that is otherwise in complete redemption of all the stock he actually owns will not be treated as constructively owning the stock actually owned by a spouse, child, grandchild or parent if:

(1) He has no personal financial interest in the corporation (prohibited interest), other than as a creditor, immediately after the redemption;

(2) He no longer serves as director, officer or employee;

(3) He doesn't acquire any prohibited interest (except by inheritance) or position within ten years after the redemption;

(4) He didn't acquire any of the redeemed stock from close family members, and didn't transfer any stock to them, within ten years before the redemption, except acquisitions or transfers not principally motivated by tax avoidance; *and*

---

18. ¶F-11101 *et seq.*; ¶3024.02 *et seq.*; TD ¶241,001
19. ¶F-11203 *et seq.*; ¶3024.04; TD ¶242,000 *et seq.*
20. ¶F-11212; ¶3024.04; TD ¶242,014

21. ¶F-11301 *et seq.*; ¶3024.05; TD ¶241,201
22. ¶F-11307; ¶3024.05; TD ¶241,211

(5) He attaches a separate statement (in duplicate) to his income tax return for the redemption year stating that he hasn't acquired any new prohibited interest (except by inheritance) and that he will notify the district director within 30 days after acquiring any new interest. (Code Sec. 302(c)(2); Reg § 1.302-4)[23]

Waiver of family attribution allows an individual to completely redeem his interest without all related persons redeeming their stock and applies only for purposes of determining that a distribution is a complete redemption. Accordingly, there is no need for the waiver if the redemption would otherwise qualify as payment in exchange for stock. (Code Sec. 302(b)(5))[24]

A partnership, estate, trust or corporation (entity) can waive family attribution if the partner, beneficiary or shareholder (related person) owns stock solely as a function of the family constructive ownership rules, such ownership is not reattributed to the entity if both the entity and the related person satisfy the conditions for a waiver and agree to be jointly and severally liable for any tax deficiency resulting from any acquisition of an interest within the ten-year period. (Code Sec. 302(c)(2)(C))[25]

¶ 3530   Redemptions not essentially equivalent to a dividend.

A redemption is not essentially equivalent to a dividend if it results in a meaningful reduction in the redeemed shareholder's proportionate interest in the distributing corporation, without regard to how it affects the distributing corporation. (Reg § 1.302-2(b))[26]

A redemption of a sole shareholder and a pro rata redemption do not reduce a shareholders' proportionate interest in the distributing corporation and cannot be essentially equivalent to a dividend.[27]

A redemption from a shareholder with over 50% of the voting power usually results in a meaningful reduction if that shareholder's voting power is reduced to 50% or less.[28]

A redemption of voting stock from a substantial minority shareholder results in a meaningful reduction if, after the redemption, the number of shareholders the redeemed shareholder must act in concert with to control the corporation is increased.[29]

A redemption of voting stock from a low percentage minority shareholder is usually treated as a meaningful reduction in interest, so long as there is some reduction in proportionate interest.[30]

Redemptions of nonvoting preferred stock from shareholders who own no common stock and no voting stock always result in a meaningful reduction in interest.[31]

The constructive ownership rules (¶3534) apply in determining the redeemed shareholder's stock ownership before and after the redemption (Code Sec. 302(c)(1)) even if no stock is actually owned after the redemption.[32]

¶ 3531   Redemptions in partial liquidation of a noncorporate shareholder.

A partial liquidating distribution in redemption of stock of a noncorporate shareholder is treated as a sale or exchange even if it is made pro rata. A redemption distribution is treated as made in partial liquidation, even if it is pro rata, if it is (1) made with respect to a noncorporate shareholder, (2) not essentially equivalent to a dividend (as determined at the corporate level), and (3) made under a plan within the tax year in which the plan is adopted or the next tax year. (Code Sec. 302(b)(4), Code Sec. 302(e)(1))[33] Partial liquidations are meant to include cases involving the genuine contraction of a corporate business.

---

23. ¶F-11313 *et seq.*; ¶3024.05; TD ¶241,401*et seq.*
24. ¶F-11311; ¶3024.05; TD ¶241,405
25. ¶F-11314; ¶3024.05; TD ¶241,403
26. ¶F-11402; ¶3024.03; TD ¶242,201
27. ¶F-11407; ¶3024.03; TD ¶242,208
28. ¶F-11418; ¶3024.03; TD ¶242,225

29. ¶F-11424; ¶3024.03
30. ¶F-11425; ¶3024.03; TD ¶242,213
31. ¶F-11429 *et seq.*; ¶3024.03; TD ¶242,218
32. ¶F-11410 *et seq.*; ¶3024.03; TD ¶242,009
33. ¶F-11500 *et seq.*; ¶3024.06; TD ¶242,604

(Reg § 1.346-1(a))[34]

If a corporation is engaged in two or more active trades or businesses for five years or more, a distribution in partial liquidation won't be essentially equivalent to a dividend if the corporation terminates one of the businesses, distributes all of the assets of the discontinued business (or its sales proceeds), and continues to operate the second business. (Code Sec. 302(e)(2), Code Sec. 302(e)(3))[35]

¶ 3532 Redemption of decedent's stock to pay death taxes.

Distributions in redemption of stock included in a decedent's gross estate for federal estate tax purposes are treated as payment for stock up to the sum of: (1) all death taxes (federal and state), including interest, and (2) funeral and administration expenses allowable as federal estate tax deductions (Code Sec. 303(a)),[36] *but only if*:

(1) The value of the redeeming corporation's stock included in the estate exceeds 35% of the decedent's adjusted gross estate; (Code Sec. 303(b)(2)(A)) (Code Sec. 303(b)(2)(B))[37]

(2) The redemption distribution takes place after the decedent's death and within three years and 90 days after the estate tax return is filed (or due, if filed early), or, in some cases, later specified dates (Code Sec. 303(b)(1));[38] and

(3) The redeemed shareholder bears the burden of the taxes or expenses. (Code Sec. 303(b)(3))[39]

¶ 3533 Stock Sales Between Related Corporations.

If shareholders control two corporations and sell stock of one controlled corporation (Issuer) to the other (Acquirer) in return for cash or other property, the sale is treated as a stock redemption. If the Acquirer is a brother corporation of the Issuer, the sale is treated as a redemption by the Acquirer. If the Issuer is a parent of the Acquirer, the sale is treated as a redemption by the Issuer. (Code Sec. 304(a)(1), Code Sec. 304(a)(2))[40] The resulting redemption is treated as payment in exchange for stock (and not as a dividend) if it qualifies under one of the exceptions listed at ¶3526. (Code Sec. 304(a))[41]

If the sale is treated as a dividend, the amount taxable to the shareholder is determined as if it were distributed *first* by the Acquiring corporation to the extent of its E&P, and *then* by the Issuing corporation to the extent of its E&P. (Code Sec. 304(b)(2))[42] The parties to transactions subject to Code Sec. 304 entered into with a principal purpose of avoiding its application to certain corporations, however, may be recast for purposes of determining the dividend amount. (Reg § 1.304-4T)[43] In the case of a *foreign* Acquirer, (a) the amount of E&P that can support a deemed dividend is limited to E&P attributable to stock of a U.S. shareholder accumulated while Acquiring was a controlled foreign corporation (CFC) (¶4623 *et seq.*) and (b) its E&P is not taken into account if more that 50% of the consequent dividend would *neither* be (i) subject to U.S. tax for the year of the dividend, *nor* includible in the E&P of a CFC (Code Sec. 304(b)(5)).[44]

If a deemed distribution from a stock sale between brother-sister corporations is treated as a dividend, (1) the stock that was sold is deemed to have been transferred by Issuing to Acquiring for stock of Issuing in a tax-free transfer to a controlled corporation, and (2) Acquiring is deemed to have redeemed the stock that is treated as having been issued to it in the constructive transfer, preventing Issuing from using the dividends-received deduction to

---

34. ¶F-11509; ¶3024.06; TD ¶242,614
35. ¶F-11516 *et seq.*; ¶3024.06; TD ¶242,608
36. ¶F-11600 *et seq.*; ¶3034.01; TD ¶243,001
37. ¶F-11605 *et seq.*; ¶3034.01; TD ¶243,013 *et seq.*
38. ¶F-11613; ¶3034.01; TD ¶243,018
39. ¶F-11617; ¶3034.01; TD ¶243,009

40. ¶F-11701 *et seq.*; ¶3044 *et seq.*; TD ¶243,301 *et seq.*
41. ¶F-11704; ¶s 3044.02, 3044.03; TD ¶243,301
42. ¶F-11706; ¶3044.03TD ¶243,305
43. ¶F-11707; ¶3044.05; TD ¶243,305
44. ¶F-11719.2; ¶F-11719.3; ¶3044.04

shelter any part of the deemed distribution. (Code Sec. 304(a)(1))[45]

A corporation is a parent if it controls another corporation. (Code Sec. 304(a)(2)) A brother-sister relationship exists where the same person or persons controls each of two corporations. (Code Sec. 304(a)(1)) Control means ownership of stock possessing at least 50% of the total combined voting power of all classes of the voting stock, or at least 50% of the total value of all classes of stock. (Code Sec. 304(c)(1))[46] Constructive ownership rules similar to those at ¶3534 apply with modifications. (Code Sec. 304(c)(3)(A))[47]

The parent-sub redemption rules apply, even if, as a result of the constructive ownership rules, a brother-sister relationship also exists.[48]

¶ 3534   Constructive ownership.

For purposes of the stock redemption rules, a person is treated as owning not only his own direct holdings, but also those of certain closely related taxpayers: (Code Sec. 302(c))

. . . An individual is considered as owning stock owned, directly or indirectly, by his spouse (unless divorced or legally separated), children (including adopted children), grandchildren and parents. (Code Sec. 318(a)(1))[49]

. . . Stock owned by or for an S corporation, partnership or estate is considered as owned proportionately by its shareholders, partners, or beneficiaries. (Code Sec. 318(a)(2)(A), Code Sec. 318(a)(5)(E)) Stock owned by or for an S corporation shareholder, partner or estate beneficiary is attributed in full to the S corporation, partnership or estate. (Code Sec. 318(a)(3)(A), Code Sec. 318(a)(5)(E))[50]

. . . Stock owned by or for a trust is considered owned by its beneficiaries in proportion to their actuarial interest in the trust. (Code Sec. 318(a)(2)(B)(i)) Stock owned by or for a trust beneficiary is attributed in full to the trust unless the beneficiary's interest in the trust is a remote contingent interest. (Code Sec. 318(a)(3)(B)(i))[1]

. . . A 50%-or-more shareholder in a C corporation is considered as owning his proportionate share of stock in other corporations owned by the C corporation. (Code Sec. 318(a)(2)(C)) A C corporation is considered as owning all the stock (except its own) owned by its 50%-or-more shareholder. (Code Sec. 318(a)(3)(C))[2]

. . . The holder of an option to buy stock is treated as the owner of the stock covered by the option. (Code Sec. 318(a)(4)) This includes an option that isn't exercisable until after the lapse of a fixed time.[3]

Stock constructively owned is considered to be actually owned for purposes of further attribution (Code Sec. 318(a)(5)(A))[4] *except* as follows (where so-called double or sidewise attribution is prohibited):

. . . Stock constructively owned by a person under the family attribution rules won't be attributed further to make another family member the constructive owner of that stock. (Code Sec. 318(a)(5)(B))[5]

⦿*illustration:* If a father and son each own 50 shares in a corporation, each is treated as owning all 100 shares. But the father's constructive ownership of the son's shares can't be attributed from the father to his daughter (who is treated as owning her father's *actual* 50 shares).

. . . Stock constructively owned by a partnership, estate, trust or corporation can't be further attributed from the partnership, etc., to make another (partner, heir, beneficiary or

---

45. ¶F-11716; ¶3044.03; TD ¶243,311
46. ¶F-11711; ¶3044.01; TD ¶243,307
47. ¶F-11720 *et seq.*; ¶3044.01; TD ¶243,323
48. ¶F-11723; ¶3044.04; TD ¶243,321
49. ¶F-11803 *et seq.*; ¶3184.02; TD ¶243,627
50. ¶F-11812 *et seq.*; ¶3184.03; TD ¶243,615 *et seq.*

1. ¶F-11827 *et seq.*; ¶3184.04; TD ¶243,618
2. ¶F-11808 *et seq.*; ¶3184.05; TD ¶243,614
3. ¶F-11834 *et seq.*; ¶3184.06; TD ¶243,632
4. ¶F-11805
5. ¶F-11804; ¶3184.07; TD ¶243,629

shareholder) the constructive owner of that stock. (Code Sec. 318(a)(5)(C))[6]

¶ 3535 Section 306 Preferred Stock Bail-Outs. ■■■■■■■■■■■■■■■■■■■■■■■■■■■■■■

Certain stock received tax-free as a stock dividend or in a substituted basis transaction is treated as Section 306 stock. A sale or other disposition of Section 306 stock, other than by redemption, generally generates ordinary income.

¶ 3536 Dispositions of Section 306 stock.

Except as discussed below, if Section 306 stock (¶3537) is redeemed, the amount paid to the shareholders is treated as a current distribution of property subject to the normal dividend rules at ¶1287 *et seq.* (Code Sec. 306(a)(2))[7]

If Section 306 stock is sold (or otherwise disposed of) to an outsider (i.e., not a redemption), the entire amount realized is treated as ordinary income to the extent that the fair market value of the stock sold on the date of distribution would have been a dividend had the corporation distributed cash instead of stock. Ordinary income treatment is limited to E&P at the time of the distribution rather than at the time of sale. (Code Sec. 306(a)(1)(A))[8] Gain is recognized from the sale to the extent the amount received exceeds the sum of the amount treated as ordinary income plus the adjusted basis of the stock disposed of. (Code Sec. 306(a)(1)(B))[9] No loss is recognized on the sale. (Code Sec. 306(a)(1)(C))[10]

The amount realized on the disposition of Section 306 stock will not be treated as a dividend if the disposition is:

. . . A complete redemption of all the shareholder's stock (Code Sec. 306(b)(1)(B));

. . . A complete termination of a shareholder's stock interest by any other disposition that leaves him without any stock actually or constructively owned (Code Sec. 306(b)(1)(A));

. . . A partial liquidation redemption from a noncorporate shareholder (Code Sec. 306(b)(1)(B));

. . . A redemption in a complete liquidation of the corporation (Code Sec. 306(b)(2));

. . . Any nontaxable disposition, e.g., an exchange of stock in a reorganization, or a gift of the tainted stock. In this case, the stock remains tainted in the transferee's hands. (Code Sec. 306(b)(3));

. . . Any disposition (including a redemption) of Section 306 stock if IRS is satisfied that federal income tax avoidance wasn't a principal purpose (i) for the distribution and disposition of the tainted stock, or (ii) if the underlying stock is disposed of before or simultaneously with the tainted stock, for the disposition of the tainted stock. (Code Sec. 306(b)(4)) Showing that the corporation that issued the Section 306 stock is widely held isn't enough to make the exception apply.[11]

¶ 3537 Stock treated as Section 306 stock.

Section 306 stock includes:

(1) Stock received as a stock dividend, other than common issued with respect to common, any part of which was nontaxable on receipt. (Code Sec. 306(c)(1)(A)) Such stock dividends are usually preferred distributed on common.[12]

(2) Stock, other than common, received in a corporate reorganization, spin-off, split-up or split-off, to the extent that (a) the transaction was substantially the same as the receipt of a stock dividend, or (b) the stock was received in exchange for Section 306 stock. (Code

---

6. ¶s F-11811, F-11814, F-11824, F-11832; ¶3184.07; TD ¶243,623 *et seq.*
7. ¶F-12106; ¶3064.02; TD ¶244,406
8. ¶s F-12103, F-12101; ¶3064.02; TD ¶244,401
9. ¶F-12103; ¶3064.02; TD ¶244,402
10. ¶F-12103; ¶3064.02; TD ¶244,403
11. ¶F-12108 *et seq.*; ¶3064.02; TD ¶244,413
12. ¶F-12122; ¶3064.01; TD ¶244,408

Sec. 306(c)(1)(B))[13]

(3) Stock (except stock described in (2) above) whose basis is determined by reference to the basis of Section 306 stock. (Code Sec. 306(c)(1)(C))[14]

🔵*observation:* Once stock is classified as Section 306 stock, the Section 306 *taint* remains in the hand of any transferee who takes the same basis as the transferor (e.g., a donee).

(4) Preferred stock (but not nonqualified preferred stock (see ¶3556)) received in a Code Sec. 351 transfer (except for certain bank transfers), provided that if cash had been distributed instead of the preferred stock, part of the cash would have been a dividend under the related corporation redemption rules (¶3531). (Code Sec. 306(c)(3)(A))[15]

Section 306 stock does not include any stock, whatever its class, that at the time of its distribution would not in any part have been a dividend if cash had been distributed instead of stock (because the corporation had no current or accumulated E&P). (Code Sec. 306(c)(2))[16]

¶ 3538   Nonliquidating Property Distributions. ■■■■■■■■■■■■

A corporation recognizes taxable gain when it makes a nonliquidating distribution (e.g., redemption, dividend) of appreciated property (other than its own obligations) to its shareholders as if the property had been sold, at the time of the distribution, to the distributee for its then fair market value. (Code Sec. 311(b)(1))[17]

A corporation recognizes no loss on a nonliquidating distribution of property. (Code Sec. 311(a)(2))[18] IRS is authorized to issue regs to prevent circumvention of the partial liquidation provision. (Code Sec. 346(b))[19]

For how nonliquidating distributions affect E&P, see ¶3523.

¶ 3539   Distribution of property subject to a liability.

If a corporation's nonliquidating distribution consists of property subject to liabilities in excess of basis, or if a shareholder assumes liabilities of the distributor corporation in connection with the distribution, then in computing the corporation's gain on the distribution (¶3538), the property's fair market value (FMV) is treated as not less than the amount of the liabilities. (Code Sec. 311(b)(2))[20] If the liability is unsecured, it is allocated among all the distributed assets (including any asset that secures another liability) according to the assets' relative FMVs.[21]

¶ 3540   Distributions of stock or stock rights.

Except for distributions of appreciated property, a corporation doesn't recognize gain or loss on distributions (not in complete liquidation) of its own stock or of rights to acquire its own stock. (Code Sec. 311(a)(1))[22]

¶ 3541   Corporate Reorganizations. ■■■■■■■■■■■■■■■■■■■■

If one corporation transfers property to another corporation solely in exchange for stock or securities of the other corporation and the exchange is made pursuant to a plan of reorganization, neither corporation will recognize gain or loss on the exchange, provided the transaction complies with strict statutory and regulatory requirements.

---

13. ¶F-12124 *et seq.*; ¶3064.01; TD ¶244,408
14. ¶F-12128; ¶3064.01; TD ¶244,408
15. ¶F-12123; ¶3064.01; TD ¶244,408
16. ¶F-12132; ¶3064.01; TD ¶244,411
17. ¶F-14004 *et seq.*; ¶3114.01; TD ¶244,203

18. ¶F-14002; ¶3114.01; TD ¶244,209
19. ¶F-14607; ¶3114.01, ¶3024.06, ¶3464.02
20. ¶s F-14005, F-14402; ¶3114.01; TD ¶244,204
21. ¶F-14006; ¶3114.01; TD ¶244,206
22. ¶F-14002; ¶3114; TD ¶244,209

¶ 3542   Conditions common to all reorganizations.

The following definitions and requirements apply to all reorganization types, with exceptions noted. Failure to meet any requirement may disqualify a reorganization and result in gain recognition and/or dividend treatment.[23]

Plan of reorganization. An exchange must be pursuant to plan of reorganization. (Code Sec. 354(a)(1); Reg § 1.368-2(c), (Reg § 1.368-2(g))[24] The plan must be adopted by each party to the reorganization (see below) and each party must include a statement on its return pursuant to regs. (Reg § 1.368-2(c))[25]

Party to a reorganization. A corporation whose stock or securities are exchanged must be a party to the reorganization for nonrecognition treatment to apply. (Code Sec. 354(a)(1))[26] This includes any corporation resulting from a reorganization and, in the case of an acquisition by one corporation of the stock or properties of another, both corporations. The parent of the acquiring corporation in a Type B, Type C, or Type G reorganization is a party to the reorganization if its stock is the consideration for the acquisition of assets or stock. A parent of the surviving corporation in a statutory merger is a party to the reorganization if its stock is used as consideration and the transaction qualifies as a Type A reorganization under Code Sec. 368(a)(2)(D) or Code Sec. 368(a)(2)(E). If assets or stock received in a Type A, Type B, Type C, or Type G reorganization are dropped down under Code Sec. 368(a)(2)(C), the corporation controlling the transferee is a party to the reorganization. (Code Sec. 368(b)) (Reg § 1.368-2(f))[27]

Continuity of interest. The regulatory continuity of proprietary interest doctrine incorporates the judicial requirement that the former target shareholders retain a significant equity participation in the target corporation after the reorganization. A proprietary interest in the target is sufficiently preserved if (1) it is exchanged for a proprietary interest in the issuing corporation, (2) it is exchanged by the acquiring corporation for a direct interest in the target corporation enterprise, or (3) it otherwise continues as a proprietary interest in the target corporation. (Reg § 1.368-1(e))[28]

Continuity of business enterprise. An acquiring corporation must either (1) continue the target's historic business (generally, its most recent business unless the most recent business was entered under the plan of reorganization), or (2) use a significant portion of the target's historic business assets in a business. (Reg § 1.368-1(d)(1), Reg § 1.368-1(d)(2)) The business may be conducted by, or the assets held through, one or more members of the acquiring corporation's qualified group, i.e., one or more chains of corporations connected through stock ownership, if the acquiring corporation has 80% control of at least one of them and each of the other corporations is controlled by one of the other corporations). (Reg § 1.368-1(d)(4)(ii))[29]

Business purpose. A transaction that is structured as a reorganization but has no business purpose is not in the nature of a reorganization and is not treated as such.[30]

The continuity of interest and continuity of business enterprise requirements do not apply to (i) recapitalizations involving a single corporation, i.e., Type E reorganizations, (¶3548).[31] or (ii) change-in-identity reorganizations, i.e., Type F reorganizations (¶3549). (Reg § 1.368-1(b))[32]

¶ 3543   Reorganizations involving investment companies.

If two or more investment companies are parties to a transaction, the transaction cannot qualify as a nonrecognition reorganization with respect to either company or the holders of its

---

23. ¶F-3500 *et seq.*; ¶3684; TD ¶232,508
24. ¶s F-4009; ¶3684.09; TD ¶232,509
25. ¶F-4118; ¶3684.09
26. ¶F-4013 *et seq.*; ¶3684.08; TD ¶232,501
27. ¶F-4013; ¶3684.08; TD ¶232,517

28. ¶s F-3501, F-3600 *et seq.*; ¶3684.10; TD ¶236,202
29. ¶F-3701 *et seq.*; ¶3684.11; TD ¶236,401
30. ¶F-3800 *et seq.*; ¶3684.12, ¶79,006.07; TD ¶236,500 *et seq.*
31. ¶F-3626; ¶3684.05; TD ¶236,221
32. ¶F-3107; ¶3684.06; TD ¶236,408

stock and securities (Code Sec. 368(a)(2)(F)(ii)),[33] unless it was a RIC,[34] REIT,[35] or a corporation that meets specific diversified investment company requirements. (Code Sec. 368(a)(2)(F)(i))[36]

¶ 3544   Type A: Merger or consolidation.

A Type A reorganization is a merger or consolidation effected under statutory law (including foreign laws). (Code Sec. 368(a)(1)(A); Reg § 1.368-2(b)(1)(ii))[37] The merger of a disregarded entity into a corporation doesn't qualify as a tax-free statutory merger or consolidation, although the merger of a corporation into a disregarded entity may qualify. (Reg § 1.368-2)[38]

¶ 3545   Type B: Acquisition of stock in exchange for stock.

A Type B reorganization is the acquisition by one corporation of stock in a second (target) corporation in exchange *solely for voting stock* of the acquiring corporation (or voting stock of its parent in the case of a triangular Type B reorganization (¶3551)), if the acquiring corporation is in *control* (¶3553) of the target immediately after the exchange. (Code Sec. 368(a)(1)(B)) An acquiring corporation that transfers property other than voting stock in connection with a Type B reorganization plan (e.g., to nonshareholders) doesn't violate the *solely for voting stock* requirement as long as the target's *stock* is acquired solely for voting stock.[39]

¶ 3546   Type C: Acquisition of a target's assets for stock.

A Type C reorganization is the acquisition by one corporation of *substantially all* of the properties of a target corporation in exchange for voting stock of the acquiring corporation (or the stock of its parent in the case of a triangular C reorganization (¶3551)). Except as noted below, liabilities assumed by the acquiring corporation are disregarded. (Code Sec. 368(a)(1)(C))[40]

There is no definition of *substantially all* of a target's properties or rules on what portion of the assets the target can safely retain.[41] For purposes of a favorable IRS ruling, the target must transfer at least 90% of the fair market value (FMV) of the net assets and at least 70% of the FMV of the gross assets that it held immediately before the transfer.[42]

A transaction won't qualify as a C reorganization unless the target, under the plan of reorganization, liquidates and distributes to its shareholders all stock, securities and other property received under the plan, as well as its other properties. IRS may waive this distribution requirement under certain conditions. (Code Sec. 368(a)(2)(G))[43]

To satisfy the *solely for voting stock* requirement, at least 80% of the FMV of property received must be acquired solely for voting stock. The remainder of the property may be acquired for cash or other property. If any cash or other property is transferred, liabilities assumed with respect to acquired properties are treated as cash. (Code Sec. 368(a)(2)(B))[44] Preexisting ownership by an acquiring corporation of a portion of the target's stock does not, in and of itself, prevent the solely for voting stock requirement from being satisfied. (Reg § 1.368-2(d)(4))[45]

---

33. ¶F-2103; ¶3684.14
34. ¶E-6001; ¶8514
35. ¶E-6500; ¶8564
36. ¶F-2101 *et seq.*; ¶3684.14
37. ¶F-2201 *et seq.*; ¶3684.01; TD ¶234,100
38. ¶F-2201.2 *et seq.*; ¶3684.01
39. ¶F-2500 *et seq.*; ¶3684.02; TD ¶234,601 *et seq.*

40. ¶F-2600 *et seq.*; ¶3684.03; TD ¶235,001
41. ¶F-2618; ¶3684.03; TD ¶235,018
42. ¶F-2618, F-2620; ¶3684.03; TD ¶235,020
43. ¶F-2629; ¶3684.03; TD ¶235,025
44. ¶F-2613; ¶3684.03; TD ¶235,014
45. ¶F-2617; ¶3684.03; TD ¶235,017

¶ 3547   Type D: Transfer of assets to subsidiary.

A Type D reorganization is the transfer by one corporation of all or part of its assets to a second corporation, if, immediately after the transfer, the transferor and/or its shareholders are in control (¶3553) of the transferee corporation *and* the transferor satisfies a distribution requirement by:

. . . distributing all of the assets (including stock and securities) of the transferee to its shareholders under a plan of reorganization as a part of the transferor's liquidation (*acquisitive* or *nondivisive* D); or

. . . distributing the stock and securities of the transferee in a tax-free spin-off, split-off or split-up (corporate separation, or *divisive* D (¶3559 *et seq.*). (Code Sec. 368(a)(1)(D))[46]

The distribution requirements of Code Sec. 368(a)(1)(D) and Code Sec. 354(b)(1)(B) are deemed satisfied even if no stock is actually distributed in cases where the same person or persons own(s) directly or indirectly all of the stock of the transferor and transferee corporations in the same proportions. Except in certain related party triangular reorganizations, if FMV is paid for the assets, the transferee is deemed to issue a nominal share of stock to the transferor, which is deemed further distributed as necessary to reflect actual ownership. (Reg § 1.368-2(l)(2))[47]

An acquiring corporation's transfer of target corporation assets to a controlled subsidiary as part of a plan of reorganization may not disqualify an otherwise qualifying D reorganization. (Reg § 1.368-2(k))[48]

A Type D reorganization may also qualify as a Type C, in which case it will be treated only as a Type D. (Code Sec. 368(a)(2)(A))[49]

¶ 3548   Type E: Recapitalization.

A Type E reorganization is a recapitalization (Code Sec. 368(a)(1)(E)) or change in the capital structure of a single corporation. A recapitalization may be achieved through an exchange of stock for stock, bonds for bonds, stock for bonds, or bonds for stock. Recapitalizations include:

. . . An issuance of preferred stock in discharge of outstanding bonds;

. . . An exchange of one class of common for another class of common, or preferred for common (provided that new preferred is not Section 306 stock (¶3534)), or vice-versa;

. . . An exchange of old bonds for new bonds with a different face value, interest rate or the like;

. . . Changes in stock or securities effected by a change in the corporate charter. (Reg § 1.368-2(e))[50]

¶ 3549   Type F: Change in Identity.

A Type F reorganization is limited to a change in identity, form or place of organization *of one corporation* (Code Sec. 368(a)(1)(F)), but may include a reincorporation as part of a plan that includes a public stock offering, a merger, or a C reorganization.[1]

¶ 3550   Type G: Bankruptcy.

A Type G reorganization is the transfer by a corporation of all or part of its assets to another corporation (including a bridge bank) under a court-approved reorganization plan in

---

46. ¶s F-2004, F-2700 *et seq.*; ¶3684.04; TD ¶237,000
47. ¶F-2708 *et seq.*; ¶3684.041;
48. ¶F-2702.1

49. ¶s F-2004, F-2700 *et seq.*; ¶3684.04; TD ¶237,000
50. ¶F-3000 *et seq.*; ¶3684.05; TD ¶235,601
1. ¶F-3100 *et seq.*; ¶3684.06; TD ¶235,801

a Title 11 or similar case (e.g., bankruptcy, receivership, or foreclosure), but only if stock or securities of the corporation to which the assets are transferred are distributed in a transaction that qualifies under Code Sec. 354, Code Sec. 355, or Code Sec. 356. (Code Sec. 368(a)(1)(G), Code Sec. 368(a)(3)(A))[2] The acquirer can use parent stock to acquire the debtor corporation in a triangular Type G reorganization. (Code Sec. 368(a)(2)(D))[3]

¶ 3551 Triangular reorganizations.

Tax free treatment applies to the following triangular reorganizations in which the acquirer's parent is a party to the transaction:

(1) *Forward triangular merger.* Where the acquirer uses parent stock to acquire *substantially all* of the target's assets (¶3546), the transaction is a forward triangular merger. If certain requirements are met, a forward triangular merger qualifies as a Type A reorganization. (Code Sec. 368(a)(2)(D))[4]

(2) *Triangular C reorganization.* Where the acquiring corporation acquires substantially all the assets of the target corporation solely in exchange for all or a part of the voting stock of the acquirer's parent, the transaction qualifies as a triangular Type C reorganization.[5] The acquiring corporation can distribute to its parent (i.e., have its parent assume) a substantial portion of the target's liabilities that it assumed without disqualifying the Type C reorganization. (Reg § 1.368-2(k)(1)(i))[6] A triangular reorganization qualifies for Type B treatment if acquirer acquires target stock solely in exchange for parent stock.[7]

(3) *Reverse triangular merger.* If the acquiring corporation acquires enough of target's stock for control and then merges into the target with the target surviving, the transaction is a reverse triangular merger. (Code Sec. 368(a)(2)(E))[8] A reverse triangular merger is tax-free despite a later sale of half of the target's operating assets.[9] If certain requirements are met, a reverse triangular merger may qualify as a Type A or Type B reorganization. (Reg § 1.368-2(k)(1)(ii))[10]

¶ 3552 Transfer of property acquired in a reorganization.

An otherwise tax-free reorganization is not disqualified by one or more later (or successive) transfers of assets or stock, provided that (i) there is continuity of business enterprise, (ii) target's corporate existence is not terminated in connection with the drop-down, and (iii) the drop-down does not cause the target to cease to be a member of the qualified group. (Reg § 1.368-2(k))[11]

¶ 3553 Control defined.

For purposes of the rules for reorganizations (other than nondivisive Type Ds), *control* is the ownership of: (i) stock possessing at least 80% of the total combined voting power of all voting stock, and (ii) at least 80% of the total number of shares of each class of nonvoting stock. (Code Sec. 368(c))[12] For nondivisive Type Ds, *control* is defined under the related corporation redemption rules (i.e., 50%, rather than 80%, ownership, see ¶3533). (Code Sec. 368(a)(2)(H)(i))[13]

If the corporate division requirements of Code Sec. 355 (¶3560) are satisfied, control isn't affected by later transfers by shareholders of the distributed controlled corporation stock or by the issuance by the corporation whose stock was distributed of additional stock. (Code

2. ¶F-3200 *et seq.*; ¶3684.07; TD ¶236,001
3. ¶F-3207; ¶3684.07; TD ¶236,007
4. ¶F-2301 *et seq.*; ¶3684.01; TD ¶234,200
5. ¶F-2650; TD ¶235,028
6. ¶F-2651 *et seq.*; ¶3684.08; TD ¶235,028
7. ¶F-2551; ¶3684.08; TD ¶234,614
8. ¶F-2401 *et seq.*; ¶3684.01; TD ¶234,400
9. ¶F-2413
10. ¶F-2400; ¶3684.01; TD ¶234,401
11. ¶F-2308, ¶F-3251; ¶3684.135; TD ¶234,209, TD ¶234,414, TD ¶235,027
12. ¶F-4502, ¶F-5500 *et seq.*; ¶3684.13; TD ¶236,701
13. ¶F-2702; ¶3684.13; TD ¶235,404

Sec. 368(a)(2)(H)(ii))[14]

¶ 3554 How shareholders are taxed in a reorganization.

If, under a plan of reorganization, the holder of stock or securities receives only stock in a corporation that's a party to the reorganization, the recipient recognizes no gain or loss. Nonrecognition also applies when securities of a corporate party to the reorganization are received in exchange for other securities, if the principal (face) amount of the securities received isn't more than the face amount given up. (Code Sec. 354(a)(1))[15] Nonqualified preferred stock (¶3556) received for stock that isn't nonqualified preferred stock is not treated as stock or securities for these purposes unless it's received in a recapitalization (¶3548) of a family-owned corporation. (Code Sec. 354(a)(2)(C))[16] Stock rights (except to acquire nonqualified preferred stock (¶3556)) (Reg § 1.356-6(a)(2))[17] not received as part of a family corporation recapitalization (¶3548) (Reg § 1.356-6(b)(1)) are treated as securities with no principal amount. (Reg § 1.354-1(e), Reg § 1.355-1(c))[18] For the treatment of nonqualified preferred stock and excess securities as boot, see ¶3556.

Type D and Type G reorganizations are not tax-free unless (i) the transferee corporation receives substantially all of the transferor's assets, and (ii) the stock, securities and other property received by the transferor, as well as its remaining assets, are distributed by the transferor under the reorganization plan. (Code Sec. 354(b))[19]

If nonrecognition would apply but for the fact that property other than stock or securities (i.e., boot (¶3556)) is also received in the exchange, gain is recognized up to the sum of the boot received. (Code Sec. 356(a)(1))[20] Gain recognized in a reorganization with boot is treated as a dividend if the exchange has the effect of a distribution (see ¶3526). The gain is treated as ordinary income to the extent of the taxpayer's ratable share of the accumulated E&P of the distributing corporation and the balance is treated as gain from the sale or exchange of property. (Code Sec. 356(a)(2))[21]

For basis of property received in the exchange, see ¶2488.

¶ 3555 How the corporate parties are taxed in a reorganization.

No gain or loss is recognized by a corporation that is a party to a reorganization (¶3542) and that exchanges property solely for stock or securities of another corporation that is also a party to that reorganization. (Code Sec. 361(a))[22] If the corporation receives other property or money (boot, see ¶3556) in addition to stock or securities, then if the corporation distributes all of the boot, it doesn't recognize gain on the exchange (but may recognize gain on the distribution of appreciated property, see below). However, if the corporation does not distribute any part of the boot, gain is recognized on the exchange but only to the extent of the undistributed boot. (Code Sec. 361(b))[23]

Gain or loss isn't recognized on the distribution of *qualified property* received under the plan of reorganization. Qualified property is stock (or the right to acquire stock) in the distributing corporation, and stock or obligations of another party to the reorganization that are received in the reorganization exchange. Gain (but not loss) is recognized on the distribution of property that isn't qualified property. (Code Sec. 361(c))[24]

For acquirer's basis in property received in the exchange, see ¶2484. For target's basis, see ¶2486.

14. ¶F-4502; ¶3684.13; TD ¶237,003
15. ¶F-4001, F-4022; ¶s 3544.01, 3544.03; TD ¶232,501
16. ¶F-4001, F-4001.1; ¶s 3544.01, 3544.03; TD ¶232,501
17. ¶F-4012.1; TD ¶232,515
18. ¶F-4012; ¶3544.06; TD ¶232,514
19. ¶s F-2701, F-3205; ¶3544.02; TD ¶235,401
20. ¶F-4017; ¶3564.02; TD ¶232,529
21. ¶F-4017; ¶3564.02; TD ¶232,533
22. ¶F-4100 et seq.; ¶3614.01; TD ¶233,001
23. ¶F-4106 et seq.; ¶3614.01; TD ¶233,003
24. ¶F-4108 et seq.; ¶3614.03; TD ¶233,007

¶ 3556   Boot.

Boot is money or the fair market value (FMV) of property other than stock or securities of a party to the reorganization (¶3542) that's received by the target in exchange for its property, or by target shareholders in exchange for their stock, under the plan of reorganization.[25] Nonqualified preferred stock received for stock other than nonqualified preferred stock is boot unless received in a recapitalization of a family-owned corporation. (Code Sec. 356(e))[26] Nonqualified preferred stock is generally preferred stock that the issuer is required to redeem, or is more likely than not to redeem, or preferred stock with a dividend rate that varies with changes in interest rates or other similar indices. (Code Sec. 351(g)(2))[27] For the effect of liabilities on characterization of property as boot, see ¶3557.

Securities in corporations not parties to the reorganization are always boot and gain is taxable to the extent of the securities' FMV. In the case of securities in corporations that are parties to the reorganization, only the excess face amount of securities received over the face amount of securities surrendered is boot. If no securities are surrendered, the FMV of any securities received is boot. (Code Sec. 354(a)(2), Code Sec. 356(d)) A stock right treated as a security having no principal amount (¶3554) isn't boot whether or not securities are surrendered in the exchange. (Reg § 1.356-3(b))[28]

¶ 3557   Assumption and transfer of liabilities.

Where a party to a reorganization (¶3542) exchanges property for stock or securities in a corporation and the corporation assumes the transferor's liabilities, the assumed liabilities are not treated as boot (¶3556) for the purpose of *recognizing* gain. (Code Sec. 357(a))[29] However, if the principal purpose for the assumption of the liabilities is tax avoidance, or is something other than a bona fide business purpose, *all the liabilities assumed* are treated as cash (i.e., boot) for purposes of both computing *and* recognizing gain. (Code Sec. 357(b))[30]

If, in the case of a Type D reorganization (¶3547) in which stock or securities of the transferee corporation are distributed in a qualifying tax-free separation under Code Sec. 355 (¶3559), the sum of the liabilities assumed exceeds the total adjusted basis of the property transferred, the excess is taxed as a gain from the sale or exchange of property (capital gain or ordinary, depending on the character of the property in the hands of the transferor). (Code Sec. 357(c))[31]

For what constitutes assumption of a liability, see ¶3516.

¶ 3558   Deductibility of reorganization costs.

Generally, expenses incurred in connection with a corporate reorganization, including the cost of borrowing, are capital expenditures, (¶1654 *et seq.*) and not deductible business expenses. If a proposed reorganization is abandoned, the costs are deductible in the year of abandonment.[32]

¶ 3559   Spin-Offs, Split-Offs and Split-Ups.

A corporate division may be accomplished on a tax-free basis in the form of a (1) *spin-off*, i.e., a pro rata distribution of a controlled corporation's stock to the distributing corporation's shareholders without requiring the shareholders to surrender any of their distributing corporation stock; (2) *split-off*, i.e., a pro rata or non pro rata distribution of a controlled corporation's stock to one or more of the distributing corporation's shareholders in exchange for stock held in the distributing corporation;

25. ¶F-4017; ¶3564.01; TD ¶231,305
26. ¶F-4001.1; ¶3564.01; TD ¶231,305
27. ¶F-1530; ¶3514.13; TD ¶231,306
28. ¶F-4021 *et seq.*; ¶3564.01; TD ¶238,006
29. ¶F-4201; ¶3574.01; TD ¶231,501
30. ¶F-4202; ¶3574.02; TD ¶231,504
31. ¶F-4203; ¶3574.03; TD ¶233,203
32. ¶L-5401; ¶L-5416; ¶2484; TD ¶301,047, TD ¶301,037

or (3) *split-up*, i.e., a transfer of all the businesses of a distributing corporation to controlled corporations followed by a distribution of the stock of the controlled corporations to the distributing corporation's shareholders and the liquidation of the distributing corporation. The distribution of controlled corporation stock to the distributing corporation's shareholders can be pro rata or non pro rata.[33]

¶ 3560 Requirements for a tax-free spin-off, split-off or split-up.

The following requirements for nonrecognition apply to spin-offs, split-offs, or split-ups.

(1) The distributing corporation (P) must distribute to its shareholders with respect to their stock, or to its security holders in exchange for their securities, solely stock or securities in a corporation (S) that it "controls" (¶3553) immediately before the distribution. (Code Sec. 355(a)(1)) Nonqualified preferred stock (¶3514) received in exchange for other than nonqualified preferred stock is not treated as stock or securities for this purpose. (Code Sec. 355(a)(3)(D))[34]

(2) The transaction must not be used principally as a device for distributing earnings and profits (E&P) of either P or S. (Code Sec. 355(a)(1)(B)) The regs identify "device factors" (the presence of which are evidence of a device) and nondevice factors, and certain distributions that aren't ordinarily considered to have been used principally as a device even though device factors are present. (Reg § 1.355-2(d))[35]

(3) There must be continuity of interest (¶3542), i.e., P's pre-distribution shareholders must end up with an amount of stock that establishes a continuity of interest in both P and S, though not necessarily proportionately (see (6), below). (Reg § 1.355-2(c)(1))[36]

(4) Both P and S (or each controlled subsidiary) must be engaged in the active conduct of a trade or business immediately after the distribution. (Code Sec. 355(b)(1)(A)) For distributions made before 2011, a corporation satisfies the active conduct of a trade or business test if and only if it is engaged in the active conduct of a trade or business (Code Sec. 355(b)(2)(A)) with all members of the corporation's separate affiliated group (SAG) being treated as one corporation. (Code Sec. 355(b)(3)(A))[37] The trades or businesses must have been actively conducted throughout the five-year period ending on the date S's stock is distributed. (Code Sec. 355(b)(2)(B))[38]

(5) The active trade or business (see 4 above) must not have been acquired during the five-year period ending on the date S's stock is distributed in a transaction in which gain or loss was recognized. (Code Sec. 355(b)(2)(C))[39]

(6) A distribution doesn't qualify as a tax-free Code Sec. 355 division if immediately after the transaction (including any series of related transactions) (1) either the distributing or controlled corporation is a disqualified investment corporation,[40] and (2) any person that did not hold 50% or more by vote or value in the disqualified investment corporation immediately before the transaction holds a 50% or greater interest (voting or value). (Code Sec. Sec. 355(g))[41]

(7) P must distribute either all its stock or securities in S, or at least an amount of S stock that's treated as "control" (¶3553). The distributions don't have to be pro rata or under a plan of reorganization. However, if P retains *any* stock or securities in S, tax avoidance must not be a principal purpose for the retention. (Code Sec. 355(a)(1)(D), Code Sec. 355(a)(2))[42]

In addition, one or more corporate business purposes must support the transaction for nonrecognition treatment to apply. (Reg § 1.355-2(b))[43] IRS established guidelines for

---

33. ¶F-4600 *et seq.*; ¶3554.01; TD ¶237,001
34. ¶F-4608; ¶3544.01; TD ¶237,002
35. ¶F-4701 *et seq.*; ¶3554.01; TD ¶237,201
36. ¶F-4613; ¶3554.03; TD ¶237,014
37. ¶F-4802 *et seq.*; ¶3554.02; TD ¶237,426.1
38. ¶F-4819; ¶3554.02; TD ¶237,403

39. ¶F-4826 *et seq.*; ¶3554.02; TD ¶237,409
40. ¶F-5403; ¶3554.035
41. ¶F-5401; ¶3554.035; TD ¶237,004.1
42. ¶F-4602 *et seq.*; ¶3544.01; TD ¶237,007
43. ¶F-4900 *et seq.*; ¶3554.03; TD ¶237,701

whether a corporate business purpose exists.[44]

¶ 3561   Boot taxed to shareholders in Sec. 355 transactions.

The receipt of boot in an otherwise tax-free spin-off, split-off or split-up (¶3560) may trigger shareholder tax. Boot includes cash and the fair market value of:

. . . Any property (including stock warrants, short-term notes, etc.) *except* (and subject to the limitations below) stock or securities (other than nonqualified preferred stock (¶3556) (Code Sec. 356(e)) in the spun-off corporation (S) (Code Sec. 356(a));

. . . Any excess in the face amount of securities of S received over the face amount of securities in distributing corporation (P) which are surrendered. (Code Sec. 355(a)(3)(A), Code Sec. 356(d)(2)(C)) Stock rights are treated as securities having no principal amounts. (Reg § 1.355-1(c))

. . . Stock in S that P acquired in a partially or wholly taxable transaction during the five-year period preceding the distribution. (Code Sec. 355(a)(3)(B))[45]

Boot received in a spin-off (where no stock or securities of P are surrendered) is treated like a Code Sec. 301 dividend (¶1288). (Code Sec. 356(b))[46]

Boot received in a split-off or split-up (where stock or securities of P are surrendered) is taxable to the recipient to the extent gain is recognized, but not in excess of the value of the boot received. (Code Sec. 356(a)(1)) If, however, the exchange "has the effect of the distribution of a dividend," it is treated as a dividend to the extent of the taxpayer's ratable share of accumulated earnings and profits. The remainder, if any, of the recognized gain is generally treated as capital gain. (Code Sec. 356(a)(2))[47] In determining whether boot has the effect of a dividend, the transaction is treated as though the shareholder had retained the P stock which he actually surrendered in exchange for S stock, and had received the boot in exchange for an amount of P stock with a value equal to the amount of the boot; the redemption rules (¶3526 *et seq.*) are then applied to determine whether the boot is treated as a dividend.[48]

No loss is recognized, whether or not boot is received. (Code Sec. 355(a), Code Sec. 356(c))[49]

For shareholders' basis in property received, see ¶2488.

¶ 3562   How distributing corporation is taxed.

No gain or loss is generally recognized by a distributing corporation (P) on its distribution of stock or securities of a corporation it controls (S) in a tax-free corporate separation (Code Sec. 355(c)(1), Code Sec. 361), with the following exceptions.

(1) The distribution is *disqualified* (as defined below), in which case P recognizes gain (but not loss) as if the property were sold for its fair market value (FMV). If the distributee assumes a liability to which the property was subject, the property's FMV will be no less than the assumed liability. (Code Sec. 355(c)(2), Code Sec. 355(d)(1) *et seq.*)[50]

(2) Pursuant to *a plan or series of related transactions*, there is an acquisition (direct or indirect) of an interest greater than or equal to 50% in either S or P following the distribution, in which case P generally must recognize gain as if it had sold the stock or securities of S to the distributee for FMV immediately before the distribution. (Code Sec. 355(e)) Regulations discuss factors for and against a finding of a plan or a series of related transactions and describe nine safe harbors to avoid gain recognition. (Reg § 1.355-7)[1]

Tax-free division treatment isn't available for distributions from one affiliated group member to another except as provided in regulations if it is part of a plan under which any person

---

44. ¶F-4902 *et seq.*; ¶3554.03; TD ¶237,702
45. ¶F-5003 *et seq.*; ¶s 3554.01, 3564.02; TD ¶238,004 *et seq.*
46. ¶F-5000 *et seq.*; ¶3564.02; TD ¶238,004
47. ¶F-5000 *et seq.*; ¶3564.02; TD ¶238,003
48. ¶F-4026; ¶3564.02; TD ¶232,534
49. ¶F-5000 *et seq.*; ¶3564.02; TD ¶238,204
50. ¶F-5201 *et seq.*; ¶s 3554.01, 3554.04; TD ¶238,205
1. ¶F-5301; ¶s 3554 *et seq.*

acquires (directly or indirectly) an interest greater than or equal to 50% in either P or S, determined after application of Code Sec. 355(e). (Code Sec. 355(f))[2]

A distribution is disqualified (unless it doesn't violate the purpose of Code Sec. 355(d) (Reg § 1.355-6(c)(4)(i))) if (1) immediately after the distribution any shareholder (or any two or more shareholders acting under a plan (Reg § 1.355-6(b)(3))) hold (actually or constructively) at least 50% of the stock of P or S, and (2) that stock was purchased (or acquired) within the immediately preceding five-year period, or was received as a distribution on P stock that was purchased (or acquired) during that period. (Code Sec. 355(c), Code Sec. 355(d))[3]

Changes in proportionate ownership attributable solely to fluctuations in the relative FMV of different classes of stock are generally not considered in determining stock ownership under Code Sec. 382. (Code Sec. 382(l)(3)(C)) In interim guidance, IRS indicated that it won't challenge a reasonable application of either a full value methodology or the hold constant principle (including certain HCP alternative methodologies) that is applied consistently.[4]

¶ 3563 Carryovers of Tax Items.

A corporation that acquires the assets of another corporation in certain tax-free reorganizations or liquidations also succeeds to and takes into account numerous tax items of the transferor (predecessor) corporation.

A predecessor's tax items are carried over to the successor corporation in a:

... Type A, C or F reorganization;

... Type D or G reorganization, but only if the transferor transfers substantially all its assets to the acquiring corporation and then (in effect) completely liquidates; or

... Complete liquidation of an 80% subsidiary. (Code Sec. 381(a))[5]

The carryover rules do not generally apply to divisive reorganizations, but items may be carried overed under general principles of corporate succession. (Reg § 1.381(a)-1(b))[6]

¶ 3564 Tax attributes that are carried over.

When the Code's carryover provisions apply, the acquiring corporation succeeds to and takes into account the following tax items of the transferor: (Code Sec. 381(c)) accounting method; amortization of bond discount or premium; capital loss carryovers; charitable contributions carryover; depreciation allowance and method; earnings and profits (E&P); employee benefit plan contributions; general business credit; installment method; inventory method; involuntary conversions; minimum tax credit; mining development and exploration expenses; net operating loss carryovers; percentage depletion on extraction of ores or minerals from waste or residue of earlier mining; personal holding company (PHC) deficiency dividend; PHC dividend carryover; real estate investment trust (REIT) or regulated investment company (RIC, or mutual fund) deficiency dividend; tax benefit items; items under Subchapter U (dealing with enterprise zones), as prescribed by regs.[7]

Tax attributes to which an acquiring corporation succeeds, including the basis of property acquired, must reflect reductions for cancellation of debt. (Reg § 1.108-7(c))[8]

¶ 3565 Tax Avoidance Acquisition Bar to Tax Benefits.

Under Code Sec. 269, any deduction, credit or other allowance may be disallowed where, for the principal purpose of tax avoidance:

... Any person or persons acquire, directly or indirectly, stock having at least 50% of the

2. ¶F-4630 *et seq.*; TD ¶237,004
3. ¶F-5202 *et seq.*; ¶3554.04; TD ¶238,404
4. ¶F-7505.1
5. ¶F-7000 *et seq.*; ¶3814.01; TD ¶240,100
6. ¶F-7005; ¶F-7013; ¶3814.01; TD ¶240,100
7. ¶F-7012, F-7098, F-7099; ¶3814.02; TD ¶240,101
8. ¶J-7404.2; ¶1084.02; TD ¶188,016.1

total combined voting power of all classes of a corporation's voting stock, or at least 50% of the total value of all classes of its stock; or

... Any corporation acquires, directly or indirectly, property of another corporation not controlled, directly or indirectly, by the acquirer (or its shareholders) immediately before the acquisition, if the acquirer takes a carryover basis in the property. (Code Sec. 269(a))[9]

IRS may also disallow tax attributes where a target that a corporation acquired in a qualified stock purchase (¶3583) *without* making a Code Sec. 338 election (¶3581) is liquidated primarily for tax avoidance or evasion, under a plan of liquidation adopted within two years after the acquisition date. (Code Sec. 269(b))[10]

¶ 3566   Limits On Use of Built-in Gains of One Corporation to Offset Losses of Another Corporation. ▬▬▬▬▬▬▬▬▬▬▬▬▬▬▬▬▬

When one corporation is acquired by another corporation, there are limits on the extent to which built-in gains of one of the corporations (gain corporation) can be used to offset the other corporation's pre-acquisition losses. Specifically, if a corporation acquires directly (or through one or more other corporations) control of another corporation, or acquires the assets of another corporation in a Type A, Type C or Type D reorganization, and either corporation is a gain corporation, then any income of either corporation attributable to recognized built-in gain within a five year period beginning on the date of the ownership change (¶3571) can't be offset by any pre-acquisition loss of the other corporation. (Code Sec. 384(a))[11] Control means stock ownership that satisfies the requirements at ¶3342. (Code Sec. 384(c)(5))[12]

Similar rules limit the use of any excess credit or net capital loss. (Code Sec. 384(d))[13]

The above offset prohibition doesn't apply to any pre-acquisition loss of any corporation if that corporation and the gain corporation were members of the same controlled group at all times during the five-year period ending on the acquisition date (or shorter period of either corporation's existence). (Code Sec. 384(b))[14]

¶ 3567   Trafficking in NOLs and Other Carryovers—Section 382 Limitation. ▬▬▬▬▬▬▬▬

If an ownership change occurs with respect to a loss corporation, that corporation's taxable income for any post-change year can be offset by pre-change losses only to the extent of a certain percent of the value of the corporation at the time of the change. Similar rules limit the use of capital loss carryovers and carryovers of certain credits.

¶ 3568   The Section 382 limitation on loss carryovers after an ownership change.

A *loss corporation* is entitled to use a net operating loss (NOL) carryover or has an NOL for the tax year in which an ownership change (¶3571) occurs (Code Sec. 382(k)(1))[15] and may offset taxable income for any tax year ending after the ownership change by pre-change loss carryforwards only to the extent of the Section 382 limitation for that year. (Code Sec. 382(a))[16] The Section 382 limitation for any post-change year is equal to the value of the loss corporation immediately before the ownership change multiplied by the long-term tax exempt rate (¶3569). (Code Sec. 382(b)(1))[17] Value for Code Sec. 382 purposes is determined under special rules. (Code Sec. 382(e)(1), Code Sec. 382(e)(2), Code Sec. 382(l)(1)(A), Code Sec. 382(l)(4))[18]

If a loss corporation has net unrealized built-in gain on the change date in excess of a defined amount, the Section 382 limitation may be increased by recognized built-in gains on

9. ¶F-7900 *et seq.*; ¶2694; TD ¶240,702
10. ¶F-7923 *et seq.*; ¶2694; TD ¶240,703
11. ¶s F-7851, F-7852; ¶3844 *et seq.*; TD ¶240,801
12. ¶F-7853; ¶3844.01; TD ¶240,813
13. ¶F-7875 *et seq.*; ¶3844.04; TD ¶240,806
14. ¶F-7860 *et seq.*; ¶3844.01; TD ¶240,804
15. ¶F-7203; ¶3824.01
16. ¶F-7201; ¶3824.01; TD ¶240,302
17. ¶F-7251; ¶3824.12; TD ¶240,314
18. ¶F-7301 *et seq.*; ¶3824.12; TD ¶240,315

an asset within the five-year period starting on the date of the ownership change (recognition period), but only if the asset was held immediately before the change date and only to the extent of the excess of the asset's fair market value over its adjusted basis on that date. Prepaid income is not treated as built-in gain. The limitation may also be increased by certain recognized Code Sec. 338 gains. (Code Sec. 382(h)(1), Code Sec. 382(h)(6))[19] The disallowed portion of a recognized built-in loss can be carried forward (but not back) like an NOL subject to the Section 382 limitation in later years as if it were a pre-change NOL. IRS guidance describes two alternative safe harbors to determine built-in income and deduction items after an ownership change.[20]

Special rules apply to determine the amount (and applicability) of the Section 382 limitation for the tax year in which the ownership change occurs. (Code Sec. 382(b)(3))[21] The Section 382 limitation doesn't apply if the old loss corporation is under the jurisdiction of a court in a bankruptcy, receivership, foreclosure, or similar proceeding (unless it elects not to have this exception apply). (Code Sec. 382(l)(5); Reg § 1.382-9(i))[22] Special rules apply for consolidated (Reg § 1.1502-90 to Reg § 1.1502-96, and Reg § 1.1502-98 to Reg § 1.1502-99) and controlled groups (Reg § 1.382-8), and for successive ownership changes. (Reg § 1.382-5(d))

¶ 3569   Long-term tax-exempt rate.

The long-term tax exempt rate is the highest of the adjusted federal long-term rates for any month in the three-calendar month period ending with the month in which the ownership change occurs. (Code Sec. 382(f))[23] The long-term tax-exempt rate for ownership changes in:[24]

Nov. 2010 is 3.86%	July 2010 is 4.01%	Mar. 2010 is 4.03%
Oct. 2010 is 3.98%	June 2010 is 4.01%	Feb. 2010 is 4.14%
Sep. 2010 is 3.99%	May 2010 is 4.03%	Jan. 2010 is 4.14%
Aug 2010 is 4.01%	Apr. 2010 is 4.03%	Dec. 2009 is 4.16%

¶ 3570   Pre-change losses and credits subject to Section 382 limitation.

The Section 382 limitation (¶3568) applies to (1) any net operating losses (NOLs) of the old loss corporation that are carried forward to the tax year ending with the ownership change or in which the change date occurs; (2) any NOL of the old loss corporation for the tax year in which the ownership change occurs to the extent the loss is allocable to the period in that year on or before the change date; (3) any recognized built-in loss for any tax year if a part of that tax year is in the recognition period (¶3568); (4) any pre-change capital loss (below); and (5) any pre-change credits (below). (Code Sec. 382(d)(1); Reg § 1.382-2(a)(2))[25] Pre-change capital losses are losses described in (1)–(3), but with respect to capital losses. (Reg § 1.383-1(c)(2))[26] Pre-change credits are excess foreign taxes under Code Sec. 904(c), unused Code Sec. 38 business credits, and the available Code Sec. 53 minimum tax credit, to the extent attributable to periods ending on or before the change date. (Reg § 1.383-1(c)(3))[27]

¶ 3571   Ownership change defined.

There is an ownership change if, immediately after any owner shift involving a 5% shareholder or an equity structure shift, the stock of the loss corporation owned by one or more 5% shareholders has increased by more the 50 percentage points over these shareholders' lowest percent ownership at any time during a three-year testing period. (Code Sec. 382(g)(1))[28]

A 5% shareholder is any person holding 5% or more by value of the stock of the corporation at any time during the testing period. (Code Sec. 382(h)(7)) The percent of stock owned is

---

19. ¶F-7340*et seq.*; ¶3824.25; TD ¶240,319 *et seq.*
20. ¶F-7340 *et seq.*; ¶3824.25; TD ¶240,321
21. ¶F-7255 *et seq.*; ¶3824.12; TD ¶240,323
22. ¶F-7700 *et seq.*; ¶3824.26; TD ¶240,325
23. ¶F-7336; ¶3824.12; TD ¶240,316

24. ¶F-7336; ¶3824.12; TD ¶240,316
25. ¶F-7363; ¶s 3824, 3824.01, 3824.25
26. ¶F-7386; ¶3834.01; TD ¶240,329
27. ¶F-7408; ¶3834.01; TD ¶240,330
28. ¶F-7441; ¶3824.02; TD ¶240,303

determined on the basis of value and nonvoting preferred stock is generally not taken into account. (Code Sec. 382(k)(6))[29] Certain nonstock interests may be treated as stock. (Reg § 1.382-2T(f)(18)(iii))[30] Special aggregation rules apply to treat groups of shareholders as single shareholders. (Reg § 1.382-2T)[31]

¶ 3572 Limitations on credit and capital loss carryforwards—Section 383 limitation.

Code Sec. 383 provides limitations on the use of unused general business credits, unused minimum tax credits, excess foreign taxes and net capital losses similar to the limits on net operating loss carryovers. If an ownership change occurs in a loss corporation, the Section 382 limitation (¶3568) for a post-change year applies to limit the amount of taxable income and regular tax liability that may be offset, respectively, by pre-change capital losses and pre-change credits (¶3570) of the new loss corporation. (Code Sec. 383; Reg § 1.383-1(b))[32]

¶ 3573 Order of loss absorption for Section 382 limitation.

A loss corporation must absorb its Section 382 limitation in the following order for each post-change year: (1) pre-change losses that are built-in capital losses recognized during that year, (2) pre-change losses that are capital loss carryovers, (3) pre-change losses that are built-in ordinary losses recognized during that year, (4) pre-change losses that are net operating loss carryovers, (5) pre-change credits for excess foreign taxes carried forward under Code Sec. 904(c), (6) pre-change credits that are unused general business credits carried over under Code Sec. 39, and (7) pre-change credits that are unused minimum tax credits under Code Sec. 53. (Reg § 1.383-1(d)(2))[33]

The losses absorb the Section 382 limitation on a dollar-for-dollar basis, but the credits must be converted to a "deduction equivalent" for this purpose. (Reg § 1.383-1(e)(2))[34]

¶ 3574 Corporate Liquidations.

If a corporation distributes its assets to its shareholders in complete liquidation, the shareholders generally recognize capital gain or loss on the receipt of the distributions. A corporation generally recognizes taxable gain or loss on the distribution or sale of property in liquidation.

¶ 3575 Shareholder's tax on liquidating distributions.

Amounts received by a shareholder in a distribution in complete liquidation of a corporation are treated as payment in exchange for the stock (i.e., capital gain or loss). (Code Sec. 331(a))[35] Gain or loss is the total amount distributed minus the shareholder's basis in his stock. (Reg § 1.331-1(b)) The amount of the distribution is the sum of the cash plus the fair market value of any other property (reduced by any liability assumed) received by the shareholder in exchange for his stock. (Code Sec. 1001(b))[36]

A shareholder who receives a series of distributions in complete liquidation of a corporation reports gain only after the cost or other basis of all of the shareholder's stock has been recovered.[37]

For basis of property received in the distribution, see ¶2490.

---

29. ¶F-7505 *et seq.*; ¶s 3824.01, 3824.10; TD ¶240,303
30. ¶F-7603; ¶3824.10; TD ¶240,312
31. ¶F-7500 *et seq.*; ¶3824.15
32. ¶F-7400 *et seq.*, ¶E-8953.1; ¶3834.01; TD ¶240,328
33. ¶F-7360, F-7405; ¶3834.01; TD ¶240,331

34. ¶F-7361, F-7404; ¶3834.01; TD ¶240,331
35. ¶F-13101; ¶3314.01; TD ¶245,401
36. ¶F-13108; ¶3314.01; TD ¶245,402
37. ¶F-13112; ¶3314.01; TD ¶245,406

¶ 3576 How corporations are taxed on liquidation.

A liquidating corporation recognizes taxable gain or loss on distributions of property as if the property had been sold to the distributee for its fair market value (FMV). (Code Sec. 336(a)) If the distributed property is subject to a liability, or if any shareholder assumes a liability of the liquidating corporation in connection with the distribution, the property's FMV is treated as not less than the amount of the liability. (Code Sec. 336(b))[38]

Exceptions apply for gain or loss on liquidating distributions made (i) by an 80%-owned subsidiary to its parent (¶3577), and (ii) in connection with tax-free reorganizations (¶3553, ¶3560). (Code Sec. 336(c))[39]

¶ 3577 Liquidation of 80% subsidiaries.

When a parent corporation completely liquidates its 80%-owned subsidiary, the *parent* (as shareholder) doesn't recognize gain or loss on the liquidating distributions (Code Sec. 332(a)), whether *cash* or other property is distributed,[40] if the following requirements are met:

(1) The parent owns at least 80% of the sub stock by vote and value on the date the plan of liquidation is adopted and until the final liquidating distribution is received. (Code Sec. 332(b)(1))[41]

(2) The distributions are made under a plan of *complete* liquidation, and in complete redemption of all of the sub's stock. (Code Sec. 332(b)(2), Code Sec. 332(b)(3))[42]

(3) The distributions are made within one taxable year of the subsidiary, or within three years from the close of the taxable year during which the first of the series of distributions under the plan of liquidation is made. (Code Sec. 332(b); Reg § 1.332-4(a))[43]

In the case of an 80% subsidiary liquidation that qualifies for nonrecognition treatment, the parent takes a carryover basis in the distributed assets. (Code Sec. 334(b)(1))[44] Special rules apply to subsidiary liquidations when the subsidiary is indebted to its parent. (Reg § 1.332-7)[45]

Where a distribution from a RIC or a REIT qualifies as a distribution in complete liquidation of the RIC or REIT under Code Sec. 332(b),[46] the corporation receiving the distribution is required to include in income as a dividend from the RIC or REIT an amount equal to the dividends-paid deduction allowable to the RIC or REIT by reason of the distribution.[47] (Code Sec. 332(c))

Minority shareholders of a subsidiary must generally recognize gain or loss under the regular liquidation rules (¶3575). (Reg § 1.332-5)[48]

¶ 3578 How 80% subsidiary is taxed on liquidating distributions.

A sub doesn't recognize any gain or loss on liquidating distributions to its 80% distributee-parent, but it does recognize gain (but not loss) on distributions to minority shareholders. (Code Sec. 336(d)(3), Code Sec. 337(a))[49] However, a C corporation generally recognizes gain on property converted to RIC or REIT property unless the RIC or REIT elects to be subject to Code Sec. 1374 (¶3365) built-in gain treatment. (Reg § 1.337(d)-7(c)(1))

38. ¶F-14401 *et seq.*; ¶3364.01; TD ¶245,201 *et seq.*
39. ¶F-14401 *et seq.*; ¶3364.01; TD ¶233,011
40. ¶F-13200 *et seq.*; ¶3324; TD ¶245,701
41. ¶F-13202 *et seq.*; ¶3324.01; TD ¶245,703
42. ¶F-13207 *et seq.*; ¶3324.01; TD ¶245,714
43. ¶F-13209; ¶3324.01; TD ¶245,712
44. ¶F-13227 *et seq.*; ¶3344.01; TD ¶245,733
45. ¶F-13216 *et seq.*; TD ¶245,737
46. ¶F-13201; ¶3324.02; TD ¶245,701
47. ¶D-3800 *et seq.*, ¶D-3828
48. ¶F-13223; ¶3324.01; TD ¶245,738
49. ¶F-14504; ¶3364; ¶3374.01; TD ¶246,201; TD ¶246,204

¶ 3579   Taxation of asset transfer to exempt entity or change to exempt entity status.

A corporation must recognize gain or loss on the transfer of its assets to a tax-exempt entity and on a change of its status to tax-exempt, subject to a number of exceptions. (Reg § 1.337(d)-4)[50]

¶ 3580   Deductibility of costs of corporate dissolution and liquidation.

Filing fees, attorney's and accountant's fees and other expenditures, including payments for tax advice, incurred in connection with the complete liquidation and dissolution of a corporation are generally deductible in full by the dissolved corporation.[1]

¶ 3581   Code Sec. 338 Election to Treat a Stock Purchase as an Asset Purchase. ▄▄▄▄

A corporate acquirer that makes a qualified stock purchase (¶3583) of the stock of another corporation (target) may be able to get a stepped-up basis for the target's assets by making a Code Sec. 338 election to treat the stock purchase as an asset purchase.

observation: The Code Sec. 338 election can best be used where the target has losses to offset gains, owns predominantly depreciated property, or will benefit from stepped-up basis through deductions for depreciation or amortization.

caution: If a Code Sec. 338 election is made, the target may have to recognize gain from the "sale" of its assets (see ¶3582). In addition, if the seller's basis in the target stock is less than the stock's fair market value, the seller must recognize gain on the sale of the stock.

For the consistency requirement, see ¶3584. For how and when to make the Code Sec. 338 election, see ¶3585. For an election where target is a member of a consolidated group, see ¶3586.

¶ 3582   Effect of Code Sec. 338 election.

If a Code Sec. 338 election is made, the target is treated (for tax purposes only) as two corporations: an "old target," and a "new target." The old target is treated as though it had sold its assets as of the close of the acquisition date for their FMV (i.e., the "aggregate deemed sale price") in a single transaction. (Code Sec. 338(a)(1); Reg § 1.338-4(a))[2]

observation: Gain or loss is recognized by old target on the deemed sale to the extent of the difference between the FMV of the old target's assets and its basis in those assets.

The new target is treated as though it had purchased all of the assets of the old target as of the beginning of the day after the acquisition date (Code Sec. 338(a)(2)), for an amount equal to the sum of: the grossed-up basis of the acquiring corporation's recently purchased stock, the basis of the acquiring corporation's nonrecently purchased stock, the target's liabilities, and other relevant items. This sum (as adjusted) is the target's "adjusted grossed-up basis" for the assets. (Code Sec. 338(b)(1), Code Sec. 338(b)(2); Reg § 1.338-5(b)(1))[3]

The acquirer may step up its basis in the target's assets by making a "gain recognition election" (on Form 8023, see ¶3585). (Code Sec. 338(b)(3); Reg § 1.338-5(d)(3))[4] Regs specify how basis is allocated among the target's assets. (Code Sec. 338(b)(5); Reg § 1.338-6)[5]

---

50. ¶F-14609 *et seq.*; ¶3374.03
1. ¶L-5500 *et seq.*; ¶2484; TD ¶301,048
2. ¶s F-8301, F-8302; ¶3384.05; TD ¶239,018

3. ¶F-8601 *et seq.*; ¶3384.09; TD ¶239,021
4. ¶F-8511; ¶3384.09; TD ¶239,023
5. ¶F-8601; ¶3384.10; TD ¶212,004.1

¶ 3583 "Qualified stock purchase" requirement.

The Code Sec. 338 election may be made only if the acquiring corporation makes a qualified stock purchase of the target. (Code Sec. 338(a))[6] A qualified stock purchase occurs when one corporation's (acquiring) purchase, in one or more transactions during a 12-month acquisition period, of another (target) corporation's stock, if the shares so purchased have at least 80% of the target's total combined voting power and at least 80% of the value of all the target's stock. (Code Sec. 338(d)(3))[7]

¶ 3584 Consistency as to purchases from target or target affiliate.

The Code provides that purchases by a purchasing corporation with respect to a target or a target affiliate must be treated consistently (all as stock purchases or all as asset purchases) if made within a consistency period (defined below). (Code Sec. 338(e), Code Sec. 338(f)) But under the regs, the consistency rules apply only where gain on the sale of an asset (or stock in the case a Code Sec. 338(h)(10) election applies) (¶3586) results in a step-up in the seller's basis in the target's stock under the consolidated return regs. Instead of resulting in a deemed election, the rules require the acquiring corporation to take a carryover basis in the acquired stock. (Reg § 1.338-5(a))[8]

⊘observation: A corporation recognizes gain on a sale in liquidation of the corporation. The consistency rules are limited to specific situations where the gain on the appreciated assets of the corporation isn't fully taxed.

The consistency period includes: (1) the one-year period before the beginning of the 12-month acquisition period, (2) that part of the acquisition period up to and including the acquisition date (i.e., the date on which the last purchase of stock needed to complete a qualified stock purchase is made) and (3) the one-year period beginning on the day after the acquisition date. (Code Sec. 338(h)(4)(A))[9]

¶ 3585 Making the Code Sec. 338 election—Form 8023.

The acquirer makes the Code Sec. 338 election on Form 8023 on or before the 15th day of the ninth month beginning after the month of the acquisition. (Code Sec. 338(g)(1), Code Sec. 338(g)(2); Reg § 1.338-2(d))[10] Once made, the election is irrevocable. (Code Sec. 338(g)(3))[11]

¶ 3586 Election by selling consolidated group to recognize gain or loss on deemed sale of target's assets—Code Sec. 338(h)(10) election.

In the case of a qualified stock purchase (¶3583) of the stock of a member of a selling consolidated return group (selling group), the acquiring corporation and the selling group can jointly elect (on Form 8023 (¶3585)) to have the selling group recognize (and report) gain or loss as though the target sold all of its assets in a single taxable transaction while still a member of the selling group. (Code Sec. 338(h)(10); Reg § 1.338(h)(10)-1(c))[12]

A Code Sec. 338(h)(10) election results in the following tax consequences:

. . . No gain or loss will be recognized by the selling group on the actual sale of target stock in a qualified stock purchase.

. . . The target is treated as if, at the close of the acquisition date but after the deemed sale, it had distributed all of its assets in complete liquidation under Code Sec. 331 (¶3576), or

---

6. ¶F-8101; ¶3384; TD ¶239,013
7. ¶F-8101; ¶3384.02; TD ¶239,002
8. ¶F-8201 *et seq.*; ¶3384.11; TD ¶239,015
9. ¶F-8917; ¶3384.11; TD ¶239,017

10. ¶F-8831 *et seq.*; ¶3384.01; TD ¶239,027
11. ¶F-8833; ¶3384.01; TD ¶239,027
12. ¶F-8820 *et seq.*; ¶3384.075; TD ¶239,031

under the 80% sub liquidation rules (¶3577).

. . . If the acquirer owns nonrecently purchased target stock, it is deemed to have made a "gain recognition election" with respect to that stock.

. . . The acquirer's adjusted gross-up basis in the target is determined under the rules described at ¶3582, with adjustments. (Reg § 1.338(h)(10)-1(d))[13]

¶ 3587　Collapsible Corporation Rules Repealed. ▰▰▰▰▰▰▰▰

The Jobs and Growth Tax Relief Reconciliation Act of 2003 (P.L. #108-27, 5/28/03) (as amended by the Tax Increase Prevention Act of 2005 (P.L. #109-222, 5/17/06)) repealed the collapsible corporation rules, effective for tax years beginning after 2002 and before 2011. Before the repeal, these rules denied capital gain treatment for shareholders' gains from the liquidation (or sale of stock) of their corporation where the profit was attributable to ordinary income assets of the corporation.

¶ 3588　Transfers to Foreign Corporations—Code Sec. 367 Transfers. ▰▰▰▰▰

Transfers of property to foreign corporations (outbound transfers) that would otherwise be tax-free under Code Sec. 351 or under the reorganization or liquidation provisions, are treated as transfers to non-corporate transferees for purposes of determining the extent to which gain is recognized on the transfer, unless an exception applies. (Code Sec. 367(c), Code Sec. 367(a)(1))[14]

Exception for foreign trade or business.

. . . Assets may be transferred for use in a transferee's active conduct of a trade or business located outside of the U.S. on a nonrecognition basis if transferor complies with reporting requirements under Code Sec. 6038B. (Code Sec. 367(a)(3)(A); Reg § 1.367(a)-2T(a))[15]

. . . Transfers of certain "tainted assets," e.g., inventory, installment obligations and accounts receivable, foreign currency, intangibles, depreciation recapture and leased property, are nonetheless subject to gain recognition. (Code Sec. 367(d); Reg § 1.367(a)-5T)[16]

. . . Gain realized on the transfer of assets of a foreign branch of a U.S. person to a foreign corporation in a Code Sec. 367 exchange is recognized to the extent necessary to recapture previously deducted losses. (Code Sec. 367(a)(3)(C); Reg § 1.367(a)-6T)[17] Therefore, a transferor with an overall foreign loss for foreign tax credit limitation purposes may be forced to recognize gain on the incorporation of a branch (with previously deducted losses).

Exceptions for certain stock transfers.

. . . The transfer of foreign corporation stock or securities by a U.S. person to another foreign corporation is not taxable under Code Sec. 367(a) if (i) the U.S. person owns less than 5% of the vote and value of the transferee stock immediately after the transfer, or (ii) the U.S. person enters into a gain recognition agreement ("GRA," see below) with respect to the transferred stock or securities. (Code Sec. 367(a)(2); Reg § 1.367(a)-3(b)(1))[18] The transfer of foreign corporation stock as part of a Type E recapitalization qualifies for nonrecognition. (Reg § 1.367(a)-3(a))[19]

. . . The transfer of U.S. stock or securities to a foreign corporation is not taxable under Code Sec. 367(a) if (i) U.S. transferors receive 50% or less of the vote and value of the transferee stock in the transaction, (ii) U.S. persons who are officers or directors of the U.S. target or 5% transferee shareholders do not own more than 50% of the transferee stock, (iii) either the U.S. transferor is not a 5% transferee shareholder, or, if the U.S. transferor is a 5% transferee shareholder, it enters into a GRA, and (iv) the transferee has been actively engaged in business for at least three years. (Reg § 1.367(a)-3(c))[20]

---

13. ¶F-8800 *et seq.*; ¶s 3384.075, 3384.09; TD ¶239,031
14. ¶F-6000 *et seq.*; ¶3674.01
15. ¶F-6101; ¶3674.02
16. ¶F-6119 *et seq.*; ¶3674.03

17. ¶F-6129 *et seq.*; ¶3674.02
18. ¶F-6202 *et seq.*; ¶3674.02
19. ¶F-6201; ¶3674.02
20. ¶F-6209 *et seq.*; ¶3674.02

The exceptions for transfers of assets used in a foreign trade or business and foreign stock do not generally apply to Code Sec. 361(a) and Code Sec. 361(b) outbound transfers incident to a reorganization. (Code Sec. 367(a)(5))[21] However, proposed regs upon which taxpayers may currently rely contain an elective exception under which, if five or fewer domestic corporations are in Code Sec. 368(c) control (¶3553) of the transferor corporation and subject to basis adjustment regs, the exceptions may apply to asset reorganizations under Code Sec. 361(a) or Code Sec. 361(b). (Prop Reg. § 1.367(a)-7)[22]

Qualification under some exceptions may require a GRA under which the U.S. transferor generally agrees to include in income any gain not recognized on the original transfer of stock or securities to the foreign corporation if the foreign transferee disposes of the stock or securities within five years. Certain nonrecognition transactions, however, are not triggering events when certain requirements are satisfied. (Reg § 1.367(a)-8)[23] The amount of gain recognized under a GRA when a disposition or other event requires recognition under more than one GRA is determined under an ordering rule. (Reg § 1.367(a)-8(c)(1)(ii))[24]

Outbound distributions of subsidiary stock under Code Sec. 355 are generally treated as exchanges and result in recognition of gain (but not loss) unless the distribution is made to a qualified U.S. person, i.e., a domestic corporation or a U.S. citizen or resident. (Code Sec. 367(e)(1); Reg § 1.367(e)-1)[25] Outbound parent-subsidiary liquidation distributions generally result in recognition of both gain and loss to the liquidating subsidiary. (Code Sec. 367(e)(2); Reg § 1.367(e)-2)[26] Code Sec. 381 applies to the carryover of certain tax attributes from the domestic corporation to the distributee foreign corporation (Reg § 1.367(e)-2(b)(3)(iii))[27]

---

21. ¶F-6207; ¶3674.02
22. ¶F-6239 *et seq.*; ¶3674.02
23. ¶F-6300 *et seq.*; ¶3674.02
24. ¶F-6300 *et seq.*; ¶3674.02

25. ¶F-6801, ¶F-6807; ¶3674.01
26. ¶F-6801 *et seq.*; ¶3374.01
27. ¶F-6912

Chapter 17 Partnerships

¶ 3700 Partnerships.

For tax purposes, a partnership is a business entity that has elected, or defaulted to, partnership classification under "check-the-box" entity classification regulations.

¶ 3701 Partnership defined.

A "partnership" includes a syndicate, group, pool, joint venture or other unincorporated organization through, or by means of which, any business, financial operation or venture is carried on if it isn't, within the meaning of the Code, a corporation, trust or estate. (Code Sec. 761(a))[1] Under the "check-the-box" entity classification regs, a partnership is a business entity, with two or more members, that isn't mandatorily classified as a corporation, and that has elected, or defaulted to, partnership tax status. (Reg § 301.7701-2(c))[2] Under default provisions, unless a domestic eligible entity elects otherwise, it's a partnership if it has two or more members. (Reg § 301.7701-3(b)(1)(i))[3] In general, an eligible entity that wishes to elect a classification other than its default classification, or that wishes to change its classification, does so by filing Form 8832. (Reg § 301.7701-3(c)(1)(i))[4] A partnership that changes to an association is deemed to contribute all of its assets and liabilities to the association in exchange for stock in it. Then, the partnership is deemed to liquidate by distributing the stock to its partners. (Reg § 301.7701-3(g)(1)(i))[5] An eligible entity classified as a partnership becomes disregarded as an entity separate from its owner when the entity's membership is reduced to one member. (Reg § 301.7701-3(f)(2))[6]

A qualified joint venture conducted by a husband and wife who file a joint return for the tax year is not treated as a partnership for tax purposes if the spouses so elect. (Code Sec. 761(f)(1)) IRS has stated that a qualified joint venture includes only businesses owned and operated by spouses as co-owners, and not in the name of a state law entity (including a general or limited partnership or limited liability company).[7] Each spouse's share of income is reported on Schedule C. The spouse's net earnings from self-employment is determined as if he were a sole proprietor. Thus, where a joint venture has real estate rental income that is excluded from self-employment income (¶3143), the spouses do not have self-employment income.[8]

For tax years of a partnership, see ¶2812.

For partnership tax returns (including Schedule K-1 (Form 1065)), see ¶4731.

¶ 3702 Electing large partnerships.

Simplified flow-through reporting (Form 1065-B) applies for an electing large partnership, i.e., a partnership with at least 100 partners in the prior tax year that elects simplified reporting under Code Sec. 771 through Code Sec. 777. (Code Sec. 775(a)(1))[9] These rules differ from the regular rules for tax partners (¶3715 et seq.), in that, for example, fewer partnership items pass through to partners (Code Sec. 772)[10] and limitations on deductions and credits generally are applied at the partnership level. (Code Sec. 773)[11]

¶ 3703 Limited liability companies (LLCs).

Limited liability companies (LLCs) are a creation of state law. LLCs are owned (in some cases managed) by members, who aren't personally liable for the LLC's debts or obligations. [12]

1. ¶B-1000 et seq.; ¶7614.01, 7614.03; TD ¶580,101
2. ¶D-1151; ¶77,014.15; TD ¶580,501
3. ¶D-1152; ¶77,014.15; TD ¶580,521
4. ¶D-1158; ¶77,014.15; TD ¶580,511
5. ¶D-1170; ¶77,014.155; TD ¶580,517
6. ¶D-1171; ¶77,014.165; TD ¶580,505
7. ¶B-1222; ¶7614.02
8. ¶A-6170.
9. ¶B-4401 et seq.; ¶7754; TD ¶594,101
10. ¶B-4402 et seq.; ¶7724; TD ¶594,112
11. ¶B-4410 et seq.; ¶7734; TD ¶594,109
12. ¶D-1150 et seq.; TD ¶582,500 et seq.

References beginning with a single letter are to paragraphs in RIA's Federal Tax Coordinator 2d and RIA's Analysis of Federal Taxes: Income. Those beginning with numbers are to paragraphs in RIA's United States Tax Reporter. Those beginning with TD are to paragraphs in RIA's Tax Desk.

598

Under the "check-the-box" entity classification rules (¶3701), if an LLC isn't mandatorily classified as a corporation, it's an "eligible entity" that may elect (on Form 8832) to be classified for tax purposes either as a partnership or as a corporation (Reg § 301.7701-2(c)), except that a single member LLC that doesn't elect to be a corporation is treated as not having any entity status, i.e., it can't be treated as a partnership. (Reg § 301.7701-2(a), Reg § 301.7701-2(c)(2)(i))[13]

☛ observation: If an LLC is characterized as a partnership for federal tax purposes, the limited liability company form will offer the flow-through of tax attributes, as well as limited liability. Pass-through of tax attributes and limited liability are also available to S corporations. S corporations are, however, subject to many restrictions, including restrictions on the number and kind of shareholders, which don't apply to limited liability companies.

¶ 3704 Family partnerships.

If capital isn't a material income-producing factor, a family member is recognized as a partner only if he contributes substantial services.[14]

If capital is a material income-producing factor in the enterprise, a valid family partnership may be created by gift of a capital interest. (Code Sec. 704(e)(1))[15]

The donee-partner's distributive share of partnership income is included in his gross income subject to two limitations:

... It must be determined after allowance of reasonable compensation for services rendered to the partnership by the donor.

... The donee's share attributable to donated capital must not be proportionately greater than the donor's share attributable to his capital. (Code Sec. 704(e)(2))[16]

A capital interest purchased from a partner by the partner's spouse, ancestor, lineal descendant or any trust for the primary benefit of such persons, is considered to be a gift of the partnership interest by the seller to the buyer. (Code Sec. 704(e)(3))[17]

A donee or purchaser of a capital interest in a family partnership isn't recognized as a partner unless the transfer to him is bona fide. (Reg § 1.704-1(e)(1)(iii))[18]

A minor child generally won't be recognized as a partner unless either: (1) the child is shown to be competent (despite legal disability under state law) to manage his or her own property, or (2) control of the child's interest is exercised by a fiduciary for the child's sole benefit, subject to any required judicial supervision. (Reg § 1.704-1(e)(2)(viii))[19]

¶ 3705 Election to be excluded from partnership rules.

Certain unincorporated organizations can elect to be excluded from the partnership rules, i.e., exempt from Subchapter K of the Code (or only some of those provisions under a partial exclusion election). The election is available only if the income of each separate member of the partnership can be adequately determined without computation of partnership taxable income. (Code Sec. 761(a); Reg § 1.761-2(a)(1))[20] The election is available for:

... "Investing partnerships" whose members own property as co-owners, reserve the right separately to dispose of their share of property, and aren't engaged in the active conduct of a business. (Reg § 1.761-2(a)(2))[21]

... "Operating agreement groups" under which a number of co-owners engage in the joint production, extraction or use of property, but not for the purpose of selling services or

13. ¶D-1167; ¶77,014.15
14. ¶B-3422; ¶7044.17; TD ¶588,713
15. ¶B-3402; ¶7044.14; TD ¶588,702
16. ¶B-3423; ¶7044.12; TD ¶588,714
17. ¶B-3426; ¶7044.11; TD ¶588,702
18. ¶B-3408; ¶7044.15; TD ¶588,706
19. ¶B-3416; ¶7044.15; TD ¶588,708
20. ¶B-1200 et seq.; ¶7614.02; TD ¶581,006
21. ¶B-1207; ¶7614.02; TD ¶581,012

property produced or extracted. (Reg § 1.761-2(a)(3))[22]

. . . Syndications formed for a short period by dealers in securities to underwrite, sell or distribute an issue of securities. (Code Sec. 761(a)(3))[23]

¶ 3706   Partnerships v. other forms of doing business.

Partnerships are "pass-through entities" —that is, their income is subject to tax only once, at the partner level. They share this characteristic with S corporations, but not C corporations (whose income is taxed twice, at the corporate and again at the shareholder level). Partnerships also offer these advantages over S corporations:

. . . There are no limitations on who may be a partner, or on how many persons may be partners, unlike an S corporation, which is subject to limitations on who may be a shareholder and on how many shareholders the corporation may have, see ¶3354.

. . . There is far greater flexibility in allocating the enterprise's profits, losses and credits (by means of special allocations, see ¶3724 *et seq.*) among partners of a partnership than among shareholders of an S corporation, see ¶3370.

. . . A partner's basis in his partnership interest, unlike a shareholder's basis in S corporation shares, includes the partner's share of partnership liabilities, see ¶3759 *et seq.*

¶ 3707   Organization and syndication fees.

No deduction is allowed to a partnership or to any partner for any amounts paid or incurred to organize a partnership or to promote the sale of, or to sell, an interest in that partnership, except as described below. (Code Sec. 709(a))[24]

A partnership may elect to deduct in the tax year it begins business up to $5,000 of its organization expenses. The $5,000 amount is reduced (but not below zero) by the amount, if any, by which the total of the organization expenses exceeds $50,000. Organization expenses in excess of the amount deductible in the year the partnership begins business are deductible ratably over the 180-month period beginning with the month in which it begins business. If a partnership is liquidated before the end of the 180-month period, any organization expenses not yet deducted may be deducted as a loss. (Code Sec. 709(b)(1))

A taxpayer (1) is deemed to have elected to expense/amortize organizational costs under Code Sec. 248 for the tax year in which the business begins, but (2) may forgo the deemed election by clearly electing to capitalize organizational expenditures on a timely filed Federal income tax return (including extensions) for the tax year in which the business begins. The choice of expensing/amortizing or capitalizing organizational expenditures is irrevocable and applies to all such expenditures. (Reg § 1.709-1T(b)(2))

Syndication expenses aren't amortizable and must be capitalized. They are expenses connected with the marketing of interests in the partnership. (Reg § 1.709-2(b)) Syndication expenses can't be deducted as a loss when the partnership is liquidated (Reg § 1.709-1T(b)(3)) or the syndication effort is abandoned.[25]

For an election to deduct start-up costs, see ¶1501.

¶ 3708   Partnership anti-abuse rules.

If a partnership is formed or used in connection with a transaction with a principal purpose of substantially reducing the present value of the partners' total tax liability in a manner that is inconsistent with the intent of subchapter K, IRS may recast the transaction as appropriate to achieve a tax result that is consistent with the intent of subchapter K.[26] These anti-abuse rules apply only with respect to federal income taxes. (Reg § 1.701-2(h))[27]

---

22. ¶B-1208; ¶7614.02; TD ¶581,013
23. ¶B-1215; ¶7614.02
24. ¶B-1301; ¶7094; TD ¶581,201

25. ¶B-1306; ¶7094.04; TD ¶581,207
26. ¶B-1251; ¶7014; TD ¶580,107
27. ¶B-1250 *et seq.*; ¶7014; TD ¶580,107

IRS also may treat a partnership as an aggregate of its partners, in whole or in part, (except as described below) as appropriate in order to carry out the purpose of any provision of the Code or regs. (Reg § 1.701-2(e)(1)) But IRS may not treat a partnership as an aggregate to the extent that:

(1) a Code or reg provision prescribes the treatment of a partnership (in whole or in part) as an entity and

(2) that treatment and the ultimate tax results, taking into account all the relevant facts and circumstances, are clearly contemplated by that provision. (Reg § 1.701-2(e)(2))[28]

¶ 3709 Treatment of Contributions to a Partnership. ▬▬▬▬▬▬

Contributions from a partner to a partnership are generally tax-free.

¶ 3710 Contributions to a partnership.

Whether contributions to a partnership's capital are made on formation of the partnership or later no gain or loss is ordinarily recognized to the partners or the partnership. (Code Sec. 721; Reg § 1.721-1) However, this rule doesn't apply where a partner acts in his individual capacity (not in his capacity as a partner) in a transaction with the partnership (¶3729); a partner contributes property to a partnership and the partnership assumes a liability of the partner, with the resulting decrease in the partner's liabilities being treated as a distribution of money to the contributing partner (¶3744); or in the situations listed at ¶3711 *et seq.*[29] Also, IRS has regulatory authority (1) to provide for gain recognition in cases where the gain would otherwise be transferred to foreign partners (Code Sec. 721(c)) and (2) to treat intangibles transferred to a foreign partnership as sold. (Code Sec. 721(d)) Depreciation recapture isn't triggered (Code Sec. 1245(b)(3), Code Sec. 1245(b)(6), Code Sec. 1250(d)(3))[30] and investment credit isn't recaptured as long as the transfer is a mere change in the form of conducting the business of the contributing partner. (Reg § 1.47-3(f)(6), Ex (5))[31]

For gain or loss on the distribution of contributed built-in gain or loss property, see ¶3752.

¶ 3711 Exchange fund partnerships.

Gain is recognized where a transfer of appreciated stocks, securities or other property is made to a partnership that would be treated as an investment company under Code Sec. 351 were the partnership a corporation. (Code Sec. 721(b)) The partnership is treated as an investment company if, after the exchange, over 80% of the value of its assets (excluding cash and nonconvertible debt) are held for investment and are readily marketable stocks or securities (or interests in REITs or in regulated investment companies). Specified categories of assets are treated as "stock and securities" and are taken into account, whether or not marketable, in determining investment company status.[32]

¶ 3712 Contribution of services.

Where a taxpayer receives a capital interest in a partnership in exchange for services, that interest is taxable compensation income to him. When the income must be recognized depends on the facts and circumstances, including whether there are any restrictions on the taxpayer's right to withdraw from the partnership or otherwise dispose of the partnership interest. (Reg § 1.721-1(b)(1))[33]

Where a taxpayer receives a profits interest in a partnership (even if substantially unvested) in exchange for services, IRS won't treat the transaction as giving rise to compensation income, unless: (1) the profits interest relates to a substantially certain and predictable stream of income from partnership assets; (2) the partner disposes of the profits interest

---

28. ¶B-1255; ¶7014; TD ¶580,109
29. ¶B-1401; ¶7214; TD ¶581,401
30. ¶s I-10311, I-10503; ¶7214.01; TD ¶223,114

31. ¶L-17418; ¶474.03; TD ¶381,409
32. ¶B-1410; ¶7214.02; TD ¶581,409
33. ¶B-1407 *et seq.*; ¶7214.01; TD ¶581,406

within two years; or (3) the profits interest is a limited partnership interest in a publicly traded partnership. Cases hold that no income is includible where the profit interest has only speculative value.[34]

¶ 3713   Partnership's basis in property contributed to it.

Property received by a partnership from a contributing partner takes the same basis in the partnership's hands as it had in the contributing partner's hands at the time of the contribution (increased by any gain recognized if the partnership is an "investment company partnership," see ¶3711). (Code Sec. 723; Reg § 1.723-1)[35]

¶ 3714   Partnership's holding period for contributed property.

A partnership's holding period for property contributed to it includes the contributing partner's holding period. (Code Sec. 1223(2); Reg § 1.723-1)[36]

¶ 3715   Partnership Income and Deductions. ▆▆▆▆▆▆▆▆▆▆▆▆▆▆▆▆▆

A partnership is essentially a conduit which passes through to each partner his share of income and deductions generated by the partnership.

¶ 3716   Partners taxed on partnership income.

The partners, not the partnership, are taxed on the partnership's income. (Code Sec. 701) The partnership only files an information return (Form 1065, see ¶4731) showing each partner's distributive share of the partnership income, gains, losses, etc. Each partner includes his share of these items on his own return. (Code Sec. 702)[37]

¶ 3717   Partnership taxable income.

Partnership taxable income is computed the same as an individual's except the following deductions aren't allowed:

. . . standard deduction (Code Sec. 63(c)(6)(D));

. . . personal exemptions;

. . . charitable contributions;

. . . nonbusiness expenses, medical expenses, alimony, retirement savings under Code Sec. 219 and taxes and interest paid to cooperative housing corporations;

. . . capital loss carryovers;

. . . net operating loss deduction;

. . . taxes paid to a foreign country or U.S. possession that can be taken as a credit or as a deduction (income and similar taxes);

. . . oil and gas well depletion. (Code Sec. 703(a)(2); Reg § 1.703-1(a)(2))[38]

¶ 3718   "Separately stated" items of income and deductions.

Partnerships are required to "state separately" —that is, to compute as separate items— certain classes of income and deductions. These are then directly "passed through" to the partnership's partners, who take them into account for tax purposes by including their distributive share of each of the classes as separate items on their tax returns. (Code Sec. 702(a))

Key items that must be separately stated are:

. . . charitable contributions;

---

34. ¶B-1408; ¶7214.01; TD ¶581,407
35. ¶B-1418; ¶7234.01; TD ¶581,411
36. ¶B-1419; ¶7234.01; TD ¶581,412

37. ¶B-1900 *et seq.*; ¶7014; TD ¶584,000 *et seq.*
38. ¶B-1901; ¶7034.01; TD ¶584,001

... dividends for which a dividends-received deduction is allowed to C corporations, or qualified dividend income eligible for long-term capital gains treatment by noncorporate taxpayers;

... foreign and U.S. possessions taxes eligible for foreign tax credit;

... income, gains and losses from the sale or exchange of unrealized receivables and substantially appreciated inventory;

... income, gain, loss, deduction or credit items that are specially allocated under the partnership agreement;

... intangible drilling and development expenses;

... long-term capital gains and losses (including separately reporting 28% rate gain and unrecaptured section 1250 gain, see ¶2605 *et seq.*);

... mining explorations expenditures;

... nonbusiness production of income expenses;

... recoveries of tax benefit items;

... Code Sec. 1231 gains and losses;

... short-term capital gains and losses;

... soil and water conservation expenses.

Partnerships must also separately state—and partners must separately take into account their distributive share of—any partnership item, if separately stating that item would result in a tax liability for any partner different from that partner's tax liability if the item weren't separately stated. (Reg § 1.702-1(a)(8))[39]

¶ 3719 Items not required to be separately stated.

After determining which of its items of income, gains, losses, deductions and credits must be separately stated, a partnership computes its taxable income or loss based on items that don't have to be separately stated. The partnership's partners, in computing their income tax liabilities, take into account their distributive shares of the partnership's nonseparately stated income or loss, as well as their distributive shares of each separately stated item. (Code Sec. 702(a)(8); Reg § 1.702-1(a)(9))[40]

¶ 3720 Character of partnership income.

Each item passed through to the partners and separately stated on their returns has the same character as if realized or incurred directly by the partnership. (Code Sec. 702(b); Reg § 1.702-1(b))[41]

¶ 3721 Consistent treatment on partner's and partnership's return— Form 8082.

A partner must, on his own return, treat a partnership item in a manner that's consistent with the treatment of that item on the partnership's return. (Code Sec. 6222(a)) A partner that treats a partnership item differently must notify IRS of the inconsistency on Form 8082. (Code Sec. 6222(b))[42]

The above consistency rule doesn't apply to certain small partnerships that aren't covered by the unified audit and review procedures for partnerships (¶4843). (Code Sec. 6231(a)(1)(B))[43]

---

39. ¶B-1903; ¶7024.01; TD ¶584,003
40. ¶B-1904; ¶7024.01; TD ¶584,004
41. ¶B-1905; ¶7024.02; TD ¶584,005

42. ¶B-1801; ¶62,214; TD ¶584,010
43. ¶T-2104; ¶62,214.10

¶ 3722   When partnership income is reported by the partners.

Each partner reports his distributive share of the partnership income, deductions and other items (including guaranteed salary and interest payments) for a partnership tax year on his individual return for his tax year within or with which the partnership tax year (discussed at ¶2812) ends. (Code Sec. 706(a); Reg § 1.706-1(a))[44]

If two partnership tax years end within a partner's individual tax year, he must report in that year his share of the partnership income for both partnership years.[45]

¶ 3723   Elections.

Elections affecting partnership taxable income must be made by the partnership except for certain elections involving discharge of indebtedness, foreign tax credits, mining exploration costs, and the election by nonresident alien individuals and foreign corporations regarding income from U.S. real property, which must be made by each partner for himself.[46]

¶ 3724   Partnership Allocations. ▄▄▄▄▄▄▄▄▄▄▄▄▄▄▄▄▄▄▄▄▄▄▄▄▄▄

A partner's distributive share of income, gain, loss, deduction or credit is controlled by the partnership agreement, unless there is no partnership agreement or the allocation in the agreement has no substantial economic effect; then the allocation is made in accordance with the partner's interest in the partnership.

¶ 3725   Allocation rules.

A partnership's allocations (the partners' distributive shares) of partnership income, gains, losses, deductions and credits are normally determined by the partnership agreement. (Code Sec. 704(a)) If, however, the partnership agreement fails to make such allocations, they must be determined in accord with the partners' interests in the partnership. (Code Sec. 704(b)(1)) If the partnership agreement does make allocations of partnership items, these will be respected for tax purposes if:

. . . they have substantial economic effect, see ¶3726; or

. . . they are in accord with the partners' interests in the partnership; or

. . . they are treated as being in accord with the partners' interests in the partnership. (Code Sec. 704(b); Reg § 1.704-1(b)(1))[47]

Special allocation rules apply to: built-in gain and loss property (¶3752); tax preferences associated with pre-'87 cost recovery property;[48] income, gains, losses, etc., with respect to property whose book value differs from its adjusted basis;[49] tax credits and credit recapture amounts;[50] creditable foreign taxes;[1] "excess percentage depletion;"[2] the basis of partnership oil and gas properties;[3] recapture income under Code Sec. 1245 and Code Sec. 1250;[4] and allocations attributable to the partnership's nonrecourse debt.[5]

Retroactive allocations—that is, allocations that give particular partners shares of partnership items of income, expense, etc., that were paid or accrued before these partners joined the partnership—aren't permitted. (Code Sec. 706(d)(1))[6]

Except to the extent provided in regs to be issued, if there is a change in any partner's interest during any partnership tax year, each partner's share of any "allocable cash basis item" is determined by assigning the appropriate portion of the item to each day in the period

44. ¶B-1701; ¶7064; TD ¶584,008
45. ¶B-1701; TD ¶584,008
46. ¶B-1907; ¶7034.02; TD ¶584,007
47. ¶B-2401; ¶7044 *et seq.*; TD ¶586,101
48. ¶B-2901
49. ¶B-2902; ¶7044.07; TD ¶586,101
50. ¶B-2903; ¶7044.07; TD ¶586,101

1. ¶B-2903.1; ¶7044.07
2. ¶B-2904; ¶7044.07; TD ¶586,101
3. ¶B-2905; ¶7044.07; TD ¶586,101
4. ¶B-2906 *et seq.*; ¶7044.07; TD ¶587,405
5. ¶B-3001 *et seq.*; ¶7044.08; TD ¶587,600
6. ¶B-3201; ¶7064.02; TD ¶588,501

to which the item is attributable. (Code Sec. 706(d)(2))

If a part of any allocable cash basis item is attributable to a period preceding the partnership tax year, it will be assigned to the first day of the tax year. (Code Sec. 706(d)(2)(C)) Any amount which would be allocated under that procedure to a person who is not a partner on the first day of the partnership's tax year is capitalized by the partnership and added to the basis of the partnership assets in accordance with the basis allocation rules of Code Sec. 755. (Code Sec. 706(d)(2)(D)) Similarly, a part of an item attributable to a period following the tax year is to be assigned to the last day of the tax year. (Code Sec. 706(d)(2)(C))

¶ 3726 Determining whether an allocation has substantial economic effect.

An allocation of partnership income, gain, loss, deduction or credit among partners has substantial economic effect if it passes a two-part test applied as of the end of the partnership year to which the allocation relates.

First, the allocation must have economic effect. (Reg § 1.704-1(b)(2)(i)) This means that it must be consistent with the underlying economic arrangement of the partners. An allocation will be treated as having economic effect only if throughout the full term of the partnership, the partnership agreement states:

(1) the partners' capital accounts are to be determined and maintained according to rules set forth in the regs (see ¶3727);

(2) when the partnership liquidates, or a partner's interest is liquidated, liquidating distributions are to be made according to the partners' positive capital account balances; and

(3) a partner with a deficit balance in his capital account after the liquidation of his partnership interest is unconditionally obligated to restore the amount of the deficit to the partnership. (Reg § 1.704-1(b)(2)(ii))[7]

Second, the economic effect of the allocation must be substantial. (Reg § 1.704-1(b)(2)(i)) The economic effect of an allocation is substantial if there's a reasonable possibility that it will affect substantially the dollar amounts to be received by the partners from the partnership, independent of the tax consequences. (Reg § 1.704-1(b)(2)(iii))[8]

⦿ *observation:* Generally speaking, the economic effect test is designed to ensure that partnership allocations of income and gain ultimately correspond to real distributions of money and property, and that allocations of deductions, losses and credits ultimately correspond to the partners' actual liabilities for partnership expenses and losses. The substantiality test is designed to ensure that the economic effects of an allocation don't arise principally from the tax character of the allocated item—for example, from the fact that an income item is tax-exempt or foreign-sourced, or that a loss is from the sale of partnership property used in its trade or business.

Final regs provide for how to test whether the economic effect of an allocation is substantial where partners are look-through entities (e.g., partnerships, S corps, trusts or estates), or members of a consolidated group. The tax consequences that result from the interaction of an allocation with the tax attributes of any person that is an owner, or in the case of a trust or estate, the beneficiary, of an interest in the partner must be taken into account. (Reg § 1.704-1(b)(2)(iii)(d)(1))[9]

¶ 3727 Partner capital account rules.

For partner capital accounts to be determined and maintained properly for purposes of the economic effect rules (see ¶3726), each partner's account must be increased by cash contributed by the partner (including cash treated as contributed when the partner assumes partnership liabilities), and by the fair market value of property contributed by the partner (net of

---

7. ¶B-2503 *et seq.*; ¶7044.03; TD ¶586,503
8. ¶B-2700 *et seq.*; ¶7044.02; TD ¶586,519

9. ¶B-2702; ¶7044.05; TD ¶586,520

liabilities secured by the property). The account must also be increased by the partner's allocable share of partnership income and gain, including tax-exempt income, book income (not tax income) for property whose book value differs from basis, and unrealized income with respect to accounts receivable and certain other accrued but unpaid items.

Each account must be decreased by cash distributed to the partner (including cash treated as distributed when the partnership assumes partner liabilities), and by the fair market value of property distributed to the partner (net of liabilities secured by the property). The account must also be decreased by the partner's allocable share of partnership expenditures that are neither deductible nor capitalizable, and partnership loss and deduction, including book (not tax) loss for property whose book value differs from basis, and unrealized deductions for accounts payable and certain other accrued but unpaid items.

Capital account adjustments may also be required when partnership property is revalued or distributed, and on the transfer of a partnership interest. For example, partnership property may be revalued (and capital accounts adjusted) if property is contributed by, or distributed to, a partner in exchange for a partnership interest. Revaluation is also allowed where a partnership interest is granted as payment for services.

An adjustment may also be required if an optional basis adjustment election is in effect (see ¶3775) and property is distributed or an interest is transferred. (Reg § 1.704-1(b)(2)(iv))[10]

¶ 3728 Partner's Dealings with Partnership.

Partners may deal with their partnerships in other than their capacity as partners. "Guaranteed payments" to partners are generally treated as made to nonpartners. Certain sales between partners and their partnerships establish the character of any gain, and require the deferral of loss.

¶ 3729 "Separate entity" transactions between partner and partnership.

If a partner provides services for or transfers property to his partnership, he may be treated as dealing with the partnership either as a member or as an outsider. If there's a related allocation and distribution of partnership income (direct or indirect), and the transaction on the whole is properly characterized as a sale or exchange between a partnership and an outsider, it will be treated in that way. (Code Sec. 707(a)(2)(A), Code Sec. 707(a)(2)(B))[11]

¶ 3730 Guaranteed payments.

Guaranteed payments are payments to a partner for services or capital *without regard to partnership income.*[12] Guaranteed payments for a partner's services or capital are treated like salary payments to employees or interest payments to creditors, not like partnership distributions. (Code Sec. 707(c); Reg § 1.707-1(c))[13]

For a guaranteed payment to be deductible as a business expense by the partnership, it must meet the business expense tests as if the payment had been made to a person who wasn't a member of the partnership. (Code Sec. 707(c))[14] In determining whether a partnership can deduct or must capitalize a guaranteed payment, the regular capital expenditure rules apply. (Code Sec. 707(c))[15]

When a partnership makes a guaranteed payment using property other than cash, it is treated as a sale or exchange of that property by the partnership on which gain is recognized, and not a partnership distribution treated as discussed at ¶3743.[16]

---

10. ¶B-2600 *et seq.*; ¶7044.04; TD ¶587,000
11. ¶B-2000 *et seq.*; ¶7074.01; TD ¶584,501
12. ¶B-2005; ¶7074.04; TD ¶584,505
13. ¶B-2006 *et seq.*; ¶7074.04; TD ¶584,505

14. ¶B-2001; ¶7074.04; TD ¶584,505
15. ¶B-2009; ¶7074.04; TD ¶584,507
16. ¶B-2009.1

¶ 3731 Losses on sales and exchanges with controlled partnership.

No deduction is allowed for losses from sales or exchanges between:

... a partnership and a person owning, directly or indirectly, over 50% of the capital interest, or profits interest, in the partnership; or

... two partnerships in which the same persons own over 50% of the capital or profits interests.

For constructive ownership rules, see ¶3733.

If property on which a loss was disallowed under the above rule is later sold by the transferee at a gain, the gain is taxable only to the extent it exceeds the loss previously disallowed. (Code Sec. 707(b)(1); Reg § 1.707-1(b)(1))[17]

¶ 3732 Gain on sale or exchange with controlled partnership.

The character of the property in the hands of the transferee, immediately after the transfer, determines the character of a *gain to the transferor* on a direct or indirect sale or exchange of property between:

... a partnership and a person owning, directly or indirectly, over 50% of the capital interest, or profits interest, in the partnership; or

... two partnerships in which the same persons own, directly or indirectly, more than 50% of the capital interest or profits interest in each.(Code Sec. 707(b)(2); Reg § 1.707-1(b)(2))[18]

Thus, if the property is a noncapital asset in the hands of the transferee, the transferor will have ordinary income on the sale. (Code Sec. 707(b)(2); Reg § 1.707-1(b)(2))[19]

For constructive ownership rules, see ¶3733.

¶ 3733 Constructive ownership of partnership interests.

In determining the percentage of ownership of partnership interests for purposes of ¶3731 and ¶3732, the constructive ownership rules for stock under Code Sec. 267(c) (¶2448) apply (substituting "capital or profits interest" for "stock"), except that a partner isn't considered as owning the interest of his partners (unless they are relatives, etc.). (Code Sec. 707(b)(3))[20]

¶ 3734 Limitations on a Partner's Deductible Loss. ▬▬▬▬▬

A partner's deduction for partnership losses may not exceed the basis of his interest in the partnership. However, partners (although not partnerships) are allowed loss carrybacks and carryovers.

¶ 3735 Limitation on partner's share of partnership loss.

A partner can deduct his distributive share of partnership *losses* only up to the amount of the adjusted basis of his interest in the partnership (¶3738 *et seq.*) at the end of the partnership's loss year. (Code Sec. 704(d))

Where a partnership has more than one class of losses (e.g., capital losses, Code Sec. 1231 losses, and operating losses) in the same year and a partner's total share of those losses exceeds the adjusted basis of his partnership interest, the limitation is allocated proportionately to each type of loss. (Reg § 1.704-1(d))

Excess losses disallowed to a partner in any year are carried over, and are deductible by him at the end of the partnership year in which the adjusted basis of the partner's interest at

---

17. ¶B-2016; ¶7074.03; TD ¶584,514
18. ¶B-2017; ¶7074.03; TD ¶584,515

19. ¶B-2017; ¶7074.03; TD ¶584,515
20. ¶B-2018; ¶7074.03; TD ¶584,516

the end of the year exceeds zero (before reduction by that year's loss). (Reg § 1.704-1(d)(4))[21]

For limits on a partner's loss under the at-risk rules, see ¶1805 *et seq.*, and under the passive activity rules, see ¶1814 *et seq.*, ¶1820, and ¶1830.

¶ 3736   Basis adjustments made before applying loss limitations.

In determining whether a partner's deductible share of partnership loss exceeds (and is thus limited by) his basis in his partnership interest (¶3735), the basis adjustments described at ¶3740 are made first. (Reg § 1.704-1(d)(2))[22]

¶ 3737   Loss carrybacks and carryovers.

A carryover or carryback of net operating losses isn't allowed to a partnership but a partner may carry back or carry over his share of the partnership's net business loss for any year to the extent it can't be used by that partner in the year it's passed through to him. (Code Sec. 702)[23]

¶ 3738   Basis of Partnership Interest.

A partner's basis for his interest in a partnership ("outside basis") depends on how he acquired it: It may be the amount of cash he contributed to the partnership, the adjusted basis of the property he contributed or the amount he paid to purchase it.

¶ 3739   Initial basis of partnership interest.

A partner's interest acquired by a tax-free contribution of money or property to the partnership has a basis equal to the amount of money plus the partner's adjusted basis for the property when contributed. (Code Sec. 722)[24] If the contributed property is subject to indebtedness or if liabilities of the partner are assumed by the partnership, the basis of the contributing partner's interest is reduced by the portion of the indebtedness assumed by the other partners. (Reg § 1.722-1)[25]

A partner's capital interest acquired for services has a basis equal to the value of the capital interest acquired. (Reg § 1.722-1)[26]

A partner's interest acquired by purchase or inheritance has a basis determined under the general basis rules (¶2463 *et seq.*). (Code Sec. 742; Reg § 1.742-1)[27]

A partner may have a divided holding period in his partnership interest, see ¶2669. (Reg § 1.1223-3)[28]

¶ 3740   Adjustments to basis of partner's interest.

The basis of a partner's interest is increased:

... by further contributions (but not by his own personal note given to the partnership);[29]

... by the cost of additional interests purchased or inherited (¶3739) (Code Sec. 742);

... by any increase in his share of partnership liabilities since the increase is treated as a contribution of money to the partnership, see ¶3760;[30]

... by his distributive share of partnership income, including tax-exempt income and any excess of net long-term capital gains over losses (Code Sec. 705(a)(1));

... by his distributive share of the excess of percentage depletion deductions over the basis of the depletable property. (Code Sec. 705(a)(1))[31]

21. ¶B-3500 *et seq.*; ¶7044.10; TD ¶589,001 *et seq.*
22. ¶B-3501 *et seq.*; ¶7044.10; TD ¶589,001
23. ¶B-3508; ¶7024.01; TD ¶589,007
24. ¶B-1502; ¶7224.01; TD ¶581,418
25. ¶B-1506; ¶7224.01; TD ¶581,422
26. ¶B-1502; ¶7224.02; TD ¶581,418
27. ¶B-1501; ¶7424.01; TD ¶581,415
28. ¶I-8934.1; ¶12,234.29; TD ¶223,556
29. ¶B-1504; ¶7054.01; TD ¶581,418
30. ¶B-1506; ¶7524; TD ¶581,422
31. ¶B-1507; ¶7054.01; TD ¶581,423

The basis of a partner's interest is reduced (but not below zero) by:

. . . the adjusted basis allocable to any part of his interest sold or otherwise transferred;[32]

. . . the amount of money and the adjusted basis of partnership property distributed to him in nonliquidating distributions (Code Sec. 705(a)(2), Code Sec. 733);[33]

. . . by any decrease in his share of partnership liabilities since the decrease is treated as a distribution of money by the partnership, see ¶3760;

. . . his distributive share of partnership losses (including capital losses) *and* nondeductible expenditures not chargeable to the capital account (Code Sec. 705(a); Reg § 1.705-1(a)) (for the partner's distributive share of losses in excess of his adjusted basis, see ¶3735);

. . . his percentage depletion deduction for partnership oil and gas property to the extent the deduction doesn't exceed his allocated proportionate share of the property's basis. (Code Sec. 705(a)(3))[34]

Regs prevent the acceleration or duplication of losses through a partnership's assumption of obligations that are not treated as resulting in a deemed cash contribution or distribution by or to the partner under the rules discussed at ¶3759. These obligations are called "Reg § 1.752-7 liabilities." Where such a liability is assumed by a partnership from a partner in a property contribution by a partner to a partnership in exchange for a partnership interest (a Code Sec. 721(a) contribution), the liability is treated as having a built-in loss (see ¶3752) equal to the amount of the liability as of the date of the partnership's assumption of the liability. (Reg § 1.752-7)[35]

Regs prevent inappropriate increases or decreases in the basis of a corporate partner's interest in a partnership resulting from the partnership's disposition of the corporate partner's stock. (Reg § 1.705-2)[36]

¶ 3741 Alternative adjusted basis computation.

The adjusted basis of a partner's interest may be determined under a "short-cut" method by reference to what would be his proportionate share of the adjusted basis of the partnership property upon a termination of the partnership (Code Sec. 705(b)) where: (1) it isn't practicable to use the regular rule, or (2) IRS is satisfied the result under the alternative method won't vary substantially from that under the regular rule. (Reg § 1.705-1(b))[37]

¶ 3742 Distributions to a Partner.

A partnership generally doesn't recognize gain or loss on a distribution to a partner, but the partner often will recognize gain or loss.

¶ 3743 Partnership's gain or loss on distribution.

No gain or loss is recognized to a partnership on a distribution to a partner of money or other property, except where a disproportionate distribution is treated as a sale by the partnership, see ¶3755. (Code Sec. 731(b)) This rule applies generally to both current and liquidating distributions.[38]

¶ 3744 Partner's gain or loss on receipt of distribution.

Gain or loss isn't recognized to a partner on receipt of a current or liquidating distribution from a partnership, except as follows:

. . . Gain is recognized to the extent that *money* (defined to include marketable securities,

32. ¶B-3805
33. ¶B-1505; ¶7334.01; TD ¶581,423
34. ¶B-1507; ¶7054.02; TD ¶581,423
35. ¶B-1506.1; ¶7524.04; TD ¶581,422.2

36. ¶B-1504.1; ¶7054.03
37. ¶B-1514; ¶7054.04; TD ¶581,428
38. ¶B-3601; ¶7314.01; TD ¶589,501

see ¶3745) distributed exceeds the adjusted basis of the partner's interest in the partnership immediately before the distribution. (Code Sec. 731(a))[39] This is treated as a gain from sale or exchange of the partner's interest. (Reg § 1.731-1(a)(3))[40] A reduction in a partner's liabilities (due either to the partnership's assumption of them or a reduction in the partner's share of partnership liabilities) is treated as a money distribution. (Code Sec. 752(b))[41]

. . . Loss is recognized to the extent the adjusted basis of the partner's interest exceeds the sum of any money, and the basis to the distributee of any unrealized receivables and inventories received if the distribution is in liquidation of the partner's interest in the partnership *and* no other property is distributed. This is treated as a loss from sale or exchange of the partner's interest in the partnership. (Code Sec. 731(a))[42]

If gain or loss is recognized under one of the above rules, the partnership may elect to, or may have to, adjust the basis of its assets, as explained at ¶3775 *et seq.*

The above rules on recognition of a partner's gains and losses don't apply to (Code Sec. 731(c); Reg § 1.731-1(c)):[43]

. . . disproportionate distributions treated as sales or exchanges of property, see ¶3755;

. . . liquidation payments made to a retiring partner or to a deceased partner's successor in interest treated as a share of income or as guaranteed payments, see ¶3769;

. . . recognition of precontribution gain under Code Sec. 737, see ¶3752.

Where a partnership took cash it would have distributed to a partner in liquidation of his interest and used it buy a house he wanted and then distributed the house to him, the partner was treated as receiving the cash as part of distribution and not the house. Thus, the attempt to reduce the partner's gain on the distribution was unsuccessful.[44]

¶ 3745 Distribution of marketable securities treated as cash.

Subject to exceptions, a distribution of marketable securities (stock and other equity instruments, evidences of indebtedness, precious metals commodities, options, forward or futures contracts, notional principal contracts and derivatives) is treated as a distribution of money. They are taken into account at their fair market value as of the date of the distribution. (Code Sec. 731(c); Reg § 1.731-2)

Gain is recognized by a distributee partner to the extent that the cash and the fair market value of the marketable securities exceeds the basis of the partner's interest in the partnership. But where a partner realizes a loss on a distribution of marketable securities, the loss isn't recognized. These rules are applied after the application of the rules that treat a shift in the partners' interests in accounts receivables and substantially appreciated inventory as a sale. (Code Sec. 731(a))[45]

The amount of marketable securities taken into account under the above rule is reduced (but not below zero) by the excess (if any) of:

(1) the partner's distributive share of the net gain that would be recognized if all marketable securities of the same class and issuer as the distributed securities held by the partnership were sold (immediately before the transaction to which the distribution relates) by the partnership for fair market value, over

(2) the partner's distributive share of the net gain that's attributable to the marketable securities of the same class and issuer as the distributed securities held by the partnership immediately after the transaction, determined using the fair market value described in (1) above. (Code Sec. 731(c)(3)(B))

All marketable securities held by the partnership are treated as marketable securities of

---

39. ¶B-3602; ¶7314.01; TD ¶589,502
40. ¶B-3602; ¶7314.01; TD ¶589,502
41. ¶B-3608; ¶7524.01; TD ¶582,002
42. ¶B-3603; ¶7314.01; TD ¶589,508

43. ¶B-3605; ¶7314.01; TD ¶589,510
44. ¶B-3612
45. ¶B-3602.1 *et seq.*; ¶7314.01; TD ¶588,035

the same class and issuer as the distributed securities. (Reg § 1.731-2(b))[46]

¶ 3746   Partner's holding period.

A partner's holding period for property distributed to him in kind includes the period the partnership held the property. (Code Sec. 735(b)) If contributed to the partnership by a partner, the recipient partner's holding period also includes the period that the property was held by the contributing partner before contribution. (Reg § 1.735-1(b))[47]

¶ 3747   Character of certain contributed property.

When a partner contributes what was an unrealized receivable in his hands to a partnership, the partnership's gain or loss on disposition of the item will still be ordinary income or loss. (Code Sec. 724(a)) The same rule applies to contributed inventory, but in this case, ordinary income or loss will result only if the assets are disposed of by the partnership within five years of the contribution. (Code Sec. 724(b))[48]

If a partner contributes a capital asset with a basis higher than its fair market value, and the partnership disposes of it within five years of the contribution, the partnership's loss will be a capital loss to the extent of the basis/value variance upon contribution. (Code Sec. 724(c))[49]

If any of the above property is disposed of by the partnership in a nontaxable disposition, the above rules apply to the substituted basis property that results. (Code Sec. 724(d)(3))[50]

¶ 3748   Partner's basis for property received in nonliquidating distributions.

The basis to a partner of property distributed to him, in kind, other than in liquidation of his partnership interest, is the same as the property's adjusted basis to the partnership immediately before the distribution. But the basis of the property to the partner may not exceed the adjusted basis of his interest in the partnership reduced by any money distributed to him in the same transaction. (Code Sec. 732(a); Reg § 1.732-1(a))[1]

¶ 3749   Partner's basis for property distributed in liquidation.

A partner's basis for property distributed in liquidation of his partnership interest is the same as the adjusted basis for his partnership interest reduced by any money distributed to him in the same transaction. However, the partner's basis in inventory and unrealized receivables cannot exceed the basis the partnership had in such items. (Code Sec. 732(b), Code Sec. 732(c); Reg § 1.732-1(b))[2]

¶ 3750   Basis adjustments to assets of corporation whose stock is distributed to corporate partner.

A corporate partner that receives a distribution of stock in another corporation ("distributed corporation") must, subject to limitations and exceptions, reduce the basis of the distributed corporation's assets if:

. . . the corporate partner "controls" (by 80% vote and value) the distributed corporation immediately after the distribution or at any time thereafter, and

. . . the partnership's adjusted basis in the stock of the distributed corporation immediately before the distribution exceeded the corporate partner's adjusted basis in such stock immediately after the distribution. (Code Sec. 732(f)(1))[3]

---

46. ¶B-3602.2; ¶7314.01
47. ¶B-3706; ¶7354.02; TD ¶589,523
48. ¶B-1420; ¶7244; TD ¶581,413
49. ¶B-1421; ¶7244; TD ¶581,414

50. ¶B-1422; ¶7244.01; TD ¶581,415
1. ¶B-3701; ¶7324.01; TD ¶589,518
2. ¶B-3702; ¶7324.01; TD ¶589,519
3. ¶B-3704; ¶7324.03

The basis reduction equals the excess described above and is applied to the property held by the distributed corporation following the distribution, if the corporate partner then has control of the distributed corporation. (Code Sec. 732(f)(1))[4]

The basis reduction cannot exceed the lesser of:

(A) the amount by which (i) the sum of the aggregate adjusted bases of the property and the amount of money of the distributed corporation exceeds (ii) the corporate partner's adjusted basis in the stock of the distributed corporation, or

(B) the adjusted basis of any property of the distributed corporation (determined before the reduction). (Code Sec. 732(f)(3))[5]

If, in applying the basis-reduction rule, the amount by which basis is to be reduced exceeds the aggregate adjusted bases of the property of the distributed corporation, then the excess is recognized by the corporate partner as long-term capital gain and increases its basis in the stock of the distributed corporation. (Code Sec. 732(f)(4))[6]

¶ 3751   Allocation of basis to distributed property when limited by basis of partner's interest.

In a current distribution in which the partner's basis in his partnership interest is less than the partnership's basis in the property distributed and in a liquidating distribution, the partner's basis in his partnership interest (reduced by any money received) must be allocated among the distributed property in the following manner:

(1) First, to any unrealized receivables and inventory items in an amount equal to the adjusted basis of each such property to the partnership. (Code Sec. 732(c)(1)(A)(i)) If the basis to be allocated is less than the sum of the adjusted bases of these properties in the hands of the partnership, a basis decrease is applied as described below. (Code Sec. 732(c)(1)(A)(ii); Reg § 1.732-1(c)(1)(i))

(2) To the extent any basis isn't allocated under (1), basis is allocated to other distributed properties. This allocation is made by assigning to each property its adjusted basis in the hands of the partnership (Code Sec. 732(c)(1)(B)(i); Reg § 1.732-1(c)(1)(ii)) and then increasing or decreasing the basis to the extent any increase or decrease in basis is required in order for the adjusted bases of the other distributed properties to equal the remaining basis under the rules described below. (Code Sec. 732(c)(1)(B)(ii); Reg § 1.732-1(c)(1)(ii))

Any basis *increase* is allocated (i) first to properties with unrealized appreciation in proportion to their respective amounts of unrealized appreciation before such increase (but only to the extent of each property's unrealized appreciation) (Code Sec. 732(c)(2)(A); Reg § 1.732-1(c)(2)(ii)) and (ii) to the extent the required increase isn't allocated under (i), in proportion to the respective fair market values of the properties. (Code Sec. 732(c)(2)(B); Reg § 1.732-1(c)(2)(ii))

Any basis *decrease* is allocated (a) first to properties with unrealized depreciation in proportion to their respective amounts of unrealized appreciation before such decrease (but only to the extent of each property's unrealized depreciation) (Code Sec. 732(c)(3)(A); Reg § 1.732-1(c)(2)(i)) and (b) to the extent the required decrease isn't allocated under (a), in proportion to the respective bases of the properties (as adjusted under (a)). (Code Sec. 732(c)(3)(B); Reg § 1.732-1(c)(2)(i))[7]

¶ 3752   Built-in gain or loss property—seven-year rule.

If the basis of property contributed to a partnership by a partner is different from the property's fair market value at the time of contribution (i.e., there is built-in gain or loss), then the following rules apply:

4. ¶B-3704; ¶7324.03
5. ¶B-3704.1; ¶7324.03
6. ¶B-3704.2; ¶7324.03
7. ¶B-3703; ¶7324.01; TD ¶589,521

If the partnership distributes property contributed to it either directly or indirectly to a partner or partners *other than the contributing partner* within seven years of the contribution, then the distributed property is treated as sold by the partnership for its fair market value at the time of the distribution, and the contributing partner must recognize any gain or loss from this constructive sale in an amount equal to the amount of gain or loss that would have been allocated to him if the property had actually been sold. (Code Sec. 704(c)(1)(B); Reg § 1.704-4(a)(5), Ex (1))[8]

Where property is distributed to the partner *who contributed the property,* the partner will recognize as gain the lesser of (a) the excess of the fair market value of the property over the adjusted basis of the partner's interest in the partnership immediately before the distribution (reduced, but not below zero, by any money also received, where money is defined to include marketable securities, see ¶3745), or (b) the partner's net precontribution gain, i.e., the gain that would have been recognized by the distributee partner under the rules discussed, above, if all property held by the partnership immediately before the distribution that had been contributed to it by the distributee partner within seven years of the distribution, was distributed to another partner. (Code Sec. 737(a), Code Sec. 737(b))[9] Distributions of property previously contributed by the distributee partner aren't taken into account for purposes of determining (a) and (b), above. (Code Sec. 737(d)(1))[10]

Special rules apply if the partnership distributes to the contributing partner property that's of "like kind" to the contributed property (within the meaning of Code Sec. 1031, see ¶2418) to limit recognition of gain by the contributing partner. (Code Sec. 704(c)(2))[11]

The rules requiring gain recognition on distributions described above do not apply when a partnership transfers all of its assets and liabilities to a partnership in exchange for an interest in the transferee partnership, and distributes the interest to its partners in liquidation as part of the same plan (a merger). With respect to a later distribution of "built-in gain" property that was transferred, the seven-year period begins when the property was originally contributed to the transferor partnership, and not from the date of the transfer to the transferee partnership. However, the merger is considered a contribution of assets, so a new seven-year period begins but only with respect to the appreciation in value that occurred while the property was held by the transferor partnership.[12]

Income, gain, loss and deductions with respect to property which was contributed to the partnership after Mar. 31, '84 is to be shared among the partners so as to take into account the difference between the property's fair market value and its basis at the time of the contribution. (Code Sec. 704(c)(1)(A)) Built-in gain or loss must be allocated using a reasonable method, i.e., the traditional method following the ceiling rule or with curative allocations, the remedial allocation method or another method appropriate to the circumstances. (Reg § 1.704-3(a)(1)) Under anti-abuse rules, an allocation isn't reasonable if made with a view to shifting the tax consequences of built-in gain or loss among partners (including indirect partners), in a way that substantially reduces the present value of the partners' aggregate tax liability. (Reg § 1.704-3(a)(10)) With respect to property contributed before Apr. 1, '84, a similar special allocation applies only if the partnership agreement so provides.[10]

If any property contributed to a partnership after Oct. 22, 2004 has a built-in loss, then:

. . . the built-in loss is taken into account only in determining the amount of items allocated to the contributing partner, and

. . . except as provided in regs, in determining the amount of items allocated to other partners, the basis of the contributed property in the hands of the partnership is treated as being equal to its fair market value at the time of the contribution. (Code Sec. 704(c)(1)(C))

If a partnership makes an installment sale of built-in gain or loss property, the installment

---

8. ¶B-3125; ¶7044.09; TD ¶588,019
9. ¶B-3171 *et seq.*; ¶7374; TD ¶588,031
10. ¶B-3178; ¶7374.03; TD ¶588,037

11. ¶B-3151 *et seq.*; ¶7044.09; TD ¶588,025
12. ¶B-3157; ¶7044.097; TD ¶588,024
13. ¶B-3103 *et seq.*; ¶7044.09; TD ¶588,001

obligation it receives is treated as built-in gain or loss property. (Reg § 1.704-3(a)(8)(ii))[14]

¶ 3753 Character of unrealized receivables and inventory to a distributee-partner.

Gain or loss on disposition of unrealized receivables and inventory by a distributee-partner is:

... in the case of *unrealized receivables*, ordinary gain or loss; (Code Sec. 735(a)(1))

... in the case of *inventory items* (whether or not substantially appreciated) sold or exchanged within five years from the date of the distribution, ordinary gain or loss. (Code Sec. 735(a)(2)) If disposed of after five years from the date of distribution, the character of the gain or loss depends upon the character of the item in the partner's hands on the date of disposition. (Reg § 1.735-1(a)(2))[15]

¶ 3754 Disproportionate Distributions. ▬▬▬▬▬▬▬▬▬▬▬▬▬▬▬

Disproportionate distributions of partnership property that includes "unrealized receivables" and "substantially appreciated inventory" (so-called "hot assets") may trigger ordinary income, gain or loss to both the partnership and its partners.

¶ 3755 Disproportionate distributions defined.

A disproportionate distribution of partnership assets to a partner is treated as a sale or exchange that may result in recognition of gain or loss to the partner and the partnership. The rule applies to all distributions, both liquidating and nonliquidating except for: (1) a distribution of contributed property to the same partner who contributed it; and (2) liquidation payments to a retiring or deceased partner that are treated as ordinary income under the rules at ¶3769. (Code Sec. 751(b))[16]

A distribution is "disproportionate" if a partner receives more than his proportionate share of partnership property in the first of the following categories and less than his proportionate share of property in the second category, or vice versa:

... "hot assets" —unrealized receivables (including recapturable deductions, certain transfers of franchises, trademarks or trade names, see ¶3756) and substantially appreciated inventory items, see ¶3757;

... other property (including money).[17]

In such a case, a partner, in effect, sells or exchanges part or all of his share in property of one category for property of the other category, see ¶3758. The general rules on partnership distributions apply to the balance of the distribution not treated as a sale or exchange. (Reg § 1.751-1(b))[18]

The partners may agree as to which particular assets in one category shall be considered to have been sold or exchanged for particular assets in the other category. Absent such an agreement, a proportionate part of each asset relinquished in one category will be considered to have been sold or exchanged for excess assets received in the other category. (Reg § 1.751-1(g))[19]

¶ 3756 "Unrealized receivables."

Unrealized receivables include any contractual or other rights to payment for:

... goods delivered, or to be delivered, to the extent the proceeds would be treated as amounts received from sale or exchange of noncapital assets;

... services rendered, or to be rendered.

14. ¶B-3100; ¶7044.09; TD ¶588,014
15. ¶B-3705; ¶7354.01; TD ¶589,522
16. ¶B-3905 *et seq.*; ¶7514.01; TD ¶591,003

17. ¶B-3905; ¶7514.01; TD ¶591,003
18. ¶B-3910 *et seq.*; ¶7514.01; TD ¶591,006
19. ¶B-3902 *et seq.*; ¶7514.01; TD ¶591,006

Such receivables are included only to the extent not previously includible in income under the method of accounting used by the partnership. (Code Sec. 751(c))[20]

Unrealized receivables also include (other than for payments to retiring partners or deceased partners under Code Sec. 736, see ¶3769): (Code Sec. 751(c))

... depreciation recapturable under Code Sec. 1245 and Code Sec. 1250;

... mine exploration deductions recapturable under Code Sec. 617;

... soil and water conservation deductions recapturable under Code Sec. 1252;

... recapturable deductions for oil, gas or certain geothermal well intangible costs under Code Sec. 1254;

... understated rental income under a Code Sec. 467 rental agrement;[21]

... DISC stock;

... stock in certain foreign corporations as described in Code Sec. 1248 (¶4626);[22]

... market discount bonds, to the extent they would give rise to ordinary income if sold by the partnership (¶1328);

... short term obligations as defined in Code Sec. 1283 (¶1330);[23]

... franchises, trademarks or trade names whose transfer is treated as a sale of a noncapital asset under Code Sec. 1253.[24]

¶ 3757 "Inventory items" and "substantially appreciated" inventory items.

Inventory items include property properly includible in inventory and property held primarily for sale to customers in the ordinary course of business (Code Sec. 751(d)(1)), as well as:

... any other property that would produce ordinary income on sale or exchange by the partnership (Code Sec. 751(d)(2)), including accounts receivable for goods or services and unrealized receivables as described at ¶3756 (Reg § 1.751-1(d)(2)(ii));

... any other property held by the partnership that would be inventory items, as defined above, if held by the selling or distributee-partner. (Code Sec. 751(d)(3)) However, this rule doesn't apply to property actually distributed to a partner. (Reg § 1.751-1(d)(2)(iii))[25]

Inventory items are "substantially appreciated" in value if the fair market value of *all* such items (including unrealized receivables) exceeds 120% of their adjusted basis to the partnership. (Code Sec. 751(b)(3)(A)) The 120% limit is computed by excluding any item acquired principally to avoid meeting it. (Code Sec. 751(b)(3)(B))

If the test is met on the basis of all inventory items, a distribution of any inventory item is a distribution of a substantially appreciated one even though the particular item may not have appreciated at all. If the test isn't met on the basis of all items, no distribution of an inventory item is a distribution of a substantially appreciated item. (Reg § 1.751-1(d)(1))[26]

¶ 3758 Gain or loss on disproportionate distribution.

If a distributee-partner receives *more* than his share of unrealized receivables and substantially appreciated inventory items and *less* than his share of other property (including money), he is considered to have sold or exchanged the portion of his share of the other property that he relinquished for the excess unrealized receivables and substantially appreciated inventory items he received. (Reg § 1.751-1(b)(2)(i), Reg § 1.751-1(b)(2)(iii))

The partnership (as constituted after the distribution) is considered to have sold or exchanged the excess other property distributed to the partner for the unrealized receivables and substantially appreciated inventory items he relinquished. (Reg § 1.751-1(b)(2)(i),

20. ¶B-3914; ¶7514.02; TD ¶591,010
21. ¶B-3916; ¶7514.02; TD ¶591,012
22. ¶B-3918; ¶7514.02; TD ¶591,011
23. ¶B-3920; ¶7514.02; TD ¶591,013
24. ¶B-3919; ¶7514.02; TD ¶591,014
25. ¶B-3921; ¶7514.02; TD ¶591,015
26. ¶B-3922; ¶7514.02; TD ¶591,016

Reg § 1.751-1(b)(2)(ii))[27]

Rules analogous to those described above apply where the distributee partner receives a disproportionate distribution of *less* than his share of unrealized receivables and substantially appreciated inventory items and *more* than his share of other property (including money). (Reg § 1.751-1(b)(3))[28]

¶ 3759 Liabilities of Partnerships and Partners. ▃▃▃▃▃▃▃▃▃▃▃▃▃▃▃▃

Changes in partners' shares of partnership liabilities are treated as cash contributions to, or distributions by, the partnership. Partners' shares of partnership liabilities depend on whether the liability is recourse or nonrecourse.

¶ 3760 Partnership liabilities.

If a partner's share of the partnership liabilities increases, or if he assumes any partnership liabilities, it's treated as a contribution of money from the partner to the partnership. (Code Sec. 752(a); Reg § 1.752-1(b))[29]

If a partner's share of the partnership liabilities decreases, or if the partnership assumes any of his liabilities, it's treated as a distribution of money to the partner. (Code Sec. 752(b); Reg § 1.752-1(c))[30]

An unassumed liability to which property is subject is considered a liability of the owner of the property (e.g., the partnership) to the extent of its fair market value. (Code Sec. 752(c))[31]

For these purposes and for determining "Reg § 1.752-7 liabilities" (see ¶3740), a liability is any fixed or contingent obligation to make payment without regard to whether the obligation is otherwise taken into account for tax purposes. Obligations include, but are not limited to, debt obligations, environmental obligations, tort obligations, contract obligations, pension obligations, obligations under a short sale, and obligations under derivative financial instruments such as options, forward contracts, and futures contracts. (Reg § 1.752-1(a)(4)(ii))[32]

¶ 3761 Share of recourse liabilities.

A partnership debt is a recourse liability to the extent that any partner bears the economic risk of loss for the liability.[33] A partner's share of a recourse liability is the part of the economic risk of loss for the liability the partner bears. (Reg § 1.752-1(a)(1))[34]

Generally, a partner bears the economic risk of loss for a partnership liability to the extent that he (or a related person) would be obligated to pay the creditor or contribute to the partnership (and wouldn't be entitled to reimbursement) in case of a constructive liquidation. (Reg § 1.752-2(b)(1))[35]

Accordingly, a recourse loan to a limited partnership was allocated solely to the general partner so the limited partners received no basis increase (¶3760). The limited partners would be liable under state law in the event the general partner defaulted, but this possibility was too remote to constitute economic risk. As a result, when the loan proceeds were distributed to a limited partner in excess of its basis in its interest, it recognized gain on the distribution, see ¶3744.[36]

¶ 3762 Share of nonrecourse liabilities.

If no partner bears the economic risk of loss for a partnership liability (e.g., unassumed mortgages), the liability is nonrecourse. (Reg § 1.752-1(a)(2)) Nonrecourse liabilities of a partnership are first allocated among all the partners to reflect their shares of:

---

27. ¶B-3910 *et seq.*; ¶7514.01; TD ¶591,003
28. ¶B-3911; ¶7514.01; TD ¶591,008
29. ¶B-1601; ¶7524.01; TD ¶582,004
30. ¶B-1602; ¶7524.01; TD ¶582,004
31. ¶B-1608; ¶7524.01; TD ¶582,007

32. ¶B-1607; ¶7524.01.
33. ¶B-1651; ¶7524.03; TD ¶582,012
34. ¶B-1653 *et seq.*; ¶7524.03; TD ¶582,011
35. ¶B-1654 *et seq.*; ¶7524.03; TD ¶582,013
36. ¶B-1655

... "partnership minimum gain" (gain on the disposition of property subject to a nonrecourse liability that exceeds its adjusted basis); and

... the gain that would be allocated to the partners under Code Sec. 704(c), or under similar principles in connection with a revaluation of partnership property, if, in a taxable transaction, the partnership disposed of all property subject to a nonrecourse liability in satisfaction of those liabilities and for no other consideration.

Any excess is allocated among the partners in proportion to their interests in partnership profits. The partnership agreement may specify the partners' profit interests as long as those interests are reasonably consistent with allocations (which have substantial economic effect) of some significant item of partnership income or gain among the partners. Alternatively, the excess may be allocated in accordance with the manner in which it's expected that the deductions attributable to the nonrecourse debt will be allocated. In addition, the excess may be allocated based on the excess gain attributable to the property securing the liability. (Reg § 1.752-3(a))[37]

¶ 3763 Transfer and Liquidation of Partnership Interest. ▬▬▬▬▬

The transfer or liquidation of a partnership interest, while generally resulting in capital gain or loss, is subject to special rules that may turn part of the gain or loss from capital to ordinary.

¶ 3764 Liquidation v. sale of partner's interest.

Withdrawal of a partner from a partnership ordinarily may be accomplished either by a retiring partner's sale or liquidation of his interest in the partnership.

Where a partner's interest is liquidated, payments are taxable to that partner as guaranteed payments or income distributions to the extent they exceed the value of his interest in the partnership property (¶3768 *et seq.*).[38]

Where a partner *sells* his interest, payments to him that exceed his basis for his interest are capital gain except to the extent of payments for unrealized receivables and inventory items (¶3765 *et seq.*). (Code Sec. 741; Reg § 1.741-1)[39]

¶ 3765 Sale or exchange of partnership interest.

If a partner sells or exchanges all or a part of his interest in the partnership after holding it for more than one-year, he may recognize ordinary income, collectibles gain (¶2607), section 1250 gain, and residual long-term capital gain or loss. (Reg § 1.1(h)-1(a)) He recognizes ordinary income to the extent (¶3766) his gain is attributable to unrealized receivables (¶3756) and inventory (¶3757). (Code Sec. 741, Code Sec. 751(a), Code Sec. 751(c))[40]

The capital gain or loss is the difference between:

... the amount realized *reduced* by the portion attributable to unrealized receivables and inventory; *and*

... the transferor-partner's adjusted basis for the partnership interest transferred *reduced* by the portion attributable to unrealized receivables and inventory. (Reg § 1.741-1(a))[41]

The seller's collectibles gain is the amount that would be allocated to him if the partnership had sold all of its collectibles for fair market value in a fully taxable transaction immediately before the sale of the interest in the entity. (Reg § 1.1(h)-1(b)(2)(ii)) The seller must take into account under Code Sec. 1(h)(6)(A)(i) in determining his unrecaptured section 1250 gain (¶2605), the amount of "section 1250 capital gain" that would be allocated to him if the

37. ¶B-1670; ¶7524.03; TD ¶582,017
38. ¶B-3811, B-4102; ¶7364.01; TD ¶590,507
39. ¶B-3801 *et seq.*; ¶7414.01; TD ¶590,501

40. ¶B-3850 *et seq.*; ¶7414.01; TD ¶590,600 *et seq.*
41. ¶s B-3802, B-3901; ¶7414.01; TD ¶590,501

partnership had sold all of its section 1250 property in a fully taxable transaction immediately before the transfer of the partnership interest. (Reg § 1.1(h)-1(b)(3)(ii)) The amount of residual long-term capital gain or loss recognized by a selling partner is the amount of long-term capital gain or loss that the partner would recognize under Code Sec. 741 (as explained above) minus (1) the collectibles gain allocable to the sold interest, and (2) the section 1250 gain allocable to the sold interest. (Reg § 1.1(h)-1(c))

¶ 3766 Ordinary gain or loss.

To the extent that money or property received by a partner in exchange for all or part of his partnership interest is attributable to his share of partnership unrealized receivables or inventory items—collectively Code Sec. 751 property—the gain or loss is ordinary income or loss. (Code Sec. 751(a))

The income or loss realized by a partner upon the sale or exchange of its interest in Code Sec. 751 property is the amount of income or loss from Code Sec. 751 property (including any remedial allocations) that would have been allocated to the partner (to the extent attributable to the partnership interest sold or exchanged) if the partnership had sold all of its property in a fully taxable transaction for cash in an amount equal to the fair market value of such property (taking into account the Code Sec. 7701(g) rule that the fair market value must be not less than the amount of the nonrecourse debt to which the property is subject) immediately before the partner's transfer of the interest in the partnership. Gain or loss attributable to Code Sec. 751 property is ordinary gain or loss. The difference between the amount of capital gain or loss that the partner would realize in the absence of Code Sec. 751 and the amount of ordinary income or loss is capital gain or loss on the sale of its partnership interest. (Reg § 1.751-1(a)(2))[42]

The basis for unrealized receivables includes all attributable costs or expenses paid or accrued but not previously taken into account under the partnership's method of accounting. (Reg § 1.751-1(c)(2)) The basis of any potential gain from the following property (treated as unrealized receivables) is zero: (1) mining exploration expenditures recapture under Code Sec. 617; (2) gain from stock of a DISC or a former DISC under Code Sec. 995(c); (3) depreciation recapture under Code Sec. 1245 and Code Sec. 1250; (4) gain from stock of a controlled foreign corporation under Code Sec. 1248(a); (5) gain from disposition of farm land under Code Sec. 1252(a)(1); (6) gain from transfers of franchises, trademarks, or trade names under Code Sec. 1253(a); or (7) oil, gas, or geothermal wells intangible drilling and development cost recapture under Code Sec. 1254. (Reg § 1.751-1(c)(5))[43]

¶ 3767 Sale of partnership business vs. sale of partnership assets.

Where *all* of the old partners sell out, whether the transaction is a sale of the partnership interests or a sale of the partnership assets generally depends on whether what was actually transferred was a going business or simply assets.[44]

¶ 3768 Payments After Partner's Death or Retirement. ██████████

When a partner either retires or dies and payments are made in liquidation of his partnership interest, the payments are broken down into several categories, which are treated as ordinary income or capital gains.

¶ 3769 Liquidation payments to retiring or deceased partners.

These payments may be for the partner's interest in the fair market value of the partnership assets, his interest in unrealized receivables or payments under an agreement akin to mutual insurance. These amounts have to be separately considered.[45]

---

42. ¶B-3901; ¶7514.01; TD ¶591,001
43. ¶B-3903; ¶7514.02; TD ¶591,002

44. ¶B-3809; TD ¶590,508
45. ¶B-4102 *et seq.*; ¶7364.01; TD ¶592,000 *et seq.*

Liquidation payments received by a retiring partner, a partner expelled from a partnership or by a deceased partner's successor in interest are treated as distributions taxable under the rules for regular distributions discussed at ¶3744 if they are for the partner's interest in partnership property, see ¶3770. (Code Sec. 736(b)(1))[46] Payments for *substantially appreciated* inventory (¶3757) may result in ordinary income under the rules governing disproportionate distributions (see ¶3758). (Reg § 1.736-1(b)(1))

Liquidation payments that aren't in exchange for partnership property are treated either as distributive shares of partnership income (if the amount is determined with regard to partnership income), or as guaranteed payments (if the amount is determined without regard to partnership income). (Code Sec. 736(a); Reg § 1.736-1(a)(3))[47]

¶ 3770 Payment for interest in partnership property.

Payments for partnership property don't include payments to a retiring or deceased general partner in a partnership in which capital isn't a material income-producing factor for (i) unrealized receivables (which for this purpose includes only accounts receivable and unbilled amounts) or (ii) goodwill (unless the partnership agreement provides for payment with respect to goodwill). (Code Sec. 736(b)(2), Code Sec. 736(b)(3))[48]

¶ 3771 Allocation of payments between income and property.

The allocation problem comes up where payments are made over two or more years. Retirement or death payments must be allocated between the portion received in exchange for partnership property and the balance, received in the form of guaranteed payments or as a distributive share of partnership income. This allocation may be made in any manner in which the remaining partners and the withdrawing partner (or a deceased partner's successor in interest) agree. However, the *total* allocated to property must not exceed the fair market value of the property at the date of death or retirement. (Reg § 1.736-1(b)(5)(iii))

In the absence of an allocation agreement, payments will be apportioned between income and property, as follows:

. . . Payments that aren't fixed in amount are first treated as made in exchange for the partner's interest in partnership property to the extent of the value of that interest. Additional amounts are ordinary income. (Reg § 1.736-1(b)(5)(ii))

. . . Payments fixed in amount and to be received over a fixed number of years are apportioned year by year in accordance with the overall ratio of property payments to total payments. (Reg § 1.736-1(b)(5)(i))[49]

A payment for goodwill is treated as a payment made in exchange for partnership property where payment for goodwill is provided by the partnership agreement. (Reg § 1.736-1(b)(3))[50]

¶ 3772 Withdrawing partner's share of final year's income.

A retiring partner must pick up his distributive share of the partnership income for the partnership year in which he retires. His share of the partnership income for the year is allocable to him only for the portion of the year he was a member of the partnership. (Reg § 1.736-1(a)(4))[1]

¶ 3773 Income of deceased partner.

The tax year of a partnership closes with respect to a deceased partner on the date of his death. Thus, partnership items for the short partnership tax year that closes on the partner's

46. ¶B-4103; ¶7364.02; TD ¶592,001
47. ¶B-4106; ¶7364.03; TD ¶592,005
48. ¶B-4104; ¶7364.02; TD ¶592,004

49. ¶s B-4109, B-4110; ¶7364.01; TD ¶592,007
50. ¶B-4105; ¶7364.02; TD ¶592,004
1. ¶B-4107; ¶7064.02; TD ¶592,006

death are included in his final return. (Code Sec. 706(c)(2))[2]

¶ 3774   Continuation of retiring or deceased partner's partner status.

A retiring partner or a deceased partner's successor in interest who receives retirement or death payments is regarded as a partner until his entire interest in the partnership is liquidated. Thus, even a two-person partnership isn't terminated until the retiring or deceased partner's interest is liquidated. (Reg § 1.708-1(b)(1)(i), Reg § 1.736-1(a)(6))[3]

¶ 3775   Special Basis Adjustments to Partnership Property. ▬▬▬▬▬▬▬

A partnership's basis in its assets ("inside basis") is unaffected by partnership distributions and transfers of partnership interests unless the partnership makes a special basis election. Under certain circumstances, the transferee of a partnership interest may elect to adjust the basis of property distributed to him as if the partnership had made the special basis election.

¶ 3776   Post-transfer adjustments to basis.

A transfer of a partnership interest by reason of a sale or exchange or the death of a partner causes a basis adjustment of the partnership's property if a basis adjustment election under Code Sec. 754 is in effect, or if the partnership has a substantial built-in loss immediately after the transfer. (Code Sec. 743(a)) A partnership is treated as having a substantial built-in loss if the partnership's adjusted basis in the partnership property is more than $250,000 more than the fair market value of that property. (Code Sec. 743(d)(1)) IRS has issued procedures for complying with the basis adjustments required in the case of substantial built-in losses.[4]

However, a contribution of cash or property to the partnership does not cause a basis adjustment to the partnership's property, regardless of whether a basis adjustment election is in effect. (Reg § 1.743-1(a))[5] If the election is in effect, the partnership's basis in its property with respect to the transferee partner is increased by any excess of the partner's basis in his interest over his share of the basis of partnership property (or decreased if his basis in his interest is lower). (Reg § 1.743-1(b))[6] Regs provide rules for allocating the basis adjustment among the partnership's assets. (Reg § 1.755-1)[7]

¶ 3777   Post-distribution adjustments to basis of undistributed property.

The basis of partnership property is not adjusted when the partnership makes a distribution to a partner unless a basis adjustment election under Code Sec. 754 is in effect, or the partnership has a "substantial basis reduction" with respect to the distribution. (Code Sec. 734(a)) A substantial basis reduction exists where the sum of (i) the amount of the partner's loss on the distribution, and (ii) the basis increase to the distributed properties is over $250,000. (Code Sec. 734(d))[8] If an adjustment is made on a partnership distribution, the partnership's basis in its retained property (1) is increased by the amount of gain recognized by the distributee partner on the distribution, and the amount by which the basis of the distributed property in the hands of the partnership before the distribution exceeds the basis of the property in the hands of the distributee partner (Code Sec. 734(b)(1)), and (2) is decreased by the amount of loss recognized by the distributee partner on the distribution and the amount by which the basis of the distributed property in the hands of the distributee partner exceeds the basis the partnership had in the property before the distribution. (Code Sec. 734(b)(2)(B))[9] Regs provide rules for allocating the basis adjustment among the partnership's assets. (Reg § 1.755-1)[10]

2. ¶B-4202; ¶7064.02; TD ¶592,502
3. ¶B-4112; ¶7084.03; TD ¶592,010
4. ¶B-4008; ¶7434; TD ¶591,511
5. ¶B-4010; ¶7434; TD ¶591,512
6. ¶B-4007 *et seq.*; ¶7434; TD ¶591,500 *et seq.*
7. ¶B-4050 *et seq.*; ¶7554; TD ¶591,526 *et seq.*
8. ¶B-4002.1; ¶7344; TD ¶591,504
9. ¶B-4002; ¶7344.01; TD ¶591,504
10. ¶B-4021 *et seq.*; ¶7554; TD ¶591,532

However, in allocating any basis reduction in partnership property under Code Sec. 734(b) as a result of a distribution, no allocation may be made to stock in a corporation that is a partner in the partnership, or to the stock of any person related to the corporation, and any amount not allocable to stock is allocated to other partnership property. Where the reduction that must be allocated to other partnership property exceeds the aggregate adjusted basis of the other partnership property immediately before the required allocation, gain is recognized by the partnership to the extent of the excess. (Code Sec. 755(c))[11]

Where the basis of a partnership's recovery property is increased as a result of a distribution of property by the partnership, the increased portion of the basis is taken into account for depreciation purposes as if it were newly purchased recovery property that is placed in service when the distribution or transfer occurs. Any applicable recovery period and method may be used to determine the recovery (depreciation) deduction for the increased portion of the basis. However, no change in determining the recovery (depreciation) deduction for the portion of the basis of recovery property for which there is no increase is allowed. (Reg § 1.734-1(e)(1))[12]

Where the basis adjustment requires a decrease in the basis of partnership recovery property, the basis decrease must be accounted for over the remaining recovery period of the property beginning with the recovery period in which the basis is decreased. (Reg § 1.734-1(e)(2))[13]

¶ 3778 Partner's basis adjustments.

Where a partnership interest is transferred and the partnership later distributes property, but hasn't made the election described at ¶3776, the transferee-partner may elect to have the basis of the property distributed to him adjusted as if the partnership had made the election. The election to make the adjustment applies only for purposes of determining the basis of distributed property (other than money) in the partner's hands. It doesn't enable the partner to amend prior income tax returns to recompute income based on an adjusted basis. (Code Sec. 732(d)) Accordingly, in computing the adjustment, no deduction is made for any depletion or depreciation of that portion of the basis of partnership property which arises from the basis adjustment, since no depletion or depreciation on the basis adjustment for the period before the distribution is allowed or allowable unless the partnership had an election in effect. (Reg § 1.732-1(d)(1)(iv))[14]

The transferee-partner may make this election only with respect to property (other than money) distributed to him within two years after he acquired his interest by transfer. (Code Sec. 732(d))[15]

The adjustment is *required* (without regard to the two-year limit) if at the time the transferee-partner acquired the transferred partnership interest all three of the following conditions existed:

(1) The fair market value of all partnership property (other than money) exceeded 110% of its adjusted basis to the partnership.

(2) Allocation of basis under Code Sec. 732(c) (general rule for allocation of basis of distributed properties) upon a liquidation of his interest immediately after the transfer of the interest would have resulted in a shift of basis from property not subject to depreciation, depletion or amortization to property that is so subject.

(3) The post-transfer adjustment would change the basis to the transferee-partner of the property actually distributed. (Code Sec. 732(d); Reg § 1.732-1(d)(4))[16]

---

11. ¶B-4054.1; ¶7554
12. ¶B-4007; ¶7344.01; TD ¶591,509
13. ¶B-4007; ¶7344.01; TD ¶591,509
14. ¶B-4029; ¶7324.01; TD ¶591,537
15. ¶B-4029; ¶7324.01; TD ¶591,537
16. ¶B-4033; ¶7324.01; TD ¶591,540

¶ 3779　Basis of unrealized receivables and inventory items distributed to a partner.

If unrealized receivables or inventory items are distributed to a *transferee partner* who has a special basis adjustment for those assets under either the post-transfer adjustment rule (¶3776) or the distributed property adjustment rule (¶3777), the partnership's adjusted basis, immediately before distribution, of any unrealized receivables or inventory items distributed to such a partner takes into account the following portions of the post-transfer or distributed property basis adjustments that the distributee partner has for those assets:

... The entire amount of the post-transfer or distributed property basis adjustments *if* the distributee-partner receives his entire share of the fair market value of the unrealized receivables or inventory items of the partnership.

... The same proportion of the post-transfer or distributed property basis adjustments as the value of the unrealized receivables or inventory items distributed to him bears to his entire share of the total value of all those items of the partnership, *if* the distributee-partner gets less than his entire share of those items. (Reg § 1.732-2(c))[17]

¶ 3780　Electing basis adjustments.

The election to adjust the basis of the partnership assets on a distribution or a sale or transfer of a partnership interest (¶3776, ¶3777) is made by the partnership filing a statement of election with the partnership return for the tax year during which the transfer of interest or the distribution of property occurs. (Code Sec. 754; Reg § 1.754-1(b))

Once made, the election applies to all current and future distributions and transfers until revoked. (Code Sec. 754; Reg § 1.754-1(a))[18]

A transferee-partner who wishes to make the distributed property adjustment (¶3778), must elect as follows:

... If the distribution includes any depreciable, depletable, or amortizable property, elect with the return for the distribution year.

... If it doesn't include any such property, elect not later than the first tax year in which the basis of any of the distributed property is pertinent in determining the transferee-partner's tax. (Reg § 1.732-1(d)(2), Reg § 1.732-1(d)(3))[19]

¶ 3781　Terminations.

A partnership ordinarily terminates only on discontinuance of operations as a partnership, or on sale or exchange of 50% or more of the total interests in the partnership.

¶ 3782　Termination of partnership.

A partnership terminates for tax purposes (whether or not it has terminated under applicable local law) when:

... it stops doing business as a partnership, or

... 50% or more of the total interest in partnership capital and profits changes hands by sale or exchange (or by distribution, unless excepted by regs) within 12 consecutive months. (Code Sec. 708, Code Sec. 761(e); Reg § 1.708-1(b)(1))[20] There has been such a change if a corporation transfers its 50% or more interest in a partnership to a new or different corporation in connection with a tax-free corporate reorganization.[21]

---

17. ¶B-4018; TD ¶591,520
18. ¶B-4023 *et seq.*; ¶7544 *et seq.*; TD ¶591,501
19. ¶B-4031; ¶7324.01; TD ¶591,538

20. ¶B-4301; ¶7084; TD ¶594,001
21. ¶B-4303; ¶7084.05; TD ¶594,004

As a result of this sale or exchange, the partnership is deemed to transfer all of its assets and liabilities to a new partnership in exchange for an interest in the new partnership, and immediately after that, the terminated partnership is deemed to distribute interests in the new partnership to the purchasing partner and the remaining partners in liquidation of the terminated partnership, either for the continuation of the business of the new partnership or for its dissolution and winding up. (Reg § 1.708-1(b)(4))[22]

The sale may be made to an existing partner or an outsider. It may be made by one or more persons. A gift, bequest, or inheritance or liquidation of a partnership interest doesn't count; nor does a contribution of property to a partnership in exchange for a partnership interest, even if this produces a 50% or more change. (Reg § 1.708-1(b)(2))[23]

¶ 3783 Split-up of partnership.

If a partnership splits up into two or more partnerships, each resulting partnership is considered a continuation of the old partnership as long as the members of the resulting partnership had more than a 50% interest in the capital and profits of the old partnership. A resulting partnership whose members had an interest of only 50% or less in the old partnership is treated as a new partnership.

If the members of none of the resulting partnerships had more than a 50% interest in the old partnership, the old partnership is considered terminated as of the date of the division, and all the resulting partnerships are treated as new partnerships. (Code Sec. 708(b)(2)(B); Reg § 1.708-1(d)(2))[24]

Any members of the original partnership who do not become members of a resulting partnership that is treated as a continuation of the original partnership are considered to have had their partnership interests liquidated as of the date of the division. (Reg § 1.708-1(d)(1))

For divisions, the resulting partnership that is treated as the divided partnership must file a return for the tax year of the partnership that has been divided and must retain the employer identification number (EIN) of the prior partnership. All other resulting partnerships that are regarded as continuing and new partnerships must file separate returns for the tax year beginning on the day after the date of the division with new EINs for each partnership. (Reg § 1.708-1(d)(2))

---

22. ¶B-4305; ¶7084; TD ¶594,006
23. ¶B-4303; ¶7084.02; TD ¶594,004

24. ¶B-4308; ¶7084.06; TD ¶594,009

Chapter 18   Trusts—Estates—Decedents

¶ 3900   Trust and Estate Income Tax Rules ▬▬▬▬▬▬▬▬▬▬▬▬▬▬▬

Trusts and estates are generally treated as separate taxpayers and, with some important qualifications, are taxed in the same way as individuals.

¶ 3901   Taxation of trusts and estates—Form 1041.

Trust and estate income is normally taxed to the fiduciary (that is, to the trust or estate itself), if retained by the trust, or to the beneficiary, if distributed. Thus, if the fiduciary passes on income to the beneficiary, the trust or estate deducts the distributed income which then becomes taxable to the beneficiary. A special yardstick called "distributable net income" (DNI) (see ¶3935 and ¶3937), is used to limit both the amount deducted by the trust or estate as a distribution and the amount taxed to the beneficiary. (Code Sec. 643, Code Sec. 651, Code Sec. 652, Code Sec. 661, Code Sec. 662)[1]

The income that's passed on to the beneficiary has the same tax attributes in the beneficiary's hands as when received by the fiduciary, see ¶3946.

Trusts and estates compute their tax under a tightly-compressed, five-bracket tax rate schedule (¶1106) that quickly reaches the top marginal rate. (Code Sec. 1(e))[2] Trusts and estates can't use the tax tables to figure their tax. (Code Sec. 3(b)(2))

⊘ caution: For treatment of trusts and estates for AMT purposes, see ¶3200 *et seq.*

A foreign trust or estate is taxed as if it were a nonresident alien individual who isn't present in the U.S. at any time, see ¶4638 *et seq.*, subject to special rules for trusts. (Code Sec. 641(b))[3]

For income tax returns of trusts and estates (Form 1041), see ¶4732 *et seq.* Beneficiaries must report items consistently with the entity's return or notify IRS (on Form 8082) of the inconsistency. (Code Sec. 6034A(c)).[4]

For the tax years of trusts and estates, see ¶2808.

¶ 3902   Election to treat revocable trust as part of estate—Form 8855.

An election can be made to have an individual's revocable trust treated as part of his estate for income tax purposes. (Code Sec. 645) If there is an executor, the trustee and the executor make the election by filing Form 8855. If there is no executor, the trustee makes the election by filing Form 8855. (Reg § 1.645-1(c))[5]

¶ 3903   Estimated tax payments by trusts and estates—Form 1041-ES.

Trusts and certain estates must make estimated income tax payments (using Form 1041-ES and vouchers) under rules similar to those that apply to individuals, with certain adjustments. (Code Sec. 6654(l)(1))[6] Trusts and estates generally have 45 days to compute their estimated tax payments under the annualization rules. (Code Sec. 6654(l)(4))[7]

Estates and grantor trusts that receive the residue of a probate estate are exempt from making estimated tax payments for their first two tax years after the date of decedent's death. (Code Sec. 6654(l)(2))[8] Charitable trusts subject to tax under Code Sec. 511 are subject to corporate, not individual estimated taxes. (Code Sec. 6654(l)(3), Code Sec. 6655(g)(3))[9]

---

1. ¶C-2600 *et seq.*, ¶C-7000 *et seq.*; ¶6414; TD ¶s 651,001, 661,001
2. ¶s C-1003 *et seq.*, C-7002 *et seq.*; ¶6414; TD ¶s 651,003, 661,003
3. ¶C-1014 *et seq.*, ¶O-10118; ¶6414; TD ¶665,501
4. ¶s C-3081, C-9081; ¶60,34A4; TD ¶665,029, TD ¶655,500
5. ¶C-1021 *et seq.*; ¶6454; TD ¶661,002
6. ¶S-5300 *et seq.*; ¶66,544.08; TD ¶658,501
7. ¶S-5304; ¶6434.08; TD ¶658,506
8. ¶s S-5302, S-5203; ¶66,544.08; TD ¶s 658,502, 666,002
9. ¶s S-5301, S-5420; ¶66,554; TD ¶658,500

References beginning with a single letter are to paragraphs in RIA's Federal Tax Coordinator 2d and RIA's Analysis of Federal Taxes: Income. Those beginning with numbers are to paragraphs in RIA's United States Tax Reporter. Those beginning with TD are to paragraphs in RIA's Tax Desk.

624

Where an electing small business trust election (see ¶3910) is effective on a date other than the first day of the trust's tax year, the trust is considered one trust for estimated tax purposes. (Reg § 1.1361-1(m)(3)(v))[10]

¶ 3904 Estimated tax payments for trusts and estates with short year.

A trust or estate with a short tax year must pay estimated tax installments on or before the 15th day of the 4th, 6th and 9th month of such tax year, and the 15th day of the first month of the following year. For a short tax year in which the trust or estate terminates, installments due before the last day of the short year must be paid, and a final installment must be paid by the 15th day of the first month following the month the short year ends.[11]

¶ 3905 Election to treat estimated tax payments as paid by beneficiary—Form 1041-T.

A trustee may elect (on Form 1041-T) to treat any part of the trust's estimated tax payments as paid by a beneficiary. Any amount so treated is considered paid or credited to the beneficiary on the last day of the trust's tax year and is considered an estimated tax payment made by the beneficiary on Jan. 15, following the trust's tax year. (Code Sec. 643(g)(1))[12]

This election is available to an estate if a tax year is reasonably expected to be its last tax year. (Code Sec. 643(g)(3))

Elect on or before the *65th day* after the tax year. (Code Sec. 643(g)(2)) Attach Form 1041-T to Form 1041 only if the election is made with Form 1041. Otherwise, file Form 1041-T separately. The election is irrevocable. (Reg § 301.9100-8(a)(4))[13]

☯️observation: The income tax return of a trust or estate is due 3 ½ months after the close of its tax year, see ¶4732. Thus the election must be made before the return due date.

¶ 3906 Trust's termination.

When a trust terminates, it ends as a separate tax entity and no longer reports gross income or claims the deductions, credits, etc. (Reg § 1.641(b)-3(d))

Though the duration of a trust may depend on the occurrence of a particular event under the trust instrument, e.g., the life beneficiary reaching a specified age, for tax purposes the trust will nevertheless continue for a reasonable period beyond this time to allow for the orderly completion of administration. (Reg § 1.641(b)-3(b))[14]

For unused deductions allowed to a beneficiary on a trust's termination, see ¶3951.

¶ 3907 Estate's termination.

An estate's status as a separate taxpayer exists only during the period of administration or settlement of the estate. (Code Sec. 641(a)(3)) This is the period actually required to perform the ordinary duties of administration, such as collecting assets and paying legacies and debts.[15] If estate administration is unduly prolonged, IRS considers the estate terminated for tax purposes after expiration of a reasonable period for performance by the executor of all the duties of administration. (Reg § 1.641(b)-3(a))[16]

For unused deductions allowed to a beneficiary on an estate's termination, see ¶3951.

---

10. ¶S-5301
11. ¶S-5311; ¶6434.08; TD ¶658,503
12. ¶S-5309; ¶66,544.08; TD ¶654,022
13. ¶S-5310; ¶6434.08; TD ¶658,510

14. ¶C-1012; ¶6414.07; TD ¶651,011
15. ¶C-7010; ¶6414.03; TD ¶661,010
16. ¶C-7011 *et seq.*; ¶6414.03; TD ¶661,010

¶ 3908　Trusts taxed as business entity.

The fact that any organization is technically cast in the trust form won't change the real character of the organization if the organization is more properly classified as a business entity under Reg § 301.7701-2. (Reg § 301.7701-4(b))[17]

¶ 3909　Liquidating trusts.

Liquidating trusts are ordinary trusts if their primary purpose is to liquidate the assets transferred to them. They are corporations if liquidation is only an incidental or ultimate intention and the primary objective is to continue normal business operations for an indefinite time. (Reg § 301.7701-4(d))[18]

¶ 3910　Electing small business trusts for holding S stock.

Electing small business trusts (ESBTs) may hold stock of an S corporation. For the portion of an ESBT consisting of S stock, the normal pass-through rules don't apply; instead, the trust is taxed at a flat rate of 35% on its taxable ordinary income as specially computed and its capital gains are taxed at the preferential rates that apply for individuals. Interest paid or accrued on debt incurred to acquire S stock is taken into account in determining the income of the S portion of an ESBT. (Code Sec. 641(c)) A grantor trust may elect to be an ESBT and if it does, the trust consists of a grantor portion, an S portion, and a non-S portion. The items of income, deduction, and credit attributable to the grantor portion are taxed to the deemed owner of that portion. The S portion is taxed under the special rules of Code Sec. 641(c), while the non-S portion is subject to the normal trust rules. (Reg § 1.641(c)-1)[19]

¶ 3911　Environmental remediation trusts.

An environmental remediation trust is treated as a grantor trust. Each contributor is taxed on the portion of the trust relating to his contributions. (Reg § 301.7701-4(e))[20]

¶ 3912　Funeral trusts—Form 1041-QFT.

A trustee of a qualified funeral trust may elect simplified tax treatment for the trust on Form 1041-QFT, if it would otherwise be treated as a grantor trust. (Code Sec. 685)[21]

¶ 3913　Multiple trusts.

If a grantor creates multiple trusts, each trust is treated as a separate taxpayer. Separate trusts may be created even though there is only one trust instrument and only one trustee.[22]

Two or more trusts are treated as one if: (1) the trusts have substantially the same grantor or grantors and substantially the same primary beneficiary or beneficiaries, and (2) a principal purpose of the trusts is avoidance of federal income tax. (Code Sec. 643(f)) However, if a trust was irrevocable on Mar. 1, '84, this consolidation rule applies only to that portion of the trust attributable to contributions to corpus after Mar. 1, '84.[23]

¶ 3914　Charitable remainder annuity trust and charitable remainder unitrust.

These types of trusts (¶2116) are not subject to income tax. However, if they have unrelated business taxable income (UBTI), they must pay an excise tax equal to 100% of the UBTI. (Code Sec. 664(c); Reg § 1.664-1(a)(1))[24]

---

17. ¶C-5003; ¶77,014.13; TD ¶651,025
18. ¶C-5015; ¶77,014.17; TD ¶651,027
19. ¶C-5700 *et seq.*; ¶6414.08; TD ¶657,500 *et seq.*
20. ¶C-5035.1; ¶77,014.12; TD ¶657,005

21. ¶C-1013.1; ¶6854; TD ¶657,018
22. ¶C-5150 *et seq.*; ¶6434.07; TD ¶651,034
23. ¶C-5154; ¶6434.07; TD ¶651,034
24. ¶C-5039; ¶6644; TD ¶651,030

¶ 3915   Pooled income fund.

A pooled income fund (PIF) formed to pay income to noncharitable beneficiaries and the remainder to charity (¶2117) generally is taxed under the trust rules[25] even if it isn't a trust under local law. (Reg § 1.642(c)-5(a)(2))[26] However, a PIF is allowed a charitable deduction for long-term capital gain that is, under the terms of its governing instrument, permanently set aside for charitable purposes during the tax year. (Code Sec. 642(c)(3); Reg § 1.642(c)-2(c)) No amount of net long-term capital gain will be considered "permanently set aside for charitable purposes" if, under the terms of the PIF's governing instrument and applicable local law, the trustee has the power, whether or not exercised, to satisfy the income beneficiaries' right to income by the payment of either (1) an amount equal to a fixed percentage of the fair market value of the PIF's assets, whether determined annually or averaged on a multiple year basis; or (2) any amount that takes into account unrealized appreciation in the value of the PIF's assets. (Reg § 1.642(c)-2(c))[27]

¶ 3916   Gross income of trusts and estates.

What would be gross income in the hands of an individual is gross income when received by a trust or estate. (Reg § 1.641(a)-2)[28]

Gross income includes income accumulated or held for future distribution under the terms of a will or trust, income that's currently distributable, income received by a decedent's estate during administration or settlement, and income that, in the fiduciary's discretion, may be either accumulated or distributed. (Code Sec. 641(a))[29]

¶ 3917   Income from real estate passing directly to heirs.

Where under local law, real property is subject to an estate's administration, the income from it is that of the estate for the period that the estate is under administration.[30]

Where state law vests legal title to decedent's real estate upon his death directly in his heirs, devisees, or other beneficiaries, income from it is taxed to the beneficiaries and not the estate. (Reg § 1.661(a)-2(e))[31]

¶ 3918   Gain or loss on distribution of property in kind.

Gain or loss is realized by a trust or estate (or the other beneficiaries) by reason of a distribution of property in kind if the distribution is in satisfaction of a right to receive a specific dollar amount, specific property other than that distributed, or income, if income is required to be distributed currently. In addition, gain or loss is realized if the trustee or executor makes the Code Sec. 643(e) election to recognize gain or loss. (Reg § 1.661(a)-2(f))[32]

Trusts and estates may not deduct a loss on property to which a Code Sec. 643(e)(3) election applies because of the rule barring losses on sales between related parties. See ¶2448.

For estates of decedents dying in 2010, if an executor uses appreciated property to satisfy a beneficiary's right to receive a pecuniary bequest, then the estate recognizes gain only to the extent the fair market value of the appreciated property on the date of the exchange exceeds the fair market value of the property on the date the decedent died. (Code Sec. 1040(a))[33]

caution: For EGTRRA sunset rules, see ¶1114.

---

25. ¶s C-2312, C-2316; TD ¶651,031
26. ¶C-5040; TD ¶651,031
27. ¶C-2316; ¶6424.03
28. ¶s C-2100 *et seq.*, C-7100 *et seq.*; ¶6414; TD ¶s 652,001, 662,001

29. ¶s C-2101, C-7101; ¶6414 *et seq.*; TD ¶s 652,001, 662,001
30. ¶C-7105; TD ¶662,009
31. ¶C-7109; TD ¶662,009
32. ¶s C-2151, C-7151; ¶6614.01; TD ¶s 652,006, 662,018
33. ¶C-7154; ¶10,404; TD ¶s 662,021

¶ 3919   Estate income from community property.

If a decedent dies leaving community property, the income from one-half of the property is taxable to the estate and the income from the other half is taxable to the surviving spouse.[34]

¶ 3920   Deductions and credits of trusts and estates.

Deductions and credits of trusts and estates are basically those allowed to individuals except for the special deduction rules discussed in the following paragraphs. (Code Sec. 641(b); Reg § 1.641(b)-1)[35]

¶ 3921   Two percent floor on miscellaneous itemized deductions.

For purposes of this floor (see ¶3110), the adjusted gross income of a trust or estate is computed the same as for an individual, except the deductions for: (1) costs paid or incurred in connection with the administration of the trust or estate (¶3922) that wouldn't have been incurred if the property weren't held in the trust or estate; (2) the trust's or estate's personal exemptions (¶3928); and (3) distribution deductions (¶3934 and ¶3936), are allowed as deductions in arriving at adjusted gross income. (Code Sec. 67(e)) Thus, these expenses aren't subject to the floor. The Supreme Court has held that investment advisory fees paid by a trust are subject to the floor if the investment advisor doesn't charge the trust more than it would charge an individual.

Amounts that wouldn't be allowable as miscellaneous itemized deductions if paid directly by an individual can't be indirectly deducted through grantor trusts. (Code Sec. 67(c); Reg § 1.67-2T(g)(1), Reg § 1.67-2T(g)(2))

¶ 3922   Administration expenses.

Reasonable amounts paid or incurred by the fiduciary of an estate or trust on account of administration expenses, including fiduciaries' fees and litigation expenses, that are ordinary and necessary in the performance of duties of administration are deductible. (Reg § 1.212-1(i)) Deductible items include commissions and legal fees, whether allocable to corpus or income.[36] For the election to deduct these expenses against income or estate tax, see ¶3925.

¶ 3923   Interest deduction.

An estate or trust may deduct interest to the same extent as an individual, see ¶1700 *et seq.* Thus, an estate or trust is subject to the bar on the deduction of "personal" interest. But otherwise deductible interest on deferred estate tax on a closely held business interest or a reversionary interest (see ¶5035) isn't subject to this limit (Code Sec. 163(h)), except that for estates of individuals dying after '97 (and, if elected, of individuals dying before '98), interest on deferred estate tax on a closely held business interest isn't deductible. (Code Sec. 163(k))[37]

¶ 3924   Expenses of exempt income.

No deduction may be taken for *any* expenses allocable to tax-exempt income. (Code Sec. 265; Reg § 1.212-1(i))[38]

¶ 3925   Election to take either income tax or estate tax deduction.

Administration expenses, including commissions and other selling expenses, and casualty and theft losses during administration may be taken either: (1) as a deduction (or as an offset

34. ¶C-7108; ¶6414.06; TD ¶662,008
35. ¶s C-2200 *et seq.*, C-7200 *et seq.*; ¶6414; TD ¶s 651,001, 661,001
36. ¶s C-2217, C-7215; ¶s 2124.09, 6424; TD ¶s 653,016, 663,014
37. ¶K-5513; ¶s 1634.013, 1634.054; TD ¶663,010
38. ¶s C-2217, C-2219, C-7217; ¶2654; TD ¶s 653,016, 663,014

against the sales price of property in determining gain or loss) in computing the estate's taxable income for *income tax* purposes, or (2) as a deduction in computing the decedent's taxable estate for *estate tax* purposes, but not both. (Code Sec. 642(g)) To take the income tax deduction, the executor should file in duplicate (a) a statement that the amount involved hasn't already been taken as a deduction for federal estate tax purposes, and (b) a waiver of the right to take it as an estate tax deduction. (Reg § 1.642(g)-1)[39]

Some items or portion of an item can be deducted for income tax purposes if the statement and waiver are filed, while a similar item or different portion of the same item can be taken for estate tax purposes. (Reg § 1.642(g)-2)[40]

Similar rules apply for purposes of the GST tax. (Code Sec. 642(g))[41]

¶ 3926 Deductions that can be claimed for both income and estate tax purposes.

The rule barring deductions for *both* income tax and estate tax purposes (¶3925) doesn't apply to obligations of the decedent for interest, taxes and expenses that are allowable as deductions in respect of a decedent as explained at ¶3970 (Reg § 1.642(g)-2), or items that qualify for deduction on the estate tax return as claims against the estate.[42]

¶ 3927 Depreciation and depletion.

Depreciation and depletion deductions of trust or estate property must be apportioned.

For a *trust*, these deductions are generally apportioned between the beneficiaries and the trustee on the basis of the trust income allocable to each. (Code Sec. 167(d), Code Sec. 611(b)(3), Code Sec. 642(e))[43] But if the trustee is required or permitted by the trust instrument or local law to maintain a reserve for the deduction, the deduction belongs to the trust to the extent that income is actually set aside for the reserve. Apart from this, the regs bar any deduction by the trust or a beneficiary that exceeds the trust's or beneficiary's allocable share of trust income. (Reg § 1.167(h)-1(b), Reg § 1.611-1(c)(4))[44]

For an *estate*, the deductions are apportioned between the estate and the beneficiaries on the basis of the estate income allocable to each, regardless of the terms of the will. (Code Sec. 167(d), Code Sec. 611(b)(4))[45]

¶ 3928 Personal exemption.

An estate is entitled to a deduction for a personal exemption of $600. (Code Sec. 642(b))[46]

A trust that's required to distribute all of its income currently has a $300 exemption (even for a year in which it makes a corpus distribution or a charitable contribution). A qualified disability trust is allowed a personal exemption amount equal to the individual personal exemption (see ¶3115) and the individual personal exemption phaseout applies to the qualified disability trust as if it was a single individual with no dependents. All other trusts deduct $100. (Code Sec. 642(b); Reg § 1.642(b)-1)[47]

---

39. ¶C-7226 *et seq.*; ¶6424.07; TD ¶s 663,025, 776,082
40. ¶C-7232; ¶6424.07; TD ¶663,025, 776,082
41. ¶C-7227; ¶6424.07; TD ¶663,026
42. ¶s C-7234, C-7235; ¶6914.04; TD ¶663,033, TD ¶776,082
43. ¶C-2222 *et seq.*; ¶6424.06; TD ¶s 653,019, 663,019

44. ¶C-2214, C-2224; ¶6424.06; TD ¶653,019
45. ¶C-7220; ¶s 1674.119, 6424.06; TD ¶663,019
46. ¶C-7207; ¶6424.01; TD ¶663,006
47. ¶C-2206; ¶6424.01; TD ¶653,004

¶ 3929   Standard deduction.

The standard deduction of a trust or estate is zero. (Code Sec. 63(c)(6)(D))[48]

¶ 3930   Net operating loss.

Trusts and estates are entitled to the net operating loss (NOL) deduction. (Code Sec. 642(d)) In computing the NOL, the charitable deduction and the deduction for distributions are disregarded. (Reg § 1.642(d)-1)[49]

¶ 3931   Charitable contributions—Form 1041-A.

An estate or trust may deduct any amount of gross income, without limitation, that, under the terms of the governing instrument is *paid* during the tax year for a charitable purpose. (Code Sec. 642(c)(1); Reg § 1.642(c)-1(a))[50] These deductions aren't subject to the 2% floor on miscellaneous itemized deductions, see ¶3110. (Code Sec. 67(b)(4)) File Form 1041-A for a trust that claims a charitable deduction under Code Sec. 642(c). Use Form 8868 for an extension, see ¶4124.

Estates are allowed to deduct any amount of gross income, without limit, which under the terms of the governing instrument is, during the tax year, permanently *set aside* for a charitable purpose. (Code Sec. 642(c)(2); Reg § 1.642(c)-2(a), Reg § 1.642(c)-2(b))[1] *Trusts* are denied the set-aside deduction, except for pooled income funds. (Code Sec. 642(c)(2), Code Sec. 642(c)(3); Reg § 1.642(c)-2(b), Reg § 1.642(c)-2(c))[2]

Contributions made out of tax-exempt income, such as state or municipal bond interest, aren't deductible. (Reg § 1.642(c)-3(b), Reg § 1.643(a)-5(b))[3]

¶ 3932   Election to accelerate charitable deduction.

A trust or estate can elect to treat a contribution actually paid in one tax year as paid in the preceding tax year. The election must be made not later than the due date (including extensions) of the income tax return for the tax year *following the tax year* to which the deductions are pushed back. Elect by attaching a statement to the return or amended return for the year to which the deductions are pushed back. (Reg § 1.642(c)-1(b))[4] (Code Sec. 642(c)(1))[5]

¶ 3933   Deduction for distributions to beneficiaries of trusts and estates.

Distributions to beneficiaries are deductible up to the "distributable net income" (DNI) of the trust or estate for the tax year. (Code Sec. 651(b), Code Sec. 661(a))[6] The distribution deduction of a trust depends on whether the trust is a simple trust or a complex trust.

A "simple" trust (¶3934) is one that makes no distribution other than of current income and the terms of which require all of its income to be distributed currently and do not provide for charitable or similar contributions. A "complex" trust (¶3936) permits accumulation of income or charitable contributions or distributes principal.

A trust may shift its character from simple to complex and vice versa. (Reg § 1.651(a)-1, Reg § 1.661(a)-1)[7]

---

48. ¶s C-2204, C-7205; ¶634; TD ¶s 653,003, 663,004
49. ¶s C-2226, C-7222; ¶6424.05; TD ¶s 653,022, 663,021
50. ¶s C-2301 *et seq.*, C-7301 *et seq.*; ¶6424.02; TD ¶s 653,023, 663,036
1. ¶C-7311; ¶6424.02; TD ¶663,036
2. ¶C-2312 *et seq.*; ¶6424.03; TD ¶653,031

3. ¶s C-2308, C-7308; ¶6424.02; TD ¶s 653,029, 663,042
4. ¶s C-2305, C-7305; ¶6424.02; TD ¶s 653,027, 663,039
5. ¶s C-2303, C-7304; ¶6424.02; TD ¶s 653,026, 663,039
6. ¶s C-2501, C-8001; ¶6514; TD ¶s 654,001, 664,001
7. ¶C-2501; ¶6514.01; TD ¶654,030

¶ 3934 Distributions deduction of a simple trust.

This deduction for a simple trust is the amount of its income for the tax year that's required to be distributed currently, up to the ceiling of its DNI for the year (¶3935). (Code Sec. 651(b)) Tax-exempt income is excluded both from accounting income and DNI in figuring the deduction. (Reg § 1.651(b)-1)[8]

¶ 3935 Distributable net income of a simple trust.

The starting point is *taxable* income, i.e., gross income minus deductions. These adjustments are then made to taxable income:

(1) Add back the deduction for personal exemption and any deduction for distributions. (Code Sec. 643(a)(1), Code Sec. 643(a)(2); Reg § 1.643(a)-1, Reg § 1.643(a)-2)

(2) Subtract any extraordinary dividends (in cash or property) and taxable stock dividends that the trustee doesn't pay or credit because he determines they are allocable to principal. (Code Sec. 643(a)(4); Reg § 1.643(a)-4)

(3) Subtract any capital gains that are allocated to principal and aren't paid, credited or required to be distributed during the tax year. Add back any capital losses, except to the extent they are taken into account in computing capital gains that are paid, credited or required to be distributed during the tax year. Add back any gain excluded under Code Sec. 1202 on the sale of qualified small business stock. (Code Sec. 643(a)(3); Reg § 1.643(a)-3(b))[9]

Gains from the sale or exchange of capital assets are included in DNI to the extent they are allocated to: (i) income; (ii) corpus, but treated consistently by the fiduciary on the trust's books, records, and tax returns as part of a distribution to a beneficiary; or (iii) corpus, but actually distributed to the beneficiary or used by the fiduciary in determining the amount that is distributed or required to be distributed to a beneficiary. (Reg § 1.643(a)-3(b))[10]

¶ 3936 Distributions deduction of a complex trust or estate.

A complex trust or estate deducts, up to its DNI ceiling for the year (¶3937), the sum of:

(1) any income for the tax year required to be distributed currently (¶3938); and

(2) any other amounts, whether income or principal, properly paid or credited or required to be distributed for that tax year (¶3939). (Code Sec. 661(a); Reg § 1.661(a)-2(a))[11]

No distributions deduction may be taken for any portion of DNI that represents an item, such as tax-exempt interest, that isn't included in the gross income of the trust or estate. (Code Sec. 661(c); Reg § 1.661(c)-1) Unless the instrument or local law requires another allocation, the distribution is considered to contain the same proportion of tax-exempt items entering into DNI as the total tax-exempt income bears to total DNI. (Code Sec. 661(b); Reg § 1.661(b)-1)[12]

¶ 3937 Distributable net income for a complex trust or estate.

The DNI of a complex trust or an estate is its taxable income with these adjustments:

(1) No deduction for distributions or personal exemption is allowed. (Code Sec. 643(a)(1))

(2) Capital gains are excluded unless: allocated to income; allocated to corpus, but treated consistently by the fiduciary as part of a distribution to a beneficiary; allocated to corpus but actually distributed to the beneficiary or used by the fiduciary in determining the amount that is distributed or required to be distributed to a beneficiary; or allowed as a

---

8. ¶C-2603 *et seq.*; ¶6514.01; TD ¶654,013
9. ¶C-2606 *et seq.*; ¶6434.01; TD ¶654,032
10. ¶C-2608; ¶6434.01; TD ¶654,034

11. ¶s C-2701, C-8101; ¶6614.01; TD ¶s 654,037, 664,001
12. ¶s C-2707, C-8107; TD ¶s 654,043, 664,036.

charitable deduction. Capital losses are excluded except to the extent they enter into a determination of any capital gains paid, credited or required to be distributed to a beneficiary during the tax year. Add back any gain excluded under Code Sec. 1202 on the sale of qualified small business stock. (Code Sec. 643(a)(3); Reg § 1.643(a)-3(b))

(3) Tax-exempt interest, reduced by allocable, nondeductible expenses, is *included* except to the extent allocable to the charitable deduction. (Code Sec. 643(a)(5); Reg § 1.643(a)-5)[13]

¶ 3938   "Income required to be distributed currently."

Income required to be distributed currently means accounting income of the trust or estate determined under the trust instrument or will and applicable local law. It doesn't include items of gross income that the fiduciary allocates to corpus. (Code Sec. 643(b))

An allocation of amounts between income and principal under applicable local law will be respected if local law provides for a reasonable apportionment between the income and remainder beneficiaries of the total return of the trust for the year, including ordinary and tax-exempt income, capital gains, and appreciation. (Reg § 1.643(b)-1)

A distribution required to be made out of income or corpus, such as an annuity, is considered to be out of currently distributable income to the extent it's paid out of income for the tax year. (Code Sec. 661(a)(1); Reg § 1.661(a)-2(b))

Currently distributable income is deductible for the tax year of the trust or estate in which it is received even though, as a matter of practical necessity, it isn't distributed until after the end of that year. (Reg § 1.651(a)-2(a), Reg § 1.651(a)-2(b))[14]

¶ 3939   "Other amounts properly paid or credited or required to be distributed."

Other amounts properly paid or credited or required to be distributed must be actually distributed or at least made available on demand by the beneficiary. Even though designated by the fiduciary as a payment of *principal* of the trust or estate, a distribution actually paid or made available is deductible by the fiduciary as a distribution of "other amounts." It isn't necessary that the distribution actually be made out of income. (Code Sec. 661(a); Reg § 1.661(a)-2(c))[15] An amount that a trust has elected to treat as an estimated tax payment by a beneficiary (¶3905) is a deductible distribution. (Code Sec. 643(g))[16]

¶ 3940   Deduction for distribution of property in kind.

Distributions of property in kind qualify for deduction as other amounts paid. (Reg § 1.661(a)-2(c)) If the trust or estate elects to recognize gain or loss (¶3918), the property distributed is taken into account at its fair market value for purposes of the distribution deduction. If the election isn't made, the property is taken into account only to the extent of the lesser of the basis of the property in the hands of the beneficiary (¶3949) or the fair market value of the property. (Code Sec. 643(e)(2), Code Sec. 643(e)(3))[17]

¶ 3941   Family support allowances—"widow's allowance."

Family support allowances (for a decedent's widow or dependent) paid by an estate under a court order or decree, or under local law, are treated as distributions deductible by the estate, subject to the regular DNI deduction ceiling. (Reg § 1.661(a)-2(e), Reg § 1.662(a)-2(c))[18]

---

13. ¶s C-2702 *et seq.*, C-8102 *et seq.*; ¶6434.01; TD ¶s 654,038, 664,030
14. ¶s C-2504 *et seq.*, C-8003 *et seq.*; ¶s 6434.03, 6514.01, 6624.01; TD ¶s 654,003, 664,003
15. ¶s C-2524 *et seq.*, C-8014 *et seq.*; ¶s 6614.01, 6624.01;
TD ¶s 654,018, 664,013
16. ¶C-2530; ¶6434.08; TD ¶654,022
17. ¶s C-2525, C-8015; ¶6434.05; TD ¶s 654,019, 664,014
18. ¶C-8011; ¶6614.01; TD ¶664,011

¶ 3942 Non-deductible distributions.

No *distributions* deduction is allowed for:

... distributions to charity (Reg § 1.663(a)-2);[19]

... the value of any interest in real estate, title to which passes directly from decedent to his heirs and devisees (Reg § 1.661(a)-2(e));[20]

... a gift or bequest of specific property or of a specific sum of money that is paid or credited all at once or in not more than three installments—an amount that can be paid only from income isn't considered a gift or bequest of a specific sum of money and is therefore includible in the distributions deduction (Code Sec. 663(a)(1));[21]

... any amount reported as a distribution in an earlier year's return because it was credited or required to be distributed in the earlier year (Code Sec. 663(a)(3); Reg § 1.663(a)-3);[22]

... any amount paid or credited within the first 65 days of the current year which the fiduciary elected to treat as paid or credited in the preceding year, see ¶3943.

¶ 3943 Election to deduct "late paid" distributions—the "65-day rule."

The fiduciary of a complex trust and the executor of an estate can elect, by checking a box on Form 1041, to treat an amount properly paid or credited within the first 65 days of any tax year of the trust as paid or credited on the last day of the preceding tax year. (Code Sec. 663(b))[23] This gives the trustee or executor time to determine income earned by the trust for the year, and the opportunity to deduct distributions of that income on the return for the year earned.

The amount to which the election applies can't exceed the greater of: (1) the entity's accounting income for the year for which the election is made, or (2) its DNI for that year, in each case reduced by any amounts paid, credited, or required to be distributed in that year other than amounts considered paid or credited in a preceding tax year by reason of the "65-day" rule. (Reg § 1.663(b)-1(a))[24]

¶ 3944 Amount taxed to beneficiary of a simple trust.

The beneficiary of a simple trust is in general taxed on the *lower* of these two items:

(1) the amount of trust income for the tax year of the trust required to be distributed to the beneficiary currently whether distributed or not; or

(2) the beneficiary's proportionate share of the trust's DNI. (Code Sec. 652(a); Reg § 1.652(a)-1)

DNI is computed as explained at ¶3935, except that for this purpose it includes tax-exempt interest minus allocable deductions. (Code Sec. 643(a)(5)) Tax-exempt income items, however, aren't taxable to the beneficiary because of the character rule explained at ¶3946. Income from sources outside the U.S. is included for foreign trusts. (Code Sec. 643(a)(6))[25]

¶ 3945 Amount taxed to beneficiary of a complex trust or estate.

The beneficiary of a complex trust or of an estate includes in gross income the sum of the following amounts, subject to the DNI ceiling (see below) and the elimination of tax-exempt items under the character rule (¶3946):

(1) income required to be distributed to him currently (though not actually distributed),

19. ¶s C-2533, C-8026; ¶6614.01; TD ¶654,027, 664,025
20. ¶C-8027; TD ¶664,026
21. ¶s C-2531 *et seq.*, C-8022 *et seq.*; ¶6614.01; TD ¶654,024, 664,021

22. ¶s C-2534, C-8028; ¶6614.01; TD ¶s 654,028, 664,027
23. ¶C-2713, ¶C-8113; ¶6634.03; TD ¶654,052, TD ¶664,047
24. ¶C-2713, ¶C-8113; ¶6634.03; TD ¶654,052
25. ¶C-3001; ¶s 6524, 6524.02, 6434.01; TD ¶655,001

which includes an annuity or other amount required to be paid out of income or corpus, to the extent it is paid out of income for the tax year; and

(2) all other amounts (whether from income or principal) properly paid, credited or required to be distributed to him for the tax year (Code Sec. 662(a))[26] including income from property distributed in-kind, see ¶3949. (Reg § 1.662(a)-3(b))

A beneficiary of a complex trust or an estate need not report as income more than his share of DNI, so that the total amount of income reported by all beneficiaries cannot exceed the total DNI of the trust or estate for the tax year. For this purpose, the beneficiaries are divided into two groups or "tiers:"

(1) The first tier is composed of beneficiaries entitled to income distributions currently, that is "income required to be distributed currently."

(2) The second tier is composed of beneficiaries receiving or entitled to receive other "noncurrent" distributions. (Code Sec. 662(a); Reg § 1.662(a)-3(c))[27]

First-tier beneficiaries report, in the aggregate, the amount of their current distributions, up to the amount of DNI for the tax year of the trust or estate, computed as explained at ¶3937 without any charitable deduction. Thus, if the total of first-tier distributions is equal to or less than DNI (without charitable deduction), each first-tier beneficiary reports his full share of the distributions. (Code Sec. 662(a)(1))[28]

But if the total of first-tier distributions exceeds DNI (without charitable deduction) each beneficiary reports an amount equal to his pro rata share of DNI (without charitable deduction). (Code Sec. 662(a)(1); Reg § 1.662(a)-2(b))[29]

Second-tier beneficiaries report, in the aggregate, the amount of their second-tier distributions up to the DNI of the trust or estate as reduced for first-tier distributions of current income. For this purpose, DNI is computed *with* allowance of any charitable deduction.

If the total of second-tier distributions equals or is less than the ceiling (DNI as reduced for first-tier distributions), each second-tier beneficiary reports his or her full share of the second-tier distributions. But, if the total of second-tier distributions exceeds the ceiling, each second-tier beneficiary reports only his pro rata share of the ceiling amount. (Code Sec. 662(a)(2); Reg § 1.662(a)-3(c))[30]

¶ 3946   Character of trust's and estate's income in beneficiary's hands.

For simple trusts, complex trusts and estates, the amounts taxable to the beneficiaries have the same character (e.g., as tax-exempt income) in the hands of the beneficiaries as the amounts had when received by the trust or estate. (Code Sec. 652(b), Code Sec. 662(b); Reg § 1.652(b)-1, Reg § 1.662(b)-1)[31]

Unless the instrument specifically allocates different classes of income to different beneficiaries, amounts distributed are treated as consisting of the same proportion of each class of items entering into the computation of DNI as the total of each class bears to the total DNI of the trust or estate. (Code Sec. 652(b), Code Sec. 662(b); Reg § 1.652(b)-1, Reg § 1.662(b)-1)[32]

Deductions that enter into the computation of DNI are allocated among the classes as follows:

. . . Deductions *directly* attributable to a particular class of income (interest, rents, dividends, capital gains, etc.) are allocated to that class.

. . . If deductions *directly* attributable to a class of income exceed that class, the excess may

26. ¶s C-3006 *et seq.*, C-9001 *et seq.*; ¶6624; TD ¶s 655,006, 665,001
27. ¶s C-3010, C-9006; ¶6624; TD ¶s 655,009, 665,005
28. ¶s C-3011 *et seq.*, C-9007 *et seq.*; ¶6624; TD ¶s 655,010, 665,006
29. ¶s C-3011, C-9008; ¶6624; TD ¶s 655,011, 665,007
30. ¶s C-3013, C-9009; ¶6624; TD ¶s 655,012, 665,008
31. ¶s C-3002, C-3016, C-9012; ¶s 6524.03, 6624.03; TD ¶s 655,002, 655,015, 665,011
32. ¶s C-3003, C-3016, C-9012; ¶s 6524.02, 6624.02; TD ¶s 655,005, 655,015, 665,011

be allocated to any other class (including capital gains) included in DNI in the manner shown below for deductions not directly attributable, except that excess deductions directly attributable to tax-exempt income cannot be used to reduce any other class of income.

... Deductions not directly attributable to a specific class of income can be allocated to any item of income (including capital gains) included in DNI, but a part must be allocated proportionately to tax-exempt income. Examples of these "neutral" deductions are trustees' commissions (both income and corpus), and state income and personal property taxes. (Reg § 1.652(b)-3)[33]

A *charitable deduction* by an estate or complex trust is allocated just before the other deductions. Allocation follows the terms of the instrument or local law, or if these are silent, the charitable deduction is allocated to each class of income items in the proportion that the total of each class bears to the total of all classes. (Reg § 1.643(a)-5(b), Reg § 1.662(b)-2)[34]

¶ 3947 Beneficiaries' separate shares treated separately.

If a complex trust or an estate accumulates income for one beneficiary and distributes principal to another beneficiary, the normal tax rules would impose a tax burden on the recipient of principal since he in effect must pay tax on income accumulated for the other beneficiary. To prevent this, the "separate share rule" treats substantially separate and independent shares of different beneficiaries of a single trust or estate as though each share represented a separate trust or estate. This applies *only* in computing DNI as a ceiling on the amount deductible by the trust or estate and taxable to the beneficiaries (Code Sec. 663(c); Reg § 1.663(c)-1(b)), and is mandatory. (Reg § 1.663(c)-1(d))[35] Code Sec. 663(c), Reg § 1.663(c)-1(a))[36] A surviving spouse's elective share is a separate share,[37] as is a pecuniary formula bequest unless it's not entitled to income or to share in appreciation or depreciation and can paid or credited in more than three installments. (Reg § 1.663(c)-4(b))[38]

¶ 3948 When a beneficiary is taxed.

Amounts required to be distributed currently are taxed to the beneficiary when they are required to be distributed even though not actually distributed. Other distributions are taxed to a beneficiary when they are made or credited, or required to be made. (Code Sec. 652(a), Code Sec. 662(a); Reg § 1.662(a)-3(a))[39]

If a beneficiary's tax year is different from that of the estate or trust, the beneficiary includes his share of the trust or estate income in his return for the tax year in which the tax year of the trust or estate ends. (Code Sec. 652(c), Code Sec. 662(c))[40]

Upon termination of an estate, a beneficiary must include in his calendar year return income received from the estate during both the estate's fiscal year and final short year where both years end within his calendar year.[41]

Where the 65-day rule is elected (¶3943), the beneficiary is considered as receiving the distribution in his tax year that includes the close of the trust's or estate's tax year in which the distribution is considered made. (Reg § 1.663(b)-1(a)(2)(ii))[42]

¶ 3949 Distributions in kind includible in a beneficiary's income.

For property distributed in kind, the amount taken into account under Code Sec. 662(a)(2) (¶3945) for purposes of determining the amount includible in the beneficiary's income and for purposes of determining his basis in the property depends on whether the estate or trust

33. ¶s C-3004, C-3017, C-9013; ¶s 6524, 6524.02, 6624.02; TD ¶s 655,005, 655,016, 665,012
34. ¶s C-3018, C-9015; ¶6624; TD ¶655,017, 665,014
35. ¶C-2711 *et seq.*; ¶6634.01; TD ¶654,047
36. ¶C-8111; ¶6634.01; TD ¶664,040
37. ¶C-8112.1; ¶6634.01; TD ¶664,042
38. ¶C-8112.2; ¶6634.01; TD ¶664,043

39. ¶s C-3025, C-9017; ¶s 6524.01, 6624.01; TD ¶s 655,020, 665,016
40. ¶s C-3026, C-9018; ¶s 6524.04, 6624.04; TD ¶s 655,021, 665,017
41. ¶C-9018; TD ¶665,017
42. ¶C-3028, ¶C-9019; ¶6634.03; TD ¶655,020

elected to recognize gain or loss on the distribution (see ¶3918).

If the estate or trust elects, the property is taken into account at its fair market value. (Code Sec. 643(e)(3))

If the estate or trust doesn't elect, the property is taken into account only to the extent of the lesser of: (1) the fair market value of the property, or (2) its basis in the hands of the beneficiary. (Code Sec. 643(e)(2))[43]

The beneficiary's basis for property distributed in kind is the adjusted basis of the property in the hands of the estate or trust immediately before the distribution, adjusted for any gain or loss recognized by the estate or trust on the distribution. (Code Sec. 643(e)(1))[44]

¶ 3950 Nontaxable gifts and bequests.

A beneficiary isn't taxable on any amount paid or credited as a gift or bequest of specific property or of a specific sum of money, and that is paid or credited all at once or in not more than three installments. (Code Sec. 663(a)(1))[45]

¶ 3951 Beneficiaries' deductions on estate or trust termination.

Beneficiaries who succeed to property of a trust or estate on its termination can deduct as a miscellaneous itemized deduction the unused deductions in excess of gross income for the last tax year of the trust or estate, other than the personal exemption and charitable contributions. The deduction is allowed only for the beneficiary's tax year in which the trust or estate terminates. It is taken into account in computing the beneficiary's items of tax preference. (Code Sec. 642(h); Reg § 1.642(h)-2(a))[46]

¶ 3952 Taxation of beneficiaries of charitable remainder trusts—CRTs.

Amounts paid to an income beneficiary of a CRT retain the character they had in the hands of the trust, with this qualification: each payment is treated as consisting of (1) ordinary income, to the extent of the trust's ordinary income for that year and undistributed ordinary income for earlier years, (2) capital gain, to the extent of capital gain for that year and undistributed capital gain (determined on a cumulative net basis) for earlier years, (3) other income (e.g., tax-exempt interest), to the extent of that income for that year and undistributed amounts for earlier years, and (4) trust corpus. (Code Sec. 664(a), Code Sec. 664(b); Reg § 1.664-1(d)(1)) Within categories (1) and (2), items are assigned to different classes to reflect rate differences (e.g., qualified dividends and different capital gain classes). (Reg § 1.664-1(d)(1)(i)(b))[47]

¶ 3953 Distribution of accumulated trust income—"throwback" rules.

The "throwback rules" tax beneficiaries on distributions of income accumulated by the trust before the year of distribution, as though the income had been distributed currently to the beneficiaries in the years received by the trust. (Reg § 1.665(a)-0A(a)(1))[48]

The throwback rules apply to foreign trusts, domestic trusts previously treated as foreign trusts (except as provided in regs), and domestic trusts created before Mar. 1, '84, that would be treated as multiple trusts under Code Sec. 643(f). (Code Sec. 665(c))

The throwback rules generally apply only to complex trusts. Estates aren't subject to the throwback rules. (Code Sec. 666; Reg § 1.665(a)-0A(d))[49]

The fiduciary of a trust subject to the throwback rules must complete Schedule J (Form

---

43. ¶s C-3009, C-9004; ¶6434.05; TD ¶s 655,008, 665,003
44. ¶s C-3009, C-9004; ¶6614.01; TD ¶s 655,008, 665,003
45. ¶s C-2531, C-8022; ¶6634.02; TD ¶s 654,024, 664,021
46. ¶s C-3033 *et seq.*, C-9053 *et seq.*; ¶6434.04; TD ¶s 655,025,

665,022
47. ¶C-3051; ¶6644.01; TD ¶655,030
48. ¶C-4001; ¶6664; TD ¶656,001
49. ¶C-4002; ¶6664; TD ¶656,002

1041) and attach it to the trust's return.[50]

¶ 3954 Distributions exempt from the throwback rules.

These distributions are exempt from the throwback rules:

• Distributions of income accumulated before birth of beneficiary or before beneficiary reaches age 21. But this exclusion doesn't apply to distributions from a foreign trust or to certain distributions from multiple trusts. (Code Sec. 665(b))[1]

• Distributions not exceeding accounting income. (Code Sec. 665(b))[2]

¶ 3955 Beneficiary's tax under throwback rules—Form 4970.

The beneficiary includes in his income for the current year:

. . . the amount of the accumulation distribution considered distributed; and

. . . the trust's income tax considered distributed. (Code Sec. 667(a), Code Sec. 666(b))[3]

The beneficiary's total tax liability for the current year is:

(1) a partial tax on the beneficiary's taxable income *reduced* by the total amounts considered distributed to the beneficiary under the throwback rules; *plus*

(2) a partial tax on the amounts considered distributed under the throwback rules (Code Sec. 667(a)); *plus*

(3) in the case of a foreign trust, a special nondeductible interest charge. (Code Sec. 667(b))[4]

The beneficiary's partial tax under (2) is computed (on Form 4970) under a special "short-cut" method and is then reduced by any estate tax or generation-skipping transfer tax attributable to the partial tax. (Code Sec. 667(b)(6))[5]

¶ 3956 Grantor or others taxed as owner of trust—grantor trust rules.

A trust grantor or another person with power over a trust or its property may be taxed on its income as the "owner" of the trust. These grantor trust rules are discussed at ¶3957 *et seq.*[6] These rules don't apply to charitable remainder trusts or pooled income funds. (Reg § 1.671-1(d)[7] These rules generally apply only to the extent they result in amounts being currently taken into account in computing the income of a U.S. citizen, resident or domestic corporation. (Code Sec. 672(f); Reg § 1.672(f)-1, Reg § 1.672(f)-2, Reg § 1.672(f)-3)

observation: Thus, the grantor trust rules generally don't apply where they would treat a foreign person as owner of the trust. This ensures that either the U.S. or the foreign jurisdiction taxes the trust income.

For this purpose, a grantor includes any person who creates a trust, or directly or indirectly makes a gratuitous transfer of property, including cash, to a trust. (Reg § 1.671-2(e))[8]

These rules may be applicable to the entire trust or, where appropriate, to only a specific portion of a trust. (Reg § 1.671-3(a))[9] If a grantor or other person is considered to be the owner of the *entire* trust, he computes his own personal income tax by taking into account all trust income, deductions and credits, as though the trust didn't exist. (Reg § 1.671-3(a)(1)) But, where a grantor is treated as owner solely because of his interest in trust *income*, he takes into account only his share of trust items that would be reported by a current income beneficiary. (Reg § 1.671-3(c))[10]

50. ¶C-4001; ¶6664; TD ¶656,001
1. ¶C-4007; ¶6664; TD ¶656,005
2. ¶C-4008; ¶6664; TD ¶656,005
3. ¶C-4101; ¶6664; TD ¶656,008
4. ¶C-4101; ¶6664; TD ¶656,009
5. ¶C-4100 *et seq.*; ¶6664; TD ¶656,009
6. ¶C-5200 *et seq.*; ¶6714; TD ¶657,000
7. ¶C-5216; ¶6714; TD ¶655,030
8. ¶C-5201; ¶6714; TD ¶657,001
9. ¶C-5207 *et seq.*; ¶6714; TD ¶657,013
10. ¶C-5209 *et seq.*; ¶6714; TD ¶657,012

For purposes of taxing the grantor as the owner of a trust, the grantor is treated as holding any power or interest held by any individual who was the spouse of the grantor at the time of the creation of the power or the interest, or who became the spouse of the grantor after the creation, but only for periods after the individual became the spouse. (Code Sec. 672(e)(1)) This rule applies only to transfers in trust made after Mar. 1, '86.[11]

A "defective grantor trust" is a trust intentionally structured so that the grantor, rather than the trust or its beneficiaries, will be taxed on the trust's income without the trust being included in the grantor's estate. A defective grantor trust can lower income taxes where the grantor is in a lower bracket than the beneficiary or some income would be accumulated in the trust and taxed at the highly compressed trust tax brackets. The grantor's payment of income tax on trust income taxed to him is not a gift to the beneficiaries. If a defective grantor trust or applicable state law requires the trustee to reimburse the grantor for the income tax on trust income, the full value of the trust property will be included in the grantor's gross estate for trusts created after Oct. 3, 2004.[12]

¶ 3957 Power to revoke.

If the grantor of a trust reserves the power to take back title to the trust funds for himself, he is considered the owner of the trust, whether or not he actually exercises that power. (Code Sec. 671, Code Sec. 676) The power to get back the trust funds may be a power to revoke, terminate, alter or amend, or to appoint. (Reg § 1.676(a)-1)

The grantor is taxed if he can exercise the power alone, if it can be exercised only by another who is regarded as a *nonadverse* party, or if it can be exercised by both the grantor and a nonadverse party together. (Code Sec. 676(a))[13] The grantor is not taxed if the power can be exercised only by or with consent of an adverse party. (Code Sec. 672(a), Code Sec. 676(a); Reg § 1.676(a)-1)[14]

An "adverse party" is any person with a substantial beneficial interest in the trust (including a general power of appointment over trust property) which would be adversely affected by the exercise or non-exercise of his power with regards to the trust. (Code Sec. 672(a)) A beneficiary is ordinarily an adverse party. (Reg § 1.672(a)-1(b)) A "nonadverse party" has either no beneficial interest, or one that is not substantial, or one which would not be adversely affected by the exercise of his power with regard to the trust. (Code Sec. 672(b); Reg § 1.672(b)-1)[15]

¶ 3958 Income for grantor, spouse or dependent.

The grantor of a trust is treated as its owner and taxed on its income, if the trust income is:

. . . distributed actually or constructively to the grantor or his spouse;

. . . held or accumulated for future distribution to the grantor or his spouse; or

. . . applied to pay premiums on life insurance policies taken out on the life of the grantor or his spouse (and not irrevocably payable to charities). (Code Sec. 677(a))

The income isn't taxable to the grantor if the application of the income to any of these purposes requires the approval of an adverse party (¶3957). (Reg § 1.677(a)-1(b))[16]

If trust income is *actually* used to support a beneficiary (other than the grantor's spouse) whom the grantor is legally obligated to support, such as his minor children, the grantor is taxable on that income. But the mere fact that trust income *may* be so used doesn't make him taxable, unless the use is discretionary with the grantor as an *individual* (not trustee). (Reg § 1.677(b)-1(d), Reg § 1.677(b)-1(e), Reg § 1.677(b)-1(f))[17]

11. ¶C-5204 *et seq.*; ¶6724.02; TD ¶657,009
12. ¶C-5200; ¶6714
13. ¶C-5301; ¶6764; TD ¶657,025
14. ¶C-5303; ¶6764; TD ¶657,025
15. ¶C-5312 *et seq.*; ¶6724.01; TD ¶657,027
16. ¶C-5401; ¶6774.01; TD ¶657,029
17. ¶C-5423; ¶6774.04; TD ¶657,033

¶ 3959   Reversionary interests.

For transfers in trust made after Mar. 1, '86, the grantor of a trust is generally taxable as the owner on its income if he has a reversionary interest in the corpus or income and, as of the inception of the trust, the value of that interest is more than 5% of the value of the trust. (Code Sec. 673(a)) The value of the reversionary interest must be determined by assuming the maximum exercise of discretion in favor of the grantor. (Code Sec. 673(c))

Any postponement of the date specified for the reacquisition of possession or enjoyment of the reversionary interest is treated as a new transfer in trust starting with the date the postponement is effective and terminating with the date prescribed by the postponement. However, income for any period isn't included in income of the grantor by reason of this rule if it wouldn't be includible in the absence of the postponement. (Code Sec. 673(d))

The grantor isn't treated as the owner where the reversionary interest takes effect on the death before age 21 of a beneficiary who (1) is a lineal descendant of the grantor, and (2) holds all present interests in the trust. (Code Sec. 673(b))[18]

¶ 3960   Power to control beneficial enjoyment (including "sprinkling" and "spray" powers).

Trust income is generally taxable to the grantor as the owner of the trust property if the beneficial enjoyment of trust corpus or income is subject to a power of disposition that may be exercised by him personally, or by a nonadverse party (¶3957), or both, and requires no consent or approval of an adverse party (¶3957). (Code Sec. 674)[19]

Similarly, the grantor will be taxed if he retains certain administrative powers, such as borrowing powers and dealing with the trust for less than full consideration. (Code Sec. 675)[20]

But certain relatively broad powers to shift benefits may be given to "independent" trustees without causing the grantor to be treated as owner. These so called "sprinkling" and "spray" powers permit the trustee to distribute, apportion or accumulate income, or to pay out corpus to or among beneficiaries (Code Sec. 674(c)), but not to add beneficiaries except to include after-born or after-adopted children. These powers vested solely in trustees won't cause the grantor to be taxed as the owner of the trust if the grantor isn't eligible as a trustee or co-trustee and no more than half the trustees vested with the power are related or subordinate parties subservient to the grantor's wishes. (Code Sec. 674(c), Code Sec. 674(d); Reg § 1.674(d)-2(b))

Also, a power to distribute, apportion or accumulate income won't subject the grantor to tax if he and his spouse (living with him) are ineligible to exercise the power as trustee or co-trustee and the power is limited by a reasonably definite external standard set forth in the trust instrument. (Code Sec. 674(d); Reg § 1.674(d)-1)[21]

¶ 3961   Person other than the grantor as owner (including "Crummey" powers).

A trustee, beneficiary, or some other person may be taxable on the income as the owner, if that person:

. . . has a power exercisable solely by himself to vest the corpus, or income from it, in himself; or

. . . has previously modified or released such a power and afterward retains control which would make the grantor taxable under the rules discussed at ¶3956 *et seq.* (Code Sec. 678)[22]

A holder of a "Crummey" power (see ¶5046) is treated as owner under the above rule.[23]

---

18. ¶C-5450 *et seq.*; ¶6734.01; TD ¶657,041
19. ¶C-5531; ¶6744; TD ¶657,000
20. ¶C-5551 *et seq.*; ¶6754; TD ¶657,057
21. ¶C-5542 *et seq.*; ¶6744; TD ¶657,055
22. ¶C-5571; ¶6784; TD ¶657,058
23. ¶C-5574; ¶6784

¶ 3962   Foreign trust grantors or other transferors—Form 3520, Form 3520-A.

If a U.S. person (e.g., a grantor) makes a transfer to a foreign trust with a U.S. beneficiary, the income of the trust (including foreign source income) will be taxed currently to the transferor as the owner of the trust. (Code Sec. 679(a)(1); Reg § 1.679-1) This rule doesn't apply where the transfer is: (a) by reason of death, (b) for fair market value, or (c) to a foreign employee benefit or charitable trust. (Code Sec. 679(a); Reg § 1.679-4)

A trust is treated as having a U.S. beneficiary for a tax year unless (1) under the terms of the trust, no part of the trust's income or corpus may be paid or accumulated during the tax year to or for the benefit of a U.S. person, and (2) if the trust is terminated at any time during the tax year, no part of the income or corpus could be paid to or for the benefit of a U.S. person. Effective Mar. 18, 2010, an amount is treated as accumulated for the benefit of a U.S. person even if the U.S. person's interest in the trust is contingent on a future event. (Code Sec. 679(c)(1))

Also effective Mar. 18, 2010:

. . . If a U.S. person directly or indirectly transfers property to a foreign trust, there is a rebuttable presumption that the trust has a U.S. beneficiary unless the U.S. person submits information as required by IRS and demonstrates to its satisfaction that requirements (1) and (2) in the above paragraph are met. (Code Sec. 679(d))

. . . If any person has the discretion to make a distribution from the trust to, or for the benefit of, any person, the trust is treated as having a U.S. beneficiary unless: (i) the trust terms specifically identify the class of persons to whom the distributions may be made; and (ii) none of those persons is a U.S. person during the tax year. (Code Sec. 679(c)(4))

. . . If any U.S. person who directly or indirectly transfers property to the trust is directly or indirectly involved in any agreement or understanding that may result in the income or corpus of the trust being paid or accumulated to or for the benefit of a U.S. person, that agreement or understanding is treated as a term of the trust. (Code Sec. 679(c)(5))

. . . For purposes of determining whether a foreign trust has a U.S. beneficiary, a loan of cash or marketable securities (or the use of any other trust property) directly or indirectly to or by any U.S. person (whether or not the U.S. person is a beneficiary under the terms of the trust) is treated as paid or accumulated for the benefit of a U.S. person, unless the U.S. person repays the loan at a market rate of interest (or pays the fair market value of the use of the property) within a reasonable period of time. (Code Sec. 679(c)(6))

The changes to the Code which became effective on Mar. 18, 2010 are meant to be consistent with already-existing regs on when a foreign trust that received property from a U.S. transferor is treated as having a U.S. beneficiary. (Reg § 1.679-2)[24]

The above rules also apply to (1) certain foreign persons who transfer property to a foreign trust and later become a U.S. person (Code Sec. 679(a)(4); Reg § 1.679-5(a)) and (2) to a U.S. person who transferred property to a domestic trust that becomes a foreign trust during the transferor's life. (Code Sec. 679(a)(5); Reg § 1.679-6(b))[25]

A foreign trust with a U.S. owner must file Form 3520-A to satisfy information reporting requirements. (Code Sec. 6048(b)(1))[26]

For tax years beginning after Mar. 18, 2010, a U.S. person who is treated as an owner of any portion of a foreign trust must provide information as IRS may require with respect to the trust. (Code Sec. 6048(b)(1))

---

24. ¶C-5600 *et seq.*; ¶6794; TD ¶657,060   26. ¶S-3645; ¶60,484; TD ¶659,024
25. ¶s C-5603.1, C-5603.2; ¶6794; TD ¶657,062

¶ 3963   Beneficiary treated as grantor to the extent of gifts to foreign grantor.

Where a foreign person would ordinarily be treated as the owner of any portion of a trust, *and* the trust has a beneficiary who is a U.S. person, the beneficiary generally is treated as the grantor of that portion to the extent the beneficiary has after Nov. 5, '90, made transfers by gift (directly or indirectly) to the foreign grantor. Gifts which are excluded from the calculation of gift tax under Code Sec. 2503(b) (generally, annual gifts of present interests of up to $13,000 for 2010 and 2011, see ¶5046) aren't included. (Code Sec. 672(f)(5); Reg § 1.672(f)-5) This rule applies even if the beneficiary wasn't a U.S. person at the time of the transfer.[27]

¶ 3964   Decedent's Income and Deductions.

A decedent's last tax year ends on his death. A cash basis decedent's final return includes only the income he actually or constructively received before he died. An accrual basis decedent's return includes income and deductions properly accruable at death (but not solely by reason of death). Post-death income and deductions "in respect of a decedent" must be reported by decedent's estate or others who acquire his rights or obligations.

¶ 3965   Income includible and deductions taken on decedent's last return.

The last tax year of a decedent ends with the day of his death. (Reg § 1.451-1(b))[28]

For a *cash basis* decedent, include only the income received, actually or constructively, up to the end of the day of death (Code Sec. 691(a); Reg § 1.451-1(b)(1), Reg § 1.691(a)-1(b)), and deduct expenses only to the extent paid before death (except for the special deduction for the unrecovered investment in an annuity contract, see ¶3966, and certain medical expenses paid within one year after death, see ¶2144).[29]

For an *accrual basis* decedent, include income and deductions computed on the accrual method. But an amount of income or deduction accrued *solely* by reason of death isn't includible on the final return. (Code Sec. 451(b), Code Sec. 461(b))[30]

¶ 3966   Deduction for unrecovered investment in annuity contract.

A decedent's unrecovered investment in an annuity contract is an itemized deduction (*not* subject to the 2%-of-AGI floor) (Code Sec. 67(b)(10)) for the decedent's last tax year, if the annuity payments cease by reason of his death. (Code Sec. 72(b)(3)(A))[31]

¶ 3967   Income in respect of a decedent (IRD, after-death income).

Income in respect of a decedent (IRD) covers income (including capital gain) which a decedent had a right to receive but that: (1) wasn't actually or constructively received by a cash basis decedent, or (2) wasn't accrued by an accrual basis decedent. IRD includes insurance renewal commissions, a monthly pension paid to deceased employee's widow, taxable distributions from a qualified employee plan or IRA, a death benefit under a deferred annuity contract, partnership income of a deceased partner (Reg § 1.742-1) and S corporation income of a deceased shareholder. (Code Sec. 1367(b)(4))[32]

¶ 3968   Installment obligations, including self-cancelling installment notes (SCINs).

Uncollected installment obligations held by the decedent and disposed of at his death are income in respect of a decedent (Code Sec. 453B(c); Reg § 1.691(a)-5(a)) and not reported on

27. ¶C-5218.31; ¶6724.03; TD ¶657,059
28. ¶C-9601; ¶6914; TD ¶579,501
29. ¶s C-9556, C-9605; ¶6914; TD ¶579,503
30. ¶s C-9606, C-9608; ¶6914.03; TD ¶579,504
31. ¶C-9608; ¶674; TD ¶579,506
32. ¶C-9505 *et seq.*; ¶s 6914, 6914.03; TD ¶578,505

the decedent's final return. (Code Sec. 691(a)(4)) The amount of the income in respect of a decedent is the excess of the face amount of the obligation over its basis in the hands of the decedent. (Code Sec. 453B(b), Code Sec. 691(a)(4)) On collecting the face amount, the executor, beneficiary or other recipient includes in gross income the same proportion of the payment that would have been reported by the decedent if he had lived and received the payment. (Reg § 1.691(a)-5(a))

If the executor or beneficiary transfers the installment obligation, the amount included in gross income for the tax year of the transfer is the fair market value of the obligation at the time of the transfer plus any excess of sales proceeds over fair market value (if it's sold) minus an amount equal to the basis of the obligation in the hands of the decedent (adjusted to reflect the receipt of any installment payments since the decedent's death). (Code Sec. 691(a)(4); Reg § 1.691(a)-5(b))

If the installment obligation is transferred to the obligor or is cancelled by the executor, any previously unreported gain from the installment sale will be recognized by the seller's estate. (Code Sec. 691(a)(5)) The result is the same where payments due on an installment note are extinguished at the holder's death under a provision contained in the sales agreement and installment note, i.e., a "death-terminating" installment note or self-cancelling installment note (SCIN).[33]

¶ 3969 Who is taxed on income in respect of a decedent?

A decedent's income in respect of a decedent (IRD) not includible on his last return must be reported, for the tax year when received, by:

. . . the decedent's estate, if it acquired the right to receive the item of income from the decedent;

. . . the person who, by reason of the decedent's death, acquires the right to the income whenever this right isn't acquired by the decedent's estate from the decedent; or

. . . the person who acquires the right from the decedent by bequest, devise or inheritance, if the amount is received after distribution by the decedent's estate of the right to the income. (Code Sec. 691(a)(1))[34]

The character of IRD is the same as it would have been in the hands of the decedent, if he had lived and received the income. (Code Sec. 691(a)(3); Reg § 1.691(a)-3(a))[35]

¶ 3970 Decedent's deductions and credits available to estate or beneficiaries.

Deductions for a decedent's business expenses, expenses for the production of income, interest, taxes, depletion and the credit for foreign taxes are available to the decedent's estate if the estate is liable for the obligation giving rise to the deduction or credit and it isn't allowable in the decedent's final (or any previous) return. If not available to the estate, the deduction or credit may be taken by the person who acquires an interest in the decedent's property from the decedent by reason of the decedent's death, or by bequest, devise or inheritance, subject to the obligation. (Code Sec. 691(b))[36]

¶ 3971 Deduction for estate tax attributable to income in respect of a decedent.

The decedent's right to income in respect of a decedent (IRD) is frequently included in his gross estate for federal estate and GST tax purposes although it's taxed as income to the recipient. As a relief, the recipient of the IRD can deduct the estate and GST tax attributable to inclusion of the right to income in the gross estate. (Code Sec. 691(c)(1); Reg § 1.691(c)-1(a)) This relief is available to an individual only if he itemizes his deductions but the deduction isn't subject to the 2%-of-AGI floor. (Code Sec. 67(b)(8))[37]

---

33. ¶C-9528; ¶6914; TD ¶578,528
34. ¶C-9501; ¶6914; TD ¶578,501
35. ¶C-9506; ¶6914.05; TD ¶578,506

36. ¶C-9551; ¶6914.04; TD ¶579,001
37. ¶C-9557 *et seq.*; ¶674; TD ¶579,007

If IRD includes capital gains or qualified dividends, the Code in effect treats the deduction as an offset against the capital gains or qualified dividends. For purposes of computing (1) the Code Sec. 1211 limitation on capital losses, (2) the maximum tax on a noncorporate tax-payer's capital gains or qualified dividends under Code Sec. 1(h), (3) the alternative tax on a corporation's capital gains, and (4) the partial exclusion of gain realized on the disposition of qualified small business stock, the amount of any gain taken into account that is treated as IRD must be reduced (but not below zero) by the amount of the allowable deduction for estate tax attributable to that gain. (Code Sec. 691(c)(4))[38]

Annuity payments received by the surviving annuitant of a joint and survivor annuity are IRD of the deceased annuitant to the extent that the payments are includible in gross income of the survivor. The portion of the estate tax attributable to the survivor's annuity is allowable as a deduction to the survivor over his life expectancy (determined under IRS tables). (Code Sec. 691(d); Reg § 1.691(d)-1(c))[39]

¶ 3972   Bankruptcy Estate for Bankrupt Individual.

The bankruptcy estate of an individual is treated as a separate taxable entity for income tax purposes, subject to special rules.

¶ 3973   Bankruptcy estate as separate taxable entity.

The separate entity rules apply if a bankruptcy case involving an *individual* debtor (not a corporation or partnership) is brought under Chapter 7 (relating to liquidations) or Chapter 11 (reorganizations) of Title 11 of the U.S. Code. (Code Sec. 1398(a))[40]

For income tax returns of bankruptcy estates (Form 1040 and Form 1041), see ¶4736.

¶ 3974   Debtor's election to close tax year.

An individual debtor can elect to close his tax year as of the day before the date the bankruptcy case commences. (Code Sec. 1398(d)(2)(A), Code Sec. 1398(d)(3)) If the election is made, the debtor's tax year that otherwise would include the commencement date is divided into two "short" tax years. The first year ends on the day before the commencement date; the second begins on the commencement date. (Code Sec. 1398(d)(2)(A))[41]

¶ 3975   Taxation of bankruptcy estate.

The gross income of the bankruptcy estate of an individual consists of: (1) any gross income of the individual debtor (other than any amount received or accrued as income by the debtor before the commencement of the case), that under the substantive law of bankruptcy (Title 11 of the U.S. Code), is property of the bankruptcy estate, and (2) the gross income of the estate beginning on and after the date the case commenced. (Code Sec. 1398(e)(1))[42]

Except as otherwise provided, the taxable income of the bankruptcy estate is computed the same as in the case of an individual. (Code Sec. 1398(c)(1))[43] The estate is allowed a personal exemption deduction equal to that of an individual (two exemptions for married debtors jointly filing for bankruptcy)[44] and the same standard deduction as married individuals filing separately. (Code Sec. 1398(c)(3)) The tax rate schedule applicable to the estate is the same as for married individuals filing separate returns. (Code Sec. 1398(c)(2))[45]

The estate succeeds to various income tax attributes of the debtor (including certain carry-overs and unused passive activity and at-risk losses). (Code Sec. 1398(g); Reg § 1.1398-1, Reg § 1.1398-2)[46]

38. ¶C-9563; ¶6914.07; TD ¶579,012
39. ¶C-9569; ¶6914.07; TD ¶579,018
40. ¶C-9701; ¶13,984; TD ¶578,001
41. ¶C-9802 *et seq.*; ¶13,984.05; TD ¶577,504
42. ¶C-9711; ¶13,984.01; TD ¶578,004

43. ¶C-9708; ¶13,984.01; TD ¶578,009
44. ¶C-9709; ¶13,984.01; TD ¶578,011
45. ¶C-9707; ¶13,984.01; TD ¶578,012
46. ¶C-9718; ¶13,984.02; TD ¶578,015

¶ 3976   Deduction of business and administrative expenses.

An amount paid or incurred by the bankruptcy estate is deductible or creditable by the estate to the same extent that the item would be by the debtor had the debtor remained in the same trades, businesses or activities after the case commenced as before and had the debtor paid or incurred the amount. (Code Sec. 1398(e)(3))[47]

The estate can deduct: (1) any administrative expense allowed under 11 U.S. Sec. 503 (11 USCS 503), and (2) any court fees and costs assessed against the estate under Chapter 123 of Title 28 of the U.S. Code. (Code Sec. 1398(h)(1))[48]

¶ 3977   Carrybacks and carryovers.

Any deduction for administrative and related expenses not used in the current year can be carried back by the estate three years and carried forward seven years (Code Sec. 1398(h)(2)), but only to a tax year of the *estate,* not of the debtor. (Code Sec. 1398(h)(2)(D))

The administrative expense carrybacks and carryovers that may be carried to a particular tax year are "stacked" after the net operating loss deductions (allowed by Code Sec. 172) are computed for the particular year. (Code Sec. 1398(h)(2)(C))[49]

If the bankruptcy estate itself incurs a net operating loss (apart from losses passing to the estate from the individual debtor), the bankruptcy estate can carry back its net operating losses not only to earlier tax years of the estate, but also to tax years of the debtor before the year in which the case commenced. (Code Sec. 1398(j)(2)(A))[50]

¶ 3978   Tax attributes on termination of estate.

On termination of the bankruptcy estate, the debtor succeeds to various tax attributes of the estate (including certain carryovers). (Code Sec. 1398(i))[1]

---

47. ¶C-9714; ¶13,984.01; TD ¶578,005
48. ¶C-9715; ¶13,984.01; TD ¶578,006
49. ¶C-9720; ¶s 1724.05, 13,984.01; TD ¶578,007

50. ¶C-9721; ¶s 1724.05, 13,984.01; TD ¶578,013
1. ¶C-9812; ¶13,984.02; TD ¶577,512

Chapter 19   Exempt Organizations

¶ 4100   Tax-Exempt Organizations.

Certain nonprofit organizations are exempt from federal income taxation, but they may be taxable on income from unrelated businesses they conduct.

Exempt organizations include:

...U.S. corporate instrumentalities organized under an Act of Congress (Code Sec. 501(c)(1));[1]

...corporations exclusively holding title to property, and collecting and remitting the income from it (less expenses) to an exempt organization (Code Sec. 501(c)(2));[2]

...religious, charitable, scientific, literary and educational organizations, organizations testing for public safety, organizations that foster national or international amateur sports competition, those organized and operated for preventing cruelty to children or animals, see ¶4102 (Code Sec. 501(c)(3)), qualified charitable risk pools, (Code Sec. 501(n)) cooperative hospital (Code Sec. 501(e)) and educational organization (Code Sec. 501(f)) service organizations;[3]

...religious and apostolic organizations, ¶4105;

...nonprofit civic organizations operated exclusively for social welfare, and local employees' associations whose net earnings are used solely for charitable, educational or recreational purposes (Code Sec. 501(c)(4));[4]

...labor, agricultural or horticultural organizations (Code Sec. 501(c)(5), Code Sec. 501(g));[5]

...chambers of commerce, business leagues, real estate boards, boards of trade or professional football leagues not organized for profit or private benefit (Code Sec. 501(c)(6));[6]

...social clubs organized for pleasure, recreation and other nonprofitable purposes (¶4107) (Code Sec. 501(c)(7)) and fraternal beneficiary societies, orders or associations operating under the lodge system and providing life, sick, accident or other benefits to members and their dependents (Code Sec. 501(c)(8));[7]

...domestic fraternal societies operating under the lodge system that don't provide payment of benefits, if their net earnings are devoted exclusively to religious, charitable, etc., and fraternal purposes (Code Sec. 501(c)(10));[8]

...voluntary employees' beneficiary associations providing benefit payments to members and their dependents (Code Sec. 501(c)(9));[9]

...local teachers' retirement fund associations (Code Sec. 501(c)(11));[10]

...certain local benevolent life insurance associations, mutual ditch or irrigation companies, mutual or cooperative telephone companies or like organizations, (Code Sec. 501(c)(12));[11]

...nonprofit cemetery companies and burial corporations (Code Sec. 501(c)(13));[12]

...credit unions and certain entities organized before Sept. 1, '57 to provide reserve funds and insure shares or deposits in building and loan associations, cooperative banks or mutual savings banks (Code Sec. 501(c)(14));[13]

...certain nonlife insurance companies (Code Sec. 501(c)(15));[14]

...farmers' cooperatives that are crop financing corporations (Code Sec. 501(c)(16));[15]

...supplemental unemployment benefit plans (SUBs) (Code Sec. 501(c)(17));[16]

---

1. ¶D-6301; ¶5014.03
2. ¶D-5801; ¶5014.04; TD ¶672,542
3. ¶D-5950 *et seq.*; ¶5014.04; TD ¶670,500 *et seq.*
4. ¶D-5100 *et seq.*; ¶5014.13; TD ¶672,501
5. ¶D-4600 *et seq.*; ¶5014.14; TD ¶672,508
6. ¶D-4800 *et seq.*; ¶5014.15; TD ¶671,501
7. ¶D-4300 *et seq.*; ¶5014.17; TD ¶671,007
8. ¶D-4304; ¶5014.19; TD ¶671,010

9. ¶D-4400 *et seq.*; ¶5014.18; TD ¶672,001
10. ¶D-5500 *et seq.*; ¶5014.20
11. ¶D-6100 *et seq.*; ¶5014.21
12. ¶D-6000 *et seq.*; ¶5014.22
13. ¶D-4900 *et seq.*; ¶5014.23
14. ¶D-5900 *et seq.*; ¶5014.24
15. ¶E-1041 *et seq.*; ¶5014.25
16. ¶D-4500; ¶5014.26

References beginning with a single letter are to paragraphs in RIA's Federal Tax Coordinator 2d and RIA's Analysis of Federal Taxes: Income. Those beginning with numbers are to paragraphs in RIA's United States Tax Reporter. Those beginning with TD are to paragraphs in RIA's Tax Desk.

... certain domestic veterans' organizations (Code Sec. 501(c)(19));[17]

... qualified employee benefit trusts (¶4319);

... trusts established by the Pension Benefit Guaranty Corporation (PBGC) in connection with a terminated plan (Code Sec. 501(c)(24));[18]

... pooled real estate investment funds of exempt organizations (Code Sec. 501(c)(25));[19]

... certain trusts created before June 25, '59, to pay benefits under a pension plan funded only by employee contributions (Code Sec. 501(c)(18));[20] black lung benefit trusts (Code Sec. 501(c)(21)); and[21] state sponsored workmen's compensation reinsurance organizations established before June 1, '96 (Code Sec. 501(c)(27)(A));[22]

... organizations (including mutual insurance companies) providing worker's compensation (Code Sec. 501(c)(27)(B));

... state sponsored high-risk health coverage organizations (Code Sec. 501(c)(26));[23] and

... qualified tuition programs. (Code Sec. 529)[24]

IRS may suspend the tax-exempt status of an organization designated or identified as a terrorist organization. (Code Sec. 501(p))[25]

For private foundations, see ¶4125 *et seq.*

¶ 4101   Feeder organizations.

An organization operated for the primary purpose of carrying on a business for profit (not just holding title to property) is taxable on all its income, even if all its profits are payable to exempt organizations. (Code Sec. 502(a); Reg § 1.502-1(a))[26]

But this type of "feeder" organization is exempt if it's controlled by and furnishes its services *solely* to: a single exempt organization, an exempt parent organization and its exempt subs, or exempt subs having a common parent. (Reg § 1.502-1(b))[27]

¶ 4102   Religious, charitable, educational and similar organizations.

A corporation, community chest, fund, foundation, or other organization is exempt if:

... it's both organized *and* operated exclusively for: religious, charitable, scientific, literary or educational (including certain child care) purposes; public safety testing; prevention of cruelty to children or animals; or fostering national or international amateur sports competition (even if it has local or regional membership); (Code Sec. 501(c)(3); Reg § 1.501(c)(3)-1(a))

... no part of its net earnings inures to benefit any private shareholder or individual; *and*

... no substantial part of its activities consists of carrying on propaganda or otherwise attempting to influence legislation, i.e., lobbying (subject to an election, see ¶4103), or intervening in any political campaign for or against any candidate (Code Sec. 501(c)(3))[28] — i.e., it can't be an "action" organization. (Reg § 1.501(c)(3)-1(c)(3)) IRS guidance shows examples of prohibited and permissible political activities of tax-exempts.[29] (For excise tax on these expenditures, see ¶4104.)

For tax years beginning after Mar. 23, 2010, special qualification requirements apply to any Code Sec. 501(c)(3) organization that operates at least one hospital facility. (Code Sec. 501(r), Code Sec. 6033(b))

IRS guidance explains when organizations providing down payment assistance to home

17. ¶D-5200 *et seq.*; ¶5014.28; TD ¶672,022
18. ¶D-5303
19. ¶D-5850 *et seq.*; ¶5014.32; TD ¶672,546
20. ¶D-5400 *et seq.*; ¶5014.27
21. ¶D-6200 *et seq.*; ¶5014.30
22. ¶5014.40
23. ¶D-6320; ¶5014.39
24. ¶A-4701; ¶5294
25. ¶D-4001A; ¶5014.44
26. ¶D-7101; ¶5024
27. ¶D-7103; ¶5024.01
28. ¶D-4101; ¶5014.05; TD ¶670,601
29. ¶D-6401; TD ¶677,001

buyers qualify for exemption.[30]

For "private foundation" presumption, see ¶4125.

¶ 4103 Lobbying expenditures election for Code Sec. 501(c)(3) organizations—Form 5768.

Certain Code Sec. 501(c)(3) organizations (other than church-related ones or private foundations) may elect (on Form 5768) to make limited lobbying expenditures without losing their exempt status. (Code Sec. 501(h))[31] The election is effective for all tax years that end after it's made, and that begin before it's revoked. (Code Sec. 501(h)(6))[32]

An electing charity's permissible lobbying expenditures for any tax year can't exceed ("general limit") the *lesser of:* (1) $1,000,000, or (2) the sum of 20% of the first $500,000 it paid or incurred for exempt purposes (including related administrative costs) for the year, plus 15% of the second $500,000, plus 10% of the third $500,000, plus 5% of any additional such expenditures. (Code Sec. 4911(c)(2); Reg § 56.4911-1(c)(1)) Also, only 25% of this lobbying amount may go to influencing legislation ("grass roots expenditures"). (Code Sec. 4911(c)(4); Reg § 56.4911-1(c)(2))[33] Charities must keep records of these expenditures (and show them on their annual returns, see ¶4124). (Reg § 56.4911-6)[34]

In any tax year an electing charity's lobbying expenditures exceed either the general or the grass roots limit, a 25% excise tax is imposed on that excess. If both limits are exceeded, the tax is imposed on the greater excess. (Code Sec. 4911(a), Code Sec. 4911(b))[35] Pay the tax on Form 4720. Use Form 8868 for an extension, see ¶4124.[36]

Also, an electing charity can lose its tax exemption if its lobbying expenditures over a four-year period exceed 150% of either limit. (Code Sec. 501(h)(1), Code Sec. 501(h)(2))[37] For the excise tax that applies if that happens, see ¶4104.

¶ 4104 Excise tax on Code Sec. 501(c)(3) organizations' political and lobbying expenditures—Form 4720.

A Code Sec. 501(c)(3) organization is subject to a two-tier excise tax on its *political expenditures.* An initial tax of 10% of the expenditure is imposed on the organization, and an initial 2 ½% tax (up to $5,000 per expenditure) is imposed on any organization manager who willfully and without reasonable cause agreed to the expenditure. (Code Sec. 4955(a), Code Sec. 4955(c)(2); Reg § 53.4955-1(b))[38] Form 4720 is used to report these taxes. Use Form 8868 for an extension, see ¶4124.[39] Additional taxes are imposed on both the organization (100%) and management (50%, up to $10,000 per expenditure) if the expenditure isn't corrected within a reasonable time. (Code Sec. 4955(b), Code Sec. 4955(c)(2))[40]

A Code Sec. 501(c)(3) organization (other than charities making the lobbying expense election (¶4103), private foundations and church-related organizations) whose *lobbying expenditures* for a tax year cause it to lose its tax exemption is subject to a 5% tax on those disqualifying amounts. The 5% tax also is imposed on any organization manager who agreed to the expenditure knowing that disqualification could result. (Code Sec. 4912)[41] Use Form 4720. Use Form 8868 for an extension, see ¶4124.[42]

IRS may also seek to enjoin a Code Sec. 501(c)(3) organization from engaging in flagrant political activities. (Code Sec. 7409(a); Reg § 301.7409-1(a))[43]

---

30. ¶D-4101
31. ¶D-6500 *et seq.,* ¶D-6571; ¶5014.12, ¶60,334; TD ¶677,020 *et seq.*
32. ¶D-6501; ¶5014.12; TD ¶677,023
33. ¶D-6507 *et seq.;* ¶49,114; TD ¶677,027
34. ¶D-6571; TD ¶677,028
35. ¶D-6532 *et seq.;* ¶5014.12, 49,114; TD ¶677,047
36. ¶S-2512; TD ¶688,030

37. ¶D-6572 *et seq.;* ¶5014.12; TD ¶677,042
38. ¶D-6421 *et seq.;* ¶49,554; TD ¶677,005
39. ¶S-2512; TD ¶688,029
40. ¶D-6421 *et seq.;* ¶49,554; TD ¶677,005
41. ¶D-6417 *et seq.;* ¶49,124; TD ¶677,017
42. ¶S-2512; TD ¶688,030
43. ¶V-2712; ¶74,094

¶ 4105 Religious or apostolic associations.

Even if an organization carries on business activities so that it can't be exempt under Code Sec. 501(c)(3) (as *exclusively* for exempt purposes), it still can be exempt as a *religious or apostolic association*. The organization may thus be exempt if it has a common or community treasury, and if its income (whether or not distributed) is taxed pro rata to its members, as a dividend received, for the organization's tax year ending with or within the member's tax year. (Code Sec. 501(d); Reg § 1.501(d)-1)[44]

observation: Exemption under Code Sec. 501(c)(3) is preferable because it means that contributions to the organization also may be deductible, see ¶2102.

¶ 4106 Civic leagues for social welfare.

A civic league is exempt if it isn't organized or operated for profit; is operated exclusively for the promotion of social welfare; no part of its net earnings inures to the benefit of any private shareholder or individual; (Code Sec. 501(c)(4)) and no substantial part of its activities consists of providing commercial-type insurance. (Code Sec. 501(m)(1))[45]

¶ 4107 Social clubs.

For a social club to be exempt, it must be organized and operated substantially for pleasure, recreation or other nonprofit purposes, its governing instruments or written policies can't provide for discrimination based on color, race or religion, and no part of its earnings may benefit any private shareholder. (Code Sec. 501(c)(7))[46]

Up to 35% of a social club's gross receipts (including investment income) may be from sources outside of its membership. Within this 35%, not more than 15% of gross receipts may be from the general public's (i.e., not members or their guests) use of the club's facilities or services.[47]

If the club fails the 35% or 15% tests (and a facts and circumstances test) in any tax year, all of its income, even amounts (reduced by allocable costs) received from members, is subject to tax in that year. (Code Sec. 277)[48]

IRS has privately ruled that a social club may carry forward its net operating losses incurred in years in which it was a tax-exempt entity to years when it is a taxable entity.[49]

¶ 4108 Nondiscrimination requirements for VEBAs and SUBs.

A VEBA or SUB won't be exempt unless it satisfies nondiscrimination rules similar to those applicable to qualified employee benefit plans (¶4325). (Code Sec. 501(c)(17)(A), Code Sec. 505(a)(1), Code Sec. 505(b)(1))[50]

¶ 4109 Political organizations—Form 1120-POL; Form 990; Form 8871; Form 8872; Form 8453-X.

A political organization is a party, committee, association, fund (including certain newsletter funds) or other organization (whether or not incorporated) that's organized and operated primarily to accept contributions and/or make expenditures for an "exempt function," e.g., influencing or attempting to influence the selection, nomination, election or appointment of any individual to public office. (Code Sec. 527(e)(1), Code Sec. 527(e)(2), Code Sec. 527(g))[1] Subject to exceptions, political organizations must (1) give notice of status electronically (use Form 8871 and Form 8453-X), (2) provide periodic reports of contributions and expenditures,

44. ¶D-5601; ¶5014.33
45. ¶D-5100 *et seq.*; ¶5014.13; TD ¶672,501
46. ¶D-4201; ¶5014.16; TD ¶671,001
47. ¶D-4206; ¶5014.16; TD ¶671,004
48. ¶D-4206; ¶5014.16; TD ¶671,001
49. ¶L-4301
50. ¶s D-4418, D-4501, D-6351; ¶5054; TD ¶672,011
1. ¶s D-5002, D-5021; ¶5274; TD ¶672,513

electronically in some cases (use Form 8872) and (3) file annual returns. Although generally tax-exempt (Code Sec. 527(a)), a political organization is taxed, at the *highest* corporate rate, on income (minus connected expenses) that isn't from its exempt function. (Code Sec. 527(b)(1), Code Sec. 527(c))[2] A political organization, whether or not tax-exempt, that has more than $100 of taxable income must file an annual income tax return on Form 1120-POL. (Code Sec. 6012(a)(6)) Only tax-exempt political organizations may have to file annual information returns. Subject to exceptions, a tax-exempt political organization (other than a qualified state or local political organization) with $25,000 or more of annual gross receipts must file Form 990. Qualified state or local political organizations must file Form 990 (see ¶4124) if they have annual gross receipts of $100,000 or more. (Code Sec. 6033(g)(1)) IRS has provided a safe harbor for establishing that a political organization's failure to report certain contributor information on Form 8872 was due to reasonable cause and not due to willful neglect.[3]

IRS has a website for political organizations to electronically file documents and allow public access and searches for contributions and expenditures.

¶ 4110   Homeowners' associations—Form 1120-H.

Associations for the management of residential real estate and condominiums and timeshare associations (but not cooperative housing corporations) that meet an organization and operation test and an income test may elect (by filing Form 1120-H) to be treated as exempt organizations. (Code Sec. 528(a), Code Sec. 528(c))[4] Electing associations are taxed at a 30% (32% for timeshare associations) rate on income other than amounts received as dues, fees or assessments from members. (Code Sec. 528(b))[5] This taxable income must be reported on Form 1120-H.[6]

¶ 4111   Loss of exemption for exempt employee trusts engaging in prohibited transactions.

Some employee trusts (including church and governmental plans) will lose or be denied their exemption from income tax (and are subject to an excise tax, see ¶4347) if they engage in "prohibited transactions." (Code Sec. 503(a)(1))[7]

A *prohibited transaction* occurs if a trust engages in an activity with its creator, a substantial contributor or person related to either, in which it:

(1) lends any part of its income or corpus without receiving adequate security and a reasonable rate of interest;

(2) pays any compensation in excess of a reasonable allowance for personal services actually rendered;

(3) makes any part of its services available on a preferential basis;

(4) makes any substantial purchase of securities or any other property for more than adequate consideration;

(5) sells any substantial part of its securities or any other property for less than adequate consideration; or

(6) engages in any other transaction that results in a substantial diversion of its income or corpus. (Code Sec. 503(b))[8]

¶ 4112   Excise tax on excess benefit transactions by disqualified persons and organization managers—Form 4720.

Penalty excise taxes are imposed on disqualified persons and organization managers who

2. ¶D-5008; ¶5274; TD ¶672,518
3. ¶S-1921; ¶5274; TD ¶672,518
4. ¶D-5701 *et seq.*; ¶5284; TD ¶672,531 *et seq.*
5. ¶D-5712; ¶5284; TD ¶672,539

6. ¶S-1922; ¶5284; TD ¶609,812
7. ¶D-6700 *et seq.*; ¶5034.01
8. ¶D-6702 *et seq.*; ¶5034.02

benefit from an excess benefit transaction with a Code Sec. 501(c)(3) or Code Sec. 501(c)(4) organization (other than a private foundation), or that was such an organization at any time within five years before the transaction. (Code Sec. 4958(a); Reg § 53.4958-1) An excess benefit transaction is one in which the exempt organization provides a benefit directly or indirectly to or for the use of a disqualified person (any person in a position to exercise substantial influence over the organization at any time during the five years before the transaction (Code Sec. 4958(f); Reg § 53.4958-4), or certain related parties, that exceeds the value of the consideration, including services, received in exchange. (Code Sec. 4958(c))[9]

The disqualified person is liable for a tax of 25% of the excess benefit (200% if the transaction is not corrected by the time a deficiency notice is mailed or the tax is assessed). (Code Sec. 4958(a)(1), Code Sec. 4958(b); Reg § 53.4958-1)[10] An organization manager (officer, director, trustee, etc.) who knowingly participates in an excess benefit transaction is liable for a tax of the lesser of 10% or $20,000. (Code Sec. 4958(a)(2), Code Sec. 4958(d)(2))[11] Distributions from a donor advised fund to a donor, donor advisor, or related person are automatically treated as excess benefit transactions. (Code Sec. 4958(c)(2)) Excess benefit transactions of Code Sec. 509(a)(3) supporting organizations are determined under special rules. (Code Sec. 4958(c)(3))[12] IRS may abate the first-tier taxes for reasonable cause. (Code Sec. 4962(b))[13] Persons liable for excess benefit transaction excise taxes report them on Form 4720. (Reg § 53.6071-1(f)) Use Form 8868 for an extension, see ¶4124.

¶ 4113 Excise tax on entities that are parties to prohibited tax shelter transactions, and on entity managers who knowingly approve prohibited tax shelter transactions.

Excise taxes are imposed on (1) certain tax-exempt entities that are parties to "prohibited tax shelter transactions" (Code Sec. 4965(a)(1)) and (2) "entity managers" of tax-exempt entities who approve the entity as a party (or otherwise cause the entity to be a party) to a prohibited tax shelter transaction and know or have reason to know that the transaction is a prohibited tax shelter transaction. (Code Sec. 4965(a)(2)) IRS has issued regs under Code Sec. 4965 that define "party" and address other aspects of the above taxes. (Reg § 53.4965-1 through Reg § 53.4965-9)[14]

¶ 4114 Tax-exempt entities must disclose participation in prohibited tax shelter transactions to IRS or face penalties—Form 8886-T.

Every tax-exempt entity described in Code Sec. 4965(c) that is a party to a prohibited tax shelter transaction (¶4113) must disclose to IRS (on Form 8886-T): (a) that the entity is a party to the prohibited tax shelter transaction; and (b) the identity of any other party to the transaction which is known to such tax-exempt entity (Code Sec. 6033(a)(2))[15] The penalty for failing to comply is $100 for each day during which such failure continues, not to exceed $50,000 with respect to any one disclosure. IRS may make a written demand on any entity or manager subject to the penalty for nondisclosure, specifying a reasonable future date by which the required disclosure must be filed. Failure to comply with the demand is subject to an additional penalty of $100 for each day after the expiration of the time specified in the demand during which such failure continues, not to exceed $10,000 with respect to any one disclosure. (Code Sec. 6652(c)(3)(B)(ii))[16] For non-plan entities, these penalties are imposed on the tax-exempt entity. For plan entities, they are imposed on the entity manager of the tax-exempt entity.

Any taxable party to a prohibited tax shelter transaction must disclose by statement to any

---

9. ¶D-6650 *et seq.*; ¶49,584; TD ¶676,500
10. ¶D-6652; ¶49,584
11. ¶D-6653; ¶49,584
12. ¶D-6654; ¶49,584
13. ¶D-6652; ¶49,624
14. ¶D-8301; ¶49,654
15. ¶S-2895; ¶60,334
16. ¶V-2538; ¶66,524.01

tax-exempt entity that is a party to the transaction that it's a prohibited tax shelter transaction. (Code Sec. 6011(g))[17]

¶ 4115 Donee organization must acknowledge and report qualified vehicle donations—Form 1098-C.

An organization that receives a charitable contribution of a "qualified vehicle" (¶2139) must provide the donor with a contemporaneous written acknowledgment of the contribution if the claimed value is more than $500, and report the information to IRS (use Form 1098-C) or face a penalty, which also applies for furnishing a false or fraudulent acknowledgment. It also must indicate whether the donee provided any goods or services in consideration for the vehicle, and, if so, a description and good faith estimate of their value, or, if they consist solely of intangible religious benefits, a statement to that effect. (Code Sec. 170(f)(12)(B))[18]

¶ 4116 Application for exemption—advance rulings—Form 1023; Form 1024.

An organization must apply in writing (on Form 1023 for Code Sec. 501(c)(3) organizations, Form 1024 for most others, and with the appropriate user fee with for an IRS ruling or determination that it's exempt from federal income tax. (Reg § 1.501(a)-1(a)(2)) A parent organization's exemption doesn't cover its subsidiary. [19] But organizations under the general control of a central organization may apply on a group basis.[20] When applying for tax-exempt status, sponsoring organizations must notify IRS of any donor advised fund they maintain or intend to maintain. (Code Sec. 508(f))

¶ 4117 Modification or revocation of exemption.

IRS may modify or revoke rulings and determination letters that granted exempt status to an organization (e.g., for failure to comply with exemption requirements, or prohibited transactions, see ¶4111). (Reg § 601.201(n)(6)) The revocation may be retroactive, in which case deficiencies and penalties may be imposed for open years.[21]

¶ 4118 Disclosure of nondeductibility of contributions.

Certain exempt organizations that aren't eligible to receive deductible contributions must expressly state that fact (in a conspicuous and easily recognizable format) in every fund-raising solicitation. (Code Sec. 6113)[22]

¶ 4119 Disclosure requirement for quid pro quo contributions.

Certain charities that are eligible to receive deductible contributions must, in connection with soliciting or receiving a quid pro quo contribution in excess of $75, inform the donor in writing that his charitable deduction is limited to the excess of his contribution over the value of the goods or services provided by the charity (with a good faith estimate, made by using any reasonable method in good faith, of the value of those goods and services). (Code Sec. 6115; Reg § 1.6115-1)[23]

¶ 4120 Disclosure of annual return and exemption application—Form 990; Form 990-PF; Form 990-T; Form 4720.

A Code Sec. 501(c) or Code Sec. 501(d) organization must make a copy of its annual returns (Form 990) for the last three years and its exempt status application and supporting documents available for inspection during business hours but religious or apostolic organizations

17. ¶S-4440; ¶60,114.023
18. ¶K-3948.2; ¶67,204; TD ¶861,084
19. ¶T-10450 *et seq.*; ¶5014.01; TD ¶670,502
20. ¶T-10481; ¶5014.01
21. ¶s T-10485, T-10486
22. ¶D-4004 *et seq.*; ¶61,134; TD ¶673,001
23. ¶s K-3101, K-3102; ¶61,154; TD ¶s 330,257, 330,259

don't have to make K-1s available. (Code Sec. 6104(a), Code Sec. 6104(b), Code Sec. 6104(d); Reg § 301.6104(d)-3)[24] The organization must provide a copy of the application without charge, except reasonable reproduction and mailing costs, to any individual who requests it. Copies must be provided within 30 days, for written requests, or immediately for in-person requests. (Code Sec. 6104(d)(1); Reg § 301.6104(d)-3) Requests don't have to be honored if the information has been made widely available or if the request is determined by IRS to be part of a harassment campaign. (Code Sec. 6104(d)(4); Reg § 301.6104(d)-2, Reg § 301.6104(d)-3)[25] These requirements apply to annual information returns (Form 990-PF and Form 4720) of private foundations, which also must disclose names and addresses of contributors. (Reg § 301.6104(d)-1(b)(4)(ii))[26] Returns of certain political organizations (¶4109) also are subject to disclosure requirements. (Code Sec. 6104(a), Code Sec. 6104(b), Code Sec. 6104(d))[27] Code Sec. 501(c)(3) organizations (¶4102) must make available for public inspection copies of their annual unrelated business income tax (UBIT) returns (Form 990-T) for the three-year period following the filing of the return. (Code Sec. 6104(d)(1)(A)(ii)) IRS has issued interim guidance on meeting this requirement pending the issuance of regs.[28]

More specifically, an organization's completed Form 990, Form 990-EZ, and Form 990-T, are available for public inspection as required by Code Sec. 6104. Schedule B (Form 990, 990-EZ, or 990-PF), Schedule of Contributors is available for public inspection for section 527 organizations filing Form 990 or 990-EZ. For other organizations that file Form 990 or 990-EZ, parts of Schedule B (990, 990-EZ, or 990-PF) may be open to public inspection.[29]

¶ 4121   Unrelated business income tax—Form 990-T.

Exempt organizations (other than U.S. corporate instrumentalities and certain other exempt organizations) are subject to a tax on income (¶4122) from any unrelated business (defined below). (Code Sec. 511(a), Code Sec. 512(a), Code Sec. 512(b)(12); Reg § 1.511-2(a)(1))[30] Form 990-T is used to report and pay the tax. (Reg § 1.6012-2(e), Reg § 1.6012-3(a)(5))[31] Imposition of this tax doesn't affect the organization's exempt status. (Code Sec. 501(b), Code Sec. 511)[32]

An unrelated business is a trade or business (i.e., carried on for the production of income, whether or not profit results) regularly carried on (including seasonally) by the organization, that isn't substantially related (aside from providing funds) to the exercise or performance of its exempt purpose or function. (Code Sec. 513(a), Code Sec. 513(c); Reg § 1.513-1)[33] An unrelated trade or business doesn't include the activity of soliciting and receiving qualified sponsorship payments (payments from a person engaged in a trade or business with respect to which the person won't get any substantial return benefit other than the use or acknowledgment of the donor's name or logo as part of a sponsored event or certain goods or services that have an insubstantial value). (Code Sec. 513(i); Reg § 1.513-4)[34] Regs provide guidance on whether a tour activity is an unrelated business. (Reg § 1.513-7)[35] Debt management plan services are an unrelated trade or business, if the organization is *not* a tax-exempt credit counseling organization. (Code Sec. 513(j))[36]

For exempt SUBs, qualified employee pension, etc., trusts, and nonexempt trusts, *any* business it regularly carries on is "unrelated." (Code Sec. 513(b))[37]

But an unrelated business doesn't include an activity where substantially all the work is performed for the organization without compensation, e.g., by volunteers. (Code Sec. 513(a)(1))[38]

---

24. ¶S-6601 *et seq.*; ¶61,044
25. ¶S-6609.1; ¶61,044
26. ¶S-6603; ¶61,044
27. ¶S-6642 *et seq.*; ¶61,044
28. ¶S-6603; ¶61,044
29. ¶S-6601 *et seq.*; ¶61,044
30. ¶D-6800 *et seq.*; ¶5114 *et seq.*; TD ¶681,000 *et seq.*
31. ¶S-2101; ¶5114; TD ¶688,501

32. ¶D-6801; ¶5114
33. ¶D-6804 *et seq.*; ¶5134.01; TD ¶681,019
34. ¶D-6819 *et seq.*; ¶5134.02; TD ¶681,026
35. ¶D-6829.1; ¶5134.03
36. ¶D-6848; ¶5134
37. ¶D-6807; ¶5134; TD ¶681,034
38. ¶D-6836; ¶5134; TD ¶681,028

The rules on assessment, collection, and penalties applicable to income tax, including estimated tax and foreign tax credit, apply. (Code Sec. 515, Code Sec. 6655(g)(3)(A); Reg § 1.511-3(a)) The corporate tax rates and filing dates apply if the organization is a corporation, and those for trusts if it's a charitable trust. (Code Sec. 511(a), Code Sec. 511(b))[39]

Tax-exempt organizations must make estimated tax payments on their unrelated business taxable income. (Code Sec. 6655(g)(3))[40]

¶ 4122   Unrelated business taxable income (UBTI) defined.

Unrelated business taxable income (UBTI) is the gross income derived from any unrelated trade or business (¶4121), less directly connected allowable deductions, but with certain exceptions (below), additions and limitations (Code Sec. 512(a), Code Sec. 512(b)), including a specific deduction of $1,000. (Code Sec. 512(b)(12))[41]

UBTI did not include gain or loss from the qualified sale, exchange, or other disposition by an eligible taxpayer of any qualifying brownfield property acquired after 2004 and before 2010. (Code Sec. 512(b)(19)(A))[42]

Social clubs, VEBAs, SUBs and veterans organizations are allowed special exclusions. (Code Sec. 512(a)(3))[43] A charitable organization's income or gain from ownership of S corporation stock is UBTI. (Code Sec. 512(e))[44]

Dividends (except certain insurance income received from a controlled foreign corporation (Code Sec. 512(b)(17))), interest, rents, royalties, annuities, payments with respect to securities loans, loan commitment fees, and gains or losses from property dispositions are excluded from UBTI, as are gains or losses from the lapse or termination of options to buy or sell securities or real property, or from the forfeiture of good-faith deposits to buy, sell, or lease real property in connection with the organization's investment activities, (Code Sec. 512(b))[45] and annual dues of up to $146 for 2010 ($148 for 2011) per member received by agricultural or horticultural organizations. (Code Sec. 512(d))[46]

But to the extent the dividends, etc., are attributable to property acquired through debt financing ("debt-financed property," see ¶4123), they *are* included in UBTI. The includible portion (computed separately for each property) equals a percentage (not over 100%) of the dividends, etc., derived from the property during the tax year, based on the ratio of: (1) the average acquisition indebtedness, to (2) the average adjusted basis of debt-financed property, for the year. (Code Sec. 514(a)(1))[47] This same percentage also is used to compute the allowable deductions for that property (other than capital loss carryovers or depreciation). (Code Sec. 514(a)(2), Code Sec. 514(a)(3))[48]

Payments of interest, rents, royalties and annuities ("specified payments") made by a controlled entity to its tax-exempt parent before 2010 were included in UBTI to the extent they exceeded fair market value. (Code Sec. 512(b)(13)(E))[49]

¶ 4123   Property acquired through debt financing—"debt-financed property."

Debt-financed property, with certain exceptions, is any property held to produce income (including gains from its disposition, as well as rents, dividends and other recurring income) (Code Sec. 514(b); Reg § 1.514(b)-1(a)), with respect to which there's an acquisition indebtedness at any time during the tax year. Securities purchased on margin by a tax-exempt trust that donated money to a university were held to be debt-financed property. As a result, income from the sale of the securities was subject to the unrelated business income tax.[50]

"Acquisition indebtedness" for any property generally means: (1) the unpaid amount of

39. ¶D-6928 *et seq.*; TD ¶681,002
40. ¶S-5421; ¶66,554; TD ¶689,001
41. ¶D-6900 *et seq.*; ¶5124; TD ¶681,004
42. ¶D-6911.3; ¶5124.01
43. ¶D-6929 *et seq.*; ¶5124; TD ¶681,034
44. ¶D-6916.1; TD ¶681,012

45. ¶D-6901 *et seq.*; ¶5124; TD ¶681,006
46. ¶D-6847; ¶5124; TD ¶681,033
47. ¶D-6901 *et seq.*; ¶5144; TD ¶682,001 *et seq.*
48. ¶s D-7007, D-7010; ¶5144; TD ¶682,001
49. ¶D-6913.2; ¶5124
50. ¶D-7012 *et seq.*; ¶5144; TD ¶682,005

indebtedness incurred by the organization in acquiring or improving the property; and (2) indebtedness incurred at other times which *but for* the acquisition or improvement wouldn't have been incurred (if incurred after the acquisition, etc., the debt must have been reasonably foreseeable at that time). (Code Sec. 514(c))[1]

Any mortgage or other lien on the acquired property is considered incurred in that acquisition, whether or not it's thus assumed by the organization. (Code Sec. 514(c)(2)(A))[2]

¶ 4124   Exempt organization returns—Form 990; Form 8868.

In general, every organization that's exempt from tax, or whose exemption application is pending, must file an annual information return (Form 990 series) and keep the records and make sworn statements as required by IRS. (Code Sec. 6033; Reg § 1.6033-2)[3] Code Sec. 509(a)(3) supporting organizations must file annual information returns (Code Sec. 6033(a)(3)(B)) containing specific information (Code Sec. 6033(l))[4] Certain exempt organizations that acquire interests in life insurance contracts must file an information return or face a penalty. (Code Sec. 6050V, Code Sec. 6724(d)(1)(B)(xiv), Code Sec. 6721(e)(2)(D))[5] For private foundations, see ¶4131.

The return must show the organization's total lobbying and political expenditures for the year (Code Sec. 6033(b)(8)), (except political expenditures of nonpolitical organizations taxed under Code Sec. 527(f) (Code Sec. 6033(e)(1)(B)(iii)))[6] and the total amount of dues and similar receipts to which the expenditures are allocable. There are exceptions for Code Sec. 501(c)(3) organizations' in-house expenditures not exceeding $2,000 (Code Sec. 6033(e)(1))[7] and certain nondeductible dues.[8]

IRS redesigned the Form 990 and its accompanying instructions for the 2008 tax year (returns filed in 2009). The revised Form 990 includes a core form to be completed by all organizations, and schedules to be completed depending on an organization's type and activities. IRS has released Publications 4740, 4741, and 4752 and has posted numerous materials on its web site to help tax-exempt organizations deal with the newly revised Form 990.

To provide many smaller organizations additional time to adapt to the new form, IRS phased in, over a three-year period (2008 – 2010), the requirement to file the new form. Beginning in 2010, most organizations with gross receipts less than $200,000 and total assets less than $500,000 may file either Form 990 or Form 990-EZ.[9]

There's no monetary penalty for failure to file Form 990-N. (Code Sec. 6652(c)(1)(E))[10]

Information returns of parent tax-exempt organizations must include information about transactions with controlled entities. (Code Sec. 6033(h))[11]

Sponsoring organizations must disclose information about donor advised funds on information returns. (Code Sec. 6033(k))

Form 990 must be for the organization's annual accounting period or if it has none, the calendar year. (Reg § 1.6033-2(b)) It must be filed on or before the 15th day of the fifth full calendar month after the close of the annual accounting period. (Reg § 1.6033-2(e))[12]

An exempt organization required to file a return on Form 990 (except for Form 990-C), Form 1041-A, Form 4720, Form 5227, or Form 8870 may obtain an automatic three-month filing extension by filing on or before the return due date a Form 8868 showing the full amount properly estimated as tax, and remitting the full amount of properly estimated unpaid tax. (Reg § 1.6081-9(a))

An exempt organization that fails to file the required information return or notice for three consecutive years will automatically lose its exempt status and must reapply to be recognized

---

1. ¶D-7040 *et seq.*; ¶5144; TD ¶682,005
2. ¶D-7043; ¶5144; TD ¶682,007
3. ¶S-2801 *et seq.*; ¶60,334; TD ¶688,001
4. ¶S-2823.1
5. ¶S-2896; ¶60,50V4
6. ¶S-2853; ¶60,334; TD ¶688,016
7. ¶s S-2858.1, S-2858.2; ¶60,334
8. ¶S-2858.3; ¶60,334
9. ¶S-2801.1; ¶60,334
10. ¶V-1907; ¶6524
11. ¶S-2862.2
12. ¶S-4928; ¶60,334; TD ¶688,003

as an exempt organization. IRS will publish and maintain a list of organizations whose status has been so revoked (Code Sec. 6033(j))[13]

Most exempt organizations must file an information return (with Form 990) on liquidation, dissolution, termination or contraction if it was exempt for any of its last five years. (Code Sec. 6043(b))[14]

Tax-exempt organizations must electronically file their Forms 990, if they have $10 million or more in total assets and file 250 or more returns a year. In addition, private foundations and charitable trusts must e-file Forms 990-PF, regardless of their asset size, if they file at least 250 returns. (Reg § 301.6033-4)[15] For other information return requirements, see ¶4745.

IRS Publication 4779 provides important information on the steps that must be taken when an exempt organization is merged or terminated including the return to be filed to inform IRS, the date by which it must be filed, information that must be disclosed on the return, required attachments to the return, and other items.

¶ 4125   Private Foundations and Donor Advised Funds.

Private foundations are generally exempt from income tax, but are subject to excise taxes, notification requirements and other restrictions.

A private foundation is any domestic or foreign religious, scientific, charitable, etc., organization described in Code Sec. 501(c)(3) (¶4102) *other than* organizations that:

(1) are "50% charities" (¶2125), except operating foundations and membership organizations (Code Sec. 509(a)(1));[16]

(2) meet detailed public support tests (Code Sec. 509(a)(2), Code Sec. 509(d));[17]

(3) operate exclusively for the benefit of one or more of the above organizations (as Type I, Type II, or Type III supporting organizations) and aren't controlled by disqualified persons (¶4127, other than foundation managers) (Code Sec. 509(a)(3));[18]

(4) are organized and operated exclusively for testing for public safety. (Code Sec. 509(a)(4))[19]

Strict accountability requirements apply to qualify as a Type III supporting organization (Code Sec. 509(f)(1));[20] and Type I and Type II supporting organizations lose their status as non-private foundations if they accept gifts from prohibited persons. (Code Sec. 509(f)(2)(A))[21]

A Code Sec. 501(c)(3) organization (other than a church or an organization whose annual gross receipts don't exceed $5,000) is presumed to be a private foundation unless it notifies IRS to the contrary (Code Sec. 508(b), Code Sec. 508(c))[22] on Form 1023 within 15 months from the end of the month it was organized. (Reg § 1.508-1(b)(2))[23]

IRS has established a specific procedure for organizations classified as supporting organizations under Code Sec. 509(a)(3) that wish to seek reclassification under Code Sec. 509(a)(1) or Code Sec. 509(a)(2).[24]

A revenue procedure provides guidance to grantor determinations of public charity status under Code Sec. 509(a)(1), Code Sec. 509(a)(2) or Code Sec. 509(a)(3), for purposes of the excise taxes imposed on grants to certain supporting organizations under Code Sec. 4942 (¶4127), Code Sec. 4945 (¶4127), and Code Sec. 4966 (¶4129).

¶ 4126   Taxable trusts and foreign organizations subject to private foundation rules—Form 1041-A; Form 5227.

Certain charitable trusts and split interest trusts, and foreign organizations meeting the

---

13. ¶S-2802; ¶60,334
14. ¶S-2883; ¶60,334; TD ¶815,008
15. ¶S-2822.2; ¶60,334; TD ¶688,001
16. ¶D-7203; ¶5074; TD ¶683,506
17. ¶s D-7204, D-7207, D-7209; ¶5074; TD ¶683,507
18. ¶D-7212 *et seq.*; ¶5074; TD ¶683,508
19. ¶D-7202; ¶5074; TD ¶670,632
20. ¶D-7211; ¶5074
21. ¶D-7211; ¶5074
22. ¶s D-7216, D-7217; ¶5074; TD ¶683,503
23. ¶T-10464; ¶5074; TD ¶683,503
24. ¶T-10492

private foundation definition (¶4125), may be subject to the private foundation excise taxes (¶4127) and rules on prohibited acts, but not the notification requirements. (Code Sec. 4947, Code Sec. 4948) File Form 1041-A for a split interest trust. Use Form 8868 for an extension, see ¶4124. Use Form 5227 to report the financial activities of a split-interest trust and to determine if it is treated as a private foundation and is subject to excise tax. Use Form 8868 for an extension, see ¶4124.[25]

¶ 4127   Excise taxes on private foundations—Form 990-PF; Form 4720.

Private foundations may be subject to the following excise taxes.

Net investment income. An *exempt* private foundation is liable for an excise tax of 2% on its net investment income for the tax year. (Code Sec. 4940(a); Reg § 53.4940-1)[26] The tax is reduced to 1% if the foundation makes certain charitable distributions (Code Sec. 4940(e))[27] and is eliminated altogether for certain operating foundations. (Code Sec. 4940(d))[28] For a *taxable* foundation, the excise tax equals the amount (if any) by which: (1) the sum of 2% of its net investment income (computed as if it were exempt) plus the unrelated business income tax (¶4122) that would have been imposed on it had it been exempt, *exceeds* (2) the income tax actually imposed on it for the tax year. (Code Sec. 4940(b))[29] Report the tax on Form 990-PF. (Reg § 53.6011-1(d))[30]

Self-dealing. An excise tax is imposed when a disqualified person (substantial contributors, foundation managers, and specified owners, family members and related entities of these, as well as government officials) (Code Sec. 4946(a)(1)) engages in any of certain acts of self-dealing with a private foundation.[31]

For *each* act of self-dealing (Code Sec. 4941(a), Code Sec. 4941(b));[32] the disqualified person (except foundation managers) is subject to an initial tax of 10% on the amount (not exceeding the amount he actually benefits) involved (Code Sec. 4941(a)(1); Reg § 53.4941(a)-1(a))[33] and a 200% additional tax if the self-dealing isn't timely corrected. (Code Sec. 4941(b)(1))[34] Any foundation manager who knowingly participates in the act is subject to an initial 5% tax. (Code Sec. 4941(a)(2))[35] and, if he refuses to agree with all or part of the correction, an additional 50% tax. (Code Sec. 4941(b)(2))[36] Managers may be jointly and severally liable, but their maximum liability for any one act is $20,000 in initial tax and $20,000 in additional tax . (Code Sec. 4941(c))[37] Report the initial taxes on Form 4720. (Reg § 53.6011-1(b)) Use Form 8868 for an extension, see ¶4124.[38]

Failure to distribute income. A foundation (other than an operating foundation) that fails to distribute its income for a tax year by the end of the *next* year is subject to an initial tax equal to 30% of the income (based on a minimum investment return) (Code Sec. 4942(a); Reg § 53.4942(a)-1(a)), which IRS may abate for reasonable cause (Code Sec. 4962(a))[39] and a 100% additional tax if the foundation fails to distribute the income by the date the initial tax is assessed or IRS issues a 90-day letter for it. (Code Sec. 4942(b))[40] Distributions by nonoperating private foundations to certain supporting organizations are not qualifying distributions. (Code Sec. 4942(g)(4))[41] Report the initial taxes on Form 4720. (Reg § 53.6011-1(b)) Use Form 8868 for an extension, see ¶4124.[42]

Excess business holdings. A foundation that has any excess business holdings is subject to an initial tax (which IRS may abate for reasonable cause) equal to 10% of those excess holdings, based on their value on the day during the tax year when those holdings were the greatest. (Code Sec. 4943(a), Code Sec. 4962)[43] If the foundation fails to timely correct its

25. ¶s D-7300 *et seq.*, D-7400 *et seq.*; ¶s 49,474, 49,484; TD ¶688,009
26. ¶D-7501; ¶49,404; TD ¶684,001
27. ¶D-7503; ¶49,404; TD ¶684,006
28. ¶D-7504; ¶49,404; TD ¶684,009
29. ¶D-7506; ¶49,404.
30. ¶S-2511; ¶60,334; TD ¶684,001
31. ¶D-7600 *et seq.*; ¶s 49,414; 49,464; TD ¶684,500
32. ¶s D-7606, D-7608; ¶49,414.02; TD ¶684,500
33. ¶D-7601; ¶49,414.02; TD ¶684,501

34. ¶D-7602; ¶49,414.02; TD ¶684,503
35. ¶D-7602; ¶49,414.02; TD ¶684,504
36. ¶D-7602; ¶49,414.02; TD ¶684,505
37. ¶s D-7603, D-7604; ¶49,414.02; TD ¶684,506
38. ¶S-2511; TD ¶684,504
39. ¶s D-7701, D-8201; ¶s 49,424, 49,614; TD ¶685,001
40. ¶s D-7701, D-7706; ¶49,424.01; TD ¶685,002
41. ¶D-7711; ¶49,424.03
42. ¶S-2511; TD ¶685,001
43. ¶s D-7800 *et seq.*, D-8201; ¶s 49,434, 49,614; TD ¶685,509

holdings, an additional 200% tax is imposed. (Code Sec. 4943(b))[44] The excess business holding tax applies to donor advised funds (Code Sec. 4943(e))[45] and the excess business holdings rules apply to certain supporting organizations. (Code Sec. 4943(f))[46] Report the initial taxes on Form 4720. (Reg § 53.6011-1(b)) Use Form 8868 for an extension, see ¶4124.[47]

Investments that jeopardize a foundation's charitable purpose. An excise tax is imposed if a foundation makes investments that jeopardize its charitable purpose. An initial tax of 10% of the amount invested is imposed on the foundation *and* on any foundation manager who knowingly participated in the investment. (Code Sec. 4944(a))[48] Additional taxes are imposed on the foundation (25%) if the investment is not timely removed from jeopardy (Code Sec. 4944(b)(1))[49] and on any manager (5%) who refuses to agree to removing the investment from jeopardy. (Code Sec. 4944(b)(2))[50] Foundation managers may be jointly and severally liable for these taxes, but the initial tax on management with respect to any one investment is limited to $10,000, and the additional tax to $20,000. (Code Sec. 4944(d))[1] The initial taxes are reported on Form 4720. (Reg § 53.6011-1(b)) Use Form 8868 for an extension, see ¶4124.[2]

Propaganda, legislative activities and other taxable expenditures. An excise tax is imposed for engaging in propaganda or legislative activities or for making other taxable expenditures. An initial tax equal to 20% of the amount of the taxable expenditure is imposed on the foundation, and a 5% initial tax is imposed on any foundation manager who willfully agreed to the expenditure. (Code Sec. 4945(a))[3] An additional tax is imposed on the foundation (100%) if the expenditure isn't timely corrected, and on any foundation manager (50%) who refuses to agree to part or all of the correction. (Code Sec. 4945(b))[4] Foundation managers may be jointly and severally liable, but the maximum tax that may be imposed on them for any one taxable expenditure is $10,000 of initial tax and $20,000 of additional tax. (Code Sec. 4945(c)) These taxes don't apply if the political expenditures tax (¶4104) applies. (Code Sec. 4955(e))[5] Report the initial taxes on Form 4720. (Reg § 53.6011-1(b)) Use Form 8868 for an extension, see ¶4124.[6]

¶ 4128 Termination of private foundation status; termination tax—Form 990-PF.

Except as otherwise provided below, an organization's status as a private foundation may terminate only if either: (1) the organization notifies IRS of its intent to terminate, or (2) the organization is guilty of willful repeated acts or omissions or of a willful and flagrant act or omission resulting in liability for any of the excise taxes on private foundations (see ¶4127), and IRS notifies the organization that it's liable for tax on termination of its status as a private foundation. (Code Sec. 507(a))[7]

The organization must pay a tax (use Form 990-PF, see ¶4131) on termination of its private foundation status. Unless abated by IRS, the tax equals the lesser of: (1) the aggregate tax benefit (as adequately substantiated by the foundation) resulting from its Code Sec. 501(c)(3) status, or (2) the value of its net assets. (Code Sec. 507(c), Code Sec. 507(g))[8]

Where there's no willful repeated acts or omissions or willful and flagrant acts or omissions resulting in private foundation excise tax liability, a private foundation's status may be terminated without imposition of the tax on termination, if: (a) it distributes all its net assets to one or more public charities that have been in existence as such for at least 60 calendar months before the distribution (IRS guidance illustrates termination under this rule); or (b) it notifies IRS of its intent to terminate, and the organization becomes a public charity for a continuous 60- month period. (Code Sec. 507(b))[9]

44. ¶D-7801; ¶49,434; TD ¶685,509
45. ¶D-7801; ¶49,434
46. ¶D-7800 et seq.; ¶49,434
47. ¶S-2511; TD ¶685,509
48. ¶s D-7901, D-7903; ¶s 49,444, 49,614; TD ¶685,503
49. ¶D-7905; ¶49,444; TD ¶685,505
50. ¶D-7906; ¶49,444; TD ¶685,507
1. ¶D-7907; ¶49,444; TD ¶685,508

2. ¶S-2511; TD ¶685,501
3. ¶D-8001; ¶s 49,454 et seq., 49,614 et seq.; TD ¶685,018
4. ¶D-8001; ¶49,454.02; TD ¶685,019
5. ¶D-8003; ¶49,554; TD ¶684,500
6. ¶S-2511; ¶s 60,114.04, 60,334; TD ¶685,017
7. ¶s D-7220, D-7222; ¶5074; TD ¶683,509
8. ¶D-7228; ¶5074
9. ¶D-7223; ¶5074

¶ 4129   Excise tax on taxable distributions from donor advised funds—Form 4720.

If a taxable distribution is made from a donor advised fund (see below):

(1) a tax equal to 20% of the amount distributed is imposed and must be paid by the donor advised fund's sponsoring organization (Code Sec. 4966(a)(1)); and

(2) a tax equal to 5% of the amount distributed is imposed if any fund manager agreed to the making of a distribution knowing that it was a taxable distribution. The tax must be paid by any fund manager who agreed to the making of the distribution. (Code Sec. 4966(a)(2))[10]

The maximum amount of tax imposed by item (2) as to any one taxable distribution is $10,000. (Code Sec. 4966(b)(2))

Subject to exceptions, a *donor advised fund* is a fund or account which is:

(1) separately identified by reference to contributions of a donor or donors,

(2) owned and controlled by a sponsoring organization, and

(3) as to which a donor (or any person appointed or designated by the donor) has, or reasonably expects to have, advisory privileges as to the distribution or investment of amounts held in the fund or account by reason of the donor's status as a donor. (Code Sec. 4966(d)(2))

¶ 4130   Excise taxes imposed on prohibited benefits received by a donor, donor advisor or related person from a donor advised fund—Form 4720.

If a distribution from a donor advised fund (¶4129) results in a donor, donor advisor, or a related person (Subsection (d) person as set forth in Code Sec. 4967(d)) receiving directly or indirectly a more than incidental benefit as a result of the distribution:

(1) A tax equal to 125% of the amount of the benefit is imposed on the advice of any Subsection (d) person to have a sponsoring organization make the distribution. The tax must be paid by the Subsection (d) person who advises that a distribution be made or who receives a benefit as a result of the distribution. (Code Sec. 4967(a)(1))

(2) A tax equal to 10% of the amount of the benefit is imposed on the agreement of any fund manager to the making of the distribution knowing that the distribution would confer a benefit described at item (1) (above). This tax must be paid by the fund manager who agreed to the making of the distribution. (Code Sec. 4967(a)(2)) However, the maximum amount of tax imposed on a fund manager as to any distribution is $10,000. (Code Sec. 4967(c)(2))[11]

Tax is not imposed as to any distribution as to which tax has been imposed under the Code Sec. 4958 excess benefit transaction rules, ¶4112. (Code Sec. 4967(b))

¶ 4131   Annual return of private foundations—Form 990-PF.

A private foundation must file an annual information return on Form 990-PF (Reg § 1.6033-2(a)(2)(i)) on or before the fifteenth day of the fifth month following the close of the tax year. (Reg § 1.6033-2(e))[12] For return disclosure requirements, see ¶4120. Certain private foundations must file returns electronically. (Reg § 301.6033-4)

---

10. ¶D-8152 *et seq.*; ¶49,664   12. ¶s S-2801, S-4928; ¶60,334; TD ¶688,021
11. ¶D-8160 *et seq.*; ¶49,674

Chapter 20   RICs (Mutual Funds), REITs, REMICs, Banks and Other Special Corporations

¶ 4200   Special Corporations and Other Entities. ████████████████████

Regulated investment companies (mutual funds), real estate investment trusts, real estate mortgage investment conduits, and certain other entities get special tax treatment.

¶ 4201   Regulated investment companies (RICs)—mutual funds.

If it makes certain distributions, a RIC (mutual fund) is taxed only on: (1) the undistributed portion of its ordinary net income, at the regular corporate rates; and (2) the undistributed portion of its net long-term capital gains, at the corporate capital gains rate. (Code Sec. 852(b))[1] The RIC isn't taxed on the amounts it distributes to shareholders, thus allowing it to pass through ordinary income, net capital gains, pre-2011 qualified dividend income eligible for capital gain treatment (see ¶1290), dividend income eligible for the corporate dividends-received deduction, and certain other items to them (see ¶1300) without any tax at the RIC level (if requirements are met). (Code Sec. 852(b))[2] For "late-paid" and year-end dividends, see ¶4203.

> ⚡*caution:* Check http://ria.thomsonreuters.com/federaltaxhandbook to see whether the pre-2011 rules have been extended.

The RIC's *undistributed* capital gains may also be designated (on Form 2439) and passed through to the shareholders (but the RIC pays tax (on Form 2438) on the retained gains). The effects of designation are that the shareholders: (1) include their shares of the undistributed capital gains in income, (2) get a credit or refund for their shares of the tax the RIC paid on these amounts (so that only one tax is paid), and (3) get a basis step-up in their shares equal to the difference between the amount of the includible capital gains from the dividend and the tax the shareholder is deemed to have paid with respect to those shares. (Code Sec. 852(b)(3)(D))[3]

A RIC is a domestic corporation that at all times in the tax year is registered with the SEC as a management company or unit investment trust, has an election in effect to be treated as a business development company under the '40 Investment Company Act, or is a mutual or common trust fund other than an "investment company" under that Act. (Code Sec. 851(a))[4] It must also meet gross income, (Code Sec. 851(b)(2))[5] diversification, (Code Sec. 851(b)(3))[6] and E&P tests, (Code Sec. 852(a)(2))[7] make certain distributions (Code Sec. 852(a)(1))[8] *and* elect on its return (Form 1120-RIC) to be taxed as a RIC. (Code Sec. 851(b)(1))[9]

¶ 4202   Real estate investment trusts (REITs).

REITs are generally taxed only on amounts not distributed to their shareholders or beneficiaries, as follows: (1) at *regular* corporate rates on undistributed earnings and profits and net capital gains, and (2) at the *highest* corporate rate on net income from foreclosure property. (Code Sec. 857(b))[10] A REIT may pass through the character of its capital gains and pre-2011 qualified dividend income eligible for capital gain treatment (see ¶1290) to its shareholders, see ¶1301. In addition, a REIT's *undistributed* capital gains may be passed through to the

---

1. ¶E-6100 *et seq.*; ¶8524.10
2. ¶E-6150; ¶8524.02
3. ¶E-6155; ¶8524.02; TD ¶173,001
4. ¶E-6001 *et seq.*; ¶8514
5. ¶E-6004; ¶8514.02

6. ¶s E-6012, E-6015; ¶8514.04
7. ¶E-6020; ¶8524.01
8. ¶E-6101; ¶8524.01
9. ¶E-6002; ¶8514.01
10. ¶E-6600 *et seq.*; ¶8574.01

References beginning with a single letter are to paragraphs in RIA's Federal Tax Coordinator 2d and RIA's Analysis of Federal Taxes: Income. Those beginning with numbers are to paragraphs in RIA's United States Tax Reporter. Those beginning with TD are to paragraphs in RIA's Tax Desk.

shareholders (on Form 2439). The REIT pays tax on the retained gains (on Form 2438) and the shareholders: (1) include their shares of the undistributed capital gains in income, (2) get a credit or refund for their shares of the tax the REIT paid on these amounts (so that only one tax is paid), and (3) get a basis step-up in their shares equal to the difference between the amount of the includible capital gains from the dividend and the tax the shareholder is deemed to have paid with respect to those shares. (Code Sec. 857(b)(3)(D))[11] For "late-paid" and year-end dividends, see ¶4203.

⚫caution: Check http://ria.thomsonreuters.com/federaltaxhandbook to see whether the pre-2011 rules have been extended.

The REIT must be a calendar-year (Code Sec. 859) corporation, trust or association that meets certain requirements as to the source of income, earnings and profits, type of its investments, nature of its activities, and its relationships with financially interested parties (Code Sec. 856(a)), and certain recordkeeping and distribution requirements. (Code Sec. 857(a)) And it must elect on its return (Form 1120-REIT) to be a REIT. (Code Sec. 856(c)(1); Reg § 1.856-2(b))[12]

⚫observation: REITs are designed to do for real estate investors what mutual funds (RICs, see ¶4201) do for investors in securities—i.e., pool resources and get a return on capital without paying a corporate tax on the gain.

For tax years beginning after May 22, 2008 and not later than May 21, 2009, certain income recognized on timber by REITs are treated as capital gains that are passed through to the REIT's shareholders. (Code Sec. 856(c))

⚫caution: Check http://ria.thomsonreuters.com/federaltaxhandbook to see whether the pre-May 21, 2009 rules have been extended.

¶ 4203   RIC (mutual fund) and REIT dividends paid after close of tax year; year-end dividends.

A RIC (¶4201) or REIT (¶4202) may elect to treat all or part of any dividend paid after the end of a tax year ("late-paid dividends") as paid during the year, if the dividend is: (1) declared before the due date of the return (REITs must state a dollar amount), and (2) paid not later than the first regular dividend date after declaration, but in no case later than 12 months after the end of the tax year. (Code Sec. 855(a), Code Sec. 858(a))[13]

A dividend declared by a RIC or REIT in October, November or December of any calendar year, that's payable to shareholders of record on a specified date in one of those months, is considered to have been paid on Dec. 31 if the dividend is actually paid during January of the following calendar year. (Code Sec. 852(b)(7), Code Sec. 857(b)(9))[14]

For shareholders' tax on these dividends, see ¶1300 (RICs) and ¶1301 (REITs).

¶ 4204   Real estate mortgage investment conduits (REMICs).

REMICs are fixed mortgage pools with multiple classes ("regular" and "residual" (Code Sec. 860G(a)(1), Code Sec. 860G(a)(2); Reg § 1.860G-1) of investment interests, that have elected REMIC status (on Form 1066). (Code Sec. 860D; Reg § 1.860D-1)[15] REMICs, which are treated as partnerships for procedural purposes (Code Sec. 860F(e))[16] generally aren't taxable. (Code Sec. 860A(a))[17] The REMIC's income is allocated to, and taken into account by, the holders of its interests. (Code Sec. 860A(b)) REMICs report on Form 1066.[18]

11. ¶E-6617.1; ¶8574.02
12. ¶s E-6501, E-6623; ¶8564.02
13. ¶s E-6201, E-6701; ¶s 8554, 8584
14. ¶s E-6202, E-6704; ¶s 8554.01, 8574.02; TD ¶172,005

15. ¶s E-6901, E-6903; ¶860A4
16. ¶E-6927; ¶860A4
17. ¶E-6917; ¶860A4
18. ¶E-7000 *et seq.*; ¶s 860A4.01, 860A4.02

Although not subject to federal income tax, a REMIC is subject to penalty taxes on: income from foreclosure property (Code Sec. 860G(c)), contributions after the start-up date (Code Sec. 860G(d)), and prohibited transactions (Code Sec. 860F(a)), and an excise tax (reported on Form 8831) on certain transfers of residual interests. (Code Sec. 860E(e))[19]

¶ 4205 Small business investment companies (SBICs).

SBICs are licensed and operated under the Small Business Investment Act of '58.[20] They are subject to these special tax rules:

. . . Loss on stock received through the conversion of convertible debentures originally acquired for long-term equity capital supplied to small business concerns is a fully deductible ordinary loss. (Code Sec. 1243)[21]

. . . An SBIC's gain or loss on sale of bonds, debentures, etc., (regardless of issuer) is ordinary gain or loss. (Code Sec. 582(c); Reg § 1.582-1(d))[22]

. . . Dividends the SBIC receives from taxable domestic corporations are 100% deductible. (Code Sec. 243(a)(2))[23]

. . . An SBIC is exempt from personal holding company tax (¶3323 *et seq.*), unless at any time in the tax year any shareholder of the SBIC owns, directly or indirectly, a 5%-or-more interest in the companies financed by the SBIC. (Code Sec. 542(c)(8))[24]

¶ 4206 Cooperatives (co-ops).

A cooperative is an entity in which the same persons are both owners and customers. Although some co-ops are *classified* as "exempt," most co-ops are taxed like any ordinary business corporation, and at the regular corporate rates, but with a specific deduction for patronage dividends, see ¶4207. (Code Sec. 1382(b)) "Exempt" farmers' co-ops also may deduct certain nonpatronage distributions. (Code Sec. 1382(c))[25]

¶ 4207 Patronage dividends and per-unit retain allocations.

Both "exempt" farmers' co-ops and nonexempt co-ops exclude (deduct) from their income amounts paid as patronage dividends or per-unit retain allocations. (Code Sec. 1381(a), Code Sec. 1382(b))[26] For deduction of nonpatronage dividends, see ¶4208. For how the patrons or shareholders treat these amounts, see ¶1302.

A patronage dividend represents distributions of net earnings among the cooperators and other patrons on the basis of each person's patronage. (Code Sec. 1388(a))[27] It may be paid in money, a certificate of indebtedness, or other property, including a qualified written notice of allocation.[28]

A per-unit retain allocation is an allocation by a co-op to a patron with respect to products marketed for him. (Code Sec. 1388(f))[29]

A written notice of allocation must disclose the dollar amount allocated to the patron and the portion that is a patronage dividend. (Code Sec. 1388(b); Reg § 1.1388-1(b))[30]

19. ¶E-6920 *et seq.*; ¶E-7106; ¶s 860A4.05, 860A4.06, 860A4.07; TD ¶162,010
20. ¶I-9541; ¶12,424
21. ¶I-9542; ¶12,424; TD ¶372,006
22. ¶I-9544
23. ¶D-2243; ¶12,424
24. ¶D-3311; ¶5424.02; TD ¶601,503
25. ¶E-1100 *et seq.*; ¶13,814.01
26. ¶E-1100 *et seq.*; ¶13,814.01
27. ¶E-1104; ¶13,814.05
28. ¶E-1120; ¶13,814.01
29. ¶E-1126; ¶13,814.14
30. ¶E-1123; ¶13,814.02

¶ 4208 Nonpatronage distributions deductible by exempt co-ops.

In addition to patronage distributions (¶4207), an "exempt" farmers' co-op may also deduct: dividends paid during the tax year on its capital stock and on any other evidence of proprietary interest in the co-op (Code Sec. 1382(c)(1); Reg § 1.1382-3(b)) distributions to patrons on a patronage basis out of earnings from nonpatronage sources (Code Sec. 1382(c)(2)(A); Reg § 1.1382-3(c), Reg § 1.1382-3(c)(3)) payments in redemption of non-qualified written notices of allocation issued to patrons on a patronage basis with respect to earnings from nonpatronage sources. (Code Sec. 1382(c)(2)(B); Reg § 1.1382-3(d))[31]

¶ 4209 Taxation of banks and other financial institutions.

Banks are generally taxed like regular corporations (Reg § 1.581-1), except that:[32]

Gains and losses from sales or exchanges of bonds, debentures, notes or certificates or other evidences of indebtedness (including any regular or residual interest in a REMIC, see ¶4204) are treated as ordinary gains and losses. (Code Sec. 582(c)(1)) Sales of stock and securities are subject to the regular wash sale provisions, see ¶2461.[33]

Interest paid or credited on deposits or CDs is deductible (special rules apply to frozen deposits).[34] But no deduction is allowed for any portion of interest expense that's allocable (comparing the bank's adjusted bases in taxable and exempt investments) to investment in tax-exempts. (Code Sec. 265(b)(1), Code Sec. 265(b)(2))[35] However, interest allocable to tax-exempts acquired (or treated as acquired) before Aug. 8, '86, is 80% deductible (100% deductible if acquired before '83). (Code Sec. 291(a)(3), Code Sec. 291(e)(1)(B))[36]

Bad debts. Banks generally must treat bad debts (e.g., losses on loans) by taking a specific deduction ("charge-off") for the debt but non-large banks can choose to deduct additions to bad debt reserves. (Code Sec. 585(a))[37] Banks using reserves must use the experience method to compute the additions. Under this method, the additions can't bring the reserve above the bank's loans outstanding at year-end, times a six-year moving average percentage (ratio of total bad debts to total outstanding loans). (Code Sec. 585(b))[38]

Losses a bank incurs on account of its deposits in other banks must be specifically deducted, whether or not it uses the reserve method for other bad debts.[39]

Worthless securities. A bad debt deduction is allowed to banks for total or partial worthlessness (¶1782) of debts evidenced by securities. (Code Sec. 582(a)) Under the charge-off method, a bank's debt is conclusively presumed to be worthless where the charge-off is made under specific orders or in conformance with established policies, of federal or state supervisory authorities, or is in accordance with a properly made "conformity" election. (Reg § 1.166-2(d))[40]

Mutual savings banks or stock associations, savings and loan associations, building and loan associations, and cooperative banks are subject to special tax rules.[41] Gain or loss from the sale or exchange of any qualifying Fannie Mae and Freddie Mac preferred stock by any applicable financial institution (those referred to in Code Sec. 582(c) or financial institution holding companies) is treated as ordinary income or loss. (§ 301 of Division A, P.L. 110-343, 10/3/2008)[42]

---

31. ¶s E-1140, E-1141, E-1142; ¶13,814.01
32. ¶E-3000 *et seq.*, ¶E-3300 *et seq.*; ¶5814
33. ¶E-3022 *et seq.*; ¶5824
34. ¶E-3105; ¶5914
35. ¶E-3108; ¶2654
36. ¶s E-3111, E-3124; ¶2914

37. ¶E-3201, ¶E-3224
38. ¶E-3227; ¶5854
39. ¶E-3139
40. ¶E-3201 *et seq.*; ¶5824
41. ¶E-3300 *et seq.*; ¶5814
42. ¶E-3022.1 *et seq.*; ¶5854

¶ 4210   Common trust funds.

A common trust fund isn't subject to tax (Code Sec. 584(b)) but must file a return (on Form 1065) and pass through its income or loss and other items attributable to each participant. (Reg § 1.6032-1)[43] A common trust fund is a fund maintained by a bank or trust company exclusively to collectively invest and reinvest moneys that it, in its capacity as a trustee, executor, administrator, guardian or custodian, contributes to the fund. (Code Sec. 584(a))[44]

¶ 4211   Taxation of insurance companies.

Life insurance companies are taxed, at the regular corporate rates, on their "life insurance company taxable income" (LICTI). (Code Sec. 801(a)(1))[45] LICTI is life insurance company gross income minus general deductions and, if applicable, the small life insurance company deduction. (Code Sec. 803(a), Code Sec. 804)[46] Gain from the redemption at maturity of certain market discount bonds is taxed under a special rule.[47]

A corporation (whether stock, mutual, or mutual benefit) is taxed as a life insurance company if: (1) it's an insurance company, (2) it's engaged in the business of issuing life insurance and annuity contracts, and (3) it meets a reserve test. (Code Sec. 816(a))[48]

Nonlife insurance companies (stock and mutual) are taxed like corporations generally (¶3303 *et seq.*), with certain deductions peculiar to insurance. Gross income is investment and underwriting income, and gain or loss from property dispositions. (Code Sec. 831, Code Sec. 832)[49] Certain small nonlife insurance companies may elect to be taxed only on investment income, (Code Sec. 831(b))[50] and others may be exempt. (Code Sec. 501(c)(15))[1]

---

43. ¶s E-3600 *et seq.*, S-4105; ¶s 5844, 60,324
44. ¶E-3600 *et seq.*; ¶5844
45. ¶E-4801; ¶8014
46. ¶E-4801 *et seq.*; ¶s 8034, 8044
47. ¶E-4819

48. ¶E-5401; ¶8164
49. ¶E-5500 *et seq.*; ¶8324.01
50. ¶E-5503; ¶8314
1. ¶D-5901

Chapter 21 Pension and Profit-Sharing Plans—401(k) Plans—Roth 401(k) Plans—IRAs—Roth IRAs— SEPs—SIMPLE Plans

¶ 4310 Employee Benefit Plans.

Qualified pension, profit-sharing and stock bonus plans offer substantial tax benefits to sponsor-employers and their employees.

The principal tax advantages are:

. . . the employer gets an immediate deduction for contributions under the plan (Code Sec. 404);[1]

. . . the income earned by funds while held under the plan is tax-exempt (Code Sec. 501(a));[2]

. . . the employee isn't taxed on his share of the fund until amounts are distributed to him (usually after retirement), ¶4338 *et seq.*, (Code Sec. 402; Reg § 1.402(a)-1);[3]

. . . qualifying "lump-sum" distributions for those born before '36 can get favorable tax treatment, ¶4339, (Code Sec. 402(d));[4]

. . . amounts transferred in a direct trustee-to-trustee transfer are excluded from income (¶4359) (Code Sec. 402(e)(6)) and eligible rollover distributions can be rolled over tax-free to eligible retirement plans (¶4359) (Code Sec. 402(c)(1));[5]

. . . tax is deferred on qualifying distributions of appreciated employer stock until the stock is sold, see ¶4340. (Code Sec. 402(e)(4))[6]

For the small-employer retirement plan start-up tax credit, see ¶2333.

¶ 4311 Pension plans.

A qualified pension plan provides systematically for the payment of definitely determinable benefits to employees (and their beneficiaries) after retirement over a period of years, usually for life.[7] Retirement benefits are generally measured by such factors as years of the employee's service and compensation received. (Reg § 1.401-1(b)(1)(i))[8] Benefits under a defined benefit plan are "definitely determinable" if they are determined actuarially, on a basis that precludes employer discretion. (Code Sec. 401(a)(25))[9] A money-purchase plan—contributions geared to a fixed formula (e.g., 10% of compensation), rather than to profits—is a pension plan if the plan "designates" its intent to be a money purchase pension plan. (Code Sec. 401(a)(27)(B); Reg § 1.401-1(b)(1)(i))[10]

Defined benefit plans also include so-called "hybrid plans," such as cash balance plans, which resemble defined contribution plans in that they determine an employee's benefit by reference to the employee's "cash balance" or other hypothetical account. Each employee's hypothetical account is the sum of the hypothetical pay credit allocations for earlier plan years, plus subsequent interest adjustments through normal retirement age. Under another type of hybrid plan called a pension equity plan (PEP), benefits typically are described as a percentage of the participant's final average pay, with the percentage determined on the basis of points received for each year of service.

For "applicable defined benefit plans" (i.e., cash balance, pension equity, and other hybrid plans), a safe harbor provides that the plans won't be treated as violating the Code and

---

1. ¶H-10000 *et seq.*; ¶4014; TD ¶280,101
2. ¶H-10500 *et seq.*; ¶4014; TD ¶280,101
3. ¶H-11006 *et seq.*; ¶4014; TD ¶280,101
4. ¶H-11200 *et seq.*; ¶4014; TD ¶280,101
5. ¶H-8250 *et seq.*; ¶s 4014.27, 4024.04; TD ¶280,101

6. ¶H-11500 *et seq.*; ¶s 4014, 4024.02; TD ¶280,101
7. ¶H-5328; ¶4014.02; TD ¶280,105
8. ¶H-5328; ¶4014.02; TD ¶280,102
9. ¶H-5328; ¶4014.10; TD ¶280,102
10. ¶s H-5205, H-5337; ¶4014.02; TD ¶280,107

References beginning with a single letter are to paragraphs in RIA's Federal Tax Coordinator 2d and RIA's Analysis of Federal Taxes: Income. Those beginning with numbers are to paragraphs in RIA's United States Tax Reporter. Those beginning with TD are to paragraphs in RIA's Tax Desk.

ERISA's age discrimination rules so long as a participant's accrued plan benefit is equal to (or greater than) that of any similarly situated, younger individual who is (or could be) a plan participant. (Code Sec. 411(b)(5))[11]

An applicable defined benefit plan also fails to meet the age discrimination rules unless it provides that the interest credit rate (or an equivalent amount) for any plan year does not exceed a "market rate of return." A plan is not treated as failing to meet the "market rate of return" requirement merely because it provides for a reasonable minimum guaranteed rate of return, or a rate of return equal to the greater of a fixed or variable rate of return. (Code Sec. 411(b)(5))[12]

In applying the Code Sec. 411(b)(1) accrual rules (sometimes referred to as the "backloading rules") to cash balance plan conversions taking place before June 29, 2005, cash balance plans that have requested or received a determination letter, and certain other plans, will not be disqualified for plan years beginning before Jan. 1, 2009, solely because the plans provided benefits based on which of two formulas (pre- or post-conversion) provided the larger benefit.[13]

¶ 4312 Profit-sharing and stock-bonus plans.

A qualified profit-sharing plan must have a definite, predetermined formula for allocating contributions made under the plan among the participants, and for distributing the funds accumulated under the plan only after a fixed number of years, the attainment of a stated age or upon the occurrence of some event (such as disability, retirement, death or severance of employment). (Reg § 1.401-1(b)(1)(ii))[14]

Contributions can be made to a qualified profit-sharing plan whether or not the employer has current or accumulated profits, and whether or not the employer is a tax-exempt organization. (Code Sec. 401(a)(27)(A))[15]

A qualified stock bonus plan provides benefits in the form of the employer-corporation's own stock. Stock bonus plans must generally satisfy the qualification requirements that apply to profit sharing plans, plus some additional requirements.[16]

¶ 4313 Paid time off (PTO) plans.

A plan may allow contributions of an employee's unused paid time off (PTO), under the employer's PTO plan, as long as certain requirements are satisfied. A "PTO plan" refers to a sick and vacation leave plan under which a participant may take paid leave without regard to whether the leave is due to illness or incapacity. If certain nondiscrimination and contribution requirements are met, then a participant does not include in gross income (i) plan contributions of the dollar equivalent of unused PTO until distributed to the participant, as provided under the rules for taxing plan contributions; and (ii) amounts paid for the dollar equivalent of unused PTO that's not contributed to the plan until the tax year in which the amount is paid to the participant.[17]

¶ 4314 Employee stock ownership plans (ESOPs).

An ESOP is a qualified defined contribution plan that is either a stock bonus plan, or a combination stock bonus and money purchase plan, that invests primarily in employer securities (Code Sec. 4975(e)(7)), and is formally designated as an ESOP.[18]

To ensure that S corporation ESOPs benefit a broad range of employees, restrictions apply

---

11. ¶H-7239.2 *et seq.*; ¶4114.33; TD ¶286,020
12. ¶H-7239.2 *et seq.*; ¶4114.33; TD ¶286,020
13. ¶H-7216.1; ¶4114.20; TD ¶286,020.1
14. ¶H-5337 *et seq.*; ¶4014.03; TD ¶280,109

15. ¶H-5337; ¶4014.03; TD ¶280,109
16. ¶H-5209; ¶4014.04; TD ¶280,111
17. ¶H-8980; H-8980.1
18. ¶H-9300 *et seq.*; ¶49,754; TD ¶280,112

under Code Sec. 409(p) that generally prohibit the accrual or allocation of S corp. stock to certain disqualified persons in an ESOP where 10% owners hold 50% or more of the interests in the S corp. (Code Sec. 409(p); Reg § 1.409(p)-1)[19]

Dividends on employer securities that are distributed from an ESOP under Code Sec. 404(k) must be reported on a Form 1099-R that does not report any other distributions, rather than on Form 1099-DIV.[20]

¶ 4315   Annuity plans.

The tax advantages of a qualified plan can be obtained without a trust by using contributions to buy retirement annuities directly from an insurance company. (Code Sec. 403(a)(1), Code Sec. 404(a)(2))[21] For Code Sec. 403(b) "tax-sheltered annuities" for employees of tax-exempt organizations and public schools, see ¶4388 *et seq.*

¶ 4316   "Thrift" and "savings" plans.

A thrift plan is in the nature of a profit-sharing plan and provides for the contribution by the participants of a specified percentage (the same for all participants) of their salaries. This employee contribution is then matched by the employer, either dollar for dollar or in some other specified manner, out of profits.[22]

A savings plan permits employees to make voluntary employee contributions which aren't limited to any specific percentage of compensation.[23]

These plans may allow withdrawal of the voluntary employee contributions (plus earnings) before retirement or termination.[24]

¶ 4317   401(k) plans—elective deferral.

Cash or deferred arrangements (CODAs), popularly known as "401(k)" plans (from Code Sec. 401(k)) allow an employee to choose whether the employer should pay a certain amount directly to the employee in cash, or should instead pay that amount on the employee's behalf to a qualified trust under a profit-sharing plan, a stock bonus plan, a pre-ERISA money purchase plan or a rural cooperative defined contribution pension plan. (Code Sec. 401(k))[25] For salary-reduction arrangements similar to 401(k) plans under SIMPLE retirement plans, SEPs established before '97, and tax-sheltered annuities, see ¶4382, ¶4381, and ¶4388.

An employee may elect to defer a maximum of $16,500 on a pre-tax basis under a 401(k) plan, SEP, or Code Sec. 403(b) tax-sheltered annuity (¶4388) for 2010 and 2011, as adjusted for inflation. (Code Sec. 402(g)(1), Code Sec. 402(g)(5))[26] Individuals who attain age 50 by the end of the plan year may make (if their plan permits (Reg § 1.414(v)-1(a)) additional pre-tax "catch-up" contributions of up to $5,500 for 2010 and 2011, as adjusted for inflation. (Code Sec. 414(v)(2)(B)(i), Code Sec. 414(v)(2)(C)) The maximum catch-up amounts apply to all qualified plans, tax sheltered annuity plans, SEPs and SIMPLE plans of an employer on an aggregated basis, as if all plans were a single plan. (Code Sec. 414(v)(2)(D))[27]

If all the requirements are met, any amount set aside under the CODA is not taxed to the employee currently but instead is taxed at the time of distribution. However, elective deferrals and designated Roth contributions (¶4375) are included in wages for purposes of social security and Medicare taxes. (Code Sec. 3121(v)(1)(A))[28]

Excess deferrals are included in the employee's gross income. (Code Sec. 402(g)(1)(A);

19. ¶H-5337; ¶4014.03; TD ¶280,109
20. ¶S-3419.1
21. ¶H-5212 *et seq.*; ¶4034; TD ¶280,113
22. ¶H-5214; TD ¶280,114
23. ¶H-5215; TD ¶280,114

24. ¶H-5313; TD ¶280,114
25. ¶H-8975 *et seq.*; ¶4014.17; TD ¶280,116
26. ¶H-9151; ¶4024; TD ¶284,025
27. ¶H-9246; ¶4144.26; TD ¶284,116
28. ¶H-4624; TD ¶544,002

Reg § 1.402(g)-1(d)(1)) They will be taxed again on distribution unless distributed to the employee in a corrective (nontaxable) distribution during the tax year or by the Apr. 15th following the close of the employee's tax year. (Code Sec. 402(g)(2)(C); Reg § 1.402(g)-1(e)(8))[29]

A 401(k) plan must meet all the normal tax qualification rules (¶4319), including the nondiscrimination rules (¶4325), and, in addition, all of the following requirements:

(1) amounts must not be distributable except by reason of (a) retirement, death, disability or other separation from employment, including certain transfers in connection with the sale of a business, (b) hardship (see below) or attainment of age 59½ (for profit-sharing or stock bonus plans), (c) in a lump sum on termination of the plan, or (d) in a lump sum, on the employer's disposition of (i) substantially all of its trade or business assets, or (ii) a subsidiary (Code Sec. 401(k)(2)(B))[30] (for loans from 401(k) plans, see ¶4343);

(2) employer contributions made under the employee's election must be nonforfeitable at all times (Code Sec. 401(k)(2)(C));[31] and

(3) a covered employee must be able to elect to have the employer make plan contributions on the employee's behalf or make the payment directly to the employee in cash (Code Sec. 401(k)(2)(A))[32] (automatic contributions are permitted for employees who don't affirmatively elect to receive cash, see below);[33]

(4) elective deferrals under the plan (as aggregated with all other plans, etc., of the employer) must be prohibited from exceeding the above indexed dollar limits;[34] and

(5) special nondiscrimination rules that require the plan to satisfy one of two "actual deferral percentage (ADP) tests," so highly compensated employees can't elect to defer a disproportionately higher amount of their salary, must be met. (Code Sec. 401(k)(3)(A))[35] Similar requirements—actual contribution percentage (ACP) tests—apply to limit employer matching or employee contributions made on behalf of highly compensated employees. (Code Sec. 401(m))[36]

A 401(k) plan is treated as meeting these requirements if it's a 'SIMPLE' plan (¶4382), that meets specified matching or nonelective contribution tests and other requirements. (Code Sec. 401(k)(11))[37]

An alternative nondiscrimination safe-harbor based on employer matching or nonelective contributions also is available. (Code Sec. 401(k)(12))[38] A 401(k) plan providing for safe harbor matching contributions won't be treated as failing to satisfy the ADP or ACP tests for a plan year where the employer sponsoring the plan reduces or suspends safe harbor nonelective contributions during the plan year because of a substantial business hardship. (Prop Reg. § 1.401(k)-3, Prop Reg. § 1.401(m)-3 ['taxpayers may rely']) [39]

Similar rules apply to employer and matching contributions under Code Sec. 401(m). (Code Sec. 401(m)(3))[40]

A nondiscrimination safe harbor applies for automatic enrollment 401(k) programs (called qualified automatic contribution arrangements 'QACAs') that meet certain contribution, vesting, and withdrawal requirements. (Code Sec. 401(k)(13)(A))

Similar rules apply for 403(b) plans, see ¶4388.

Generally, requirements for safe harbor 401(k) plans (i.e., those satisfying certain contribution, notice, and vesting requirements) also apply to QACAs. (Reg § 1.401(k)-3(a)(2), Reg § 1.401(m)-3(a))[41]

29. ¶H-9155 *et seq.*; ¶s 4014.176, 4154.015; TD ¶284,024 *et seq.*
30. ¶H-9201 *et seq.*; ¶4014.17
31. ¶H-8975.12; ¶4014.17; TD ¶284,003
32. ¶H-8975.12; ¶4014.17; TD ¶284,003
33. ¶H-9053.1I; TD ¶284,007
34. ¶s H-9150, H-9159; ¶4014.17; TD ¶284,003
35. ¶H-6579 *et seq.*; ¶4014.17; TD ¶284,003

36. ¶H-6555 *et seq.*; ¶4014.212; TD ¶284,042
37. ¶H-9087; ¶4014.1735; TD ¶284,022
38. ¶H-9053.1; ¶4014.21; TD ¶284,003
39. ¶H-9053.1D *et seq.*; ¶4014.178; TD ¶284,010
40. ¶H-9050 *et seq.*; ¶4014.176; *et seq.* TD ¶284,042
41. ¶H-9053.1H; ¶4014.179;¶4014.214

To be a QACA, a plan must uniformly apply the qualified percentage (i.e., an initial minimum automatic elective deferral of 3% of compensation through the end of the plan year following the year of initial participation, increasing by 1% for each of the next three plan years, not ever to exceed 10% of compensation) to all eligible employees. The qualified percentages are minimums, and a QACA can provide for higher percentages (but not more than 10%). (Reg § 1.401(k)-3(j)(2))[42]

A Code Sec. 401(k) plan can include a qualified Roth contribution program; see ¶4375.

An in-service distribution on account of hardship may only be made if the employee has 'an immediate heavy financial need' and the distribution is 'necessary to meet such need.' But a distribution may be considered for hardship only to the extent that, as shown by the employee, the need can't be relieved by certain alternate sources, e.g., loans, insurance. (Reg § 1.401(k)-1(d)(2))[43]

401(k) plans may permit hardship distributions for the medical, tuition, funeral etc. expenses of a named plan beneficiary, or of a person who has an unconditional right to all or a part of the participant's account balance on the participant's death.[44]

Hardship distributions are not rollover-eligible, see ¶4359.

For the special rules that apply to qualified hurricane distributions and qualified disaster recovery assistance distributions from, and rollovers to, 401(k) (and other qualified) plans, see ¶4344.

For the small-employer retirement plan start-up tax credit, see ¶2333. For the saver's credit for lower-income taxpayers' elective contributions to 401(k) plans, see ¶2371.

¶ 4318   Defined contribution and defined benefit plans.

Certain rules governing employee benefit plans specifically apply either to 'defined contribution plans' or to 'defined benefit plans.'

A 'defined contribution plan' provides for individual accounts for participants and for benefits based on those accounts. (Code Sec. 414(i)) Included are money purchase pension plans, profit-sharing plans and stock bonus plans.

A 'defined benefit plan' is a pension plan other than a defined contribution plan. (Code Sec. 414(j)) It provides for the payments of definitely determinable benefits to the employee over a period of years, usually for life, after retirement. (Reg § 1.401-1(b)(1)(i))[45]

Employers with 500 or fewer employees may establish a combined defined benefit-401(k) plan (a 'DB(k) plan'). (Code Sec. 414(x)(2))[46]

¶ 4319   Qualification requirements for a qualified employee plan.

The chief requirements for tax qualification of an employee benefit plan and tax-exempt trust are:

(1) The plan must be a definite written program[47] that's communicated to the employees. (Reg § 1.401-1(a)(2))[48]

(2) The plan must be established by the employer for the *exclusive* benefit of the employees or their beneficiaries. (Code Sec. 401(a)(1))[49]

(3) The plan must generally provide that benefits can't be assigned, except for transfers

---

42. ¶H-9053.1H; ¶4014.179;¶4014.214
43. ¶H-9211 *et seq.*; ¶4014.17
44. ¶H-9211 *et seq.*; ¶4014.17
45. ¶H-5200 *et seq.*; ¶s 4014.02, 4014.03; TD ¶280,100
46. ¶H-9252; ¶4144.27
47. ¶H-5301; ¶4014.05; TD ¶286,001
48. ¶H-5303; ¶4014.05
49. ¶H-5304; ¶4014.09; TD ¶286,001

under a qualified domestic relations order (QDRO) and judgments or settlements for certain ERISA crimes and violations. (Code Sec. 401(a)(13); Reg § 1.401(a)-13(g)(2))[50]

(4) The plan must meet special tests based on coverage and eligibility of employees to participate (¶4323).

(5) The plan must not discriminate in favor of highly compensated employees with respect to contributions or benefits (¶4325).

(6) The plan must be properly funded (¶4330), and must meet certain vesting requirements (¶4322).

(7) Under a defined benefit plan, forfeitures must not be applied to increase the benefits of the employees. (Code Sec. 401(a)(8))[1]

(8) A pension plan (and certain other plans) must in general pay a married participant's benefits in the form of a qualified joint and survivor annuity (QJSA), unless the participant elects otherwise (with written spousal consent). The monthly survivor benefit must be at least 50% of the joint benefit. (Code Sec. 417(b))[2] Plans that offer a QJSA must offer, as an option, a joint and survivor benefit that provides at least a 75% survivor benefit. (Code Sec. 417(a)(1)(A), Code Sec. 417(g)) Plans subject to the QJSA requirements must provide, to a participant who waives the QJSA, the chance to elect a qualified optional survivor annuity (QOSA), and must provide a written explanation to participants of the QOSA's terms and conditions. (Code Sec. 417(a)(1)(A)(ii))[3]

(9) In the event of a merger or consolidation with, or transfer of assets or liabilities to, any other plan, each participant must be entitled to a termination benefit after the merger, etc., at least equal to his pre-merger termination benefit. (Code Sec. 401(a)(12))[4]

(10) The plan may not provide for contributions or benefits that exceed specified overall limitations (Code Sec. 401(a)(16))[5] (¶4328).

(11) The plan must provide that benefit payments begin (unless otherwise elected) no later than the 60th day after the plan year in which occurs the latest of: (a) the date the participant reaches age 65 (or earlier retirement age), (b) the 10th anniversary of the employee's participation in the plan, or (c) the date the participant terminates service. (Code Sec. 401(a)(14); Reg § 1.401(a)-14(a))[6]

Qualified pension plans may allow employees age 62 or older to receive in-service distributions (i.e. receive plan benefits before retirement). (Code Sec. 401(a)(36); Reg § 1.401(a)-1(b)(1)(i))[7]

(12) The plan must provide certain required minimum distribution rules (Code Sec. 401(a)(9) (¶4345).

(13) A pension plan can't allow withdrawal of employer contributions before termination of employment, or of the plan.[8] But employer contributions accumulated in a profit-sharing plan may be distributed after a fixed number of years (not less than two years). (Reg § 1.401-1(b)(1)(ii))[9] A profit-sharing plan may also permit withdrawal of employer contributions for hardship[10] or by participants with at least 60 months of participation.[11]

(14) Every plan must provide that a distributee of an eligible rollover distribution may elect to have the distribution transferred directly to an eligible retirement plan (¶4359). (Code Sec. 401(a)(31)(A); Reg § 1.401(a)(31)-1)[12] Plans also must adhere to certain involuntary cash-out rollover rules (see ¶4359). (Code Sec. 401(a)(31)(B))

(15) The plan can't reduce plan benefits (including death or disability) to account for post-

50. ¶H-8200 *et seq.*; ¶4014.14
1. ¶H-7502; ¶4014.11; TD ¶286,032
2. ¶H-8611; ¶4174.02
3. ¶H-8623.1 *et seq.*; ¶4174.02; ¶4174.035
4. ¶H-8800 *et seq.*; ¶4014.07
5. ¶H-5901 *et seq.*; ¶4154; TD ¶282,001
6. ¶H-8271; ¶4014.15; TD ¶286,034

7. ¶H-8273.2; ¶4014.141
8. ¶H-5310; TD ¶286,003
9. ¶H-5346; TD ¶280,109
10. ¶H-5348
11. ¶H-5346
12. ¶H-8250 *et seq.*; TD ¶144,037

separation social security benefit increases. (Code Sec. 401(a)(15))[13]

(16) A plan may take into account only the first $245,000 for 2010 and 2011 (as indexed for inflation) of each employee's annual compensation. (Code Sec. 401(a)(17))[14]

(17) Defined benefit plans other than government plans must meet minimum participation requirements (¶4323) (Code Sec. 401(a)(26)) in addition to the coverage and eligibility requirements (¶4324).[15]

(18) If a plan member elects to have an eligible rollover distribution paid directly to a specified eligible retirement plan, the plan must make the distribution in the form of direct trustee-to-trustee transfer. (Code Sec. 401(a)(31))[16]

(19) A qualified trust that's a retirement plan must provide that the survivors of a participant who dies while performing qualified military service are entitled to any additional benefits (other than benefit accruals relating to the period of qualified military service) under the plan as if the participant had resumed and then terminated employment on account of his death. (Code Sec. 401(a)(37)) Employers operating retirement plans in compliance with this requirement, have until the last day of the first plan year beginning on or after Jan. 1, 2010 (Jan. 1, 2012 for governmental plans) to amend their plans. (2008 Heroes Act §104(d)(2))

For the cash-out requirements under the minimum survivor annuity rules, which allow participant accounts of $5,000 or less to be distributed, the present value of plan benefits is calculated using the "applicable mortality table" and the "applicable interest rate." (Code Sec. 417(e)(3)) The "applicable interest rate" is the adjusted first, second, and third segment rates for the month before the distribution date (or as IRS regs prescribe), with a transition rule that phases in the use of the segment rates ratably over five years.[17] The "applicable mortality table" is a mortality table, modified as appropriate by IRS, based on the mortality table specified for the plan year. There is no transition rule for the applicable mortality table.[18]

¶ 4320 Distributions pursuant to domestic relations orders.

The rules prohibiting the assignment or alienation of qualified plan benefits do not apply to the creation, assignment, or recognition of a right to any benefit payable with respect to a participant under a domestic relations order that is determined to be a "qualified domestic relations order" (i.e., a "QDRO, "). (Code Sec. 401(a)(13)(B)) A domestic relations order is any judgment, decree, or order (including approval of a property settlement agreement) that: (i) relates to the provision of child support, alimony payments, or marital property rights to a spouse, former spouse, child, or other dependent of the participant, and (ii) is made under a state domestic relations law (including a community property law). (Code Sec. 414(p)(1))[19]

The term "qualified domestic relations order," which (i) provides an exception to the anti-alienation rules, and (ii) may place the responsibility for the taxation of plan distributions on an alternate payee who is a spouse or former spouse of a plan participant, means a "domestic relations order" (see above) that: (1) creates or recognizes the existence of an alternate payee's right, or assigns to an alternate payee (see below) the right, to receive all or a portion of a plan participant's benefits payable under a plan, (2) clearly specifies certain facts, such as the amount or percentage of, and manner that, the participant's benefits are to be paid to the alternate payee, and (3) does not alter the amount or form of benefit. Code Sec. 414(p)(1)(A)) Code Sec. 414(p)(2)) Code Sec. 414(p)(3))[20]

For purposes of the rules on QDROs, an "alternate payee" includes any spouse, former

---

13. ¶H-5311; ¶4014.22; TD ¶286,022
14. ¶H-5919; ¶4014.18; TD ¶280,505
15. ¶H-5700 *et seq.*; ¶4014.25; TD ¶286,007
16. ¶H-8251; ¶4014.27

17. ¶H-8705.1; ¶4174.06
18. ¶H-8704; ¶4174.06
19. ¶H-8207; ¶H-8208; ¶141,005
20. ¶H-8209; ¶4144.20

spouse, child, or other dependent of a participant who is recognized by a qualified domestic relations order as having a right to receive all, or a portion of, the benefits payable under a plan with respect to the participant. Code Sec. 414(p)(8)) (Code Sec. 72(t)(2)(G)(i))[21]

A spouse (or former spouse) who has a right to receive all or a part of a distribution under a QDRO as an alternate payee, is treated as the distributee of any distribution received under the QDRO. However, a distribution to a participant's non-spouse dependent (who also may be an alternate payee) is taxed to the participant. Code Sec. 402(e)(1)(A)) Similar rules apply to distributions from Code Sec. 457 plans. Code Sec. 414(p)(12))[22]

Lump-sum distributions made to alternate payees who are spouses (or ex-spouses) of participants are eligible for preferential tax treatment (see ¶4339) so long as the distributions would qualify for the preferential tax treatment if made to the participant. Further, any amounts paid or distributed under a qualified plan to an alternate payee who is the spouse (or former spouse) of the participant under a QDRO may be rolled over (see ¶4359 *et seq.*) as if the alternate payee were the participant. Thus, a QDRO distribution made to an employee's spouse (or former spouse) as an alternate payee is an eligible rollover distribution. Code Sec. 402(e)(1)(B))[23]

In the case of a distribution made to the spouse (or former spouse) of the plan participant as alternate payee under a QDRO, net employee contributions (together with other amounts treated as the participant's investment in the contract) are apportioned between the participant and the alternate payee. The apportionment is made pro rata, on the basis of the present value of all benefits of the participant under the plan and the present value of all benefits of the alternate payee under the plan (as alternate payee with respect to the participant under a QDRO). Code Sec. 72(m)(10))[24]

¶ 4321 Incidental benefits.

Life or accident and health insurance features that are incidental to the primary benefit of a qualified plan, may be included to a limited extent. (Reg § 1.401-1(b)(1)(i), Reg § 1.401-1(b)(1)(ii))[25]

¶ 4322 Vesting of benefits.

Plans must provide that a participant's right to his accrued benefit (defined below) vests at certain rates during the years of his employment. Benefits derived from employee contributions must be 100% vested at all times. (Code Sec. 411(a); Reg § 1.411(a)-1(a)(2)) Benefits derived from employer contributions must become nonforfeitable when the employee reaches normal retirement age (defined below). (Code Sec. 411(a)) The plan also must meet one of two alternative minimum vesting standards for vesting in benefits derived from employer contributions before normal retirement age: (1) a five-year cliff schedule requiring full vesting after five years of service, or (2) a three-to-seven year graded schedule requiring 20% vesting after three years of service and 20% additional vesting in each of the following years. (Code Sec. 411(a)(2); Reg § 1.411(a)-3T) Slightly faster vesting (three-year cliff or two-to-six year graded) applies to all employer contributions (non-elective employer contributions as well as matching contributions). (Code Sec. 411(a)(12), Code Sec. 411(a)(2)(B))[26]

The accelerated three-year cliff or two-to-six year graded vesting schedule applies to *all* employer contributions in a defined contribution plan (non-elective employer contributions as well as matching contributions). (Code Sec. 411(a)(2)(B))[27] A plan may have one vesting schedule for employer nonelective contributions for plan years beginning before Jan. 1, 2007,

21. ¶H-11116.1; TD ¶145,513.2
22. ¶H-11008; TD ¶145,513.2
23. ¶H-11439; TD ¶144,022
24. ¶H-11049; TD ¶141,040
25. ¶H-8104 *et seq.*; ¶4014.13; TD ¶280,105
26. ¶H-7400 *et seq.*; ¶s 4114, 4114.01; TD ¶286,028
27. ¶H-7410 ; ¶4114.01

and another vesting schedule for these contributions for plan years beginning after Dec. 31, 2006, if certain requirements are met.[28]

Accrued benefit means the participant's annual benefit (or its actuarial equivalent) starting at normal retirement age (defined benefit plans) or the balance in the participant's account (defined contribution plans). (Code Sec. 411(a)(7)(A))[29]

Normal retirement age is the earlier of the time a participant attains normal retirement age under the plan or the later of: (1) the time the participant reaches age 65, or (2) the 5th anniversary of the individual's participation in the plan. (Code Sec. 411(a)(8))[30]

IRS regs allow plans to set normal retirement age lower than age 65, so long as this age isn't earlier than the earliest age that is reasonably representative of the typical age for the industry in which the covered workforce is employed. The regs establish age 62 (coinciding with the rule allowing in-service distributions to employees age 62 or older, see ¶4319) as a safe harbor for this requirement. (Reg § 1.401(a)-1(b)(2))[31]

¶ 4323 Coverage and eligibility requirements.

A qualified plan other than a government plan must meet special tests designed to ensure adequate coverage of rank and file employees and avoid discrimination.

The plan must, on at least one day in each quarter of its tax year, either: (1) benefit 70% of the employees who aren't "highly compensated" (¶4326), (2) benefit a percentage of nonhighly compensated employees that is at least 70% of the highly compensated benefiting, or (3) meet a test under which the average benefit for the nonhighly compensated is at least 70% of the average benefit for the highly compensated. (Code Sec. 410(b)(1)) This "average benefits test" also requires that the plan benefit employees under a nondiscriminatory classification. (Code Sec. 410(b)(2))[32] However, a plan maintained by an employer that has no employees other than highly compensated employees for a year is treated as meeting the coverage requirement for the year. (Code Sec. 410(b)(6)(F))[33]

A qualified plan can't require as a condition of participation that any employee complete a period of service extending beyond the later of the date he: (1) reaches age 21, or (2) completes one year of service (or two years, if the plan provides full and immediate vesting for all participants). (Code Sec. 410(a)(1)(A), Code Sec. 410(a)(1)(B)(i))[34]

¶ 4324 Minimum participation requirement—the 50-employee/40% test.

A defined benefit plan other than a governmental plan isn't qualified unless, on each day of the plan year, the plan benefits at least the lesser of (a) 50 employees of the employer, or (b) the greater of 40% of employees, or 2 employees (or 1 employee if there is only 1 employee). (Code Sec. 401(a)(26)(A))[35] Instead of meeting the test on each day of the plan year, compliance on a single representative "snapshot" day during the year is sufficient. (Reg § 1.401(a)(26)-7(b))[36]

¶ 4325 Contributions or benefits must be nondiscriminatory.

Contributions or benefits under a plan other than a governmental plan must not discriminate in favor of "highly compensated employees", see ¶4326. (Code Sec. 401(a)(4))[37] To comply, a plan must satisfy three requirements: (1) either the contributions or benefits under the plan must be nondiscriminatory in amount, (2) the plan's optional forms of benefit, ancillary

---

28. ¶H-7412.4.
29. ¶H-7200 *et seq.*; ¶4114.06; TD ¶286,020
30. ¶H-7404; ¶4114.08; TD ¶286,027
31. ¶H-7404; ¶4114.08; TD ¶286,027
32. ¶H-5410 *et seq.*; ¶s 4104.11, 4104.12; TD ¶286,006

33. ¶H-5410; ¶4104.12
34. ¶s H-5804, H-5807 *et seq.*; ¶4104.02; TD ¶286,008
35. ¶H-5701 *et seq.*; ¶4014.25; TD ¶286,007
36. ¶H-5704; ¶4014.25
37. ¶H-6100 *et seq.*; ¶4014.19; TD ¶286,010

benefits (e.g., disability benefits), and other rights and features (e.g., plan loans and invest-ment alternatives) must be made available to employees in a nondiscriminatory manner, and (3) the effect of the plan under certain plan amendments, grants of past service credit, and plan terminations must be nondiscriminatory. (Reg § 1.401(a)(4)-1(b))[38] Defined benefit plans can be cross-tested for discrimination on the basis of equivalent employer contributions to profit-sharing plans, and vice versa. (Reg § 1.401(a)(4)-8) "Catch-up" elective deferrals by older employees (¶4317) are not subject to nondiscrimination requirements, above, but all eligible employees must have the opportunity to make these "catch-up" contributions (the "universal availability" requirement). (Code Sec. 414(v)(3)(B))[39]

¶ 4326 Who is a highly compensated employee.

A highly compensated employee is an employee who (1) was a 5% owner at any time during the determination year or the preceding year, or (2) for the preceding year, received more than $110,000 for 2010 and 2011 in compensation from the employer and, if the employer elects, also was in the "top-paid group" (top 20%) of employees for that year. (Code Sec. 414(q))[40]

¶ 4327 Plans covering self-employed persons (Keogh plans).

A person who is a "self-employed individual," i.e., derives "earned income" from a busi-ness or profession that he owns or conducts, or who has earned income from a partnership in which he is a partner, or has other self-employment income (such as director's fees), can establish and be covered by a qualified retirement plan (sometimes called a Keogh plan). (Code Sec. 401(c)(1))[41] Earned income for this purpose consists essentially of earnings attribu-table to personal services, whether from a sole proprietorship, partnership or other unincor-porated venture, derived from the trade or business with respect to which the plan is estab-lished. (Code Sec. 401(c)(2), Code Sec. 401(d))[42]

¶ 4328 Overall limitations on plan contributions and benefits.

A plan can't be qualified if it provides for contributions or benefits that exceed the overall limitations described below.

Benefits under a defined benefit plan will disqualify the plan if the "annual benefit" for each participant beginning at age 65 exceeds the lesser of: (1) $195,000 for 2010 and 2011, but actuarially reduced if benefit begins before age 62, and raised if it begins after age 65), or (2) 100% of the participant's average compensation for his three high consecutive years of active plan participation. (Code Sec. 415(b); Reg § 1.415(b)-1(a)(1))[43] The maximum dollar benefit is reduced if the employee has less than ten years of plan participation when retirement bene-fits begin. (Code Sec. 415(b)(5)) This reduction doesn't apply to pro rata benefit increases under a terminating plan if there is no discrimination in favor of highly compensated employ-ees. (Code Sec. 4980(d)(4)(C))[44] Neither the dollar nor the percentage limitation applies if the annual benefit payable under a defined benefit plan doesn't exceed $10,000 and the employer has never had a defined contribution plan in which the employee participated. (Code Sec. 415(b)(4))[45]

Annual additions under a defined contribution plan may not exceed the lesser of: (1) $49,000 for 2010 and 2011, or (2) 100% of the participant's compensation. (Code Sec. 415(c)(1)) Annual additions include employer contributions, employee contributions other than qualified cost-of-living contributions to a defined benefit plan (Code Sec. 415(k)(2)(A)),

---

38. ¶H-6350 *et seq.*; ¶4014.19; TD ¶286,010
39. ¶H-9247.1; ¶4144.26; TD ¶284,119
40. ¶H-6702; ¶s 4144.21, 4154.015; TD ¶286,012
41. ¶s H-5218, H-9500 *et seq.*; ¶4014.24; TD ¶284,500 *et seq.*
42. ¶H-9512 *et seq.*; ¶4014.24; TD ¶284,522
43. ¶H-5950; ¶4154.02; TD ¶287,002
44. ¶H-5962; ¶4154.02
45. ¶H-5965; ¶4154.02; TD ¶282,002

and employee forfeitures. (Code Sec. 415(c); Reg § 1.415(c)-1(a)(1))[46]

Mandatory employee contributions that are made to a defined benefit plan are treated as contributions made to a defined contribution plan, and are therefore subject to the Code Sec. 415(c) contribution limit. An individual medical account that is part of a pension or annuity plan under Code Sec. 401(h), and an account established to provide post-retirement medical benefits or life insurance for a key employee under Code Sec. 419A(d)(1), are treated as defined contribution plans, so that contributions to these accounts are also subject to the Code Sec. 415(c) limit.[47]

Special rules apply the limits to certain ESOPs. (Code Sec. 415(c)(6); Reg § 1.415(c)-1(f))[48]

Benefits provided to alternate payees under any qualified domestic relations order (QDRO) relating to a participant's benefits must be aggregated with benefits provided to the participant from all defined benefit and defined contribution plans in applying the Code Sec. 415 limitations.[49]

¶ 4329   Additional qualification requirements for "top-heavy" plans.

A "top-heavy" plan is one that primarily favors officers, shareholders, partners and other key employees. If more than 60% of the accrued benefits in a defined benefit plan, or more than 60% of the aggregate of the account balances in a defined contribution plan, are for "key employees," the plan is top-heavy and must meet additional requirements for minimum vesting, and minimum benefits or contributions for non-key employees, in determining contributions or benefits. (Code Sec. 416(a))[50] SIMPLE retirement plans (¶4382) and Code Sec. 401(k) plans that meet safe-harbor nondiscrimination requirements, aren't subject to the top-heavy rules. (Code Sec. 416(g)(4)(G), Code Sec. 416(g)(4)(H))[1]

Vesting requirements. For any plan year for which a plan is a top-heavy plan, an employee's rights to accrued benefits must be 100% vested after three years of service or, at the employer's option, 20% vested after two years' service and 20% in each of the following years (100% vested after six years of service). (Code Sec. 416(b))[2]

Minimum benefits or contributions. A top-heavy defined benefit plan must provide a minimum annual retirement benefit, not integrated with social security, for each non-key employee equal to the lesser of: (1) 2% of the participant's average compensation for years in the testing period multiplied by his years of service with the employer, or (2) 20% of his average compensation in the years in the testing period. (Code Sec. 416(c)(1))[3]

In a defined contribution plan, the employer must contribute for each non-key employee not less than 3% of that employee's compensation (including employer matching contributions). (Code Sec. 416(c)(2))[4]

¶ 4330   Minimum funding requirements.

To qualify for tax advantages, defined benefit plans and money purchase plans (including target benefit plans) must meet minimum funding standards. To the extent the minimum funding standard is not met, the employer must pay nondeductible taxes on the amount of the deficiency until the deficiency is eliminated.

A plan is treated as satisfying the minimum funding standard for a plan year if:

(1) for a single-employer defined benefit plan, the employer makes contributions to, or

---

46. ¶H-6000 *et seq.*; ¶4154.06; TD ¶287,003
47. ¶H-6000 *et seq.*; ¶4154.06; TD ¶287,003
48. ¶H-6016; ¶4154.09
49. ¶s H-5950, H-6000, H-8217 *et seq.*; ¶4154.02
50. ¶H-8000 *et seq.*; ¶4164; TD ¶286,002

1. ¶H-8001 *et seq.*; ¶4164.02; TD ¶286,002
2. ¶H-7423; ¶4164.04; TD ¶286,030
3. ¶H-8025; ¶4164.05; TD ¶286,025
4. ¶H-8032; ¶4164.06; TD ¶286,026

under, the plan for the plan year which, in total, are not less than the minimum required contribution for the plan year;

(2) for a single-employer money purchase plan, the employer makes contributions to, or under, the plan for the plan year, which are required under the plan's terms; and

(3) for a multiemployer plan, the employers make contributions to, or under, the plan, for any plan year which, in the aggregate, are sufficient to ensure that the plan does not have an accumulated funding deficiency as of the end of the plan year. (Code Sec. 412(a)(2))[5]

For single-employer defined benefit plans, the minimum required contribution generally depends on whether the value of plan assets covers the plan's "funding target," which is the present value of all benefits accrued, earned, or otherwise allocated to years of service before the first day of the plan year. (Code Sec. 430(d)(1); Reg § 1.430(d)-1(b)(2))[6]

If the value of plan assets (less any prefunding balance or funding standard carryover balance) is less than the funding target, the minimum required contribution is the sum of the plan's target normal cost and the shortfall and waiver amortization charges for the plan year. (Code Sec. 430(a)(1); Reg § 1.430(d)-1(b)(2)) If the value of plan assets (less any prefunding balance or funding standard carryover balance) equals or exceeds the funding target, the minimum required contribution is the plan's target normal cost for the plan year reduced (but not below zero) by the amount of the excess. (Code Sec. 430(a)(2); Reg § 1.430(d)-1(b)(2))

A plan's target normal cost is the present value of the benefits that are expected to accrue or to be earned during the plan year, plus any plan-related expenses expected to be paid from plan assets, and less any mandatory employee contributions expected to be made during the plan year. (Code Sec. 430(b)(1)(A); Reg § 1.430(d)-1(b)(1))[7]

Typically, a plan will have a funding shortfall for a plan year if its funding target for the year exceeds the value of the plan's assets. The shortfall amortization base for a plan year is (1) the plan's funding shortfall, less (2) the present value, determined using one of several permissible rates, of the total of the shortfall amortization installments that have been determined for the current plan year and any succeeding plan years. The total of these installments is referred to as the shortfall amortization charge.[8]

Generally, shortfall amortization installments are the amounts necessary to amortize the plan's shortfall amortization base for any plan year, in level annual installments over the seven-year period beginning with the plan year in which the shortfall occurs. For any two plan years in the 2008–2011 plan-year period, however, instead of amortizing their plans' shortfall amortization bases over seven years, plan sponsors may make an "extended amortization election" allowing the shortfall amortization base to be amortized over (1) nine years, using the "2 + 7" amortization schedule, or (2) 15 years, using the 15-year amortization schedule. (Code Sec. 430(c)(2)(D))[9]

Plans in "at risk status" (generally, plans that are less than 80% funded) must use additional actuarial assumptions to determine their funding target and target normal cost. (Code Sec. 430(i); Reg § 1.430(i)-1)[10]

Finally, underfunded defined benefit plans must also satisfy funding-based limits on the accrual and payment of benefits, such as plant shutdown benefits, plan amendments that increase liabilities for benefits, the payment of accelerated benefit distributions, etc. (Code Sec. 436; Reg § 1.436-1)[11]

---

5. ¶H-7601; ¶4124.20
6. ¶H-7752.1; ¶4304
7. ¶H-7751.1; ¶4304.01
8. ¶H-7751.3; ¶H-7751.2; ¶4304.01

9. ¶H-7751.2A; ¶4304.011
10. ¶H-7759.1 *et seq.*; ¶4304.01*et seq.*
11. ¶H-7730.5 *et seq.*; ¶4364.04*et seq.*

¶ 4331 Returning veteran's pension rights.

An employee who returns to a civilian employer following qualified military service is entitled to restoration of certain qualified plan benefits that would have accrued but for the absence due to military service. Qualified military service of a reemployed person must not be treated as a break in service, and must be considered service with the employer for purposes of determining the nonforfeitability and the accrual of the individual's benefits. (Code Sec. 414(u)(8)(B))[12] "Make-up" contributions in excess of the usual contribution and deduction limits for the year made, and suspension of plan loan repayment during uniformed service do not cause loss of a plan's qualified status. (Code Sec. 414(u)(1); Code Sec. 414(u)(4))[13] Plans must permit returning employees to make additional elective deferrals and employee contributions, and must make matching contributions that would have been required had the deferral been made during the period of military service. (Code Sec. 414(u)(2)(A)) Report make-up contributions on Form W-2 or a separate statement identifying the type of plan, years involved, and amounts.[14]

For retirement plans that are subject to Code Sec. 414(u): (1) an individual receiving a differential wage payment (¶3004) has to be treated as an employee of the employer making the payment; (2) the differential wage payment has to be treated as compensation; and (3) the plan won't be treated as failing to meet certain nondiscrimination requirements by reason of any contribution or benefit that is based on the differential wage payment (but other nondiscrimination requirements apply). (Code Sec. 414(u)(12)(A)) Despite (1), an individual is treated as having been severed from employment during any period he is performing service in the uniformed services for purposes of the limitation on in-service distributions for: elective deferrals under a Code Sec. 401(k) plan; amounts attributable to a salary reduction agreement under a Code Sec. 403(b) tax-sheltered annuity; amounts contributed to a Code Sec. 403(b)(7) custodial account; and amounts deferred under a Code Sec. 457(b) eligible deferred compensation plan. (Code Sec. 414(u)(12)(B))

Death benefits. Qualified retirement plans, including Code Sec. 403(b) tax-deferred annuities and Code Sec. 457(b) plans, must provide that, where a plan participant dies while performing qualified military service, the participant's survivors are entitled to any additional benefits (other than benefit accruals relating to the period of qualified military service) that would have been provided under the plan had the participant resumed employment and then terminated employment on account of death. The types of additional benefits subject to this requirement include accelerated vesting, ancillary life insurance benefits, and other survivor's benefits provided under a plan that are contingent on a participant's termination of employment on account of death. However, benefit accruals for the period of qualified military service are excepted from these additional benefits. Thus, benefit accruals (whether benefit accruals under a defined benefit plan or contributions under a defined contribution plan) are not required to be imputed for the period of qualified military service in determining death benefits that are based on a deceased participant's accrued benefit.[15]

¶ 4332 How to get IRS approval of plan—Form 5300; Form 5307.

Although advance IRS approval isn't required, it's desirable and customary to seek it by requesting a determination letter on special forms issued by IRS (e.g., Form 5300).[16]

Master and prototype plans. Instead of establishing a plan on its own, an employer may adopt (use Form 5307) a qualified plan using an IRS-approved master or prototype plan prepared and sponsored by trade or professional associations, banks, insurance companies or

12. ¶H-9951; TD ¶286,040
13. ¶H-9952 *et seq.*; TD ¶286,041 *et seq.*
14. ¶H-9956; TD ¶286,041

15. ¶H-9963*et seq.*; TD ¶286,040
16. ¶T-10500 *et seq.*; ¶4014.01

regulated investment companies (mutual funds).[17] IRS has adopted a system of remedial amendment cycles for issuing determination letters for individually designed plans, and six-year amendment/approval cycles for pre-approved plans.[18]

For the small-employer retirement plan start-up tax credit, see ¶2333.

¶ 4333 Employee contributions and employer matching contributions.

A plan may require an employee to contribute to the plan, as a condition to participation, or it may permit such contributions, or both, if no discrimination results.[19]

Employee contributions and employer matching contributions under defined contribution plans (and those under a defined benefit plan treated as made under a defined contribution plan) must meet a nondiscrimination test that restricts the extent to which the actual contribution percentage (ACP) of eligible highly compensated employees can exceed the ACP for all other eligible employees. (Code Sec. 401(m), Code Sec. 414(k)(2)) The current year ACP for highly compensated employees is compared to the previous year's, or, electively, the current year's ACP for other employees. (Code Sec. 401(m)(2)) The ACP test can be satisfied using a safe-harbor. (Code Sec. 401(m)(11))[20] "SIMPLE" plans (¶4382) are deemed to satisfy the ACP test. (Code Sec. 401(m)(10))[21]

Defined contribution plans generally must allow participants to immediately diversify any employee contributions or elective deferrals invested in employer securities into at least 3 other investment options. For employer contributions, other than elective deferrals, invested in employer securities, the same diversification rights must be given to participants with at least 3 years of service, or each beneficiary of such participants or deceased participants. (Code Sec. 401(a)(35)) A plan is not treated as holding employer securities to which the diversification rules apply if the securities are held by either a registered investment company or a regulated pooled investment vehicle. (Code Sec. 401(a)(35)(H)(i)(I))[22]

Individuals with diversification rights must be offered the opportunity to divest the employer securities and reinvest in another investment at least quarterly.[23]

An ESOP won't lose its exemption from the application of the diversification rules just because it receives rollover contributions of amounts from another plan that are held in a separate account. The exemption continues to apply even if those amounts were attributable to contributions that were subject to Code Sec. 401(k) or Code Sec. 401(m) in the other plan.[24]

¶ 4334 Ceiling on deductions for contributions to pension and annuity plans.

Subject to applicable limits (see following) an employer can deduct its timely paid (¶4337) contributions to a qualified plan. (Code Sec. 404(a); Reg § 1.404(a)-1(b))[25] However, the plan to which the contribution is made must be in existence by the end of the employer's tax year.[26]

The employer may choose one of three alternative special ceilings on annual deductions for contributions to a pension or annuity plan, to get the largest deduction:[27]

(1) The "level cost" ceiling permits a deduction equal to an amount necessary to provide for all participating employees the remaining unfunded cost of their past and current service credits, distributed as a level amount (or level percentage of compensation) over the entire future remaining service of each employee. If the remaining unfunded cost with

17. ¶T-10631; ¶4014.01
18. ¶H-8760 *et seq.*
19. ¶H-6556.1 *et seq.*; ¶4014.21
20. ¶H-6565; ¶4014.21
21. ¶H-6565; ¶4014.21
22. ¶4014.12

23. ¶H-8071; ¶4014.12
24. ¶H-8072; ¶4014.12
25. ¶H-10001; ¶4044.01; TD ¶280,500
26. ¶H-10021; ¶4044.02; TD ¶280,518
27. ¶H-10102 *et seq.*; ¶4044.04; TD ¶281,006

respect to any three individuals is more than 50% of the total remaining unfunded cost, the unfunded cost attributable to those three must be distributed over at least five tax years. (Code Sec. 404(a)(1)(A)(ii))

(2) The "normal cost" ceiling permits the employer to deduct contributions equal to (a) the "normal cost" (cost of credits for current services determined as though past service credits had been properly funded), plus (b) an amount necessary to amortize the cost of past service or supplementary or annuity credits provided by the plan in equal annual payments (until fully amortized) over ten years. (Code Sec. 404(a)(1)(A)(iii))

(3) If the minimum funding standard (¶4330) exceeds the "level cost" or "normal cost" ceiling applicable to the plan, the employer can deduct the amount necessary to satisfy the minimum funding standard. (Code Sec. 404(a)(1)(A)(i))

The single-employer defined benefit plan contribution deduction limit for any tax year is the greater of:

(i) the excess (if any) of (A) the sum of: the plan's funding target, the plan's target normal cost, and a cushion amount for a plan year, over (B) the value of plan assets (determined under Code Sec. 430(g)(3)) as of the valuation date for the plan year (Code Sec. 404(o)(2)(A)); over

(ii) the minimum required contribution for the plan year. (Code Sec. 404(o))[28]

The multiemployer defined benefit plan contribution deduction limit is the excess (if any) of:

(a) 140% of the plan's current liability (as determined under Code Sec. 431(c)(6)(C)); over

(b) the value of the plan's assets (as determined under Code Sec. 431(c)(2)). (Code Sec. 404(a)(1)(D))[29]

The maximum annual deduction under the above ceilings, however, cannot generally exceed the full funding limitation for the year (Code Sec. 404(a)(1)(A)).[30] Money purchase and target benefit plans also are subject to the 25%-of-compensation deduction limit that applies to profit-sharing plans (¶4335). (Code Sec. 404(a)(3)(A)(v))[31]

Contributions in excess of the amount deductible (except contributions to SIMPLE plans (¶4382) for household workers (Code Sec. 4972(c)(6))) are subject to a nondeductible 10% excise tax in certain cases (Code Sec. 4972), but may be carried over and deducted in later years, subject to the above limitations. (Code Sec. 404(a)(1)(E))[32]

¶ 4335   Ceiling on deductions for contributions to profit-sharing and stock bonus plans.

The special ceiling on deductions for contributions under a profit-sharing, stock-bonus, or "SIMPLE" plan is 25% of the aggregate compensation (exclusive of qualified plan contributions) paid or accrued during the tax year for all employees participating in the plan. (Code Sec. 404(a)(3)(A); Code Sec. 404(m)(1); Reg § 1.404(a)-9(c)) Contributions in excess of this limit may be carried over and deducted in a later year to the extent that contributions for that later year are below the applicable percentage limit for that year. (Code Sec. 404(a)(3)(A)(ii))[33]

The percentage of compensation limit on deductible contributions to a stock bonus or profit-sharing plan for a self-employed individual (Keogh plan) is 25% of "earned income," which is

---

28. ¶H-10102.1; ¶4044.02
29. ¶H-10102.2; ¶4044.02
30. ¶H-10105 *et seq.*; ¶4044.04; TD ¶281,006

31. ¶H-10102; ¶4044.07; TD ¶281,006
32. ¶H-10125 *et seq.*; ¶4044.04; TD ¶280,500
33. ¶H-10202; ¶4044.06; TD ¶281,302

25% of net earnings from self-employment less the self-employment tax deduction and deductible qualified plan contributions. (Code Sec. 404(a)(8)(B))[34]

Elective deferrals (¶4317) are not subject to the deduction limits for stock bonus and profit sharing plans, combination defined contribution and defined benefit plans, or ESOPs. (Code Sec. 404(n))[35] Compensation includes elective deferral amounts, amounts deferred to a cafeteria plan, and certain pre-disability compensation. (Code Sec. 404(a)(12))[36]

¶ 4336   Deduction ceiling for combinations of qualified plans.

If there is a mixture of one or more defined contribution plans and one or more defined benefit plans, or any combination of two or more pension trusts, annuity plans, and stock bonus or profit-sharing trusts, an overall limit on deductible contributions applies. Under this limitation, the total amount deductible for *all* plans is the greater of: (1) 25% of the compensation (exclusive of qualified plan contributions) paid or accrued during the tax year to the beneficiaries of the various trusts or plans, or (2) the total contributions to the trusts or plans to the extent those contributions don't exceed the amount necessary to satisfy the Code Sec. 412 minimum funding standards. The amount necessary to satisfy the Code Sec. 412 minimum funding standard must not be less than the plan's funding shortfall under Code Sec. 430. (Code Sec. 404(a)(7)(A))

The 25% limit does not apply if the only amounts contributed to the defined compensation plan are elective deferrals. (Code Sec. 404(a)(7)(C)(ii))[37] Further, the combined plan limit applies only to employer contributions to one or more defined contribution plans to the extent the contributions exceed 6% of the compensation otherwise paid or accrued to plan beneficiaries during the tax year.[38]

In determining the limit on deductions where there is a combination of one or more defined benefit and one or more defined contribution plans, any defined benefit plan guaranteed by the PBGC is not taken into account. (Code Sec. 404(a)(7)(C)(iv))

¶ 4337   Timely payment requirement.

A contribution actually must be paid to the trust or under the plan to be deductible. (Code Sec. 404(a))[39] However, payments (including those made to "SIMPLE" plans (¶4382) (Code Sec. 404(m)(2)(B)), made after the end of a year are considered paid on the last day of the year if paid by the employer no later than the due date of its tax return (including extensions). (Code Sec. 404(a)(6))[40] This applies to both cash and accrual employers, even if other accrual requirements are not met. (Reg § 1.404(a)-1(c))[41]

¶ 4338   How employees are taxed.

Apart from certain "lump-sum" payments qualifying for the preferential tax treatment (¶4339 *et seq.*), and "rollovers" (¶4359), distributions from a qualified plan (reported to recipients on Form 1099-R) generally are taxed to the employee under the annuity rules (¶1357 *et seq.*) in the year distributed or otherwise made available to the employee. (Code Sec. 402(a); Reg § 1.402(a)-1(a)) Thus, the excess of the distribution (cash or fair market value of property) over the amount of any after-tax plan contributions made by the employee, is ordinary income. (Code Sec. 402; Reg § 1.402(a)-1(a)(1)(i))[42]

Certain early (¶4344) distributions are subject to penalty.

34. ¶H-10204; ¶4044.08; TD ¶281,305
35. ¶H-10202; ¶4044.08; TD ¶281,302
36. ¶H-10203; ¶4044.08; TD ¶281,303
37. ¶H-10120 *et seq.*; ¶4044.09; TD ¶281,014
38. ¶H-10120

39. ¶H-10010; ¶4044.01; TD ¶280,506
40. ¶H-10016; ¶4044.01; TD ¶280,513
41. ¶H-10017; ¶4044.01; TD ¶280,513
42. ¶H-11006 *et seq.*; ¶4024; TD ¶141,002

¶ 4339   Preferential treatment for certain lump-sum distributions.

Distributions from a qualified plan to an employee or his beneficiaries, that are lump-sum distributions, are taxable as ordinary income, subject to special elections for pre-'74 capital gain treatment and/or ten-year forward averaging for those born before '36.

A lump-sum distribution eligible for preferential tax treatment is a distribution or payment from an exempt trust or annuity within one tax year of the recipient of the balance to the credit of the participant (excluding amounts payable to an alternate payee under a qualified domestic relations order (QDRO; see ¶4320), which separately can qualify for lump-sum treatment to the alternate payee): (1) on account of an employee's (other than a self-employed's) separation from service; or (2) after attaining age 59½ (regardless of his separation from service); or (3) on account of his death; or (4) on account of disability. (Code Sec. 402(e)(4)(D))[43]

A participant who reached age 50 before '86 (or an individual, estate or trust that receives a distribution with respect to that employee) is permitted:

(1) to elect capital gains treatment at a flat 20% rate without regard to the phase-out of elective capital gains treatment of distributions for pre-'74 plan participation, and

(2) to elect ten-year averaging at '86 tax rates with respect to a lump-sum distribution. This election (use Form 4972) can only be made once with respect to an employee.[44]

¶ 4340   Lump-sum distributions of securities of employer corporation.

If a lump sum distribution consists in part of securities of the employer, the net unrealized appreciation in value of the securities while held by the trust is not taxed to the recipient at the time of distribution. But the same amount also is excluded from the recipient's basis in the securities, so that it's taken into account for tax purposes if and when the securities are later disposed of in a taxable transaction. The distributee, however, has the right to elect, on the tax return on which a distribution is required to be included, to have this rule not apply, i.e., to include any net unrealized appreciation in income. (Code Sec. 402(e)(4)(B); Reg § 1.402(a)-1(b)(1))[45] Net unrealized appreciation that isn't included in income at the time of distribution is long-term capital gain when it's realized in a later taxable transaction. (Reg § 1.402(a)-1(b)(1)(i))[46]

¶ 4341   Tax on current payments for life insurance protection.

The cost of current life insurance protection under a life insurance contract purchased with employer contributions to a qualified plan (or earnings thereon) is income to the insured employee for the tax year of purchase, where the benefits are payable to him or his beneficiaries. (Code Sec. 72(m)(3); Reg § 1.72-16(b)) The taxable amount is generally determined under IRS's "Table 2001," carried at IRS Notice 2002-8. [47]

¶ 4342   Tax on failure to notify participants of benefit-accrual reduction.

Defined benefit plans and individual account plans subject to minimum funding standards are subject to an excise tax of $100 per day per participant, subject to an overall dollar limit, for failure to provide written notice to any participant, employee organization, or alternate payee under a qualified domestic relations order within a reasonable time when the plan is amended to provide for a significant reduction in the rate of future benefit accrual. (Code

---

43. ¶H-11200 *et seq.*; ¶4024.03; TD ¶142,001
44. ¶H-11229; ¶4024.03; TD ¶142,028
45. ¶s H-11501, H-11503; ¶4024.02; TD ¶142,058
46. ¶H-11510; TD ¶142,063
47. ¶H-10507 *et seq.*; ¶724.24; TD ¶141,081

Sec. 4980F(a); Reg § 54.4980F-1)[48] Plans with fewer than 100 participants or that offer participants the option to choose between a new benefit formula and the old one may be able to use a simplified notice form or be exempted by IRS from the notice requirements. (Code Sec. 4980F(e)(2)(A))[49]

¶ 4343 Loans from qualified plans.

A loan from a qualified plan isn't treated as a taxable distribution to the plan participant only if it must be repaid within five years (except for certain home loans), and doesn't exceed the *lesser* of: (1) $50,000, or (2) the greater of (a) ½ of the present value of the employee's nonforfeitable accrued benefit under the plan, or (b) $10,000. If a plan loan (when added to the employee's outstanding balance of all other plan loans at the time the loan is made and the highest outstanding loan balance during the year before the loan was made) exceeds these limits, the excess is treated (and taxed) as a plan distribution (¶4338). The entire amount of a plan loan that isn't required to be repaid within five years (except for certain home loans) is treated as a plan distribution. (Code Sec. 72(p))[50] The outstanding balance of a plan loan is treated as distributed if the borrower fails to make a scheduled loan repayment installment before any allowable grace period expires. (Reg § 1.72(p)-1, Q&A 10(b))[1] Loan repayment following a deemed distribution increases the participant's investment in the contract (basis). (Reg § 1.72(p)-1, Q&A 21)[2]

A plan loan must be amortized in substantially level payments, at least quarterly, over its term. (Code Sec. 72(p)(2)(C))[3] The level amortization requirement doesn't apply while the employee is on leave without pay for up to one year. (Reg § 1.72(p)-1, Q&A 9)[4]

Special rules applied to plan loans that were made before Jan. 1, 2007 to individuals who were affected by hurricanes Katrina, Rita, or Wilma. Similar rules apply to plans loans relating to the Kansas and Midwestern disaster areas. (Code Sec. 1400Q(c)(1))[5]

For loans as prohibited transactions, see ¶4347.

¶ 4344 Penalty for premature distributions—Form 5329.

Early withdrawals from a qualified retirement plan, SIMPLE plan, or IRA result in an additional tax (reported on Form 5329) equal to 10% of the amounts withdrawn that are includible in gross income. (Code Sec. 72(t)(1)) The additional tax applies to all withdrawals unless specifically excepted. Exceptions include distributions (i) made on or after age 59½; (ii) made to a beneficiary or estate on or after death; (iii) attributable to disability; (iv) from a qualified plan after an employee's separation from service in or after the year in which he attains age 55 (this rule does not apply to IRAs); (v) not in excess of the amount allowable as a medical expense deduction for the year, whether or not the distributee itemizes; (vi) that are part of a series of substantially equal periodic (annual or more frequent) payments (made after separation from service if from a qualified plan) for the life (or life expectancy) of the employee or the joint lives (or joint life expectancies) of the employee and his beneficiary; (vii) from an IRA not exceeding amounts paid for medical insurance by IRA owners who have received unemployment compensation for at least 12 weeks (or could have except for being self-employed); (viii) from an IRA for qualified higher education expenses; (ix) from an IRA for qualified "first-home" purchases, subject to $10,000 lifetime cap; (x) from a qualified plan to an alternate payee under a qualified domestic relations order (QDRO ¶4320; this rule does not apply to IRAs); and (xi) made on account of an IRS tax levy. (Code Sec. 72(t)(2), Code Sec. 72(t)(3))[6]

---

48. ¶H-7374
49. ¶H-7368
50. ¶H-11067 *et seq.*; ¶724.23; TD ¶141,049 *et seq.*
1. ¶H-11070; ¶724.23; TD ¶141,049
2. ¶724.23; TD ¶141,049

3. ¶H-11068; ¶724.23; TD ¶141,054
4. ¶H-11068.1; ¶724.23; TD ¶141,067
5. ¶H-11067.2; ¶14,00Q4; TD ¶141,053.1
6. ¶H-11100 *et seq.*; ¶724.22; TD ¶145,501

For transfers of an IRA to a spouse (or former spouse) under a divorce or separation instrument, see ¶4357.

Taxpayers who used the annuitization or amortization methods to compute substantially equal payments can make a one-time switch to the required minimum distribution method, which generally requires smaller annual distributions, without triggering the 10% penalty.[7]

The additional tax is 25%, rather than 10% on amounts received from a SIMPLE retirement account (¶4382) during the employee's first two years of participation. (Code Sec. 72(t)(6))[8]

The tax applies to certain involuntary cash-outs and deemed distributions. It doesn't apply to amounts distributed from unfunded deferred compensation plans of tax-exempt employers or state and local government employees, i.e., Code Sec. 457 plans.[9]

The 10% early withdrawal tax does not apply to distributions from a governmental defined benefit pension plan to a qualified public safety employee (e.g., firefighter or policeman) who separates from service after age 50. (Code Sec. 72(t)(10))

The 10% additional tax also does not apply to any "qualified reservist distribution" made to individuals ordered or called to active duty for more than 179 days (or an indefinite period) after Sept. 11, 2001. (Code Sec. 72(t)(2)(G)(i))[10] Recipients of such distributions may, at any time during the two-year period beginning on the day after the end of the active duty period, make contributions to their IRAs in an aggregate amount not to exceed the amount of the distribution (i.e., they may make "pay back" contributions). The regular IRA dollar contribution limits don't apply to "pay back" contributions, but these contributions aren't deductible. (Code Sec. 72(t)(2)(G)(i))[11]

¶ 4345   Required minimum distributions.

A qualified plan must provide that the employee's entire interest will be distributed, starting Apr. 1 of the calendar year following the later of the year in which he: (a) reaches age 70 ½ or (b) retires (except for 5% owners), no later than over (i) his life, (ii) his life and the life of a designated beneficiary, (iii) a period of not more than his life expectancy, or (iv) a period of not more than his life expectancy and that of a designated beneficiary. (Code Sec. 401(a)(9)(A), Code Sec. 401(a)(9)(C)) (Similar rules apply to IRAs, see ¶4357.) A qualified plan may provide that the required beginning date for all employees (including non-5% owners) is Apr. 1 of the calendar year following the calendar year in which the employee attained age 70½.[12]

Where distributions to a participant have begun, but he dies before his entire interest has been distributed, his remaining interest must be distributed at least as rapidly as under the method of distribution in effect at the date of his death. (Code Sec. 401(a)(9)(B)(i)) Where he dies before receiving any required plan distributions, his entire interest must be distributed within five years after his death, except where the employee's interest: (1) is distributed over the life of a designated beneficiary (or over a period not extending beyond the life expectancy of the beneficiary) and the distributions begin no later than one year after the date of the employee's death (Code Sec. 401(a)(9)(B)(ii), Code Sec. 401(a)(9)(B)(iii)), or (2) is distributed over the life of the surviving spouse (or over a period not extending beyond his life expectancy), and the distributions begin no later than the date on which the employee would have reached age 70½. If the surviving spouse dies before payments must begin, then the 5-year rule applies as if the surviving spouse were the employee. (Code Sec. 401(a)(9)(B)(iv))

If the 5-year payout rule applies to an account with respect to any decedent, the 5-year

7. ¶H-11107
8. ¶H-12377; TD ¶282,815
9. ¶H-11101; ¶724.22

10. ¶H-11116; ¶724.22; TD ¶145,513.1
11. ¶H-11116.1; TD ¶145,513.2
12. ¶H-8275.1 *et seq.*; ¶4014.15; TD ¶144,300

period is determined without regard to calendar year 2009, for which RMDs were not required. (Code Sec. 401(a)(9)(H)(ii)(II)) For example, for an account with respect to an individual who died in 2007, the five year period ends in 2013 instead of 2012. (Committee Report)

Failure to make the required distributions is subject to an excise tax (report on Form 5329) equal to 50% of the minimum amount that should have been distributed over the amount actually distributed. (Code Sec. 4974(a))[13]

Lifetime distributions. The RMD for each year is found by dividing the account balance as of the end of the preceding year by the age-based factor from the table in Reg § 1.401(a)(9)-9, Q&A 2. Portions of this table are excerpted below (the full table goes to age 115).

Uniform Lifetime Table

Employee's Age	Distribution Period	Employee's Age	Distribution Period
70	27.4	84	15.5
71	26.5	85	14.8
72	25.6	86	14.1
73	24.7	87	13.4
74	23.8	88	12.7
75	22.9	89	12.0
76	22.0	90	11.4
77	21.2	91	10.8
78	20.3	92	10.2
79	19.5	93	9.6
80	18.7	94	9.1
81	17.9	95	8.6
82	17.1		
83	16.3		

This table is used for lifetime distributions of the account owner regardless of the identity of the beneficiary or age differential between account owner and designated beneficiary, unless the account owner's spouse is the sole beneficiary and is more than 10 years younger than the account owner, in which case the distribution period may be measured by the joint life and last survivor life expectancy of the employee and spouse, using the life expectancies in the joint and last survivor table of Reg § 1.401(a)(9)-9, Q&A 3.[14]

Determination of designated beneficiary. The account owner's designated beneficiary is determined based on the beneficiaries designated as of the account owner's date of death who remain beneficiaries on Sept. 30 of the year following the year of the account owner's death. Any beneficiary eliminated by distribution of the benefit or through disclaimer (or otherwise) during the period between the account owner's death and Sept. 30 of the year following the year of death is disregarded in determining the designated beneficiary for purposes of calculating RMDs. (Reg § 1.401(a)(9)-4, Q&A 4(a)) Except for certain trusts (see below), only an individual may be a designated beneficiary for purposes of the RMD rules. (Reg § 1.401(a)(9)-4, Q&A 3)[15]

Trusts as beneficiaries. An underlying beneficiary of a trust may be treated as the account owner's designated beneficiary for RMD purposes when the trust is named as the beneficiary of a retirement plan or IRA, if certain requirements are met (e.g., documentation of the underlying beneficiaries of the trust must be provided timely to the plan administrator, and beneficiaries of the trust can be identified). (Reg § 1.401(a)(9)-4, Q&A 6(b), Reg § 1.401(a)(9)-4, Q&A 5)[16]

---

13. ¶H-8500 *et seq.*; ¶49,744; TD ¶145,515
14. ¶H-8279; ¶4014.153

15. ¶H-8278; ¶4014.153
16. ¶H-8278.4; ¶4014.153

Post-death distributions. For non-annuity-type payouts after the death of the account owner:

. . . If the account has a designated beneficiary, and the account owner died before his required beginning date (generally, April 1 following the year in which the account owner attains age 70 ½), the remaining account balance may be paid out over the remaining life expectancy of the beneficiary, using the life expectancy of the beneficiary in the Single Life Table of Reg § 1.401(a)(9)-9, Q&A 1.

. . . If the account has a designated beneficiary, and the account owner died after the date he was required to begin receiving distributions, the remaining account balance may be paid out over the longer of the remaining life expectancy of the beneficiary or the remaining life expectancy of the account owner. In either instance, the life expectancy for post-death RMDs is determined using the Single Life Table of Reg § 1.401(a)(9)-9, Q&A 1.

. . . If the account does not have a designated beneficiary: (1) If the account owner dies after his required beginning date (generally, April 1 following the year in which the IRA owner attains age 70-1/2), the remaining balance is paid out over the remaining life expectancy of the account owner, using the Single Life Table of Reg § 1.401(a)(9)-9, Q&A 1. (2) If the account owner dies before his required beginning date, the account balance must be paid out no later than 5 years after the year of the owner's death. (Reg § 1.401(a)(9)-3, Q&A 1, Reg § 1.401(a)(9)-5, Q&A 5)[17]

The 50% excise tax on failures to make RMDs is waived during the first five years after the year of the account owner's death before the required beginning date if the entire benefit is distributed by the end of the fifth year following the year of death. (Reg § 54.4974-2, Q&A 4)

Annuity type distributions. Separate rules apply to annuity type required distributions, namely defined-benefit (i.e., pension) plan RMDs, as well as annuity contracts purchased from firms such as insurance companies to make RMDs from other qualified plans and IRAs. (Reg § 1.401(a)(9)-6) Under these rules, distributions of an employee's entire interest must be paid in the form of periodic annuity payments for the employee's or beneficiary's life (or the joint lives of the employee and beneficiary) or over a comparable period certain. The payments must be nonincreasing or only increase as provided in the regs. (Reg § 1.401(a)(9)-6, Q&A 1)[18]

¶ 4346 Excise tax on employer reversions—Form 5330.

An "employer reversion" from a qualified plan (except for certain exempt employers and government plans) is, in addition to being includible in the employer's gross income, also subject to a 50% excise tax (20% in certain cases). (Code Sec. 4980(a), Code Sec. 4980(b), Code Sec. 4980(c)(1), Code Sec. 4980(d)) Pay with Form 5330 filed no later than the last day of the month following the month in which the reversion occurred.[19]

¶ 4347 Excise tax on prohibited transactions—Form 5330.

An excise tax is imposed on a disqualified person who takes part in a prohibited transaction with a qualified plan, IRA, or medical savings account. The tax (report on Form 5330 each year for each transaction (Reg § 54.6011-1(b))) is 15% of the amount involved in the prohibited transaction for each tax year (or part of the year) in the taxable period. And if the prohibited transaction isn't timely corrected, the disqualified person must pay an additional tax of 100% of the amount involved. (Code Sec. 4975(a), Code Sec. 4975(b)) The Eighth Circuit has held that certain transactions are "self-correcting," automatically avoiding the second tier 100% tax, but IRS disagrees.[20] Neither level of tax is imposed on a fiduciary acting only

17. ¶H-8279.8; ¶4014.153
18. ¶H-8280; ¶4014.153
19. ¶H-8900 *et seq.*; ¶49,804; TD ¶286,004
20. ¶H-12510; TD ¶287,501

as such. (Code Sec. 4975(a))[21]

Providing investment advice through an "eligible investment advice arrangement" to participants and beneficiaries of a defined contribution plan who direct the investment of their accounts under the plan and to beneficiaries of IRAs (as well as HSAs, Archer MSAs, and Coverdell education savings accounts) is exempt from the prohibited transaction rules. (Code Sec. 4975(d)(17))[22]

Other transactions also are exempt from the prohibited transaction rules, including certain transactions between plans and service providers, for adequate consideration (Code Sec. 4975(d)(20)), certain cross trades of securities between a plan and a party in interest (Code Sec. 4975(d)(22)), and certain otherwise prohibited transactions involving the sale or exchange of securities and commodities between the plan and a party in interest that are corrected within 14 days (Code Sec. 4975(d)(23)).

¶ 4348   Transfers to health benefits accounts before 2014.

Before Jan. 1, 2014, excess pension assets may be transferred to a retiree health benefit account without being treated as either a prohibited transaction or a reversion to the employer if certain conditions are met. (Code Sec. 420(a))[23]

Single-employer plans can use excess pension assets to fund future retiree health benefits by making qualified future transfers to retiree health benefit accounts, providing that certain minimum cost requirements are maintained. Similar rules apply to "collectively bargained transfers" to fund collectively bargained retiree health liabilities. A qualified future transfer or collectively bargained transfer must meet the requirements applicable to qualified transfers, with certain modifications to the requirements, one of which is the minimum cost requirement. (Code Sec. 420(f))

For qualified future transfers, the minimum cost requirement is satisfied if, during the transfer period and the four subsequent years, the annual average amount of employer costs is not less than applicable employer cost determined for the transfer. For collectively bargained transfers, the minimum cost requirement is satisfied if each collectively bargained group health plan provides that the collectively bargained employer cost for each tax year in the collectively bargained cost maintenance period is not less than the amount specified by the collective bargaining agreement.

Qualified transfers may satisfy the minimum cost requirement by satisfying the minimum cost requirement that applies to a collectively bargained transfer. (Code Sec. 420(c)(3)(A))[24]

Multiemployer plans may transfer excess pension assets to retiree health accounts. (Code Sec. 420(a); Code Sec. 420(e)(5)) The funding rules for defined benefit plans (see ¶4330) are integrated into the rules on the transfer of excess pension assets to retiree health accounts. (Code Sec. 420(e)(2), Code Sec. 420(e)(4)) Further, any assets transferred in a qualified transfer to a retiree health account will not be treated as assets in the plan for purpose of the minimum contribution rules. (Code Sec. 430(l))[25]

¶ 4349   Distributions from governmental retirement plans for health and long-term care insurance for public safety officers.

Public safety officers may exclude from income governmental retirement plan distributions that don't exceed accident, health or long-term care insurance premiums for themselves, their spouses, and dependents, if the distributions are paid directly to insurers. The exclusion is limited to $3,000 per year. (Code Sec. 402(l), Code Sec. 403(a), Code Sec. 403(b), Code

21. ¶H-12514 *et seq.*; ¶49,754; TD ¶287,501
22. ¶H-12558.1; ¶49,754.01
23. ¶H-8163; ¶4204

24. ¶H-8173; ¶4204.01
25. ¶H-8164; ¶4204.06

Sec. 457(a))[26]

Further, the accident or health plan receiving the payments of qualified health insurance premiums may be a self-insured plan.[27]

¶ 4350   Plans that fail to qualify or that lose qualified status.

The following rules apply to a plan that fails to qualify or loses its qualified status:

Contributions to the trust by an employer are included in the gross income of the employee. (Code Sec. 402(b)) The employee must report the value of his interest in the employer's contributions the first time his interest isn't subject to substantial risk of forfeiture, or is transferable free of such risk, whichever occurs first. (Reg § 1.402(b)-1)[28]

An employer's contributions are deductible in the tax year in which an amount attributable to the contribution is includible in the gross income of employees participating in the plan (Code Sec. 404(a)(5)), even if the employer is an accrual basis taxpayer.[29]

The amount actually distributed or made available to the employee or other distributee (beneficiary, etc.) is taxable in the year distributed or made available under the regular annuity rules (¶1357 *et seq.*), with a minor exception for distribution of trust income before the annuity is to begin. (Code Sec. 402(b)(2))[30]

Premiums paid by an employer for an annuity contract not purchased under a qualified annuity plan (¶4315), are included in the employee's gross income. Amounts actually paid or made available to any employee-beneficiary under the nonqualified annuity contract are taxed under regular annuity rules. (Code Sec. 403(c))[31]

¶ 4351   Retirement Savings Plans for Individuals (IRAs).

Employees and self-employed individuals who aren't active participants in an employer-maintained retirement plan can set aside and deduct up to $5,000 for 2010 and 2011, for contributions to an individual retirement account (IRA), or for the purchase of individual retirement annuities or endowment contracts. An individual who is an active participant in an employer plan (or whose spouse is) can't make deductible IRA contributions unless his adjusted gross income is below specified levels (¶4352).

An individual retirement account (IRA) is a trust (or custodial account) created or organized in the U.S. with a written governing instrument.[32] The assets of the account must be invested in a trusteed or custodial account with a bank, savings and loan association, credit union or other qualified person. (Code Sec. 408(a)(2))[33]

IRAs may be set up by employers for employees and by unions for members if these employer- and association-sponsored IRAs separately account for the interest of each participant (or his spouse). (Code Sec. 408(c); Reg § 1.408-2(c))[34] Qualified retirement plans, tax-sheltered annuities, and government retirement plans may allow employees to make voluntary contributions to separate IRA or Roth IRA accounts or annuities. (Code Sec. 408(q))[35]

Individuals who turn age 50 before the close of the tax year may increase the maximum permitted annual contribution by $1,000. (Code Sec. 219(b)(5)(B))[36]

Except for rollover contributions (¶4359) the maximum amount that may be contributed to IRAs for any individual for the 2010 and 2011 tax years is $6,000 ($5,000 + $1,000 catch-up

26. ¶H-11089; ¶4024.02; TD ¶141,090.1
27. ¶H-11091
28. ¶H-3200 *et seq.*; ¶4024.01; TD ¶135,506
29. ¶H-3677 *et seq.*; ¶4044.16; TD ¶277,506
30. ¶H-3246; ¶4024.01; TD ¶135,505
31. ¶H-3249; ¶4034.05; TD ¶135,506

32. ¶H-12201; ¶4084.02; TD ¶283,041
33. ¶H-12202 *et seq.*; ¶4084.02
34. ¶s H-12212, H-12213; ¶4084.02; TD ¶283,045
35. ¶H-12280; ¶4084.07
36. ¶H-12215; ¶2194.01; TD ¶283,001

contribution). (Code Sec. 408(a)(1), Code Sec. 408(b)(4), Code Sec. 219(b)(1)(A), Code Sec. 219(b)(5)(A), Code Sec. 219(b)(5)(D))[37]

IRA funds can't be used to buy life insurance. (Code Sec. 408(a)(3))[38] IRA contributions may not be invested in "collectibles" (except for certain coins and bullion), the acquisition of which is treated as an includible distribution (and possibly subject to premature distribution penalties). (Code Sec. 408(m))[39]

Individual retirement annuities are nontransferable flexible premium annuity or endowment contracts issued by an insurance company. (Code Sec. 408(b))[40]

No tax is paid on income earned on contributions until the retirement savings are distributed or retirement bonds are cashed, at which time the distributions or retirement bond proceeds are taxable (Code Sec. 408(d)(1))[41] though the tax-free "rollover" provisions (¶4359) may apply. Rules penalize excess contributions, premature (before age 59½) distributions (¶4344), and certain distributions deferred beyond age 70½ (¶4357).

For deductible contributions, see ¶4352; for nondeductible contributions to traditional IRAs, see ¶4354.

For Roth IRAs, see ¶4367 *et seq.* For the saver's credit for lower-income taxpayers' contributions to IRAs, see ¶2371.

¶ 4352 Deduction for IRA.

An individual who isn't an active participant in certain employer-sponsored retirement plans, and whose spouse isn't an active participant, can deduct, for a tax year, cash contributions to an IRA for that year, up to the lesser of: (1) $5,000 for 2010 and 2011, plus a catch-up contribution, if eligible, see ¶4351, or (2) 100% of the compensation that's includible in his gross income for that year. (Code Sec. 219(b)(1))[42] For spousal IRAs, see ¶4355.

If the individual (or his spouse) is an active plan participant (for any part of a plan year in his tax year), and has adjusted gross income (AGI) that exceeds an "applicable dollar limit," the IRA deduction limit is reduced (but not below zero) by an amount (rounded to the next lowest multiple of $10) that bears the same ratio to the dollar limit on the deduction that his (and his spouse's if a joint return is filed) AGI (determined without regard to the IRA deduction and with certain other modifications), minus the applicable dollar limit, bears to $10,000 ($20,000 for joint return filers, except for non-active plan participants whose spouses are active plan participants). (Code Sec. 219(g)(1), Code Sec. 219(g)(2), Code Sec. 219(g)(3)(A), Code Sec. 219(g)(7)(B)) But the maximum IRA deduction can't be reduced below $200 unless the applicable dollar limit is reduced to zero. (Code Sec. 219(g)(2)(B))[43] The applicable dollar limit is higher than the usual limit for an individual who is not an active participant in an employer plan during any part of the year, but whose spouse is an active plan participant. The higher limit does not apply to the active-participant spouse. (Code Sec. 219(g)(7))[44] The income limits for deductible contributions for active participants in an employer sponsored plan and non-active participants whose spouses are active participants (but not for marrieds filing separately) are indexed for inflation.

For 2010, for joint filers, the deduction phaseout begins at modified adjusted gross income (AGI) of $89,000 and is fully phased-out at modified AGI of $109,000 ($90,000 to $110,000 for 2011). For 2010 and 2011, for single filers, or heads of households, the deduction phaseout begins at modified AGI of $56,000 and is fully phased-out at modified AGI of $66,000. For marrieds filing separately, the deduction phaseout begins at modified AGI of zero, and is fully phased-out at modified AGI of $10,000. Finally, for a non-active participant whose spouse is

37. ¶H-12215; ¶2194.01; TD ¶283,001
38. ¶H-12201; ¶4084.02
39. ¶H-12259; ¶4084.03; TD ¶143,012
40. ¶H-12208 *et seq.*; ¶4084.02; TD ¶283,042
41. ¶H-12253; ¶4084.03; TD ¶143,003
42. ¶H-12215; ¶2194; TD ¶283,001
43. ¶H-12217; ¶2194.02; TD ¶283,002
44. ¶H-5300; ¶408A4; TD ¶283,002*et seq.*

an active participant, the deduction phaseout for 2010 begins at modified AGI of $167,000 and is fully phased-out at modified AGI of $177,000 ($169,000 to $179,000 for 2011).

Spouses who file separate returns and live apart at all times during the year aren't treated as married for purposes of the IRA deduction phase-out. (Code Sec. 219(g)(4))[45]

"Compensation" means wages, salaries, commissions, tips, bonuses, professional fees and other amounts received for personal services. It doesn't include earnings from property, such as interest, rents and dividends, or pension and annuity payments or other deferred compensation. Only compensation includible in gross income is used. (Code Sec. 219(f)(1))[46] Compensation includes taxable alimony paid under a decree of divorce or separate maintenance. Compensation also includes any differential wage payments (¶3004). (Code Sec. 219(f)(1))[47]

The amount shown on Form W-2 as "Wages, tips, other compensation," less any amount shown as distributions from nonqualified plans can be used as "safe harbor" compensation. [48]

The "compensation" of a self-employed individual includes net earnings from self-employment reduced by any allowable deduction for contributions on his behalf to a tax-qualified plan, e.g., a Keogh plan. (Code Sec. 219(f)(1))[49] A self-employed individual's net earnings from self-employment are also reduced by the deduction allowed for one-half of the self-employment tax (¶1755). (Code Sec. 219(f)(1), Code Sec. 401(c)(2)(A)(vi))[50]

Combat pay excluded under Code Sec. 112 (¶1225) is treated as if it were includible compensation for IRA purposes. (Code Sec. 219(f)(7))[1]

No deduction is allowed for contributions for the benefit of an individual for the tax year he attains age 70½ or any later year. (Code Sec. 219(d)(1))[2]

The IRA must be established no later than the due date (*not* including extensions) of the taxpayer's income tax return for the year the deduction is claimed. To be deductible for the preceding tax year, the contribution also must be made by that date. (Code Sec. 219(f)(3))[3]

No part of a premium (under an IRA endowment policy) that's used to buy life insurance is deductible. (Code Sec. 219(d)(3))[4]

No deduction is permitted for a rollover contribution (¶4359) (Code Sec. 219(d)(2))[5] or for any contribution to an "inherited" IRA —one acquired by other than the surviving spouse as a result of the death of the employee-participant. (Code Sec. 219(d)(4))[6]

¶ 4353   Active participant defined.

An individual who (or whose spouse) is an active participant in a qualified pension, profit-sharing, stock bonus or annuity plan, government plan, tax-sheltered annuity plan, SEP, SIMPLE retirement plan, or certain other trusts can't make deductible IRA contributions unless his adjusted gross income falls with the dollar limits at ¶4352. (Code Sec. 219(g))[7]

An individual is an active participant for any tax year in which he's eligible to participate in a defined benefit plan, or any year in which employer or employee contributions or forfeitures are added to his account in a defined contribution plan.[8]

¶ 4354   Nondeductible IRA contributions—Form 8606.

An active participant in a qualified plan who may not be eligible to make deductible contributions either in whole or in part to an IRA (see ¶4353), can make (use Form 8606)

45. ¶H-12217; ¶2194.02; TD ¶283,002
46. ¶H-12226; ¶2194.01; TD ¶283,012
47. ¶H-12232; ¶2194.01; TD ¶283,018
48. ¶H-12226; TD ¶283,012
49. ¶H-12226; TD ¶283,012
50. ¶s H-9514, H-12228; TD ¶284,523
1. ¶H-12215.1 *et seq.*; TD ¶283,018.1

2. ¶H-12234; ¶2194.01; TD ¶283,020
3. ¶H-12233; ¶2194.01; TD ¶283,019
4. ¶H-12236; ¶2194.01; TD ¶283,022
5. ¶H-12235; TD ¶283,021
6. ¶H-12237; ¶2194.01; TD ¶283,023
7. ¶H-12217 *et seq.*; ¶2194.02; TD ¶283,006
8. ¶H-12220 *et seq.*; ¶2194.02; TD ¶283,007

designated nondeductible contributions (DNCs) to an IRA for a tax year (Code Sec. 408(o)(2)(C)(i)) up to the due date (*without* extensions) for the taxpayer's income tax return for that year. (Code Sec. 408(o)(3))[9]

The amount of any DNCs made in any tax year on behalf of an individual is limited to the excess of: (1) the lesser of $5,000 in 2010 and 2011, plus an additional $1,000 for those 50 and over, see ¶4351, or 100% of compensation (including the higher-earning spouse's compensation (¶4355)), over (2) the amount allowable as a deduction for IRA contributions by active participants. (Code Sec. 408(o)(2)(B)(i))[10]

A taxpayer can elect to treat an otherwise deductible contribution as a DNC, thereby increasing, to that extent, his DNC limit for that year. (Code Sec. 408(o)(2)(B)(ii))[11]

DNCs and deductible contributions may be made to the same IRA.[12]

¶ 4355 Special IRA deduction rules for married taxpayers.

Married taxpayers can each make deductible contributions to separate IRAs, subject to the deduction phase-out rules at ¶4352 that apply if either or both are active participants in an employer retirement plan for any part of the tax year.[13]

An individual who files a joint return and has less taxable compensation than his spouse may contribute to a spousal IRA and deduct the lesser of (1) $5,000 in 2010 and 2011, plus an additional $1,000 for those 50 and over, see ¶4351, or (2) the sum of (a) that individual's includible compensation for the tax year, plus (b) the includible compensation of the individual's spouse reduced by the sum of the spouse's allowable IRA deduction, designated nondeductible IRA contribution, and Roth IRA contribution for that tax year. (Code Sec. 219(c))[14]

¶ 4356 Penalties for excess contributions—Form 5329.

An individual who contributes more to an IRA than he is entitled to deduct must pay (use Form 5329) a 6% excise tax on the excess *every year*. The tax for any particular year, however, can't exceed 6% of the value of the IRA (as of the close of the tax year). (Code Sec. 4973(a))

An excess contribution to an IRA is the sum of: (1) the excess of the amount contributed for the tax year (*other than* a contribution to a Roth IRA or a rollover contribution), over the amount allowable as a deduction for the contribution, plus (2) any excess contribution for the preceding tax year, *reduced by* the sum of taxable distributions for the tax year, distributions for the tax year of excess contributions after the due date of the return, and the excess (if any) of the maximum amount allowable as a deduction for the tax year, over the amount contributed to the IRA for the tax year (without regard to any deduction for a preceding year's excess contribution), *including* the amount contributed to a Roth IRA. (Code Sec. 4973(b))[15]

There's no 6% penalty for the year of the contribution (or any other year) if the taxpayer is allowed no IRA deduction for the excess *and* withdraws the excess (together with any net income earned on it) by the due date for filing his income tax return for the year the excess contribution was made. (Code Sec. 4973(b))[16]

For tax on excess contributions to Roth IRAs, see ¶4369.

9. ¶s H-12238, H-12240; ¶4084.01; TD ¶283,024
10. ¶H-12239; ¶4084.01; TD ¶283,025
11. ¶H-12240; ¶4084.01; TD ¶283,027
12. ¶H-12238; ¶4084.01; TD ¶283,024
13. ¶H-12217; ¶2194.02; TD ¶283,002
14. ¶s H-12230, H-12231; ¶2194.01; TD ¶s 283,016, 283,017
15. ¶H-12242 *et seq.*; ¶49,734; TD ¶283,030
16. ¶H-12247 *et seq.*; ¶49,734; TD ¶283,031 *et seq.*

¶ 4357   Distributions from IRAs and individual retirement annuities.

Payouts from an IRA can be made without penalty once the participant attains age 59½ (or earlier in the case of death, disability, annuitized payments, certain medical-related distributions, higher education expenses, certain first-time homebuyer expenses, and IRS levies, see ¶4344). These distributions can be made in a lump-sum or in installments and are taxable as ordinary income under the annuity rules (see ¶1357 *et seq.*), when received, except that distributions are tax-free if reinvested (i.e., "rolled over," see ¶4359 *et seq.*) within 60 days into that or another IRA. (Code Sec. 408(d)(3)(A))[17] (If not reinvested, the distribution is taxable in the year received, not the year in which the 60-day rollover period ends.)[18] A distribution from a SIMPLE retirement plan (¶4382) can't be rolled over tax-free except to another SIMPLE plan during the employee's first two years of participation in the plan. (Code Sec. 408(d)(3)(G))

caution: Although an IRA account can be used as a source for an interest-free "loan" (of up to 60 days), this can be done only once in a one-year period, see ¶4360.

Amounts distributed from an IRA are included in gross income under the Code Sec. 72 annuity rules. (Code Sec. 408(d)(1)) In applying the annuity rules, all IRAs (other than Roth IRAs) are treated as one contract, all distributions made during any tax year are treated as one distribution, and the value of the contract, income on the contract, and investment in it are determined at the end of the calendar year in which the tax year begins. (Code Sec. 408(d)(2))[19] Part of an individual's withdrawal from an IRA is excludible if he previously made nondeductible IRA contributions. The excludible part is (the amount withdrawn × [aggregate nondeductible IRA contributions ÷ aggregate balance on the last day of the tax year of all IRAs of the individual]). For purposes of the calculation, IRAs include all of the taxpayer's traditional IRAs, SEPs and SIMPLE IRAs.[20]

A loss in an individual's traditional IRA is recognized only when *all* amounts have been distributed from *all* of the individual's traditional IRAs, and the amounts distributed are less than the individual's unrecovered basis (total nondeductible contributions) in his traditional IRAs.[21] For how to claim the loss, see ¶3110. For losses from Roth IRAs, see ¶4373.

Distributions from an IRA are reported on Form 1099-R. Distribution recipients who at any time made nondeductible contributions to a IRA (¶4354), must file Form 8606.

The transfer of an interest in an IRA (but not the distribution of funds from an IRA) to a spouse under a divorce or separation instrument isn't taxable (the transferred IRA is treated as the spouse's). (Code Sec. 408(d)(6))[22] Roth IRAs (¶4367 *et seq.*) are treated separately. (Code Sec. 408A(d)(4))

For the tax on early distributions from an IRA, see ¶4344.

Distribution of a participant's entire interest in his IRA (other than a Roth IRA, see ¶4373) must be made under rules similar to the Code Sec. 401(a)(9) required distribution rules for qualified plans (¶4345), (Code Sec. 408(a)(6), Code Sec. 408(b)(3)) except that required distributions from an IRA can't be deferred beyond age 70-½ due to the account owner's not being retired (Code Sec. 401(a)(9)(C)(ii)(II)), see ¶4319. While the required minimum distribution must be separately calculated for each IRA an individual has, the amounts may then be totalled, and the total distribution taken from any one or more of the individual's IRAs. Failure to make the required distributions results in a nondeductible excise tax payable (on Form 5329) by the recipient. The tax is 50% of the excess of the minimum amount that should

---

17. ¶H-12253; ¶4084.03; TD ¶143,003
18. ¶s H-11460, H-12253; ¶4084.03; TD ¶144,034
19. ¶H-12253; ¶4084.03; TD ¶143,003

20. ¶H-12253; ¶4084.03; TD ¶143,003
21. ¶H-12255; TD ¶143,005
22. ¶H-12261; ¶4084.03; TD ¶143,013

have been distributed over the amount actually distributed. (Code Sec. 4974(a))[23] IRS can waive the 50% tax if the shortfall in the amount distributed is due to "reasonable error" and reasonable corrective steps are taken. (Code Sec. 4974(d))[24]

¶ 4358 Exemption of IRA from tax.

Income earned by an IRA is tax-exempt until distribution. This tax exemption doesn't apply to the unrelated business income tax, see ¶4121. Engaging in a prohibited transaction causes loss of the exemption. (Code Sec. 408(e))[25] Certain nominal gifts, free banking services, and free group term life insurance offered by banks for opening and contributing to an IRA are exempted from the prohibited transaction rules.[26]

If the owner of an individual retirement annuity borrows any money under, or by use of, the annuity contract, the contract stops being an individual retirement annuity as of the first day of the tax year, and the owner must include in income for that year an amount equal to the fair market value of the contract on the first day of the year. (Code Sec. 408(e)(3)) If the individual for whom an IRA is established uses the account or any portion of it as security for a loan, that portion is treated as distributed to that individual. (Code Sec. 408(e)(4))

¶ 4359 Tax-free rollovers from qualified plans.

A tax-free rollover from a qualified plan is any portion of the balance of an employee's credit in a qualified trust paid to the employee in an "eligible rollover distribution," any portion of which the employee then transfers to an "eligible retirement plan." (Code Sec. 402(c)(1))[27] A distribution must be rolled over within 60 days after receipt to be tax-free, but IRS may waive the 60-day rollover period for equitable reasons, including cases of casualty, disaster, or other events beyond an individual's control (Code Sec. 402(c)(3), Code Sec. 408(d)(3); Reg § 301.7508A-1(c)(1)) such as bank error, if certain conditions are met.[28]

An "eligible rollover distribution" is any distribution to an employee of all or any portion of the balance to the credit of the employee in a qualified trust. (Code Sec. 402(c)(4)) An "eligible rollover distribution" does *not* include:

(1) any distribution that's one of a series of substantially equal periodic payments made (at least annually) for (a) the life (or life expectancy) of the employee, or the joint lives (or joint life expectancies) of the employee and the employee's designated beneficiary, or (b) a specified period of ten years or more (Code Sec. 402(c)(4)(A));

(2) any distribution to the extent it is a required distribution under Code Sec. 401(a)(9); (Code Sec. 402(c)(4)(B); Reg § 1.402(c)-2) and

(3) any hardship distribution. (Code Sec. 402(c)(4)(C), Code Sec. 403(b)(8)(B))[29]

©️*caution:* An eligible rollover distribution from a qualified plan is subject to 20% withholding, unless there is a direct trustee-to-trustee transfer, see ¶3036.

Amounts transferred in a direct trustee-to-trustee transfer (¶4319) are excludable from income for the tax year of the transfer. (Code Sec. 402(e)(6))[30]

Certain payments can't be rolled over, e.g., corrective distributions of excess 401(k) contributions, loans treated as deemed distributions, and dividends paid on employer securities. (Reg § 1.402(c)-2, Q&A 4) However, where a plan loan offset amount is treated as a default, it is an eligible rollover distribution that may be rolled over tax–free to an IRA. (Reg § 1.402(c)-2, Q&A 9)[31]

---

23. ¶H-8501; ¶49,744; TD ¶145,515
24. ¶H-8508; ¶49,744
25. ¶H-12214; ¶4084.03; TD ¶283,044
26. ¶H-12530
27. ¶H-11402; ¶4024.04; TD ¶144,001

28. ¶H-11452; ¶H-11452.2; ¶4024.04; TD ¶144,034
29. ¶H-11406; ¶4024.04; TD ¶144,006
30. ¶H-11403; ¶4024.04; TD ¶144,003
31. ¶H-11415; ¶4014.27; TD ¶144,016

Taxpayers who receive "qualified settlement income" from the Exxon Valdez litigation during a tax year may contribute up to $100,000 of this income to an eligible retirement plan (see below) in which the qualified taxpayer is a beneficiary, so long as the contribution is made by the end of the tax year in which the income was received.[32]

An "eligible retirement plan" is: (1) an individual retirement account (not a Roth IRA), (2) an individual retirement annuity (other than an endowment contract), (3) a qualified trust, (4) an annuity plan, (5) a Code Sec. 403(b) annuity, and (6) a governmental section 457 plan. If any portion of an eligible rollover distribution is attributable to payments or distributions from a designated Roth account (see ¶4375), then an eligible retirement plan with respect to that portion includes only (a) another designated Roth account, and (b) a Roth IRA. (Code Sec. 402(c)(8)(B))[33]

If noncash property (e.g., securities) is distributed, the employee can sell the property and roll over the proceeds. There's no gain or loss recognized on the sale if the full proceeds are rolled over. (Code Sec. 402(c)(6)(A))[34] If cash is distributed, it must be recontributed as cash.[35]

Plan administrators must inform recipients of potential rollovers in writing ("a section 402(f) notice") of the applicable rollover rules, no less than 30 days, and no more than 90 days before making an eligible rollover distribution (but the 30-day time period may be waived by a participant in certain cases, and a summary notice procedure also is available). (Code Sec. 402(f); Reg § 1.402(c)-2, Q&A 2, Reg § 1.402(f)-1, Q&A 2(b)) IRS has provided a model safe harbor explanation of this notice.[36]

Where a participant with a small accrued benefit (a nonforfeitable accrued benefit whose present value is $5,000 or less) is terminating his employment with the company sponsoring the plan, the plan may provide for the distribution of the employee's benefit without his consent, or the consent of his spouse (a "mandatory distribution" or an "involuntary cash-out distribution"). Such mandatory distributions must follow the automatic rollover rules. Under these rules, plans with mandatory distribution provisions must transfer the amount of the distribution to an IRA of a designated trustee or issuer where:

. . . the distribution of a nonforfeitable accrued benefit is more than $1,000, but no more than $5,000; and

. . . the plan participant (or beneficiary) receiving the distribution does not elect to have the distribution paid directly to another qualified plan or IRA (a direct rollover), and does not elect to receive the distribution himself. (Code Sec. 401(a)(31)(B))[37]

The plan administrator must also notify the distributee in writing, either separately or as part of the section 402(f) notice (see above), that the distribution may be transferred without cost or penalty to another IRA.[38]

For rollovers of after-tax contributions, see ¶4362.

¶ 4360   Other types of rollovers.

Permissible types of tax-free 60-day rollovers, besides those covered at ¶4359, include:

. . . Rollovers from one type of IRA (individual retirement account or individual retirement annuity) to the same or another type. But these rollovers may be made no more than once in a one-year period. (Code Sec. 408(d)(3))[39] Qualified rollovers from an IRA to a Roth IRA are disregarded for purposes of the one-year rule. (Code Sec. 408A(e)) However, a distribution from a SIMPLE retirement plan (¶4382) can't be rolled over tax-free except to another SIMPLE plan during the employee's first two years of participation in the plan. (Code

---

32. ¶H-8251; ¶4024.04; TD ¶144,037
33. ¶H-11440; ¶4024.04; TD ¶144,023
34. ¶H-11448; ¶4024.04; TD ¶144,028
35. ¶H-11402; TD ¶144,001

36. ¶H-11455; ¶4024.04; TD ¶144,053
37. ¶H-8251.3; ¶4014.27; TD ¶144,037.1
38. ¶H-8251.6; TD ¶144,053
39. ¶H-11460 *et seq.*; ¶4084.03; TD ¶144,055

Sec. 408(d)(3)(G))

... From one type of IRA (individual retirement account or individual retirement annuity) to an eligible retirement plan (¶4359) (limited to amount which would otherwise be included in gross income). (Code Sec. 408(d)(3)(A)(ii))

... Eligible rollover distributions from a Code Sec. 403(b) plan to an eligible retirement plan (¶4359) and from an eligible retirement plan to a Code Sec. 403(b) plan. (Code Sec. 402(c)(8)(B), Code Sec. 403(b)(8)(A)(ii))

... Eligible rollover distributions from a Code Sec. 457 plan to an eligible retirement plan (¶4359) and from an eligible retirement plan to a Code Sec. 457 plan. (Code Sec. 402(c)(8)(B), Code Sec. 457(e)(16))

For taxable rollovers to Roth IRAs, see ¶4363.

¶ 4361   Partial rollovers.

When an employee elects to roll over less than his entire distribution:

(1) the portion not rolled over is taxed under the regular rules for taxing ordinary income. Ten-year forward averaging and/or capital gains treatment, where applicable, for lump-sum distributions (¶4339) don't apply if any part of the lump-sum distribution is rolled over; (Code Sec. 402(c)(1), Code Sec. 402(d)(4)(K), before amended by Sec. 1401(a), P.L. 104-188, 8/20/96)

(2) the basis recovery rules of Code Sec. 72(e) apply to a distribution that's rolled over under Code Sec. 402(c); and

(3) any net unrealized appreciation in employer securities attributable to nondeductible employee contributions is subject to tax immediately.[40]

¶ 4362   Rollovers of after-tax contributions.

Generally, only otherwise taxable amounts of an eligible rollover distribution may be rolled over. However, the "nontaxable" portion of a eligible rollover distribution (attributable to after-tax employee contributions) may be rolled over to the extent that the "taxable" portion is rolled over to (1) an IRA, or (2) to a defined contribution plan or tax-sheltered Code Sec. 403(b) annuity) that will account separately for the taxable and nontaxable portions. In such a case, the amount transferred is treated as consisting first of the portion of the distribution that would be includible in income were it not for the rollover. (Code Sec. 402(c)(2))[41]

¶ 4363   Qualified plan to Roth IRA rollovers.

Distributions from qualified retirement plans, tax-sheltered Code Sec. 403(b) annuities, and governmental Code Sec. 457 plans may be rolled over directly into a Roth IRA, generally subject to the usual rules that apply to rollovers from a traditional IRA into a Roth IRA (see ¶4371). For example, a rollover from a qualified retirement plan into a Roth IRA is includible in gross income (except to the extent it represents a return of after-tax contributions), and the 10% early distribution tax does not apply. (Code Sec. 408A(e)) A rollover from a qualified plan, etc., to a Roth IRA doesn't count for purposes of the one-per-year rule.[42] The rollover also can be made through a distribution from the plan that's then contributed (rolled over) to the Roth IRA within 60 days. In either case, the amount rolled over must be an eligible rollover distribution.

For tax years beginning before 2010, an individual could not make a qualified rollover

---

40. ¶H-11405 *et seq.*; ¶4024.04; TD ¶144,005   42. ¶H-11444; ¶4024.04; TD ¶144,005.5
41. ¶H-12290.17; ¶408A4

contribution to a Roth IRA from an eligible retirement plan (other than another Roth IRA) if, for the year the eligible rollover distribution is made, his modified adjusted gross income (AGI) exceeded $100,000 or he was married and filed a separate return.[43]

For the tax treatment of amounts rolled into a Roth IRA from an eligible retirement plan that are later distributed within 5 years, see ¶4374.

¶ 4364   One-time IRA to HSA rollovers.

Taxpayers may make a one-time-only tax-free rollover, via direct trustee-to-trustee-transfer, from an IRA to a Health Savings Account (HSA) (¶1529). (Code Sec. 408(d)(9)) The rollover amount is nondeductible and is limited to the otherwise maximum deductible HSA contribution amount, computed on the basis of the type of coverage under the taxpayer's high deductible health plan (HDHP) at the time of the contribution. The rollover reduces the otherwise allowable HSA contribution amount.

Generally, only one rollover may be made during a taxpayer's lifetime, but if one is made during a month in which he has self-only coverage as of the first day of the month, an additional rollover may be made during a subsequent month within the tax year in which he has family coverage. (Code Sec. 408(d)(9)(C)(ii))

If a taxpayer does not remain an eligible individual (except because of death or disability) during the testing period (begins with the month of the contribution and ends on the last day of the 12th month following that month), the amount of the IRA distribution that would otherwise have been includible is taxed to him and is subject to a 10% penalty tax. The amount is includible in income for the tax year of the first day during the testing period that the taxpayer is not an eligible individual. (Code Sec. 408(d)(9)(D))[44]

A qualified HSA funding distribution may be made from a traditional IRA or a Roth IRA, but not from an ongoing SIMPLE IRA or SEP IRA. Further, a qualified HSA funding distribution must not exceed the IRA or Roth IRA account owner's maximum annual HSA contribution.[45]

¶ 4365   Surviving spouse's rollover of distribution from decedent.

A surviving-spouse beneficiary may elect to treat the entire beneficiary interest in the decedent's IRA as the spouse-beneficiary's own IRA if he or she is the sole beneficiary of the IRA and has an unlimited right to withdraw amounts from it. However, this requirement is not satisfied if a trust is named beneficiary of the IRA even if the spouse is sole beneficiary of the trust. (Reg § 1.408-8, Q&A 5(a)) The election is made by the surviving spouse redesignating the account as an account in her name as IRA owner rather than as beneficiary. Alternatively, a surviving spouse is deemed to have made the election if, at any time, either of the following occurs: (1) any amount required to be distributed to the surviving spouse as beneficiary is not timely distributed, or (2) any additional amount is contributed to the IRA. (Reg § 1.408-8, Q&A 5(b)) If the election is made, the surviving spouse is considered the IRA owner for all purposes under the Code. (Reg § 1.408-8, Q&A 5(c))[46]

A surviving spouse may also roll a distribution from a qualified plan, annuity, or IRA over to any other qualified plan, annuity, or IRA in which the surviving spouse participates that accepts rollover contributions. (Code Sec. 402(c)(9), Code Sec. 408(d)(3)(C))[47]

---

43. ¶H-12290.16; ¶408A4; TD ¶283,317
44. ¶H-12253.1A; ¶4084.03; TD ¶143,003.1A
45. ¶H-12253.1B; ¶4084.03; TD ¶143,003.1B

46. ¶H-12264.7; TD ¶143,024
47. ¶H-11467 *et seq.*; ¶4084.03; TD ¶144,065

¶ 4366 Rollover by beneficiary other than surviving spouse.

Distributions from qualified plans, tax-sheltered annuities (¶4388 *et seq.*), and Code Sec. 457 government plans may be rolled over (in a direct trustee–to–trustee transfer, see ¶4319) to a non-spouse beneficiary's IRA that's established for the purpose of receiving the distribution. This "recipient IRA" is treated as an inherited IRA, and so is subject to the required minimum distribution (RMD) rules that apply to inherited IRAs of nonspouse beneficiaries (¶4345). To the extent provided by IRS, the change applies to benefits payable to a trust maintained for a designated beneficiary to the same extent it applies to the beneficiary. (Code Sec. 402(c)(11), Code Sec. 403(a)(4)(B), Code Sec. 457(e)(16)(B))[48]

¶ 4367 Roth IRAs. ◼◼◼◼◼◼

Taxpayers can make nondeductible contributions to Roth IRAs. Qualified distributions from Roth IRAs are tax-free and penalty-free. Roth IRAs aren't subject to the post-age 70-½ required distribution rules. Traditional IRAs can be rolled over penalty-free (but not tax-free) into Roth IRAs.

¶ 4368 Roth IRAs—overview.

A Roth IRA is an IRA that is designated as a Roth IRA when it's established (Code Sec. 408A(b)); it's treated as a traditional IRA (¶4351 *et seq.*) except to the extent that special rules apply to it. (Code Sec. 408A(a)) Contributions to a Roth IRA aren't deductible (Code Sec. 408A(c)(1)), and are limited based on modified adjusted gross income (¶4369). Qualified distributions from a Roth IRA aren't included in income (Code Sec. 408A(d)(1)) and other distributions are treated as a return of investment to the extent of contributions to Roth IRAs (¶4373). (Code Sec. 408A(d)(4)) Rollovers from traditional IRAs to Roth IRAs are taxable, but not subject to the 10% premature distribution penalty tax. (Code Sec. 408A(d)(3))[49] (Reg § 1.408A-3, Reg § 1.408A-4, Reg § 1.408A-5)

Use Form 5305-R, Form 5305-RA, and Form 5305-RB to set up Roth trust, custodial, and annuity accounts, respectively, with financial institutions.

¶ 4369 Contributions to Roth IRAs.

An individual can make annual nondeductible contributions to a Roth IRA in amounts up to $5,000 for 2010 and 2011, plus an additional $1,000 for those 50 and older, or 100% of compensation, if less, reduced by the amount of contributions for the tax year made to all other IRAs (Code Sec. 408A(c)(1), Code Sec. 408A(c)(2)) but not reduced by contributions to a SEP (¶4377) or SIMPLE plan (¶4382) (Code Sec. 408A(f)(2); Reg § 1.408A-3, Q&A 3(c))[50] The allowable contribution phases out ratably (in $10 increments) over the following levels of modified adjusted gross income (AGI):

- For joint filers, $167,000 to $177,000 for 2010 ($169,000 to $179,000 for 2011);
- For married persons filing separately, $0 to $10,000 for 2010 and 2011; and
- For single taxpayers and heads of household, $105,000 to $120,000 for 2010 ($107,000 to $122,000 for 2011).

However, a $200 contribution may be made if the phase-out lowers the contribution limit to under $200 but more than $0. (Code Sec. 408A(c)(3)(A), Code Sec. 408A(c)(3)(B); Reg § 1.408A-3, Q&A 3(b))

AGI for purposes of the Roth IRA contribution phaseout is defined as it is for traditional

48. ¶H-11437; ¶H-11438; TD ¶144,020; TD ¶144,021
49. ¶H-12290 *et seq.*; ¶408A4; TD ¶283,300 *et seq.*
50. ¶H-12290.7; ¶408A4; TD ¶283,306 *et seq.*

IRA purposes (¶4352), except that it does not include income resulting from the conversion from a traditional IRA to a Roth IRA (¶4371). (Code Sec. 408A(c)(3)(C)(i); Reg § 1.408A-3, Q&A 5, Reg § 1.408A-3, Q&A 6(b))[1]

🅡*observation:* The modified AGI-based contribution limits for Roth IRAs apply whether or not the taxpayer is a participant in a qualified retirement plan.

Roth IRA contributions for a year must be made by the unextended tax return due date for the contribution year. (Code Sec. 408A(c)(7); Reg § 1.408A-3, Q&A 2(b))[2] Unlike traditional IRAs, contributions are permitted after age 70½. (Code Sec. 408A(c)(4))[3] For rollover contributions, see ¶4371.

A 6% excise tax is imposed each year on excess contributions to an IRA (¶4356). Similar rules apply to a Roth IRA. (Code Sec. 4973(f))[4]

Any contribution distributed from a Roth IRA before the due date of the individual's tax return is treated as an amount not contributed. (Code Sec. 4973(f))[5]

For the saver's credit for lower-income taxpayers' contributions to Roth IRAs, see ¶2371.

A recipient of a military death gratuity or Servicemembers' Group Life Insurance (SGLI) proceeds can contribute the amounts received (reduced by any amounts contributed to a Coverdell education savings account, ¶2207) to a Roth IRA as qualified rollover contributions. The requirement that only one tax-free rollover contribution can be made to a Roth IRA during any one-year period (¶4360) doesn't apply. The rollover has to be made within one year of receipt of a payment. (Code Sec. 408A(e)(2))

¶ 4370 Recharacterizing (changing the nature of) IRA contributions.

A taxpayer may elect to recharacterize an IRA contribution, that is, treat a contribution to one type of IRA (Roth IRA or traditional IRA) as made to a different type of IRA. (Code Sec. 408A(d)(6); Reg § 1.408A-5)

🅡*observation:* The recharacterization election allows a contribution to a traditional IRA to be treated as made to a Roth IRA, or a contribution to a Roth IRA to be treated as made to a traditional IRA. It also allows a taxpayer to "reverse" a traditional-IRA-to-Roth IRA conversion (¶4371), in other words, treat the conversion as if it had never been made.

To make the recharacterization election:

... The taxpayer must notify the trustees of the first (distributing) and second (receiving) IRAs of his election to recharacterize a contribution (regular or conversion), i.e., that he is electing for tax purposes to treat the contribution as having been made to the second IRA, instead of the first IRA. The taxpayer must provide the trustees with specified information (including the type and amount of the contribution being recharacterized) sufficient to effect the recharacterization transfer.

... The contribution (regular or conversion) originally made to first IRA, plus net income (if any) allocable to the contribution (Reg § 1.408A-10, Reg § 1.408A-5, Q&A 2(c)), must be transferred from the first IRA to the second IRA via a trustee-to-trustee transfer.

... The trustee-to-trustee transfer must be made on a timely basis. (Reg § 1.408A-5, Q&A-6)[6]

An IRA contribution for a tax year may be recharacterized as late as six months after the unextended due date for filing the return for that year. (Reg § 301.9100-2(b))[7]

---

1. ¶H-12290.9; ¶408A4; TD ¶283,310
2. ¶H-12290.14; ¶408A4; TD ¶283,315
3. ¶H-12290.13; ¶408A4; TD ¶283,314
4. ¶H-12242.1; ¶49,734; TD ¶283,032

5. ¶H-12242.1; ¶49,734; TD ¶283,032
6. ¶H-12290.22; ¶408A4; TD ¶283,328
7. ¶H-12290.23A; TD ¶283,331

A recharacterization election cannot be revoked after the transfer. (Reg § 1.408A-5, Q&A 6(b))

The contribution that is being recharacterized is treated as having been originally contributed to the second IRA on the same date and (in the case of a regular contribution) for the same tax year that the contribution was made to the first IRA. (Reg § 1.408A-5, Q&A 3)

⚠️ *caution:* For the limit on *reconversion* to a Roth IRA following a recharacterization from a Roth IRA to a traditional IRA, see ¶4372.

¶ 4371   Conversions of traditional IRAs to Roth IRAs—Form 8606.

After 2009, taxpayers, including marrieds filing separately, may convert amounts in a traditional IRA to amounts in a Roth IRA without regard to their modified adjusted gross income (AGI) or filing status.[8] The conversion may be done in one of three ways:

(1) Rollover to a Roth IRA of a distribution from a traditional IRA within 60 days of the distribution.

(2) Trustee-to-trustee transfer from the trustee of the traditional IRA to the trustee of the Roth IRA.

(3) Transfer of an amount in a traditional IRA to a Roth IRA maintained by the same trustee. (Code Sec. 408A(d)(3)(C); Reg § 1.408A-4, Q&A 1(b))

Amounts from a SEP-IRA (¶4378) or a SIMPLE IRA (¶4357) also may be converted to a Roth IRA, but a conversion from a SIMPLE IRA may be made only after the 2-year period beginning on the date on which the taxpayer first participated in any SIMPLE IRA maintained by the taxpayer's employer. (Reg § 1.408A-4, Q&A 4)

The conversion is subject to tax (report on Form 8606) as if it were distributed from the traditional IRA and not recontributed to another IRA (¶4357) (Code Sec. 408A(d)(3)(A)(i)), but isn't subject to the 10% premature distribution tax. (Code Sec. 408A(d)(3)(A)(ii); Reg § 1.408A-4, Q&A 7)[9] Unless a taxpayer elects otherwise, however, none of the gross income from a 2010 conversion is included in income in 2010; half of the income resulting from the conversion is includible in gross income in 2011 and the other half in 2012. (Code Sec. 408A(d)(3)(A))[10]

When a traditional individual retirement annuity is converted to a Roth IRA, the amount treated as distributed is the FMV of the annuity contract on the date it is converted. Similarly, when a traditional IRA holding an annuity contract as an account asset is converted to a Roth IRA, the amount that is treated as distributed with respect to the annuity contract is the FMV of the annuity contract on the date the annuity contract is converted (i.e., distributed or treated as distributed from the traditional IRA). (Reg § 1.408A-4, Q&A 14(a))[11]

¶ 4372   Reconversion to Roth IRA.

A person who has converted an amount from a traditional IRA to a Roth IRA (¶4371) may not only transfer the amount back to a traditional IRA in a recharacterization (¶4370), but may later reconvert that amount from a traditional IRA to a Roth IRA, and, under certain circumstances, have his resulting income fixed at the time of the reconversion.

An IRA owner who converts an amount from a traditional IRA to a Roth IRA and then transfers that amount back to a traditional IRA by way of a recharacterization can't reconvert that amount from the traditional IRA to another Roth IRA before the beginning of the tax year following the tax year in which the amount was converted to a Roth IRA or, if later,

---

8. ¶H-12290.16A; ¶408A4; TD ¶283,317.1
9. ¶H-12290.20; ¶408A4; TD ¶283,326 *et seq.*

10. ¶H-12290.20B
11. ¶H-12290.20A; ¶408A4.

the end of the 30-day period beginning on the day on which the IRA owner transfers the amount from the Roth IRA back to a traditional IRA by way of a recharacterization. This timing rule applies regardless of whether the recharacterization occurs during the tax year in which the amount was converted to a Roth IRA or the following tax year. (Reg § 1.408A-5, Q&A 9(a)(1))

☺ *observation:* This restriction prevents a taxpayer from recharacterizing a Roth IRA as a traditional IRA if the market value of the IRA has been substantially reduced, e.g., because of a sharp decline in the market value of stocks held in the IRA, and then immediately reconverting to a Roth IRA to take advantage of the lower market value in determining the income to be reported from the conversion.

A reconversion made before the later of the beginning of the next tax year or the end of the 30-day period that begins on the day of the recharacterization is treated as a failed conversion, subject to correction through a recharacterization back to a traditional IRA. (Reg § 1.408A-5, Q&A 9(a)(1)) A failed conversion results in a distribution from the traditional IRA that's subject to tax (and possibly penalty tax) followed by a regular contribution to the Roth IRA. To the extent it exceeds the annual contribution limit, the amount treated as a regular contribution to the Roth IRA is treated as an excess contribution subject to the excise tax under Code Sec. 4973. (Reg § 1.408A-4, Q&A 3(b), Reg § 1.408A-4, Q&A 1(d), Reg § 1.408A-5, Q&A 9(a)(1)) For purposes of the reconversion timing rules, above, a failed conversion resulting from not having satisfied the statutory requirements is treated as a conversion in determining when an IRA owner may make a reconversion. (Reg § 1.408A-5, Q&A 9(a)(2))

¶ 4373   Distributions from Roth IRAs—Form 8606.

Qualified distributions. Qualified distributions from Roth IRAs aren't included in income. (Code Sec. 408A(d)(1)) These are distributions made after the five-tax-year period beginning with the first tax year for which the taxpayer or the taxpayer's spouse made a contribution to a Roth IRA established for the taxpayer, including a qualified rollover contribution from an IRA other than a Roth IRA (Code Sec. 408A(d)(2)(B)), and that are made:

(1) on or after attaining age 59½,

(2) at or after death (to a beneficiary or estate),

(3) on account of disability, or

(4) for a first-time home purchase expense under Code Sec. 72(t)(2)(F). (Code Sec. 408A(d)(2)(A), Code Sec. 408A(d)(5); Reg § 1.408A-6, Q&A 1)[12]

The five-year period for qualified distributions isn't recalculated when a Roth IRA owner dies. The five-year period for a beneficiary's inherited Roth IRA is determined independently of the period for any other Roth IRA that the beneficiary may have, except that the 5-year period for a spousal beneficiary with both an inherited Roth IRA and his own Roth IRA ends with the earlier of the five-year periods. (Reg § 1.408A-5, Q&A 7)

Corrective distributions made by the return due date, plus extensions, for the tax year of the contribution aren't qualified distributions. (Code Sec. 408A(d)(2)(C); Reg § 1.408A-6, Q&A 2)[13]

Nonqualified distributions. Distributions that aren't qualified distributions are treated as made first from contributions to all of an individual's Roth IRAs and are nontaxable to that extent; distributions in excess of contributions are taxable. (Code Sec. 408A(d)(4))[14]

Order of distributions. Distributions are treated as made from contributions to the Roth

---

12. ¶H-12290.28; ¶408A4; TD ¶283,337
13. ¶H-12290.30; ¶408A4; TD ¶283,338

14. ¶H-12290.34; ¶408A4; TD ¶283,342

IRA to the extent that the distribution, when added to all previous distributions from the Roth IRA, doesn't exceed the total amount of all contributions. (Code Sec. 408A(d)(4)(B)(i)) Contributions are treated as withdrawn in the following order: first, contributions other than qualified rollover contributions (i.e., qualified conversions, see ¶4371); second, qualified rollover contributions (on a FIFO basis); third, a distribution allocable to a qualified rollover contribution is allocated first to the part of the contribution required to be included in gross income. (Code Sec. 408A(d)(4)(B)(ii); Reg § 1.408A-6, Q&A 8)[15] All of a taxpayer's Roth IRAs are treated as a single Roth IRA. (Code Sec. 408A(d)(4)(A), Code Sec. 408(d)(2))

If the taxpayer withdraws all amounts from all of his Roth IRAs, a loss is recognized if the amounts distributed are less than his unrecovered basis (regular and conversion contributions).[16] For how to claim the loss, see ¶3110.

Report Roth IRA distributions on Form 8606, Part III.

Roth IRAs aren't subject to the required minimum distribution rules of Code Sec. 401(a)(9)(A) or the incidental benefit requirements of Code Sec. 401(a) (¶4345). Instead, after the Roth IRA owner's death, the distribution rules in Reg § 1.408-8 apply as though the Roth IRA owner died before his required beginning date. Thus, the entire Roth IRA must generally be distributed within five years of the owner's death unless it is distributed over the life expectancy of a designated beneficiary, and distributions commence prior to the end of the calendar year following the year of the owner's death. Where the sole beneficiary of a Roth IRA is the Roth IRA owner's surviving spouse, the spouse may delay distributions until the Roth IRA owner would have reached age 70½, or may treat the Roth IRA as his or her own. (Reg § 1.408A-6, Q&A 14(b)) (Code Sec. 408A(c)(5))[17]

For the 10% early distribution penalty tax, see ¶4374. For distributions from designated Roth accounts, see ¶4375.

¶ 4374   10% premature distribution tax on Roth IRA distributions.

As with other IRAs (¶4344) the Code Sec. 72(t) 10% early withdrawal tax applies to the portion of an early withdrawal that is includible in income. In addition, however, a distribution from a Roth IRA is subject to the early withdrawal tax as if it *were* includible in income, if that distribution (or any portion of it): (1) is allocable (under rules at ¶4373) to a "qualified rollover contribution;" and (2) is made within the five-tax year period beginning with the tax year for which the contribution was made. However, the 10% tax applies only to the extent that the amount of the qualified rollover contribution was includible in income. (Code Sec. 408A(d)(3)(F))[18]

¶ 4375   Designated Roth (Roth 401(k)) Accounts ▬▬▬▬▬

An employer's Code Sec. 401(k) plan (¶4317) or Code Sec. 403(b) annuity (¶4388) may include a qualified Roth contribution program (i.e., a "Roth 401(k)") that allows participants to elect to have all or part of their elective deferrals treated as Roth contributions—that is to make "designated Roth contributions." (Code Sec. 402A) Designated Roth contributions, which are currently includible in income, aren't subject to the AGI based phaseouts for regular Roth IRA contributions (¶4369). Qualified distributions are excludable from income. (Code Sec. 402A(d))[19]

Designated Roth contributions. These are elective contributions under a 401(k) plan that are:

---

15. ¶H-12290.35; ¶408A4; TD ¶283,343
16. ¶H-12255; TD ¶143,005
17. ¶H-12290.42; ¶408A4; TD ¶283,351

18. ¶H-12290.38; ¶408A4; TD ¶283,346
19. ¶H-12295.1 *et seq.*; ¶402A4; TD ¶283,400 *et seq.*

(1) designated irrevocably by the employee when he makes the cash or deferred arrangement (CODA) election as designated Roth contributions;

(2) treated by the employer as includible in the employee's income when he would have received the contribution in cash had he not made the CODA election (e.g., by treating the contributions as wages subject to applicable withholding requirements); and

(3) maintained by the plan in a separate account. (Code Sec. 402A(b)(2); Reg § 1.401(k)-1(f)(1), Reg § 1.401(k)-1(f)(2))

A 401(k) plan can't provide for designated Roth contributions unless it also offers pre-tax elective contributions. (Reg § 1.401(k)-1(f)(1)(i))

A designated Roth contribution must satisfy the requirements that apply to elective contributions made under a qualified CODA (i.e., a 401(k) plan), such as the nonforfeitability and distribution restrictions for elective contributions, and the Code Sec. 401(k) ADP (actual deferral percentage) test; see ¶4317. (Reg § 1.401(k)-1(f)(3))

For tax years beginning after Dec. 31, 2010, governmental section 457 plans may add designated Roth accounts. Code Sec. 402A(e)(1)(C))

Rollovers. For distributions made before Sept. 28, 2010, direct rollovers from a designated Roth account could be made only to another designated Roth account under a qualified retirement plan (or Code Sec. 403(b) annuity) or to a Roth IRA, and only to the extent the direct rollover is permitted under the Code Sec. 402(c) rules (¶4359). (Reg § 1.401(k)-1(f)(4)(ii)) A designated Roth distribution to an employee may be rolled over by him into a Roth IRA (or to a designated Roth account) within a 60-day period. (Reg § 1.402A-1, Q&A 5.)

For distributions made after Sept. 27, 2010, employers may amend their 401(k) (or 403(b)) plans to allow participants to transfer an eligible rollover distribution (ERD) to their designated Roth account in the plan. (Code Sec. 402A(c)(4)) An ERD is a distribution (1) made after Sept. 27, 2010, (2) from a non-designated Roth account in the same plan, (3) because of an event that triggers an ERD from the plan; and (4) otherwise meets the rollover requirements.

For tax years beginning after 2010, similar rules apply to governmental section 457 plans that have added designated Roth accounts. (Code Sec. 402A(e)(1)(C))

The participant must include in gross income the amount that would be includible in gross income if it were not part of a qualified rollover distribution. (Code Sec. 402A(c)(4)(A)(i))

Any amount that would be includible in a taxpayer's gross income for the 2010 tax year due to the rollover of an ERD to a designated Roth account is included in gross income ratably over the two-year period beginning in the taxpayer's 2011 tax year. However, the taxpayer may elect to not have this two-year deferral apply, and so then would include the entire taxable portion in gross income in the 2010 tax year. An election not to take the two-year tax deferral for an ERD made in 2010 may not be changed after the extended due date of the 2010 income tax return. (Code Sec. 402A(c)(4)(A)(iii))

The two-year tax deferral on rollovers to a designated Roth account in 2010 must be accelerated if the individual receives distributions from that designated Roth account in 2010 or 2011. Acceleration is also required if the individual dies before 2012, unless a surviving spouse acquires the entire account and elects to continue the deferral. (Code Sec. 402A(c)(4)(D))

Any distribution from an applicable retirement plan (other than from a designated Roth account) that is contributed in a qualified rollover contribution to the designated Roth account, is not taken into account as a designated Roth contribution. (Code Sec. 402A(c)(4)(C))

Distributions from designated Roths. A qualified distribution from a designated Roth is excluded from income if it meets the requirements for qualified distributions from Roth IRAs (¶4373), with the following differences:

... A distribution for a first-time home purchase isn't excluded. (Code Sec. 402A(d)(2)(A)

... the five-year period necessary for a distribution to be excluded begins on the first day of the employee's tax year for which he first had designated Roth contributions made to the plan. If a direct rollover is made from a designated Roth account under another plan, the five-year period begins on the first day for which the employee first had designated Roth contributions made to the other plan, if earlier. (Reg § 1.402A-1, Q&A 4)

... Designated Roth accounts are subject to the lifetime required minimum distribution (RMD) rules of Code Sec. 401(a)(9)(A) and Code Sec. 401(a)(9)(B) (¶4345). (Reg § 1.401(k)-1(f)(4)(i)) By contrast, a regular Roth IRA is not subject to the Code Sec. 401(a)(9)(A) lifetime RMD rules (¶4373).

A distribution from a designated Roth account that is not a qualified distribution is taxable to the distributee under the Code Sec. 72 rules, *not* under the regular Roth IRA ordering rules (¶4373). (Reg § 1.402A-1, Q&A 3)

¶ 4376 Deemed IRAs.

Qualified plans, Code Sec. 403(b) annuities (¶4388), and governmental Code Sec. 457 plans may include a deemed IRA, which is a separate account or annuity in a qualified employer plan to which plan participants may make voluntary IRA or Roth IRA contributions.

The qualified plan must elect to allow employees to make voluntary employee contributions (designated as such by the employees) to a separate account or annuity (meeting the requirements for a traditional IRA or Roth IRA) established under the plan. However, the general requirement that IRA assets not be commingled does not apply to deemed IRAs. (Code Sec. 408(q))[20]

SEPs (see ¶4377) and SIMPLE IRAs (¶4382) cannot be used as deemed IRAs. (Reg § 1.408(q)-1(b))[21]

Contributions to a deemed IRA are treated as contributions to an IRA, and not as contributions to the qualified employer plan. Thus, a deemed IRA contribution is in addition to the $16,500 (for 2010 and 2011) maximum amount that can be contributed to a 401(k) plan (excluding catch-up contributions). (Code Sec. 408(q)(1))

The ceilings on modified adjusted gross income that limit a taxpayer's ability to make Roth IRA contributions or deductible contributions to a regular IRA also apply to voluntary contributions to a deemed IRA. (Code Sec. 408(q)(1)(B); Reg § 1.408(q)-1(f)(4))[22]

A deemed IRA isn't subject to the rules that apply to the qualified employer plan, so contributions to a deemed IRA are not taken into account in applying those rules to any other contributions under the plan. Thus, deemed IRA contributions don't count against the 100% of income or dollar limit on annual additions to defined contribution plans. (Reg § 1.408(q)-1(c))

¶ 4377 Simplified Employee Pensions (SEPs)

An employer can make deductible contributions on behalf of its employees to a simplified employee pension (SEP). These deductible employer contributions are excluded from the gross income of the employee.

---

20. ¶H-12280; ¶4084.07; TD ¶283,080
21. ¶H-12280; ¶4084.07; TD ¶283,080

22. ¶H-12284; TD ¶283,084

¶ 4378   Simplified employee pension (SEP) defined.

A SEP is an individual retirement account or individual retirement annuity (IRA, see ¶4351), established by an employer by filing Form 5305-SEP, in which:

(1) The employer contributions are made only under a definite written allocation formula that is executed within the time for making a deductible contribution (¶4379)[23] that specifies (a) the requirements that an employee must satisfy to share in an allocation, and (b) how the allocated amount is computed. (Code Sec. 408(k)(5))[24]

(2) Employer contributions for a year must be made to each SEP of each employee who has reached age 21, performed service for the employer during at least three of the immediately preceding five years and has received at least $550 in compensation (for 2010 and 2011). (Code Sec. 408(k)(2))[25]

(3) The employer contributions don't discriminate in favor of highly compensated employees. (Code Sec. 408(k)(3)(A))[26]

(4) The employer contributions aren't conditional on the retention in the plan of any portion of the amounts contributed. (Code Sec. 408(k)(4))[27]

(5) The employer doesn't restrict employee withdrawals. (Code Sec. 408(k)(4)(B))[28]

(6) Elective deferrals made by each highly compensated employee under a salary reduction arrangement may not exceed the average of the deferral percentage of all other eligible employees multiplied by 1.25. (Code Sec. 408(k)(6)(A)(iii))[29]

Employer contributions are discriminatory unless they bear a uniform relationship to the first $245,000 (for 2010 and 2011) of the compensation (including self-employed income) of each employee maintaining the SEP. (Code Sec. 408(k)(3)(C))[30]

Employees covered by a collective bargaining agreement and nonresident aliens may be excluded from participation in the plan and from the discrimination test under certain conditions. (Code Sec. 408(k)(3)(B))[31]

Maximum allowable contributions made by an employer to a SEP on behalf of an employee for any year cannot exceed the lesser of: (1) 25% of compensation (limited by the annual compensation limit, see ¶4319) from the employer includible in the employee's gross income for the year (determined without regard to the employer's contributions to the SEP), or (2) the dollar limitation for defined contribution plans ($49,000 for 2010 and 2011, see ¶4328). (Special calculations are needed for self-employeds, like those for Keogh plans, see ¶4327.) Employee elective deferrals to a SEP (¶4381) do not count towards the limit. Where the SEP is integrated with social security, the dollar limitation in (2) is reduced by the amount taken into account above the integration level, in the case of a highly compensated employee. (Code Sec. 402(h)(2))[32]

¶ 4379   Employer's deduction for contributions to a SEP.

A contribution by an employer to a SEP is deductible for a tax year if made on account of that year and not later than the time prescribed for filing the return for that year plus extensions.[33] The deduction can't exceed 25% of the compensation paid to the employees during the calendar year, up to the defined contribution plan limit (¶4328). Contributions that exceed this limit can be carried over to, and deducted in, succeeding tax years in order of

23. ¶H-12303; ¶4084.05; TD ¶282,306
24. ¶H-12310; ¶4084.05; TD ¶282,306
25. ¶H-12305; ¶4084.05; TD ¶282,302
26. ¶H-12306; ¶4084.05; TD ¶282,303
27. ¶H-12309; ¶4084.05; TD ¶282,305
28. ¶H-12309; ¶4084.05; TD ¶282,305

29. ¶H-12321; ¶4084.05; TD ¶282,315
30. ¶H-12307; ¶4084.05; TD ¶282,304
31. ¶H-12306; TD ¶282,303
32. ¶s H-12308, H-12311; ¶4084.05; TD ¶282,307
33. ¶H-12312 *et seq.*; ¶4084.05; TD ¶282,311

time. (Code Sec. 404(h))[34]

An employer may elect to use either the calendar year or, subject to such terms and conditions as IRS may prescribe, its own tax year as the computation period for purposes of determining contributions to a SEP. (Code Sec. 408(k)(7)) If the calendar year is used, contributions made for a year are deductible for the employer's tax year with which or within which the calendar year ends. If the employer's "regular" tax year is used, contributions are deductible for that tax year. For purposes of deductibility, contributions are treated as if they were made for a tax year if the contributions are made on account of the tax year and are made not later than the time prescribed by law for filing the return for the tax year, plus extensions. (Code Sec. 404(h)(1)(A), Code Sec. 404(h)(1)(B))[35] Special rules apply where the employer also contributes to other plans. (Code Sec. 404(h)(2), Code Sec. 404(h)(3))[36]

¶ 4380 Employee's treatment of SEP contributions and withdrawals.

Contributions made to a SEP by an employer on behalf of an employee are excluded from the employee's gross income, up to the deduction limits at ¶4379. (Code Sec. 402(h)(1)) Contributions in excess of those limits are taxed to the employee in the year made. (Code Sec. 402(h)(2))[37] Payments made from the SEP are taxed to the recipient under the IRA rules (¶4357). (Code Sec. 402(h)(3))[38]

¶ 4381 Salary reduction SEPs (SARSEPs).

Employers can no longer establish salary reduction SEPs. However, a SEP that's maintained by an employer (except for tax-exempt or governmental employers) with no more than 25 employees at any time during the year before a particular tax year may include a salary reduction arrangement with the SEP for that year, if the plan as in effect on Dec. 31, '96 had a salary reduction arrangement. Not less than 50% of the participating employees must be able to elect to have the employer either make contributions to the SEP on his behalf or pay him cash. The amount of the elective deferrals for any year must satisfy the CODA deferral limits, including catch-up contributions for those age 50 and over (¶4317). Also, the SEP must provide for distribution of excess contributions. (Code Sec. 408(k)(6))[39]

For the saver's credit for lower-income taxpayers' elective contributions to SEPs, see ¶2371.

¶ 4382 "SIMPLE" Retirement Plans.

An employer with 100 or fewer employees that doesn't have a qualified plan can establish a "SIMPLE" (savings incentive match plan for employees) retirement plan, without having to meet most requirements for qualified plans.

¶ 4383 Employers eligible to adopt SIMPLE retirement plans.

A "SIMPLE retirement plan" can be adopted (use Form 5305-SIMPLE, Form 5304-SIMPLE if there's no designated financial institution, or Form 5305-SA for a SIMPLE individual retirement custodial account) by an employer with 100 or fewer employees who received at least $5,000 of compensation from the employer for the preceding year (Code Sec. 408(p)(2)(C)(i)(I)) that doesn't have another employer-sponsored retirement plan (including a SEP or annuity plan), except for a collectively bargained plan covering employees ineligible to participate in the SIMPLE plan, to which contributions were made or benefits accrued for the year. (Code Sec. 408(p)(2)(D))[40] "Employee" includes a self-employed individual. (Code Sec. 408(p)(6)(B)) A qualifying employer that maintains a SIMPLE plan but later

34. ¶H-12315; ¶4044.08; TD ¶282,309
35. ¶H-12317; ¶4044.08; TD ¶282,311
36. ¶H-12318 *et seq.*; ¶4084.05; TD ¶282,312
37. ¶H-12311; ¶4084.05; TD ¶282,307
38. ¶H-12319.3; TD ¶143,001
39. ¶H-12321; ¶4084.05; TD ¶282,314
40. ¶H-12351; ¶4084.06; TD ¶282,801

fails to qualify may continue to maintain the plan for two years after its last year of eligibility, subject to certain restrictions for acquisitions, dispositions and similar transactions. (Code Sec. 408(p)(2)(C)(i)(II), Code Sec. 408(p)(10))[41]

¶ 4384   "Qualified salary reduction arrangements" under SIMPLE plans.

Employees designate contributions to be made to a SIMPLE plan under a "qualified salary reduction arrangement." This is a written arrangement under which an employee may elect to have the employer make elective employer contributions (expressed as a percentage of compensation, or, if the employer permits, a specific dollar amount) to a SIMPLE retirement account on behalf of the employee, or to the employee directly in cash. The amount that an employee may elect for any year can't exceed $11,500 for 2010 and 2011, as indexed for inflation. (Code Sec. 408(p)(2)(A)(i), Code Sec. 408(p)(2)(A)(ii), Code Sec. 408(p)(2)(E))[42] SIMPLE 401(k) or SIMPLE IRA participants who are age 50 or over by the end of the plan year may make additional catch-up contributions of up to $2,500 for 2010 and 2011. (Code Sec. 414(v)(2)(B)(ii), Code Sec. 414(v)(2)(C))[43]

For the saver's credit for lower-income taxpayers' elective contributions to SIMPLE plans, see ¶2371.

The employer must make either:

(1) a matching contribution equal to the amount the employee contributes, up to 3% (Code Sec. 408(p)(2)(C)(ii)(I)) of the employee's compensation for the year, or, electively, as little as 1% in no more than two out of the previous five years, if the employer timely notifies the employees of the lower percentage (Code Sec. 408(p)(2)(C)(ii)(II))[44] ; or

(2) a nonelective contribution of 2% of compensation for each employee eligible to participate who has at least $5,000 of compensation from the employer for the year. (Code Sec. 408(p)(2)(B)(i))[45]

No other contributions may be made. (Code Sec. 408(p)(2)(A)(iv), Code Sec. 408(p)(8)) Elective employer contributions must be made no later than 30 days after the month for which the contributions are to be made. (Code Sec. 408(p)(5)(A)(i)) Matching contributions and nonelective contributions must be made by the deductible contribution due date for the year. (Code Sec. 408(p)(5)(A)(ii))[46]

"Compensation" is wages for income tax withholding purposes plus the amount of the employee's elective deferrals (Code Sec. 408(p)(6)(A)(i)) (for a self-employed person, net self-employment earnings (under Code Sec. 1402(a)) without regard to the SIMPLE retirement plan provisions. (Code Sec. 408(p)(6)(A)(ii)) For purposes of determining contributions to a SIMPLE plan, the definition of compensation includes wages paid to domestic workers, even though those amounts are not subject to income tax withholding. (Code Sec. 408(p)(6)(A)(i))

The compensation taken into account for purposes of determining the amount of the 2% nonelective contribution can't exceed the limit on compensation (under Code Sec. 401(a)(17), see ¶4319) that may be taken into account for the year. (Code Sec. 408(p)(2)(B)(ii))[47]

¶ 4385   SIMPLE retirement account defined.

A "SIMPLE retirement account" into which employer contributions under a SIMPLE retirement plan are made), is an individual retirement account or annuity (Code Sec. 408(p)(1)) for which the only contributions allowed are contributions under a "qualified

41. ¶H-12352.1; ¶4084.06; TD ¶282,801
42. ¶H-12357; ¶4084.06; TD ¶282,803
43. ¶H-9244.1; ¶4144.26; TD ¶284,114
44. ¶H-12359; ¶4084.06

45. ¶H-12360; ¶4084.06
46. ¶H-12364; ¶4084.06; TD ¶282,809
47. ¶H-12358; ¶4084.06

salary reduction arrangement" and that meets certain vesting, participation and administrative requirements (Code Sec. 408(p)(1)(A)). Employees' rights to all SIMPLE account contributions must be nonforfeitable. (Code Sec. 408(p)(3)) All employees (except those who can be excluded from a qualified plan (Code Sec. 408(p)(4)(B)) who received at least $5,000 in compensation from the employer during any two preceding years (Code Sec. 408(p)(4)(A)(i)), and are reasonably expected to receive at least $5,000 in compensation during the current year (Code Sec. 408(p)(4)(A)(ii)) must be eligible either to elect to make a salary reduction contribution or receive nonelective contributions. (Code Sec. 408(p)(4)(A))[48]

¶ 4386 Contributions to SIMPLE retirement accounts.

Employer contributions to SIMPLE accounts are deductible in the employer's tax year with which (or within which) the calendar year for which the contributions were made ends. (Code Sec. 404(m)(1); Code Sec. 404(m)(2)(A)) Contributions are treated as made for the tax year if they are made (a) on account of that year, and (b) not later than the time for filing that year's tax return (including extensions). (Code Sec. 404(m)(2)(B))[49]

observation: "Employer contributions" include elective contributions, matching contributions, and nonelective contributions.

Contributions to simplified employee pensions are excluded from the employee's income similar to the rules for SEPs under Code Sec. 402(h)(1) (¶4380). Employees aren't entitled to a deduction for employer contributions made on their behalf to a SIMPLE retirement account. (Code Sec. 219(b)(4)) Any elective contributions under a SIMPLE retirement plan are included in the sum of elective deferrals, subject to an annual limit on the amount that can be excluded from income. (Code Sec. 402(g)(3)(D))[50] Matching contributions on behalf of self-employed persons aren't treated as employer elective contributions for this purpose. (Code Sec. 408(p)(9))[1]

observation: Thus, matching SIMPLE contributions for a self-employed person don't count toward the annual limit on elective deferrals (¶4317).

SIMPLE plans may also incorporate an automatic enrollment arrangement (ACA), which permits an employer to make contributions to an employee's SIMPLE IRA without the employee having made an affirmative election to participate in the plan.[2]

¶ 4387 SIMPLE retirement account distributions.

Rules similar to those for distributions from simplified employee pensions (SEPs), apply to SIMPLE retirement accounts. (Code Sec. 402(k)) Thus, they are taxed under the rules relating to IRAs in the year of distribution. (Code Sec. 402(h)(3))[3] For tax-free rollovers of SIMPLE retirement account distributions, see ¶4357.[4] For early withdrawal penalties for SIMPLE account distributions, see ¶4344.[5]

¶ 4388 Tax-Sheltered 403(b) Annuities. ▬▬▬▬▬▬

Employees of tax-exempt educational, charitable, religious, etc., organizations, or public schools get special tax advantages from annuities bought for them by the exempt employers.

Tax-sheltered annuities offer benefits similar to those under a qualified employee plan. The tax isn't imposed when the annuity is bought, but is deferred until payments are received.

---

48. ¶H-12361; ¶4084.06; TD ¶282,807
49. ¶H-12372; ¶4084.06; TD ¶282,811
50. ¶H-12373; TD ¶282,813
1. ¶H-12357; ¶4084.06

2. ¶H-12365.1
3. ¶H-12374; ¶4084.06; TD ¶282,814
4. ¶H-12375; TD ¶282,816
5. ¶H-12377; TD ¶282,815

(Code Sec. 403(b); Reg § 1.403(b)-1)[6] These annuities may be bought only for common law employees of certain exempt educational, charitable, religious, etc., employers, and by or for certain self-employed ministers. (Code Sec. 403(b)(1)(A))[7] The annuity must be nonforfeitable (except for failure to pay premiums) and nontransferable. (Code Sec. 403(b)(1)(C); Reg § 1.401-9(b)(3))[8] Certain elective deferral limits must be met if the annuity is part of a salary reduction arrangement (¶4390). (Code Sec. 403(b)(1)(E))[9] Also, except for annuities bought by church employers, certain nondiscrimination tests must be met. (Code Sec. 403(b)(1)(D), Code Sec. 403(b)(12))[10] Tax-sheltered annuities are treated as defined contribution plans for purposes of the contribution limits (¶4328).[11]

Up to $100,000 in "qualified settlement income" relating to the Exxon Valdez litigation may be contributed by qualified taxpayers to 403(b) plans, see ¶4359.

IRS regs have reduced the extent to which the 403(b) rules differ from the rules for arrangements such as 401(k) plans and 457(b) plans. Included among these changes are the requirement that a 403(b) plan be operated in accordance with a written plan document, and that the 403(b) plan meet a nondiscrimination "universal availability" requirement. (Reg § 1.403(b)-1 through Reg § 1.403(b)-11)[12]

¶ 4389   How tax-sheltered annuity arrangements work.

Employees of a qualifying employer can get a prescribed amount of their compensation in the form of a tax-sheltered annuity. The employee pays no immediate tax on the amount the employer pays for the annuity, but is taxed under the regular annuity rules (¶1357 *et seq.*) when the annuity payments are made. (Code Sec. 403(b)(1))[13]

The tax deferral is denied for distributions attributable to contributions made under a salary reduction agreement (¶4390), unless the annuity provides that payments may be paid only: (1) when the employee attains age 59½, separates from employment, dies, or becomes disabled, or (2) in the case of hardship. (Code Sec. 403(b)(11)) (The premature distribution penalty applies, ¶4344). (Code Sec. 72(t)) The contract may not provide for the distribution of any income attributable to such contributions in the case of hardship. (Code Sec. 403(b)(11))[14] Tax-sheltered annuities are subject to the loan rules at ¶4343. (Code Sec. 72(p)(4)(A))[15]

For rollovers to and from Code Sec. 403(b) plans, see ¶4359 and ¶4360.

¶ 4390   Tax-sheltered annuity salary-reduction agreements.

An employee of a qualifying employer can agree to reduce his salary or forego an increase as a means of contributing to a 403(b) plan. The rules that apply to cash or deferred arrangements under Code Sec. 401(k) (¶4317) determine how often a salary reduction may be entered into, the compensation to which the agreement applies, and the ability to revoke the agreement.[16]

All of the employer's employees (except those covered by a CODA or an eligible Code Sec. 457 plan for tax-exempt and governmental employers) must get a chance to elect to have the employer contribute more than $200 under the salary reduction agreement, on a nondiscriminatory basis, if *any* employee may so elect. (Code Sec. 403(b)(12)(A))[17] The employee's elective deferrals for a year can't exceed the CODA limits, including catch-up contributions for those age 50 or over (¶4317). (Code Sec. 403(b)(1)(E); Reg § 1.403(b)-4(c))[18]

---

6. ¶H-12400 *et seq.*; ¶4034.04; TD ¶135,506
7. ¶s H-12402, H-12409; ¶4034.04
8. ¶H-12415; ¶4034.04
9. ¶H-12427 *et seq.*; ¶4034.04
10. ¶H-12420; ¶4034.04
11. ¶H-12454 *et seq.*; ¶4034.04; TD ¶284,029
12. ¶H-12400 *et seq.* ¶4034 *et seq.* TD ¶284,701 *et seq.*

13. ¶H-12431
14. ¶H-12430; ¶4034.04
15. ¶H-11066; ¶724.23
16. ¶H-12419.1; ¶4034.04
17. ¶H-12420; ¶4034.04
18. ¶H-12427; ¶4034.04

A 403(b) plan can include a qualified Roth contribution program (see ¶4375).

The term "salary reduction agreement" includes a plan or arrangement whereby a payment will be made if the employee:

... elects to reduce compensation pursuant to a cash or deferred election as defined at Reg § 1.401(k)-1(a)(3);

... elects to reduce compensation pursuant to a one-time irrevocable election made at or before the time of initial eligibility to participate in the plan or arrangement (or pursuant to a similar arrangement involving a one-time irrevocable election); or

... agrees as a condition of employment (whether the condition is set by statute, contract, or otherwise) to make a contribution that reduces the employee's compensation. (Reg § 31.3121(a)(5)-2(a))[19]

For the saver's credit for lower-income taxpayers' contributions to 403(b) annuities, see ¶2371.

¶ 4391 Tax-sheltered annuity contribution limit.

If a qualifying employer buys a tax-sheltered annuity for an employee and employee's rights are nonforfeitable, the premium paid is not taxable to the employee at that time, up to the applicable limit for a defined contribution plan under Code Sec. 415 (¶4328). (Code Sec. 403(b)(1), Code Sec. 415(c)(1), Code Sec. 415(k)(4); Reg § 1.403(b)-3(b)(3))[20]

Special limits apply for contributions by church plans. (Code Sec. 415(c)(7))

¶ 4392 "Includible compensation" and "years of service."

"Includible compensation" means the amount of compensation received by the employee from the qualified employer that is includible in his gross income (without regard to the exclusion for certain foreign source earned income) for the most recent period ending not later than the close of the employee's tax year that can be counted as one "year of service" and which precedes the tax year by no more than five years. Amounts contributed by the employer for tax-sheltered annuities are not included. Elective deferrals and any amount contributed or deferred by the employer at the employee's election that is excluded from income under Code Sec. 125 or Code Sec. 457 are included. (Code Sec. 403(b)(3))[21]

"Includible compensation" doesn't include any compensation *earned* when the employer wasn't a qualified employer. But it's immaterial whether the employer was qualified when the compensation is actually *received* by the employee.[22]

Similar rules apply to compensation received from "eligible employers." (Reg § 1.403(b)-2(b)(11)

The employee's "years of service," which can't be less than one, includes one year for each full year he was a full-time employee of the organization buying the annuity for him, plus a fraction of each year, as prescribed by regs, for each full year he was a part-time employee, or for each part of a year he was a full- or part-time employee. (Code Sec. 403(b)(4))[23]

An employee's years of service equals the aggregate of the annual work periods during which he is employed by the eligible employer. (Reg § 1.403(b)-4(e))

---

19. ¶H-4650; TD ¶544,018
20. ¶H-12439; ¶4034.04
21. ¶H-12443; ¶4034.04

22. ¶H-12443; ¶4034.04
23. ¶H-12444 *et seq.*; ¶4034.04

Chapter 22 Farmers

¶ 4500 Farmers.

Farmers get tax breaks not generally available to others: three-year income averaging, a generally longer NOL carryback period, favorable accounting and inventory methods, income deferrals, capital gain-ordinary loss treatment and the deduction of items normally capitalized.

¶ 4501 Farmers' income and expenses—Schedule F (Form 1040).

A farmer's gross income includes cash and the fair market value of goods received ("barter income") from crops, produce, poultry and livestock. (Reg § 1.61-4(c)) The value of produce consumed by the farmer and his family isn't included, but expenses incurred in raising that produce can't be deducted.[1]

Farmers may deduct the ordinary and necessary expenses of operating a farm for profit—e.g., rent, labor, feed (¶4515), fertilizer (¶4516). (Reg § 1.162-12(a))[2] For required capitalization of certain expenses, see ¶4519. Where farming isn't engaged in for profit, see ¶1780.

¶ 4502 Three-year averaging for farming or fishing income—Schedule J.

An individual (including a partner in a partnership and a shareholder of an S corporation, but not including an estate or trust) engaged in a farming or fishing business may elect three-year averaging of "elected farm income" (below) for regular income tax (but not for employment tax) purposes. If the election is made, the tax for the year is equal to the sum of (1) the tax computed on taxable income reduced by elected farm or fishing income, and (2) the increase in tax that would result if taxable income for the three prior tax years were increased by an amount equal to one-third of the elected farm or fishing income. Any adjustment under this provision for any tax year is taken into account in applying this provision for any later tax year. (Code Sec. 1301(a), Code Sec. 1301(b)(3); Reg § 1.1301-1(b)) Taxable income for prior years can be less than zero, but in that case any amount that may provide a benefit in another tax year (such as an NOL) is added back in determining base year taxable income. (Reg § 1.1301-1(d)(2))[3]

Elect by filing Form 1040, Schedule J with a return for the election year (including a late or amended return if the time for filing for a credit or refund has not expired). An individual may change or revoke a previous election, if the period of limitation on filing a claim for credit or refund has not expired for the election year. (Reg § 1.1301-1(c))

"Elected farm income" means the amount of taxable income for the tax year attributable to any farming or fishing business that's specified in the election to average farm or fishing income (Code Sec. 1301(b)(1)(A); Reg § 1.1301-1T(e)(2)) including farm wages paid to an S shareholder (Reg § 1.1301-1(e)(1)), income of fishing-boat crew members compensated by a share of the boat's catch or a share of the catch proceeds (Reg § 1.1301-1T(e)(1)) and certain crop-share income. (Reg § 1.1301-1(b)(2)) Gain from the sale or other disposition of property (other than land) regularly used by the taxpayer in a farming or fishing business for a substantial period is treated as attributable to that farming business. (Code Sec. 1301(b)(1)(B); Reg § 1.1301-1(e)(1)(ii)(A))[4] A landlord is engaged in a farming business for farm averaging purposes for rental income based on a share of production (not fixed rent) from a tenant's farming business determined under a written agreement entered into before the tenant begins significant activities on the land. Similar rules apply to fishing-boat lessors

---

1. ¶N-1151; ¶1624.340; TD ¶116,001
2. ¶N-1301; ¶1624.340; TD ¶297,501

3. ¶N-1500 *et seq.*; ¶13,014; TD ¶119,001 *et seq.*
4. ¶N-1500 *et seq.*; ¶13,014; TD ¶s 119,003, 119,004

References beginning with a single letter are to paragraphs in RIA's Federal Tax Coordinator 2d and RIA's Analysis of Federal Taxes: Income. Those beginning with numbers are to paragraphs in RIA's United States Tax Reporter. Those beginning with TD are to paragraphs in RIA's Tax Desk.

who share in the catch. (Reg § 1.1301-1T(b)(3)) Tobacco quota payments don't qualify for income averaging.[5]

Electing income averaging does not cause the taxpayer's AMT to increase because regular tax liability for determining the AMT is computed as though the election had not been made, see ¶3201.

Qualified taxpayers (such as fishermen) may report qualified settlement income (interest, punitive damages) received from the '89 Exxon Valdez oil spill civil action using 3-year income averaging under Code Sec. 1301. Such income also may be used to make contributions (not exceeding $100,000) to retirement accounts, and is not subject to FICA or SECA tax. (Sec. 504, Div C, P.L. 110-343, 10/3/2008)

¶ 4503 Three- or five-year NOL carryback.

Although net operating losses (NOLs) generally may be carried back only two years, a taxpayer engaged in the business of farming gets a three-year carryback for NOLs (other than those that qualify for the five-year carryback, below) attributable to federally declared disasters (Code Sec. 172(b)(1)(F)(ii)(III))[6], see ¶1842. And "farming losses" (any NOL attributable to the income and deductions of a farming business, but not in excess of the taxpayer's NOL for the year; qualified disaster losses aren't included) may be carried back five years (Code Sec. 172(b)(1)(G)) (and forward for the regular 20-year period).[7] Farmers may elect (by the due date, including extensions, for the loss year, or, if a timely return was filed, on an amended return within six months of the original return due date) not to have the five-year carryback apply, in which case the regular NOL rules apply (¶1842); once made, the election is irrevocable for that year. (Code Sec. 172(i)(3))[8]

¶ 4504 Limitation on deduction of farm losses

For tax years beginning after 2009, the farming loss of a taxpayer, other than a C corporation, is limited for any tax year in which any applicable subsidies are received. The loss is limited to the greater of (a) $300,000 ($150,000 for a married person filing separately), or (b) the taxpayer's total net farm income for the prior five tax years. Applicable subsidies are (1) any direct or counter-cyclical payments under title I of the Food, Conservation, and Energy Act of 2008 (or any payment elected in lieu of any such payment), or (2) any Commodity Credit Corporation (CCC) loan. (Code Sec. 461(j))[9] For partnerships and S corporations, the limit is applied at the partner or shareholder level. (Code Sec. 461(j)(5))

Total net farm income is an aggregation of all income and loss from farming businesses for the prior five tax years. Any loss that is disallowed under this rule in a particular year is carried forward to the next tax year and treated as a deduction attributable to farming businesses in that year. Farming losses due to fire, storm, or other casualty, or disease or drought, are disregarded for purposes of calculating the limitation. (Code Sec. 461(j))

¶ 4505 Farmers' accounting methods.

Farmers (unless listed at ¶4510) may use the cash method (¶4506), the accrual method (¶4509), the crop method (¶4512), or a "hybrid" method combining any of these methods if it clearly reflects income (¶2817). (Reg § 1.61-4, Reg § 1.446-1(c), Reg § 1.471-6(a))[10]

While most taxpayers who produce, buy or sell merchandise must use inventories (and therefore the accrual method, see ¶2863), farmers may choose not to, except to the extent they

5. ¶N-1501 *et seq.*; ¶13,014; TD ¶s 119,003, 119,004
6. ¶M-4305.2; ¶1724.436; TD ¶356,011
7. ¶M-4305.3; ¶1724.437; TD ¶356,012

8. ¶M-4305.4; ¶1724.437; TD ¶356,013
9. ¶N-1331; ¶4614.78; TD ¶297,701
10. ¶N-1010 *et seq.*; ¶s 614.053, 4464.09; TD ¶118,001

are subject to the uniform capitalization rules (¶4519). (Reg § 1.471-6(a))[11] But a farmer who does use inventories must use the accrual method at least for purchases and sales.[12] However, IRS has excepted the following from having to account for inventories or use an accrual method of accounting: (1) any business with average annual gross receipts of $1 million or less; and (2) taxpayers whose principal business activity is not mining, manufacturing, wholesale trade, retail trade, or information industries, for all of their trades or businesses, if average annual gross receipts are $10 million ($5 million for C corporations) or less, see ¶2818.

¶ 4506   Cash method farmers.

Cash method farmers include income in the year actually or constructively received, whichever is earlier (¶2819). Gross income includes receipts of: (1) proceeds from sales of *raised* livestock or produce; (2) profits from the sale of any *purchased* property, including livestock, (3) breeding fees, (4) fees from renting teams, machinery or land, (5) taxable subsidy and conservation payments, (6) crop insurance proceeds, and (7) all other gross income. (Reg § 1.61-4(a))[13] For deferral of insurance proceeds and forced livestock sales, see ¶4508.

Expenses are ordinarily deductible in the year paid (other than the cost of animals and plants bought for resale, see ¶4507). (Reg § 1.61-4(a))[14] For feed expenses, see ¶4515, and for pre-paid expenses, see ¶4517. An option to accelerate the receipt of any payment under a production flexibility contract that is payable under the FAIR Act of 1996 as in effect on Dec. 17, '99 won't accelerate the recognition of income unless the option is exercised. (Sec. 525 of P.L. 106-170) The constructive receipt rules also don't apply to options to receive payments under the Farm Security and Rural Investment Act of 2002.[15]

¶ 4507   Cash method farmer's deduction of costs of purchased animals and plants—election to deduct in year bought or year sold.

Cash method farmers generally deduct the costs of animals and plants bought for resale only in the year the animals or plants are disposed of. (Reg § 1.61-4(a)) But for these animals and plants, a farmer may elect to deduct the costs either for the year they are purchased or for the year they are sold, if the method chosen clearly reflects income:

... baby chicks and pullets bought for raising and resale;

... hens bought for commercial egg production;

... seeds and young plants (other than Christmas trees and timber) bought for further development and cultivation before sale. (Reg § 1.162-12)[16]

The farmer makes the election by deducting the cost for the first year in which he buys the items. Once the farmer elects this option—which is a method of accounting—he must use it consistently until IRS consents to a change (¶2838).[17]

¶ 4508   One-year deferral elections for cash method farmers—"disaster" receipts.

A cash method farmer can elect to defer reporting certain insurance proceeds and federal disaster payments (including payments under Title II (but not Title I) of the '88 Disaster Assistance Act) until the tax year after the year of the destruction or damage to, or inability to plant, the crops, if he shows that under his practice, the income from the crops would be reported in a later year. To elect, check box in Part I on Schedule F and attach a statement to the return (or amended return) for the year payments are received. (Code Sec. 451(d);

11. ¶N-1100 et seq.; ¶4714.73; TD ¶118,002
12. ¶N-1017; TD ¶118,009
13. ¶N-1013; ¶614.054; TD ¶118,002
14. ¶614.054; TD ¶297,500

15. ¶N-1152.1; ¶4514.039
16. ¶s N-1021, N-1022; TD ¶118,007
17. ¶N-1022; TD ¶118,007

Reg § 1.451-6)[18]

One-year deferral also may be elected for income from livestock sold on account of a drought, flood or other weather-related condition so severe the sale had to take place in an earlier year than normal. Elect on a statement attached to the return for the sale year. (Code Sec. 451(e)(1); Reg § 1.451-7(g)) However, if the period for buying replacement property for such livestock under the involuntary conversion rules is extended to four years from the end of the year of sale (see ¶2438), the election of one-year deferral is valid if made during that replacement period. (Code Sec. 451(e)(3))[19] (For involuntary conversions, see ¶2432.)

¶ 4509   Accrual method farmers.

Accrual farmers include farm income for the year earned, regardless of when payment is received, and deduct farm expenses for the year the "all events test" is met (¶2824 *et seq.*). Inventories must be used (¶4513). (Code Sec. 461(h); Reg § 1.61-4(b), Reg § 1.446-1(c))[20]

An accrual farmer's gross income for a tax year is the sum of: (1) the sales price of all livestock and other products held for sale that are sold during the year, (2) the inventory value of the livestock, etc. (i.e., the proceeds from the disposition of livestock, etc., during the year, plus the inventory value of livestock, etc., not sold at the end of the year, reduced by the inventory value of livestock, etc., on hand at the start of the year, and by the cost of any livestock, etc., bought during the year and included in inventory), (3) miscellaneous farm receipts, e.g., fees from breeding or from renting teams, (4) all subsidy and conservation payments includible that year, plus (5) gross income from all other sources. Crop shares are included in the year they are reduced to money or its equivalent. (Reg § 1.61-4(b))[21]

¶ 4510   When accrual accounting is mandatory for farmers.

Corporations (except as noted below) and any partnership in which a corporation is a partner must use the accrual method of accounting to compute their taxable income from farming (as must tax shelters, which include farm syndicates, see ¶4511). Raisers and harvesters of nut and fruit trees are covered by this rule, but nurseries, sod farms and raisers and harvesters of other types of trees aren't. (Code Sec. 447(a))[22]

The mandatory accrual rule doesn't apply to:

(1) S corporations. (Code Sec. 447(c)(1))

(2) A "family corporation" (family members own at least 50% of (a) the total combined voting power of all voting stock, and (b) the total number of shares of all other classes of stock) other than one whose gross receipts exceed $25 million for any tax year. (Code Sec. 447(c)(2), Code Sec. 447(d)(2))[23] Two- or three-family corporations must meet special ownership tests, and must have been engaged in farming since Oct. 4, '76. (Code Sec. 447(h))[24]

(3) A corporation whose gross receipts (or any predecessor's) don't exceed $1 million for any tax year. (Code Sec. 447(c)(2), Code Sec. 447(d)(1))[25]

(4) Certain corporations (and partnerships having a corporate partner) engaged in growing sugar cane, any plant with a pre-productive period of two years or less, or, if an (irrevocable) election made for the first tax year beginning after '86 is in effect, any other plant (other than any citrus or almond tree). And, for all ten tax years ending with the first tax year beginning after '75, the corporation (or partnership) must have used an "annual accrual method" of accounting for the trade or business. (Code Sec. 447(g))[26]

---

18. ¶N-1024 *et seq.*; ¶s 614.054, 4514.171; TD ¶118,005
19. ¶N-1031 *et seq.*; ¶4514.176; TD ¶118,003
20. ¶N-1017; ¶4614.15; TD ¶118,009
21. ¶N-1014, N-1017; ¶614.051; TD ¶118,009
22. ¶N-1036 *et seq.*; ¶4474; TD ¶118,012

23. ¶s N-1036, N-1040; ¶4474; TD ¶118,012
24. ¶N-1056; ¶4474; TD ¶118,013
25. ¶N-1036; ¶4474; TD ¶118,012
26. ¶N-1049; ¶4474; TD ¶118,012

¶ 4511   Tax shelters and farming syndicates.

All tax shelters, including farming syndicates, must use the accrual method. (Code Sec. 448(a)(3))[27] For pre-paid expenses, see ¶4517. For uniform capitalization rules, see ¶4519. For tax shelter losses for AMT purposes, see ¶3210.

A farming syndicate is any partnership (or other noncorporate enterprise) or S corporation engaged in the business of farming if:

. . . at any time, interests in the partnership, etc., have been offered for sale in an offering required to be registered with any federal or state agency having authority to regulate the offering of securities for sale; or

. . . more than 35% of the losses during any periods are allocable to limited partners or limited entrepreneurs (Code Sec. 464(c)); or

. . . it's a tax shelter. (Code Sec. 461(i)(3), Code Sec. 461(i)(4))[28]

¶ 4512   Crop method.

A farmer may, with IRS consent, use the crop method to report income from crops (other than timber) for which the process of planting, harvesting and sale isn't completed within the same tax year. (Reg § 1.61-4(c))[29] Under this method, all expenses of the crop (including expenses of seed or young plants) are charged, and all crop receipts are credited, to a crop account. Profit (or loss) is realized and included in income (or loss deducted) only in the year the crop is harvested and disposed of. (Reg § 1.61-4(c), Reg § 1.162-12(a))[30]

¶ 4513   Farmers' inventories.

A farmer using inventories (¶4514) *must* inventory:

. . . all livestock and poultry, raised or purchased, held primarily for sale (Reg § 1.61-4(b));

. . . all harvested and purchased farm products held for sale, feed, or seed, such as grain, hay ensilage, concentrates, cotton, tobacco;

. . . supplies, unless only small amounts are on hand;

. . . if in the hatchery business, eggs in incubation and growing and pre-market chickens. (Inventories *may* be used for hens primarily held for egg production which are also held for sale after their egg-producing life.)[31]

Livestock held for dairy, breeding, sporting or draft purposes may be inventoried at the taxpayer's election. But raised livestock must be inventoried by farmers using the unit-livestock-price method. (Reg § 1.61-4(b), Reg § 1.471-6(f))[32]

¶ 4514   Inventory valuation methods for farmers.

Methods that farmers use to value inventory include:

. . . *Cost method* (¶2869). (Reg § 1.471-3)[33]

. . . *Lower-of-cost-or-market method* (¶2870). (Reg § 1.471-4)[34]

. . . *Farm price method.* Each item, raised or purchased, is valued at its market price less estimated direct cost of disposition. A farmer using this method must use it for all his

---

27. ¶G-2456; ¶4484; TD ¶118,001
28. ¶G-2456 *et seq.*; ¶4644; TD ¶442,023
29. ¶N-1018 *et seq.*; ¶614.056; TD ¶118,010
30. ¶N-1019; ¶614.056; TD ¶118,010

31. ¶N-1102; ¶614.057; TD ¶298,001
32. ¶s N-1109, N-1113; ¶s 614.057, 4714.73; TD ¶298,001
33. ¶N-1106; ¶s 614.057, 4714.41, 4714.73; TD ¶298,003
34. ¶N-1107; ¶s 614.057, 4714.51; TD ¶298,004

inventory, but may use the unit-livestock-price method for livestock. (Reg § 1.471-6(d))[35]

... Unit-livestock-price method. Livestock is reasonably classified according to kind and age. A standard unit price is used for each animal within a class. Unit prices must reflect costs capitalized under the uniform capitalization rules, see ¶4519. Once established, the accounting methods used to determine unit prices and to classify animals must be consistently applied in all future tax years. Users of this method must annually reevaluate their unit prices and adjust them to reflect increases or decreases in the costs of raising livestock. IRS consent isn't required for these adjustments; however it is required for other changes in classification or unit prices. (Reg § 1.471-6(f))[36]

¶ 4515 Feed.

The cost of feed is a deductible business expense. (Reg § 1.162-12(a))[37] A cash method farmer may deduct in the year paid, the cost of feed his livestock will consume that year. Payments for feed to be used in the next tax year ("pre-paid feed") aren't deductible until the year of consumption, except the farmer may deduct pre-paid feed expenses in the payment year if: (1) the payment represents a purchase and not a deposit, (2) the advance payment is for a business purpose and not merely for tax avoidance, *and* (3) deduction in the payment year doesn't materially distort income.[38] For pre-paid farm expenses generally, see ¶4517.

¶ 4516 Fertilizer.

The cost of acquiring fertilizer, lime, marl, and other materials used to enrich, neutralize, or condition farmland, and the costs of applying them, are deductible in the year the costs are paid or incurred if the benefit doesn't last beyond one year. If the benefit lasts substantially more than a year the costs generally are capitalized but the farmer may elect to deduct them in the year paid or incurred (Code Sec. 180(a))[39] by deducting them on his return for that year. (Code Sec. 180(c); Reg § 1.180-2)[40] The election to deduct isn't allowable for costs of preparing land not previously used for farming by the taxpayer or his tenant. (Code Sec. 180(b); Reg § 1.180-1(b))[41]

If fertilizer expenses are capitalized, the taxpayer may deduct a portion of the capitalized amounts for each year the benefits last. The portion deducted each year need not be the same if benefits are clearly greater in the early years.[42]

¶ 4517 Pre-paid farm expenses.

A cash method taxpayer's current deduction for pre-paid farm expenses (i.e., for feed, seed, fertilizer, and similar farm supplies that won't be used until a later tax year) is limited to one-half of his other deductible farming expenses for the year (for a special rule for feed, see ¶4515). The "excess" part (i.e., over that one-half amount) isn't deductible until the year the supplies are used. (Code Sec. 464(f)(1), Code Sec. 464(f)(2))[43] This rule also applies to farming syndicates (required to use the accrual method, see ¶4511). (Code Sec. 464(a))[44]

But this limit *doesn't apply* if the taxpayer's (or a family member's) principal home (within the meaning of Code Sec. 121, see ¶2442) is a farm or his principal business is farming, if: (1) for the three preceding tax years, his total pre-paid farm expenses are less than 50% of his total other deductible farm expenses, or (2) for the current year, his pre-paid farm expenses are more than 50% of his other farm expenses because of a change in business operations

35. ¶N-1112; ¶s 614.057, 4714.73; TD ¶298,005
36. ¶N-1113; ¶s 614.057, 4714.73; TD ¶298,006
37. ¶N-1311; ¶1624.340; TD ¶297,514
38. ¶N-1312; ¶1624.340; TD ¶297,515
39. ¶N-1306; ¶1804; TD ¶297,510
40. ¶N-1307; TD ¶297,511
41. ¶N-1306; TD ¶297,510
42. ¶N-1306; TD ¶297,510
43. ¶N-1319 *et seq.*; ¶4644; TD ¶297,519
44. ¶N-1319 *et seq.*; ¶4644; TD ¶297,519

attributable to extraordinary circumstances. (Code Sec. 464(f)(3))[45]

¶ 4518   Pre-productive period expenses.

The taxpayer has the option to either deduct or capitalize certain costs of developing and operating his farm and crops (e.g., taxes, interest, upkeep) during its pre-productive period (Reg § 1.162-12(a))[46] (subject to the uniform capitalization rules, see ¶4519). But he can't deduct any capital expenditures.[47] The pre-productive period begins when the farmer first acquires the seed or plant, and ends when the plant produces marketable quantities or is reasonably expected to be sold or otherwise disposed of. (Code Sec. 263A(e)(3))[48]

¶ 4519   Application of uniform capitalization rules to farmers and ranchers.

Farmers and ranchers are subject to the uniform capitalization rules for taxpayers generally (¶1660) with respect to the production, growing, or raising of property that:

... is produced by a farmer required to use the accrual method (¶4510), (Code Sec. 263A(a), Code Sec. 263A(d)(1); Reg § 1.263A-4(a), Reg § 1.263A-4(b)) or

... has a pre-productive period (¶4518), of more than two years. (Code Sec. 263A(d)(1)(A)(ii))

For taxpayers not required to use the accrual method, the uniform capitalization rules *don't apply* to costs related to any animal, or plant with a pre-productive period of two years or less, which is produced by a taxpayer in a farming business. (Code Sec. 263A(d)(1)(A); Reg § 1.263A-4(a)(2))[49] The preproductive period is the period before the first marketable crop or yield, for plants that have more than one crop or yield (e.g., the orange tree); the period before a crop or yield is disposed of, for the crop or yield of a plant that will have more than one crop or yield (e.g., the orange); or, for any other plant, the period before it is disposed of. (Reg § 1.263A-4(b)(2)) IRS has published a noninclusive list of plants with preproductive periods in excess of 2 years.[50]

For exception for replanting because of casualties, see ¶4520. For election out of the uniform capitalization rules, see ¶4521.

¶ 4520   Exception to uniform capitalization rules for replanting because of casualties.

The uniform capitalization rules (¶4519) don't apply to costs incurred for the replanting, cultivation, maintenance and development of plants bearing an edible crop for human consumption (including citrus or almond) that were lost or damaged (while in the taxpayer's hands) by freezing temperatures, disease, drought, pests, or casualty (replanting costs). (Code Sec. 263A(d)(2)(A); Reg § 1.263A-4(e)(1), Reg § 1.263A-4(e)(4))[1]

This casualty exception generally applies to the costs of the person owning ("owner") the plants at the time of the loss or damage. But costs paid or incurred by another person (payor) in any tax year also may qualify if in that year: (1) the owner has a more-than-50% equity interest in the plants, and (2) the payor owns any of the remaining equity interest in them *and* materially participates in their planting, maintenance, cultivation or development. (Code Sec. 263A(d)(2)(B); Reg § 1.263A-4(e)(2))[2]

---

45. ¶N-1319; ¶4644; TD ¶297,520
46. ¶N-1302; ¶1624.349; TD ¶298,009
47. ¶N-1303; ¶1624.349; TD ¶298,009
48. ¶N-1074; TD ¶298,009

49. ¶N-1071 et seq.; ¶263A4; TD ¶298,011
50. ¶N-1071.1; ¶263A4.15
1. ¶N-1081; ¶1624.339; TD ¶298,014
2. ¶N-1082; ¶263A4; TD ¶298,014

¶ 4521   Farmers' election to have uniform capitalization rules not apply.

Except as noted below, a farmer may elect to have the uniform capitalization rules at ¶4519 *not* apply to any plant produced in his farm business (Code Sec. 263A(d)(3)(A)), so he may currently deduct all otherwise deductible preproductive costs.[3]

If the taxpayer or any related person (as specially defined) makes the election, he must use Code Sec. 168(g)(2) alternative (i.e., straight-line) depreciation for all his property used predominantly in the farming business that was placed in service in any tax year during which the election is in effect (Code Sec. 263A(e)(2)(A); Reg § 1.263A-4(d)(4)(ii)) and follow other requirements in the regs. (Reg § 1.263A-4(d)(4))[4]

If the election is made, any plant with respect to which amounts would have been capitalized *but for* the election is treated as Code Sec. 1245 property (if it's not otherwise Code Sec. 1245 property). (Code Sec. 263A(e)(1)(A)(i); Reg § 1.263A-4(d)(4)(i)) Deductible amounts that *but for* the election would have been capitalized are treated as depreciation deductions for Code Sec. 1245 purposes (Code Sec. 263A(e)(1)(A)(ii), Code Sec. 263A(e)(1)(B)) so that they are recaptured as ordinary income when the product is disposed of, see ¶2695.[5]

The election can't be made for any item attributable to the planting, maintenance or development of any citrus or almond grove (or part of a grove) that's incurred before the close of the fourth tax year beginning with the tax year the trees were planted. For this purpose, the portion of a grove planted in one tax year must be treated separately from the portion planted in another tax year. (Code Sec. 263A(d)(3)(C); Reg § 1.263A-4(d)(2))[6]

Elect out of UNICAP by not applying the rules of Code Sec. 263A to determine the capitalized costs of plants produced in a farming business and by applying the rules of Reg § 1.263A-4(d)(4) on the original return for the first tax year capitalization of Code Sec. 263A costs is required. For partnerships or S corporations, the election is made by the partner, shareholder, or member. (Code Sec. 263A(d)(3)(D); Reg § 1.263A-4(d)(3)(i)) A taxpayer that does not make the automatic election described above must get IRS consent (¶2838) to change accounting methods. (Reg § 1.263A-4(d)(3)(ii))[7] The election can't be made by farmers who must use the accrual method of accounting, see ¶4510. (Code Sec. 263A(d)(3)(B))[8]

¶ 4522   Soil and water conservation and erosion prevention costs.

Farmers may deduct currently, as business expenses, certain outlays for soil and water conservation or erosion prevention that are incurred to maintain the farm and preserve its normal productivity, and not to increase its value or convert it to a new use. Costs that result in the acquisition of depreciable property must be capitalized.[9]

A farmer may elect to deduct certain nondepreciable expenditures for conservation, etc., with respect to land he uses for farming (Code Sec. 175(a)) if the expenditures are consistent with a federal or state approved conservation plan. (Code Sec. 175(c)(3))[10] Qualifying expenditures include (1) costs of: treating or moving earth (e.g., leveling, terracing or restoring fertility); constructing and protecting diversion channels, drainage ditches, earthen dams; eradicating brush; planting windbreaks; producing vegetation primarily to conserve soil or water, or prevent soil erosion and (2) expenses paid or incurred for endangered species recovery, including site-specific management actions under the Endangered Species Act of '73. (Code Sec. 175(c); Reg § 1.175-2(a), Reg § 1.175-2(b)(2)) Costs of draining or filling wetlands or for center pivot irrigation systems don't qualify. (Code Sec. 175(c)(3)(B)) Nor does

---

3. ¶N-1084; ¶263A4; TD ¶298,015
4. ¶N-1090; ¶263A4; TD ¶298,015
5. ¶N-1093; ¶263A4; TD ¶298,015
6. ¶N-1089; ¶263A4; TD ¶298,015

7. ¶N-1087; ¶263A4; TD ¶298,016
8. ¶N-1085; ¶263A4; TD ¶298,015
9. ¶N-1401; ¶1754; TD ¶299,001
10. ¶N-1402; ¶1754.02; TD ¶299,002

the election apply to depreciable assets. (Reg § 1.175-1)[11]

The amount of conservation, etc., expenses a farmer may deduct in any tax year under this election can't exceed 25% of his gross income from farming for the year. Any excess may be carried over to and deducted in the next tax year (subject to that year's 25% ceiling). (Code Sec. 175(b); Reg § 1.175-5(b))[12]

Elect by deducting the expenses on the return for the first tax year they are incurred. (Reg § 1.175-6(a))[13] IRS consent is needed to elect for a year other than that first year. (Code Sec. 175(d)(2))[14] Once the election is made, a farmer must continue to deduct all qualifying expenditures (subject to the 25% ceiling) unless IRS consents to a change. (Code Sec. 175(e))[15]

A farmer must recapture as ordinary income (use Form 4797) part of the conservation, etc., expenses if the farm land is disposed of after being held for less than 10 years. (Code Sec. 1252)[16]

¶ 4523   Depreciation for farm property—Form 4562.

A farmer may take depreciation deductions (on Form 4562) on property used in a farming business (Code Sec. 168(b)(2)(B)), including: buildings (except his dwelling); farm machinery; other physical property (not including land); orchards (trees and vines bearing fruits or nuts); and draft, breeding, sporting or dairy livestock (unless inventoried). (Reg § 1.167(a)-6(b))[17]

Farm property generally is depreciated under MACRS using the 150% declining balance method, but straight line applies to nonresidential real property, trees or vines bearing fruits or nuts. (Code Sec. 168(b)(1)(B), Code Sec. 168(b)(2)(B), Code Sec. 168(b)(3)(A), Code Sec. 168(b)(3)(B))[18]

The cost of *purchased* dairy, etc., livestock may be recovered under MACRS. The cost of *raised* livestock may be either deducted (but costs so deducted can't be included in depreciable basis) (Reg § 1.61-4(a), Reg § 1.162-12(a)) or capitalized as the taxpayer chooses.[19] But accrual method farmers using inventories can't depreciate any purchased dairy, etc., livestock that's inventoried. (Reg § 1.167(a)-6)[20]

¶ 4524   Unharvested crop sold with land.

Gain or loss on an unharvested crop sold, exchanged, or compulsorily or involuntarily converted with the underlying land qualifies under the capital gain-ordinary loss rule of Code Sec. 1231 (¶2684 *et seq.*), if: (1) the land was used in the taxpayer's trade or business and was held for the long-term capital gain holding period (¶2667), *and* (2) the land and crops are sold at the same time and to the same person. (Code Sec. 1231(b)(4)) It doesn't matter how long the *crops* were held, or their state of maturity. (Reg § 1.1231-1(f))[21]

¶ 4525   Dispositions of converted wetlands or highly erodible croplands.

Gain on the disposition of land used for farming that is converted wetland or highly erodible cropland is ordinary income. Loss is long-term capital loss. (Code Sec. 1257)[22]

¶ 4526   Dispositions of breeding, dairy, sporting, draft livestock.

Gains and losses from the sale, exchange, or involuntary conversion of animals held for draft, breeding, dairy, or sporting purposes qualify for capital gain-ordinary loss treatment

---

11. ¶s N-1406, N-1407; ¶1754.02; TD ¶299,002
12. ¶N-1415; ¶1754.02; TD ¶299,015
13. ¶N-1420; TD ¶299,020
14. ¶N-1421; ¶1754; TD ¶299,021
15. ¶N-1422; TD ¶299,022
16. ¶N-1423; ¶12,524; TD ¶299,023

17. ¶N-1304; ¶1674.035; TD ¶298,501
18. ¶L-8912; ¶1684.01; TD ¶267,014
19. ¶s N-1020, N-1350 *et seq.*; ¶1624.339; TD ¶298,501
20. ¶N-1351; ¶1674.035; TD ¶298,501
21. ¶N-1206; ¶12,314.13; TD ¶117,012
22. ¶N-1424 *et seq.*; ¶12,574; TD ¶299,024

under Code Sec. 1231 (¶2684 *et seq.*) as follows:

... cattle and horses held for 24 months or more from the date of acquisition;

... other livestock (except poultry) held for 12 months or more from the date of acquisition. (Code Sec. 1231(a), Code Sec. 1231(b)(3); Reg § 1.1231-2(a))[23]

Inventorying the livestock doesn't preclude Code Sec. 1231 treatment if the animal is held for the required purposes and relevant period and not for sale to customers.[24]

¶ 4527 Like-kind exchange of livestock.

The trading of livestock may qualify as a tax-free like-kind exchange (¶2418 *et seq.*) if the exchanged animals are the same sex. (Code Sec. 1031(e); Reg § 1.1031(e)-1)[25]

¶ 4528 Special farm payments.

Conservation programs. Unless the taxpayer elects out (Code Sec. 126(c)), gross income doesn't include the excludable part of payments received under certain conservation programs specified in Code Sec. 126(a)(1) to Code Sec. 126(a)(8) or received under Code Sec. 126(a)(9) Agriculture Department programs affecting small watersheds found by IRS to be similar to those programs. (Code Sec. 126(b))[26] Part or all of the cost-share payments made under the Forest Health Protection Program (FHPP) may qualify for the Code Sec. 126 exclusion.

Pledge of crops to secure CCC loan. Farmers who pledge part or all of their production to secure a Commodity Credit Corporation (CCC) loan can make a special election to treat the loan proceeds as income in the year received and obtain a basis in the commodity for the amount reported as income. Thus, instead of a loan, the money advanced to the farmer may be treated as the sales price of the commodity pledged for the loan. Elect by reporting the CCC loan proceeds as income on Schedule F, Form 1040 for the year the loan is received and attaching a statement to the return showing the details of the CCC loan.[27]

Payments under the Tobacco Transition Payment Program. Eligible tobacco quota holders may receive total payments of $7 per pound of quota in 10 equal annual payments in fiscal years 2005 through 2014 in exchange for the termination of tobacco marketing quotas and related price support. Payments are proceeds from a sale of the owner's tobacco quota and may be reported on the installment method under Code Sec. 453 or deferred under the like-kind exchange rules of Code Sec. 1031 (if the owner otherwise qualifies).[28]

---

23. ¶s N-1209, N-1223; ¶s 12,314, 12,314.12; TD ¶117,001
24. ¶N-1209; TD ¶117,001
25. ¶N-1215; ¶10,314.04; TD ¶117,002

26. ¶N-1181; ¶1264; TD ¶116,002
27. ¶N-1164; ¶774.03; TD ¶221,008
28. ¶N-1152.5

Chapter 23 Foreign Income—Foreign Taxpayers—Foreign Currency Transactions

¶ 4610 Foreign Income of U.S. Taxpayers.

U.S. taxpayers—U.S. citizens, U.S. residents, U.S. (domestic) corporations and other taxable U.S. entities—ordinarily are fully taxable on their income from outside the U.S., subject to special exemptions and other special treatment for particular taxpayers, and particular kinds and sources of income. Nonresident aliens, foreign corporations and other foreign entities, however, are taxed only on their income that is effectively connected with a U.S. trade or business, and certain passive income derived from U.S. sources. Nonresidents who gave up U.S. citizenship or terminated long-term U.S. residency are subject to special expatriation tax rules.

¶ 4611 Foreign income of U.S. citizens and resident aliens.

U.S. citizens, whether they reside in the U.S. or abroad, are generally subject to U.S. income tax on their income from sources outside the U.S. (Reg § 1.1-1(b))[1] with exemptions for foreign earned income and housing costs (¶4612), income from U.S. possessions (¶4618), and certain allowances for U.S. government employees (¶4619). For the foreign tax credit, see ¶2375 *et seq.* For when a foreign corporation's *undistributed* income is taxed to its U.S. shareholders, see ¶4623, ¶4630, and ¶4631. For a resident alien's U.S. income, see ¶4635.

Every person born or naturalized in the U.S. and subject to its jurisdiction is a U.S. citizen. A foreigner who has filed a declaration of intent to become a citizen but who hasn't yet been admitted to citizenship by a final order of a naturalization court is an alien. (Reg § 1.1-1(c))[2]

¶ 4612 Partial exclusion for foreign earned income.

For any tax year in which an individual "qualifies" (¶4615), he may elect (¶4617) to exclude from gross income $80,000 (as adjusted for inflation, see below) of foreign earned income. (Code Sec. 911(a), Code Sec. 911(b)(2))[3] For a *separate* exclusion for foreign housing costs, see ¶4613.

An individual's "foreign earned income" is his earned income from foreign sources attributable to services he performed during the period he "qualifies." (Code Sec. 911(b)(1)(A))[4] Earned income means wages and other amounts received as compensation (i.e., not as a distribution of profits) for personal services actually rendered. This includes cash, the fair market value of property, and allowances or reimbursements (including taxable moving expense reimbursements) attributable to performing those services (Code Sec. 911(d)(2)(A); Reg § 1.911-3(e)(5)) and, where both personal services and capital are material income-producing factors in the taxpayer's noncorporate business, a reasonable allowance (up to 30% of his share of the net profits) as compensation for personal services. (Code Sec. 911(d)(2)(B))[5] A "stacking rule" limits the benefits of the earned income and housing costs exclusions by subjecting taxpayers using these exclusions to the same U.S. tax rates as individuals in the U.S. Any income above the exclusion amount under Code Sec. 911 is taxed (under the regular tax and the alternative minimum tax) by applying to that income the tax rates that would have applied had the individual not elected the Code Sec. 911 exclusions. Special rules are used to calculate both the regular tax and alternative minimum tax where the net capital

---

1. ¶O-1001 *et seq.*; TD ¶190,501
2. ¶O-1003; TD ¶190,503
3. ¶O-1100 *et seq.*; ¶9114 *et seq.*; TD ¶191,000 *et seq.*

4. ¶O-1140 *et seq.*; ¶9114.01; TD ¶191,024
5. ¶O-1111, ¶O-1117 *et seq.*; ¶s 9114.01, 9114.06 *et seq.*; TD ¶191,019

References beginning with a single letter are to paragraphs in RIA's Federal Tax Coordinator 2d and RIA's Analysis of Federal Taxes: Income. Those beginning with numbers are to paragraphs in RIA's United States Tax Reporter. Those beginning with TD are to paragraphs in RIA's Tax Desk.

gain exceeds the individual's taxable income for a tax year. (Code Sec. 911(f))[6]

An individual's foreign earned income exclusion for a tax year can't exceed his foreign earned income (¶4612) for the year, as computed on a daily basis at an annual rate of $91,500 for 2010, as indexed for inflation ($92,900 for 2011). (Code Sec. 911(b)(2)(A), Code Sec. 911(b)(2)(D))[7]

Where an individual is entitled to both the foreign earned income exclusion (¶4612) and foreign housing costs exclusion (¶4613) and/or deduction (¶4614) for a tax year, his foreign earned income exclusion is the *lesser* of: (a) $80,000 (as indexed), multiplied by the number of days in the tax year on which he "qualified" (¶4615), and divided by the number of days in the year, or (b) his foreign earned income as reduced by the foreign housing costs exclusion for the year. (Reg § 1.911-3(d)(2), Reg § 1.911-4(d))[8]

For married couples, the exclusion (and ceiling) is computed separately for each spouse based on the income attributable to the spouse's services. If the spouses file separate returns, each may exclude the amount of his foreign earned income attributable to his services, subject to the ceilings. If the spouses file a joint return, the sum of those separate amounts may be excluded. (Reg § 1.911-5(a)(2))[9]

¶ 4613 Partial exclusion for foreign housing costs.

A qualified individual (¶4615) may elect (¶4617) to exclude from gross income a part of his housing costs paid or incurred as a result of his foreign employment. (Code Sec. 911(a)(2))[10] For deduction of nonemployer-provided housing expenses, see ¶4614. For how the stacking rule applies where the foreign earned income exclusion or foreign housing costs exclusion applies, see ¶4612.

A qualified individual who elects the housing costs exclusion may not claim less than the full amount of the allowable exclusion. (Reg § 1.911-4(d)(1))[11]

The amount of housing costs eligible for exclusion in a tax year is the excess of: (1) the individual's housing expenses for the year, over (2) 16% of the amount (computed on a daily basis) of the foreign earned income exclusion limitation (¶4612) i.e., the base housing amount—*multiplied* by the number of days in the tax year within the individual's period of foreign residence or presence. (Code Sec. 911(c)(1)) The exclusion of foreign housing expenses in excess of the base housing amount is limited to 30% of the taxpayer's foreign earned income exclusion. IRS has used its authority to adjust this limit by listing high-cost areas in which taxpayers can deduct or exclude a higher portion of their housing costs. (Code Sec. 911(c)(2))[12]

> **Illustration:** Thus, the maximum amount of the foreign housing cost exclusion is $12,810 for 2010 ($91,500 × 30%) − ($91,500 × 16%). For 2011, it's $13,006 ($92,900 × 30%) − ($92,900 × 16%).

Where spouses reside together and both claim a foreign housing costs exclusion (or deduction), they may compute their exclusion separately or jointly. Spouses who file separate returns must make separate computations, but they may allocate the housing expenses between them. (Reg § 1.911-5(a)(3)(i)) Where spouses reside apart, they both may exclude (or deduct) their respective housing cost amounts if their tax homes (¶4615) aren't within reasonable commuting distance of each other and neither spouse's residence is within a reasonable commuting distance of the other spouse's tax home. If the spouses' tax homes or residences *are* within reasonable commuting distance, only one spouse may exclude (or deduct) his

6. ¶O-1101.1; ¶9114; TD ¶191,001.1
7. ¶O-1102; ¶9114.12; TD ¶191,004
8. ¶O-1102 *et seq.*; ¶s 9114.01, 9114.12; TD ¶191,004
9. ¶O-1115; ¶9114.09; TD ¶191,006

10. ¶O-1161 *et seq.*; ¶9114.02; TD ¶191,001
11. ¶O-1168; ¶9114.02; TD ¶191,001
12. ¶O-1166; ¶9114.02; TD ¶191,028

housing cost amount. In either case, and whether they file separately or jointly, the amount of the housing costs exclusion (or deduction) is determined separately for each spouse. (Code Sec. 911(d)(3); Reg § 1.911-5(a)(3)(ii))[13]

Also, only housing expenses for the abode bearing the closest relationship to the taxpayer's tax home, or to a second foreign household for his spouse and dependents who don't reside with him because of adverse living conditions, qualify for the exclusion. (Code Sec. 911(c)(2)(B); Reg § 1.911-4(b)(5)(i))[14]

¶ 4614 Deduction for foreign housing expenses not provided by employer.

A qualified individual (¶4615) may deduct foreign housing expenses that aren't attributable to employer-provided amounts. (Code Sec. 911(c)(3)(A))[15] The deduction is limited to the individual's foreign earned income for the tax year which isn't otherwise excluded from gross income under either the foreign earned income (¶4612) or foreign housing costs (¶4613) exclusions. (Code Sec. 911(c)(3)(B)) Any unused housing expenses may be carried over and deducted in the next tax year, subject to that year's limits. (Code Sec. 911(c)(4)(C))[16]

¶ 4615 Who qualifies for the foreign earned income/housing costs exclusions?

A taxpayer "qualifies" for the foreign earned income (¶4612) and housing costs (¶4613) exclusions for a tax year if his "tax home" (below) is in a foreign country *and* he is either:

. . . a U.S. citizen who meets a *foreign residence test.* To meet this test, the individual must be a bona fide *resident* of one or more foreign countries for an uninterrupted period including an entire tax year. (Code Sec. 911(d)(1)(A))[17] (A resident alien who's a national of a "treaty" country may qualify.) [18] or

. . . a U.S. citizen or resident who meets a *foreign presence test* (with an exception for emergency situations). To meet this test, the individual must, in any period of 12 consecutive months, be *present* in one or more foreign countries during at least 330 full days. (Code Sec. 911(d)(1)(B)) This means *physically* present, including time while on vacation or unemployed.[19]

An individual's "tax home" is his home for purposes of deducting away-from-home travel expenses (¶1544). He has no "tax home" in a foreign country for any period his abode is in the U.S. (Code Sec. 911(d)(3)) But the fact that an individual is temporarily present in the U.S. or maintains a U.S. dwelling (even if used by his spouse or dependents) doesn't necessarily mean his abode is in the U.S. (Reg § 1.911-2(b))[20] For married couples, if both spouses "qualify," each may elect the exclusion or deduction. (Reg § 1.911-5(a)(1))[21]

¶ 4616 Denial of double deduction, exclusion or credit.

No deduction, exclusion or credit, including any credit or deduction for foreign or possessions taxes (¶2375 *et seq.*), is allowable to the extent the deduction, etc., is allocable to or chargeable against foreign income excluded from gross income under the foreign earned income (¶4612) or housing costs (¶4613) exclusions. (Code Sec. 911(d)(6))[22]

---

13. ¶s O-1174, O-1175; ¶9114.02; TD ¶191,032
14. ¶O-1164; ¶9114.02; TD ¶191,033
15. ¶O-1171; ¶9114.02; TD ¶191,030
16. ¶O-1173; ¶9114.02; TD ¶191,030
17. ¶O-1250 *et seq.*; ¶9114.04; TD ¶191,506

18. ¶O-1271; ¶9114.04; TD ¶191,509
19. ¶O-1300 *et seq.*; ¶9114.05; TD ¶191,501
20. ¶s O-1202, O-1203, O-1250 *et seq.*
21. ¶O-1351; ¶9114.09; TD ¶191,006
22. ¶O-1112; ¶9114.11; TD ¶191,002

¶ 4617 Electing foreign earned income and housing costs exclusions— Form 2555 and Form 2555-EZ.

The foreign earned income (¶4612) and housing costs (¶4613) exclusions won't apply unless elected. (Code Sec. 911(a)) Each exclusion must be elected separately, on Form 2555 attached to the taxpayer's return for the first tax year it is to apply. (Reg § 1.911-7(a)(1), Reg § 1.911-7(a)(2)(i)) (Form 2555-EZ may be used for the foreign earned income exclusion if none of the individual's income was from self-employment, his total foreign earned income didn't exceed the $80,000 (see ¶4612) amount *and* he doesn't have business/moving expenses or claim the foreign housing costs exclusion or deduction.)[23]

Once either exclusion is elected for a year, it's effective for that year and all later years, unless revoked (Code Sec. 911(e))[24] or the taxpayer claims the foreign tax credit.[25]

¶ 4618 Income from certain U.S. possessions—exemption for individuals.

An individual who is a bona fide resident of American Samoa for the entire tax year is exempt from U.S. tax on his income (except for amounts earned as an employee of the U.S.) from sources within, or effectively connected with his conduct of a trade or business within American Samoa, Guam or the Commonwealth of the Northern Mariana Islands (CNMI). Form 4563 is used to claim the exemption. An individual who is a bona fide resident of Guam or CNMI for the entire tax year must file a return with the possession and is not subject to U.S. tax. (Code Sec. 931(a), Code Sec. 931(d); Reg § 1.931-1; Former Code Sec. 935; Reg § 1.935-1)

Special rules apply to determine if a person is a bona fide possessions resident and if income is possessions source income. (Code Sec. 937; Reg § 1.937-1, Reg § 1.937-2)[26]

An individual (regardless of citizenship) who is a bona fide resident of Puerto Rico for the entire tax year is exempt from U.S. tax on income from Puerto Rican sources, *except* amounts received for services performed for the U.S. government. But no deductions (other than for personal exemptions) or credits are allowed (i.e., from *taxable* non-Puerto Rican source income) for items attributable to the excluded amounts. (Code Sec. 933(1))[27]

A U.S. citizen who gives up Puerto Rican residence after being a bona fide resident there for at least two years may exclude from gross income for the year of change in residence, any income from Puerto Rican sources attributable to the period before the change (including amounts received *after* that year), to the extent allowed above. (Code Sec. 933(2); Reg § 1.933-1(b))

A U.S. citizen (or resident) who derives income from the Virgin Islands (VI) but is *not a bona fide resident* there for the entire tax year must file two identical returns, one with the U.S. and one with the VI (Form 8689). The individual's is taxed in the VI on the proportion of his adjusted gross income (AGI) from VI sources and the VI tax (if any) is credited against his total U.S. tax liability (¶2375 *et seq.*). (Code Sec. 932(a), Code Sec. 932(b); Reg § 1.937-1, Reg § 1.932-1)[28]

An individual who is a *bona fide VI resident* for the entire tax year (or files a joint return with a person who is a VI resident for the entire tax year) files a VI return and pays VI tax on his worldwide income for that year. If the individual properly files and reports all his income from all sources on a VI tax return and pays the VI tax, he is not subject to tax in the U.S. (Code Sec. 932(c)(4); Reg § 1.932-1)[29] For a joint return, resident status is based on the

23. ¶O-1351 *et seq.*; ¶9114.13; TD ¶191,036
24. ¶O-1351, O-1353; TD ¶191,039
25. ¶O-1354; TD ¶191,040
26. ¶O-1085 *et seq.*, ¶O-10987 *et seq.*, ¶O-1402 *et seq.*, ¶O-1432

et seq.; ¶9374 *et seq.*
27. ¶O-1450 *et seq.*; ¶9314.04
28. ¶O-1471; ¶9314.05
29. ¶O-1472 *et seq.*; ¶9314.05

residence of the spouse with the greater AGI for the year, without regard to community property laws. (Code Sec. 932(d))

¶ 4619 Exemption for certain U.S. government employees' allowances.

Certain allowances are exempt from tax. These include (a) cost-of-living allowances received by U.S. government civilian officers and employees (including judicial employees) stationed outside the continental U.S. (except Alaska) (Code Sec. 912(2)),[30] (b) amounts received as allowances or otherwise under: Chapter 9 of Title I of the '80 Foreign Service Act; Section 4 of the '49 Central Intelligence Agency Act; Title II of the Overseas Differentials and Allowances Act; or Subsection (e) or (f) of the first section of, or Section 22 of, the '46 Administrative Expenses Act (Code Sec. 912(1)),[31] and (c) allowances to a Peace Corps volunteer or volunteer leader and members of his family under Section 5 or 6 of the Peace Corps Act, *except:* termination payments, leave allowances, allowances to members of the family of a volunteer leader who is training in the U.S. and the part of an allowance designated as basic compensation. (Code Sec. 912(3)),[32] Recruitment incentives given because of station location, foreign post or service differentials, or allowances that are part of a salary are not exempt.[33]

¶ 4620 U.S. beneficiaries of foreign trusts.

A U.S. beneficiary is taxed on a foreign trust's foreign- and U.S.-source income, at the time it becomes distributable. (Code Sec. 643(a)(6), Code Sec. 652(a))[34] Distributions to the U.S. beneficiary of accumulated trust income are subject to the trust throwback rules (¶3953 *et seq.*)[35] and a nondeductible interest charge. (Code Sec. 668)[36] Loans to a U.S. beneficiary or related party generally are treated as distributions. (Code Sec. 643(i)) For loans made and uses of property after Mar. 18, 2010, any use of trust property by a U.S. grantor, U.S. beneficiary, or any U.S. person related to a U.S. grantor or U.S. beneficiary is treated as a distribution of the fair market value (FMV) of the use of the property to the U.S. grantor or U.S. beneficiary. (Code Sec. 643(i)(1)) A subsequent return of property treated as a distribution under Code Sec. 643(i) is disregarded for tax purposes. (Code Sec. 643(i)(3)) The rule treating the use of a foreign trust's property by the U.S. grantor, U.S. beneficiary or any related U.S. person as a distribution to the U.S. grantor or U.S. beneficiary does not apply to the extent that the trust is paid the FMV of the use of the property within a reasonable period of time of the use. (Code Sec. 643(i)(2)(E))[37]

¶ 4621 Domestic corporations—taxation of U.S. and foreign income.

A domestic corporation (i.e., created or organized in, or under the law of, the U.S. or any state) is subject to U.S. tax on its income from both foreign and U.S. sources (except for IC-DISCs, see ¶4622). (Code Sec. 63, Code Sec. 7701(a)(4))[38] It may also be taxed on the *undistributed* income of a controlled foreign corporation (¶4623) or certain types of PFICs (¶4630, ¶4631) in which it's a shareholder.[39]

¶ 4622 Interest charge domestic international sales corporations (IC-DISCs)

A qualifying corporation that elects (on Form 4876-A) to be an IC-DISC (also referred to as a "DISC") can defer income attributable to $10 million or less of qualified export receipts. However, the DISC's shareholders are subject to an interest charge (reported on Form 8404) equal to the shareholder's DISC-related deferred tax liability for the year × the base period T-

30. ¶H-3133; ¶9124.01; TD ¶138,034
31. ¶H-3135; TD ¶138,036
32. ¶H-3136; ¶9124.02; TD ¶138,037
33. ¶H-3134; TD ¶138,035
34. ¶C-3021; ¶6524; TD ¶655,003

35. ¶C-4003; ¶s 6664, 6684; TD ¶656,002
36. ¶C-4107 *et seq.*; ¶6684; TD ¶656,009
37. ¶C-4107.1; ¶6684; TD ¶656,002
38. ¶O-1006
39. ¶s O-2600 *et seq.*, O-3600 *et seq.*; TD ¶601,516

bill rate. (Code Sec. 995(f))[40] An IC-DISC must file Form 1120-IC-DISC.[41]

Certain DISC income (e.g., taxable income attributable to qualified export receipts that exceed $10 million) and certain other items trigger dividend income taxable to the DISC shareholders. (Code Sec. 995(b)(1))[42]

¶ 4623 Tax on U.S. shareholders of controlled foreign corporations (CFCs).

If a foreign corporation is a CFC (¶4624) for an uninterrupted period of 30 days or more during its tax year, every person who is a "U.S. shareholder" (¶4624) of the CFC at any time that year, and who owns stock in the CFC on the last day of its tax year, must report (on Form 5471, see ¶4660) his pro rata share of the foreign corporation's undistributed earnings ("Subpart F income," see ¶4625) for that year. (Code Sec. 951(a)(1); Reg § 1.951-1(a)) A U.S. shareholder's pro rata share, which depends on his interest in the various classes of the corporation's stock, is determined under special rules. (Reg § 1.951-1(e))[43]

A CFC's "U.S. shareholders" are also taxed on their pro rata shares of the CFC's:

. . . increase during the tax year in earnings invested in U.S. property (to the extent not included as Subpart F income) (Code Sec. 951(a)(1)(B));[44]

. . . previously excluded income withdrawn from investment in less developed countries (under the rules in effect before the Tax Reduction Act of '75) (Code Sec. 951(a)(1)(A)(ii));[45]

. . . previously excluded Subpart F income withdrawn from foreign base company shipping operations for that year (Code Sec. 951(a)(1)(A)(iii));[46] and

. . . decrease in investments in export trade assets. (Code Sec. 970(b))[47]

The tax on a U.S. shareholder on the increase in earnings invested in U.S. property during the tax year is applied by taxing the U.S. shareholder on the lesser of (1) the U.S. shareholder's pro rata share of the average amount of U.S. property (calculated by basis) held (directly or indirectly) by the CFC as of the close of each quarter of the tax year, less that portion of the CFC's earnings and profits attributable to amounts included previously in that shareholder's gross income under this rule or under any of the other CFC rules and (2) the shareholder's pro rata share of the CFC's applicable earnings. (Code Sec. 956)[48]

¶ 4624 Controlled foreign corporation (CFC) defined.

A CFC is a foreign corporation more than 50% (25%, for insurance companies) of whose stock *by vote or value* is, on any day in the corporation's tax year, owned (directly or indirectly) by "U.S. shareholders." (Code Sec. 957(a), Code Sec. 957(b)) A "U.S. shareholder" is a U.S. citizen or resident, or a U.S. corporation, partnership, estate or trust, that owns, directly or indirectly, more than 10% of the corporation's voting stock. (Code Sec. 951(b))[49]

¶ 4625 What is Subpart F income?

A CFC's Subpart F income consists of:

(1) Income derived from insuring (or reinsuring) certain foreign risks. (Code Sec. 953)[50]

(2) Foreign base company income (FBCI), which is

. . . (a) Foreign personal holding company income (FPHCI). This includes investment income such as dividends, interest, rents, royalties and annuities; gains from certain

---

40. ¶s O-2020 *et seq.*, O-2108 *et seq.*; ¶9914 *et seq.*
41. ¶S-1917
42. ¶O-2115 *et seq.*; ¶9954.01
43. ¶s O-2600 *et seq.*, O-2701; ¶9514.01
44. ¶O-2546 *et seq.*; ¶9564.01
45. ¶O-3309; ¶s 9514.01, 9554

46. ¶O-2531; ¶s 9514.01, 9554.01
47. ¶O-2536 *et seq.*; ¶9704.01
48. ¶O-2546 *et seq.*; ¶9564.01
49. ¶O-2300 *et seq.*; ¶9574.01
50. ¶O-2404 *et seq.*; ¶9534.01

property and commodities transactions, certain personal services income, and certain other passive type income. Exceptions apply for certain income received from related parties or as part of an active business. For tax years of foreign corporations beginning before Jan. 1, 2010, and tax years of U.S. shareholders with or within which such tax years of foreign corporations end, interest, rent, and royalties received or accrued from a CFC which is a related person will not be treated as FPHCI to the extent attributable or properly allocable to income of the related person which is not subpart F income or treated as effectively connected with a U.S. trade or business if deductions for those amounts don't create a deficit which reduces the subpart F income of the related CFC payor or another CFC.

caution: Check http://ria.thomsonreuters.com/federaltaxhandbook to see whether the pre-2010 rules have been extended.

. . . (b) Foreign base company sales, services, and oil-related income. (Code Sec. 952(a)(2), Code Sec. 954(c)(6), Code Sec. 954; Reg § 1.954-1, Reg § 1.954-2)[1]

(3) Income from operations in compliance with an unsanctioned international boycott. (Code Sec. 952(a)(3))[2]

(4) The amount of any illegal (under the U.S. Foreign Corrupt Practices Act) payment made (directly or indirectly) by or for the CFC to a government official, employee or agent in fact. (Code Sec. 952(a)(4))[3]

(5) Income (reduced by allocable deductions and taxes) from a foreign country during any period that Code Sec. 901(j) (which denies any credit for taxes paid to certain foreign countries, see ¶2377) applies to that country. (Code Sec. 952(a)(5))[4]

For tax years of foreign corporations beginning before 2010 (and for tax years of U.S. shareholders with or within which any such tax year of the foreign corporation ends), exceptions apply for certain income derived in the active conduct of a banking, financing, or similar business, or in the conduct of an insurance business. (Code Sec. 953(e)(10), Code Sec. 954(h)(9))[5]

caution: Check http://ria.thomsonreuters.com/federaltaxhandbook to see whether the pre-2010 rules have been extended.

Also, in any tax year when the sum of the CFC's FBCI and insurance income exceeds 70% of its gross income, *all* of its income for the year is treated as FBCI or insurance income (subject to the "high foreign tax" exception, below). (Reg § 1.954-1(d)(6)) If this sum is less than 5% of the CFC's gross income or $1,000,000 (whichever is less), *none* of the CFC's income is FBCI or insurance income. (Code Sec. 954(b)(3); Reg § 1.954-1(b))[6]

Any item of FBCI or insurance income that is subject to an effective rate of foreign tax which is greater than 90% of the maximum U.S. corporate rate may, at the election of the CFC's controlling U.S. shareholders, be excluded from Subpart F income. (Code Sec. 954(b)(4); Reg § 1.954-1(d))[7]

¶ 4626   Disposition of CFC stock.

Gain from the sale, exchange or redemption (under Code Sec. 302, see ¶3526 *et seq.*) of stock in, or from the liquidation of, a foreign corporation is (to the extent of its post-'62 earnings and profits attributable to that stock) taxable as ordinary dividend income *if:*

---

1. ¶O-2424 *et seq.*; ¶9544 *et seq.*
2. ¶O-2528; ¶9524.02
3. ¶O-2529; ¶9524.03
4. ¶O-2530; ¶9524.04

5. ¶O-2423.1, O-2480.3
6. ¶O-2508 *et seq.*; ¶9544.01
7. ¶O-2520 *et seq.*; ¶9544.01

... the selling or exchanging shareholder is a U.S. citizen or resident, or a domestic partnership, corporation, trust or estate; *and*

... the shareholder was a "U.S. shareholder" (¶4624) of the corporation at some time during the five-year period ending on the date of the sale, etc.; *and*

... the foreign corporation was a CFC (¶4624) at some time during the period the shareholder was a "U.S. shareholder," during that five-year period. (Code Sec. 1248(a))[8]

This dividend treatment may also apply to certain distributions or dispositions with respect to a *domestic* corporation, e.g., where the domestic corporation was formed or availed of principally for holding (directly or indirectly) stock of one or more foreign corporations. (Code Sec. 1248(e), Code Sec. 1248(f))[9]

This dividend treatment doesn't apply to Code Sec. 303 redemptions, amounts otherwise treated as dividends, ordinary income, short-term capital gains, or gains from sales made by non-U.S. persons. (Code Sec. 1248(g)) Nor does it apply to gifts or other transfers that don't result in recognized gain.[10]

There is a ceiling on the tax on the "dividend" income for an individual shareholder who held the stock for the long-term holding period (¶2667). (Code Sec. 1248(b))[11]

¶ 4627   Sales of patents, etc, to a foreign corporation.

A U.S. citizen or resident, or a domestic partnership, corporation, trust or estate, that sells (or exchanges) a patent, invention, formula or process, or similar property right to a foreign corporation in which the seller owns (directly, indirectly or constructively) stock with over 50% of the combined voting power of all classes of stock must treat *as ordinary income* any gain recognized on that sale (exchange). (Code Sec. 1249)[12]

¶ 4628   U.S. shareholders in a passive foreign investment company— Form 8621.

A U.S. shareholder in a PFIC (¶4629) may defer the U.S. tax (with respect to that investment) until he disposes of the PFIC stock or receives an "excess distribution." At that time, the shareholder must pay U.S. tax, plus interest, based on the value of the tax deferral (unless the PFIC is a qualified electing fund, see ¶4630). (Code Sec. 1291(a)(1), Code Sec. 1291(a)(2)) All gain recognized and all distributions are ordinary income, allocated ratably to each day the shareholder held the stock. (Code Sec. 1291(a)(1)(A), Code Sec. 1291(a)(1)(B))[13] Report the distributions and dispositions on Form 8621.[14]

An "excess distribution" is a current year distribution received by a shareholder on PFIC stock, to the extent the distribution exceeds its ratable portion of 125% of the average amount so received during the three preceding years. (Code Sec. 1291(b))[15]

Portions of distributions that aren't "excess distributions" are taxed under the normal rules for corporate distributions, see ¶1287 *et seq.* (Code Sec. 1291(a)(1)(B))[16]

A transfer of stock on which gain otherwise wouldn't be recognized under these rules is nevertheless treated as gain on the sale or exchange of that stock. (Code Sec. 1291(f))[17]

A PFIC shareholder may claim both direct and indirect ("deemed") foreign tax credits (¶2375 *et seq.*) with respect to these dispositions and distributions. (Code Sec. 1291(g))[18]

For a special mark-to-market election, see ¶4631.

---

8. ¶s O-2801, O-2807; ¶12,484 *et seq.*
9. ¶O-2805
10. ¶O-2803; ¶12,484.01
11. ¶O-2811; ¶12,484.02
12. ¶O-2900 *et seq.*; ¶12,494
13. ¶s O-2200 *et seq.*, O-2218, O-2228; ¶12,914.01
14. ¶O-2228
15. ¶O-2225; ¶12,914.01
16. ¶O-2218
17. ¶O-2239; ¶12,914.01
18. ¶O-2253 *et seq.*; ¶12,914.01

The CFC rules override the PFIC rules. Thus, amounts that could be included in gross income under the CFC rules (¶4623) are not included under the PFIC rules. (Code Sec. 951(c))[19]

Effective on Mar. 18, 2010, unless otherwise provided by IRS, each U.S. person who is a shareholder of a PFIC must file an annual information return containing information as IRS may require. IRS has announced that until further guidance is issued, PFIC shareholders that were not otherwise required to file Form 8621 annually before Mar. 18, 2010 will not be required to file an annual report for tax years beginning before Mar. 18, 2010. (Code Sec. 1298(f))[20]

¶ 4629   Passive foreign investment company (PFIC) defined.

A PFIC is any foreign corporation if: (1) at least 75% of its gross income for its tax year is passive, or (2) at least 50% of the assets it held during the year produce passive income. (Code Sec. 1297(a)) The 50% test is based on the adjusted basis of the corporation's assets if the corporation isn't publicly traded and is a controlled foreign corporation or elects to have the test based on the adjusted basis of the corporation's assets. The test is applied on the basis of the value of the corporation's assets if the corporation is publicly traded for the tax year or the test isn't required to be applied based on the adjusted basis of the corporation's assets. (Code Sec. 1297(e))[21] For treatment as a qualified electing fund, see ¶4630. For how the PFIC's shareholders are taxed, see ¶4628.

A passive foreign investment company (PFIC) isn't treated as a PFIC with respect to a U.S. shareholder who owns at least 10% of the stock, if the company is a controlled foreign corporation (CFC). (Code Sec. 1297(e))[22]

¶ 4630   Qualified electing fund (QEF) status avoids PFIC treatment—Form 8621.

A PFIC (¶4629) is treated as a qualified electing fund (QEF) with respect to a particular shareholder if he so elects (as explained below) and the PFIC complies with the requirements prescribed by regs for determining its ordinary earnings and net capital gain (under Reg § 1.1293-1(a)(2)(i)) and any other necessary information. (Code Sec. 1295)[23]

A U.S. investor in a PFIC makes the QEF election by attaching a completed Form 8621 to his timely filed income tax return (original or amended) for that year. (Code Sec. 1295(b)(2); Reg § 1.1295-1(e)) The investor must reflect in the Form 8621 the information provided by the PFIC in its annual information statement. (Reg § 1.1295-1(f)(1))

If the election is made, the shareholder's U.S. tax on disposition of the stock or receipt of an excess distribution won't be increased by any interest charge (that applies to PFICs, see ¶4628). (Code Sec. 1291(d)(1))[24] But the electing shareholder must currently include in income his share of the PFIC's earnings and profits (with appropriate basis adjustments for amounts not distributed and previously taxed distributions). The fund's ordinary income and net capital gain are passed through to the shareholder as ordinary income and long-term capital gain. (Code Sec. 1293) A 10% corporate shareholder is allowed a foreign tax credit on its share of the PFIC's earnings. (Code Sec. 1293(f))[25]

¶ 4631   Mark-to-market election for PFIC stock.

A shareholder of a passive foreign investment company (PFIC) may make a mark-to-market election for marketable PFIC stock and avoid the non-QEF rules described at ¶4628.

---

19. ¶O-2605; ¶9514.03
20. ¶O-2201.1; ¶12,984
21. ¶O-2202 *et seq.*; ¶12,974
22. ¶O-2219.1

23. ¶O-2268; ¶12,954
24. ¶O-2262 *et seq.*; ¶12,954
25. ¶O-2262; ¶12,934

(Code Sec. 1296, Code Sec. 1291(d)) Regs explain when stock is marketable PFIC stock. (Reg § 1.1296-2)

The election is made by filing Form 8621 with an annual original or amended return filed before the return due date (including extensions). Special rules apply for how the election is made by a controlled foreign corporation on behalf of its shareholders. (Reg § 1.1296-1(h)(1))[26] The election is effective for indirect shareholders who hold PFIC shares through a partnership, trust or estate and is effective only for the shareholder making the election, for all stock of the corporation for which the election is made. (Reg § 1.1296-1(b))[27]

If the election is made, the shareholder includes in income each year an amount equal to the excess, if any, of the fair market value of the PFIC stock as of the close of the tax year over the shareholder's adjusted basis in the stock. The shareholder is allowed a deduction for the lesser of the excess, if any, of the adjusted basis of the PFIC stock over its fair market value as of the close of the tax year, or the "unreversed inclusions" with respect to the PFIC stock—the excess, if any, of the mark-to-market gains for the stock included by the shareholder for earlier tax years, including any amount which would have been included for any earlier tax year but for the Code Sec. 1291 interest on tax deferral rules, over the mark-to-market losses for the stock that were allowed as deductions for earlier tax years. (Code Sec. 1296)[28]

Amounts included in income or deducted under the mark-to-market election, as well as gain or loss on the actual sale or other disposition of the PFIC stock, are treated as ordinary income or loss. (Code Sec. 1296(c)(1))[29]

¶ 4632   Recognition of gain on transfers to certain foreign entities.

Except as provided in regs, gain is recognized upon a transfer of appreciated property by a U.S. person to a foreign estate or trust to the extent its fair market value exceeds its basis in the hands of the transferor. (Code Sec. 684) Regs except transfers to foreign grantor trusts, exempt charitable trusts, certain transfers by reason of death of the U.S. transferor, transfers to unrelated foreign trusts for fair market value, transfers of stock by a domestic corporation to a foreign trust if the domestic corporation doesn't recognize gain on the transfer under Code Sec. 1032. (Reg § 1.684-3) In addition, gain is not recognized upon a distribution to a trust on an interest held by the trust in a corporation, partnership, investment trust, liquidating trust, or environmental remediation trust. (Reg § 1.684-3(f))

If a U.S. person transfers property to a domestic trust and for any reason the domestic trust becomes a foreign trust and neither is treated as owned by any person under the grantor trust rules, the domestic trust is deemed to have transferred all of its assets to a foreign trust. The domestic trust has to immediately recognize gain unless one of the above exceptions applies at that time. (Reg § 1.684-4)

For transfers after 2009, the gain recognition rule applies to transfers at death to a nonresident alien. (Code Sec. 684(a))[30]

⊘*caution:* For EGTRRA sunset rules, see ¶1114.

⊘*caution:* Check http://ria.thomsonreuters.com/federaltaxhandbook to see whether the pre-2010 rules have been extended.

For gain recognition on transfers to a foreign corporation, see ¶3588. For gain recognition on transfers to foreign partnerships, see ¶3710.

---

26. ¶O-2217.7; ¶12,964
27. ¶O-2217.7; ¶12,964
28. ¶O-2217.1; ¶12,964
29. ¶O-2217.1; ¶12,964
30. ¶C-1020; ¶6844

¶ 4633   Tax sanctions for international boycott activities— Form 5713.

Participation in or cooperation with an international boycott can result in: (1) reduction of the allowable foreign tax credit, ¶2375 *et seq.*, (Code Sec. 908), (2) reduced deferral under the DISC rules, ¶4622, (Code Sec. 995(b)(1)(F)), and (3) a CFC's undistributed earnings being currently taxed to its U.S. shareholders, ¶4625, (Code Sec. 952(a)(3)) Taxpayers must report (on Form 5713) boycott operations and requests to participate or cooperate. (Code Sec. 999)[31]

¶ 4634   Resident Aliens Taxed as U.S. Persons. ▬▬▬▬▬▬▬▬▬▬

A resident alien individual generally is subject to U.S. tax in the same manner as a U.S. citizen.

¶ 4635   Resident aliens as U.S. persons.

Resident aliens are generally taxed just like U.S. citizens on their U.S. and foreign source income. (Reg § 1.871-1(a))[32] An alien individual is treated as a U.S. resident for any calendar year in which he (1) meets a lawful permanent residence ("green card") test, (2) meets a "substantial presence" test (¶4636), or (3) makes the "first year election" (¶4637). (Code Sec. 7701(b)(1)(A))[33] For nonresident aliens, see ¶4638 *et seq.*

¶ 4636   Substantial presence test—Form 8843, Form 8840.

Subject to certain exceptions, an individual meets the substantial presence test (i.e., is a U.S. resident), for any calendar (current) year if:

(1) he is present in the U.S. on at least 31 days during the year, *and*

(2) the sum of the number of days he was present in the U.S. during the current year and the two preceding calendar years, when multiplied by the applicable multiplier (1 for the current year, ⅓ for the first preceding year, and ⅙ for the second preceding year), is at least 183. (Code Sec. 7701(b)(3)(A))[34]

An individual isn't present in the U.S. on any day on which he's exempt (e.g., foreign official, teacher) or his medical condition prevents him from leaving the U.S. (Code Sec. 7701(b)(3)(D), Code Sec. 7701(b)(5)) File Form 8843 to claim the exemption. (Reg § 301.7701(b)-8(b)(2)(i))[35]

An individual who otherwise meets the substantial presence test can avoid being treated as a U.S. resident that year if he: (1) is present in the U.S. on fewer than 183 days during the year, and (2) files a "closer connection statement" on Form 8840 which establishes that for the year, he has a tax home (¶1544) in a foreign country to which he has a closer connection than to the U.S. (Code Sec. 7701(b)(3)(B); Reg § 301.7701(b)-8(b)(1)(i)) If the individual is required to file Form 1040 or 1040NR, the statement must be attached to the return for the relevant tax year. An individual who doesn't have to file a return should send the form to the IRS center in Philadelphia, PA by the due date (including extensions) for filing an income tax return for the calendar year for which the statement applies. (Reg § 301.7701(b)-8(c))[36]

¶ 4637   "First year" election to be taxed as a U.S. resident.

A qualifying alien who arrives in the U.S. too late in a calendar year to meet the substantial presence test (¶4636) may elect (on a statement attached to the return) to be taxed as a U.S. resident for part of that first (election) year if he meets the substantial presence test in

---

31. ¶O-3500 *et seq.*; ¶9994.01
32. ¶O-1008; ¶8714.01; TD ¶190,502
33. ¶O-1051; ¶8714; TD ¶190,509
34. ¶O-1057; ¶8714; TD ¶190,510
35. ¶s O-1062, O-1080; ¶8714; TD ¶190,515 *et seq.*
36. ¶s O-1063, O-1081; ¶8714; TD ¶190,516

the next calendar year. (Code Sec. 7701(b)(4); Reg § 301.7701(b)-4(c)(3))[37] For joint return election where one spouse is a nonresident alien, see ¶4705.

¶ 4638 Taxation of Nonresident Aliens and Foreign Corporations. ▬▬▬▬▬

A nonresident alien or foreign corporation is taxed at a 30% (or lower treaty) rate on investment income from U.S. sources and, if engaged in a U.S. trade or business, at regular U.S. rates on income effectively connected with that business. Otherwise the nonresident alien or foreign corporation is exempt from U.S. tax.[38]

A foreign taxpayer also may be subject to the accumulated earnings tax (¶3316 *et seq.*), the personal holding company tax (¶3323 *et seq.*), (Reg § 1.881-1(e))[39] a branch profits tax (¶4644), a transportation tax (¶4646), and the alternative minimum tax (¶3200 *et seq.*).

For allowance of deductions and credits, see ¶4647.

¶ 4639 Nonresident alien individuals and foreign corporations.

A *nonresident alien individual* is an individual who isn't a U.S. citizen or resident. (Code Sec. 7701(b)(1)(B)) Aliens who are bona fide residents of Puerto Rico, Guam, American Samoa or the Northern Mariana Islands for the entire tax year are generally taxed like resident aliens (Code Sec. 876)[40] (except for income from these possessions, see ¶4618).

A *foreign corporation* is one that's organized outside the U.S. or under any law other than that of the U.S., a state or the District of Columbia. (Code Sec. 7701(a)(3), Code Sec. 7701(a)(4), Code Sec. 7701(a)(9))[41]

A corporation created or organized in or under the law of American Samoa or the Virgin Islands isn't treated as foreign for any tax year if: (1) at all times that year less than 25% (by value) of its stock is owned (directly or indirectly) by foreign persons; (2) at least 65% of its gross income for the last three tax years (or shorter period of existence) is shown to IRS's satisfaction to be effectively connected with a trade or business in either the possession or the U.S.; *and* (3) no substantial part of its income is used (directly or indirectly) to satisfy obligations to persons who are not bona fide residents of that possession or the U.S. (Code Sec. 881(b)(1); Reg § 1.881-5(c))

A corporation formed in Guam or the Commonwealth of the Northern Mariana Islands (CNMI) is treated as foreign if: (a) at all times during the tax year, less than 25% in value of its stock is owned (directly or indirectly) by foreign persons and (b) at least 20% of its gross income is shown to IRS's satisfaction upon examination to have been derived from sources within the possession for the three-year period ending with the close of the preceding tax year of the corporation (or for such part of the period it was in existence). (Reg § 1.881-5(d))[42]

¶ 4640 Tax on income "effectively connected" with a U.S. business.

A foreign corporation or nonresident alien engaged in a U.S. business (¶4641), at any time in the tax year is taxed at regular U.S. rates on taxable income "effectively connected" with that business—i.e., the gross income effectively connected with the U.S. business, less allowable deductions (¶4647). (Code Sec. 871(b), Code Sec. 882(a))[43] For tax on income that is not effectively connected with a U.S. trade or business, see ¶4642.

All *U.S.-source* income, gain, or loss (other than periodical income and capital gains and losses) derived by a nonresident alien or foreign corporation engaged in a U.S. business any time in the tax year is treated as "effectively connected." (Code Sec. 864(c)(3))[44]

37. ¶O-1051, ¶O-1072 *et seq.*; ¶8714; TD ¶190,529
38. ¶s O-10101, O-10301; ¶s 8714.01, 8814 *et seq.*
39. ¶O-10300 *et seq.*; ¶8824; TD ¶641,002
40. ¶s O-1010, O-1086; ¶s 8714, 8764, 9314 *et seq.*; TD ¶630,110
41. ¶O-10360; ¶8814.01; TD ¶632,005
42. ¶O-10361; ¶s 8814.01, 8814.02; TD ¶632,005
43. ¶s O-10501, O-10601, O-10602; ¶8644 *et seq.*; TD ¶641,001
44. ¶O-10604; ¶8644 *et seq.*; TD ¶642,006

Foreign-source income treated as "effectively connected" is limited to the items below to the extent the item is attributable to an office or other fixed place of business in the U.S.:

. . . Rents, royalties and gains on intangible personal property derived from an active licensing business.

. . . Dividends, interest or gain from stock or obligations derived from an active banking, financing or trading business.

. . . Certain inventory sales attributable to a U.S. sales office.

. . . Items that are economically similar to the above items on this list. (Code Sec. 864(c)(4))[45]

¶ 4641   What is "engaging in a U.S. business"?

A nonresident alien who performs personal services in the U.S. in the tax year engages in business in the U.S. that year (so he's taxed on the compensation income) *unless* his compensation for those services is $3,000 or less, he's in the U.S. for 90 days or less, *and* he works for a foreign person. (Code Sec. 864(b))[46] Special rules apply to foreign students, trainees, etc. (Code Sec. 871(c), Code Sec. 872(b)(3))[47]

An alien isn't subject to U.S. tax on compensation received for services as an employee of a foreign government or international organization, *except* where the services are primarily in connection with the foreign government's commercial activities, or where the alien is an employee of a "controlled commercial entity." (Code Sec. 893)[48]

If a partnership, estate or trust is engaged in a U.S. business, the entity's foreign partners or beneficiaries are considered so engaged. (Code Sec. 875)[49]

¶ 4642   U.S.-source income not "effectively connected" with U.S. business—30% tax.

Nonresident aliens and foreign corporations are taxed at a flat 30% (or lower treaty rate) on this income, if U.S.-source and not "effectively connected" with a U.S. business:

. . . Interest (other than original issue discount (OID) and certain portfolio and bank account interest), dividends, rents, salaries, wages, premiums, annuities, compensations, remunerations, emoluments and other fixed or determinable annual or periodical gains, profits and income. (Code Sec. 871(a)(1)(A), Code Sec. 881(a)(1))

. . . Payments on bonds with OID, and amounts received on their disposition, that are ordinary income under the OID rules (¶1315 *et seq.*). (Code Sec. 871(a)(1)(C), Code Sec. 881(a)(3))

. . . Amounts includible in income of residual REMIC interest holders. (Code Sec. 860G(b)(1)) Special rules apply for this type of income, including rules regarding allocations by partnerships that hold residual REMIC interests. (Reg § 1.860G-3)

. . . 85% of Social Security benefits paid to nonresident aliens. (Code Sec. 871(a)(3))

. . . Gains on sale or exchange of patents, copyrights and the like, where payments are contingent on productivity, etc. (Code Sec. 871(a)(1)(D), Code Sec. 881(a)(4))

. . . Certain types of gambling winnings (but not winnings from blackjack, baccarat, craps, roulette or big six wheel, except to the extent provided in regs). (Code Sec. 871(j))

. . . Gains from the disposal, with a retained economic interest, of timber, coal or iron ore. (Code Sec. 871(a)(1)(B))[50]

---

45. ¶O-10622; ¶8644.02; TD ¶642,011
46. ¶O-10502; ¶8644.01; TD ¶630,114
47. ¶O-10503; ¶s 8714.03, 8724.03; TD ¶630,116

48. ¶O-11829; ¶8934; TD ¶647,005
49. ¶s O-10504, O-10505; ¶8754; TD ¶641,510
50. ¶O-10201 *et seq.*; ¶s 8714.02, 8814.02; TD ¶632,001 *et seq.*

The 30% tax does not apply to dividends paid by a foreign corporation with effectively connected income. (Code Sec. 871(i)(2)(D)) Also exempt are interest related RIC dividends that would not be subject to withholding and short-term capital gains. (Code Sec. 871(k), Code Sec. 881(e))

No deductions are allowed against this income. The 30% tax is on the *gross* amount. (Code Sec. 873, Code Sec. 882(c))[1] (But if a nonresident alien has a U.S. spouse, the couple can, effectively, elect to be taxed at regular rates, see ¶4705.)

Non-"effectively connected" long- and short-term capital gains (except as listed above) aren't taxed to foreign corporations (Code Sec. 881), and are taxed to nonresident aliens only if they are present in the U.S. for at least 183 days in the tax year. (Code Sec. 871(a)(2))[2]

¶ 4643 Election for investment income from U.S. real property.

A nonresident alien or foreign corporation may elect to treat certain income from U.S. real property held for investment as effectively connected with the conduct of a U.S. business. (Code Sec. 897(a), Code Sec. 871(d), Code Sec. 882(d)) The foreign taxpayer is thus taxed at regular U.S. rates (not 30%) on net rather than gross income, and can take depreciation deductions, etc., see ¶4640.[3] Elect on a statement attached to the income tax return for the election year. (Reg § 1.871-10(d)(1)(ii))[4]

¶ 4644 Branch profits tax on foreign corporations— Form 1120F.

A foreign corporation engaged in a U.S. trade or business through a branch office in the tax year is liable for a branch profits tax (and regular income tax) equal to 30% of the year's "dividend equivalent amount" (pay on Form 1120F). (Code Sec. 884(a); Reg § 1.884-1(a)) The "dividend equivalent amount" is the corporation's effectively connected earnings and profits (E&P), *reduced* (not below zero) by any increase for the year in its U.S. net equity (i.e., amounts reinvested in the U.S. business), and *increased* (within limits) by any decrease for the year in its U.S. net equity (i.e., amounts remitted to the foreign head office). (Code Sec. 884(b); Reg § 1.884-1(b))[5]

If a foreign corporation is subject to the branch profits tax for any tax year (whether any branch profits tax is actually due), *income* tax withholding (see ¶4662 *et seq.*), isn't required on any dividends it pays out of its E&P for that year. (Code Sec. 884(e)(3))[6]

observation: The branch profits tax is the counterpart of the withholding tax, at the shareholder level, on dividends paid by a U.S. sub to its foreign parent, ¶4642.

The branch profits tax won't be imposed on a foreign corporation for the year it completely terminates its U.S. trade or business, except where there is a corporate liquidation or reorganization, or a Code Sec. 351 incorporation. The corporation must waive the statute of limitations for the year (on Form 8848 attached to the income tax return). (Reg § 1.884-2T, Reg § 1.884-2T(a)(2)(i))[7]

The branch profits tax doesn't apply if it's inconsistent with existing U.S. income tax treaties, if the foreign corporation is a qualified resident of the treaty country, except for treaty shopping situations. (Code Sec. 884(e)(1); Reg § 1.884-1(g))[8]

1. ¶O-10641, O-10648; ¶s 8734, 8814.02; TD ¶641,004
2. ¶O-10231; ¶s 8714.02, 8814.02; TD ¶630,132
3. ¶O-10615 *et seq.*; ¶8714.04; TD ¶642,016
4. ¶O-10619; TD ¶642,018
5. ¶O-11300 *et seq.*; ¶8844
6. ¶s O-11982, O-11454; ¶8844
7. ¶O-11356 *et seq.*; ¶8844
8. ¶O-11390 *et seq.*; ¶8844

¶ 4645   Branch-level interest tax.

If a foreign corporation is engaged in a U.S. trade or business (or has gross income treated as "effectively connected"), interest (including original issue discount) paid by the corporation's U.S. trade or business (i.e., its U.S. branch) is treated as if it were paid by a U.S. corporation (i.e., the U.S. branch is treated as a sub)—i.e., it's subject to the 30% tax discussed at ¶4642. (Code Sec. 884(f)(1)(A); Reg § 1.884-4(a)(1), Reg § 1.884-4(b)(1)) To the extent the amount of interest allowable as a deduction in computing the foreign corporation's taxable "effectively connected" income exceeds the amount of interest paid by its U.S. branch, the foreign corporation is liable for the withholding tax discussed at ¶4663 (pay on Form 1120F) on "any interest" which is or is treated as "effectively connected" with a U. S. trade or business. (Code Sec. 884(f)); Reg § 1.884-4(a)(2)) This treatment doesn't apply where the payor and recipient meet certain residency standards. (Code Sec. 884(f)(3))[9]

¶ 4646   4% tax on transportation income.

A 4% tax is imposed on the U.S.-source gross transportation income of foreign corporations and nonresident aliens. (Code Sec. 887(a)) Income subject to this 4% gross-basis tax isn't subject to the 30% tax (¶4642) or the regular U.S. tax on "effectively connected" income (¶4640). (Code Sec. 887(c))[10]

¶ 4647   Deductions and credits of foreign corporations and nonresident aliens.

Foreign corporations and nonresident aliens generally may take deductions only to the extent related (under regs) to "effectively connected" income (¶4640). (Code Sec. 873(a), Code Sec. 882(c)(1)(A); Reg § 1.882-5) Regs provide rules for how interest deductions are allocated to effectively connected income. (Reg § 1.882-5)[11] But these deductions are allowed whether or not related to that income: for charitable contributions; and for nonresident aliens, for nonbusiness casualty and theft losses, and personal exemptions (limited). (Code Sec. 873(b), Code Sec. 882(c)(1)(B))[12]

Credits also generally are allowable only if attributable to "effectively connected" income, except for certain credits (e.g., for taxes withheld at source, earned income credit). (Code Sec. 874(b), Code Sec. 882(c)(2); Reg § 1.874-1)[13]

Generally, a return (see ¶4656 *et seq.*) must be filed in order to get the benefit of an otherwise allowable deduction or credit. (Code Sec. 874(a), Code Sec. 882(c)(2); Reg § 1.882-4(a)(2))[14] The regs require the return be timely filed. However, IRS may waive the deadlines in certain cases. (Reg § 1.874-1(b)(2), Reg § 1.882-4(a)(3)(ii))[15]

¶ 4648   Is income from U.S. or foreign sources?

Specific rules are used to determine the source of the following types of income:

Compensation—where the services were performed. (Code Sec. 861(a)(3), Code Sec. 862(a)(3); Reg § 1.861-4)[16]

Interest—where the debtor is located. Before 2011, an exception applied under which interest paid by a resident alien individual or a domestic corporation was not U.S. source income if at least 80% of its income was income from an active foreign business. The exception was repealed, subject to separate transition rules (1) for certain pre-Aug. 10, 2010 obligations and (2) for a portion of the interest paid by existing 80/20 companies that satisfied the pre-2011

9. ¶O-11376 *et seq.*; ¶8844
10. ¶O-11501; ¶8634.03; TD ¶644,501
11. ¶O-10641, ¶O-10648, ¶O-10649; ¶s 8734, 8824; TD ¶641,004
12. ¶O-10243, O-10648; ¶s 8734, 8824; TD ¶641,004

13. ¶s O-10643, O-10675; ¶8824; TD ¶641,006
14. ¶s O-10644, O-10676; TD ¶641,007
15. ¶O-10645.1, O-10676.1
16. ¶O-10931.1 *et seq.*; ¶8614.15 *et seq.*; TD ¶633,004

requirements. (Code Sec. 861(a)(1), Code Sec. 862(a)(1)), Code Sec. 862(a)(2)' Code Sec. 872(i)(2), Code Sec. 872(l)[17]

Dividends—where the corporation is incorporated. But dividends from a foreign corporation are U.S.-source unless less than 25% of all its income for the last three years is effectively connected with a U.S. business. Before 2011, an exception applied under which dividends paid by a domestic corporation were not subject to withholding if at least 80% of its income was income from an active foreign business. The exception was repealed, subject to a transition rule for a portion of the dividends paid by existing 80/20 companies that satisfied the pre-2011 requirements. (Code Sec. 861(a)(2), Code Sec. 862(a)(2))[18] For payments made after Sept. 13, 2010, dividend equivalents, such as substitute payments under a securities lending agreement and payments under notional principal contracts are treated as dividends from U.S. sources. (Code Sec. 871(m)(1)) (Code Sec. 871(m)(2))[19]

Rents and royalties—where the property is used. (Code Sec. 861(a)(4), Code Sec. 862(a)(4))[20]

Sales of personal property—where the seller resides. (Code Sec. 865(a)) Special rules apply to the sale of depreciable and intangible property (Code Sec. 865(c), Code Sec. 865(d)), and to inventory. (Code Sec. 865(b)) Income from the sale of any personal property (other than inventory sold for use or disposition outside the U.S.) that's attributable to a nonresident's U.S. office is U.S.-source income. Sales of certain property by a U.S. resident through a foreign office is foreign-source if at least a 10% foreign tax is paid on it. (Code Sec. 865(g))[21]

Sales of real property or natural resources—location of the property or resource. (Code Sec. 861(a)(5), Code Sec. 862(a)(8))[22]

Transportation income from transportation that either begins or ends in the U.S. (but not both) is half foreign- and half U.S.-source. (Code Sec. 863(c)(2)(A))[23]

International communications income of a U.S. person is half foreign- and half U.S.-source. (Code Sec. 863(e)(1)(A)) A foreign person's international communications income is foreign-source, except where it is attributable to an office or fixed place of business in the U.S. (Code Sec. 863(e)(1)(B))[24]

Space and ocean activity income of a U.S. person is U.S.-source, while that of a foreign person is foreign-source. (Code Sec. 863(d)(1))[25]

Insurance income from insuring U.S. risks is U.S.-source. (Code Sec. 861(a)(7))[26]

¶ 4649 Allocating deductions between U.S. or foreign source income.

Under IRS regs deductions other than interest are allocated or apportioned based on the factual relationship of deductions to gross income. (Reg § 1.861-8)[27] Interest is attributed on the basis of the taxpayer's assets or under another permitted method. (Reg § 1.861-9T)[28]

¶ 4650 Dispositions of U.S. real property—FIRPTA rules.

A gain or loss of a nonresident alien or foreign corporation from the disposition of a U.S. real property interest (USRPI) is treated as effectively connected with a U.S. trade or business. (Code Sec. 897(a)(1))[29] For reporting, see ¶4660, and withholding, see ¶4671.

A USRPI includes: (1) an interest in real property located in the U.S. or the Virgin Islands, and (2) any interest (other than solely as a creditor) in any U.S. corporation unless it's shown

17. ¶O-10906 *et seq.*; ¶8614.01; TD ¶633,002
18. ¶s O-10228, O-10926 *et seq.*; ¶8614.10 *et seq.*; TD ¶633,003 *et seq.*
19. ¶O-10930B *et seq.*; ¶8714.02 *et seq.*
20. ¶O-10936; ¶8614.22; TD ¶633,005
21. ¶O-10948 *et seq.*; ¶8654 *et seq.*; TD ¶633,011
22. ¶O-10945; ¶s 8614.24, 8974; TD ¶633,023
23. ¶O-10941; ¶8634.03; TD ¶633,020
24. ¶O-10984; ¶8634.04
25. ¶O-10976; ¶8634.04
26. ¶O-10985; ¶8614.27
27. ¶O-11000 *et seq.*; ¶8614.29
28. ¶O-11000 *et seq.*; ¶8614.29
29. ¶O-10700 *et seq.*; ¶8974; TD ¶643,001

not to have been a U.S. real property holding corporation (USRPHC) during the five-year period ending on the date of disposition. (Code Sec. 897(c)(1)(A))[30]

Foreign taxpayers that hold USRPIs indirectly (e.g., as shareholders, partners or beneficiaries of a corporation, partnership, estate or trust that owns the property) are also, when they dispose of their interest in the entity, subject to U.S. tax on any gain attributable to the entity's USRPIs. (Code Sec. 897(g); Reg § 1.897-7T)[31]

Special rules apply to foreign taxpayers who hold interests in RICs and REITs that would otherwise be USRPIs. The special rules do not apply to RICs after Dec. 31, 2009 (although look-through and withholding rules apply after this period). (Code Sec. 897(h))[32]

⚠️*caution:* Check http://ria.thomsonreuters.com/federaltaxhandbook to see whether the pre-2010 RIC rules have been extended.

Gain is recognized even if the disposition is a transfer to paid-in surplus or a capital contribution to a foreign corporation. (Code Sec. 897(j))[33] For exception, see ¶4651.

¶ 4651   Election by foreign corporation to be treated as a U.S. corporation.

A foreign corporation protected by treaty (with respect to USRPIs) may elect to be treated as a U.S. corporation for purposes of the FIRPTA rules (¶4650), including reporting and withholding (¶4671) (Code Sec. 897(i))[34] if the corporation: is a U.S. real property holding corporation (¶4650) (Reg § 1.897-8T(b)), holds the USRPI at the time of the election, and submits an election statement in proper form. (Reg § 1.897-3(b))[35]

¶ 4652   Tax treaties—Form 8833.

Tax treaties typically exempt or reduce U.S. tax on certain business, compensation and investment income. (Code Sec. 894(a))[36] IRS Publication 515 lists the treaty countries and the benefits available for the residents of each country.[37] A taxpayer who takes a return position that a treaty overrules or otherwise modifies the Code and reduces any tax incurred at any time, must disclose that return position on Form 8833 attached to the return. Disclosure is waived for certain treaty-based return positions. (Code Sec. 6114(a); Reg § 301.6114-1)[38]

¶ 4653   Giving up U.S. citizenship or terminating long-term residency before June 17, 2008— Form 8854.

A nonresident alien individual described below, who within the 10-year period immediately preceding the close of the tax year lost U.S. citizenship, is subject to alternative expatriate income tax graduated rates for the year (if this alternative tax, after reducing it for the payment of foreign taxes, is greater than the ordinary tax on nonresident aliens to which he would be subject). (Code Sec. 877(a)(1)) The alternative expatriate income tax applies if:

(1) the individual's average annual net income tax for the period of five tax years ending before the date of the loss of U.S. citizenship is greater than an inflation adjusted amount that is $145,000 for 2010 ($147,000 for 2011);

(2) the individual's net worth as of the date in (1) is $2,000,000 or more; or

(3) the individual: (i) fails to certify under penalty of perjury that he has met the requirements of the Code for the five preceding tax years, or (ii) fails to submit evidence of his compliance as IRS may require. (Code Sec. 877(a)(2)) The certification is made on Form

30. ¶O-10735 *et seq.*; ¶8794; TD ¶643,016
31. ¶O-10733 *et seq.*; ¶8974; TD ¶643,014
32. ¶O-10734, O-10753; ¶8974; TD ¶643,015, 643,016
33. ¶O-10702; ¶8974; TD ¶643,006
34. ¶O-10810 *et seq.*; ¶8974.01; TD ¶643,029
35. ¶O-10812; ¶8974.01; TD ¶643,029
36. ¶O-15000 *et seq.*; ¶8944; TD ¶630,107
37. ¶O-12029 *et seq.*; ¶8944; TD ¶192,010
38. ¶O-15010 *et seq.*; ¶61,144; TD ¶192,006

8854.

An expatriate subject to the alternative tax must provide an annual statement on Form 8854.[39]

The average income tax and net worth tests don't apply to certain individuals. (Code Sec. 877(c)) Individuals who are subject to the alternative tax must file information statements during the 10-year period. (Code Sec. 6039G)

In addition, individuals must provide notice of their expatriation on and file an information statement (using Form 8854) in order to expatriate. (Code Sec. 7701(n)) After expatriation, individuals may be taxed as U.S. citizens or residents if they satisfy a substantial presence test. (Code Sec. 877(g)(1))[40]

¶ 4654 Giving up U.S. citizenship or terminating long-term residency after June 16, 2008

Under a mark-to-market deemed sale rule, property of certain U.S. citizens who relinquish their U.S. citizenship and certain long-term U.S. residents who terminate their U.S. residency after June 16, 2008 is treated as sold on the day before the expatriation date for its fair market value.

The "mark-to-market" tax is imposed on the net unrealized gain in the property as if the property had been sold for its fair market value on the day before the expatriation or residency termination. Any gain is taken into account at that time without regard to other Code provisions, and any loss generally is taken into account to the extent otherwise provided in the Code, except that the wash sale rules of Code Sec. 1091 don't apply. Net gain on the deemed sale is recognized to the extent it exceeds an inflation adjusted amount that is $627,000 in 2010 ($636,000 in 2011). (Code Sec. 877A(a)(2), Code Sec. 877A(a)(3)) Subsequent gains or losses that are realized are to be adjusted for the gains and losses taken into account under the deemed sale rules, without regard to the exemption. (Code Sec. 877A(a)(2))

While the mark-to-market tax applies to most types of property interests held on the date of citizenship relinquishment or residency termination, deferred compensation items, interests in nongrantor trusts, and specified tax deferred accounts are excepted from the tax but are subject to special rules. (Code Sec. 877A(c))

Covered expatriates. The tax applies to U.S. citizens who relinquish citizenship and long-term residents who terminate U.S. residency, if they meet the average annual net income tax test, net worth test, or failure to certify test described at ¶4653. (Code Sec. 877A(g)(1)(A)) However, an exception applies under the average annual net income tax or net worth tests for (1) an individual who was born as a dual citizen of the U.S. and another country; on the expatriation date continues to be a citizen of, and is taxed as a resident of, the other country; and has been a U.S. resident (under the substantial presence test), for not more than 10 tax years during the 15 tax-year period ending with the tax year in which the expatriation date occurs and (2) an individual who gives up his U.S. citizenship before becoming 18 ½ years old; and was a U.S. resident (under the substantial presence test) for not more than 10 tax years before the relinquishment date. (Code Sec. 877A(g)(1)(B))

Election to defer tax on expatriation. An individual may irrevocably elect, on a property-by-property basis, to defer payment of the mark-to-market tax imposed on the deemed sale of property. Interest is charged for the period the tax is deferred. The deferred tax generally is due when the return is due for the tax year in which the property is disposed of. (Code Sec. 877A(b)(1))

---

39. ¶O-11701 *et seq.*; ¶8774; TD ¶644,701 *et seq.*   40. ¶O-11701.2 *et seq.*; ¶8774; TD ¶644,701.2 *et seq.*

¶ 4655　Corporate and partnership expatriations (inversions)

Special rules apply where a domestic corporation or partnership is succeeded by a foreign corporation or partnership under a plan. These rules apply where (in the case of a corporation) substantially all of the domestic corporation's assets are transferred to a foreign entity and the former owners receive the following percentage interests in the transfer:

. . . Where the former owners own 80% or more of the interests, the successor entity is treated as a domestic entity

. . . Where the former owners own 60% or more of the interests, the taxable income of the expatriated entity cannot be less than the gain on the expatriation transaction. Similar rules apply to certain post-expatriation transactions with certain related entities. (Code Sec. 7874(a), Code Sec. 7874(b), Code Sec. 7874(e); Reg § 1.7874-1, Reg § 1.7874-2T) Thus these gains cannot be offset by losses or credits. (Code Sec. 7874(d))

An exception applies for where the entity (including certain related parties) has substantial activities in the country in which the successor entity is organized. (Code Sec. 7874(a))[41]

¶ 4656　Returns Relating to Foreign Taxpayers. ▬▬▬▬▬▬▬▬

U.S. income tax returns must be filed by nonresident alien individuals and foreign corporations engaged in a U.S. business. Information returns are required for certain foreign transactions.

¶ 4657　Return of nonresident alien individual—Forms 1040NR and 1040NR-EZ.

A nonresident alien individual must file a U.S. tax return (Form 1040NR, or, for certain nonresident aliens with no dependents, Form 1040NR-EZ) for any tax year he was engaged in business in the U.S. (which includes most employees, see ¶4641), whether his income met the minimum (exemption amount); his tax was fully paid by withholding; or he claims tax treaty benefits. (Reg § 1.6012-1(b))[42] He must file to claim any deductions or to get a refund. (Reg § 1.6012-1(b)(2)(i))[43]

Form 1040NR and Form 1040NR-EZ are due by the 15th day of the sixth month (i.e., June 15), or fourth month (April 15, if the alien had wages subject to wage withholding) after the end of the year. (Reg § 1.6072-1(c))[44]

¶ 4658　Departing alien—"sailing permits" (Form 1040C, Form 2063).

An alien (resident or nonresident) leaving the U.S. generally must get a "certificate of [tax] compliance" ("sailing permit"), except for most tourists, students and foreign government personnel. (Code Sec. 6851(d)(1); Reg § 1.6851-2(a)(2)) The alien uses Form 1040C if he has income subject to U.S. tax (and Form 1040NR if required, see ¶4657), and Form 2063 if he has no taxable income. (Reg § 1.6851-2(b))[45]

¶ 4659　Return of foreign corporation—Form 1120F.

A foreign corporation must file a U.S. income tax return (Form 1120F) if it was engaged in business in the U.S., or its tax was not fully satisfied by withholding, or it claims tax treaty benefits (a statement claiming the benefits must be attached to the return) or a refund. Otherwise, no return is required. (Reg § 1.6012-2(g))[46]

A foreign corporation must file the return on or before the 15th day of the third month

---

41. ¶F-5700 *et seq.*; ¶78,744; TD ¶236,900 *et seq.*
42. ¶s S-1750, S-1752, S-1755; ¶60,124.02; TD ¶190,533
43. ¶S-1756; TD ¶630,104

44. ¶S-4703; ¶60,724; TD ¶630,104
45. ¶S-1760 *et seq.*; ¶68,514.04; TD ¶630,104
46. ¶S-1910; ¶s 8814, 60,124.03; TD ¶609,808

(sixth month if it has no U.S. office or place of business) following the close of the tax year. (Code Sec. 6072(b), Code Sec. 6072(c))[47] A foreign corporation that maintains an office in the U.S. may apply for both the automatic and the blanket filing extensions discussed at ¶4728.[48]

¶ 4660 Information returns—Form 5471; Form 5472; Form 926; Form 8865

A U.S. person who controls a foreign corporation for at least 30 consecutive days in his tax year must furnish IRS with certain information concerning the foreign corporation (on Form 5471). (Code Sec. 6038; Reg § 1.6038-2(a)) Similar reporting rules apply to U.S. partners that control foreign partnerships. (Code Sec. 6038; Reg § 1.6038-3)[49] "Control" means more than 50% ownership (by total vote or total value) of the corporation's stock. (Reg § 1.6038-2(b))[50] A person controls a partnership if the person owns, directly or indirectly, more than a 50% interest in the partnership. (Code Sec. 6038(e)(3)(A); Reg § 1.6038-3(b)) Use Form 8865 for partnership reporting.[1]

The organization or reorganization of, or acquisition of stock in, a foreign corporation must be reported (on Form 5471) by certain U.S. persons. (Code Sec. 6046; Reg § 1.6046-1)[2]

If a U.S. corporation, or a foreign corporation engaged in a U.S. trade or business, is controlled by a foreign person at any time in the tax year, it must maintain records and furnish IRS with certain information (on Form 5472) concerning specified transactions with related parties in that year. A separate form is required with respect to each related party. (Code Sec. 6038A(a), Code Sec. 6038C; Reg § 1.6038A-1, Reg § 1.6038A-2, Reg § 1.6038A-3)[3] To be in "control," the foreign person must own: (1) stock with at least 25% of the total combined voting power of all classes of voting stock, or (2) at least 25% of the total value of shares of all classes of stock. (Code Sec. 6038A(c)(1))[4]

Each U.S. person transferring property to a foreign corporation or partnership in specified tax-free exchanges or distributing property in complete liquidation to a non-U.S. person must report the transfer to IRS (on Form 926 for corporations, Form 8865 for partnerships) (Code Sec. 6038B; Reg § 1.6038B-1, Reg § 1.6038B-2)[5] A U.S. person must report (on Form 8865) an acquisition or disposition of an interest in a foreign partnership if he holds a 10% or greater interest in the partnership either before or after the event. (Code Sec. 6046A; Reg § 1.6046A-1)[6]

Foreign investors in U.S. real property must report their direct ownership interests to IRS. (Code Sec. 6039C)[7]

¶ 4661 Return of foreign partnership.

A foreign partnership isn't required to file a partnership return (Form 1065), if it doesn't have gross income that is (or is treated as) effectively connected with the conduct of a trade or business within the U.S. (ECI) and does not have gross income (including gains) derived from sources within the U.S.(U.S.-source income). Subject to exceptions, a foreign partnership that has ECI or has U.S.-source income that is not ECI must file a partnership return for its tax year. (Code Sec. 6031(e); Reg § 1.6031(a)-1(b)(1)) A foreign partnership (other than a with-holding foreign partnership) that has $20,000 or less of U.S.-source income and has no ECI during its tax year need not file a partnership return if, at no time during the partnership tax year, 1% or more of any item of partnership income, gain, loss, deduction, or credit is allocable in the aggregate to direct U.S. partners. The U.S. partners must directly report their shares of the allocable items of partnership income, gain, loss, deduction, and credit.

47. ¶S-4704
48. ¶S-5024
49. ¶S-3585; ¶60,384; TD ¶815,503
50. ¶S-3588; ¶60,384; TD ¶815,503
1. ¶S-3585.3
2. ¶S-3602 *et seq.*; ¶60,464; TD ¶815,501

3. ¶S-3510 *et seq.*; ¶60,38A4; TD ¶815,504
4. ¶S-3580; ¶6038A4; TD ¶815,504
5. ¶S-3629 *et seq.*; ¶60,38B4; TD ¶815,506
6. ¶S-3643; ¶60,46A4, ¶60,38B4; TD ¶815,506
7. ¶S-3502 *et seq.*; ¶60,39C4; TD ¶815,508

(Reg § 1.6031(a)-1(b)(2))

If a partnership is not a withholding foreign partnership and one or more withholding agents file the required Forms 1042 and 1042-S and pay the associated withholding tax, (1) a foreign partnership with U.S.-source income but no ECI and no U.S. partners is not required to file a partnership return, and (2) a foreign partnership with U.S.-source income and one or more U.S. partners but no ECI must file a partnership return. However, such a partnership need file Schedules K-1 only for its direct U.S.partners and for its passthrough partners through which U.S. partners hold an interest in the foreign partnership. (Reg § 1.6031(a)-1(b)(3))[8]

¶ 4662　Tax Withholding on Payments to Foreign Taxpayers.

The payor or person controlling the amount subject to withholding (the withholding agent), must withhold a 30% tax (or lower rates in certain cases) at source from certain U.S.-source amounts (e.g., interest and dividends) paid to nonresident aliens and foreign corporations.

¶ 4663　When withholding agent must withhold tax on payment to foreign payee.

Any person having the control, receipt, custody, disposal, or payment of specified items of income (¶4667) (a "withholding agent") must deduct and withhold U.S. income tax from those items, to the extent they are gross income from U.S. sources of foreigners subject to withholding (¶4665). (Code Sec. 1441(a))

The amount of tax to be deducted and withheld on an item is 30% unless a reduced rate applies by treaty (subject to an exception) or because the item is a scholarship or fellowship, or the item is specified compensation that's exempt from such withholding. (Code Sec. 1441(a)) In determining the withholding tax rate that applies to investment income earned in Guam by a nonresident alien, Guam is treated as part of the U.S.[9] Regs explain how to claim reduced withholding under a treaty. (Reg § 1.1441-6)[10]

A withholding agent must withhold the 30% tax on a payment made to a foreign payee, unless the agent can reliably associate the payment with documentation that the payment can be treated as made to a U.S. payee, or a foreign beneficial owner entitled to a reduced rate. (Reg § 1.1441-1(b)(1)) But the withholding agent need not withhold where the foreign person assumes responsibility for withholding on the payment as a (1) qualified intermediary (QI); (2) U.S. branch of a foreign person (or U.S. possessions financial institution treated as one); or (3) withholding foreign partnership or authorized foreign agent. (Reg § 1.1441-1(b)(2)) These persons provide a withholding agent with a withholding certificate Form W-8IMY.

Withholding by qualified intermediary. A QI is typically a foreign financial institution that enters into an agreement with IRS under which it acts as a withholding agent that determines the extent of its withholding obligation, as described above. (Reg § 1.1441-1(e)(5)) A QI is subject to the withholding and reporting provisions applicable to withholding agents and payors under the Code Sec. 1441 *et seq.* withholding, Code Sec. 6001 *et seq.* information reporting and the backup withholding and other withholding rules, except to the extent provided under the agreement. (Reg § 1.1441-1(e)(5)(iii))

However, the QI generally doesn't have to withhold if it doesn't assume primary withholding responsibility and has provided a valid withholding certificate and correct withholding statements to a withholding agent from which it receives an amount subject to that withholding.[11]

8. ¶S-2717.1
9. ¶O-1411
10. ¶O-12037
11. ¶O-11900 *et seq.*; ¶14,414 *et seq.*

Withholding foreign trusts and partnerships may similarly enter into agreements with IRS under they may act as withholding agents, as described above.[12]

¶ 4664 Reporting withholding—Form 1042, Form 1042-S.

Form 1042 is an annual form that's used: (a) to report tax withheld and tax deposited that a withholding agent (¶4663) had to report on all Forms 1042-S (see below) for the preceding year; and (b) as a cover sheet for remitting Form 1042-S. It must be filed with IRS on or before Mar. 15 of the year following the year in which the income was paid, even though no tax was required to be withheld during a given year, if the withholding agent is required to file any Forms 1042-S for the year. (Reg § 1.1461-1(b)(1))

A withholding agent (other than an individual who is not acting in the course of a trade or business with respect to a payment) must make an information return on Form 1042-S for each recipient of an amount subject to Code Sec. 1441 withholding (¶4663 et seq.), that was paid during the preceding year. But any person that withholds or is required to withhold under Code Sec. 1441 must file Form 1042-S for the payment withheld upon, whether or not that person is engaged in a trade or business, and whether or not the payment is an amount subject to reporting. (Reg § 1.1461-1(c)(1)(i))

One copy of Form 1042-S is filed with IRS on or before Mar. 15 of the year following the year in which the amount subject to reporting was paid, with a transmittal form. Another copy of Form 1042-S must be furnished to the recipient for whom the form is prepared on or before Mar. 15 of the year following the year in which the amount was paid. The withholding agent must retain a copy of each Form 1042-S. (Reg § 1.1461-1(c)(1)(i))[13]

¶ 4665 Which foreigners are subject to withholding

The following foreigners are subject to withholding at source on their U.S.-source income:

... nonresident alien individuals (Code Sec. 1441(a)) (even if an election is made to be treated as a U.S. resident for joint return purposes). (Reg § 1.1441-1(c)(3)(ii))

... a foreign corporation subject to U.S. income tax, other than a corporation created or organized in or under the laws of Guam, American Samoa, the Northern Mariana Islands, or the Virgin Islands if certain requirements are met. (Code Sec. 1442(c))

... a foreign partnership (but Reg § 1.1441-1(c)(6) applies concepts of payee and beneficial owner to determine if a payment is made to a foreign person). (Code Sec. 1441(a))

A withholding agent generally determines if a payee is a U.S. or foreign person on the basis of a withholding certificate (Form W-8) or a Form 8233 (indicating foreign status of the payee or beneficial owner) or a Form W-9 (indicating U.S. status of the payee). (Reg § 1.1441-1(b)(2)(i))

No withholding is required on payments to a foreign partnership or foreign corporation if IRS is satisfied that withholding would impose an undue administrative burden and that tax collection won't be jeopardized. (Code Sec. 1441(d), Code Sec. 1442(b))[14]

¶ 4666 How to claim exemption from withholding—Forms W-9, 8233, W-8, W-8EXP

Absent actual knowledge or reason to know otherwise, a withholding agent (¶4663) may treat a payee as a U.S. person, for whom withholding is not required, where the payee is required to furnish a Form W-9, and furnishes a Form W-9 under the backup withholding rules, which includes the payee's taxpayer identification number (TIN). A U.S. branch of a foreign person may establish its status as a foreign person exempt from Code Sec. 6001

12. ¶O-12005.8, ¶O-12014.2; ¶14,414 et seq.
13. ¶S-3495.1; ¶14,414

14. ¶O-11900 et seq.; ¶14,414 et seq.

information reporting rules and backup withholding by providing a withholding certificate on Form W-8. (Reg § 1.1441-1(d))

Where a payee is not required to furnish a Form W-9, the withholding agent may (absent knowledge or reason to know otherwise) rely on a certificate of U.S. status, i.e., an exemption certificate, or a Form W-9 (or a substitute form) that is signed under penalties of perjury by the payee and contains the name, residence address, and TIN of the payee. (Reg § 1.1441-1(d))

A withholding agent that makes a payment to an intermediary, a flow-through entity, or a U.S. branch, may treat the payment as made to a U.S. payee to the extent that, prior to the payment, the withholding agent can reliably associate the payment with: (a) a Form W-9 attached to a valid intermediary, flow-through, or U.S. branch withholding certificate, or (b) a Form W-8 that evidences an agreement to treat a U.S. branch as a U.S. person. (Reg § 1.1441-1(d)(4))

To obtain an exemption from withholding on compensation for personal services of a nonresident alien individual by reason of a tax treaty, a separate withholding certificate must be submitted to each withholding agent from whom payments are to be received, for each of the nonresident's tax years. If the withholding agent is satisfied that an exemption from withholding is warranted, it accepts the certificate and forwards it to IRS within five days. The exemption from withholding becomes effective for payments made at least 10 days after a copy of the accepted withholding certificate is forwarded to IRS. (Reg § 1.1441-4(b)(2)(i))

The statement claiming exemption is made on Form 8233, an acceptable substitute for that form, or such other form as IRS may prescribe. (Reg § 1.1441-4(b)(2)(ii))

Foreign governments use Form W-8EXP to claim exemption from withholding.[15]

¶ 4667 What income items are subject to and exempt from withholding.

The gross amounts of these items of income (from U.S. sources) are subject to withholding:

. . . Interest (other than original issue discount (OID) and certain portfolio and bank account interest), dividends, rent, salary, wages, premiums, annuities, compensations, remunerations and emoluments.

. . . Other fixed or determinable annual or periodical gains, profits and income.

. . . Gains from lump-sum employee plan distributions.

. . . Original issue discount (OID) on sale, exchange, or retirement of corporate or governmental bonds.

. . . Gains from contingent payments with respect to patents and other intangibles sold or exchanged. (Code Sec. 1441(b), Code Sec. 1442(a))

. . . Gains from the disposal of timber, coal, or domestic iron ore with retained economic interests. (Code Sec. 1441(b); Reg § 1.1441-2(c))

. . . Social Security benefits paid to nonresident aliens, but only to the extent of 85% of those benefits. (Code Sec. 871(a)(3)(A))

. . . Amounts paid when a U.S. real property interest is acquired from a foreign person (¶4671). (Code Sec. 1445(a))

. . . Amounts includible in the gross income of the holder of a residual interest in a REMIC. (Code Sec. 860G(b)(1))

These items are exempt from withholding:

. . . The items listed above to the extent they are gross income from foreign sources. (Code Sec. 1441(b); Reg § 1.1441-3(a))

15. ¶O-11964; ¶14,414.02

. . . Any item of income (other than compensation for personal services) which is effectively connected with the conduct of a U.S. business and taxed at regular U.S. tax rates. (Code Sec. 1441(c)(1), Code Sec. 1442(a)) Use Form W-8ECI to claim exemption. Amounts received as an annuity under a qualified employee benefit plan that are exempt from U.S. tax because they are attributable to the nonresident alien's foreign employment (including temporary U.S. employment for an employer located abroad) and at least 90% of the persons in the plan are U.S. citizens or residents. (Code Sec. 1441(c)(7)) Where the withholding agent is *not* the employer who established the plan, the recipient files a duplicate statement with the withholding agent, who must forward the duplicate with and attached to the Form 1042S filed by the withholding agent. (Reg § 1.1441-4(g))[16]

. . . RIC dividends that are paid out of interest that would not be subject to withholding and short-term capital gains are exempt from withholding if certain requirements are satisfied. (Code Sec. 1441(c)(12))

¶ 4668 Wage withholding for compensation for personal services of a nonresident alien individual.

Compensation paid for personal services performed by a nonresident alien individual, which is otherwise "wages" and which is effectively connected with a U.S. trade or business, is subject to regular graduated income tax withholding under Code Sec. 3402. (Reg § 31.3401(a)(6)-1(a))[17]

Employers must (except for students and business apprentices from India) compute nonresident alien employees' wage withholding by adding an additional amount to their wages to offset an assumed standard deduction incorporated into withholding tables.[18]

The following aren't wages subject to regular wage withholding:

(1) wages paid for services performed outside the U.S. by a nonresident alien individual other than a resident of Puerto Rico; (Reg § 31.3401(a)(6)-1(b))

(2) remuneration paid to Canadian and Mexican residents who enter or leave the U.S. at frequent intervals and are engaged in transportation service or in service on international projects; (Reg § 31.3401(a)(6)-1(c))

(3) wages paid to Puerto Rican residents for services performed in Puerto Rico for an employer other than the U.S. government;

(4) wages paid for services performed outside the U.S., but not in Puerto Rico, by a Puerto Rican resident for an employer other than the U.S. government if the individual does not expect to be a Puerto Rican resident during the entire tax year;

(5) compensation paid for services performed outside the U.S. by a nonresident alien individual who is a resident of Puerto Rico as an employee of the U.S. government, if the individual does not expect to be a Puerto Rican resident during the entire tax year; (Reg § 31.3401(a)(6)-1(d)) or

(6) wages exempt from tax by law or treaty. (Reg § 31.3401(a)(6)-1(f))

To get exemptions under (2), (4) or (5) above, the employee must furnish a statement in duplicate to his employer confirming that he's entitled to it. The statement must be dated, identify the tax year to which it relates, be signed by the employee, and contain (or be verified by) a written declaration that it is made under penalty of perjury. (Reg § 31.3401(a)(6)-1)[19]

---

16. ¶O-11902; ¶14,414
17. ¶O-11988 *et seq.*; ¶14,414.06

18. ¶H-4529.1
19. ¶O-11988 *et seq.*; ¶14,414.06

¶ 4669   Compensation subject to 30% withholding.

Although U.S. source compensation paid to a nonresident alien individual may be exempt from the definition of wages, and thus exempt from the regular graduated income tax withholding of Code Sec. 3402 (see ¶4668), the flat 30% withholding rate under Code Sec. 1441 (see ¶4663) applies to all forms of salaries, compensation, remuneration, etc. received by a nonresident alien individual to the extent these items of income are gross income from U.S. sources (Code Sec. 1441(a), Code Sec. 1441(b)), as well as to amounts paid as compensation for personal services that are effectively connected with the conduct of a U.S. trade or business. (Code Sec. 1441(c)(1)) Except that such Code Sec. 1441 withholding doesn't apply, if that compensation (Code Sec. 1441(c)(4)):

(1) is subject to withholding as "wages" under Code Sec. 3402 (see ¶4668).

(2) would be subject to graduated tax withholding as wages under Code Sec. 3402, except that it is specifically exempted from wages by Code Sec. 3401(a), with certain exceptions.

(3) is for services performed by Canadian or Mexican residents who enter or leave the U.S. at frequent intervals.

(4) is exempt from tax by law or treaty. (Reg § 1.1441-4(b)(1)) Where the exemption is by treaty the nonresident alien must submit a statement to each withholding agent from which amounts are to be received on Form 8233 (or an acceptable substitute); (Reg § 1.1441-4(b)(2))

(5) is paid as a commission or rebate by a ship supplier to a nonresident alien individual who is employed by a nonresident alien individual, foreign partnership or foreign corporation in the operation of ships of foreign registry, for placing orders for ship supplies; or

(6) is exempt from withholding under Code Sec. 3402 due to the Code Sec. 3402(e) "all-or-nothing rule," if the employee and employer enter into a voluntary nonwage withholding agreement. (Reg § 1.1441-4(b)(1))[20]

observation: Items (3) and (4) above are also exempt from regular wage withholding, see ¶4668.

¶ 4670   Withholding by partnerships with respect to foreign partners— Form 8813, Form 8804, Form 8805.

A partnership must pay a withholding tax if it has "effectively connected taxable income" for the tax year (whether or not the income is distributed), any part of which is allocable to a foreign partner. (Code Sec. 1446(a)) Unless the partner can show that the tax will be lower, the partnership must withhold at the highest rate of U.S. tax to which the foreign partner would be subject on the effectively connected taxable income allocable to the foreign corporate or noncorporate partner. (Code Sec. 1446(b); Reg § 1.1446-3, Reg § 1.1446-6) The partnership must determine the status of its partners based on Forms W-8 or W-9 filed by the partners. In the absence of documentation of a partner's status, the partnership must follow the presumptions in the regs. (Code Sec. 1446(b); Reg § 1.1446-1) Special rules apply to publicly traded partnerships and tiered partnerships. (Reg § 1.1446-4, Reg § 1.1446-5)[21]

The partnership must pay the withheld amount in installments based on the estimated tax requirements (¶3349) together with a Form 8813. The partnership must also report the partnership's total withholding liability for its year on Form 8804 and notify each foreign partner of his share thereof on Form 8805. (Reg § 1.1446-3)[22]

A domestic partnership must withhold on amounts subject to withholding (¶4667) that are

---

20. ¶O-11988 *et seq.*; ¶14,414.06
21. ¶O-12100 *et seq.*; ¶14,464; TD ¶634,030
22. ¶S-2718 *et seq.*; TD ¶634,031

not effectively connected income and are includible in the gross income of a partner that is a foreign person. A U.S. partnership must withhold when any distributions (including guaranteed payments) that include amounts subject to withholding are made. To the extent a foreign partner's distributive share of income subject to withholding has not been actually distributed to the foreign partner, the partnership must withhold on the partner's distributive share of the income on the earlier of the date the Form K-1 is mailed or otherwise furnished to the partner, or the due date for furnishing the K-1. If a partnership withholds on a distributive share before the amount is actually distributed to the partner, then withholding is not required when the amount is later distributed. (Reg § 1.1441-5(b)(2))[23]

¶ 4671 U.S. real property dispositions—Form 8288, Form 8288-A, Form 8828-B.

U.S. tax must be withheld when a foreign investor disposes of a USRPI (¶4650) (Code Sec. 1445(a))[24] including certain interests in a partnership, trust, or estate that directly or indirectly owns a USRPI. (Code Sec. 1445(e)(5); Reg § 1.1445-11T(b))[25]

The amount to be withheld generally is 10% of the amount realized on the disposition. (Code Sec. 1445(a)) The amount realized is the sum of cash received (not including any stated or unstated interest or original issue discount), the fair market value of any other property received, and any liability assumed by the transferee (e.g., buyer) or to which the USRPI was subject. (Reg § 1.1445-1(g))[26]

The withholding obligation is generally imposed on the transferee, (Code Sec. 1445) who must report the amounts withheld and pay them over (to IRS) by the 20th day after transfer. (Reg § 1.1445-1(c)) Form 8288 and Form 8288-A are used for this purpose. Foreign transferees are required to include their taxpayer identification numbers (TINs) on withholding tax returns.[27]

Withholding isn't required if the transferor gives the transferee a sworn "nonforeign affidavit" showing the transferor's U.S. taxpayer identification number and stating that he isn't a foreign person (Code Sec. 1445(b)(2); Reg § 1.1445-2(b)), or a sworn "non-USRPHC affidavit" stating that it's not a U.S. real property holding corporation,[28] *unless* (in either case) the transferee knows the affidavit is false. (Code Sec. 1445(b)(7))[29] For dispositions of USRPIs after July 30, 2008, a transferor may furnish the affidavit to a qualified substitute, rather than to the transferor directly. (Code Sec. 1445(b)(9))[30]

Nor does withholding apply if the USRPI is acquired by the transferee as his residence, and the amount realized doesn't exceed $300,000. (Code Sec. 1445(b)(5))[31]

IRS will issue a certificate excusing or reducing withholding if the transferor is exempt from U.S. tax, or if either the transferor or transferee agrees to pay the tax and gives security for its payment. (Reg § 1.1445-3(e)) A certificate gotten before a transfer notifies the transferee that no withholding, or reduced withholding, is required. A certificate gotten after the transfer may authorize a normal or early refund. (Use Form 8288-B to request a certificate.)[32]

¶ 4672 Withholdable payments to foreign financial institutions and other foreign entities

Generally effective for payments made after Dec. 31, 2012, Code Sec. 1471 through Code Sec. 1474 provide for withholding taxes to enforce reporting requirements on specified foreign accounts owned by specified U.S. persons or by U.S. owned foreign entities. There are rules

---

23. ¶O-12010; ¶14,414
24. ¶O-13001; ¶14,454; TD ¶644,002
25. ¶O-13035 *et seq.*; ¶14,454; TD ¶644,020
26. ¶O-13002; ¶14,454; TD ¶644,002
27. ¶S-5662; ¶14,454; TD ¶644,006

28. ¶O-13010 *et seq.*; ¶14,454; TD ¶644,007
29. ¶O-13013; TD ¶644,010
30. ¶O-13011
31. ¶O-13016; ¶14,454; TD ¶644,007
32. ¶O-13021 *et seq.*, S-5664; ¶14,454; TD ¶644,016

for withholdable payments to foreign financial institutions and those for withholdable payments to other foreign entities. The rules don't apply to any obligation outstanding on Mar. 18, 2012, or from the gross proceeds from any disposition of the obligation.

Payment to foreign financial institutions. Generally for payments made after Dec. 31, 2012, a withholding agent must deduct and withhold a tax equal to 30% of any withholdable payment made to a foreign financial institution that does not meet certain requirements. (Code Sec. 1471(a)) A "withholdable payment" is non-effectively connected (1) U.S. source fixed or determinable annual or periodical income, (2) gross proceeds from the sale of property that produces interest and dividend income and (3) interest on deposits with foreign branches of a domestic commercial bank (which is otherwise non-U.S. source income). (Code Sec. 1473(1)) To avoid this 30% withholding requirement, a "foreign financial institution" must either enter into a Code Sec. 1471(b) agreement with IRS or satisfy one of several alternatives regarding reporting information on U.S. accounts. (Code Sec. 1471(a))

Annual reporting is also required as to account balances and gross receipts and withdrawals from any U.S. accounts. (Code Sec. 1471(c)(1))

U.S. accounts. A U.S. account is any financial account which is held by one or more "specified U.S. persons" or a "U.S. owned foreign entity" (with an exception where all accounts held by a natural person do not exceed $50,000). (Code Sec. 1471(d)(1)) A specified U.S. person is any U.S. person other than (i) a corporation whose stock is regularly traded on an established securities market or members of its "expanded affiliated group" and (ii) certain entities that are exempt or have a special status and government bodies. (Code Sec. 1473(3)) A "U.S. owned foreign entity" is a foreign entity with one or more substantial U.S. owners, applying a more than 10% ownership of stock by vote or value test to a corporation; a more than 10% of capital or profits interests test to a partnership; any interest in a grantor trust; and under regs, any specified U.S. person with more than a 10% interest in a trust. (Code Sec. 1471(d)(1))

Payments to other foreign entities. Generally for payments made after Dec. 31, 2012, a withholding agent must deduct and withhold a tax equal to 30% of any withholdable payment made to a nonfinancial foreign entity if the beneficial owner of the payment is a nonfinancial foreign entity that does not meet specified requirements. (Code Sec. 1472(a)) Withholding is not required if the payee or the beneficial owner of the payment provides the withholding agent with either a certification that the foreign entity does not have a substantial U.S. owner, or provides the withholding agent with the name, address and TIN of each substantial U.S. owner. (Code Sec. 1472(b))

Withholding does not apply to any payment beneficially owned by a publicly traded corporation or a member of an expanded affiliated group of a publicly traded corporation. Nor does it apply to any payment beneficially owned by any: (1) entity organized under the laws of a U.S. possession, which is wholly owned by one or more bona fide residents of that possession; (2) foreign government, political subdivision thereof, or wholly owned agency or instrumentality of any foreign government or political subdivision thereof; (3) international organization or any wholly owned agency or instrumentality thereof; (4) foreign central bank of issue; (5) any other class of persons identified by IRS for these purposes; or (6) payments identified by IRS as posing a low risk of U.S. tax evasion. (Code Sec. 1472(c))

¶ 4673 Individuals must file disclosure statement for "specified foreign financial asset" with return

For tax years beginning after Mar. 18, 2010, individuals with an interest in a "specified foreign financial asset" during the tax year must attach a disclosure statement to their income tax return for any year in which the aggregate value of all such assets is greater than $50,000. (Code Sec. 6038D(a)) In addition, IRS may require disclosure for any domestic entity formed or availed of for purposes of holding, directly or indirectly, specified foreign financial assets. (Code Sec. 6038D(f))

"Specified foreign financial assets" are: (1) depository or custodial accounts at foreign financial institutions, and (2) to the extent not held in an account at a financial institution, (a) stocks or securities issued by foreign persons, (b) any other financial instrument or contract held for investment that is issued by or has a counterparty that is not a U.S. person, and (c) any interest in a foreign entity. (Code Sec. 6038D(b))

Individuals who fail to make the required disclosures are subject to a penalty of $10,000 for the tax year. An additional $10,000 penalty per each 30 days of failure to disclose (or fraction of such 30-day period) applies if the failure to disclose continues for more than 90 days after IRS notifies an individual by mail of his failure to disclose, up to a $50,000 maximum penalty. (Code Sec. 6038D(d)) No penalty is imposed where an individual can establish that the failure was due to reasonable cause and not willful neglect. A foreign law prohibition against disclosure of the required information doesn't constitute reasonable cause. (Code Sec. 6038D(g))

To the extent IRS determines that an individual has an interest in one or more foreign financial assets, and he doesn't provide sufficient information to enable IRS to determine the aggregate value of such assets, the aggregate value of the identified foreign financial assets is presumed to exceed $50,000 for purposes of assessing the penalty. (Code Sec. 6038D(e))

IRS is given authority to issue regs necessary to carry out the intent of these rules, including exceptions for nonresident aliens and specified classes of assets and exceptions to avoid duplicative reporting requirements. (Code Sec. 6038D(h))

¶ 4674   Foreign Currency Rules. ████████████████████████████████████

Transactions involving foreign currency must be expressed in U.S. dollars for U.S. tax purposes.

¶ 4675   Functional currency.

All U.S. taxpayers are required to make all federal income tax determinations in their "functional currency," (Code Sec. 985(a))[33] on a transaction-by-transaction basis.[34]

"Functional currency" generally means the U.S. dollar. (Code Sec. 985(b)(1)(A)) "Qualified business units" (QBUs) that conduct a significant part of their activities in an economic environment with a non-dollar currency in which they keep their books and records use that currency (Code Sec. 985(b)(1)(B))[35] unless the taxpayer elects (on Form 8819) to use the dollar as the QBU's functional currency. (Code Sec. 985(b)(3); Reg § 1.985-2)[36]

A QBU is any separate and clearly identified unit (or activity) of a trade or business of a taxpayer which maintains separate books and records. (Code Sec. 989(a); Reg § 1.989(a)-1(b)(2)(ii)) A corporation is a QBU. A partnership, trust or estate is a QBU of a partner or beneficiary. An individual is not a QBU. (Reg § 1.989(a) 1(b)(2)(i))[37]

Any foreign business entity—whether a branch or a sub—that uses a nondollar functional currency must use a profit-and-loss method to translate the results of its operations into U.S. dollars, at the "appropriate exchange rate." (Code Sec. 987)[38]

¶ 4676   Foreign currency gains and losses; section 988 transactions.

Foreign currency gain or loss attributable to a "Section 988 transaction" must generally be computed separately and be treated as interest income or expense, as the case may be. (Code

---

33. ¶G-6900 *et seq.*; ¶9854 *et seq.*
34. ¶G-6901
35. ¶G-6901 *et seq.*; ¶9854 *et seq.*

36. ¶G-6918 *et seq.*; ¶9854.01
37. ¶G-6912; ¶9854
38. ¶G-6966 *et seq.*; ¶9874 *et seq.*

Sec. 988(a)(1)(A), Code Sec. 988(a)(2))[39] However, a taxpayer may elect to treat the foreign currency gain or loss attributable to certain of these transactions as capital gain or loss. (Code Sec. 988(a)(1)(B); Reg § 1.988-3(b))[40]

Recognition of foreign currency gain or loss requires a closed and completed transaction, such as the payment of a liability.[41]

The source of these gains and losses is determined by reference to the residence of the taxpayer or QBU on whose books the relevant asset, liability or item of income or expense is properly reflected. (Code Sec. 988(a)(3); Reg § 1.988-4)[42] There are special rules for certain related corporations (Code Sec. 988(a)(3)(C))[43] currency swaps[44] and hedging transactions. (Code Sec. 988(d)(2))[45]

A "section 988 transaction" is any of specified transactions if the amount the taxpayer is entitled to receive, or is required to pay, by reason of the transaction is either: (1) denominated in terms of a nonfunctional currency; or (2) determined by reference to the value of one or more nonfunctional currencies. (Code Sec. 988(c)(1)(A))[46]

The Code Sec. 988 rules apply to transactions entered into by an individual only to the extent the expenses properly allocable to them satisfy Code Sec. 162, Code Sec. 212(1) or Code Sec. 212(2). An individual who disposes of foreign currency in a personal transaction doesn't recognize gain by reason of fluctuations in exchange rates during the period the taxpayer held the currency, unless the gain exceeds $200.[47]

¶ 4677   Reporting Gifts from Foreign Persons. ▮▮▮▮▮

U.S. persons must report certain gifts from foreign persons.

¶ 4678   Reporting foreign gifts— Form 3520.

If the value of the aggregate "foreign gifts" (see below) received by a U.S. person (other than an exempt Code Sec. 501(c) organization) exceeds a threshold amount (see below), the U.S. person must report each "foreign gift" to IRS. (Code Sec. 6039F(a)) Form 3520 is used to report these gifts.

Different reporting thresholds apply for gifts received from (a) nonresident alien individuals or foreign estates, and (b) foreign partnerships or foreign corporations. For gifts from a nonresident alien or foreign estate, reporting of gifts over $5,000 is required only if the aggregate amount of gifts from that person exceeds $100,000 during the tax year. For gifts from foreign corporations and foreign partnerships, the reporting threshold amount is an inflation adjusted aggregate amount of gifts of $14,165 for tax years beginning in 2010 ($14,375 for 2011).

"Foreign gifts" include any amounts received from a person that isn't a U.S. person the recipient treats as a gift or bequest. The term doesn't include any qualified tuition or medical payments made on behalf of a U.S. person (under Code Sec. 2503(e)(2)) or any distribution that was properly disclosed under Code Sec. 6048(c)). (Code Sec. 6039F(b))[48]

39. ¶s G-7001 *et seq.*, G-7028; ¶9884 *et seq.*
40. ¶G-7024 *et seq.*; ¶9884.01
41. ¶G-7001
42. ¶G-7029; ¶9884.01
43. ¶O-4504; ¶9884.01
44. ¶G-7021 *et seq.*; ¶9884.01
45. ¶G-7027 *et seq.*; ¶s 9884.01, 9884.02
46. ¶G-6988 *et seq.*; ¶9884.01
47. ¶G-7047; ¶9884.01
48. ¶S-3649.1, ¶S-3649.5; ¶60,39F4; TD ¶746,002

Chapter 24   Returns and Payment of Tax

¶ 4700   Returns and Payment of Tax. ▬▬▬▬▬▬▬▬▬▬▬▬▬▬▬▬▬▬▬▬▬▬

An individual taxpayer must file an income tax return if his gross income equals or exceeds a specified amount. Married taxpayers may file a joint return. Corporations, trusts and estates must also file income tax returns. A partnership files an information return of income. Payors and others must file information returns to report specified payments, sales, etc. Times, places and methods of paying tax are specified.

¶ 4701   Who must file individual income tax returns?

An income tax return must be filed by every individual U.S. citizen and resident alien (including an alien who is a bona fide resident of Puerto Rico during the entire tax year) (Reg § 1.1-1(b), Reg § 1.6012-1(a)(1)) and nonresident or dual-status alien married to a U.S. citizen or resident at year-end who elects to be treated as a resident alien (Reg § 1.6013-6(a))[1] who has gross income (including excluded homesale gain and foreign earned income (Code Sec. 6012(c)) that equals or exceeds the following amounts:

	2010
(1) Single (Code Sec. 6012(a)(1)(A)(i))	$9,350
—65-or-over (Code Sec. 6012(a)(1)(B))	10,750
(2) Married filing joint return (Code Sec. 6012(a)(1)(A)(iv))	18,700
—one 65-or-over (Code Sec. 6012(a)(1)(B))	19,800
—both 65-or-over (Code Sec. 6012(a)(1)(B))	20,900
(3) Married filing separate return (Code Sec. 6012(a)(1)(A))	3,650
(4) Head of Household (Code Sec. 6012(a)(1)(A)(ii))	12,050
—65-or-over (Code Sec. 6012(a)(1)(B))	13,450
(5) Surviving spouse (Code Sec. 6012(a)(1)(A)(iii))	15,050
—65-or-over (Code Sec. 6012(a)(1)(B))	16,150

If an individual can be claimed as a dependent, that individual/dependent must file a return if (a) his unearned income exceeds $950 for 2010 plus any additional standard deduction (¶3112), or (b) his total gross income is more than the standard deduction (¶3112). (Code Sec. 6012(a)(1)(C)(i))[2] A married dependent whose spouse files a separate return and itemizes deductions must file if he has gross income of $5 or more.[3] But, no return is required for a child where the parent elects (¶3139) to include the child's income on the parent's return. For 2010, the election is available if the child's income exceeds $950 and is less than $9,500. (Code Sec. 1(g)(7)(A))[4]

The filing threshold in (2), above, applies only if the spouses, at the end of the tax year, had the same household as their home (Code Sec. 6012(a)(1)(A)(iv)) and no other taxpayer could claim an exemption for either spouse. (Code Sec. 6012(a)(1)(A))

Individuals who file a short year return due to a change in accounting period must file a return if gross income received during the short year equals or exceeds $3,650 for 2010, prorated in the ratio that the months of the short year bear to 12. (Reg § 1.6012-1(a)(2)(v))[5]

The following may have to file an income tax return even though they have gross income

---

1. ¶S-1701; ¶60,124.02; TD ¶570,201
2. ¶S-1705; ¶60,124; TD ¶570,204
3. ¶S-1705; TD ¶570,204

4. ¶S-1704.1; ¶14.11; TD ¶568,400
5. ¶S-1707; ¶60,124; TD ¶570,206

References beginning with a single letter are to paragraphs in RIA's Federal Tax Coordinator 2d and RIA's Analysis of Federal Taxes: Income. Those beginning with numbers are to paragraphs in RIA's United States Tax Reporter. Those beginning with TD are to paragraphs in RIA's Tax Desk.

below the levels listed above: individuals who received tips from which social security tax wasn't withheld;[6] individuals receiving advance payment of the earned income credit (¶2349) for tax years beginning before 2011; (Code Sec. 6012(a)(8))[7] individuals owing AMT;[8] employees of certain religious and other church-controlled organizations, if they receive more than $108.28 of compensation from the organization during the year;[9] individuals receiving income from U.S. possessions;[10] nonresident aliens (NRAs)[11] but not NRAs who earn less than the personal exemption;[12] individuals who change their citizenship or country of residence during the year;[13] individuals who must pay a tax with respect to an IRA, qualified retirement plan, Archer MSA, health savings account, Coverdell education savings account, or qualified tuition program (if filing only for this reason, use Form 5329 by itself);[14] individuals who owe uncollected payroll tax on group-term life insurance;[15] individuals who must pay a tax resulting from recapture of credits;[16] and certain self-employed individuals (¶4713).

The individual filing thresholds for a decedent's final return aren't reduced or prorated. [17]

¶ 4702   Individual income tax returns—Forms 1040, 1040A, and 1040EZ.

U.S. citizens and residents use Form 1040 (Reg § 1.6012-1(a)(6)), Form 1040A (Reg § 1.6012-1(a)(7)(i)), or Form 1040EZ. Form 1040A may be used by a taxpayer in any filing status who: (1) has income only from wages, salaries, tips, interest, ordinary dividends, capital gain distributions, taxable scholarships and fellowship grants, pensions, annuities, IRAs, unemployment compensation, taxable social security and railroad retirement benefits, and Alaska Permanent Fund dividends; (2), can only claim certain adjustments to gross income (educator expenses, IRA deduction, student loan interest deduction, and tuition and fees deduction); (3) doesn't itemize deductions; (4) has taxable income less than $100,000; and (5) has only certain tax credits. Form 1040A may be used even if the taxpayer owes alternative minimum tax (AMT).[18]

Single or married filing jointly taxpayers under 65 who aren't blind can use Form 1040EZ if they claim no dependents, have income only from wages, salaries, tips, taxable scholarships or fellowships, unemployment compensation, Alaska Permanent Fund Dividends, and interest (of $1,500 or less), no adjustments to gross income, no itemized deductions, taxable income of less than $100,000 and no tax credits other than the earned income credit (EIC) (but no advance payment of the EIC) or the Making Work Pay credit.[19]

¶ 4703   E-filing individual returns.

Tax preparers can e-file current year returns (Form 1040, Form 1040A and Form 1040EZ) (but not after Oct. 15 even with a filing extension) and Form 4868 automatic filing extensions for individual taxpayers,[20] including returns that show a balance due.[21] However an electronic return can't be filed for returns for years other than the current tax year, amended returns, returns that cover fiscal year tax periods, or in certain other situations.[22]

An electronic return is a composite return consisting of data transmitted to IRS electronically and of paper documents (filed later) that can't be electronically transmitted, such as an individual income tax declaration for an individual *e-file* return (use Form 8453), documents prepared by third parties, etc.[23] IRS has developed procedures for accepting signatures in

6. ¶S-1709; ¶60,124; TD ¶570,208
7. ¶S-1710; ¶60,124; TD ¶570,209
8. ¶S-1716; ¶60,124; TD ¶570,215
9. ¶S-1718; ¶60,124; TD ¶570,217
10. ¶S-1704.3; ¶60,124.02; TD ¶570,207
11. ¶S-1750 *et seq.*; ¶60,124.02
12. ¶S-1755
13. ¶S-1758
14. ¶S-1708.1; ¶60,124; TD ¶570,203

15. ¶S-1708.1; ¶60,124; TD ¶570,208
16. ¶S-1708.1; ¶60,124; TD ¶570,203
17. ¶C-9602, ¶C-9603; ¶60,124.04; TD ¶579,501
18. ¶S-1715; ¶60,114.01; TD ¶570,214
19. ¶S-1715; ¶60,114.01; TD ¶570,214
20. ¶S-1601; ¶60,114.08; TD ¶572,010
21. ¶S-1617; ¶60,114.08; TD ¶572,029
22. ¶S-1604; TD ¶572,009
23. ¶S-1601.2 *et seq.*; ¶60,114.08; TD ¶572,005

digital or electronic form. (Code Sec. 6061(b))[24] Tax practitioners can e-file individual income tax returns only if the returns are signed electronically using 1 of 2 methods: either a self-select Personal Identification Number (PIN) or a practitioner PIN. Practitioner PINs require the use of Form 8879, which is retained by the electronic return originator (ERO).[25] For how to submit payments for electronic returns on Form 1040-V, see ¶4720.

¶ 4704 Husband and wife—joint or separate returns.

Married persons have the choice of filing a joint return (reporting their combined taxable income) (Code Sec. 6013(a))[26] or separate returns. (Code Sec. 1(d))[27] Neither a return prepared and executed by IRS nor a Form 870 waiver is a valid election to file a joint return.[28]

☑observation: Filing separately may save taxes due to the floors on some deductions (e.g., medical expenses, miscellaneous itemized deductions, casualty losses). Each floor is measured against adjusted gross income (AGI), so if either spouse has high amounts of these expenses, measuring them against a separate AGI can produce a larger deduction than if measured against joint AGI. But, any advantages may be offset by many restrictive rules for separate filers.

Separate returns. Each spouse is liable only for his own tax and penalties.[29]

Joint returns. Except as noted at ¶4708 to ¶4710, each spouse is jointly and severally liable for the full amount of the tax, penalties (other than civil fraud (¶4883)), and interest arising out of their joint return, regardless of the amount of his separate taxable income. (Code Sec. 6013(d)(3)) Only the spouse committing fraud can be subjected to fraud penalties.[30]

¶ 4705 Qualifying for joint returns.

Spouses may file a joint return even if only one has income (Code Sec. 6013(a))[31] and even if they have different accounting *methods.* But they must be legally married as of the *end* of the tax year. (Code Sec. 6013(d))[32] If the spouses filed a joint return during their "marriage" and later get an annulment, they must refile as separate unmarried persons.[33]

A joint return *can't* be filed if:

. . . *either spouse was a nonresident alien* (NRA) at any time during the tax year (Code Sec. 6013(a)(1))[34] but where 1 spouse is an NRA for the entire year (Code Sec. 6013(g)) or where an NRA spouse becomes a U.S. resident during the tax year (Code Sec. 6013(h)), spouses can file a joint return if they agree to subject their worldwide income to U.S. taxation;[35]

. . . *the spouses have different tax years,* except when 1 spouse dies, see ¶4707.

¶ 4706 Changing from joint to separate returns and vice versa.

Once a joint return has been filed, spouses may revoke it by filing separate returns up until the return's due date. After the due date, they can't switch. (Reg § 1.6013-1(a))[36]

☑observation: A couple may file jointly in 1 year and separately in another.

A married couple who filed separate returns may switch to a joint return after the due date if: (a) the joint return is filed within 3 years from the original due date (without extension),

24. ¶S-4518; ¶60,614
25. ¶S-1617.3
26. ¶S-1801; ¶60,134 *et seq.*; TD ¶570,601
27. ¶A-1502; ¶14.01; TD ¶566,002
28. ¶S-1827
29. ¶V-8504; TD ¶570,903
30. ¶V-8502; ¶s 60,134.05, 66,534.11; TD ¶570,901
31. ¶S-1801; ¶60,134; TD ¶570,601
32. ¶S-1803; ¶60,134.03; TD ¶570,602
33. ¶A-1609; ¶60,134.03; TD ¶566,509
34. ¶S-1802; ¶60,134; TD ¶570,601
35. ¶A-1800 *et seq.*; ¶60,134.01; TD ¶567,501
36. ¶S-1831; ¶60,134.01; TD ¶570,622

and (b) neither spouse has, with respect to his previously filed separate return, petitioned the Tax Court, filed a suit for refund, or entered into a closing agreement or final compromise. (Code Sec. 6013(b); Reg § 1.6013-2(b))[37]

¶ 4707   Joint return for year spouse(s) dies.

A joint return may be filed for a husband and wife where their tax years start on the same day and end on different days because of the death of either or both (unless the survivor remarries before the end of his tax year). The joint return must be made with respect to the tax year of each. (Code Sec. 6013(a)(2))[38] For when to file, see ¶4716.

recommendation: File a joint return to get the benefits of the joint return rates, to use up decedent's net operating loss, capital loss, or charitable contribution carryforwards or other expiring deductions or credits, if the survivor has income or can generate income before the end of the survivor's tax year.

A surviving spouse may file a joint return for the deceased and surviving spouse if: the deceased spouse didn't previously file a return for the tax year; an executor/administrator hasn't been appointed by the time the joint return is made; and an executor/administrator hasn't been appointed before the due date for filing the return of the surviving spouse (including extensions). (Code Sec. 6013(a)(3))[39]

observation: The return for the year before the year of death also is subject to these rules if the decedent died before filing a return for that year.

If an executor or administrator is appointed on or before the filing due date, the surviving spouse *can't* file a joint return for the decedent. Only the fiduciary can act for the decedent, so both the fiduciary and the surviving spouse must sign the joint return. Even if the surviving spouse properly filed a joint return (because no fiduciary had been appointed by the due date), the fiduciary may disaffirm (revoke) the joint return by filing a *separate* return for the decedent within 1 year after the due date (including extensions). Any "joint" return improperly filed by the survivor or disaffirmed by the fiduciary is treated as a *separate* return of the survivor. (Code Sec. 6013(a)(3))[40] For when survivor can use joint return *rates*, see ¶3132.

¶ 4708   Elective relief from joint tax liability (innocent spouse rule)—Form 8857.

Unless an exception to innocent spouse relief (¶4711) applies, an individual who has filed a joint return may elect (use Form 8857) relief from joint and several liability (¶4704) under innocent spouse procedures. (Code Sec. 6015(a)(1)) Under IRS procedures, an individual will be relieved of liability for tax (and interest, penalties, etc.) for a tax year to the extent the liability is due to an understatement if: (a) a joint return was filed for the tax year; (b) there's an understatement of tax on the return due to the other spouse's erroneous items; (c) the individual shows that, in signing the return, he didn't know or had no reason to know of the understatement; (d) under the facts and circumstances, it would be inequitable to hold the individual liable for the deficiency; and (e) the individual elects the benefits of the innocent spouse rules, by filing Form 8857 (separately from the tax return) and the required attached statement, no later than 2 years after IRS has begun collection activities against the individual. (Code Sec. 6015(b)(1))[41]

observation: Innocent spouse relief isn't available for unpaid liabilities that were properly reported on a joint return, because in that situation there's no understatement of tax. However, equitable relief (¶4710) may be available.

37. ¶S-1829; ¶60,134.01; TD ¶570,620
38. ¶S-1805; ¶60,134; TD ¶570,603
39. ¶S-1806; ¶60,134; TD ¶570,604

40. ¶S-1806; ¶60,134; TD ¶570,605
41. ¶V-8506 *et seq.*; ¶60,154.01; TD ¶570,904

A spouse who knew or had reason to know of the understatement, but shows that he didn't know or have reason to know of its *extent*, can be relieved of liability to the extent of the understatement of which he didn't know or have reason to know. (Code Sec. 6015(b)(2))[42]

Special innocent spouse relief applies to a spouse of a partner in a partnership subject to unified partnership audit procedures (¶4842). The 9th Circuit held that the Tax Court couldn't review IRS's refusal to act on a relief claim until the completion of the partnership level audit. (Code Sec. 6230(a)(3), Code Sec. 6230(c)(5))[43]

A spouse in a community property state who files a separate return and doesn't include the proper amount of community income on the return, unless it is inequitable to hold the other spouse liable. (Code Sec. 66)[44] Any determination of innocent spouse relief is made without regard to the operation of community property laws. (Reg § 1.6015-1(f)(1))[45] For a spouse's separate liability election, see ¶4709.

Upon receipt of a request for relief (¶4709; ¶4710), IRS must send a notice to the nonrequesting spouse's last known address informing that spouse of the requesting spouse's claim for relief. (Reg § 1.6015-6(a)(1)) The nonrequesting spouse may file a protest and receive an IRS appeals conference regarding a determination. IRS's procedures protect domestic abuse victims who fear retaliation for applying for innocent spouse relief.[46] The nonrequesting spouse may also intervene to support the requesting spouse's innocent spouse claim.[47]

¶ 4709 Separate liability ("allocation of liability") election—Form 8857.

An individual who files a joint return and meets certain eligibility requirements can elect to limit his liability for any deficiency. This "separate liability" election may be made in addition to the innocent spouse election (¶4708). (Code Sec. 6015(a)(2))[48] Separate liability relief is available only for unpaid liabilities resulting from understatements; refunds aren't authorized. (Reg § 1.6015-3(c)(1))[49]

An individual can elect only if, when the election is filed, he's no longer married to, or is legally separated from, the spouse with whom the joint return was filed, or wasn't a member of the same household as that spouse at any time during the previous 12-month period. If IRS shows that assets were transferred between spouses in a fraudulent scheme joined in by both spouses, a separate liability election of either spouse is invalid. (Code Sec. 6015(c)(3)(A))[50]

To elect, file Form 8857 (separately from the return) with specified attached statement no later than 2 years after IRS begins collection activity against the electing spouse. (Code Sec. 6015(c)(3)(B); Reg § 1.6015-5)[1]

Except as provided below, an electing spouse's liability for any deficiency that IRS assesses won't exceed the portion of the deficiency properly allocable to that spouse. (Code Sec. 6015(c)(1), Code Sec. 6015(d)(3)(A))[2] The liability is generally allocated between the spouses in proportion to the net items taken into account in determining the deficiency as if separate returns were filed. (Code Sec. 6015(d)(1))[3] But, the limitation on an electing spouse's tax liability is increased by the value of property transferred to that spouse by the nonelecting spouse principally to avoid tax, which is rebuttably presumed (except for divorce or separate maintenance transfers) to be the case for transfers made anytime after 1 year before the first letter of proposed deficiency is sent. (Code Sec. 6015(c)(4))[4] Also, except where a joint return was signed under duress, the election doesn't apply to the extent that IRS has evidence that the electing spouse had *actual* knowledge of an item giving rise to all or part of a deficiency

---

42. ¶V-8516; ¶60,154.01; TD ¶570,905
43. ¶T-2261.1, ¶U-2148; ¶62,304
44. ¶A-5016 *et seq.*; ¶664; TD ¶573,602
45. ¶V-8511
46. ¶V-8550
47. ¶U-2152
48. ¶V-8533; ¶60,154.02; TD ¶570,933

49. ¶T-5513
50. ¶V-8534; ¶60,154.02; TD ¶570,934
1. ¶V-8536; ¶60,154.02; TD ¶570,936
2. ¶V-8537; ¶60,154.02; TD ¶570,941
3. ¶V-8539; ¶60,154.02; TD ¶570,939
4. ¶V-8538; ¶60,154.02; TD ¶570,938

allocable to the other spouse. (Code Sec. 6015(c)(3)(C))[5]

¶ 4710   Equitable relief for spouses—Form 8857.

If under all the facts and circumstances it's inequitable to hold a spouse liable for any portion of any unpaid tax or deficiency, and relief isn't available under the innocent spouse (¶4708) or separate liability election (¶4709) rules, IRS may relieve that spouse of liability for that unpaid tax or deficiency (Code Sec. 6015(f); Reg § 1.6015-4) and in limited cases may issue a refund. To request equitable relief, file Form 8857 (separately from the tax return) with specified attached statement. (Reg § 1.6015-5(a))

All of the following threshold conditions must be met to be considered for this relief:

(1) a joint return must have been filed for the tax year and the liability for which relief is sought, subject to limited exceptions, is attributable to the nonrequesting spouse;

(2) relief isn't available under Code Sec. 6015(b) or Code Sec. 6015(c);

(3) relief must be applied for no later than 2 years after IRS's first collection activity with respect to the individual. (Reg § 1.6015-5(b)(1)) But, the Tax Court has invalidated this 2-year time limit (but IRS and the Seventh Circuit disagree with the decision);

(4) the liability is unpaid when relief is requested. However, relief in the form of a refund of liabilities may be available for certain post-request installment payments;

(5) no assets were transferred between joint filers (spouses) as part of a fraudulent scheme;

(6) no disqualified assets were transferred to the individual by nonrequesting spouse (if there were, relief is available only to the extent the liability exceeds their value); and

(7) the individual didn't file the joint return with fraudulent intent.[6]

Equitable relief ordinarily is granted to an individual who meets the above-listed threshold requirements where: (a) the joint return liability was unpaid at the time the return was filed; (b) at the time relief is requested, the individual is no longer married to, or is legally separated from, the spouse with whom the joint return was filed, or has not been a member of the same household as that spouse during the 12-month period ending on the date the relief is requested; (c) when the return was signed, the individual didn't know, and had no reason to know, that the tax would not be paid. The individual must show that it was reasonable to believe that the other spouse would pay the reported liability (partial relief may be available); and (d) the individual will suffer economic hardship (determined by IRS under rules similar to those in Reg § 301.6343-1(b)(4)) if relief isn't granted.

The Tax Court uses a de novo standard to review IRS's denial of a claim for equitable relief (but IRS opposes the use of this standard).[7]

Relief only applies to the tax liability shown on the return (before adjustments), and is only available to the extent the unpaid tax is attributable to the nonrequesting spouse. IRS lists factors for and against granting relief.[8]

¶ 4711   Exceptions to innocent spouse relief.

Innocent spouse relief (¶4708, ¶4709, ¶4710) isn't available: (1) for liabilities other than income taxes, (e.g. domestic service employment taxes, see ¶3031), that are reported on a joint federal income tax return (Reg § 1.6015-1(a)(3))[9]; (2) for a tax year for which the spouse seeking relief has entered into an offer in compromise or a closing agreement with IRS that disposes of the liability (Reg § 1.6015-1(c))[10]; or (3) if a spouse transferred assets to the other spouse as part of a fraudulent scheme to defraud IRS or another third party. (Reg § 1.6015-

5. ¶V-8549; ¶60,154.02; TD ¶570,949
6. ¶V-8553; ¶60,154.04
7. ¶V-8554; ¶60,154.04; TD ¶570,954

8. ¶V-8554; ¶60,154.04; TD ¶570,954
9. ¶V-8501; ¶60,154
10. ¶V-8506.1A; ¶60,154

1(d))[11]

¶ 4712 Returns for minors and incompetents.

Returns for minors and others who are incapable of filing their own returns should be filed for them by their guardians or fiduciaries. A minor may make his own return. (Reg § 1.6012-3(b)(3))[12] For the election to claim a child's income on a parent's return, see ¶3139.

¶ 4713 Self-employed individuals' tax returns—Form 1040 and Schedule SE.

Individuals (except nonresident aliens) who have $400 or more net earnings from self-employment (¶3143) have to file Form 1040 (including Form 1040, Schedule SE) even if the individual's gross income is less than the filing thresholds (¶4701). (Code Sec. 6017) The self-employment tax (¶3140), which is in addition to the income tax, is reported on Form 1040 and paid as part of the income tax.[13]

¶ 4714 Decedent's final return.

A final income tax return must be filed for a deceased person who would be required to file if alive, for the part of the year up to the date of death. A decedent's final return is filed by the person entrusted with his property (e.g., the estate's executor or administrator). (Code Sec. 6012(b)(1))[14] For refunds, see ¶4849.[15] For a joint return by a surviving spouse, see ¶4707.

recommendation: Even though a final return may not otherwise be required, file one to claim any refund due for tax withheld from salary or for estimated tax paid.

Personal exemptions (¶3116) and the standard deduction (¶3112) allowed on a decedent's final income tax return aren't reduced because the return is for a short year.[16] For when the return is due, see ¶4716. For the income and deductions reportable on the return, see ¶3964.

¶ 4715 U.S. military and civilian employees dying in combat/ terrorist attacks.

If a military or civilian employee of the U.S. dies as a result of wounds or injury sustained in a terrorist or military action, income tax won't apply for the year of death and any earlier year beginning with the last year ending before the year in which the wounds or injury were sustained. (Code Sec. 692(c)(1)) IRS has outlined procedures for determining whether a terrorist or military action has occurred. Refund of withheld or estimated taxes may be claimed by filing Form 1040, or, if one had already been filed, Form 1040X. On joint returns, the tax liability must be allocated between the deceased and surviving spouses.[17]

¶ 4716 When and where to file individual returns.

Income tax returns (including self-employment tax returns and a decedent's final return (¶4714)) of U.S. citizens and resident aliens must be filed on or before the 15th day of the fourth month following the end of the tax year (Apr. 15 for calendar year taxpayers). (Code Sec. 6072(a); Reg § 1.6072-1(a)(1), Reg § 1.6072-1(b))[18] For when a nonresident alien's return must be filed, see ¶4657.

caution: However, calendar year taxpayers have until Apr. 18, 2011 to file their 2010 returns because Apr. 15, 2011 falls on a Friday on which a D.C. holiday is observed.

---

11. ¶V-8506.1A; ¶60,154; TD ¶570,935
12. ¶S-1704.1; ¶s 60,124, 60,124.04; TD ¶570,211
13. ¶S-1717; ¶s 14,024 *et seq.*, 60,174; TD ¶570,216
14. ¶C-9601, S-2003; ¶60,124.04; TD ¶570,212, TD ¶579,501

15. ¶T-5710; ¶60,124.04; TD ¶802,039
16. ¶C-9602 *et seq.*; TD ¶579,507
17. ¶C-9660; ¶6924; TD ¶579,601
18. ¶S-4701 *et seq.*; ¶60,724; TD ¶570,219 *et seq.*

A "short period return" must be filed by the 15th day of the fourth month following the end of the short period. (Reg § 1.6071-1(b))[19]

File as specified on the return form (or instructions). For an individual, this usually is the service center for the place where the individual lives.[20]

¶ 4717   Extensions of time for filing individual returns—Form 4868.

File Form 4868 to get an automatic extension of 6 months for filing (until Oct. 15 for a calendar year taxpayer). (Reg § 1.6081-4)[21] The form must show the full amount properly estimated as tax for the year but it needn't be accompanied by payment of the balance of the tax estimated to be due. (Reg § 1.6081-4(b))[22] (Failure to include the balance due won't affect the filing extension, but interest on the balance will still be charged, and a penalty for failure to pay may be imposed.)[23] IRS also accepts extension requests by e-filing.[24] For extension of time to pay, see ¶4721; for installment payments, see ¶4722. IRS can terminate an automatic extension on 10 days' notice. (Reg § 1.6081-4(d))[25]

Extensions can't exceed 6 months unless the taxpayer is abroad. (Code Sec. 6081(a))[26]

For automatic extensions obtained by merely making a credit card payment, see ¶4720.

¶ 4718   Extensions for citizens or residents with tax homes outside the U.S.—Form 4868; Form 2350.

A U.S. citizen or resident whose tax home and abode is outside the U.S. and Puerto Rico (Reg § 1.6081-5(a)(5)) and a U.S. citizen or resident in military or naval service on duty outside the U.S. and Puerto Rico (Reg § 1.6081-5(a)(6)), get automatic extensions until the 15th day of the sixth month after the end of the tax year. A statement should be attached to the return which shows that the taxpayer qualified for this extension. (Reg § 1.6081-5(b)) For these taxpayers, the automatic 6-month extension for individuals (¶4717) runs concurrently with the 2-month extension of time to file. (Reg § 1.6081-4(a))

illustration: On Apr. 15, T, a U.S. citizen using the calendar year, has a tax home outside the U.S. and Puerto Rico. T's tax return and tax payment are due on June 15. If T files Form 4868 by June 15 and pays any estimated unpaid tax, T has until Oct. 15 to file.

U.S. citizens or resident aliens who expect to qualify for the foreign earned income exclusion (¶4612) (and owe no tax), but not until more than 2 months after the regular return due date, should file extension request Form 2350 by that due date. (Reg § 1.911-7(c)(2))[27]

¶ 4719   Deadline and collection extensions for taxpayers serving in a combat zone or affected by a declared disaster, terrorist or military action.

Individuals serving in the U.S. armed forces in an area designated by the President as a "combat zone" (¶1225) or in a 10 USC §101(a)(13) "contingency operation" can suspend the period of time to perform various tax actions (e.g., tax return filing). (Code Sec. 7508) The suspension also applies to individuals serving in support of the Armed Forces in a combat zone, or acting under the Armed Forces' direction. These individuals are allowed extra time to perform tax acts (e.g., filing of any income, estate, gift, excise or employment tax return, or filing a claim for credit or refund) and the period is extended for the determination and assessment of their federal tax liability. (Code Sec. 7508(a)(1)) The suspension includes (1) any period of continuous hospitalization as a result of injury received while serving in the

19. ¶S-4701; ¶60,724; TD ¶570,219
20. ¶S-5100 *et seq.*; ¶60,914; TD ¶570,225
21. ¶S-5011; ¶60,814.03; TD ¶570,301
22. ¶S-5013; ¶60,814.03; TD ¶570,301
23. ¶s S-5010, S-5011; ¶60,814.03; TD ¶570,301

24. ¶S-1606; ¶60,814.03; TD ¶570,301
25. ¶S-5009; ¶60,814.03; TD ¶570,301
26. ¶S-5003; ¶60,814.04; TD ¶570,302
27. ¶S-5020; ¶9114.13; TD ¶570,305

combat zone, and (2) time in missing in action status plus a 180-day period after the termination of service or hospitalization.[28]

IRS may allow taxpayers affected by a Code Sec. 165(h)(3)(C)(i) "federally-declared" disaster or a Code Sec. 692(c)(2) terrorist or military action to extend for up to 1 year (1) the timely performance of acts under Code Sec. 7508(a)(1) (including filing any income, estate, gift, excise, or employment tax return); (2) the amount of any interest, penalty, additional amount, or addition to tax due for periods after the disaster date; and (3) the amount of any tax credit or refund.[29] (Code Sec. 7508A) IRS has specified acts subject to postponement,[30] (Reg § 301.7508A-1) including disasters occurring in 2010.[31]

On notice to IRS, the collection of income tax of a servicemember falling due before or during his military service is to be deferred for up to 180 days after termination of the taxpayer's service (or his release from it), if his ability to pay the tax is materially affected by the military service. No interest or penalty will accrue for this deferment period because of the nonpayment of any deferred amount. Also, the running of the statute of limitations against the collection of any deferred amount, by seizure or otherwise, is suspended for the period of service plus 270 days.[32] For rules granting tax relief for a decedent who was a military or civilian U.S. employee who died in combat or a terrorist attack, see ¶4715.

¶ 4720 Payment of taxes due—Form 1040-V.

The tax is due on the original due date for filing the return despite any extensions of time for *filing* the return. (Code Sec. 6151(a); Reg § 1.6151-1(a))[33] If IRS computes the tax, the tax due date is the later of the thirtieth day after the date IRS mails the tax bill or the tax return due date. (Reg § 1.6151-1(b))[34] The automatic filing extension for taxpayers with a tax home and abode, or in military service, outside the U.S. (¶4718), also extends the time for payment. (Reg § 1.6081-5(a))[35] For treatment of extension requests without full payment, see ¶4717.

Taxpayers with a balance due on a return can use a payment voucher Form 1040-V to make their payments, make a credit card payment by phone or by Internet, or make a payment using the electronic federal tax payment system (EFTPS).[36] Make tax payments by check or money order payable to the U.S. Treasury. Receipt of the check is payment, if the check is honored. IRS will accept personal checks or money orders drawn on any U.S. financial institution if the check or money order is payable in U.S. currency at par. Express, telegraphic, and similar money orders are also acceptable. (Reg § 301.6311-1)[37]

Taxes (including interest and penalties) also may be paid by any commercially acceptable means that IRS deems appropriate by regs, including credit or debit cards approved by IRS in the manner and in accordance with IRS forms, etc. (Code Sec. 6311(a), Code Sec. 6311(d)(1); Reg § 301.6311-2) Taxpayers can: (1) authorize IRS to debit their checking or savings account for the unpaid balance, or (2) make credit or debit card payments through tax software, by phone, or through the Internet. IRS doesn't set or collect any fees for credit or debit card payments, but convenience fees may be charged by these service providers: Official Payments Corp. (1-800-UPAY-TAX; www.officialpayments.com), RBS World Pay (1-888-9-PAYTAX; www.payUSAtax.com), and Link2Gov Corp. (1-888-PAY-1040 or on the Web at www.pay1040.com). All individuals, whether filing on paper or electronically, may use this system to charge taxes to American Express, Discover, VISA, or MasterCard accounts. The option to pay taxes by credit or debit card applies to payments with automatic extensions of time to file and to estimated tax payments. Taxpayers who charge a payment with an automatic extension request or who charge an estimated tax payment do not need to file the

28. ¶S-8007; ¶75,084; TD ¶138,018
29. ¶S-8502; ¶75,08A4; TD ¶868,531 *et seq.*
30. ¶S-8012; ¶75,08A4; TD ¶570,306
31. ¶S-8501.13; TD ¶570,317.4
32. ¶S-8001; ¶63,014.04; TD ¶904,001

33. ¶S-5451; ¶61,514; TD ¶570,226
34. ¶S-5454; ¶61,514
35. ¶S-5064; ¶60,814
36. ¶S-5454.1
37. ¶S-5752; ¶63,114; TD ¶559,802

respective paper Form 4868 or Form 1040-ES.[38]

Tax payment by credit or debit card is deemed made when the issuer properly authorizes the transaction, provided payment is actually received by IRS in the ordinary course of business and isn't returned due to error resolution processing. (Reg § 301.6311-2(b))[39]

Where quarterly estimated tax payments (¶3150) aren't necessary, payments are generally made with the individual's return (¶4716).[40]

¶ 4721   Extension of time for paying individual income tax—Form 1127.

Apply on Form 1127 for a reasonable extension of time (not to exceed 6 months, unless taxpayer is abroad) to pay the tax. (Code Sec. 6161(a)(1)) File on or before the date prescribed for payment of the tax. (Reg § 1.6161-1(c)) IRS grants extensions only on a satisfactory showing that payment on the due date will result in undue hardship (more than an inconvenience), e.g., that taxpayer would have to sell property at a great financial sacrifice (i.e., below fair market value) to pay the tax. (Reg § 1.6161-1(b))[41]

¶ 4722   Installment payments of individual income tax— Form 9465.

To request an agreement to pay installments, attach Form 9465 to the front of the balance-due return. A fee of $105 ($52 if the fee is directly debited from the taxpayer's bank account; and $43 for certain low-income taxpayers), (Reg § 300.1(b)),[42] interest and a late-payment penalty apply, see ¶4875.

IRS must enter into an installment agreement requested by an *individual* whose aggregate tax liability (without interest, penalties, additions to tax, and additional amounts) isn't more than $10,000; and who (or whose spouse for joint return liability) hasn't failed to file or to pay income tax, or entered into another installment agreement, during any of the preceding 5 tax years, if IRS determines that the taxpayer is financially unable to pay the liability in full when due (and the taxpayer submits information that IRS may require to make this determination). The agreement must require full payment within 3 years, and the taxpayer must agree to comply with all Code provisions while it's in effect. (Code Sec. 6159(c); Reg § 301.6159-1(c)) IRS grants installment agreement requests to taxpayers who agree to pay a balance due of $25,000 or less within a 5-year period, without requiring a collection manager's approval.[43]

IRS may (but isn't required to, except as noted above) enter into an agreement that allows a taxpayer to make payment of any tax in installments if it determines that the agreement will facilitate full or partial collection of the tax. (Code Sec. 6159(a); Reg § 301.6159-1(a)) IRS may disregard frivolous submissions of installment payment applications. (Code Sec. 7122(f))[44]

An individual who had an automatic 6-month extension of time to file without paying the tax estimated to be due (¶4717), but can't pay by the extended due date, should use Form 9465 to arrange an installment agreement.[45]

¶ 4723   Amended income tax returns—Form 1040X.

Amended income tax returns (on Form 1040X) may be filed to claim a refund (¶4851) after an original return has been filed if the period of limitations is open. (Reg § 301.6402-3(a)(2))[46] Amended returns can't be filed electronically.[47]

---

38. ¶S-5756.1A *et seq.*, ¶S-1629.1; ¶63,114; TD ¶559,803
39. ¶S-5756.4
40. ¶S-5200 *et seq.*
41. ¶S-5851; ¶61,614; TD ¶570,305
42. ¶T-10021; ¶61,594; TD ¶901,006

43. ¶V-5010 *et seq.*; ¶61,594; TD ¶901,006 *et seq.*
44. ¶V-5010; ¶61,594; TD ¶901,006
45. ¶s S-5020, V-5010 *et seq.*; ¶61,594; TD ¶570,227
46. ¶S-5151.5; ¶s 60,114.01, 64,024.15; TD ¶805,006
47. ¶S-1604; TD ¶572,011

¶ 4724 Corporate returns.

Every corporation that is subject to federal income tax, and that's in existence during any portion of a tax year, must file an income tax return for that year (or portion), regardless of the amount of its gross income or whether it has taxable income. (Code Sec. 6012(a)(2); Reg § 1.6012-2(a))[48] A corporation that has merely received a charter doesn't have to file if it furnishes a statement to IRS that it hasn't perfected its organization, has transacted no business, and has received no income from any source. (Reg § 1.6012-2(a)(2))[49]

After a corporation ceases business and dissolves, retaining no assets, it must make a return for that fractional part of the year during which it was in existence. But retention of even a small amount of cash keeps the corporation alive for filing purposes until the cash is distributed or paid. (Reg § 1.6012-2(a)(2))[50] A receiver, trustee in bankruptcy or dissolution, or assignee that has control and custody of all (or substantially all) of a corporation's business or property must make the return in the same manner as the corporation would. (Code Sec. 6012(b)(3))[1]

If a corporation fails to file a required return, IRS may make a return for it. (Code Sec. 6020)[2]

¶ 4725 Who signs corporate returns.

The return and all related documents requiring a signature on behalf of the corporation, must be signed by the president, vice-president, treasurer, assistant treasurer, chief accounting officer (controller) or any other officer duly authorized to sign. If a return is made for the corporation by a trustee, receiver or assignee, that fiduciary must sign. (Code Sec. 6062)[3]

¶ 4726 Corporate income tax forms—Form 1120.

Most domestic corporations file Form 1120 as their income tax return. (Reg § 1.6012-2(a)) Form 1120, Schedule PH must be attached if the corporation is a personal holding company (¶3323 *et seq.*). (Reg § 1.6012-2(b))[4] (For foreign corporation returns, see ¶4659.)

A regulated investment company (mutual fund) uses Form 1120-RIC,[5] a real estate investment trust, Form 1120-REIT,[6] a political organization, Form 1120-POL, a homeowners association, Form 1120-H,[7] and a designated settlement fund, Form 1120-DF.[8] Insurance companies use Form 1120L (life) or Form 1120-PC (property and casualty).[9]

An S corporation uses Form 1120S, which must show information on actual and constructive distributions to shareholders. (Code Sec. 6037(a); Reg § 1.6012-2(h)) The corporation must, on or before the date it files the return, furnish this information to anyone who was a shareholder during the tax year. (Code Sec. 6037(b))[10]

Small corporations (less than $250,000 in gross receipts and less than $250,000 in assets) don't have to complete Schedules L, M-1, and M-2 of Form 1120; or Schedules L and M-1 of Form 1120S.[11] Large corporations (reporting total assets of $10 million or more on Form 1120, Schedule L), must file the more detailed Schedule M-3 instead of M-1. M-3 filers must file Schedule B reporting information about allocations, transfers of interest, cost sharing arrangements, and changes in methods of accounting.[12]

---

48. ¶s S-1900, S-1901, S-1908; ¶60,124.03; TD ¶609,801
49. ¶S-1908; ¶60,124.03; TD ¶609,801
50. ¶S-1909; ¶60,124.03; TD ¶609,803
1. ¶S-2014; ¶60,124.04; TD ¶803,056
2. ¶S-1004; ¶60,204; TD ¶570,104
3. ¶S-4508; ¶60,614; TD ¶609,801.1
4. ¶s S-1902, S-1903; ¶60,124.03; TD ¶609,801
5. ¶S-1920; ¶8514.09

6. ¶S-1919; ¶8564.10
7. ¶S-1921, S-1922; ¶5284, ¶60,124; TD ¶609,811, TD ¶609,812
8. ¶S-1925; ¶468B4
9. ¶S-1904; ¶60,124.03; ¶8314
10. ¶s S-1905, S-1906; ¶60,374; TD ¶628,002
11. ¶S-1902; TD ¶609,806
12. ¶S-1902.1; TD ¶609,801

Beginning with the 2010 tax year, corporations (filing Form 1120), insurance companies (filing Form 1120L or Form 1120PC), and foreign corporations (filing Form 1120F) with both uncertain tax positions and at least $100 million of assets have to file Schedule UTP if they or a related party issued audited financial statements. Schedule UTP requires a concise description of each uncertain *federal* tax position for which the taxpayer or a related entity recorded a reserve on financial statements (or which no reserve was recorded because of an expectation to litigate). Tax positions taken *before 2010* do not have to be reported. A separate Form 8275 need not be filed to avoid accuracy-related penalties with respect to the tax position other than a reportable transaction. For 2010 tax years, IRS isn't making other entities filing Form 1120 series (e.g., REITs), pass-through entities, or tax-exempt organizations to file Schedule UTP. A corporation doesn't have to file Schedule UTP for a *short tax year* that ends in 2010. Schedule UTP is phased in over 5 years, the $100 million asset threshold is reduced to $50 million in 2012 and to $10 million in 2104. IRS has announced rules under which it will seek workpapers that document the completion of Schedule UTP.[13]

Electronic filing. A corporation that files at least 250 returns of any kind in the aggregate, including information returns, during the calendar year ending with or within its tax year must file its income tax return (all members of the Form 1120 and Form 1120S series of returns) electronically if it has assets of $10 million or more. Exemptions apply for forms that can't be filed electronically (e.g., a Form 1120 for a taxpayer that has changed its accounting period), and where IRS waives the requirement for undue hardship. To get a waiver, corporations file a written request complying with Notice 2010-13. All members of a controlled group must file electronically if the controlled group in the aggregate files at least 250 returns (including information returns). Failure to file electronically when required to do so is deemed to be a failure to file a return. (Reg § 301.6011-5)[14] For returns filed after 2009, IRS will allow a filer 10 calendar days from the date of first transmission to perfect a rejected e-file return for resubmission. For returns that can't be accepted for processing electronically, the filer generally has ten days to file a paper return. (Notice 2010-13)

¶ 4727 When and where to file corporate income tax returns.

Domestic corporations (including RICs, REITs, S corporations) must file their returns on or before the 15th day of the third month after the end of the tax year (Mar. 15 for a calendar year corporation). (Code Sec. 6072(b); Reg § 1.6037-1(b))[15] For extensions, see ¶4728.

"Short period" returns must be filed by the 15th day of the third month after the end of the short period. If a corporation dissolves and distributes all its assets, its final return is due by the 15th day of the third *full* month after the dissolution or liquidation.[16]

File as directed on the form's instructions. (Code Sec. 6091(b)(2)(A); Reg § 1.6091-2(c)) Hand-carried returns may be filed with any person assigned the responsibility to receive hand-carried returns in the local IRS office (i.e., the office in which the corporation has its principal place of business). (Code Sec. 6091(b)(4); Reg § 1.6091-2(d)(2))[17]

¶ 4728 Extensions for filing corporate returns—Form 7004.

Automatic six-month extensions—Form 7004. A corporation (including an S corporation, an affiliated group planning to file a consolidated return, see ¶3342, and a foreign corporation with a U.S. office) can get an automatic 6-month extension by filing a Form 7004 that shows its estimated tax liability by the original due date. (Reg § 1.6081-3)[18] But this won't extend the time for *paying* the tax, see ¶4729. (Reg § 1.6081-3(c))[19] IRS can terminate the extension

13. ¶S-4462.1; TD ¶816,030
14. ¶S-1941; ¶60,114.022
15. ¶S-4704; ¶s 60,374, 60,724
16. ¶S-4710; ¶60,724
17. ¶S-5104; ¶60,914
18. ¶S-5027 *et seq.*; ¶60,814.02; TD ¶609,802
19. ¶S-5027; ¶60,814.02; TD ¶609,802

on 10 days' notice. (Code Sec. 6081(b); Reg § 1.6081-3(d))[20]

Blanket extensions. A domestic corporation that transacts business and keeps its records outside the U.S. or Puerto Rico, or whose principal income is from sources within U.S. possessions, and a resident foreign corporation, may file its return up to the 15th day of the sixth month after the end of the tax year. A statement setting forth the qualifying facts must be attached to the return. (Reg § 1.6081-5(a)(2), Reg § 1.6081-5(a)(4), Reg § 1.6081-5(b))[21]

¶ 4729 Payment of corporate tax; extensions—Form 1127, Form 1138.

Pay in full on or before the due date (without extension) for filing the return (¶4727). (Code Sec. 6151(a))[22] For corporate estimated tax, see ¶3346 *et seq.*

Six-month extension for undue hardship—Form 1127. An extension (up to 6 months) for making a payment of corporate income tax may be granted by IRS at the taxpayer's request (on Form 1127) by the payment due date on a showing of undue hardship (¶4721). Late applications won't be considered. (Code Sec. 6161(a); Reg § 1.6161-1)[23]

Loss carryback expected—Form 1138. A corporation that expects a net operating loss in a current year can get an extension for paying the *preceding* year's tax based on the expected carryback (Code Sec. 6164(a)), by filing Form 1138. (Reg § 1.6164-1) The extension expires the last day of the month for filing the current year return or, if an application for a tentative carryback refund (Form 1139, see ¶4852) is filed before that date, on the date IRS sends notice that the refund is allowed or disallowed. (Code Sec. 6164(d))[24]

¶ 4730 Tax deposits—Form 8109.

Unless an exemption applies, a corporation has to make electronic deposits of all depository taxes using the Electronic Federal Tax Payment System (EFTPS) if the aggregate annual deposits of certain taxes by the corporation exceed $200,000 or if the corporation was required to use EFTPS in 2009. For EFTPS deposits to be timely, the corporation has to initiate the transaction at least 1 business day before the deposit is due. (Reg § 31.6302-1(h)(2)(ii))[25]

Corporations that aren't required to use EFTPS must make their income and estimated tax payments by depositing them with an authorized depositary by the return due date (¶4727) (Code Sec. 6302; Reg § 1.6302-1(a))[26] and report the deposits on the return.[27] For the requirement to make tax deposits by electronic funds transfer (EFT), see ¶3029. Deposits not made by electronic funds transfer must be accompanied by Form 8109 deposit coupons (but, IRS will no longer maintain the paper coupon system after 2010).[28] Deposits are timely if mailed (¶4754) at least 2 days before the due date. (Code Sec. 7502(e)(2))[29]

¶ 4731 Partnership income tax return—Form 1065, Schedule K-1; Form 7004.

Partnerships (except foreign partnerships with no or de minimis U.S. source gross income and no gross income effectively connected with a U.S. trade or business) (Reg § 1.6031(a)-1(b))) must file Form 1065 (Form 1065-B for electing large partnerships) to report gross income and deductions for the tax year. (Code Sec. 6031(a), Code Sec. 6031(e); Reg § 1.6031(a)-1(a))[30] Certain tax-exempt bond partnerships are exempt from this requirement.[31] (Reg § 1.6031(a)-1(a)(3)(ii)) A foreign partnership that is otherwise exempt from filing must file a return to make any partnership election, (Reg § 1.6031(a)-1(b)) and a foreign or domestic partnership must file to elect out of the Code's partnership rules.

20. ¶S-5009; ¶60,814.02
21. ¶S-5064; ¶60,814.01
22. ¶S-5451; ¶61,514
23. ¶S-5850 *et seq.*; ¶61,614; TD ¶659,018
24. ¶S-5865 *et seq.*; ¶61,644; TD ¶804,016 *et seq.*
25. ¶S-5623; ¶63,014; TD ¶559,853
26. ¶s S-5601, S-5604, S-5607; ¶63,014; TD ¶609,202
27. ¶S-5601
28. ¶S-5601; ¶63,014; TD ¶609,202
29. ¶T-10777; ¶s 63,014, 75,024
30. ¶S-2701; ¶60,314; TD ¶596,001
31. ¶S-2708

(Reg § 1.6031(a)-1(c))

A partnership needn't file a partnership return for any period before it has taxable income or incurs deductible expenses. (Reg § 1.6031(a)-1(a)(3))[32] Nor does it file if it doesn't have any gross income that is effectively connected with the conduct of a U.S. trade or business, or any U.S. source gross income. (Reg § 1.6031(a)-1(b)(1))[33]

Form 1065 must be filed by the 15th day of the fourth month after the end of the partnership's tax year (Apr. 15 for a calendar year partnership). (Code Sec. 6072(a))[34] For an automatic 5-month extension of time for filing a partnership return, use Form 7004. The extension doesn't extend the time for filing a partner's return. (Reg § 1.6081-2T)[35]

Every partnership required to file a return must furnish (by its tax return due date, with extensions) Form 1065, Schedule K-1, containing information from the return to every person who was a partner (or who held a partnership interest as a nominee for another person) at any time during the partnership's tax year. The Form 1065, Schedule K-1 has to indicate whether a partner contributed built-in gain or loss property during the tax year. An "electing large partnership" (¶3702) must provide this information by Mar. 15th following the end of its tax year. (Code Sec. 6031(b); Reg § 1.6031(b)-1T(a))[36] (The nominee must in turn give the information it gets to the other person (Code Sec. 6031(c)(2); Reg § 1.6031(c)-1T(h)) and furnish the partnership with specified information about that person.) (Code Sec. 6031(c)(1); Reg § 1.6031(c)-1T(a))[37]

Certain large partnerships must file Form 1065, Schedule M-3 instead of Form 1065, Schedule M-1. M-3 filers must complete Form 1065, Schedule C to report related party transactions, allocations, transfers of interest, cost sharing arrangements and changes in accounting methods.[38]

Electronic filing requirement. Partnerships with more than 100 partners must file Form 1065 and Form 1065, Schedule K-1 electronically, unless IRS excludes them from electronic filing. Hardship waivers are available. (Reg § 301.6011-3)[39]

¶ 4732   Returns of trusts and estates—Form 1041, Schedule K-1, Form 7004, etc.

Trusts (¶4733) and estates (¶4734) must file income tax and information returns.[40]

If there are *joint* fiduciaries, a return by one will suffice if he states in the return that he has sufficient knowledge of the facts to make the return and that it is true to the best of his knowledge and belief. (Reg § 1.6012-3(c))[41]

The fiduciary who prepares the income tax return filed by the trust or estate must furnish to beneficiaries (or their nominees) receiving distributions or to whom an income item is allocated, a Form 1041, Schedule K-1 or a substitute that contains the same information. This must be furnished on or before a return is filed with IRS, and a copy must be filed with Form 1041. (Code Sec. 6034A(a)) (If a nominee is given this information, he must furnish it to his beneficiary, and he must furnish to the estate or trust specified information about the beneficiary.) (Code Sec. 6034A(b))[42]

Income tax returns that must be filed by estates, domestic trusts, and foreign trusts having an office or place of business in the U.S. must be filed on or before the 15th day of the fourth month following the end of the tax year. (Reg § 1.6072-1(a)(1)) Foreign trusts and estates of nonresident aliens that don't have an office or place of business in the U.S. must file on or before the 15th day of the sixth month following the end of the tax year. (Reg § 1.6072-1(c))[43]

---

32. ¶S-2701; ¶60,314; TD ¶596,001
33. ¶S-2717.1; ¶60,314
34. ¶S-4923; ¶60,724; TD ¶596,016
35. ¶S-5030; ¶60,814; TD ¶596,017
36. ¶S-2710; ¶60,314; TD ¶596,008
37. ¶S-2740; ¶60,314; TD ¶596,014

38. ¶S-1902.1
39. ¶S-1350 *et seq.*; ¶60,114.065; TD ¶596,025
40. ¶s S-2004, S-2007; ¶60,124.04; TD ¶659,000
41. ¶S-2002; ¶60,124.04; TD ¶659,001
42. ¶s S-2019, S-2020; ¶60,34A4; TD ¶659,011
43. ¶S-4707; ¶60,724; TD ¶667,002, TD ¶659,013

Trusts (¶4733) and estates (¶4734) get an automatic 5-month extension to file Form 1041 by filing Form 7004 showing the full amount properly estimated as tax by the trust's return due date. A trust's or an estate's automatic extension doesn't extend the beneficiary's return due date. (Reg § 1.6081-6T)[44] IRS can terminate a trust's or an estate's automatic extension on 10 days' notice. (Reg § 1.6081-6T(a))[45] *Payment* extensions must be separately applied for under the rules at ¶4721.

¶ 4733 Income tax returns of trusts—Form 1041; Form 1041–A.

A trustee must file on Form 1041 if the trust isn't tax-exempt and if the trust has: (a) any taxable income for the year; (b) gross income of $600 or more; or (c) any beneficiary who is a nonresident alien. (Code Sec. 6012(a)(4), Code Sec. 6012(a)(5))[46]

Trust income taxable to the grantor or other "owner" must be reported on a separate statement attached to Form 1041, except that alternative reporting methods are available, if certain requirements are met. The alternatives available depend on whether the trust is treated as owned by 1 grantor, or by 2 or more grantors (which in the latter case may require a Form 1099 to be provided by the trustee along with a statement showing trust income items, deductions and credits). (Reg § 1.671-4(b))[47]

Split-interest trusts must file Form 1041-A even if the trust must currently distribute all net income. (Code Sec. 6034(a))[48]

¶ 4734 Income tax returns of estates—Form 1041.

The executor or administrator must file Form 1041 if gross income for the estate's tax year is $600 or more (Code Sec. 6012(a)(3)) *or* if any beneficiary is a nonresident alien. (Code Sec. 6012(a); Reg § 1.6012-3(a)(1)(iii))[49] A fiduciary doesn't have to file a copy of the will for income tax purposes unless IRS *requests* a copy. (Reg § 1.6012-3(a)(2))[50]

The executor who probates the entire will (in the state the decedent was domiciled) files Form 1041 reporting all the income. Any out-of-state (i.e., ancillary) executor *also* files a Form 1041, but it shows only the gross income received by the ancillary fiduciary and the deductions attributable to that income. (Reg § 1.6012-3(a)(3))[1]

¶ 4735 Extension for making elections.

Two automatic extensions are available for taxpayer elections, if the taxpayer takes corrective action within the extension period:

(1) An automatic *12-month extension* for certain regulatory elections specified in Reg § 301.9100-2(a)(2). The more widely applicable ones are: the election to use a tax year other than the required tax year (¶2813); the election to use the LIFO inventory method (¶2874), and the election to adjust basis on partnership transfers and distributions (¶3780). The extension is available regardless of whether the taxpayer timely filed its return for the year the election should have been made. (Reg § 301.9100-2(a)(1))[2]

(2) An automatic *6-month extension* for regulatory elections and statutory elections which are required to be made by the due date of the return or the due date of the return *including extensions,* for taxpayers who timely filed the return for the year in which the election should have been made. (Reg § 301.9100-2(b))[3]

Nonautomatic extensions of time are available for regulatory elections that don't qualify for

44. ¶S-5032; ¶60,814.05; TD ¶659,014; TD ¶667,004
45. ¶S-5009; ¶60,814.05
46. ¶S-2007; ¶60,124.04; TD ¶659,003
47. ¶S-2009 *et seq.*; ¶6714; TD ¶659,004
48. ¶S-2806; ¶60,344

49. ¶S-2004; ¶60,124.04; TD ¶667,001
50. ¶S-2006; ¶60,124.04; TD ¶667,009
1. ¶S-2005; ¶60,124.04; TD ¶667,008
2. ¶S-4819; ¶78,054.02
3. ¶S-4821; ¶78,054.02

an automatic extension, if the taxpayer shows IRS that he acted reasonably and in good faith, and that granting relief won't prejudice IRS's interests. (Reg § 301.9100-3(a)) A request for a nonautomatic extension is generally a request for a letter ruling, and is submitted under those procedures, with the applicable user fee. (Reg § 301.9100-3(e)(5))[4]

The grant of an extension of time to make an election isn't a determination that the taxpayer is otherwise eligible to make the election. (Reg § 301.9100-1(a))[5]

¶ 4736　Income tax returns of individual bankruptcy estates—Form 1041.

The debtor-in-possession or trustee, if one is appointed, for a bankruptcy estate for an individual under Chapter 7 or 11 must file an income tax return (Form 1041) if the estate's gross income equals at least the sum of the exemption amount plus the basic standard deduction for unmarried taxpayers who weren't surviving spouses or heads of household. (Code Sec. 6012(a)(8), Code Sec. 6012(a)(9)) This amount is $9,350 for 2010 ($9,500 for 2011).[6]

¶ 4737　Information returns—Form 1099, etc. and filing dates.

Taxpayers must report certain of their activities with third parties on prescribed returns and statements. These information returns are filed with IRS and in some cases furnished to the third parties.[7] For electronic filing, see ¶4753.

Payors (including nominees, see ¶4738) report their payments for a calendar year by filing an appropriate Form 1099 (or permitted substitute form) for payee (with a Form 1096 transmittal statement) after Sept. 30 of the calendar year of the payment (but not before the payor's final payments for the year) and on or before the next Feb. 28. (Reg § 1.6042-2(c), Reg § 1.6044-2(d), Reg § 1.6049-1(c))[8] However, returns filed electronically aren't due until Mar. 31 after the end of the calendar year to which they relate. (Code Sec. 6071(b); Reg § 31.6071(a)-1(a)(3)(i))[9] For filing extension, see ¶4746. For payee statements, see ¶4742.

¶ 4738　Nominees and middleman returns.

If reportable interest or dividends are paid to any person who, as middleman or nominee, then pays them over to the actual (or beneficial) owner, the original payor (corporation, bank, etc.) must file an information return (Form 1099) with respect to the nominee, who must file another Form 1099 with respect to the actual or beneficial owner. (Code Sec. 6042(a)(1)(B), Code Sec. 6049(a)(2); Reg § 1.6042-2(a)(1)(iii), Reg § 1.6049-4(b)(3))[10]

A nominee is any payee who isn't the actual owner of the dividend or interest, but who would be required to furnish his taxpayer identification number (¶4752) to the payor for inclusion on the *payor's* return. Nominees include banks, trust companies, etc., and, with respect to dividends, dealers and brokers. (Reg § 1.6042-2(a)(2), Reg § 1.6049-1(a)(2))[11] Special reporting rules also apply for payments to joint payees (Reg § 1.6041-1(c)); and payments on behalf of another. (Reg § 1.6041-1(e))

¶ 4739　Dividend reporting—Form 1099-DIV, Form 5452, Form 1099-PATR.

A payor (including nominees, see ¶4738) must file a Form 1099-DIV for each person to whom it pays "reportable" dividends aggregating $10 or more during the calendar year. (Code Sec. 6042(a), Reg § 1.6042-2(a)(1)) Dividends qualifying for preferential tax rates must be differentiated from nonqualified dividends.[12] For payee statements, see ¶4742.

---

4. ¶S-4823; ¶78,054.02
5. ¶S-4815.1; ¶78,054.02
6. ¶C-9700 *et seq.*, S-2016; ¶60,124; TD ¶578,021
7. ¶s S-2900 *et seq.*, S-4930; TD ¶811,000
8. ¶S-4930; ¶s 60,424, 60,494; TD ¶811,003
9. ¶S-1305; ¶S-4930; ¶60,414.06
10. ¶S-2904 *et seq.*; ¶s 60,424, 60,494; TD ¶811,007
11. ¶s S-2904 *et seq.*, S-3003 *et seq.*; ¶s 60,424, 60,494; TD ¶811,008
12. ¶S-2901; ¶60,424; TD ¶811,001

Reportable dividends are corporate "dividends" (¶1287 *et seq.*) and substitute dividends (e.g., payments in lieu of dividends that brokers pay on short sales). (Code Sec. 6042(b)(1))[13] Nontaxable dividends are reported on Form 5452.[14]

Cooperatives (¶4206) report *patronage dividends* aggregating $10 or more to any payee in a calendar year on Form 1099-PATR. (Code Sec. 6044(a)(1); Reg § 1.6044-2(b))[15]

¶ 4740 Reporting interest—Form 1099-INT.

Every person (including nominees, see ¶4738) who pays $10 or more of reportable interest to any person (except certain payees) in a calendar year must report the payments (Code Sec. 6049(a)(1), Code Sec. 6049(d)) on Form 1099-INT.[16] For payee statements, see ¶4742.

Reportable interest is interest on: (a) obligations issued publicly or in registered form (other than a short-term obligation held by a corporation), (b) deposits with banks or brokers, and (c) amounts held by insurance or investment companies. (Code Sec. 6049(b)(1))[17] Reportable interest also includes original issue discount (¶4741); amounts includible in gross income with respect to regular real estate mortgage investment conduits interests (¶4204) (Code Sec. 6049(d)(6)(A)(i), Code Sec. 6049(d)(7)(A));[18] and interest paid on tax-exempt bonds. But interest on obligations issued by a natural person isn't "reportable." (Code Sec. 6049(b)(2))[19]

¶ 4741 Reporting original issue discount (OID)—Form 1099-OID, Form 8281.

Original issue discount (OID) of $10 or more on any obligation must be reported by the issuer (or nominee, see ¶4738) as a payment of interest. (Code Sec. 6049(d)(6)) Form 1099-OID is used to report the OID, and any interest actually paid on the obligation.[20] In addition, Form 8281must be filed by certain issuers of publicly-offered debt instruments having OID, within 30 days after issuance. (Code Sec. 1275(c)(2); Reg § 1.1275-3(c))[21]

⚫/observation: The one-time reporting requirement on Form 8281 is in addition to the annual information reporting on Form 1099-OID.

¶ 4742 Payee statements—Form 1099.

Payors of reportable dividends (and payments in lieu of dividends) and interest (including OID) must furnish payees with specified written statements of the amount reported to IRS (i.e., Copy B of Form 1099 sent to IRS). This generally must be done, either in person or in a "statement mailing," on or before Jan. 31 of the year following the calendar year for which the payor's Form 1099 was required. (Reg § 1.6042-4(d)(1), Reg § 1.6044-5(b), Reg § 1.6049-3(c)(1)) However, if payees consent, Form 1099 statements may be furnished electronically.[22]

¶ 4743 Business payments of $600 or more—Form 1099-MISC.

With limited exceptions, every person, corporate or otherwise, engaged in a trade or business who, in the course of that business, makes payments aggregating $600 or more to another person (e.g., an independent contractor) in a calendar year must file an information return (Form 1099-MISC) setting forth the name and address of the payee and the amount paid, and furnish a statement to the payee. Reportable payments are: rent, salaries, wages, premiums, annuities, compensations, remunerations, emoluments, or other fixed or determinable gains, profits and income. For payments made after 2011, reporting also applies to gross proceeds paid in consideration for property or services. (Code Sec. 6041; Reg § 1.6041-

13. ¶S-2910, ¶S-3724; ¶60,424; TD ¶811,010
14. ¶S-2914; ¶60,424; TD ¶811,012
15. ¶S-2951; ¶60,444; TD ¶811,021
16. ¶S-3001 *et seq.*; ¶60,494; TD ¶811,501
17. ¶S-3011 *et seq.*, ¶S-3023 *et seq.*; ¶60,494; TD ¶811,512
18. ¶s S-3073, S-3087; ¶60,494; TD ¶811,537.
19. ¶s S-3040, S-3042; ¶60,494; TD ¶811,523
20. ¶s S-3073, S-3074; ¶60,494; TD ¶811,530
21. ¶S-3080 *et seq.*; ¶12,714.06; TD ¶811,536
22. ¶S-2927 *et seq.*; ¶s 60,424, 60,444, 60,494; TD ¶811,015

1)[23] A payor also has to report taxable prizes and awards of $600 or more (that aren't paid for services rendered) on Form 1099-MISC.[24]

This rule doesn't apply to transactions covered by other information return rules (e.g., for dividends, see ¶4739), or most payments to corporations (for payments made before Dec. 12, 2011). (Reg § 1.6041-3)[25] For payments made after Dec. 31, 2011, notwithstanding any IRS reg issued before Mar. 23, 2010, for purposes of reporting business payments, a person includes any corporation that is not exempt from tax under Code Sec. 501(a). (Code Sec. 6041(h))[26] For payments made after 2011, IRS can prescribe regs, etc. as may be appropriate or necessary to carry out the purposes of these rules, including rules to prevent duplicative reporting. (Code Sec. 6041(i))[27]

IRS has issued guidance on how the above requirements may be met for payments made with credit cards or debit cards.[28]

¶ 4744　Mortgage interest (and points) received—Form 1098.

A person ("interest recipient") who receives interest, or reimburses interest overpayments, aggregating $600 or more for a calendar year on a mortgage must report (on Form 1098) those receipts or reimbursements, even if the interest is received on behalf of another. This applies to any person (including cooperative housing corporations) who, in the course of his trade or business (except governmental recipients), receives interest on a mortgage secured all or in part by real property, where the payor of record is an individual. (Code Sec. 6050H; Reg § 1.6050H-1, Reg § 1.6050H-2(a))[29] The return must also include any points received in the year that were paid directly by the buyer (including certain points paid by or charged to the seller). (Code Sec. 6050H(b)(2)(C); Reg § 1.6050H-1(f))[30]

¶ 4745　Other information returns.

...*Abandonment or foreclosure of property held as security* for a business loan must be reported by the lender on Form 1099-A (Code Sec. 6050J; Reg § 1.6050J-1T) (unless related to a discharge of debt reported on Form 1099-C, below).[31]

...*Accelerated death benefits* paid to any individual must be reported by the payor (Code Sec. 6050Q) on Form 1099-LTC.[32]

...*Acquiring corporation in taxable acquisition* must file information returns with IRS and furnish statements to shareholders if a shareholder of the acquired corporation recognizes gain or loss in whole or in part due to the acquisition. (Code Sec. 6043A(a))[33]

...*Alcohol and biodiesel fuel tax benefits, Code Sec. 34 credit for farming, off-highway and certain other nontaxable uses of fuel*—information return required by persons claiming alcohol or biodiesel fuel tax benefits or a Code Sec. 34 credit, providing information on the benefits or credit. (Code Sec. 4104(a))[34]

...*Attorney's fees* paid in the course of a trade or business that aren't reportable as wages or under Code Sec. 6041 (¶4743) (or would have to be reported under Code Sec. 6041 but for the $600 limitation), whether or not the services are performed for the payor (Code Sec. 6045(f); Reg § 1.6045-5) and whether or not the attorney is the exclusive payee, on Form 1099-MISC. (Reg § 1.6045-5)[35]

...*Banks and online payment networks* ("payment settlement entities") will have to report

23. ¶S-3655 et seq.; ¶s 60,414, 60,414.06; TD ¶814,001
24. ¶S-3658; TD ¶814,002
25. ¶S-3676; ¶60,414.06; TD ¶814,001
26. ¶S-3656.A1; ¶60,414.035; TD ¶814,001.A1
27. ¶S-3656.A2; ¶60,414.035; TD ¶814,001.A2
28. ¶S-3656.1, J-9325; ¶34,064
29. ¶S-3901 et seq.; ¶60,50H4; TD ¶814,054
30. ¶S-3907 et seq.; TD ¶814,065
31. ¶S-4200 et seq.; ¶60,50J4; TD ¶816,001
32. ¶S-3440; ¶60,50Q4
33. ¶S-4317; ¶6043A4; TD ¶815,010
34. ¶S-4466; ¶41,044
35. ¶S-3851; ¶60,454.06; TD ¶814,087

credit card sales to IRS and participating merchants on Form 1099-K for calendar years beginning after 2010. (Code Sec. 6050W) Persons required to make these returns can match TINs under IRS procedures.[36]

... *Barter exchanges* through which at least 100 exchanges of property or services are made during the calendar year report each exchange on Form 1099-B. (Code Sec. 6045; Reg § 1.6045-1(e))[37]

... *Brokers* must report each sale of securities, commodities, and forwards or futures contracts the broker effects for its customers, on Form 1099-B. (Code Sec. 6045; Reg § 1.6045-1(c), Reg § 1.6045-2)[38] For options granted or acquired after 2012, brokers will have to report information relating to the lapse of, or a closing transaction with respect to, an option on certain securities. (Code Sec. 6045(h))[39] For real estate reporting persons, see below. brokers also must report customer's adjusted basis and character of gain or loss for sales of certain securities acquired after 2010. (Code Sec. 6045(g))[40] Also, brokers that transfer "covered securities" (as defined in Code Sec. 6045(g)(3)) to other brokers will have to provide statements to other brokers starting 2011. (Code Sec. 6045A)[41]

... *Cash of more than $10,000,* including certain cash equivalents (e.g., cashier's checks, foreign currency) received in connection with a trade or business must be reported by the recipient (Code Sec. 6050I(a), Code Sec. 6050I(d); Reg § 1.6050I-1(a)(1), Reg § 1.6050I-1(c)(1)) within 15 days after receipt. Use Form 8300 (Reg § 1.6050I-1(e)), except that banks file Form 4789 and casinos, under special rules (Reg § 1.6050I-1(d)(2)) file Form 8362 (certain Nevada casinos file Form 8852) to report cash from gaming activities.[42] Special rules apply for cash installment payments. (Reg § 1.6050I-1(b))[43]

... *Change in control or recapitalization of a corporation* generally must be reported on Form 8806 showing the parties to the transaction, the fees involved, the changes in capital structure and any other information IRS requires. (Code Sec. 6043(c))[44]

... *Charitable organization required to acknowledge gift of auto, plane, or boat* (¶2139) must provide the information required on Form 1098-C to IRS. (Code Sec. 170(f)(12)(D))[45]

... *Charitable property disposition* by the donee within 3 years of contribution must be reported on Form 8282 by the charity, if the deduction claimed for the property exceeds $5,000 (but disposition of items appraised for $500 or less doesn't have to be reported). (Code Sec. 6050L; Reg § 1.6050L-1)[46]

... *Commodity Credit Corporation (CCC)* must report market gain associated with the repayment of a CCC loan, regardless of whether the taxpayer repays the loan with cash or uses CCC certificates in repayment of the loan, on Form 1099-G. (Code Sec. 6039J)[47]

... *Direct sales of consumer goods* of $5,000 or more to any 1 buyer in a calendar year must be reported by the seller (Code Sec. 6041A) on Form 1099-MISC.[48]

... *Discharge of debt (including student loans) by banks, and certain other financial entities and organizations that have a significant lending trade or business* of $600 or more must be reported to IRS, on Form 1099-C. (Code Sec. 6050P; Reg § 1.6050P-1, Reg § 1.6050P-2)[49]

... *Donee of qualified intellectual property* (¶2106) must file annual information return (Form 8899) of net income from property for each specified tax year of the donee. (Code Sec. 6050L(b)(1); Reg § 1.6050L-2)[50]

... *Education-related payments* received (or billed) by higher education institutions for qualified tuition and related expenses; qualified tuition refunded to an individual (Form

36. ¶S-3699.18; ¶60,50W4; TD ¶814,088
37. ¶S-3700 *et seq.*; ¶60,454; TD ¶814,037
38. ¶S-3700 *et seq.*; ¶60,454; TD ¶814,023
39. ¶S-3747; ¶60,454.08; TD ¶814,207
40. ¶S-3741 *et seq.*; ¶60,454.08; TD ¶814,201
41. ¶S-3761 *et seq.*; ¶60,45A4; TD ¶814,301
42. ¶S-4000 *et seq.*; ¶60,50I4 *et seq.*; TD ¶814,074
43. ¶S-4019 *et seq.*; ¶60,50I4.02; TD ¶814,084

44. ¶S-4308; ¶60,434; TD ¶815,006
45. ¶K-3948.1; ¶S-2872.1
46. ¶S-2873; ¶60,50L4; TD ¶688,033
47. ¶N-1171.1; ¶60,39J4
48. ¶S-3677; ¶60,41A4; TD ¶814,020
49. ¶S-4251 *et seq.*; ¶60,50P4; TD ¶816,008
50. ¶S-2882.1; ¶60,50L4; TD ¶688,042

1098-T) (Reg § 1.6050S-1); and interest of $600 or more received from an individual for a calendar year on an educational loan (Form 1098-E) must be reported. (Code Sec. 6050S; Reg § 1.6050S-3)[1] In general, for educational loans, lenders must also report amounts (in addition to all other interest paid) attributable to capitalized interest and loan origination fees.[2] Statements to students and borrowers may be provided electronically if conditions are met. (Reg § 1.6050S-2(a)(1), Reg § 1.6050S-4(a))[3]

... *Employer-owned life insurance contracts* issued after Aug. 17, 2006, must be reported on Form 8925 by applicable policyholders. (Code Sec. 6039I)[4]

... *Education savings distributions* (certain) from Coverdell ESAs[5] and qualified tuition programs or 529 plans are reported on Form 1099-Q.[6]

... *Executors* of estates of decedents dying after 2009 must report (with the decedent's final income tax return (¶4714), or later as specified by regs (Code Sec. 6075(a))) information including the adjusted basis, decedents' holding period, and recipients of certain large property transfers at death. (Code Sec. 6018)[7]

☑/caution: For EGTRRA sunset rules, see ¶1114.

... *Fishing boat operators* must report on Form 1099-MISC certain crew payments. (Code Sec. 6050A; Reg § 1.6050A-1)[8]

... *Fish purchased for resale* for cash are reported on Form 1099-MISC for each seller by every person engaged in the trade or business of purchasing fish for resale. (Code Sec. 6050R)[9]

... *Foreign financial accounts* must be reported on Form TD F 90-22.1 (FBAR) by any person with a financial interest in or signature authority over the account, if the aggregate value of these accounts exceeds $10,000 at any time during the calendar year. FBAR is due by June 30 of the year following the year that the account holder meets the $10,000 threshold. Persons with signature authority over, but no financial interest in, a foreign account have until June 30, *2011* to file the FBAR that otherwise would have been due on June 30, 2010.[10]

... *Gift tax return filers* must furnish donees a written statement with information about the return filer and the gift property for post-2009 transfers. (Code Sec. 6019(b))[11]

☑/caution: For EGTRRA sunset rules, see ¶1114.

... *IRA (and Roth IRA) contributions and withdrawals* must be reported by the IRA trustees or issuer (Code Sec. 408(i), Code Sec. 408A(d)(3)(D)), on Form 5498.[12] The trustee also must report on Form 5498 that a minimum distribution is required (but not the amount) for a calendar year. (Reg § 1.408-8, Q&10)[13] For required distributions, additional information must be provided to the IRA owner by Jan. 31 of the required distribution year.[14]

... *Issuers* of specified securities (i.e., stocks, bonds, commodity contracts, and other financial instruments) have to provide information starting in 2011 about organizational actions (e.g., stock splits, mergers, acquisitions, etc.) that affect basis. (Code Sec. 6045B)

... *Liquidating corporations* report the adoption of the plan of liquidation on Form 966,[15] and liquidating distributions (Code Sec. 6043(a)) on Form 1099-DIV.[16]

... *Long-term care payments* made under a long-term care insurance contract to any individual must be reported by the payor (Code Sec. 6050Q) on Form 1099-LTC.[17]

1. ¶S-3430 *et seq.*; ¶60,50S4; TD ¶816,500 *et seq.*
2. ¶S-3436; ¶60,50S4.01
3. ¶S-1370; ¶60,50S4.01
4. ¶S-3246; ¶60,39I4
5. ¶S-3428
6. ¶S-3422; TD ¶147,110
7. ¶S-2310; ¶60,184.03
8. ¶S-3695; ¶60,50A4; TD ¶816,024
9. ¶S-3695.1; ¶60,50R4
10. ¶S-3650; ¶60,114.06
11. ¶S-2206; ¶60,194; TD ¶746,006.1
12. ¶S-3391; ¶4084.04; TD ¶813,032
13. ¶S-3392.1; ¶4084.04; TD ¶813,033.1
14. ¶S-3392.2; ¶4084.04; TD ¶813,033.1
15. ¶S-4314; ¶60,434; TD ¶815,009
16. ¶S-4315; ¶60,434; TD ¶815,009
17. ¶S-3440; ¶60,50Q4

. . . *Medical savings account and health savings account contributions and distributions* must be reported by the trustee on Form 5498-SA and Form 1099-SA. (Code Sec. 220(h))[18]

. . . *Mortgage credit certificate* (MCC) information is reported (on Form 8329) by each person who makes a "certified indebtedness" loan under an MCC program. (Reg § 1.25-8T(a))[19] Each state or political subdivision with MCC programs reports (on Form 8330) the amount of MCCs issued each quarter. (Code Sec. 25(g); Reg § 1.25-4T)[20]

. . .

Mortgage insurance premiums aggregating $600 or more for any calendar year must be reported on Form 1098 by any person who, in the course of a trade or business, received the premiums. (Code Sec. 6050H(h)(1), Reg § 1.6050H-3T)[21]

. . . *Outbound Code Sec. 355 distributions* (¶3559) and outbound Code Sec. 332 corporate liquidations (Reg § 1.6038B-1(e))[22] are reported on Form 926.

. . . *Parent tax-exempt organizations* that are controlling organizations (under Code Sec. 512(b)(3)) report transactions with controlled entities on Form 990-T. (Code Sec. 6033(h))[23]

. . . *Partnership interest sales or exchanges* attributable to unrealized receivables, inventory, collectibles, or Code Sec. 1250 gain are reported by partnerships on Form 8308. (Code Sec. 6050K; Reg § 1.1(h)-1(e), Reg § 1.6050K-1(a)(1))[24] The partnership doesn't have to file until it's notified of the exchange (Code Sec. 6050K(c)(2)), i.e., when it either receives written notification required from the transferor, or has knowledge of it. (Reg § 1.6050K-1)[25]

. . . *Pension, profit-sharing plans* file annual return/report forms in the Form 5500 series (Code Sec. 6058(a)),[26] file Form 5310A to notify IRS of a merger, consolidation or division of the plan, (Code Sec. 6057(b)(4))[27] and make returns and reports of designated Roth contributions. (Code Sec. 6047(f))[28] Certain 1-participant plans with total assets of $250,000 or less are exempt from filing the annual return.[29] All annual reports—including any accompanying statements and schedules—are filed electronically with DOL and in a format that can be displayed on the Internet.[30]

. . . *Political organizations* except for certain state and local committees under Code Sec. 527 must file an initial notice of status (Form 8871) (Code Sec. 527(i))[31], and periodic reports of contributions and expenditures (Form 8872) (Code Sec. 527(j)(2)), which can be filed on-line at www.irs.gov/polorgs with an IRS-supplied user ID and password).[32]

. . . *Real estate* reporting persons (as specially defined) must report real estate transactions on Form 1099-S, including the sale of a condominium unit or stock in a cooperative housing unit. For a transaction involving a residence, the return must include any portion of real property tax treated as imposed on the buyer. Reporting isn't required for sales of principal residences for $250,000 or less ($500,000 or less for married sellers) (regs can permit higher amounts) if the reporting person receives specified written assurances (on IRS's certification form) from the seller by Jan. 31 following the year of sale. (Code Sec. 6045(e); Reg § 1.6045-4)[33] Reportable real estate transactions also include sales or exchanges (completed after May 28, 2009) of standing timber for lump-sum payments. (Reg § 1.6045-4(b)(2)(i)(E), Reg § 1.6045-4(s))[34]

. . . *Refunds of state and local income tax* of $10 or more must be reported by the state or

---

18. ¶H-1328.1; ¶2204.02; TD ¶288,105
19. ¶S-4206; ¶254.02; TD ¶816,011
20. ¶S-4207; ¶254.02; TD ¶816,012
21. ¶S-3923; ¶60,50H4; TD ¶814,074.1
22. ¶S-3640.1; ¶S-3640.1A
23. ¶S-2862.2; ¶60,334
24. ¶S-2725 *et seq.*; ¶60,50K4; TD ¶591,019
25. ¶S-2734 *et seq.*; ¶60,50K4; TD ¶591,022
26. ¶S-3351; ¶s 4014.01, 60,584; TD ¶813,001

27. ¶s S-3383, S-3384; ¶s 4014.01, 60,574; TD ¶813,028
28. ¶S-3400.1
29. ¶S-3357; TD ¶813,010
30. ¶S-3400.1
31. ¶S-2858.7
32. ¶S-2858.9
33. ¶S-3800 *et seq.*; ¶60,454.04; TD ¶814,040 *et seq.*
34. ¶S-3813; ¶60,454.04; TD ¶814,045

local tax authority/payor on Form 1099-G. (Code Sec. 6050E; Reg § 1.6050E-1)[35]

... *Royalty payments* that aggregate $10 or more per year per payee (including nominees) must be reported unless the payee is a corporation, exempt organization or government (Code Sec. 6050N), on Form 1099-MISC. Where a publisher pays royalties to an author's agent and the agent subtracts his commission and expenses, both parties must report the gross royalties on Form 1099-MISC, unreduced by the subtracted amounts.[36]

... *Stock transfers under incentive stock options (ISOs) and employee stock purchase plans (ESPPs)* have to be reported by corporations on Form 3921. (Code Sec. 6039(a); Reg § 1.6039-1)[37]

... *Sick pay* (nonwage) paid by a third party to an employee must be reported by the third party to the employee's employer. (Code Sec. 6051(f)(1); Reg § 31.6051-3(a))[38]

... *Simplified employee pension (SEP) contributions* must be reported by the SEP trustee or issuer of a SEP endowment contract (Code Sec. 408(l)) on Form 5498.[39]

... *Sponsoring organizations* (defined in Code Sec. 4966(d)(1), ¶4129), on their annual information returns (Form 990-T), must include information relating to donor advised funds (DAFs, ¶4125) owned by an organization at the end of the tax year. (Code Sec. 6033(k))[40]

... *Supporting organizations* (defined in Code Sec. 509(a)(3)) must file annual information returns listing supported organizations, the type of supporting organization, and a certification that the organization that it isn't controlled by 1 or more disqualified persons. (Code Sec. 6033(l))[41]

... *Tips* must be reported by employees to employers on Form 4070. (Code Sec. 6053(a); Reg § 31.6053-1(b)(2))[42] Large food and beverage establishments (more than 10 employees on a typical business day) must report to IRS (on Form 8027) and to employees, tips reported by the employees to the employer plus the excess (as specially allocated) of 8% of the establishment's gross receipts (as specially defined) over the amount of tips thus reported by the employees. The 8% can be reduced to not below 2%, on application to IRS. (Code Sec. 6053(c)(3); Reg § 31.6053-3)[43] For 2007-2011, employers meeting certain requirements may elect to participate in a voluntary tip reporting program (Attributed Tip Income Program or ATIP).[44] An employer doesn't have to report tips that aren't reported to the employer until it receives a Code Sec. 3121(q) Notice and Demand. Then, the employer reports them on its next Form 941.[45]

... *Unemployment insurance benefit* payments of $10 or more must be reported by the payor on Form 1099-G. (Code Sec. 6050B; Reg § 1.6050B-1)[46]

¶ 4746   Extension of time for information returns—Form 8809.

Use Form 8809 to request a 30-day extension to file the following forms: W-2 series, 1042-S, 1098 series, 1099 series, 5498 series, and 8027. Approval is automatic for 30-day extension requests (no signature or explanation needed). Detailed explanation and signature are required for requests beyond the original 30-day extension. (Reg § 1.6081-8(d))[47] Automatic extension is also available to file SSA's copy of Forms W-2 and W-3. (Reg § 31.6081(a)-1) Make a written application (don't use Form 8809) to request an extension of up to 30 days for furnishing the payee statement, see ¶4742.[48]

35. ¶S-3690; ¶60,50E4; TD ¶816,020
36. ¶S-3684 *et seq.*; ¶60,50N4; TD ¶816,016
37. ¶S-3206.1 *et seq.*; ¶60,394; TD ¶812,015.1 *et seq.*
38. ¶S-3173; ¶60,514; TD ¶812,013
39. ¶S-3399 *et seq.*; ¶4084.05; TD ¶813,035
40. ¶S-2862.3; ¶60,334
41. ¶S-2823.1; ¶60,334
42. ¶H-4344; ¶60,534; TD ¶532,011
43. ¶S-3250 *et seq.*; ¶60,534; TD ¶812,054
44. ¶H-4344.3 *et seq.*
45. ¶H-4344.1; TD ¶559,526
46. ¶S-3694; ¶60,50B4; TD ¶816,023
47. ¶S-5049; ¶60,814.07
48. ¶s S-5041, S-5042; ¶60,814.07; TD ¶811,015

¶ 4747 Material advisors must disclose reportable transactions and maintain lists—Form 8918; Form 13976.

Each material advisor with respect to any reportable transaction (as defined in Code Sec. 6707A(c), see ¶4892) must make a return on Form 8918 setting out: information identifying and describing the transaction; information describing any potential tax benefits expected to result from the transaction; and any other information that IRS requests. (Code Sec. 6111(a); Reg § 301.6111-3(a)) The form should be filed by the last day of the month following the calendar quarter in which the person becomes a material adviser.[49] For the penalty for failure to meet this requirement, see ¶4894.

A material advisor is any person who provides any material aid, assistance, or advice with respect to organizing, managing, promoting, selling, implementing, insuring, or carrying out any reportable transaction, and who directly or indirectly derives gross income in excess of a threshold amount (or such other amount prescribed by IRS) for that assistance or advice. (Code Sec. 6111(b)(1)(A); Reg § 301.6111-3(b)) A person becomes a material adviser when (1) he makes a tax statement, (2) he receives (or expects to receive) the minimum fees, and (3) the transaction is entered into by the taxpayer.[50]

The threshold amount is $50,000 for a reportable transaction substantially all of the tax benefits from which are provided to natural persons, and $250,000 in any other case. (Code Sec. 6111(b)(1)(B); Reg § 301.6111-3(b)(3))

Each material advisor must maintain a list with respect to any reportable transaction. The list must identify each person for whom the advisor acted as a material advisor for the transaction and contain any other information as IRS regs may require. The list may (but is not required to) be kept on Form 13976. (Code Sec. 6112(a); Reg § 301.6112-1)[1]

¶ 4748 Participation in confidential tax avoidance transactions—Form 8886.

Taxpayers must disclose (on Form 8886 due with an original or amended return reporting participation) their participation in "reportable transactions," by attaching an information statement to their income tax returns, including:

. . . listed transactions (i.e., transactions that have been specifically identified by IRS as tax avoidance transactions such as "sale in/lease-out transactions" or SILOs, certain offsetting currency transactions solely used to import losses but not gains);

. . . confidential transactions offered under conditions of confidentiality and for which the taxpayer has paid an advisor a minimum fee;

. . . transactions with contractual protection;

. . . loss transactions resulting in a taxpayer claiming a tax loss exceeding specified amounts; and

. . . transactions of interest (i.e., transactions that are the same or substantially similar to transactions identified by IRS). (Reg § 1.6011-4) Transactions of interest include certain charitable contributions of real property interests ("successor member interests") that involve inflated valuations, "toggling" grantor trust transactions where grantor trusts are purportedly terminated and recreated to generate large losses, certain sales of interests in charitable remainder trusts that result in the grantor or other non-charitable recipient receiving the value of the trust while claiming to recognize little or no taxable gain, and certain transaction involving blocker partnerships to avoid the inclusion of income of lower-tier controlled foreign corporations.[2]

---

49. ¶S-4401, ¶S-4401.4; TD ¶817,005
50. ¶S-4401.2; TD ¶817,003

1. ¶S-4408.1; ¶61,124
2. ¶S-4427.1, ¶S-4427.15, ¶S-4427.24; ¶61,114

A copy of Form 8886 must be sent to the IRS Office of Tax Shelter Analysis (OTSA). For penalties, see ¶4892. Taxpayers also must disclose participation in listed transactions involving estate tax (Reg § 20.6011-4), gift tax (Reg § 25.6011-4), employment tax (Reg § 31.6011-4), excise tax related to private foundations and certain other tax exempts (Reg § 53.6011-4), excise taxes relating to qualified pension and other plans under Code Sec. 4971 through Code Sec. 4980F (Reg § 54.6011-4), and excise taxes relating to public charities. (Reg § 56.6011-4) Confidential corporate tax shelters also are subject to the tax shelter registration rules of Code Sec. 6111. Affected transactions are listed transactions and other tax-structured transactions as specially defined. (Reg § 301.6111-2)[3]

¶ 4749　Reporting qualified residence interest on seller-provided financing.

A return on which taxpayer claims a deduction for qualified residence interest (¶1730) on seller-provided financing must show the name, address and taxpayer identification number (TIN) of the person (the seller) to whom the interest is paid or accrued on Form 1040, Schedule A. Any person who receives or accrues interest from seller-provided financing must include on Form 1040, Schedule B for the tax year in which the interest is so received or accrued the name, address and TIN of the person liable for the interest. (Code Sec. 6109(h))[4]

¶ 4750　Preparer's duty in preparation of returns.

A tax return preparer (¶4751) must:

. . . *sign the return* in the manner prescribed by IRS in forms, instructions or other appropriate guidance. (Code Sec. 6695(b)) If the return isn't signed electronically, he has to sign the completed return before it is presented to the taxpayer for signature. If the preparer is unavailable for signature, another preparer must review the entire return and sign it. (Reg § 1.6695-1(b)(1)) Preparers may sign original or amended returns, or extension requests, as a return preparer with a rubber stamp, mechanical device, or computer software program. The method used must contain either a facsimile of the preparer's signature or the preparer's printed name.[5]

. . . *enter a preparer ID number (PTIN) on any return filed after 2010.* (Code Sec. 6109(a)(4)) All compensated preparers (including preparers who already have PTINs) have to be registered on the on-line registration system (on the Tax Professional's page at irs.gov) or by submitting a paper Form W-12 (4 to 6 weeks of response time). Receipt of a PTIN will be immediate after successful online registration. These preparers have to renew PTINs annually and pay the associated user fee ($64.25 for 2011). Preparers who aren't CPAs (or LPAs in certain states as listed on irs.gov), attorneys, or enrolled agents have to satisfy competency testing and continuing education requirements. After 2010, all tax return preparers have to comply with standards of conduct set by Circular 230. As part of its return preparer compliance campaign, IRS sent approximately 10,000 letters to preparers and visited thousands of preparers to remind them of these standards for preparers.[6]

. . . *enter an address where the return was prepared* on any return he prepares; if there's a partnership or employment arrangement between 2 or more preparers, the identifying number of the partnership or employer must also appear on the return or claim for refund. The identifying number of a preparer (whether an individual, corporation, or partnership) who employs or engages 1 or more persons to prepare returns or refund claims is that preparer's employer identification number (EIN). (Reg § 1.6109-2(a))[7]

. . . *furnish the taxpayer with a completed copy of any tax return* no later than when the return is presented for signature. (Code Sec. 6107(a)) The same rule applies to a return

---

3. ¶S-4419.1; ¶61,114; TD ¶817,002　　　　　6. ¶S-1522; ¶61,094; TD ¶867,012
4. ¶S-1524 *et seq.*; ¶61,094　　　　　　　　7. ¶S-1523; ¶61,094; TD ¶867,012
5. ¶S-4603, ¶S-4604; ¶66,954; TD ¶867,010

prepared for a nontaxable entity (i.e., partnership or S corporation). (Reg § 1.6107-1(a))[8]

... *retain for 3 years a completed copy of each return* or a list of the name and TIN of each taxpayer for whom a return was prepared (Code Sec. 6107(b));[9]

... *retain a record of the name, TIN, and principal place of work of each income tax return preparer* employed or engaged by the preparer/employer during each July 1 through June 30 period. (Reg § 1.6060-1(a)(1))[10]

... *for returns filed after 2010, electronically file* individual income tax returns (which for this purpose includes estate and trust returns), unless the preparer neither prepares nor reasonably expects to prepare 10 or more individual income tax returns in a calendar year. (Code Sec. 6011(e)) But, IRS is phasing this requirement in over two years. Tax return preparers will have to e-file beginning: Jan. 1, 2011, for preparers anticipating preparing 100 or more federal individual or trust tax returns during the year; and Jan. 1, 2012, for preparers anticipating preparing 11 or more federal individual or trust tax returns during the year.[11]

¶ 4751 Tax return preparer defined.

A tax return preparer is any person, including a partnership or corporation, who, in return for compensation, prepares, or employs or engages another to prepare, all or a substantial portion of any tax return or refund claim under the Internal Revenue Code. (Code Sec. 7701(a)(36)(A)) A *signing* tax return preparer is the individual tax return preparer who has the primary responsibility for the overall substantive accuracy of the preparation of the return or refund claim. (Reg § 301.7701-15(b)(1))

A *nonsigning* tax return preparer is any tax return preparer who is not a signing tax return preparer but who prepares all or a substantial portion of a return or claim for refund for events that have occurred at the time the advice is rendered. Time spent on advice that is given after events have occurred that represents less than 5% of the individual's aggregate time with respect to the position giving rise to the understatement is not taken into account. Examples of nonsigning tax return preparers are preparers who provide advice to a taxpayer or another preparer when that advice leads to a position or entry that is a substantial portion of the return. (Reg § 301.7701-15(b)(2)(i))[12]

A person may also be a "preparer" of a related return if an entry on a return he actually prepared (e.g., partnership or S corporation return) is directly reflected on the related return (e.g., partner's or shareholder's return), and the entry is a substantial portion of the related return. (Reg § 301.7701-15(b)(3)(iii))[13]

A portion of a return prepared by a nonsigning tax return preparer won't be "substantial" if, aggregating all schedules, etc., he prepared, that portion involves amounts of gross income, deductions, or amounts on which credits are based that are: (1) less than $10,000, or (2) less than $400,000 *and* less than 20% of the gross income (adjusted gross income, for individuals) as shown on the return. (Reg § 301.7701-15(b)(3)(ii)(A))[14]

A tax consultant is a "preparer" even though he may do no more than review a return already prepared by the taxpayer.[15] A person is a "preparer" if he supplies enough information and advice so that completion of a return is a mere mechanical or clerical matter (Reg § 301.7701-15(c))[16] but not if he merely furnishes typing, reproducing or other mechanical assistance with respect to preparing a return. (Code Sec. 7701(a)(36)(B)(i);

8. ¶S-1102; ¶61,074; TD ¶867,015
9. ¶V-2675; ¶61,074; TD ¶867,014
10. ¶V-2676; ¶60,604; TD ¶867,013
11. ¶S-1601; ¶60,114.075; TD ¶572,002
12. ¶S-1107; ¶77,014.24; TD ¶867,002

13. ¶S-1117; TD ¶867,002
14. ¶S-1116; TD ¶867,006
15. ¶S-1109; TD ¶867,004
16. ¶S-1109; ¶61,074; TD ¶867,004

Reg § 301.7701-15(f)(1)(viii)) A person who provides a computerized return preparation service is a preparer if his computer programs provide substantive tax determinations, but not if his services are limited to mechanical calculations and processing.[17]

¶ 4752 Taxpayer identification number (TIN)—Form SS-5.

Any person who files a return, statement, or other document must include his own TIN (Code Sec. 6109(a)(1))[18] and the TIN of any other person, as required by the form or instructions to the form. (Code Sec. 6109(a)(3); Reg § 301.6109-1(c))[19] Thus, an alimony payor's return must include the payee's TIN. (Use Form W-9 to request another person's TIN.)[20] A child to whom the kiddie tax rules, ¶3135 *et seq.*, apply for any tax year must provide his parent's TIN on his (child's) tax return for that year. (Code Sec. 1(g)(6))[21]

Social security numbers (SSNs) are used to identify most individuals, sole proprietors not otherwise required to use employer identification numbers (EINs), and grantor trusts. (Code Sec. 6109(d); Reg § 301.6109-1(a))[22] To get an SSN, file Form SS-5 with the Social Security Administration. (Reg § 301.6109-1(d)(1))[23]

Aliens who aren't eligible for SSNs must use IRS individual taxpayer identification numbers (ITINs). (Reg § 301.6109-1(a)) Use Form W-7 to request an ITIN.[24] Prospective adoptive parents who have had a child placed in their household by an authorized placement agency and meet certain other requirements may apply (use Form W-7A) for a temporary (2-year) adoption taxpayer identification number (ATIN) for the child (unless the child is an alien eligible to get an ITIN) to satisfy filing requirements (but not for earned income credit purposes (¶2344)). (Reg § 301.6109-3)[25]

Other entities use the EIN. (Reg § 301.6109-1(a)) Taxpayers can request an EIN instantly through http://www.irs.gov by entering the required information. Taxpayers may also apply for an EIN by phone, mail, or fax. (Reg § 301.6109-1(d))[26] All employers, whether corporations, partnerships or sole proprietors, must get and use EINs for reporting employment and excise taxes.[27] Large food and beverage establishments use a 15-digit identifying number for tip reporting. (Reg § 31.6053-3(a)(5))[28]

Buildings that have been or will be allocated a low-income housing credit must be assigned a building identification number (BIN) by the applicable state housing credit agency.[29]

Foreign transferors of U.S. real property interests (USRPIs) (and transferees where applicable) must provide their TINs on withholding tax returns, applications for withholding certificates, and other required notices and elections. Foreign persons must have TINs for placement on any return, statement, or other document required by the regs under Code Sec. 897 or Code Sec. 1445. (Reg § 301.6109-1(b)(2)(vi))[30]

¶ 4753 Magnetic media and electronic filing—Form 4419.

Certain information returns *must* be filed on magnetic media. (Code Sec. 6011(e)(2)(A))[31] There are exceptions for certain low-volume filers (fewer than 250 returns), but partnerships with more than 100 partners (counting any person who is a partner at any time during its tax year) must file on magnetic media. (Reg § 301.6011-3)[32] Electronic filing satisfies the magnetic media requirement. Hardship waivers (request on Form 8508) are available. (Code

---

17. ¶S-1110; ¶61,075; TD ¶867,005
18. ¶S-1502; ¶61,094; TD ¶570,106
19. ¶S-1531; ¶61,094; TD ¶861,050
20. ¶S-1535; ¶2154.03; TD ¶861,050
21. ¶S-1544
22. ¶S-1505; ¶61,094; TD ¶570,106
23. ¶S-1581; ¶61,094; TD ¶570,106
24. ¶S-1508.1; ¶61,094; TD ¶570,106

25. ¶S-1504.6 *et seq.*; ¶61,094.01; TD ¶570,110
26. ¶S-1582 *et seq.*; ¶61,094; TD ¶659,009
27. ¶S-1505; ¶61,094
28. ¶S-3289; TD ¶812,039
29. ¶S-1521; ¶424.70
30. ¶S-1508
31. ¶S-1301; ¶60,114.07; TD ¶861,061
32. ¶S-1350; ¶60,114.065; TD ¶596,025

Sec. 6011(e)(2)(B))[33] For employee benefit plan years beginning on or after Jan. 1, 2009 (i.e., for returns due to be filed on or after July 31, 2010), all annual reports—including any accompanying statements and schedules—must be filed electronically under the EFAST program (¶4745).[34]

For returns the due date for which (determined without regard to extensions) is after Mar. 18, 2010, the numerical limitation (the 250–or–more–return rule, discussed above) doesn't apply to any return filed by a financial institution for tax for which the institution is liable as a withholding agent under Code Sec. 1461 or Code Sec. 1474(a)). (Code Sec. 6011(e)(4))[35]

Submit Form 4419 at least 30 days before the return due date to apply to transmit information returns electronically/magnetically.[36] The due dates for filing paper information returns with IRS also apply to magnetic media filings, but not to electronic filing. For magnetic media, Form 1098, forms in the Form 1099 series, and Form W-2G must be submitted to IRS postmarked by Feb. 28. For electronic filing, however, the due date for information returns is Mar. 31.[37] A transmittal statement on Form 4804 must accompany magnetic media; Form 4804 isn't required for electronic filers.[38]

Individuals and organizations with 25 or more trucks, tractors or other heavy vehicles used on highways have to file excise tax Form 2290 electronically.[39]

For electronic filing of income tax returns, see ¶4703 for individuals, ¶4726 for corporations, and ¶4731 for partnerships.

¶ 4754   Timely mailing as timely filing and paying.

A return, claim, statement, document or payment (except a tax deposit) that must be filed or made by a certain date generally is considered timely filed or made if it has a timely postmark. (Code Sec. 7502(c)(1))[40] This also applies to claims for credit or refund made on a late-filed original return. (Reg § 301.7502-1(f))[41]

For the timely mailing rule to apply, the return, etc., must be: (1) deposited in the U.S. mail in a properly addressed envelope or wrapper with sufficient postage; (Code Sec. 7502(a)(2)(B)) (2) postmarked on or before the prescribed filing or payment date (Code Sec. 7502(a)(2)(A)) (returns postmarked after the due date are considered filed when received by IRS); and (3) actually delivered by U.S. mail to the proper place. (Code Sec. 7502(a)(1))[42]

Some courts permit delivery to be proven by the so-called common-law "mailbox rule" (i.e., when mail is properly addressed and deposited in the U.S. mails, with postage duly prepaid on it, there is a rebuttable presumption that it was received by the addressee in the ordinary course of the mail).[43]

Under authority to expand the timely-mailing rule to include certain private delivery services, (Code Sec. 7502(f)) IRS has designated the following as services for which the timely-mailing-as-timely filing rule also applies: *DHL* Same Day Service, DHL Next Day 10:30 AM, DHL Next Day 12:00 PM, DHL Next Day 3:00 PM, and DHL 2nd Day Service; *FedEx* Priority Overnight, FedEx Standard Overnight, FedEx 2 Day, FedEx International Priority, and FedEx International First; *UPS* Next Day Air, UPS Next Day Air Saver, UPS 2nd Day Air, UPS 2nd Day Air A.M., UPS Worldwide Express Plus, and UPS Worldwide Express.[44]

The postmark stamp date on the mailing envelope overrides the postmark stamp date on a Certificate of Mailing (P.S. Form 3817).[45] If a private postage meter is used, the postmark

33. ¶S-1314; ¶60,114.07
34. ¶S-1630 *et seq.*; ¶S-3351
35. ¶S-1302; ¶60,114.07; TD ¶861,061
36. ¶S-1311
37. ¶S-1305; TD ¶861,062
38. ¶S-1308; TD ¶861,062
39. ¶W-6456
40. ¶T-10751; ¶75,024; TD ¶570,237
41. ¶T-10752.1; ¶75,024
42. ¶T-10751 *et seq.*; ¶75,024; TD ¶570,237
43. ¶T-10774 *et seq.*
44. ¶T-10781; ¶75,024; TD ¶570,238
45. ¶T-10762

isn't enough. The document must actually be received by the proper office or officer not later than the time the postmark indicates it ordinarily would be received. If it is actually received later, taxpayer can prove timely mailing only by showing: (1) that the document was deposited in the mail before the last collection that was postmarked (by the U.S. Post Office) on the last day for filing; and (2) that the delay in receiving the document was due to delay in transmission of the mail; and (3) the cause of the delay. (Reg § 301.7502-1(c)(1)(iii)(B))[46]

In general, an electronically filed tax return (¶4703) isn't considered filed until IRS acknowledges the electronic portion of the return as accepted and a signature has been received either electronically or on Form 8453 or Form 8453-OL. But, certain taxpayers can pick their own 5-digit personal identification number (PIN) and don't have to file Form 8453.[47]

¶ 4755 Effect of registered or certified mail.

The date of registration is considered to be the postmark date, (Code Sec. 7502(c)(1)(B)) and registration is prima facie evidence the return, etc., was delivered to the agency, officer or office to which addressed. (Code Sec. 7502(c)(1)(A))[48] The date of the U.S. postmark on the sender's receipt is treated as the postmark date of a document sent by certified mail (Reg § 301.7502-1(c)(2)), and proof that a properly postmarked certified mail sender's receipt was properly issued and that the envelope or wrapper was properly addressed is prima facie evidence that the document was properly delivered. (Reg § 301.7502-1(e)(1))[49]

¶ 4756 Due date on Saturday, Sunday or holiday.

If a due date falls on Saturday, Sunday or legal holiday, there is an automatic extension of time to the next succeeding day that isn't a Saturday, Sunday or legal holiday. The rule applies to *all acts* required to be performed under the Code both by the *taxpayer* and IRS. "Legal holiday" includes: (1) the legal holidays throughout the state or possession where the office at which the act to be performed is located even if not a legal holiday in the state or possession where the taxpayer resides, and (2) all legal holidays in the District of Columbia (D.C.) (Code Sec. 7503), i.e.: New Year's Day—Jan. 1; Inauguration Day—Jan. 20 (every fourth year); Martin Luther King, Jr.'s birthday—third Monday in Jan.; President's Day—third Monday in Feb.; Emancipation Day—Apr. 16; Memorial Day—last Monday in May; Independence Day—July 4; Labor Day—first Monday in Sept.; Columbus Day—second Monday in Oct.; Veterans Day—Nov. 11; Thanksgiving Day—fourth Thursday in Nov.; Christmas Day—Dec. 25. If a holiday in D.C. falls on Sunday, the next day is a holiday in D.C. When a legal holiday in D.C. (other than Inauguration Day) falls on a Saturday, it's treated as falling on the preceding Friday.[50]

¶ 4757 How to get a copy of a tax return— Forms 4506, 4506T, 4506T-EZ.

Use Form 4506.[1] IRS charges $57 for each return requested. Use Form 4506-T to request free tax return transcripts, tax account transcripts, W-2 information, 1099 information, verification of non-filing, or a record of account.[2] For a free Form 1040 series tax return transcript, use Form 4506T-EZ or IRS's telephone automated system to order. Transcripts requested under the automated system can't be mailed to a third party.

46. ¶T-10763; TD ¶570,237
47. ¶S-1609; ¶S-1617.3; ¶60,114.08; TD ¶572,018
48. ¶T-10762.3; ¶75,024; TD ¶570,237
49. ¶T-10776.1; TD ¶570,237

50. ¶T-10790 *et seq.*; ¶75,034; TD ¶570,240
1. ¶S-6407; ¶s 61,034, 61,034.09
2. ¶S-6409; ¶61,034

Chapter 25 Deficiencies—Refunds—Penalties

¶ 4800   Tax Audits, Deficiencies and Assessments. ▀▀▀▀▀▀▀▀▀▀▀▀▀▀

IRS makes certain preliminary cursory checks of every return filed; it selects returns for audit based on various criteria. Once IRS finishes an audit, a taxpayer has various alternatives it can pursue to resolve any disputed items.

¶ 4801   Mathematical, etc., check of returns.

IRS checks every return for math errors and computes tax using figures on the return. If the taxpayer made a computational error resulting in a tax underpayment, IRS sends a corrected computation and a notice and demand for payment of any balance due (which doesn't entitle the taxpayer to go to Tax Court) (Code Sec. 6213(b)(1)) or reduces any refund. (Reg § 601.105(a)) Failure to include a correct TIN on the return, as required under Code Sec. 21 (child care credit), Code Sec. 24 (child credit), Code Sec. 25A (higher education credit), Code Sec. 32 (earned income credit (EIC)), and Code Sec. 151 (personal exemptions), is treated as a math or clerical error and assessed accordingly. If EIC is claimed on net earnings from self-employment, failure to pay the proper amount of self-employment tax is treated as a math error. So is failing to provide IRS with certain information after improperly claiming EIC. (Code Sec. 6213(g)(2)) IRS may treat an EIC claim on a noncustodial parent's return as a math error. (Code Sec. 6213(g)(2)(M))[1] Adjustments to make an S corporation shareholder's return consistent with the corporation's return are treated as resulting from math or clerical error. (Code Sec. 6037(c)(3))[2] Similar rules apply when estate and trust beneficiaries file returns inconsistent with the entity's. (Code Sec. 6034A(c)(3))[3] A taxpayer's federal income and estate tax returns may also be checked against his state or foreign tax returns.[4]

¶ 4802   Check against information returns.

IRS compares the taxpayers' income tax returns against information returns, such as wage, interest and dividend statements, under a document matching program (Information Returns Program). If there is a mismatch, IRS sends the taxpayer a computer-generated notice (CP-2000), which must describe the basis for, and identify, any amounts of taxes, additions, interest or penalties claimed to be due. (Code Sec. 7522) The notice, which isn't a demand for payment, can be challenged by the taxpayer, who has the burden of proof. IRS also matches information filed by pass-through entities (partnerships, S corporations, and trusts) to what the partners, shareholders, and beneficiaries report on their own returns.[5]

¶ 4803   Returns selected for examination.

IRS selects returns for examination, e.g., based on discrepancy with information returns (¶4802), the filing of frivolous returns, random sampling (National Research Program (NRP)), etc. IRS's computerized "discriminant function" (DIF) technique ranks and selects returns having the greatest audit potential. In fiscal year 2009, IRS audited 1% of all individual returns that were filed in the previous year.[6]

¶ 4804   Individual taxpayers average deductions.

---

1. ¶T-3628; TD ¶836,017
2. ¶D-1801; TD ¶614,724
3. ¶C-3081; ¶C-9081; ¶62,134.02; TD ¶655,501, 665,029

4. ¶T-1001; TD ¶655,501; TD ¶665,029
5. ¶s T-1003, T-1004; ¶75,224; TD ¶821,003
6. ¶T-1023, T-1060 *et seq.*; TD ¶821,004

References beginning with a single letter are to paragraphs in RIA's Federal Tax Coordinator 2d and RIA's Analysis of Federal Taxes: Income. Those beginning with numbers are to paragraphs in RIA's United States Tax Reporter. Those beginning with TD are to paragraphs in RIA's Tax Desk.

2008 Average Deductions Claimed Based on Adjusted Gross Income

Adjusted Gross Income in Thousands of Dollars

AGI	$0-15	$15-30	$30-50	$50-100	$100-200	$200-250	$250 & up
Medical	7,931	7,074	6,153	7,102	9,269	21,554	37,143
Taxes paid	3,025	3,146	3,830	6,050	10,798	18,164	50,267
State & local tax*	797	1,032	1,653	3,162	6,357	11,804	40,151
Income taxes only	1,234	1,259	1,894	3,562	7,096	13,333	46,308
Gen. sales tax only	506	738	1,058	1,553	2,483	3,590	6,382
Contributions	1,341	2,024	2,189	2,693	3,757	5,895	20,930
Interest	9,607	9,245	9,055	10,659	13,734	18,570	27,865
Total itemized (after limitation)	15,741	15,669	16,259	20,568	28,923	42,471	96,458

* State and local taxes are the total of both income taxes and general sales taxes.

observation: RIA computed these averages from IRS's latest available statistics.

¶ 4805   Market Segment Specialization (MSSP) audit guidelines.

These provide revenue agents and tax examiners with a broad and detailed review of the way a particular industry (e.g., attorneys, taxicabs, air charters, trucking, bed and breakfasts) works and the things an agent should be looking for when reviewing a return from within that industry. The guides are available to practitioners and others.[7]

¶ 4806   Industry Issue Resolution, Audit Tiers and Pre-Filing Programs.

IRS's Industry Issue Resolution Program exists to provide guidance to resolve frequently disputed or burdensome issues common to any size business taxpayers.[8] Taxpayers under the jurisdiction of IRS's Large Business and International Division (called the Large and Mid-Size Business Division until Oct. 1, 2010) may request that IRS examine specific issues relating to returns before they're filed. If the issues are resolved before filing, the taxpayer and IRS can make a pre-filing agreement.[9] IRS also has an audit tiers program that focuses audit resources on high risk tax issues and prioritizes these issues into three tiers.[10]

¶ 4807   Settlement initiatives.

IRS periodically offers qualifying taxpayers who have participated in various tax shelters or who have otherwise taken tax positions that IRS considers abusive an opportunity to settle on terms that are more favorable than could result if the parties litigated.[11] IRS will consider voluntary taxpayer disclosures in determining whether cases will be criminally prosecuted.[12]

¶ 4808   Types of examinations (audits); time and place.

IRS fixes the time and method of examination, which must be reasonable under the circumstances. (Code Sec. 7605(a); Reg § 301.7605-1(a)) Depending on the amounts and sources of income and the nature of the taxpayer's business, an examination may be at: (1) an IRS office, with the taxpayer bringing (office audit) or mailing (correspondence audit) his records (Reg § 601.105(b)(2)(ii)), or (2) the office of the taxpayer (or his representative) (field audit).

---

7. ¶T-10161.1   10. ¶T-1040
8. ¶T-9974   11. ¶M-5977
9. ¶T-9552   12. ¶V-3829

(Reg § 601.105(b)(3))[13]

IRS generally won't conduct the audit at the taxpayer's place of business if the business is so small that doing so essentially requires the taxpayer to close the business.[14] The taxpayer may ask to have the audit transferred, e.g., to the district where his books and records are kept. IRS also may initiate a transfer, but the taxpayer may ask to keep the original site. (Reg § 301.7605-1(e), Reg § 301.7605-1(g))[15] IRS can't use financial status or economic reality examination techniques (so-called "lifestyle" audits) to determine the existence of any unreported income unless it has a reasonable indication that there is a likelihood of unreported income. (Code Sec. 7602(e))[16]

¶ 4809   Taxpayer's rights in an examination.

Before or at an initial in-person interview (other than criminal investigations), IRS must give the taxpayer an explanation (written or oral) of the audit process (and assessment and collection) and his rights under that process. (Code Sec. 7521(b)(1))[17] A taxpayer has the right to: be represented by an advisor (¶4810); make certain audio (but generally not videotape) recordings of meetings (on advance notice) with the IRS agent (Code Sec. 7521(a)(1)); claim additional deductions not claimed on the return; ask that a particular technical question raised in the examination be referred to IRS's National Office for technical advice; not be subjected to unnecessary examinations (¶4812); and claim constitutional rights if questioned about possible criminal violations.[18]

¶ 4810   Who can represent the taxpayer?

The taxpayer's representative may be an attorney, CPA, enrolled agent, enrolled actuary or any other person permitted (under Circular 230 Reg § 10.3) to represent taxpayers before IRS, who isn't disbarred or suspended from practice before IRS (IRS may censure (publicly reprimand), suspend, impose a monetary penalty (as explained in detailed IRS guidance), or disbar any practitioner from practice before IRS if he is shown to be incompetent or disreputable, refuses to comply with any of the Circular 230 requirements, or with intent to defraud, willfully and knowingly misleads or threatens a client or prospective client[19]), and who has a written power of attorney (on Form 2848) executed by the taxpayer. Absent a summons, IRS can't require the taxpayer to accompany the representative. (Code Sec. 7521(c))[20]

If, during an interview, the taxpayer clearly states a desire to consult with a representative, IRS must suspend the interview for that purpose. (Code Sec. 7521(b)(2))[21]

Where legal advice of any kind is sought from a professional legal adviser in his capacity as such, the communications relating to that purpose, made in confidence by the client, are protected from disclosure by himself or by the legal adviser unless he waives the protection.[22] The work product privilege protects written statements, private memoranda and personal recollections, prepared or formed by an adverse party's counsel in the course of his legal duties, that aren't protected by the attorney-client privilege. The First Circuit has held that it doesn't protect tax accrual workpapers.[23]

An attorney-client privilege of communications applies for other federally authorized tax practitioners with respect to tax advice (except for tax shelters) in any non-criminal tax matter or proceeding. (Code Sec. 7525)[24] An individual can check a box on his return to authorize IRS to communicate with his paid preparer (¶4751) about math error notices and the status of a refund or payment but must sign a power of attorney for representation on

---

13. ¶T-1090 *et seq.*; ¶76,054; TD ¶821,011
14. ¶T-1094; ¶75,214; TD ¶821,011
15. ¶T-1102; TD ¶821,015
16. ¶T-1076; ¶76,024; TD ¶821,010
17. ¶T-1122 *et seq.*; ¶75,214; TD ¶821,016
18. ¶s T-1120 *et seq.*, T-1129 *et seq.*; ¶76,024.10; TD ¶821,017 *et seq.*

19. ¶T-10930
20. ¶s T-1124, T-1127; ¶75,214; TD ¶821,018
21. ¶T-1127; ¶75,214; TD ¶821,017
22. ¶T-1314
23. ¶T-1330
24. ¶T-1334; ¶75,254

examination matters, underreported income, appeals and collections notices.[25]

¶ 4811   IRS's power to summon persons and records.

IRS can issue a summons for a taxpayer's testimony and records (Code Sec. 7602(a), Code Sec. 7602(b)) for a legitimate purpose, if IRS doesn't make unreasonable demands.[26] The summons (Form 2039) must describe with reasonable certainty the books and records sought (Code Sec. 7603), and set the time for examination—not less than ten days from the summons date. (Code Sec. 7605(a))[27] If the taxpayer intentionally disregards the summons, IRS can apply to the district court (or U.S. Commissioner) for an order directing compliance. (Code Sec. 7604(b))[28]

IRS may issue a summons ("third-party summons") to a person other than the taxpayer (e.g., his employer, or a "third-party recordkeeper," such as his bank) for testimony and records bearing on its examination of the taxpayer. (Certain communications (see ¶4810) are privileged.) Subject to exceptions, within three days of the service of a summons on a third-party, but no later than the 23rd day before the day fixed in the summons as the day when the records are to be examined, IRS must send by registered or certified mail a notice of the summons, including a copy of the summons, and an explanation of the taxpayer's right to institute a suit to quash the summons. (Code Sec. 7609(a)(1); Reg § 301.7609-1) If the taxpayer intervenes in a proceeding to enforce a third-party summons, the running of the assessment period for the taxpayer is suspended for the period during which a proceeding, and any appeal, as to the enforcement of the summons is pending. (Code Sec. 7609(e)(1); Reg § 301.7609-5(b)) IRS generally can't contact any third parties without providing reasonable notice in advance to the taxpayer. (Code Sec. 7602(c)(1); Reg § 301.7602-1)[29]

With some exceptions, IRS may not issue, or begin any action to enforce, any summons to produce or analyze any tax-related computer software source code. (Code Sec. 7612)[30] A summons can't be issued (or enforced) against a person for whom a Justice Department referral is in effect (i.e., criminal tax prosecution is recommended). (Code Sec. 7602(d))[31]

¶ 4812   One examination rule—unnecessary examinations.

Unnecessary examinations are barred. IRS may make only one inspection of a taxpayer's books and records for each tax year unless the taxpayer requests otherwise, or IRS notifies him *in writing* that an additional inspection is necessary (Code Sec. 7605(b)), or IRS suspects fraud. (Code Sec. 6212(c)) Re-examination also is permitted if the taxpayer doesn't file a timely Tax Court petition after receiving a 90-day letter (¶4826) for the year.[32]

¶ 4813   National Taxpayer Advocate—Taxpayer Assistance Orders (TAOs).

The Office of the Taxpayer Advocate is headed by the National Taxpayer Advocate, who reports directly to the Commissioner. (Code Sec. 7803(c)(1)) Its functions are to assist taxpayers in resolving problems with IRS, identify areas where taxpayers have problems dealing with IRS, propose changes in IRS administrative practices to mitigate these identified problems; and identify potential legislative changes that may do so. (Code Sec. 7803(c)(2)(A))

The National Taxpayer Advocate is responsible for the appointment of local taxpayer advocates. (Code Sec. 7803(c)(2)(D)) On taxpayer's application (on Form 911 or in a signed written statement containing the information prescribed in regs). (Reg § 301.7811-1(b)(1)) to the Office of the Taxpayer Advocate, the National Taxpayer Advocate (or his designee) can issue a Taxpayer Assistance Order (TAO) if he determines that the taxpayer is suffering (or will suffer) significant hardship because of IRS's administration of the tax laws, or if the taxpayer

---

25. ¶S-6405.3
26. ¶s T-1201, T-1212 *et seq.*; ¶76,024 *et seq.*; TD ¶822,001
27. ¶s 76,024.04, 76,054; TD ¶822,002
28. ¶T-1357; ¶76,044; TD ¶822,012

29. ¶T-1250 *et seq.*; ¶76,094; TD ¶822,013
30. ¶T-1290; ¶76,124; TD ¶822,200
31. ¶s T-1205, T-1206; ¶76,024; TD ¶822,004
32. ¶T-1425 *et seq.*; ¶76,024.10; TD ¶822,022

meets such other requirements provided in regs. (Code Sec. 7811(a)(1))[33]

¶ 4814 User fees for IRS rulings or determinations.

IRS charges taxpayers a separate user fee for each request for a ruling, closing agreement, installment agreement or similar service. (Code Sec. 7528)[34]

¶ 4815 Proposed deficiencies—revenue agent's report (RAR).

An IRS examiner may propose adjustments to a taxpayer's return before *determining* a deficiency (¶4825), (which generally doesn't exist until IRS issues a statutory notice of deficiency—"90-day letter," see ¶4826).[35] The agent will discuss the proposed adjustments with the taxpayer to settle the case informally. The taxpayer can agree to the adjustments or argue they should be modified ("unagreed" case) before the examiner submits his report (revenue agent's report, or RAR). Once the RAR is submitted, the taxpayer can discuss and settle the case only in an Appeals Office conference (¶4818).[36]

In an unagreed field audit case, the agent prepares a report explaining the proposed adjustments. After review by the district review staff, the RAR is sent to the taxpayer with a transmittal letter ("30-day letter," see ¶4816). (Reg § 601.105(c)(2)(i))[37] In an office audit, the taxpayer will usually be informed of the examiner's findings and given an opportunity to agree at the end of the interview. If he doesn't agree, he may request an immediate meeting with an appeals officer. If the taxpayer doesn't request an immediate conference, or it isn't practicable, the RAR (and 30-day letter) will be mailed to him. (Reg § 601.105(c)(1)(ii))[38]

¶ 4816 The 30-day letter.

The examiner's report that IRS sends, along with a transmittal ("30-day letter") to a taxpayer who rejects the examiner's findings from a field or office audit must show the basis for and amount of any proposed adjustments. (Code Sec. 7522(a), Code Sec. 7522(b)(3)) The letter also explains the appeal procedures and asks a taxpayer to indicate, within 30 days, whether he will accept the findings and sign a waiver of restrictions on assessment (Form 870, which allows IRS to collect the deficiency without issuing a 90-day letter (¶4826), and limits the taxpayer's appeal to a claim or suit for refund (no Tax Court petition)), request an Appeals Office conference (¶4818; or do nothing and IRS will send a 90-day letter. (Reg § 601.105(d)(1))

IRS must include an explanation of the entire process from examination through collection with respect to a proposed deficiency (including the assistance available to the taxpayer from the National Taxpayer Advocate, ¶4813, at various points in the process) with any first letter of proposed deficiency that allows the taxpayer an opportunity for administrative review in the IRS Office of Appeals.[39]

¶ 4817 Early referral to Appeals.

Any taxpayer may request early referral of one or more unresolved issues from either the examination or collection division, to the IRS Office of Appeals. (Code Sec. 7123(a))[40]

¶ 4818 Appeals Office conference.

The taxpayer can get an Appeals Office conference by sending a written request (in response to a 30-day letter, see ¶4816) and any required protest (¶4819) to IRS.[41] The Appeals

---

33. ¶T-10200 *et seq.*; ¶78,114 *et seq.*; TD ¶821,023
34. ¶T-10000 *et seq.*; ¶76,557.401
35. ¶T-1550 *et seq.*; TD ¶823,502
36. ¶T-1550 *et seq.*; TD ¶824,001
37. ¶T-1601; TD ¶823,502

38. ¶T-1604 *et seq.*; TD ¶823,505 *et seq.*
39. ¶T-1601 *et seq.*; TD ¶823,503
40. ¶T-1709; ¶71,234; TD ¶824,001
41. ¶T-1711; TD ¶824,002

Office proceedings are informal and testimony isn't under oath, although the taxpayer may be asked to submit affidavits. (Reg § 601.106(c))[42] An Appeals Office conference still is available to a taxpayer even after IRS has issued a 90-day letter (¶4826), e.g., where the taxpayer ignored the 30-day letter or where the assessment period was about to expire (or the taxpayer requested the 90-day letter). If the taxpayer then files a Tax Court petition (income, estate or gift tax case) or pays the additional tax assessed (other taxes), he can get an Appeals conference. (Reg § 601.106(a)(1))[43]

¶ 4819　Protest.

An oral request is enough to get Appeals consideration in all office or correspondence audit cases. In a field audit case, a written protest is: *required* if the total amount of the proposed increase in tax (including penalties), proposed overassessment or claimed refund, or compromise offer, exceeds $10,000 for any tax period; *optional* (but a statement of issues is required) if that total amount is between $2,500 and $10,000; and *not required* if it is less than $2,500. (Reg § 601.106(a)(1)(iii)(a))[44] The 30-day letter (¶4816) contains instructions for the protest (Reg § 601.105(d)(2)) and spells out the required information.[45]

¶ 4820　Appeals Office settlement authority; nonbinding mediation and arbitration.

The Appeals Office has authority to settle all factual and legal issues raised by the examiner's report (RAR, see ¶4815) or the taxpayer's protest (¶4819) (Reg § 601.106(f)(2))[46] as long as the case isn't docketed in the Tax Court. (Reg § 601.106(a)(2))[47] If no settlement is reached, IRS will prepare a 90-day letter (¶4826).[48] Under procedures prescribed by IRS, either the taxpayer or IRS Office of Appeals can request nonbinding mediation on any issue that is still unresolved after the conclusion of appeals procedures, or unsuccessful attempts to enter into a closing agreement or a compromise. (Code Sec. 7123(b)(1))[49] In addition, a taxpayer and IRS can jointly request binding arbitration of factual issues unresolved after the conclusion of appeals procedures, or unsuccessful attempts to enter into a closing agreement or a compromise. (Code Sec. 7123(b)(2))[50]

¶ 4821　Execution of Appeals Office settlement—Form 870, Form 890.

If the taxpayer accepts IRS's position in full, with no concessions, he signs a Form 870 (Form 890, in gift, estate or generation-skipping transfer tax cases), waiving restrictions on assessment (¶4832). (Reg § 601.106(d)(2))[1] For concessions, see ¶4822.

¶ 4822　Settlement with concessions—Form 870-AD, Form 890-AD.

If the Appeals Office makes any concessions, a Form 870-AD (Form 890-AD, in gift or estate tax cases) is executed stating that: the settlement is subject to acceptance by IRS; on acceptance it won't be reopened by IRS absent fraud, malfeasance, concealment or misrepresentation of a material fact, an important mathematical mistake, or an excessive tentative NOL carryback; *and* the taxpayer waives his right to file a claim for refund (other than from an NOL carryback) for any years covered by the agreement.[2]

¶ 4823　Final closing agreements—Form 866, Form 906.

The taxpayer and IRS may conclusively settle a tax dispute by entering into a final agreement to close either a tax year that has ended (use Form 866) (Code Sec. 7121(a);

42. ¶T-1720
43. ¶s T-1710, T-1900 *et seq.*
44. TD ¶824,008
45. ¶T-1602 *et seq.*; TD ¶824,009
46. ¶T-1721; TD ¶824,003
47. ¶T-1725; TD ¶824,003
48. ¶T-1732; TD ¶824,003
49. ¶T-1733; ¶71,234; TD ¶824,003.1
50. ¶T-1756
1. ¶T-1731; TD ¶824,005
2. ¶T-3401 *et seq.*; TD ¶824,006

Reg § 301.7121-1(b)(2), Reg § 601.202(a)(2))[3] or a *specific transaction,* past or future (use Form 906). (Reg § 601.202(a)(2))[4] The agreement is irrevocable (except for fraud, malfeasance or misrepresentation of a material fact) and binds *both* parties. (Code Sec. 7121(b))[5]

¶ 4824 Compromise—Form 656, Form 433-A, Form 433-B.

Civil or criminal tax cases can be compromised by IRS, after assessment, before referral to the Department of Justice (after referral, compromise can be only by the Attorney General). (Code Sec. 7122(a))[6] IRS may compromise tax liabilities on any of these grounds: (1) doubt as to collectibility, (2) doubt as to liability, (3) to promote effective tax administration because either (a) collection of the full amount would cause economic hardship for the taxpayer, or (b) compelling public policy or equity considerations justify compromise. (Reg § 301.7122-1(b)) To make an offer, file Form 656 (which has a box allowing a taxpayer to designate someone to assist while IRS is processing the offer) and, except for offers based solely on doubt as to liability, Form 433-A (individuals) or Form 433-B (businesses) (sole proprietors file must file both of the latter forms) and pay the $150 processing fee that generally applies. (Reg § 301.7122-1(d)(1)) IRS may disregard frivolous offer submissions. (Code Sec. 7122(f))[7]

¶ 4825 Deficiency defined.

A deficiency is the amount by which a taxpayer's correct tax liability is more than the excess of: (1) the tax shown on the return (math or clerical errors corrected), plus (2) the amounts previously assessed (or collected without assessment) as a deficiency, over (3) the amount of any rebates (credits, refunds, or other repayments). (Code Sec. 6211(a), Code Sec. 6213(b)) The correct tax and the tax shown on the return are computed without regard to credits for estimated taxes and taxes withheld under Code Sec. 31 (i.e., on wages, including excess social security withholdings, and back-up withholding). (Code Sec. 6211(b)(1)) In determining a deficiency, any excess of the additional child tax credit for families with three or more children, the gasoline and special fuel tax credit under Code Sec. 34, the earned income credit, and the Code Sec. 53(e) alternative minimum tax refundable credit, over the tax imposed by subtitle A (without taking into account those credits) and any excess of those credits shown by the taxpayer on the return over the amount shown as tax on the return (without taking into account those credits) is taken into account as a negative amount of tax. (Code Sec. 6211(b)(4)) If no return was filed, or if a return doesn't show any tax, the deficiency equals the entire amount of the correct tax. Additional taxes reported on an amended return filed after its due date are treated as "tax shown" ((1) above), not deficiencies. (Reg § 301.6211-1(a))[8] If a taxpayer elects to have IRS compute the tax, IRS's computation of tax imposed is the "tax shown" on the return. (Code Sec. 6211(b)(3))[9] Where a deficiency on a joint return is challenged by only one spouse, the deficiency as to that spouse is reduced by any tax collected from the other spouse.[10]

¶ 4826 Notice of deficiency—"90-day letter."

A statutory notice of deficiency ("90-day letter") tells a taxpayer that IRS has determined a deficiency (in income, estate or gift tax, or excise tax on private foundations or pension plans). This is the only notice IRS will issue for that determination.[11] It must describe the basis for and identify the amounts (if any) of tax, interest, additional amounts, additions to tax and assessable penalties (for exceptions, see ¶4828). (Code Sec. 7522(a))[12] and be sent by certified or registered mail to the taxpayer at his last known address.[13] After receiving the letter, the taxpayer can: pay the deficiency, not pay and seek to rescind it, pay and file a

3. ¶T-9500; ¶71,214 *et seq.*; TD ¶841,011
4. ¶T-9524; ¶71,214; TD ¶841,012
5. ¶T-9507; ¶s 71,214.07, 71,214.08; TD ¶841,005
6. ¶T-9600 *et seq.*; ¶71,224 *et seq.*; TD ¶842,001
7. ¶T-9601; ¶71,224; TD ¶842,012
8. ¶T-1501 *et seq.*; ¶62,114 *et seq.*; TD ¶822,501
9. ¶T-1506; ¶62,114.01; TD ¶822,501
10. ¶T-1507; TD ¶822,501
11. ¶T-2701; ¶62,114; TD ¶831,001
12. ¶T-2714; ¶75,224; TD ¶831,004
13. ¶T-2801; ¶62,124; TD ¶831,004

refund claim (¶4851), take no action (let tax be assessed) and then file a compromise offer (¶4824), or file a Tax Court petition (¶4860).[14]

⊘*observation:* A taxpayer can go to Tax Court only when IRS issues a 90-day letter.

All 90-day letters must include the date determined by IRS as the last day on which the taxpayer may file a petition with the Tax Court, ¶4860. (Code Sec. 6213(a)) But the Tax Court says that failure to include the date doesn't necessarily invalidate the letter.[15] Notices must include information about interest (Code Sec. 6631) and penalties (Code Sec. 6751).[16]

¶ 4827   Time for making assessments.

Unless the taxpayer and IRS sign a closing agreement (¶4823), or the taxpayer voluntarily pays the deficiency or signs a Form 870 (¶4816), or IRS determines collection is in jeopardy (¶4830), or in the case of court ordered restitution (¶4829), IRS can't assess deficiencies in income, estate, and gift taxes, and the excise taxes on private foundations and qualified pension, etc., plans until after the taxpayer has had an opportunity to make a Tax Court appeal. (Code Sec. 6213(a))[17]

¶ 4828   Assessment of interest and penalties.

Interest may be assessed when the underlying tax is collectible. (Code Sec. 6601(g))[18] For income, estate, gift and certain excise taxes, the negligence and fraud penalties are assessed like deficiencies (¶4827). So are the delinquency penalties (¶4874, ¶4875), but only if attributable to a deficiency and not if measured by the tax shown on the return. The penalty for estimated tax underpayments (¶3118, ¶3352) is assessed as a deficiency only if no return is filed. (Code Sec. 6665(b); Reg § 301.6659-1(c))[19]

The normal assessment and collection rules don't apply to the penalties for promoting an abusive tax shelter (¶4890) or for aiding and abetting a tax understatement (¶4886). A taxpayer may delay collection of these penalties by paying at least 15% of the penalty and filing a claim for refund of it, within 30 days of notice and demand for payment. If IRS denies the claim, the taxpayer has 30 days to sue for refund in a district court (where IRS may counterclaim for the unpaid penalty amount). The normal procedures also don't apply to the penalty for filing a frivolous return (¶4898). (Code Sec. 6703(b), Code Sec. 6703(c))[20]

¶ 4829   Assessment of restitution payments.

For restitution ordered by a court after Aug. 16, 2010, IRS can assess and collect restitution for unpaid taxes owed by defendants in criminal tax cases as if it were a tax. (Code Sec. 6201(a)(4))[21] Court-ordered restitution can be assessed, or a court proceeding for the amount can be begun without assessment, at any time. (Code Sec. 6501(c)(11))[22]

¶ 4830   Jeopardy assessment and termination of a tax year.

If IRS believes assessment or collection of a deficiency will be jeopardized by delay, it can immediately assess the deficiency (plus interest and penalties) and demand payment. (Code Sec. 6861(a); Reg § 301.6861-1(a)) But, within 60 days after the assessment, IRS must issue the taxpayer a 90-day letter (¶4826) if it hasn't already done so. (Code Sec. 6861(b))[23] IRS Chief Counsel must pre-approve jeopardy assessments. (Code Sec. 7429(a)(1)(A))[24]

IRS can presume the collection of income tax is in jeopardy if an individual who has

14. ¶T-2738; TD ¶831,009
15. ¶T-2701.1; ¶62,134; TD ¶831,009
16. ¶T-2714.1, ¶T-2714.2; ¶67,514, ¶66,314
17. ¶T-3601; ¶62,134; TD ¶836,002
18. ¶T-3646; ¶66,014.01; TD ¶836,011
19. ¶T-3638 *et seq.*; ¶66,654; TD ¶836,012

20. ¶V-5650; ¶67,034
21. ¶T-3639; ¶62,014
22. ¶T-4172; ¶65,014.149
23. ¶T-3700 *et seq.*; ¶68,614 *et seq.*; TD ¶837,002
24. ¶T-3733.1; ¶74,294

physical possession of more than $10,000 in cash or cash equivalents denies ownership of it and doesn't claim it belongs to another identifiable person who acknowledges ownership. (Code Sec. 6867(a), Code Sec. 6867(d); Reg § 301.6867-1(f)(2), Reg § 301.6867-1(f)(3)) The entire amount of the cash is presumed to represent income of the possessor for the year and is taxable at the highest individual tax rate. (Code Sec. 6867(b)) The possessor is treated as the taxpayer for assessment and collection purposes (unless the true owner comes forward), but not for purposes of administrative or judicial review of the assessment. (Code Sec. 6867(b), Code Sec. 6867(c); Reg § 301.6867-1(c), Reg § 301.6867-1(d), Reg § 301.6867-1(f)(4))[25]

IRS can also terminate a tax year and demand immediate payment of income taxes for the current and preceding year, if it finds that a taxpayer plans to leave (or remove his property from) the U.S. quickly, conceal himself or his property in the U.S., or do any other act that would prejudice the collection of those taxes ("termination assessment"). Within 60 days after the due date (with extensions) of the taxpayer's return for the full tax year or, if later, the date the return is actually filed, IRS must issue a 90-day letter to the taxpayer for the full year. (Code Sec. 6851(a), Code Sec. 6852(a))[26] There are procedures for administrative and judicial review of jeopardy and termination assessments (Code Sec. 7429)[27] and for stay of collection. (Code Sec. 6863)[28]

observation: A jeopardy assessment is used only where IRS makes its determination *after* the end of the tax year to which it relates. In a termination assessment, the determination is made *before* the related tax year ends or *before* the due date to file a return and pay the tax.

¶ 4831 Assessments in bankruptcy or receivership proceedings.

IRS may make an immediate assessment of any deficiency in income, estate and gift taxes, and certain excise taxes, whether or not a notice of deficiency (90-day letter, see ¶4826) has been issued in these situations: (1) on the debtor's estate in a case under Title 11 of the U.S. Code (bankruptcy cases); (2) on the debtor, but only if liability for the tax becomes res judicata under a determination in a Title 11 case; or (3) on the appointment of a receiver for the taxpayer in any receivership proceeding. (Code Sec. 6871(a), Code Sec. 6871(b))[29]

¶ 4832 General three-year statute of limitations on assessments.

Generally (for exceptions, see ¶4834, ¶4837), all taxes must be assessed: (1) within three years after the date the return was filed (below), or (2) if the tax is payable by stamp, within three years after the date any part of the tax was paid. (Code Sec. 6501(a))[30] A return filed before the filing deadline is considered filed on the due date. (Code Sec. 6501(b)(1))[31] But a return of tax withheld (from wages or at source) for any period ending with or within a calendar year is, if filed before Apr. 15 of the next calendar year, considered filed *on* Apr. 15. (Code Sec. 6501(b)(2); Reg § 301.6501(b)-1(b))[32] The assessment period for a late-filed return starts on the day after the actual filing, whether the lateness is due to taxpayer's delinquency, or under a filing extension granted by IRS. (Code Sec. 6501(a))[33] If within 60 days before the limitations period expires, IRS receives an amended return that shows an increase in tax liability, IRS has 60 days from the receipt to assess the additional tax. (Code Sec. 6501(c)(7))[34]

The assessment period for items of a partnership, S corporation, trust or estate that are passed through to and reported by the partners, shareholders or beneficiaries, respectively, is based on their returns (not the partnership's, etc.), as specifically codified in Code Sec.

25. ¶T-3726 *et seq.*; ¶68,674; TD ¶837,006
26. ¶T-3717 *et seq.*; ¶68,514
27. ¶T-3735 *et seq.*; ¶74,294; TD ¶837,009
28. ¶T-3757 *et seq.*; ¶68,634 *et seq.*; TD ¶903,002
29. ¶T-3802; ¶68,714; TD ¶837,007

30. ¶T-4001; ¶65,014;TD ¶838,001
31. ¶T-4002; ¶65,014.09; TD ¶838,002
32. ¶T-4010; ¶65,014.09; TD ¶838,002
33. ¶T-4003; ¶s 65,014.01, 65,014.02; TD ¶838,002
34. ¶T-4209.1; ¶65,014.28; TD ¶838,030

6501(a).[35] Subject to exceptions and special rules, the period for assessing tax attributable to a partnership item (or affected item), for a partnership tax year won't expire before the date that is three years after the later of: (1) the date the partnership return was filed, or (2) the last day for filing the return for that year (without regard to extensions). (Code Sec. 6229(a)) Courts have held that this special rule cannot shorten the general limitation period.[36]

If a taxpayer makes (or revokes) an election to have the alcohol fuel credit, enhanced oil recovery credit, employer social security credit for taxes paid on employee tips, work opportunity credit, the new qualified plug-in electric drive motor vehicle credit, the alternative motor vehicle credit, the qualified alternative fuel vehicle refueling (QAFVR) property credit, the credit for production of low sulfur diesel fuel, or the "orphan drug" credit apply for a tax year, the assessment period for a deficiency due to the election (or revocation) won't expire until one year after IRS is notified of the election or revocation. (Code Sec. 6501(m))[37]

¶ 4833 Expiration of the limitations period as a bar to assessment.

A taxpayer who claims that the assessment of a tax is barred by the expiration of the limitations period (¶4832) must raise the issue and has the burden of proof.[38]

¶ 4834 Six-year assessment period.

Over-25% omissions. The assessment period is six years for income tax (or estate, gift or excise tax) returns that omit from gross income (or gross estate, total gifts made in the return period, or excise tax) more than 25% of the gross income (or gross estate, total gifts or excise tax) that is reported. In applying these tests, capital gains and losses aren't netted; only gains are taken into account. These "omissions" don't include amounts for which adequate information is given on the return or attached statements. (Code Sec. 6501(e)) For this purpose, gross income, as it relates to a trade or business, means the total of the amounts received or accrued from the sale of goods or services, without reduction for the cost of those goods or services. Regs (which have been held invalid by the Tax Court) clarify that, outside the trade or business context, gross income has the same meaning as under Code Sec. 61(a) and thus any basis overstatement that leads to an understatement of gross income constitutes an omission. (Reg § 301.6501(e)-1T(a)(1))[39]

Personal holding company tax on a personal holding company (PHC) that didn't file a PHC schedule with its income tax return may be assessed within six years after the income tax return was filed. (Code Sec. 6501(f))[40]

Understatements due to foreign financial assets. For returns filed after Mar. 18, 2010 and for any other return for which the Code Sec. 6501 assessment period has not yet expired as of Mar. 18, 2010, a 6-year limitations period applies for assessment of tax on understatements of income attributable to foreign financial assets. This limitations period applies if there is an omission of gross income in excess of $5,000, and the omitted gross income is attributable to an asset for which information reports are required under Code Sec. 6038D (¶4673), applied without regard to the dollar threshold and certain exceptions. (Code Sec. 6501(e)(1)(A))[41] The extended limitations period rule for foreign financial asset omissions is also applicable where a partnership omits such foreign financial assets. (Code Sec. 6229(c)(2))[42]

Both the special definition of gross income for a trade or business and the rule treating adequately disclosed items on the return (or attachment) as not omitted (see over-25% omissions above) also apply for foreign financial asset omissions. (Code Sec. 6501(e)(1)(B))

35. ¶T-4020 *et seq.*; ¶65,014.04; TD ¶838,005
36. ¶T-4018; ¶62,294; TD ¶838,003
37. ¶T-4014.1; ¶65,014
38. ¶T-4030; ¶65,014.01; TD ¶838,007

39. ¶T-4201 *et seq.*; ¶65,014.15; TD ¶838,016
40. ¶T-4218; ¶65,014.29; TD ¶838,026
41. ¶T-4210.1; ¶65,014.155
42. ¶T-4215; ¶62,214.08

¶ 4835   Assessment period for carrybacks to and carryovers from closed years.

A deficiency attributable to a taxpayer's carryback of a net operating loss (NOL), capital loss, or business credit may be assessed at any time before expiration of the period applicable to the year the loss was sustained or the credit earned. (Code Sec. 6501(h), Code Sec. 6501(j))[43] A deficiency attributable to a foreign tax credit carryback may be assessed up to one year after the credit year's assessment period expires. (Code Sec. 6501(i))[44] Where a credit carryback results from the carryback of an NOL, capital loss or other credit carryback from a later year, a deficiency for the carryback year can be assessed at any time before the expiration of the period for the later year. (Code Sec. 6501(j))[45]

¶ 4836   Assessment period for unreported listed transactions.

If a taxpayer fails to include on any return or statement for any tax year any information with respect to a listed transaction (as defined at ¶4892) that's required under Code Sec. 6011, the time for assessment of any tax as to that transaction won't expire before one year after the earlier of: (1) the date the required information is furnished to IRS, or (2) the date a material advisor meets the Code Sec. 6112 list-maintenance requirements as to a request by IRS under Code Sec. 6112(b) relating to the transaction with respect to the taxpayer. (Code Sec. 6501(c)(10))[46] Taxpayers can rely on proposed regs or previously issued guidance to start the one-year period above. (Prop Reg. § 301.6501(c)-1, [Taxpayers may rely])

¶ 4837   When the assessment period remains open.

The assessment period is open indefinitely where a taxpayer:

. . . fails to file a required return (Code Sec. 6501(c)(3)), but the assessment period starts to run if a trust or partnership return is filed by a taxpayer later held to be a corporation (Code Sec. 6501(g)(1)) or an exempt organization return is filed by an organization later held to be taxable (Code Sec. 6501(g)(2));[47]

. . . files a false or fraudulent income, gift or estate tax return with intent to evade tax. (Code Sec. 6501(c)(1)) The Tax Court has held that an income tax return preparer's fraud keeps a taxpayer's income tax return open indefinitely under this rule, even if the taxpayer had no intent to evade taxes.[48] Filing a later amended, nonfraudulent return won't starting the normal three-year assessment period running;[49]

. . . willfully attempts in any manner to defeat and evade taxes (Code Sec. 6501(c)(2));[50]

. . . fails to pay any part of a tax required to be paid by stamp (Code Sec. 6501(a); Reg § 301.6501(a)-1);[1]

. . . for gift tax, fails to show or adequately disclose (1) any gift of property (or increase in taxable gifts) whose value is determined under the special valuation rules or (2) any post-Aug. 5, '97 gift. (Code Sec. 6501(c)(9); Reg § 301.6501(c)-1(e), Reg § 301.6501(c)-1(f))[2] Filing an amended return with required information will get the limitation period running for a prior gift that wasn't adequately disclosed.[3]

. . . is subject to the tax for termination of private foundation status, see ¶4128.[4]

IRS says that a responsible person liable for the trust fund recovery penalty is subject to an unlimited assessment period where the employer has committed fraud, willfully attempted to evade tax, or failed to file an employment tax return.[5] The penalties for promoting abusive

43. ¶T-4034; ¶65,014.28; TD ¶838,008
44. ¶T-4042; ¶65,014.28; TD ¶838,009
45. ¶T-4039; ¶65,014.28; TD ¶838,009
46. ¶T-4163; ¶65,014.147; TD ¶838,055
47. ¶T-4101 *et seq.*; ¶s 65,014.05, 65,014.06, 65,014.14; TD ¶838,012 *et seq.*
48. ¶T-4127; ¶65,014.13; TD ¶838,014

49. ¶T-4209; ¶65,014.04; TD ¶838,014
50. ¶T-4141; ¶65,014.13; TD ¶838,015
1. ¶T-4122; TD ¶838,001
2. ¶T-4147; ¶65,014.28; TD ¶838,022
3. ¶T-4148
4. ¶T-4143
5. ¶T-4029.1

tax shelters, or for aiding and abetting an understatement, can be assessed at any time,[6] as can the penalty (but not the tax) imposed on a return preparer for willful tax understatements,[7] and certain restitution in criminal tax cases (¶4829).[8]

For information required under certain provisions, the assessment period for tax as to any event or period to which the information relates won't expire before the date that is 3 years after the information is given to IRS. The provisions include Code Sec. 6038, Code Sec. 6038A, Code Sec. 6038B, Code Sec. 6046, Code Sec. 6046A, and Code Sec. 6048. For returns filed after Mar. 18, 2010 and for other returns for which the Code Sec. 6501 assessment period had not yet expired as of Mar. 18, 2010: (1) if a failure is due to reasonable cause and not willful neglect, the above suspension rule applies only to items related to that failure (2) the suspension rule refers to "tax return, event, or period" not "event or period" and (3) the suspension rule is extended to failure to provide timely information returns required with regard to a passive foreign investment company (PFIC) under Code Sec. 1295(b) or under Code Sec. 1298(f) and to the self-reporting of foreign financial assets information required under Code Sec. 6038D. (Code Sec. 6501(c)(8))[9]

¶ 4838   Voluntary extension of the assessment period—Form 872.

At any time *before* expiration of the assessment period (¶4832), a taxpayer and IRS can agree in writing (usually on one of the Form 872 series) to extend the assessment period (except for estate taxes). They can also enter into successive agreements further extending the period. (Code Sec. 6501(c)(4))[10]

observation: Form 872 is generally referred to by IRS as a *"consent."* Tax practitioners sometimes refer to it as a *"waiver,"* which technically means a Form 870, ¶4821.

Restricted consent. A restricted consent postpones the close of the tax year with respect to an unsettled issue. It is used where some issues are resolved, but settlement of others must await the establishment of an IRS position through a court decision, etc., or where other equally meritorious circumstances exist.[11]

Indefinite consent—Form 872-A. A taxpayer whose case is before the Appeals Office (¶4818) can execute Form 872-A, which is an indefinite extension.[12] It expires 90 days after: (1) Appeals receives notice (on Form 872-T) of the taxpayer's desire to terminate the extension, (2) IRS mails Form 872-T to the taxpayer, or (3) IRS mails a 90-day letter.[13]

IRS must notify the taxpayer of his right to refuse to extend the assessment limitations period, or to limit the extension to particular issues or a particular time period, on each occasion the taxpayer is requested to provide consent. (Code Sec. 6501(c)(4)(B))[14]

¶ 4839   Suspension of the assessment period.

A 90-day letter (¶4826) suspends the assessment period. It stops running on the date IRS mails the letter, and doesn't resume until 60 days after: (1) the 90-day period (150 days if the letter is addressed to a person outside the U.S.) if no petition is filed, or (2) the Tax Court's decision becomes final if a petition is filed. (Code Sec. 6503(a))[15] A taxpayer's application for a Taxpayer Assistance Order (¶4813) also suspends the assessment period, up to the date the National Taxpayer Advocate makes a decision. (Code Sec. 7811(d))[16]

IRS's mailing of a notice of adjustment suspends the statute of limitations on the making of assessments for the longer of (1) the period during which IRS is prohibited from making the assessment, or (2) if a proceeding in respect of the notice of adjustment is placed on the docket

---

6. ¶s T-4125, T-4126; ¶67,034; TD ¶838,027
7. ¶T-4145; ¶66,964; TD ¶838,011
8. ¶T-4172; ¶65,014.149
9. ¶T-4146; ¶65,014.28
10. ¶T-4400 *et seq.*; ¶65,014.17 *et seq.*; TD ¶838,034
11. ¶T-4445; TD ¶838,034

12. ¶T-4402; TD ¶838,036
13. ¶T-4457 *et seq.*; TD ¶838,036
14. ¶T-4403; ¶65,014; TD ¶838,035
15. ¶T-4300 *et seq.*; ¶65,034.01; TD ¶838,043
16. ¶T-4324; ¶78,114.01; TD ¶838,045

of the Tax Court, until the decision of the Tax Court becomes final, and for 60 more days. (Code Sec. 6234(e)(2))[17] The assessment period is suspended in Tax Court employment tax determinations. (Code Sec. 7436(d)(1))[18]

For returns of corporations being examined under the coordinated examination program or a successor program, the issuance of a "designated summons" or a related summons also suspends the assessment period, pending final resolution of its enforcement. (Code Sec. 6503(j); Reg § 301.6503(j)-1)[19]

¶ 4840   Request for prompt assessment—Form 4810.

The normal three-year assessment period can be cut to 18 months *at the taxpayer's request* (use Form 4810) for an income tax return of a decedent or an estate, or for a return of a dissolved or dissolving corporation. (Code Sec. 6501(d))[20]

¶ 4841   Statutory (mitigation) and judicial relief for barred years.

Generally, after the period for assessment or refund has run, IRS can't make an assessment and a taxpayer can't get a refund. But an otherwise closed year may be reopened under the Code's "mitigation" provisions under certain circumstances. (Code Sec. 1311, Code Sec. 1312, Code Sec. 1313)[21] Relief from the limitation periods may be available in the district court or Court of Federal Claims if the statutory mitigation conditions aren't met, under equitable recoupment (closed year's overpayment or underpayment used to offset open year's deficiency or refund, see ¶4860 for Tax Court's authority to do this)[22] estoppel[23] or election.[24]

¶ 4842   Unified Audit and Review for Partnerships. ■■■■■■■■■■■■■■■■■■■■■

IRS generally can't adjust partnership items on a partner's return except through a unified entity-level proceeding. A decision in the unified proceeding binds all of the partners and permits IRS to make the necessary corresponding adjustments on their individual returns. Simplified procedures apply for electing large partnerships.

¶ 4843   Unified audit and review procedure for partnerships and partners.

The tax treatment of any partnership item (¶4844), and the applicability of any penalty, addition to tax or additional amount which relates to an adjustment to a partnership item, is generally determined at the partnership level, in one unified proceeding. This applies at both the administrative and judicial levels. (Code Sec. 6221; Reg § 301.6221-1(c)) Partnership level determinations include all the legal and factual determinations that underlie the determination of any penalty, addition to tax, or additional amount (other than partner level defenses). (Reg § 301.6221-1(c))[25]

No assessment of a deficiency attributable to any partnership item may be made before the end of the 150th day after IRS issues a notice of final partnership administrative adjustment (FPAA, see ¶4846) to the tax matters partner (TMP, see ¶4845) or, if the TMP files a Tax Court petition in that 150-day period, before the Tax Court decision becomes final. (Code Sec. 6225(a))[26] However, IRS can make an earlier assessment in certain abusive tax shelter situations. (Reg § 301.6231(c)-1)[27]

These rules generally apply to any partnership (except certain small partnerships, see ¶4847) required to file a partnership return (Form 1065), and to any entity that, for the year it filed a partnership return, either wasn't a partnership or wasn't in existence for the full

17. ¶T-3554; ¶62,344
18. ¶T-4301.1; ¶74,364
19. ¶T-4333 *et seq.*; ¶65,034.04; TD ¶838,046
20. ¶T-4500 *et seq.*; ¶65,014.16; TD ¶838,032
21. ¶T-5000 *et seq.*; ¶13,134; TD ¶823,507
22. ¶T-5200 *et seq.*; ¶65,144; TD ¶444,531
23. ¶T-5300 *et seq.*; ¶74,338.400
24. ¶T-5400 *et seq.*; ¶74,338.424
25. ¶T-2100 *et seq.*; ¶62,214; TD ¶825,001
26. ¶T-4015; ¶62,254; TD ¶838,003
27. ¶T-6517; ¶62,214; TD ¶804,012

year. (Code Sec. 6231(a)(1), Code Sec. 6233; Reg § 301.6233-1)[28] A REMIC (¶4204) is treated as a partnership for these purposes. (Code Sec. 860F(e))[29] Special consistency and audit rules apply for electing large partnerships (¶3702) and their partners. (Code Sec. 6240 through Code Sec. 6255)[30] IRS may rely on the partnership return in determining whether the unified audit rules apply. (Code Sec. 6231(g))[31]

The unified proceedings usually begin when IRS notifies the partnership that its return has been selected for audit. Or the TMP may file (use Form 8082) a request for an administrative adjustment for the partnership. The request is treated as a substituted return (correcting errors) or a claim for refund. (Code Sec. 6227(a))[32] Special deficiency procedures apply to a partner's "oversheltered return" (one that shows no taxable income and a net loss from a partnership). (Code Sec. 6234)[33]

¶ 4844   What are "partnership items"?

A "partnership item" is any item that must be taken into account for the partnership's tax year, to the extent regs provide the item is more appropriately determined at the partnership level than at the partner level (Code Sec. 6231(a)(3)), including: items of income, gain, loss, deduction or credit; expenditures not deductible in computing taxable income (e.g., charitable contributions); any partner's tax preference items; tax-exempt income; partnership liabilities; amounts needed to enable the partnership or the partners to compute the investment credit (or recapture), at-risk amounts or depletion; and items relating to contributions to or distributions from the partnership, and transactions between a partner and the partnership (e.g., guaranteed payments). (Reg § 301.6231(a)(3)-1(a))[34] In some contexts, courts have held that amounts at risk were not partnership items.[35]

¶ 4845   Tax matters partner (TMP).

The tax matters partner (TMP) acts on behalf of the partners in the unified partnership proceedings. The TMP is: (a) the general partner the partnership designates as such on its return (Form 1065) (Form 1066, for a REMIC (Reg § 1.860F-4(d))) or (b) if no designation is made, the general partner with the largest profits interest in the partnership at the end of the tax year. (Code Sec. 6231(a)(7)) IRS may select a general partner (or limited partner, if no general partner is eligible) (Reg § 301.6231(a)(7)-1(p)) as TMP if no designation is made under (a), above, and it is impracticable (under regs) (Reg § 301.6231(a)(7)-1(o)) to use (b). (Code Sec. 6231(a)(7); Reg § 301.6231(a)(7)-1(n))[36] The other partners generally must receive notice from the TMP of both IRS's and the TMP's actions. (Code Sec. 6223(g); Reg § 301.6223(g)-1)[37]

¶ 4846   Final partnership administrative adjustment (FPAA).

If after auditing the partnership IRS concludes that adjustments to the return are needed, it will issue a "final partnership administrative adjustment" (FPAA), which must be sent to the TMP and to "notice partners" IRS knows are eligible to receive notice. (Code Sec. 6223(a))[38] The TMP has 90 days from when the FPAA was mailed to file a petition for judicial review of the FPAA. (Code Sec. 6226(a)) If the TMP doesn't file within that time, any notice partner can file the partnership petition within the next 60 days. (Code Sec. 6226(b)(1)) Detailed procedures govern the conduct of the partnership-level proceeding (Code Sec. 6224; Reg § 301.6224(a)-1, Reg § 301.6224(c)-3)[39] assessments (Code Sec. 6225, Code Sec. 6229; Reg § 301.6229(b)-1), judicial review of FPAAs (Code Sec. 6226, Code Sec. 6228;

28. ¶T-2101; ¶62,214; TD ¶825,005
29. ¶E-6927; ¶860A4.04; TD ¶825,004
30. ¶T-2300 *et seq.*; ¶62,404; TD ¶825,501 *et seq.*
31. ¶T-2108.1; ¶62,214.10; TD ¶825,007
32. ¶T-2201; ¶62,214.06; TD ¶825,201
33. ¶T-3551 *et seq.*; ¶62,344

34. ¶T-2110; ¶62,214; TD ¶825,009
35. ¶T-2111
36. ¶T-2121; TD ¶825,023
37. ¶T-2151; TD ¶825,056
38. ¶T-2156 *et seq.*; TD ¶825,217
39. ¶T-2156 *et seq.*; ¶62,214; TD ¶825,029

Reg § 301.6226(f)-1) and other matters.[40]

¶ 4847 Exception for certain small partnerships.

The unified audit rules at ¶4843 *et seq.* don't apply to a "small" partnership (unless it elects them under procedures set forth by regs). (Reg § 301.6231(a)(1)-1(b)(2)) A partnership is "small" for a tax year if it has ten or fewer partners, each of whom is an individual (other than a nonresident alien), a C corporation, or an estate of a deceased partner. (Code Sec. 6231(a)(1)(B)(i); Reg § 301.6231(a)(1)-1(a)(1), Reg § 301.6231(a)(1)-1(a)(3))[41]

¶ 4848 Refunds; Tax Litigation. ▬▬▬▬▬▬▬▬▬▬▬

A taxpayer can recover an overpayment as a credit or a refund by properly filing a claim and, if the claim is denied, bringing suit. A taxpayer who has been issued a 90-day letter can go to Tax Court without first paying the disputed tax.

¶ 4849 Overpayments—recovery by refund or credit.

An overpayment is the excess of the amount paid (or withheld) as tax over the taxpayer's correct tax liability. It includes the part of a correct tax paid after the applicable assessment period has run. (Code Sec. 6401)[42] An overpayment can be recovered as a refund or credit, generally only by the taxpayer who paid the tax. But IRS may first credit the overpayment (including interest) against *any* of the taxpayer's past due tax liability (including interest, additions, penalties). (Code Sec. 6402(a); Reg § 301.6402-3(a)(5))[43] For offset against nontax debts, see ¶4850. Electronic filers may elect (on Form 8453) to have their refunds deposited directly into their bank accounts. Paper filers elect direct deposit by filling in the appropriate blanks on the "Refund" lines of Form 1040. In either case, use Form 8888 to direct deposit a refund into two or three accounts including IRAs.[44] A refund may be claimed for a deceased taxpayer. Attach Form 1310 (not needed for surviving spouse filing jointly with decedent) to the decedent's final return (¶4714).[45]

¶ 4850 Overpayments applied to child support and other nontax debts.

If a state notifies the Treasury that a taxpayer owes any child support payments, it must first apply the taxpayer's overpayment (including earned income amounts) to those past-due obligations, before making any refund or credit. (Code Sec. 6402(c))[46] If a federal agency notifies the Treasury of any past-due, legally enforceable nontax debt a taxpayer owes the agency, IRS must apply the balance (i.e., after the child support offset) of the taxpayer's overpayment to that nontax debt. (Code Sec. 6402(d))[47] Refunds can be offset by state income tax debts. (Code Sec. 6402(e))[48] Any overpayment remaining after these three permitted reductions can be reduced to recover overpayments made to the taxpayer under state family aid plans approved under part A of Title IV of the Social Security Act. (Code Sec. 6402(f))[49] A spouse should file Form 8379 to prevent her share of a joint return refund from being used to satisfy the other spouse's obligations.

¶ 4851 Refund claim.

To get a refund, a taxpayer must file a timely (¶4856) written claim. For income, gift and federal unemployment taxes, a separate claim must be made for each tax year or period. (Reg § 301.6402-2(a), Reg § 301.6402-2(d))[50] Official forms are:

40. ¶T-2215 *et seq.*; TD ¶825,224
41. ¶T-2104, T-2109; ¶62,214.10; TD ¶825,003, 825,008
42. ¶T-5500 *et seq.*; ¶64,014; TD ¶801,006
43. ¶T-5600 *et seq.*, T-5700 *et seq.*; ¶64,024; TD ¶803,012
44. ¶T-5610; TD ¶802,011
45. ¶T-5710; TD ¶802,039
46. ¶T-6013 *et seq.*; ¶64,024.26; TD ¶803,022
47. ¶T-6023 *et seq.*; ¶64,024.23; TD ¶803,026
48. ¶T-6038; ¶64,024
49. ¶T-6037; TD ¶803,029
50. ¶T-6702; ¶s 64,024, 64,024.08; TD ¶805,002

... Form 1040X (amended U.S. individual income tax return). (Use Form 1040, Form 1040A, or Form 1040-EZ *only* for refund of overwithheld taxes or excess estimated taxes.) (Reg § 301.6402-3(a)(2), Reg § 301.6402-4)

... Form 1120 or Form 1120X (original or amended corporate income tax return). (Reg § 301.6402-3(a)(2))

... Amended returns for taxpayers who filed a form other than Form 1040, Form 1040A, Form 1040-EZ or Form 1120 (e.g., a return for an estate or trust). (Reg § 301.6402-3(a)(4))

... Form 843 for refunds of non-income taxes (Reg § 601.105(e)(1)), except excise taxes reported on Form 720, Form 730, or Form 2290. Form 720X and Form 8849 are used for excise tax refund claims.[1]

IRS must explain disallowances of refund claims (Code Sec. 6402(j)) and it now notifies taxpayers whose refunds have been frozen under its questionable refund program..[2]

¶ 4852   Quick refund for carrybacks and claim of right— Form 1045; Form 1139.

A taxpayer who reports a carryback of a capital loss, net operating loss (NOL), business credit, or capital loss from a section 1256 contract under Code Sec. 1212(c) on his return can quickly recover a refund based on the carryback by filing Form 1045 (individuals) or Form 1139 (corporations) *on or after* the date the return for the loss or credit year is filed, and within 12 months after the end of the tax year *from which* the carryback is made. (Code Sec. 6411(a); Reg § 1.6411-1(b)(1))[3] This procedure also applies to overpayments attributable to a "claim of right" adjustment (¶2862), where the amount of repayment in any one year exceeds $3,000. (Code Sec. 6411(d))[4] IRS has 90 days from the later of the date the claim is filed or the last day of the month the loss year return is due (with extensions), to make any credit or refund. (Code Sec. 6411(b); Reg § 1.6411-3)[5]

IRS's determination is tentative. If the claim is rejected, the taxpayer can't sue but must first file a standard refund claim. (Code Sec. 6411(a); Reg § 1.6411-3(c)) Even if IRS grants the refund, it can later examine the loss year return and the refund application. IRS may assess any part of the refund it finds excessive, without issuing a 90-day letter. (Code Sec. 6213(b)(3))[6]

¶ 4853   Quick refunds of corporate estimated tax overpayments— Form 4466.

A corporation that overpaid estimated tax (¶3346 *et seq.*) can get a refund within 45 days after filing Form 4466. (Code Sec. 6425(b)(1), Code Sec. 6425(b)(2); Reg § 1.6425-1(b)) The form must be filed *after* the corporation's tax year ends and *on or before* the 15th day of the third month after the year ends (or before the corporation first files its income tax return for that year, if earlier). (Code Sec. 6425(a)(1); Reg § 1.6425-1(c)(1)) The corporation's estimated tax overpayment must be at least 10% of its revised expected annual tax, *and* at least $500. (Code Sec. 6425(b)(3)) If a refund is excessive, an addition to tax equal to the underpayment interest rate (¶4867), times the excessive amount is imposed. (Code Sec. 6655(h))[7]

¶ 4854   Protective refund claims.

A protective refund claim is a regular refund claim (on the regular form, see ¶4851) filed merely to keep a particular claim alive. It's generally used where IRS has a settled view adverse to a taxpayer on an issue being litigated by other taxpayers. A protective refund claim is usually filed just before the refund claim period expires. It will keep the taxpayer's claim alive (i.e., protect his right to sue) for the additional period from the date of filing to the

---

1. ¶T-6707 *et seq.*; ¶64,024 (Excise); TD ¶805,004 *et seq.*
2. ¶T-5618.1; ¶64,024; TD ¶802,018
3. ¶T-6501 *et seq.*; ¶64,114; TD ¶804,001
4. ¶T-6522; ¶64,114; TD ¶804,015

5. ¶T-6509; ¶64,114; TD ¶804,007
6. ¶T-6513; ¶62,134.02; TD ¶836,002
7. ¶T-6600 *et seq.*; ¶s 64,254, 66,554; TD ¶804,500 *et seq.*

date of rejection plus the refund suit period.[8]

¶ 4855   Interest on overpayments.

Interest on overpayments is allowed. (Code Sec. 6611(a)) The interest (compounded daily) runs from the date of the overpayment (below) to a date not more than 30 days before the refund is made (or to the (unextended) return due date for the amount against which the overpayment is credited). (Code Sec. 6611(b))[9] But no interest is payable on a refund arising from an original income, employment, excise, estate or gift tax return made within 45 days after the later of the return due date (without extensions) or the date it was filed. (Code Sec. 6611(e)(1); Reg § 301.6611-1(g))[10] If a refund arising from an amended return or refund claim is issued within 45 days, no interest is payable for that up-to-45 day period. (Code Sec. 6611(e)(2))[11] For refunds or credits arising from an adjustment initiated by IRS, the interest period is reduced by 45 days. (Code Sec. 6611(e)(3))[12]

For refunds of withheld taxes for: (1) returns due after Mar. 18, 2010, (2) claims for refund filed after Mar. 18, 2010, and (3) IRS initiated adjustments if the refunds are paid after Mar. 18, 2010, the grace period during which the government isn't required to pay interest on overpayments is increased from 45 days to 180 days for overpayments resulting from excess amounts deducted and withheld under chapter 3 of the Code (Code Sec. 1441 through Code Sec. 1464 (withholding on nonresident aliens and foreign corporations)) or chapter 4 of the Code (Code Sec. 1471 through Code Sec. 1474). (Code Sec. 6611(e))

With respect to returns filed after the due date (with extensions), no interest is payable for the period preceding the actual filing date. (Code Sec. 6611(b)(3))[13] And, no interest is payable on an estate's overpayment unless it shows that the interest (and refund) won't escheat to the state. (Code Sec. 6408)[14] IRS also won't pay interest when it refunds a conditional or advance payment of taxes.[15]

The overpayment rate for corporations except C corporations with large overpayments is the short-term AFR plus two percentage points. But, the overpayment rate for individuals is the short-term AFR plus 3 percentage points (i.e., the same as the underpayment rate, see ¶4867). (Code Sec. 6621(a)(1))[16] Recently the overpayment rate for corporations has been 3% (Apr. 1, 2009—Dec. 31, 2010).[17] For C corporations, the rate is reduced to the short-term AFR plus 0.5 percentage points, to the extent the overpayment for any period exceeds $10,000. (Code Sec. 6621(a)(1))[18] Recently, this rate has been 1.5% (Apr. 1, 2009—Dec. 31, 2010).[19]

The overpayment date for taxes withheld or paid as estimated taxes is the unextended due date of the return. (Code Sec. 6513(b))[20]

A deposit that is returned to a taxpayer is treated as a payment of tax for any period to the extent (and only to the extent) attributable to a disputable tax for that period. (Code Sec. 6603(d)(1)) However, the interest on the return of such a deposit is payable only at the short-term AFR rate compounded daily. (Code Sec. 6603(d)(4))[21]

Overpayments resulting from the carryback of an NOL, net capital loss, business credit, or foreign tax credit, are considered not to have been made before the "filing date" for the tax year in which the loss or credit arose or the foreign tax was in fact paid or accrued. (Code Sec. 6611(f))[22] Similarly, where a business credit carryback is attributable to an NOL, etc., carryback from a later year, the overpayment is considered not to have been made before the filing date for that later year. (Code Sec. 6611(f)(3))[23]

8. ¶T-6742; ¶64,024.17; TD ¶805,033
9. ¶s T-8008, T-8031, T-8034; ¶66,114; TD ¶807,006
10. ¶T-8024; ¶66,114; TD ¶807,012
11. ¶T-8027; ¶66,114; TD ¶807,015
12. ¶T-8028; ¶66,114; TD ¶807,016
13. ¶T-8008; ¶66,114; TD ¶807,006
14. ¶s T-8063, T-8065; ¶64,084; TD ¶807,044
15. ¶T-8046; ¶66,114

16. ¶T-8002; ¶66,214; TD ¶807,001
17. ¶T-8003.1; ¶66,214; TD ¶807,001
18. ¶T-8002; ¶66,214; TD ¶807,001
19. ¶T-8003.2; ¶66,214; TD ¶807,001
20. ¶T-7530; ¶s 66,114, 65,134; TD ¶806,026
21. ¶S-5804.3; ¶66,034.01; TD ¶807,006.1
22. ¶T-8049 *et seq.*; ¶66,114; TD ¶807,034
23. ¶T-8051; ¶66,114; TD ¶807,035

¶ 4856   Deadline for refund claims.

A claim for credit or refund of a tax paid by *return* must be filed within the later of: (1) three years from the date the return was timely or untimely filed (or the due date if filed earlier), or (2) two years from the date the tax was paid. If the required return wasn't filed, the claim must be filed within two years from when the tax was paid. (Code Sec. 6511(a))[24] This limitations period has been held to apply to telephone excise tax refund claims.[25] A refund claim filed on a Form 1040X after the limitations period expired was allowed where it was found to be amendment to an original timely claim, rather than an untimely new claim. For the prohibited transaction excise tax (¶4347), the relevant return is the plan's annual Form 5500, not Form 5330 on which the tax is reported.[26] A remittance accompanying an automatic filing extension is a tax payment for this purpose.[27]

However, a longer refund claim period applies in these cases:

. . . If a taxpayer and IRS execute one of the Form 872 series extending the assessment period (see ¶4838), the claim can be filed within six months after the expiration of the extended assessment period. (Code Sec. 6511(c)(1))[28]

. . . For an overpayment resulting from carryback of an NOL, net capital loss, or business credit, the period expires three years after the time the return is due (including extensions) for the year the loss or credit arose, not the year to which it's carried back. The Federal Circuit has held that this exception does not apply to a year to which a net capital loss is carried over. (Code Sec. 6511(d)(2), Code Sec. 6511(d)(4))[29] If the overpayment is attributable to a carryback from a later year, the period expires three years after the time for filing the return (including extensions) for that later year. (Code Sec. 6511(d)(4))[30]

. . . For an overpayment resulting from the payment or accrual of foreign taxes for which a foreign tax credit is allowed, the claim period is ten years. (Code Sec. 6511(d)(3))[31]

. . . For an overpayment resulting from a bad debt or from worthless securities, the claim period is seven years. (Code Sec. 6511(d)(1))[32]

. . . For self-employment tax claims attributable to Tax Court employment status proceedings, the claim period is two years after the calendar year in which the Tax Court determination becomes final. (Code Sec. 6511(d)(7))[33]

. . . For credit or refund claims filed after June 17, 2008 for retired military personnel who receive disability determinations from the Dept. of Veterans Affairs (VA), the refund claim filing period is extended for one year after the date of a disability determination from the VA (if later than the time allowed under the general refund limitations period). (This would apply to cases where an individual receives includible retirement benefits that are later retroactively determined to have been service-connected disability benefits excludable from income.) But, the extended time period doesn't apply for any tax year beginning more than five years before the date of the disability determination. (Code Sec. 6511(d)(8))[34]

Also, under certain circumstances, the limitations period is suspended during any period an individual is unable to manage his financial affairs by reason of his medically-determinable physical or mental impairment. (Code Sec. 6511(h))[35]

---

24. ¶T-7501 *et seq.*; ¶65,114; TD ¶806,001
25. ¶T-7504.1
26. ¶T-7524; ¶65,114.04; TD ¶806,022
27. ¶S-5801.4; TD ¶806,031
28. ¶T-7574; ¶65,114.09; TD ¶806,068
29. ¶T-7554; ¶s 65,114.11, 65,114.13; TD ¶806,050

30. ¶T-7563; ¶65,114.13; TD ¶806,058
31. ¶T-7569; ¶65,114.12; TD ¶806,063
32. ¶T-7552; ¶65,114.10; TD ¶806,049
33. ¶T-7573.1; ¶65,114.155; TD ¶806,067
34. ¶T-7573.2; ¶65,114.16; TD ¶806,076
35. ¶T-7506; ¶65,114; TD ¶806,008

¶ 4857 Refund suit period.

A taxpayer *must* file a refund claim with IRS before starting a suit for refund (or credit). (Code Sec. 7422(a))[36] The refund suit can't be started *before* six months from filing the claim (unless IRS acts on the claim in that period), or *after* two years from the date IRS mails a notice of disallowance. (Code Sec. 6532(a)(1)) The taxpayer can waive (on Form 2297) issuance of this notice and the two-year period will start on the date the waiver is filed. (Code Sec. 6532(a)(3)) Also, the taxpayer and IRS can execute a Form 907 extending the two-year period. (Code Sec. 6532(a)(2))[37]

¶ 4858 Limits on amount of refund or credit.

If a claim is filed within three years from the time the return was filed, the refund or credit is limited to the portion of tax paid during the three years (plus the period of any filing extension) immediately preceding the filing of the claim. (Code Sec. 6511(b)(2)(A))[38] If the claim wasn't filed within the three-year period, the refund or credit is limited to the portion of the tax paid during the two years immediately preceding the filing of the claim. (Code Sec. 6511(b)(2)(B)) This two-year limitation also applies if a claim, but no return, was filed. (Reg § 301.6511(b)-1(b)(1)(iii))[39] Where no claim is filed and a refund or credit is allowed within three years from the time the return was filed, the refund or credit is limited to the portion of the tax paid during the three years immediately before the allowance. If the refund or credit is not allowed within that three-year period, it's limited to the portion of the tax paid during the two years immediately before the allowance. (Code Sec. 6511(b)(2)(C))[40] The Tax Court cannot refund taxes that a non-filer paid more than two years before a deficiency notice was mailed. (Code Sec. 6512(b)(3))[41]

For purposes of determining the amount of an individual taxpayer's refund or credit under these rules, the refund claim periods described above are suspended during any period when the individual is unable to manage his financial affairs (see ¶4856). (Code Sec. 6511(h))[42]

¶ 4859 Tax litigation.

A taxpayer may go to:

. . . the Tax Court to set aside a deficiency determined by IRS (¶4860) (Code Sec. 6214(a));[43]

. . . a U.S. district court or the U.S. Court of Federal Claims to recover an overpayment of taxes (after filing a refund claim) (Code Sec. 6532(a));[44]

. . . a U.S. district court or the U.S. Court of Federal Claims to determine the correct amount of (or for a refund of) the estate's estate tax liability, even if it wasn't fully paid due to a Code Sec. 6166 election. (Code Sec. 7422(j)(1))[45]

. . . the Tax Court, the district court for the DC Circuit or the U.S. Court of Federal Claims for a declaratory judgment on the tax status of a charity or foundation (Code Sec. 7428(a));[46]

. . . the Tax Court for a declaratory judgment on retirement plan qualification (Code Sec. 7476(a)),[47] eligibility for deferral of estate tax on a closely held business interest (Code Sec. 7479),[48] or the value of certain gifts made. (Code Sec. 7477; Reg § 301.7477-1);[49]

. . . the Tax Court for review of IRS's failure to abate interest (Code Sec. 6404(g));[50]

. . . the Tax Court for a worker classification determination in certain cases. (Code

36. ¶T-6701; ¶74,224; TD ¶808,006
37. ¶T-9034; ¶65,324.01; TD ¶808,017
38. ¶T-7537; ¶65,114.07; TD ¶806,037
39. ¶s T-7546, T-7547; ¶65,114.07
40. ¶T-7548; ¶65,114.07; TD ¶806,045
41. ¶T-7578
42. ¶T-7537; ¶65,114; TD ¶806,008
43. ¶U-2100 *et seq.*; ¶s 62,144 *et seq.*, 74,414 *et seq.*

44. ¶s U-4000 *et seq.*, U-6000 *et seq.*; ¶74,224 *et seq.*; TD ¶802,019
45. ¶T-9007.1; ¶74,224; TD ¶808,004
46. ¶s U-3800 *et seq.*, U-4116, U-6005; ¶74,284
47. ¶U-3700 *et seq.*; ¶74,764
48. ¶U-3851 *et seq.*; ¶74,794
49. ¶U-3880; ¶74,774
50. ¶U-2129.1; ¶64,044

Sec. 7436)[1]

. . . a district court to enjoin IRS from assessing and collecting a tax in certain cases (¶4910), or to get damages for IRS's unauthorized collection activities or failure to release a lien. (Code Sec. 7432, Code Sec. 7433)[2]

. . . a bankruptcy court to sue for up to $1 million in damages for willful IRS violations of automatic stay or discharge in bankruptcy. (Code Sec. 7433(e))[3]

For taxpayers other than certain large partnerships, corporations, and trusts, IRS has the burden of proof in any court proceeding with respect to any factual issue relevant to ascertaining a taxpayer's liability for any tax imposed by subtitle A or B of the Code, e.g., income and self-employment, gift, estate, and generation-skipping transfer taxes, if the taxpayer: introduces credible evidence with respect to the issue; has complied with the substantiation requirements; has maintained all required records; and has cooperated with reasonable IRS requests. (Code Sec. 7491(a))[4] IRS has the burden of production (i.e., to come forward initially with evidence) in any court proceeding with respect to the liability of any individual for any penalty imposed by the Code. (Code Sec. 7491(c))[5] The Supreme Court has declined to review a Second Circuit decision holding that a shift of the burden of proof to IRS didn't require the Tax Court to adopt the estate's valuation method.

¶ 4860   The Tax Court.

To get Tax Court review of a deficiency, a taxpayer must file a petition with the Tax Court at Washington, D.C., in response to a 90-day letter (see ¶4826) from IRS, within 90 days (150 days if the letter is addressed to a person outside the U.S.) after the letter is mailed (i.e., postmarked). A petition is treated as timely if it's filed with the Tax Court on or before the last date specified by IRS in the 90-day letter for filing it. (Code Sec. 6213(a))[6]

The Tax Court's jurisdiction generally is limited to the review (without a jury) of deficiencies asserted by IRS (and not paid when the 90-day letter is issued). It can order payment of a refund if it determines the taxpayer overpaid. (Code Sec. 6512(b)) But it can't grant equitable relief. The Tax Court has jurisdiction to order a refund of any amount collected while IRS was prohibited from collecting a deficiency by levy or court proceeding but only if a timely petition for a redetermination of the deficiency has been filed and only with respect to the deficiency at issue. (Code Sec. 6213(a))[7] The Tax Court has jurisdiction, which the Supreme Court has held is exclusive, to review IRS's failure to abate interest to taxpayers within certain net worth limits who bring an action within 180 days of IRS's final adverse determination, and to order abatement if IRS abused its discretion. (Code Sec. 6404(i))[8] It can also determine worker classification in certain cases and, according to it, the correct amount of employment taxes that relate to such determinations. (Code Sec. 7436)[9] It has jurisdiction to determine innocent spouse relief when a deficiency has been issued and the taxpayer elects regular or separate innocent spouse relief or requests equitable relief, but it can't rule on the timeliness of an assessment in reviewing a denial of innocent spouse relief. (Code Sec. 6015(e)) The Tax Court has held that it could adjudicate a taxpayer's claim for spousal relief even though her former spouse intervened and later filed for bankruptcy, triggering an automatic stay.[10] The Tax Court generally is barred from determining whether the tax for any period not before it has been overpaid or underpaid. However, it may apply the doctrine of equitable recoupment, even though, according to the Tax Court, it lacks subject matter jurisdiction over the type of tax to which the equitable recoupment claim is directed. (Code Sec. 6214(b))[11] The Tax Court has exclusive jurisdiction over appeals of Collection Due Process hearings (¶4905).

1. ¶U-2143; ¶74,364
2. ¶s V-5801, V-6113; ¶s 74,324, 74,334; TD ¶903,010
3. ¶V-5820 *et seq.*; ¶74,334
4. ¶U-1351; ¶74,914
5. ¶U-1331; ¶74,914
6. ¶U-2300 *et seq.*; ¶62,134 *et seq.*

7. ¶U-2134.1; ¶s 65,124, 74,424; TD ¶806,072
8. ¶U-2129.1; ¶64,044
9. ¶U-2143; ¶74,364
10. ¶U-2148; ¶75,214
11. ¶U-2138; ¶62,144.02

¶ 4861   Settlement after Tax Court petition is filed.

IRS District Counsel will refer all docketed Tax Court cases to the Appeals Office for consideration of settlement (unless Appeals issued the deficiency notice, in which case there will be no referral if there is little likelihood that all or part of the case can be settled in a reasonable period of time). Counsel and Appeals can agree otherwise, work together, or transfer the case back and forth to promote efficient disposition of the case. The taxpayer-petitioner and/or his representative will be notified as to who has the case and the settlement authority.[12] If the taxpayer and IRS agree on a settlement, they enter into a written agreement stipulating the amount of any deficiency or overpayment. This stipulation is filed with the Tax Court which will enter a decision in accordance with it. (Reg § 601.106(d)(3)(i))[13]

¶ 4862   Small tax claims in Tax Court.

Special informal procedures apply, at a taxpayer's election and with the Tax Court's concurrence, to any Tax Court case where neither the amount (including any additions to tax, additional amounts and penalties) of the deficiency disputed nor of any claimed overpayment exceeds $50,000 (the Tax Court has held that the limit includes tax, interest and penalties and applies to the total owed for all years in a single proceeding). The taxpayer thus gets the court's decision faster and more easily, but gives up the right to appeal. (Code Sec. 7463)[14]

¶ 4863   Appeals from Tax Court, district court and U.S. Court of Federal Claims.

Decisions of the Tax Court and U.S. district courts are appealable to the U.S. Court of Appeals.[15] The appeal is made generally in the circuit where the taxpayer's legal residence (for appeals from Tax Court)[16] or the trial court (for appeals from district courts) is located.[17] U.S. Court of Federal Claims decisions may be appealed to the Court of Appeals for the Federal Circuit.[18] Appeals from U.S. Courts of Appeals are to the U.S. Supreme Court.[19]

¶ 4864   Recovery of attorneys' fees and costs.

Taxpayers whose net worth doesn't exceed specified limits, who meet other requirements, and who prevail against the U.S. in court (or at the administrative level) may be awarded reasonable litigation and administrative costs (including the costs of recovering the award). (Code Sec. 7430) For 2009 and 2010, the limit on attorney fee recoveries is $180 per hour. (Code Sec. 7430(c)(1)) To avoid an award of fees, IRS must establish that its position was substantially justified. (Code Sec. 7430(c)(4)(B)) Administrative costs can be awarded from the date IRS sends the "30-day letter." (Code Sec. 7430(c)(2)) IRS losses on similar issues in other circuits are taken into account in determining whether its position was substantially justified (Code Sec. 7430(c)(4)(B)(iii)), and costs can be awarded where a taxpayer makes an offer, IRS rejects it and later gets a judgment equal to or less than the offer. (Code Sec. 7430(c)(4)(E)(i); Reg § 301.7430-7)[20]

¶ 4865   Interest and Penalties.

Interest is charged on underpayments of tax. Various civil and criminal penalties are imposed on taxpayers (and/or return preparers) who violate the tax law.

12. ¶T-1901 *et seq.*; TD ¶832,003
13. ¶T-1909; TD ¶832,004
14. ¶U-3600 *et seq.*; ¶74,536.1704
15. ¶s U-3417, U-5000 *et seq.*; ¶s 74,336.12, 74,824
16. ¶U-5202; ¶74,824
17. ¶U-5401
18. ¶U-6001; ¶74,336.10
19. ¶s U-5700 *et seq.*, U-7000 *et seq.*; ¶74,336.15
20. ¶U-1240 *et seq.*; ¶74,304

¶ 4866   Interest on underpayments.

Interest is generally payable whenever any tax or civil penalty isn't paid when due (Code Sec. 6601(a)), even if the taxpayer has been granted an extension of time to pay the tax. (Code Sec. 6601(b)(1); Reg § 301.6601-1(a)) There's no interest on late payments of estimated tax (Code Sec. 6601(h)) (but for comparable penalty computations, see ¶3159 (individuals) and ¶3352 (corporations)) or unemployment tax. (Code Sec. 6601(i))[21] Interest is payable on an erroneous refund or credit. (Code Sec. 6602)[22]

¶ 4867   Interest rate on underpayments.

The rate of interest on tax underpayments and penalties is keyed to the short-term applicable federal rate (AFR) for the first month of the previous calendar quarter (Code Sec. 6621(a)(2)), and is compounded daily.[23] Recently, this rate has been 4% (Apr. 1, 2009—Dec. 31, 2010).[24] If a C corporation's tax underpayment for any tax period exceeds $100,000, a higher interest rate (short-term AFR plus five percentage points) applies for the period after the 30th day after a notice (or proposed notice) of deficiency. Recently this rate has been 6% (Apr. 1, 2009—Dec. 31, 2010). (Code Sec. 6621(c)(3); Reg § 301.6621-3)[25] A net interest rate of zero applies to equivalent amounts of underpayments and overpayments. (Code Sec. 6621(d)) Taxpayers request interest netting on Form 843.[26]

¶ 4868   Interest accrual period.

Interest on unpaid tax liabilities runs from the last day prescribed by the Code for payment (disregarding extensions or any installment payment agreement) (Code Sec. 6601(b)(1)), to the date paid. (Code Sec. 6601(a)) However, where the tax is paid within 21 days after notice and demand (10 business days if the amount is $100,000 or more), interest stops on the date of the notice and demand. (Code Sec. 6601(e)(3))[27] (For payments to stop interest, see ¶4869.) Also, where a taxpayer consents to immediate assessment (by signing one of the Form 870 waiver of assessment series, see ¶4821) and IRS doesn't make notice and demand for payment within 30 days of the filing of that consent, interest stops running during the period beginning immediately after that 30th day and ending with the date of the notice and demand. (Code Sec. 6601(c))[28]

Interest on civil penalties runs from the date of notice and demand if not paid within 21 days after that date (10 business days for amounts of $100,000 or more). (Code Sec. 6601(e)(2)(A)) But for the penalties for failure to file, valuation misstatement (income tax) or understatement (estate or gift tax), substantial understatement, negligence, and (except for returns due (without extension) before '89) fraud, the interest period begins on the *return* due date (with extensions). In either case, the interest stops on the date the penalty is paid. (Code Sec. 6601(e)(2)(B))[29]

¶ 4869   Deposits to prepay and/or stop the running of interest.

A cash deposit made in conformity with IRS rules may be used to pay income, gift, estate, or generation-skipping tax or certain excise taxes that have not yet been assessed at the time of the deposit. (Code Sec. 6603(a)) The amount of the deposit that is later used by IRS to pay tax is treated as a tax payment at the time of the deposit, for purposes of determining whether the taxpayer owes interest on an underpayment of tax. (Code Sec. 6603(b)) Interest may be allowed on the return of all or part of such a deposit, see ¶4855.[30]

21. ¶V-1000 *et seq.*; ¶66,014; TD ¶852,001
22. ¶T-9108; ¶66,024; TD ¶852,008
23. ¶s V-1101, V-1104; ¶66,214; TD ¶851,001
24. ¶V-1102; ¶66,214; TD ¶851,001
25. ¶V-1106 *et seq.*; ¶66,214; TD ¶851,005

26. ¶V-1301.1; ¶66,014; TD ¶851,008
27. ¶V-1200 *et seq.*, ¶V-1300; ¶66,014.02; TD ¶853,001
28. ¶V-1307; ¶66,014.02; TD ¶853,002
29. ¶V-1225; ¶66,014.02; TD ¶853,018
30. ¶S-5804 *et seq.*; ¶66,034; TD ¶853,009 *et seq.*

¶ 4870 How other year's tax payments affect interest.

Interest on a deficiency isn't eliminated when the deficiency is eliminated by a net operating loss (NOL), net capital loss or business credit carryback (or a foreign tax credit carryback arising in a tax year beginning after Aug. 5, '97). It accrues from its original due date to the filing date for the tax year in which the carryback arose (or, with respect to any portion of a credit carryback attributable to a carryback from a later year, to the filing date for that later year). (Code Sec. 6601(d))[31]

An underpayment of tax in one year may be paid by crediting against it an overpayment of tax in another year. (Code Sec. 6402(a)) No interest accrues on any portion of the underpayment so paid for any period after the return due date (*without* extension) for the overpayment year or, if later, when the offsetting return is filed. This rule doesn't apply to the extent the zero rate (¶4867) applies. (Code Sec. 6601(f))[32]

When a taxpayer elects to apply an overpayment to the following year's estimated taxes, the overpayment will be applied to unpaid installments of estimated tax due on or after the date(s) the overpayment arose, in the order in which they are required to be paid to avoid an estimated tax penalty. IRS will assess interest on a later determined deficiency for the overpayment year only from the date(s) that the overpayment is applied to the following year's estimated taxes.[33]

¶ 4871 Abatement of interest, penalties and additions to tax—Form 843.

IRS has discretion to abate any interest that was assessed because of a deficiency attributable to any unreasonable error or delay by an IRS officer or employer acting in his official capacity when performing a managerial or ministerial act, or that is due on a notice of deficiency to the extent any error or delay in payment is attributable to an IRS employee or officer being erroneous or dilatory in performing a managerial or ministerial act, but only if no significant aspect of the error or delay can be attributed to the taxpayer involved. (Code Sec. 6404(e)(1); Reg § 301.6404-2)[34]

IRS must abate any portion of any penalty or addition to tax attributable to erroneous written advice (as specifically defined) (Reg § 301.6404-3(c)(1)) furnished to a taxpayer by an IRS officer or employee acting in an official capacity in response to a specific written request. The taxpayer must have reasonably relied on the advice (Code Sec. 6404(f)(1), Code Sec. 6404(f)(2)(A)), and the portion of the penalty or addition to tax must not have resulted from his failure to provide adequate or accurate information. (Code Sec. 6404(f)(2)(B))[35]

Make the abatement request on Form 843 (as annotated and with certain attachments as required by the regs). (Reg § 301.6404-3(d))[36]

For taxpayers affected by a federally declared disaster or a terroristic or military action, IRS may postpone the deadlines for performing various tax acts for a period of up to one year. The postponement period may be disregarded in determining the amount of interest due for periods after the disaster date. (Code Sec. 7508A(a)(2))[37]

¶ 4872 Interest and penalty suspension for failing to notify individual of liability.

Subject to exceptions (including a gross misstatement such as a substantial omission of items to which the six-year statute of limitation applies (see ¶4834), a gross valuation misstatement (see ¶4881), undisclosed reportable transactions, and listed transactions (see ¶4892)), the imposition of interest and penalties with respect to any failure relating to a

31. ¶V-1302; ¶66,014.03; TD ¶853,015
32. ¶V-1301; ¶66,014.03
33. ¶V-1210; TD ¶853,013
34. ¶T-3951 *et seq.*; ¶64,044; TD ¶837,514

35. ¶T-3908 *et seq.*; ¶64,044; TD ¶837,504
36. ¶T-3914 *et seq.*; TD ¶837,503
37. ¶T-3973; ¶75,08A4; TD ¶837,623

timely filed individual income tax return must be suspended if, before the end of the 36-month period beginning on the date the return is filed or, if later, the date it's due (without extensions), IRS fails to provide a notice to the taxpayer specifically stating the taxpayer's liability and the basis for the liability. The suspension period begins on the day after the end of the 36-month period and ends on the date that's 21 days after IRS provides the notice. Where a taxpayer files an amended return (or other written document) showing additional tax liability, the 36-month period for IRS to issue the required notice of liability (and avoid interest or penalty suspension) is restarted. (Code Sec. 6404(g); Reg § 301.6404-4)[38]

¶ 4873   When reasonable cause excuses civil penalties.

Certain civil penalties won't be imposed if the taxpayer's failure to perform the required act was due to reasonable cause—e.g., reliance on tax expert or IRS advice, irregularities in mail delivery, death or serious illness, unavoidable absence, casualty, disaster. Generally, a taxpayer who challenges IRS's imposition of a civil penalty has the burden of showing that his failure was due to reasonable cause and not willful neglect.[39]

No accuracy-related (¶4876 *et seq.*) or fraud (¶4883) penalty applies as to any portion of an underpayment for which the taxpayer shows reasonable cause and that he acted in good faith. (Code Sec. 6664(c)(1); Reg § 1.6664-4) A taxpayer's failure to disclose a reportable transaction (¶4748) is a strong indication of failure to act in good faith. (Reg § 1.6664-4(d))[40]

The reasonable cause exception generally doesn't apply to an underpayment attributable to a substantial or gross valuation overstatement as to charitable deduction property. But, this bar doesn't apply to a substantial valuation overstatement if the claimed value of the property was based on a qualified appraisal made by a qualified appraiser, and the taxpayer made a good faith investigation of the value of the contributed property. (Code Sec. 6664(c)(2))[41]

¶ 4874   Failure to file income, estate or gift tax returns when due.

The penalty is 5% of the amount of tax required to be shown on the return (less any earlier payments and credits) for the first month (Code Sec. 6651(b)(1)), plus an additional 5% for each month (or fraction of a month) the failure continues without reasonable cause (¶4873), but not more than 25%. (Code Sec. 6651(a)(1))[42] There's a minimum penalty for failure to file any income tax return within 60 days of the due date (including extensions), except if due to reasonable cause and not willful neglect. This minimum penalty is the lesser of $135 or the amount of tax required to be shown on the return. (Code Sec. 6651(a))[43] The failure-to-file penalty (5%) is reduced (but not below the above minimum) by the amount of any failure-to-pay penalty (½%, see ¶4875) for that month. (Code Sec. 6651(c)(1)) The 25% ceiling is applied to each penalty before making this reduction.[44] If the failure to file is fraudulent, the penalty is increased to 15% per month (or fraction), up to a 75% cap. (Code Sec. 6651(f))[45]

¶ 4875   Failure to pay tax.

A penalty is imposed on a taxpayer who, without reasonable cause (¶4873) fails to pay the tax shown on a return or an assessed deficiency of that tax by the prescribed date. The penalty is ½% of tax shown (or assessed) for each month (or fraction of a month) that it isn't paid (but not more than 25%). (Code Sec. 6651(a)(2), Code Sec. 6651(a)(3))[46] A substitute return prepared by IRS is a return. (Code Sec. 6651(g)(2); Reg § 301.6020-1(b)(3))[47] The penalty is increased to 1% per month or fraction (up to 25% penalty maximum) if the tax isn't paid within ten days after IRS serves notice of levy. (Code Sec. 6651(d))[48] The penalty is

---

38. ¶V-1401, ¶V-1601.2, ¶V-1401, V-1601.2; ¶64,044; TD ¶s 837,509, 852,006
39. ¶V-1776 *et seq.*, ¶V-2750 *et seq.*; ¶66,644; TD ¶868,500 *et seq.*
40. ¶V-2060; TD ¶863,001
41. ¶V-2237; ¶66,644; TD ¶863,001
42. ¶V-1750 *et seq.*; ¶66,514.01; TD ¶861,001

43. ¶V-1752; ¶66,514.01; TD ¶861,001
44. ¶V-1791; ¶66,514.01; TD ¶861,001
45. ¶V-1753; ¶66,514.01
46. ¶V-1671 *et seq.*; ¶66,514.01; TD ¶862,501
47. ¶V-1685; ¶60,204; TD ¶862,515
48. ¶V-1683; ¶66,514.01; TD ¶862,513

reduced to ¼% per month for individuals paying in installments. (Code Sec. 6651(h))[49] An individual who gets an automatic extension of time for *filing* is subject to the penalty (absent reasonable cause) if any additional payment due with the extended return *either*: (1) exceeds 10% of the total shown on Form 1040, *or* (2) isn't paid by the extended filing date. (Reg § 301.6651-1(c)(3))[50]

¶ 4876   Accuracy-related penalty.

An "accuracy-related" civil penalty applies if any portion of an understatement of tax on a tax return is due (absent reasonable cause, see ¶4873) to: negligence (¶4877), substantial income tax valuation misstatements (¶4878), income tax understatements (¶4879), estate or gift tax valuation understatements (¶4881), pension liability overstatements (¶4882), disallowance of benefits due to lack of economic substance (¶4896), or undisclosed foreign financial asset understatements (¶4880). (Code Sec. 6662(a), Code Sec. 6662(b), Code Sec. 6664(c)(1); Reg § 1.6662-2(a))[1] :

The accuracy-related penalty doesn't apply to any portion of an underpayment for which the fraud penalty (¶4883) is imposed or to the portion of any underpayment which is attributable to a reportable transaction understatement on which the Code Sec. 6662A reportable transaction understatement penalty is imposed, except: (i) for purposes of determining whether an underpayment is substantial or (ii) where the 40% gross valuation misstatement penalty applies. (Code Sec. 6662(b))[2] Also, it only applies if a return is filed by the taxpayer (not by IRS). (Code Sec. 6664(b); Reg § 1.6662-2(a))[3]

¶ 4877   Negligence.

The "accuracy-related" penalty is imposed if any part of an underpayment of tax is due either to negligence or to disregard of rules or regs but without intent to defraud. The penalty is 20% of the portion of the underpayment attributable to the negligence, etc. (Code Sec. 6662(a), Code Sec. 6662(b)(1)) For rules common to all accuracy-related penalties, see ¶4876. "Negligence" includes any failure to make a reasonable attempt to comply with the law or to exercise ordinary and reasonable care in preparing a tax return, as well as failure to keep adequate books and records or to substantiate items properly. "Disregard" includes any careless, reckless or intentional disregard. (Code Sec. 6662(c); Reg § 1.6662-3(b))[4]

The penalties are not imposed for a position with respect to an item (other than a reportable transaction) that is contrary to a revenue ruling or a notice (other than a proposed rulemaking) published in the IRB, if the position has a realistic possibility of being sustained on its merits. (Reg § 1.6662-3(a)) The penalty for disregard of rules or regs isn't imposed where a position is contrary to a rule or reg if the position is disclosed and has a reasonable basis, the taxpayer keeps adequate books and records and substantiates items properly; and, in the case of a position contrary to a reg, the position represents a good faith challenge to the reg. (Reg § 1.6662-3(c), Reg § 1.6662-7(c))[5]

¶ 4878   Misstating value or basis of property on income tax return.

The accuracy-related penalty is imposed on a taxpayer who makes any of these "substantial valuation misstatements": (Code Sec. 6662(b)(3))

. . . any value (or adjusted basis) claimed on an income tax return that is 150% or more of the correct figure (Code Sec. 6662(e)(1)(A));

. . . Code Sec. 482 transfer price adjustments where the price for any property (or its use) or services on an income tax return is 200% or more, or 50% or less, of the correct figure—

49. ¶V-1684; ¶66,514; TD ¶862,514
50. ¶V-1681; ¶66,514
1. ¶V-2000 *et seq.*; ¶66,624; TD ¶863,000
2. ¶V-2002; ¶66,624; TD ¶865,004

3. ¶V-2051; ¶66,624; TD ¶863,001
4. ¶V-2105; ¶66,624; TD ¶863,005.5
5. ¶V-2106 *et seq.*; ¶66,624.02; TD ¶863,005.6

transactional penalty (Code Sec. 6662(e)(1)(B)(i); Reg § 1.6662-6(b));

. . . a net increase in taxable income for a tax year (without regard to carryovers) resulting from all Code Sec. 482 adjustments in the transfer price of any property (or its use) or services, that (with certain adjustments) exceeds the lesser of $5 million or 10% of the taxpayer's gross receipts—net adjustment penalty. (Code Sec. 6662(e)(1)(B)(ii), Code Sec. 6662(e)(3); Reg § 1.6662-6(c))[6]

The penalty equals 20% of the portion of any income tax underpayment that results from the misstatement (except to the extent the fraud penalty is imposed) (Code Sec. 6662(a), Code Sec. 6662(b))—40% if the misstatement is gross (the above 200%, 150%, 50% and $5 million/10% figures are, respectively, 400%, 200%, 25% or $20 million/20%, or the correct value or basis is zero). (Code Sec. 6662(h); Reg § 1.6662-5(g))[7]

The penalty doesn't apply unless the amount of the underpayment for the tax year attributable to all these misstatements for the year exceeds $5,000 ($10,000 for corporations other than S corporations or personal holding companies). (Code Sec. 6662(e)(2))[8] Reasonable cause (¶4873) excuses the penalty. There's no disclosure exception. (Code Sec. 6664(c)(1); Reg § 1.6662-5(a))[9] Strict appraisal requirements apply to overvalued charitable gifts. (Code Sec. 6664(c)(2), Code Sec. 6664(c)(3))[10]

¶ 4879   Penalty on substantial understatements of income tax.

The 20% accuracy-related penalty is imposed on any portion of an underpayment of tax that (absent reasonable cause, see ¶4873) is attributable to any substantial understatement of income tax, self-employment tax (¶3140 *et seq.*), (Code Sec. 6662(a), Code Sec. 6662(b)(1); Reg § 1.6662-4(b)(3))[11] or unrelated business income tax (¶4121).[12] For rules common to all accuracy-related penalties, see ¶4876. For corporate taxpayers (other than S corporations and personal holding companies), an understatement is substantial if the amount of the understatement exceeds the lesser of (1) 10% of the tax required to be shown on the return for that tax year (or $10,000 if that is greater), or (2) $10 million. For other taxpayers, an understatement is substantial if it exceeds the greater of $5,000 or 10% of the tax required to be shown on the return. (Code Sec. 6662(d)(1); Reg § 1.6662-4(b)(1))[13]

An understatement is the excess of (a) the tax amount required to be shown on the return, over (b) the tax amount that's shown (or withheld) reduced by any rebate. (Code Sec. 6662(d)(2)(A); Reg § 1.6662-4(b)(2), Reg § 1.6662-4(b)(3))[14] The understatement is reduced to the extent attributable to any item (other than tax shelter items, see below) for which:

. . . there is or was substantial authority for how the taxpayer treated it (Code Sec. 6662(d)(2)(B)(i)), or

. . . the relevant facts affecting the item's tax treatment are adequately disclosed either on the return (IRS each year lists which items on the return qualify) or on a Form 8275 (Form 8275-R if the taxpayer's position is contrary to a reg) attached to the return *and* there's a reasonable basis (¶4877) for the taxpayer's treatment of the item. (Code Sec. 6662(d)(2)(B)(ii); Reg § 1.6662-4(f)) A corporation doesn't have a reasonable basis for its tax treatment of an item attributable to a multi-party financing transaction if the treatment doesn't clearly reflect its income. (Code Sec. 6662(d)(2))[15]

For tax shelter items, a noncorporate taxpayer's understatement is reduced only to the extent there is or was substantial authority for that treatment *and* he reasonably believed his

6. ¶V-2200 *et seq.*; ¶66,624; TD ¶863,010
7. ¶V-2206 *et seq.*; ¶66,624; TD ¶863,010
8. ¶V-2205; ¶66,624; TD ¶863,010
9. ¶V-2234; ¶66,644; TD ¶863,001
10. ¶V-2237; ¶66,644; TD ¶863,011

11. ¶V-2150 *et seq.*; ¶66,624; TD ¶863,014
12. ¶V-2151; TD ¶863,014
13. ¶V-2159; ¶66,624.03; TD ¶863,014
14. ¶V-2154; ¶66,624.03; TD ¶863,015
15. ¶s V-2154, V-2167 *et seq.*; ¶66,624.04; TD ¶863,017

treatment was more likely than not proper. There's no disclosure exception. Corporate tax-payers get no reduction. (Code Sec. 6662(d)(2)(C); Reg § 1.6662-4(g))[16]

"Substantial authority" exists for the tax treatment of an item (only if the weight of the authorities supporting the treatment is substantial in relation to the weight of authorities supporting contrary positions (in light of the pertinent facts and circumstances). (Reg § 1.6662-4(d)(3)(i))[17]

¶ 4880 Penalty on undisclosed foreign financial assets understatement.

For tax years beginning after Mar. 18, 2010, a 40% penalty is imposed on any understate-ment attributable to an undisclosed foreign financial asset. (Code Sec. 6662(j)(3)) The term "undisclosed foreign financial asset" includes all assets subject to information reporting re-quirements under Code Sec. 6038 (return of U.S. person who controls a foreign corporation or partnership), Code Sec. 6038B (return of U.S. person making certain "outbound" transfers to foreign entities), Code Sec. 6038D (self-reporting required for "specified foreign financial assets"), Code Sec. 6046A (return of U.S. person who acquires, disposes of, or has substantial changes in, foreign partnership interests), or Code Sec. 6048 (certain information reporting as to foreign trusts) for which the required information wasn't provided by the taxpayer as required under the applicable reporting provisions. (Code Sec. 6662(j)(2)) An understatement is attributable to an undisclosed foreign financial asset if it is attributable to any transaction involving the asset. (Code Sec. 6662(j)(1))[18]

¶ 4881 Penalty for understating value of property on gift or estate tax return.

If the value of any property claimed on any gift or estate tax return is 65% or less of the correct value, the 20% accuracy-related penalty (¶4876) is imposed on an underpayment of tax that's attributable to that understatement. (Code Sec. 6662(a), Code Sec. 6662(b)(5), Code Sec. 6662(g)(1)) The penalty is increased to 40% for gross misstatements—i.e., the claimed value is 40% or less of the correct figure. (Code Sec. 6662(h)(1), Code Sec. 6662(h)(2)(C))[19] The penalty applies only if the portion of the underpayment attributable to all these undervalua-tions for the tax period exceeds $5,000. (Code Sec. 6662(g)(2))[20]

¶ 4882 Overstatement of pension liabilities.

A taxpayer who (absent reasonable cause, see ¶4873) substantially overstates pension liabilities for a tax year is subject to the accuracy-related penalty (¶4876) if the overstatement results in an income tax underpayment of $1,000 or more. (Code Sec. 6662(a), Code Sec. 6662(b)(4), Code Sec. 6662(f)(2))[21] The penalty equals 20% of the underpayment (40% for "gross" overstatements). (Code Sec. 6662(a), Code Sec. 6662(h)(1))[22] Pension liabilities are substantially overstated if the actuarial determination of the liabilities taken into account in computing the contribution deduction (¶4334) is at least 200% of the correct amount. (Code Sec. 6662(f)(1)) The overstatement is "gross" if it's 400% or more of the correct figure. (Code Sec. 6662(h)(2)(B))[23]

¶ 4883 Fraud.

Fraudulent underpayment of tax required to be shown on a return results in a civil penalty of 75% of the portion of the underpayment attributable to fraud. (Code Sec. 6663(a))[24] The fraud penalty can be imposed only if a return is filed (not by IRS). (Code Sec. 6664(b))[25] It

16. ¶V-2154; ¶66,624.04
17. ¶V-2161, ¶V-2163; ¶66,624.04; TD ¶863,016
18. ¶V-2276; ¶66,624.13; TD ¶863,001
19. ¶s V-2251, V-2252; ¶66,624 (Estate & Gift), ¶66,624.10; TD ¶863,013
20. ¶V-2251; ¶66,624 (Estate & Gift), ¶66,624.10; TD ¶863,013

21. ¶V-2270 *et seq.*; ¶66,624.09; TD ¶863,012
22. ¶V-2272; ¶66,624.09; TD ¶863,012
23. ¶V-2263; ¶s 66,624, 66,624.09; TD ¶863,012
24. ¶V-2300 *et seq.*; ¶s 66,634, 66,534; TD ¶865,001
25. ¶V-2051; ¶66,634; TD ¶865,001

won't be imposed where the taxpayer shows reasonable cause (¶4873) for the underpayment, and that he acted in good faith. (Code Sec. 6664(c)(1))[26] Imposition of the fraud penalty on any part of an underpayment precludes imposition of any of the accuracy-related penalties (¶4876) on that same part. (Code Sec. 6662(b))[27] If IRS establishes that any part of an underpayment is attributable to fraud, the entire underpayment is treated as attributable to fraud, except for any part the taxpayer establishes (by a preponderance of the evidence) isn't so attributable. (Code Sec. 6663(b))[28]

¶ 4884   Trust fund recovery penalty for responsible persons.

Willful failure to collect or account for and pay over a tax or willful attempt to evade or defeat a tax, by a "responsible person" required to collect, account for, and pay over the tax carries a civil "trust fund recovery penalty" equal to 100% of the total tax evaded or not accounted for and paid over. (Code Sec. 6672) IRS can't assess the penalty without notifying a responsible person of its intent to do so at least 60 days before making notice and demand for the penalty (unless collection is in jeopardy). (Code Sec. 6672(b)) A "responsible person" is an officer or employee of the corporation, or a partner or employee of a partnership, who is under a duty to perform the act at issue. (Code Sec. 6671(b))[29] Unpaid volunteer board members of exempt organizations who aren't involved in day-to-day financial activities and don't know about the penalized failure are exempt from the penalty, unless that results in no one being liable for it. (Code Sec. 6672(e))[30] For tax years beginning before 2011, the penalty applies to an employer's failure to make advance earned income credit payments to an employee who had a valid certificate in effect (Code Sec. 3507(d)(4)) unless the employer had properly withheld and deposited all income and FICA taxes for the employee. (Reg § 31.3507-1(c)(4))[31]

IRS must disclose, at the written request of a responsible person, the names of other responsible persons and the collection activities related to them. (Code Sec. 6103(e)(9))[32] Responsible persons who pay more than their proportionate share of tax have the right to recover the excess from other responsible persons. (Code Sec. 6672(d))[33]

¶ 4885   Penalty for filing erroneous refund claim.

If a claim for refund or credit of income tax (other than one relating to the earned income credit) is made for an "excessive amount," the person making the claim is liable for a penalty equal to 20% of the excessive amount. (Code Sec. 6676(a)) An "excessive amount" is the amount by which the claimed refund or credit exceeds the allowable amount. (Code Sec. 6676(b)) The penalty doesn't apply if it is shown that the claim for the excessive amount has a reasonable basis. (Code Sec. 6676(a)) But the reasonable basis exception doesn't apply to transactions entered into after Mar. 30, 2010 that lack economic substance (¶4896). (Code Sec. 6676(c)) The penalty doesn't apply to any portion of the excessive amount that's subject to an accuracy-related penalty imposed under Code Sec. 6662 (¶4876) or Code Sec. 6662A (¶4893) or a fraud penalty under Code Sec. 6663 (¶4883). (Code Sec. 6676(c))[34]

¶ 4886   Penalty for aiding and abetting understatement of tax liability.

A penalty of $1,000 ($10,000 for a corporation) (Code Sec. 6701(b))[35] is imposed on any person who aids or assists, procures or advises with respect to the preparation or presentation of any portion of a return, affidavit, claim or other document connected with any matter arising under the internal revenue laws, and who knows (or has reason to believe) that the portion will be used in connection with any material matter arising under those laws, and knows that an understatement of another person's tax would result from that use (Code

26. ¶V-2060; ¶66,644; TD ¶865,001
27. ¶V-2002; ¶66,624; TD ¶865,004
28. ¶V-2302; ¶66,634; TD ¶865,001
29. ¶V-1700 *et seq.*; ¶66,724; TD ¶864,001
30. ¶V-1703.1; TD ¶864,009

31. ¶V-1702; TD ¶864,003
32. ¶S-6313.1; TD ¶864,024
33. ¶V-1730; TD ¶864,024
34. ¶V-2291; ¶66,764
35. ¶V-2352; ¶67,104; TD ¶867,030

Sec. 6701(a)) even if there is no actual understatement.[36] The penalty applies whether or not the taxpayer knew of or gave consent to the understatement. (Code Sec. 6701(d))[37] The term "advises" includes the actions of lawyers and accountants who counsel a particular course of action[38] and appraisers who falsely or fraudulently overstate the value of property in a qualified appraisal (of property for which a charitable contribution is claimed, see ¶2138). (Reg § 1.170A-13(c)(3)(iii))[39]

⊘*observation:* Unlike the return preparer penalties which apply only to "paid" preparers (¶4887), the aiding and abetting penalty applies regardless of whether a fee is charged.

¶ 4887   Return preparer understatement penalties.

If a tax return preparer prepares a return or refund claim for which any part of a tax liability understatement is due to an "unreasonable position" and the preparer knew or should have known of the position, the preparer must pay a penalty for each return or claim equal to the greater of $1,000 or 50% of the income derived (or to be derived) by the preparer with respect to the return or claim. (Code Sec. 6694(a)(1)) In the case of a position with respect to a reportable transaction (to which Code Sec. 6662A applies, ¶4893) or a tax shelter, a position is unreasonable if it wasn't reasonable to believe that the position would more likely than not be sustained on its merits. In other cases, a position is unreasonable if (1) there wasn't substantial authority for it or (2) for a position that was disclosed in the return or in a statement attached to the return (under Code Sec. 6662(d)(2)(B)(ii)(I)), there was no reasonable basis for it. (Code Sec. 6694(a)(2); Reg § 1.6694-2(a)(1)) However, there's no penalty if it is shown that there was reasonable cause for the understatement and the preparer acted in good faith. (Code Sec. 6694(a)(3); Reg § 1.6694-2(e))[40]

"Tax return preparer" means any person who is a tax return preparer under the rules at ¶4751. An individual is a tax return preparer subject to the penalty if the individual is primarily responsible for the position on the return or claim for refund giving rise to an understatement. There is only one individual within a firm who is primarily responsible for each position on the return or claim for refund giving rise to an understatement. If there is a signing tax return preparer under the rules at ¶4751, he will generally be considered the person primarily responsible for all of the positions on the return or claim for refund giving rise to an understatement, unless, based on credible information from any source, it's concluded that the signing tax return preparer isn't primarily responsible for the position. If there is no signing tax return preparer for the return or claim for refund within the firm or if it's concluded that the signing tax return preparer isn't primarily responsible for the position, the nonsigning tax return preparer within the firm with overall supervisory responsibility for the position giving rise to the understatement generally will be considered the tax return preparer who is primarily responsible for the position for purposes of the penalty unless, based on credible information from any source, it's concluded that another nonsigning tax return preparer within that firm is primarily responsible for the position. (Reg § 1.6694-1(b))[41]

A tax return preparer who prepares a return or refund claim for which any part of a tax liability understatement is due to "willful or reckless conduct" must pay a penalty for each return or claim equal to the greater of (1) $5,000; or (2) 50% of the income derived (or to be derived) by the tax return preparer for preparing the return or claim. (Code Sec. 6694(b); Reg § 1.6694-3(a)) "Willful or reckless conduct" is conduct by the tax return preparer which is a willful attempt to understate the tax liability on the return or claim, or a reckless or intentional disregard of rules or regulations. (Code Sec. 6694(b)(2); Reg § 1.6694-3(b), Reg § 1.6694-3(c)) A penalty payable by a person due to willful or reckless conduct in connection with a return or refund claim is reduced by the penalty paid by that person due to

36. ¶V-2351 *et seq.*; ¶67,014; TD ¶867,027
37. ¶V-2354; ¶67,014; TD ¶867,027
38. ¶V-2353; ¶67,014; TD ¶867,027
39. ¶V-2351; TD ¶867,032
40. ¶V-2631 *et seq.*; ¶66,944
41. ¶V-2632 *et seq.*; ¶66,944

an unreasonable position. (Code Sec. 6694(b)(3); Reg § 1.6694-3(f))[42]

IRS has provided lists of the documents covered by the above penalties.[43]

¶ 4888   Penalty for valuation misstatements attributable to incorrect appraisals.

A penalty is imposed on any person who: (A) prepares a property appraisal and knows, or reasonably should have known, that the appraisal would be used in connection with a return or a refund claim, and (B) the claimed property value on the return or refund claim that is based on the appraisal results in a substantial valuation misstatement under Code Sec. 6662(e), a gross valuation misstatement under Code Sec. 6662(h) (¶4878), or a substantial estate or gift tax valuation understatement under Code Sec. 6662(g). (Code Sec. 6695A(a))[44] No penalty, however, will be imposed if the person satisfies IRS that the value established in the appraisal was more likely than not the proper value. (Code Sec. 6695A(c)) The amount of the penalty equals the lesser of 125% of the gross income for preparing the appraisal received by the person who prepared it or an amount that is the greater of: (a) 10% of the underpayment attributable to the misstatement, or (b) $1,000. (Code Sec. 6695A(b))

¶ 4889   Other penalties on tax return preparers.

A tax return preparer who fails to perform the duties described at ¶4750 is subject to these civil penalties (up to a maximum $25,000 per calendar year for any single type of failure):

. . . $50 for each failure to sign a return as required. (Code Sec. 6695(b))[45]

. . . $50 for each failure to show his taxpayer ID number or PTIN as required. (Code Sec. 6695(e))[46]

. . . $50 for each failure to furnish completed copy of return to the taxpayer. (Code Sec. 6695(a))[47]

. . . $50 for each failure to retain a copy of a prepared return or to include it on a list of prepared returns. (Code Sec. 6695(d))[48]

. . . $50 for each failure to retain and make available a record of the preparers employed or engaged, plus $50 for each failure to include a required item in the record required to be retained and made available. (Code Sec. 6695(e))[49]

. . . $500 (with no annual maximum) for each check with respect to taxes issued to a taxpayer that the preparer endorses or otherwise negotiates, except where the preparer is a bank and deposits the check to the taxpayer's account in the bank. (Code Sec. 6695(f))[50]

. . . $100 for each failure to follow regulatory due diligence requirements as shown on Form 8867 in claiming the earned income credit. (Code Sec. 6695(g); Reg § 1.6695-2(b))[1]

Improper disclosure or use of information by return preparers is subject to a civil penalty of $250 for each improper disclosure or use ($10,000 maximum per calendar year), (Code Sec. 6713(a))[2] as well as a criminal penalty. (Code Sec. 7216)[3] Regs provide exceptions to these penalties (Reg § 301.7216-1(a), Reg § 301.7216-2)[4] and additional exceptions where the taxpayer consents. Consents may permit disclosure of social security numbers to foreign preparers where adequate safeguards are provided. (Reg § 301.7216-3)[5]

IRS may get a district court to enjoin a preparer from engaging in specific misconduct, but only if an injunction is appropriate to prevent recurrence of the misconduct. If the court finds that the preparer has continually or repeatedly engaged in this misconduct and an injunction isn't sufficient to prevent the preparer's interference with proper tax administration, it can

42. ¶V-2630; ¶66,944
43. ¶V-2631.3; ¶66,944
44. ¶V-2691; ¶66,95A4
45. ¶V-2673; ¶66,954; TD ¶867,016
46. ¶V-2677; ¶66,954; TD ¶867,016
47. ¶V-2674; ¶66,954; TD ¶867,016
48. ¶V-2675; ¶66,954; TD ¶867,016
49. ¶V-2676; ¶66,954; TD ¶867,016
50. ¶V-2671; ¶66,954; TD ¶867,018
1. ¶V-2677.1; ¶66,954
2. ¶V-2678; ¶67,134; TD ¶867,035
3. ¶V-3308; ¶72,164; TD ¶871,010
4. ¶V-2678; ¶V-3309 *et seq.*; ¶72,164; TD ¶871,010
5. ¶V-3317; ¶72,164

enjoin him from practicing. (Code Sec. 7407(b))[6]

¶ 4890   Abusive tax shelters and conduct.

A person who promotes an abusive tax shelter is subject to a penalty equal to the lesser of $1,000 or 100% of the gross income derived or to be derived from the activity. However, if an activity on which the penalty is imposed involves a false or fraudulent statement, the penalty equals 50% of the gross income derived or to be derived by that person from the activity. (Code Sec. 6700(a))[7] IRS may seek an injunction to stop any action or failure to take action:

(1) that is subject to penalty under Code Sec. 6700, Code Sec. 6701 (aiding or abetting an understatement, see ¶4886), Code Sec. 6707 (failure to furnish information regarding reportable transactions, see ¶4894), and Code Sec. 6708 (failure to provide list of advisees with respect to reportable transactions, see ¶4891) or

(2) in violation of any requirement imposed by regs issued under Section 330 of Title 31 of the U.S. Code (rules regulating the practice of taxpayer representatives before the Department of the Treasury), i.e., the Circular 230 rules. (Code Sec. 7408)[8]

¶ 4891   Penalty for failure to provide reportable transaction advisee list.

Any person required under Code Sec. 6112 to maintain a list of advisees with respect to reportable transactions (see ¶4747) who fails to make that list available to IRS on its written request within 20 business days after the date of the request is liable for a $10,000 per day penalty for each day of that failure after the 20th day. This penalty isn't imposed, however, for any day that the failure to provide the list is due to reasonable cause. (Code Sec. 6708(a))[9]

¶ 4892   Penalty imposed for failure to report reportable transactions.

A penalty is imposed on any person who fails to include on any return or statement any information regarding a reportable transaction that's required under Code Sec. 6011 (see ¶4748) to be included with the return or statement. (Code Sec. 6707A(a); Reg § 301.6707A-1T(a)) The penalty is 75% of the decrease in tax shown on the return resulting from the transaction (or which would have resulted if the transaction were respected) subject to a maximum of $10,000 for natural persons and $50,000 for others (increased to $100,000 and $200,000 respectively if a listed transaction is involved). The minimum penalty per transaction is $5,000 for natural persons and $10,000 for others. (Code Sec. 6707A(b)) The status of transactions as reportable transactions and listed transactions is determined under regs under Code Sec. 6011. (Code Sec. 6707A(c); Reg § 1.6011-4(b))

IRS can rescind all or a portion of a penalty imposed under Code Sec. 6707A if (a) the violation relates to a reportable transaction that is not a listed transaction and (b) rescission would promote compliance with the Code and effective tax administration. (Code Sec. 6707A(d)) The rescission also applies to any penalty imposed on a material advisor under Code Sec. 6707 (¶4894) (Code Sec. 6707(c)) Temporary regs list factors considered in determining whether to grant rescission requests. (Reg § 301.6707A-1T(d)) IRS procedures establish how to request rescission.[10]

¶ 4893   Penalty for understatements regarding reportable transactions.

A 20% accuracy-related penalty applies for reportable transaction understatements. (Code Sec. 6662A(a)) The penalty is 30% for any portion of any reportable transaction understatement for which specified disclosure rules are not met. (Code Sec. 6662A(c)) A reportable transaction understatement is the sum of (1) the amount of the increase (if any) in taxable

---

6. ¶V-2679 *et seq.*; ¶74,074; TD ¶867,033
7. ¶V-2403; ¶67,004
8. ¶V-2451; ¶74,084

9. ¶V-2503; ¶67,084
10. ¶V-2531 *et seq.*; ¶67,07A4; TD ¶866,501

income resulting from a difference between (a) the proper tax treatment of an item subject to the penalty rules and (b) the taxpayer's treatment of the item (on the taxpayer's tax return), multiplied by the highest noncorporate rate (or corporate tax rate, in the case of a corporation), and (2) the amount of the decrease (if any) in the total amount of income tax credits which results from a difference between (a) the taxpayer's treatment of an item subject to the penalty rules (on the taxpayer's tax return) and (b) the proper tax treatment of the item. (Code Sec. 6662A(b)(1)(B)) The penalty doesn't apply to any part of an understatement on which the 40% penalty for transactions that lack economic substance (¶4896) is imposed. (Code Sec. 6662A(e)(2)(B))[11]

For this purpose, any reduction in the excess of deductions allowed in the tax year over gross income for the year, and any reduction in the amount of capital losses which would (without regard to the capital loss carryover rules) be allowed for the year, is treated as an increase in taxable income. (Code Sec. 6662A(b)(1))

An item is subject to the penalty rules if the item is attributable to any listed transaction and any reportable transaction (other than a listed transaction) if a significant purpose of the transaction is federal income tax avoidance or evasion. (Code Sec. 6662A(b)(2)(B)) Listed and reportable transactions are defined under the Code Sec. 6707A penalty rules for reportable transactions for which disclosure is required (see ¶4892) (Code Sec. 6662A(d))

Except as provided in regs, no tax treatment included with an amendment or supplement to a tax return is taken into account in determining the amount of any reportable transaction understatement if the amendment or supplement is filed after the earlier of the date the taxpayer is first contacted by IRS regarding the examination of the return or any other date specified by IRS. (Code Sec. 6662A(e)(3))

A limited reasonable cause exception applies if certain disclosure, substantial authority and reasonable belief requirements are met. (Code Sec. 6662A(d))[12] But this exception doesn't apply to any part of a reportable transaction understatement which is attributable to a transaction that lacks economic substance under Code Sec. 7701(o) or fails to meet the requirements of any similar rule of law (¶4896). (Code Sec. 6664(d)(2))[13]

¶ 4894   Material advisor's penalty for not reporting reportable transactions.

A material advisor who fails to file a timely information return required under Code Sec. 6111(a) (¶4747), or who files a false or incomplete information return, for a reportable transaction (including a listed transaction) is subject to a penalty of $50,000 for each failure. But, if the failure relates to a listed transaction, the penalty increases to the greater of: (1) $200,000, or (2) 50% of the gross income received by the advisor that is attributable to aid, assistance, or advice provided for the listed transaction before the date the advisor files an information return including the transaction. If the reporting failure for a listed transaction is due to an intentional failure or act, the 50% of gross income penalty amount (item 2 above) is increased to 75% of gross income. (Code Sec. 6707(a), Code Sec. 6707(b)) Reportable and listed transactions are defined under Code Sec. 6707A(c) (see ¶4892). (Code Sec. 6707(d))[14]

¶ 4895   Penalties for tax-exempts acting as tax shelter accommodation parties.

Certain tax-exempt entities are subject to penalties for participating in a prohibited tax-shelter transaction as accommodation parties, see ¶4113. An exempt organization that participates in a reportable transaction (including a listed transaction) in order to shelter its own tax liability from tax is subject to disclosure rules. (Code Sec. 6033(a)(2), Code Sec. 6652(c)(3))

---

11. ¶V-2283; ¶66,62A4
12. ¶V-2281; ¶66,62A4; TD ¶868,101
13. ¶V-2284; ¶66,644.01
14. ¶V-2500; ¶67,074

¶ 4896   Penalty for transaction lacking economic substance.

For underpayments attributable to transactions entered into after Mar. 30, 2010, a 20% penalty applies to an underpayment attributable to any disallowance of claimed tax benefits by reason of a transaction lacking economic substance (as defined in Code Sec. 7701(o), see below), or failing to meet the requirements of any similar rule of law. (Code Sec. 6662(b)(6)) The penalty rate is increased to 40% if the taxpayer doesn't adequately disclose the relevant facts affecting the tax treatment in the return or a statement attached to the return. (Code Sec. 6662(i)(1)) An amended return or supplement to a return is not taken into account if filed after the taxpayer has been contacted for audit or such other date as IRS specifies. (Code Sec. 6662(i)(3)) No reasonable cause and good faith exception applies. (Code Sec. 6664(c)(2)) This provision doesn't apply to personal transactions of individuals, only to transactions entered into in connection with a trade or business or an activity engaged in for the production of income. (Code Sec. 7701(o)(5)(B)) The penalty also doesn't apply to any portion of an underpayment on which a fraud penalty is imposed (¶4883).[15]

Economic substance. For transactions entered into after Mar. 30, 2010 and for underpayments, understatements, and refunds and credits attributable to transactions entered into after Mar. 30, 2010, a transaction is treated as having economic substance only if (apart from Federal income tax effects): (1) the transaction changes in a meaningful way the taxpayer's economic position, and (2) the taxpayer has a substantial purpose for entering into the transaction. (Code Sec. 7701(o)(1)) Any State or local income tax effect which is related to a Federal income tax effect is treated in the same manner as a Federal income tax effect. (Code Sec. 7701(o)(3)) A purpose of achieving a favorable accounting treatment for financial reporting purposes isn't taken into account as a non-Federal-income-tax purpose if the origin of the financial accounting benefit is a reduction of Federal income tax. (Code Sec. 7701(o)(4))

A taxpayer may rely on factors other than profit potential to show that a transaction results in a meaningful change in the taxpayer's economic position or that the taxpayer has a substantial non-Federal-income-tax purpose for entering the transaction. Code Sec. 7701(o) doesn't require or establish a minimum return that will meet the profit potential test. But, if a taxpayer relies on profit potential, the present value of the reasonably expected pre-tax profit must be substantial in relation to the present value of the expected net tax benefits that would be allowed if the transaction were respected ("the pre-tax profit to tax benefit ratio test"). (Code Sec. 7701(o)(2)(A)) Fees and other transaction expenses are considered as expenses in determining pre-tax profit. IRS is to issue regs requiring foreign taxes to be treated as expenses in determining pre-tax profit in appropriate cases. (Code Sec. 7701(o)(2)(B))

The economic substance doctrine is defined as the common law doctrine under which tax benefits under subtitle A with respect to a transaction aren't allowed if the transaction doesn't have economic substance or lacks a business purpose. (Code Sec. 7701(o)(5)(A)) Whether the doctrine is relevant to a transaction is determined in the same manner as if Code Sec. 7701(o) hadn't been enacted. (Code Sec. 7701(o)(5)(C))[16]

¶ 4897   Information return penalties.

A payor who, without reasonable cause, fails to timely file a required information return (¶4737 *et seq.*) in the required manner (e.g., on magnetic media), or fails to include all of the information required to be shown on the return, or includes incorrect information, is subject to a $50 penalty for each return, up to a $250,000 calendar year maximum ($100,000 if the payor's gross receipts for the year don't exceed $5 million). (Code Sec. 6721(a), Code Sec. 6721(d)(1)(A), Code Sec. 6724(a); Reg § 301.6721-1(a)(2)) The penalty and maximum are

---

15. ¶V-2271; ¶66,624.12; TD ¶863,001   16. ¶M-5901; ¶77,014.35

reduced to $15 per return ($75,000 maximum—$25,000 if gross receipts test is met) if corrected within 30 days from the required filing date, or to $30 per return ($150,000 maximum—$50,000 if gross receipts test is met) if corrected on or before Aug. 1 of the calendar year of the required filing date. For information returns required to be filed after 2010, the penalty is $100 for each return, up to a $1,500,000 calendar year maximum ($500,000 if gross receipts don't exceed $5 million), (Code Sec. 6721(a), Code Sec. 6721(d)(1)(A)) and the penalty and maximum are reduced to $30 per return ($250,000 maximum—$75,000 if gross receipts test is met) if corrected within 30 days from the required filing date, or to $60 per return ($500,000 maximum—$200,000 if gross receipts test is met) if corrected on or before Aug. 1. (Code Sec. 6721(b), Code Sec. 6721(d))[17] A payor who, without reasonable cause, fails to timely furnish a payee statement to the person prescribed, fails to include all of the required information on the statement, or includes incorrect information, is subject to a penalty of $50 for each such statement, up to a $100,000 calendar year maximum ($100 up to a $1,500,000 calendar year maximum for statements required after 2010, subject to reductions for correction within specified periods). (Code Sec. 6722(a), Code Sec. 6722(b), Code Sec. 6724(a))[18] However, subject to exceptions, the above penalties are increased *with no calendar year maximum* if the failure is due to intentional disregard. (Code Sec. 6721(e), Code Sec. 6722(c))[19]

The penalties won't apply to a de minimis number of information returns that don't include all the required information, or that include incorrect information, if the failure is corrected by Aug. 1 of the calendar year in which the required filing date occurs. This exception for any calendar year is limited to ten information returns or, if greater, ½% of the total number of such returns the payor is required to file that year (Code Sec. 6721(c)), and doesn't apply to returns that aren't due on Feb. 28 or Mar. 15. (Reg § 301.6721-1(d)(4))[20] Also, no penalty will be imposed solely by reason of any failure to comply with the rules requiring filing on magnetic media (¶4753) except (1) to the extent the failure is with respect to more than 250 returns or (2) in the case of a partnership having more than 100 partners, to the extent the failure occurs with respect to more than 100 information returns. (Code Sec. 6724(c); Reg § 301.6721-1(a)(2)(ii)) But, for returns due after Mar. 18, 2010, failures by financial institutions to file returns described in Code Sec. 6011(e)(4) (¶4753) on magnetic media can trigger a penalty without regard to the number of returns involved. (Code Sec. 6724(c))[21]

The penalties described above apply to information returns required under:

... Code Sec. 110(d) (qualified lease construction allowances for short-term leases).

... Code Sec. 264(f)(5)(A)(iv) (natural-person-as-holder exception to the disallowance of the deduction of interest buildup on certain life insurance and annuity contracts).

... Code Sec. 338(h)(10)(C) (relating to elective recognition of gain or loss).

... Code Sec. 408(i) (individual retirement accounts (IRAs) or annuities).

... Code Sec. 1060(b) or Code Sec. 1060(e) (information required of transferors and transferees with respect to applicable asset acquisitions).

... Code Sec. 4101(d) (relating to fuels taxes).

... Code Sec. 6039(a) (transfers of stock from exercises of incentive stock options and certain purchases from employee stock purchase plans).

... Code Sec. 6041(a) (payments of $600 or more).

... Code Sec. 6041(b) (collection of foreign items).

... Code Sec. 6041A(a) (payments by recipients of services) or Code Sec. 6041A(b) (returns of direct sellers).

... Code Sec. 6042(a)(1) (corporate dividends).

... Code Sec. 6043A(a) (taxable mergers and acquisitions).

---

17. ¶V-1803 *et seq.*; ¶s 67,214, 67,244.01; TD ¶861,053 *et seq.*
18. ¶V-1814 *et seq.*; ¶s 67,224, 67,244.01; TD ¶861,066 *et seq.*
19. ¶s V-1811 *et seq.*, V-1816 *et seq.*; ¶s 67,214, 67,224;

TD ¶861,063
20. ¶V-1809; ¶67,214; TD ¶861,059
21. ¶V-1810; ¶67,214; TD ¶861,060

... Code Sec. 6044(a)(1) (patronage dividends).

... Code Sec. 6045(a) (transactions, including real estate transactions, reportable by brokers).

... Code Sec. 6045(d) (certain "substitute payments" made to brokers on behalf of customers in connection with short sales).

... Code Sec. 6045B(a) (organizational actions affecting the basis of a "specified security" after Dec. 31, 2010).

... Code Sec. 6047(d) (employers, plan administrators, etc.).

... Code Sec. 6049(a)(1) (payments of interest).

... Code Sec. 6050A(a) (payments made by certain fishing boat operators).

... Code Sec. 6050H(a) (payments of $600 or more in a calendar year of mortgage interest that is received in the course of a trade or business).

... Code Sec. 6050H(h)(1) (mortgage insurance premiums of $600 or more in a calendar year).

... Code Sec. 6050I(a) (receipts of more than $10,000 in cash in one transaction (or two or more related transactions) that are received in the course of a trade or business).

... Code Sec. 6050I(g)(1) (receipt of more than $10,000 in cash by court clerks as bail).

... Code Sec. 6050J(a) (foreclosures and abandonments of property held as security for business loans).

... Code Sec. 6050K(a) (certain exchanges of partnership interests).

... Code Sec. 6050L(a) (certain dispositions of donated property).

... Code Sec. 6050N(a) (payments of royalties).

... Code Sec. 6050P(a) (discharges of debt by certain financial and government entities).

... Code Sec. 6050Q (relating to certain long-term care benefits).

... Code Sec. 6050R (cash payments by purchasers of fish for resale).

... Code Sec. 6050S (payments for qualified tuition and related expenses and deductible payments of interest on qualified education loans).

... Code Sec. 6050T (credit for health insurance costs of eligible individuals).

... Code Sec. 6050U (for charges or payments for qualified long-term care insurance contracts, under combined arrangements).

... Code Sec. 6050V (applicable insurance contracts in which certain exempt organizations hold interests).

... Code Sec. 6050W (for calendar years beginning after 2010 for returns relating to payment card transactions and third party network transactions).

... Code Sec. 6051(d) (tax withheld).

... Code Sec. 6052(a) (wages paid in the form of group-term life insurance).

... Code Sec. 6053(c)(1) (certain tips from "large food or beverage establishments"). (Code Sec. 6724(d)(1))

¶ 4898   Other civil penalties relating to information reporting and other items.

Other civil penalties are provided for:

... failure to file information returns for dividend payments under $10 (Code Sec. 6652(a));

... failure to, file actuarial report of pension plan (¶4745) (Code Sec. 6692);[22]

... failure to file annual return for a pension plan (¶4745) (Code Sec. 6652(f));[23]

... failure to file annual return for an exempt organization or private foundation (¶4124)

---

22. ¶V-1971; ¶66,924   23. ¶V-1971; ¶66,524

(Code Sec. 6652(c));[24]

. . . failure by split-interest trust to file an information return (Code Sec. 6652(c)(2));[25]

. . . failure by an exempt organization to report excise tax on personal benefit contracts (Code Sec. 170(f)(10)(F)(iii));

. . . failure by any person, under a duty to comply with Code Sec. 6104(d) requirements relating to public inspection of, and provision of copies of, exempt organization annual returns or exempt status application materials (Code Sec. 6652(c)(1)(C), Code Sec. 6652(c)(1)(D));[26]

. . . failure to file fringe benefit plan return (¶4745) (Code Sec. 6652(e));[27]

. . . failure to provide a written explanation to the recipient of a qualified rollover distribution (Code Sec. 6652(i));[28]

. . . failure to file report on deductible employee contributions (Code Sec. 6652(g));[29]

. . . failure to file notification of change of status of pension plan (¶4745), (Code Sec. 6652(d)(2));[30]

. . . failure to file registration statement of pension plan (¶4745) (Code Sec. 6652(d)(1)),[31] or to give a plan participant a statement of the information in the statement (Code Sec. 6690);[32]

. . . failure to file individual retirement account, simple retirement account reports, Archer MSA, HSA, CESA, and qualified tuition program, reports (Code Sec. 6693);[33]

. . . overstatement reported on return by IRA participant of the amount of designated nondeductible contributions (Code Sec. 6693(b));[34]

. . . failure to keep records for reporting on pension, annuity, etc., payments subject to withholding (Code Sec. 6704(a));[35]

. . . failure to notify recipients of plan distributions of their option to elect out of withholding (Code Sec. 6652(i));

. . . failure by a corporation that issues qualified small business stock to make prescribed reports to IRS (Code Sec. 6652(k));[36]

. . . failure to file certain returns for foreign corporations, partnerships (Code Sec. 6679)[37] and trusts (Code Sec. 6677);[38]

. . . failure to file information returns in connection with foreign corporations and partnerships (¶4660) (Code Sec. 6038(b), Code Sec. 6038(c), Code Sec. 6038A(d), Code Sec. 6038B(c), Code Sec. 6038C(c));

. . . failure to include tax information with passport or green card applications (Code Sec. 6039E(c));

. . . failure to keep records, furnish information, or file DISC returns (¶4622) (Code Sec. 6686);[39]

. . . failure to keep records, furnish information or file returns for a FSC (or former FSC) (Code Sec. 6686);

. . . failure to meet FIRPTA reporting requirements (Code Sec. 6652(f));[40]

. . . failure to file notice of redetermination of certain foreign taxes (Code Sec. 6689);[41]

. . . failure to withhold tax on U.S. income of certain foreign persons (¶4662 *et seq.*) (Code Sec. 1463);[42]

---

24. ¶V-2714; ¶66,524; TD ¶861,032
25. ¶V-2716; ¶66,524
26. ¶V-2718; ¶s 66,524, 66,854; TD ¶861,032
27. ¶V-1973; ¶66,524; TD ¶861,037
28. ¶V-1984; ¶66,524; TD ¶861,037
29. ¶V-1980; ¶66,524
30. ¶V-1971; ¶66,524; TD ¶861,037
31. ¶V-1971; ¶66,524; TD ¶861,037
32. ¶V-1972; ¶66,904
33. ¶V-1974 *et seq.*; ¶66,934; TD ¶861,037

34. ¶V-1981; ¶66,934; TD ¶283,028
35. ¶V-1986; ¶67,044; TD ¶868,006
36. ¶V-1843; ¶66,524
37. ¶V-1903; ¶66,794; TD ¶861,049
38. ¶V-1901; ¶66,774; TD ¶861,046
39. ¶V-1912; ¶66,864
40. ¶V-1909; ¶66,524; TD ¶861,049
41. ¶V-1983; ¶66,894; TD ¶861,049
42. ¶O-11903; ¶14,614.01

... failure to disclose a treaty-based position taken on a return that overrules or otherwise modifies the tax law (¶4652) (Code Sec. 6712);[43]

... failure by individual who loses U.S. citizenship or terminates U.S. residency (¶4653) to file expatriate information statement (Code Sec. 6039G(d));

... failure by an exempt organization to disclose that information it is offering to sell or soliciting money for is available free from the federal government (Code Sec. 6711);[44]

... failure by an exempt organization to disclose that fund-raising solicitations are nondeductible as charitable contributions (¶4119) (Code Sec. 6710);[45]

... failure by an exempt organization to make the required disclosure for quid pro quo contributions of $75 or more (¶4119) (Code Sec. 6714);[46]

... willful failure to make available for inspection or provide copies of, a return or application for exemption of certain exempt organizations (Code Sec. 6685);[47]

... any repeated or willful and flagrant act or failure to act by any person who becomes liable for any excise tax on a private foundation by reason of the act or failure to act (Code Sec. 6684);[48]

... making a negligent or fraudulent misstatement in connection with the issuance of a mortgage credit certificate or failing to file the required report (¶4745) (Code Sec. 6709);[49]

... failure to file a partnership return (¶4731) exposes the partnership to a penalty of $195 ($89 for tax years beginning before 2010) per month per partner (Code Sec. 6698);[50]

... failure to file an S corporation return exposes the S corporation to a penalty of $195 ($89 for tax years beginning before 2010) per month per shareholder (Code Sec. 6699);[1]

... failure to file returns with respect to qualified rental housing projects (Code Sec. 42(l)(2), Code Sec. 6652(j));[2]

... failure to deposit taxes (an IRS procedure explains how IRS applies deposits in determining the penalty when there is a shortfall) (Code Sec. 6656(a))[3] (including deposits required to be made by electronic funds transfer (EFT, see ¶3029);[4]

... use of any commercially acceptable instrument to pay taxes, if the amount isn't duly paid (bad check penalty is expanded to cover electronic payments for instruments tendered after July 2, 2010) (Code Sec. 6657);[5]

... failure to pay stamp taxes (Code Sec. 6653);[6]

... claiming excessive gasoline tax rebates (Code Sec. 6675);[7]

... filing a frivolous income tax return or submitting a position identified as frivolous on IRS's list of frivolous positions (Code Sec. 6702);[8]

... use of Tax Court primarily for delay or where: taxpayer's position is frivolous or groundless, he hasn't exhausted administrative remedies or he has instituted a frivolous or groundless claim for damages against the U.S. (Code Sec. 6673);[9]

... failure to supply taxpayer identification numbers (Reg § 301.6723-1(a));[10]

... failure to report tips (¶4745) (Code Sec. 6652(b));[11]

... failure by broker to provide back-up withholding notice (Code Sec. 6705);[12]

... failure to file information return for change in control or recapitalization of corporation (¶4745) (Code Sec. 6652(l));[13]

... making a false statement that results in reduced amounts of withholding (Code

---

43. ¶V-1908; ¶67,124; TD ¶868,011
44. ¶V-2705; ¶67,114; TD ¶861,032
45. ¶V-2701; ¶67,104; TD ¶861,032
46. ¶V-2703; ¶67,144; TD ¶861,032
47. ¶V-2718; ¶66,854
48. ¶V-2721; ¶66,844; TD ¶868,005
49. ¶V-1998; ¶67,094; TD ¶861,040
50. ¶V-1762 *et seq.*; ¶66,984; TD ¶861,041
1. ¶V-1763.1; ¶66,994; TD ¶861,042.1
2. ¶V-1996; ¶66,524; TD ¶861,039
3. ¶V-1652; ¶66,564; TD ¶862,005

4. ¶V-1658
5. ¶V-1687; ¶66,574; TD ¶868,001
6. ¶V-2722; ¶66,530.40
7. ¶V-2726; ¶ 66,754 (Excise); TD ¶868,012
8. ¶V-2551; ¶67,024; TD ¶866,001
9. ¶V-2601; ¶66,734; TD ¶836,014
10. ¶V-1821 *et seq.*; ¶67,234; TD ¶861,050
11. ¶V-1745; ¶66,524; TD ¶861,038
12. ¶V-1842; ¶67,054; TD ¶861,079
13. ¶V-1845; ¶66,524; TD ¶861,031.2

Sec. 6682),[14] or relates to the applicability of backup withholding. (Code Sec. 6682)[15]

¶ 4899 Damages for filing fraudulent information return.

A person who is the subject of a fraudulent information return may sue the filer for damages of the greater of (1) $5,000, or (2) actual damages plus costs, and, in the court's discretion, reasonable attorney's fees. The court must specify the correct amount, if any, that should have been reported on the return. (Code Sec. 7434)[16]

¶ 4900 Criminal tax evasion.

Tax evasion is a felony punishable by a fine of up to $100,000 ($500,000 for a corporation) and/or up to five years' imprisonment, plus costs of prosecution. The elements of the crime are willfulness, an attempt to evade tax and additional tax due. (Code Sec. 7201)[17]

¶ 4901 Other criminal penalties.

Any person who willfully aids or assists in, or procures, counsels or advises the preparation or presentation of a materially false or fraudulent return, affidavit, claim or other document, is subject to a criminal penalty of up to $100,000 ($500,000 for a corporation) and/or up to three years' imprisonment, plus costs of prosecution. (Code Sec. 7206(2))[18]

Any federal officer or employee, IRS contractor or certain other persons with access to tax returns and return information who willfully inspects any tax return or return information without authorization is subject to a criminal fine of not more than $1,000 and imprisonment of not more than one year, or both. (Code Sec. 7213A)[19]

Other criminal penalties (fines and/or imprisonment) are imposed for willful failure to: (1) file a return (Code Sec. 7203);[20] (2) pay a tax (Code Sec. 7203);[21] (3) collect or pay over a tax as required (Code Sec. 7202);[22] (4) keep proper records (Code Sec. 7203);[23] (5) supply tax information (Code Sec. 7203);[24] or (6) furnish a W-2 to employees in the manner, at the time or with the information required, or willful filing of a false or fraudulent W-2. (Code Sec. 7204)[25] Criminal penalties are also imposed for: willful filing of a false or fraudulent return (Code Sec. 7207);[26] failure to obey a summons (Code Sec. 7210);[27] and various other offenses relating to returns, statements, stamp taxes, etc.[28]

¶ 4902 Tax Collection.

IRS has broad tax collection powers, including seizure and sale of a taxpayer's property (levy and distraint) and liens.

¶ 4903 Collection procedures.

Within 60 days after a tax has been assessed, IRS must send the taxpayer a notice of the amount assessed and a demand for payment, before it can start administrative collection proceedings. (Code Sec. 6303(a), Code Sec. 6331(a))[29] The taxpayer usually gets at least ten days from a date stated in the notice and demand to pay the tax, unless IRS finds that collection is in jeopardy. (Code Sec. 6331(a); Reg § 301.6331-1(a)(3))[30] Taxpayers suffering undue hardship can get an extension of time for paying the assessed taxes. For installment

---

14. ¶V-1741; ¶66,824; TD ¶868,002
15. ¶V-1743; ¶66,824; TD ¶868,004
16. ¶S-4470 *et seq.*; TD ¶810,501
17. ¶V-4100 *et seq.*; ¶72,014 *et seq.*; TD ¶871,001
18. ¶V-3113; ¶72,064; TD ¶871,009
19. ¶V-3305.1; ¶72,13A4
20. ¶V-3002; ¶72,034; TD ¶871,015
21. ¶V-3001; ¶72,034; TD ¶871,015
22. ¶V-3017; ¶72,024; TD ¶871,008

23. ¶V-3007; ¶72,034; TD ¶871,015
24. ¶V-3008; ¶72,034; TD ¶871,013
25. ¶V-3013; ¶72,044
26. ¶V-3114; ¶72,074; TD ¶871,013
27. ¶V-3503; ¶72,104; TD ¶871,014
28. ¶V-3500 *et seq.*; TD ¶871,014
29. ¶s V-5003, V-5004; ¶s 63,014.03, 63,314.01; TD ¶901,013
30. ¶V-5007; ¶63,314.01; TD ¶901,014

agreements, see ¶4904.[31] IRS must send delinquent taxpayers a written notice of the amount of the delinquency at least annually. (Code Sec. 7524)[32]

IRS may pay rewards to informers (whistleblowers) for information on tax law violations.[33]

¶ 4904 Agreements for installment payments of tax—Form 9465.

IRS may enter into a written agreement with a taxpayer for that taxpayer to satisfy liability for *any tax* in installment payments. (Code Sec. 6159(a); Reg § 301.6159-1(a))[34] An individual who owes $10,000 or less and meets other conditions can force IRS to enter into an installment agreement. (Code Sec. 6159(c))[35] A taxpayer uses Form 9465 (attached to his balance due return) to request an installment agreement.[36] IRS may require the taxpayer to agree to certain terms and conditions. (Reg § 301.6159-1(b)(1))[37] Individuals can also apply online by completing an Online Payment Agreement on IRS's website. A user fee is imposed for entering into, or restructuring or reinstating, an installment agreement. (Reg § 300.0, Reg § 300.1, Reg § 300.2)[38] See ¶4722.

🅡🅘🅐 ***observation:*** Submit the fee with the first installment payment, not with the Form 9465 request. A reminder notice (Form 521) sent to the taxpayer will reflect this.

The agreement remains in effect for its term unless the taxpayer fails to comply with it. (Code Sec. 6159(b)(2); Reg § 301.6159-1(b)(3)) However, IRS may modify or terminate the agreement under certain circumstances after 30 days' notice to the taxpayer. (Code Sec. 6159(b); Reg § 301.6159-1(e)(4))[39]

¶ 4905 Seizure and sale of a delinquent taxpayer's property—levy and distraint.

IRS has power to collect taxes by levy and distraint. This means it may seize any property (unless it's exempt) of a delinquent taxpayer (whether held by the taxpayer or someone else), sell it, and apply the proceeds to pay the unpaid taxes.[40] The property seized may be real, personal, tangible, or intangible, including receivables, evidences of debt, securities (Code Sec. 6331(a)) and, to the extent they exceed a specified amount, present and future wages. (Reg § 301.6331-2(c)) There are exemptions for certain kinds of income (Code Sec. 6334(d)) and property (e.g., clothing, tools) (Code Sec. 6334(a); Reg § 301.6334-3(d)), and a complete exemption for a taxpayer's principal residence unless a judge or magistrate approves the levy in writing. (Code Sec. 6334(a)(13)(B)) There also is an exemption for real property used as a residence by a taxpayer, or any nonrental real property of the taxpayer used by any other individual as a residence, if the amount of the levy is $5,000 or less (Code Sec. 6334(a)(13)(A)), as well as an exemption for tangible personal property or real property (other than real property which is rented) used in a trade or business of an individual taxpayer, unless collection is in jeopardy, or the levy is approved in writing by authorized IRS personnel. (Code Sec. 6334(a)(13)(B)) Levy is prohibited where an installment agreement is pending or in effect (Code Sec. 6331(k); Reg § 301.6331-4). Levy also is barred for unpaid divisible taxes (provided a portion of the taxes is paid and other conditions are met). (Code Sec. 6331(i)). (Code Sec. 6331(k)) Regs enumerate exemptions. (Reg § 301.6334 1)[41]

IRS must give the taxpayer 30 days' advance written notice before it can levy on any of his property, except where collection is in jeopardy. (Code Sec. 6331(d))[42]

Subject to exceptions, IRS may not levy against a person's property or right to property unless it gives the person a notification in writing of his right to, and the opportunity for, a pre-levy Collection Due Process hearing with IRS (a CDP hearing). (Code Sec. 6330(a)(1);

31. ¶V-5009; TD ¶901,015
32. ¶V-5009.2; TD ¶901,002
33. ¶T-1030; ¶76,234; TD ¶444,043
34. ¶V-5010; ¶61,594; TD ¶901,006
35. ¶V-5012; ¶61,594; TD ¶901,007
36. ¶V-5010; ¶61,594; TD ¶901,006

37. ¶V-5011; ¶61,594; TD ¶901,006
38. ¶T-10020 *et seq.*; ¶61,594; TD ¶901,006
39. ¶V-5015 *et seq.*; ¶61,594; TD ¶901,006
40. ¶V-5100 *et seq.*; ¶63,314 *et seq.*; TD ¶902,001
41. ¶V-5200 *et seq.*; ¶s 63,314.03, 63,314.05; TD ¶902,006
42. ¶V-5253 *et seq.*; ¶63,314.01; TD ¶902,505

Reg § 301.6330-1(a)(1)) The exceptions relate to jeopardy levies, levies to collect from state tax refunds, and persons subject to employment tax levies who made a previous recent hearing request as to unpaid employment taxes. (Code Sec. 6330(f)) The notice—the Collection Due Process Hearing Notice (CDP Notice)—must be given at least 30 days before the day of the first levy with respect to the unpaid tax for the tax period. (Code Sec. 6330(a)(2)) A person who receives a CDP Notice may request a hearing (use Form 12153) with the IRS Office of Appeals within the 30-day period beginning on the day after the date of the CDP Notice. (Code Sec. 6330(b)(1); Reg § 301.6330-1(b)(1), Reg § 301.6330-1(c)(1)) A person who requests a CDP hearing can, within 30 days of the date it was made, appeal the determination reached at the hearing. (Code Sec. 6330(d); Reg § 301.6330-1(f)) The Tax Court has sole jurisdiction over all CDP appeals. (Code Sec. 6330(d)(1)) IRS can disregard frivolous requests for a hearing before a levy is made. (Code Sec. 6330(g))[43]

A penalty (plus costs and interest) applies if the person fails or refuses to surrender the property. (Code Sec. 6332(d))[44] If IRS is unable to sell the seized property for the minimum price it establishes, it can return the property to the taxpayer and add the cost of the unsuccessful sale to the unpaid tax liability. (Code Sec. 6335(e)(1)(D))[45]

Salary and wages and certain other payments are subject to continuous levy. (Code Sec. 6331(e); Code Sec. 6331(h)(1))[46]

¶ 4906   Wrongful seizures.

If IRS wrongfully levies on property, it may, on written request, return the specific property seized (or the proceeds from its sale) or the amount of money levied on (Code Sec. 6343(b)), with interest (Code Sec. 6343(c)). IRS may also return (without interest) property, including money deposited in the Treasury, that has been levied on if IRS determines that: (1) the levy was premature or otherwise not in accordance with its administrative procedures (Code Sec. 6343(d)(2)(A)); (2) the taxpayer has agreed to pay off the underlying tax liability in installments, unless the agreement provides otherwise (Code Sec. 6343(d)(2)(B)); (3) the return of the property will make collection of the underlying tax liability easier (Code Sec. 6343(d)(2)(C)); or (4) the return of the property is in the taxpayer's best interests, as determined by the National Taxpayer Advocate (¶4813), and IRS, and the taxpayer or the National Taxpayer Advocate consent. (Code Sec. 6343(d)(2)(D); Reg § 301.6343-3)[47]

¶ 4907   Third-party remedies for wrongful IRS seizures.

If IRS wrongfully seizes property of a person other than the taxpayer, the third party may sue for its return (or the sale proceeds, if it has been sold) (Code Sec. 7426), but must start the suit within nine months of the levy. (Code Sec. 6532(c)(1)) The Supreme Court held that Code Sec. 7426(a)(1) is the exclusive remedy for third-party levy claims.[48] The third party may also recover damages (subject to limits, see ¶4908) if the action results in a finding that any IRS officer or employee recklessly, intentionally, or negligently disregarded any Code or reg provision. (Code Sec. 7426(h)) Regs spell out procedures for claiming damages. (Reg § 301.7426-2)[49] The owner (or his heirs, etc.) of any realty sold to satisfy a tax liability can redeem the property at any time within 180 days after the sale. (Code Sec. 6337(b)(1))[50]

¶ 4908   Damages for unauthorized IRS collection actions.

If any IRS officer or employee recklessly, intentionally or negligently disregards a Code or reg section in connection with collection of tax, the taxpayer may bring a civil suit for damages against the U.S. in a district court. Damages are limited to the lesser of (1) $1

43. ¶V-5271-*et seq.*; ¶63,304; TD ¶902,522
44. ¶V-5116; ¶63,314.04
45. ¶V-5437; ¶63,354.01
46. ¶V-5214, ¶V-5216; ¶63,314.01; TD ¶902,214, TD ¶902,216
47. ¶V-5136, ¶V-5137; TD ¶902,005; TD ¶903,008
48. ¶V-5120, ¶V-5126; ¶s 65,324.04, 74,264; TD ¶903,007
49. ¶V-5135; ¶74,264; TD ¶903,007
50. ¶V-5424; ¶63,354.03; TD ¶903,007

million ($100,000 for negligence) or (2) the actual, direct economic damages thus sustained plus the costs of the action. (Code Sec. 7433; Reg § 301.7433-1)[1] A taxpayer may petition a bankruptcy court for damages (subject to the above limits) if, in connection with any collection of tax, an IRS officer or employee willfully violates any provision of 11 USCS 362 (relating to the automatic stay arising when a debtor files for bankruptcy) or 11 USCS 524 (relating to the effect of a bankruptcy discharge, which operates as an injunction against commencement or continuation of actions to collect a discharged debt as a personal liability of the debtor). (Code Sec. 7433(e); Reg § 301.7433-2)[2]

¶ 4909 Collection period.

IRS must generally start distraint or court proceedings within ten years after assessment (Code Sec. 6502(a)). But if no return is filed, a collection suit may be brought at any time, without assessment. (Code Sec. 6501(c)(3))[3] The collection period may be extended in connection with installment agreements, (Code Sec. 6502(a); Reg § 301.6502-1)[4] or suspended under various circumstances. (Code Sec. 6330(e)(1); Reg § 301.6330-1(g))[5]

¶ 4910 Injunctions against tax collection.

Injunctions against collection of taxes are generally barred. But exceptions apply during the period allowed to file a Tax Court petition or, where a petition has been filed, before the Tax Court's decision becomes final, and where an individual other than the taxpayer sues to recover property wrongfully seized and in other cases. (Code Sec. 7421(a))[6]

¶ 4911 Federal tax liens.

Federal tax liens are claims against a taxpayer's property for payment of delinquent taxes (including any interest, additional amounts, additions to tax, assessable penalties, or accrued costs).[7] There are various federal tax liens, including:

. . . general tax lien, which applies to all property, both real and personal, tangible and intangible including a tenancy by the entirety and an heir's interest in an estate even though he later attempts to disclaim it (Code Sec. 6321; Reg § 301.6321-1);[8]

. . . gift tax lien (Code Sec. 6324(b); Reg § 301.6324-1(b));[9]

. . . estate tax lien (Code Sec. 6324(a); Reg § 301.6324-1(a));[10]

. . . special lien for deferred estate tax attributable to a farm or other closely held business (Code Sec. 6324A; Reg § 20.6324A-1, Reg § 301.6324A-1);[11]

. . . special lien for recapture of estate tax attributable to special use valuation of a farm or closely held business (Code Sec. 6324B; Reg § 20.6324B-1);[12]

. . . generation-skipping transfer tax lien. (Code Sec. 2661; Reg § 26.2662-1(f))[13]

IRS must give written notice of its filing of a notice of lien (NFTL), to the person whose property is to be subject to the lien, not more than five days after it files the notice of lien (Code Sec. 6320(a); Reg § 301.6320-1(a))[14] IRS must hold a Collection Due Process hearing with respect to the filing if the taxpayer timely requests one (use Form 12153). (Code Sec. 6320(b)(1); Reg § 301.6320-1(b)) But IRS can disregard frivolous requests for a hearing before a lien is filed. (Code Sec. 6320(c))[15] Regs explain how a request for a withdrawal of a federal tax lien is made. (Reg § 301.6323(j)-1)[16]

---

1. ¶V-5800 *et seq.*; ¶74,334; TD ¶903,010
2. ¶V-5820; ¶74,334; TD ¶903,011
3. ¶V-5600 *et seq.*; ¶65,024 *et seq.*; TD ¶901,025
4. ¶V-5604 *et seq.*; ¶65,024; TD ¶901,026
5. ¶V-5277; ¶63,304; TD ¶902,527
6. ¶V-5701; ¶74,214 *et seq.*
7. ¶V-5900 *et seq.*; TD ¶911,000 *et seq.*
8. ¶V-5902 *et seq.*; ¶63,214 *et seq.*; TD ¶911,023

9. ¶V-6042; ¶63,244 (Estate & Gift); TD ¶911,026
10. ¶V-6044; ¶63,244 (Estate & Gift); TD ¶911,027
11. ¶V-6046; ¶63,24A4 (Estate & Gift); TD ¶911,029
12. ¶V-6051; ¶63,24B4 (Estate & Gift); TD ¶911,031
13. ¶V-6053; TD ¶911,033
14. ¶V-6001; ¶63,204
15. ¶V-6005; ¶63,204
16. ¶V-6134; ¶63,234.18

¶ 4912　Priority of tax liens.

Priority of tax liens is governed by federal, not state, law.[17] The general rule is that a lien first in time is first in right.[18] But a tax lien is subordinated to certain later liens that arise either before notice of the tax lien (Form 668) is filed, or before the other lienor has actual knowledge of it. This protects purchasers for adequate consideration without actual notice, mortgagees, pledgees and other lienors whose rights arose before notice of the tax lien was filed. (Code Sec. 6323(a); Reg § 301.6323(a)-1)[19] It also protects certain interests arising even after the notice was filed, e.g., attorney's liens and certain security interests. (Code Sec. 6323(b); Reg § 301.6323(b)-1)[20]

The special gift and estate tax liens don't have to be filed to be superior to claims arising after the special lien arises. But certain later purchasers and creditors are protected. (Code Sec. 6324A(d)(3), Code Sec. 6324B(c)(1))[21]

IRS may withdraw a notice of lien if it was filed prematurely or otherwise not in accordance with its administrative procedures, and for certain other reasons. (Code Sec. 6323(j)(1)) At the taxpayer's request, IRS must make reasonable efforts to notify credit reporting agencies and creditors specified by the taxpayer of the withdrawal of the notice. (Code Sec. 6323(j)(2))[22]

¶ 4913　Taxes in bankruptcy or receivership proceedings.

A receiver in a receivership proceeding must give IRS notice of the receivership. (Code Sec. 6036) (Use Form 56) But a bankruptcy trustee, debtor-in-possession, or other like fiduciary in a bankruptcy proceeding needn't give notice (Reg § 301.6036-1(a)(1)(i)), because notice under the Bankruptcy Rules is sufficient.[23] The filing of a federal bankruptcy petition (but not the start of a state receivership proceeding) automatically stays any tax proceedings against the taxpayer-debtor.[24] The running of the assessment period is suspended from the date a bankruptcy or receivership proceeding is instituted until 30 days after IRS has received notice of the proceeding, but the suspension may not exceed two years. (Code Sec. 6872; Reg § 301.6872-1)[25]

Although a taxpayer's bankruptcy triggers an immediate assessment (¶4831) collection of the tax is stayed while the taxpayer-debtor's assets are under the control of a federal or state court in bankruptcy or receivership proceedings.[26] With some exceptions, debtor relief proceedings don't discharge the taxpayer's liability for taxes or interest (including certain post-petition interest).[27]

¶ 4914　Transferee's liability for transferor's unpaid taxes.

A transferee is liable for a taxpayer-transferor's unpaid taxes (and interest and penalties) where: (1) the transfer is void or voidable under rules of equity,[28] (2) transferee liability is imposed by statute,[29] or (3) transferee liability arises under contract.[30] Transferees include a donee, heir, legatee, devisee or distributee of a decedent's estate, a shareholder of a dissolved corporation, the assignee or donee of an insolvent person, certain fiduciaries, a successor in a tax-free corporate reorganization, and various other classes of distributees. (Code Sec. 6901(h); Reg § 301.6901-1(b))[31] IRS must assess the (first) transferee within one year after the limitations period against the transferor has run. (Code Sec. 6901(c)(1))[32]

17. ¶V-6324; ¶63,234; TD ¶913,001
18. ¶V-6301; ¶63,214.04; TD ¶913,001
19. ¶s V-6400 *et seq.*, V-6426 *et seq.*; ¶63,234 *et seq.*; TD ¶913,002
20. ¶V-6401; ¶63,234; TD ¶913,003
21. ¶s V-6455, V-6456; ¶63,244 (Estate & Gift); TD ¶911,028
22. ¶V-6134; TD ¶911,021.1
23. ¶S-4103; ¶60,364; TD ¶817,504
24. ¶U-1220; ¶68,714

25. ¶T-4323; ¶68,724; TD ¶838,050
26. ¶V-7301 *et seq.*; ¶68,714; TD ¶838,050
27. ¶V-7335 *et seq.*; ¶68,734
28. ¶s V-9100 *et seq.*, V-9200 *et seq.*; ¶69,014 *et seq.*
29. ¶V-9300 *et seq.*; ¶69,014 *et seq.*
30. ¶V-9400 *et seq.*; ¶69,014.02
31. ¶V-9001; ¶69,014.01
32. ¶V-9801; ¶69,014.10

¶ 4915 Early discharge of executor's personal liability.

An executor or administrator can be discharged from personal liability for estate tax as early as nine months after the estate tax return is due (or filed, if later) if he makes a written request to IRS to determine the estate tax liability, and any tax determined to be due is paid (or a bond is posted if the payment period was extended). (Code Sec. 2204(a))[33] A trustee or other fiduciary can get a similar discharge. (Code Sec. 2204(b))[34] An executor or administrator can also request (on Form 5495) early discharge from personal liability for a decedent's income and gift taxes. (Code Sec. 6905(a))[35]

33. ¶s T-4511, T-4512; ¶22,044 (Estate & Gift)
34. ¶T-4513; ¶22,044 (Estate & Gift)

35. ¶T-4518; ¶69,054

Chapter 26　Estate, Gift and Generation-Skipping Transfer Taxes

¶ 5000　Estate Tax. ▰▰▰▰▰▰▰▰▰▰▰▰▰▰▰▰▰▰▰▰

The federal estate tax is imposed on the transfer of an individual's property at death and on other transfers considered to be the equivalent of transfers at death. The tax is imposed on the "taxable estate," which is the value of the total property transferred or considered transferred at death (the "gross estate"), reduced by various deductions. The tax is computed under a unified rate schedule under which lifetime taxable gifts and transfers at death are taxed on a cumulative basis.

Transfer taxes are in a state of flux. The Economic Growth and Tax Relief Reconciliation Act of 2001 (EGTRRA) repealed the estate tax and the generation-skipping transfer (GST) tax for estates of individuals dying in 2010 (but it did not repeal the gift tax for 2010 (see ¶5037)). However, under the EGTRRA "sunset rule" (see ¶1114) the pre-EGTRRA rules return after 2010 unless Congress provides otherwise.

Under pre-EGTRRA law, there was no gift tax and no estate tax on the first $675,000 of combined transfers during life or at death, for gifts made and individuals dying in 2001. These two taxes were tied together under a unified system having a top rate of 55%. EGTRRA substantially increased the $675,000 exemption in stages after 2001. For individuals dying in 2006 through 2008, the exemption was $2 million. It rose to $3.5 million for individuals dying in 2009. EGTRRA also changed the unified system so that the gift tax exemption amount remained at $1 million for all years after 2001.

Under the EGTRRA "sunset rule," the exemption will be $1 million for both estate and gift tax purposes in 2011. The top estate and gift tax rate reverts to 55% in 2011.

For basis rules for inherited property that applied for decedents dying before 2010, and will apply again for decedents dying after 2010 under the EGTRRA sunset provisions, see ¶2512. For basis of property acquired from a decedent dying in 2010, see ¶2523.

For other transfer tax changes under the EGTRRA sunset rule, see ¶1114.

In determining the tax on estates of individuals who at death were citizens or residents of the U.S., the entire estate is considered. (Code Sec. 2033)[1] For nonresident aliens, see ¶5036.

The paragraphs that follow explain how the estate tax is computed, what items are within reach of the tax, valuations issues, allowable deductions, credits against the tax, and other items.

¶ 5001　Computation of estate tax—Form 706.

First, compute a tentative tax under the unified rate schedule at ¶1113 on the total of: (1) the amount of the taxable estate (¶5017), and (2) the total amount of taxable gifts made by the decedent after '76 that aren't includible in his gross estate. (Code Sec. 2001(b)(1)) Then reduce this amount by the amount of gift tax payable on the decedent's post-'76 gifts to get the gross estate tax payable (before credits). (Code Sec. 2001(b)(2))

The net estate tax payable is the gross estate tax minus the unified credit, and allowable credits for state death taxes, gift taxes on pre-'77 gifts, estate taxes on earlier transfers and foreign death taxes (¶5029 *et seq.*). (Code Sec. 2010, Code Sec. 2011, Code Sec. 2012, Code Sec. 2013, Code Sec. 2014)[2]

The estate of a "qualified decedent" who was an armed forces member or victim of terrorism, or an astronaut who died in the line of duty, is entitled to compute its estate tax liability

---

1. ¶R-1010 *et seq.*, ¶R-2000 *et seq.*; ¶20,314 *et seq.*, ¶20,334 *et seq.*;　　2. ¶R-7001 *et seq.*; ¶20,014.02; TD ¶780,501
　　TD ¶761,001

References beginning with a single letter are to paragraphs in RIA's Federal Tax Coordinator 2d and RIA's Analysis of Federal Taxes: Income. Those beginning with numbers are to paragraphs in RIA's United States Tax Reporter. Those beginning with TD are to paragraphs in RIA's Tax Desk.

under a special estate tax rate schedule containing lower rates, which in many cases results, in no tax being owed. (Code Sec. 2201)[3]

¶ 5002   Property owned by decedent.

The gross estate of a decedent includes the value of all property owned by him at his death. (Code Sec. 2033; Reg § 20.2033-1(a))[4]

¶ 5003   Gifts within three years of death—Form 706, Schedule G.

An individual who transferred an interest in, or relinquished a power over, any property, within three years of death, must include the value of the property in his gross estate to the extent it would have been included in his gross estate under Code Sec. 2036 (transfers with retained life estate, etc., ¶5005), Code Sec. 2037 (transfers taking effect at death, ¶5007), Code Sec. 2038 (revocable transfers, ¶5008), or Code Sec. 2042 (life insurance proceeds, ¶5015), if the interest or relinquished power had been retained. (Code Sec. 2035(a))[5] This rule doesn't apply to any bona fide sale for full and adequate consideration. (Code Sec. 2035(d))

¶ 5004   Gift tax "gross-up"—Form 706, Schedule G.

Gift tax paid by the decedent, his estate or his donees on gifts made by decedent or his spouse including, according to the Tax Court, deemed gifts under Code Sec. 2519 (¶5047) within three years of decedent's death is included in his gross estate. But gift tax paid by the spouse on the spouse's share of decedent's gifts under the gift-splitting rules isn't included. (Code Sec. 2035(b))[6] The gift tax gross-up rule does not apply to the payment of a gift tax by a nonresident alien within three years of death.[7]

¶ 5005   Retained life estate—Form 706, Schedule G.

A decedent's gross estate includes transfers under which he retained the possession or enjoyment of, or the right to the income from, the transferred property. (Code Sec. 2036(a)(1); Reg § 20.2036-1)[8]

The decedent's gross estate also includes transfers where he retained the right to designate the person(s) to possess or enjoy the transferred property or its income. (Code Sec. 2036(a)(2))[9]

These rules don't apply to any bona fide sale for full and adequate consideration. (Code Sec. 2036(a))

A decedent who transfers property during life to a trust and retains the right to an annuity, unitrust, or other income payment from, or retains the use of an asset in, the trust has retained the right to income from all or a specific portion of the property transferred. The includible amount is that portion of the trust corpus, valued as of the decedent's death (or the alternate valuation date, if applicable) necessary to yield that annual payment (or use) applying the appropriate Code Sec. 7520 interest rate in effect on the date of death (or alternate valuation date). (Reg § 20.2036 1(c)(2))[10]

Under IRS guidance, corpus of an irrevocable trust that a grantor created during life is not includible in his gross estate under Code Sec. 2036 on account of the grantor having retained the power, exercisable in a nonfiduciary capacity, to acquire property held by the trust by substituting other property of equivalent value.[11]

IRS has had mixed results in getting assets transferred to family limited partnerships (FLPs) included in the transferor's gross estate under the foregoing rules but with less success more recently. For example, the Tax Court held that a transferor's gross estate did

---

3. ¶R-7011; ¶22,014; TD ¶780,510
4. ¶R-2001; ¶20,334; TD ¶761,001
5. ¶R-2201 *et seq.*; ¶20,354; TD ¶763,001
6. ¶s R-2210, R-2211; ¶20,354; TD ¶763,010
7. ¶R-8006

8. ¶R-2400 *et seq.*; ¶20,364; TD ¶764,001
9. ¶R-2450; ¶20,364; TD ¶764,002
10. ¶R-2408.1; ¶20,364
11. ¶R-2454.1

not have to include, in a 2009 case involving millions of dollars in asserted estate tax deficiencies, stock transferred to an FLP, and, in a 2010 case involving an asserted deficiency of almost $5 million, a transfer of timberland and an interest in a family limited partnership (whose partners were her extended family members) holding timberland to an FLP (whose partners were her more immediate family members), because the transfers were bona fide sales for an adequate and full consideration in money or money's worth.[12]

¶ 5006 Retention of voting rights in stock of a controlled corporation—Form 706, Schedule G.

Retention of voting rights in stock of a controlled corporation is a retention of the enjoyment of the transferred stock. The value of the transferred stock is included in the decedent's gross estate. (Code Sec. 2036(b))[13]

¶ 5007 Transfers taking effect at death—Form 706, Schedule G.

If a decedent transfers property during his lifetime, but the transferee cannot possess or enjoy the property except by surviving the decedent, and the decedent retained a significant reversionary interest (exceeding 5% of the value of the transferred property immediately before the decedent's death), then the value of the property is includible in decedent's gross estate. This rule doesn't apply to any bona fide sale for full and adequate consideration. (Code Sec. 2037)[14]

¶ 5008 Revocable transfers—Form 706, Schedule G.

The decedent's gross estate includes his lifetime transfers if the enjoyment of the transferred property was subject at his death to any change through the exercise by him of a power to *alter, amend, revoke or terminate*. This includes any power affecting the time or manner of enjoyment of property or its income. (Code Sec. 2038(a)(1)) This rule doesn't apply to any bona fide sale for full and adequate consideration.[15]

Includible revocable transfers include savings bank (Totten) trusts that are revocable in form,[16] and custodial accounts where the donor is custodian.[17]

Under IRS guidance, corpus of an irrevocable trust that a grantor created during life is not includible in his gross estate under Code Sec. 2038 on account of the grantor having retained the power, exercisable in a nonfiduciary capacity, to acquire property held by the trust by substituting other property of equivalent value.[18]

¶ 5009 Qualified terminable interest property (QTIP).

Qualified terminable interest property (QTIP) for which the estate tax (¶5022) or gift tax (¶5047) marital deduction was elected is includible in the estate of the donee spouse at its then fair market value unless the donee disposed of any part of the qualifying income interest for life. (Code Sec. 2044) The property is treated as passing from the surviving spouse. (Code Sec. 2044(c)) Where a predeceased spouse's estate made an unnecessary QTIP election that did not reduce its estate tax liability, steps may be taken so that the unneeded election will be treated as null and void for federal estate, gift, and generation-skipping transfer tax purposes. As a result, the property won't have to be included in the survivor's estate.[19]

The surviving spouse's executor may recover the estate taxes caused by the inclusion from the persons to whom the property passes at the surviving spouse's death, unless the surviving spouse's will specifically indicates an intent to waive the right of recovery. (Code

---

12. ¶R-2421.1
13. ¶R-2436; ¶20,364; TD ¶764,032
14. ¶R-2500 *et seq.*; ¶20,374; TD ¶765,000
15. ¶R-2600 *et seq.*; ¶20,384 *et seq.*; TD ¶765,501

16. ¶R-2621; TD ¶765,520
17. ¶R-2620; ¶20,384.03; TD ¶765,519
18. ¶R-2612.1
19. ¶R-2900 *et seq.*; ¶20,444; TD ¶777,032

Sec. 2207A(a))[20]

¶ 5010   Powers of appointment—Form 706, Schedule H.

If the decedent possessed a general power of appointment (created after Oct. 21, '42) at the time of his death, the property subject to the power is included in his gross estate. (Code Sec. 2041(a))[21] A "general" power is one exercisable in favor of the decedent, his estate, his creditors, or the creditors of his estate. (Code Sec. 2041(b)(1))[22]

¶ 5011   Jointly-held property—Form 706, Schedule E.

Joint ownership acquired through gift, bequest, devise, or inheritance from another. The decedent's fractional share of the property is included in the gross estate. (Reg § 20.2040-1(a)(1))[23]

Joint ownership created by co-owners. Except for husband-wife tenancies (¶5012), the *entire* value of the property is included in the co-owner's gross estate except the part, if any, attributable to the consideration in money or money's worth furnished by the other joint owner(s). Consideration furnished by the surviving joint owner(s) doesn't include money or property acquired from the decedent for less than a full and adequate consideration in money or money's worth. (Reg § 20.2040-1(a)(2))[24]

Tenancy in common. Only the value of decedent's undivided share of the property is included in his gross estate.[25]

¶ 5012   Spouses' jointly-held property—Form 706, Schedule E.

If an interest in property created after '76 is held by a decedent and his spouse as tenants by the entireties or as joint tenants with right of survivorship (if the decedent and his spouse are the only joint tenants), one half of the value of the jointly-owned interest will be included in the estate of the decedent spouse regardless of which spouse furnished the original consideration. (Code Sec. 2040(b)) Where the surviving spouse isn't a U.S. citizen, this rule applies only if the property passes in a qualified domestic trust (QDOT, ¶5025). (Code Sec. 2056(d)(1)(B), Code Sec. 2056(d)(2))[26]

Thus, the survivor gets a new basis for one-half of the property, see ¶2517.

¶ 5013   Community property.

The value of the interest in community property vested in the decedent by state law—ordinarily, half of the community property—is included in the decedent spouse's estate.[27]

¶ 5014   Annuities—Form 706, Schedule I.

The value of an annuity or other payment receivable by a beneficiary is included in the decedent's gross estate if, under the contract or agreement, either:

(1) an annuity or other payment was payable to decedent, either alone or with another person(s), for decedent's life or for any period not ascertainable without reference to his death or for any period that doesn't in fact end before his death, or

(2) the decedent possessed, for one of the periods in (1), above, the right to receive such an annuity or other payment, either alone or with another. (Code Sec. 2039(a))

---

20. ¶R-6439 *et seq.*; ¶s 20,444, 20,564.08, 22,07A4, 25,194; TD ¶778,135
21. ¶R-3000 *et seq.*; ¶20,414; TD ¶767,301
22. ¶R-3006; ¶20,414; TD ¶767,319
23. ¶s R-2705, R-2709; ¶20,404; TD ¶766,005

24. ¶R-2700 *et seq.*; ¶20,404; TD ¶766,005
25. ¶R-2707; ¶20,334.15; TD ¶766,006
26. ¶R-2724 *et seq.*; ¶20,404; TD ¶766,019 *et seq.*
27. ¶R-2800 *et seq.*; ¶s 20,334.16, 20,334.17; TD ¶766,022

The amount included is an amount proportionate to the part of the purchase price contributed by the decedent. Contributions made by an employer are considered made by the employee if made by reason of his employment. (Code Sec. 2039(b))[28]

¶ 5015   Life insurance—Form 706, Schedule D.

Proceeds of insurance on the decedent's life receivable by the executor or administrator, or payable to the decedent's estate, are includible in his gross estate. (Code Sec. 2042(1)) The estate needn't be specifically named as the beneficiary. (Reg § 20.2042-1(b)(1))[29]

Proceeds of insurance on the decedent's life not receivable by or for the benefit of the estate are includible if the decedent possessed at his death or transferred within 3 years of death any incidents of ownership in the policy, exercisable either alone or with any other person. (Code Sec. 2042(2)) "Incidents of ownership" include the power to change the beneficiary, to revoke an assignment, to pledge the policy for a loan, etc. (Reg § 20.2042-1(c)(2)), and certain reversionary interests. (Reg § 20.2042-1(c)(3))[30]

¶ 5016   Group term life insurance—Form 706, Schedule D.

An employee can prevent inclusion in his estate (under the rule at ¶5015) of the proceeds of group term life insurance furnished by his employer by transferring the insurance before his death, if:

(1) the group policy and applicable state law permit the employee to make an absolute assignment of all his incidents of ownership, and

(2) the employee irrevocably assigns all policy rights.[31]

¶ 5017   Computing the taxable estate.

To get the taxable estate, deduct the following from the gross estate:[32]

. . . Funeral expenses. (Code Sec. 2053(a)(1))

. . . Administration expenses, such as executors' and administrators' commissions, attorneys', accountants' and appraisers' fees, and court costs. (Code Sec. 2053(a)(2); Reg § 20.2053-3)

. . . Claims against the estate, including property taxes accrued before the decedent's death, unpaid income and gift taxes, and medical expenses of the decedent paid by his estate after his death (to the extent not claimed as an income tax deduction, see ¶2144). (Code Sec. 2053(a)(3); Reg § 20.2053-6)

. . . Transfers in satisfaction of claims by the decedent's former spouse. (Code Sec. 2043(b)(2))

. . . Indebtedness on property if the total value of the property is included in the gross estate. (Code Sec. 2053(a)(4))

. . . Casualty and theft losses. (Code Sec. 2054)

. . . Transfers to charitable and similar organizations (Code Sec. 2055), see ¶5019.

. . . Transfers to surviving spouse (marital deduction) (Code Sec. 2056), see ¶5020.

. . . State death taxes (Code Sec. 2058), see ¶5026.

For an item to be deductible as a debt, claim, or expense it must also be allowable by the jurisdiction under which the estate is being administered. (Code Sec. 2053(a))[33] Under regs that apply for estates of decedents dying after Oct. 19, 2009, post-death events are taken into account in determining the deductible amount of a claim or other expense under Code Sec.

28. ¶R-4401 *et seq.*; ¶20,394; TD ¶768,054
29. ¶R-4002 *et seq.*; ¶20,424.01; TD ¶768,002
30. ¶R-4006 *et seq.*; ¶20,424 *et seq.*; TD ¶768,008
31. ¶R-4033; TD ¶768,032

32. ¶R-5400 *et seq.*; ¶s 20,514, 20,534, 20,544, 20,554, 20,564; TD ¶776,001
33. ¶R-5404; ¶20,534 *et seq.*; TD ¶776,003

2053 and deductions generally are limited to amounts actually paid by the estate in satisfaction of deductible claims and expenses. Exceptions apply for claims against the estate with respect to which there is an asset or claim includible in the gross estate that is substantially related to the claim against the estate and for claims against the estate that, collectively, do not exceed $500,000 (not including those deductible as ascertainable amounts). Although both exceptions provide an opportunity to claim a deduction at the time of filing the estate tax return, in each case, the amount of the deduction is subject to adjustment to reflect post-death events, consistent with the general approach of the regs. (Reg § 20.2053-1, Reg § 20.2053-4)[34]

¶ 5018   Income v. estate tax deduction.

Many estate administration expenses can qualify as an estate tax deduction on the estate tax return and as an income tax deduction, or an offset against the sales price of property in determining gain or loss, on the estate's income tax return. But the estate is entitled to an income tax deduction or offset only if an estate tax deduction for the item is waived. (Code Sec. 642(g))[35] For the election to take an income tax or estate tax deduction, see ¶3925.

¶ 5019   Deductions for charitable bequests—Form 706, Schedule O.

Deductions are allowed (on Form 706, Schedule O) for the value of property included in the gross estate and transferred by decedent during life or by will to or for the use of the U.S., any state, political subdivision thereof, or the District of Columbia, and to various types of charitable organizations (Code Sec. 2055(a)) including foreign ones.[36]

Strict requirements apply where the charitable bequest is of an income interest or a remainder interest. (Code Sec. 2055(e))[37]

¶ 5020   Marital deduction—Form 706, Schedule M.

A marital deduction is allowed (on Form 706, Schedule M) for the value of all property included in the gross estate that passes to the decedent's surviving spouse in a manner qualifying for the deduction. (Code Sec. 2056(a))[38] For terminable interests, see ¶5021. For where surviving spouse isn't a U.S. citizen, see ¶5025.

¶ 5021   Terminable interests and the marital deduction—Form 706, Schedule M.

With certain exceptions (see, e.g., ¶5022), a terminable interest doesn't qualify for the marital deduction if another interest in the same property passed from the decedent to some other person for less than adequate and full consideration in money or money's worth and by reason of its passing that other person or his heirs may enjoy part of the property after the termination of the surviving spouse's interest. (Code Sec. 2056(b)(1); Reg § 20.2056(b)-1(c)) A terminable interest is one that will terminate or fail after a certain period of time, the happening of some contingency, or the failure of some event to occur. (Reg § 20.2056(b)-1(b))[39]

¶ 5022   Qualified terminable interest property (QTIP) election—Form 706, Schedule M.

Property in which a spouse is given only a life estate may qualify for the marital deduction as an exception to the terminable interest rule (¶5021) if the executor elects (by listing the property on Form 706, Schedule M and deducting its value) to have all or part of the property so qualify and the surviving spouse has a "qualifying income interest for life." A surviving spouse has such an interest if:

---

34. ¶R-5403; TD ¶776,002
35. ¶R-5507; ¶20,534; TD ¶776,082
36. ¶R-5700 *et seq.*; ¶20,554 *et seq.*; TD ¶777,000

37. ¶R-5735 *et seq.*; ¶s 20,554, 20,554.14, 20,554.16; TD ¶777,035
38. ¶R-6000 *et seq.*; ¶20,564 *et seq.*; TD ¶778,001
39. ¶R-6300 *et seq.*; ¶20,564; TD ¶778,049

(1) the surviving spouse is entitled for life to all the income from the property, payable at least annually, or the spouse has a usufruct interest for life in the property, and

(2) no person (including the spouse) has a power to appoint any part of the property to any person other than the surviving spouse during the surviving spouse's life. (Code Sec. 2056(b)(7))[40]

A surviving spouse's interest can meet the "all income" requirement if the spouse is entitled to income as determined by applicable local law that provides for a reasonable apportionment between the income and remainder beneficiaries of the trust's total return. (Reg § 20.2056(b)-5(f)(1), Reg § 20.2056(b)-7(d)(2))[41]

QTIP treatment isn't defeated merely because the spouse's income interest is contingent on the executor making a QTIP election. (Reg § 20.2056(b)-7(d)(3))[42]

An annuity, including one arising under community property law, where only the surviving spouse has the right to receive payments before the death of that surviving spouse qualifies and the QTIP election is treated as made with respect to it unless the executor otherwise elects. (Code Sec. 2056(b)(7)(C))[43]

Certain individual retirement accounts (IRAs) qualify. (Reg § 20.2056(b)-7(h), Ex 10) A revenue ruling explains how total return concepts affect QTIP deductions for IRAs.[44]

Partial QTIP elections that relate to a fractional or percentage share of the property are allowed. (Reg § 20.2056(b)-7(b)(2))[45] Protective QTIP elections are possible. (Reg § 20.2056(b)-7(c))[46]

For inclusion of the qualified terminable interest property in the surviving spouse's estate, see ¶5009.

¶ 5023   Effect of death taxes on amount of marital deduction.

Federal estate or other death taxes payable out of the marital share reduce the amount of the bequest that qualifies for the marital deduction. (Code Sec. 2056(b)(4)(A))

The spouse's interest can be completely absolved from the burden of the tax by a provision in decedent's will that is effective under local law. In such a case, death taxes won't affect the amount of the deduction.[47]

¶ 5024   Effect of administration expenses on amount of marital deduction

The marital deduction is reduced by estate transmission expenses paid from the marital share (Reg § 20.2056(b)-4(d)(2)) but not by estate management expenses attributable to and paid from the marital share unless those expenses are deducted on the estate tax return under Code Sec. 2053. (Reg § 20.2056(b)-4(d)(3)) The marital deduction is reduced to the extent estate management expenses are paid from the marital share and are attributable to other property. (Reg § 20.2056(b)-4(d)(4)) Estate transmission expenses are expenses that wouldn't have been incurred but for the necessity of collecting the decedent's assets, paying his debts and death taxes, and distributing his property. They include any administration expense that is not a management expense. (Reg § 20.2056(b)-4(d)(1)(ii)) Management expenses are those incurred in connection with the investment of estate assets or with their preservation or maintenance during a reasonable period of administration. (Reg § 20.2056(b)-4(d)(1)(i))[48]

---

40. ¶R-6393; ¶20,564.08; TD ¶778,100
41. ¶R-6355
42. ¶R-6400; ¶20,564.08; TD ¶778,115
43. ¶R-6413 *et seq.*; ¶20,564.08; TD ¶778,125
44. ¶R-6422; TD ¶778,129

45. ¶R-6431; ¶20,564.08; TD ¶778,106
46. ¶R-6430; TD ¶778,105
47. ¶R-6612 *et seq.*; ¶20,564.17; TD ¶778,145
48. ¶R-6608; ¶20,564.05; TD ¶778,142

¶ 5025 Marital deduction where surviving spouse isn't a U.S. citizen—qualified domestic trust (QDOT) requirement.

No marital deduction is allowed if the surviving spouse isn't a U.S. citizen (Code Sec. 2056(d)(1)(A); Reg § 20.2056A-1(a)), unless the property passes (or is treated as passing) to the spouse in a QDOT (Code Sec. 2056(d)(2))—a trust that satisfies certain requirements (Code Sec. 2056A; Reg § 20.2056A-2) or the spouse timely becomes a citizen. (Code Sec. 2056(d)(4); Reg § 20.2056A-1(b))[49]

An estate tax is imposed (use Form 706-QDT) on any distribution (other than an income or a hardship distribution (Reg § 20.2056A-5(c))) from the trust before the date of the surviving spouse's death and on the value of the property remaining in the trust on the date of death of the surviving spouse (Code Sec. 2056A(b)(1)) (or the date the trust ceases to qualify). (Code Sec. 2056A(b)(3))[50]

¶ 5026 Deduction for state death taxes

The value of the taxable estate is determined by deducting from the gross estate any estate, inheritance, legacy, or succession taxes actually paid to any state or the District of Columbia for any property included in the gross estate, but not including any taxes paid for the estate of a person other than the decedent. (Code Sec. 2058)

⚠ caution: This deduction won't apply for estates of individuals dying after 2010 if the EGTRRA sunset kicks in (see ¶1114). Instead, the prior law credit for state death taxes would apply.

¶ 5027 Value of property included in the gross estate.

The value of property included in the gross estate is the fair market value of the property at the date of the decedent's death (or at the alternate valuation date, see below). (Code Sec. 2031; Reg § 20.2031-1)[1]

Regs provide rules for valuing specific types of properties including: stocks and bonds (Reg § 20.2031-2); business interests (Reg § 20.2031-3); notes (Reg § 20.2031-4); household and personal effects (Reg § 20.2031-6); and life insurance and annuity contracts. (Reg § 20.2031-8) Under IRS guidance, an interest in a restricted management account (RMA) (an agreement allowing a bank to manage assets for a fixed term that can't be altered in exchange for a reduced fee) is valued for transfer tax purposes without any reduction or discount for the restrictions imposed by the RMA agreement.[2] The Eleventh Circuit has held that in determining the estate tax value of holding company stock, the company's value is reduced by the entire built-in capital gain tax liability as of the date of death.[3]

An executor may elect (on Form 706, Schedule U) to exclude from the gross estate up to 40% of the value of land subject to a qualified conservation easement meeting certain requirements and subject to a dollar cap of $500,000. (Code Sec. 2031(c)) If a qualified conservation easement is granted after the decedent's death but on or before the due date (including extensions) for the estate tax return, an estate tax charitable deduction is allowed, but only if no income tax charitable deduction is allowed to any person with respect to the grant. (Code Sec. 2031(c)(9))[4]

⚠ observation: The rules for qualified conservation easements would be changed for estates of individuals dying after 2010 if the EGTRRA sunset rule kicks in, see ¶5000.

The fair market value of annuities (other than commercial annuities), life estates, term of years, remainders, and reversions is determined under IRS tables, which include an interest

---

49. ¶R-6201 *et seq.*; ¶s 20,564, 20,56A4; TD ¶778,027
50. ¶R-7081 *et seq.*; ¶20,56A4.02; TD ¶781,501
1. ¶R-1006; ¶20,314; TD ¶751,005

2. ¶P-6748.2
3. ¶P-6366.2
4. ¶R-4700 *et seq.*; ¶20,314.13; TD ¶773,400

rate component and, if applicable, a mortality component.

The annuity tables typically are used to value lottery winnings and structured settlement payments.[5]

The executor can elect (irrevocably, on Form 706) to use an alternate valuation date rather than the decedent's date of death to value the property included in the gross estate. This alternate date is generally six months after decedent's death or earlier date of sale or distribution. (Code Sec. 2032(a))[6] Alternate valuation can be elected only if its use decreases both the value of the gross estate and the combined estate and generation-skipping transfer tax liability. (Code Sec. 2032(c); Reg § 20.2032-1(b)(1))[7]

observation: The executor can't elect in order to step up the basis of assets that increase in value after death (for example, where there would otherwise be no estate tax cost to the increased valuation because the marital deduction eliminates any tax).

IRS says that alternate valuation cannot be used to achieve a discount for restrictions placed on stock in a post-death reorganization.[8]

¶ 5028 Special-use valuation of farm or other business real property—Form 706, Schedule A-1.

If certain conditions are met, an executor may elect (irrevocably, on Form 706, Schedule A-1) to value qualified real property used for farming purposes or in a trade or business on the basis of the property's value for its actual use, rather than on its highest and best use. The total decrease in the value of all real property under this election may not exceed $1,020,000 for individuals dying in 2011. (Code Sec. 2032A)[9] The resulting estate tax savings may be recaptured (use Form 706-A) under certain conditions. (Code Sec. 2032A(c))[10]

¶ 5029 Unified credit against estate tax.

The credit for estates of individuals dying in 2011 is $345,800 (Code Sec. 2010(a)) (assuming the EGTRRA sunset kicks in, see ¶5000) but can't exceed the estate tax imposed. (Code Sec. 2010(c)) The effect is to exempt up to $1 million from estate taxation for individuals dying in 2011.[11]

The credit is reduced by 20% of the amount of the pre-'77 $30,000 gift tax exemption allowed for gifts made before '77 and after Sept. 8, '76. (Code Sec. 2010(b))[12]

¶ 5030 Credit for tax on prior transfers—Form 706, Schedule Q.

Credit is allowed (on Form 706, Schedule Q) against the estate tax for federal estate tax paid by the estate of another decedent (the transferor) on the transfer of property to the present decedent from that transferor where the transferor died within ten years before, or within two years after, the present decedent's death. (Code Sec. 2013)[13]

Where a transferor decedent was denied a marital deduction because the surviving spouse wasn't a U.S. citizen or where the estate tax on qualified domestic trust distributions applied (see ¶5025), the surviving spouse decedent is allowed a credit for the estate tax paid by the transferor decedent, or by the trust, without regard to when the transferor decedent died. (Code Sec. 2056(d)(3))[14]

5. ¶P-6679.1
6. ¶R-5002; ¶20,324; TD ¶773,001
7. ¶R-5001; ¶20,324; TD ¶773,001
8. ¶R-5022.1
9. ¶R-5200 *et seq.*; ¶20,32A4; TD ¶771,001

10. ¶R-5301; ¶20,32A4; TD ¶771,053
11. ¶R-7100 *et seq.*; ¶20,104; TD ¶781,801
12. ¶R-7103; ¶20,104; TD ¶781,804
13. ¶R-7300 *et seq.*; ¶20,134; TD ¶782,500 *et seq.*
14. ¶R-7301; ¶20,564; TD ¶782,515

¶ 5031   Credit for gift taxes paid on pre-'77 gifts.

Credit for gift taxes paid on pre-'77 gifts is allowed against the estate tax where gifts were made by a decedent before '77 of property included in his gross estate. (Code Sec. 2012(a))[15]

¶ 5032   Credit for foreign death taxes—Form 706, Schedule P.

Credit is allowed (on Form 706, Schedule P), subject to certain limits, against the estate tax for estate, inheritance, legacy, or succession taxes actually paid to any foreign country or U.S. possession. (Code Sec. 2014)[16]

¶ 5033   Return requirements—Form 706.

An executor must file an estate tax return Form 706 if the decedent's gross estate at death exceeds the amount effectively exempted by unified credit ($1 million for estates of individuals dying in 2011, assuming the EGTRRA sunset kicks in see ¶5029). This dollar amount is reduced by certain gifts made by the decedent. (Code Sec. 6018(a)(1), Code Sec. 6018(a)(3))[17]

¶ 5034   When to file estate tax return.

File within nine months after the date of death. (Code Sec. 6075(a))[18]

IRS will grant an automatic 6-month extension to file Form 706 and may grant a 6-month discretionary filing extension (1) for estates that didn't seek an automatic extension, (2) to file Form 706-NA for the estates of nonresident alien, and (3) to file specialized estate tax forms for various recapture estate taxes (e.g., Form 706-A for recapture of special use valuation). (use Form 4768 for all extensions). An executor who is abroad can request a longer discretionary extension. (Reg § 20.6081-1)[19]

¶ 5035   When to pay tax.

The estate tax must be paid at the time for filing the return. Filing extensions don't extend the time for payment, (Reg § 20.6151-1)[20] but extensions of time to pay can be granted (use Form 4768) for reasonable cause. (Code Sec. 6161(a)(1))[21]

Special extensions (elected on Form 706) are available where a future interest is included in the estate (Code Sec. 6163)[22] or where the estate consists largely of a closely-held business. (Code Sec. 6166)[23]

The estate tax on distributions made from qualified domestic trusts (QDOTs, see ¶5025), before the surviving spouse's death is due on Apr. 15 of the year following the calendar year the taxable event occurs. (Code Sec. 2056A(b)(5))[24]

¶ 5036   Estates of nonresident aliens—Form 706-NA.

Decedents who were neither U.S. citizens nor U.S. residents are taxed only on the transfer of property situated within the U.S. With that exception, the make-up of the gross estate is the same as that for a U.S. citizen or resident. (Code Sec. 2103)

The same rate schedule that applies to the estates of U.S. citizens (¶1113) applies to the estates of nonresident aliens. (Code Sec. 2101(b))

A marital deduction is allowed under the principles of the regular marital deduction rules (¶5020 *et seq.*), with respect to U.S. property. (Code Sec. 2106(a)(3)) Other deductions are also

15. ¶R-7501; ¶20,124; TD ¶783,001
16. ¶R-7400 *et seq.*; ¶20,144; TD ¶782,801
17. ¶S-2300 *et seq.*; ¶60,184; TD ¶751,015
18. ¶S-4902; ¶60,754; TD ¶783,508
19. ¶S-5035.1; ¶60,814; TD ¶783,509

20. ¶S-5851; ¶61,514; TD ¶783,513
21. ¶S-5900 *et seq.*; ¶61,614; TD ¶783,514
22. ¶S-5910; ¶61,634; TD ¶782,807
23. ¶S-6000 *et seq.*; ¶61,664 *et seq.*; TD ¶784,001
24. ¶R-7085 *et seq.*; ¶20,56A4.02; TD ¶781,506

allowed, within limits. (Code Sec. 2106)

A unified credit of $13,000 is allowed against the estate tax of nonresident aliens, with an alternative credit computations for estates of certain residents of U.S. possessions (Code Sec. 2102(b)(1), Code Sec. 2102(b)(2)), and to the extent required under certain treaty obligations of the U.S. (Code Sec. 2102(b)(3)(A)) The $13,000 is reduced by any gift tax unified credit allowed. (Code Sec. 2102(b)(3)(B))

Credits are also allowed for estate tax on prior transfers and gift tax on certain pre-'77 gifts. (Code Sec. 2102(b)(5))[25]

An estate tax return on Form 706-NA must be filed for the estate of every nonresident not a U.S. citizen if the value of the part of the estate in the U.S. exceeds $60,000 (Code Sec. 6018(a)(2)), reduced by: (1) the amount of adjusted taxable gifts made by the decedent after '76, and (2) the amount of any pre-'77 specific exemption allowed for gifts made by the decedent after Sept. 8, '76. (Code Sec. 6018(a)(3))[26] The time for filing the return is the same as for U.S. citizens or residents, see ¶5034.

Expatriates and former long-term residents who gave up citizenship or terminated residency before June 17, 2008. A tougher expatriate estate tax is imposed on the transfer of a taxable estate of a decedent nonresident non-U.S. citizen who dies during the 10-year period that he is subject to the expatriate alternative tax described at ¶4659. (Code Sec. 2107(a))[27]

Expatriates and former long-term residents who gave up citizenship or terminated residency after June 16, 2008. A special transfer tax (the "Code Sec. 2801 tax") is imposed on any U.S. citizen or resident who receives any "covered gift or bequest" from a "covered expatriate," see ¶4653. (Code Sec. 2801(a)) The tax applies to any covered gift or bequest valued in excess of the annual exclusion amount in effect for gift tax purposes in the year of the transfer ($13,000 for 2010 and 2011). (Code Sec. 2801(c)) The amount of the Code Sec. 2801 tax is determined by multiplying the value of the covered gift or bequest by the greater of (i) the highest estate tax rate listed in the Code Sec. 2001(c) rate table in effect on the date the transferee receives the covered gift or bequest, or (ii) the highest gift tax rate listed in the Code Sec. 2502(a) rate table in effect on that date. (Code Sec. 2801(a)) IRS intends to issue a new Form 708, on which to report the receipt of gifts and bequests that are subject to the Code Sec. 2801 tax on covered gifts and bequests[28]

¶ 5037   Gift Tax. ◼◼◼◼◼◼◼◼◼

The gift tax is imposed on the transfer of money or other property by gift. For gifts made in 2010, the gift tax is in effect (but the estate tax is not, see ¶5000). For gifts made and decedents dying after 2010, the gift tax is integrated with the estate tax under a "unified" rate schedule that imposes a single tax on transfers during life and at death (see ¶5000).

The tax is imposed on the transfer, not on the property transferred. It applies even though the property transferred may be exempt from income or other taxes. (Code Sec. 2501(a); Reg § 25.2501-1, Reg § 25.2511-1(a), Reg § 25.2511-2)[29]

Gifts made by a person who, in a tax year, makes no gift of a present interest with a value of over $13,000 (for 2010 and 2011) to any one person, and who makes no gifts of future interests, aren't subject to tax, see ¶5046 (and no gift tax return need be filed, see ¶5054).

¶ 5038   Who must pay gift tax?

The gift tax must be paid by the person (the donor) who makes the gift. (Code Sec. 2501(a); Reg § 25.2511-2(f)) It applies only to donors who are individuals (Reg § 25.2501-1(b)) but a gift by a corporation may be treated as a gift by the shareholders. (Reg § 25.2511-1(h)(1))[30]

---

25. ¶R-8000 *et seq.*; ¶21,014.02; TD ¶786,000 *et seq.*
26. ¶S-2302; ¶60,184; TD ¶783,504
27. ¶R-8033; ¶21,074
28. ¶R-8100; ¶28,014

29. ¶Q-1000 *et seq.*; ¶s 25,009, 25,014; TD ¶701,002
30. ¶s Q-1000 *et seq.*, Q-2400 *et seq.*; ¶s 25,014, 25,114; TD ¶714,000

If the donor fails to pay the tax when due, the donee is also liable for the tax to the extent of the value of his gift. (Code Sec. 6324(b); Reg § 25.2502-2, Reg § 301.6324-1(b))[31]

These rules apply to a U.S. citizen or resident no matter where the gift property (tangible or intangible) is situated. (Code Sec. 2501(a); Reg § 25.2501-1(a), Reg § 25.2511-3(a))[32]

A nonresident who's not a U.S. citizen is subject to gift tax only if the gift property is real estate or tangible personal property and is situated in the U.S. at the time of the gift. (Code Sec. 2501(a), Code Sec. 2511(a); Reg § 25.2511-1(b), Reg § 25.2511-3(a)) A nonresident generally isn't subject to tax on a gift of intangible property. (Code Sec. 2501(a)(2))

For a special transfer tax for expatriates and former long-term residents who gave up citizenship or terminated residency after June 16, 2008, see ¶5036.

¶ 5039   What is a gift?

All transactions whereby property or property rights are gratuitously bestowed upon another are gifts. (Reg § 25.2511-1(c)) Each transfer made in 2010 to a trust that is not treated as wholly owned by the donor or the donor's spouse under the grantor trust is considered to be a transfer by gift of the entire interest in the property. (Code Sec. 2511(c))

A gift isn't complete (i.e., taxable), until the donor parts with dominion or control over the transferred property or property interest. He must be left without power to change the disposition of the property either for his own benefit or for that of others. (Reg § 25.2511-2(b))[33]

There's no gift tax on a transfer to a political organization. (Code Sec. 2501(a)(5))[34]

¶ 5040   Educational or medical payment exclusion.

The gift tax doesn't apply to amounts paid by one individual:

(1) on behalf of another individual directly to a qualifying educational organization as tuition for that other individual. (Code Sec. 2503(e); Reg § 25.2503-6(b)(2))

(2) on behalf of another individual directly to a provider of medical care as payment for that medical care. (Code Sec. 2503(e); Reg § 25.2503-6(b)(3)) Payments for medical insurance qualify for this exclusion. (Reg § 25.2503-6(b)(3))

These exclusions are available in addition to the annual gift tax exclusion (¶5046). (Reg § 25.2503-6(a))[35] No gift tax return is required. (Code Sec. 6019)[36]

Contributions to qualified tuition programs (¶2209 *et seq.*) and CESAs (¶2205 *et seq.*) don't qualify for the Code Sec. 2503(e) tuition exclusion but, instead, are treated as present gifts that can qualify for the gift tax annual exclusion including by electively spreading contributions in a single year over a five-year period. A contributor isn't subject to gift tax on distributions from qualified tuition programs and CESAs. (Code Sec. 529(c), Code Sec. 530(d)(3)) A transfer by reason of a change in the designated beneficiary under a qualified tuition program, or a rollover to the account of a new beneficiary, is subject to gift and GST taxes unless the new beneficiary is: (1) assigned to the same generation as, or a higher generation than, the old beneficiary; and (2) a member of the old beneficiary's family. (Code Sec. 529(c)(5)(B))

¶ 5041   Below-market loans.

If a below-market (or interest-free) loan is a "gift loan" (that is, a below-market loan where the forgoing of interest is in the nature of a gift), it's treated as: (1) a loan to the borrower/donee in exchange for an interest-paying note, and (2) a gift to the borrower of the

31. ¶V-9301; ¶63,244; TD ¶702,001
32. ¶Q-1016; ¶s 25,014, 25,114 *et seq.*; TD ¶703,002
33. ¶Q-3004; ¶25,114.01; TD ¶711,005

34. ¶Q-3201; ¶25,014; TD ¶716,015
35. ¶Q-5250 *et seq.*; ¶25,034; TD ¶732,501
36. ¶S-2201; ¶25,014; TD ¶746,001

funds to pay the interest. The amount of the gift equals:

... the forgone interest—excess of interest payable at the applicable federal rate (¶1116) over actual interest payable—if the loan is a demand loan, or

... the excess of the amount loaned over the present value (using a discount rate equal to the applicable federal rate) of all payments required under the terms of the loan, if the gift loan is a term loan. (Code Sec. 7872)[37]

For demand loans, the gift is treated as made on the last day of the calendar year. (Code Sec. 7872(a)) For term loans, the gift is treated as made on the date the loan was made. (Code Sec. 7872(b))[38]

These rules don't apply to certain gift loans between individuals that don't exceed $10,000. (Code Sec. 7872(c)(2))[39]

If the outstanding balance of a gift loan made between individuals is $100,000 or less, the amount of interest treated as retransferred by the borrower to the lender each year doesn't exceed the borrower's net investment income for that year. If the net investment income is $1,000 or less, the amount treated as retransferred is zero. (Code Sec. 7872(d)(1))[40]

¶ 5042   Joint ownership of property.

A gift may result where property is placed in joint ownership with someone other than a spouse or where joint ownership with someone other than a spouse ends.[41]

If an individual with his own funds buys property and has the title conveyed to himself and others as joint tenants, with rights of survivorship, but which rights may be defeated by any joint tenant severing his interest, there is an immediate gift to the other joint tenants of equal shares of the property. (Reg § 25.2511-1(h)(5))[42]

An individual doesn't make a gift when he opens a joint bank account with his own funds for himself and another but he can regain the entire fund without the other's consent. A gift is made only when the other person withdraws money for his own benefit. (Reg § 25.2511-1(h)(4)) Similar rules apply for joint brokerage accounts and U.S. savings bonds.[43]

¶ 5043   Qualified disclaimers.

A qualified disclaimer (an irrevocable and unqualified refusal to accept ownership, made in writing by a specified deadline) with respect to any interest in property has the effect of treating that interest, for gift (and estate and generation-skipping transfer tax) purposes, as if it had never been transferred to the disclaimant. (Code Sec. 2518) And the disclaimant isn't treated as having made a gift to the person to whom the interest passes by reason of the disclaimer. (Reg § 25.2518-1(b))[44]

¶ 5044   Amount of the gift.

The amount of the gift is the money given or, if property is given, the property's value as of the date of the gift. (Code Sec. 2512(a))[45]

The market value of annuities (other than commercial annuities), unitrust interests, life estates, term of years, remainders, and reversions transferred by gift is determined by use of standard or special Code Sec. 7520 actuarial factors. (Reg § 25.2512-5(a), Reg § 25.7520-1(a)) These factors are derived by using the appropriate Code Sec. 7520 interest rate[46] and, if applicable, the mortality component for the valuation date of the interest that's being valued. These factors appear in IRS issued tables. (Reg § 25.2512-5T(d)(1))[47]

---

37. ¶Q-2150 *et seq.*; ¶78,724; TD ¶155,001 *et seq.*
38. ¶Q-2150; ¶78,724; TD ¶155,003
39. ¶Q-2165; ¶78,724; TD ¶155,027
40. ¶J-2905; ¶78,724; TD ¶155,005
41. ¶Q-2900 *et seq.*; ¶25,114; TD ¶714,501
42. ¶Q-2906; ¶25,114; TD ¶714,507

43. ¶Q-2921 *et seq.*; TD ¶714,519
44. ¶Q-2350 *et seq.*; ¶25,184 *et seq.*; TD ¶713,012
45. ¶Q-1200; ¶25,124; TD ¶741,000
46. ¶P-6619
47. ¶P-6615; ¶25,124; TD ¶521,501

¶ 5045   Taxable gifts.

Taxable gifts are the gifts made during the calendar year after the annual exclusion (¶5046), and reduced by allowable deductions (¶5047, ¶5048). (Code Sec. 2503(a), Code Sec. 2503(b))[48]

¶ 5046   Annual exclusion.

The first $13,000 of gifts of a present interest made by a donor *to each donee* in 2010 and 2011 is excluded from the amount of the donor's taxable gifts. (Code Sec. 2503(b))[49] For 2010, the first $134,000 of gifts made by a donor to a spouse who isn't a U.S. citizen is excluded ($136,000 for 2011). (Code Sec. 2523(i)(2))[50]

No annual exclusion is allowed for gifts of future interests (Code Sec. 2503(b); Reg § 25.2503-2), e.g., reversions or remainders. (Reg § 25.2503-3)[1] A district court has held that a married couple's gifts of interests in a limited liability company to their children didn't qualify for gift tax annual exclusions because they were gifts of future interests. Likewise, the Tax Court has held that a married couple's gifts of interests in a limited partnership to their adult children did not qualify for gift tax annual exclusions because they were gifts of future interests.[2]

A "Crummey" power (in general, a trust beneficiary's noncumulative right to withdraw a specified amount of trust principal within a limited period) makes a transfer to the trust a gift of a present interest.[3]

A transfer for the benefit of a *minor* isn't considered a gift of a future interest if the property and its income:

(1) may be expended by or for the benefit of the minor before he reaches 21, and

(2) any balance not so expended *will pass to the minor* when he reaches 21, or if he dies before 21 will go either to his *estate* or as he may appoint under a general power of appointment. (Code Sec. 2503(c); Reg § 25.2503-4(a))[4]

Gifts to minors made through custodians designated under Uniform Acts for gifts or transfers to minors qualify for the annual exclusion.[5]

¶ 5047   Marital deduction.

A marital deduction is allowed for the value of all qualifying gifts made by one spouse to the other if the donee spouse is a U.S. citizen (with some exceptions) and the gift isn't a nondeductible "terminable interest." (Code Sec. 2523)[6]

Qualified terminable interest property (QTIP) qualifies for the deduction if the donee spouse receives income payments for life and no person has a power to appoint any part of the property to anyone other than the donee spouse during that spouse's life. (Code Sec. 2523(f))[7]

For an increased exclusion for transfers to noncitizen spouses, see ¶5046.

If an estate (¶5022) or gift tax QTIP marital deduction is taken, the QTIP property is included in the spouse's estate on her death (¶5009). However, transfer tax is accelerated if the spouse makes a gift of her income interest. Under Code Sec. 2519, if a spouse makes a gift of any portion of her qualifying income interest in the QTIP trust, she is deemed to make a transfer of the entire value of the remainder.[8]

---

48. ¶Q-1000; ¶25,034; TD ¶744,008
49. ¶Q-5000 *et seq.*; ¶25,034; TD ¶731,002
50. ¶Q-5003; ¶25,034; TD ¶731,003
1. ¶Q-5100 *et seq.*; ¶25,034; TD ¶731,008
2. ¶Q-5104.1
3. ¶Q-5112; ¶25,034; TD ¶731,022

4. ¶Q-5201 *et seq.*; ¶25,034; TD ¶732,001
5. ¶Q-5212; ¶25,034; TD ¶732,014
6. ¶Q-6100 *et seq.*; ¶25,234; TD ¶734,001
7. ¶Q-6300 *et seq.*; ¶25,234; TD ¶736,001
8. ¶Q-6315; ¶25,194; TD ¶764,007

¶ 5048   Charitable gifts.

Charitable gifts and certain similar gifts are deducted in arriving at taxable gifts for the calendar year. (Code Sec. 2522)[9] The Tax Court has upheld a gift tax valuation formula that produced a higher gift tax charitable deduction than was originally reported. This occurred after IRS challenged the value of units in a limited liability company that was funded with stock and the formula caused noncharitable donees to get less units and charitable donees to get more.[10]

¶ 5049   Split gifts to third parties by married donors.

A husband and wife may consent to have their gifts to others treated as if made one-half by each (Code Sec. 2513(a); Reg § 25.2513-1) if:

. . . both spouses are U.S. citizens or residents on the date of the gift (Code Sec. 2513(a));

. . . both spouses consent (on Form 709) to have all gifts made to others in the calendar year treated as split gifts (Code Sec. 2513(a), Code Sec. 2513(b), Code Sec. 2513(c); Reg § 25.2513-1(b)(5));

. . . the consenting spouses are married to each other on the date of the gift and don't remarry during the remainder of the calendar year. (Code Sec. 2513(a))[11]

Each spouse is liable, jointly and severally, for the *entire* gift tax for the period in which he or she consents to split gifts. (Code Sec. 2513(d); Reg § 25.2513-4)[12]

Gifts of community property to a third party are generally considered to have been made one half by each spouse.[13]

¶ 5050   Gift tax on "estate freeze" transfers (Chapter 14 rules).

For gift tax valuation purposes, certain interests retained by the transferor after a transfer to a family member are disregarded. (This ensures that a high gift tax will be imposed on the transferred interest at the time of the transfer.) These Chapter 14 (of the Code) rules apply to:[14]

. . . transfers of interests in corporations and partnerships;

. . . transfers of interests in trusts (other than certain trusts known as GRATs, GRUTs, and qualified personal residence trusts);

. . . buy-sell agreements and options; and

. . . lapsing rights.

¶ 5051   Gift credit/unified credit against gift tax.

For 2010, there's a gift tax credit of $330,800. For 2011, a unified credit of $345,800 is allowed against gift tax on gifts made by a U.S. citizen or resident. The credit effectively exempts the first $1,000,000 of transfers. The credit against tax on gifts in a calendar period is reduced by the sum of all amounts allowable as a credit in preceding calendar periods. (Code Sec. 2505)[15]

¶ 5052   How to compute gift tax if no gifts made before current year.

If a person has *not* made any taxable gifts (in excess of annual exclusions and deductions and the pre-'77 specific lifetime exemption) before the calendar year for which the tax is being

9. ¶Q-6000 *et seq.*; ¶25,224; TD ¶733,001
10. ¶Q-1983.2
11. ¶Q-7000 *et seq.*; ¶25,134; TD ¶743,001
12. ¶V-8505 *et seq.*; ¶25,134; TD ¶746,007

13. ¶Q-2929 *et seq.*; ¶25,134.01; TD ¶743,001
14. ¶Q-3350; ¶s 27,014, 27,024, 27,034, 27,044; TD ¶721,002
15. ¶Q-8005; ¶25,054; TD ¶744,004

computed, the gift tax is computed as follows:[16]

(1) Determine the aggregate value of the total gifts made during the calendar year for which the tax is being computed. If the donor is married, and he and his wife have consented to split their gifts to third parties, only half of the gifts he made to third parties plus half of the gifts, if any, she made to third parties are included in computing his total gifts. (A separate gift tax computation is made for the wife, and the other half of the husband's gifts to third parties plus the other half of the wife's gifts to third parties are included in computing the wife's total gifts.)

(2) Deduct from the amount in (1), above, any amounts qualifying for the year's annual exclusion (¶5046).

(3) From the excess of (1) over (2), above, subtract the amount of charitable (¶5048) and marital (¶5047) gifts.

(4) Compute a gift tax on the excess of (1) over the sum of (2) and (3); for gifts made during 2010, use the rate schedule at ¶1113.

(5) Subtract from the gift tax computed in (4), the allowable unified credit.

¶ 5053 Cumulative computation where gifts were made before current year.

Previous taxable gifts affect the amount of gift tax imposed on gifts made in the current year. These taxable gifts are taken into account whether they were made before '77 or after '76. (Code Sec. 2502) In general the gift tax (before unified credit) is the excess of: (1) a tentative tax computed under the unified rate schedules on the aggregate sum of taxable gifts for the current calendar year for which the tax is being computed *and* taxable gifts (made after June 6, '32) for all preceding years, over (2) a tentative tax computed under the unified rate schedule on the aggregate sum of the taxable gifts (made after June 6, '32) for all of the years preceding the current calendar year for which the tax is being computed. (Code Sec. 2502(a)) The gift tax payable is the excess of the tentative tax in (1) over the tentative tax in (2) reduced by the unified credit allowable.

¶ 5054 Gift tax returns—Form 709.

Any individual who makes gifts to any one donee during a calendar year which aren't fully excluded under the $13,000 annual exclusion for 2010 (and 2011) must file a gift tax return (Form 709). A return must be filed even if no tax is payable. (Reg § 25.6019-1(f)) But no return is required to report a qualified transfer for educational or medical costs (¶5040), most charitable transfers, or a transfer that qualifies for the marital deduction (¶5047) (Code Sec. 6019), except that a return must be filed to make a QTIP (¶5047) election. (Reg § 25.6019-1(a))[17] The return is due on Apr. 15 of the year following the year the gifts were made. (Code Sec. 6075) A different rule applies if the donor has died.[18] An extension for filing the income tax return automatically extends the time for filing the gift tax return for the same calendar year. (Code Sec. 6075(b)(2)) Use Form 8892 to request an extension of time to file Form 709 when not applying for an extension to file an income tax return or to make a payment of gift (or GST) tax when applying for an extension of time to file Form 709. (Reg § 25.6081-1)[19]

¶ 5055 Generation-Skipping Transfer Tax.

A "generation-skipping" transfer (GST) tax is imposed on transfers outright or in trust to beneficiaries more than one generation below the transferor's generation at a flat rate, equal to the maximum gift and estate tax rate. The GST tax does not apply for estates of decedents dying in 2010 but there is uncertainty over how it will apply after 2010. The uncertainty stems from whether the EGTRRA sunset rule will kick in, see ¶1114 and ¶5000.

---

16. ¶Q-8010 *et seq.*; ¶25,009 *et seq.*; TD ¶744,008
17. ¶S-2200 *et seq.*; ¶s 25,014, 60,194; TD ¶746,001

18. ¶S-4901; ¶60,754; TD ¶746,009
19. ¶S-5035; ¶s 60,754, 60,814; TD ¶746,010

¶ 5056   Transfers subject to tax.

The generation-skipping tax is imposed on every generation-skipping transfer. (Code Sec. 2601)

The GST tax generally applies to generation-skipping transfers made after Oct. 22, '86. (Tax Reform Act of '86 (TRA '86) § 1431(a)) However, it doesn't apply to any generation-skipping transfer from a trust that was irrevocable on Sept. 25, '85. The exception doesn't apply to a transfer made out of corpus added to the trust after Sept. 25, '85. (TRA '86 § 1433(b)(2)(A))

A generation-skipping transfer is any one of three taxable events: (1) a *taxable termination* of an interest in a trust if, after the termination, all interests in the trust are held by or for the benefit of persons two or more generations below that of the transferor (trustee pays the GST tax on taxable terminations on Form 706GS(T)), (2) a *taxable distribution* of income or principal from a trust to or for the benefit of a person two or more generations below that of the transferor (transferee pays the tax on Form 706GS(D), the trustee must file Form 706GS(D-1)), and (3) a *direct skip,* which is a transfer of an interest in property to or for the benefit of a person two or more generations below that of the transferor (transferor pays tax with Form 709 for lifetime direct skips, executor pays with Form 706 and attached Form 706, Schedule R or Form 706, Schedule R-1, for direct skips occurring at death). (Code Sec. 2611(a), Code Sec. 2612) (Use Form 8892 to request an extension of time to file Form 709 when not applying for an extension to file an income tax return or to make a payment of GST tax when applying for an extension of time to file Form 709.) In determining whether there is a generation-skipping transfer, a special rule "steps up" the generation of an individual (or the descendants of an individual) with a deceased parent that's a descendant of the transferor's parent. (Code Sec. 2651(e)(1); Reg § 26.2651-1)[20]

¶ 5057   Exemptions from tax.

Every individual is allowed a $1 million exemption (for transfers in 2011, assuming the EGTRRA sunset kicks in, see ¶1114 and ¶5000) which may be allocated to any property transferred. (Code Sec. 2631) Married couples may treat transfers as made one-half by each spouse, in effect giving them a combined $2 million exemption (for transfers in 2011). (Code Sec. 2652(a)(2))[21] Once a transfer is designated as exempt, all later appreciation in the value of the exempt property is also exempt.[22] The tax doesn't apply to lifetime transfers (except for certain transfers in trust) that are exempt from gift tax because of the annual exclusion (¶5046) or the exclusion for certain tuition and medical expense payments (¶5040). (Code Sec. 2642(c)(3)) For lifetime transfers, the available GST exemption is automatically allocated to a direct skip under Code Sec. 2632(b), and to indirect skips made after Dec. 31, 2000 under Code Sec. 2632(c), unless the individual elects out of the automatic allocation under Code Sec. 2632(b)(3) and Code Sec. 2632(c)(5), respectively. The automatic allocation under Code Sec. 2632(c) also applies to an indirect skip occurring upon the post-2000 termination of an estate tax inclusion period. (Code Sec. 2632(c)(4)) Regs provide details about these elections. (Reg § 26.2632-1)[23]

caution: Some of these GST technical rules would be altered if the EGTRRA sunset rule kicks in, see ¶5000.

---

20. ¶R-9500 *et seq.*; ¶s 26,014, 26,114, 26,124 *et seq.*; TD ¶791,001
21. ¶R-9551; ¶s 26,014, 26,314; TD ¶791,004

22. ¶R-9557; ¶26,324; TD ¶791,004
23. ¶R-9501 *et seq.*; ¶26,424; TD ¶791,001

INDEX

References are to paragraph [¶] numbers.

A

Annuities and annuity contracts — Cont'd
. qualified employee plans — Cont'd
.. premature distributions 1370
. "secured" annuities 1372
. separate contract treatment, partial annui-
       tization of annuities 1367
. starting date 1366; 1367
. tax-free exchange 2417
. trusts 2116; 2119;
                                                                    3914
. unrecovered investment in 3966
. unrelated business taxable income 4122
. "unsecured" private annuities 1372
. variable 1362
. withholding on . . . . 3035 et seq.
Anti-churning rules 1908; 1976
Appellate division conference . . . . 4818 et seq.
Appliances, household
. credit for energy efficient 2338
Applicable asset acquisition 2472
Applicable federal rate
. below-market interest rate loans 5041
. leases and rentals 1600
. overpayments of tax, interest on 4855
. table of 1116
. underpayments of tax, interest on 4867
. unstated interest 1312
Appraisals of property
. casualties 1796; 3110
. charitable gifts 2138; 4878
.. itemized deductions 3110
.. overstatement of value 4873
.. "Statement of Value" for gifts of art 2140
. cost of 2168; 5017
. penalty for valuation misstatements 4888
Appreciated property
. charitable contribution of . . . . 2107; 2129 et
                                                                    seq.
. corporate distribution of
      generally 3538
.. earnings and profits, effect on 3523
. financial positions, constructive sale of 2637; 2638
. gift of 2683
. passive activity, disposition of as 1819
. reacquisition by donor, basis 2514
Arbitrage bonds 1334
Arbitration of tax disputes 4820
Archer medical savings account (MSA)
. contributions to
.. adjusted gross income computation 3102
.. deductibility 1528
. distributions from
.. exclusion for 1382
. employer contributions to 1258
. Medicare Advantage Medical Savings Ac-
      counts 1530
Architectural barriers
. disabled access credit 2324
. removal expenses 1667; 2324;
                                                                    2695

Armed Forces *See also "Reservists"*
. combat zone compensation, exempt wages 3006
. Coverdell ESAs, rollover of military death
      gratuity or Service members' Group
      Life Insurance payments to 2207
. dependency exemption, effect of depen-
      dency allotments on 3124
. disability pension, exclusion for 1286
. dying in combat or terrorist attacks
.. death benefits under qualified retirement
      plans 4331
.. estate tax computation 5001

Armed Forces *See also "Reservists"* — **Cont'd**
. dying in combat or terrorist attacks — Cont'd
.. Roth IRA contributions 4369
.. tax relief 4715
. earned income credit 2345; 2346
. exclusions and allowances 1225
. extensions of time 4719
. first-time homebuyer credit 2370
. "missing status" spouse 3132
. moving expenses 1653
. principal residence, exclusion of gain on
      sale 2442; 2443;
                                                                    2445
. veterans' benefits 1226
Artists
. creative, expenses of 1638; 1660
. performing, expenses of 3105
Assessments
. bankruptcy proceedings 4831; 4913
. bar to, expiration of limitation period 4833
. "designated summons," issuance of 4839
. local benefit, for 1760
. mathematical error on return 4801
. open assessment period 4837
. period, assessment . . . . 4834 et seq.
. prompt assessment, request for 4840
. restitution payments 4829
. statute of limitations on . . . . 4832 et seq.
. suspension of assessment period 4839
. time for making 4827
. unrelated business income tax 4121
. unreported listed transactions 4836
. voluntary extension of assessment period 4838
Assets
. capital and noncapital . . . . 2616 et seq.
. in reorganizations *See "Reorganizations"*
. partnership, adjustment to basis . . . . 3713 et seq.
Assignment
. benefits of qualified plans 4319
. income, of 1201
. personal injury liability, of, accepting 1387
Assistance orders, taxpayer 4813
Associations, shares in 3512
Assumption of liabilities
. basis 2465; 2485;
                                                                    2488
. controlled corporations, transfers to 3515; 3516
. corporate distributions
      generally 3539
.. earnings and profits, effect on 3523
. dividends, determination of amount 1294
. exempt organizations 4123
. like-kind exchanges 2422
. liquidations 3576
. mortgages 2465
. partnerships 3740; 3760
. reorganizations
      generally 3557
.. Type C 3546
. shareholders 3521
. unstated interest, exception to rules 1314
"At risk" limitations
      generally . . . . 1804 et seq.
. activities "at risk" 1806
. alternative minimum tax 3202
. amounts considered "at risk" 1808
. business investment credit 2307
. real property, rules for 1810
. recapture of previously allowed losses 1809
. taxpayers subject to rules 1805
Attorneys
. audit by IRS, representing taxpayer 4810

    References are to paragraph [¶] numbers.

Motion picture films
. amortization 1977
. depreciation 1908; 1927;
. . . . 1961
. domestic production activities, deduction
. . . . . for 1616
. election to expense production costs 1967
. . recapture rules 2695
Moving expenses
. *generally* . . . . 1645 et seq.
. above-the-line-expenses 1647
. armed forces 1653
. distance test 1648
. equipment and machinery 1514
. foreign moves 1650
. reimbursement of
. . allowances for, armed forces members 1225
. . qualified moving expense reimbursement 1250
. . withholding on 3006
. relocation allowances and loans 1206; 1215
. self-employed persons 1645
. 78-week test 1649
. 39-week test 1649
. time for deduction 1646; 1652
. United States, moves to 1651
Multiple corporations . . . . 3341 et seq.
Multiple support agreements, personal ex-
. . . . . emptions 3123
Multiple trusts 3913
Mutual insurance companies 4100

N

Nanny tax 3030; 3031
National Guard
. travel expenses 3102
National Health Service Corps Loan Re-
. . . . **payment Program** 1392
Native Americans *See "Indian employment*
. . . . *credit"; "Indian reservation property"*
Natural resources
. capital expenditures 1623; 1625
. depletion deduction . . . . 1979 et seq.
. depreciation 1902
. royalties 1347
. sales and exchanges 4667
. source of income 4648
Negligence
. damages against IRS for 4906; 4907
. penalty 4877
Net earnings from self-employment 3143
Net operating loss
. *generally* . . . . 1840 et seq.
. acquiring corporation 3564
. alternative minimum tax 3212
. ATNOLD (alternative tax net operating loss
. . . . deduction) 3212
. bankruptcy estate 3977
. carrybacks and carryovers
. . *generally* . . . . 1842 et seq.
. . disaster losses 1844
. . election to forego carryback 1845; 3212
. . elective 3-, 4- or 5-year carryback 1843
. . farmers 4503
. . Gulf Opportunity Zone losses 1844
. . intervening year modifications 1850
. . Madoff-style schemes, losses from 1800
. . refunds 4852; 4855
. . social clubs 4107
. . successor corporation's use of 3564
. change in ownership . . . . 3567 et seq.
. common trust funds 1841

Net operating loss — Cont'd
. computation
. . *generally* . . . . 1846 et seq.
. . corporate taxpayers 1848
. . noncorporate taxpayers 1847
. deduction 1846; 1849
. definition 1841
. dividends-received deduction, effect on 3311
. estates and trusts 1841; 3930
. Gulf Opportunity Zone losses 1844
. partnerships 1841; 3717;
. . . . 3737
. personal holding companies 3324
. self-employment tax 3143
. specified liability losses 1842
Net worth method of determining income . . . 2857
New markets tax credit 2331
New York Liberty Zone
. business employee credit 2303
. qualified zone property
. . bonus first year depreciation allowance 1933; 3207
. . leasehold improvement property
. . . MACRS depreciation 1914; 1925;
. . . . 1932; 1934
. . MACRS depreciation
. . . leasehold improvement property 1914; 1925;
. . . . 1932
90-day letter 4815; 4826;
. . . . 4838; 4860
No-additional-cost services, excludable
. . . . **fringe benefit, as** 1245
Nominees, information returns
. *generally* 4738
. partnerships 4731
. trusts and estates 4732
Nonbusiness bad debts 1856; 1857
Nonbusiness expenses . . . . 2166 et seq.
Non-cash compensation 1216; 3004
Noncompetition agreement
. amortization 1977; 1978
. basis of 2471; 2472
. capital asset, as 2627
Nonconventional fuel credit 2341
Nondiscrimination rules
. cafeteria plans 1271
. employer-provided child care credit 2332
. 401(k) plans 4317
. group-term life insurance 1264
. health savings accounts (HSAs) 1529
. pension and profit-sharing plans 4311; 4319;
. . . . 4325 et seq.
. simplified employee pensions (SEPs) 4378
. small employer pension plan startup credit . . . 2333
. supplemental unemployment benefit plans
. . . . (SUBs) 4108
. tax-exempt organizations 4108
. tax-sheltered annuities 4388
. tuition reductions 2217
. voluntary employee beneficiary associa-
. . . . tions (VEBAs) 4108
Nonpayroll taxes, withholding . . . . 3032 et seq.
Nonprofit organizations . . . . 4100 et seq.
Nonqualified deferred compensation
. . . . **plans** 1277
. funding triggers 1278
. from tax-indifferent entities 1279
Nonrecognition of gain or loss . . . . . . 2400; 2413 et
. . . . seq.
Nonrecourse debt
. allocation rules 3725
. assumption of liabilities 3516
. at-risk rules 1808

Original issue discount — Cont'd
. deductibility . . . . 1743; 1751 et
                                                        seq.
. defined 1316
. interest income, inclusion as . . . . 1315 et seq.
. reporting requirements 4741
. short-term obligations 1330
. stated redemption price at maturity 1318
. tax-exempt bonds 2636
. withholding 4667
Orphan drug credit 2330
Outbound transfers 3588
Overall foreign losses (OFLs) 2381
Overpayments
. interest on 4855
. refunds *See "Refunds"*

P

Paid time off (PTO) plans 4313
PALs *See "Passive activity loss rules"*
Parachute payments *See "Golden para-*
    chute payments"
Parent-sub controlled groups 3341; 3533
Parking
. fees 1559; 1561;
                                                        2121
. qualified transportation fringe benefits 1249
Parsonage rental allowance 1228
Participation
. active participation
. . at-risk activities 1806
. . passive losses, rental real estate 1836; 1837
. material participation *See "Material partici-*
    pation"
. pension and profit-sharing plans 4326
Partnerships
    generally . . . . 3700 et seq.
. accounting methods 2818
. allocations
    generally . . . . 3724 et seq.
. . change in partnership interests 3725
. . liabilities 3762
. . retirement or death payments 3771
. . substantial economic effect, determina-
    tion of 3726
. alternative minimum tax 3200; 3202
. anti-abuse rules 3708
. assessments, limitation period on 4832
. assets, sale of v. sale of partnership busi-
    ness 3767
. at-risk rules 1806
. audit of, unified audit and review . . . . 4708; 4842 et
                                                        seq.
. basis
    generally . . . . 2481; 3775 et
                                                        seq.
. . adjustments to basis of partner's interest 3740; 3741;
                                                        3751
. . adjustments to basis of partnership prop-
    erty . . . . 3775 et seq.
. . alternative adjusted basis computation 3741
. . contributed property . . . . 3713 et seq.
. . incorporation, basis after 2491
. . "inside" basis 3775
. . liquidating distributions, partner's basis of
    property received in 3749
. . loss limitations, basis adjustments made
    before applying 3736
. . nonliquidating distributions, partner's ba-
    sis of property received in 3748
. . "outside" basis 3738

Partnerships — Cont'd
. basis — Cont'd
. . partnership interest . . . . 3738 et seq.
. . stock distributions to corporate partner,
    basis adjustments in connection with 3750
. capital accounts of partners 3727
. capital contributions 3710
. contributions to
    generally . . . . 3709 et seq.
. . built-in gain or loss property 3752
. . character of contributed property 3747
. controlled partnership, sales and ex-
    changes with 3731; 3732
. deceased partner's successor in interest,
    payments to . . . . 3768 et seq.
. deductions of
    generally . . . . 3715 et seq.
. . separately stated items 3718
. deferred compensation from 1279
. defined 3701
. discharge of indebtedness income 1399
. distributions
    generally . . . . 3742 et seq.
. . basis, allocation of 3751
. . basis adjustments . . . . 3777 et seq.
. . built-in gain or loss property 3752
. . disproportionate . . . . 3754 et seq.
. . gain or loss . . . . 3743 et seq.
. . holding period 3746
. . liquidations 3749
. . marketable securities 3745
. . nonliquidating 3748
. . stock distributions to corporate partner,
    basis adjustments in connection with 3750
. . termination of partnership 3782
. domestic production activities, deduction
    for 1615
. electing large partnerships 3702; 4731
. electronic filing requirement 4731
. exclusion from rules, election 3705
. expatriations (inversions) 4655
. family partnerships 3704; 5005
. farming 4510
. final year's income
. . deceased partner 3773
. . retired partner 3772
. foreign partners, effectively connected in-
    come, withholding on distributions 4670
. foreign partnerships
. . domestic partnerships succeeded by (in-
    versions) 4655
. . returns 4661; 4731
. . withholding 4665
. foreign tax credit 2375
. guaranteed payments 3730; 3769;
                                                        3771
. holding period
. . contributed property 3714
. . interest in partnership 2669
. husband and wife partnership 3701
. income of . . . . 3715 et seq.
. incorporation, basis of property after 2491
. information returns 4745; 4753
. interest in
. . amortization 1978
. . appreciated financial positions, construc-
    tive sales 2637; 2638
. . basis . . . . 3738 et seq.
. . changes in, effect on allocation of part-
    nership items 3725
. . constructive ownership 3733
. . holding period 2669

References are to paragraph [¶] numbers.

References are to paragraph [¶] numbers.